PARKER AND MELLOWS:

THE MODERN LAW OF TRUSTS

D1585745

PARKER AND MELLOWS:

THE MODERN LAW OF TRUSTS

Ninth Edition

by

A. J. OAKLEY, M.A., LL.B., T.E.P.,
of Lincoln's Inn, Barrister-at-Law,
Sometime Fellow of Trinity Hall, Cambridge

LONDON
SWEET & MAXWELL
2008

First Edition by Profs D. B. Parker & A. R. Mellows	1966
Second Edition "	1970
Third Edition "	1975
Fourth Edition "	1979
Fifth Edition "	1983
Sixth Edition by A. J. Oakley	1994
Second Impression	1995
Third Impression	1997
Seventh Edition by A. J. Oakley	1998
Second Impression	2000
Eighth Edition by A. J. Oakley	2003
Second Impression	2005
Ninth Edition	2008

Published in 2008 by
Sweet & Maxwell Ltd of
100 Avenue Road, Swiss Cottage,
London NW3 3PF
http://www.sweetandmaxwell.co.uk
Computerset by Interactive Sciences Ltd,
Gloucester
Printed in the Netherlands by
Krips of Meppel

A CIP catalogue record for this book is available
from the British Library
ISBN–9780421945906

No natural forests were destroyed
to make this product;
only farmed timber was used.

PREFACE

In the preface to the first edition of this work in 1966, its authors stated that the law of trusts "is a branch of the law which is developing at a rapid pace and which is highly relevant to modern conditions, not merely to a bygone age". The accuracy of this statement was demonstrated by the fact that four further editions rapidly followed, culminating in the fifth edition in 1983. The unexpected and untimely death of Professor Parker in 1987, just when the authors might have been expected to have been thinking about a further edition, delayed the production of the sixth edition until 1994. That edition, the seventh, the eighth, and this ninth edition have been entrusted to me. It is now 25 years since an edition was produced by Professor Parker and Professor Mellows and the work has somehow since more than doubled in length. It is therefore inevitable that the proportion of the text which remains in the form in which it was actually written by them is now much reduced. However, the format and the contents of the work remain largely unchanged and the debt which this edition owes to their erudition and scholarship will be apparent to anyone familiar with the editions produced by them and will continue to be apparent for many editions to come.

This edition follows exactly the same order as its predecessor save that I have deleted the final chapter on Exporting Trusts and divided its contents between the chapter on The Appointment, Retirement and Removal of Trustees and the chapter on The Taxation of a Trust on the basis that this material is no longer only relevant to trusts which are exported. A particular objective of this edition has been the removal of out of date material or, in some marginal cases, its relegation to the footnotes. For ease of reference, numbered paragraphs have been introduced for the first time.

The most important legislative development since the last edition has been the enactment of the Charities Act 2006, which has meant that the majority of the chapter on Charitable Trusts has had to be amended and reformulated. Substantial legislative reform to every single one of the taxes considered in the chapter on The Taxation of a Trust has necessitated amendments to the whole of that chapter and to parts of a number of other chapters, while there has also been legislative reform in the area of Pension Trusts. The long anticipated legislation on Perpetuities and Accumulations is to be enacted in 2009 while the proposal for the enactment of legislation to restrict the use of Trustee Exemption Clauses has been abandoned. The two most important judicial developments have been provided by the decision of the Privy Council in *Barlow Clowes International v. Eurotrust International*, which has clarified the definition of dishonesty for the purposes of the imposition of "liability for dishonest assistance", and by the decision of the House of Lords in *Stack v. Dowden* concerning the beneficial entitlements of cohabitees. However, many other significant judgments have been handed down at all levels.

Since the publication of the previous edition of this work, I have dedicated myself exclusively to full time practice at the Chancery Bar but I continue to hope not only that this work is no less academic for now being written by a full time practitioner but also that it has benefited from the insights which I have acquired as a result of my practice.

I would like to thank Professor Mellows for continuing to repose his confidence in me by entrusting me with this further edition, for which I alone am responsible. I would also like to renew my thanks to the many friends and colleagues with whom I have discussed the subject matter of this work over the years for the benefit of their ideas and criticisms. I would also like to thank my clerks for their forbearance while this edition was being prepared and to thank my wife, Margaret Halliwell, for her help. Finally, I would like to thank the publishers for producing the Index and the Tables of Cases, Statutes, and Statutory Instruments and for their general efficiency.

The law has been stated from the sources which were available to me on April 30, 2008.

A. J. Oakley
4–5 Gray's Inn Square,
Gray's Inn

May 13, 2008

CONTENTS

12. PENSION TRUSTS   554

13. THE APPOINTMENT, RETIREMENT AND REMOVAL OF TRUSTEES   600

14. THE ADMINISTRATION OF TRUSTS   639

15. THE TAXATION OF A TRUST   697

16. APPORTIONMENTS   752

17. INCOME FROM THE TRUST FUND   772

TABLE OF CASES

TABLE OF STATUTES

TABLE OF STATUTORY INSTRUMENTS

CHAPTER 1

INTRODUCTION

I. THE TRUST TODAY

The modern trust is the direct successor of the medieval use. Ever since the **1–001** use was first invented, it has been impossible for any property lawyer to give a comprehensive service to his client unless he has had a thorough grasp of the law governing the creation, operation and determination of uses and, later on, of trusts. This is as true today as it has ever been; indeed, it is arguably more so. This is the case because, throughout their history, the use and the trust have been employed by lawyers because they are devices capable of circumventing inconvenient rules of law.

1. *The Historical Background*

It was during the early medieval period that the practice first arose of **1–002** owners of property transferring that property to third parties[1] to the use[2] either of the owners themselves or of some other person who was intended to benefit. The effect of such a transfer was that the third parties became the owners of the property in the eyes of the law but held their legal title to the property for the benefit of the transferor and/or any other intended beneficiary.

The fact that the law regarded the third parties as the owners of the property meant that, in the event that they failed to comply with the terms of the use, neither the transferor nor the other intended beneficiaries had any remedy in any of the Royal Courts which had been established by then.[3]

---

[1] Property transferred by way of use was virtually always put in the name of more than one third party so that on the death of any one of them the other(s) would take the property by survivorship; this avoided difficulties, principally in relation to the incidence of taxation but also in relation to enforceability, which would otherwise have arisen if a sole trustee had died. It is still the almost invariable practice to have more than one trustee when the property is transferred to natural persons rather than to a trust corporation although, where a trust is created by declaration rather than by transfer, there is only likely to be one initial trustee; however, today the death of a sole trustee will only cause any difficulties in the relatively unlikely event that there is no documentary evidence of the terms on which he is holding the trust property.

[2] The expression comes from the Latin *ad opus*.

[3] By early in the thirteenth century, three courts had been established to deal with specific distinct areas of the Royal jurisdiction. These courts became known as the Court of King's Bench, the Court of Common Pleas, and the Court of Exchequer; they were collectively known as the Courts of Common Law and the body of rules which they enforced was known as the Common Law. They continued in existence until 1875 when they were abolished and their jurisdiction was transferred to the Supreme Court of Judicature.

However, in such circumstances a complaint could be made by way of petition to the King in Council. At first the practice of the Council was to instruct its principal officer, the Chancellor, who was at that time also the King's principal minister, to investigate the matter and recommend an appropriate remedy, which the Council then put into effect. In due course,[4] however, the quantity of petitions of this and other types which reached the hands of the Chancellor brought about the establishment of what eventually became known as the Court of Chancery, a jurisdiction of the Chancellor quite separate from, although complementary to, that of the original Royal Courts.[5]

The Court of Chancery habitually protected those beneficially entitled under uses (and later on those beneficially entitled under trusts). This was one of the first, and remains the best, of the examples of the Chancellor developing rules of law distinct from those which had been developed by the original Royal Courts. Later on[6] the different rules developed by successive Chancellors were formulated and became known as the rules of Equity, of which the trust has always been the principal institution.

1–003   The earliest situations in which uses were employed were generally of a temporary nature. Until 1290, a freeholder who wished to alienate land in the modern sense, that is to say transfer his entire interest in his land to a transferee, had to surrender the land in question to his feudal lord so that the latter could make the appropriate feudal grant to the transferee.[7] Between surrender and re-grant the lord held the land to the use of the transferee. Uses also had to be employed, both before and after 1290, by anyone who wished to transfer his land into the name of himself and another; he had to put the land into the name of a third party who would hold it to his use pending a transfer back into joint names (this was necessary because until as recently as 1926 it was not possible for anyone to convey land to himself[8]). Further, there are examples of Crusaders about to depart for the Holy Land[9]

---

[4] Probably before the end of the fourteenth century.

[5] Initially the jurisdiction of the Chancellor was of an extraordinary nature. However, towards the end of the fifteenth century the number of petitions was increasing steadily and the sixteenth century saw such a dramatic increase that the Chancellor could scarcely cope. A substantial part of this increase consisted of petitions from defrauded beneficiaries of uses, making the rise of the use both a cause and an effect of the establishment of this separate jurisdiction. By the end of the sixteenth century, what can by then be described as the Court of Chancery had to all intents and purposes ceased to be an extraordinary court. It continued in existence alongside the Courts of Common Law until 1875 when, like them, it was abolished and its jurisdiction was transferred to the Supreme Court of Judicature.

[6] Towards the end of the seventeenth century, principally by Lord Nottingham who was Chancellor from 1675 to 1682.

[7] For this reason such an alienation (technically known as an alienation by substitution) required the consent of the feudal lord. The transferor could alternatively make the appropriate feudal grant himself but this did not transfer his entire interest in the land to the transferee; instead this created a fresh rung in the feudal ladder and the transferor became the feudal lord of the transferee. This did not affect his existing responsibilities to his own feudal lord and, consequently, this form of alienation (technically known as subinfeudation) could be carried out as of right. The Statute Quia Emptores 1290 changed the situation completely by prohibiting subinfeudation and permitting substitution without the consent of the feudal lord, thus establishing the right of free alienability which has ever since been enjoyed by all those absolutely entitled to freehold land.

[8] It is now possible by virtue of Law of Property Act 1925, s.72(3).

[9] And others about to embark on hazardous journeys.

transferring their lands to third parties to hold for them until they returned or for their rightful heirs in the event that they did not do so.[10]

However, it soon came to be realised that uses could equally be employed on a permanent basis. An early example is provided by grants of land made to the Franciscan Friars, who were forbidden by their Order from owning land, shortly after they arrived in England in 1224.[11] Other permanent situations quickly followed.

1–004

During the thirteenth century the Crown made strenuous attempts to avoid land being given to corporations (the usual donees being the ever increasing number of ecclesiastical foundations). A series of statutes known collectively as the Statutes of Mortmain[12] purported to impose prohibitions on such gifts with a view to preventing land being taken out of circulation more or less indefinitely, something which had the effect of depriving feudal lords of most, if not all, of their revenue from the lands in question.[13] The effect of these statutes was for over a century able to be avoided by the employment of a use; until 1391,[14] a transfer of the land in question to third parties to the use of the corporation which was the intended donee was effective to circumvent these prohibitions.

More significantly, until 1540,[15] all freehold land automatically descended to the heir of a deceased person; it was simply not possible for the latter to make any alternative disposition of such land by will. However, this inability could be circumvented by a landowner transferring any land which he wished to leave away from his heir to third parties during his lifetime; they would hold the land to the use of the transferor for the remainder of his life and thereafter to the use of the intended beneficiary. This enabled the landowner to continue to derive the whole of the benefit from his land for as long as he lived; following his death, the third parties would automatically hold the land for and would normally convey it to the intended beneficiary.

However, the reason why uses were most frequently employed in the medieval period was for the purpose of avoiding feudal inheritance taxes; such uses were one of the earliest examples of what are now known as "tax avoidance schemes". These taxes principally affected the heirs of anyone who held land from his feudal lord as a tenant in knight service (by the fourteenth century[16] this had become and until 1661 remained the basic tenure by means of which land was held by persons other than subsistence

1–005

---

[10] Since the odds were substantially against the Crusader returning and he was in any event likely to be absent for many years, such transfers were in practice more likely to be permanent than temporary.

[11] Such a grant was made to the municipal corporation of Oxford to the use of the Friars in 1225.

[12] Culminating in the Statute De Viris Religiosis 1279.

[13] By this time most of the feudal taxes worth collecting were levied on inheritances. Corporations die much more infrequently than natural persons and medieval ecclesiastical foundations never died at all (at least not until Henry VIII decided to dissolve the Monasteries in the sixteenth century)—hence the name "mortmain" ("dead hand").

[14] When the device was prohibited by statute (15 Ric. II (1391), c.5).

[15] Prior to the enactment of the Statute of Wills 1540.

[16] Originally this had been the tenure of the aristocratic military class, the descendants of the leaders of the army which had come to England with King William the Conqueror in 1066.

farmers and agricultural labourers[17]).These feudal inheritance taxes differed depending on whether the heir of the tenant in knight service in question was an adult or a minor.

An heir who was an adult could not claim his inheritance until he had paid a fixed sum and, originally, a year's profits of the land in question to his future feudal lord. By the fourteenth century, the former liability had ceased to have much significance due to the effects of inflation and the latter liability which, because it was related to the annual value of the land, kept pace with inflation, only arose where the feudal lord in question was the King.[18] This obviously meant that the latter liability became an increasingly important source of income for the King.

The position of an heir who was a minor, a situation which, due to the very limited life expectancy which then prevailed, was likely to occur at least every other generation, was considerably worse. The future feudal lord would be entitled to use the land for his own exclusive benefit[19] until the minor reached the age of majority.[20] This liability had originally been not unreasonable since it compensated the feudal lord for the inability of the minor heir to render the services in exchange for which the land had originally been granted; however, by the fourteenth century, as a result of inflation these services were no longer worth collecting, rendering the liability increasingly unreasonable. To make matters worse, the minor heir also had either to submit to the feudal lord's choice of a spouse or, if he or she could not endure the thought of spending a lifetime locked in the arms of the person chosen, to compensate the lord for the value of the marriage to him.[21] Further, if the feudal lord in question was the King, the minor also had to make a payment of half a year's profits of the land on attaining his or her majority.[22] Although these liabilities benefited all feudal lords, they again principally benefited the King because, apart from the additional payment payable to him, he alone was always feudal lord and never tenant.

All these potential liabilities could be avoided if a tenant in knight service conveyed his land to third parties during his lifetime to the use of himself during the remainder of his life and thereafter to the use of his heir. He would continue to derive the whole of the benefits from his land for as long as he lived and, following his death, the third parties would transfer the land to the heir—in the case of an adult heir, straightaway; in the case of a minor heir, when he or she came of age. The heir thus received the land as

---

[17] The impact of feudal inheritance taxes on the latter was much less significant.

[18] As a result of the Statute of Marlborough 1267, c.16.

[19] This right was formally recognised in the Assize of Northampton 1176, c.4. However, Magna Carta 1215, cc.4, 5 subsequently prohibited feudal lords from destroying the capital value of the inheritance but they remained entitled to the whole of the income which it produced.

[20] 21 for males and 14 for females (unless the death occurred when the female was already over 14 and unmarried, in which case she came of age at 16 or upon earlier marriage).

[21] The lord could not put forward the most unattractive girl he could find in the hope that the infant would refuse and so give the lord a right to compensation. Magna Carta 1215, c.3 contained a list of defects in a potential spouse which prevented her from being put forward.

[22] Prior to Magna Carta 1215, c.3, this payment had had to be made to all feudal lords.

surely as if the tenant in knight service had retained legal title to that land until his death; however, because the heir had not actually received the land by way of inheritance, the feudal lord was not entitled to any of the payments or other rights set out above.

Because uses therefore had the effect of depriving feudal lords in general   **1–006** and the King in particular[23] of a substantial proportion of their feudal revenues, the existence of uses understandably became increasingly unpopular with the Crown. Henry VIII consequently attempted to take away the advantages conferred on the heirs of tenants in knight service by the employment of uses by enacting the Statute of Uses 1536.[24] Although the effects of this Statute were draconian,[25] its effects were relatively short-lived.[26] The right to leave freehold land by will was progressively re-established by statute[27] and all the feudal taxes which uses had been employed to avoid were subsequently abolished.[28] Further by the eighteenth century the use had been re-established under the name of the trust.[29]

---

[23] Both because of his additional rights and because of the fact that he alone was always lord and never tenant (the benefits to other feudal lords were over time largely cancelled out by the liabilities of their own heirs to their own feudal lords, particularly where the latter was the King).

[24] This legislation "executed" the use by transferring the legal title to its subject matter from the third parties in whom the latter had been vested to the beneficiary. As a result, the last two devices described in the text ceased to work because the effect of the Statute was that the transferor remained entitled to the land on his death.

[25] The Statute obviously re-imposed all the feudal taxes discussed in the text. This was of course the whole object of the exercise but the Statute also had the effect of preventing anyone from leaving freehold land, not just land held in knight service, away from his heir. This took away powers which had been regarded as a common right for more than a century and left freeholders unable to leave any of their freehold land to their younger children, thus preventing them from meeting some of the most serious obligations which morality and natural affection placed on them. This caused great unrest and a step back had to be taken almost immediately by the enactment of the Statute of Wills in 1540. This enabled two-thirds of land held in knight service and all land held in any other tenures to be left by will but did not, however, enable the beneficiaries of the will to escape the feudal taxes.

[26] Its most controversial effect was removed by the Statute of Wills 1540 (see the previous footnote) and the feudal taxes which it re-imposed disappeared when tenure in knight service was abolished by the Tenures Abolition Act 1661. Although the remaining effects of its provisions were, as will be seen below, rapidly circumvented by the ingenuity of lawyers, the Statute of Uses nevertheless remained in force until the end of 1925 and during this period considerable care had to be taken in drafting in order to avoid its provisions.

[27] By the Statute of Wills 1540 (see n.25 above) subject to restrictions in the case of tenure in knight service which were removed by the latter's abolition by the Tenures Abolition Act 1661.

[28] By the Tenures Abolition Act 1661.

[29] The Statute of Uses was held only to "execute" the first of two or more successive uses; second and subsequent uses were neither executed by the Statute nor valid at common law. Consequently, if land was transferred "unto and to the use of" third parties (to the third parties to their own use) "to the use of" the intended beneficiary, the third parties retained the legal title to the land in question and were regarded by the common law as its absolute owners. The intended beneficiary under the second or subsequent use was consequently as unprotected at common law as the beneficiaries of all uses had been before the Statute of Uses. The Chancellor, therefore, once again intervened to protect the beneficiaries of second or subsequent uses. Such uses were subsequently renamed trusts to distinguish them from the uses which were "executed" by the Statute of Uses. The result of all this was that the third parties held the legal title to the land in question on trust for the intended beneficiaries in exactly the same way as they had done before the Statute of Uses. The Statute of Uses had thus been avoided by the simple expedient of adding the words "and to the use of". This was acknowledged by Lord Hardwicke

The lawyers then found a number of further situations in which trusts could be usefully employed.

1–007　　In the eighteenth and nineteenth centuries trusts were employed by wealthy landowners in order to tie up their wealth for the benefit of succeeding generations of their families and also in order to make provision for all their dependants. Under the traditional form of settlement which developed,[30] the land in question was vested successively in the eldest son of each generation, generally only for his lifetime, but the trustees of the settlement were given overriding powers to raise capital for the benefit of all the other members of the family.[31]

Trusts were also employed in order to avoid another rule of the common law, which was in principle of general application, that a married woman could not hold property in her own right during the marriage[32]; this rule could also be overcome by vesting her property in trustees to hold on trust for her. Further, during the nineteenth century, trusts paid a significant role in the development of unincorporated associations such as clubs, friendly societies and trade unions; because such bodies are not themselves legal entities and so cannot hold property, they would not have developed in the way that they have had it not been possible for their property to be held by trustees on their behalf.[33] Finally, in the twentieth century, trusts once again came to be used as a means of creating "tax avoidance schemes", a role which they continue to retain, subject to the ever-increasing attacks of the legislature, in this new century.[34]

2. *The Principal Uses of the Trust Today*

1–008　The many and varied purposes for which trusts are employed today will now be summarised. They may be classified as family, commercial or social

---

L.C. in *Hopkins v. Hopkins* (1738) 1 Atk. 581 at 591, where he said "by this means a Statute made upon great consideration . . . has had no other effect than to add at most three words to a conveyance" (a statement which not only overlooks the other very significant consequences of the Statute of Uses but also puts into question the ability of Lord Hardwicke to count).

[30] A succinct description of settlements of this kind (generally known as "strict settlements") can be found in *Megarry's Manual of the Law of Real Property*, 8th edn (London, Sweet & Maxwell, 2002), pp.247–249.

[31] This system however prevented the land from being developed since not only did no one person have the power to dispose of or deal with the land in order to do so but also the son with the interest in possession for the time being had no interest in utilising its income for that purpose either. The end result was consequently often a situation of total sterility. During the nineteenth century, when land became necessary for development following the industrial revolution, the powers of the eldest son (or other beneficiary in possession) for the time being were therefore very considerably extended and full powers of disposal and management were finally conferred by the Settled Land Act 1882, which formed the basis of the Settled Land Act 1925.

[32] This restriction seems to date from the beginning of the thirteenth century. In its final form, all the personalty owned by a wife on marriage, or acquired by her thereafter, became the absolute property of her husband; he was also entitled to manage and to take the profits of her freehold land, which by law became vested in both of them. However, the property of the married woman nevertheless passed in accordance with her will or the appropriate intestacy rules on her death. The restriction was finally taken away by the Married Women's Property Act 1882.

[33] See *post*, para 3–107.

[34] See *post*, paras 1–014, 6–047–6–049.

purposes, although the majority fall within more than one category. The first six purposes set out below are primarily but not exclusively family purposes, the next three are virtually entirely commercial purposes, and the final three, particularly the last one of all, the provision of pensions for retired persons and their dependants, have elements of all three classifications.

(1) To enable property, particularly land, to be held for persons who cannot themselves hold it. Although the legal title to land cannot be vested in a minor, there is no objection to land being held on trust for such a person. Indeed the legislature has adopted this particular route, providing that a purported conveyance of a legal estate in land to a minor operates as a declaration that the land is held in trust for that person.[35]   **1–009**

(2) To enable a person to make provision for dependants privately. The most obvious examples are any provision made by a man for his mistress or his illegitimate child. During his lifetime he can make such provision without publicity but an express testamentary gift in favour of a mistress or an illegitimate child by will may well become public knowledge. Once probate has been obtained, a will becomes a public document and is therefore open to public inspection— indeed tabloid journalists routinely inspect the wills of famous persons in the hope of finding embarrassing information of this type. A trust created other than by will, on the other hand, escapes publicity of this type provided that the person making such provision either settles property on the intended beneficiaries during his lifetime or creates what is known as a secret trust[36] in their favour in his will.   **1–010**

(3) To tie up property so that it can benefit persons in succession. It is of course always possible to make an outright gift of property to a parent in the hope and expectation that on the parent's death that property will go to his children but there is no guarantee that it will actually do so; the parent may fall out with the children or die bankrupt. On the other hand, a gift of property to trustees to hold on trust for the parent for life and, subject to that, for the children will ensure[37] that the children derive a benefit. It is admittedly not normally possible to ensure that the person ultimately entitled will receive the actual property which is settled, since the trustees will   **1–011**

---

[35] Trusts of Land and Appointment of Trustees Act 1996, Sch.1, para.1. Before this Act came into force on January 1, 1997, such a conveyance operated as an agreement for valuable consideration to create a settlement of that land on the minor and in the meantime to hold the land on trust for him (Settled Land Act 1925, s.27); any conveyances which were operating in this way on January 1, 1997 thereafter also took effect as declarations of trust.

[36] See *post*, para 4–051.

[37] Unless the parent and children agree, after all the children have reached the age of majority, to bring the trust to an end prematurely.

almost always have the power to sell it and re-invest the proceeds. But it is possible to ensure that the person ultimately entitled does at the very least receive whatever assets are derived from that property.

1–012

(4) To protect family property from wastrels and spendthrifts. A person may feel that an outright gift of money to a surviving spouse or child will lead to the money being rapidly dissipated. On the other hand, a gift of that money to trustees to hold on trust to pay either the income or only a limited proportion of the capital to the surviving spouse or child will probably prevent this happening. Flexibility can be preserved by giving the trustees a discretion as to the amount (if any) of income or capital which they may pay over at any one time; another possibility is for property to be given to trustees to hold on trust for a beneficiary in such a way that the property will be preserved from the beneficiary's creditors in the event that he becomes bankrupt.[38]

1–013

(5) To make a gift to take effect in the future in the light of circumstances which have not yet arisen and so cannot yet be known. A person who has three young daughters may choose to set up a trust in his will whereby a sum of money is given to trustees for them to distribute among the daughters, either as they think fit or having regard to certain stated factors. They might, for example, in due course decide to give one-quarter each to two of the daughters who had achieved financial stability and one-half to the third daughter who had not done so.

1–014

(6) To minimise the incidence of income tax, capital gains tax and inheritance tax. A high proportion of the numerous possible "tax avoidance schemes" which have been devised involve a trust in one way or another.[39] One example will suffice for the moment. At present a person with a high income[40] will pay income tax at the higher rate of 40 per cent on any investment income. However, substantial tax savings can be made if the higher rate taxpayer transfers an investment to trustees to be held on trust for other members of his family who are of more modest means and so either pay no income tax at all or pay income tax at the basic rate of, at present, 20 per cent.[41] While the income of the trust is subject to income tax at the maximum rate in the hands of the trustees, the beneficiaries can recover all or some of that tax so as to bring the amount of tax paid down to their own rate. The potential saving

---

[38] This device is known as a protective trust; see *post*, paras 8–003–8–022.

[39] Such schemes "involve" trusts because in the majority of cases they will necessitate either the setting up of a trust or the breaking of an existing trust or a combination of the two.

[40] In 2008–2009, income tax is payable at 40 per cent on any taxable income (that is on the balance of the taxpayer's income after the deduction of any personal allowances to which he is entitled) over £36,000.

[41] In 2008–2009, payable on taxable income up to £36,000. In the years immediately prior to 2008–2009, there was also a starting rate of 10 per cent but the basic rate was 22 per cent.

varies depending on the nature of the investment.[42] Only rarely[43] is
the tax saved less than 20 per cent of the income (the difference
between the 40 per cent tax otherwise payable and the 20 per cent
basic rate of tax) and no income tax will ultimately be paid at all in
respect of income other than income from shares[44] paid to any
member of the family who does not have enough other income to
use up his annual personal allowance.[45] However, it must be noted
that these figures do not take into account the administration
expenses of the trust which have to be borne out of the taxed income
of the trust before any income is distributed to any of the beneficiaries; consequently, the actual saving is invariably a little less
than the potential saving.

(7) To enable two or more persons to own land. One of the more curious   **1–015**
features of English land law is that, if two or more persons wish to
own land jointly, they cannot be the absolute legal and beneficial
owners of that land; up to four of them can be the legal owners but
all beneficial interests have to take effect behind a trust.[46] Since the
Second World War, it has become increasingly common for married
couples (and for that matter unmarried couples living in a de facto
relationship) to have the family home vested in their joint names
—indeed, building societies and banks normally make any mortgage advance by means of which the property is to be acquired
conditional on this being done. Substantially more than half the
residential property in the country must now be owned jointly in
this way; this means that, technically, well over half the houses in
the country are now held on trust, a fact which would probably
surprise most of their occupants.[47]

(8) To facilitate investment through unit trusts and investment trusts.   **1–016**
The objective of such trusts is to enable the small investor to acquire
a small stake in a large portfolio of investments and thus to spread
his risk across a substantial range of stocks and shares. Further, such
portfolios are sufficiently large for their investments to be super-

---

[42] Income from shares, bank interest, and other sorts of income such as rental income are now
taxed at different rates.

[43] Where dividend income arising under a discretionary trust is paid to a basic rate taxpayer,
in which case the total tax payable is, in 2008–2009, 23.5%.

[44] Income from shares necessarily bears tax of at least 10%.

[45] In 2008–2009, £5,435.

[46] This will be a trust of land under the Trusts of Land and Appointment of Trustees Act 1996.
Before this Act came into force on January 1, 1977, the trust in question would either have been
a trust for sale or a settlement under the Settled Land Act 1925. All pre-existing trusts for sale
have been converted into trusts of land but pre-existing settlements under the Settled Land Act
1925 continue, although no new ones can be created.

[47] This has come to be so much a matter of course that some solicitors are now thought to
have given up explaining the provisions of conveyances of land which declare the trusts upon
which the property is to be held; if this is indeed the case, the fact that the property is to be held
on trust may never even have been mentioned to its purchasers.

vised on a full-time basis. The importance of investment vehicles of this kind for the small investor cannot be overestimated.[48]

In the case of a unit trust, the promoter, usually the future manager, of the unit trust invites the public to subscribe for units of a fixed initial value. The funds so obtained are invested in the stock market, either entirely generally or with at least the majority of the holdings being in a particular nominated sphere, such as in oil companies, or in a particular geographical location, such as the Far East. The investments so purchased are vested in trustees, usually in a trust corporation. The trustees receive the income from the investments which, after payment of the trustees' administration expenses and the remuneration of the manager (usually a percentage of the value of the fund), either are distributed among the investors in proportion to the number of units held or are reinvested to increase the total value of the fund and so of the individual units in it. The manager, who is responsible for selecting the original investments and changing them when he feels this to be appropriate, is obliged to buy back the units at any time at a price fixed by reference to the total value of the fund at any one time. He will offer for sale any units so bought back at a slightly higher price. There are consequently at any one time two different prices at which units are respectively bought back and sold.

An investment trust works in a broadly similar way with two important distinctions. First, the fund is not divided into units so that the capital subscribed can be of any amount which the manager is prepared to accept. Secondly, the individual investors can only deal with their investments on a stock exchange (the manager is not under any obligation to buy the investments back); this consequently means that the price paid will depend on market forces rather than being directly related to the total value of the fund at any one time.

1–017   (9) To enable companies to raise finance from investors on the security of debentures and bonds.

The principal assets of trading companies are their stock in trade, which is continuously bought and sold and so, unlike retained property such as their premises or plant, is not susceptible of being the subject matter of a fixed mortgage or charge.[49] Stock in trade can instead be used as security for funds advanced under what is known as a debenture, or floating charge, which attaches itself to whatever relevant assets the trading company holds at any one time. The interests of the debenture holders, the persons who advance the funds in exchange for the appropriate interest in the

---

[48] Many unit trusts and investment trusts are incorporated in which case they are governed not by trust law but by the Companies Act 2006. All such investment vehicles are in any event subject, in addition to the normal provisions of trust law and company law, to special legislation designed to protect the public against fraud.
[49] The subject matter of fixed mortgages and charges, which also includes residential property mortgaged to the bank or building society which advanced funds for its purchase or improvement, cannot in practice be sold without the mortgage or charge first being paid off.

debenture stock in question, are often protected by having any substantial assets which are subject to those debentures transferred to trustees, usually a trust corporation, on trust for them.

In the same sort of way, funds subscribed to United Kingdom financial institutions, against the issue of what are known as Euro-bonds, for investment throughout Europe and the assets in which the funds raised are subsequently invested are held by the financial institution in question on trust for the subscribers.

(10) To make provision, particularly by will, for causes or for non-human **1–018** objects. By means of a trust money can be donated for the further-ance of education or for the purpose of maintaining a beloved animal such as a favourite dog or cat.

(11) To protect the environment. The Environment Agency has adopted **1–019** the practice of requiring, as a condition of issuing waste manage-ment licences issued under the Environmental Protection Act 1990, that the holders of licences settle on trust adequate sums by way of provision in respect of their duties and obligations under the licences and in particular those relating to the aftercare of the site once the tipping of waste has ceased. The sums settled are payable for the purpose of satisfying any expenses incurred by the Agency in satisfying any such obligations but are returned to the licence holder once those obligations have been satisfied.[50] In other jurisdic-tions, such trusts are of even greater significance.[51]

(12) Last, but by no means least, to provide pensions for retired persons **1–020** and their dependants. This is today by far the most significant purpose of all, both because of the scale of funds which are now devoted to it[52] and because of its immense importance for every member of society other than the fortunate few who have never needed to work. Nothing shows this importance more clearly than the repeated, and so far not very successful, efforts made by the present government to persuade the populace as a whole that it is necessary for everyone to make some provision for his or her retire-ment in addition to the increasingly inadequate pension paid by the state.

---

[50] See *Environment Agency v. Hillridge* [2003] EWHC 3023 (Ch).

[51] Canada has developed what is known as "the 'trusteed' environmental fund" in order to provide some form of assurance for the state that, following the termination of some envir-onmentally harmful activity such as mining or logging, the post-closure land reclamation will be adequately financed. The party carrying out the activity makes periodic payments to trustees who invest these payments for return; and the accumulated fund is the primary or immediate source for meeting the costs of land reclamation (see Waters, *Equity, Fiduciaries and Trusts 1993* (ed. Waters, 1993), p.383). This is similar to the English practice, although on a substantially larger scale. The United States of America has developed an analogous "public trust doctrine", under which each State has a fiduciary obligation to ensure that the public lands which constitute the coastline, the bays of the sea, and the tidal rivers and their beds are made continuously available for the members of the public at large. But English law has no obvious need for any such doctrine since all such lands are already vested in the Crown.

[52] The net value of the investment assets of pension schemes constitutes a very substantial proportion of the available investment capital of the country.

Since the Second World War pension schemes have increasingly been regarded as an essential part of virtually every contract of employment. Pension schemes for employees are either non-contributory, in which case the whole of the money is provided by the employer, or contributory, in which case both the employer and the employee pay into the fund. Their importance for employees is demonstrated by the furore which has accompanied the recent increasing tendency by employers to reduce pension provision because of its ever increasing cost.[53] In the vast majority of cases, pension funds provided for employees are held by trustees with the objective, usually but sadly not always[54] achieved, of assuring the employee that his pension will in fact be forthcoming and that in the meantime his employer cannot in any way dispose of the money.

Pensions are also an important factor for the self-employed, who take out personal pension schemes, facilitated by generous tax concessions (such schemes are also available to employees who either are not members of a pension scheme by virtue of their employment or wish to "top-up" the pension provision made by their employer's scheme). The funds contributed towards such pension schemes are typically paid to insurance companies for investment in insurance policies but can also be held in the form of investments by trustees, in such cases usually by trust corporations.

1–021   All the illustrations which have just been given concern trusts which have been deliberately created in order to achieve the purpose in question. However, trusts can also arise in other ways. The court will in certain circumstances infer the existence of a relationship of trustee and beneficiary where the owner of property has intentionally carried out some other transaction (such trusts are known as "resulting trusts"). The court is also able to impose a relationship of trustee and beneficiary as a result of some type of misconduct by the person who is held to be a trustee (such trusts are known as "constructive trusts").

1–022   The multiple purposes for which trusts can be and are employed today emphasise the importance of the trust in modern law and society. They also make it apparent that one of the greatest advantages of trusts is the flexibility of purpose for which they can be used. Another is the fact that the

---

[53] In 1998 pension schemes lost 10% of their income as a result of the withdrawal of a tax credit to which they had previously been entitled in respect of their income from company distributions. The cost of paying pensions has also progressively increased because of the ever-increasing longevity of the members of pension schemes.

[54] The systematic looting by the late Robert Maxwell of the pension fund established to provide pensions for ex-employees of The Daily Mirror caused great concern among employees in general; pension fund administration then became the subject of a Committee of Inquiry, the Pensions Law Reform Committee, which reported in the autumn of 1993 and came down on the side of continuing to utilise the trust vehicle. A more recent problem has been caused by companies becoming bankrupt and leaving the pension fund with insufficient resources to pay future pensions in full; this problem has. at least in theory, been resolved for the future by the creation of a central fund to bail out the pension funds in question (although whether its resources will prove sufficient for the purpose remains to be seen) but the position of those who had already lost their pensions has not yet been satisfactorily resolved.

rules which govern trusts are by and large the same whatever the purpose for which they are employed. The remainder of this book attempts to explain those rules.

II. THE DEFINITION OF A TRUST

1. *Suggested Definitions*

Considerable difficulty has been found in providing a comprehensive defini-   1–023
tion of a trust, but various attempts have been made. The following definitions deserve consideration.

(A) Lord Coke's Definition

Lord Coke defined a trust as "a confidence reposed in some other, not   1–024
issuing out of the land but as a thing collateral thereto, annexed in privity to
the estate of the land, and to the person touching the land, for which cestui
que trust has no remedy but by subpoena in the Chancery".[55] Some of this
language may require elucidation. When Coke says that a trust is collateral
to land, not issuing out of it, he means that a trust differs from a legal
proprietary interest. Traditionally, a legal proprietary interest has continued
to subsist even after a purchase for value without notice of that interest,
whereas an equitable proprietary interest such as that of a beneficiary under
a trust does not do so and is, for that reason, collateral (this remains accurate
save in the case of interests in registered land whose continued existence
does not normally depend on whether they are legal or equitable). When
Coke says that a trust is annexed in privity to the estate, he means that the
trust will only continue so long as the estate continues and, when he says
that a trust is annexed in privity to the person, he means that a purchaser for
value of the legal estate without notice of the trust will (subject to the same
exception) take free from its provisions.

It has, however, to be said that some objections can be made to Coke's
formulation. First, what is a "confidence"? This expression does not explain
precisely the meaning of "trust". Secondly, the definition imports the idea of
a reliance placed by one person on another. This may not be universally
correct. The *cestui que trust* (or "beneficiary") may be a babe in arms or
unborn or for some other reason wholly ignorant of the trust. The trust in
such cases may still be effective (and normally will be) but the *cestui que trust*
will place no "reliance" whatever on the trustee. Thirdly, Coke's definition
applies only to land, whereas the subject-matter of a trust has always also
been able to be personal chattels. Finally, his definition is procedurally out
of date, although he can hardly be blamed for that! The Court of Chancery
no longer exists and the entire Supreme Court of Judicature now has jurisdiction in equity matters.[56]

Nevertheless, this early definition is undoubtedly worth a mention subject
to the criticisms which have been made, it is at least as useful as most of the
modern definitions.

---

[55] Co. Litt. 272b.
[56] Supreme Court of Judicature (Consolidation) Act 1925, s.4(4).

(B) Sir Arthur Underhill's Definition

1–025   Sir Arthur Underhill, the original author of the leading practitioners' work which is now known as Underhill and Hayton, *Law of Trusts and Trustees*, described a trust as "an equitable obligation binding a person (who is called a trustee) to deal with property over which he has control (which is called trust property), for the benefit of persons (who are called beneficiaries or *cestuis que trust*[57]), of whom he may himself be one and any one of whom may enforce the obligation". In the current edition of this work, this description has been changed to: "an equitable obligation, binding a person (called a trustee) to deal with property (called trust property) owned by him as a separate fund, distinct from his own private property, for the benefit of persons (called beneficiaries or, in old cases, *cestuis que trust*[58]), of whom he may himself be one and any one of whom may enforce the obligation".[59]

As a comprehensive definition of all kinds of trusts, it may be objected that neither version of this one in terms covers charitable trusts or, further, makes any provision for the so-called "trusts of imperfect obligation",[60] such as a trust "for the maintenance and support of my dog Winston"—this may well amount to a valid trust but is a trust of imperfect obligation because Winston cannot enforce it. The successive editors of what is now Underhill and Hayton have, however, pointed out that, even though charitable trusts are outside the scope of the work, they are in any event covered by the definition, simply because such a trust is for the benefit of persons, namely the public, on whose behalf the Attorney-General may intervene.[61] They have also stated that trusts of imperfect obligation are not referred to because they are acknowledged to be "anomalous".[62]

(C) A Judicial Definition

1–026   *Lewin on Trusts*,[63] the other main practitioners' work, refers to a rather more comprehensive definition which was set out by an Australian judge, Mayo J., in *Re Scott*.[64] According to this formulation:

"the word 'trust' refers to the duty or aggregate accumulation of obligations that rest upon a person described as trustee. The responsibilities are in relation to property held by him, or under his control. That property he will be compelled by a court in its equitable jurisdiction to administer in the manner lawfully prescribed by the trust instrument, or where there be no specific provision written or oral, or to the extent that such provision is invalid or lacking, in accordance with equitable principles. As a consequence the administration will be in such a manner that the consequential

---

[57] This is the plural: *"Cestuis que trustent"* is "hopelessly wrong": Sweet (1910) 26 L.Q.R. 196.

[58] This is the plural: *"Cestuis que trustent"* is "hopelessly wrong": Sweet (1910) 26 L.Q.R. 196.

[59] Underhill & Hayton, *Law of Trusts and Trustees*, 18th edn (London, Lexis Nexis, 2006), p.2. The definition was approved by Cohen J. in *Re Marshall's Will Trusts* [1945] Ch. 217 at 219 and by Romer L.J. in *Green v. Russell* [1959] 2 Q.B. 226 at 241.

[60] See *post*, para 8–093.

[61] *op.cit.*, 5, n.2; see *post*, para 11–001.

[62] *ibid.*; see *post*, para 3–093.

[63] 18th edn (London, Sweet & Maxwell, 2008), pp.4–5.

[64] [1948] S.A.S.R. 193 at 196.

benefits and advantages accrue, not to the trustee, but to the persons called *cestuis que trust*, or beneficiaries, if there be any, if not, for some purpose which the law will recognise and enforce. A trustee may be a beneficiary, in which case advantages will accrue in his favour to the extent of his beneficial interest."

(D)   The Definition in the Recognition of Trusts Act 1987

The Recognition of Trusts Act 1987 was enacted in order to incorporate into   **1–027** English law the provisions of The Hague Convention on the Law Applicable to Trusts and their Recognition. This international convention contains the following definition of a trust in Article 2:

"For the purposes of this Convention, the term 'trust' refers to the legal relationships created—inter vivos or on death—by a person, the settlor, when assets have been placed under the control of a trustee for the benefit of a beneficiary or for a specified purpose. A trust has the following characteristics—

(a)   the assets constitute a separate fund and are not part of the trustee's own estate;
(b)   title to the trust assets stands in the name of the trustee or in the name of another person on behalf of the trustee;
(c)   the trustee has the power and the duty, in respect of which he is accountable, to manage, employ or dispose of the assets in accordance with the terms of the trust and the special duties imposed upon him by law.

The reservation by the settlor of certain rights and powers, and the fact that the trustee may himself have rights as a beneficiary, are not necessarily inconsistent with the existence of a trust."

The purpose of the Convention was twofold: first, to provide rules by which the courts of signatory states can uniformly determine the jurisdiction by whose laws trusts with international dimensions are governed (this aspect of the Convention will be considered in detail in Chapter 23) and, secondly, to provide some means of dealing with trusts in jurisdictions where the trust concept is unknown. When property situated in such jurisdictions becomes the subject matter of a trust, problems potentially arise because it can be extremely difficult to convince the authorities of the jurisdiction in question that the trustees are not the beneficial owners of the trust property.

In commercial terms, the principal potential difficulty relates to the issue of Eurobonds by United Kingdom financial institutions to raise funds for the purpose of investment throughout Europe. The funds subscribed and the assets in which they are invested are held on trust for the subscribers. This can cause problems where the funds are invested in those jurisdictions in mainland Europe where the trust concept is unknown. The insolvency of the trustees may cause the authorities in any of these jurisdictions in which trust assets are situated to attempt to take the trust assets for the benefit of the trustees' creditors. Alternatively, where the trustees lend the funds sub-scribed to organisations situated in any of these jurisdictions, doubts may be cast on the ability of the trustees to sue those organisations if the latter default on the loans.

In non-commercial terms, the principal difficulty relates to testamentary dispositions by the increasingly large number of English people who own holiday homes in jurisdictions where the trust concept is unknown. Such owners are quite likely to deal with those homes in the same way as with the rest of their property and leave them by will to their executors and trustees on trust for their surviving spouses and/or their children. The immediate reaction of the authorities of the jurisdiction in question will unquestionably be to treat the trustees as the beneficial owners of the property, something which has potentially adverse fiscal consequences; this is because in many of the jurisdictions of this type the rate of Inheritance Tax payable is deter-mined by how closely the beneficiary is related to the testator[65] and many trustees will inevitably not be in any way related to their testator. Other difficulties can also arise.[66]

The definition set out above is therefore intended to provide the necessary explanation of the nature of a trust in a form which is capable of being applied to and being comprehensible in a large number of different legal systems. For this reason, its format inevitably not only has to include references to a number of features of a trust which are not mentioned in the definitions already considered but also cannot include specific references to features which apply only to English law, such as the fact that the trustee is compellable by a court acting under its equitable jurisdiction. This defini-tion, like the Australian judicial definition referred to in *Lewin on Trusts*, does not roll off the tongue as easily as the one propounded by Sir Arthur Underhill. Nevertheless, its comprehensive nature cannot be disputed and no trust recognised by English law falls outside the four corners of this most recent of the many attempts to define a trust.[67]

---

[65] In Spain, probably the country which contains the largest number of holiday homes owned by English people, this factor determines both the tax free allowance and the rate of tax charged. If the tax free sum to which spouses, ascendants and descendants are entitled is treated as 2X and the rate of tax payable by them is treated as 2Y, then the tax free sum to which more distant relatives are entitled is X and the rate of tax payable by them is 3Y, while beneficiaries who are not related in any way to the testator have no tax free sum whatever and pay tax at the rate of 4Y. The situation is broadly similar, although less extreme, in France.

[66] There may be other adverse fiscal consequences. If the trustees are beneficially entitled to other property in the same jurisdiction, the local Revenue may well try to aggregate the income and capital taxes payable on the trust property with that payable on their own property, thus producing a higher marginal rate of tax (most European countries have many more different rates of tax than the United Kingdom and the top rate is usually substantially higher; in Spain in 2007 it was 58%, which applied to both income tax and capital gains tax). Further, such jurisdictions never recognise the existence of the beneficiaries' equitable interests because there is no way in which they can be protected on the relevant Property Register. This can prejudice the beneficiaries in the event of a dispute between them and the trustees, particularly if the trustees are resident in the jurisdiction in question.

[67] For judicial definitions, see *Sturt v. Mellish* (1743) 2 Atk. 610 at 612, *per* Lord Hardwicke L.C.; *Burgess v. Wheate* (1759) 1 Eden 177 at 223, *per* Lord Mansfield C.J.; *Re Williams* [1897] 2 Ch. 12 at 19 (CA), *per* Lindley L.J. As to the meaning of "trust" and "trustee" in Trustee Act 1925, see *ibid.* s.68(17).

2. *The Essential Elements of a Trust*

All the definitions which have just been considered point to a number of 1–028
essential elements, all of which must be present in order for a trust to be
effectively constituted.

(A) Property Subject to the Trust
No valid trust can be created unless there is some identifiable property 1–029
subject to the trust over which the trustees have control. Any property
whatever can form the subject matter of a trust, whether that property be
tangible, such as a freehold or leasehold interest in land or a collection of
books or silver (English law calls such property "a chose in possession"), or
intangible, such as a share in a company or the benefit of a contractual
obligation (English law calls such property "a chose in action"). It is evident
from these illustrations that it makes no difference whether the property in
question is realty or personalty. Furthermore, it makes no difference whether
the interest subject to the trust is a legal interest or an equitable interest. If
the legal title to property is held by trustees on trust, the interests of the
beneficiaries in that property are necessarily equitable. If any beneficiary
assigns his equitable interest to a third party to hold on quite different trusts,
that equitable interest will constitute the subject matter of the second trust
(technically a sub-trust and therefore subject to certain special rules which
will be considered later[68]); the legal title to the property will nevertheless
remain vested in the original trustees.[69]

However, property subject to a trust must be capable of being identified. 1–030
Consequently a liability cannot, without more, be the subject matter of a
trust. If a creditor suggests to his debtor and the debtor agrees that, instead
of repaying the loan, the debtor should hold the sum in question on trust for
a third party, a valid trust will only arise if the debtor segregates the
appropriate sum from his other assets by, for example, opening a new bank
account for the purpose. If he does so, the trust will then be of the segregated
assets, not of the liability. If, on the other hand, he fails to do so, something
which in practice is highly likely since if the debtor had the assets to
segregate he could equally easily have repaid the loan on the spot, the third
party will be unable to point to any property subject to any trust and so will
have no remedy.[70]

(B) One or More Trustees
There must be one or more trustees in whom title to the trust property is 1–031
vested. In principle, any number of persons may be trustees but this basic

---

[68] See *post*, para 4–018.

[69] See *Gilbert v. Overton* (1804) 2 H. & M. 110.

[70] Exactly this situation arose in *M'Fadden v. Jenkyns* (1842) 1 Ph. 153; however, despite the fact
that all three parties had clearly intended the debtor to be the trustee, Lord Lyndhurst L.C.
generously found that the effect of the agreement was that the creditor held his right to sue the
debtor on trust for the third party, thus providing her with a remedy against his personal
representatives. The creditor can of course create such a situation intentionally; in *Barclays Bank
v. Willowbrook International* (1987) 1 F.T.L.R. 386, a creditor charged to the bank a debt which was
due to be repaid and the Court of Appeal held that any repayments made by the debtor were
held by the creditor on constructive trust for the bank.

rule is now subject to a number of statutory restrictions which will be discussed in detail later on.[71] Briefly, there can be no more than four trustees of either a non-charitable trust of land[72] or a trust of property of any type for a minor which was created as the result of a death and where no trustees were appointed by the will in question.[73]

1–032   If a trust is created by a person during his lifetime (in which case it is said to have been created *"inter vivos"*), there may well be no trustee other than the person who has created the trust, who is known as its settlor; in such circumstances, he will have created the trust by declaration, by simply declaring that from then on he is holding the property in question on trust for the objects in question. Alternatively, and necessarily if a trust is created as the result of a death (in which case it is said to have been created *"mortis causa"*), the trust may be created by transfer; in this case the trustees will be those persons (normally more than one in order to avoid the problems which might arise if a sole trustee died) to whom the settlor or the deceased has transferred the property in question; in the case of an *inter vivos* trust, the settlor will frequently be one of the initial trustees. If a settlor attempts to create an *inter vivos* trust by purporting to transfer property to trustees who are neither named nor identified or to persons who are already dead, no valid trust will have been created. If, on the other hand, a testator fails to nominate any trustees in his will, his personal representatives will hold the property in question as trustees until other trustees are appointed.

1–033   Once a trust has been validly constituted, it cannot thereafter fail for want of a trustee since anyone in whom the trust property comes to be vested, other than a bona fide purchaser for value of a legal interest in the property without notice of the interests of the beneficiaries[74] (or, in the case of registered land, the statutory equivalent[75]), will be bound by that trust and so will be a trustee of the property.

(C) An Equitable Obligation

1–034   The trustees must be under an equitable obligation, often described as a fiduciary duty, to deal with the trust property for the persons, purposes or objects defined by the settlor or testator—if they are not under any duty to do anything at all, there cannot be a trust (this does not prevent trustees being given completely unfettered discretions as to whether and, if so, how to deal with the trust property; their duty in such cases consists of being obliged to consider from time to time what, if anything, they should do[76]). This equitable obligation not only imposes on the trustees potential personal liabilities to the beneficiaries, liabilities which can be both penal and

---

[71] See *post*, para 13–049.
[72] Trustee Act 1925, s.34(3).
[73] Administration of Estates Act 1925, s.42.
[74] The one person whose interests are always preferred to those of the beneficiaries of a trust (see *Basset v. Nosworthy* (1673) Rep.Temp.Finch 102, where this time honoured rule was laid down by Lord Nottingham L.C.). For this reason, such a person has traditionally been known as "equity's darling".
[75] A bona fide purchaser for valuable consideration (other than marriage consideration) claiming under a registered disposition (Land Registration Act 2002, ss.28–31, 129(1), 132(1)); some commentators jocularly refer to such a person as "the Registrar's darling".
[76] See *post*, Chapter 5.

extremely stringent[77]; it also binds the trust property itself in the hands of anyone who has not taken free of the interests of the beneficiaries in that property for the reasons stated above.

(D) One or More Beneficiaries

No trust can exist without one or more beneficiaries (or *cestuis que trust*) for whose benefit the property is held. The trustees may also be some or all of the beneficiaries (most co-owners of land hold the land in question as trustees on trust for themselves[78]) but a sole trustee cannot also be the sole beneficiary—in this event, there would simply be no trust.

    The precise nature of the interest of a beneficiary in the trust property has always been difficult to define.[79] On the one hand, the beneficiary has a proprietary interest in the subject matter of the trust because he can recover it from anyone into whose hands it passes other than a bona fide purchaser for value of a legal interest in that property without notice of the interest of the beneficiary (or, in the case of registered land, the statutory equivalent); his right is, therefore, clearly more than what is known as a right *in personam*, a merely personal right. On the other hand, given that, if the property does reach the hands of such a person, it cannot be recovered by the beneficiary, whose only option will then be to bring a personal action against his trustees for breach of trust, his interest is certainly not what is known as a right *in rem*, an indefeasible proprietary interest. The best view is that the interest of a beneficiary is a true hybrid—substantially more than a right *in personam* but substantially less than a right *in rem*. This is reflected by the decided cases, which regard the beneficiary as owner of the trust property for some purposes but not for others. Thus in *Baker v. Archer-Shee*,[80] the beneficiary was held to be the real owner of the trust assets for income tax purposes. On the other hand, in *Schalit v. Joseph Nadler*,[81] a beneficiary whose trustees had granted a lease of the trust property was held unable to distrain (take chattels found on the land) in order to satisfy the rent due under that lease. The Divisional Court stated that "[t]he right of the *cestui que trust* whose trustee has demised property subject to the trust is not to the rent, but to an account from the trustees of the profits received from the trust".[82] Both decisions appear to be in accordance with principle.

1–035

1–036

3. *"Trusts in the Higher Sense" and "Trusts in the Lower Sense"*

As Lord O'Hagan once said,[83] there is no magic in the word "trust", which can mean different things in different contexts. For example, a person may be in a position of trust without being a trustee in the equitable sense and terms such as "anti-trust" or "trust territories" are not intended to relate to a trust enforceable in a court of equity. By the same token, a trust in the

1–037

---

[77] See *post*, paras 10–046–10–152.

[78] Law of Property Act 1925, ss.34, 36 as amended by Trusts of Land and Appointment of Trustees Act 1996, Sch.2, paras 3, 4.

[79] See Latham (1954) 32 Can B.R. 520 on the question generally.

[80] [1927] A.C. 844.

[81] [1933] 2 K.B. 79.

[82] *ibid*. at 83.

[83] In *Kinloch v. Secretary of State for India in Council* (1882) 7 App. Cas. 619 at 630.

conventional legal sense may be created without actually using the word "trust".[84] In each case it is necessary to consider whether the latter type of trust was or was not intended.[85]

This is exactly what had to be decided in *Tito v. Waddell (No. 2)*,[86] a case which Megarry V.-C. aptly described as "litigation on a grand scale".[87] The case involved Ocean Island, a small island in the Pacific, called Banaba by its inhabitants, who were unsurprisingly known as Banabans. The island had formerly been part of the Gilbert and Ellice Islands Protectorate and subsequently became a Crown Colony. At the beginning of the twentieth century, phosphate was discovered on the island and royalties for mining the phosphate were duly paid to the islanders. As time passed, the Banabans understandably sought increases in the royalty payments. Some increases were paid but they were considerably less than the amounts claimed by the Banabans. The latter continued to make various claims of a political and an international nature; however, when those claims finally failed, they brought proceedings, claiming that the rates of royalties payable in respect of certain transactions had been less than the proper rates and that accordingly the Crown, as the responsible authority, was subject to a trust or fiduciary duty for the benefit of the Banabans or their predecessors and was liable for breach of that duty.

1–038   The question as to whether there was indeed such a trust or fiduciary duty involved the construction of various agreements and ordinances as well as other documents. In the event, it was held that there was neither a trust nor a fiduciary duty. The essential elements of the decision for the purposes of any definition of a trust[88] appear to be as follows:

(1) Although the word "trust" had occasionally been used with reference to the Crown or its agents, that did not create a trust which was enforceable in the courts (what Megarry V.-C. described as a "trust in the lower sense" or "true trust") but rather a trust "in the higher sense", by which was meant a governmental obligation which was not enforceable in the courts.[89]

(2) Such a trust "in the higher sense" could only be discharged under the direction of the Crown.[90] There might be many means available of persuading the Crown to honour its governmental obligations, for example, by means of international pressure, but even if its obligations were higher than normal obligations they were not enforceable by the court.[91]

---

[84] *Tito v. Waddell (No. 2)* [1977] Ch. 106 at 211, *per* Megarry V.-C.

[85] See *post*, paras 3–002–3–012.

[86] [1977] Ch. 106.

[87] *ibid*. at 123. The report of the judgment of Megarry V.-C. runs to 241 pages. The Vice-Chancellor also held a view of the *locus in quo* (the Pacific island in question).

[88] For other aspects of the decision, see *post*, paras 10–082, 22–062.

[89] Adopting the language of Lord Selborne L.C. in *Kinloch v. Secretary of State for India in Council* (1882) 7 App. Cas. 619 at 625.

[90] *Tito v. Waddell (No.2)* [1977] Ch. 106 at 216.

[91] *ibid*. at 217.

(3) Although some of the ordinances imposed statutory duties on the Crown, they did not also impose fiduciary obligations. As will be seen later on,[92] in some cases a person may be in a fiduciary position even though he is not a fiduciary in the proper sense of the word (such as a trustee, an agent, a company director or a partner) and such a person will be liable if he is in breach of his fiduciary obligations. A relationship giving rise to fiduciary obligations may be either legal or equitable or purely statutory but it must be a relationship with enforceable legal consequences.[93] However, as Megarry V.-C. specifically held, "a trust in the higher sense or governmental obligation lacks this characteristic and where the primary obligation itself is one which the courts will not enforce, then it [cannot] of itself give rise to a secondary obligation which is enforceable by the courts".[94]

(4) If a duty is imposed by statute (such as the ordinances in this case) to perform certain functions, that statute will not, as a general rule, also impose fiduciary obligations nor is it to be presumed that it does so. It has to be affirmatively shown that such obligations are indeed imposed.[95]

Suffice it to say that this book is concerned with "trusts in the lower sense" or "true trusts" and with those situations which give rise to enforceable fiduciary obligations. 1–039

4. *Sources of the Law of Trusts*

It has already been seen[96] that trusts emerged as a re-establishment of uses some 150 years after the enactment of the Statute of Uses 1536 and that those beneficially entitled under uses and, later, under trusts were only ever protected in the Court of Chancery. The early Chancellors were usually bishops rather than lawyers and, in exercising the residue of judicial power left in the hands of the King after the establishment of the Courts of Common Law, they acted as keepers of the King's conscience, giving or withholding a remedy to the persons who petitioned them on the basis of their view what the conscience of the petitioner and the respondent in question demanded. At that stage it could fairly be said that, in so far as the Court of Chancery had any rules at all, they varied according to the views of each Chancellor. Indeed, decisions of the Court of Chancery were not even formally recorded until the middle of the sixteenth century—the earlier 1–040

---

[92] See *post*, para 10–047 *et seq.*
[93] [1977] Ch. 106 at 224.
[94] *ibid.* at 225.
[95] *ibid.* at 235. See also *Swain v. The Law Society* [1983] A.C. 598 (in exercising a statutory power the Law Society was performing not a private duty but a public duty for breach of which there was no remedy in breach of trust or equitable account); see further *post*, p.282.
[96] See *ante*, paras 1–001—1–007.

activities of the Chancellors can only be reviewed on the basis of the petitions received by them and any decrees endorsed on those petitions.

1–041   Even so, however, it is clear from other records that successive Chancellors gradually extended the protection given to those beneficially entitled under uses. Initially a use was enforceable only as against the third parties to whom the property had been originally transferred subject to that use; however, in 1465 it was laid down that a use would also be enforced against any transferee of the property in question who had notice of the use,[97] in 1483 the Chancellor stated that a use would also be enforced against any heir of the third parties who inherited the property in question,[98] and in 1522 it was said that a use would also be enforced against anyone to whom the third parties had given the property in question whether or not that person had notice of the use[99] (later on, Lord Nottingham was to consolidate these developments by enunciating[100] the time honoured rule to which reference has already been made[101] that the interests of the beneficiaries of a trust bind the whole world other than a bona fide purchase for value of a legal interest in the property without notice of the interest of the beneficiaries).

1–042   These extensions of the protection given to those beneficially entitled under uses constituted some of the earliest substantive principles of what later came to be known as the rules of equity. By the middle of the sixteenth century the typical Chancellor was a lawyer rather than a bishop. At about the same time the decisions of the Court of Chancery began to be formally recorded and, in due course, to be the subject matter of law reports. Consequently, at the beginning of the seventeenth century, Lord Ellesmere (1596–1617) was able to begin to develop the rules of equity into a code of principles and the later work of Lord Nottingham (1673–1682) in systematising those rules earned him the title of "the father of equity".

The rules of equity were therefore developed by the Chancellors rather than by the legislature and even today the rules of equity are principally derived from decided cases rather than from statute—in this jurisdiction the law of trusts has never been codified.[102]

1–043   Nevertheless, as early as 1677 the legislature intervened to establish mandatory formal requirements for the creation of *inter vivos* trusts of land and of interests under pre-existing trusts[103] and in 1837 similarly intervened to

---

[97] Y.B. 5 Edw. IV, Mich., Pl. 16.

[98] Y.B. 22 Edw. IV, Pasch., Pl. 18.

[99] Y.B. 14 Hen. VIII, Mich. Pl. 5, fol. 7.

[100] In *Basset v. Nosworthy* (1673) Rep.Temp.Finch 102.

[101] See *ante*, paras 1–033, 1–036.

[102] This is also true of the vast majority of the jurisdictions where the law of trusts has been established as part of the common law, such as the common law jurisdictions of the United States of America, Canada and the Caribbean and the remaining jurisdictions of the old Commonwealth such as Australia, New Zealand and Hong Kong. It is only where the law of trusts has been introduced into Commonwealth jurisdictions whose pre-existing law was not common law, such as India, Jersey, and Guernsey, or into jurisdictions which have never had anything to do with the common law, such as Liechtenstein, The Netherlands and the non-common law Caribbean jurisdictions, that it has been necessary for that law to be codified (a few off-shore jurisdictions, such as Belize and the Turks & Caicos Islands, have also codified their law of trusts for marketing purposes).

[103] Statute of Frauds 1677, ss.3, 7 and 9.

establish mandatory formal requirements for wills which obviously applied to all trusts *mortis causa*.[104] Provisions of this type, in an amended form, still exist today.[105]

The legislature has also, during the last 150 years, increasingly intervened   **1–044** in relation to such matters as the appointment and removal of trustees and the administrative duties and powers of trustees. The pattern of these legislative interventions is typified by the provisions of the Trustee Act 1925 and the Trustee Act 2000. Provisions governing the appointment and removal of trustees[106] are mandatory; the provisions of the trust deed or will in question are relevant only to the extent that the statutory provisions specifically so provide.[107] Provisions imposing specific duties on trustees[108] are also mandatory, although the trustees in question may nevertheless escape liability for any breach of these provisions if the trust deed or will in question contains a valid exemption clause on which they can rely.[109] On the other hand, provisions conferring powers on trustees[110] generally[111] apply only to the extent that a contrary intention is not expressed in the trust deed or will in question[112]; such contrary intentions can either enlarge or reduce the statutory powers in question.

These are the sources of the law of trusts with which this book has to deal.

III. THE DISTINCTION BETWEEN TRUSTS AND OTHER LEGAL CONCEPTS

1. *Contract*

English law recognises two types of contract, the simple contract (a contract   **1–045** constituted as a result of the existence of an offer and acceptance, intention to create legal relations, and consideration) and the specialty contract (a contract constituted by virtue of being in a deed), often also described as a covenant.

---

[104] Wills Act 1837, s.9. see *post*, para 4–006.

[105] See, *post*, paras 4–006–4–050.

[106] Trustee Act 1925, ss.34–40. See *post*, Chapter 13.

[107] In that, for example, the settlor or testator can nominate who is to appoint new or additional trustees (see Trustee Act 1925, s.36(1)(a)).

[108] Such as the duty of care imposed by Trustee Act 2000, ss.1–2 and Sch.1; see *post*, para 14–002 *et seq.*

[109] See *post*, para 22–078 *et seq.*

[110] Such as the powers of maintenance and advancement contained in Trustee Act 1925, ss.31–32; see *post*, paras 17–035, 18–006.

[111] There are some exceptions; see, for example, Trustee Act 1925, s.14 (power of trustees to give receipts).

[112] Trustee Act 1925, s.69 (2), which applies to all the relevant remaining provisions of that Act. Trustee Act 2000 so provides in respect of each relevant Part (see ss.6, 9, 26 governing respectively Parts II, III and IV) and some further sections (see ss.28(1), 29(5)).

Until the enactment of the Contracts (Rights of Third Parties) Act 1999 on November 11, 1999, the general rule, to which there were exceptions, was that neither a simple contract[113] nor a specialty contract[114] was enforceable by a person who was not a party to that contract. These rules were in stark contrast with the rule that a trust has always been able to be enforced by a beneficiary who was not a party to the instrument creating the trust (indeed, it is very unusual for beneficiaries to be parties to such instruments save in the case where the settlor is also a beneficiary). However, the rigidity of the general rule was mitigated by the possibility of creating a trust of the benefit of the contract in question.

1–046 It has always been (and remains) the law that, if one of the parties to either form of contract expressly or impliedly contracts as trustee for a third party, that third party is entitled to the benefit of the contract by virtue of being the beneficiary of a trust. The party who contracted as trustee can obviously enforce the contract on behalf of the third party anyway[115] but, in the event that he does not do so, the third party can sue as *cestui que trust* joining the trustee as co-claimant or, if he declines to be joined in that capacity, as co-defendant.[116]

1–047 It has also always been (and still is) possible for a person who has not originally contracted as a trustee subsequently to create a trust of the benefit of a contract for a third party either by declaring a trust of its benefit or by assigning the contract to trustees to hold on trust. Such a trust may be created either gratuitously or pursuant to the provisions of a contract between the original contracting party and the third party (whether or not a trust has actually been created is a question of construction).[117] Even where the contract in question is incapable of being assigned because, for example, it is a contract for the provision of personal services, a trust can nevertheless be declared of its benefit unless this is specifically prohibited by the contract[118]; but in such a case the third party would not be permitted to put the subject matter of the trust, the non-assignable contract, at risk by attempting

---

[113] The general rule seems to have been firmly established as a result of the decisions of the House of Lords in *Midland Silicones v. Scruttons* [1962] A.C. 446 and *Beswick v. Beswick* [1968] A.C. 58; it was subject to a number of recognised exceptions founded in statute but, apart from Law of Property Act 1925, s.56 (which applies only to land), they had (and have) no particular relevance to the law of trusts.

[114] *Cannon v. Hartley* [1949] Ch. 213, *Beswick v. Beswick* [1968] A.C. 98 at 102–105. The same statutory exceptions applied (and apply). However, a deed poll, a deed to which only the covenantor is named as a party, could and can be enforced by anyone with whom he purports to make that deed.

[115] In which case he can recover on behalf of the third party beneficiary the damages suffered by the latter as well as the nominal damages suffered by himself (see *Gregory and Parker v. Williams* (1817) 3 Mer. 582; *Lloyd's v. Harper* (1880) 16 Ch. D. 290).

[116] *Vandepitte v. Preferred Accident Insurance Corporation of New York* [1933] A.C. 70 at 79. This principle does not entitle a beneficiary to institute proceedings in tort for negligence on behalf of his trust by joining the trustees in this way (see *Bradstock Trustee Services v. Nabarro Nathanson* [1995] 1 W.L.R. 1405 at 1411); outside the contractual area, the right of a beneficiary to intervene in proceedings is limited to cases where the position of the trustees has been compromised by virtue of a breach of trust, a conflict of interest and duty, or some other exceptional circumstances (see *Hayim v. Citibank* [1987] A.C. 730 at 747–748).

[117] *Don King Productions v. Warren* [2000] Ch. 291.

[118] *ibid.* at 320–322 (Lightman J.), 335 (C.A.).

himself to enforce it against the other original party in the ways indicated in the previous paragraph.[119]

However, Section 1 of the Contracts (Rights of Third Parties) Act 1999 **1–048** provides that a third party to a contract who is identifiable may enforce any term of that contract in his own right provided that either the contract so provides or the term in question purports to confer a benefit on him and it does not appear, on a proper construction of that term, that the parties did not intend him to be able to do so. A third party will be identifiable if he is expressly identified by name, or is a member of an identified class, or answers a specific description; there is no requirement that he should have been in existence at the date of the contract.[120] The Act applies automatically to both simple contracts and specialty contracts entered into on or after May 11, 2000, six months after the Act was passed.[121]

The enactment of this legislation does not of course prevent a party to a **1–049** contract either from expressly or implied contracting as a trustee, or from making a declaration of trust of the benefit of a contract, or from assigning that benefit to trustees on trust. Contracting expressly as a trustee or subsequently creating a trust of the benefit of a contract has never given rise to any difficulties. The real difficulty before the legislation was to know when a trust of the benefit of a contract was to be implied; this difficulty obviously survives in the case of those contracts to which the legislation does not apply. In this respect, simple contracts and specialty contracts require separate consideration.

The series of decisions in which the courts have considered whether or not a trust of the benefit of a simple contract is to be implied,[122] which were examined in detail in previous editions of this book,[123] are not particularly easy to reconcile. However, it appears from the later decisions such as *Re*

---

[119] *ibid.*

[120] This is particularly important in the case of specialty contracts because the beneficiaries of trusts of after acquired property which are the subject matter of a covenant to settle are more often than not unborn at the time when the covenant is entered into; see *post*, para 5–084 *et seq*.

[121] The Act also applied to contracts entered into during that six month period if the contracts in question contained an express provision to that effect; Contracts (Rights of Third Parties) Act 1999, s.10.

[122] *Re Flavell* (1883) 25 Ch. D. 89 (trust implied of the benefit of a provision in articles of partnership whereby the surviving partner was to pay an annuity to the widow of his co-partner); *Les Affreteurs Reunis S.A. v. Leopold Walford (London)* [1919] A.C. 801 (charterer held to have contracted with the shipowner as trustee for the charterer's broker, thus enabling the charterer to sue the shipowner for the commission payable under the contract to the broker); *Harmer v. Armstrong* [1934] Ch. 65 (specific performance ordered of a contract for the sale of the copyright in certain periodicals which had been entered into for the benefit of the plaintiff); *Vandepitte v. Preferred Accident Insurance Corporation of New York* [1933] A.C. 70 (P.C.) (third party motor insurance policy issued by the defendant which covered all persons driving the car with the consent of the owner not entered into by the latter as trustee for his daughter who, while driving the care with the consent of the owner, had negligently injured the plaintiff; had the owner been a trustee and the contract had therefore been enforceable by his daughter, the plaintiff would have been subrogated to her rights under the relevant British Columbian legislation); *Re Schebsman* [1944] Ch. 83 (see below); *Swain v. The Law Society* [1983] A.C. 598 (see below).

[123] See the 7th (1998) edition, pp.19–23.

Schebsman[124] (now over 60 years ago) and *Swain v. The Law Society*[125] (now over 25 years ago), which are summarised in the footnotes, that the courts have increasingly turned their backs on the earlier authorities and are now most reluctant to interpret a contract as creating a trust in the absence of the clearest possible evidence that a trust was intended. This view derives further support from the significant fact that no reliance was placed on the trust concept by the members of the House of Lords when they were deciding *Beswick v. Beswick*,[126] also summarised in the footnotes. These decisions would remain applicable in the relatively unlikely event that an action were now brought to enforce a simple contract entered into before May 11, 2000; however, only contracts of option entered into before that date are likely still to be executory and few if any of those are likely to be in favour of third parties.

1–050 However, these decisions are also in principle still applicable to later contracts in any situations in which the provisions of the Contracts (Rights of Third Parties) Act 1999 do not apply.

Given that the trend of the recent authorities is against implying trusts of the benefit of a simple contract, it seems inconceivable that a trust of the benefit of such a contract would be implied in the two situations where the

---

[124] [1944] Ch. 83. A company agreed with one of its employees that, in consideration of his retirement, it would pay certain sums to him during his lifetime and after his death to his wife and child. He subsequently became bankrupt and died soon afterwards. The question then arose as to whether his trustee in bankruptcy could "intercept" the money which the employers were willing to pay to the wife and child. The Court of Appeal held that the employee had not entered into the contract as a trustee for his wife and child. Du Parcq L.J. said (at 104) that, unless an intention to create a trust was clearly to be collected from the language used and the circumstances of the case, the court ought not to be "astute" to discover implications of any such intention. The wife and child, therefore, could not enforce the contract against the company (however, the court went on to hold that the trustee in bankruptcy could not intercept the payments because the employee would not have been able to do so; consequently, the company was free to comply with the terms of the contract and make the required payments).

[125] [1983] A.C. 598. The Law Society had under its statutory powers arranged a master policy for the provision of indemnity insurance, something which was compulsory for all practising solicitors. It had been agreed that a proportion of the commission earned by the insurance brokers should be paid to The Law Society, which would apply it for the benefit of the profession as a whole. Two solicitors claimed that The Law Society was a trustee of the benefit of the master policy contract for the benefit of all individual solicitors and was, therefore, accountable for the proportion of the commission which it received. Reliance was placed on the fact that the policy contract stated that the policy was being entered into "on behalf of" solicitors and former solicitors, words which, it was claimed, imputed an intention to create a trust. The House of Lords held that these words were clearly insufficient to express a trust and did not necessarily imply one. Lord Brightman said (at 621): "it would indeed, be surprising if a society of lawyers, who above all might be expected to make their intention clear in a document they compose, should have failed to express the existence of a trust if that was what they intended to create."

[126] [1968] A.C. 58. A nephew was employed by his uncle in the latter's business as a coal merchant. An agreement was made between them whereby the uncle assigned the business to the nephew in return for the nephew's promise to pay the uncle £6/10/- a week for the rest of his life and, after his death, to pay an annuity of £5 a week to his widow. The nephew complied with this agreement during his uncle's lifetime but after his death made only one payment to the widow. The House of Lords held that the widow had no claim against him in her personal capacity because she was not a party to the contract; however, she was held to be entitled to obtain specific performance of the contract as her husband's administratrix.

Act expressly provides that it does not apply.[127] These situations are: first, where, in the absence of an express provision providing that the third party may enforce the contract, it does not, on a proper construction of a term of the contract purporting to confer a benefit on him, appear that the parties intended him to be able to enforce it; and, secondly, where the third party in question is not identifiable. This seems inconceivable because, in none of the authorities referred to above, was there the slightest doubt that the third parties were intended to benefit from the contract and in all of them the third parties were clearly identifiable.

However, section 2 of the Act provides that, where a third party has rights under section 1, the parties to a contract may not rescind it without his consent where the third party has communicated to the person who is bound by the term in question his assent to that term. It must follow as a necessary corollary of this provision that, at least so far as the Act is concerned, the parties to the contract can rescind any contract conferring rights on a third party under section 1 where the third party has not so communicated his consent. But any such rescission by a person who actually held the benefit of the term in question on trust for the third party would be a breach of that trust by him. Consequently, if the third party only finds out about the existence of the term in question after the parties have purported to rescind the contract, it will remain highly relevant whether or not there is such a trust.[128] Such a situation may appear somewhat far-fetched in respect of simple contracts but, as will be seen below, it certainly is not in relation to specialty contracts. However, it nevertheless remains as unlikely as it was before the enactment of the Contracts (Rights of Third Parties) Act 1999 that any trust of the benefit of a simple contract will now be implied.

Specialty covenants for the benefit of third parties are, typically, covenants   **1–051**
between a settlor and his trustees to settle on trust what is known as after-acquired property, property which had not yet come into existence when the covenant was entered into. While there is in principle no reason why the intended beneficiaries of the trust should not also be parties to the covenant in question, in which case it has always been clear that they can enforce that covenant as against the settlor,[129] in practice those beneficiaries will almost always be third parties to the covenant.

Prior to the enactment of the Contracts (Rights of Third Parties) Act 1999, it was accepted and established that the beneficiaries could enforce the covenant against the settlor by joining the trustees as co-claimants or co-defendants if there was an express or implied trust of the benefit of the specialty contract[130]; however, there was a great deal of controversy as to when such a trust could be implied. In the absence of such a trust, it was accepted and established that the beneficiaries were unable to compel the trustees to enforce the covenant against the settlor.[131] It was also established that the trustees would be directed not to enforce the covenant against the

---

[127] Contracts (Rights of Third Parties) Act 1999, s.1.
[128] See Halliwell [2003] Conveyancer 192.
[129] *Cannon v. Hartley* [1949] Ch. 213.
[130] As in *Fletcher v. Fletcher* (1844) 4 Hare 67.
[131] *Re d'Angibau* (1880) 15 Ch.D. 228.

settlor if they sought the directions of the court.[132] Although it has been argued that the courts were wrong to restrain the parties to a covenant from exercising their legal rights to sue under that covenant if they wished to do so,[133] the likely consequences of such an exercise suggested that the established state of the law should be upheld.[134]

1–052   However, the effect of the enactment of the Contracts (Rights of Third Parties) Act 1999 has unquestionably been to permit such beneficiaries to enforce the covenant directly against the settlor where that Act is applicable. To what extent does the pre-existing law remain relevant following the enactment of the Contracts (Rights of Third Parties) Act 1999? It is of course much more likely than in the case of simple contracts that specialty contracts entered into before May 11, 2000 are still outstanding; it is obviously possible for after-acquired property which such specialty contracts covenanted to settle on trust to be acquired by the settlor only after that date. In such circumstances, it will obviously remain crucial whether or not there is a trust of the benefit of the specialty contract.

1–053   In respect of such contracts entered into on or after that date, the position seems to be as follows. No trust could arise where the beneficiaries were unidentifiable, since any such trust would be void for uncertainty of objects.[135] On the other hand, it could certainly be decided as a matter of construction that the settlor did not intend the beneficiaries to be able to enforce the term of the covenant purporting to confer a benefit on them; but in such circumstances, it would be wholly inconsistent with such a decision to uphold the existence of an implied trust of the benefit of the specialty contract and the existence of such a trust is therefore inconceivable.

1–054   However, it is certainly possible for a beneficiary only to find out about the existence of the specialty contract after the settlor has purported to rescind it under section 2 of the Contracts (Rights of Third Parties) Act 1999. The settlor may initially conceal the existence of the covenant (as happened in the leading case,[136] where he concealed it until after his death[137]) and later purport to rescind it. Another possibility is that the beneficiary may not be born or may not attain the age of majority until after the settlor has purported to rescind the covenant. In such circumstances, it will obviously continue to be highly relevant whether or not there is a trust of its benefit. Further, even where the Contracts (Rights of Third Parties) Act 1999 is applicable to a specialty contract, there are some circumstances in which the existence or non-existence of a trust of the benefit of that contract may determine precisely who is beneficially entitled to the property to be settled.[138] Consequently, the pre-existing law remains relevant in a number of circumstances even where the specialty contract in question was entered into after May 11, 2000 and obviously remains relevant where it was entered

---

[132] *Re Pryce* [1917] 1 Ch. 234; *Re Kay* [1939] Ch. 329; *Re Cook's Settlement Trusts* [1965] Ch. 92.

[133] Particularly by Elliott (1960) 76 L.Q.R. 100.

[134] See *post*, paras 5–104–5–110.

[135] See *post*, para 3–029 *et seq.*

[136] *Fletcher v. Fletcher* (1844) 4 Hare 67.

[137] The beneficiaries were the settlor's illegitimate sons and it seems tolerably clear that the settlor did not wish anyone to become aware of their existence until after his death.

[138] See Halliwell [2003] Conveyancer 192.

into before that date. That pre-existing law is best considered in the context of the general rules governing the ways in which a trust can be completely constituted.[139]

2. Debt

It has already been seen that a liability cannot, without more, be the subject matter of a trust and that a debtor will only be able to create a valid trust of the sum owed in favour of his creditor or of a third party if he segregates the appropriate amount from his other assets.[140] Such a trust will clearly come into existence where the debtor makes an express declaration of trust in respect of duly segregated assets. The effect of the creation of such a trust will be to give its beneficiary an advantage over the other creditors of the debtor in the event of his bankruptcy—this is because the proprietary right of the beneficiary will enjoy priority over the purely personal rights of any unsecured general creditors. For this reason, in the event that the debtor does subsequently become insolvent, such a trust will be vulnerable to challenge under the Insolvency Act 1986[141] on the grounds that it amounts to preferential treatment (technically known as a "preference") of the beneficiary vis-à-vis the general creditors. However, if consideration is given to the possibility of the debtor's insolvency at the time when the debt is first created, it is sometimes possible for the creditor to obtain a priority which cannot be successfully challenged.

1–055

There is in principle no reason why the same transaction should not give rise to both a trust and a debt; a loan for a specific purpose can be made in such a way that the sum advanced will be held on trust for the lender unless and until that purpose is carried out. This was specifically held by the House of Lords in *Barclays Bank v. Quistclose Investments*.[142] Quistclose Investments advanced money to a company for the purpose of paying a dividend on its shares. The advance was made on the basis that the money was to be used only for this purpose but the company became insolvent before the dividend had been paid. The House of Lords held that arrangements for the payment of a debtor's creditors by a third person were capable of giving rise to a trust unless and until the creditors were paid.[143] Once they were paid, the third person would become no more than an unsecured creditor of the debtor. However, there was "no difficulty in recognising the co-existence in one transaction of legal and equitable rights and remedies".[144] If instead the creditors were not paid and the purpose for which the money had been advanced therefore failed, the money would, as between the debtor and the third party, still be held on trust by the debtor for the third party.

1–056

The potential advantages of such a trust for the person advancing the money are demonstrated by the facts of the two leading cases. In *Barclays Bank v. Quistclose Investments*, the principal creditor of the company was the

1–057

---

[139] See *post*, paras 5–104–5–119.
[140] See *ante*, para 1–030.
[141] s.239 in the case of companies, s.340 in the case of individuals. See *post*, paras 7–056–7–061.
[142] [1970] A.C. 567.
[143] [1970] A.C. 567 at 580.
[144] *ibid.* at 581.

bank with whom the money advanced by Quistclose Investments had been deposited. If Quistclose Investments was merely an unsecured creditor of the company, it would enjoy no priority over any other creditors, the money in the bank would belong to the company, and the bank would be entitled to set off the credit balance of the account against the much larger amount owed to it by the company.[145] If, on the other hand, the money was held on trust for Quistclose Investments, its proprietary interest in that money would be capable of enjoying priority over the rights of the bank. In *Twinsectra v. Yardley*[146] the claimant had made a loan on the basis that the sum advanced was paid to the borrower's solicitors, who gave an undertaking to the claimant to utilise the loan money solely for the acquisition of property on behalf of the borrower and for no other purpose. In breach of that undertaking, the solicitors transferred most of that money to another solicitor; he disbursed the funds transferred to him in accordance with the instructions of the borrower but not all of those funds were spent on the acquisition of property. If the arrangement between the parties had given rise to a trust, the claimant would be able both to recover the product of the disbursements made by the other solicitor[147] and to seek to impeach the conduct of that solicitor because of his involvement in what would then amount to a breach of trust.[148] In each of these two cases, the House of Lords upheld the existence of a trust and the creditor obtained the consequential advantages.

1–058   It is theoretically possible for the parties to an arrangement of this type to have expressly agreed that, in the event that the specific purpose fails, the recipient of the money will hold it on trust for the person who paid it; in that event, the trust in his favour will obviously be an express trust. In practice, however, there is unlikely to have been any such express agreement; there was not in either of the two cases considered above. In that event, *Twinsectra v. Yardley* establishes that any failure of the purpose will give rise to a resulting trust of the money in favour of the person who paid it. Since this is generally the way in which what have become known as *Quistclose* trusts take effect, the various situations in which such trusts have been found to exist are best considered in the context of the general rules governing resulting trusts.[149]

1–059   Where no *Quistclose* trust has arisen, the liability of a debtor, whether the debt in question is contractual or non-contractual, is of course only a personal liability and does not confer any proprietary rights on the creditor. In *Re Sharpe (a Bankrupt)*[150] the bankrupt purchased a property with the help of a sum lent to him by his aunt as part of an arrangement whereby the aunt was to live in the property for the rest of her life. Browne-Wilkinson J., while finding in her favour on another ground, rejected her claim to a beneficial interest in the property by virtue of her loan advance, holding that where

---

[145] Banks have a statutory right to amalgamate the balances of the different accounts held with them.
[146] [2002] UKHL 12, [2002] 2 A.C. 164.
[147] The claimant would have an equitable proprietary interest in that product by virtue of the trust; see *post*, para 22–147.
[148] This aspect of the case is discussed *post*, para 16–175.
[149] See *post*, paras 9–053–9–075.
[150] [1980] 1 W.L.R. 219.

"moneys are advanced by loan there can be no question of the lender being entitled to an interest in the property".[151] He distinguished on the grounds of its "very special" facts the earlier decision in *Hussey v. Palmer*[152] where, in a similar situation, the Court of Appeal had been unable to agree as to whether the payment in question had been made by way of loan or by way of direct contribution to the building of an extension and had, by a majority, imposed a constructive trust on the basis of a principle[153] which is no longer regarded as good law.[154] While it is sometimes difficult to decide, in the context of family arrangements, whether a particular payment has been made by way of loan or by way of contribution to the acquisition of the property in question, once the intention of the parties has actually been established the two possibilities are mutually exclusive.

3. *Estates of Deceased Persons*

(A) Personal Representatives and Trustees Compared
In one sense it can indeed be said that the legal personal representative—an   **1–060**
executor in the case of a person nominated as such in a will, otherwise an administrator—of a deceased person is a trustee for the creditors of the deceased and for the beneficiaries who are entitled to his assets; after all, he holds the real and personal estate for their benefit rather than for his own benefit. Further, by virtue of section 69 of the Trustee Act 1925, the provisions of that Act also apply to personal representatives[155]; so do the provisions of the Trustee Act 2000.[156] However, it would be an error to equate the legal position of personal representatives with that of trustees because certain differences still persist, primarily as the result of other statutory provisions.

Thus, while an action by a beneficiary to recover trust property or in   **1–061**
respect of any breach of trust cannot, in the absence of fraud or the retention of the property by the trustee,[157] be brought after six years,[158] personal representatives are subject to a different period of limitation, namely 12 years for a claim to personal estate[159] and six years for actions to recover arrears of interest in respect of legacies.[160] However, the exception relating to fraud and to property retained by the trustee applies just as much to personal representatives as it does to trustees.[161] The authority of personal representatives in handling pure personalty is several, whereas that of

---

[151] *ibid.* at 223.
[152] [1972] 1 W.L.R. 1286.
[153] That a constructive trust is a general equitable remedy which can be invoked in order to do justice in the individual case. See *post*, paras 10–035, 10–310.
[154] See *post*, para 10–310.
[155] See also Administration of Estates Act 1925, ss.33, 39.
[156] Trustee Act 2000, s.35(1).
[157] Limitation Act 1980, s.21(1).
[158] *ibid.*, s.21(3) and see *post*, para 22–046.
[159] *ibid.*, s.22.
[160] *ibid.*
[161] *ibid.*. See also *post*, para 22–040.

trustees is joint.[162] Consequently, one of a number of personal representatives can give a valid title to a purchaser or pledgee of pure personalty whereas one of a number of co-trustees cannot, the intervention of all the trustees being necessary. However, the authority of personal representatives over realty (which since 1925 for this purpose been defined as including leasehold land[163]) is, like that of trustees, joint.[164] Since July 1, 1995, this applies just as much to contracts as to conveyances[165] (previously one of a number of personal representatives could enter into a valid contract for the sale of land).

1–062   The functions of personal representatives are also different from those of trustees. The duty of trustees is to administer a trust on behalf of beneficiaries, some of whom may be minors or unborn, and this may be a long continuing process since many years may elapse before a trust is brought to an end. On the other hand, the primary duty of personal representatives is to wind up the estate, first by paying the debts and any inheritance tax which is payable and, secondly, by transferring the net assets to whoever is entitled to receive them; this will be either the persons absolutely beneficially entitled to those assets under the will or intestacy in question[166] or any trustees nominated by the deceased, who more often than not will be the personal representatives themselves, to be held on the relevant trusts.

1–063   Further, whereas a beneficiary has an equitable interest in the trust property as soon as a trust takes effect,[167] a legatee or devisee or intestate successor has neither a legal nor an equitable proprietary interest whilst the assets of the estate remain in course of administration. At that stage such persons have only the right to require the deceased's estate to be duly administered by the personal representatives.[168] It therefore follows that, although a personal representative has, like a trustee, fiduciary duties to perform, those duties are owed to the estate as a whole; it does not, therefore, necessarily follow that the duty of an executor in the course of administering an estate is subject to the trustee's duty to hold an even balance as between the different beneficiaries.[169] It was accordingly held in *Re Hayes's Will Trusts*[170] that, where executors had exercised a testamentary power of sale in favour of one of the children of the testator at the price at which the

---

[162] *Jacomb v. Harwood* (1751) 2 Ves. Sen. 265; *Attenborough v. Solomon* [1913] A.C. 76. It was recommended many years ago that the power should also be joint in the case of personal representatives (Law Reform Committee on the Powers and Duties of Trustees (23rd Report, Cmd. 8733 (1982) but this recommendation has never been enacted. For the historical reasons for the existing rule, see 1 *Spence's Equitable Jurisdiction* (1846), p.578 and *Collier v. Hollinshead* (1984) 272 E.G. 941.

[163] Administration of Estates Act 1925, ss.3(1), 54.

[164] *ibid.*, s.2(2).

[165] Law of Property (Miscellaneous Provisions) Act 1994, s.16.

[166] Considered in more detail *post*, para 13–018.

[167] At any rate, in the case of a "fixed trust", but not in the case of a "discretionary trust"; see *post*, para 6–133.

[168] *Commissioner of Stamp Duties (Queensland) v. Livingston* [1965] A.C. 694; *Eastbourne Mutual B.S. v. Hastings Corporation* [1965] 1 W.L.R. 861; *Lall v. Lall* [1965] 1 W.L.R. 1249; *Re Leigh's Will Trusts* [1970] Ch. 277.

[169] *Re Hayes's Will Trusts* [1971] 1 W.L.R. 758 at 764 and see *post*, para 16–001 for discussion of the duties of trustees in this respect.

[170] [1971] 1 W.L.R. 758.

property had been valued for the purposes of estate duty,[171] his other children could not attack the valuation on the ground that the executors had not considered the question of holding an even balance between him and them.

(B) When Personal Representatives Become Trustees

Personal representatives remain personal representatives indefinitely unless **1–064** the grant to them is limited or is revoked by the court.[172] However, where a will nominates the persons who are acting as personal representatives also to be the trustees of all or part of the assets comprised in the estate, it is not always easy to determine the precise moment when, and the circumstances in which, they cease to hold the assets in question as personal representatives and instead hold them as trustees. What has to be determined is whether or not the personal representatives have exhausted all their duties and functions as such and have consequently taken on themselves the character of trustees. In principle, this will occur as soon as they have paid all funeral and testamentary expenses, discharged all debts and liabilities, and satisfied all the gifts of specific items of property or of specific sums of money. Once that has been done, what is known as the deceased's residuary estate will have been established and the personal representatives will cease to hold as such the assets which comprise it and will instead hold those assets on trust for the beneficiaries entitled to receive them.[173]

Where the beneficiaries in question, who may be or may include the **1–065** personal representatives themselves, are absolutely entitled to the residuary estate, the assets in question will normally then be transferred to them; indeed, in such circumstances, the beneficiaries have the right to call for such a transfer to be made[174] or alternatively to require the trustees to retire from their trusteeship.[175] This is one of the reasons why it is important to know precisely when the personal representatives become trustees. Where the trusts are to continue, this is also important for a number of further reasons: first, because the trustees can then exercise their statutory powers to appoint new trustees in their place[176]; secondly, because tax will then be payable on the assets in question on a different basis[177]; and, thirdly, because in the case of trusts of land, the trustees will be obliged to consult with any beneficiaries of full age before disposing of the land in question.[178]

The personal representatives will make any transfer of land to the bene- **1–066** ficiaries by executing in their favour a document known as an assent.[179]

---

[171] One of the predecessors of inheritance tax. Such valuations tend to be lower than the open market value.

[172] See *Attenborough v. Solomon* [1913] A.C. 76.

[173] *Re Ponder* [1921] 2 Ch. 59; *Re Pitt* (1928) 44 T.L.R. 371.

[174] Under the Rule in *Saunders v. Vautier* (18410 Cr. & Ph. 240; see *post*, para 19–019.

[175] Under Trusts of Land and Appointment of Trustees Act 1996, s.19; see *post*; para 13–072. In contrast, personal representatives can only be removed by the court.

[176] *Re Cockburn's Will Trusts* [1957] Ch. 438.

[177] The amount of any liability to income tax and capital gains tax may be affected.

[178] Under *ibid.*, s.11(1), trustees of land are under an obligation to consult with any beneficiaries of full age and, in so far as is consistent with the general interests of the trust, give effect to the wishes of those beneficiaries or the majority of them (however, this obligation is in practice often excluded by the will or trust deed in question).

[179] By virtue of Administration of Estates Act 1925, s.36(4).

Such a document also has to be executed where the personal representatives are themselves the beneficiaries in question and where their status is merely changing from that of personal representatives to trustees. Until 1964 it was generally accepted that no such documents were necessary in the latter two cases but in that year this generally accepted practice was rejected[180]; this had the extremely inconvenient effect of rendering technically defective the title to any land which had been administered in accordance with what had since 1925 been regarded as the accepted practice but virtually all such titles must now have long since been put in order.[181] It has always been clear that assents in writing are not necessary in the case of pure personalty[182] and so can be implied and taken to have occurred as soon as the administration of the estate in question has been completed.

4. *Agency*

1–067   The relationship between principal and agent has some resemblances to the relationship between trustee and beneficiary. For example, agents are liable to their principals, as are trustees to their beneficiaries, for any secret profits made out of the property or business entrusted to them and in such circumstances their respective positions may coincide.[183] The main difference, from which various other consequences follow, is that the relationship between principal and agent is primarily that of creditor and debtor. Consequently, while a trustee has full title to the property vested in him,[184] an agent has not; while an agent acts on behalf of his principal and subject to his control, a trustee does not[185]; and, while agency is based on agreement, it is not necessary that there should be—and indeed there is usually not—any agreement between a trustee and his beneficiary.

5. *Equitable Charges*

1–068   An equitable charge is created where specific property is appropriated to the discharge of some debt or other obligation without there being any change in ownership either at law or in equity.[186]

The distinction between an equitable charge and a trust is that an equitable charge merely imposes a liability on the property which is subject to it

---

[180] In *Re King's Will Trusts* [1964] Ch. 542. However, the Court of Appeal subsequently decided that an assent to the vesting of an equitable interest in land does not need not to be in writing but can be inferred by conduct (*Re Edwards's Will Trusts* [1982] Ch. 30).

[181] By the process, which was often both time-consuming and expensive, of obtaining the necessary written assent, sometimes many years after the estate in question had been administered. Only where the title to the land in question is still unregistered, which is now only possible if there has been no disposition, other than a change of trustees, since 1964, is it possible for there still to be any technical defect in title of this type.

[182] Because Administration of Estates Act 1925, s.36 applies only to realty (defined, for this purpose, as including leasehold land).

[183] See *post*, paras 10–047, 10–057.

[184] See *ante*, para 1–029.

[185] See *post*, para 14–101.

[186] *London County and Westminster Bank v. Tompkins* [1918] 1 K.B. 515 at 528.

whereas a trust imposes a fiduciary character on the owner of the property.[187] This has a number of consequences. If property is held subject to an equitable charge and the chargee satisfies the charge, he will hold the property beneficially,[188] whereas a trustee will, on the termination of the trust, hold the property on resulting trust.[189] Again, a chargee is not accountable for rents and profits during the subsistence of the charge,[190] whereas a trustee is.[191] On the other hand, there is a basic similarity in that both an equitable charge and a trust are equitable interests and may therefore be overridden, that is to say destroyed, by a bona fide purchaser for value of the legal estate without notice[192] or, in the case of registered land, the statutory equivalent.[193]

6. Conditions

A condition may, in certain carefully defined circumstances, operate as a trust. Property may be given to a person on condition that he does something or confers a benefit on somebody. But it is only if that condition can, or must necessarily, be fulfilled or satisfied out of the property that it will take effect as a trust.[194] This will not be its effect if the duty is merely collateral.[195]   **1–069**

7. Powers

The basic distinction between a trust and a power is that a trust is imperative whereas a power is discretionary. Almost all trusts involve the exercise of powers or discretions by the trustees. In many cases this does not affect beneficial entitlement. So, depending on the circumstances of the particular trust, the trustees will often have a number of powers of an administrative nature; examples are powers to vary the investments of the trust,[196] to grant a lease of property which is subject to the trust,[197] to settle claims,[198] to apply income for the support of a minor beneficiary or to accumulate it,[199] to apply   **1–070**

---

[187] *Cunningham v. Foot* (1878) 3 App. Cas. 974 at 992–993, *per* Lord O'Hagan.
[188] *Re Oliver* (1890) 62 L.T. 533.
[189] See *post*, para 9–076.
[190] *Re Oliver* (1890) 62 L.T. 533.
[191] See *post*, para 22–009.
[192] *Parker v. Judkin* [1931] 1 Ch. 475.
[193] A bona fide purchaser for valuable consideration (other than marriage consideration) claiming under a registered disposition (Land Registration Act 2002, ss.28–31, 129(1), 132(1)).
[194] *Att.-Gen. v. Wax Chandlers Co.* (1873) L.R. 6 H.L. 1; *Cunningham v. Foot* (1878) 3 App. Cas. 974 at 995, *per* Lord O'Hagan.
[195] See *Re Brace* [1954] 1 W.L.R. 955 (no trust was held to arise when a house was devised to a daughter on condition that "she provides a home" for another daughter); *Swain v. The Law Society* [1983] A.C. 598 (the words "on behalf of" were held not to express or imply a trust; see *ante*, para 1–038 and *post*, para 10–049). Compare *Re Frame* [1939] Ch. 700 (a condition in a will that a legatee should adopt the testator's daughter was held to constitute a trust); *Re Niyazi's Will Trusts* [1978] 1 W.L.R. 910 (the words "on condition that" were held apt to create a trust).
[196] See *post*, para 14–055.
[197] Trusts of Land and Appointment of Trustees Act 1996, s.6(1)
[198] Trustee Act 1925, s.15.
[199] See *post*, para 17–019.

to the court for guidance as to the execution of the trust,[200] and to insure trust property.[201] Administrative powers are also commonly given to other persons designated in the trust instrument; the power most commonly conferred on persons other than the trustees is the power to remove trustees and to appoint new ones in their place[202] (where a trust has what is known as a protector, a person nominated by, and usually a confidante of, the settlor in order to control the exercise of some or all of the powers which the trustees would otherwise have, such a power is normally granted to him instead). These, and other, administrative powers which can be conferred by the trust instrument on trustees and other persons will each be the subject of detailed discussion later on. It must be stressed at this stage, and cannot be stressed too often, that it is fundamental to the nature of a trust that its trustees should not be puppets dangling at the end of a string pulled by the settlor or the beneficiaries[203] but should instead be persons with the right and the ability to exercise an independent judgment in respect of a wide variety of issues.

1–071   The powers and discretions which can be conferred on trustees and other persons are not, however, limited to the type of administrative matters considered in the previous paragraph; they can also extend to beneficial entitlement to the trust property. Trustees (and other persons) can be given powers to select who will receive the benefit of the capital subject to the trust and/or the income produced by that capital. Such a power of selection can be exercisable either, first, in favour of anyone in the world or, secondly, in favour of specific persons or defined classes of persons to which the persons making the selection can additionally be given a power to add or, thirdly, in favour of anyone in the world except specific persons or defined classes of persons.[204] Alternatively, the beneficiaries or classes of beneficiaries may be determined once and for at the outset and the pre-trustees merely be given a discretion to determine how much each of them is actually to receive and/or, in relation to income, whether it is distributed or accumulated.[205] Where powers relating to the existence and extent of beneficial enjoyment are conferred on persons who are not themselves trustees, such persons are known as donees of a power (a protector is in principle no more than the donee of various powers; the difference in practice is that his powers are likely to be much more extensive, sometimes even more extensive than those of the trustees). In such circumstances, the trustees hold the property

---

[200] See *post*, para 14–121.

[201] Trustee Act 1925, s.19, as amended by Trustee Act 2000, which removed pre-existing restrictions as to the value of the cover.

[202] See *post*, para 13–075.

[203] It is in this respect that the position of a normal trustee differs from that of a nominee trustee, who in the absence of contrary agreement is under an express or implied obligation to comply in all respects with the beneficiary's directions (there is only ever one beneficiary or two or more joint beneficiaries, which amounts to the same thing, in a nominee trust). As a result, the nominee trustee is entitled to a complete indemnity from the beneficiary not limited, as is the case with a normal trustee, to the value of the trust property.

[204] Such powers are known respectively as general powers, special powers, and intermediate (or hybrid) powers. The third category, the intermediate (or hybrid) power and the possibility of adding to the persons or classes of persons in whose favour a special power may be exercised have evolved relatively recently; neither was clearly established until the decision in *Re Manisty's Settlement* [1974] Ch. 17.

[205] See *post*, para 6–001.

for whatever beneficiaries and to whatever extent the donee of the power in question indicates. The precise nature and interrelation of powers and discretions of this type are discussed fully later on.[206] For present purposes, all that is necessary is an outline of the different categories of trusts and powers which relate to beneficial entitlement.

Where a person not only has the right but is also under an obligation to **1–072** make a selection relating to the beneficial enjoyment of property, he is said to hold a "trust power", an apparently contradictory term which indicates that, contrary to the basic distinction between trusts and powers, the power in question is imperative rather than discretionary. Rather confusingly, two quite distinct situations are now described as giving rise to the creation of a trust power: first, where a trustee is under a duty to make a selection relating to the beneficial enjoyment of property vested in him (this situation was traditionally and is still more usually described as a discretionary trust); and, secondly, where a person who is not a trustee is under a duty to make a selection relating to the beneficial enjoyment of property which is not vested in him (this situation was traditionally and is still sometimes described as a "power in the nature of a trust"). Given the very considerable differences between trusts and powers and, to a lesser extent, the differences between powers and discretions, it is most unfortunate that what were formerly described as discretionary trusts and powers in the nature of a trust can now both be described by the same name; the confusion thus potentially caused has often materialised and on at least one occasion has extended even to the members of the House of Lords.[207]

A trust power, whether it is what was formerly described as a discre- **1–073** tionary trust or what was formerly described as a power in the nature of a trust, can only arise where the selection in question has to be made from an already defined class of persons; however, as a result of the decision of the House of Lords in *McPhail v. Doulton*,[208] it is no longer necessary for all the members of that class to be actually ascertainable. In this situation, it has always been held that, in the event that the person entitled to make the selection fails to do so, the court can and will step in to decide the beneficial enjoyment of the property in question; in other words, if a trust power is not exercised, the court can and will execute that power. Traditionally, the court has done so by dividing the capital or income in question equally between all the members of the class. However, now that it is no longer necessary for all the beneficiaries in whose favour a trust power can be exercised to be ascertainable, this is no longer always possible; in such circumstances, the court has to have recourse to three other possible methods of executing a trust power which were envisaged by the House of Lords in *McPhail v. Doulton*.[209] However, in the 30 years which have elapsed since the decision in that case, there has as yet been no reported case in which a court has actually had to do this.

---

[206] See *post*, para 6–001.
[207] Particularly in *McPhail v. Doulton* [1971] A.C. 424.
[208] [1971] A.C. 424.
[209] [1971] A.C. 424 at 457; see *post*, para 3–040.

1–074   Where, on the other hand, a person has the right, but is not under any obligation, to make a selection relating to the beneficial enjoyment of property, he is said to hold a mere power. The traditional view was that, in the event that the person entitled to make the selection failed to do so, the court could not step in and decide the beneficial enjoyment of the property in question; in other words that, when a mere power was not exercised, that power could not be executed by the court. However, a distinction has more recently been drawn between mere powers held by trustees and, in some circumstances, by other persons in a fiduciary position[210] (described for this purpose as "fiduciary powers") and mere powers held by anyone else (described as "non-fiduciary powers" or "personal powers"). It has been stated[211] that, in the event that a fiduciary power is not exercised, the court will in appropriate circumstances step in and execute that power by having recourse to at least one and possibly all three of the additional methods of executing a trust power which were envisaged by the House of Lords in *McPhail v. Doulton*[212] (once again there has as yet been no reported case in which a court has had to do this). However, the court is still unable to step in and execute a non-fiduciary or personal power.

1–075   Precisely which of the various different kinds of trusts and powers outlined above has been created in any given case is a question of construction of the language of the deed or will in question. Such instruments should ideally be drafted in such a way as to leave no room for doubt. However, in the majority of the cases which have come before the courts, the wording of the instrument in question has given rise to considerable doubt and that doubt has consequently had to be resolved by the application of a number of rules of construction developed for the purpose. These rules and the other important distinctions between trusts and powers, particularly the different rights of the beneficiaries of a trust and the persons in whose favour a power is able to be exercised, will be discussed fully later on.[213]

---

[210] See *post*, para 6–050.
[211] In *Mettoy Pension Trustees v. Evans* [1990] 1 W.L.R. 1587; *post*, para 6-067.
[212] [1971] A.C. 424 at 457.
[213] See *post*, para 6–001.

CHAPTER 2

THE CLASSIFICATION OF TRUSTS

I. STATUTORY, EXPRESS, IMPLIED, RESULTING AND CONTRUCTIVE TRUSTS

Trusts may be created either, first, by statute—these are statutory trusts; or, **2–001** secondly, where a settlor or testator intentionally creates a relationship of trustee and beneficiary—these are express trusts; or, thirdly, where a settlor or testator carries out some intentional act other than the creation of a relationship of trustee and beneficiary from which the court infers a relationship of trustee and beneficiary—these are implied or resulting trusts; or, fourthly, by operation of law, where a relationship of trustee and beneficiary is imposed by the court as a result of the conduct of the trustee—these are constructive trusts.[1]

1. *Statutory Trusts*

A number of trusts have been created by statute, either expressly or by **2–002** implication. A large number of these are set out in the Schedules 1 and 2 to the Trusts of Land and Appointment of Trustees Act 1996.[2] Those which are most likely to be relevant for the purposes of this book are as follows:

(1) Under section 34 of the Law of Property Act 1925, as amended by the Trusts of Land and Appointment of Trustees Act 1996,[3] whenever land is conveyed or left by will to persons in undivided shares, that land vests in the first four persons named in the conveyance or the personal representatives respectively on trust for all the grantees beneficially as tenants in common in equity.

(2) Under section 36 of the Law of Property Act 1925, as amended by the Trusts of Land and Appointment of Trustees Act 1996,[4] whenever land is conveyed or devised to persons as joint tenants, it vests

---

[1] For a well-known classification, see *Cook v. Fountain* (1676) 3 Swanst. 585, *per* Lord Nottingham L.C. Compare *Soar v. Ashwell* [1893] 2 Q.B. 390 and *Re Llanover Settled Estates* [1926] Ch. 626.

[2] These Schedules contained the amendments to the various statutes which comprise the Property Legislation of 1925 which were necessary in order to replace by trusts of land the trusts for sale imposed by that 1925 legislation.

[3] Sch.2, para.3.

[4] Sch.2, para.4.

in the first four persons named in the conveyance or the personal representatives respectively on trust for all the grantees beneficially as joint tenants in equity.

(3) Under section 33 of the Administration of Estates Act 1925, as amended by the Trusts of Land and Appointment of Trustees Act 1996,[5] on the death of a person intestate, his property vests in his personal representatives on trust to be divided between his surviving spouse, if any, and his issue or other relatives in the proportions specified by the legislation.[6]

2. *Express Trusts*

2–003　Express trusts arise where a settlor or testator intentionally creates a relationship of trustee and beneficiary; this may be done either orally or by deed or by writing or by will.[7] A trust will be regarded as express even where the settlor or testator has expressed himself ambiguously if the court concludes, upon a true construction of the instrument in question, that a trust was what was intended by the settlor; consequently, words of prayer, entreaty or expectation, collectively known as precatory words, may be held to have created an express trust.[8] Further, a power to distribute property among a class of persons may be construed as indicating an intention to create an express trust in favour of that class if there is no gift over in default of appointment. In each case the question is entirely one of construction of the relevant instrument.[9]

3. *Implied or Resulting Trusts*

2–004　Implied or resulting trusts arise where a settlor or testator carries out some intentional act other than the creation of a relationship of trustee and beneficiary from which the court infers that a relationship of trustee and beneficiary has been created. Such trusts consequently arise from the unexpressed but presumed intention of the settlor or testator. The two alternative names stem from the fact that not only are they implied by the court but also often cause the beneficial interest thereunder to "result" to the settlor or to his estate or to the residuary beneficiaries or intestate successors of the testator. Implied or resulting trusts arise in two sets of circumstances. The first are where one person transfers property to another or into the joint names of himself and that other or pays, wholly or in part, for the purchase of property which is vested either in the name of another or in the joint names of himself and that other; in such circumstances, there is a presumption that no gift was intended and so the property is held on trust for the payer or, in the case of a joint purchase, for the two of them in proportion to their contributions (this is, however, only a presumption and can be rebutted

---

[5] Sch.2, para.5.
[6] See *post*, para 13–018.
[7] See *post*, para 4–005 for cases where writing is necessary.
[8] See *post*, para 3–003.
[9] See *post*, para 6–055.

by the counter-presumption of advancement when the parties are in one of a number of established relationships or by affirmative evidence of the payer's intention to make an outright beneficial transfer). The second set of circumstances are where a settlor or testator who creates an express trust fails fully to dispose of the whole of his beneficial interest in the property in question; in such circumstances, the court will imply that so much of the beneficial interest as is undisposed of will be held on trust for the settlor himself or his estate, or for the residuary beneficiaries or intestate successors of the testator.[10]

4. Constructive Trusts

Constructive trusts arise by operation of law. Unlike all other trusts, a **2–005** constructive trust is imposed by the court as a result of the conduct of the trustee and therefore arises quite independently of the intention of any of the parties. To give a very well known illustration, where an express trustee of leasehold property used his position to induce the landlord, who had refused to renew the lease to the trust, to renew the lease in his own favour instead, a constructive trust was imposed on him whereby he held the new lease on the same trusts as he had held the old one—his attempt to obtain a personal advantage for himself was regarded as hostile to the interests of the beneficiaries and was therefore contrary to the duty of loyalty which he, as an express trustee, owed to them.[11]

II. SIMPLE AND SPECIAL TRUSTS

1. Simple Trusts

A simple trust arises where a trustee is simply a repository of the trust **2–006** property with no active duties to perform.[12] If a settlor or testator vests property in trustees to be held on trust for a nominated beneficiary absolutely, the trust is a simple trust. The only duty which the trustee has to perform is to transfer the whole or some part of the property to the beneficiary if the latter so directs.[13] In such a case, he is known as a bare trustee.

2. Special Trusts

A special trust arises where the trustee is appointed to carry out a purpose **2–007** designated by the settlor or testator and is therefore obliged to exert himself actively in the performance of the trust.[14] Consequently, he is known as an active trustee. Therefore, if the trust created is for the trustee to collect the

---

[10] *Westdeutsche Landesbank Girozentrale v. Islington L.B.C.* [1996] A.C. 669 at 708. See further *post*, Chapter 9.
[11] *Keech v. Sandford* (1726) Sel.Cas. Ch. 61 and see also generally *post*, para 10–118.
[12] Underhill and Hayton, *Law of Trusts and Trustees* 17th edn (London, Lexis Nexis, 2006), pp.76–77.
[13] See *Christie v. Ovington* (1875) 1 Ch.D. 279; *Re Cunningham and Frayling* [1891] 2 Ch. 567.
[14] Underhill and Hayton, *op. cit.*, pp.77–78.

rents and profits of the trust property, to pay the cost of repairs to and insurance of that property out of these rents and profits, to pay whatever is left to a nominated beneficiary for his lifetime and then, on that person's death, to hold the property on trust for someone else absolutely, the trust will be a special one until the death of the life tenant; this is because during that period the trustee has active duties to perform. However, on the death of the life tenant, the trust will become a simple trust and the trustee will become a bare trustee because the only duty still binding on him will be to transfer the trust property to the ultimate beneficiary in the manner and to the extent that he is directed by the latter.

Special trusts are subdivided into ministerial trusts and discretionary trusts. The former require for their performance no more than ordinary business intelligence on the part of the trustees, for example, the collection of the rents and profits of the trust property and their distribution in accordance with the instructions of the settlor or testator. The latter require the exercise of a discretion on the part of the trustees. This will be the case and the trust in question will be discretionary where funds are transferred to the trustees for them to divide up at their absolute discretion between a number of local charities such as a dogs' home, a cats' home, and a body such as the Salvation Army. A trust will also be discretionary where the trustees have a discretion to determine whether and if so, how much, income should be paid to each of the members of a class of beneficiaries nominated by the settlor or testator.[15]

III. EXECUTED AND EXECUTORY TRUSTS

2–008   In this context, the terms "executed" and "executory" are used in a partic-ular technical sense. A trust is regarded as executed in this sense when all the terms of the trust are specified in the trust instrument or in the declara-tion which has constituted that trust. A trust is, on the other hand, regarded as executory in this sense when, although the trust property is vested in the trustees or is the subject matter of an enforceable agreement to vest that property in them, that instrument or declaration requires the execution of a further instrument setting out the detailed terms of the trust. The distinction between the two is that, in the case of an executed trust, the settlor has, in the language of the nineteenth century, been his own conveyancer[16] whereas, in the case of an executory trust, he has not. A conventional, if old-fashioned, example of an executory trust is marriage articles from which a formal marriage settlement is later to be prepared.[17] A modern example is an occupational pension scheme established, as most pensions schemes are, by an interim deed of trust which provides for the subsequent execution of a definitive deed of trust. In one such case,[18] the definitive deed of trust was duly executed but its validity was challenged when questions arose as to the entitlement to surplus funds. Scott J. in fact found the definitive deed to be

---

[15] See post, Chapter 6.
[16] Egerton v. Brownlow (1853) 4 H.L.C. 1 at 210, per Lord St Leonards.
[17] For further discussion, see post, para 5–078.
[18] Davis v. Richards & Wallington Industries [1990] 1 W.L.R. 1511.

valid but stated that, had he not done so, the interim deed would nevertheless have been upheld as a valid executory trust capable of being executed by a court order; this would have had the effect of providing rules corresponding to those in the definitive deed by means of which the questions as to the surplus funds would have been able to have been resolved. Another very recent example[19] is where a testator provided for one-third of his residuary estate to be held on discretionary trust for such of the members of a class of persons as his trustees should determine but did not specify the trusts on which that property was to be held.

IV. COMPLETELY AND INCOMPLETELY CONSTITUTED TRUSTS

A trust is described as completely constituted when it has been perfectly   2–009
created by either the settlor declaring himself to be a trustee of the property in question or the settlor or testator vesting that property in the intended trustees by means of the appropriate formalities so that nothing more remains to be done by him. Both executed and executory trusts are inevitably completely constituted trusts. But if, on the other hand, something still remains to be done by the settlor or testator, the trust in question is imperfect and is said to be incompletely constituted; this is another way of saying that, because there is as yet no valid trust, no interest of a proprietary nature has yet vested in the beneficiary. This will be the case where the settlor has undertaken to vest title to the trust property in the intended trustees but has not actually transferred the property in question. In such circumstances, the only conceivable remedies of the beneficiaries will be a direct or indirect contractual action against the settlor; they will have no proprietary remedy against the trustees.[20]

V. FIXED AND DISCRETIONARY TRUST

Discretionary trusts have already been mentioned as one of the two types of   2–010
"special trusts". They must also be contrasted with fixed trusts, which are trusts in favour of pre-determined beneficiaries or classes of beneficiaries. In the case of a fixed trust, each of the beneficiaries is entitled in equity to a fixed pre-determined share of the trust property at the appropriate time and he may enforce his rights to that share against the trustees. In the case of a discretionary trust, on the other hand, the trustees will have to exercise one or more of the discretions vested in them by the settlor or testator before any individual beneficiary has a right to any part of the trust property. The discretion vested in the trustees may merely be that of deciding in what proportions, if any, the trust property is to be divided among the members of a pre-determined class; at the other extreme, the discretion vested in the trustees may be that of deciding the membership of the class itself. Whatever

---

[19] *Pengelly v. Pengelly* [2008] [2007] EWHC (Ch) 3227, [2008] 3 W.L.R. 66.
[20] For further discussion, see *post*, para 5–084.

the discretion, unless and until it is exercised, no individual beneficiary or potential beneficiary has any proprietary rights.[21]

VI. Private and Public Trusts

2–011   A private trust aims to benefit one or more persons who have either been defined by the settlor or testator or are to be determined in the future in the manner which the settlor or testator has provided. A public or charitable trust, on the other hand, aims to bring about or to support some purpose which will be of benefit to society or to some considerable section of society. Because of their public nature, charitable trusts enjoy a number of privileges not shared by private trusts; in particular, they do not have to comply with the requirements of certainty of objects or of the rule against perpetuity and, most important of all today, are exempt from payment of most local and national taxes.[22]

VII. New Classifications?

2–012   The traditional classification of implied, resulting and constructive trusts, which has generally been thought to be workable, has been the subject of considerable judicial comment in the last 40 years. The effect of these comments on these types of trusts will be analysed in detail in due course in the appropriate chapters. However, these possible changes to the traditional classification of trusts merit some brief discussion here.

2–013   In the first place, it has been contended that the two recognised sets of circumstances in which implied or resulting trusts arise should respectively be classified as "presumed" and "automatic" resulting trusts. According to this distinction, suggested by Megarry J. in *Re Vandervell's Trusts (No.2)*,[23] a presumed resulting trust arises when a purchase or transfer is made in the name of another person but not on any express trust; in these circumstances, there is a presumption that that other holds the property in question on resulting trust for the purchaser or transferor but this implied or presumed intention can be rebutted either by other legal presumptions or by evidence to the contrary.[24] An automatic resulting trust, on the other hand, arises where a transfer has been made on trusts which have left the whole or some part of the beneficial interest undisposed of (because, for example, those are in some way ineffective or incomplete); in this situation the transferee of the property in question automatically holds it on resulting trust for the transferor to the extent that the beneficial interest has not been disposed of. In such a case, according to Megarry J., the resulting trust "does not depend on

---

[21] They do, however, have a right to compel the due administration of the trust and can share in the fund on a premature determination. See *post*, para 6–133.

[22] The distinctions are discussed *post*, para 11–003.

[23] [1974] Ch. 269, at 294, 295. The actual decision of Megarry J. was reversed by the Court of Appeal at [1974] Ch. 269 but the Court of Appeal made no comment on the judge's formulation.

[24] See *post*, para 9–020 for the ways in which it may be rebutted.

any intentions or presumptions, but is the automatic consequence of [the transferor's] failure to dispose of what is vested in him".[25]

The distinction between "presumed" and "automatic" resulting trusts **2–014** appears at first sight to accord with common sense; however, it is fair to say that, just as what Megarry J. described as a presumed resulting trust is said to be created by implication as the result of a purchase in or transfer into the name of another, so an intention can be said to be implied on the part of a settlor or testator that the settled property should result to him to the extent that he has failed to dispose of it. The implication of an intention in the second type of resulting trusts does not actually appear to be markedly more artificial than in the first type of resulting trusts. Precisely this argument was adopted in *Westdeutsche Landesbank Girozentrale v. Islington L.B.C.*[26] by Lord Browne-Wilkinson, who reasserted the traditional view that both types of resulting trusts are examples of trusts giving effect to the common intention of the parties; he said that he was not convinced that Megarry J. had been right to suggest that the second type of resulting trust does not depend on intention but operates automatically.[27]

Lord Browne-Wilkinson's view is certainly preferable to the view of **2–015** Megarry J.[28] However, a further definition of resulting trusts has also been propounded,[29] namely that such trusts require nothing more and nothing less than a transfer of property in circumstances in which the provider of that property did not intend to benefit the recipient. This definition seems highly convincing,[30] at least so far as the two recognised categories of resulting trusts are concerned.[31] Its influence can be seen in the decision of the Privy Council in *Air Jamaica v. Charlton*,[32] where Lord Millett, while accepting that resulting trusts arise by operation of law and give effect to intention, emphasised that a resulting trust "arises whether or not the transferor intended to retain a beneficial interest—he almost always does not—since it responds to the absence of any intention on his part to pass a beneficial interest to the recipient". These observations seem successfully to blend the new definition into the view propounded by Lord Browne-Wilkinson, which of course unquestionably represents English law at present.

In the second place, there have been a number of attempts to bring the **2–016** concepts of resulting and constructive trusts closer together with a view to changing the basic attitude of English law towards the constructive trust.

---

[25] [1974] Ch. 269 at 294.

[26] [1996] A.C. 669 at 708.

[27] Lord Browne-Wilkinson went on to say that, if a settlor or testator has expressly, or by necessary implication, abandoned any beneficial interest in the trust property, there will be no resulting trust; the interest in question will instead vest in the Crown as *bona vacantia*.

[28] Birks [1996] R.L.R. 3 at 11 regards Lord Browne-Wilkinson's view as "correct", despite the fact that it led to the rejection of his own argument that a resulting trust should arise whenever money is paid under a mistake or under a condition which is not subsequently satisfied.

[29] By Chambers, *Resulting Trusts* (Oxford, Clarendon Press, 1997).

[30] His extrapolation of that definition dealing with the nature of *Quistclose* trusts was, however, reviewed and rejected by Lord Millett in *Twinsectra v. Yardley* [2002] UKHL 12, [2002] 2 A.C. 164; see *ante*, para 1–057 and *post*, para 9–066.

[31] Chambers, *op.cit.*, also classifies as resulting trusts a large number of other situations which most commentators regard as having nothing whatever to do with resulting trusts.

[32] [1999] 1 W.L.R. 1399 at 1412.

These attempts were largely initiated by Lord Denning M.R. in a series of cases decided by the Court of Appeal in the years immediately before and after 1970. In *Cooke v. Head*[33] he stated that "whenever two parties by their joint efforts acquire property to be used for their joint benefit, the courts may impose or impute a constructive or resulting trust",[34] while in *Hussey v. Palmer*[35] he said this:

"the plaintiff alleged that there was a resulting trust. I should have thought that the trust in this case, if there was one, was more in the nature of a constructive trust: but this is more a matter of words than anything else. The two run together."[36]

2–017   The expressed intention of Lord Denning M.R. was to convert the constructive trust into a remedy for unjust enrichment, as it has long since been in the common law jurisdictions of the United States of America and is now also, to a much more restricted extent, in the common law jurisdictions of Canada, in New Zealand and in some offshore jurisdictions (constructive trusts of this type are generally known as remedial constructive trusts). Thus in *Hussey v. Palmer*, immediately following the passage which has just been cited, Lord Denning M.R. continued:

"By whatever name it is described, it is a trust imposed by law whenever justice and good conscience require it. It is a liberal process, founded upon large principles of equity . . . It is an equitable remedy by which the court can enable an aggrieved party to obtain restitution."[37]

English law had hitherto regarded the constructive trust as "an institutional obligation attaching to property in certain specified circumstances",[38] one of which was mentioned when constructive trusts were defined at the beginning of this chapter.[39] Despite the efforts of Lord Denning M.R., this remains the situation at present—in this jurisdiction, his approach has generally been rejected in subsequent decisions in which the traditional approach towards the constructive trust has been reasserted.[40]

2–018   However, this traditional approach has not been universally adopted. In 1990 the Court of Appeal stated[41] that "there is a good arguable case" that circumstances may arise in which "the court will be prepared to impose a constructive trust *de novo* as a foundation for the grant of equitable remedy by way of account or otherwise", classifying such a trust as a "remedial

---

[33] [1972] 1 W.L.R. 518.

[34] *ibid.* at 520.

[35] [1972] 1 W.L.R. 1286.

[36] *ibid.* at 1289.

[37] *ibid.* at 1289–1290.

[38] D.M.W. Waters in *Equity and Contemporary Legal Developments* (ed. Goldstein, Jerusalem, 1992) 457 at 463.

[39] See *ante*, para 2–005.

[40] *Burns v. Burns* [1984] Ch. 317; *Grant v. Edwards* [1986] Ch. 638; *Ashburn Anstalt v. Arnold* [1989] Ch. 1; *Halifax Building Society v. Thomas* [1996] Ch. 217; *Re Polly Peck (No.2)* [1998] 3 All E.R. 812 at 827.

[41] In *Metall und Rohstoff A.G. v. Donaldson Lufkin & Jenrette* [1989] 1 Q.B. 391 at 473–474.

constructive trust". Subsequently, in 1996, Lord Browne-Wilkinson said[42] that "the remedial constructive trust, if introduced into English law, may provide a more satisfactory road forward . . . However, whether English law should follow the United States and Canada in adopting the remedial constructive trust will have to be decided in some future case where the point is directly in issue." It has been made abundantly clear by the Court of Appeal on a number of occasions[43] that the contention that English law should adopt the remedial constructive trust cannot be maintained other than in the House of Lords. In *Twinsectra v. Yardley*[44] counsel for the claimant[45] would have argued for its adoption, admittedly as an argument of last resort, had the House not accepted the existence of a *Quistclose* trust.[46] There can, therefore, be not the slightest doubt that the House of Lords will one day soon be called upon to decide whether to return to the trail blazed by the Court of Appeal immediately before and after 1970 or to retain the more traditional approach adopted before and after that period.

Whatever the fate of this possible new development, however, the series of decisions handed down immediately before and after 1970 has had a lasting influence on the law governing joint enterprises entered into by the members of a family unit. It is in this area of the law that the concepts of resulting and constructive trusts have been brought closer together as a result of the development of what has become known as "the common intention constructive trust", which contains elements of both resulting trusts and constructive trusts. **2–019**

If two or more persons make direct contributions to the acquisition of a property, usually but not necessarily a property in which they intend to live together, the principles of resulting trusts will give each of them a beneficial interest in proportion to his respective contribution, provided that the contrary is not stated in the conveyance by means of which the property is conveyed to one or more of them. Additionally or alternatively, if a person is encouraged by another to believe that he will acquire a beneficial interest, or an enhanced beneficial interest, in a property, again usually but not necessarily[47] a property in which they are living together, as a result of making contributions of a less direct nature towards the repayment of the mortgage or the subsequent improvement of the property (a straightforward illustration is the payment by one of the parties of all the day to day household expenses so that the other can more easily make the repayments of the mortgage), any attempt subsequently to deprive that party of the enhanced beneficial interest which he or she has been encouraged to expect will be regarded as unconscionable and will lead either to the imposition of a constructive trust or to the invocation of the principle of equitable proprietary estoppel.[48] **2–020**

---

[42] In *Westdeutsche Landesbank Girozentrale v. Islington L.B.C.* [1996] 669 at 716.

[43] Among many other occasions, in *Twinsectra v. Yardley* [1999] Lloyd's Rep. Bank 438 and *Bank of Credit and Commerce International (Overseas) v. Akindele* [2001] Ch. 437.

[44] [2002] UKHL 12, [2002] 2 A.C. 164.

[45] Who included the author of this edition.

[46] See *ante*, para 1–057 and *post*, para 9–066.

[47] An case where the joint enterprise was of a purely commercial nature was *Yaxley v. Gotts* [2000] Ch. 162.

[48] See particularly *Lloyds Bank v. Rosset* [1991] 1 A.C. 107, discussed *post*, para 10–296.

2–021   This development has in no sense undermined the traditional categories of resulting and constructive trusts which have already been mentioned. What it has done is to produce a new type of trust which contains features of both types of trust and it is thought that this may in the end lead to the development of a general principle of unconscionability to replace both the "common intention constructive trust" and the principle of equitable proprietary estoppel (indeed it has now been held that an equitable proprietary estoppel will give rise to the imposition of a constructive trust where there has been unconscionable conduct[49]). For the moment, however, the "common intention constructive trust" has undoubtedly brought closer together certain aspects of resulting and constructive trusts which are now co-existing in a manner which, while clearly defined and wholly justifiable, could not possibly have been anticipated 60 years ago.

---

[49] *Yaxley v. Gotts* [2000] Ch. 162.

CHAPTER 3

THE ESSENTIAL INGREDIENTS OF A TRUST

This and the two following chapters consider the requirements for the **3–001**
creation of a valid non-charitable trust. The essential ingredients for the
creation of a trust are that the provisions of the trust should manifest what
are known as the three certainties and that there should be some beneficiary
who is capable of enforcing those provisions. These requirements, and some
anomalous exceptions to the requirement that there should be a beneficiary,
are considered in this chapter along with various purported trusts which do
not or may not satisfy these requirements. The following chapter considers
the circumstances in which the creation of a trust must satisfy certain formal
requirements and the chapter following that considers the different ways in
which a trust may be constituted in order to render that trust enforceable by
its beneficiaries.

I. THE THREE CERTAINTIES

In *Knight v. Knight*[1] Lord Langdale laid down the principle that three certain- **3–002**
ties are required for the creation of a trust: first, the words used must be so
couched that, taken as a whole, they may be deemed to be imperative
("certainty of intention"); secondly, the subject matter of the trust must be
certain ("certainty of subject matter"); and, thirdly, the persons or objects
intended to be benefited must also be certain ("certainty of objects").

1. *Certainty of Intention*

The first of the essential ingredients for the effective creation of a trust is, **3–003**
therefore, certainty that its settlor or testator intended to impose binding
obligations on his chosen trustees. In this respect, Equity looks to his intention rather than to the form of what he has actually done. No particular form
of words is required for the creation of a trust. While a specific direction that
the trustees hold the property "on trust" for the intended beneficiaries is
highly desirable, the use of some such formulation is not essential. As will
be considered in detail below, it is possible for what are known as precatory
words, words which in terms express merely a desire, belief, recommendation or hope, to be held to create a trust if the requisite intention can be
clearly deduced from the expressions used by the settlor or testator. Nor is
the use of the words "in trust" actually decisive, although it obviously

---

[1] (1840) 3 Beav. 148 at 173. It is not normally possible to introduce extrinsic evidence in order
to aid the process of construction (see *Rabin v. Gerson Berger Association* [1986] 1 W.L.R. 526).

normally will be. In *Harrison v. Gibson*[2] it was stated that the "mere fact that the testator has used the words 'in trust' is not in itself inconsistent with an intention on his part that his wife should be the absolute beneficial owner". However, both in that case and in *Re Harding*,[3] it was decided that those words were in fact incompatible with an absolute gift and in the latter case it was stated[4] that what the judge in *Harrison v. Gibson* seemed to have had in mind was the distinction between "the 'trust' which a layman might think results from the appointment of executors" on the one hand, and a limited gift, on the other.

(A) The Changing Attitude of the Courts to Precatory Words

3–004 It is important to note that the attitude of the courts to the requirement for certainty of intention has changed over time.

3–005 Before the middle of the nineteenth century, the courts tended to take the view that any expression of desire or hope or the like on the part of a testator was imperative and therefore created a binding trust. Indeed it is possible to see in the older cases an intention being attributed to a testator which had the effect of creating an artificial certainty of intention where no such certainty existed at all. This practice derived from a rule relating to executors. Until the passing of the Executors Act 1830, an executor of a deceased person was permitted to take any part of the latter's estate which had not been disposed of by his will.[5] It was obviously unsatisfactory that executors were able to do this and the Court of Chancery therefore endeavoured to find some reason for intervening in order to make an executor into a trustee of any property which had not been disposed of and would seize on any expression of hope or desire in order to negative the presumption that the executor was intended to take beneficially. Although there was no reason for the same attitude to be adopted in the case of *inter vivos* transactions, the Court of Chancery nevertheless did so and regarded any precatory words of this type as sufficiently certain to create a trust even though the alleged trustee was not an executor and the settlor had completely disposed of all the property which was subject to the trust.

3–006 This ceased to be necessary once the Executors Act 1830 had provided for executors to hold any property which had not been disposed of for the next-of-kin unless the testator had shown an intention that the executor should take beneficially. Consequently, when expressions such as "desire", "wish", and "full confidence" received fresh consideration later in the nineteenth century, there was a change of approach.[6] One of a number of illustrative decisions was *Re Adams and Kensington Vestry*,[7] where a testator had given all his real and personal estate to his wife "in full confidence that she would do what was right as to the disposal thereof between my children". The Court

---

[2] [2005] EWHC 2957 (Ch), [2006] 1 W.L.R. 1212, *per* Hart J. at [13].

[3] [2008] EWHC 3 (Ch), [2008] 1 W.L.R. 361, *per* Lewison J. at [11].

[4] *ibid.* at [10].

[5] At that time, and indeed until 1858, estates of deceased persons were administered by the ecclesiastical courts rather than by the royal courts.

[6] Perhaps the earliest case which illustrates the new approach was *Lambe v. Eames* (1871) L.R. 6 Ch. 597 (property to be at disposal of widow "in any way she may think best for the benefit of herself and family").

[7] (1884) 27 Ch.D. 394.

of Appeal held that, by virtue of these words, the widow took an absolute interest in the property unfettered by any trust in favour of the children. The court also stated that some of the previous cases had gone very far and had unjustifiably given words a meaning beyond that which they could possibly bear if looked at in isolation. This well-known authority was by no means the first decision of its type; by the time it was decided, the change of approach had already occurred and beneficiaries were no longer being made into trustees unless this was clearly intended by the settlor or testator.

(B) The Modern Test
As a result of this change of approach, the intention of the settlor or testator   **3–007** became all-important. While it is still possible for the use of precatory words to be held to have created a trust in appropriate circumstances, the necessary intention has to be established by construction of the instrument. However, the question of what constitute appropriate circumstances can be partic- ularly difficult to establish in practice; this cannot be considered in a vacuum but can only as a result of a careful examination of all the words used in the instrument in question.[8] This proposition, which to modern eyes appears somewhat self-evident, was formulated by Lindley L.J. in *Re Hamilton*[9] in the following way: "You must take the will which you have to construe and see what it means, and if you come to the conclusion that no trust was intended you say so, although previous judges have said the contrary on some wills more or less similar to the one you have to construe."[10]

(C) Illustrations of the Modern Test
It would be both a difficult and, probably also a pointless exercise to   **3–008** consider even a small number of the many decided cases which illustrate the modern rule. However, at the risk of making the subject seem rather easier than it actually is, two cases, one on each side of the line, can appropriately be considered. On the one hand, in *Re Diggles*[11] a testatrix gave all her property to her daughter and to the latter's heirs and assigns, stating "And it is my *desire*[12] that she allows to A.G. an annuity of £25 during her life"; the

---

[8] Administration of Justice Act 1982, s.21, now provides that extrinsic evidence, including evidence of the testator's intention, may be admitted to assist in the interpretation of a will: (a) in so far as any part of it is meaningless; (b) in so far as the language used in any part of it is ambiguous on the face of it; and (c) in so far as evidence, other than evidence of the testator's intention, shows that the language used in any part of it is ambiguous in the light of the surrounding circumstances. It is also provided (*ibid.*, s.20) that the court has jurisdiction to rectify a will if satisfied that it is so expressed that it fails to carry out the testator's intention in consequence of a clerical error or of a failure to understand his instructions.

[9] [1895] 2 Ch. 370 at 373. See also *Re Williams* [1897] 2 Ch. 12 at 14 and *Comiskey v. Bowring-Hanbury* [1905] A.C. 84 at 89.

[10] Some doubt may possibly have been cast on this impeccable principle by *Re Steele's Will Trusts* [1948] Ch. 603; where Wynn-Parry J. held that the words in question had the same meaning as they had been held to have in *Shelley v. Shelley* (1868) L.R. 6 Eq. 540. This decision is obviously capable of indicating that, where identical words to those before the court had been held in a previous case to create a trust, that case should be followed unless it was clearly wrongly decided; that approach is obviously very different from construing the instrument in question on its merits even if other earlier decisions are taken into account. However, if this is indeed the basis on which Wynn-Parry J. was proceeding, it is not easy to support his view.

[11] (1888) 39 Ch.D. 253.

[12] Emphasis added.

Court of Appeal held that no trust to pay this money had been imposed on the daughter.[13] On the other hand, in *Comiskey v. Bowring-Hanbury*[14] (which may also be usefully compared with the decision in *Re Adams and Kensington Vestry*[15]), the testator gave all his property to his wife "absolutely *in full confidence*[16] that she will make such use of it as I would have made myself and that at her death she will devise it to such one or more of my nieces as she may think fit". The House of Lords held that, on a true construction of the whole will, the words "in full confidence" had created a trust. There may be some doubt about the correctness of the actual decision, given that the significance of the preceding word "absolutely" may perhaps not have been fully appreciated and taken into account; however, this decision of the highest authority nevertheless underlines the rule that in the last analysis the question is that of construing the instrument as a whole.[17]

3–009   A more recent illustration of some interest, which involved the winding-up of a company, is *Re Kayford*[18] in which rather different considerations arose. The company in question carried on a mail order business whose customers sent with their orders either the full price or a deposit on account. Difficulties arose over the supply and delivery of goods and so the company opened a separate bank account called a "Customers' Trust Deposit Account" into which all payments subsequently made by customers were paid and were only withdrawn when the goods ordered had been delivered; the idea of this was that, in the event that the company had to go into liquidation, the payments made by customers in respect of goods which had not yet been delivered could be returned to them. When the company did subsequently go into liquidation, the question arose as to whether the money in the bank account was indeed held in trust for those customers or instead formed part of the general assets of the company and so was available for all its creditors, who obviously included the customers. Megarry J. had no doubt that the facts showed that there was a trust; consequently, the sums paid had remained in the beneficial ownership of those who sent them until the goods ordered were delivered.[19]

---

[13] Nor was any trust held to have been created in the following cases: *Lambe v. Eames* (1871) L.R. 6 Ch. 597 ("in any way she may think best"); *Re Hutchinson and Tenant* (1878) 8 Ch.D. 540 ("have confidence"); *Mussoorie Bank v. Raynor* (1882) 7 App. Cas. 321 ("feeling confident"); *Re Hamilton* [1895] 2 Ch. 370 ("wish"); *Hill v. Hill* [1897] 1 Q.B. 483 ("request"); *Re Williams* [1897] 2 Ch. 12 ("fullest trust and confidence"); *Re Connolly* [1910] 1 Ch. 219 ("specially desire"); *Re Johnson* [1939] 2 All E.R. 458 ("request"); *Swain v. The Law Society* [1983] 1 A.C. 598 ("on behalf of").

[14] [1905] A.C. 84.

[15] (1884) 27 Ch.D. 394; see also *Re Williams* [1897] 2 Ch. 12.

[16] Emphasis added.

[17] A trust was held to have been created in the following cases: *Re Steele's Will Trusts* [1948] Ch. 603, ("request" but see above); *Re Endacott* [1960] Ch. 232 ("for the purpose of").

[18] [1975] 1 W.L.R. 279; see *post*, para 9–063.

[19] Megarry J. emphasised that the general rule is that, if money is sent to a company for goods which are not delivered, the sender is merely a creditor of the company unless a trust has been created. However, he held at 282 that in this case there was a trust whereupon "the obligations in respect of the money are transformed from contract to property, from debt to trust". He also indicated that a trust of this kind might not be effective in favour of trade creditors; however, in the case before him, the court was only concerned with the interests of members of the public.

The requirement of certainty of intention therefore requires that the requi- **3–010** site intention to create a trust appears from the words in the instrument.[20] The words used are, however, relevant not simply for the purpose of decid- ing whether a trust or a mere moral obligation has been created; those words may also lead other possible conclusions, namely that a power of appoint- ment has been created,[21] or that the Crown may be administering property in its hands in the exercise of its governmental functions without a trust having been created at all[22] (as has already been seen, the mere fact that the word "trust" has been used in relation to the Crown is not decisive[23]).

All the decisions to which reference has so far been made involved private **3–011** trusts. In contrast, where the intention which is derived from in the instru- ment is an intention to create a charitable trust, then, as the House of Lords confirmed in *I.R.C. v. McMullen*,[24] any ambiguity should receive a "benig- nant" construction if this is at all possible.[25] However, it was not found necessary to resort to such a construction in that case.

(D) The Effect of Uncertainty of Intention

If an intention to create a trust cannot be derived from the words used in the **3–012** instrument but only, at the most, some form of moral obligation, the effect of the consequential uncertainty of intention is that there is no trust. Conse- quently, the donee will take the property beneficially[26] (unless of course the words are construed as having given rise to a power of appointment[27]).

2. *Certainty of Subject Matter*

The second of the essential ingredients for the effective creation of a trust is **3–013** that its subject matter is certain. The property subject to the trust must either be clearly defined or be capable of ascertainment. This requirement has a number of aspects.

(A) The Property Subject to the Trust

It must be possible to establish exactly what property is subject to the **3–014** trust.

In *Palmer v. Simmonds*,[28] a testatrix left her residuary estate to her husband **3–015** "for his own use and benefit" but subject to a trust on his death "to leave the bulk of my residuary estate" to four named relatives. This trust was held to fail for uncertainty of subject-matter and so the husband took the property

---

[20] The question whether a trust or a power has been created is considered *post*, para 6–055.

[21] *ibid.*

[22] As a "trust in the higher sense"; see *Tito v. Waddell (No.2)* [1977] Ch. 106 at 216, *ante*, para 1–037.

[23] *ibid.* at 212. The Crown can be a trustee but only if it deliberately chooses so to do: *ibid.*, *Civilian War Claimants Association v. The King* [1932] A.C. 14 at 27; *Nissan v. Attorney-General* [1970] A.C. 179 at 223.

[24] [1981] A.C. 1. The facts are set out *post*, para 11–084.

[25] *ibid.* at 14.

[26] See the cases cited *ante*, n.13.

[27] See *post*, para 6–055.

[28] (1854) 2 Drew 221; compare *Bromley v. Tryon* [1952] A.C. 265.

absolutely. A similar result occurred in *Sprange v. Barnard*[29]; the testatrix left stock to her husband "for his sole use, and all that is remaining in the stock, that he has not necessary use for, to be equally divided between" her brothers and sisters. In both *Palmer v. Simmonds* and *Sprange v. Barnard* the conclusion was reached that the testator had intended the donee to receive an absolute interest on which the failed trusts were subsequently to be engrafted; consequently, in both of these cases, the husband took the property in question absolutely.[30]

3–016   However, apparently absolute gifts have sometimes instead been construed as conferring only a limited interest on the initial beneficiary; such a construction avoids uncertainty of subject matter in respect of the subsequent trusts. In *Re Last*[31] the testatrix left all her property to her brother, providing that "at his death anything that is left, that came from me" was to pass to certain other specified persons. This limitation was very similar to that in *Sprange v. Barnard* but it was in fact construed as conferring merely a life interest on the brother; consequently, on his death, all the property was held on the trusts specified by the testatrix. Similarly, in the earlier case of *Re Thomson's Estate*[32] a testator left all his property to his widow "to be disposed of as she may think proper for her own use and benefit" but, "should there be anything remaining of the said property or any part thereof" on her death, it was to be held on various trusts. Hall V.-C. held that the widow had a life interest together with a power to dispose of the property during her lifetime but no testamentary power so to do; consequently, any property not disposed of during her lifetime was held on the further specified trusts. These decisions are obviously only justifiable on the basis that the intention of the testator was indeed to confer no more than a limited interest on the initial beneficiary.

3–017   Another method of avoiding uncertainty of subject matter is for the court to find some way of ascertaining what the subject matter of a potentially uncertain trust actually is. In *Re Golay's Will Trusts*[33] the testator directed his trustees to permit a beneficiary to "enjoy one of my flats during her lifetime and to receive a reasonable income from my other properties". Ungoed-Thomas J. upheld the gift, holding that the yardstick of "reasonable income" indicated by the testator was not what he or some other person subjectively considered to be reasonable but what he identified objectively as "reasonable income", something which the court could therefore quantify. This conclusion was undoubtedly inconsistent with other contemporaneous decisions on certainty[34] but does seem to be consistent with the more recent

---

[29] (1789) 2 Bro.C.C. 585.

[30] This was by virtue of the rule generally known as the Rule in *Hancock v. Watson* [1902] A.C. 14 (formerly known as the Rule in *Lassence v. Tierney* (1849) 1 Mac. & G. 551). This establishes that, where there is an absolute gift of property in the first instance and the necessary intention subsequently to impose trusts on that property can be established, then in the event that the trusts fail for any reason the property is not held on a resulting trust for the settlor or his estate but will vest absolutely in the person to whom the property was first given absolutely.

[31] [1958] P. 137.

[32] (1879) 13 Ch.D. 144.

[33] [1965] 1 W.L.R. 969.

[34] Such as *Re Kolb's Will Trusts* [1962] Ch. 531 (a reference to "blue-chip" securities was held to be uncertain and consequently an investment clause was held to be void for uncertainty).

practice of the courts in trying to avoid, if at all possible, holding dispositions to be void for uncertainty, particularly in respect of expressions such as
"reasonable" or "satisfactory".[35]

(B)   The Part of the Property Subject to the Trust
Problems have also arisen in connection with attempts to declare trusts of   3–018
some certain but unidentified part of a larger holding.

(1)   Tangible property
The situation with tangible property is relatively clear. In *Re London Wine*   3–019
Company,[36] wine dealers sent letters to purchasers of wine confirming that
they were the sole beneficial owners of the wine which they had bought and
paid for; however, no steps were taken to segregate the wine in question
from the general mass of stock held by the dealers. It was held that no trust
had arisen so that the purchasers had no proprietary rights in the wine as
against the holders of a floating charge which the dealers had granted over
their entire assets. This decision remains a useful illustration of the general
principle but, because it concerned a sale rather than a gift, its result would
now be different because of the Sale of Goods (Amendment) Act 1995, which
makes such purchasers tenants in common of the general mass of stock.
However, this provision will not avail anyone in the position of the purchasers in *Re Goldcorp Exchange*.[37] They had purchased but had not taken
delivery of unascertained bullion; save for a small group whose bullion had
indeed been segregated, there was no identifiable property whatever to
which any trust could attach and the remaining purchasers thus remained
unsecured creditors in the bullion company's insolvency.

(2)   Intangible property
The position with intangibles is more controversial. In *Hunter v. Moss*[38] a   3–020
declaration of trust in respect of 50 shares in a company in which the settlor
held 950 shares was upheld on the basis that any identification of the
particular 50 shares held on trust was unnecessary and irrelevant. At first
instance, the principle enunciated in *Re London Wine Company* was confined
to tangible property since "ostensibly similar or identical assets may in fact
have characteristics which distinguish them from other assets in the
class"[39]—as the judge[40] said, some of the wine might have become corked or
might have deteriorated in some other way. He then went on to state that a
declaration of trust in respect of £1,000 in a bank account with a current
balance superior to £1,000 would also be effectual. Although the principle
thus enunciated must clearly be confined to intangible property similar to
the choses in action held by the settlor in respect of the shares and the

---

[35] See particularly *McPhail v. Doulton* [1971] A.C. 424, *post*, para 3–053 and, in relation to
expressions such as "reasonable" or "satisfactory' ", *Sudbrook Trading Estates v. Eggleton* [1983]
A.C. 444 and *Graham v. Pitkin* [1992] 1 W.L.R. 403.
[36] [1986] Palmer's Company Cases 123.
[37] [1995] 1 A.C. 74. (Privy Council on appeal from New Zealand).
[38] [1994] 1 W.L.R. 452.
[39] [1993] 1 W.L.R. 934 at 940.
[40] Colin Rimer, Q.C. sitting as a Deputy High Court Judge.

imaginary bank account, it nevertheless caused some surprise. It had hitherto been thought that trusts of such choses in action would only be valid if the settlor declared a trust either of his entire interest in the chose in action or of a fixed proportion of it[41] (in other words, on the facts of *Hunter v. Moss*, a trust of one-nineteenth of the shares held in the company in question) so that thereafter they would be held on trust for the settlor and the beneficiary in the appropriate proportions.

3–021   The settlor appealed to the Court of Appeal where Dillon L.J.[42] simply held that *Re London Wine Company* was "a long way from the present" case and concluded that "[j]ust as a person can give by will a specified number of his shares in a certain company, so equally, in my judgment, he can declare himself a trustee of 50 of his ordinary shares and that is effective to give a beneficial proprietary interest to the beneficiary under the trust". This analogy between a bequest and a declaration of trust has been the subject of fierce criticism.[43] The effect of a will is to vest the whole estate of the testator in his executors to be administered; consequently, a legatee acquires merely an equitable chose in action until the administration has been completed, at which point he will receive whatever shares are allocated to him by the executors. The effect of a declaration of trust, on the other hand, is to vest an immediate proprietary interest in the beneficiary; this necessitates some immediate means of determining which shares are subject to the trust. How otherwise can it be determined, in the event that the trustee subsequently deals with the shares by, for example, selling 50 of them, with whose shares he has actually dealt—his own, those of the beneficiary, or a rateable proportion of the shares of each of them?

3–022   Whether or not these criticisms are actually justified, there can be no doubt that the decision in *Hunter v. Moss* is the law at present and it has since been applied in *Holland v. Newbury*[44] by Neuberger J., who upheld a trust where a dealer in securities was holding unidentified shares in identified companies as the nominee of various of its clients. This latter decision made clear that the crucial distinction is indeed whether the property in question is tangible or intangible (this was the distinction which had been adopted at first instance in *Hunter v. Moss* but Dillon L.J. had made no reference whatever to it in the Court of Appeal). Thus it is apparently now possible to declare a trust of a fixed sum in a bank account with a balance superior to that amount.

3–023   Nevertheless it must be emphasised that, even in the case of intangible property, where funds should have been segregated but have not been, there will still be no trust simply because there is no identifiable trust property at all. This occurred in *MacJordan Construction v. Brookmount Frostin*[45] where under the provisions of a building contract 3 per cent of each stage payment was to be retained from but held on trust for the builder; however, the fund

---

[41] See Underhill & Hayton, *Law of Trusts and Trustees*, 17th edn (London, Lexis Nexis, 2006), para 8–14.

[42] [1994] 1 W.L.R. 452 at 458, 459. This was an unreserved judgment with which the other two members of the court simply agreed.

[43] By Hayton in 110 L.Q.R. (1994) 335 and in Underhill & Hayton, *Law of Trusts and Trustees*, 17th edn (London, Lexis Nexis, 2006), para 8–20.

[44] (1997) *The Times*, July 18, 1997.

[45] (1991) 56 B.L.R. 1.

which it was envisaged should be constituted to hold these retentions was never set up and so there was nothing to form the subject matter of the intended trust. Similarly, in *Hemmens v. Wilson Browne*,[46] a document purporting to give one party the right to call on the other party for a payment of £110,000 at any time was held not to have created a trust either because there was no identifiable fund which could conceivably form its subject matter.

(C) What Property is Held on Trust for Which Beneficiary

Another aspect of uncertainty of subject matter arises where it is clear what property is intended to be subject to the trust but some or all of the beneficial interests are unascertained in the sense that it is not clear what property is held on trust for which beneficiary.   **3–024**

In *Curtis v. Rippon*[47] the testator left all his property to his wife "trusting   **3–025** that she should, in fear of God, and in love of the children committed to her care, make such use of it as should be for her own and their spiritual and temporal good, remembering always, according to circumstances, the Church of God and the poor". There was no doubt what property was subject to the trust but the beneficial interest was to be taken by an ascertained beneficiary, subject to the right of others to unascertained parts of it. The rights of the latter were held to fail and the ascertained beneficiary took everything under the Rule in *Hancock v. Watson*.

Where, on the other hand, all the beneficial interests are unascertained, the   **3–026** trust will fail completely. Thus, in *Boyce v. Boyce*[48] a testator devised two houses to trustees on trust to convey to Maria "whichever house she may think proper to choose or select" and to convey the other house to Charlotte. Maria died in the lifetime of the testator and was thus of course unable to make her choice. The court held that it was impossible to establish which house was held on trust for Charlotte (it is impossible to fault this decision as a matter of construction but it might have been easier to reach the opposite conclusion had there been more than two houses—the consequential direction to convey the "others" to Charlotte could have been construed as "the houses not chosen by Maria"). As a result the houses were held on resulting trust for the testator's residuary estate (the Rule in *Hancock v. Watson* did not apply since there had been no absolute gift of the houses to the trustees in the first instance). In contrast, in *Re Steel*,[49] the testator directed that his residue was to be divided between legatees who had only received "small amounts"; Megarry V.-C. rather generously held that this gift was valid on the basis that the words were merely explaining the testator's motives and ordered the residue to be divided between all the legatees equally whatever the size of their legacies.

(D) The Effect of Uncertainty of Subject Matter

When a trust fails for uncertainty of subject matter then, assuming that there   **3–027** is certainty of intention, a trust will obviously have been intended; consequently, the basic rule is that the failure of the trust on the grounds of

---

[46] [1995] Ch. 223.
[47] (1820) 5 Madd. 434.
[48] (1849) 6 Sim. 476.
[49] [1979] 1 Ch. 218.

uncertainty of subject matter will not enable the potential trustees to take beneficially unless the principle generally known as the Rule in *Hancock v. Watson*[50] applies. This rule applies where there is an absolute gift of property in the first instance and the certainty of intention necessary subsequently to impose trusts on that absolute gift can be established. In those circumstances, in the event that the trusts fail for any reason, the property will vest absolutely in the person to whom the property was first given. In every other case, the property is in principle held on resulting trust for the person who made the absolute gift. This will be the settlor if he is alive; if he is not, and necessarily where the absolute gift was made by will, the resulting trust will be in favour of the residuary beneficiary, or, if there is no gift of residue, in favour of the persons entitled to the estate under the intestacy rules.

3–028   However, there is some authority for the proposition that the court may apply the maxim "equality is equity" and divide the entirety of the beneficial interest equally between the beneficiaries.[51] Cases involving joint bank accounts held by husband and wife are the best known situation in which this maxim is applied when, after dissolution of the marriage, it is found impracticable to divide the fund meticulously between them.[52] However convenient and "equitable" this may be, it is somewhat difficult to justify in principle the application of the maxim in a case involving uncertainty as to the actual beneficial interest taken by the objects of a trust; it is, therefore, somewhat doubtful whether these decisions can actually be justified.

3. *Certainty of Objects*

3–029   The third of the essential ingredients for the effective creation of a trust is that its objects are either certain or are capable of being rendered certain. When this is not the case, the consequences are exactly the same as in the case of uncertainty of subject matter: unless the Rule in *Hancock v. Watson* applies, in which case the potential trustees will be entitled to take the trust property beneficially, that property will be held on resulting trust for the settlor or his estate. However, it should be observed that only private trusts are subject to the certainty of objects requirement. A charitable trust will be upheld despite the fact that its objects are uncertain provided that a paramount intention of charity can be upheld[53]; in such circumstances, what is known as a *cy-près* scheme can be made to enable the trust property to be devoted to defined charitable purposes.

3–030   Three possible tests for certainty of objects have been canvassed by the courts: first, that the objects of a private trust will only be certain if it is possible to draw up a complete list of the objects of the trust (this has become known as "the complete list test"); secondly, that the objects of a private trust will be certain if it is possible to say of any given person that he is, or is not, an object of the trust (this has become known as "the given postulant test"); and, thirdly, that the objects of a private trust will be certain

---

[50] [1902] A.C. 14 (formerly known as the Rule in *Lassence v. Tierney* (1849) 1 Mac. & G. 551).
[51] See *Doyley v. Attorney-General* (1735) 2 Eq.Cas.Abr. 194.
[52] See *Jones v. Maynard* [1951] Ch. 572; *Rimmer v. Rimmer* [1953] 1 Q.B. 63.
[53] See *post*, para 11–118.

if it is possible to show that one identifiable person is clearly an object of the trust (this test has become known as "the one person test").

(A) The Position Prior to *McPhail v. Doulton*[54]

(1) The scope of the complete list test

Prior to the decision of the House of Lords in *McPhail v. Doulton* in 1970, all private trusts had to comply with the complete list test; consequently, their objects were only certain if it was possible to draw up a complete list of them. This requirement had originally been laid down in *Morice v. Bishop of Durham*[55] early in the nineteenth century. At this time virtually all trusts were fixed trusts, that is to say trusts in favour of pre-determined beneficiaries or classes of beneficiaries, each of whom is entitled to a fixed predetermined share of the trust property.[56]   **3–031**

However, following the subsequent development of discretionary trusts, whose trustees determine in what proportions, if any, the trust property is to be divided among members of a pre-determined class and sometimes even decide the membership of the class itself, the Court of Appeal confirmed in *I.R.C. v. Broadway Cottages Trust*[57] that such trusts were also subject to the same requirement. In that case, trustees held funds on trust to apply the income for the benefit of all or any of a class of beneficiaries as they might think fit. It was held, as a matter of construction of the trust deed, that a trust had been created in favour of the specified class. That trust was consequently void for uncertainty on the ground that the whole of the class was at any given time unascertainable; the whole range of objects eligible for selection had to be ascertained or be capable of ascertainment at all times. The expressed principle underlying this decision was that the court, if called upon to execute the trust, could only do so on the basis of equal division, something which would not be possible unless the identity of all the members of the class could be ascertained.   **3–032**

(2) The scope of the given postulant test

On the other hand, mere powers only had to comply with the given postulant test; consequently, their objects were certain if it was possible to say of any given person that he was, or was not, an object of the mere power (it will be remembered[58] that a person is said to hold a mere power if he has a right, but is not under any obligation, to make a selection relating to the beneficial enjoyment of property).   **3–033**

The given postulant test had originally been formulated by Harman J. in *Re Gestetner Settlement*.[59] In that case, capital was held on trust for such member or members of a specified class as the trustees might think fit. The specified class comprised certain named individuals; any person living or thereafter born who was a descendant of the settlor's father or uncle; any spouse, widow or widower of any such person; five charitable bodies; any   **3–034**

---

[54] [1971] A.C. 424.
[55] (1804) 9 Ves.Jr. 399, affirmed (1805) 10 Ves.Jr. 522.
[56] See *ante*, para 2–010.
[57] [1955] Ch. 20; see also *Re Sayer* [1957] Ch. 423.
[58] See *ante*, para 1–070.
[59] [1953] Ch. 673.

former employee of the settlor or his wife; the widow or widower of any such employee; and any director or employee of a named company. Harman J. held that it was unnecessary in a power of this kind to establish that the objects were all capable of ascertainment. It was simply necessary to be able to say of any given person that he was, or was not, an object of the power. The trustees did not have "to worry their heads to survey the world from China to Peru"[60] to find out who was within the designated class. There was no difficulty in ascertaining whether or not any given postulant was a member of the class. Consequently, the mere power in question was held to be valid.

3–035   The combined effect of this decision and the slightly later decision in *I.R.C. v. Broadway Cottages Trust*[61] was to establish a crucial difference between discretionary trusts and mere powers, since the former had to comply with the complete list test and the latter only had to comply with the given postulant test. Given the factual similarity between the two, this caused considerable problems when the courts had subsequently to consider the proper construction of gifts which would be void if they were construed as having created discretionary trusts but valid if they were construed as having created mere powers. These difficulties were undoubtedly the principal reason why the House of Lords eventually assimilated the position of discretionary trusts and mere powers in *McPhail v. Doulton*.[62]

(3) The scope of the one person test

3–036   Gifts subject to the donee satisfying a condition precedent clearly had to comply only with the one person test; consequently, their objects were certain if it was possible to show that one identifiable person was clearly an object of the gift. Thus in *Re Allen*[63] a testator left property to the eldest of his nephews "who shall be a member of the Church of England and an adherent to the doctrine of that Church"; this gift was held to be valid on the basis that, whatever the precise meaning of the conditions, it was perfectly possible for a claimant to show that he fell within them. This remains the law today.

3–037   Following the formulation of the given postulant test in *Re Gestetner Settlement*,[64] it was also contended on a few occasions, most notably by Lord Denning M.R.,[65] that test should be interpreted in the same way as the one

---

[60] *ibid.* at 688–689. This expression was incorrectly attributed by Harman J. to Alexander Pope (see *Re Baden's Trust Deeds* [1969] 2 Ch. 388 at 397, *per* Harman L.J.); the words are in fact those of Samuel Johnson.

[61] [1955] Ch. 20; see also *Re Sayer* [1957] Ch. 423.

[62] [1971] A.C. 424.

[63] [1953] Ch. 810.

[64] [1953] Ch. 673.

[65] In the Court of Appeal in *Re Gulbenkian's Settlement Trusts* [1968] 1 Ch. 126 at 34; see also, *per* Winn L.J. at 138 (the limitation is discussed *post* in the text). It was also used in *Re Gibbard* [1967] 1 W.L.R. 42 at 47–48, where Plowman J. upheld a power to appoint to "any of my old friends", and in *Re Leek* [1967] Ch. 1061 at 1073 where Buckley J. upheld a power to appoint to "such other person as the company may consider to have a moral claim upon you" (the Court of Appeal held ([1969] 1 Ch. 563) that the gift in question was a trust rather than a power and so was void because it was impossible to ascertain all the members of the class. The one person test still applies to individual gifts subject to the donee satisfying a condition precedent or answering a particular description; see *post*, para 3–050.

person test. But the more strict interpretation of the given postulant test, under which, if it was impossible to ascertain whether or not a given individual was within the class, the power would fail despite the fact that other classes of persons were clearly within it, was supported by the preponderance of authority[66] and was finally confirmed definitively by the House of Lords in *Re Gulbenkian's Settlement Trusts*.[67]

That case involved the construction of a clause in a work of precedents   **3–038** then much used by the legal profession. The clause provided that a special power of appointment could be exercised for the maintenance and personal support of all or any one or more of the following persons as the trustees should in their absolute discretion think fit: the settlor's son; any wife, children or remoter issue of the son; and any persons in whose house or apartments or in whose company or under whose care and control or by whom the husband might from time to time be employed or residing.

The clause had been considered before in *Re Gresham's Settlement*,[68] where   **3–039** Harman J. had held it void for uncertainty on the grounds that there might be a number of persons of whom it could not be determined whether they were or were not within the dragnet of this unusually constructed clause; he had distinguished his own decision in *Re Gestetner Settlement* because there, despite the fact that not all the persons within the specified class were actually known, it could be said whether any given person was or was not within the class. But in *Re Gulbenkian's Settlement Trusts* the House of Lords overruled *Re Gresham's Settlement* and held that the clause before them was sufficiently certain to satisfy the test laid down in *Re Gestetner Settlement*. Lord Upjohn, in affirming the latter test, rejected the application of the one person test which had been advocated by Lord Denning M.R. in the Court of Appeal.[69]

(B) The Effect of *McPhail v. Doulton*[70]

In *McPhail v. Doulton*[71] in 1970, the majority of the House of Lords overruled   **3–040** the test laid down in *I.R.C. v. Broadway Cottages Trust* and held that discretionary trusts had to comply only with the given postulant test, not with the complete list test. The case for rigid requirements for trusts which had been made in *I.R.C. v. Broadway Cottages Trust*, namely that their imperative nature necessarily required that all their objects should be known, was admittedly a persuasive one; indeed it had been restated in the House of Lords by Lord Upjohn in the intervening decision of the House of Lords in *Re Gulbenkian's Settlement Trusts*.[72] However, Lord Wilberforce indicated in

---

[66] *Re Coates* [1955] Ch. 495 (for any friends his wife might feel that he had forgotten); *Re Sayer Trust* [1957] Ch. 423 (power in favour of employees, ex-employees, widow, children and "dependants"); in both these cases the power was held to be valid despite the application of the stricter test.

[67] [1970] A.C. 508, applied in *Re Denley's Trust Deed* [1968] Ch. 373.

[68] [1956] 1 W.L.R. 573, followed in *Re Allan* [1958] 1 W.L.R. 220, where the same clause had been utilised.

[69] Lord Donovan reserved his opinion on this point.

[70] [1971] A.C. 424.

[71] [1971] A.C. 424.

[72] [1970] A.C. 508 The point was restated by Lord Hodson in his dissenting speech in *McPhail v. Doulton* [1971] A.C. 424 at 442.

McPhail v. Doulton that the law should take account of practicalities, particularly the narrow distinction between discretionary trusts (which he also described as "trust powers") and mere powers.

3–041   Lord Wilberforce also rejected as inappropriate the theory specifically postulated in *I.R.C. v. Broadway Cottages Trust* that the court can only execute a trust by ordering equal distribution in which every beneficiary shares: "equal division among all may, probably would, produce a result beneficial to none", being "surely the last thing the settlor ever intended".[73] Lord Wilberforce stated that, if the trustees failed to execute the trust, the court would instead do so "in the manner best calculated to give effect to the settlor's . . . intentions". He envisaged this being done in one of three ways: either by appointing new trustees, or by directing persons representative of the classes of beneficiaries to prepare a scheme of distribution, or, should the proper basis for distribution be apparent, by directing the trustees how to distribute the fund.[74] (This does not of course mean that equal distribution will never again be ordered; in the case of a small class of beneficiaries whose entire membership is known, it is almost inevitable that equal distribution will still be ordered. It is, therefore, likely that the novel powers of the court outlined by Lord Wilberforce will only in fact be used where it is not possible to ascertain the entire membership of the class of beneficiaries in question, that is to say in the case of discretionary trusts which would have been void for uncertainty but for the decision in *McPhail v. Doulton*). This fundamental change in judicial attitudes enabled the certainty of objects requirements for discretionary trusts and for powers to be equated; the criterion for both is whether or not it can be said of "any given postulant" that he is a member of the class of potential beneficiaries.

3–042   However, the fact that the test for certainty of objects in mere powers and discretionary trusts has now been assimilated does not mean that mere powers and discretionary trusts have themselves been assimilated. As will be seen in a later chapter,[75] the basic distinction between the two remains. The court will not normally compel the exercise of a mere power and, when it is exercised, will interfere only where that power is exercised improperly or, possibly, capriciously. On the other hand, in the event that the trustees do not exercise their discretion under a discretionary trust, the court will do so in the manner thought most appropriate to carry out the settlor's intentions. Moreover, as a result of this distinction, "a wider and more comprehensive range of inquiry"[76] as to the range of possible objects is called for in the case of discretionary trusts than in the case of mere powers.

(C)   Outstanding Questions

3–043   Despite the decision in *McPhail v. Doulton*, a number of aspects of certainty of objects have not yet been finally resolved.

(1)   The scope of the given postulant test

3–044   While *McPhail v. Doulton* has established that the given postulant test is the appropriate test for certainty of objects of both discretionary trusts and mere

---

[73] [1971] A.C. 424 at 451.
[74] *ibid.* at 457.
[75] See *post*, Chapter 6.
[76] *McPhail v. Doulton* [1971] A.C. 424, *per* Lord Wilberforce at 457.

powers, there is in other respects still some room for debate as to the applicability of the test.

(a) Fixed trusts The first question is whether the given postulant test **3–045** only applies to the type of trust which was under consideration in *McPhail v. Doulton*, that is to say only to discretionary trusts, or also applies to fixed trusts.

In the editions of this work which were prepared by Professors Parker and Mellows,[77] it was contended that there seems to be no reason in principle why the given postulant test should not also apply to fixed trusts. Just as an order for distribution (not necessarily, as has been seen, on the basis of equal division) can be made by the court in the case of a discretionary trust, so also, it might be thought, could such an order be made in the case of a fixed trust where one or more of the beneficiaries are not ascertainable.[78] (The point is conceded to be "more academic than real", arising only in the almost inconceivable case of a trust for objects which could not be fully ascertained also containing a provision for distribution to them in equal or some other definite shares.)

However, the more general view, which is shared by the author of this edition, is that the "given postulant" test does not apply to fixed trusts, in respect of which it is still necessary to be able to draw up a complete list of the objects.[79] It is generally thought, contrary to the view already considered, that, if the trust property is to be divided among a class of beneficiaries in fixed shares, it would be wholly contrary to the intention of the settlor for the court to order any other form of division; on this basis, it is essential that all the possible beneficiaries should be capable of being ascertained by the time at which any distribution of capital or income has to be made.

(b) "Powers in the nature of a trust" It has already been seen that **3–046** discretionary trusts are today often known as trust powers; this is largely, if not entirely, because they were so described by Lord Wilberforce in *McPhail v. Doulton*. However, the same name is also used to denote powers whose donees are under an obligation to exercise them. Such powers are also known as "powers in the nature of a trust".[80] Where such a power is found

---

[77] See, for example, the fifth and last of those editions (1983) at p.79. See also Matthews [1984] Conv. 22.

[78] The authors' reading of Lord Wilberforce's speech was that the new test applies to all trusts. Furthermore, it was contended that it would be regrettable if this were not so, because a discretionary trust is a trust, despite the fact that such trusts have close affinities with powers.

[79] See, for example, Hanbury & Martin, *Modern Equity*, 17th edn (London, Sweet & Maxwell, 2005), para 3–025; Underhill & Hayton, *Law of Trusts and Trustees*, 17th edn (London, Lexis Nexis, 2007), para 8–42.

[80] The terminological confusion caused by the fact that the expression "trust power" is now used to describe two factually similar but legally quite distinct types of gift has already been mentioned (see *ante*, para 1–072). Hanbury & Martin, *Modern Equity*, 17th edn (London, Sweet & Maxwell, 2005), para 3–037 suggests that it may have been the two meanings of "trust power" which caused the discrepancy between the majority and the minority in *McPhail v. Doulton*, the majority having in mind the modern discretionary trust and the minority the old style power in the nature of a trust.

to exist, the court will execute the power in the event that its donee fails to exercise it.

3–047   Such a case was *Burrough v. Philcox*.[81] The testator left property on trust for his two children for life and, subject thereto, to their issue but further declared that, if both his children should die without issue, the surviving child should have the power to dispose by will of the property "among my nephews and nieces or their children, either all to one of them or to as many as my surviving child shall think proper". The surviving child died without so appointing. Lord Cottenham L.C. held that, "when there appears a general intention in favour of a class, and a particular intention in favour of individuals of a class to be selected by another person, and the particular intention fails from that selection not being made, the Court will carry into effect the general intention in favour of the class".[82] He held that the words used evinced a general intention of this type consequently the court could execute the power on behalf of its donee by dividing the property equally among all the members of the class (had he not found a general intention of this type, the property would have passed on a resulting trust for those entitled to the residuary estate of the testator).

3–048   With which test for certainty of objects do such powers in the nature of a trust have to comply? If it is still the case that the court would automatically execute such a power by dividing the property equally between all the members of the class, then it ought to follow that the test is the same as that for fixed trusts; in this case, according to the general view that the appropriate test for fixed trusts is the complete list test,[83] it will be necessary for it to be possible to draw up a complete list of the members of the class at the appropriate time. If, on the other hand, the remarks of Lord Wilberforce in *McPhail v. Doulton* as to the ways in which the court can now execute a discretionary trust[84] also apply to powers in the nature of a trust, then there will be no need for the complete list test to apply and such limitations will presumably also be governed by the given postulant test.

3–049   This question is in fact somewhat academic since powers in the nature of a trust are almost invariably in favour of small groups of beneficiaries, usually, as in *Burrough v. Philcox*, the members of a family. Gifts of this type will inevitably satisfy either test for certainty of objects and in practice, the court would almost inevitably order equal distribution quite irrelevant of whether or not this was actually obligatory. It has admittedly been argued that powers in the nature of a trust should be regarded as fixed trusts subject to defeasance by exercise of the power of selection and, as a result, must still be governed by the test appropriate to fixed trusts.[85] However, because of the factual similarity between powers in the nature of a trust and discretionary trusts, it seems as a matter of principle to be more appropriate that such powers should today also be governed by the given postulant test on the already mentioned assumption that, whenever the entire membership of the class is known, equal division will in fact be ordered.

---

[81] (1840) 5 Myl. & Cr. 72.

[82] *ibid*.

[83] The contrary view was adopted in earlier editions of this work (see *ante*, para 3–045).

[84] See *ante*, para 3–041.

[85] In Hanbury & Martin, *Modern Equity*, 17th edn (London, Sweet & Maxwell, 2005), para 3–037.

(c) Gifts subject to a condition precedent and individual gifts The one   3–050
person test clearly still applies to gifts subject to the donee satisfying a
condition precedent. This is illustrated by *Re Tuck's Settlement Trusts*,[86] where
requirements that the principal beneficiary for the time being under a
settlement had to be of the Jewish faith and, if married, be married to an
approved Jewish wife were held by the majority of the Court of Appeal[87] to
be conditions precedent and consequently valid under the one person
test.

The one person test has now also been extended to gifts made to individ-   3–051
uals who answer a particular description.[88] In *Re Barlow's Will Trust*[89] the
testatrix provided that "any friends of mine who may wish to do so" might
purchase any of her paintings at their probate valuation. This limitation was
not expressed in the form of a condition precedent; however, it nevertheless
amounted to a series of gifts to any individuals who answered a particular
specified description. Browne-Wilkinson J. held that, had this been a gift to
a class and therefore had had to satisfy the given postulant test, it would
have been void; it would obviously also have been void if it had had to
satisfy the complete list test. However, he regarded the limitation as creating
a series of individual gifts in the form of options exercisable by any person
who qualified as a "friend"; since there might be persons who could, on any
conceivable test, prove that they were friends, the limitation was valid.

While the applicability of the one person test to conditions precedent and   3–052
other analogous gifts is clearly established, it would certainly not be easy for
the court to decide whether any individual did in fact qualify in such
circumstances; any doubts as to qualification would, therefore, presumably
lead to the automatic disqualification of the claimant. However, this is not
necessarily an objection to the existence of the test since, as will be seen in
the next section, this is now arguably also the case with the given postulant
test.

(2) Conceptual and evidential certainty

In *Re Gulbenkian's Settlement Trusts*,[90] Lord Upjohn posed the distinction   3–053
between conceptual certainty and evidential certainty; this distinction was
also adopted in *McPhail v. Doulton*.[91] Objects will be conceptually uncertain
if the exact meaning of the definition used contains any linguistic or semantic uncertainty, if in other words it is impossible to say what the words in
question actually mean. If this is the case, the gift in question will be wholly
void unless the court can resolve the conceptual uncertainty in some way.
Only where objects are conceptually certain does any question of evidential
certainty arise; this is the question of whether, on the facts, it can be
established whether or not the objects satisfy the relevant test for certainty

---

[86] [1978] Ch. 49.
[87] Lord Russell of Killowen and Eveleigh L.J.; Lord Denning M.R. adopted a different
approach, discussed *post*, para 3–065.
[88] Conditions subsequent are subject to a stricter test; the situations in which such a condition
will operate must be wholly clear from the outset. For a recent discussion, see *Re Tepper's Will
Trusts* [1987] Ch. 49.
[89] [1978] 1 W.L.R. 278.
[90] [1970] A.C. 508 at 524.
[91] [1971] A.C. 424 at 457.

of objects; if it cannot be so established, the gift in question will also be rendered wholly void.

3–054   (a) The complete list test The complete list test requires total certainty. Any form of conceptual or evidential uncertainty will render the gift in question void.

On the assumption that fixed trusts are still governed by the complete list test, a fixed trust for the settlor's "old friends" in equal shares would be likely to be conceptually uncertain[92]; this is simply because the expression used is capable of so many different interpretations.[93]

On the same assumption, the objects of a fixed trust will be evidentially uncertain if it is impossible to list all the members of the class at the appropriate time. However, there is never any difficulty about a trust for one person for life followed by a gift in remainder to his children in equal shares; even if the life tenant has no children at the time at which the trust is constituted, it will become clear whether or not he has any children and, if so, how many not later than nine months after the determination of his life interest upon his death.[94] But the sort of classes of beneficiaries which were established in *Re Gestetner Settlement*,[95] *Re Gulbenkian's Settlement*[96] and *McPhail v. Doulton*[97] cannot conceivably satisfy the "complete list" test because of the impossibility of determining between how many persons the capital or income has to be divided. Having said that, provided that it is possible to establish the maximum number of possible beneficiaries, it does not matter that the continued existence or present whereabouts of some of the possible members of the class cannot be discovered; the shares payable to any such beneficiaries can be paid into court to await either their appearance or definitive proof that they did not in fact qualify.[98] All that is necessary is that the list which is able to be drawn up at the appropriate time is, on a balance of probabilities, complete.

3–055   (b) The one person test The one person test does not require any conceptual certainty whatever. This follows inexorably from *Re Barlow's Will Trust*[99] where Browne-Wilkinson J. held that, had the gift to "any friends of mine" been governed by either the complete list test or the given postulant test, it would have been void for conceptual uncertainty. That did not prevent him from upholding the gift.

---

[92] This was stated by Browne-Wilkinson J. in *Re Barlow's Will Trusts* [1970] 1 W.L.R. 278 at 281–282.

[93] However, such an expression would satisfy the more diluted test advocated by Lord Denning M.R. (see *ante*, n.65), provided that one "old friend" of the settlor could be clearly identified—this was specifically held by Browne-Wilkinson J. in *Re Barlow's Will Trusts* [1979] 1 W.L.R. 278 in respect of a series of individual gifts with a condition precedent or description attached, to which the more diluted test was held to be applicable.

[94] The point at which the children's interest would vest in possession (each child having acquired a vested interest in interest on his birth); the nine-month extension is made so that any posthumous children can be included.

[95] [1953] Ch. 673.

[96] [1970] A.C. 508.

[97] [1971] A.C. 424.

[98] See Emery (1982) 98 L.Q.R. 551.

[99] [1978] 1 W.L.R. 278.

The only evidential certainty required by the one person test is that it must be possible for that one person to show that he satisfies the criteria of the gift in question. Thus the gift in *Re Allen*[100] was upheld because, whatever the precise meaning of the words "a member of the Church of England and an adherent to the doctrine of that Church", it was perfectly possible for a claimant to show that he fell within them.

(c) **The given postulant test** The effect of conceptual and evidential uncertainty in relation to the given postulant test had to be considered in *Re Baden's Deed Trusts (No.2)*,[101] the sequel to *McPhail v. Doulton* in which the test laid down by the House of Lords had to be applied to the terms of the trust in question. The trust deed in question directed the trustees to apply the net income of the fund in making at their absolute discretion grants to or for the benefit of any of the officers and employees or ex-officers or ex-employees of a specified company or to any relatives or dependants of any such persons. The Court of Appeal held that this class satisfied the given postulant test but the members of the court agreed neither as to the correct interpretation of the test nor, consequently, as to the conceptually certain meaning of the two problematic words, "relatives" and "dependants".

3–056

Of the three members of the Court of Appeal, Stamp L.J. alone interpreted the given postulant test strictly, holding that the test would only be satisfied if it was possible to say either "yes" or "no" to any person who could conceivably present himself to the trustees.[102] On the other hand, both Sachs L.J. and Megaw L.J. seemed to broaden the test laid down by the House of Lords. Sachs L.J. held that, provided that the class was conceptually certain, the gift could never fail for evidential uncertainty; the burden of proof was on the postulant and, if he could not positively prove that he was within the class, then he was outside it.[103] Megaw L.J. held that, if it could be said with certainty that a substantial number of objects did fall within the class, then it did not matter that, as regards a substantial number of other persons, the answer had to be that "it is not proven whether they are in or out".[104]

3–057

All three views are susceptible of criticism. The interpretation advocated by Stamp L.J. in practice does not fall far short of a return to the complete list test expressly rejected in *McPhail v. Doulton*; according to this interpretation, while there is no need for the trustees actually to draw up a list, it has to be admitted that those otherwise entitled to the property subject to a discretionary trust will be able to upset that trust whenever they can come up with one person whose claim to be a member of the class cannot be proven one way or the other. On the other hand, the interpretations adopted by both Sachs L.J. and Megaw L.J. move some considerable way towards the one person test specifically rejected in *Re Gulbenkian's Settlement Trusts*. The interpretation adopted by Sachs L.J. could undoubtedly lead to there being only one beneficiary within the class but only if the expression used was conceptually certain, something which is not actually required in the case of

3–058

---

[100] [1953] Ch. 810.
[101] [1973] Ch. 9.
[102] *ibid.* at 28.
[103] *ibid.* at 19.
[104] *ibid.* at 24.

gifts subject to the one person test.[105] The interpretation adopted by Megaw L.J. would admittedly require a substantial number of persons rather than just one to fall within the class; however, it is unclear whether or not conceptual certainty would also be required.

3–059   Having expressed these differing views as to the interpretation of the given postulant test, the members of the Court of Appeal all accepted that, no matter what meaning was given to "dependants", the trust would be both conceptually and evidentially certain.[106] Sachs and Megaw L.JJ. held that the trust would also be conceptually certain even if the widest possible meaning, "descendants from a common ancestor", was attributed to "relatives" and that there was no evidential difficulty about ascertaining whether any given postulant was a relative.[107] Stamp L.J., on the other hand, held that, if such a meaning was given to "relatives", the trust would fail because of the impossibility of saying that any given postulant was not a relative of a past or present officer or employee of the company; he consequently interpreted "relatives" as meaning "statutory next-of-kin", an expression which is on any view both conceptually and evidentially certain.[108]

3–060   It is not easy to determine the precise effect of Re Baden's Deed Trusts (No.2) so far as conceptual certainty is concerned. There has been little or no subsequent judicial discussion of this aspect of the interpretation of the test laid down in Re Gulbenkian's Settlement Trusts and McPhail v. Doulton. The limitation in Re Baden's Deed Trusts (No.2) was of course complex and it must not be thought that problems of this kind will often arise; however, it must not be forgotten that, in Re Barlow's Will Trust,[109] Browne-Wilkinson J. held that, had the gift to "any friends of mine" been a gift to a class and therefore had had to satisfy the given postulant test, it would have been void for conceptual uncertainty. Other illustrations of conceptual uncertainty are to be found in cases prior to McPhail v. Doulton where it was plain that there was, and would still be, conceptual uncertainty of objects.

3–061   Thus in Re Astor's Settlement Trusts,[110] which concerned the newspaper The Observer, a settlement provided for income to be applied at the trustees' discretion among a number of non-charitable purposes including the "maintenance of good understanding, sympathy and co-operation between nations" and "the preservation of the independence and integrity of newspapers" and other such purposes for the protection of newspapers. Roxburgh J. held that the objects listed above were void for uncertainty and that for this and other reasons the trusts were void; he said that purposes must be stated in phrases which embody definite concepts and, moreover, the means by which the trustees are to attain them must be prescribed with a

---

[105] See ante, para 3–055.
[106] [1973] Ch. 9 at 20, 22, 30.
[107] ibid. at 21, 22.
[108] ibid. at 28–30. "Relatives" has traditionally been construed as "statutory next-of-kin" if this is necessary to save a gift; however, an appointment by the trustees in favour of relatives who are not statutory next-of-kin is nevertheless valid, which signifies that, in the event that the court were called upon to execute the trust because of a default by the trustees, distribution would necessarily be among a narrower class than that available to the trustees (see Re Poulton's Will Trusts [1987] 1 W.L.R. 795).
[109] [1978] 1 W.L.R. 278.
[110] [1952] Ch. 534. See also post, para 3–061.

sufficient degree of certainty. Similarly, in *Re Endacott*[111] the Court of Appeal held that a trust which was in effect for a purpose regarded by the trustees as "useful" was void for uncertainty because it was not clear what "utility" meant.

It is also generally thought that a discretionary trust in favour of "persons   **3–062** having a moral claim" on the settlor would also be void for conceptual uncertainty because of the impossibility of defining "moral claim". Admittedly, in *Re Leek*[112] a limitation in favour of "such persons as the [donee of the power in question] may consider to have a moral claim" on the settlor was held by Buckley J. to be sufficiently certain, a view which was supported by Harman L.J. in the Court of Appeal by way of dictum.[113] However, it is arguable that the restriction of the class to such persons as a specified individual or individuals regards as having such a moral claim makes the issue more, rather than less, conceptually uncertain, unless that restriction is regarded as a valid delegation in the manner considered below.

(d) Can conceptual uncertainty be cured by delegation? *Re Leek*[114]   **3–063** raises a question of general importance, which can arise in all cases in which conceptual certainty is required, as to the extent to which conceptual uncertainty can be cured by a provision that the matter is to be settled by the decision of either the trustees or of some third party.

The orthodox view is that a question of fact can be delegated for resolu-   **3–064** tion in this way[115] but not a question of law, since the jurisdiction of the court to decide matters of law cannot be ousted.[116] For present purposes, this suggests that, while an issue of evidential uncertainty could be delegated by the settlor to the trustees[117] or to some third party for resolution, an issue of conceptual uncertainty could not be so delegated.[118] However, in *Dundee General Hospital Board of Management v. Walker*,[119] the House of Lords held, on a Scottish appeal, that a proviso that a legacy was only to be paid to a hospital if the trustees of the will "were in their sole and absolute discretion"

---

[111] [1960] Ch. 232.
[112] [1967] Ch. 1061 (Buckley J.) [1969] 1 Ch. 563 (C.A.).
[113] As the words in square brackets indicate, Buckley J. actually held that this limitation had created a mere power. At that time, only mere powers were subject to the given postulant test and, on appeal, the Court of Appeal instead found that the limitation had created a discretionary trust which, under the then law, was void for uncertainty because it was impossible to satisfy the complete list test (such a discretionary trust would of course now also be subject to the given postulant test).
[114] [1967] Ch. 1061 (Buckley J.) [1969] 1 Ch. 563 (C.A.).
[115] *Re Coxen* [1948] Ch. 747.
[116] *Re Wynn* [1952] Ch. 271.
[117] *Re Coxen* [1948] Ch. 747. This case concerned a condition subsequent; a provision that the trustees should be able to determine whether or not the testator's widow had "ceased permanently to reside" at a particular property was upheld. See also *Re Burton* [1955] Ch. 82 at 95.
[118] *Re Jones* [1953] Ch. 125. This case also concerned a condition subsequent; a provision that the "uncontrolled opinion" of the trustees should determine whether or not the testator's daughter had "social or other relationship" with a named person was held to be void for uncertainty.
[119] [1952] 1 All E.R. 896. This decision was considered in *Re Jones* [1953] Ch. 125 (*supra*) but was distinguished on the grounds that it concerned a condition precedent whereas *Re Jones* concerned a condition subsequent.

satisfied that the hospital had not been placed under state control made the trustees the sole judges of this question; therefore, there could be no appeal to the courts from their decision unless they had considered the wrong question or failed to consider the right question in a proper manner. This decision suggests that a question of law can now be referred to a third party for decision, in which case there seems no reason why an issue of conceptual uncertainty should not similarly be delegated.

3–065   This impression is confirmed by some remarks of Lord Denning M.R. in *Re Tuck's Settlement Trusts*,[120] which concerned conditions precedent in a settlement that the principal beneficiary for the time being had to be of the Jewish faith and, if married, be married to an approved Jewish wife. The settlement provided that any dispute as to the conditions was to be referred to the Chief Rabbi for decision. The majority of the Court of Appeal found that these conditions were conditions precedent; consequently, they did not need to be conceptually certain anyway and so were valid.[121] Lord Denning M.R., however, held that, in the event that there was any conceptual uncertainty in the conditions, this was cured by the reference to the Chief Rabbi.[122] If this view is correct, the further question arises as to whether it is necessary for the person to whose decision the resolution is delegated to be someone who, like the Chief Rabbi, can be regarded as having some expertise in this respect or can be anyone at all. This may be relevant in any consideration of the question mentioned above as to whether the restriction of a class to such persons as a specified individual or individuals regards as having a moral claim on a settlor makes the gift in question more or less conceptually uncertain.

3–066   In any event, this matter cannot yet be regarded as settled, particularly in the light of the fact that Lord Denning's remarks were subsequently overlooked in the rather inadequately reported *Re Wright's Will Trusts*.[123] However, there is clearly considerably more possibility than hitherto that issues of conceptual uncertainty can now be cured in this way.

(3)   Administrative unworkability

3–067   In *McPhail v. Doulton*,[124] Lord Wilberforce added a third class of potential uncertainty, where "the meaning of the words used is clear but the definition of beneficiaries is so hopelessly wide as not to form 'anything like a class' so that the trust is administratively unworkable" (he gave as an example "all the residents of Greater London"). A discretionary trust was indeed struck down for this reason in *R. v. District Auditor, ex p. West Yorkshire Metropolitan County Council*,[125] where the local authority resolved to create a trust "for the benefit of any or all or some of the inhabitants of the County of West Yorkshire" for various specific purposes. Given that there were 2,500,000 potential beneficiaries, the court, while prepared to assume without deciding that "inhabitant" was sufficiently conceptually certain, held that the trust was void for administrative unworkability on the grounds that the

---

[120] [1978] Ch. 49.
[121] *ibid., per* Lord Russell of Killowen at 63–64, *per* Eveleigh L.J. at 64–65.
[122] *ibid.* at 60, 62.
[123] [1981] Law Society Gazette Reports 841.
[124] [1971] A.C. 424 at 457.
[125] (1986) 26 R.V.R. 24. See Harpum (1986) 45 C.L.J. 391.

class was much too large. It was also accepted in *Re Harding*[126] that a private trust for such a large class as the black community in four London Boroughs would be administratively unworkable and therefore void.

While the concept of administrative unworkability thus clearly applies to discretionary trusts, there has been considerable debate over whether or not it also applies to mere powers.   3–068

In *Blausten v. I.R.C.*,[127] the trustees had power to introduce to the class of beneficiaries any person other than the settlor. An argument that this power was void for administrative unworkability was rejected on the ground that, although the trustees had this admittedly wide power, it could only be exercised with the written consent of the settlor and hence only during his lifetime. Therefore, it could not be said that the settlor had failed to set "metes and bounds" to the beneficial interests which he intended to create or to permit to be created under the settlement. Buckley L.J. therefore clearly assumed, admittedly only by way of dictum, that the concept of administrative unworkability did apply to mere powers.   3–069

However, this reasoning is difficult to reconcile with subsequent decisions. In *Re Manisty's Settlement*,[128] the trustees had a mere power to add beneficiaries and to benefit the persons so added and this power was exercisable in favour of anyone in the world except the settlor, his wife and some other persons. Templeman J. held that this power did not fail for administrative unworkability even though there were no expressed restrictions on its operation by the trustees; he preferred the view that a mere power could not be void on the grounds of breadth of numbers but only if its terms were capricious. Megarry V.-C. in *Re Hay's Settlement Trusts*[129] also took the view that a mere power would not be administratively unworkable on the grounds of mere numbers on the basis that this should not inhibit the trustees in its exercise and would not prevent the courts from controlling them. He did however state that a discretionary trust as broad as the power in that case ("to or for the benefit of any person or persons whatsoever or to any charity" with only the settlor, her husband, and the trustees excluded) would have been void as administratively unworkable. Subsequently, in *Re Beatty's Will Trusts*[130] a mere power given to trustees in favour of "such person or persons as they think fit" was held valid, this time without any mention of the possibility of it being administratively unworkable at all.   3–070

At this stage, it seemed tolerably clear that the concept of administrative unworkability did not apply to mere powers. However, as will be seen in a later chapter,[131] the duties of the donee of a mere power and the remedies available to the objects of such a power have now been the subject of an important review in *Mettoy Pensions Trustees v. Evans*[132]; this decision envisages the adaptation of the remedies available for the enforcement of discretionary trusts for the purpose of enforcing mere powers. It has therefore   3–071

---

[126] [2008] EWHC 3 (Ch), [2008] 1 W.L.R. 361, *per* Lewison J. at [13].
[127] [1972] Ch. 256.
[128] [1974] Ch. 17.
[129] [1982] 1 W.L.R. 202.
[130] [1990] 1 W.L.R. 1503.
[131] See *post*, para 6–140.
[132] [1990] 1 W.L.R. 1587.

been suggested[133] that this may cause the concept of administrative unworkability to be applied to at least some types of mere powers. It obviously remains to be seen whether this is yet another consequence of this important decision.

(4) Capriciousness

3–072   Another possible ground of potential uncertainty is capriciousness, a concept developed by Templeman J. in *Re Manisty's Settlement*,[134] in which he upheld a mere power of very considerable breadth. He held that the exercise of the process of selection by discretionary trustees and by the donees of powers may be rendered practically impossible if the terms of the discretionary trusts and powers in question are capricious. He gave as an example of a capricious power one in favour of "the residents of Greater London", not because of the number of objects of the power but "because the terms of the power negative any sensible intention on the part of the settlor" and any "sensible consideration by the trustees of the exercise of the power". "If the settlor intended and expected the trustees would have regard to persons with some claim on his bounty or some interest in an institution favoured by the settlor, or if the settlor had any other sensible intention or expectation, he would not have required the trustees to consider only an accidental conglomeration of persons who have no discernible link with the settlor or with any institution."[135]

3–073   Because the example given by Templeman J. of a capricious power was exactly the same as the example given by Lord Wilberforce in *McPhail v. Doulton* of an administratively unworkable discretionary trust, it was originally thought that the two concepts were the same,[136] the former being applicable to mere powers and the latter being applicable to discretionary trusts. However, it is now clear that the concept of capriciousness applies both to discretionary trusts and to powers. In *R. v. District Auditor, ex p. West Yorkshire Metropolitan County Council*,[137] the discretionary trust held void for administrative unworkability because the 2,500,000 inhabitants of West Yorkshire constituted too large a class was held not to be capricious since the County Council had every reason for wishing to benefit the inhabitants of West Yorkshire. The concepts of administrative unworkability and capriciousness are therefore apparently distinct, the former but not the latter being limited to breadth of numbers. No discretionary trust or mere power has yet been set aside on the grounds of capriciousness; it will be interesting to see whether this ever occurs.

(5) Duty to survey the field

3–074   Given that, save in the case of a fixed trust, the identity of all the objects of a trust or a power will not necessarily be known, the trustees of a discretionary trust and those entitled to exercise a power in the nature of a trust or a mere power cannot be obliged to consider the claims of every possible

[133] By Gardner (1991) 107 L.Q.R. 214.
[134] [1974] Ch. 17.
[135] *ibid.* at 27.
[136] See Emery (1982) 98 L.Q.R. 551.
[137] (1986) 26 R.V.R. 24.

object. In *McPhail v. Doulton*[138] Lord Wilberforce stated that the trustees of a discretionary trust "ought to make such a survey of the range of objects or possible beneficiaries as will enable them to carry out their fiduciary duty" and emphasised that a "wider and more comprehensive range of enquiry is called for" in the case of discretionary trusts than in the case of mere powers. Where the possible objects number thousands or hundreds of thousands, the trustees must assess "the size of the problem" in a businesslike manner.[139] A more detailed account of the duties of discretionary trustees was provided by Megarry V.-C. in *Re Hay's Settlement Trusts*[140] in the following passage.

"The trustee must not simply proceed to exercise the power in favour of such of the objects as happen to be at hand or claim his attention. He must first consider what persons or classes of persons are objects of the power . . . : what is needed is an appreciation of the width of the field, and thus whether a selection is to be made merely from a dozen or, instead, from thousands or millions. . . . Only when the trustee has applied his mind to the 'size of the problem' should he then consider in individual cases whether, in relation to other possible claimants, a particular grant is appropriate. In doing this, no doubt he should not prefer the undeserving to the deserving but he is not required to make an exact calculation whether, as between deserving claimants, A is more deserving than B."

This duty, considerably broader than had hitherto been thought,[141] has so far been applied only to trustees of discretionary trusts but would presumably also be applied to the donees of powers in the nature of a trust. The duties of a donee of a mere power "cannot be more stringent than those for a discretionary trust".[142] It will be remembered[143] that mere powers are divided into fiduciary powers (basically mere powers held by trustees) and non-fiduciary or personal powers (mere powers held by anyone else). A donee of a non-fiduciary mere power is under no obligation to do anything at all and so cannot possibly have any duty to survey the field. On the other hand, in *Mettoy Pension Trustees v. Evans*,[144] it was stated that a donee of a fiduciary mere power must consider periodically whether or not he should exercise the power, the range of objects of the power, and the appropriateness of individual appointments. As will be seen in a later chapter,[145] a donee of a fiduciary power is consequently "to some extent subject to the control of the courts in relation to its exercise"[146]; as a result, powers held by fiduciaries may well in some respects have been assimilated to discretionary

3–075

---

[138] [1971] A.C. 424 at 457.
[139] *Re Baden's Deed Trusts (No.2)* [1973] Ch. 9 at 20, *per* Sachs L.J.
[140] [1982] 1 W.L.R. 202 at 209–210.
[141] In *Re Gestetner* [1953] Ch. 672 at 688, Harman J. had stated that "there is no obligation on the trustees to do more than consider from time to time the merits of such persons of the specified class as are known to them".
[142] *Re Hay's Settlement Trusts* [1982] 1 W.L.R. 202 at 209–210.
[143] See *ante*, para 1–074.
[144] [1990] 1 W.L.R. 1587.
[145] See *post*, para 6–140.
[146] *Mettoy Pension Trustees v. Evans* [1990] 1 W.L.R. 1587 at 1614.

trusts. However, the precise scope of the duties which were enunciated in *Mettoy Pension Trustees v. Evans* must await further clarification.

II THE BENEFICIARY PRINCIPLE

3–076   The last of the essential ingredients for the effective creation of a trust is that there should be some beneficiary capable of enforcing it. As Grant M.R. stated in *Morice v. Bishop of Durham*,[147] "there must be someone in whose favour the court can decree performance". This requirement does not apply to charitable trusts, which can be enforced by the Attorney-General. However, private trusts which do not satisfy the beneficiary requirement will not generally be enforced; "a court of equity does not recognise as valid a trust which it cannot both enforce and control".[148]

3–077   The qualification "generally" is necessary for two reasons. First, some trusts which are on the face of things for some purpose rather than for the direct benefit of any beneficiary capable of enforcing them have in fact been construed as outright gifts to some person or persons, the purpose being construed merely as an expression of the motive for the gift. Trusts construed in such a way necessarily satisfy the beneficiary requirement; thus a trust for the planting of trees on an estate for shelter has been held to be for the benefit of whoever was entitled to that estate,[149] and trusts for the education of children have been held to be a trust for their benefit[150] Secondly, it has been held[151] that a trust which, despite the fact that it is expressed in the form of a purpose, is directly or indirectly for the benefit of one or more ascertainable individuals satisfies the beneficiary requirement, provided that all its terms comply with the relevant certainty requirements.

3–078   Further, there are a number of anomalous cases in which non-charitable purpose trusts have been upheld even though there has been no human beneficiary capable of enforcing them. Such trusts are often described as trusts of imperfect obligation on the grounds that, although they will not be enforced, the courts will not forbid their performance if the trustees wish to carry them out. In *Re Endacott*[152] these cases were said to fall into the following categories: trusts for the erection or maintenance of monuments or graves; trusts for the saying of masses in jurisdictions where such trusts are not regarded as charitable; trusts for the maintenance of particular animals; trusts for the benefit of unincorporated associations (although, due to subsequent developments in the law, many trusts for the benefit of unincorporated associations are now valid anyway); and miscellaneous cases (a few further cases which do not fit into any of the other categories). The decisions which have established these anomalous exceptions have been

---

[147] (1804) 9 Ves. 399 at 405.
[148] *Re Astor's Settlement Trusts* [1952] Ch. 534 at 549.
[149] *Re Bowes* [1896] 1 Ch. 507.
[150] *Re Andrew's Trust* [1905] 2 Ch. 48; *Re Osoba* [1979] 1 W.L.R. 247.
[151] In *Re Denley's Trust Deed* [1969] 1 Ch. 373.
[152] [1960] Ch. 232.

described as "concessions to human weakness or sentiment"[153] and it is clear that they will not now be extended.[154]

1. *The General Rule*

Trusts for non-charitable purposes are generally void for two different   **3–079** reasons: first, because there is no one who can enforce them; and, secondly, because the courts are unable to control the execution of such trusts. This rule was originally established in *Morice v. Bishop of Durham*,[155] which concerned a gift of residue to the Bishop of Durham to be applied by him "for such objects of benevolence and liberality as [he] in his own discretion shall most approve of". Grant M.R. held that this gift failed, saying[156] that "there can be no trust, over the exercise of which this Court will not assume a control, for an uncontrollable power of disposition would be ownership, and not trust". On appeal, Lord Eldon L.C. added[157] that the court had to be in a position both to execute the trust if the trustees for any reason did not do so and to prevent maladministration of the trust. Both these reasons are eminently justifiable; since it is the lack of enforceability which in practice inhibits judicial control, they are also linked.

The first in a line of important decisions which reconsidered the whole   **3–080** question of trusts for non-charitable purposes was *Re Astor's Settlement Trusts*,[158] whose objects included "the establishment, maintenance and improvement of good understanding, sympathy and co-operation between nations", "the preservation of the independence and integrity of newspapers" and "the promotion of freedom of the press" (the trust was intended to facilitate the continued independence of the newspaper *The Observer*, which had been founded by the Astor family). This case has already been considered in relation to certainty of objects; the conclusion which was reached, that these objects were conceptually uncertain, was however only a secondary ground for the decision that the trusts were ineffective. The primary question considered by the court was whether, irrelevant of whether or not the objects were certain, the trusts would have been effective as non-charitable purpose trusts. Roxburgh J. concluded that the general principle was that gifts on trust must have a beneficiary or *cestui que trust*, to which principle the anomalous cases to which reference has already been made constituted exceptions. He suggested that these cases should, following the view of Underhill,[159] be regarded as concessions to human weakness or sentiment; however, he held that they could not be used to justify the proposition that a court of equity would recognise as an equitable obligation a direction to apply funds in furtherance of enumerated non-charitable purposes in a manner which no court could control.[160]

---

[153] *Re Astor's Settlement Trusts* [1952] Ch. 534 at 547.
[154] *Re Endacott* [1960] Ch. 232 at 250–251.
[155] (1804) 9 Ves. 399 (1805) 10 Ves. 522.
[156] (1804) 9 Ves. 399 at 404–405.
[157] (1805) 10 Ves. 522 at 539–540.
[158] [1952] Ch. 534.
[159] See now Underhill & Hayton, *Law of Trusts and Trustees*, 17th edn (London, Lexis Nexis, 2007), para 8.155.
[160] [1952] Ch. 534 at 547.

3–081   The views of Roxburgh J. were applied in *Re Shaw*,[161] another decision at first instance, where the main question was whether trusts in the will of George Bernard Shaw which provided that his residuary estate was to be used for 21 years in experimentation in the possible reform of the English alphabet of 26 letters by its substitution for a phonetic alphabet of 40 letters were valid charitable trusts. In the event it was held that they were not charitable trusts and the question then arose as to whether they could be valid as non-charitable purpose trusts. Harman J. held that they were also invalid as such since they lacked any *cestui que trust*.

3–082   Subsequently, the compass of non-charitable purpose trusts seemed to have been firmly confined by the decision of the Court of Appeal in *Re Endacott*.[162] The testator had given his residuary estate to the North Tawton Parish Council "for the purpose of providing some useful memorial to myself". The court held that this trust did not fall within the "anomalous" classes of trusts of imperfect obligation since it was of too wide and uncertain a nature to qualify. Harman L.J. affirmed the views on this type of trusts which had been expressed by Roxburgh J. in *Re Astor's Settlement Trusts*. He said[163]: "I applaud the orthodox sentiments expressed by Roxburgh J. and I think, as I think he does, that though one knows there have been decisions which are not satisfactorily classified but are merely occasions when Homer has nodded, yet the cases stand by themselves and ought not to be increased in number nor indeed followed except where the one is exactly like the other." He added that he could not think that a case of this kind, that of providing outside a church an unspecified and unidentified memorial, was the kind of instance which should be added to these "troublesome, anomalous and aberrant" cases.

3–083   Similarly, one of the reasons why the Court of Appeal held in *R v. District Auditor ex p. West Yorkshire Metropolitan Council*[164] that a discretionary trust to apply £400,000 for one of four purposes "for the benefit of any or some of the inhabitants of" West Yorkshire was void was because it was a non-charitable purpose trust.

3–084   As will be seen later on,[165] a number of trusts for unincorporated associations, where the subject matter of the gift was to be held on trust for the purposes of the association as a quasi-corporate entity, have been held void on the grounds of perpetuity. Such cases are primarily concerned with perpetuity and are best dealt with under that heading. However, in one of the leading cases, *Leahy v. Attorney-General for New South Wales*,[166] Viscount Simonds, although concluding that the gift in question was indeed prima facie void for perpetuity, was clearly of the opinion that such a purpose trust would be void in any event because of the lack of any cestui que trust to enforce it. He said[167]:

---

[161] [1957] 1 W.L.R. 729.
[162] [1960] Ch. 232.
[163] *ibid.* at 250–251.
[164] [1986] R.V.R. 24.
[165] See *post*, para 3–096.
[166] [1959] A.C. 457.
[167] *ibid.* at 478.

"If the words 'for the general purposes of the association' were held to import a trust, the question would have to be asked, what is the trust and who are the beneficiaries? A gift can be made to persons (including a corporation) but it cannot be made to a purpose or to an object; so also a trust may be created for the benefit of persons as cestuis que trust but not for a purpose or object unless the purpose or object be charitable. For a purpose or object cannot sue but, if it be charitable, the Attorney-General can sue to enforce it."[168]

Thus, the question raised in cases such as *Re Astor's Settlement Trusts* and *Re Shaw*, namely whether the categories of the anomalous trusts of imperfect obligation could be extended to other non-charitable purposes which complied with the requirement for certainty of objects, was clearly answered in the negative both by the Court of Appeal in *Re Endacott* and by the Privy Council in *Leahy v. Attorney-General for New South Wales*.

While the reasoning which has been adopted, namely that the lack of a **3–085** *cestui que trust* to enforce such trusts puts their execution outside the control of the courts, appears to be unimpeachable, that does not necessarily mean that the present position is entirely satisfactory. At present, the law permits a person to give his property to human beings, whether they are good or bad, to give that property to charity, and even to set up trusts for the various anomalous purposes recognised by the law, such as for his dogs and cats or for the promotion of foxhunting. But, it seems that, as a general rule, a person cannot dedicate his property to a social experiment falling outside the confines of the law of charity if that experiment is defined in terms of some purpose, no matter how certain that purpose may be[169] (this proposition of course assumes that it is only possible to construe the gift in terms of a purpose; as was stated at the outset, the beneficiary requirement will be satisfied if the gift can instead be construed as an outright gift to some person or persons, in which case the purpose is construed merely as an expression of the motive for the gift[170]).

2. *The Qualification Established by* Re Denley's Trust Deed[171]

The qualification "as a general rule" had to be added because, according to **3–086** the decision of Goff J. in *Re Denley's Trust Deed*,[172] there may in certain circumstances be a way out of this difficulty. In that case Goff J. held that the basic rule laid down in *Morice v. Bishop of Durham* was confined to purpose trusts which were "abstract or impersonal"; consequently, he held that a trust which, although it was expressed in the form of a purpose, was directly

---

[168] In *Re Lipinski's Will Trusts* [1976] Ch. 235, Oliver J. argued (at 246) that this was not intended as an exhaustive statement or to do more than indicate the broad division of trusts into those where there are ascertainable beneficiaries (whether for particular purposes or not) and trusts where there are none.

[169] See Marshall (1953) 6 C.L.P. 151;.Kiralfy (1950) 14 Conv. (N.S.) 374; Sheridan (1953) 17 Conv. (N.S.) 46.

[170] See *Re Bowes* [1896] 1 Ch. 507; *Re Andrew's Trust* [1905] 2 Ch. 48; *Re Osoba* [1979] 1 W.L.R. 247. See also *Re Sanderson's Trust* (1857) 3 K. & J. 497 at 503.

[171] [1969] 1 Ch. 373.

[172] [1969] 1 Ch. 373.

or indirectly for the benefit of one or more ascertainable individuals was nevertheless valid, provided that all its terms satisfied the relevant certainty requirements.

3–087   In *Re Denley's Trust Deed*,[173] the expressed purpose of the trust was the maintenance of a sports ground, primarily for the benefit of the employees of a company and secondarily for the benefit of such other persons as the trustees allowed to use it. Goff J. held the trust to be valid on the basis that it was an express private trust in favour of ascertainable human beneficiaries by whom it could necessarily be enforced. However commendable this approach may be as an attempt to "liberalise" the law, there must nevertheless be some doubt as to whether it is actually correct. The trust in *Re Denley's Trust Deed*s was, as a matter of construction, clearly framed as a purpose; it could not be construed as an outright gift to the employees of the company and any other persons whom the trustees allowed to use the sports ground. Consequently, despite the fact that the trust was for their benefit, the purpose of the trust was its dominant factor; consequently, if that purpose was non-charitable (which it clearly was), it should have failed unless it could be brought within the recognised anomalous exceptions.

3–088   *Re Denley's Trust Deed* was nevertheless followed in *Re Lipinski's Will Trusts*,[174] where the testator left his residuary estate to trustees for an unincorporated recreational association, which was not charitable, for the purpose of constructing and improving buildings for that association. Oliver J. held that this was a valid purpose trust, principally because the beneficiaries, the members of the association, were ascertainable and so could enforce the purpose. As a matter of construction, *Re Lipinski's Will Trusts* may well be a stronger case than *Re Denley's Trust Deed* because of the fact that it was a gift to an unincorporated association and was thus also able to be upheld on that basis,[175] something which was not possible in *Re Denley's Trust Deed*. The conclusion arrived at in *Re Denley's Trust Deed* was also accepted by Megarry V.-C. in *Re Northern Developments (Holdings)*.[176] Subsequently, however, in *Re Grant's Will Trusts*,[177] Vinelott J. expressed the view that *Re Denley's Trust Deed* did not involve a purpose trust at all but rather a discretionary trust. However, this view is not really consistent either with the lengthy discussion of purpose trusts in *Re Denley's Trust Deed* or with the subsequent interpretation of that decision by Oliver J. and Megarry V.-C.; consequently, it does not appear to be an acceptable explanation of that decision.

3–089   If the view expressed in *Re Grant's Will Trusts* is for this reason discounted, the decision in *Re Denley's Trust Deed* and the other two first instance decisions in which it has been applied indicate that this type of non-charitable purpose trust may be treated as a valid express private trust for

---

[173] [1969] 1 Ch. 373.
[174] [1976] Ch. 235.
[175] It was held that it was valid as a gift in favour of an unincorporated association with a superadded discretion; see *post*, para 3–107.
[176] (1978) unreported; see (1985) 101 L.Q.R. 280.
[177] [1980] 1 W.L.R. 360.

the incidental benefit of ascertainable beneficiaries, albeit for a particular purpose. Whether *Re Denley's Trust Deed* rightly or wrongly decided, there is little doubt that, as will be seen in the final section of this chapter,[178] that decision has been the impetus for the enactment of purpose trust legislation in a large number of off-shore jurisdictions.

It must, however, be re-emphasised that in this jurisdiction, despite the   3–090
fact that the rationale on which such trusts have been upheld is that they incidentally benefit identifiable persons, those persons have no right to call for the trust property. Consequently, such trusts are quite distinct from those trusts which, although they are on the face of things for some purpose rather than for the direct benefit of any beneficiary capable of enforcing them, have in fact been construed as outright gifts to some person or persons, the purpose being construed merely as an expression of the motive for the gift.[179] It must also be emphasised that the rule that a valid power cannot be deduced from what is intended to be a trust applies just as much to non-charitable purpose trusts as to any other type of trust[180]; if a trust is intended, it cannot be treated as a power. That does not of course prevent the express creation of powers for non-charitable purposes but such powers impose no obligations on their donees to exercise them.

It should be added that it is generally thought that any non-charitable   3–091
purpose trusts which are upheld in accordance with the decision in *Re Denley's Trust Deed*[181] must comply with the rule against inalienability, one of the aspects of the rule against perpetuities which restricts the duration of the anomalous trusts which take effect as exceptions to the beneficiary principle (this rule is referred to in the next section[182] and considered in detail in a later chapter[183]). However, whether such trusts are so restricted has not yet actually had to be decided since, both in *Re Denley's Trust Deed* and in the two reported cases in which that decision has been applied, the trusts in question were expressly limited so that they could take effect only within the relevant perpetuity period; those trusts therefore necessarily complied with the rule against inalienability.

Finally, it must be emphasised that, despite the decision in *Re Denley's*   3–092
Trust Deed, it is nevertheless, from a practical point of view, inadvisable in this jurisdiction to endeavour to provide expressly for the establishment of a non-charitable purpose trust, other than one falling within the existing anomalous exceptions; this will only cease to be the case in the event that legislation validating non-charitable purpose trusts is enacted here. In the meantime, the simplest solution to the problem remains what it has always been: the formation of a company to carry out the non-charitable purpose in question (the permissible objects of companies are not subject to any of the

---

[178] See *post*, para 3–139.
[179] See *Re Bowes* [1896] 1 Ch. 507; *Re Andrew's Trust* [1905] 2 Ch. 48; *Re Osoba* [1979] 1 W.L.R. 247. See also *Re Sanderson's Trust* (1857) 3 K. & J. 497 at 503.
[180] See *I.R.C. v. Broadway Cottages Trust* [1955] Ch. 20 at 36; *Re Endacott* [1960] Ch. 232 at 246. This principle is not affected by *McPhail v. Doulton* [1971] A.C. 424 (see *ante*, para 3–040).
[181] [1969] 1 Ch. 373.
[182] See *post*, para 3–096.
[183] See *post*, para 7–044.

restrictions which apply to non-charitable trusts) and the subsequent transfer of the relevant property to that company.[184]

3. The Anomalous Cases

3–093 As has already been mentioned, the situations in which non-charitable
purpose trusts have been upheld even though there has been no human
beneficiary capable of enforcing them have been said[185] to fall into the
following categories: trusts for the erection or maintenance of monuments or
graves; trusts for the saying of masses in jurisdictions where such trusts are
not regarded as charitable; trusts for the maintenance of particular animals;
trusts for the benefit of unincorporated associations; and miscellaneous
cases (a few further cases which do not fit into any of the other categories).

3–094 It also seems that these exceptions will only be upheld if the trust in
question is contained in a will. Indeed, it has also been said that the will
must be drafted in such a way that any of the property not expended on the
non-charitable purpose will fall into residue.[186] This is allegedly because in
such circumstances an order can be made whereby the trustees undertake to
carry out the non-charitable purpose with the residuary legatees being given
leave to apply to the court if the trustees fail to do so; this of course makes
the trust in question indirectly enforceable in that the trustees have a choice
between carrying out the specified purpose and transferring the property to
the residuary legatees. However, the residuary legatees or intestate successors can clearly be given such leave to apply even if the will is not drafted
in this way; consequently, there seems no reason in principle why such a
provision should be necessary or why the subject matter of the trust should
not be the residue itself.[187]

3–095 The existence of these anomalous cases, particularly the miscellaneous
cases, contrasts markedly with the willingness of the courts to strike down
as capricious trusts for the management of property in a manner which
confers no obvious benefit on anyone. Such a case was *Brown v. Burdett*,[188]
where a gift of a house on trust to block up its windows and doors for 20
years was held to be void. There is no possible justification for this difference
in attitude; its explanation may be that the anomalous exceptions are
regarded as "concessions to human weakness or sentiment".[189] The present
state of the authorities really requires a review either by the House of Lords

---

[184] An independent committee on Charity Law and Voluntary Organisations set up by the
National Council of Social Services under the chairmanship of Lord Goodman which reported
in 1976 recommended that trusts for non-charitable purposes should be valid. Its proposals on
charitable trusts bear a considerable resemblance to the much more recent proposals which
formed the basis of the Charities Act 2006 but the latter proposals made no reference whatsoever to non-charitable purpose trusts.

[185] *Re Endacott* [1960] Ch. 232; the Court of Appeal adopted the classification put forward in
J.H.C. Morris & W.B. Leach, *The Rule against Perpetuities*, 2nd edn (London, Stevens & Sons,
1964), p.306.

[186] *Re Thompson* [1934] Ch. 342 at 344; *Re Astor's Settlement Trusts* [1952] Ch. 534 at 546.

[187] See *Re Endacott* [1960] Ch. 232 at 240.

[188] (1882) 21 Ch.D. 667.

[189] *Re Astor's Settlement Trusts* [1952] Ch. 534 at 547.

or by the legislature (such a review could usefully also encompass the decision in *Re Denley's Trust Deed*[190]).

These non-charitable purpose trusts are also subject to a further require-   **3–096** ment, namely that the property subject to the trust must not be rendered inalienable.[191] This principle is one of the aspects of the rule against perpetuities, which will be considered in detail in a later chapter.[192] If, at the time when the trust comes into effect, there is any possibility, no matter how remote, that it is capable of continuing for longer than the appropriate perpetuity period, then the trust will be void.

The testator may specify a perpetuity period consisting of one or more   **3–097** nominated lives in being plus 21 years or of any fixed period of years up to 21 years.[193] The nominated lives in question can be those of the persons related in some way to the trust or its purposes; alternatively, the testator can use what is known a "royal lives clause", specifying the perpetuity period by reference to the lives of the Royal Family—an example of such a clause is one specifying a period "ending at the expiration of 21 years from the death of the last survivor of all the lineal descendants of his late Majesty King George VI[194] who shall be living at the time" when the trust comes into effect. Only human lives can be specified[195] otherwise it would be open to an eccentric settlor to tie up property indefinitely by settling it on trusts limited by reference to the lives of tortoises or other animals noted for their longevity. Alternatively, the testator may prefer to specify "such period as the law allows" in which case, assuming that there are no relevant lives, the perpetuity period will be 21 years. If no period is specified at all, the trust will be void unless it must necessarily determine one before the end of the perpetuity period, which in most cases will mean within 21 years.

(A) Trusts for the Erection or Maintenance of Monuments or Graves

A trust for the erection of a particular monument or for the maintenance of   **3–098** a particular grave is not charitable but it has been held that such a trust may nevertheless take effect as a non-charitable purpose trust. In *Trimmer v. Danby*[196] a legacy of £1,000 left by the painter Turner to his executors "to erect a monument to my memory in St Paul's Cathedral" was upheld. There is no requirement that the monument or tombstone be for the testator personally. In *Musset v. Bingle*[197] a somewhat bizarre gift for the erection of a monument to the testator's widow's first husband was also upheld. It

---

[190] [1969] 1 Ch. 373.
[191] *Carne v. Long* (1860) 2 De G.F. & J. 75 at 80.
[192] See *post*, para 7–044.
[193] *Re Dean* (1899) 41 Ch.D. 552 at 557.
[194] The father of the present Queen. Consequently, the royal lives in question are those of H.M. Queen Elizabeth II, her descendants, and the descendants of her late sister, H.R.H. Princess Margaret. It is also probably just about possible still to use H.M. King George V (the grandfather of the present Queen), although the number of his descendants is now very considerable. It is certainly unsafe to specify the descendants of any previous sovereign. One potential difficulty about such clauses today is the fact that "descendants" now includes illegitimate descendants, who are not necessarily identifiable. But there seems no reason why future "royal lives clauses" should not be expressly restricted to legitimate descendants.
[195] *Re Kelly* [1932] I.R. 255 (Supreme Court of the Republic of Ireland).
[196] (1856) 25 L.J.Ch. 424.
[197] [1876] W.N. 171.

does, however, seem that the monument must be of a funerary nature if it is to fall within the scope of this exception.[198] The question of perpetuity has not been raised in any of the cases involving the construction of monuments on the basis that it will inevitably be carried out as soon as is reasonably practicable after the testator's death and thus well within the perpetuity period.

3–099   In contrast, perpetuity is an issue in relation to trusts for the maintenance of monuments and graves. Thus in *Re Hooper*[199] a gift to trustees for the upkeep of graves and monuments for "so long as they can legally do so" was held to be valid for 21 years but would clearly have been void for perpetuity if it had not been so restricted. Indeed in *Musset v. Bingle*[200] it had been agreed that a perpetual trust to maintain the monument which was to be erected was void for perpetuity. However, as will be seen in the next part of this section,[201] there are certain other methods whereby the maintenance of monuments and graves for longer periods can be achieved.

3–100   In the judgments in these cases the courts made clear that the trustees in question could not be compelled to erect the relevant monument or to keep up the relevant grave but that, if they decided to do so, they would not be restrained. On the other hand, if the trustees are unwilling to perform the trust, they will hold the trust property on resulting trust for the testator's estate; any surplus left after the purpose has been carried out will be held in the same way. The trust property will also "result" to the testator's estate on the determination of the period stipulated in the instrument for the duration of the trust or of the relevant perpetuity period, as the case may be.

(B)   Trusts for the Saying of Masses

3–101   It was uncertain for a long time whether or not trusts for the saying of masses were charitable but this point was finally settled in *Re Hetherington*,[202] where such trusts were held to be charitable provided that the masses in question are open to the public. However, in the event that this condition is not satisfied in any individual case, as would be the case where the masses were to be celebrated for the members of a cloistered and contemplative religious order and/or in a private chapel to which the public were not admitted,[203] the trust in question would clearly be valid as a non-charitable purpose trust provided that it complies with the rule against inalienability by being limited to take effect only within the perpetuity period.[204]

(C)   Trusts for the Maintenance of Particular Animals

3–102   Gifts for the maintenance of animals in general are charitable.[205] However, gifts for the maintenance of one or more particular animals are not; such

---

[198] See *Re Endacott* [1960] Ch. 232.
[199] [1932] 1 Ch. 38, following *Pirbright v. Salwey* [1896] W.N. 86 (a gift of consols for application "so long as law permitted" to keep up a burial enclosure was held valid for 21 years).
[200] [1876] W.N. 171.
[201] See *post*, para 3–106.
[202] [1990] Ch. 1.
[203] Trusts for such orders are not regarded as charitable; *Gilmour v. Coats* [1949] A.C. 426.
[204] *Bourne v. Keane* [1919] A.C. 815 at 874–875.
[205] See *post*, para 11–090.

gifts can only take effect, if at all, as non-charitable purpose trusts. Thus in *Pettingall v. Pettingall*,[206] the testator bequeathed £50 a year to his executor to provide for the testator's favourite black mare. It was held that the executor could perform the testator's wishes and might keep the surplus for his own purposes. It was also indicated that, if the executor failed to look after the mare, the beneficiaries could apply to the court to reconsider the arrangement but that, subject to that possibility, the trust was to last for the animal's lifetime. Similarly, in *Re Dean*[207] there was a bequest of an annual sum for the maintenance of the testator's horses and hounds for a period of 50 years, if any of the horses and hounds should so long live. This was also held to be valid; the trustees were clearly at liberty to carry out the terms of the gift although the beneficiaries, being dumb, could not compel them to do so. *Re Dean* is an explicit authority—not all the early cases in this area of the law are particularly explicit—that a non-charitable purpose trust for the upkeep of a given animal may be valid notwithstanding the fact that by its nature it is not enforceable by the beneficiary.

Few of the cases on animals deal adequately with the question of perpetuity. Judicial notice is sometimes taken of the fact that the expected life of the animal in question is less than the 21-year period.[208] In the large majority of cases, the animals will inevitably survive the testator for a time much shorter than 21 years and it seems convenient and not at all improper that, if a period is not stipulated in the trust instrument, the trust should not fail if the contemplated duration of the life of the animal in question falls short of the 21-year period. However, this does not justify either of the cases mentioned above. Horses can certainly live for more than 21 years and so the decision in *Pettingall v. Pettingall* that the trust was to last for the animal's lifetime could undoubtedly have contravened the rule against inalienability, depending of course on how old the mare was at the time of the testator's death. Further, the fixed period of 50 years established in *Re Dean* does not constitute one of the permissible perpetuity periods and the horses, if not the hounds, could certainly have survived for more than 21 years. The only correct and safe approach to follow with trusts of this kind is, therefore, to limit the duration of the trust by reference to nominated lives in being or alternatively to use some expression like "for such period as the law allows". **3–103**

(D) Trusts for the Benefit of Unincorporated Associations
The existence of this category has always been regarded as somewhat doubtful.[209] The view has been expressed in some quarters that some types of trusts for the benefit of unincorporated associations[210] depend for their validity on the existence of a further anomalous exception to the beneficiary principle. This was thought to be the case where such trusts were held to **3–104**

---

[206] (1842) 11 L.J.Ch. 176.

[207] (1889) 41 Ch.D. 552.

[208] *Re Haines* (1925), *The Times*, November 7, 1952 (life of cat approximately 16 years) but this may be wrong—see Morris & Leach, *The Rule against Perpetuities*, 2nd edn (London, Stevens & Sons, 1962), p.323 and compare *Re Kelly* [1932] I.R. 255 at 260–261.

[209] Morris & Leach, *op. cit.* in their classification comment that "this group is more doubtful".

[210] Discussed more fully *post*, para 3–107.

have been made by way of endowment (one of a number of ways in which gifts in favour of unincorporated associations can be construed) since such an endowment is likely to have been intended to be perpetual, the adoption of this construction will generally lead to the gift being held to be void for perpetuity.[211] But if a trust has been established which satisfies the rule against perpetuities (because, for example, it is held to have been intended to benefit only the existing members[212]), it will also have to satisfy the beneficiary principle. Prior to the decision in *Re Denley's Trust Deed*,[213] it was sometimes thought that such a trust could only do so by virtue of being a further anomalous exception to that principle. However, if the decision in *Re Denley's Trust Deed* is in fact correct, any need for the existence of this particular exception to the beneficiary principle will now have disappeared. Only if that decision is rejected, therefore, will this exception have any further role to play.

(E) Miscellaneous Cases

3–105   From time to time anomalous cases have cropped up which do not fit into any of the other categories. Of these cases, the Court of Appeal in *Re Endacott*[214] referred only to *Re Catherall*,[215] where Roxburgh J. had upheld a gift to a vicar and churchwardens for a suitable memorial to the testator's parents and sisters whether or not it was charitable. No doubt was cast on this decision in *Re Endacott*, although Lord Evershed M.R. said that the decision could in any event be justified on the grounds that the purposes in question were charitable.[216] However, this certainly cannot be said of the best known of these miscellaneous cases, *Re Thompson*,[217] which concerned a gift of £1,000 to be applied towards the promotion and furtherance of fox-hunting. The residuary legatee, Trinity Hall Cambridge, wished to carry out the testator's wishes in so far as this was legally possible but, as a charity, felt obliged to object to the enforcement of this trust. The gift, which complied with the rule against inalienability, was nevertheless upheld by analogy with *Pettingall v. Pettingall*.[218] Neither this decision nor the other authorities in which trusts of this type have been upheld[219] can be supported. Nor can the apparent preparedness of the courts to allow in principle a number of further trusts of this type which in the event were held void on the grounds of perpetuity.[220] None of these authorities is likely to be

---

[211] As in *Leahy v. Attorney-General for New South Wales* [1959] A.C. 457.

[212] As in *Re Drummond* [1914] 2 Ch. 90.

[213] [1969] 1 Ch. 393.

[214] [1960] Ch. 232.

[215] (June 3, 1959) unreported.

[216] [1960] Ch. 232 at 249.

[217] [1934] Ch. 342.

[218] (1842) 11 L.J.Ch. 176.

[219] *Re Catherall* (June 3, 1959) unreported but referred to in *Re Endacott* [1960] Ch. 232 at 248–249, (discussed *ante*, p.107); *Re Gibbons* [1917] 1 I.R. 448 (a trust for property to be disposed of "to [the testator's] best spiritual advantage as conscience and sense of duty may direct", which was upheld where the executors were Roman Catholic priests and were prepared to perform the trust by constructing a church and saying masses in it for the testator's soul).

[220] *Re Nottage* [1895] 2 Ch. 649 (trust to endow an annual cup for yacht racing); *Re Gassiott* (1901) 70 L.J.Ch. 242 (trust to keep a portrait in repair); *Re Lawlor* [1934] V.L.R. 22 (Supreme Court of Victoria, affirmed by the High Court of Australia *sub nom. Roman Catholic Archbishop of Melbourne v. Lawlor* (1934) 51 C.L.R. 1) (trust to found a Catholic newspaper).

followed; in this respect the miscellaneous cases are distinct from those in the other categories, which will be applied but not extended.[221]

4. *Maintenance of Monuments and Tombs for Longer than the Perpetuity Period*

It has already been seen that a trust for the maintenance of monuments and graves will be valid as a non-charitable purpose trust if its duration is limited to the perpetuity period. It is also possible for a testator to ensure that a perpetual trust for this purpose is valid.[222] However, the ways in which this may be achieved are both complex and somewhat heavy-handed. The first possibility is to set up a trust for the maintenance of the whole of the churchyard containing the monument or tomb in question; this is a valid charitable trust[223] and so will succeed in bringing about the maintenance of the monument or tomb for ever. The second possibility is to make a gift to one charity with a gift over to another charity if the monument or tomb is not kept in repair; this will be successful provided that no binding obligation is actually imposed on the first charity to maintain the monument or tomb in question.[224] What used to appear to be a third possibility probably no longer works.[225]

3–106

5. *Gifts for the Benefit of Unincorporated Associations*

An unincorporated association has been defined as "two or more persons bound together for one or more common purposes, not being business purposes, by mutual undertakings each having mutual duties and obligations, in an organisation which has rules which identify in whom control of it and its funds rests and on what terms and which can be joined or left at

3–107

---

[221] *Re Endacott* [1960] Ch. 232 at 250–251, *per* Harman L.J.

[222] It may also be possible to take advantage of Parish Councils and Burial Authorities (Miscellaneous Provisions) Act 1970, s.1, which authorises local authorities and burial authorities to make an agreement to maintain graves and so forth for a period not exceeding 99 years but this possibility is nothing to do with the law of trusts.

[223] *Re Pardoe* [1906] 2 Ch. 184.

[224] In *Re Tyler* [1891] 3 Ch. 252, a sum of stock was given to the trustees of the London Missionary Society with a gift over to the Blue Coat School if the Society failed to keep a tomb in repair. Since both the donees were charitable bodies, the perpetuity rule did not apply to them but the question still remained as to whether the condition in question (that is to say, for the maintenance of the tomb) contravened the rule. It was held by the Court of Appeal that, since the testator had not actually required the Society to maintain the tomb, the condition was valid. On the other hand, in *Re Dalziel* [1943] Ch. 277, where both donees were also charities, it was held that the condition in question amounted to a positive direction that the income was to be applied in the first instance to the maintenance of the mausoleum in question and not merely as in *Re Tyler*, a moral obligation; the trust therefore failed.

[225] Because the only apparent justification for the decision which established this possibility (*Re Chardon* [1928] Ch. 464, which was followed in *Re Chambers Will Trusts* [1950] Ch. 267 but was distinguished in *Re Wightwick's Will Trusts* [1950] Ch. 260) was that the gift in question had conferred a determinable interest on the cemetery company in question. Determinable interests were not then subject to the rule against perpetuities but now are as a result of Perpetuities and Accumulations Act 1964, s.12; consequently, such a gift could not now enable the monument or tomb in question to be maintained for longer than the perpetuity period anyway.

will".[226] Because an unincorporated association is not a legal person, its property necessarily has to be vested in some or all of its members as trustees. Where its purposes are charitable, such trusts do not give rise to any difficulties. Charitable trusts have to comply neither with the requirement of certainty of objects, nor with the beneficiary principle, nor with the rule against perpetuities. All of these requirements have to be satisfied, however, when the purposes of an unincorporated association are not charitable, giving rise to very considerable theoretical difficulties.

3–108   It was formerly thought that a gift of property to a non-charitable unincorporated association could only be construed in two possible ways. Both these constructions are still possible but have become uncommon; virtually all such gifts are now construed in accordance with a third possible construction enunciated by Cross J. in *Neville Estates v. Madden*[227] and considerably developed in subsequent decisions.

3–109   The first possible construction was and is that the gift has been made to the persons who were the members of the association on the date that it was made. Such a gift may be outright, in that title to the property in question passes immediately to the members as tenants in common or joint tenants, or may vest the property in trustees for the members as beneficial tenants in common or joint tenants. Either way, if they are tenants in common they can take their share while, if they are joint tenants, any member can sever his share and then claim it, whether or not he remains a member. Where such a trust exists, its objects must be sufficiently certain but it will clearly comply with the beneficiary principle and will not offend the rule against perpetuities.[228] However, this construction is not without theoretical difficulties: any member who subsequently leaves will retain his share unless he assigns it to the other members with the appropriate formalities[229]; no member who subsequently joins will acquire any interest in the property in question; and, where the members are tenants in common, the share of any member who dies will devolve according to his will or intestacy. In practice, these theoretical difficulties have generally been ignored.

3–110   The second possible construction was and is that the gift has been made by way of endowment for the unincorporated association. Such a gift necessarily has to take effect by way of trust. Any such endowment is likely to have been intended to be perpetual; consequently, the adoption of this

---

[226] *Conservative and Unionist Central Office v. Burrell* [1982] 1 W.L.R. 522, *per* Lawton L.J. at 525. The case was concerned with the meaning of "unincorporated association" for the purposes of taxation legislation but this definition seems to be of general application. Underhill & Hayton, *Law of Trusts & Trustees*, 17th edn (London, Lexis Nexis, 2007), para 8.186 questions whether it is in fact necessary that the association should be able to be joined and left at will on the basis that the existence of rules restricting membership should not negative the existence of an unincorporated association.

[227] [1962] Ch. 832.

[228] It is not particularly likely that a trust will be utilised if the intention of the donor is really only to benefit the existing members. The intention to exclude future members has been far from clear in some of the decided cases such as *Re Drummond* [1914] 2 Ch. 90, *Re Prevost* [1930] 2 Ch. 383 and *Re Turkington* [1937] 4 All E.R. 501; such cases would today probably be regarded as falling within the more recently developed third possible construction.

[229] Where a trust exists, writing will be required by virtue of Law of Property Act 1925, s.53(1)(c); see *post*, para 4–008.

construction will generally lead to the gift being held to be void for perpetuity.[230] However, if a trust has been established which satisfies the rule
against perpetuities, it will undoubtedly be valid provided that its objects
are sufficiently certain. Such a trust will satisfy the beneficiary principle by
virtue of the decision in *Re Denley's Trust Deed*,[231] assuming of course that
that case was correctly decided (prior to that decision, it was sometimes
thought that such trusts constituted one of the anomalous exceptions to the
beneficiary principle[232]). Some trusts have been held to satisfy the rule
against perpetuities on the grounds that they were intended to benefit only
the existing members of the unincorporated association.[233] In principle, it
must also be possible to satisfy the rule against perpetuities by expressly
providing that the property is to be held on trust for the benefit of the
unincorporated association until the end of the perpetuity period and then
be held for some ascertained person (such as the estate of the donor) or some
charitable purpose. Such cases were obviously exceptional.

In practice, therefore, prior to the decision in *Neville Estates v. Madden*, gifts   **3–111**
to unincorporated associations were only valid if the first possible construction was adopted; consequently, there was a presumption in favour of this
construction. Where there was a gift "for the general purposes of the association", then, although those words appeared to seek to impose a perpetual
trust which would consequently be void, they could be disregarded by the
court as having virtually no meaning; this would enable the first construction to be adopted. This was not, however, always possible. In *Leahy v.
Attorney-General for New South Wales*,[234] a ranch was left "upon trust for such
order of nuns of the Catholic Church or the Christian Brothers as my
executors and trustees shall select". This gift was prima facie valid as a gift
to the individual members of the order chosen. However, the Privy Council
held that the presumption was rebutted: first, because of the improbability
of a beneficial gift to the members of the order who happened to be alive at
the date of the death of the testator; and, secondly, because of the nature of
the property. As an intended endowment for the benefit of the order as a
continuing society, the trust would therefore have been void for perpetuity
but for a saving legislative provision in a New South Wales statute.

The absence of any effective method of making gifts for the present and   **3–112**
future members of unincorporated associations was hardly satisfactory and
was eventually remedied by the enunciation in *Neville Estates v. Madden*[235] of
a third possible construction. This is that there may be:

"a gift to the existing members not as joint tenants, but subject to their
respective contractual rights and liabilities towards one another as members
of the association. In such a case a member cannot sever his share. It will

[230] *Re Macaulay's Estate* (1933) [1943] Ch. 435; *Leahy v. Att.-Gen. for New South Wales* [1959] A.C.
457.
[231] [1969] 1 Ch. 393.
[232] See *ante*, para 3–104.
[233] *Re Drummond* [1914] 2 Ch. 90 was a case of this kind. These trusts might equally well have
been classified as falling within the first possible construction and, like such trusts, would today
probably be regarded as falling within the third possible construction.
[234] [1959] A.C. 457.
[235] [1962] Ch. 832.

accrue to the other members on his death or resignation, even though such members include persons who became members after the gift took effect. If this is the effect of the gift, it will not now be open to objection on the score of perpetuity or uncertainty unless there is something in its terms or circumstances or in the rules of the association which precludes the members at any given time from dividing the subject of the gift between them on the footing that they are solely entitled to it in equity."[236]

Thus the members of an unincorporated association have the possibility of enjoying rights in property in a new manner distinct from the traditional joint tenancy and tenancy in common (whether this is, strictly speaking, a form of co-ownership is not entirely clear).

3–113   Where a gift to an unincorporated association is construed in this way, the property in question is held by some or all of the individual members (or, of course, by independent trustees) on trust to be applied in accordance with the contract between the members contained in the rules of the association. This apparently resolves the technical difficulties caused by the adoption of the first possible construction in that any member who leaves or dies will lose his share in the property of the association without any need for any formal disposition and any new member of the association will be able to enjoy the benefit of its property without any need for any transfer of any share to him. Precisely how the statutory formal requirements of the Law of Property Act 1925 and the Wills Act 1837 which will be considered in a later chapter[237] are actually satisfied has never been made entirely clear; signed acceptance by each member of rules drafted in an appropriate form would presumably cause the member to be bound by the trusts during his membership[238] but certainly would not suffice to deprive him of his share on his death.[239] The answer may be that, by entering into the contract contained in the rules, each member estops himself (and, after his death, his personal representatives) from relying on the absence of the statutory formalities to claim his proportion of the property of the association.

3–114   The objects of trusts of this type must of course be sufficiently certain.[240] However, such trusts will clearly satisfy the beneficiary principle. Further, it has been held that they will satisfy the rule against perpetuities provided that the members are entitled under the rules (if necessary as a result of exercising a power in the rules to change them) to bring the association to an end and to divide its property between themselves; the combined effect of the decisions which have been reached means that there is now little chance of a gift of this type being void for perpetuity.

3–115   In *Re Recher's Will Trusts*,[241] the testatrix left part of her residuary estate to a specified "Anti-Vivisection Society" (a non-charitable unincorporated

---

[236] *ibid.* at 849, *per* Cross J.

[237] See *post*, Chapter 4.

[238] Because his signed acceptance would presumably satisfy the formal requirements of Law of Property Act 1925, s.53(1)(c).

[239] Because his signed acceptance certainly would not satisfy the formal requirements of the Wills Act 1837.

[240] The trusts in question will almost inevitably be discretionary trusts and so will be governed by *McPhail v. Doulton* [1971] A.C. 424.

[241] [1972] Ch. 526.

association). Had the society not ceased to exist before her death, the gift would have been upheld as a valid non-charitable purpose trust. Brightman J. stated that, where the subscriptions of the members of an unincorporated association are held as an accretion to its funds to be applied in accordance with its rules, any gifts or legacies to the association will, in the absence of any words purporting to impose a trust, be held on the same basis. The rules of the association could have been changed by the unanimous agreement of the members. Therefore, it would have been irrelevant that it existed for the promotion of some purpose rather than for the benefit of the members themselves, since they could nevertheless vote to change the rules in order to abandon this purpose and to divide the assets between themselves.

Re Lipinski's Will Trusts[242] concerned a gift to an unincorporated associa-   **3–116**
tion "in memory of my late wife to be used solely in the work of constructing the new buildings for the association and/or improvement to the said
buildings". The purpose specified was within the powers of the association
and, despite the fact that the gift was to be used "solely" for this purpose,
Oliver J. held that the members would not thereby be prevented from
abandoning the specified purpose and instead dividing the assets between
themselves. Consequently, the gift was valid as a non-charitable purpose
trust for the benefit of the members of the association.

In *News Group Newspapers v. SOGAT 82*,[243] the local branches of the union   **3–117**
SOGAT 82 were held to be unincorporated associations capable of seceding
from the union and dissolving themselves; consequently, a sequestration
order issued against the union was held not to apply to funds held by its
local branches.

Finally, in *Universe Tankships Inc. of Monrovia v. International Transport*   **3–118**
Workers Federation,[244] the House of Lords held that a payment by shipowners
into the fund maintained by the Federation took effect as an accretion to that
fund by way of outright gift rather than a contribution on trust (in which
case, it would have been void). In the Court of Appeal,[245] Megaw L.J. had
emphasised that, even if there is no provision for the amendment of the
rules of an association, they can nevertheless be "altered at will by the
unanimous agreement of the contracting parties".

There is now a strong presumption that an unincorporated association   **3–119**
holds its property in this way; gifts to unincorporated associations will
therefore not now normally be construed either as gifts to the members of
the association in question[246] or as gifts for the purposes of its endowment.
However, the third possible construction is not actually all-embracing.

This construction cannot be applied unless there is a set of rules to provide   **3–120**
the necessary contract between the members. This was emphasised by
Lawton L.J. in *Conservative and Unionist Central Office v. Burrell*.[247] This was
why the third possible construction could not have been adopted in *Leahy v.*

---

[242] [1976] Ch. 235.
[243] [1986] I.C.R. 716.
[244] [1983] 1 A.C. 366.
[245] [1981] I.C.R. 129 at 159.
[246] *Re Grant's Will Trusts* [1980] 1 W.L.R. 360 at 365.
[247] [1982] 1 W.L.R. 522 at 525.

Attorney-General for New South Wales[248]; no such contract existed between the members of the religious orders. Consequently, even on the basis of this construction, the gift would still have had to be held to be an intended endowment and, but for statute, void for perpetuity.

3–121   Nor can this construction be applied when the members are unable to divide the assets between themselves. In *Re Grant's Will Trusts*,[249] Vinelott J. held that a gift to "the Labour Party Property Committee for the benefit of the Chertsey Headquarters of the Chertsey and Walton Constituency Labour Party" could not be construed as a gift to the members of the Constituency Party. They did not have the power to alter their rules, which were under the control of the National Labour Party. Although this did not of itself give rise to any problems of perpetuity (because the rules provided, in the last resort, for a resulting trust for the original subscribers), the members were clearly unable to dispose of the property among themselves.[250] Vinelott J. held that, consequently and in any event, the gift amounted to a trust for the purposes specified and not, as in *Re Lipinski's Will Trusts*,[251] a gift for the members of the Constituency Party for those purposes; for this reason, the gift was void for perpetuity. It has admittedly been suggested that the requirement that the members should be able to divide the property between themselves is unnecessary provided that they have the right "to ensure that the funds are used to pay for general expenses benefiting them as members".[252] However, the requirement clearly exists at present.

3–122   It should be noted that the way in which a gift to an unincorporated association is construed can have some effect on what happens to the assets of the association in the event of its dissolution. In the highly unlikely event that the first possible construction is adopted, those assets will be the property of those who were the members of the association on the date that the gift was made. In the only slightly less unlikely event that the second possible construction is adopted and the gift to the association has, therefore, taken effect as a valid trust by way of endowment, such a trust will necessarily be limited to take effect only within the perpetuity period; it will, therefore, inevitably contain some provisions as to what is to happen to the property thereafter and, in such circumstances, dissolution of the association will presumably mean that it will devolve in accordance with these provisions. In the highly likely event that the third possible construction is adopted, there are three possibilities: first, that each asset is held on resulting trust for whoever gave it to the association in the first place; secondly, that the assets are divided between those who were the members of the association on the date of its dissolution; and, thirdly, that the assets go to the Crown as *bona vacantia*. As will be seen in a later chapter,[253] although there is at present a conflict of authority between a number of first instance

---

[248] [1959] A.C. 457.

[249] [1980] 1 W.L.R. 360.

[250] The National Labour Party was entitled to alter the rules so as to require the property to be transferred to itself.

[251] [1976] Ch. 235.

[252] Underhill & Hayton, *Law of Trusts and Trustees*, 17th edn (London, Lexis Nexis, 2007), para 8.191.

[253] See *post*, para 9–083.

decisions, it is now generally accepted[254] that the resulting trust analysis is no longer appropriate, that the general rule is for equal division between the members of the association, and that *bona vacantia* is only relevant when the association in question has become moribund in that all, or all but one of the members have resigned or died.

Finally, where a gift is made to a body which does not satisfy the defini-   **3–123** tion of an unincorporated association because of the absence of the necessary mutual obligations contained in its rules, the gift will take effect by way of mandate or agency. In *Conservative and Unionist Central Office v. Burrell*,[255] the Court of Appeal held that the Conservative Party was not an unincorporated association for the purposes of taxation legislation because of the absence of any contractual link between a contributor of funds and their recipient; Brightman L.J. correspondingly characterised the recipient of the funds as the agent of the contributor for the purpose of dealing with the funds in accordance with the object or mandate for which the contribution was made. He said this[256]:

"So far as the money is used within the scope of the mandate, the recipient discharges himself vis-à-vis the contributor. The contributor can at any time demand the return of his money so far as not spent, unless the mandate is irrevocable, as it might be or become in certain circumstances. But once the money is spent, the contributor can demand nothing back, only an account of the manner of expenditure. No trust arises, except the fiduciary relationship inherent in the relationship of principal and agent. If, however, the recipient were to apply the money for some purpose outside the scope of the mandate, clearly the recipient would not be discharged. The recipient could be restrained, like any other agent, from a threatened misapplication of the money entrusted to him, and like any other agent could be required to replace any money misapplied."

This analysis is not without difficulties. Precisely who is the beneficial   **3–124** owner of the money until it is spent? Presumably the contributor unless and until the mandate becomes irrevocable by, for example, the money being mixed in the larger fund administered by the recipient. What happens if the mandate thereafter cannot be carried out or is carried out leaving a surplus? At first instance,[257] Vinelott J. took the view that in such circumstances there would be an implied obligation to return the fund to the subscribers in proportion to their original contributions (anonymous gifts and contributions to raffles would devolve as *bona vacantia*). Do the rights of the contributor survive a change in the identity of the person administering the fund? And, finally, how can testamentary gifts be brought within the framework of

---

[254] As a result of the decision in *Re Bucks Constabulary Fund Friendly Society (No.2)* [1979] 1 W.L.R. 936. However, the view expressed by Walton J. in this case is inconsistent with, but generally regarded as preferable to, the view expressed by Goff J. in *Re West Sussex Constabulary's Benevolent Fund Trusts* [1971] Ch. 1. These and other authorities are discussed *post*, para 9–083.

[255] [1982] 1 W.L.R. 522.

[256] *ibid.* at 529.

[257] [1980] 3 All E.R. 42 at 63–64.

mandate or agency when "no agency could be set up at the moment of death between a testator and his chosen agent"?[258]

3–125   Whatever the answers to these questions, it is at least clear that there are considerable differences between the mandate or agency analysis and the treatment of gifts to unincorporated associations. It has been suggested that it might be appropriate for the mandate or agency theory to be extended to those gifts to unincorporated associations which, according to the rules which have already been discussed, are void.[259] Whether that theory is extended in this, or indeed in any other, way obviously remains to be seen.

III. PURPORTED TRUSTS

3–126   The final section of this chapter considers a number of situations in which trusts have been created which have been held not to satisfy one of the three certainties or the beneficiary requirement or which arguably do not do so. Some of the situations of this type arise where the way in which the trust in question has been operated is wholly inconsistent with the provisions of the trust deed; such purported trusts are often described as sham trusts. Other situations of this type have arisen as the result of the intentional creation by the legislatures of offshore jurisdictions of types of trusts which do not satisfy one or more of the three certainties and/or the beneficiary requirement.

1. *Sham Trusts*

3–127   In the discussion of certainty of intention with which this chapter commenced it was assumed that a conclusion that an instrument manifests sufficient certainty of intention will be conclusive. However, it is not impossible for the words of the instrument to be held to be a sham in the sense that the settlor never had the slightest intention of parting with his pre-existing beneficial interest in the property in question.[260] In such circumstances his intention will instead have been to prevent some third party, usually his creditors, his estranged or former spouse, or his dependants, from obtaining access to the settled assets. Where a trust is found to be a sham, the settled property will be held still to be vested beneficially in the settlor or his estate and will therefore be available to meet the claims of the creditors, spouse, or dependants in question.

(A)   Total Shams
3–128   In practice the purported creation of a trust is only likely to be capable of being a total sham where that trust has purportedly been created by declaration. It is difficult to see how the purported creation of a trust by transfer could be regarded as a total sham unless title to the property in question is

---

[258] [1982] 1 W.L.R. 522 at 530. Brightman L.J. thought that the answer to this problem was not difficult to find but no one else has yet succeeded in finding it (see Smart [1987] Conv. 415).
[259] See Creighton [1983] Conv. 15.
[260] See Matthews [2007] Trust Law International 191.

capable of passing on delivery, in other words unless it is cash, bearer bonds, bearer shares, gold bars, or valuable personal chattels such as paintings. If the property in question is instead land or shares and title to that property has been transferred in accordance with the appropriate formal requirements, those formalities are likely to be conclusive, rendering a finding of total sham improbable. In such circumstances, any sham which is found to exist is likely to be held to be of the different type considered below, namely a partial sham.

However, a total sham was held to exist in *Midland Bank v. Wyatt*,[261] where   **3–129** a husband and wife executed a declaration of trust, of whose precise effect the wife was unaware, in respect of their matrimonial home, which was mortgaged to the bank; this declared that the equity in the matrimonial home, in other words the value of the property which remained after deducting the amount of the mortgage debt, was held as to one half for the wife and as to the other half for their daughters. The husband subsequently raised further loans from the bank secured on the matrimonial home on the basis that he was still entitled to one half of the equity; he was able to do so because he did not reveal the existence of the declaration of trust either to the bank or to his solicitors until the former sought to realise its security.

The judge[262] held that the husband had never had any intention of giving   **3–130** an interest in the property to his daughters but had declared the trust in order to safeguard his family from commercial risk. He therefore held that, irrelevant of whether the husband's motives were dishonest or fraudulent or simply based on mistaken advice, the declaration of trust was a pretence or sham in accordance with the definition of sham propounded by Diplock L.J. in *Snook v. London and West Riding Investments*[263]: "acts done or documents executed by the parties to the 'sham' which are intended by them to give to third parties or to the court the appearance of creating between the parties legal rights and obligations different from the actual legal rights and obligations (if any) which the parties intended to create". Although Diplock L.J. there required all parties to have been involved in the sham, unsurprisingly in the context of what was a bilateral transaction for value, the judge held that, in the context of a supposed settlement where only the settlor is in effect providing value, there is no requirement that all the parties to the transaction held to be a sham should have had a common interest or a common intention. Given that the unawareness of the wife was therefore irrelevant, the judge held that the declaration of trust was void and unenforceable[264]; the husband had consequently retained his beneficial interest in the house throughout and the bank was entitled to enforce its security over it.

Subsequently, however, in *Shalson v. Russo*,[265] Rimer J., following an inter-   **3–131** vening decision of the Royal Court of Jersey,[266] held, contrary to what had been stated in *Midland Bank v. Wyatt*, that it was necessary for all parties to

---

261 [1995] 1 F.L.R. 696.
262 D.E.M. Young, Q.C. sitting as a Deputy Judge of the High Court.
263 [1967] 2 Q.B. 786, 802.
264 The trust was also held to be voidable under Insolvency Act 1986, s.423. See *post*, para 7.056.
265 [2003] EWHC 1637 (Ch), [2005] Ch. 281.
266 *Re Esteem Settlement* [2003] J.L.R. 188.

have been involved in the sham. He therefore held that, in the case of a settlement executed by a settlor and a trustee, the trust in question will only be a sham if both settlor and trustee so intended.[267] Although the trust in *Midland Bank v. Wyatt* had been created by a declaration by two settlors, one of whom had been unaware of the consequences of what she was doing, rather than by a settlor and a trustee, the decision in *Shalson v. Russo* is clearly inconsistent with the decision in *Midland Bank v. Wyatt*, although the two decisions are of equal status as a matter of precedent. However, whether or not *Midland Bank v. Wyatt* remains good law, it is clearly still possible for there to be a total sham where the sole settlor or all the settlors of a trust purportedly created by declaration have no intention to create a trust at all; this must also be possible where both settlor and trustee have no such intention in the case of a trust whose subject matter is property whose title is capable of passing on delivery.

(2) *Partial shams*

3–132   The other type of sham is generally known as a partial sham.[268] Such a sham occurs where a trust has been created and duly carried into effect by a transfer of its subject matter from settlor to trustees but the provisions and *modus operandi* of the trust lead to the conclusion that it is a sham. However, the decision in *Shalson v. Russo*[269] concerned an alleged partial sham and therefore establishes that the trust in question will only be a sham if both settlor and trustee so intended.[270] A decision that a trust is a partial sham does not cast any doubt on the intention of the settlor to create a trust; the sham instead relates to the stated objects of the trust in that the beneficial interests supposedly vested in persons other than the settlor are held to be shams. However, such a decision produces exactly the same result as a decision that a trust is a total sham since the trust property is equally available to satisfy any claims which anyone may have against the settlor.

3–133   There is in principle no reason why the claims in question should not, as in *Midland Bank v. Wyatt*, be the claims of the settlor's creditors. However, for the first five years following the creation of the trust, his creditors are highly likely to be able to set aside the trust, whether or not it is a sham, under the Insolvency Act 1986[271]; only thereafter will creditors need to have recourse to the doctrine of partial sham and this is relatively unlikely. In all the claims which have been litigated to date in the trust context,[272] it has instead been the settlor's estranged or former spouses and/or children who have brought

---

[267] *ibid.*, at 340–342.
[268] Mowbray 8 T.L.I. (1994) 68 prefers the expression "illusory trust".
[269] [2003] EWHC 1637 (Ch), [2005] Ch. 281 at 340–342.
[270] *ibid.*, at 340–342.
[271] See *post*, para 7–056.
[272] *Rahman v. Chase Bank (CI) Trust Co.* 1991 J.L.R. 103 (Royal Court of Jersey); *Re Marriage of Ashton* (1986) 11 Fam.L.R. 457; *Re Marriage of Goodwin* (1990) 14 Fam.L.R. 801; *Re Marriage of Davidson* (1990) 14 Fam.L.R. 817 (all Family Court of Australia). Such claims have also been made in English proceedings in the Family Division for ancillary relief, in other words for financial provision following divorce, where off-shore trusts have been alleged to be shams and their subject matter consequently available to provide that financial provision; see *A v. A and St. George's Trustees* [2007] EWHC 99 (Fam), [2007] 2 F.L.R. 467 (similar claims have also been made in such proceedings relating to sham companies (also known as *alter ego* companies); see

claims to the trust property on the basis that it is in reality still vested in the settlor or, if he is dead, in his testate or intestate successors. But in *R. v. Allen*[273] criminal sanctions were imposed on a settlor in respect of his failure to disclose to the Inland Revenue his beneficial interest in the subject matter of two trusts of which he was not formally a beneficiary but which the jury decided were shams of this type.

(a) **Effective retention of control by the settlor** Allegations of partial   3–134
sham are most likely where the trustees have slavishly followed the directions of the settlor and/or, contrary to the provisions of the trust, have
continued to apply some or all of the trust property either directly or
indirectly for his benefit. The trusts which were determined to be shams of
this type in *R. v. Allen*[274] had only two beneficiaries, both charities, powers
given to the trustees to add further beneficiaries having not been exercised.
Nevertheless, the companies of which the trusts were the sole shareholders
owned the settlor's house and paid all the living expenses of both him and
his family and it was on this basis that he was convicted. The facts of the
leading trust case of this type, the decision of the Royal Court of Jersey in
Rahman v. Chase Bank (C.I.) Trust Co.,[275] are less extreme in that the settlor
had expressly retained certain rights under the settlement in question but
they are nevertheless comparable.

Under the provisions of a settlement set up in 1977, the settlor had   3–135
retained during his lifetime a power of appointment over the whole of the
trust property exercisable with the consent of the trustees and a power of
appointment over a third of the current assets of the trust in each 12-month
period exercisable without their consent; the latter power thus enabled him
to bring the trust to an end in any 10-year period. Although provision was
made for the distribution of trust capital and income in default of any
appointment by the settlor and on his death, in the interim the trustee was
empowered to pay or apply the capital or income to or for the benefit of the
settlor and was directed to have regard exclusively to his interests in determining whether or not to do so. Further, most of the trustee's administrative
powers required the prior written consent of the settlor. The trustee made no
independent investment decisions and invariably complied with the settlor's directions. Further, the settlor drew money and made distributions
from the fund of which the trustee was only later informed and often
directly instructed the trust banks in respect of investments. Following the
settlor's death intestate, his widow contended that the trust was void and

---

Nicholas v. Nicholas (1984) 5 F.L.R. 285; *Cruttenden v. Cruttenden* [1990] 2 F.L.R. 361; *Green v. Green* [1993] 1 F.L.R. 236).

[273] [2000] Q.B. 744, where the Criminal Division of the Court of Appeal rejected a challenge to the validity of the direction on the basis of which the jury had convicted (the challenge was not renewed on the subsequent unsuccessful appeal to the House of Lords, reported at [2002] 1 A.C. 509).

[274] [2000] Q.B. 744 (CA), [2002] 1 A.C. 509.

[275] 1991 J.L.R. 103. See Hayton [1992] J.Int.P. 3; Mowbray [1994] Trust Law International 68, [1992] Brownbill [1992] J.Int.P. 13. Other relevant authorities are: three decisions of the Family Court of Australia in *Re Marriage of Ashton* (1986) 11 Fam.L.R. 457; *Re Marriage of Goodwin* (1990) 14 Fam.L.R. 801; *Re Marriage of Davidson* (1990) 14 Fam.L.R. 817; also *Hess v. Line Trust Corporation* (1998) 2 B.O.S. 385 (Court of Appeal of Gibraltar) and *Re WKR Trust* (2000) unreported but see [2001] P.C.B. 111 (Zurich District Court, Switzerland).

that he had consequently died absolutely entitled to the trust property which, therefore, devolved according to the relevant intestacy rules.[276] One of the two grounds[277] on which this claim succeeded was the fact that the settlor had at all times remained in total control of the trust property, something which was held to show that he had never intended the trust to have legal effect.

3–136   The facts of this case may appear extreme to the uninitiated. However, although it must admittedly be rare for a settlor to be able to deal directly with the assets of a trust in this way, the actual provisions of the settlement were not at all unusual in the context of off-shore settlements, particularly where, as in this case, the settlor in question is not from a common law jurisdiction and is unlikely fully to understand the nature of a trust. This decision, therefore, caused great concern in many off-shore jurisdictions. It has admittedly since become clear that no attack of this type will succeed where the trustees have taken possession and control of the trust assets and there are positive examples of them exercising independent control over those assets rather than simply responding on demand to every request made by the settlor.[278] These concerns must also have been alleviated by the subsequent decisions both in Jersey[279] and in this jurisdiction[280] that a trust will only be a partial sham if both settlor and trustee so intended. Nevertheless, a number of off-shore jurisdictions have also attempted to prevent partial shams of this type from being upheld by enacting legislation providing that the retention, possession, or acquisition of a whole series of powers by settlors and the existence of provisions requiring their consent to any act or abstention will not invalidate a trust.[281] Such legislation will clearly work in the courts of the jurisdictions in question; however, it cannot be guaranteed to do so if any attack on the validity of the trust is mounted elsewhere in a jurisdiction in which some or all of the trust property is actually situated.[282]

3–137   **(b) Disguised wills** A different type of partial sham arises where a person purports to settle property on trust during his lifetime with the objective not of depriving anyone of anything but of avoiding the expense of a will and the subsequent administration of his estate. In *Re Pfrimmer*,[283] a settlor vested four properties in himself, his wife, their son and their son-

---

[276] Both she and the various defendants to the action (basically his children by former marriages) were beneficiaries under the trust; however, she stood to inherit more if the subject matter of the trusts devolved on the basis that he had died intestate than she was likely to receive under the trust.

[277] The other was based on a rule of Norman Customary Law then (but not now) operable in Jersey.

[278] See *Shalson v. Russo* [2003] EWHC 1637 (Ch), [2005] Ch. 281 at 340–342

[279] *Re Esteem Settlement* [2003] J.L.R. 188

[280] *Shalson v. Russo* [2003] EWHC 1637 (Ch), [2005] Ch. 281 at 340–342.

[281] The Cook Islands had in fact already done so in (The Cooks Islands) International Trusts Act (1984), s.13C. The Bahamas subsequently did so in (The Bahamas) Trustee Act 1998, s.3 and that provision has been widely copied by, among others, Jersey in Trusts (Jersey) Law 1984, s.9A (added in 2004).

[282] This is an endemic problem of creative trust legislation which is inherently vulnerable to being ignored in any other jurisdiction whose courts regard it as infringing what they regard as fundamental principles of trust law.

[283] [1936] 2 D.L.R. 460 (Court of Appeal of Manitoba, Canada).

in-law on immediate trusts, under which he and his wife were entitled to all the revenue from the properties until sale or other disposal, which they appeared to be able to initiate; in the event of sale, they also appeared to be entitled to the proceeds and whatever remained at the death of the survivor of the husband and wife was to be held on trust for their grandchildren. The deceased subsequently made a will disposing of one of the properties and the furniture in another one. The trust could probably have been held void for uncertainty of subject matter[284] but the Court of Appeal of Manitoba actually held that the deceased had not absolutely parted with his interest in the property; consequently, this was not a trust and could only take effect if at all as a will. In the event, which seems highly unlikely, that it complied with the formal requirements for a will, it would be valid; otherwise, the later will would have effect according to its terms and the remaining properties would pass on a partial intestacy.

The problem here was not that the settlor had retained a life interest, which is not uncommon in some jurisdictions,[285] but that he had in reality not disposed of anything at all and so not only was in complete control of his property but, as the subsequent will showed, intended that he should be.[286] The off-shore legislation referred to above has also attempted to prevent partial shams being upheld on this ground.

(c) **Blind trusts** The facts of *R. v. Allen*[287] demonstrate that a partial sham can also arise where a settlor has transferred property to trustees on trust intending that the persons who benefit from the trust should be quite different from the beneficiaries whose names appear in the trust instrument (the latter are, as in *R. v. Allen*, usually charities). In effect, the settlor is giving property to his trustees to hold for a discretionary class which is not closed; the original objects are charities who will in practice never receive a penny and the real objects are added later.[288] Unless and until they are added,[289] the trust is in effect a partial sham[290] and the trust property is consequently held on resulting trust for the settlor or his estate.[291] It is, therefore, not a prerequisite of such a sham being upheld that the subject matter of the trust is, as in *R. v. Allen*, being applied for the benefit of the settlor, or his family, or indeed of anyone else; however, this fact will undoubtedly make that conclusion easier to reach.

Trusts of this type are often known as blind trusts (quite distinct from the type of blind trust that has recently become fashionable in political circles whereby the work of politicians is funded without them having any control

3–138

---

[284] See *ante*, para 3–013.

[285] It would be pointless today under English law since the entire settled property would fall into the estate of the settlor for inheritance tax purposes. See *post*, para 15–059.

[286] This decision was applied by the Court of Appeal of Singapore in *Hiranand v. Harilela* (2000) 3 I.T.E.L.R. 297.

[287] [2000] Q.B. 744 (C.A.), [2002] 1 A.C. 509 (H.L.).

[288] See *Steele v. Paz* (1995) 1 B.O.S. 338 (Court of Appeal of the Isle of Man).

[289] In *Steele v. Paz* they were to be added not by the trustees but by the protector (see *post*, para 6–029) and could not on the face of things be so added because no protector had been appointed.

[290] This argument does not appear to have occurred to anyone in *Steele v Paz*. Instead, the court appointed a protector who was then able to add the real beneficiaries.

[291] See *post*, para 9–051.

of the assets in question) or "Red Cross" trusts (because the named charitable beneficiary has in practice often been the Red Cross, as indeed one of them was in *R. v. Allen*). The reasons for proceeding in this way, apart from the blatant and illegal tax evasion which was being practised in *R. v. Allen*, can either be to avoid the tax which would otherwise be payable on the creation of the settlement or to avoid a challenge to the trusts which are really intended.

2. *Purpose Trusts*

3–139　It will be recalled[292] that trusts for non-charitable purposes are generally void for two different reasons: first, because there is no one who can enforce them; and, secondly, because the courts are unable to control the execution of such trusts. Both these reasons are eminently justifiable; since it is the lack of enforceability which in practice inhibits judicial control, they are also linked. It will also be recalled[293] that in *Re Denley's Trust Deed*[294] Goff J. held that such trusts are void only where the purpose in question is "abstract or impersonal" and that a trust which, although it is expressed in the form of a purpose, is directly or indirectly for the benefit of one or more ascertainable individuals is nevertheless valid, provided that all its terms satisfy the relevant certainty requirements. This decision seems to have been the impetus for the enactment of legislation[295] in a large number of off-shore jurisdictions[296] permitting not only purpose trusts of this kind[297] but also purpose trusts where there are no such ascertainable individuals[298]; such trusts can be and have been employed for a wide variety of purposes.[299] Whether the lack of enforceability or the lack of judicial control is the principal reason for the existence of the general rule is perceived as crucial to the debate about the potential enforceability in this jurisdiction of purpose trusts of this type which have been created off-shore.

---

[292] See *ante*, para 3–79.

[293] See *ante*, para 3–86.

[294] [1969] 1 Ch. 373.

[295] The trust legislation already enacted in Liechtenstein in 1928 and in Nauru in 1960 was in terms broad enough to permit the creation of purpose trusts, although this was probably unintentional, at least in the case of Liechtenstein.

[296] Although The Cook Islands introduced legislation of this type in 1984, this was not taken seriously; it was Bermuda which really set the ball rolling by enacting the widely copied Trusts (Special Provisions) Act 1989, subsequently redrafted and substantially amended in 1998; see *post*, para 3–140.

[297] See Matthews in *Trends in Contemporary Trust Law* (ed. Oakley, 1996) 1.

[298] See Matthews [1998] Trust Law International 98 and in *Extending the Boundaries of Trusts* (ed. Hayton, 2002) 203; Duckworth, [1999] Trust Law International 158; Hayton 117 L.Q.R. (2001) 96; Parkinson [2002] C.L.J. 657.

[299] See Matthews in *Trends in Contemporary Trust Law* (ed. Oakley, 1996) 1. Use of these trusts for what was at one stage their principal commercial purposes, for off balance-sheet transactions carried out by means of special purpose vehicles, is now less common, at least by listed companies, following the crackdown on accounting standards which followed a number of spectacular corporate collapses in the United States of America in 2002 caused by the inaccuracy of those corporations' on-shore balance sheets which had been resulted from the use of the trusts for these purposes.

The first significant and therefore the most influential legislation of this   **3–140**
type was Bermudan, the Trusts (Special Provisions) Act 1989,[300] whose
original form[301] was widely copied elsewhere. Typically,[302] such legislation
permits trusts to have any non-charitable purposes which are sufficiently
certain, lawful and not contrary to public policy[303]; however, it is necessary
for a person known as an enforcer,[304] who generally cannot also be one of
the trustees, to be appointed by the trust deed to enforce the non-charitable
purposes in the event that any such enforcement proves to be necessary. The
existence of an enforcer independent of the trustees was obviously intended
to address one of the two traditional objections to the existence of non-
charitable purpose trusts, the absence of anyone who can enforce such
trusts. However, this is less than entirely convincing, at least from the point
of view of English law, because of the fact that the enforcer will necessarily
be nominated by the settlor and, consequently, is hardly likely to enforce the
trusts if that would be contrary to the wishes of the latter; it is, therefore, not
immediately obvious that there is any real judicial control whatsoever of
trusts of this kind.

Possibly for this reason, subsequent Bermudan legislation,[305] which has   **3–141**
also been copied elsewhere, has removed the absolute requirement for an
enforcer; instead the Supreme Court of Bermuda can make orders for the
enforcement of the trust on the application of the settlor,[306] of any enforcer
that there may nevertheless be, of any trustee, and of any one else whom the
court considers to have a sufficient interest. This reform, at least superficially, appears to be intended rather to address the other traditional objection to the existence of non-charitable purpose trusts, the absence of any
judicial control. The question which this raises is, therefore, rather whether
there is any realistic possibility of anyone, other than the settlor, the trustees
and any enforcer that there may be, even finding out about the existence of
the trust; only if this is possible will there be anyone other than those
persons who will ever be in a position to ask the court to consider whether
or not he has a sufficient interest to enforce the trust. Admittedly the
Attorney-General of Bermuda may make such an application if he can

---

[300] See Anderson in *Equity, Trusts and Fiduciaries 1993* (ed. Waters, 1993) p.99. Although The
Cook Islands had introduced legislation of this type in 1984, this was not taken seriously; it was
Bermuda which really set the ball rolling by enacting this legislation.

[301] It was subsequently redrafted and substantially amended in 1998.

[302] See (Jersey) Trusts (Jersey) Law 1984 Articles 10A, 10B and 10C (added in 1996) and (Isle
of Man) Purpose Trusts Act 1996, ss.1–5, both of which are similar to the original Bermudan
legislation.

[303] The original Bermudan legislation restricted permissible purposes to those which are
"specific, reasonable and possible" and "not under the law immoral, contrary to public policy
or unlawful", as does the Manx legislation; the Jersey legislation instead permits any purposes
other than those which are contrary to the law of Jersey. The amended Bermudan legislation
referred to in the text below merely requires the purposes to be sufficiently certain to allow the
trust to be carried out, to be lawful, and not to be contrary to public policy.

[304] Also one of the alternative names for a protector (see *post*, para 6–031); "enforcer" is
presumably utilised in the context of purpose trusts to distinguish the role played in that
context from that played by a protector in the normal sense of that expression.

[305] The (Bermuda) Trusts (Special Provisions) Act 1989 was subsequently redrafted and
substantially amended in 1998; the current provisions are ss.12A–12D.

[306] In the absence of contrary provision in the trust instrument (something which is probably
advisable).

satisfy the court that no one else is able and willing to do so but how is he to find out about the existence of the trust in the first place in order to be able to do so?

3–142   The current Bermudan legislation also permits purpose trusts to last for ever.[307] It will be recalled[308] that it is generally thought that any non-charitable purpose trusts which are upheld in accordance with the decision in *Re Denley's Trust Deed*[309] must comply with the rule against inalienability and, therefore, cannot last for longer than the common law perpetuity period of a nominated life or lives in being plus 21 years. If this is indeed English law, there seems no reason why legislation enacted by an off-shore jurisdiction permitting purpose trusts to last for up to a stated statutory perpetuity period of a fixed number of years[310] should not be regarded as satisfying this requirement; English law has long permitted such a period[311] for the purposes of the rule against remoteness, although admittedly not for the purposes of the rule against inalienability.[312] But a perpetual purpose trust cannot conceivably comply with the policy on which the existence of rule against inalienability is based.

3–143   It is, therefore, somewhat questionable whether any of these types of purpose trusts would be enforceable in this jurisdiction in the event that this proved to be necessary.[313] There is of course not the slightest doubt that they would be enforceable in the courts of the jurisdiction pursuant to whose legislation they had been created. The question is whether, in the event that some of the assets of a purpose trust of one of these types were situated in England and Wales, the trustees would be able to resist a claim in the courts of England and Wales to those assets brought by the creditors of the settlor or by his estranged or former spouses and/or children on the basis that the assets were still beneficially owned by him or by his estate.

3–144   Those who doubt whether such trusts would be enforceable in the English courts stress the absence of anyone with a right to enforce the trust who has any real interest in doing so and the absence of any equitable ownership for the duration of the purpose trust, in other words the absence of anyone capable of exercising the Rule in *Saunders v. Vautier*[314]; where such trusts are capable lasting for ever, that is a further reason for questioning whether they would be upheld by the English courts. Those who assert that such trusts would be enforceable here rely on the Recognition of Trusts Act 1987,[315] whereby the courts of England and Wales are bound to recognise any trust which is valid according to its applicable law unless that law is manifestly

---

[307] (Bermuda) Trusts (Special) Provisions) Act 1989, s.12A(2) (as amended in 1998).

[308] See *ante*, paras 3–91, 3–96–3–97.

[309] [1969] 1 Ch. 373.

[310] Jersey originally permitted a period of up to 100 years, although since 2006 all Jersey trusts, including purpose trusts, have been capable of lasting for ever. The Isle of Man originally permitted and still permits a period of up to 80 years.

[311] At present 80 years, although the Law Commission has proposed that this should be increased to 125 years and this is to be enacted in 2009.

[312] See *post*, para 7–044.

[313] See the series of articles by Matthews and Duckworth summarised in Matthews 12 T.L.I. (1998) and Duckworth 13 T.L.I. (1999) 158; also Matthews in *Extending the Boundaries of Trusts* (ed. Hayton, 2002) 203, Hayton 117 L.Q.R. (2001) 96, Parkinson [2002] C.L.J. 657.

[314] (1841) Cr. & Ph. 240; see *post*, para 19–019.

[315] See *post*, para 23–039.

incompatible with public policy. It is self-evident that this question turns on whether the absence of enforceable rights and of equitable ownership and, where relevant, the failure to comply with the rule against inalienability is or is not incompatible with public policy.

3. *STAR Trusts*

Even less orthodox are two types of trusts known as STAR trusts[316] which **3–145** have been introduced in the Cayman Islands. The legislation there permits the creation of purpose trusts which cannot be enforced in any way by anyone other than the person(s) appointed for this purpose by or pursuant to the trust deed, who are also known as enforcer(s), or by the persons appointed for this purpose by the court (if there is at any time no enforcer, the trustees are under a duty to apply to the court for one to be appointed). The fact that only companies licensed to conduct trust business in the Cayman Islands can be trustees of a STAR trust provides, or at any rate is meant to provide, some form of comfort for settlors. Thus far, apart from the fact that the relevant legislation is more explicit in this respect, this type of STAR trust does not in practice greatly differ from the original Bermudan legislation although it is obviously different from the amended form of that legislation. But the legislation also permits trusts for human beneficiaries which cannot be enforced in any way by anyone other than the enforcer(s) or the persons appointed for this purpose by the court. Despite the fact that the beneficiaries are named as such, they have no right either to enforce the trust, or to make any claim against the trustees or the enforcer(s), or to assert any right to the trust property. This deprives those beneficiaries of any right to any information either about the existence of the trust or about its subject matter and administration, although the legislation does envisage the possibility of there being, as well as one or more enforcers, a protector who can be given a right to information about the subject matter and administration of the trust. Both types of STAR trusts are also capable of lasting for ever.[317]

The doubts which have been expressed as to whether purpose trusts of this type would be enforceable in the English courts are considerably reinforced in the case of STAR trusts with human beneficiaries because of the fact that the rights of such beneficiaries to enforce trusts under which they are entitled have been stated to be quite fundamental to the nature of a trust and a core requirement of its enforceability by the English courts.[318] Indeed the debate as to the enforceability of off-shore purpose trusts has largely been conducted with reference to STAR trusts.[319] While it obviously cannot be predicted with any certainty how the English courts would deal with a

---

[316] The name is an acronym derived from the legislation by which these trusts were originally introduced, the Special Trusts (Alternative Regime) Law 1997; this has now become (Cayman Islands) Trusts Law 2001, ss.95–109. See Matthews [1998] Trust Law International 98; Duckworth [1999] Trust Law International 158.

[317] (Cayman Islands) Perpetuities Law (1999 Revision), s.13(1).

[318] See, for example, *Armitage v. Nurse* [1998] Ch. 241 at 253 *per* Millett L.J.

[319] The debate between Matthews and Duckworth in Trust Law International, of which [1998] Trust Law International 98 and Duckworth [1999] Trust Law International 158 were the culmination, was conducted in this context.

challenge to a STAR trust in the event that one were ever made, in principle it is considered that such a challenge ought to be successful.

4. VISTA Trusts

3–146   Trusts known as VISTA trusts,[320] which are unorthodox in quite different respects, have been introduced in the British Virgin Islands. The objective of these trusts is to enable their trustees to be completely exonerated from any responsibility or liability for the management of any companies of which the trusts are the shareholders. Professional trustees are perceived as being increasingly unwilling to become involved in corporate structures of this kind because, under orthodox principles of trust law, they are potentially liable to the beneficiaries if anything goes wrong[321] and are probably unable effectively to exclude that liability by means of trustee exemption clauses.[322] The idea of VISTA trusts is to address this perceived reluctance by leaving the management of the companies entirely to their directors so that any potential liabilities are imposed only on the latter. Further, not only do the trustees have no control whatsoever over the appointment and reappointment of the directors; the directors can oblige the trustees to retain the shares in the company in question for so long as the directors think fit. The subject matter of VISTA trusts is limited to shares in British Virgin Islands international business companies; thus, in order for the shares of any company incorporated anywhere else to be held in a VISTA trust, it is necessary for such a company to be created and interposed between the external company and the trust. Both this restriction and the fact that only the holder of a trust licence in the British Virgin Islands can be a trustee of a VISTA trust are clearly intended to benefit the economy of the British Virgin Islands rather than to provide any form of comfort for settlors or beneficiaries.

It must also be doubtful whether a VISTA trust would be enforceable in the English courts in the event that this proved to be necessary. This is because of the fact that the obligation of a trustee to account to his beneficiaries has also been stated to be quite fundamental to the nature of a trust and a core requirement of its enforceability[323]; indeed this obligation is arguably even more fundamental than the ability of a beneficiary to enforce his trust. While it again obviously cannot be predicted with any certainty how the English courts would deal with a challenge to a VISTA trust in the event that one were ever made, in principle it is considered that such a challenge ought to be successful.

---

[320] The name is again an acronym derived from the legislation by which these trusts were originally introduced, the Virgin Islands Special Trusts Act 2003; see Moerman, [2004] Trust Law International 67.

[321] By virtue of *Bartlett v. Barclays Bank Trust Co. (No.2)* [1980] Ch. 515; see *post*, para 14–066.

[322] See *post, ibid.*

[323] See, for example, *Armitage v. Nurse* [1998] Ch. 241 at 253 *per* Millett L.J.

CHAPTER 4

THE FORMAL REQUIREMENTS FOR THE CREATION
OF A TRUST

I. Capacity to Create a Trust

Any person who has a power of disposition over a particular type of **4–001**
property can generally create a trust of it. Accordingly, any person over the
age of 18[1] who is not suffering from mental incapacity may create an express
trust of any property which is capable of disposition and may also create a
trust of certain types of property of which he cannot dispose—an example
of the latter type of property is a pension granted by a company to a retired
director on the basis that it is non-assignable; the director may nevertheless
be able to create a valid trust of the benefit of that agreement. Full capacity
is, therefore, required before a fully binding express trust can be created;
however, any property validly transferred under a trust which is subsequently held to be void is generally held by its recipient on resulting trust
for the incapable settlor.

The position concerning settlors who lack mental capacity has recently **4–002**
been amended. Until September 30, 2007, this depended on whether a
receiver had been appointed under sections 94 and 99 of the Mental Health
Act 1983 on the grounds that the settlor was incapable of managing his
affairs; once a receiver had been appointed, it was generally thought that
any trust purportedly created by the patient would be void.[2] Since October
1, 2007, the position is instead governed by the Mental Capacity Act 2005
(which came into force on that date) and depends on whether there is a
subsisting order under sections 16 and 18 of that Act making decisions
concerning the patient's property; where there is such an order, it is thought
that any trust purportedly created by the patient which is inconsistent with
the order will equally be void. However, the Court of Protection has power
to direct the settlement of any property of such a person for his own benefit
or for the benefit of others.[3] There is also a similar power to direct the
execution of a will on behalf of such a person.[4] These powers must be
exercised in the best interest of the persons on behalf of whom they are

---

[1] Family Law Reform Act 1969, s.1(1).
[2] There was no authority under the 1983 Act; however, this was the effect of *Re Walker* [1905]
1 Ch. 160, *Re Marshall* [1920] 1 Ch. 284 and *Re Beaney* [1978] 1 W.L.R. 770 at 772, all decisions
on the old law of lunacy.
[3] Mental Capacity Act 2005, ss.16(1)(b), 16(2)(a), s.18(1)(h). These provisions replaced similar
provisions in Mental Health Act 1983, ss.95, 96.
[4] *ibid.*

made and in accordance with the general principles in section 1 of the Mental Capacity Act 2005.[5]

4–003   However, even where no receiver had been appointed or, now, no order has been made, a trust will nevertheless be set aside if it can be shown that the settlor did not have the capacity to understand the nature of the act in which he was engaged when it was explained to him—the extent of understanding required is relative to the transaction which is to be effected and varies with its circumstances.[6] It appears that the burden of proof will, at the outset, always lie on the person seeking to set the trust aside; however, where there is a long history of mental illness, this burden will easily be able to be discharged and will then effectively be reversed, since the court will then require evidence that the settlor created the trust during a lucid interval.[7] Where a trust is set aside for this reason, any property transferred will be held by the recipient on a resulting trust for the settlor. It must, however, be emphasised that no trust created for valuable consideration will be set aside where the person providing the consideration was unaware of the incapacity of the settlor at the time when the trust was made.[8]

4–004   A person under the age of 18 cannot hold land[9] although he can certainly hold an equitable interest in land and will do so in the event of a purported conveyance of a legal estate to him, since this takes effect as a declaration of trust in his favour.[10] Consequently, while a minor cannot create a settlement of a legal estate in land, for no such estate can be vested in him, he can create a trust of such property as he does hold, including a trust of an equitable interest in land. Any trust which he does create is voidable until shortly after he attains the age of 18; if he does not repudiate it then, the trust will become fully binding upon him.[11] However, in order to create even a voidable trust, a minor must be old enough to appreciate the nature of his act. If he is too young to do so, his act is void and property which has been transferred is held by the recipient on a resulting trust[12] for the minor.[13]

II. THE STATUTORY REQUIREMENT OF WRITING

4–005   It has already been seen that an express trust can be constituted *inter vivos* either by declaration, where the settlor declares that specific property vested

---

[5] *ibid.*, s.16(3); as to best interests, see s.4. Under the previous law, the court had principally consider what the patient would have been likely to have done if he had not been incapable; *Re T.B.* [1967] Ch. 247; *Re D.(J.)* [1982] Ch. 237.

[6] *Re Beaney* [1978] 1 W.L.R 770; *Simpson v. Simpson* [1992] 1 F.L.R. 601 (both cases in which *inter vivos* gifts which upset the balance of the settlor's estate were held to be void).

[7] See *Cleare v. Cleare* (1869) 1 P. & D. 655; *Chambers and Yatman v. Queen's Proctor* (1840) 2 Curt. 415.

[8] *Price v. Berrington* (1851) 3 Mac. & G. 486.

[9] Law of Property Act 1925, s.1(6) Family Law Reform Act 1969, s.1.

[10] Trusts of Land and Appointment of Trustees Act 1996, Sch.1, para. 1 (this replaced Settled Land Act 1925, s.27, under which such a conveyance operated as an agreement for valuable consideration to create a settlement of the land on the minor).

[11] *Edwards v. Carter* [1893] A.C. 360.

[12] See *post*, para 9–051.

[13] Formerly it was possible, under the Infant Settlements Act 1855, for a minor female aged 17 or over to make a binding settlement (this was at the time when the age of majority was 21); however, there was no obvious point in preserving this right when the age of majority was reduced to 18 and so it was abolished by the Family Law Reform Act 1969, s.11(a).

in him is thereafter the subject matter of a trust, or by transfer, where a settlor transfers specific property to trustees for them to hold on trust, the latter method being the only way of constituting a testamentary trust. The creation of trusts by either of these methods is subject to certain statutory rules concerning formalities, testamentary trusts being governed by the Wills Act 1837 and *inter vivos* trusts being governed by the Law of Property Act 1925.

1. *The Statutory Provisions governing Testamentary Trusts*

Testamentary trusts are governed exclusively by the provisions of the Wills Act 1837,[14] Section 9 of which[15] provides that no will is valid unless it satisfies the following conditions: first, it must be in writing and signed by the testator or by some other person in his presence and by his direction; secondly, it must appear that the testator intended by his signature to give effect to the will; thirdly, that signature must be made or acknowledged by the testator in the presence of two or more witnesses present at the same time; and, fourthly, each witness must either attest and sign the will or acknowledge his signature in the presence of the testator (but not necessarily in the presence of any other witness), no particular form of attestation being necessary.

4–006

The formal validity of any trust whose terms are entirely contained within a will is determined entirely by whether or not that will was executed in accordance with this provision; testamentary trusts of this type therefore do not require any further consideration in this section. It is, however, possible for a will executed in accordance with this provision to constitute a trust whose existence and/or terms are not revealed on the face of the will. The validity of such trusts is governed by the doctrine of secret trusts, which will be considered in detail in the next section.[16]

4–007

2. *The Statutory Provisions governing Inter Vivos Trusts*

The principal statutory provision governing the creation of *inter vivos* trusts is section 53 of the Law of Property Act 1925. Its wording has been the subject of detailed analysis by the courts and therefore needs to be set out in full.

4–008

"(1) Subject to the provisions hereinafter contained with respect to the creation of interests in land by parol—

    (a) no interest in land can be created or disposed of except by writing signed by the person creating or conveying the same, or by his agent thereunto lawfully authorised in writing, or by will, or by operation of law;

---

[14] Law of Property Act 1925, s.55 in effect requires the transaction in question to be made by will rather than in accordance with the formal requirements of that Act by providing that nothing in s.53, the provision which lays down the formal requirements for the creation of trusts, is to invalidate dispositions by will.

[15] As substituted by section 17 of the Administration of Justice Act 1982.

[16] See *post*, para 4–051 *et seq*.

(b) a declaration of trust respecting any land or any interest therein must be manifested and proved by some writing signed by some person who is able to declare such trust or by his will;

(c) a disposition of an equitable interest or trust subsisting at the time of the disposition, must be in writing signed by the person disposing of the same, or by his agent thereunto lawfully authorised in writing or by will.[17]

(2) This section does not affect the creation or operation of resulting, implied or constructive trusts."

(A) The Different Formal Requirements of this Provision

4–009   Paragraphs a and c of subsection 1 require the transaction in question to be in writing; therefore any failure to comply with this requirement makes the transaction in question wholly void. However, the writing need not in all cases contain every detail—if the assignee is to hold subject to some fiduciary duty, the writing need not comprise particulars of the trust.[18] Nor does it seem to be necessary that the writing should all be contained in one document; a number of documents may be joined together for the purpose of satisfying the statute, provided that they are sufficiently connected.[19]

4–010   On the other hand, paragraph b of subsection 1 requires only evidentiary writing so that any failure to comply with this requirement does not make the transaction in question wholly void but merely unenforceable. This has two consequences: first, that the transaction is and remains valid unless and until one of the parties specifically raises the absence of the writing[20]; secondly, the necessary evidentiary writing can take the most diverse forms[21] and be provided at any time and quite unintentionally, provided that it does contain all the terms of the trust.

4–011   A further difference is that the writing required by paragraphs a and c can be signed either by the grantor or by an agent of the grantor who has been

---

[17] To be effective, a disposition under s.53(1)(c) must be unconditional; see *Chandler v. Clark* [2003] EWCA Civ. 1249, [2003] 1 P. & C.R. 239.

[18] *Re Tyler* [1967] 1 W.L.R. 1269.

[19] *Re Danish Bacon Company Staff Pension Fund Trusts* [1971] 1 W.L.R. 268; Megarry J. stated that this was a novel question on which there appeared to be no previous direct authority.

[20] This can presumably be done at any time, even long after the creation of the trust. In principle, this means that there is nothing to stop a settlor who has created an *inter vivos* trust of land without the necessary formalities (or, more realistically, his trustee in bankruptcy or the residuary beneficiaries of his estate) from recovering the land in question at any time. However, any beneficiary who had acted to his detriment would inevitably be able to resist such a claim by relying on an equitable proprietary estoppel (see *post*, para 5–055). Further, it may now follow from *Pennington v. Waine* [2002] EWCA Civ 227, [2002] 1 W.L.R. 2075 (see *post*, para 5–032) that it would be regarded as unconscionable for the residuary beneficiaries so to do even if the beneficiary had not acted to his detriment; however, this decision actually concerned the complete constitution of trusts, not their formalities; see Halliwell [2003] Conveyancer 192.

[21] For example, it may be provided by correspondence (*Foster v. Hale* (1798) 3 Ves.Jun. 696), by a recital in an instrument (*Re Hoyle* [1893] 1 Ch. 84), by an answer to what used to be known as interrogatories, now known as requests for further information (*Hampton v. Spencer* (1693) 2 Vern. 288), or even by a telegram (*McBlain v. Cross* (1871) 25 L.T. 804). It remains to be seen whether it would today also be held capable of being provided by a fax, a type of document which it is notoriously easy to forge. Under the present law, an e-mail would not be regarded as having been signed.

duly authorised in writing, while the writing required by paragraph b can be signed only by the grantor.

(B) The Scope of the Different Paragraphs

Paragraphs a and b of subsection 1 are expressed to apply only to interests   **4–012** in land; paragraph c, on the other hand, is not expressly so restricted. However, the definitions section of the Law of Property Act 1925,[22] provides that "equitable interests" means "all the other interests and charges in or over land", unless the context otherwise requires. The question of whether this definition does restrict the scope of paragraph c to interests in land or whether, on the other hand, the context does otherwise require, has not been specifically addressed by an English court.[23] It is generally thought that the context does otherwise require; were this not the case, paragraph c would be superfluous since every situation falling within it would already have been caught by paragraph a, something which cannot possibly have been the intention of the legislature. Moreover, the House of Lords applied paragraph c to a relevant disposition of pure personalty in *Grey v. Inland Revenue Commissioners*[24] without any objection being raised, a decision which must resolve the question in this jurisdiction unless and until it is specifically raised.

A further difficulty is the apparent overlaps between paragraphs a, b, and   **4–013** c of subsection (1), which respectively deal with the creation or disposition of any interest in land, any declaration of a trust of land, and any disposition of a subsisting equitable interest or trust. The distinction thus drawn between the creation and the disposition of interests must be applied in the light of the fact that, when property is owned legally and beneficially by the same person, he holds only a legal interest therein, not a separate equitable interest as well.[25] Consequently, when such a person confers an equitable interest in that property on someone else, he is not disposing of an existing equitable interest therein but creating a new one. This is capable of falling within paragraphs a and b but not within paragraph c, which clearly relates only to the disposition of a "subsisting" equitable interest, that is to say one existing separately from the legal estate. This, however, only rules out any overlap between paragraph b and paragraph c; there may nevertheless be overlaps between, on the one hand, paragraph a and, on the other hand, paragraphs b and c.

The fact that, on the face of things, there seems to be a clear overlap   **4–014** between paragraph a and paragraph c, in that a disposition of a subsisting

---

[22] s.201(1)(x).

[23] It was considered by the High Court of Australia in *Adamson v. Hayes* (1973) 130 C.L.R. 276, where the members of the court disagreed. Menzies J. held that the equivalent Western Australian provision was restricted to interests in land, whereas Gibbs J. held that it was not. The remaining judges did not specifically mention this point but, since Walsh and Stephen JJ. agreed with Gibbs J. in other respects, the Australian commentators have concluded that they also rejected the view of Menzies J. and that there was therefore a majority against the provision being so restricted.

[24] [1960] A.C. 1.

[25] *Commissioner of Stamp Duties (Queensland) v. Livingston* [1965] A.C. 694 (Privy Council on appeal from the High Court of Australia).

equitable interest in or trust of land is caught by both of them, has no significance in this jurisdiction since the formal requirements of the two paragraphs are identical.[26]

4–015   Potentially more problematic is the fact that a declaration of trust respecting land appears to fall within both paragraph a and paragraph b, which have different formal requirements; such a trust supported only by evidentiary writing signed by the settlor appears to be void under paragraph a and valid under paragraph b. Once again there is no English authority.[27] If this overlap exists, paragraph b is in effect superfluous, something which again cannot possibly have been the intention of the legislature. It is thought that the potential difficulty could and should be resolved by reading paragraph a as if it said "no interest in land can be created or disposed of *otherwise than by the declaration of a trust* except by writing . . . " (the italicised words being interpolated). However, unless and until this matter is actually considered by a court, there must be a certain amount of doubt as to whether a declaration of trust of land which is not in writing and is supported only by evidentiary writing signed by the settlor is actually valid.

(C)   The Exception in Subsection 2

4–016   The exception contained in section 53(2) qualifies the whole of section 53(1). Consequently, the creation or operation of implied, resulting or constructive trusts does not have to comply with the formal requirements of the section. This provision is applied extremely literally. It clearly exempts such trusts from having to comply with section 53(1)(b). This is illustrated by *Hodgson v. Marks*,[28] where an elderly widow was persuaded by her lodger to convey her house into his name on the spurious grounds that this would prevent him from being turned out of it after her death. He subsequently sold and conveyed the property to third parties without revealing that he had no beneficial interest in that property. The Court of Appeal decided that, as he had held the property on resulting trust for the widow, such a trust arose without any need to comply with the statutory formalities required by section 53(1)(b) and so was capable of binding the third parties.[29] The

---

[26] This is undoubtedly why the question has never been raised. The only way of escaping from this conclusion is to hold that paragraph a is confined to legal interests in land. This was held by Menzies J. in *Adamson v. Hayes* (1973) 130 C.L.R. 276 but the majority of the High Court of Australia (Walsh, Gibbs and Stephen JJ.) took the opposite view. However, none of them specifically mentioned the possible overlap, which would be significant only in Queensland, whose equivalent of paragraph c unusually requires only evidentiary writing—the legislation in the remaining Australian jurisdictions is similar to s.53(1)(c).

[27] The Australian decisions are mutually inconsistent. In *Adamson v. Hayes* (1973) 130 C.L.R. 276, Gibbs and Stephen JJ. expressly and Walsh J. implicitly but not Menzies J. held that there was such an overlap but the opposite view was subsequently taken at first instance in *Secretary, Department of Social Security v. Jones* (1990) 95 A.J.R. 615 (Supreme Court of Western Australia), where a declaration of trust of land was held only to fall within paragraph b.

[28] [1971] Ch. 892.

[29] It was in fact held to bind the third parties on the grounds that the widow had an overriding interest under s.70(1)(g) of the Land Registration Act 1925 by virtue of her actual occupation of the house. This remains the position under ss.29, 30 and Sch.3, para.2, of the Land Registration Act 2002, unless it is held that her occupation would not have been obvious on a reasonably careful inspection of the land and the purchasers had no actual knowledge of it.

equivalent provision in the Law of Property (Miscellaneous) Provisions Act 1989,[30] which exempts such trusts from having to comply with the formal requirements for contracts of the sale of land, has been held not to apply to equitable proprietary estoppel interests where it is unconscionable for their existence to be denied.[31] However, although resulting, implied and constructive trusts can come into existence and operate without any need for writing, any disposition of an interest arising under such a trust must comply with section 53(1)(c)—this is demonstrated by the decision of the House of Lords in *Grey v. I.R.C.*,[32] where what was being disposed of by the settlor was an interest arising under a resulting trust.

3. *The Effect of the Statutory Provisions governing Inter Vivos Trusts*

(A) The Creation by Declaration of a Trust of Property Vested in the Settlor

If the interest in the property in question held by the settlor is a legal interest, the effect of the statutory provisions depends on whether it is in land or in pure personalty. If it is an interest in land,[33] section 53(1)(b) applies on any view; consequently, the declaration of trust will require evidentiary writing signed by the settlor, in default of which the declaration will be unenforceable. Signature by an agent is insufficient.[34] The appropriate writing will still be required even if the land in question is situated out of the jurisdiction and no writing is necessary according to the *lex situs*; this is because this is a rule of evidence which must be complied with in an English court.[35] If, on the other hand, the property is an interest in pure personalty, none of the statutory provisions applies and so the declaration of trust will be able to be made entirely orally. It is indeed rather surprising that a declaration of trust requires the appropriate writing even if it relates to as little as a square foot of land while a declaration of trust of millions of pounds worth of cash or investments does not; however, that is what the statutory provisions provide.

4–017

If, on the other hand, the interest in the property in question held by the settlor is an equitable interest,[36] the result is exactly the same with one further complication. The equitable interest in question must necessarily be taking effect behind an existing trust so that what the settlor will in reality be declaring is a sub-trust. The effect of this may depend on whether the

4–018

---

[30] s.2(5).

[31] *Yaxley v. Gotts* [2000] Ch. 162.

[32] [1960] A.C. 1. See *post*, para 4–027.

[33] This includes freehold and leasehold property: Law of Property Act 1925, s.205(1)(ix).

[34] If, contrary to what was suggested above, there is indeed an overlap between s.53(1)(a) and s.53(1)(b), the former provision will also apply, requiring the declaration of trust to be in writing signed by the settlor or by an agent of the settlor duly authorised in writing, in default of which the declaration will be void.

[35] *Rochefoucauld v. Boustead* [1897] 1 Ch. 196 at 207.

[36] This includes freehold and leasehold property (Law of Property Act 1925, s.205(1)(ix)) and also apparently a share in the proceeds of sale of land (Law of Property (Miscellaneous) Provisions) Act 1989, s.2(6)).

sub-trust declared is passive or active.[37] If it is passive, there is binding authority[38] (although contrary views have been expressed[39]) that the settlor of the sub-trust will "disappear from the picture" and drop out so that his trustees will hold the property directly on trust for the intended beneficiary of the sub-trust[40]; if it is active, there is further authority[41] (and it is generally agreed) that the settlor of the sub-trust will not drop out and will hold his own subsisting interest on trust for the intended beneficiary of the sub-trust.

4–019   So far as formalities are concerned, the conventional view[42] is that, if the settlor does drop out, his purported declaration of trust will be treated as amounting to a disposition of his subsisting equitable interest under the original trust; consequently, section 53(1)(c) will apply, requiring the declaration of sub-trust to be in writing signed by the settlor or by an agent of the settlor duly authorised in writing, in default of which the declaration will be void. According to this view, a declaration of a passive sub-trust (but not an active sub-trust) requires writing under section 53(1)(c). This is not particularly significant in the case of a sub-trust of land, where evidentiary writing under section 53(1)(b) is necessary on any view,[43] but immensely significant in the case of a sub-trust of pure personalty, which would otherwise require no formality whatever. An alternative view has been put forward[44] that all declarations of sub-trust, whether active or passive, have to comply with section 53(1)(c) whether the settlor drops out or not; this view thus requires writing in even more cases than the conventional view. However, it is thought that the conventional view should be adopted until such time as the

---

[37] It will be regarded as passive where the settlor has declared that his entire interest under the existing trust is to be held for the intended beneficiary of the sub-trust; where, on the other hand, the settlor has either declared that only a part of his interest under the existing trust is to be held for that beneficiary or has reserved some duties which in effect restrict the nature of the interest being given to him (the example which is always given is a declaration of trust to pay the rents and profits of the trust property to the intended beneficiary, thus restricting his rights to call for the capital), it will be regarded as active. It is unclear whether an apparently passive sub-trust for persons by way of succession is passive or active; however, it is suggested that the better view is that of Fry L.J. in *Re Lashmar* [1891] 1 Ch. 258 (by way of dictum) that it is passive.

[38] This was stated in *Grainge v. Wilberforce* (1889) 5 T.L.R. 436 at 437 and held by the Court of Appeal in *Re Lashmar* [1891] 1 Ch. 258.

[39] By Green in (1984) 37 M.L.R. 385. This view has also been expressed in some of the common law jurisdictions of the United States of America and seems to be supported in Australia by some remarks of Dixon J. in *Comptroller of Stamps (Victoria) v. Howard Smith* (1936) 54 C.L.R. 614 (High Court of Australia).

[40] This has also been held to be the effect of the creation of a constructive sub-trust as the result of a specifically enforceable contract for the sale of an equitable interest; see *Oughtred v. I.R.C.* [1960] A.C. 206 at 240 *per* Lord Radcliffe, *Re Holt's Settlement* [1976] 1 Ch. 100 at 116 pe Megarry J., *Neville v. Wilson* [1997] Ch. 144 (CA) and *post*, paras 4–043–4–047. However, the mere fact that a third party has contributed the purchase price and therefore has an interest under a resulting trust in such a specifically enforceable contract does not cause the purchaser to drop out and the vendor to hold the subject matter of the contract on constructive trust directly for the third party; this was held, on a somewhat inadequate citation of authority, in *Nelson v. Greening & Sykes (Builders)* [2007] EWCA Civ. 1358.

[41] *Onslow v. Wallis* (1849) 1 Mac. & G. 506.

[42] See Battersby [1979] Conv. 17.

[43] If, contrary to what was suggested above, there is indeed an overlap between s.53(1)(a) and s.53(1)(b), this will make no difference at all.

[44] By Green in (1984) 37 M.L.R. 385.

question is considered by a court (it has never had to be considered in relation to the Law of Property Act 1925).

(B) The Creation by Transfer of a Trust of Property Vested in the Settlor

In this case, the settlor must vest the property in question in the trustees on the intended trusts by the appropriate formalities.   **4–020**

(1) Legal interests

If the interest in the property in question held by the settlor is a legal interest, the formalities depend on the nature of the property.   **4–021**

Registered land or any interest in registered land must be transferred by the appropriate land transfer form and duly registered in the name of the trustees in the Land Register,[45] whereas unregistered land must be transferred by deed.[46] The transfer or deed in question will normally set out the trusts on which the interest in land in question is to be held; if it does not do so, those trusts should have been set out in a separate document which complies with section 53(1)(b)[47]—in default, the trustees will hold the property on resulting trust for the settlor.   **4–022**

Choses in possession, that is to say personal chattels, can be transferred either by delivery of the chattel with the appropriate intention to give or by deed[48]; the trusts on which they are to be held can be communicated orally.   **4–023**

Choses in action must in principle be assigned in accordance with section 136 of the Law of Property Act 1925[49] but the assignment of some specific choses[50] in action is instead governed by their own specific legislative provisions.[51] However, a transfer which has not been made in accordance with these formal requirements may nevertheless take effect in equity by virtue of the Rule in *Re Rose*[52] where the settlor has done everything within his power to bring about the transfer; it may also, more controversially, take effect in equity where it would be unconscionable for the settlor to deny its existence.[53]   **4–024**

---

[45] Land Registration Rules 2003, r.58.

[46] Law of Property Act 1925, s.52.

[47] The only situation where this is now actually necessary is where the trusts in question are secret (see *post*, para 4–051 *et seq.*, 4–103); see *Re Baillie* (1886) 2 T.L.R. 660, a case of a half secret trust—the absence of writing has never been raised in respect of a fully secret trust. If there is indeed an overlap between s.53(1)(a) and s.53(1)(b), the writing in question will instead have to comply with s.53(1)(a).

[48] See *Cochrane v. Moore* (1890) 25 Q.B.D. 57. However, if the trust is being constituted pursuant to a contract for the sale of goods, the legal title will pass in accordance with the legislation governing sales of goods.

[49] This provision requires the assignment to be in writing signed by the assignor and for express notice in writing to be given to the debtor or other person from whom the assignor would have been able to claim the debt or other chose in action.

[50] Such as shares, copyrights, certain types of insurance policies, and bills of exchange.

[51] Most shares are transferred simply by filling in the appropriate share transfer form, sometimes printed on the back of the share certificate itself, and sending it to the Registrar of the company in question for entry on the Register of Shareholders.

[52] [1952] Ch. 499. See *post*, para 5–026.

[53] *Pennington v. Waine* [2002] EWCA Civ. 227, [2002] 1 W.L.R. 2075 (see *post*, para 5–032 and Halliwell [2003] Conveyancer 192).

(2) Equitable interests

4–025   If the interest in the property in question held by the settlor is an equitable interest, then, no matter what the nature of the property, its transfer will constitute a disposition of a subsisting equitable interest; consequently, both the actual transfer and the trusts on which the equitable interest are to be held will have to be in writing complying with section 53(1)(c). An equitable interest can also be assigned under section 136 of the Law of Property Act 1925 on the basis that it is a chose in action.[54]

(C) The Creation of a Trust by the Settlor Giving Instructions to his Trustees

4–026   In all the examples considered so far the settlor in question has himself dealt with property vested in him. It is now necessary to consider the situation where a settlor who is beneficially entitled to property under a trust gives instructions to his trustees to deal with that property in some way in order to vest his interest in a third party.

(1) Where the settlor directs his trustees to hold on trust for a third party

4–027   This situation had to be considered by the House of Lords in *Grey v. I.R.C.*[55] Trustees were holding shares as the nominees of the settlor, who was therefore beneficially entitled to those shares under a resulting trust. The settlor, having made six settlements in favour of his grandchildren, orally directed the trustees to hold the shares on the trusts of those settlements. The trustees then executed six written declarations of trust in similar form, each of which recited their legal ownership of the shares, the settlor's oral direction, and their acceptance of the trust reposed in them by that direction. This apparently pointless exercise was an ingenious scheme to avoid payment of the *ad valorem* stamp duty which was then normally chargeable on a transfer of shares into a settlement. Stamp duty is payable only on documents so none would be payable if the oral directions of the settlor had passed his beneficial interest in the shares to the trustees. However, the House of Lords upheld the Inland Revenue's argument that the directions of the settlor were in fact dispositions by him of his subsisting equitable interest in the shares and so were within section 53(1)(c); because the directions had not been made in writing as required by that paragraph, they had not been effective at the time. Consequently, the directions had only became effective later on when the trustees had executed the written declarations of trust and so stamp duty was payable on those written declarations.

4–028   The decision depended entirely on the correct interpretation of the word "disposition" in section 53(1)(c). It had been persuasively argued on behalf of the settlor that section 53 was merely a consolidation of three provisions of the Statute of Frauds 1677, sections 3, 7 and 9. There is a general principle that consolidating statutes are not to be interpreted as changing the pre-existing law unless the words are too clear to admit of any other construction. On this basis, the term "disposition" had to be interpreted in the same

---

[54] This will require the assignment to be in writing signed by the assignor and for express notice in writing to be given to the trustee in question.

[55] [1960] A.C. 1.

way as the expression "grants and assignments" found in section 9 which, it was contended, would not cover the directions given by the settlor.[56] However, the House of Lords held that section 53 could not be regarded as a true consolidation of the three sections of the Statute of Frauds. The Law of Property Act 1925 was undoubtedly a consolidating statute but what it had consolidated was the Law of Property Act 1922 and the Law of Property (Amendment) Act 1924, the latter of which had repealed the three sections of the Statute of Frauds 1677 and re-enacted them in an altered form. In the absence of any direct link between section 9 of the Statute of Frauds 1677 and section 53(1)(c), it was inadmissible to allow the construction of the word "disposition" to be limited or controlled by any meaning which could conceivably be attached to "grants and assignments" in section 9 of the Statute of Frauds. Consequently the word "disposition" had to be given the wide meaning which it bears in normal usage.[57]

The effect of this decision is that, if at the start of a transaction a person **4–029** has a subsisting equitable interest and at the end of that transaction no longer has that interest, there will have been a disposition and the paragraph will have to be complied with.[58] Only two exceptions to this rule have subsequently emerged. First, it has been established that a disclaimer of an equitable interest is not caught by section 53(1)(c) and so does not have to be made in writing. This was held in *Re Paradise Motor Company*,[59] where a verbal disclaimer by a person to whom shares had been given in such a way as to give him an equitable interest in those shares was held to be effective and therefore disentitled him from claiming in the liquidation of the company in question. Secondly, it has been stated that the paragraph does not apply to a right commonly given by pension schemes to employees who are not yet in receipt of their pensions to nominate a person to receive a payment in the event of their death.

(2) Where the settlor directs his trustees to transfer the trust property to a third party beneficially

This situation occurred in *Vandervell v. I.R.C.*,[60] the first of three cases which **4–030** arose out of an endowment in favour of the Royal College of Surgeons whose ramifications were insufficiently investigated in advance.[61] Vandervell had during his lifetime been a very successful businessman. He was beneficially entitled to virtually all the shares in a private products company which he ran and he could declare dividends as and when he pleased.

---

[56] It was, as Lord Radcliffe said, a "nice question" whether or not this type of direction would have been caught by section 9; the point had never been decided and perhaps never would be.

[57] [1960] A.C. 1 at 17–18.

[58] If there is indeed an overlap between s.53(1)(a) and s.53(1)(c), paragraph a will also apply where the subject matter is land but this in practice makes no difference whatever.

[59] *Re Paradise Motor Company* [1968] 1 W.L.R. 1125, where a verbal disclaimer by a person to whom shares had been given in such a way as to give him an equitable interest in those shares was held to be effective and therefore disentitled him from claiming in the liquidation of the company in question.

[60] [1967] 2 A.C. 291.

[61] An incisive statement of the facts can be found in the judgment of Lord Denning M.R. in *Re Vandervell's Trusts (No.2)* [1974] Ch. 269 at 316–318; this decision of the Court of Appeal was the final stage of the third of the three cases.

Further, in 1949 he had formed a trust company for the benefit of his children and had transferred money and shares to that company to be held on trust for them. In 1958 he decided to respond to an appeal for funds by the Royal College of Surgeons by founding a chair of pharmacology at a cost of £150,000.[62] In the hope of making this endowment in a tax efficient way,[63] he directed the bank which held the shares in his products company on trust for him to transfer those shares to the College; however, the shares were not transferred as an outright gift but subject to an option enabling the trust company to re-purchase the shares for £5,000 (a figure considerably less than their market value) at any time within five years. It was intended that, once sufficient dividends had been declared and paid on the shares to provide £145,000, the trust company would exercise the option, pay the remaining £5,000 and reacquire the shares, which could then be used for other purposes. Between 1958 and 1961 the products company declared dividends on the shares which were more than sufficient to endow the chair at the College.[64]

4–031   Unfortunately, however, Vandervell had not by 1961 specified the trusts on which the trust company was to hold the option (it appeared that he had not made up his mind whether the option should be held in trust for his children or for the employees of his company). The Revenue therefore argued that Vandervell was liable to surtax on the dividends[65] on the basis that he had throughout retained a beneficial interest in the shares. By a majority of three to two, the House of Lords held that, because no trusts of the option had yet been declared, the option was held on resulting trust for Vandervell himself and he had therefore been rightly assessed to surtax. This conclusion, which has nothing to do with formalities, was sufficient to dispose of the case.

4–032   However, for present purposes, what is important is the Revenue's alternative argument, which was indeed argued first, that section 53(1)(c) had not been complied with. At the outset Vandervell had undoubtedly held the equitable beneficial interest in the shares which were in the name of his bank. According to the Revenue, he had never transferred that equitable interest to the College in the manner required by section 53(1)(c); consequently, the beneficial interest was still vested in him and he was for that

---

[62] Well over £2,000,000 when converted to 2008 values using the Retail Prices Index.

[63] Any dividends declared by the company would be subject to deduction at source of the tax payable on company distributions (then 6s.8d. in the pound—33.33 per cent) and would then be subject to surtax (the name then given to what is now known as the higher rate of income tax) in the hands of the shareholders (in Vandervell's case at 50 per cent). The total tax payable by Vandervell on any dividends would thus have been 83.33 per cent. The purpose of vesting the shares in the Royal College of Surgeons was to remove any liability of Vandervell to surtax and to enable the College, as a charity, to recover the 33.33 per cent tax already paid on the company distributions. That way a third of the endowment would be being provided out of tax already paid. This scheme would have worked perfectly had Vandervell not failed fully to divest himself of his beneficial interest in the shares.

[64] The dividends amounted to over £266,000; after tax at source, the College received about £175,000 plus the £5,000 payable under the option and it was envisaged that it would also be able to reclaim the tax deducted at source.

[65] Amounting, ultimately, to the whole amount of the dividends. The initial demand was for £250,000 in respect of the first two years of assessment; a further assessment was no doubt made in respect of the third year. The surtax was payable by virtue of the Income Tax Act 1952, s.415.

reason liable to surtax on the dividends declared thereon. The House of Lords rejected this contention, holding that section 53(1)(c) has no application where the holder of the equitable interest also controls the legal interest and intends that both should be transferred to a third party beneficially. In other words, section 53(1)(c) only applies to the disposition of an existing equitable interest when that interest is both before and after the disposition vested in someone other than the holder of the legal interest. The House had little alternative but to reach this conclusion since otherwise nominees would no longer have been able to pass a beneficial interest to a third party in the absence of a written disposition by or on behalf of the beneficiary.[66] However, the reasons enunciated in support of this conclusion are less than wholly convincing.

Two of the speeches can be immediately dismissed. Lord Reid[67] simply refused to give any reasons whatever for his decision on this point. Lord Wilberforce[68] held that Vandervell had done everything in his power to transfer his beneficial interest and so could rely on the Rule in *Re Rose*[69] which gives effect in equity to transfers which a settlor has done everything within his power to bring about; however, this argument in fact begged the question because Vandervell had only done everything in his power if he did not have to use writing—precisely the question in issue.[70]

4–033

The remaining argument, by Lord Upjohn,[71] merits more serious consideration. He had recourse to the mischief rule of statutory interpretation and held that section 53(1)(c) had been enacted to prevent fraud on those who were truly beneficially entitled; consequently, he held that it could not apply to an absolutely entitled beneficiary like Vandervell, who could control his trustees. Since the only person whom such a person could possibly defraud was himself, there could, therefore, be no grounds for invoking the section where such an absolute beneficial owner wanted to deal with the legal estate. Lord Pearce agreed with the speech of Lord Upjohn and Lord Donovan[72] reached the same conclusion without bothering to make any specific reference to the rules of statutory interpretation. Lord Upjohn's argument therefore found favour with at least three members of the House and is not wholly unconvincing. However, the mischief rule of statutory interpretation is only supposed to be invoked where there is some ambiguity or lacuna in the provision in question, something which is certainly not the case with section 53(1)(c).[73]

4–034

---

[66] In particular, the practice whereby brokers who are holding shares on behalf of their clients can and do resell them on the strength of oral instructions would have required some reconsideration in the event that the House of Lords had reached the opposite conclusion.

[67] [1967] 2 A.C. 291 at 307.

[68] *ibid.* at 329–330.

[69] See *post*, para 5–026.

[70] See Jones 24 C.L.J. (1968) 19.

[71] [1967] 2 A.C. 291 at 311.

[72] *ibid.* at 317–318.

[73] Nor is this argument wholly consistent with the decision in *Grey v. I.R.C.* Lord Upjohn admittedly took great pains to confine his argument to the situation where the settlor intended to deal with the legal title and so the *rationes decidendi* of the two decisions are wholly distinct; however, that does not alter the fact that the settlor in *Grey v. I.R.C.* was also absolutely beneficially entitled to the subject matter of the trust and s.53(1)(c) was nevertheless held to apply.

4–035   Thus far, it appeared that the decision of the House of Lords on the formalities argument was best regarded as having been taken on policy grounds. Much more recently, it has instead been suggested that the decision can be justified by recourse to the doctrine of overreaching, in other words that the transfer of the shares by the bank to the Royal College of Surgeons for value (the option contract to retransfer them) overreached Vandervell's beneficial interest into the benefit of that option contract[74]; if this analysis is correct, neither Vandervell's instructions to the bank nor the subsequent overreaching of his interest when the bank complied with those instructions fell within section 53(1)(c).[75] However, whatever the grounds for the decision, it has to be admitted that the conclusion reached does at least have the merit of being clear: where a settlor directs his trustees to transfer the trust property to a third party with the intention that that third party should take both the legal and the beneficial interest in the property, the settlor does not have to comply with section 53(1)(c).

(3)   Where the settlor directs his trustees to declare new trusts in favour of a third party

4–036   This situation occurred in *Re Vandervell's Trusts (No.2)*.[76] These proceedings were a direct consequence of the decision in *Vandervell v. I.R.C.* that the option was held on resulting trust for Vandervell between 1958 and 1961. It will be recalled that during this period the trusts on which the option to repurchase was held had not been specified and the option itself had not been exercised. At the end of that period, in October 1961, the trust company exercised the option and paid the £5,000 payable thereunder to the Royal College of Surgeons from the funds of the children's settlement. The trust company, therefore, became the legal owners of the shares themselves, no longer merely of the option to re-purchase them. All subsequent dividends were paid to the trust company and held on the trusts of the children's settlement. But even at this stage Vandervell made no express declaration of the trusts on which the shares or the dividends should be held. It was not until March 1964 (when judgment was given at first instance in *Vandervell v. I.R.C.*[77]) that it occurred to anyone that he might have retained an interest under a resulting trust.[78] Subsequently, in January 1965,[79] he did execute a deed transferring to the trust company such interest as he might have in the shares or dividends and expressly declaring that the trust company was to hold them on the trusts of the children's settlement. The Revenue accepted

---

[74] Nolan [2002] C.L.J. 169.

[75] Vandervell could also validly have revoked those instructions prior to the bank acting on them; however, a transfer by the bank without notice of any revocation would not have been a breach of trust and so would have been effective to overreach Vandervell's interest; *Leslie v. Baillie* (1843) 2 Y. & C.C.C. 91.

[76] [1974] Ch. 269.

[77] [1966] Ch. 261.

[78] Plowman J. so held (the decision of the Special Commissioners which was under appeal to him had found Vandervell liable on a different ground).

[79] The first day of the hearing of the appeal to the Court of Appeal from the decision of Plowman J. (see [1966] Ch. 261).

that this deed was effective to divest Vandervell of any interest in the shares or dividends.[80]

Re *Vandervell's Trusts (No.2)* concerned the period between October 1961 **4–037** and January 1965. The Revenue, on the basis that Vandervell had not divested himself of his interest in the shares or the option until January 1965, assessed his estate to surtax in respect of the dividends received by the trust company during this period.[81] In order to be able to pay this tax, his executors therefore had to claim from the trust company all the dividends from the shares which had been paid to that company during this period (the children were not beneficiaries of Vandervell's will because he had thought that he had made sufficient provision for them under their settlement). The Revenue sought and failed to be joined to these proceedings (their unsuccessful attempt was also taken to the House of Lords[82]) but, pending their conclusion, the executors' appeal against the surtax assessment was stood over.

It has already been seen that the £5,000 payable under the option was **4–038** provided out of the children's settlement and that thereafter all the dividends received by the trust company were transferred to the children's settlement and treated as part of its funds. Furthermore, during this period the solicitors for the trust company had written a letter to the Revenue stating that the shares which the company had purchased would be held on the trusts of the children's settlement. The Revenue admitted that these dealings, all of which had been done with Vandervell's approval, showed that he and the trust company intended that the shares should be held on trust for the children's settlement; however, they argued that this intention was in fact unavailing and that the shares and dividends had in fact been held on trust for Vandervell until January 1965 for the following reasons: first, until October 1961, Vandervell had had an equitable interest under a resulting trust—this was indisputable since the House of Lords had so held in *Vandervell v. I.R.C.*[83]; secondly, he himself had never disposed of that interest until January 1965; and, thirdly and in any event, any disposition prior to January 1965 would necessarily have been an oral disposition of an equitable interest which, by virtue of section 53(1)(c), had to be in writing.

This argument succeeded before Megarry J. but the Court of Appeal **4–039** rejected it as fallacious. The court held, *inter alia*,[84] that the dealings with the dividends during this period not only showed an intention to create but actually amounted to the declaration of a trust of the shares in favour of the children's settlement which, because its subject matter was pure personalty,

---

[80] Vandervell subsequently died early in 1967, aware of the result of *Vandervell v. I.R.C.* (the House of Lords handed down its decision on November 24, 1966) but not of the subsequent proceedings which were to drag on for more than seven years after his death until the Court of Appeal gave judgment in *Re Vandervell's Trusts (No.2)* on July 3, 1974.

[81] Amounting to the frivolity of £628,229, well over £9,000,000 when converted to 2008 values using the Retail Prices Index.

[82] *Re Vandervell's Trusts* [1971] A.C. 912. This meant that, paradoxically, the executors had to fight the Revenue's battle on its behalf because they would be liable for the surtax if the Revenue ultimately succeeded.

[83] [1967] 2 A.C. 291. See *ante*, para 4–031.

[84] Other aspects of their decision are discussed *post*, paras 5–012, 5–018, 5–066.

could be created without writing.[85] Section 53(1)(c) was, therefore, irrelevant. Leave to appeal to the House of Lords against this decision was granted but in the end no appeal was in fact made. This was presumably a cause of great relief to the Vandervell trustees but was perhaps unfortunate for the development of the law since the decision of the Court of Appeal has given rise to the following difficulties.

4–040   Some of these difficulties concern other requirements for the creation of a valid express private trust each of which is considered elsewhere. It is questionable whether a valid trust of the shares could have been completely constituted.[86] Further, even if such a trust could have been constituted, it is not easy to find the certainty of intention which was a necessary prerequisite of its creation.[87] While there is no doubt that both Vandervell and the trust company intended that the shares should be held on trust for the children's settlement, it is difficult to infer that Vandervell could have intended to dispose or did dispose of his equitable interest under the resulting trust of the option in 1961 when he was totally unaware that he had such an interest until the first instance decision in *Vandervell v. I.R.C.* was handed down in March 1964.

4–041   However, it is the remaining difficulty which is relevant for present purposes. Even if a trust could have been completely constituted and the necessary intention can be inferred to have existed any time prior to January 1965,[88] why did the decision in *Grey v. I.R.C.*,[89] where the settlor had similarly been trying to dispose of an interest under a resulting trust, not oblige Vandervell to dispose of his equitable interest in writing in accordance with section 53(1)(c)?[90] The Court of Appeal actually held that Vandervell's interest under the resulting trust had been extinguished when the gap in the beneficial ownership which had given rise to it was filled by the creation or declaration of a valid trust. In other words, the gap in the beneficial ownership had only existed until the option was exercised; as soon as this had occurred, a valid trust of the shares was created in favour of the children's settlement.

4–042   This proposition can be interpreted in two ways. It is possible to confine its effect to the situation where an option is held on trust; in this case *Re Vandervell's Trusts (No.2)* merely decides that, where an option is held on resulting trust, a direction by the beneficiary to the trustees to declare new trusts of the property which they receive as a result of exercising the option does not require writing under section 53(1)(c).[91] However, the formulations of principle in the judgments are not actually restricted to options and so at least suggest that, where any property of any type is held on resulting trust,

---

[85] Law of Property Act 1925, s.53(1)(b) applies only to trusts of land. See *ante*, para 4–008.

[86] See *post*, paras 5–012, 5–018.

[87] See *ante*, para 3–002.

[88] When Vandervell executed the deed which the Revenue accepted was effective to deprive him of any beneficial interest.

[89] [1960] A.C. 1. See *ante*, para 4–027.

[90] See the summary of the argument by Stephenson L.J. in *Re Vandervell's Trusts (No.2)* [1974] Ch. 269 at 322–323. This particular point had not been argued before Megarry J. at first instance.

[91] Where the subject matter is land, s.53(1)(b) (or, in the event of an overlap, s.53(1)(a)) would apply to such a declaration of trust.

a direction by the beneficiary to the trustees to declare new trusts of that property does not require writing under section 53(1)(c); if this is indeed the case, then it is not easy to see any satisfactory distinction[92] between *Re Vandervell's Trusts (No.2)* and *Grey v. I.R.C.*, where a similar direction by the beneficiary of a resulting trust to the trustees to hold the property on new trusts was held to require writing.

(D   The Creation of a Trust as a result of a Specifically Enforceable Contract of Sale

This possibility depends on section 53(2) which provides that section 53 as a whole does not apply to the creation or operation of resulting, implied or constructive trusts.[93] It was contended in *Oughtred v. I.R.C.*[94] that this provision enables equitable interests to be disposed of without any need for writing where the disposition in question is by way of constructive sub-trust arising as the result of the formation of a specifically enforceable contract of sale. In this case, shares in a private company had been settled on trust for a mother for life and subject to that for her son. In order to enable each of them to own shares in the company absolutely, they agreed to exchange other shares in the same company to which the mother was already absolutely entitled for the son's equitable remainder, thus enlarging her life interest into absolute ownership. A contract for the sale of shares in a private company, unlike the majority of contracts for the sale of pure personalty, is specifically enforceable; this is because damages would not be an adequate remedy for the loss of the shares. The effect of any specifically enforceable contract is that the vendor holds its subject matter on a constructive trust for the purchaser, who therefore acquires an immediate equitable interest therein.[95] So the contract between mother and son automatically gave rise to a constructive trust (strictly speaking, because its subject matter was a subsisting equitable interest, a constructive sub-trust) under which the son held his equitable remainder on trust for his mother.

4–043

It was argued that, as a result of the creation of this passive sub-trust, the son had "disappeared from the picture" and dropped out,[96] causing his equitable remainder to pass to his mother; since, by virtue of section 53(2), no writing was necessary for the creation of this constructive sub-trust, the mother had, therefore, acquired an absolute beneficial interest in the shares without the use of any instrument on which stamp duty could be levied. The trustees had admittedly subsequently transferred the legal title to the shares to her but it was argued that this had transferred only a bare legal title, in respect of which only a nominal duty of 50p was payable.

4–044

The majority of the House of Lords, however, accepted the Revenue's contention that the latter transfer had to be stamped ad valorem. The reasoning behind this decision was stated by Lord Jenkins, who held that, if the subject matter of a sale is such that the full title to it can only be

4–045

---

[92] Unless there is some forensic difference between telling trustees "to hold on new trusts" and telling them "to declare new trusts".

[93] See *ante*, para 4–016.

[94] [1960] A.C. 206.

[95] See *post*, para 10–333.

[96] This was stated in *Grainge v. Wilberforce* (1889) 5 T.L.R. 436 at 437 and held by the Court of Appeal in *Re Lashmar* [1891] 1 Ch. 258. See *ante*, para 4–018.

transferred by an instrument, then any instrument executed by way of transfer ranks for the purposes of stamp duty as a conveyance upon sale. He stated that, in the case of a contract for the sale of land, "a constructive trust in favour of the purchaser arises on the conclusion of the contract for sale, but (so far as I know) it has never been held on this account that a conveyance subsequently executed in performance of the contract is not stampable ad valorem on a transfer on sale".[97]

4–046   The attempt to save stamp duty therefore failed without any need for the majority of the House of Lords to consider the scope of section 53(2). However Lord Radcliffe, who dissented, had to do so; he accepted the contention that the mother had acquired the equitable remainder without any writing having been used.[98] On the other hand, Lord Cohen (also dissenting) and Lord Denning (the only one of the majority to mention the point) both stated by way of dicta[99] that, although the constructive sub-trust had come into existence without any need for writing, the interest arising thereunder could not be transferred without complying with section 53(1)(c). This view, which at first sight appears consistent with *Grey v. I.R.C.*, in fact overlooks the point that authority,[100] admittedly not binding on the House of Lords, establishes that the son "disappeared from the picture", something which must have caused his interest to pass to his mother automatically by operation of law. Consequently, the view of Lord Radcliffe has always seemed preferable and has now been adopted definitively.

4–047   The first decision in which this view was subsequently adopted was in *Re Holt's Settlement*,[101] where Megarry J. held that, when beneficiaries of a trust agree for valuable consideration to a variation of the beneficial interests, their existing interests (which are necessarily equitable) are varied without any need for any writing. Further support was provided by the remarks of two members of the Court of Appeal in *D.H.N. Food Distributors v. Tower Hamlets L.B.C.*[102] and of Lord Wilberforce in *Chinn v. Collins*.[103] Lord Radcliffe's view was, however, definitively accepted by the Court of Appeal in *Neville v. Wilson*.[104] All the shares in a private company were owned beneficially by a second private company but in order to qualify the two directors for office each held the legal title to 60 shares as the second company's

---

[97] [1960] A.C. 206 at 240.

[98] *ibid.* at 228.

[99] *ibid.* at 230; at 233.

[100] *Grainge v. Wilberforce* (1889) 5 T.L.R. 436 at 437; *Re Lashmar* [1891] 1 Ch. 258. See *ante*, para 4–018.

[101] [1976] 1 Ch. 100 at 116.

[102] [1976] 1 W.L.R. 852. Goff L.J. at 865 and Shaw L.J. at 867 accepted that, where the transaction in question is not a gift, an equitable interest in land could pass without writing.

[103] [1981] A.C. 533 at 548, where he stated that, as soon as there was an agreement for the sale of the equitable interest in shares in a public company held by nominees followed by payment of the price, "the equitable title passed at once to the purchaser". This contract was not even specifically enforceable so that this enunciation of principle is even wider than that of Lord Radcliffe. However, Hanbury & Martin: *Modern Equity*, 17th edn (London, Sweet & Maxwell, 2005) p.91 notes the fact that this principle led to the imposition of liability for capital gains tax.

[104] [1997] Ch. 144. A contrary view had earlier been expressed by Chadwick J. by way of dictum in *United Bank of Kuwait v. Sahib* [1997] Ch. 107 but the question was not raised on the subsequent appeal which was heard by a differently constituted Court of Appeal after argument but before judgment in *Neville v. Wilson*.

nominee. These shares were, as the result of an oral agreement, included in the subject matter of an agreement made by all the shareholders of the second company to distribute all the shares in the first company to them in proportion to their shareholdings; consequently, the two directors had entered into a specifically enforceable contract to assign the subsisting equitable interests in the shares. The Court of Appeal merely had to consider the validity of the contract; no issue arose as to the effect of sub-trusts. Nourse L.J.[105] analysed the speeches in *Oughtred v. I.R.C.* and held that the analysis of Lord Radcliffe was "unquestionably correct". Consequently, because of the existence of the constructive sub-trust and the effect of section 53(2), the oral contract was not rendered ineffective by section 53(1)(c). This approval of Lord Radcliffe's view must therefore also establish that, where an equitable interest becomes subject to a constructive sub-trust as a result of the creation of a specifically enforceable contract of sale, that equitable interest will, by virtue of section 53(2), immediately vest in the purchaser without any need for writing.[106] However, since only specifically enforceable contracts have this effect, this possibility is now limited to contracts for the sale of shares in private companies and of rare chattels[107]; the only other specifically enforceable contracts, contracts for the sale of land, now have to be in writing anyway.[108]

4. Equity will not Allow a Statute to be Used as an Instrument of Fraud

The courts will not allow the statutory provisions which have just been considered (any more than they would allow their predecessors, the relevant provisions of the Statute of Frauds 1677), to be applied in such a way as to achieve a fraudulent purpose. A basic equitable maxim is that equity will not allow a statute to be used as a "cloak" or "engine" for fraud. It of course cannot be doubted that a major, if not the major, objective of all the statutory provisions which have been reviewed is the prevention of fraud and was the primary reason for the enactment of the first of them—the Statute of Frauds. But it is easy to visualise a situation where an automatic application of the statutory provisions would have the unintended effect of allowing fraud by one party to succeed and in such circumstances the court will intervene in order to protect the other party under the umbrella of the equitable maxim set out above.   **4–048**

Thus in *Bannister v. Bannister*,[109] the defendant sold and conveyed two adjoining cottages to the plaintiff on the basis that she could continue to occupy one of them rent free for as long as she wished. When he subsequently sought to evict her on the basis that the conveyance did not mention her right of occupation, she successfully counterclaimed for a declaration   **4–049**

---

[105] At 157, giving the judgment of the court.

[106] However, this will cease to be the case if a different view is ever taken of the effect of a passive sub-trust. See *ante*, para 4–018.

[107] The only type of contracts for the sale of pure personalty which are specifically enforceable; contracts for the sale of property which is readily available on the open market, such as shares in a public company and normal chattels, are not specifically enforceable because damages will always be an adequate remedy for the purchaser.

[108] Under the Law of Property (Miscellaneous Provisions) Act 1989, s.2.

[109] [1948] 2 All E.R. 133 [1948] W.N. 261.

that the plaintiff held the cottage on trust for her for her lifetime. The Court of Appeal classified as fraudulent the conduct of the plaintiff in attempting to rely on the absence of the writing which section 53(1)(b) of the Law of Property Act 1925 requires for the creation of the interest claimed by the defendant and imposed a constructive trust under which he held the property on trust for her for her lifetime. This and the other relevant authorities will be considered more fully in the chapter on constructive trusts.[110]

4–050   The principle that equity will not allow a statute to be used as an instrument of fraud has also been relied on by the courts as the justification for the existence of the doctrine of secret trusts. Such trusts arise when an intending settlor makes a gift of property in his will or leaves an existing will unrevoked or dies intestate on the strength of an undertaking by the person entitled under his will or intestacy to hold whatever property he receives on trust for a third party. In such circumstances, the court will enforce performance of the undertaking at the suit of the third party despite the fact that this involves admitting evidence which does not comply with section 9 of the Wills Act 1837. This has been justified on the basis that otherwise the person who made the undertaking would be being allowed to benefit from his own fraud. However, this work adopts the alternative view, which has been relied on by the courts in the majority of the more recent authorities, that the justification for the admission of such evidence is that secret trusts operate outside the will, so that the provisions of the Wills Act have nothing whatever to do with them. Nevertheless, this is a convenient moment to examine the rules governing secret trusts, which are discussed in detail in the next section.[111]

III. SECRET TRUSTS

4–051   As was mentioned in the previous section, a secret trust arises when an intending settlor makes a gift of property in his will[112] or leaves an existing will unrevoked[113] or dies intestate[114] on the strength of an undertaking by the person entitled under his will or intestacy to hold whatever property he receives on trust for a third party. In such circumstances the court will enforce performance of the undertaking at the suit of the third party. There are two types of secret trusts, fully secret trusts and half secret trusts. A trust is fully secret when both the existence of the trust and its terms are concealed; such a trust therefore arises where the property which is the subject

---

[110] See *post*, para 10–273.

[111] See *post*, para 4–051 *et seq.*

[112] This is what occurs in the overwhelming majority of cases of secret trusts. The earliest cases, *Crook v. Brooking* (1688) 2 Vern. 50 and *Pring v. Pring* (1689) 2 Vern. 99 were cases of this kind, as were *McCormick v. Grogan* (1869) L.R. 4 H.L. 82 and *Blackwell v. Blackwell* [1929] A.C. 318, which are respectively the leading cases on fully secret and half secret trusts.

[113] This occurred in *Tharp v. Tharp* [1916] 1 Ch. 142.

[114] This occurred in *Sellack v. Harris* (1708) 5 Vin.Abr. 512, pl.31. See also *Re Gardner* [1920] 2 Ch. 523, where there was a partial intestacy (a wife made a will which merely left her property to her husband for life; she died possessed only of personalty and he therefore also took the interest in remainder under the intestacy rules; both interests were held to be subject to a fully secret trust communicated and accepted after the date of the will).

matter of the trust is, on the face of the will, left to the recipient absolutely or where the settlor has died intestate. On the other hand, a trust is half secret when the existence of a trust is revealed but its terms are concealed; such a trust therefore arises where the property which is the subject matter of the trust is, on the face of the will, left to the recipient as a trustee. The advantages of a secret trust are that a testator can conceal the true objects of his benevolence from public view—a will is, of course, a public document—and can also, in the case of a fully secret trust, alter those objects at any time before his death simply by communicating with the secret trustee.

Secret trusts depend for their efficacy on the intervention of equity. This intervention is, on the face of things, directly contrary to the important statement of principle contained in section 9 of the Wills Act 1837. This provision, which was summarised at the beginning of the previous section,[115] requires wills to be in writing signed by the testator, or some other person in his presence and by his direction, in the presence of two witnesses both present at the same time, who also sign. It was enacted for an obvious and important reason of policy—to ensure that false claims cannot be generated after the death of a testator when he is in no position to refute them. Such a policy can undoubtedly operate in an extremely harsh way but the courts have, rightly, always been reluctant to admit as evidence in proceedings concerning the administration of an estate any documents which fail to comply with these formal requirements.   **4–052**

It is almost inevitable that the existence of secret trusts will only be able to be proved by evidence which does not comply with these requirements; the whole object of the exercise is to exclude the identity of the beneficiary from the formally attested documents admitted to probate. Inevitably, therefore, the evidence of the communication, acceptance and terms of the secret trust in question will be either oral or contained in a document which has not been properly signed and attested. The existence of secret trusts, therefore, involves a departure both from the letter and the spirit of the Wills Act and consequently, as might be expected, various justifications for their existence have been suggested by the courts. Since several of the rules governing the operation of secret trusts stand or fall depending upon the justification which is adopted, it is necessary to discuss them before considering these rules.   **4–053**

1. *The Theoretical Justification for the Existence of the Doctrine of Secret Trusts*

(A) Fraud

It has often been stated that the justification for the existence of the doctrine of secret trusts is that, if evidence of the terms of the trust were not admitted contrary to the provisions of the Wills Act, the result would be fraud. However, there has been considerable judicial disagreement as to the nature of this fraud. Some judges have found this fraud in the ability of the intended trustee to take the property beneficially if evidence of the terms of   **4–054**

---

[115] See *ante*, para 4–006.

the trust is not admitted. Others have instead found it in the consequential failure to observe the intentions of the testator and the consequential destruction of the beneficial interests arising under the trust.

(1) By the intended trustee

4–055 The view that the potential fraud stems from the ability of the intended trustee to take the property beneficially is normally expressed in this way. If evidence of the terms of the trust were not admitted contrary to the provisions of the Wills Act, the person who received the property under the will or intestacy in question would be able to disregard his undertaking to the intending settlor and take the property beneficially.

4–056   This was the argument adopted by the members of the House of Lords in *McCormick v. Grogan*.[116] The testator made a will leaving all of his property to Grogan. When near to death, he summoned Grogan, told him of the will and said that a letter would be found with it. However, he did not seek to obtain any undertaking from him in respect of the letter, which named various persons to whom the testator wished Grogan to give money and the amount of the intended gift to each, concluding with these words:

"I do not wish you to act strictly to the foregoing instructions, but leave it entirely to your own good judgment to do as you think I would if living and as the parties are deserving, and as it is not my wish that you should say anything about the document there cannot be any fault found with you by any of the parties should you not act in strict accordance with it."

4–057   One of the named persons whom Grogan decided to exclude brought an action claiming that Grogan held the property on secret trust to give effect to the provisions of the letter. This action failed on the grounds that the testator had imposed no legally binding obligation upon Grogan. The members of the House of Lords clearly stated that the doctrine of secret trusts was established so as to prevent any possibility of fraud by the secret trustee. Lord Hatherley L.C. said that the doctrine of secret trusts "involves a wide departure from the policy which induced the legislature to pass the Statute of Frauds,[117] and it is only in clear cases of fraud that this doctrine has been applied—cases in which the Court has been persuaded that there has been a fraudulent inducement held out on the part of the apparent beneficiary in order to lead the testator to confide to him the duty which he undertook to perform".[118] This line of reasoning is a possible justification for the existence of the doctrine when, as in *McCormick v. Grogan*, the trust in question is fully secret. In such a case, unless evidence of the trust is admitted contrary to the provisions of the Wills Act, the intended trustee will be able to take the property beneficially and so will clearly profit from his own misconduct.

---

[116] (1869) L.R. 4 H.L. 82. A similar view had been expressed over a century earlier in *Drakeford v. Wilks* [1747] 3 Atk. 539 and was subsequently repeated by Lord Davey in *Re French* [1902] 1 I.R. 172, 230 (an appeal to the House of Lords from the Court of Appeal of Ireland).

[117] Prior to the enactment of the Wills Act 1837, the formal requirements for wills were contained in the Statute of Frauds 1677.

[118] (1869) L.R. 4 H.L. 82 at 89.

However, this line of reasoning cannot normally justify the existence of **4–058**
half secret trusts. In such a trust, the intended trustee takes the property as
a trustee on the face of the will. Therefore, if the court declined to admit
evidence of the terms of the half-secret trust, he would not take the subject
matter beneficially but would clearly hold the property in question on trust
for whoever was entitled to the testator's residuary estate[119] or for his
statutory next-of-kin.[120] On the face of things, therefore, there is no way in
which such an intended trustee could profit by failing to carry out his
promise to the testator, unless of course he were himself the residuary
beneficiary or intestate successor of the testator. It is not entirely clear
whether he would in such circumstances be entitled to take the property as
residuary beneficiary or intestate successor if the half secret trust failed but
it is suggested that in principle he should be able to do so on the grounds
that in such a situation he would be claiming the property not as a trustee
but in a different capacity of which the testator must necessarily have been
aware. On this assumption, an intended trustee holding property under a
half secret trust would be enabled to profit by failing to carry out his
undertaking to the testator and so the admission of evidence contrary to the
terms of the Wills Act could be justified by the fraud argument. But this
argument will obviously not apply to the vast majority of half secret trusts
simply because the intended trustee will not normally be the appropriate
residuary beneficiary or intestate successor. Consequently in such circumstances there would be no possibility whatsoever of the intended trustee
taking the subject matter beneficially if evidence of the trust were not
admitted contrary to the provisions of the Wills Act. Thus, in normal circumstances, the argument based on the fraud of the secret trustee cannot justify
the existence of half secret trusts.

(2) On the testator and the beneficiaries
The alternative view is that the fraud in question is committed on the   **4–059**
testator and the beneficiaries by reason respectively of the failure to observe
the intentions of the former and of the destruction of the beneficial interests
of the latter. This view is normally expressed in this way. If evidence of the
terms of the trust were not admitted contrary to the provisions of the Wills
Act, the testator would be defrauded in that, on the faith of the promise
made by the secret trustee, he had either made or left unrevoked a disposition of his property. In the same sort of way, the beneficiaries of the secret
trust would be defrauded in that they would be deprived of their beneficial
interests.

This argument (which of course applies just as much to fully secret trusts   **4–060**
as to half secret trusts) emerged as early as 1748 in *Reech v. Kennegal*,[121]
where Lord Hardwicke L.C. admitted evidence contrary to the Statute of
Frauds "in respect of the promise and of the fraud upon the testator in not
performing it". This view was expressed even more clearly in the Irish case

---

[119] Whatever is left after payment of the testator's debts and after any specific gifts made in
the will.
[120] *Re Pugh's Will Trusts* [1967] 1 W.L.R. 1262.
[121] (1748) 1 Ves. 123. See also the review of the early authorities by Hargrave, *Juridical
Arguments and Collections* (1801) Vol. II, p.912.

of *Riordan v. Banon*[122] in a passage which was subsequently cited with approval by Hall V.-C. in *Re Fleetwood*[123]: "The testator, at least when his purpose is communicated to and accepted by the proposed legatee, makes the disposition to him on the faith of his carrying out his promise and it would be a fraud in him to refuse to perform that promise."

4–061   While the authorities so far discussed all emphasised the fraud on the testator, Lord Buckmaster emphasised rather the fraud on the beneficiaries in the leading case of *Blackwell v. Blackwell*.[124] Blackwell left in his will £12,000 to five persons "upon trust . . . to apply for the purposes indicated by me to them". In fact the money was to be used to maintain his mistress and illegitimate son. His deceived wife and child brought an action against the five legatees claiming that no valid trust for these purposes existed. Their counsel raised the argument that fraud could not justify the admission of evidence of the terms of a half secret trust contrary to the provisions of the Wills Act because there was no possibility of a half secret trustee taking the property beneficially. Counsel for the legatees relied not on principle but on the previous practice of the courts manifested in cases such as *Re Fleetwood*. The House of Lords upheld the existence of the doctrine of half secret trusts. Lord Buckmaster (with whose speech Lord Hailsham L.C. concurred) said that "a testator having been induced to make a gift on trust in his will in reliance on the clear promise by the trustee that such trust will be executed in favour of certain named persons, the trustee is not at liberty to suppress the evidence of the trust and thus destroy the whole object of its creation, in fraud of the beneficiaries".[125] A similar view was expressed by Lord Warrington of Clyffe.[126]

4–062   The emphasis placed in the authorities just discussed on the failure to observe the intentions of the testator and the destruction of the beneficial interests is deceptively simple and is, superficially, quite attractive. In fact, however, such arguments are completely circular. To refer to the terms of the secret trust as the "wishes of the testator" and to describe those entitled under the secret trust as "beneficiaries" begs the question; only if evidence of the terms of the trust is admitted contrary to the provisions of the Wills Act is it appropriate to describe the terms of the secret trust as the wishes of the testator and to refer to those entitled thereunder as its beneficiaries. It is not possible to use as a justification for admitting evidence contrary to the provisions of the Wills Act facts which can only be proven if such evidence is admitted. Consequently it is impossible to regard this argument as a valid justification for the existence of the doctrine of either fully secret trusts or half secret trusts.

(B)   That Secret Trusts Operate Outside the Will

4–063   Given that fraud can justify only the existence of fully secret trusts, if half secret trusts are to be accepted as valid some other possible justification

---

[122] (1876) 10 Ir.Eq. 469 (Court of Chancery of Ireland).
[123] (1880) 15 Ch.D. 594 at 606–607.
[124] [1929] A.C. 318.
[125] *ibid.* at 328–329.
[126] *ibid.* at 342.

must be sought. One does indeed exist in the totally different approach adopted by Viscount Sumner, another member, and therefore a minority,[127] of the House of Lords in *Blackwell v. Blackwell*. He stated that the provisions of the Wills Act have nothing whatsoever to do with the doctrine of secret trusts and that it is inappropriate to state that evidence of their existence is adduced contrary to the provisions of the Wills Act. He said that it is "communication of the purpose to the legatee, coupled with acquiescence or promise on his part, that removes the matter from the provisions of the Wills Act and brings it within the law of trusts, as applied in this instance to trustees, who happen also to be legatees".[128] In other words, secret trusts operate wholly outside the will or intestacy in question and so are governed not by the rules of probate but by the rules of the law of trusts, which in no way prevent the introduction of oral evidence (other, possibly, than in the case of trusts of land). This argument will obviously also apply both to fully secret trusts and to half secret trusts.

The notion that secret trusts so operate wholly outside the will or intes-   **4–064** tacy had in fact been referred to many years earlier by Lord Westbury in *Cullen v. Attorney-General for Ireland*.[129] This notion suggests that the enforcement of secret trusts is dependant upon fraud only to the extent that the basic duty of trustees to carry out their obligations as such is dependant on general equitable principles. A similar conclusion may perhaps be drawn from one of the more recent cases on secret trusts, *Re Snowden*,[130] where Megarry V.-C. held that the standard of proof necessary to establish the existence of a secret trust is the ordinary civil standard of proof required to establish an ordinary trust, not the higher standard necessary for rectification claims, on the grounds that "the whole basis of secret trusts . . . is that they operate outside the will, changing nothing that is written in it, and allowing it to operate according to its tenor, but then fastening a trust on to the property in the hands of the recipient".[131] Thus, according to these authorities, the justification for the existence of secret trusts, whether fully secret or half secret, is that such trusts operate wholly outside the will or intestacy in question. This proposition requires close examination.

(1) The problem
Clearly, a secret trust cannot operate completely independently of the will in   **4–065** question simply because the will alone can vest the subject matter of the trust in the secret trustee. To take an extreme example, if the will itself is invalid, the secret trust will fail with it for lack of subject matter. Therefore, the rules of probate clearly have some role to play. The crucial question is at

---

[127] Lord Hailsham L.C., Lord Buckmaster and Lord Warrington of Clyffe had expressed the view set out above. The remaining member of the House of Lords, Lord Carson, simply agreed (at 343) with "all the views expressed" in the three speeches delivered without expressing any preference as between the different opinions expressed in them.

[128] [1929] A.C. 318 at 339.

[129] (1866) L.R. 1 H.L. 190 at 198 (on appeal from the Court of Appeal in Chancery of Ireland).

[130] [1979] Ch. 528.

[131] *ibid.* at 535.

what point the rules of probate cease to operate and are superseded by the rules of the law of trusts.

(2) The crucial situations

4–066   This question can only be answered by an examination of the situations where the rules of probate and the rules of the law of trusts are in conflict. There are three such situations: when the secret trustee or secret beneficiary has attested the will, when the secret trustee or secret beneficiary has predeceased the testator or intestate, and where the secret trustee disclaims the gift in his favour. An examination of these situations suggests that the only possible answer is that the rules of probate govern the vesting of the subject matter of the secret trust in the secret trustee, while the rules of the law of trusts govern any matter concerning the operation of the secret trust.

4–067   **(a) Attestation** Section 15 of the Wills Act 1837 provides that a legacy to an attesting witness is ineffective, whereas, as a matter of the law of trusts, there is no reason why the trust deed should not be signed by the trustees or beneficiaries. What happens if the secret trustee or the secret beneficiary attests the will?

4–068   In *Re Young*[132] one of the beneficiaries under a half secret trust attested the will. Danckwerts J. held that, since the trust arose outside the will, section 15 of the Wills Act 1837 was quite irrelevant and so the beneficiary could take his interest. This conclusion is consistent with the possible principle suggested above and presumably would also apply in the case of a fully secret trust (there is no authority on this point).

4–069   No case has yet been reported in which a secret trustee has attested the will. However, if the possible principle suggested above is correct, this matter should be governed by the rules of probate since it concerns the vesting of the legacy. A legatee who takes beneficially on the face of the will is clearly caught by section 15. Therefore, if a fully secret trustee attested the will, the legacy to him would be ineffective and so the secret trust would fail for lack of subject matter (unless, presumably, the property nevertheless vested in the secret trustee under the intestacy rules, in which case he would undoubtedly be bound to perform the trust). On the other hand, a legatee who takes as a trustee on the face of the will is not caught by section 15.[133] Therefore, if a half secret trustee attested the will, the legacy to him would be effective and so the half secret trust would not fail by reason of his attestation. This discrepancy between fully secret and half secret trusts is, admittedly, a little odd; however, there are in fact many examples of discrepancies of this kind.

4–070   **(b) Predecease** Section 25 of the Wills Act 1837 provides that, subject to certain exceptions which are not here material, a gift in a will lapses if the

---

[132] [1951] Ch. 344.
[133] *Cresswell v. Cresswell* (1868) L.R. 6 Eq. 69.

recipient predeceases the testator. Similarly, no one who predeceases an intestate can possibly take any of his property under the intestacy rules. What therefore happens if the secret trustee or secret beneficiary predeceases the testator or intestate?

If the secret trustee predeceases the testator or intestate, the result once **4–071** again seems to differ depending on whether the trust in question is fully secret or half secret. In *Re Maddock*[134] Cozens-Hardy L.J. stated, by way of dictum, that if a fully secret trustee predeceases the testator, the legacy will lapse and the secret trust will fail for lack of subject matter. This conclusion is another example of probate principles being applied to the vesting of the legacy. On the other hand, it has always been clear that a gift to a person who takes as a trustee on the face of a will will not lapse by reason of his predecease.[135] Thus, if a half secret trustee predeceases the testator, this principle will presumably apply and the secret trust will, therefore, not fail.

Much more controversy surrounds the situation where the secret benefici- **4–072** ary predeceases the testator or intestate. This occurred in *Re Gardner (No.2)*.[136] Romer J. held that a beneficiary under a secret trust acquires an interest in the trust property as soon as the trust is communicated to and accepted by the secret trustee. Thus, the beneficiary had acquired an interest before his death and that interest naturally passed to his personal representatives for the benefit of those entitled under his will or intestacy.

This decision has been rightly criticised on the grounds that a beneficiary **4–073** under a trust acquires no interest in the trust property until the trust has been completely constituted in accordance with the rules discussed in the next chapter.[137] Since this could not possibly have occurred until the trust property vested in the secret trustee at the death of the testatrix, the beneficiary could not have acquired an interest prior to his death. Indeed, in *Kasperbauer v. Griffith*[138] the Court of Appeal specifically stated, admittedly in a quite different context,[139] that a secret trust takes effect on the death of the testator. It is therefore generally accepted that this case was wrongly decided.[140]

It is of course quite impossible to justify the reasoning which led **4–074** Romer J. to his conclusion. If, however, it is accepted that the trust became completely constituted at the death of the testator, what has to be considered is the effect of completely constituting a trust in favour of a person who is already dead—that is, after all, what actually happened in *Re Gardner (No.2)*. If, as the authorities so far discussed suggest, the rules of probate govern the vesting of the legacy in the secret trustee while the rules of the law of trusts

---

[134] [1902] 2 Ch. 220.
[135] *Re Smirthwaite's Trusts* (1871) L.R. 11 Eq. 251.
[136] [1923] 2 Ch. 230.
[137] See *post*, Chapter 5.
[138] (1997) [2000] W.T.L.R. 333 at 343.
[139] In respect of the right of both the testator and the intended trustee to change his mind before the former's death.
[140] See, for example, the views of Hayton in Hayton & Marshall, *Commentary and Cases on the Law of Trusts and Equitable Remedies*, 12th edn (London, Sweet & Maxwell, 2005), para 2–139.

govern any matter concerning the operation of the secret trust, this issue falls to be determined by application of the rules of the law of trusts.

Is, therefore, there any rule of the law of trusts which provides that it is not possible to constitute a trust in favour of a dead person? The authorities on the effect of constituting a trust in favour of someone whom the settlor knows to be dead are indecisive.[141] However, that is not the situation under discussion; that question is what is the effect of constituting a trust in favour of someone whom the settlor thinks is alive but is in fact dead. This question is totally devoid of authority. If such a trust were valid, it would necessarily have to take effect in favour of those entitled under the dead beneficiary's will or intestacy; if this is the case, for this reason rather than the reasoning adopted by Romer J., *Re Gardner (No.2)* was correctly decided. However, the overwhelming view of the commentators is that such a trust would be wholly void[142]; if this is the case, then *Re Gardner (No.2)* was indeed wrongly decided. Whatever view is taken (and in the light of the weight of academic opinion, the second view seems almost inevitable), that view should clearly apply whether the trust in question is, as in *Re Gardner (No.2)*, fully secret or is half secret.

4–075   **(c) Disclaimer** Where a person who is nominated as a trustee declines to act, the court will appoint another to act in his stead.[143] Thus it seems that, if a half secret trustee declines to act, the court will appoint a replacement trustee and the secret trust will, therefore, not fail.

4–076   However, a disclaimer of a testamentary gift by a person who takes beneficially on the face of the will causes the legacy to fail[144]; on this basis a disclaimer by a fully secret trustee will necessarily have this effect. This will not be a problem if the purpose of the disclaimer is to enable the secret trustee to take not under the disclaimed testamentary gift but rather as residuary beneficiary or intestate successor. Such clearly unconscionable conduct will inevitably lead to the imposition of a constructive trust on the basis of the principle enunciated in *Bannister v. Bannister*,[145] which was discussed earlier on. Consequently the secret trustee will hold the property which passes to him under the residuary gift or intestacy on constructive trust to perform the secret trust.

However, where the disclaiming fully secret trustee takes no other benefit under the will or intestacy of the testator, such a disclaimer will produce a conflict between the rule of probate that a disclaimer of a legacy by a person who takes beneficially on the face of the will causes the legacy to fail and the

---

[141] Prior to the enactment of the Property Legislation of 1925, there was some authority that it was not possible to constitute a trust in favour of a dead person (*Re Tilt* (1896) 74 L.T. 163, applying *Re Corbishley's Trusts* (1880) 14 Ch.D. 846). However, it is questionable whether these authorities are still good law. Since 1925, a grantee is presumed to take the greatest interest that his grantor was able to give him (Law of Property Act 1925, s.60(1)) and so arguably will take an interest not only for himself but also for those entitled under his will or intestacy.

[142] See *ante*, n.140.

[143] The power of the court so to appoint trustees stems both from statute (Trustee Act 1925, s.41(1)) and from its inherent jurisdiction (see *Dodkin v. Brunt* (1868) L.R. 6 Eq. 580).

[144] *Townson v. Tickell* (1819) 3 B. & Ald. 31.

[145] [1948] W.N. 261. See *ante*, para 4–049.

rule of the law of trusts that equity will not permit a trust to fail for want of a trustee. This conflict has been the subject of opposing dicta: in *Re Maddock*,[146] Cozens-Hardy L.J. suggested that a fully secret trust would fail in such a situation, while in *Blackwell v. Blackwell*[147] Lord Buckmaster said that the court would intervene to prevent such a result. There is something to be said for each view: in favour of the view of Cozens-Hardy L.J. is the proposition that probate principles should govern the vesting of the legacy on the other hand, in favour of the view of Lord Buckmaster is the fact that a court would undoubtedly be extremely reluctant to permit a trustee who had agreed to act as such to destroy a completely constituted trust by disclaiming his office. It remains to be seen which view is finally adopted.

(3) Conclusion

The discussion of these three difficult areas shows that it is perfectly possible   **4–077**
to decide which rule to apply in situations where there is a conflict between the rules of probate and the rules of the law of trusts. It is therefore suggested that this view, as laid down by Viscount Sumner in *Blackwell v. Blackwell*,[148] is both correct and workable. Indeed, nearly all the authorities decided since *Blackwell v. Blackwell* which have just been discussed[149] support the view that secret trusts operate wholly outside the will or intestacy in question. As has already been seen, this view alone is a satisfactory justification for the existence both of fully secret and of half secret trusts. It is therefore suggested that the theoretical justification for the existence of the doctrine of secret trusts is that such trusts operate wholly outside the will or intestacy in question. The enforceability of such trusts in equity is, therefore, no more dependant upon fraud than is any other type of trust. For these and other reasons, it will later be suggested that secret trusts are in fact express trusts.

2. *The Prerequisites of Secret Trusts*

In *Kasperbauer v. Griffith*,[150] the Court of Appeal held that a secret trust will   **4–078**
come into existence if the following three requirements are satisfied: an intention by the testator to create a trust, satisfying the traditional requirement of three certainties which have already been considered,[151] namely certain language in imperative form, certain subject matter and certain objects or beneficiaries; secondly, the communication of the trust to the intended trustee; and, thirdly, acceptance of the trust by the intended trustee, an acceptance which can take the form of silent acquiescence. Secret trusts must also satisfy the other requirements for the creation of a valid

---

[146] [1902] 2 Ch. 220.
[147] [1929] A.C. 318.
[148] [1929] A.C. 318
[149] The only decision clearly contrary to this conclusion is *Re Gardner (No.2)*, the reasoning of which is on any view clearly incorrect.
[150] (1997) [2000] W.T.L.R. 333 at 343.
[151] See *ante*, Chapter 3.

private trust, in that there must be a beneficiary capable of enforcing the trust and that that trust must be completely constituted. The extent to which the formal requirements discussed earlier in this chapter apply to secret trusts is more debateable.

(A)   The Three Certainties

(1)   Certainty of Intention

4–079   This was which was in issue in *Kasperbauer v. Griffith*.[152] The testator said at a family meeting attended by his wife and his children by a former marriage that he intended to leave his house and his lump sum pension benefit to his wife on the basis that the lump sum would pay off or reduce the mortgage; the house was to be sold within a year of his death and the proceeds divided between the children; his remaining property was to go to his children. A secret trust was alleged to have arisen as a result of the testator saying, in response to a suggestion from the son that this should be written down, that his wife "knew what she had to do". The wife said nothing whatever during the meeting. The testator subsequently changed his mind and made a will in a slightly different form as a result of which the wife received both the house and the lump sum without having to discharge the mortgage out of it and the children received effectively nothing. The judge held that it was not the intention of the testator to impose any binding obligation on his wife and so there was no secret trust. The Court of Appeal upheld his decision, holding that the testator's words were equivocal and were at least consistent with the belief and intention that only a moral obligation was being imposed on the wife. They added that his subsequent change of mind was also consistent with this conclusion.

4–080   The question of whether there was certainty of intention to create a trust is quite distinct from the question of whether a fully secret or a half secret trust has been created. Where a secret trust has arisen as the result of an intestacy, the trust in question is necessarily fully secret.[153] Where a secret trust has arisen as the result of a will, whether the trust in question is fully secret or half secret is determined entirely on the basis of the contents of the will.

4–081   Where the property in questions vests beneficially in the intended trustee under the provisions of the will in question so that the legatee takes the property as beneficial owner on the face of the will, the trust in question will be a fully secret trust. This requirement is satisfied despite the presence of phrases such as "in the hope that he will use the property for certain purposes which I have communicated to him" or "imposing no trust upon him". Provided that such expressions are, as is highly likely, held to be

---

[152] (1997) [2000] W.T.L.R. 333.

[153] *Sellack v. Harris* (1708) 5 Vin. Abr. 512, pl.31; *Re Gardner* [1920] 2 Ch. 523, where the intestacy in question was partial (a wife had made a will which merely left her property to her husband for life; she died possessed only of personalty and he therefore also took the interest in remainder under the intestacy rules; both interests were held to be subject to a fully secret trust).

insufficiently certain to create a trust on the face of the will, any secret trust which is found to exist will, despite their presence, be fully secret.[154]

Where, on the other hand, the property in question vests non-beneficially 4–082 in the intended trustee under the provisions of the will in question so that the legatee takes the property as a trustee on the face of the will, the trust in question will be a half secret trust.[155] For this requirement to be satisfied, the testator must use an expression which imposes an obligation to hold the property upon trust.

(2) Certainty of subject matter

The basic rule governing certainty of objects, that the property subject to the 4–083 trust must either be clearly defined or be capable of ascertainment,[156] unquestionably applies to secret trusts. In one case[157] a testator, whose earlier wills had divided his assets between all three of his adult children, by

---

[154] An interesting point which has yet to arise in a reported case is whether expressions of this type, although insufficiently certain to create a trust, may nevertheless have an effect upon the rules governing communication of the terms of the trust to the secret trustee. Communication of a fully secret trust may normally be made either before or after the execution of the will provided that it takes place during the lifetime of the testator and may normally be either written or oral. If the will contains some expression such as "in the hope that he will use the property for certain purposes which I have communicated to him in writing", do those words, although imposing no trust upon the face of the will, nevertheless invalidate any communication which is subsequent to the execution of the will and/or any communication which, whether before or after the communication of the will, is oral? (This would undoubtedly be the case if the trust in question were half secret—see *Re Keen* [1937] Ch. 236 and *Re Spence* [1949] W.N. 237, both discussed in the text, *post* para 4–093, although such cases are readily distinguishable because in a half secret trust such expressions on the face of the will are necessarily effective to impose a trust and therefore must inevitably limit the trust so imposed.) It is clear that a court will admit evidence of a fully secret trust despite the fact that the will in question expressly states that no trust is imposed on the legatee (*Re Spencer* (1887) 57 L.T. 519, where the will contained the words "relying but not by way of trust upon their applying the said sum in or towards the object or objects communicated to them" and a fully secret trust was upheld). In the light of such authorities and the fact that it has been suggested that fully secret trusts operate wholly outside the will in question, it is suggested that in a fully secret trust the presence of such expressions on the face of the will should not have the effect of limiting the permissible ways of communication of the terms of the trust. Nevertheless it would be extremely interesting to see how the courts dealt with this question.

[155] It is necessary to distinguish half secret trusts from the cases where the probate doctrine of incorporation by reference arises. If the testator on the face of his will makes a disposition of property for the purposes set out in a named existing and identifiable document, then that document is deemed to be incorporated into the will and is admitted to probate as part of the will even though it does not itself comply with the formal requirements of the Wills Act (see, for example, *In the goods of Smart* [1902] P. 238). In fact, this doctrine has on occasions been argued to be the theoretical justification for the doctrine of half secret trusts (see Matthews [1979] Conveyancer 360). Adoption of this argument would indeed explain the otherwise inexplicable and much criticised rule that in a half secret trust communication of the terms of the trust must be made before or contemporaneously with the making of the will in question. However, apart from the fact that there seems to be no authority whatsoever in support of such an argument, its acceptance would involve either extending the probate doctrine of incorporation by reference to oral communications or alternatively requiring communication of the terms of a half secret trust to be in writing (in which case *Blackwell v. Blackwell* was wrongly decided). Neither of these possibilities seems to be consistent either with principle or with precedent and it is therefore suggested that this argument is not an acceptable justification for the doctrine of half secret trusts.

[156] See *ante*, para 3–013.

[157] *Margulies v. Margulies* (2000) reported only as Law Tel Document AC7200857.

his last will left all his assets to his eldest child absolutely and, in a later letter to him, signed and witnessed in his presence, stated that "you should feel free to keep my estate for your own benefit or dispose of it at your absolute discretion". An attempt by another child to uphold the existence of a secret trust failed on the grounds of uncertainty of subject matter; there was simply no indication of what property formed the subject matter of any trust. This fact reinforced the conclusion that there had been no certainty of intention either.

4–084   However, where specific property has been referred to by the testator, the courts appear to be prepared to allow much more flexibility in the case of secret trusts than would otherwise be permitted. In *Ottaway v. Norman*,[158] a testator devised his bungalow to his housekeeper and bequeathed her £1,500 and half his residuary estate. Before the death of the testator, she had agreed to leave the bungalow and whatever money was left at her own death to the testator's son. However, in the event she left all her property away from the son, who brought an action against her executor for a declaration that her estate was subject to a trust in his favour. Brightman J. duly held that the bungalow was subject to a fully secret trust in favour of the son. However, he held that there was no valid secret trust of the residue of the money. His Lordship was prepared to assume, without deciding, that it was possible to impose a secret trust under which the secret trustee could deal as he liked with the subject matter during his lifetime and then leave anything that was left to a third party. However, even on that assumption, he held that the terms of the alleged trust were far too unclear. The housekeeper had not been placed under any obligation to keep the money subject to the alleged trust separate from her own funds and, in any event, it was unclear precisely what was meant by money in this context. This decision has several novel features.

4–085   It is unusual to find a secret trust where the obligation imposed on the trustee is to enjoy the property left to him for his lifetime, either as in this case by occupying it or by receiving the income therefrom, and then to leave it on in his will to a third party. However, there is no particular reason for objection to be made to this,[159] at least where the property which is subject to this obligation is clearly ascertainable (as the bungalow in *Ottaway v. Norman* clearly was).

4–086   The other novel feature of *Ottaway v. Norman* is that Brightman J. was prepared to assume, without deciding, that a secret trust is also feasible where the secret trustee is entitled to dispose of the property at will and need only leave anything that is left to a third party. If this is indeed the case, then this will amount to a modification of the normal rules governing certainty of subject matter which were considered in the previous chapter.[160] At present a similar modification appears to apply only to the constructive trusts which arise as a result of mutual wills when the first party to die has left a will made in accordance with the agreement between him and the

---

[158] [1972] Ch. 698.

[159] At the time of the decision, objection could have been taken by reason of the fact that such a secret trust evaded the provisions of the Settled Land Act 1925. However, no further settlements subject to this Act can now be created as a result of the Trusts of Land and Appointment of Trustees Act 1996.

[160] See *ante*, para 3–013.

survivor. As will be seen in the chapter on constructive trusts,[161] although such trusts clearly embrace both the property left to the survivor by the first party to die and whatever property of the survivor is subject to the agreement,[162] the survivor is nevertheless entitled, in the absence of any agreement to the contrary,[163] to dispose freely of any or all of that property during his lifetime[164]; only whatever remains at his death has to be left to the ultimate beneficiary of the mutual wills.[165] The nature of such trusts has been considered judicially on various occasions[166] but none of the explanations given is really satisfactory; the only answer seems to be to regard such trusts as an entrenched anomaly. The type of secret trust envisaged by Brightman J. would move secret trusts into the murky area which has caused such conceptual difficulties in the case of mutual wills. It is much to be hoped that no such secret trusts will ever be upheld so that the doctrine of secret trusts can be spared this sort of conceptual confusion. That does not alter the fact that the judgment in *Ottaway v. Norman* clearly envisages this possibility.

(3) Certainty of objects

There does not actually appear to have been any secret trust case in which   **4–087**
this has been an issue. However, it has never been doubted that this requirement is the same in secret trusts as in all other trusts; it therefore depends on whether the trust in question is fixed or discretionary.[167] All secret trusts which have had to be considered in reported cases have in fact been fixed trusts.

(B) The Communication of the Trust to the Intended Trustee

The rules governing the communication of a secret trust to the intended   **4–088**
trustee differ depending on whether the trust in question is fully secret or half secret.

(1) Fully secret trusts

The rules governing communication of a fully secret trust emerge from *Moss*   **4–089**
v. Cooper[168] and *Re Boyes*.[169] Before his death, the testator must ask the legatee to hold the legacy on trust for a third party. It does not matter whether the communication of the trust to the legatee takes place before or

---

[161] See *post*, para 10–313. See also *Constructive Trusts*, 3rd edn (London, Sweet & Maxwell, 1997), pp.263–272.

[162] *Re Hagger* [1930] 2 Ch. 190.

[163] As in *Re Green* [1951] Ch. 148.

[164] *Birmingham v. Renfrew* (1937) 57 C.L.R. 666 at 689, *per* Dixon J. (High Court of Australia); *Re Goodchild (decd.)* [1996] 1 W.L.R. 694 at 700, *per* Carnwath J.

[165] *Birmingham v. Renfrew, ibid.*, does admittedly envisage the possibility of the ultimate beneficiary restraining a disposition by the survivor which is calculated to defeat the mutual wills. However, in practice this will only be feasible where the subject matter of the mutual wills is or includes a specific asset and not where, as is normally the case, it is the residuary estate of both parties.

[166] *Birmingham v. Renfrew* (1937) 57 C.L.R. 666 at 689, *per* Dixon J. (High Court of Australia); *Re Goodchild (decd.)* [1996] 1 W.L.R. 694 at 700, *per* Carnwath J. (not considered on appeal at [1997] 1 W.L.R. 1216).

[167] See *ante*, para 3–029.

[168] (1861) 1 J. & H. 352.

[169] (1884) 26 Ch.D. 531.

after the execution of the will provided that it takes place during the lifetime of the testator—communication by a letter received after the death of the testator is not sufficient since the legatee then has no opportunity to refuse to act. Nor does it matter that the legatee does not know the precise terms of the trust—a testator may hand the legatee a sealed envelope to be opened after his death[170] or reserve the details of the trusts for future communication provided such communication occurs before his death. These rules equally apply in the case of a secret trust arising as the result of an intestacy (where no will has been made because the intestate has asked his intestate successor to hold the property which he receives on trust for a third party).

4–090   However, in *Kasperbauer v. Griffith*[171] the Court of Appeal stated that it is open to the testator or intestate to change his mind before the gift takes effect on his death; he could, therefore, either vary the terms of the secret trust or cancel it completely. In practice, of course, clear evidence of any change of mind, particularly of the latter type, would be required otherwise it would be far too easy for the intended trustee to defeat the testator's intentions by alleging that the latter had cancelled the secret trust. However, in the event that the court were satisfied that he had done so, the intended trustee would then of course take beneficially.

4–091   Problems sometimes arise where the testator leaves a legacy to two or more persons jointly and fails to communicate with all of them. Special rules have been developed to deal with this situation. These rules are generally stated in the form laid down by Farwell J. in *Re Stead*.[172] Where the property is left to the legatees as tenants in common, only those legatees with whom the testator has communicated are bound—the others take their shares in the property beneficially. Where, on the other hand, the property is left to the legatees as joint tenants, then, if the testator has communicated with any of the legatees prior to the execution of the will, all the legatees are bound by the trust; on the other hand, if the testator does not communicate with any of the legatees until after the execution of the will, only those with whom he does communicate are bound—the others take their shares beneficially.

4–092   The cases which are alleged to establish these peculiar rules have been examined in detail by Perrins.[173] He argues convincingly that this formulation of the rules was based on a misunderstanding of the earlier cases, from which a different rule in fact emerges. In his view, the only question is whether the gift to all the legatees was induced by the agreement to act of any of them; if it was, all are bound but, if it was not, then only those who have agreed to act are bound—the others take their shares beneficially. In his opinion, neither the type of co-ownership nor the time of communication is decisive in determining whether or not the necessary inducement has occurred, although it will obviously be more difficult to show inducement where the legatees are tenants in common and well-nigh impossible to show it where communication is subsequent to the execution of the will. It is not

---

[170] *Re Boyes* (1884) 26 Ch.D. 531 (where the letters were not in fact handed to the intended trustee before the death of the testator and so the communication was held to be unsuccessful); *Re Keen* [1937] Ch. 236 (actually a case of a half secret trust).

[171] (1997) [2000] W.T.L.R. 333 at 343.

[172] [1900] 1 Ch. 237 at 241.

[173] 88 L.Q.R. (1972) 225.

possible to fault Perrins' analysis of the authorities. However, it remains to be seen whether the courts will adopt his rule in preference to the more traditional ones.

(2) Half secret trusts

Before or contemporaneously with the making of the will, the testator must   **4–093** ask the legatee to hold the legacy on trust for a third party. This rule was established by dicta of the members of the House of Lords in *Blackwell v. Blackwell*,[174] was reiterated, also by way of dicta, by the Court of Appeal in *Re Keen*,[175] and was applied, apparently without any contrary argument from counsel, in *Re Bateman's Will Trusts*.[176] It is difficult to see any justification for making this distinction between half secret trusts and fully secret trusts (where, as has already been seen, communication and acceptance may occur at any time prior to the death of the testator); if there was going to be a difference between the two, the rule should arguably be the other way round because there is much more chance of something going wrong where the secret trustee is absolutely beneficially entitled on the face of the will than where he is named as a trustee on its face. It is, therefore, suggested that the rule governing fully secret trusts should be applied also to half secret trusts so as to permit communication and acceptance at any time prior to the death of the testator.[177] However, at present the rule of English law is quite clear—communication and acceptance must occur before or contemporaneously with the making of the will.

However, the form of communication made must not be contrary to the   **4–094** express provisions of the will. In *Re Keen*,[178] the testator left £10,000 to two persons "to be held upon trust and disposed of by them among such person, persons or charities as may be notified by me to them or either of them during my lifetime". Before the execution of the will, he had handed a sealed envelope containing the name of the intended beneficiary to one of the legatees. The Court of Appeal held that it did not matter that the testator had given the legatee his instructions in a sealed envelope which was not to be opened until after his death. However, the Court held that the express provisions of the will contemplated only a future communication and so the communication before the date of the will was contrary to the express provisions of the will and consequently ineffective. (Of course, any communication made after the date of the will in accordance with its provisions would also have been ineffective since communication after the date of the will is impermissible in the case of a half secret trust). Similarly, in *Re Spence*,[179] the testator left property to four persons "to be dealt with in accordance with my wishes which I have made known to them". In fact the

---

[174] [1929] A.C. 318.
[175] [1937] Ch. 236.
[176] [1970] 1 W.L.R. 1463.
[177] This has been done in Ireland *Re Browne* [1944] Ir.R. 90 (High Court of the Republic of Ireland) and in most of the common law jurisdictions of the United States of America (see *Scott on Trusts*, 4th edn (New York, Aspen Publishers, 1989 and subsequent cumulative supplements), para.55.8).
[178] [1937] Ch. 236.
[179] [1949] W.N. 237.

testator had communicated only with some of the legatees and this communication was also held to be contrary to the express provisions of the will and therefore ineffective.

4–095   It is not clear whether, in the case of a half secret trust it is open to the testator to change his mind before the gift takes effect on his death in the way envisaged by the Court of Appeal in *Kasperbauer v. Griffith*,[180] where the trust in question would have been fully secret had it been upheld. If the testator cannot communicate his intentions after the date of the will, there is no obvious reason why he should be able to change his intentions at that stage either. If it is indeed thus not possible for him to do so, this constitutes a further objection to the existing law.

4–096   Problems can arise where the testator (without having made an express provision as in *Re Spence*) leaves a legacy to two or more persons jointly and fails to communicate with all of them. Of course all the legatees will quite clearly be trustees and so the only question which arises is whether those with whom the testator failed to communicate hold their share of the property on trust for the communicated purpose or for the residuary beneficiary or intestate successor. There seems to be no reported half secret trust case in which this problem has actually arisen. Presumably the issue would be determined by application of the rules which apply in this situation to fully secret trusts—the nature of these rules is at present uncertain since, as has already been seen,[181] Perrins has recently challenged the established formulation of the rules.

(C) Acceptance of the Trust by the Intended Trustee

4–097   The requirement that a secret trust must be accepted by the intended trustee is the same for fully secret and half secret trusts. The legatee must agree to hold the legacy on trust for a third party but he will be deemed to have done so unless he positively refuses—silence constitutes assent for this purpose.[182] This was confirmed by the Court of Appeal in *Kasperbauer v. Griffith*[183]; consequently, had there been certainty of intention in that case, the wife would have been bound despite the fact that she had said nothing. However, knowledge that the testator intended to create a secret trust is not enough in the absence of any agreement on the part of the alleged secret trustees to honour its terms.[184]

4–098   However, the Court of Appeal also stated in *Kasperbauer v. Griffith*[185] that the intended trustee can validly renounce his acceptance at any time before the death of the testator or intestate; however, this can presumably only be done by communicating that renunciation to the testator or intestate at a

---

[180] (1997) [2000] W.T.L.R. 333 at 343.
[181] See *ante*, para 4–091.
[182] *Paine v. Hall* (1812) 18 Ves. 475.
[183] (1997) [2000] W.T.L.R. 333 at 343.
[184] This was held by the Court of Appeal of Singapore in *Hiranand v. Harilela* (2000) 3 I.T.E.L.R. 297, 3 *Butterworths Offshore Service* 483. It had to be assumed that the executors and beneficiary of what turned out to be the testator's last will had known that he had intended to make a later will in favour of someone else which was in fact invalid for lack of formality. A claim by a beneficiary of the later invalid will that its provisions nevertheless took effect as a fully secret trust on the basis of this knowledge was rejected.
[185] (1997) [2000] W.T.L.R. 333 at 343.

time when the latter is still in a position to make alternative arrangements. If the testator or intestate makes no alternative testamentary provision following a valid renunciation by the intended trustee, the subject matter of the secret trust will then presumably devolve as if there were no secret trust.

(D) Satisfaction of the Beneficiary Principle

It has already been seen that no private trust can exist without one or more beneficiaries for whose benefit the trust property is held[186] and that, as a general rule, that beneficiary must be capable of enforcing the trust.[187] Although the Court of Appeal did not specifically refer to these requirements in *Kasperbauer v. Griffith*,[188] it undoubtedly applies to both fully secret and half secret trusts.   **4–099**

It is obviously not possible for the sole trustee of a fully secret trust also to be its sole beneficiary. However, where there is a plurality of fully secret trustees, there is nothing to stop one of them being the sole beneficiary nor, where there is a plurality of beneficiaries, is there anything to stop a sole fully secret trustee from being included among them. This latter proposition was upheld expressly in *Irvine v. Sullivan*,[189] where a legatee who took absolutely on the face of the will was held to be entitled to take whatever surplus remained after observing the testator's instructions to pay various pecuniary legacies. It also follows from *Ottaway v. Norman*,[190] where the question was not raised explicitly but a fully secret trust in favour of the secret trustee for life, with remainder over to the testator's son, was held to be valid.   **4–100**

It is equally obvious that it is not possible for the sole trustee of a half secret trust also to be its sole beneficiary. In principle, it might be thought that, where there is a plurality of half secret trustees, there is nothing to stop one of them being the sole beneficiary and that, where there is a plurality of beneficiaries, there is nothing to stop a sole half secret trustee from being included among them. However, this does not appear to be the law. According to the decision of the Court of Appeal in *Re Rees' Will Trusts*,[191] a half secret trustee cannot be one of the secret beneficiaries since such a beneficial interest would be contrary to the express provision of the will that he takes the property as a trustee.[192] On the basis that, as has already been suggested, secret trusts operate outside the will, it is not easy to justify this harsh rule, which must undoubtedly lead to the frustration of the intentions of the testator. Considerable doubts as to its validity were expressed by Pennycuick J. in *Re Tyler*,[193] although his Lordship conceded that he would have been bound by *Re Rees' Will Trusts* if the point had arisen for decision.   **4–101**

---

[186] See *ante*, para 1–035.
[187] See *ante*, para 3–076 *et seq.*
[188] (1997) [2000] W.T.L.R. 333.
[189] (1869) L.R. 8 Eq. 673.
[190] [1972] Ch. 698.
[191] [1950] Ch. 204.
[192] This rule was also stated by way of dicta in *Irvine v. Sullivan* (1869) L.R. 8 Eq. 673, which actually concerned a fully secret trust.
[193] [1967] 1 W.L.R. 1269 at 1278.

(E) Complete Constitution of the Secret Trust

4–102   Nor did the Court of Appeal specifically refer in *Kasperbauer v. Griffith*[194] to the requirement that a secret trust become completely constituted by the subject matter of the secret trust being vested in the secret trustee under the will or intestacy of the deceased.[195] However, this requirement clearly applies to both fully secret and half secret trusts. If it were not complied with, as would be the case if the will were not executed in accordance with section 9 of the Wills Act and so was void, the secret trust, despite complying with the three requirements actually listed in *Kasperbauer v. Griffith*,[196] would have no subject matter and so would be completely ineffective. It has already been seen[197] that a secret trust may also not become completely constituted because the secret trustee or secret beneficiary has witnessed the will or has died before the testator, or because the secret trustee disclaims his interest under the will.

(F) Formalities

4–103   It may also be necessary for the communication and acceptance of a secret trust to comply with the formal requirements of section 53(1) of the Law of Property Act 1925. This would mean that a secret trust of land would, under section 53(1)(b), have to be "manifested and proved by some writing signed by some person who is able to declare such trust", while a secret trust of a subsisting equitable interest would, under section 53(1)(c), have to be "in writing signed by the person disposing of the same, or by his agent thereunto lawfully authorised in writing". This question did not arise in *Kasperbauer v. Griffith*[198] but would have done had the necessary intention been held to exist. Whether section 53(1) has to be complied with depends on whether secret trusts are or are not express trusts (if they are not and are instead either implied, resulting, or constructive trusts, they would be exempt from the formal requirements of section 53(1) by virtue of section 53(2)).

4–104   The authorities are inconclusive. In *Re Baillie*,[199] a half secret trust of land was held to be ineffective because of the absence of the necessary writing. That decision suggests that half secret trusts, at least, are express trusts. On the other hand, fully secret trusts of land have been upheld in the absence of the necessary writing—most recently in *Ottaway v. Norman*,[200] although neither in this nor in any of the other reported cases has the absence of this writing actually been raised. At first sight, this might be thought to suggest, if only by virtue of the silence of the courts, that fully secret trusts are not express trusts. However, any such conclusion would in fact be unsound. The absence of evidentiary writing must be specifically pleaded; if it is not so pleaded, then the absence of the writing will not be a bar to the success of

---

[194] (1997) [2000] W.T.L.R. 333.

[195] See *post*, para 5–006 *et seq.*

[196] (1997) [2000] W.T.L.R. 333.

[197] See *ante*, paras 4–067–4–074.

[198] (1997) [2000] W.T.L.R. 333.

[199] (1886) 2 T.L.R. 660 (this was of course a decision on the pre-existing provision, Statute of Frauds 1677, s.7).

[200] [1972] Ch. 698.

the action.[201] Consequently, the fact that fully secret trusts have been upheld in the absence of the evidentiary writing required by section 53(1)(b) is totally irrelevant to the question of whether such writing is actually necessary because in none of the authorities was the absence of the necessary writing pleaded. And, although in *Gold v. Hill*[202] section 53(1)(c) was stated to be inapplicable to a secret trust of rights arising under a pension trust, that is not in fact relevant either; such rights are not within section 53(1) anyway.[203]

What then is the nature of secret trusts? Most commentators, on the **4–105** strength of *Re Baillie* and the fact that half secret trusts, unlike fully secret trusts, appear on the face of the will, seem to accept that half secret trusts are express trusts. However, the general view seems to be that no fully secret trust can ever fail for lack of writing, simply because of the maxim that a statute cannot be used as an instrument of fraud; for this reason, many commentators have classified fully secret trusts as constructive trusts.[204] Indeed this classification was assumed by Nourse J. by way of dictum in *Re Cleaver*,[205] a case which actually concerned mutual wills, and was upheld by the Court of Appeal in *Kasperbauer v. Griffith*[206]; however, in neither case was there any argument to the contrary, nor did the issue arise, nor was there any reference to half secret trusts.

Apart from the fact that it seems contrary to principle to distinguish in this **4–106** way between fully secret and half secret trusts,[207] the proposition that no fully secret trust can ever fail for lack of writing is in fact unsound. Obviously no fully secret trustee would be allowed to profit by raising the absence of the necessary writing as the basis of a claim to take the property beneficially. The clearly unconscionable conduct involved in any attempt to do this would inevitably lead to the imposition of a constructive trust on a quite different ground, namely the principle enunciated in *Bannister v. Bannister*.[208] But there remains the possibility that a fully secret trustee who admits that he is holding the property which he has received under the will

---

[201] *North v. Loomes* [1919] 1 Ch. 378 (actually a decision on Statute of Frauds 1677, s.4 (subsequently Law of Property Act 1925, s.40, now repealed by Law of Property (Miscellaneous Provisions) Act 1989, s.2); however s.53(1)(b), like s.40 and Statute of Frauds 1677, s.4, requires only evidentiary writing and is generally thought to be governed by the same principles). A specific decision on the predecessor of s.53(1)(b), Statute of Frauds 1677, s.7, where the point presently under discussion did not arise, is *Foster v. Hale* (1798) 3 Ves.Jun. 696, which concerned the question of what type of writing would satisfy the provision.

[202] [1999] 1 F.L.R. 54.

[203] *Re Danish Bacon Company Staff Pension Fund* [1971] 1 W.L.R. 248 at 256.

[204] See, for example, the view of Hayton in Hayton & Marshall, *Commentary and Cases on the Law of Trusts and Equitable Remedies* 12th edn (London, Sweet & Maxwell, 2005), p.121, repeated in the current edition of *Underhill and Hayton, Law of Trusts and Trustees* 17th edn (London, Lexis Nexis, 2006), p.317, where it is stated that "secret trusts should be categorised as constructive trusts".

[205] [1981] 1 W.L.R. 939 at 947.

[206] (1997) [2000] W.T.L.R. 333.

[207] This view was adopted by Hayton in *Hayton and Marshall: Cases and Commentary on the Law of Trusts*, 9th edn (London, Sweet & Maxwell, 1996), p.105, n.31: "since the court is recognising and enforcing a testator's express trust why not call a spade a spade?" but this is no longer his view (see *ante*, n.204). A more ambivalent view is expressed by Martin in Hanbury & Martin: *Modern Equity*, 17th edn (London, Sweet & Maxwell, 2005), pp.168–169.

[208] [1948] 2 All E.R. 133, [1948] W.N. 261; discussed *ante*, para 4–049.

or intestacy in question but cannot point to the writing required by section 53(1) will find himself confronted by opposing claims from the beneficiaries of the secret trust and the testator's residuary beneficiary or his statutory next-of-kin. In this situation, the maxim that a statute cannot be used as an instrument of fraud will be of no assistance whatever and the result will be determined by whether fully secret trusts are constructive trusts, in which case the property will go to the beneficiaries of the secret trust, or express trusts, in which case because of the absence of the necessary writing it will go to his residuary beneficiary or the statutory next-of-kin.

4–107 It is, therefore, necessary to decide as a matter of principle whether secret trusts are express trusts or constructive trusts. In the case of both fully secret and half secret trusts the testator clearly intends to create a relationship of trustee and beneficiary. This suggests that, as a matter of definition, both fully secret and half secret trusts should be classified as express trusts. This view is strengthened if, as has already been suggested, the theoretical justification for the existence of the doctrine of secret trusts is not fraud but the fact that such trusts operate wholly outside the will or intestacy in question. It is accordingly suggested that all secret trusts are express trusts and so must comply with section 53(1) of the Law of Property Act 1925. However, it has to be admitted that there is as yet no general agreement on this question, which must, therefore, await definitive resolution by the courts.

3. The Effect of the Creation of a Secret Trust

(A) Fully Secret Trusts

4–108 Where all the requirements for the creation of a fully secret trust are satisfied, the beneficiary will be able to enforce that trust in the same way as any other trust, not only against the fully secret trustee but also against any successor in title to the fully secret trustee who has not taken the property in question free of the equitable interest of the beneficiary. If no property vests beneficially in the intended trustee, the fully secret trust will simply fail for want of subject matter. If property vests under the will or intestacy in question but there is no trust because, for example, of a lack of certainty of intention or because the same person is sole trustee and sole beneficiary, the person in whom the property vests will take it absolutely under the will. However, where there has been a failure of communication, the situation is less straightforward. If the intended trustee does not hear of the existence of the secret trust until after the death of the testator, he will take the property beneficially even though it can be proved that the testator intended that a secret trust should be imposed upon him. This was held in *Wallgrave v. Tebbs*.[209] However, if the legatee agrees during the lifetime of the testator to hold the property on trust but is not informed of the beneficial interests before the death of the testator, then he will hold the property on trust for whoever is entitled to the testator's residuary estate or for his statutory next-of-kin. This was held in *Re Boyes*.[210] Although the question has never arisen,

---

[209] (1855) 2 K. & J. 313.
[210] (1884) 26 Ch.D. 531.

it is suggested that this would be the case even if the legatee were himself entitled to the residuary estate or were the intestate successor in question.

The effect of attestation by, or the predecease of, the beneficiary of a fully   **4–109** secret trustee was considered in an earlier previous part of this section.[211] If, as was suggested there, the theoretical justification for the existence of the doctrine of secret trusts is that such trusts operate wholly outside the will in question, then the effect of the occurrence of either of these events will be governed by the rules of the law of trusts. Attestation of the will by the beneficiary will, therefore, be irrelevant but the effect of the predecease of the beneficiary will depend on what the relevant rule of the law of trusts actually is. *Re Gardner (No.2)*[212] decided that in such circumstances the beneficial interest would devolve according to the beneficiary's will or intestacy; this decision undoubtedly constitutes the present law but has been universally condemned by the commentators.

If, on the other hand, the theoretical justification for the existence of secret   **4–110** trusts is fraud, any secret trust which can be proved to have been the subject of the necessary communication and acceptance will presumably be regarded as taking effect as part of the will in question; if this is indeed the case, the probate rules will presumably apply rather than the rules of the law of trusts. In this event, attestation of the will by the secret beneficiary will therefore prevent him from taking beneficially under the will while the predecease of the secret beneficiary will unquestionably bring the doctrine of lapse into play; in both cases, the fully secret trustee will therefore presumably hold whatever property he receives on trust for whoever is entitled to the testator's residuary estate or for his statutory next-of-kin.

(B) Half Secret Trusts

Where all the requirements for the creation of a half secret trust are satisfied,   **4–111** the beneficiary will be able to enforce that trust in the same way as any other trust, not only against the half secret trustee but also against any successor in title to the half secret trustee who has not taken the property in question free of the equitable interest of the beneficiary. However, if the testator asks the intended trustee to hold a particular sum on trust and in fact leaves him a larger sum, only the sum in respect of which the trustee undertook to act will be subject to the secret trust; the residue will be held by him on trust for whoever is entitled to the testator's residuary estate or for his statutory next-of-kin. This was held in *Re Cooper*.[213] More generally, if no property vests beneficially in the intended trustee under the will, the half secret trust will simply fail for want of subject matter. If the trust fails for any other reason, the intended trustee will not take the property beneficially but will hold it on trust for whoever is entitled to the testator's residue or for his statutory next-of-kin. This was held in *Re Pugh's Will Trusts*.[214] It is suggested that the half secret trustee should be able to take the property beneficially if he is himself entitled to the residuary estate or is the intestate successor in question,

---

[211] See *ante*, paras 4–067–4–074.
[212] [1923] 2 Ch. 230.
[213] [1939] Ch. 580.
[214] [1967] 1 W.L.R. 1262.

although this may be contrary to the spirit, if not the letter, of the already criticised decision of the Court of Appeal in *Re Rees' Will Trusts*.[215]

4–112   The effect of attestation by, predecease of, and disclaimer by a half secret trustee were considered in an earlier part of this section.[216] If, as was suggested there, the theoretical justification for the existence of the doctrine of secret trusts is that such trusts operate wholly outside the will in question, then the effect of the occurrence of any one of these three events will be governed by the rules of probate and will, therefore, be irrelevant. If, on the other hand, the theoretical justification for the existence of secret trusts is fraud, any secret trust which can be proved to have been the subject of the necessary communication and acceptance will presumably be regarded as taking effect as part of the will in question; if this is indeed the case, the probate rules will presumably still apply with exactly the same results.

---

[215] [1950] Ch. 204.
[216] See *ante*, paras 4–067–4–074.

CHAPTER 5

THE CONSTITUTION OF A TRUST

I. INTRODUCTION

An express trust is completely constituted either by an effective transfer of **5–001** the trust property to trustees or by an effective declaration of trust. The implications of this principle were clearly brought out by Turner L.J. in his classic judgment in *Milroy v. Lord*[1] when he said:

"In order to render a voluntary settlement valid and effectual, the settlor must have done everything which according to the nature of the property comprised in the settlement was necessary to be done in order to render the settlement binding upon him. He may, of course, do this by actually transferring the property to the persons for whom he intends to provide and the provision will then be effectual and it will be equally effectual if he transfers the property to a trustee for the purposes of the settlement, or declares that he himself holds it on trust for those purposes and if the property is personal, the trust may, as I apprehend, be declared either in writing or parol but, in order to render the settlement binding, one or other of these modes must, as I understand the law of this court, be resorted to, for there is no equity in this court to perfect an imperfect gift."

The latter part of this passage emphasises the crucial difference between **5–002** a completely constituted trust and an incompletely constituted trust. Only when a trust is completely constituted is it binding on the settlor; in other words, only in such circumstances is a trust enforceable by the beneficiaries, whose equitable proprietary interest in the trust property will then be binding not only upon the settlor but also against any third party into whose hands the trust property may come other than a bona fide purchaser of a legal interest in that property for value without notice (or the statutory equivalent).

Trusts which are completely constituted are divided into executed and **5–003** executory trusts; an executed trust arises when the settlor has defined in the trust instrument precisely what interests are to be taken by the beneficiaries, whereas an executory trust arises where the instrument or declaration requires the subsequent execution of a further instrument whose terms it does not itself define precisely.

When, on the other hand, a trust has not been completely constituted, **5–004** there is in effect no trust enforceable by the beneficiaries, who, therefore,

[1] (1862) 4 De G.F. & J. 264 at 274.

have no equitable proprietary interest whatever. Their position is often illustrated by reference to equitable maxims, a recourse which is at best unhelpful and at worst potentially confusing. The straightforward proposition that, if the settlor has failed completely to constitute the trust, equity will not do so for him is often expressed by reference to the equitable maxim that "equity will not perfect an imperfect gift" (however, this maxim is somewhat imprecise because of the number of exceptions to the basic rule which equity has permitted). In such circumstances, the incompletely constituted trust can only be enforced under the law of contract; the rights of the beneficiaries depend on the existence of a binding contract enforceable either by them or on their behalf. In the absence of such a contract, they have no rights whatsoever and are, therefore, often described as volunteers. This is in accordance with another equitable maxim that "equity will not assist a volunteer"; this maxim is not merely imprecise but positively confusing because of the failure of equity clearly to define precisely who is regarded as a volunteer for this purpose.

5–005   This chapter, therefore, involves the consideration of three questions: first, the circumstances in which a trust will be held to be completely constituted; secondly, the distinction between executed and executory trusts; and, thirdly, the circumstances in which, where a trust is incompletely constituted, the beneficiaries will have a contractual remedy.

II. WHEN WILL A TRUST BE COMPLETELY CONSTITUTED?

1. By Transfer of the Trust Property To Trustees

(A)   Legal Interests

5–006   If the subject matter of the proposed trust is a legal estate or interest, the transfer of the trust property must be effective to vest that estate in the trustees. Consequently the basic rule, to which there are some exceptions,[2] is that the settlor must comply with all the formalities required for a complete transfer of the property in order to give the trustees full legal title thereto. Exactly the same rule applies where the transfer is made with the intention of making a gift; the donor must comply with all the formalities required for a complete transfer of the property in order to give the donee full legal title to that property.

5–007   So if the subject matter of the trust or gift is land, a deed is necessary[3] followed, in the case of registered land, by registration of the transfer on the Land Register[4]; if it is a copyright, then what is necessary is writing signed by or on behalf of the assignor[5]; if it is a bill of exchange or other negotiable instrument, then whether it is payable to the bearer or to the holder, delivery and the appropriate form of indorsement are necessary[6]; if it is shares in a

---

[2] See *post*, paras 5–036–5–072.
[3] Law of Property Act 1925, s.52.
[4] Land Registration Act 2002, ss.29, 30.
[5] Copyright, Designs and Patents Act 1988, s.90(3), re-enacting Copyright Act 1956, s.36(3).
[6] See *Antrobus v. Smith* (1806) 12 Ves. 39; *Jones v. Lock* (1865) 1 Ch. App. 25.

company other than bearer shares,[7] the correct form of transfer is necessary followed by registration of the transfer in the Share Register of the company in question[8]; if it is the benefit of a right of action, writing is necessary, followed by notice in writing to the other party[9]; and, finally, if it is a chattel, either a deed of gift[10] or an intention to give together with a delivery of possession is necessary, although any such personal delivery must be effective.[11]

The requirement that the full legal title be transferred to the trustees is illustrated by a number of decisions involving the transfer of shares. In *Milroy v. Lord*[12] itself, the intending settlor had covenanted to transfer bank shares to the defendant on trust for the plaintiff. The defendant already had a general power of attorney to transfer the shares into his own name at any time but neither he nor the settlor actually did so prior to the settlor's death, which had the effect of revoking the power of attorney. Since neither the settlor nor the defendant was any longer in a position to make the necessary transfer, the shares therefore remained the settlor's property; consequently, they formed part of his residuary estate and could not successfully be claimed by the plaintiff. Similarly, in *Re Fry*[13] the intending settlor, who was domiciled in the United States of America, executed transfers of shares in a limited company, partly by way of gift to his son and partly to a trust. The company were unable to register the transfers because the consent of the Treasury had not been obtained under the Defence Regulations then operative. The forms required for obtaining this consent were sent to the settlor, who signed and returned them but died before the consent was given. Romer J. held that the trust had not been completely constituted prior to the settlor's death; consequently the shares did not pass either to the son or to the trust but, as in *Milroy v. Lord*, formed part of the settlor's residuary estate. In order to perfect the transaction it would apparently have been necessary for the donor to have effected confirmatory transfers after the consent had been given.[14]

These two decisions establish that, for so long as something remains to be done by a settlor in order to render a voluntary transfer effective, that

5–008

5–009

---

[7] The rights attached to bearer shares vest in whoever has physical possession of the share certificates.

[8] *Milroy v. Lord* (1862) 4 De G.F. & J. 264, see also *post*, p.138. The relevant Act is the Stock Transfer Act 1963, s.1.

[9] Law of Property Act 1925, s.136.

[10] *Jaffa v. Taylor Gallery* (1990) *The Times*, March 21, 1990, where a trust of a painting was held to have been completely constituted without physical delivery to the trustees, one of whom was abroad, on the grounds that the formal declaration of trust contained in the deed transferred title to the painting to the trustees.

[11] See *Re Cole* [1964] Ch. 175, which concerned an alleged delivery of furniture by a husband to his wife when the two were living together in a common establishment. The Court of Appeal held that this did not unequivocally establish either a change in possession or a delivery of the furniture; accordingly, there was no effected or perfected gift to her, the court rejecting the contention that a perfect gift of chattels can be constituted simply by showing them to the donee and speaking the appropriate words of gift.

[12] (1862) 4 De G.F. & J. 264. The classic statement of the law made by Turner L.J. at 274 is set out: *ante*, para 5–001 and *post*, para 5–020.

[13] [1946] Ch. 312.

[14] *ibid.* at 316.

transfer will remain abortive.[15] However, some subsequent decisions have established a number of glosses on that basic rule, at least some of which are extremely questionable. These glosses apparently enable an ineffective transfer nevertheless to take effect in equity and to bring about the complete constitution of a trust in that way. These glosses will be considered in detail later in this section.[16]

5–010   Further, it is in any event questionable how far it is possible to reconcile the authorities already discussed with the decision in *Re Vandervell's Trusts (No.2)*,[17] whose facts have already been considered. Lord Denning M.R., as an alternative ground for his decision that the shares in the products company were held on trust for the children's settlement, was of the opinion[18] that Vandervell had made a perfect gift to the trust company of the dividends on the shares "so far as they were handed over or treated by him as belonging to the trust company for the benefit of the children". In reaching this conclusion, his Lordship purported to follow *Milroy v. Lord* itself.

5–011   It has already been seen that, in *Milroy v. Lord* an attempt to create a trust of bank shares was held to have been ineffective because legal title to the shares had never been vested in the intended trustee and, as a result, the shares finished up in the hands of the settlor's residuary legatees. However, during the settlor's lifetime, the dividends payable on the shares had been paid by the bank to the intended trustee by virtue of the power of attorney which he held; he had paid these dividends on to the beneficiary who had in turn used them to purchase shares in a quite different company. It was held that the settlor should be treated as having made a perfect gift of the dividends to the beneficiary; the settlor's residuary legatees therefore had no claim to the shares in the other company which had been purchased with the dividends.

5–012   It is not easy to see how this decision can justify the conclusion reached by Lord Denning M.R. in *Re Vandervell's Trusts (No.2)*. The settlor in *Milroy v. Lord* had given the intended trustee a power of attorney to collect the dividends and so must inevitably have intended them to be held for the beneficiary, whereas Vandervell had not even been aware that he had still retained an equitable interest in the option relating to the shares of his products company at the time when he had made the supposedly perfect gift of the dividends to the trust company. The two decisions thus seem readily distinguishable.

(B) Equitable Interests

5–013   The decisions already discussed are illustrations of the important principle that, if the subject matter of a trust or a gift is a legal interest, the transferor must vest the legal title to the property in the trustee or donee. The same principle applies to the transfer of an equitable interest. It is not, of course, necessary for the transferor to procure a conveyance of the legal interest (which will be held by the trustees); all that is necessary is that he should

---

[15] See also *Letts v. I.R.C.* [1951] 1 W.L.R. 201, which concerned a direction by a father to a company to allot shares direct to his children.

[16] See *post*, paras 5–020–5–035.

[17] [1974] Ch. 269. See *ante*, paras 4–036–4–042.

[18] *ibid.* at 321.

make a perfect assignment of his interest, which in this case will be necessarily and universally required to be in writing by virtue of section 53(1)(c) of the Law of Property Act 1925.[19] This assignment will, where a trust is being constituted, be followed by a direction to the trustees to hold for the future its subject matter on trust for the assignee.[20] This is as much as the transferor of an equitable interest is able to do.

However, the fact that this at least must be done is shown by the decision   **5–014**
of the Court of Appeal in *Re McArdle*.[21] In this case, some brothers and sisters were entitled under the will of their father to a house after the death of their mother, who lived in the house with one of the brothers and his wife. After the wife had effected various improvements to the house, all the brothers and sisters signed a document addressed to her, stating that "in consideration of your carrying out certain alterations to the property, we hereby agree that the executors shall repay to you from the estate when distributed the sum of £488" in settlement of the amount spent on improvements. The court held, in effect, that this document was neither one thing nor the other. If it was intended to create a contract, the contract lacked consideration since the only possible consideration was past. If, on the other hand, it was an attempted gift, that gift was imperfect because the donors had not done what was necessary to make the gift complete; it was still necessary for them to authorise the executors to make the necessary payment and, unless and until they did so, the gift remained ineffective.

2. *By Declaration of Trust*

By far the most common method of completely constituting a trust is for the   **5–015**
settlor to transfer the trust property to trustees in the manner just described. However, it is equally effective for a settlor to make a declaration of trust that he is from the moment of the declaration a trustee of the property in question for the intended beneficiaries. Any words which clearly express the intention to create a present and irrevocable trust will give rise to the creation of a completely constituted trust—it is not necessary for an effective declaration of trust that the settlor should say in terms "I hereby declare myself to be a trustee".

That does not alter the fact that the necessary intention must be satisfacto-   **5–016**
rily shown. In *Jones v. Lock*[22] a father put a cheque, presumably payable to himself, into the hands of his infant son, saying: "Look you here, I give this to baby; it is for himself". He then took back the cheque and put it away but subsequently reiterated his intention of giving the amount of the cheque to his son. Shortly afterwards he died and the cheque was found among his effects. Lord Cranworth L.C. held that there was neither an effective transfer by way of gift nor a valid declaration of trust. It was quite impossible to regard the somewhat theatrical exercise enacted by the father as a delivery

---

[19] See *Kekewich v. Manning* (1851) De G.M. & G. 176 (assignment of an equitable reversionary interest in shares); *Gilbert v. Overton* (1864) 2 H. & M. 110 (assignment of an agreement for lease); and *ante*, para 4–008.

[20] See *Grey v. I.R.C.* [1960] A.C. 1 (direction to trustees to hold on trust may take effect as an assignment), discussed *ante*, para 4–027.

[21] [1951] Ch. 669.

[22] (1865) 1 Ch. App. 25.

of the moneys represented by the cheque. To effect a perfect transfer, he should have paid the cheque, presumably after the necessary endorsement,[23] into a bank account opened either in the name of his son or in the name of trustees on behalf of his son. Nor had he made a valid declaration of trust, since no inference that he had made himself a trustee could be deduced from his words and actions.

5–017   In all such cases, it is a question of construction whether the words used, taking into account the surrounding circumstances, amount to a clear declaration of trust. So in *Paul v. Constance*,[24] acknowledged[25] to be a "borderline case", the words used by the deceased were "[T]he money is as much yours as mine", words which he had often repeated to the plaintiff, a woman with whom he had lived for a number of years. He was referring to money in a bank account which had been opened to hold a sum paid to him by way of compensation for an industrial injury; however, the account also contained their joint bingo winnings and the only withdrawal ever made had been used for their joint benefit. The Court of Appeal held, distinguishing *Jones v. Lock*, that the words, taken with the use which had been made of the account during the deceased's lifetime, amounted to a present irrevocable declaration that the plaintiff was entitled to half the balance of the account.[26]

5–018   Thus far the law appears reasonably clear. However, the requirements established by the authorities discussed so far seem to have been relaxed materially in *Re Vandervell's Trusts (No.2)*.[27] The Court of Appeal managed to find an effective declaration of trust of the shares in question by the trust company in favour of a settlement for the benefit of Vandervell's children from the following facts: first, that the trust company had used £5,000 from the children's settlement for the purposes of exercising an option to re-purchase the shares; secondly, that thereafter all the dividends received by the trust company had been paid into the bank accounts of the children's settlement and subsequently treated as part of the funds of that settlement; and, thirdly, that the solicitors for the trustee company had written to the Inland Revenue stating that the shares would be held on the trusts of the settlement. None of these facts, least of all the third, seems to indicate a present irrevocable declaration of trust[28]; further, as Stephenson L.J. expressly indicated, it is not easy to see how a limited company such as the trust company could have declared a trust by parol or conduct or, for that matter, could have declared a trust at all without a resolution of its board of

---

[23] A cheque can, as a negotiable instrument, be endorsed by the holder (the person in whose favour it is drawn) either to bearer (by the holder signing the cheque on the back) or in favour of a specified person X (by the holder writing on the back of the cheque "Pay X" and signing it). However, modern personal cheques tend to bear the words "ACCOUNT PAYEE" which means that they are payable only to the original holder. Whether or not cheques have to be paid into a bank account or can be cashed over the counter at the branch of the bank at which the account of the drawer of the cheque is held depends on whether or not they are crossed (modern personal cheques invariably are).

[24] [1977] 1 W.L.R. 527.

[25] *ibid.* at 532, *per* Scarman L.J.

[26] See also *T. Choithram International S.A. v. Pagarani* [2001] 1 W.L.R. 1, discussed *post*, para 5–023.

[27] [1974] Ch. 269. The facts are stated in detail *ante*, paras 4–036–4–042.

[28] The question was not argued before Megarry J. at first instance.

directors[29] (this need to find an effective declaration of trust only of course arose because the Court of Appeal had resolved the question of how Vandervell could have disposed of the equitable interest which the House of Lords had held still to be vested in him[30] without using the writing required by section 53(1)(c) of the Law of Property Act 1925 in favour of the trust company in the equally questionable way which has already been considered[31]). It is not considered that the courts are likely often to be so generous to settlors.

Finally, it should be recalled that, if the subject matter of a declaration of trust is land, the requirements of section 53(1) of the Law of Property Act 1925 will need to be complied with. This certainly requires evidentiary writing in accordance with section 53(1)(b), in default of which the trust in question will be valid but unenforceable. Further, if there is indeed an overlap between section 53(1)(b) and section 53(1)(a), the declaration of trust will actually have to be made in writing in accordance with the latter provision, in default of which the trust in question will be wholly void.[32]   **5–019**

3. By an Ineffective Transfer Taking Effect in Equity

(A) The General Rule

Where it is clear that the settlor intended to create a trust by transfer but has used an ineffectual method of transfer, the general rule is that this ineffectual transfer will not be interpreted as taking effect in equity as an effectual declaration of trust. In *Milroy v. Lord*[33] itself, Turner L.J., immediately after the passage from his judgment which has already been cited,[34] continued[35]:   **5–020**

"The cases, I think, go further to this extent: that if the settlement is intended to be effectuated by one of the modes to which I have referred, the court will not give effect to it by applying another of these modes. If it is intended to take effect by transfer, the court will not hold the intended transfer to operate as a declaration of trust, for then every imperfect instrument would be made effectual by being converted into a perfect trust."

This principle was applied in *Richards v. Delbridge*.[36] The deceased, the owner of certain leasehold premises, indorsed and signed on the lease the following memorandum: "This deed and all thereto I give to [the intended transferee] from this time forth, with all the stock-in-trade". The Court of Appeal held that there was no perfected transfer, since the indorsement had not been made with the formalities necessary for a deed and so was ineffective to transfer the leasehold interest. Nor, in the circumstances, could the indorsement take effect as a declaration of trust.   **5–021**

---

[29] *ibid.* at 323.
[30] In *Vandervell v. I.R.C.* [1967] 2 A.C. 291. See *ante*, paras 4–030–4–035.
[31] See *ante*, paras 4–036–4–042.
[32] See *ante*, paras 4–010–4–015.
[33] (1862) 4 De G.F. & J. 264.
[34] See *ante*, para 5–001.
[35] (1862) 4 De G.F. & J. 264 at 275.
[36] (1874) L.R. 18 Eq. 11.

5–022   The existence of this principle does not, however, mean that a settlor who intends to create a trust by transfer cannot expressly declare himself to be trustee of the subject matter pending that transfer. If he does so, he will himself be the trustee of a completely constituted trust of the subject matter unless and until he transfers that property to the intended trustees. Thus in *Re Ralli's Will Trusts*,[37] a settlor entered into a covenant to transfer any existing or after-acquired property to the trustees of her marriage settlement; the deed of settlement stated that it was "the intention" of the parties that all such property "shall become subject in equity to the settlement". The settlor failed to transfer to the trustees certain property caught by the covenant which, although existing during the settlor's lifetime, did not vest in possession in her until after her death. Buckley J. held that, although no completely constituted trust of the property had arisen by transfer, the settlor had declared herself to be a trustee of any such property pending transfer; consequently this completely constituted trust arising by declaration of trust could be enforced by the beneficiaries of the marriage settlement against the settlor's personal representative.

(B)   Where a Settlor who is One of a Number of Trustees Declares a Trust

5–023 In *T. Choithram International S.A. v. Pagarani*,[38] the settlor, who knew that he was dying of cancer, wished to create a philanthropic foundation before his death. To this end, one month before his death, he arranged a ceremony at his bedside in which he executed the requisite deed of trust, of which he and nine other persons, three of whom were present, were to be the trustees, and purported orally to make an immediate absolute gift to the foundation of his shareholdings and credit balances in four British Virgin Islands' companies. Although the minutes of a meeting of each of these companies held later that day recorded that the trustees of the foundation were now the holders of the assets in question, the settlor did not vest those assets in the other trustees prior to his death and it was, therefore, contended that the trust was incompletely constituted (in which case the assets would have devolved under the settlor's intestacy).

5–024   The Privy Council,[39] whose opinion was delivered by Lord Browne-Wilkinson, held that the settlor had satisfied the criteria for the creation of a trust by declaration (this decision is consistent with the authorities on creating trusts by declaration which have already been considered[40]). However, on the face of things the settlor was instead purporting to create a trust of which he was one of a number of trustees by transfer. The Board held that there was in principle no distinction between a settlor declaring himself to be sole trustee and one of a number of trustees.[41] In both cases it would be equally unconscionable for him subsequently to be able to resile from his declaration of trust (this statement, although unobjectionable in its context,

---

[37] [1964] Ch. 288. See also *Middleton v. Pollock* (1876) 2 Ch.D. 194, where effective declarations of trust were made.

[38] [2001] 1 W.L.R. 1. See Halliwell [2003] Conveyancer 192.

[39] On appeal from the Court of Appeal of the British Virgin Islands.

[40] See *ante*, paras 5–015–5–019.

[41] [2001] 1 W.L.R. 1 at 12.

has since unjustifiably been interpreted much more broadly[42]). Consequently, the trust was completely constituted.

It was clearly crucial to this decision that the execution of the deed of trust   5–025
and the oral gift formed part of one composite transaction; any special
factors, such as any intention of the settlor, whether expressed or implied
from the circumstances, that no trust should arise until the moment of
transfer of the subject matter to the other trustees, would have led to a
different result. It must also be remembered that, if the subject matter had
been land, the requirements of the equivalent of section 53(1) of the Law of
Property Act 1925 would have had to be complied with. Since the members
of the Privy Council can hardly be blamed for the wholly objectionable
manner in which their decision has since been extended,[43] that decision is
therefore supportable. This was anyway not a case in which an ineffective
transfer has been held to take effect as an effective declaration of trust
because it was held that there had been a declaration of trust by the settlor.
However, it is obviously unlikely that similar circumstances will arise very
often.

(C)   Where a Settlor has Done All in his Power to Transfer the Property

Where a settlor has done everything within his power in order to render a   5–026
transfer effective but something has yet to be done by a third party, the
transfer will be immediately valid in equity; consequently, although it will
remain ineffective to pass the legal title unless and until the third party does
whatever remains to be done by him, the transferor will in the meantime
hold the subject matter of the transfer on the trusts of the settlement.[44] This
was established by the decision of the Court of Appeal in *Re Rose*[45] in which
an earlier unconnected first instance decision, coincidentally also bearing
the name *Re Rose*,[46] was applied and followed. Not surprisingly, the rule so
established is known as the Rule in *Re Rose*.

In the first case named *Re Rose*,[47] a testator had made a specific bequest of   5–027
shares but subsequently before his death executed a share transfer in respect
of the same shares in favour of the legatee. Because these were shares in a
private company, its directors had the right to refuse to register the transfer
and did not actually register it until after the death of the testator. The
question then arose as to whether the legatee had taken the shares *inter vivos*
or could only take them, if at all, *post mortem*.[48] Jenkins J. held that, because
the testator had done everything in his power to transfer the shares

---

[42] See *Pennington v. Waine* [2002] 1 W.L.R. 2075; *post*, para 5–032.

[43] See *post*, para 5–032.

[44] Since this trust does not arise out of any express or implied intention of the transferor or
the beneficiaries, it must therefore, necessarily be brought into existence by operation of law
and should therefore be classified as a constructive trust (see *post*, para 10–339).

[45] [1952] Ch. 499.

[46] [1949] 1 Ch. 78.

[47] [1949] 1 Ch. 78.

[48] This mattered because the bequest was conditional on the shares not having been transferred to the legatee prior to the testator's death; it was, therefore, possible to argue that the
transfer *inter vivos* was ineffective to pass any title but nevertheless sufficient to defeat the
testamentary gift, thus preventing the legatee from receiving the shares at all.

inter vivos, from that moment he held the shares on trust for the transferee; consequently, the legatee had taken the shares *inter vivos*.

5–028   This decision was followed and applied by the Court of Appeal in the second case named *Re Rose*.[49] Two transfers of shares in a private company, one by way of gift to the transferor's wife and the other to trustees on trust, were not registered until three months later. The transferor subsequently died at a point when estate duty was payable if the transfers had only been effective on registration but not if they were effective on execution.[50] Were the transfers effective upon execution or upon registration? The Court of Appeal held that, once the transferor had executed the transfers in the appropriate form, the transferor had done everything in his power which was necessary to vest the legal interest in the shares in the transferees. Consequently, from that moment the transfers were effective in equity and the transferor consequently held the legal title to the shares on trust for the transferees until they subsequently acquired legal title thereto upon registration of the transfers. Therefore no estate duty was payable.

5–029   The conclusion reached in these two decisions is not easy to reconcile either with the passages from the judgment of Turner L.J. in *Milroy v. Lord*[51] which have been set out above or with the decision in *Re Fry*[52] which has already been considered.[53] In the second case named *Re Rose*, the Court of Appeal held that the remarks of Turner L.J. only applied where the transfer in question had not been carried out in the appropriate way (this was admittedly the situation under consideration in *Milroy v. Lord*[54] but no such restriction was actually mentioned by Turner L.J.); on the other hand, *Re Fry* was distinguished on the basis that there the transferor had not done all in his power to vest the property in the transferees, apparently because in order to perfect the transaction he would have had to have effected confirmatory transfers after the consent had been given. Neither of these distinctions is particularly convincing.

5–030   Difficulties also arise in relation to the role of the third party. Some third parties have a merely formal role in that they have no effective discretion to refuse to act—those responsible for registering a transfer of registered land or the transfer of shares in a public company clearly fall within this category. Is the Rule in *Re Rose* limited to situations such as these or does it also operate where the third party in question is able to decline to act? In both the

---

[49] [1952] Ch. 499.

[50] A gift made *inter vivos* within a prescribed minimum period prior to death is treated as forming part of the estate of the deceased for the purpose of calculating the tax payable on his estate. Under the present system of Inheritance Tax, a gift is exempt if made *inter vivos* more than seven years before death; if made more than three years before death, the tax is progressively reduced. At the time of *Re Rose*, the relevant period for Estate Duty had just been increased to five years without any progressive reductions but the testator's estate was subject to transitional provisions which produced the result stated in the text.

[51] (1862) 4 De G.F. & J. 264 at 274–275.

[52] [1946] Ch. 312.

[53] See *ante*, para 5–008.

[54] The settlor had covenanted to transfer bank shares to the defendant on trust for the plaintiff. The defendant already held a general Power of Attorney to transfer shares of the settlor so the settlor merely handed over the share certificates to him. However, neither he nor the settlor ever procured the entry in the books of the bank which was necessary for the transfer of the legal title.

cases named *Re Rose*, the directors of the companies in question were indeed entitled to refuse to register the share transfers and in the first case actually refused to do so for over 18 months. Although the point was not specifically considered, the two decisions must, therefore, establish that the rule will indeed operate even where the third party in question is entitled to decline to act. However, in this respect, it is once again difficult to reconcile the Rule in *Re Rose* with the decision in *Re Fry*.

Notwithstanding the doubts expressed in the previous two paragraphs, the Rule in *Re Rose* is unquestionably English law at the present time. The rule was applied by Lord Wilberforce in *Vandervell v. I.R.C.*[55] in order to justify his conclusion as to the scope of section 53(1)(c) of the Law of Property Act 1925.[56] More recently in *Mascall v. Mascall*[57] it was held that delivery by the transferor of registered land to the transferee of a duly executed transfer form and the land certificate will bring the rule into operation so that, pending the registration of the transferee's title, the transferor will hold the land in question on trust for the transferee.[58] Further in *Brown & Root Technology v. Sun Alliance and London Assurance Co.*[59] it was held that an assignment of a lease which had been duly executed with the consent of the landlord but had not even been stamped *ad valorem*, never mind presented to the Land Registry, had taken effect in equity under the rule.[60] The Rule in *Re Rose*, therefore, constitutes an established, although questionable, exception to the general rule that equity will not regard an ineffective transfer as taking effect in equity as a declaration of trust.   5–031

(C)   Where it is Unconscionable for the Transferor to Change his Mind
The wholly novel proposition that an ineffective transfer will take effect in equity where it is unconscionable for the transferor to change his mind was established by the Court of Appeal in *Pennington v. Waine*.[61] A donor intended to transfer 400 shares in a private company to her nephew. Having consulted the company's auditors, she duly signed the necessary transfer form but this was never delivered either to the company or to the nephew; had it been delivered to the company, the other shareholders would have had a right of pre-emption. She also wished him to become a director, which required him to hold at least one share, and they both signed a form agreeing to his appointment. After her death, the question arose as to whether the 400 shares formed part of the donor's residuary estate or were held on trust for the nephew. On the face of things, because of her failure to deliver the share transfer form, she had neither transferred the shares to him   5–032

---

[55] [1967] 2 A.C. 271. See *ante*, para 4–030.
[56] This argument actually begged the question being considered by the House of Lords (see Jones (1966) 24 C.L.J. 19) but that does not alter the fact that Lord Wilberforce applied the Rule in *Re Rose*.
[57] (1984) 50 P. & C.R. 119.
[58] Consequently, it was too late for the transferor to revoke his gift of the land in question to his son, who at the time of the purported revocation had had the transfer stamped *ad valorem* but had not yet presented it to the Land Registry.
[59] [1996] Ch. 51. This question did not arise in the subsequent appeal: (1996) 75 P. & C.R. 223.
[60] This prevented the original tenant from exercising a right to bring the lease to an end which could not be exercised following an effective assignment.
[61] [2002] 1 W.L.R. 2075. See Halliwell [2003] Conveyancer 192.

nor done all in her power to do so. However, the Court of Appeal held that the delivery of a share transfer form could be dispensed with in some circumstances. It would have been unconscionable for the donor to have recalled what she clearly intended to have been a gift once the nephew had signed the form agreeing to become a director. Consequently thereafter she, and after her death her estate, held the 400 shares on constructive trust for the nephew.

5–033   This decision seems to have been based on a complete misunderstanding of the decision of the Privy Council in *T. Choithram International S.A. v. Pagarani*.[62] Lord Browne-Wilkinson had there held that it would be as unconscionable for a settlor who had declared a trust when he was one of a number of trustees subsequently to resile from his declaration of trust as it would be if he had declared himself to be sole trustee.[63] In this context he stated[64] that, although equity would not aid a volunteer, it would not strive officiously to defeat a gift. The Court of Appeal[65] seized on the latter statement as authority for upholding the gift in *Pennington v. Waine*, completely overlooking the fact that in *T. Choithram International S.A. v. Pagarani* Lord Browne-Wilkinson had held that there had been a declaration of trust; in contrast, in *Pennington v. Waine*, the donor had neither declared a trust nor made a gift nor done everything in her power to make a gift. Further, in *T. Choithram International S.A. v. Pagarani* the Privy Council had upheld the declaration of an express trust, not as Arden L.J. suggested in *Pennington v. Waine*,[66] a constructive trust.

5–034   It is apparent that the result reached by the Court of Appeal in *Pennington v. Waine* is not supported by *T. Choithram International S.A. v. Pagarani*; in fact the Court of Appeal's decision contradicts every single previous authority, including all the cases in which the Rule in *Re Rose* has been applied.[67] Indeed Clarke L.J. acknowledged that hard cases make bad law.[68] It is, therefore, suggested that *Pennington v. Waine* was wrongly decided and should not be followed. However, at least for the moment, it constitutes a second exception to the general rule that equity will not regard an ineffective transfer as taking effect in equity as a declaration of trust.

5–035   If *Pennington v. Waine* is followed, it is conceivable that that decision could be interpreted in such a way as to affect the formalities rules which have already been discussed.[69] Failure to comply with section 53(1)(b) of the Law of Property Act 1925, which requires a trust of land to be evidenced in writing, makes the transaction in question unenforceable rather than wholly void. While any beneficiary who had acted to his detriment on the basis of an oral declaration of trust would inevitably be able to uphold that trust by

---

[62] [2001] 1 W.L.R. 1. See Halliwell [2003] Conveyancer 192.
[63] *ibid.* at 12.
[64] *ibid.*
[65] [2002] 1 W.L.R. 2075 at 2089 (Arden L.J.), 2105 (Clarke L.J.).
[66] *ibid.* at 2088.
[67] Arden L.J. and Clarke L.J. both stated that it was not crucial to the decision in the second case named *Re Rose* that in that case the share transfers had been delivered (*ibid.* at 2091 and 2103) but these statements are entirely speculative and, it is suggested, wrong in principle.
[68] *ibid.* at 2093.
[69] See *ante*, para 4–008 *et seq.*

relying on an equitable proprietary estoppel,[70] until now a beneficiary who has not so acted has been unable to prevent the settlor (or, more realistically his trustee in bankruptcy or his residuary beneficiaries) from recovering the land in question at any time. But it may now follow from *Pennington v. Waine* that it would be regarded as unconscionable for such a person to do so even if the beneficiary had not acted to his detriment. It is to be hoped that this does not turn out to be a further consequence of this controversial decision. However, it does not seem that the decision could operate in a similar way in respect of a failure to comply with section 53(1)(c) of the Law of Property Act 1925 since such a failure renders the disposition in question wholly void and reliance on such a provision in the absence of detriment does not appear to be capable of being classified as unconscionable.

4. *By Virtue of Other Exceptions to the Rule in* Milroy v. Lord

(A)   The Rule in *Strong v. Bird*[71]
The decision in *Strong v. Bird* itself had nothing to do with the complete   **5–036**
constitution of trusts; it concerned the release of debts. The defendant had borrowed £1,000 from his stepmother, who lived in his house paying him £212.50[72] a quarter for board. They agreed that the debt should be paid off by the deduction of £100 from each quarter's payment. Deductions of this amount were duly made for two quarters but on the third quarter-day the stepmother generously refused to hold to the agreement any longer and paid the full £212.50 board on each subsequent quarter-day until her death four years later, in other words long after the whole of the loan would have been repaid had the deductions continued. She had appointed the defendant as sole executor of her will, which he duly proved. One of the beneficiaries of the stepmother's residuary estate then claimed that the defendant still owed the balance of the debt to the estate. At common law it had long been established that a debt can no longer be enforced after the death of the creditor if the creditor has appointed the debtor as one of his executors[73] (the debtor does not actually have to prove the will provided that he has survived the testator and has not renounced his executorship; his right to do so suffices[74]). Although in principle the debtor nevertheless remains liable to the estate in equity, in *Strong v. Bird* Jessel M.R. held that equity will deny any claim by those entitled to the debt under the will of the creditor where the creditor intended to release the debt during his lifetime and, up until the moment of his death, had a continuing intention so to do. This was readily demonstrated in *Strong v. Bird* by the fact that the stepmother had continued to pay the full £212.50 per quarter; consequently, the defendant did not have to pay the debt to those entitled to the stepmother's residuary estate). There does not appear to be any requirement that the appointment of the debtor as executor should occur after the release of the debt because, although the point does not appear to have been specifically raised, this principle was

---

[70] See *post*, para 5–055 *et seq*.
[71] (1874) 18 Eq. 315.
[72] In fact, of course, the pre-decimalisation equivalent, £212 10s.
[73] At least since *Wankford v. Wankford* (1704) 1 Salk. 299.
[74] *Re Applebee* [1891] 3 Ch. 422.

applied by the Court of Appeal in *Re Pink*,[75] where the debtor had been appointed executor before the testator released the debt.

5–037　　The developed Rule in *Strong v. Bird* extends this principle to gifts and establishes that, where an ineffective gift has been made *inter vivos* and the donor maintains up until the time of his death a continuing intention to give that property to the donee, the requirement for the transfer of legal title by donor to donee can be fulfilled if the legal title vests in the donee as executor of the donor by operation of law on the death of the donor. In other words, the appointment by the donor of the intended donee as his executor perfects the intention of the donor and completes the gift, displacing by virtue of being first in time the equity of anyone else who is entitled to the property in question under the will of the donor. This was held in *Re Stewart*[76] where a husband had bought some bonds which he intended to give to his wife; however, he died before they had actually been delivered to him and so he was unable to assign them to her in his lifetime. Her appointment as one of five executors, coupled with his continuing intention to give the bonds to her, was held to be sufficient to perfect the gift. However, it has been held that the effect of the rule is limited to specific existing property[77]; thus a continuing unfulfilled intention to make a gift of a sum of money will not be perfected by the intended donee subsequently becoming the donor's executor. This restriction to specific existing property also makes it questionable whether the rule is applicable to a residuary gift.

5–038　　Further, both the immediate intention and the continuing intention to make a gift *inter vivos* must be established. An intention to do so only on death is clearly insufficient.[78] In *Re Freeland*[79] the owner of a car promised to give it to the plaintiff whom she subsequently appointed as one of her executrices. However, she did not actually purport to give it to her and, subsequently, she lent it to the defendant, the other executrix. The Court of Appeal held that the absence of any immediate intention to make the gift prevented the rule from applying and, even if there had been such an intention, the making of the loan was inconsistent with any continuing intention to do so. Similarly, in *Re Wale*,[80] a settlement recited that the settlor had transferred the trust property to the trustees but in fact the settlor never did so; she subsequently forgot all about the settlement and treated the property which she had not transferred to the trustees as her own. She subsequently appointed the trustees as two of her three executors. It was argued that this perfected the gift but Upjohn J. held that she lacked the continuing intention to transfer the property which was necessary in order for the Rule in *Strong v. Bird* to apply.

5–039　　Thus far it is just about possible to justify the existence of the rule. Even though the vast majority of testators will necessarily be unaware of its

---

[75] [1912] 2 Ch. 528.

[76] [1908] 2 Ch. 251.

[77] *Re Innes* [1910] 1 Ch. 188.

[78] *Re Hyslop* [1893] 3 Ch. 522 (actually a case on the release of a debt).

[79] [1952] Ch. 110.

[80] [1956] 1 W.L.R. 1346. There was also held to be no such intention in *Re Eiser's Will Trusts* [1937] 1 All E.R. 244, where the creditor subsequently took security for the amount of the debt.

existence, an executor is at least expressly nominated by his testator. However, it is less easy to justify the subsequent extension of the rule to administrators. This occurred in *Re James*[81] where the deceased had, on the earlier death of his father, handed over the title deeds of his father's house to his father's housekeeper. This was of course insufficient to vest the legal title to the house in the housekeeper (which would have necessitated a deed) but she continued to live there until the son died and it was clear that he had at all times intended her to have the house. When he died intestate, she obtained appointment as his administratrix and so the legal title to the house became vested in her by operation of law. It was held that this fortuitous occurrence brought the Rule in *Strong v. Bird* into operation and thus perfected the incomplete gift to her.

No administrator is ever nominated by the deceased. Who becomes **5–040** administrator depends, in principle, on the order of preference set out in the Non-Contentious Probate Rules and, as between relatives of the same degree or, in the absence of any relatives, other beneficiaries of a will, it is often a matter of pure chance which of them ends up as administrator. It, therefore, seems highly unreasonable that that person should obtain an advantage over the other beneficiaries by reason of his appointment. This was indeed precisely the reason why the original common law rule relating to the release of debts was never applied to administrators. Exactly these criticisms of *Re James* were forcefully made in *Re Gonin (deceased)*[82] by Walton J., who doubted the decision in that case. However, since both counsel had accepted its correctness, Walton J. nevertheless applied it to an ineffective gift *inter vivos* of a house and its furniture by a mother to the daughter who had devoted her life to caring for her parents; however, on the facts, he held that sufficient continuing intention had been made out in respect only of the furniture and not of the house.

Other uncertainties remain. It is probable that, like the common law rule, **5–041** the rule in *Strong v. Bird* gives the executor or administrator priority only over those beneficially entitled to the estate and not over the creditors of the estate; however, this has never been the subject of judicial comment in this jurisdiction.[83] Nor does it appear to have been expressly decided whether the rule applies where the imperfect gift is in favour of the executor or administrator as trustee rather than beneficially. However, in *Re Wale*,[84] where the rule was not in fact applied, no objection was made on the grounds that in that case the executors would have taken as trustees. Consequently, it appears highly likely that the rule in *Strong v. Bird* does indeed apply in such circumstances. For present purposes, it should be emphasised that it is only if this is the case that the Rule in *Strong v. Bird* will be capable of operating in such a way as to constitute an otherwise incompletely constituted trust.

---

[81] [1935] Ch. 449.
[82] [1964] Ch. 288.
[83] The question has been considered in Australia; see *Bone v. Stamp Duty Commissioner* (1974) 132 C.L.R. 38 at 53 (High Court of Australia).
[84] [1956] 1 W.L.R. 1346.

(B) The Principle Enunciated in *Re Ralli's Will Trusts*[85]

5–042   In this case, a settlor entered into a covenant to transfer any existing or after-acquired property to the trustees of her marriage settlement. At the time of this settlement, she already held existing property caught by this covenant, namely an interest in remainder in the residue of her father's estate subject to the prior life interest of her mother. She never assigned this interest to the trustees of the marriage settlement at any time prior to her death 32 years later. Her mother actually survived her so that it was over four years after her death before her interest in remainder vested in possession. At that point the sole trustee of her father's will was, fortuitously, also the sole trustee of the marriage settlement. He was, therefore, in the former capacity holding on trust for her an interest which she should have assigned to him in the latter capacity. The question therefore arose as to whether this fortuitous occurrence had the effect of completely constituting a trust of the interest in favour of the beneficiaries of the marriage settlement.

5–043   As has already been seen,[86] Buckley J. actually held, as a matter of construction, that the settlor had declared herself to be a trustee for her marriage settlement of any property caught by the covenant pending transfer of that property to the trustees. Thus her interest in remainder had, ever since the date of the marriage settlement, been subject to a completely constituted trust in favour of that settlement. Its beneficiaries could, therefore, obviously enforce this trust without any need to rely on the fact that the interest had fortuitously vested in their trustee in another capacity. This decision on construction was obviously enough to dispose of the case. However, Buckley J. went on to hold that, since the interest in question had fortuitously reached the hands of the person to whom the settlor should have transferred it, the trust of that property in favour of the beneficiaries of the marriage settlement had by this means also become completely constituted, this time by transfer rather than by declaration. He went on to say that it was totally irrelevant how the property had come into the hands of the person to whom it should have been transferred; the mere fact, fortuitous though it was, that the property had reached his hands was sufficient to have completely constituted the trust. Nor was it of any significance that the result of the case would, on this ground, have been different had anyone other than the trustee of the marriage settlement been the trustee of the will.

5–044   It does not seem appropriate to regard the statements of Buckley J. merely as a further extension of the Rule in *Strong v. Bird*. It is admittedly of no great significance that the person whose hands the property had reached had no beneficial interest therein—it has never been expressly held that the Rule in *Strong v. Bird* is limited to beneficial gifts to executors and administrators and, as has already been indicated, no objection was taken in *Re Wale*[87] to the applicability of the rule on this ground. But it is questionable whether the Rule in *Strong v. Bird* is applicable to a residuary gift, given its restriction to

---

[85] [1964] Ch. 288.
[86] See *ante*, para 5–022.
[87] [1957] 1 W.L.R. 1346.

specific existing property.[88] Further, the trustee in question does not appear to have been either the executor or the administrator of the settlor and no evidence was either required or given that the settlor had had any continuing intention of transferring the property in question to the trustees of her marriage settlement at any time during the 32 years which had elapsed between the creation of the settlement and her death. It is, therefore, clear that virtually none of the established requirements of the Rule in *Strong v. Bird* was actually satisfied in *Re Ralli's Will Trusts*.

It therefore seems more appropriate to regard the statements of Buckley J. as authority for the existence of a wholly distinct principle which can be formulated in the following way: if property of any type reaches without impropriety[89] the hands of a person to whom it should already have been transferred as a trustee inter vivos, the trust in question will become completely constituted by transfer whether or not there is any continuing intention on the part of the settlor that this should occur. Since it seems from the judgment of Buckley J. that his statements were intended by him to amount to a second *ratio decidendi* rather than merely *obiter dicta*, this distinct principle may well represent the present law, if it does, it will therefore also be capable of operating so as to constitute an otherwise incompletely constituted trust.

5–045

However, it must also be said that any such principle appears to be inconsistent with the earlier decision in *Re Brooks's Settlement Trusts*,[90] which was not cited to Buckley J. In this case, under the terms of a voluntary settlement the settlor had covenanted to transfer to the trustees any property which he might acquire under his parents' marriage settlement. A bank was trustee of both settlements so that, when a sum was subsequently appointed to the settlor as a result of the exercise of the powers contained in the marriage settlement, that sum was already in the hands of the trustees to whom he had covenanted to transfer it. At that time, for reasons which will be considered later in this section,[91] neither the trustees nor the beneficiaries of the voluntary settlement could have enforced against the settlor his covenant to transfer that sum. Consequently Farwell J. held that, despite the coincidence of trustees, the settlor was entitled to receive the sum appointed to him. In the light of this decision, it must therefore be questionable whether the novel principle enunciated by Buckley J. in *Re Ralli's Will Trusts* does indeed actually represent the law; it remains to be seen which of the two decisions is followed in future.

5–046

(C) *Donationes Mortis Causa*
The rules governing *donationes mortis causa*, or death bed gifts, can also have the effect of constituting an otherwise incomplete transfer. Three general

5–047

---

[88] See *Re Innes* [1952] 1 Ch. 188, *ante*, para 5–037.
[89] This point was particularly emphasised by Buckley J. His principle would therefore clearly not have applied in the event that the property had reached the hands of the trustee as the result of a disposition of property in breach of trust.
[90] [1939] 1 Ch. 993.
[91] See *post*, paras 5–104–5–110.

requirements for such a gift were identified in *Sen v. Headley*[92] by Nourse L.J., reformulating similar statements in earlier authorities.[93]

"First, the gift must be made in contemplation, although not necessarily in expectation, of impending death. Secondly, the gift must be made upon the condition that it is to be absolute and perfected only on the donor's death, being revocable until that event occurs and ineffective if it does not. Thirdly, there must be a delivery of the subject matter of the gift, or the essential indicia of title thereto, which amounts to a parting with dominion and not mere physical possession over the subject matter of the gift."

(1) The gift must have been made in contemplation of impending death

5–048   All that is necessary is that the donor contemplated his impending death at the time of the gift; there is no requirement that he is expecting to die in the immediate future. Although the point has never been expressly decided in England,[94] the test seems to be subjective and not objective. It is the donor's own state of mind, not the actual circumstances, which is material. Moreover, the title of the donee will not be invalidated if the donor dies from some cause other than the disease from which he knew that he was suffering.[95] In *Wilkes v. Allington*,[96] the donor was suffering from an incurable disease and made the gift knowing that he had not long to live. As things turned out, he lived an even shorter time than he had thought, because he died two months later from pneumonia. The gift, however, remained valid.

(2) The gift must have been conditional on the death of the donor

5–049   The gift must be made subject to the condition that it is to be absolute and perfected only on the death of the donor; the gift must, therefore, be revocable at all times prior to his death and ineffective if the donor does not in fact die as contemplated. In this respect a *donatio mortis causa* is different from other types of gift inter vivos; the latter are absolute whereas a *donatio mortis causa* is necessarily conditional on death. The condition is not usually expressed in so many words but an inference to this effect will usually be drawn from the fact of the illness of the donor.[97] This of course means not only that the subject matter of the gift will revert to the donor if he recovers from his illness but also that he can revoke his gift at any time during his

---

[92] [1991] Ch. 425 at 431.

[93] Particularly *Cain v. Moon* [1896] 2 Q.B. 283 at 286 *per* Lord Russell of Killowen C.J.

[94] It appears that an objective test has been adopted in Canada; see 81 L.Q.R. (1965) 21 and the Canadian cases cited *post*, n.95.

[95] It need not, perhaps, necessarily be illness, though it normally is. Nor apparently need the donor be *in extremis*. The contrary suggestion is made in *Thomson v. Meechan* [1958] D.L.R. 103, but this seems incorrect. For a similar suggestion, see *Canada Trust Co. v. Labrador* [1962] O.R. 151. See also 81 L.Q.R. (1965) 21.

[96] [1931] 2 Ch. 104. See also *Mills v. Shields* [1948] I.R. 367 (death from suicide). *Re Dudman* [1925] Ch. 553 held contemplation by the deceased of suicide to be insufficient but, since this case was decided before the Suicide Act 1961 provided that suicide was and is no longer a crime, it is arguable, but by no means certain, that a *donatio mortis causa* made in such circumstances may now be valid.

[97] *Re Lillingston* [1952] 2 All E.R. 184.

lifetime.[98] The donor will be regarded as having expressly revoked his gift if he resumes dominion over it[99]; there is also some authority for the proposition that it will also be sufficient if the donor simply informs the donee of his intention to revoke.[100] However, a purported revocation by will will not suffice simply because the will does not take effect until the death of the testator, by which time the donee will have become unconditionally entitled.[101] But the fact that the gift is conditional in this sense does not detract from the basic requirement that, for a *donatio mortis causa* to be effective, it must, like any other gift, be a present gift and not a gift to take effect at some time in the future.[102]

(3)   There must have been some form of delivery from donor to donee
The donor must have delivered to the donee either the subject matter of the   5–050
gift or the means or part of the means by which the subject matter can be obtained. The nature of this requirement varies according to the nature of the subject matter of the *donatio mortis causa* but it is in all cases a pre-condition that the donor intended to part with dominion of the subject matter rather than merely physical possession of what has been delivered[103]; this question is ultimately a matter of fact.

No difficulties normally arise in the case of personal property which is   5–051
capable of physical delivery. Handing the chattel itself to the donee will not only constitute delivery[104] but will also pass the legal title. Sufficient delivery will also occur if the donee is given some means of obtaining the chattel such as the keys of a cupboard in which it is stored.[105] The circumstances of the delivery must also be sufficient to demonstrate that the donor can no longer interfere with the subject matter of the gift.[106]

However, some items of personal property, such as a bank account, are   5–052
choses in action and so are incapable of physical delivery.[107] In such circumstances, the gift will be ineffective unless the donee can compel the personal representative of the deceased to complete the gift of the chose in action to him. The essential pre-condition which, according to the conventional formulation, must be satisfied is that the donor must have delivered to the donee whatever document constitutes the essential evidence of his title to

---

[98] *Staniland v. Willott* (1850) 3 Mac. & G. 664.

[99] *Bunn v. Markham* (1816) 7 Taunt. 224 at 231.

[100] *Jones v. Selby* (1710) Prec.Ch. 300 at 303. Resuming mere possession for the purpose of ensuring safe custody of the subject matter is not enough; *Re Hawkins* [1924] 2 Ch. 47.

[101] *Jones v. Selby* (1710) Prec.Ch. 300.

[102] *Re Ward* [1946] 2 All E.R. 206.

[103] *Birch v. Treasury Solicitor* [1951] Ch. 298.

[104] See *Re Cole* [1964] Ch. 175.

[105] *Re Mustapha* (1891) 8 T.L.R. 160; see also *Re Lillingston* [1952] 2 All E.R. 184.

[106] *Re Craven's Estate* [1937] Ch. 423 at 427, where the delivery of one of two duplicate keys was held to be insufficient. However, the fact that a donor had possibly retained a second set of car keys which he was too ill to use was held to be insignificant in *Woodard v. Woodard* [1995] 3 All E.R. 980, as was the retention by a donor of a set of keys to a house to which he knew he would not return in *Sen v. Headley* [1991] Ch. 425.

[107] Some choses in action, such as bearer shares and bearer bonds, are of course transferable by delivery. Delivery of such choses in action will therefore be sufficient to constitute an effective *donatio mortis causa* and so also will delivery of the key of a box containing them; *Re Wasserberg* [1915] 1 Ch. 195.

the chose in action in question. This test was applied in *Re Weston*[108] where a dying man had handed over to his fiancée his Post Office Savings Book; this action was held sufficient to constitute an effective *donatio mortis causa* of the savings recorded in it. In the course of his judgment, Byrne J. expressed the view that the document in question must also contain all the essential terms on which the subject matter of the chose in action was held. However, it is easy to visualise circumstances in which a strict application of this rule would work injustice, although it did not do so in *Re Weston* itself. Consequently, the Court of Appeal was clearly right expressly to disapprove this view in *Birch v. Treasury Solicitor*,[109] which concerned a similar gift of a bank deposit pass-book. The correct approach to be followed is, in the words of Evershed M.R. in that case, that delivery must be made of the "essential indicia of title, possession or production of which entitles the possessor to the money or property purported to be given".[110] This principle was applied by the Court of Appeal in *Sen v. Headley*,[111] where the authorities on *dona-tiones mortis causa* of choses in action were reviewed particularly fully.

5–053   However, *Sen v. Headley* actually concerned an attempted *donatio mortis causa* of land. In that case, three days before his death the deceased had, with the necessary intention, delivered to the donee the only key to the steel box which contained the title deeds to his unregistered house and land; she already had a set of keys to the house in question and after the deceased's death found the box in a cupboard. Land is, of course, if anything more incapable of physical delivery than a chose in action and in *Duffield v. Elwes*[112] Lord Eldon L.C. had appeared to suggest that land cannot be the subject matter of a *donatio mortis causa*. However, in *Sen v. Headley* the Court of Appeal stated that anomalies do not justify anomalous exceptions, that to make a distinction in the case of land would be to make just such an exception, and that a *donatio mortis causa* of land was "neither more nor less anomalous than any other".[113] Consequently, since the Court of Appeal in *Birch v. Treasury Solicitor* had extended rather than restricted the operation of the doctrine of *donationes mortis causa*, the court held that land is indeed

---

[108] [1902] 1 Ch. 680. A similar conclusion was reached in *Darlow v. Sparks* [1938] 2 All E.R. 235 in respect of national savings certificates and, rather more unexpectedly, in *Re Mead* (1880) 15 Ch.D. 651, in respect of a cheque drawn by a third party in favour of the donor (unexpected because the cheque was capable of being endorsed; the decision would be unexceptionable in respect of a modern cheque stated to be "A/C Payee only" and so not endorsable). However, a cheque drawn by the donor in favour of the donee is not sufficient to take effect as a *donatio mortis causa* because such a cheque is simply a revocable order to the bank to make payment to the payee which will inevitably be revoked by the donor's death (*Re Leaper* [1916] 1 Ch. 579).

[109] [1951] Ch. 298.

[110] *ibid.* at 311.

[111] [1991] Ch. 425. See Halliwell [1991] Conv. 307.

[112] (1827) 1 Bli. (N.S.) 497.

[113] [1991] Ch. 425 at p.440. Every *donatio mortis causa* circumvented the Wills Act 1837 and the fact that *inter vivos* transfers of land were subject to statutory formalities not applicable to pure personalty did not constitute a more substantial obstacle since any trust needed to give effect to any *donatio mortis causa* would be a resulting or constructive trust and so exempt from those formalities anyway (the trust would presumably be a resulting trust if the personal representatives of the donor agreed to be bound by the *donatio mortis causa* subject to proof of its constituent elements but a constructive trust if they sought to rely on the provisions of the Wills Act 1837 to deny its existence).

capable of passing by way of a *donatio mortis causa*. The court then went on to hold that the fact that the donor also had a set of keys to the house and had obviously retained the theoretical ability to deal with the title to it despite the delivery of the key to the donee did not, on the facts, amount to a retention of dominion. The *donatio mortis causa* was therefore upheld. However, it is obviously unlikely that anything less than delivery of the deeds (or, in the case of registered land, an official copy of the entries on the Land Register[114]) or the means of obtaining them will ever be held to constitute an appropriate delivery in respect of land.

Finally, it must be emphasised that, in the case both of choses in action   **5–054** and of land, the legal title to the property in question will not be automatically acquired by the donee as a result of a delivery in the manner prescribed. The gift of whatever property is represented by whatever has been delivered will still be imperfect. The effect of establishing a *donatio mortis causa* is instead that the donor's personal representatives will be compelled to perfect the gift.[115] It is, therefore, in the case of *donationes mortis causa* of choses in action and of land that equity, contrary to the Rule in *Milroy v. Lord*, compels the completion of what would otherwise be an incomplete gift.

(D)   The Doctrine of Equitable Proprietary Estoppel[116]

(1)   The nature of the doctrine
If the doctrine of estoppel were still limited to the sense in which it has   **5–055** traditionally been generally applied, it would barely be worthy of mention here. Since the traditional form of the doctrine operated only defensively so as to prevent a party from asserting rights of his which, but for that doctrine, he would have been able to assert, it could obviously not operate so as to perfect an imperfect gift or complete an incompletely constituted trust.[117]

---

[114] This possibility was not specifically envisaged by the Court of Appeal but must follow from their finding that it did not matter that the donor had retained the theoretical ability to deal with his title. If the proprietor of registered land which is mortgaged has no more than a copy of the Charge Certificate and the Land Certificate is held by the Land Registry, delivery of the copy of the Charge Certificate will presumably suffice; however, this situation can only arise if the land was mortgaged under the Land Registration Act 1925 prior to the coming into force of the Land Registration Act 2002, which abolished Charge Certificates and replaced Land Certificates by official copies of the entries on the registered title).

[115] *Re Dillon* (1890) 44 Ch.D. 76 at 82–83.

[116] See *Phipson on Evidence* 16th edn (London, Sweet & Maxwell, 2005), 116–124 (see also its cumulative supplements); K.J. Gray and S.F. Gray, *Elements of Land Law* 4th edn (London, Lexis Nexis, 2004), 474–520; Halliwell, *Equity and Good Conscience* 2nd edn (London, Old Bailey Press, 2004), Chap. 2; M. Pawlowski, *The Doctrine of Proprietary Estoppel* (London, Sweet & Maxwell, 1996); M. Spence, *Protecting Reliance* (Oxford, Hart Publishing, 1999).

[117] This was predominantly so in a case of so-called promissory estoppel but the traditional distinctions between promissory estoppel and equitable proprietary estoppel have been eroded by recent authorities. See particularly *Taylors Fashions v. Liverpool Victoria Trustees Company* (1976) [1982] Q.B. 133N; *Amalgamated Investment & Property Company v. Texas Commerce International Bank* [1982] Q.B. 84 (leave to appeal to the House of Lords was subsequently not granted [1982] 1 W.L.R. 1). One distinction which must nevertheless remain is that promissory estoppel, unlike equitable proprietary estoppel, is not permanent in its effect. The promisor can resile from his position if he gives the promisee notice which provides him with a reasonable opportunity of resuming his former position; see *Re Vandervell's Trusts (No.2)* [1964] Ch. 269 at 301, *per* Megarry J.

However, the modern principle of equitable proprietary estoppel can be used offensively, "as a sword" as it is sometimes described, in order to perfect an imperfect gift if, for example, the donor has stood by and watched the donee improve property or do other acts to his detriment on the supposition that there has been or will be an effective gift.

5–056　　　　The doctrine appears to be of early origin[118] but until relatively recently had evolved in the form of three separate overlapping categories of cases: first, cases concerning imperfect gifts; secondly, cases concerning common expectations, where parties have consistently dealt with one another in such a way as to cause one of them to rely on a shared supposition that he would acquire rights of some kind in the land of the other; and, thirdly, cases of unilateral mistake, where the owner of land has stood by and allowed another person to act to his detriment on a mistaken belief that he has a legally enforceable interest in the land in question. The principles established by these three groups of authorities have now been synthesised into the modern principle of proprietary estoppel. The key decision in this process seems to have been *Taylor Fashions v. Liverpool Victoria Trustees Company*.[119] In this case Oliver J. rejected the notion that the principle was narrowly confined to the three categories of cases already mentioned. Instead his Lordship found support in these three groups of cases for "a much wider jurisdiction to interfere in cases where the assertion of strict legal rights is found by the courts to be unconscionable".[120] He therefore held that the purchasers of a freehold reversion were estopped from claiming to have taken free for want of registration of options to renew leases which, at the time of their grant, were wrongly thought by conveyancers not to be registrable. The most recent summary of the present law by the Court of Appeal may be found in *Uglow v. Uglow*.[121]

5–057　　　　As a result of this synthesis, it is now clear that a successful claim of proprietary estoppel involves four elements: first, an assurance or a representation by the owner of or the person entitled to some form of property, usually but not necessarily land; secondly, reliance on that assurance or representation by the person to whom it is made; thirdly, some unconscionable disadvantage or detriment suffered by the person to whom the assurance or representation is made; and, fourthly, failure to satisfy the minimum equity which is necessary in order to do justice to the person to whom the assurance or representation is made and in order to avoid an unconscionable or disproportionate result.

5–058　　　　The first element will be satisfied when the owner of the property in question, expressly or by necessary implication, raises in another person an expectation that that person will obtain some interest or entitlement in that property which he would not otherwise have; it is sufficient if the assurance is that its maker will enter into a binding contract relating to the property in question with the other person.[122] The assurance can range from an express request to incur expenditure through encouragement or incitement so to do,

---

[118] See *Foxcroft v. Lester* (1703) 2 Vern. 456.
[119] (1976) [1982] Q.B. 133N.
[120] *ibid.* at 147.
[121] [2004] EWCA Civ. 987, [2004] W.T.L.R. 1183.
[122] *Cobbe v. Yeoman's Row Management Ltd* [2006] EWCA Civ. 1139, [2006] 1 W.L.R. 2964 at 2978 *per* Mummery L.J.

to silent abstention from the assertion of rights, although in the last case the owner of the property obviously has to be shown to have at least some knowledge of the mistaken belief of the other person. The latter must establish both this first element and the third element, namely that he has acted to his detriment; if he can do so, it is for the maker of the assurance to disprove the second element, that the other person acted in reliance on the assurance.[123] The fourth element is a negative one, namely that, despite the fact that the first three elements have been satisfied, no remedy will be awarded if the equity of the person to whom the assurance or representation has been made has been satisfied by the benefits which he has in fact already received.[124]

Where such an equitable proprietary estoppel has arisen, the court enjoys very considerable flexibility in that a remedy can be provided appropriate to the circumstances of each individual case. Such remedies range from the grant of an unqualified estate in fee simple or lesser interest in or over land such as a lease, or an easement through the grant of a right to occupy the land to the grant of monetary compensation—obviously only the latter is possible in the case of property other than land; it is also possible for a grant of a right in or a right to occupy land to be combined with a grant of monetary compensation.[125] The doctrine is of course still developing and not only is there an increasing overlap between the doctrine of equitable proprietary estoppel and the "common intention constructive trust" (as will be seen in the chapter on constructive trusts[126]) but also an equitable proprietary estoppel has been held itself to give rise to a constructive trust where it is unconscionable for the estopped party to deny its existence.[127] **5–059**

The terminology employed in the majority of the cases decided prior to *Taylor Fashions v. Liverpool Victoria Trustees Company* would be likely to be very different if those cases were to recur today. However, there is no doubt whatsoever that all the cases in which equitable proprietary estoppels were upheld would still be decided in the same way and they consequently remain important as illustrations of the situations, formerly quite distinct, which today fall within the doctrine of equitable proprietary estoppel. The difference today is that the enunciation of a broader general jurisdiction means that equitable proprietary estoppels are now likely to be upheld in situations in which this would not formerly have been the case. **5–060**

(2) The relevance of the doctrine for the constitution of trusts

For the purposes of the complete constitution of trusts, what are important are the cases concerning imperfect gifts. A useful starting point is *Dillwyn v. Llewelyn*[128] where a father put his son into possession of land without a conveyance. It was intended that the son should build a house on the land. **5–061**

---

[123] *Wayling v. Jones* (1993) 60 P. & C.R. 170 (CA) at 173 *per* Balcombe L.J., citing *Greasley v. Cooke* [1980] 1 W.L.R. 1306 (CA).

[124] *Uglow v. Uglow* [2004] EWCA Civ. 97, [2004] W.T.L.R. 1183 at 1192 *per* Mummery L.J.; *Sledmore v. Dalby* (1996) 72 P. & C.R. 196 (CA).

[125] *Gillett v. Holt* [2001] Ch. 210 (CA); *Jennings v. Rice* [2002] EWCA Civ. 159, [2002] W.T.L.R. 367.

[126] See *post*, para 10–291 *et seq.*

[127] *Yaxley v. Gotts* [2000] Ch. 162.

[128] (1862) 4 De G.F. & J. 517.

The son successfully claimed that the land should be formally conveyed to him. Lord Westbury L.C. said: "If A puts B in possession of a piece of land and tells him 'I give it to you that you may build a house on it', and B, on the strength of that promise, with the knowledge of A, expends a large sum of money in building a house accordingly, I cannot doubt that the donee acquires a right from the subsequent transaction to call on the donor to perform that contract, and complete the imperfect donation which was made." In other words, the subsequent acts of the donor gave the donee a right which he did not acquire from the original gift. In the much more recent decision in *Pascoe v. Turner*,[129] the parties had lived together in a house as man and wife and the man had encouraged or acquiesced in the woman improving the house in the belief that it belonged to her. He was ordered to execute a conveyance of the house to her. In both these cases, the donee took an estate in fee simple. However, as has already been mentioned, the estate or interest of the donee depends on the circumstances of the case. Thus, in *Inwards v. Baker*,[130] the donee was held to be entitled to remain in occupation for as long as he wished.

5–062   All the cases discussed so far were cases between the donee and the donor (or the latter's estate). *E.R. Ives Investments v. High*,[131] on the other hand, was a case between the donee and a successor in title of the donor for value. In that case, the donee, the defendant, was allowed a right of way for as long as the plaintiff and his successors in title maintained the foundations of a building on the defendant's land; this was because the plaintiff's predecessors in title, by licensing the defendant to use the yard in question, had encouraged him to build a garage on his own adjoining land in such a position that it could only be entered from the yard, something which had created an estoppel in his favour. It was also held that the equitable interest which had arisen as a result of this estoppel was not subject to the rules regarding the registration of land charges,[132] which of course only apply to unregistered land; consequently, the equitable interest was governed by the equitable doctrine of notice and bound the whole world other than a bona fide purchaser for value of a legal interest without notice. Interests protected by proprietary estoppel are also capable of binding the successors in title of the party originally estopped where the land in question is registered—this is specifically provided by the Land Registration Act 2002.[133] However, whether such an interest will be so binding depends on the general principles of registered conveyancing; it will, therefore, only be binding if it has been protected on the register unless its holder has an interest which overrides the registration of the title of the third party by virtue of his actual occupation of the land.[134]

5–063   These decisions were applied in *Crabb v. Arun District Council*[135] where there was an agreement "in principle", not amounting to a binding contract,

---

[129] [1979] 1 W.L.R. 431.
[130] [1965] 2 Q.B. 29. See also *Ward v. Kirkland* [1967] Ch. 194, where a perpetual easement of drainage was granted.
[131] [1967] 2 Q.B. 289.
[132] Under what is now the Land Charges Act 1972.
[133] Land Registration Act 2002, s.114.
[134] Land Registration Act 2002, Sch.1, para.3, Sch.3, para.3.
[135] [1976] Ch. 179.

that the plaintiff should have a right of access, in reliance on which he sold the front portion of his land without reserving a right of way over it giving access to the back portion. The Court of Appeal held that this was a case of equitable proprietary estoppel and that he was therefore entitled to an easement or licence[136]; he had been encouraged to act to his detriment by the defendant's conduct.[137] Similarly, in *Jones v. Jones*[138] a father had led his son to believe that a house would be his home for the rest of his life, on the basis of which expectation the son had given up his job and moved in. It was held that he could pray in aid the doctrine of estoppel proprietary estoppel and that both the father and his administratrix were estopped from turning the son out during his lifetime. Again in *Re Sharpe*,[139] where an aged aunt had lent money for the purchase of a house by her nephew on the basis that she could live there with him and his wife, it was held that an irrevocable licence to occupy the house had arisen in favour of the aunt until such time as the loan was repaid.

Further, as has already been seen, although the person who is seeking to rely on equitable proprietary estoppel must establish both the existence of the assurance and that he has acted to his detriment, it is for the maker of the assurance to establish that the other did not act in reliance on it. Thus in *Greasley v. Cooke*,[140] assurances had been given that the defendant could remain in a house, where she had not only been employed as a maid for more than 40 years but had also lived with one of the children of the family as man and wife; it was held that these assurances raised an equity in her favour and it was to be presumed that she had acted on the faith of those assurances. The plaintiffs failed to rebut this presumption.[141]

5–064

It used to be thought that the conduct of the owner of the property in question could only be held to give rise to the inequitable consequences which are a necessary ingredient of establishing a proprietary estoppel if he was aware of the true facts. This is certainly still a requirement for the type of cases traditionally classified as cases of unilateral mistake. However, it no longer appears to be essential for the type of cases under discussion at present, cases concerning imperfect gifts.[142]

5–065

Admittedly Megarry J. did uphold the existence of such a requirement at first instance in *Re Vandervell's Trusts (No.2)*.[143] He refused to find an estoppel, pointing out that, although Vandervell had concurred in the dealings with the moneys and shares carried out by the trust company[144] following the exercise of the option, the company had not been able to show that he

5–066

---

[136] An easement according to Lord Denning M.R. and Lawton L.J.; an easement or licence according to Scarman L.J.

[137] One of the acts to his detriment was the sale of land separate from the land over which the access was to be granted. Normally, the acts involve expenditure in relation to the actual land intended to be disposed of.

[138] [1977] 1 W.L.R. 438.

[139] [1980] 1 W.L.R. 219.

[140] [1980] 1 W.L.R. 1306.

[141] Lord Denning M.R. said (at 1311) that the incurring of expenditure of money or other prejudice was not a necessary element. However, this appears to be far too wide a generalisation; see at 1313 *per* Dunn L.J.

[142] Nor is it for cases concerning common expectation.

[143] [1974] Ch. 269 at 301.

[144] These dealings are referred to *ante*, para 5–018.

even knew that he was the beneficial owner of the option at the time of its exercise. However, the question was not fully argued before Megarry J. and the opposite view was subsequently taken in the Court of Appeal. The court was of the opinion that, if Vandervell had been alive, his concurrence in these dealings would have estopped him from denying the existence of a beneficial interest vested in the children's settlement of which the trust company was trustee; consequently, his executors could be in no better position. This was admittedly not the only ground on which the Court of Appeal decided the case[145] and it might, therefore, be a mistake to read too much into these remarks about proprietary estoppel. In particular, knowledge cannot possibly be, as the Court of Appeal appeared to suggest, totally irrelevant.

5–067   The better view must, therefore, be the intermediate position adopted by Oliver J. in *Taylors Fashions v. Liverpool Victoria Trustees Company*[146] where he held that knowledge of the true position by the party alleged to be estopped was merely one of the relevant factors in the overall inquiry. He held that the essential question was whether, in the particular circumstances, it would be unconscionable for a party to be permitted to deny that which, knowingly or unknowingly, he had allowed or encouraged another to assume to his detriment.[147] Accordingly, the principle could apply where, at the time the expectation was encouraged, both parties (not just the representee) were acting under a mistake of law as to their rights. He therefore held that the purchasers of a freehold reversion were estopped from claiming to have taken free for want of registration of options to renew leases which, at the time of their grant, were wrongly thought by conveyancers not to be registrable.[148] This decision, which, as has already been seen, set the doctrine of proprietary estoppel on its present course, obviously did not involve the law of trusts but must nevertheless have had an effect on it.

(3) The impact of the doctrine on the law of trusts
5–068   The doctrine of equitable proprietary estoppel gives rise to a number of potential difficulties for the law of trusts.

The first relates to cases involving the incidence of taxation such as the second case named *Re Rose*.[149] Were the gift or trust in such a case to have arisen as a result of the doctrine of equitable proprietary estoppel, it would have to be determined whether the gift or trust in question was to be regarded as having been constituted at the time when the gift was made, the trust created, or on the occurrence of the subsequent events which created the estoppel. In this case, the position is relatively straightforward since the latter would certainly seem to be the correct approach.[150]

---

[145] See *ante*, para 5–018.

[146] (1976) [1982] Q.B. 133N.

[147] See also *Amalgamated Investment & Property Company v. Texas Commerce International Bank* [1982] Q.B. 84 (leave to appeal to the House of Lords was subsequently not granted: [1982] 1 W.L.R. 1).

[148] See also *Thomas Bates & Son v. Wyndhams (Lingerie)* [1981] 1 W.L.R. 505; estoppel applied where the mistake was a unilateral rather than a common mistake.

[149] [1952] Ch. 499, discussed *ante*, para 5–018.

[150] In this respect, see generally: Jackson (1965) 81 L.Q.R. 84; Poole (1968) 38 Conv. (N.S.) 96; Sunnucks (1968) 118 New L.J. 769.

In other respects, however, the position is more doubtful. In *Williams v.*   **5–069**
Staite,[151] Cumming-Bruce L.J. considered, without finding it necessary to
decide, that the rights of an equitable licensee for life did not necessarily
crystallise when his rights came into existence but only when the court came
to determine what interest he had in the property, since the court might well
decide that, as a result of his conduct, he had forfeited an interest to which
he otherwise would have been entitled. Lord Denning M.R. shared the
opinion that, in an extreme case an equitable licence might be revoked on
the grounds of misconduct.[152] However, he actually held that the conduct of
the licensees, which involved excessive user and bad behaviour, was not of
a kind to bring the equity established in their favour to an end; their
behaviour could instead be remedied by an award of damages. While it may
be regarded as debatable whether or not an established equity can be
forfeited in this way, it does at least seem clear that, when a person is
asserting a right to an equity for the first time, his conduct may be taken into
account in deciding whether to uphold such a right; this is no more than an
application of the basic maxim that "he who comes to equity must come
with clean hands".[153]

There can be no doubt that, when an equity is being so asserted for the   **5–070**
first time, virtually everything must be dependant on the facts of the case.
Having said that, however, in cases where the party with the benefit of the
equity has not been in any way guilty of misconduct, such as *Re Sharpe*,[154]
it is absolutely essential that his rights are held to have arisen at the time of
the transaction in question. This is because it is only in this event that a
subsequent breach of those rights by the other party caused by, for example,
a disposition of the property in question to a third party will be able to be
appropriately remedied; priority over that third party will only be able to be
asserted if the equity was indeed in existence prior to any order of the
courts.[155] It therefore seems that there is a distinction between, on the one
hand, the undeniable existence of an equity prior to any decision of the court
which can be relied on in order to confer any necessary priority over third
parties and, on the other hand, the manner in which the court may choose,
in the exercise of its discretion in the light of all the facts, to implement that
equity.

(4) Conclusion

Some of the aspects of the scope of the doctrine of proprietary estoppel and   **5–071**
the consequences of its utilisation in fiscal and conveyancing terms have still
to be finally clarified. Nevertheless, the doctrine is clearly one of the most
significant movements occurring in the contemporary law of real property.
The extent to which its development will increase the extent to which equity
will constitute trusts which would otherwise be incompletely constituted
remains to be seen. Nevertheless, there can be no doubt that the development of this doctrine has increased both the importance of this particular

---

[151] [1979] Ch. 291.
[152] *ibid.* at 297.
[153] Goff L.J. was of this opinion in *Williams v. Staite* [1979] Ch. 291 at 299.
[154] [1980] 1 W.L.R. 219. The facts were stated *ante*, para 5–063.
[155] *ibid.* at 225.

exception and the possibilities of a trust becoming completely constituted thereby.

(E) Statutory Exceptions

5–072   Since January 1, 1997 there has only been one statutory exception to the rule that equity will not constitute a trust which would otherwise be incompletely constituted. A trust will be constituted by statute as a result of a purported conveyance of a legal estate in land to a minor. Because such an estate can only be held by an adult,[156] the conveyance will, by virtue of the Trusts of Land and Appointment of Trustees Act 1996,[157] operate as a declaration that the land is held in trust for the minor in question.[158]

III. THE DISTINCTION BETWEEN EXECUTED AND EXECUTORY TRUSTS

5–073   Completely constituted trusts may be either executed or executory trusts and it is still in some circumstances important to distinguish not only between these two categories of trusts but also between the two of them and trusts which are incompletely constituted. An executed trust arises when the settlor has defined in the trust instrument precisely what interests are to be taken by the beneficiaries.[159] An executory trust, on the other hand, arises where the will or deed in question vests the trust property in the trustees or personal representatives but the interests to be taken by the beneficiaries remain to be delimited in some subsequent instrument pursuant to the general intention of the settlor or testator.[160] However, this general intention must be sufficiently clear. The directions as to the trusts to be defined must not be too ambiguous; if they are, there will be no executory trust either.[161] This is particularly so in the case of a will since a testator cannot leave it to someone else to make his will for him.[162]

---

[156] Law of Property Act 1925, s.1(6).

[157] Sch.1, para.1. Before this Act came into force on January 1, 1997, such a conveyance operated as an agreement for valuable consideration to create a settlement of that land on the minor and in the meantime to hold the land on trust for him (Settled Land Act 1925, s.27); any conveyances so operating on January 1, 1997 thereafter also take effect as declarations of trust.

[158] Prior to January 1, 1997, there was also a second exception arising out of the fact that it was not possible to create a settlement of a legal estate in land pursuant to the Settled Land Act 1925 without the use of two documents—a trust instrument and a vesting document (either a deed or an assent). The use of only one document did not pass the legal estate but such a document operated as a trust instrument and, therefore, took effect as an enforceable trust pending the execution of the vesting deed by the trustees. However, pursuant to Trusts of Land and Appointment of Trustees Act 1996, s.2(1), no further settlements under the Settled Land Act 1925 can now be created; consequently, this exception only survives to the extent that any such settlement created before January 1, 1997 still has no vesting deed, a possibility which will become less and less likely with the passage of time.

[159] See *Egerton v. Brownlow* (1853) 4 H.L.C. 1 at 210, *per* Lord St. Leonards.

[160] See *Davis v. Richards & Wallington Ltd.* [1990] 1 W.L.R. 1511 at 1537 where Scott J. approved the definition in these terms found in *Underhill and Hayton, Law of Trusts and Trustees* 17th edn (London, Lexis Nexis, 2006), 87. A leading authority is *Sackville-West v. Viscount Holmesdale* (1870) L.R. 4 H.L. 543; see also *Norton on Deeds* 2nd edn (1928), 674–694.

[161] *Re Flavel's Will Trusts* [1969] 1 W.L.R. 444.

[162] *ibid.*, at 446; *Pengelly v. Pengelly* [2007] EWCA 3227 (Ch), [2008] 3 W.L.R. 66 at [10].

1. *The Nature of the Distinction*

Historically the practical importance of the distinction between executed **5–074** and executory trusts has related to their construction although in that respect the position today is no longer of as much importance as it used to be.[163] The construction of an executed trust is governed by strictly interpreted rules of law, whereas executory trusts are construed more liberally and always with a view to carrying out the true intention of the settlor. This may be illustrated by comparing two cases.

In *Re Bostock's Settlement*,[164] the settlor had omitted certain words of **5–075** limitation which, had they been inserted, would have given an estate in fee simple to the beneficiaries. It was held that, in the absence of those words, the beneficiaries took only a life estate notwithstanding the fact that it was probably intended that they should have taken an estate in fee simple. This was a case of an executed trust and, in the absence of the necessary technical expressions, the limitation was construed according to strict rules of law.

On the other hand, in *Glenorchy v. Bosville*[165] the testator had devised real **5–076** property to trustees upon trust to convey the estate, after the marriage of his grand-daughter, to her use for life, remainder to the use of her husband for life, remainder to the use of the issue of her body. Under the rule of construction known as the Rule in *Shelley's Case*,[166] the grand-daughter would, if this had been an executed trust, have taken an estate in fee tail (a now obsolete estate of freehold[167] which cannot as such be alienated[168] and can descend only to the heirs of the body of the original tenant). However, since this was an executory trust, the court was able to look at the true intention of the testator. His intention had clearly been to provide for the children of the marriage; consequently, it was held that the trustees should, regardless of the Rule in *Shelley's Case*, convey the property to the grand-daughter for life, with remainder to her first and other sons for an estate in fee tail and an ultimate remainder to her daughter for an estate in fee simple.

These cases illustrate the practical importance of the distinction between **5–077** executed and executory trusts in matters of construction. One case, *Re Arden*,[169] does admittedly suggest that it could be argued that the distinction is not anything like as clear-cut. In that case it was held, in effect, that the use of an non-technical expression by the creator of an executed trust gave the court a loophole which enabled it to apply a construction which accorded with the real intentions of the settlor. The settlor had used the word "absolutely"; Clauson J. held that the use of this word entitled him to decide that the beneficiary in whose favour it had been used took an equitable fee

---

[163] See *post*, para 5–078.

[164] [1921] 2 Ch. 469.

[165] (1733) Cas. t. Talb. 3; see also *Papillon v. Voice* (1728) P. Wms. 471.

[166] (1581) 1 Co.Rep. 88B. This case does not apply to instruments taking effect after 1925; see *post*, p.149.

[167] No estates in fee tail have been able to be created since 1996; pre-existing estates nevertheless continue: Trusts of Land and Appointment of Trustees Act 1996, Sch.1, para. 5.

[168] A tenant for an estate in fee tail in possession can nevertheless generally convert his estate into an estate in fee simple.

[169] [1935] Ch. 326.

simple even though, if that word had been omitted, it was acknowledged that he would only have taken a life interest. If this decision is correct, which is in fact somewhat questionable, the position may be somewhat different from that stated above, namely that a non-technical expression which is present in a document may be given a technical meaning even in an executed trust, while the absence of any such expression—as in *Re Bostock's Settlement*[170]—will still nevertheless produce the effect prescribed by strict rules of law.

2. *The Special Treatment of Marriage Articles*

5–078   One class of executory trusts has always been given special treatment. These are executory trusts which arise under marriage articles. In such cases the presumption is that the intention of the settlor was to provide for the issue of the marriage so that, despite any technical rules of construction, the husband and wife will normally take life interests,[171] a presumption which will apply unless it is clear that the parties intended to create some other type of interest. This presumption is a strong one and will only be rebutted by the clearest evidence to the contrary. It was particularly significant in the application of the Rule in *Shelley's Case*. In a limitation of land before 1926 for a person for life, remainder to the heirs of his body, that person would have taken an estate in fee tail by virtue of the rule of construction established in that case. But if an executory trust on these lines was contained in marriage articles, the court would strive to avoid this construction and would give that person only a life estate; had this not been done, that person would have been able immediately to bar the estate in fee tail, that is to say bar the interests of his successors in title including his own issue, by converting his own interest into an estate fee simple.

5–079   However, in the case of other types of executory trusts, which normally only arise under the provisions of wills, the court, while as always construing the instrument as a whole in order to ascertain the true intention of the settlor, would consider the question of construction on its merits. So, in the ancient case of *Sweetapple v. Bindon*,[172] a testator gave the then substantial sum of £300 to trustees upon trust to invest it in the purchase of land and to settle the land to "the only use of" a person and her children and, in the event that that person died without issue, "the land to be divided between her brothers and sisters then living". Since this was an executory trust under a will, the question of construction was approached on the basis that there was no overriding necessity to give that person a life interest; consequently, it was held that she took an estate in fee tail.

3. *The Modern Significance of the Distinction*

5–080   What has been stated above is still applicable as a matter of principle but, along with the authorities cited, must now be read subject to the effect of the

---

[170] [1921] Ch. 469.
[171] *Jervoise v. Duke of Northumberland* (1820) 1 Jac. & W. 559 at 574; *Trevor v. Trevor* (1720) 1 P. Wms. 622.
[172] (1706) 2 Vern. 536.

legislation of the twentieth century. The Property Legislation of 1925 had two effects on instruments taking effect on or after January 1, 1926: first, it abolished the rule in *Shelley's Case*[173]; and, secondly, it removed any necessity for the use of words of limitation for the purpose of creating an estate in fee simple.[174] The distinction still had to be borne in mind thereafter because of the continuing necessity for words of limitation for the creation of estates in fee tail[175]; however, this too has ceased to have any relevance since January 1, 1997, given that the Trusts of Land and Appointment of Trustees Act 1996 has prevented the creation of any further estates in fee tail on or after that date.[176]

The modern significance of the distinction is therefore somewhat less. **5–081** Marriage articles are now rare, presumably because, in so far as marriage settlements are still created at all, they are highly likely to have been set up at least partly for the purpose of tax avoidance, something which requires all the documents involved to have been carefully thought out and prepared in advance. However, there is one respect in which the distinction between executed and executory trusts is still potentially extremely important today in the field of construction. Most pension schemes are initially established by an interim deed of trust which provides for the subsequent execution of a definitive deed of trust later on. In *Davis v. Richards & Wallington Industries*,[177] following the initial execution of an interim deed, the definitive deed was subsequently duly executed; however, the validity of the latter deed was challenged when questions arose as to the entitlement to surplus funds. Scott J. in fact found the definitive deed to have been valid. However, he stated that, had he not done so, he would have upheld the interim deed as a valid executory trust capable of being executed by a court order; this would have enabled the court to provide rules corresponding to those in the definitive deed by means of which the questions relating to the surplus funds would have been able to have been resolved. Given the importance of pension schemes today, their potential reliance on the doctrine of executory trusts is therefore extremely significant.

Further the distinction between executory and executed trusts can still be **5–082** relevant in respects other than matters of construction. In *Pengelly v. Pengelly*,[178] decided as recently as 2007, the testator left one-third of his net residuary estate to his trustees "upon such trusts as they shall in their absolute discretion decide for a class of beneficiaries as they shall decide" to select from a defined class[179]; his will went on to provide that "the settlement shall be established by a deed executed by my Trustees not later than two years after my death". On the face of things the settlement was therefore to be created not by the testator but by the trustees; this would have the effect of making them settlors as well which would in turn create a number of potential fiscal problems. In the event, however, it was held that the

---

[173] Law of Property 1925, s.131.
[174] *ibid.* s.60.
[175] *ibid.* s.130.
[176] Sch.1, para. 5.
[177] [1990] 1 W.L.R. 1511.
[178] [2008] [2007] EWHC 3227, (Ch), [2008] 3 W.L.R. 66.
[179] On the face of the will the membership of the class was wholly unrestricted but the court rectified the will to restrict membership to a defined class.

testator had by his will created a valid executory trust; consequently, the discretionary trust was established on his death and all that the trustees would do by means of their deed was to delimit the precise terms of that trust.

5–083   Similarly, where a settlor or testator has manifested an intention to create an immediate charitable trust but further steps may have to be taken in order to put into effect the charitable intention which he has expressed, that trust will also amount to an executory trust and will be immediately established. This was specifically held by the Court of Appeal in *Harris v. Sharp*,[180] where a memorandum manifesting such an intention was signed by a settlor in respect of property already held by the intended trustees, the settlor's solicitors; the settlor subsequently seemed to have changed his mind[181] but the Court of Appeal held that a valid charitable trust had already been created.

IV. When a Trust is Incompletely Constituted, When will the Intended Beneficiaries have a Contractual Remedy?

5–084   Where no completely constituted trust has arisen either as a result of the effective transfer of the intended trust property to the trustees or as a result of a declaration of trust by the settlor and where the intended beneficiaries are unable to rely on any of the exceptions to the rule that equity will not perfect an imperfect gift, the only possibility open to them will be to rely on the law of contract. There are a number of situations where a contractual remedy will enable the intended beneficiaries either to bring about the complete constitution of the trust or, in default, obtain common law damages. The possibility that they will be able to do so has been considerably enhanced by the enactment of the Contracts (Rights of Third Parties) Act 1999.[182]

5–085   This does not mean that a contractual remedy will always be available to the intended beneficiaries. Where there is neither a completely constituted trust nor a contractual remedy, the trust in question is said to be voluntary and the beneficiaries are said to be volunteers. It is a long-established equitable maxim that "equity will not assist a volunteer".[183] Although this maxim is invariably relied on by the courts whenever an intended beneficiary is denied a remedy, its utilisation adds nothing and is a source of potential confusion. The maxim neither denies a remedy to a beneficiary who already has one nor provides a remedy to a beneficiary who does not have one. Consequently, it does no more than state the obvious, namely that, if a beneficiary can point neither to the existence of a completely constituted trust nor to the existence of any form of contract enforceable either by him

---

[180] (1989) [2003] T.L.I. 41, [2003] W.T.L.R. 1541.

[181] He had signed the memorandum between his conviction and his subsequent sentencing for defrauding another charity; its execution was clearly intended to be and was used in mitigation but he was nevertheless sent to prison.

[182] See *ante*, paras 1–045–1–059.

[183] *Ellison v. Ellison* (1802) 6 Ves. 656 at 662, *per* Lord Eldon L.C.; see also *Jefferys v. Jefferys* (1841) Cr. & Ph. 138.

or on his behalf, then equity will not assist him. More significantly, the existence of the maxim has hindered the development of the law since, unfortunately but predictably, the courts have tended to utilise it as a substitute for reasoned analysis of whether or not in any particular case any contractual remedy is actually available to the intended beneficiary.

The contractual remedies available to the intended beneficiaries of an **5–086** incompletely constituted trust may arise either under a simple contract (a contract constituted as a result of the existence of offer and acceptance, intention to create legal relations, and consideration) or under a specialty contract (a contract constituted by virtue of being contained in a deed, often also described as a covenant).

The contract entered into by the settlor may be a straightforward contract **5–087** to settle some of his existing property, that is to say property of which he is already able to dispose.[184] However, there is normally little reason for a settlor to enter into such a contract in respect of existing property.[185] Such property can be the subject of a valid assignment, of a valid declaration of a trust, and of a valid contract to assign or declare a trust. Consequently, if the subject matter of a proposed trust is existing property, the settlor can just as easily constitute the trust immediately by transfer to trustees or by declaration as enter into a contract so to do.

For this reason, most contracts of this type (and most of the cases which **5–088** have come before the courts) have concerned property which has not yet come into existence. Such property is generally known as after-acquired property. It cannot be the subject of a valid assignment, which is at law wholly void,[186] although equity will treat the assignment of after-acquired property made in exchange for valuable consideration as a contract to assign or declare a trust if and when the property is acquired.[187] Nor can after-acquired property be the subject of a valid declaration of trust,[188] although equity will enforce this declaration of trust in favour of anyone who has provided valuable consideration if and when the property is acquired.[189] Further, an express contract to assign or declare a trust if and when the property is acquired will be enforced whether it is a simple contract and is consequently supported by valuable consideration or merely a speciality contract; a simple contract of this type will be enforced both in equity and

---

[184] Such cases were *Williamson v. Codrington* (1750) 1 Ves.Sen. 511 (covenant to settle a plantation); *Fletcher v. Fletcher* (1844) 4 Hare 167 (covenant to settle £60,000); and *Re Cavendish Browne's Settlement Trusts* [1916] W.N. 341 (covenant to settle property to which the settlor was entitled under the wills of persons who had already died).

[185] In both *Williamson v. Codrington* and *Fletcher v. Fletcher*, the reason was undoubtedly the fact that the beneficiaries were the illegitimate children of the settlors, who clearly wished to avoid embarrassing publicity until after their own deaths.

[186] *Holroyd v. Marshall* (1862) 10 H.L.C. 191 (assignment by way of mortgage of machinery which in the future might be substituted for existing machinery); *Re Tilt* (1896) 40 Sol.Jo. 224 (assignment of an expectancy under the intestacy of a person who was still alive); *Re Ellenborough* [1903] 1 Ch. 697 (assignment of an expectancy under the will of a person who was still alive).

[187] *Holroyd v. Marshall* (1862) 10 H.L.C. 191 at 211, 220.

[188] *Williams v. C.I.R.* [1965] N.Z.L.R. 395 (Court of Appeal of New Zealand) (declaration of trust of the first £500 of the net income arising under a life interest in each of four future years).

[189] *Ellison v. Ellison* (1802) 6 Ves.Jun. 656 at 662; *Williams v. C.I.R.* [1965] N.Z.L.R. 395 (Court of Appeal of New Zealand).

at common law,[190] while a speciality contract of this type will be enforced at common law,[191] but not in equity.[192] All of this means that, where the subject matter of a proposed trust is after-acquired property, the settlor will have no option but to enter into what either is or is deemed by equity to be a contract to settle the property in question if and when it is acquired.

5–089   Because of this significant distinction between existing and after-acquired property, it is important to note that, for this purpose, existing property is not confined to property which has already vested in possession and is thus available for the immediate enjoyment of the person entitled thereto. Existing property also includes property which has not yet come into possession, either because the interest is vested in interest, in other words awaiting the determination of some prior interest (an example is the interest of a person who is absolutely entitled in remainder during a preceding life tenancy) or contingent (an example is the interest of a person entitled to property at the age of 30 when he has not yet attained that age). Further, existing property includes existing choses in action (an example is the right to recover book-debts arising in the course of a business[193]) and the right to exercise an existing power of appointment only at some future time (an example is an already granted power of appointment which is exercisable only by will).

5–090   After-acquired property, on the other hand, is property in respect of which only the future will determine whether or not the person in question ever acquires any rights at all (examples are the possibility of receiving property (including the right to exercise a power of appointment[194]) under the will[195] or intestacy[196] of someone who is still alive or under an as yet unexercised power of appointment, the possibility of receiving future royalties payable in respect of a copyright or a mining operation,[197] and the possibility of acquiring future book-debts arising in the course of a business[198]).

5–091   Consequently, while a settlor may validly assign an equitable remainder to trustees on trust, declare a trust[199] of that interest, or enter into either a simple or a specialty contract to make such an assignment or declaration of trust, his possible courses of action in respect of the payments which he hopes to receive such as the royalties on a book or a mine are much more

---

[190] The simple contract will not be enforceable at common law if the valuable consideration in question is marriage, which is not regarded as valuable consideration at law. However, a simple contract supported by marriage consideration will nevertheless be enforceable in equity; see *Pullan v. Koe* [1913] 1 Ch. 9, *post*, para 5–097.

[191] *Cannon v. Hartley* [1949] Ch. 213. See *post*, para 5–104.

[192] *Jefferys v. Jefferys* (1841) Cr. & P. 138.

[193] As in *Barclays Bank v. Willowbrook International* [1987] 1 F.T.L.R. 386.

[194] *Re Ellenborough* [1903] 1 Ch. 697.

[195] *Re Tilt* (1896) 40 Sol.Jo. 224.

[196] *Re Parkin* [1892] 3 Ch. 510.

[197] *Coulls v. Bagot's Trustee* [1967] 40 A.L.J.R. 471.

[198] *Tailby v. Official Receiver* (1888) 13 App. Cas. 523. A further example which the author of this edition has encountered in practice is any new tenancy or monetary compensation given for the future surrender of a protected tenancy of residential property such as a tenancy under the Rent Act 1977 (the right to remain in occupation under such a tenancy is not itself a proprietary interest but merely consists of the right to resist eviction and so cannot itself be the subject of an assignment or a declaration of trust); another example would be similar rights in relation to a business tenancy protected under Part II of the Landlord and Tenant Act 1954.

[199] Strictly speaking, a sub-trust. See *ante*, para 4–018.

restricted. He cannot validly either assign or declare a trust of such payments, although a purported assignment or declaration of trust will be regarded by equity as a contract to assign or declare a trust if and when the property is acquired; however, he can enter into either a simple contract (enforceable both at law[200] and in equity) or a specialty contract (enforceable only at law) to make such an assignment or declaration of trust.

1. *A Simple Contract to Create the Trust*

If the settlor and the beneficiary have entered into a simple contract for the creation by the settlor of a completely constituted trust in favour of the beneficiary, then both parties to the contract will be entitled to the appropriate contractual remedies. The beneficiary will also be so entitled if he is a third party to the contract in question who is entitled to enforce that contract under the Contracts (Rights of Third Parties) Act 1999.[201]   **5–092**

(A)   A Simple Contract Recognised both at Common Law and in Equity

Where the consideration provided by the beneficiary is money or money's worth, then the existence of the contract will be recognised both at common law and in equity. Consequently both settlor and beneficiary will be able to obtain damages for breach of contract or, if the contract in question is capable of being specifically enforced, an order for specific performance.   **5–093**

Where specific performance is available, the property in question will in equity immediately become subject to the trust. Thus, if the settlor contracts with the beneficiary for money or money's worth to transfer land to trustees to hold on trust for him, in equity the land will immediately become subject to the trust and the beneficiary will be able to obtain an order for specific performance of this contract; thus he will be able to oblige the settlor to transfer the land to the trustees in exchange for the money or money's worth in question. This remedy will also be available to the beneficiary where the subject matter of the intended trust is pure personalty for whose loss equity regards damages as an inadequate remedy; this will be the case where the subject matter is a chattel not readily available on the open market, such as a rare painting, a rare antique, a vintage motor vehicle, or shares in a private company.   **5–094**

Where, on the other hand, the contract in question is not capable of being specifically enforced because damages are an adequate remedy for the loss of the subject matter of the intended trust, the beneficiary will be limited to common law damages for breach of contract. These damages will be payable directly to the beneficiary rather than to the intended trustees, although there will obviously be nothing to prevent the beneficiary from himself paying the sum in question on to the trustees and thus creating a completely constituted trust of the money.   **5–095**

---

[200] Provided that the consideration is money or money's worth rather than marriage consideration.

[201] See *ante*, paras 1–045–1–054.

5–096   These principles apply not only to existing property but also to after-acquired property if and when it is acquired. In *Holroyd v. Marshall*,[202] following the sale of machinery in a mill, the purchaser assigned the machinery to a trustee on trust for the vendor if he should pay £5,000 to the purchaser and if not on trust for the purchaser. The deed of assignment included both the existing machinery and any after-acquired machinery which might be added to or substituted for the original machinery. The House of Lords held that, as soon as any further machinery was acquired, it vested immediately in equity in the trustee on these trusts and thus could not be the subject of execution by the creditors of the vendor. It has been established by subsequent authorities that this will occur even in the case of property in respect of which specific performance would not normally be ordered provided that the valuable consideration has already been furnished by the beneficiary.[203] Thus in *Re Gillott's Settlement*[204] debtors agreed with their creditors that any income which they received should within three days of receipt be paid to a trustee on various trusts for both debtors and creditors. It was held that an equitable interest in each payment received by the debtors vested immediately in the trustee so that the trust of each payment was immediately completely constituted. The majority of the decided cases, however, concern marriage consideration, a type of valuable consideration which is not recognised by the common law, and so will be discussed separately.[205]

(B)   A Simple Contract Recognised Only in Equity
5–097   In one particular situation not recognised by the common law, equity will imply both a contract for the creation by the settlor of a completely constituted trust in favour of the beneficiary and the consideration necessary for that contract on the part of the beneficiary. This occurs where the beneficiary can bring himself within a marriage consideration. Where a settlement in consideration of marriage is made either before the marriage or contemporaneously with the celebration of the marriage or subsequent to the marriage pursuant to an agreement made prior to the marriage, equity implies that the settlor, the spouses, and the children and more remote descendants of the marriage are parties to a contract in respect of which they have given consideration. Any of the persons thus deemed to be a party to this implied contract can enforce any of the obligations arising thereunder, not only the original obligation of the settlor to create the settlement in question but also any obligations of the spouses to transfer any of their existing or after-acquired property to the trustees to be held on the trusts of the settlement. Any such obligation is capable of being specifically enforced even where damages would normally be an adequate remedy for the loss of the property in question. In the case of a marriage settlement, common law damages are never an adequate remedy for the simple reason that they are not available

---

[202] (1862) 10 H.L.C. 191.
[203] Principally by the House of Lords in *Tailby v. Official Receiver* (1888) 13 App. Cas. 523 (a case concerning an assignment by way of mortgage rather than an assignment to trustees on trust).
[204] [1934] Ch. 97. See also *Re Lind* [1915] 2 Ch. 345 and *Re Haynes' Will Trusts* [1949] Ch. 5.
[205] See *post, infra*.

in an action by the beneficiaries[206]—the common law does not recognise marriage consideration.

These principles are illustrated by the case of *Pullan v. Koe*.[207] A wife was given a sum of money which was caught by a covenant to settle after-acquired property into which both she and her husband had entered in their marriage settlement. The sum was never transferred to the trustees and part of the money was eventually invested in bonds which were held at a bank in the name of the husband. Following his death, the bonds came into the hands of his executor. Any action by the trustees on the covenants had by then become statute barred. However, it was held that the money received by the wife had been subject to the trusts of the marriage settlement from the moment of its receipt. Consequently, the children of the marriage could specifically enforce the simple contract implied by equity and thus bring about the transfer of the bonds by the executor to the trustees.

5–098

Normally the only persons within the marriage consideration are the spouses, the children and the more remote descendants of the marriage.[208] However, there is some, admittedly somewhat ambiguous, authority that, in certain circumstances, illegitimate children and children of an earlier or subsequent marriage of one of the spouses may be brought within the marriage consideration if their interests are so "interwoven" with the interests of the children of the marriage in consideration of which the settlement was made that the interests of the latter cannot be enforced without also enforcing the interests of the former. This was suggested in *Attorney-General v. Jacobs-Smith*[209] and was supported by Buckley J. in *Re Cook's Settlement Trusts*.[210]

5–099

However, *Re Cook's Settlement Trusts*[211] also shows that this extension will apparently not be extended any further. In that case, an attempt was made to establish a similar principle to enable an intended beneficiary who is specially an object of the intended trust or is within the consideration of the deed of settlement to enforce any obligations contained therein. (This alleged principle bears some resemblance to the former doctrine of "meritorious consideration", a principle analogous to marriage consideration which existed at least until the end of the eighteenth century[212]; the latter principle was based on the natural love and affection between parent and child and consequently could be utilised by the latter to enforce settlements made by the former.) Sir Francis Cook had entered into a settlement, which was not in consideration of marriage, in which he had covenanted with his father

5–100

---

[206] Common law damages will of course be available in an action by the trustees to enforce any covenants entered into by either the settlor or the spouses.

[207] [1913] 1 Ch. 9.

[208] *MacDonald v. Scott* [1893] A.C. 642 at 650 establishes that "issue" includes both children and more remote issue such as grandchildren and great-grandchildren.

[209] [1895] 2 Q.B. 341 at 354, *per* Kay L.J.

[210] [1965] Ch. 902. See also *Re D'Avigdor-Goldsmid* [1951] Ch. 1038 at 1053 (overruled on other grounds: [1953] A.C. 347).

[211] [1965] Ch. 902.

[212] This is generally thought to be the basis on which a covenant to settle a plantation on illegitimate children was enforced in *Williamson v. Codrington* (1750) 1 Ves.Sen. 511 and is one of the possible explanations of the decision in *Fletcher v. Fletcher* (1844) 6 Hare 67 (see Jones (1965) 24 C.L.J. 46 at 49).

and with the trustees that, in the event that he sold certain valuable paintings which had been transferred to him by his father, he would pay over the proceeds of sale to the trustees to be held on the trusts of the settlement, ultimately for the benefit of his children. He subsequently purported to give one of the paintings to his then wife who wished to sell it. Buckley J. refused to accept the alleged principle, holding that the equitable exception to the rule that equity will not assist a volunteer is confined to persons within the marriage consideration. Having consequently held that the children could not enforce the covenant against Sir Francis, he then went on to hold, for reasons that will be considered later but which no longer necessarily constitute the law,[213] that the trustees ought not to enforce the covenant against him either.

5–101   Because at the time when a marriage settlement is entered into, it is not normally known whether or not there will actually be any issue of the marriage, therefore, it is usual to insert an ultimate remainder in favour of the statutory next-of-kin of one of the spouses. Such persons are not within the marriage consideration and cannot enforce any of the obligations arising under the marriage settlement. This is illustrated by *Re Plumptre's Settlement*.[214] The husband and wife, on the occasion of their marriage, covenanted with their trustees to settle the wife's after-acquired property for the benefit of herself and her husband successively for life, then for the issue of the marriage, and then for the wife's next-of-kin. The husband bought certain stock in the wife's name and the wife afterwards sold it and invested the proceeds of sale in other stock. She then died without issue, leaving her husband as her administrator. It was held that the next-of-kin, because they were volunteers, could not enforce the wife's covenant against her husband as administrator. It was also held that the trustees could not sue for damages for breach of covenant because the claim was statute-barred.[215]

5–102   Finally, it should be noted that, if the settlement is made after marriage and not in pursuance of an ante-nuptial agreement, it will be wholly voluntary. This is because, although there may be consideration between husband and wife, that consideration would not be their marriage—such being past —but consideration of some other kind to which their children would be strangers.[216] This was expressly held in *Green v. Paterson*,[217] which was applied in *Re Cook's Settlement Trusts*.

2. *A Specialty Contract or Covenant to Create the Trust*

5–103   Specialty contracts or covenants to settle property on trust have traditionally played an important role in settlements of all types. Not only have settlors

---

[213] See *post*, para 5–108.

[214] [1910] 1 Ch. 609. See also to a like effect *Re D'Angibau* (1880) 15 Ch.D. 228.

[215] Any such action subsequently appeared to have become impossible whether or not it was statute-barred because of the decisions in *Re Pryce* [1917] 1 Ch. 234, *Re Kay's Settlement* [1939] Ch. 329 and *Re Cook's Settlement Trusts* [1965] Ch. 902; however, those decisions now no longer necessarily represent the law so the issue of limitation has once again become relevant. See *post*, para 5–108.

[216] Such as the consideration provided in *Re Cook's Settlement Trusts*.

[217] (1886) 32 Ch.D. 95.

commonly entered into covenants to create entirely new trusts by transfer-ring existing or after-acquired property to trustees on trust; trusts which have already been completely constituted have regularly included cove-nants by the beneficiaries to transfer their existing or after-acquired property to the trustees to be held on the trusts of the settlement. This is illustrated by the cases which have already been discussed in this section. When a cove-nant to create a trust is entered into in exchange for valuable consideration, it will be enforceable in accordance with the principles which were con-sidered in the immediately preceding part of this section. This part of this section is concerned with the situation where a covenant has been entered into other than for valuable consideration. In such circumstances, the bene-ficiaries will inevitably be in a weaker position. Their only possibilities are to attempt to enforce the covenant themselves or to show that there is a completely constituted trust in their favour of its benefit.[218]

(A)   Enforcement of the Covenant by the Beneficiaries

The beneficiaries will be able to maintain an action at common law against the settlor on the covenant to settle if the covenant to settle purports to be made with them as covenantees and is either a deed poll (a deed to which only the settlor is a party) or a deed inter partes (a deed to which the settlor and others are parties) to which the beneficiaries are either parties or are made parties by section 56 of the Law of Property Act 1925 (which applies only where the subject matter is land).[219] In *Cannon v. Hartley*[220] a husband, wife and daughter were all parties to a deed of separation in which the father covenanted to settle on himself, the wife and the daughter one half of any property which he might receive under the will of either of his parents. Having received such property, he refused to settle it. The daughter was held to be entitled to maintain against him an action for damages for breach of covenant. Since she had given no value, she was clearly unable to obtain specific performance. However, the fact that, because she was a volunteer, equity declined to assist her did not mean that equity would frustrate her right at common law to enforce a covenant to which she was a party. She consequently recovered, by way of damages, the value of the interest which she should have received under the settlement. Thus, while this remedy will not enable the trust to be completely constituted, the beneficiaries will be able to recover compensation for the loss of the interest which they would have obtained under that trust.   **5–104**

The beneficiaries will also be able to maintain an action at common law against the settlor on the covenant to settle if they can bring themselves with the provisions of the Contracts (Rights of Third Parties) Act 1999. Section 1 of that Act provides that a third party to a contract who is identifiable may enforce any term of that contract in his own right provided that either the   **5–105**

---

[218] These possibilities have been the subject of an immense body of periodical literature, of which the principal articles are (in chronological order): Elliott (1960) 76 L.Q.R. 100; Hornby (1962) 78 L.Q.R. 228; Lee (1969) 85 L.Q.R. 213; Barton (1976) 92 L.Q.R. 236; Meagher & Lehane (1976) 92 L.Q.R. 427; Rickett (1979) 32 C.L.P. 1 and (1981) 34 C.L.P. 189; Friend [1982] Conv. 280.

[219] See the review of the authorities by Lord Upjohn in *Beswick v. Beswick* [1968] A.C. 98 at 102–105.

[220] [1949] Ch. 213.

contract so provides or the term in question purports to confer a benefit on him and it does not appear, on a proper construction of that term, that the parties did not intend him to be able to do so. A third party will be identifiable if he is expressly identified by name, or is a member of an identified class, or answers a specific description. There is no requirement that he should have been in existence at the date of the contract; this is very important for present purposes because the beneficiaries of trusts of after-acquired property which are the subject matter of a covenant to settle are more often than not unborn at the time when the covenant is entered into. The Act applies automatically to specialty contracts entered into on or after May 11, 2000, six months after the Act was passed.[221]

5–106   This provision will normally be applicable to covenants to settle property on trust. The beneficiaries will necessarily be identifiable, since otherwise the trust in question would be void for uncertainty of objects.[222] Consequently, those beneficiaries will normally be able to enforce the covenant against the settlor and obtain damages for breach of covenant. However, there are a number of circumstances where this will not be possible. First, it could be decided as a matter of construction that the settlor did not intend the beneficiaries to be able to enforce the term of the covenant purporting to confer a benefit on them. Secondly, the covenant may have been entered into before May 11, 2000 (it is obviously possible for after-acquired property which was the subject matter of a covenant entered into before that date to be acquired by the settlor only after that date). Thirdly, the beneficiaries may only find out about the existence of the covenant after the settlor has purported to rescind it under section 2 of the Contracts (Rights of Third Parties) Act 1999[223] (this possibility is not as far-fetched as it might appear since the settlor may initially conceal the existence of the covenant[224] and later purport to rescind it; alternatively, he may purport to rescind the contract before a relevant beneficiary has been born or has attained the age of majority). In all these situations, the pre-existing law will remain relevant.

5–107   In such circumstances, the beneficiaries will nevertheless be able to enforce the covenant indirectly if there is a completely constituted trust of its benefit of the type considered in the next part of this section. In the absence of any such trust, they will clearly have no direct means of enforcing the covenant. This somewhat obvious proposition was confirmed by the Court of Appeal in *Re d'Angibau*,[225] where the eventual beneficiaries under a

---

[221] Contracts (Rights of Third Parties) Act 1999, s.10. The Act will also apply to contracts entered into during that six-month period if the contracts in question contain an express provision to that effect.

[222] See *ante*, para 3–029.

[223] This section provides that, where a third party has rights under Section 1, the parties to a contract may not rescind it without his consent where he has communicated his assent to the term in question to the person bound by that term. It must follow as a necessary corollary of this provision that, at least so far as the Act is concerned, they can rescind the contract where he has not so communicated his consent.

[224] In *Fletcher v. Fletcher* (1844) 4 Hare 67, *post*, para 5–113, the settlor concealed the existence of the covenant throughout his lifetime and it was only discovered among his papers some years after his death; the beneficiaries were his illegitimate sons and it seems tolerably clear that he did not wish anyone to become aware of their existence until after his death.

[225] (1880) 15 Ch.D. 228.

marriage settlement, the wife's next-of-kin, who were of course not within the marriage consideration, were held unable to enforce a covenant by the wife to transfer an equitable remainder to the trustees of the settlement.

Consequently, the only remaining option of the beneficiaries will be to attempt to enforce the covenant indirectly by means of an action by the trustees on the covenant at law against the settlor. It is clear that the beneficiaries cannot compel the trustees to bring such an action (in the absence of a trust of the benefit of the covenant and of any simple or specialty contract to which they are parties, they are clearly in no position to compel anyone to do anything and are undoubtedly volunteers). However, given that the trustees have an undoubted right of action at law against the settlor, it might be thought that they would be entitled to exercise that right of action if they so chose and hold any damages recovered from the settlor on trust for the beneficiaries. This is not in fact the case. It has long been established that, if the trustees seek the directions of the court,[226] they will be directed not to sue the settlor on the covenant. Indeed, this rule is so well established that there is now no need for the trustees to trouble to obtain any directions—the present authorities provide them with a complete defence to any action for breach of trust.[227]

5–108

The three relevant authorities are *Re Pryce*,[228] *Re Kay's Settlement*[229] and *Re Cook' Settlement Trusts*.[230] None of them contains any reasoned discussion of exactly why the trustees must not enforce the covenant. It has been argued[231] that there is no reason for equity thus to restrain parties to a covenant from exercising their legal rights thereunder if they wish to do so.[232] However, it seems that the consequences of such an action would not ultimately favour the beneficiaries. Even on the assumption that the trustees would be able to obtain substantial damages for breach of covenant (an

5–109

---

[226] Something which trustees habitually do before embarking on legal proceedings to avoid any risk of being made personally responsible for the costs in the event that they were subsequently held not to have been properly incurred.

[227] See *Re Ralli's Will Trusts* [1964] Ch. 288 at 301–302.

[228] [1917] 1 Ch. 234. The trustees of a marriage settlement sought directions from the court as to whether they were bound to enforce in favour of the wife's next-of-kin (who were the only persons beneficially entitled other than the wife) a covenant by the wife to settle after-acquired property. Eve J. held, correctly, that the next-of-kin could not obtain relief directly and that, consequently, there was no reason for equity to give them relief indirectly by an order to the trustees to enforce the covenant. He then went on to hold, without further discussion, that they were bound not to enforce the covenant (this conclusion was not in fact necessary, since the negative answer to the question which Eve J. was asked was, strictly speaking, "the trustees are not bound to sue" rather than "the trustees are bound not to sue"; this is one of the grounds on which the decision has been criticised by Elliott (1960) 76 L.Q.R. 100).

[229] [1939] Ch. 329. The trustees of a voluntary settlement sought directions whether they should or should not take proceedings in favour of the ultimate beneficiaries against the settlor on her covenant to settle after-acquired property and were directed by Simonds J. not to do so. The question put to him envisaged three possible answers: "the trustees must sue", "the trustees may sue", "the trustees must not sue"; consequently, his direction to the trustees not to sue clearly constitutes his *ratio decidendi*.

[230] [1965] Ch. 902.

[231] Particularly by Elliott (1960) 76 L.Q.R. 100.

[232] Because of the risk of being held personally liable for the costs, no trustee would be likely to do so unless the beneficiaries were members of his family or had agreed to indemnify him fully.

assumption which, although it has been doubted,[233] is in fact supported both by principle[234] and by precedent[235]), there is no reason why these damages should be held on the trusts of the settlement. In a situation where, as is being assumed, there is not a completely constituted trust of the benefit of the covenant, it appears that any damages arising from any action on the covenant would be held by the trustees not on trust for the beneficiaries but on resulting trust for the settlor.[236] Since any action brought by the trustees against the settlor would thus result in the damages payable being held on resulting trust for the person paying them, equity is clearly correct to prohibit such a circuitous action. Consequently, for this reason *Re Pryce, Re Kay's Settlement* and *Re Cook's Settlement Trusts* were, in this respect, correctly decided.

5–110   It thus follows that the beneficiaries will not be able to enforce a covenant to settle indirectly by means of an action by the trustees on the covenant at law against the settlor and thus, in the absence of a completely constituted trust and of any simple or specialty contract which they can enforce, they will have no means either of bringing about the complete constitution of the trust of the benefit of the covenant or of obtaining any compensation for the settlor's failure to comply with his covenant to settle.

(B) A Completely Constituted Trust of the Benefit of the Covenant

5–111   As has already been indicated, where the beneficiaries are unable to enforce a covenant to settle in any other way, they will nevertheless be able to enforce that covenant indirectly if there is a completely constituted trust of its benefit. There is no objection in principle to such a trust. Any chose in action can be the subject matter of a trust and so a settlor is certainly capable of declaring that the right which, by means of his covenant, he has conferred upon the trustees to enforce the covenant against him should be held on trust for the beneficiaries of the intended trust. If such a trust can be found to have been created, then, although the trust of the property which the settlor covenanted to settle will remain incompletely constituted unless and until he transfers that property to the trustees, the beneficiaries will nevertheless be entitled to enforce the completely constituted trust of the benefit of the covenant. This trust will be enforceable in the same way as any other completely constituted trust; the beneficiaries will be able to request the trustee to enforce the covenant against the settlor[237] and, if he declines so to do, they will be able either to bring an action to compel him to do so or to sue the settlor directly on the covenant joining the trustee as a co-defendant to the action.[238]

---

[233] See Marshall (1950) 3 C.L.P. 30.

[234] The fact that a party to an action at law is a trustee cannot be a ground for limiting him to nominal damages for the simple reason that the common law does not recognise trusts. For this reason, it should not matter that the trust is in fact incompletely constituted or that the property to be settled is after-acquired.

[235] *Re Cavendish-Browne's Settlement Trusts* [1916] W.N. 341. An analogous authority involving a trust of the benefit of a simple contract is *Lloyd's v. Harper* (1880) 16 Ch.D. 290.

[236] See Underhill & Hayton, *Law of Trusts and Trustees* 17th edn (London, Lexis Nexis, 2007), pp.228–231.

[237] *Lloyd's v. Harper* (1880) 16 Ch.D. 290.

[238] *Les Affreteurs Reunis v. Leopold Walford* [1919] A.C. 801.

The existence or non-existence of such a trust will be crucial in the   **5–112**
situations where the Contracts (Rights of Third Parties) Act 1999 is not
applicable to a covenant.[239] Further, whether or not that legislation is applicable, there are some circumstances in which the existence or non-existence
of a trust of the benefit of that covenant may determine precisely who is
beneficially entitled to the property to be settled.[240] If, for example, the
covenant is to settle after-acquired property on persons as joint tenants, even
if the latter have a right of action on the covenant, they will not have a
proprietary right which they are capable of severing unless and until the
property is acquired and vested in the trustee. Consequently, if one of them
dies before that time, the other will take the entire property by survivorship.
If, on the other hand, the benefit of the covenant is the subject matter of a
completely constituted trust, they will each have an immediate proprietary
right which they will be able to sever so as to prevent the property passing
by survivorship; it will instead devolve according to the will or intestacy of
each of them.

The principal difficulty lies in determining exactly when a trust of the   **5–113**
benefit of a contract will arise. In *Fletcher v. Fletcher*[241] a settlor covenanted
with trustees that, if either or both of his two illegitimate sons survived him,
his executors should, within 12 months of his death, pay to the trustees
£60,000 which was to be held on trust for such of the two as reached the age
of 21. The existence of the deed was never revealed by the settlor either to
the trustees or to his sons; he retained the deed in his possession until his
death and it was only discovered some years later among his papers. Only
one of the sons both survived the settlor and reached the age of 21; he
sought to enforce the covenant against the executors. Wigram V.-C. held that
the settlor had clearly vested in the trustees the right to sue his executors for
£60,000. He held that this was sufficient to produce a completely constituted
trust of the benefit of the covenant, which could be enforced by the son.

This decision, which is supported by other contemporaneous author-   **5–114**
ities,[242] has been interpreted in a variety of ways. However, it has to be seen
against the background of the rules which at that time governed certainty of
intention (the question of when a settlor will be held to have had sufficient
intention to constitute a trust[243]). Until the middle of the nineteenth century,
the courts tended to take the view that any expression of desire or hope or
the like on the part of the settlor was imperative and therefore created a
binding trust. Given that the settlor had clearly intended his sons to receive
the benefit of the covenant after his death, it was perhaps not unreasonable,
in the light of the view then habitually adopted as to certainty of intention,

---

[239] See *ante*, para 5–105.
[240] See Halliwell [2003] Conveyancer 192.
[241] (1844) 4 Hare 67.
[242] None of these authorities contains as clear a statement of principle as that contained in
Fletcher v. Fletcher; consequently, all have been the subject of different explanations. Wigram
V.-C. himself relied on *Clough v. Lambert* (1839) 10 Sim. 74 and *Williamson v. Codrington* (1750)
1 Ves.Sen. 511 (although this decision is equally explicable as based on "meritorious consideration" (see *ante*, n.200)). *Watson v. Barker* (1843) 6 Beav. 283 and *Cox v. Barnard* (1850) 8 Hare 310
have also been described as cases of this type, although the better explanation for the latter, as
well as for the much later inadequately reported *Re Cavendish-Browne's Settlement Trusts* [1916]
W.N. 341 may well be the presence of a covenant for further assurance.
[243] See *ante*, para 3–003.

for Wigram V.-C. to have found a completely constituted trust of the benefit of the covenant.

5–115 However, following the modification of the rules governing certainty of intention which took place towards the end of the nineteenth century,[244] it is difficult to see how any such intention could today be deduced from the facts of *Fletcher v. Fletcher*. Certainly no such trust has been upheld in any of the cases subsequent to the change in the certainty of intention rule in which arguments based on *Fletcher v. Fletcher* have been raised. Admittedly in one of those cases, *Re Cook's Settlement Trusts*,[245] Buckley J. distinguished *Fletcher v. Fletcher* not on this ground but on the basis that the covenant which he was considering related to after-acquired property, something which was also the case in three other decisions in which *Fletcher v. Fletcher* was not applied.[246] Given that after-acquired property can undoubtedly form the subject matter of a covenant,[247] there seems no good reason for this distinction[248] nor is it consistent with other authorities. In *Davenport v. Bishopp*,[249] Knight-Bruce V.-C. indicated that it was possible for there to be a completely constituted trust of the benefit of a covenant to settle after-acquired property, a view which is confirmed by other authorities in which promises to pay uncertain sums on uncertain future dates arising under simple contracts have been held capable of forming the subject matter of a trust.[250]

5–116 Consequently, the distinction of *Fletcher v. Fletcher* on the grounds of lack of certainty of intention seems clearly preferable to the distinction adopted by Buckley J. in *Re Cook's Settlement Trusts*; the latter case is better explained on the grounds that there was no intention to create a trust of the benefit of Sir Francis Cook's covenant in favour of his children but merely an intention to create a trust if and when its subject matter came into existence and was duly transferred to the trustees. On this basis, a completely constituted trust of the benefit of a covenant to settle either existing or after-acquired property must certainly be capable of being found today if the settlor has clearly manifested the appropriate intention[251] by, for example, stating expressly that, pending transfer of the intended trust property, "the benefit of the covenant to settle shall be held by the trustees on the trusts of the settlement". All the commentators would be likely to agree that the use of this

---

[244] *ibid.*

[245] [1965] Ch. 902. The facts were considered *ante*, para 5–100.

[246] *Re Plumptre's Settlement* [1910] 1 Ch. 609; *Re Pryce* [1917] 1 Ch. 234; *Re Kay's Settlement* [1939] Ch. 329.

[247] See *ante*, para 5–088.

[248] See Barton (1976) 92 L.Q.R. 236 and Meagher & Lehane (1976) 92 L.Q.R. 427.

[249] (1843) 2 Y. & C.C.C. 451 at 460.

[250] *Lloyd's v. Harper* (1880) 16 Ch.D 290 (Lloyd's was held to be entitled to sue as trustee for the benefit of all those with whom an underwriter had entered into contracts of insurance); *Royal Exchange Assurance v. Tomlin* [1928] Ch. 179 (trust of the benefit of a promise to pay a sum only in the event of a person's death before a certain date upheld).

[251] It has been questioned whether the relevant intention should be that of the settlor or of the trustees, since it is the latter who hold the chose in action which is the subject matter of the trust. However, in the case of a covenant to settle other than for value, the better view is that the relevant intention should be that of the settlor (see *The Restatement of Trusts* (2nd edn), para. 26; Rickett (1979) 32 C.L.P. 1; Feltham (1982) 98 L.Q.R. 17).

wording would give rise to a completely constituted trust of the benefit of the covenant in question.

However, there is no general agreement as to what, if any, other situations **5–117** should be found to give rise to such a trust. On the one hand, it has been contended that such a trust should never be found in the absence of some clear indication of the type exemplified above that this was indeed the intention of the settlor.[252] This view has the merit of being consistent with the modern rule as to certainty of intention and with all the modern authorities; however, it involves distinguishing *Fletcher v. Fletcher* in one of the ways mentioned above and undoubtedly enables settlors to go back on voluntary covenants to settle where the beneficiaries cannot enforce those covenants directly.[253] On the other hand, it has been contended that such a trust should be implied into every covenant to settle.[254] This view is clearly inconsistent with the vast majority of the decided cases[255] but does prevent voluntary covenants to settle from ever becoming unenforceable and, therefore, meaningless.[256]

Between these two extreme views, various intermediate positions have **5–118** been suggested. It has been argued[257] that such a trust should be implied where the covenant in question gives rise to a debt[258] but not otherwise.[259] It has also been argued[260] that such a trust should be implied where the deed in question merely consists of one covenant, on the basis that, since the deed would otherwise be futile, this must be taken to be the intention of the settlor, but that, on the other hand, such a trust should not be implied in the case of lengthy settlements,[261] where the intention of the settlor in relation to individual covenants is necessarily unclear.[262]

However, despite the bewildering variety of views which have been **5–119** expressed,[263] there is absolutely no doubt that at present, for whatever reason, a completely constituted trust of the benefit of a covenant will not be found in the absence of some clear manifestation of the appropriate intention of the settlor; it certainly has to be admitted that only this view seems

---

[252] This view has been adopted in successive editions of this work, of Hanbury & Martin, *Modern Equity* and of Pettit, *Equity and the Law of Trusts*.

[253] See Feltham (1982) 98 L.Q.R. 17.

[254] See Elliott (1960) 76 L.Q.R. 100; Hornby (1962) 78 L.Q.R. 228.

[255] Other than *Fletcher v. Fletcher* and the other cases referred to *ante*, n.242.

[256] See *The Restatement of Trusts* (2nd edn), para. 26 and Feltham (1982) 98 L.Q.R. 17.

[257] By Friend [1982] Conv. 280.

[258] Which will be the case where the subject matter of the covenant is existing money.

[259] In other words, where the subject matter of the covenant is either specific and presently existing property other than money or after-acquired property.

[260] By Hayton in Hayton & Marshall, *Commentary and Cases on the Law of Trusts and Equitable Remedies* 12th edn (London, Sweet & Maxwell, 2005), p.244. Hayton goes on to say "that this would be the position, anyhow, under the Contracts (Rights of Third Parties) Act 1999 if the covenant was created after May 10, 2000"; admittedly the beneficiary of the intended trust could almost certainly then enforce the covenant but that is not technically the same as being able to enforce a completely constituted trust.

[261] Such as marriage settlements, where covenants to settle are invariably made in favour of both persons within the marriage consideration and of persons outside it.

[262] The settlor cannot be taken to have intended to create such a trust in favour of persons outside the marriage consideration.

[263] Those mentioned in the text are only a sample.

to be consistent with the modern rule as to certainty of intention. Only in these circumstances will beneficiaries who are unable to enforce a covenant to settle in any other way nevertheless be able to enforce that covenant indirectly by relying on the existence of such a trust.

CHAPTER 6

DISCRETIONS AND POWERS

I. THE NATURE OF DISCRETIONS AND POWERS

1. *Generally*

Almost all trusts[1] involve the exercise of powers of a largely administrative nature, either conferred expressly by the trust instrument or implied into it by statute; whether or not the powers are exercised is a matter of discretion. Such powers arise whether the trust in question is fixed or discretionary. Discretionary trusts, but not fixed trusts, additionally involve the exercise of discretions of a entirely dispositive nature. This follows from the basic distinction between fixed and discretionary trusts,[2] namely that each of the beneficiaries of a fixed trust is entitled in equity to a fixed pre-determined share of the trust property at the appropriate time and may enforce his rights to that share against the trustees; on the other hand, before any individual beneficiary of a discretionary trust has a right to any part of the trust property, the trustees have to exercise one or more of the discretions vested in them by the settlor or testator. The immense majority of discretionary trusts also confer powers of a dispositive nature exercisable by the trustees, by the settlor, by one or more of the beneficiaries or by some third party who is often described as the protector of the settlement in question[3]; the exercise of these powers is also capable of conferring proprietary rights on individual beneficiaries of the discretionary trust.

6–001

It is discretions and powers of a dispositive nature with which this chapter is principally concerned. However, a few words about powers of an administrative nature are also necessary. Such powers are normally conferred only on trustees, although their exercise is sometimes made subject to the control of the settlor, one or more of the beneficiaries or, in the case of discretionary trusts, of the protector of the settlement. Among the powers generally granted are the following: powers to deal with the investment of the trust property by making and transposing investments[4] (these powers now[5] confer all the powers of an absolute owner[6]; this includes the power to

6–002

---

[1] Only nominee trusts do not do so. Trustees are nominees where they are bare trustees for a sole beneficiary and additionally have agreed with their beneficiary to follow his instructions in all respects; in return, they are entitled to be indemnified by the beneficiary against any liabilities which they may incur to third parties (see *Hardoon v. Belilios* [1901] A.C. 118).

[2] See *ante*, para 2–010.

[3] See *post*, para 6–029.

[4] See *post*, para 14–055.

[5] Since the Trustee Act 2000 came into force.

[6] Trustee Act 2000. s.3(1).

make investments in land[7]; powers to settle claims[8]; powers to apply to the court for guidance as to the execution of the trust[9]; powers to insure trust property[10]; powers during a minority either to advance income for the maintenance of the infant beneficiary or to accumulate that income[11]; and powers to advance capital for the benefit of any beneficiary.[12] All these powers, and many more, will be implied by statute into every trust instrument unless they are expressly excluded.

6–003   The last two powers mentioned, the powers of maintenance and advancement, although administrative in nature, are of course dispositive in effect and can be used to achieve the same results as purely dispositive discretions and powers. They are, therefore, much more relevant to the subject matter of this chapter than are the purely administrative powers. So are the vital powers to replace some or all of the existing trustees and appoint new ones which are generally conferred on the settlor of an *inter vivos* trust and, subject to that, on the existing trustees or indeed on anyone else at all—in the absence of any express provision, statute confers these powers on the existing trustees although, in such circumstances, beneficiaries of full age who are between them absolutely entitled to the trust property are now also entitled to exercise them.[13] These latter powers are important for the somewhat obvious reason that it is the persons appointed trustees as a result of their exercise who will normally be able to exercise the dispositive powers thereafter.

6–004   Two final points must be stressed. First, most of the principles discussed in this chapter are applicable to all the discretions and powers conferred by the trust instrument or by statute, whether those discretions and powers are administrative or dispositive in nature. Secondly, it is fundamental to the nature of a trust that a trustee, or for that matter anyone else who is exercising discretions and powers, should not be a puppet at the end of a string pulled by the settlor or by the beneficiaries[14]; he must instead be a person who can and will exercise an independent judgment over a wide

---

[7] Trustee Act 2000, s.8; the powers conferred on trustees of land by Trusts of Land and Appointment of Trustees Act 1996, s.6(1) have been amended to bring them into line with the Trustee Act 2000. Similar powers are held by whoever has the power of investment under a settlement subject to the Settled Land Act 1925; although no new settlements of this type have been able to arise since 1996; continuing settlements of this type are not trusts of land and their position is still governed by the Settled Land Act 1925, s.41.

[8] Trustee Act 1925, s.15, as amended by Trustee Act 2000, s.40(1), Sch.2, Pt. II, para. 20.

[9] See *post*, para 14–121.

[10] Trustee Act 1925, s.19, as substituted by Trustee Act 2000, s.34(1).

[11] See *post*, para 17–035.

[12] See *post*, para 18–006.

[13] See *post*, para 13–042. The latter powers were conferred on absolutely entitled beneficiaries by Trusts of Land and Appointment of Trustees Act 1996, ss.19, 20. However, they may be (and in practice generally are) excluded by the trust instrument. Although they prima facie apply to trusts created prior to 1997, in the case of such trusts they can also be excluded by a deed executed thereafter by the settlor or by the surviving settlors of full capacity.

[14] It is in this respect that the position of a trustee differs from that of a nominee, a bare trustee who is generally under an express or implied contractual obligation to comply in all respects with the directions of the beneficiaries. A bare trust is one where property is held directly on trust for a body corporate or one or more beneficiaries of full age absolutely. However, not all trustees whose beneficiaries are of full age and between them absolutely entitled to the trust property are bare trustees. A trustee who holds property by way of succession for persons who are between them absolutely beneficially entitled is certainly not a bare trustee and must act in

field. In this respect, the fact that a trustee has been appointed by the settlor, by someone else who has been given an express power so to do such as a protector, or by beneficiaries of full age who are between them absolutely entitled to the trust property does not enable him to escape from liability for breach of trust if he fails to exercise his own independent judgment; however, while he will certainly be at risk if he blindly follows the instructions of the settlor or a protector, he will not be at any risk if he follows instructions given to him by beneficiaries of full age who are between them absolutely entitled to the trust property.

2. *Aspects of Discretions*

(A)   Generally

Discretions of a dispositive nature arise under discretionary trusts, trusts in favour of such of the members of a class, either pre-determined or selected by the trustees, as the trustees in their absolute discretion determine from time to time. Where the class is pre-determined, there are two possibilities: the trustees may merely have the discretion to decide to whom and in what proportions the trust property, or the income arising from that property in any particular year, is to be distributed (this type of trust is known as an exhaustive discretionary trust); alternatively, the trustees may have the discretion both whether to make any distribution at all and, in the event that they decide to do so, to whom and in what proportions (this type of trust is known as a non-exhaustive discretionary trust[15]). Where the trustees also have the right to determine the membership of the class (or add to the membership of a pre-determined class), they obviously have yet a third discretion.   **6–005**

In all three cases, no individual beneficiary or potential beneficiary of the trust has any right to any part of the trust property unless and until the trustees have exercised in his favour one or more of the discretions vested in them by the settlor or testator. However, individual or potential beneficiaries do have the right to compel the trustees to administer the trust properly[16]; this includes a right to have their claims properly considered from time to time by the trustees.[17] They may also, under what is known as the Rule in *Saunders v. Vautier*,[18] join together to wind-up the trust although this is only possible if they are all ascertained and of full age and are between them absolutely entitled to the subject matter of the trust; if these requirements are satisfied, it does not matter that the interests of some of them are deferred or contingent or wholly dependant on the exercise of discretions by the trustees in their favour.   **6–006**

---

such a way as to protect the interests both of the tenant for life and of the remainderman. However, both his beneficiaries and the beneficiaries of a bare trust have the right to terminate the trust at any time by calling for the transfer of the trust property to them.

[15] A discretionary trust can only be non-exhaustive during whatever accumulation periods are permitted.

[16] See *post*, para 19–013.

[17] See *ante*, para 3–074.

[18] (1841) Cr. & Ph. 240; see *post*, para 19–019.

6–007   Whether a trust in fact confers a discretion on its trustees is a question of construction which is not always easy to resolve. Fixed, rather than discretionary, trusts were upheld in each of the following three cases.

In *Re Sanderson's Trust*,[19] the trustees were directed to apply the whole or any part of the income "for and towards maintenance, attendance and comfort" of a specified person. Page-Wood V.-C. held that the trustees had no discretion and must apply such part of the income as was necessary for his maintenance, attendance and comfort of that person. The author of this edition recently relied on this decision in order to compromise proceedings arising out of a gift on trust "to utilise a maximum of one-third of my residuary estate for the purposes of rehousing my father for the rest of his lifetime or for so long as he shall wish to reside in such accommodation". This was done on the basis that the trustees equally had no discretion and therefore had to use whatever part of a third of the residuary estate proved to be necessary in order to rehouse the father.[20] In neither of these two cases was it relevant that the trust in question was for a purpose; this was because of the general rule that trusts of this type are regarded as absolute gifts to the person in question with the purpose being merely their motive.[21]

However, the fact that the trust in question was for a purpose might perhaps have been regarded as relevant in the rather more controversial decision in *Re Bowes*[22] that a trust to expend funds "in planting trees for shelter" on an estate which, although held by the testator during his lifetime, had become vested in another on his death, which had created an absolute beneficial interest in favour of the latter; he was, therefore, held to be entitled to call for the money and spend it on whatever he liked. The only real justification for this decision appears to be the fact that, since he could not be compelled to plant trees on his own land, the only other option was to hold that the trust was void for lack of a beneficiary to enforce it so that, on balance, the conclusion reached appears closer to what the testator presumably intended.

(B) For How Long are Discretions Exercisable?

6–008   Although the discretions vested in trustees obviously permit very considerable flexibility, they nevertheless cannot be exercised indefinitely but only within a reasonable time. What is reasonable depends on the facts of each case. In *Re Gulbenkian's Settlement Trusts (No.2)*,[23] the trustees learned in April 1957 of a decision[24] which cast doubt on the validity of a provision of the trust instrument relating to the accumulation of income. They therefore retained the income without accumulating it. The doubt raised was not actually resolved until the decision of the House of Lords in *Re Gulbenkian's*

---

[19] (1857) 3 K. & J. 497.

[20] In both cases, there are obvious difficulties about certainty of subject matter (see *ante*, para 3–013); this point was not raised before Page-Wood V.-C. and was not particularly relevant to the issue before him, which was what was to happen to the surplus of the income not so expended. The possibility of it being raised in the more recent proceedings was one of the bases on which the proceedings were settled.

[21] See *Re Osoba* [1979] 1 W.L.R. 247.

[22] [1896] 1 Ch. 507.

[23] [1970] Ch. 408.

[24] *Re Gresham's Settlement* [1956] 1 W.L.R. 573, subsequently overruled.

Settlement Trusts (No.1)[25] in October 1968. The question then arose as to whether the trustees were still entitled to exercise their discretion in respect of income which had been accruing ever since 1957. Plowman J. held that in the circumstances the trustees' retention of the income was not unreasonable; consequently, they could still exercise their discretion in respect of the whole of the accrued income. It therefore follows that, provided the surrounding circumstances make it reasonable for them so to do, trustees can retain income as income for some time and only then decide whether or not to accumulate it.

On the other hand, if the trustees do not exercise their discretion within a reasonable time, the consequences differ depending on whether or not the trustees were obliged to exercise it, in other words whether the discretion in question arose by virtue of a trust power or mere power. In the former case, the trustees will have been under an obligation to exercise their discretion; consequently, it will not be extinguished by lapse of time. Accordingly, the trustees will be able to exercise it at any time, no matter how much later, and, if they fail to do so, the court will direct them so to do[26] or, in default, execute the trust in one of the ways laid down by Lord Wilberforce in *McPhail v. Doulton*.[27] In the latter case, on the other hand, while the trustees will have been under a duty to consider whether or not to exercise their discretion, they will not have been under any duty actually to exercise it; in such circumstances, any failure to exercise their discretion within a reasonable time will cause it to be lost and, consequently, no longer exercisable.[28] Any income which they could have distributed will therefore either have to be turned into capital by being accumulated or, if this is no longer possible,[29] will have to be given to whichever beneficiary is next entitled under the trust.   6–009

(C) To What Extent can Discretions be Delegated?

While there is no restriction on the ability of settlors and testators to confer discretions on their trustees and on other persons, there are restrictions on the ability of the latter to delegate those discretions to others. The basic position is that matters involving a decision on a matter of policy, or importance, which would include a decision as to whether or not a person is to benefit and, if so, to what extent, cannot be delegated,[30] but that ancillary decisions taken in order to give effect to the trustees' decision can be delegated.[31] So, if the trustees in the exercise of their discretion decide to give a beneficiary £500, they are entitled to leave to their solicitor the decision as to whether to pay that sum by cheque or in cash. Otherwise impermissible delegation is of course capable of being authorised by the terms of the trust instrument but in the case of discretions, as distinct from powers, this is not normally done.   6–010

---

[25] [1970] A.C. 508 and see *ante*, para 3–038.
[26] *Re Locker's Settlement Trusts* [1978] 1 All E.R. 216.
[27] [1971] A.C. 424 at 457; *ante*, para 3–040.
[28] *Re Gourju's Will Trusts* [1943] Ch. 24; *Re Wise* [1896] 1 Ch. 281; *Re Allen-Meyrick's Will Trusts* [1966] 1 W.L.R. 499.
[29] At present, accumulation is permitted only for limited periods; see *post*, para 7–046.
[30] *Re May* [1926] 1 Ch. 136; *Re Mewburn* [1934] Ch. 112; *Re Wills' Will Trusts* [1959] Ch. 1.
[31] *Att.-Gen. v. Scott* (1750) 1 Ves.Sen. 413; *Re Hetling and Merton's Contract* [1893] 3 Ch. 269.

3. *Aspects of Powers*

(A) The Basic Definition of Powers

6–011   While powers are most frequently found as provisions in trust instruments, they can exist outside a trust and it is, therefore, necessary to consider them as a separate concept. A power can be said to be the right to exercise, in respect of property belonging to another, one or more of the rights which are the normal incidents of ownership. Some differences between trusts and powers are immediately apparent. For example, a trust is necessarily equitable, while a power may or may not be. Thus a power of attorney to convey a legal estate and a power of sale over a legal estate exercisable by a mortgagee are both legal; on the other hand, a power affecting the beneficial entitlement to property is now necessarily equitable.[32] But the primary basis of the distinction is of course that a trust is imperative, whereas a power is not. The distinction may be shown by contrasting a trust for sale and a power of sale. Where land is given by deed *inter vivos* or by will to trustees on express trust for sale, then the trustees will be under a duty to sell the land, even though statute now implies a power to postpone sale in every case.[33] On the other hand, where there is merely a power of sale, whether in a deed *inter vivos* or a will, the person in whom the power is vested will not be compelled to exercise it.

(B) Powers in the Trust Context

6–012   Concentrating on the dispositive powers which are the principal subject matter of this chapter rather than the administrative powers to which reference has already been made, there has been a general tendency to make trusts more and more flexible, which is of course one of the reasons why discretionary trusts have become more popular than fixed trusts. Two of the more recent developments have been to include what are generally known as overriding powers of appointment and powers to alter the class of beneficiaries.

(1) Overriding powers of appointment

6–013   Where property is settled on discretionary trusts, it necessarily follows that no one has an immediate interest in possession either as to income or as to capital; this is also the effect of a settlement on fixed trusts for persons who are not *sui juris*. In such circumstances, it has become the normal practice to vest in the trustees, or where appropriate in the protector, a power, exercisable at any time before any beneficiary obtains an absolute interest in the capital of the trust, for the following purposes: first, to permit some or all of the existing trusts to be revoked and for new trusts to be declared in favour of the same, or sometimes slightly different, beneficiaries; and/or, secondly, to permit the trust property to be transferred to the trustees of other settlements under which the same, or sometimes slightly different, persons are beneficially entitled. Such powers are generally known as overriding powers of appointment.

---

[32] LPA 1925, s.1(7).
[33] Trusts of Land and Appointment of Trustees Act 1996, s.4(1).

The first of these powers enables the trusts of a settlement to be modified   **6–014**
in the light of subsequent events with a view particularly to avoiding for as
long as possible anyone obtaining an interest in possession and so giving
rise to the deemed disposal for the purposes of capital gains tax which such
an event inevitably brings with it.[34] The second of these powers enables the
trust to be wound-up without having to give any of the beneficiaries an
interest in possession in the process, although in this case such a deemed
disposal cannot be avoided.[35] Well drawn overriding powers of appointment[36] normally also contain a modified form of the statutory power of
advancement (which would be implied anyway in the absence of contrary
intention); this power will be exercised in order to vest property in one or
more of the beneficiaries absolutely,[37] something which will also give rise to
a deemed disposal.

Any trust which contains an overriding power of appointment will inevi-   **6–015**
tably also contain an ultimate absolute beneficial gift in favour of some
person or persons who is or are already *sui juris*. No one ever has the
slightest intention that these persons, who are generally known as default
beneficiaries, should ever obtain an interest in possession save in the
unlikely event that all the other beneficiaries are wiped out by some unforeseen disaster such as an air crash or a terrorist bomb. They are there for two
purposes: first, to forestall the sort of argument which succeeded in *Vandervell v. I.R.C.*[38] that the ultimate beneficiary is in fact the settlor, something
which can affect not only, as in that case, the incidence of income tax but also
the incidence of inheritance tax[39] (for the same reason, the settlor and his
present and future spouse also have to be excluded from the class of
beneficiaries in whose favour the power can be exercised); and, secondly, to
forestall any argument that the trustees have for any moment of time in
effect, even though not on the face of things, been holding on trust for one
of the earlier beneficiaries absolutely, something which would trigger an
undesired deemed disposal.

It will be apparent from the contents of the previous two paragraphs that   **6–016**
the utilisation of overriding powers of appointment is a complicated affair.
The most elaborate precautions have to be taken: first, in order to ensure that
what is being done is within the powers which have been conferred on the
trustees, which are in turn subject to various overriding rules of law, such as
the various rules against perpetuities and accumulations which will be
discussed in the next chapter[40]; and, secondly, to avoid any undesirable or
unexpected fiscal consequences. These difficulties multiply when overriding

---

[34] See *post*, para 15–136.
[35] Because the trustees will be holding the property on trust for the trustees of the other
settlement absolutely; see *post*, p.638.
[36] An excellent example are the overriding powers of appointment which are explained and
set out in the precedents included in Kessler, *Drafting Trusts and Will Trusts* (it is particularly
important always to use the most recent edition of this work; the current one is the 8th edn
(London, Sweet & Maxwell, 2007).
[37] Powers of advancement can also be used to make resettlements (see *Pilkington v. I.R.C.*
[1964] A.C. 612) but this is not necessary where the settlement in question also contains an
overriding power of appointment.
[38] [1967] 2 A.C. 191; see *ante*, para 4–030.
[39] See *post*, para 13–059.
[40] See *post*, Chapter 7.

powers of appointment are being used on a second or subsequent occasion because of the need to act in a way which is consistent not only with the provisions of the original settlement but also with the modifications which have already been made. Dealing with such clauses is, therefore, one of the most difficult and one of the most stimulating aspects of modern discretionary trusts.

(2) Powers to alter the class of beneficiaries

6–017   The decision in Re Manisty's Settlement[41] established, resolving previous doubts in this respect, that there is in principle no objection to a settlor conferring powers on the trustees, or for that matter on any protector, which permit the alteration of the class of beneficiaries, either by addition to or by subtraction from the pre-existing class.

What was actually in issue in that case was a power to add persons to the existing class of beneficiaries. The settlement was a discretionary trust for the benefit of the children and remoter issue of the settlor. The trustees purported to exercise a power to bring other persons into that class by bringing in the settlor's mother and any person who in the future might become the settlor's widow. Templeman J. held that such a power could indeed be validly conferred on trustees and that their exercise of it was therefore valid.[42] Such powers provide a useful means of providing for people whose existence has been overlooked or whose financial situation suddenly changes for the worse.

However, the settlement also conferred a power on the trustees to exclude any individual members of the existing class of beneficiaries. Such a power is even more useful because it enables the settlor initially to declare a very wide class of beneficiaries and at the same time give his trustees power to exclude anyone within that class if this becomes necessary at any later stage (as it often does, usually as a result of the introduction of new legislation adversely affecting the fiscal liabilities of the settlor, the trust or the beneficiaries). Templeman J. was equally prepared to accept the validity of this sort of power.

Needless to say, exactly the same precautions have to be taken in the exercise of this type of power as in the exercise of overriding powers of appointment.

(C) To What Extent can Powers be Delegated?

6–018   There is no doubt that a settlor or testator can give a power of appointment to a trustee or indeed to anyone else—even a general power of appointment given by a testator to his trustees cannot be impugned as a delegation of testamentary disposition.[43] The basic rule governing the extent to which trustees or others can delegate the powers which have been given to them is the same as in the case of discretions: matters involving a decision on a matter of policy, or importance, which would include a decision as to

---

[41] [1974] Ch. 17; see also *Blausten v. I.R.C.* [1982] Ch. 256 and *Re Hay's Settlement Trusts* [1982] 1 W.L.R. 202, discussed *ante*, para 3–074.

[42] The decision was consistent with the earlier approval by the House of Lords in *Pilkington v. I.R.C.* [1964] A.C. 612 of the exercise of a power of advancement which took effect by way of resettlement; see *post*, para 18–037.

[43] *Re Beatty's Will Trusts* [1990] 1 W.L.R. 1503; see Davies, 107 L.Q.R. (1991) 211.

whether or not a person is to benefit and, if so, to what extent, cannot be delegated,[44] but ancillary decisions taken in order to give effect to the trustees' decision can be delegated.[45] However, the instrument by which a power is conferred can expressly authorise delegation of its exercise and modern overriding powers of appointment generally contain provisions to this effect.[46] Occasionally, powers can also be delegated by virtue of express statutory provisions.[47] Where there is no such express authority, it seems that delegation can still be made effectively where there is an implied power to this effect in the instrument creating the power but not otherwise.

So far as powers to determine beneficial entitlements are concerned, the question of delegation most often arises where there is a power to appoint a fund among a number of beneficiaries and the donee of the power wishes to make an appointment not in favour of a particular beneficiary absolutely but instead on trust for him. It is clear that the donee of the power cannot appoint the fund on discretionary trusts, even if all the beneficiaries of the discretionary trust in question are beneficiaries of the original settlement, unless this is expressly or impliedly authorised in the trust instrument (most modern overriding powers of appointment specifically so provide[48]). This is because an unauthorised appointment on discretionary trusts amounts to the donee of the power delegating to the trustees of the new trust the power to decide what each beneficiary of the discretionary trust will in fact receive.[49] Similarly if, in the absence of such authorisation, an appointment is made on protective trusts[50] (which has the effect of conferring a life interest which, in the event of on the life tenant's bankruptcy, will determine and be replaced by discretionary trusts), the appointment of the life interest will be valid but the discretionary trusts will be void in the event that they replace the life interest.[51] However, it is accepted that any appointment on trust which is validly made in accordance with the terms of the power may also confer a power of advancement on the trustees, even if the trustees of the original settlement did not have one or did not have one as broad; to this extent at least, an appointment may confer an additional discretion on the trustees of a new settlement.[52] The different question of the extent to which

6–019

---

[44] *Re May* [1926] 1 Ch. 136; *Re Mewburn* [1934] Ch. 112; *Re Wills' Will Trusts* [1959] Ch. 1.

[45] *Att.-Gen. v. Scott* (1750) 1 Ves.Sen. 413; *Re Hetling and Merton's Contract* [1893] 3 Ch. 269.

[46] See the overriding powers of appointment set out in Kessler, *Drafting Trusts and Will Trusts* (it is particularly important always to use the most recent edition of this work; the current one is the 8th edn (London, Sweet & Maxwell, 2007).

[47] An example of statutory authority to delegate is that conferred by Trusts of Land and Appointment of Trustees Act 1996, s.9, which enables trustees of land to delegate their powers of management; see also *post*, para 14–101.

[48] See the overriding powers of appointment set out in Kessler, *Drafting Trusts and Will Trusts* (it is particularly important always to use the most recent edition of this work; the current one is the 8th edn (London, Sweet & Maxwell, 2007).

[49] *Re Morris' Settlement* [1951] 2 All E.R. 528; *Re Hay's Settlement Trusts* [1982] 1 W.L.R. 202.

[50] See *post*, para 8–003.

[51] *Re Boulton's Settlement Trusts* [1928] Ch. 703; *Re Morris' Settlement* [1951] 2 All E.R. 528; *Re Hunter* [1963] Ch. 72.

[52] This was specifically held in *Re Morris' Settlement* [1951] 2 All E.R. 528, a decision which was accepted to be correct in *Re Wills' Will Trusts* [1959] Ch. 1 and in *Pilkington v. I.R.C.* [1964] A.C. 612.

trustees can delegate their powers of management and administration and appoint agents to act on their behalf is considered in later chapters.[53]

4. *Distinctions between Discretions and Powers of Appointment*

6–020   It has already been seen that the practical effect of the exercise of discretions and of powers of appointment is very similar. Deciding which of the two has been created is often far from straightforward. In *Bond v. Pickford*[54] the trustees were given the power to "apply capital for the benefit of any one or more of the beneficiaries by allocating or appropriating to such beneficiary such sum or sums out of or investments forming part of the capital of the trust fund" as they thought fit. Nourse J. held that this power of "allocation or appropriation" was akin to a limited special power of appointment. Conclusions of this type, however marginal they may be, may nevertheless be important because there are three significant practical differences between discretions and powers of appointment.

(A) Payments from the Trust Fund

6–021   The first difference relates to payments from the trust fund. Strictly speaking, a discretion deals with funds which are already in hand, whereas a power of appointment governs money which will arise or become payable in the future. An analogy can usefully be drawn with the operation of a railway with each train representing a payment.

The exercise of a discretion in favour of a beneficiary takes place after a train or a number of trains have already reached the marshalling yard and are under the control of the marshaller (that is to say, after a payment of funds or a number of payments of funds have reached the hands of the trustees); in such circumstances, the marshaller has to decide down which of a number of possible tracks to send the individual wagons making up the train or trains (that is to say, the trustees have to decide which of the beneficiaries should receive the whole or some part of each payment received).

On the other hand, the exercise of a power of appointment in favour of a beneficiary amounts to setting the points towards a particular track. This action does not of course in itself cause a train to come along and go down that particular track (that is to say, the exercise of the power of appointment in favour of the beneficiary does not of itself cause any payment to be made to him). However, whenever a train comes along (that is to say, whenever funds become available for payment), that train will go down that track (that is to say, the funds will be paid to that particular beneficiary) without any further action or decision being taken for so long as the points remain set in that direction (that is to say, for so long as the appointment remains unrevoked).

6–022   This difference is particularly important when, as is generally the case, the funds subject to the power are the income of the trust fund. In the case of a

---

[53] See *post*, paras 13–088, 14–101.
[54] [1982] S.T.C. 403; the subsequent appeal to the Court of Appeal is reported only in *The Times*, May 24, 1983.

discretion, a separate decision has to be taken on each occasion on which any income is available for distribution. This latter point may be illustrated by *Wilson v. Turner*.[55] In that case the trustees had a power to pay or apply income arising from the trust fund to or for the maintenance of an infant beneficiary.[56] They did not make a conscious decision on each occasion but merely handed over the income to the infant's father. The Court of Appeal held that the payments so made had to be repaid to the trust fund. Had the trustees instead from time to time actively considered the merits of the case and consciously decided to apply the income for the maintenance of that infant, their decision would have been valid.[57] If, on the other hand, income is subject to a power of appointment, then, once an appointment has been made, all income arising will go to the beneficiary to whom it has been appointed without any further decision having to be taken.

(B) Formalities
The second difference between a discretion and a power of appointment is   6–023
in relation to formalities. No formality whatever is required for the exercise of a discretion, simply because the discretion is exercised at the moment when the decision is taken to do so.[58] On the other hand, although in principle no formality is necessary for the exercise of a power of appointment either, in practice some formality is almost always prescribed in the instrument by which the power is conferred. Where this is the case, the formal requirements in question have to be strictly complied with. Consequently, if a power of appointment is to be exercised by deed, it cannot be exercised by will[59] and a power which is to be exercised by will cannot be exercised by any instrument which is not a will.[60] Further, where a power has to be exercised within a particular time, it will only be validly exercised by will if the testator has died by then.[61]

However, there are some exceptions to this basic rule. If the donor of the   6–024
power not only specifies the type of instrument by which the power is to be exercised, such as a deed or will, but also specifies particular formalities to be observed in the execution of that instrument, such as signature in the presence of several witnesses, the requirements stipulated by him are sometimes modified by statute. Section 159 of the Law of Property Act 1925 provides that, in the case of a power which has to be exercised by deed, any deed exercising it will be formally valid if executed in the presence of at least two witnesses; similarly, in the case of a power which has to be or is

---

[55] (1883) 22 Ch.D. 521.

[56] The statutory power of maintenance is considered *post*, para 17–035.

[57] A further illustration of the same principle is *Re Greenwood* (1911) 105 L.T. 509.

[58] It is theoretically possible for the donor of the power to prescribe some formal requirement for the exercise of any discretion arising thereunder but it is most unlikely that this would ever be done.

[59] *Lord Darlington v. Pulteney* (1797) 3 Ves.Jr. 384; *Lady Cavan v. Doe* (1795) 6 Bro.P.C. 175; *Re Phillips* (1884) 41 Ch.D. 417.

[60] *Reid v. Shergold* (1805) 10 Ves.Jr. 370; *Re Evered* [1910] 2 Ch. 147.

[61] *Cooper v. Martin* (1867) L.R. 3 Ch.App. 47. However, this will not actually prevent the power being exercised *inter vivos* by then where this is a permissible alternative.

exercised by will, any will which complies with the provisions of the Wills Acts[62] will be effective to do so.[63]

6–025　　It can, therefore, generally be said that the exercise of a discretion requires only a metaphysical act, whereas the exercise of a power of appointment requires a physical act by the appointor. It should, however, be stressed that questions of formality must not be confused with any requirement that the consent of any person must be obtained prior to exercise. The exercise of both a discretion and a power of appointment can be made subject to various consents being first obtained, and any purported exercise made without those consents will be ineffective.

(C)　Revocability

6–026　The third difference between discretions and powers of appointment relates to revocability. When a discretion is exercised, its effect is to confer upon the beneficiary a right to a sum which is in hand. The beneficiary has the right to demand payment, and payment is in fact usually made to him promptly. It is then too late for the person exercising his discretion to seek to change his mind and to recall the money.[64] On the other hand, a power of appointment looks towards the future. It can, therefore, clearly be expressed to be revocable and in this event, subject always to the terms of the instrument by which the power was conferred, the appointment can be revoked and a new appointment made without any limit.

6–027　　Whether a power is actually revocable at all depends on the terms of the instrument by which it is created. Most modern overriding powers of appointment[65] deal with this question expressly, usually by providing that powers may be exercised either revocably or irrevocably; however, there is obviously nothing to stop a settlor or testator from providing that any particular power can only be exercised irrevocably. In the absence of any express or implied provision dealing with the matter, it seems to be assumed that a power can be exercised in either of the two ways. But if, on the exercise of a power which is capable of being exercised in either of the two ways, nothing is said as to whether it is being exercised revocably or irrevocably, there seems to be a presumption that the power is being exercised irrevocably.[66]

---

[62] Wills Act 1837, s.10; Wills Act 1963, s.2.

[63] A possible further exception to the general principle that formal requirements must be strictly observed is that equity has in certain cases perfected the imperfect exercise of a power in a somewhat similar way to that in which equity will perfect an imperfect gift (see *ante*, para 5–020); broadly speaking, equity has done this where the donee of the power intended to exercise it and his exercise of the power was in order to satisfy a moral obligation (see *Chapman v. Gibson* (1791) 3 Bro.C.C. 229; *Garth v. Townsend* (1869) L.R. 7 Eq. 220; *Kennard v. Kennard* (1872) L.R. 8 Ch.App. 227). However, there are no recent examples of this exception and it cannot be assumed that it would now necessarily would be applied.

[64] It is theoretically possible for the donor of the power to provide that the donees of the discretion could change their minds between the exercise of the discretion and the payment over of the sum to the beneficiary in question but it is most unlikely that this would ever be done.

[65] See the overriding powers of appointment set out in Kessler, *Drafting Trusts and Will Trusts* (it is particularly important always to use the most recent edition of this work; the current one is the 8th edn (London, Sweet & Maxwell, 2007).

[66] Assuming that this presumption does in fact exist, it must clearly be able to be rebutted by implication in appropriate circumstances.

It is of course apparent that a discretion and revocable power of appoint-   6–028
ment can both be used to achieve the same general effect. Suppose, for
example, that someone has the right to dispose of the income of a fund and
wishes that for the year 2009 it should go to Charles; for the year 2010 it
should go to Douglas; and for the year 2011 it should go to Edward. If what
the donor has is a discretion, a decision can be made at or after the end of
2008 in favour of Charles; at or after the end of 2009, in favour of Douglas;
and, at or after the end of 2010, in favour of Edward. If, on the other hand,
what the donor has is a revocable power of appointment, at the beginning
of 2009 the income can be revocably appointed to Charles; at the beginning
of 2010, that appointment can be revoked and a new revocable appointment
be made in favour of Douglas; and, at the beginning of 2011, the appointment can again be revoked and a new revocable appointment made in
favour of Edward. The result so far as the beneficiaries in question are
concerned is the same in both cases. If, as is likely in the case of modern trust
instruments, the donors are trustees and have the option of taking either
course of action, they are likely to be influenced in their choice as to how to
proceed by fiscal considerations.

5. *The Exercise of Discretions and Powers by Third Parties*

It has already been seen that discretions and powers can be vested not only   6–029
in the two parties whose existence is necessary to the existence of any trust,[67]
namely one or more trustees and one or more beneficiaries (each of the two
being able to be and very often being[68] both trustee and beneficiary) but also
in the settlor, even though he is neither trustee nor beneficiary, and in third
parties who have no other connection with the trust in question.

There has long been a tendency for certain powers to be vested in settlors   6–030
and in individual beneficiaries. Traditional settlements for persons by way
of succession have habitually given the settlor or the initial tenant for life a
power to choose which of a number of potential remaindermen will take at
the end of the life interest—a typical formulation would be a gift "to trustees
to hold on trust for my wife for life and subject to that for such of our
children as I the settlor [or she my wife] may by will or by deed appoint and
in default of appointment for all our children in equal shares absolutely".
Powers of this type are also sometimes given to persons who are otherwise
totally unconnected with the settlement.

However, in recent years it has become increasingly common, particularly   6–031
in trusts created in off-shore jurisdictions, for much more substantial powers
to be conferred on a person who is generally known as "the protector" of the
settlement in question; it is important to emphasise, however, that such a
person is just as much a donee of powers as a person with more restricted
powers.[69] Initially, substantial powers of this type tended to be of a negative,

---

[67] See *ante*, para 1–035.

[68] Every property which is jointly owned will, under Law of Property Act 1925, ss.34 and 36,
be held by its co-owners as trustees at law on trust for themselves as either joint tenants or
tenants in common in equity.

[69] See generally Waters in *Trends in Contemporary Trust Law* (ed. Oakley, 1996), p.63; Duckworth, [2006] Trust Law International 180, 235.

rather than a positive, nature in that they merely enabled protectors to veto the ways in which the trustees exercised the powers vested in them, although such powers of veto were admittedly often backed up by a power to remove the existing trustees and appoint new ones in their place. However, it is now normal for a protector to be given positive, rather than merely negative, powers both to determine the beneficial interests and to direct the trustees how to exercise the administrative powers vested in them.[70]

6–032   The expression "protector of the settlement" is actually derived from the Fines and Recoveries Act 1833 and originally denoted a person who, in certain circumstances, had to give his approval to a now virtually obsolete estate in land known as an estate in fee tail being converted into an estate in fee simple.[71] However, none of the characteristics of a modern protector is derived from this statute. Further, there is not the slightest need for a person with the sort of substantial powers referred to in the previous paragraph to be given any specific title whatever by the trust instrument and, even if such a person is given some specific title, there is no requirement that he be described as a protector. Other names, such as an enforcer, a nominator or a committee,[72] are also commonly employed, the name enforcer being particularly common in respect of the novel types of purpose trusts which, as has already been seen,[73] have been the subject of legislative development in some of the off-shore jurisdictions.[74] However, for present purposes, all such persons will be described as protectors.

6–033   Where an off-shore jurisdiction has made specific reference to protectors by that or any other name,[75] the legislation in question has tended also to regulate in certain respects their powers and potential liabilities and any such regulation is of course definitive in the jurisdiction in question. However, many jurisdictions, such as England and Wales, have no legislation

---

[70] (The Bahamas) Trustee Act 1998, s.81 specifically envisages a whole series of such powers being given to protectors.

[71] An estate in fee tail devolves on the successive heirs of the body of the original tenant in fee tail. However, such an estate can be converted into an estate in fee simple, a process known as barring the entail; this has the effect of depriving the next person in line of his inheritance. A tenant in fee tail in possession has, since 1833, been able to bar his entail by an inter vivos conveyance of the land in fee simple or, since 1925, by his will. But a tenant in fee tail who does not have an interest in possession has only ever been able to do this inter vivos and then only with the consent of the person known as the protector of the settlement. That person will now always be the holder of the interest in possession for the time being or, in default, the court; however, until 1926, settlors were entitled to nominate up to three persons of their choice to act as protector of the settlement and that possibility is the basis of the modern usage of the expression. Estates in fee tail do still exist but sadly no more can now be created as a result of the Trusts of Land and Appointment of Trustees Act 1996, Sch.1, para. 5.

[72] See the British Virgin Islands Trustee Ordinance 1994, s.86 ("protector, nominator, committee or any other name").

[73] See ante, para 3–139.

[74] The most influential legislation was (Bermuda) Trusts (Special Provisions) Act 1989, subsequently redrafted and substantially amended in 1998; see also (Jersey) Trusts (Jersey) Law 1984 Articles 10A, 10B and 10C (added in 1996), which are similar to the original Bermudan legislation. Much more revolutionary was (Cayman Islands) Special Trusts (Alternative Regime) Law 1997, now (Cayman Islands) Trusts Law 2001, ss.95–109 (because of the name of the original legislation, such trusts are known as STAR trusts). All these statutes use the expression "enforcer").

[75] Other examples are (Belize) Trusts Act 1992, s.16 ("protector"); (Cook Islands) International Trusts Act 1984, s.2 ("protector").

which contains any reference to the rights and duties of protectors and the legislation of jurisdictions in off-shore jurisdictions which has created the novel types of purpose trusts is not generally applicable to other types of trusts there either. In such circumstances, the position of protectors is governed exclusively by the contents of the trust instrument in question. This was specifically held in Bermuda, one of the jurisdictions which has never had any relevant legislation other than that concerning purpose trusts, in one of the very few cases in which the position of protectors has yet had to be considered, *Von Knieriem v. Bermuda Trust Company*[76]; the same approach was adopted, although not explicitly, in the other leading case, the decision of the Court of Appeal[77] of the Isle of Man in *Steele v. Paz*.[78]

No matter what the precise powers conferred on any particular protector actually are, however, his appointment is for one purpose and one purpose only, namely to enable the trustees to be directed and controlled in the exercise of their discretions in the way desired by the settlor. It is because the settlors of trusts subject to English law are likely to know, and consequently have confidence in, their chosen trustees, and because such trustees are anyway likely to be reasonably susceptible to the influence of the settlor and the beneficiaries, that protectors have not yet become particularly common in such trusts. The frequent utilisation of protectors in off-shore trusts is precisely because in practice such trusts have to have locally based trustees whom neither the settlor nor the beneficiaries is even likely to know, never mind trust. While it is usually inadvisable for either a resident settlor of an off-shore trust or resident beneficiaries to be among its trustees,[79] the same risks do not automatically attach to having a resident settlor as protector; however, having the settlor as protector is still not generally recommended.[80] But there is no risk at all in having a third party protector from the settlor's "home" jurisdiction; indeed the settlor's local lawyer often fulfils this role in the same way as he would fulfil the role of an on-shore trustee.[81] Such a protector can readily be informed of the wishes of the person who will necessarily have appointed him (and who *in extremis* will often be able to remove and replace him); this will normally mean that the trustees' discretions are exercised in accordance with the settlor's wishes not

6–034

---

[76] (1994) 1 *Butterworths Offshore Cases and Materials* 116 (see Matthews, 9 Trust Law International (1995) 108).

[77] Technically known as "the Staff of Government Division".

[78] (1995) 1 *Butterworths Offshore Cases and Materials* 338.

[79] This is because Her Majesty's Revenue and Customs may then contend that the person in question is in control of the trust and attempt to tax him on its income and its capital gains, thus defeating the whole object of the exercise. This happened in *I.R.C. v. Schroder* [1983] S.T.C. 480, where it was unsuccessfully claimed that this was the result of the settlor having the power to appoint trustees and protectors. Further, under the present law, a majority of off-shore trustees is necessary even where the settlor was non-resident at the time when the trust was created.

[80] Where the settlor is resident, the income of the trust will be taxable as his income if he as protector has the power to direct its application. Further, whatever his residence, there is a risk, particularly if the powers given to the protector are very extensive, that it may be contended that the level of control thus retained by the settlor makes the trust a sham; see *ante*, para 3–127.

[81] This has been the case in the majority of the reported cases on protectors where the protector has been a third party.

only during the settlor's lifetime but more or less indefinitely since the protector will continue in office after the settlor's death and is likely to have the power to nominate a successor.

6–035   The presence of a protector will also generally be advantageous for the beneficiaries, at any rate after the settlor's death. But this will not necessarily be the case during the settlor's lifetime, whether the protector is the settlor himself or someone else. In *Von Knieriem v. Bermuda Trust Company*,[82] the trust property comprised a substantial minority holding in a company which was in turn the holding company of a major pharmaceutical group. The settlor was the moving spirit of this holding company but, due to a boardroom struggle, had to face the possibility that he would be voted off its board of directors. The protector, the settlor's lawyer and personal friend, sought assurances from the trustee, a Bermuda trust company, that it would delegate its votes to him and thus enable him to vote for the settlor. The trust company, apparently under some pressure from the beneficiaries who seem to have been less enthusiastic about the settlor, refused to do so. So the protector simply removed the trustee and appointed another Bermudan trust company as trustee in its place. The court held that both the removal and the appointment were valid and granted the protector an order[83] that the shares be transferred to the new trustee. The position of the settlor was therefore preserved contrary to the wishes of the beneficiaries, who were also deprived of any possibility of recourse against the original trust company.[84] However, in the light of a subsequent decision[85] that such powers are normally[86] fiduciary powers, beneficiaries in this position might well now be able successfully to contend that any exercise by the protector of his powers which could be shown not to be in their interests was void.

6–036   In any event, the exercise by a protector of his powers is not wholly devoid of control. As will be seen later on,[87] the exercise of any power can be set aside in the event that the donee commits fraud on the power or makes a relevant mistake and these rules must apply as much to protectors as to other donees of powers. In this respect, it will be significant whether the power in question is a fiduciary power or a personal power; such authorities as there are[88] suggest that powers will be fiduciary powers unless they can be used for the personal benefit of the individual protector, something which is only likely to be the case if he is also a beneficiary. However, in the absence of dishonesty, it does not appear that a protector

---

[82] (1994) 1 *Butterworths Offshore Cases and Materials* 116 (see Matthews, 9 Trust Law International (1995) 108).

[83] Where, as in this case, the protector had no statutory authority to seek the aid of the court, the basis of his right to do so is not entirely clear but has not been questioned in any of the relevant authorities (see also *Re X's Settlement* (1994) 1 *Butterworths Offshore Cases and Materials* 600 (Jersey) and *Re Omar's Family Trust* [2000] W.T.L.R. 713 (The Cayman Islands)).

[84] Who could not possibly be held liable for breach of trust if it had been sacked against its will.

[85] *Re Osiris Trustees and Goodways* (1999) 3 Butterworths Offshore Service 257 (Isle of Man).

[86] This is not the case where the protector is also one of the beneficiaries.

[87] See *post*, para 6–102.

[88] Apart from the authorities already referred to, see *Rawson Trust Co. v. Perlman* (1990) 1 Butterworths Offshore Service 31 at 50–52 (The Bahamas).

can be held liable to compensate the beneficiaries for his actions except where relevant legislation so provides.[89] But where a protector is dishonest, he can certainly be dismissed by the court[90] and he will be liable to return to the trust any trust property for whose misappropriated he has been responsible, whether that property was received by him or by a third party.[91]

6. Reasons for Creating Discretions and Powers

(A) Flexibility

As was mentioned in Chapter 1,[92] a settlor or testator often wishes to make a present disposition but to confer a benefit at some time in the future in the light of the circumstances then pertaining, circumstances which have not yet arisen and which therefore necessarily cannot be known. A person who is creating a trust for his children or remoter issue may wish the amount, if any, which each receives to depend on his or her conduct, financial need and/or success. A much larger payment may be justified in the case of a beneficiary who is a student or who is training for entry into a profession or vocation than in the case of a sibling of his who is already well established in business. Alternatively, a person may have definitively decided to devote funds to charitable purposes but may wish the particular recipients of his bounty to be selected according to the social or other needs which seem most pressing at the time in the future when the funds become available. However, it must not be thought that the fact that discretions have been vested in trustees necessarily means that the objects of the trust must be treated unequally. A father who creates a trust for his children or more remote issue leaves the trustees entirely free to treat them all alike if the trustees wish to do so; equally, the trustees are free to treat them unequally whether or not one of the special circumstances which the father may have had in mind occurs.

6–037

(B) Continuing Control of the Property

(1) By the settlor as such

A settlor of a trust has no formal legal right to any control over the trust property by virtue of the fact that he was the settlor; indeed, he does not as such even the right to have his wishes listened to. However, there is nothing to stop the settlor of an inter vivos trust appointing himself as one of the original trustees and this is extremely common in the case of on-shore trusts,

6–038

---

[89] Only the (United States of America) Restatement (Second) of Trusts (1959), s.185 specifically envisages such liability, although jurisdictions such as The Bahamas and The British Virgin Islands, which exonerate protectors when acting in good faith, may well be regarded as envisaging such liability in the absence of good faith.

[90] *Re The Frieburg Trust* [2004] 6 I.T.E.L.R. 1078 (Jersey)

[91] He will be potentially liable for what is known as "dishonest assistance" and "knowing receipt" respectively; see *post*, para 10–153.

[92] See *ante*, para 1–013.

although usually inadvisable in the case of off-shore trusts.[93] Further, even where the settlor is not one of the original trustees, he will generally be able to direct and control the trustees in the exercise of their discretions during his lifetime. He will undoubtedly have been responsible for choosing the original trustees and they are obviously likely to listen to his views. Indeed, in the case of off-shore trusts, settlors generally have the power to remove the trustees and appoint new ones in their place without having to show cause; however, such powers have been held to be fiduciary powers[94] and so their exercise will be voidable if they are not exercised in the interests of the beneficiaries but, for example, in the interests of the settlor himself.

(2) By the settlor as the donee of powers

6–039 As has just been seen, the settlor of an inter vivos trust may well have the power to remove the trustees and appoint new trustees in their place without having to show cause. It has also already been seen[95] that traditional settlements for persons by way of succession have habitually given the settlor a power to choose which of a number of potential remaindermen will take at the end of the initial life interest and that there is no reason in principle why the settlor should not appoint himself as the initial protector, although this also is not usually recommended.[96] A further type of power which is occasionally vested in the settlor of an *inter vivos* trust is a power to revoke the settlement in question. The exercise of such a power will necessarily take away any fiscal advantages which the creation of the settlement was intended to achieve and so, where the settlor remains subject to the tax regime of his home jurisdiction, there are now fewer[97] circumstances where its exercise will have any point. However, the existence, as distinct from the exercise, of such a power cannot now[98] of itself adversely affect the existence of a settlement and there is, therefore, now no reason why such powers should not be included, as they often are in off-shore jurisdictions.

(3) By means of the use of a third party protector

6–040 It has also already been seen[99] that the purpose of appointing a protector is to enable the trustees to be directed and controlled in the exercise of their

---

[93] This is because Her Majesty's Revenue and Customs may then contend that the person in question is in control of the trust and attempt to tax him on its income and its capital gains, thus defeating the whole object of the exercise. This happened in *I.R.C. v. Schroder* [1983] S.T.C. 480, where it was unsuccessfully claimed that this was the result of the settlor having the power to appoint trustees and protectors. Further, under the present law, a majority of off-shore trustees is necessary even where the settlor was non-resident at the time of the creation of the trust.

[94] *Re Osiris Trustees and Goodways* (1999) 3 *Butterworths Offshore Services* 257 (Isle of Man).

[95] See *ante*, para 6–038.

[96] Because of the risk that it may be contended, particularly if the powers given to the protector are very extensive, that the level of control thus retained by the settlor makes the trust a sham; see *ante*, para 3–127.

[97] The decision in *Melville v. I.R.C.* [2000] S.T.C. 628 established that the exercise of a power of revocation could enable capital gains tax which would otherwise have arisen on the creation of a settlement to be held over; however, that decision was in this respect reversed by legislation in 2002.

[98] It could conceivably have done so before the effect of the decision in *Melville v. I.R.C.* [2000] S.T.C. 628 was reversed.

[99] See *ante*, para 6–031.

discretions in the way desired by the settlor; where the protector is neither the settlor nor a beneficiary of a settlement, his appointment will normally mean that the trustees' discretions are exercised in accordance with the settlor's wishes not only during the settlor's lifetime but more or less indefinitely since, once the settlor is dead, each protector is likely to have the power to nominate his successor.

(4) By means of letters of wishes

A less direct means by which settlors can control the ultimate devolution of the trust property is by means of letters of wishes.[100] As their name suggests, these are documents which exist outside the formal trust documents. They set out the wishes of the settlor but are not binding on the trustees.[101] Further, as will be seen later on,[102] at present the beneficiaries are not normally entitled to see them.   6–041

A genuine letter of wishes, by which the settlor provides additional guidance for the trustees of a discretionary trust who have little contact with and may well not know all the members of a class of beneficiaries, is not only not objectionable; it can be extremely helpful. Such non-binding guidance can be very useful for both settlor and trustees, although less so for beneficiaries even in the event that they are actually allowed to see the document in question.   6–042

However, in off-shore jurisdictions, letters of wishes can play rather differ-ent roles. Deeds of trust tend to be standard form documents used in hundreds of cases and often take the form of a declaration of trust by the off-shore trustees stating that a nominal sum has been transferred to them to be held on the trusts in question rather than a deed of settlement executed by the settlor. In such circumstances, letters of wishes are often the only docu-ments which reveal the identity of the true settlor and the true beneficiaries. They, therefore, enable the existence of the settlement and the interests of the beneficiaries thereunder to be concealed both from any creditors, and dependants and fiscal authorities who might be interested in discovering them.[103] This admittedly does not prejudice either the settlor or the beneficiaries.   6–043

Letters of wishes are also used off-shore for more sinister purposes. Tailored letters of wishes are sometimes used to convince settlors unfamiliar with the nature of discretionary trusts, usually but not always settlors from non-common-law jurisdictions with a less than perfect command of English, that their wishes will in fact be followed when the reality is that those wishes are not binding. In these circumstances, if the trust deed were held to be a sham and the settlor were held to have intended the letter of wishes to have been binding on the trustees, the letter of wishes could be regarded as constituting the true trusts. This would admittedly only be likely to cause any immediate problems if the settlor had expressed the wish that income or   6–044

---

[100] See Matthews [1995] Offshore Tax Planning Review 181.

[101] *Bank of Nova Scotia Trust Co. (Bahamas) v. Ricart de Barletta* (1985) 1 *Butterworths Offshore Service* 5, 8–9.

[102] See *post*, para 14–026.

[103] See the description of a settlement of this type in *Re T.R. Technology Investment Trust* [1988] B.C.L.C. 256, 263–264.

capital should be paid to him or to his spouse (for settlors in most jurisdictions, this would effectively make all income and capital gains taxable in their hands on-shore). However, the consequential loss of secrecy could obviously also in the long-term prejudice the interests of other beneficiaries.

6–045 Even worse, letters of wishes are occasionally pure shams, either because their terms have not been explained to the settlor or because they have been signed by dummy settlors who request the trustees to take into account the wishes of a settlor whose name has not even yet been inserted in the appropriate space on the standard form letter[104]; the latter type of sham letters of wishes obviously often accompany potentially sham trusts.[105] If the trust deed were held to be a sham and a much less precise letter of wishes obliged the trustees to follow the instructions of the settlor, he could be regarded as having retained a life interest in the trust property; if, on the other hand, both the trust deed and the letter of wishes were held to be a sham, there would be no trust at all and the trust property would be deemed to have been held on resulting trust for the settlor at all times. Both results would, in addition to the income tax and capital gains tax consequences already mentioned, expose settlors in most jurisdictions to inheritance tax on the entire trust property on their deaths and, in civil law jurisdictions, would also expose the assets much more readily to attacks by their forcible heirs, the persons in such jurisdictions whom it is not possible to disinherit.

6–046 Nevertheless, these abusive uses of letters of wishes should not be allowed to detract from the extremely useful function of a genuine letter of wishes in enabling the settlor to provide non-binding guidance for the trustees and thus control, at least to some extent, the devolution of the trust property.[106]

(C) Fiscal Considerations
6–047 Despite the obvious advantages already discussed, it is nevertheless fiscal considerations which are still, despite the repeated attacks on the fiscal efficacy of discretionary trusts, usually the principal reason for their creation.

In the United Kingdom, income tax is a so-called "progressive tax" in that it is imposed on the "slices" of a person's taxable income or capital gains at a progressively increasing rate. Each person is entitled to receive the first "slice" of his income free of tax.[107] The next "slice" is taxable at what is known as "the starting rate" of, at present, 10 per cent, although since April 6, 2008 this rate has only been applicable to unearned income and not to earned income; the next "slice" is taxable at what is known as "the basic

---

[104] See the facts of *West v. Lazard Brothers & Co. (Jersey)* [1993] Jersey L.R. 165, 201–205.

[105] See *ante*, para 3–127.

[106] See *ante*, para 1–012.

[107] The amount of this "slice" is calculated by means of personal allowances, which vary according to the personal circumstances of the individual. For the year 2008–09, each person under 65 was entitled to a personal allowance of £5,435. Additional allowances are available to pensioners, which vary depending on their age and marital status, and also in certain other circumstances. The size of these allowances is reviewed annually in each Budget and listed in the Finance Act by means of which each Budget is brought into effect.

rate" of, at present, 20 per cent; and the residue is taxable at what is known as "the higher rate" of, at present, 40 per cent.[108] Capital gains tax was, until April 5, 2008, also a progressive tax[109] but is now imposed on such part of a person's taxable capital gains in each year as exceeds his annual exemption[110] at a fixed rate of 18 per cent. Inheritance tax was originally a progressive tax but has long since been imposed at a fixed rate of 40 per cent on the balance of a person's estate (which for this purpose includes any property disposed of other than for value during the seven years immediately prior to his death) after deduction of his lifetime allowance, generally known as his nil rate sum,[111] and of any other assets which are exempt from inheritance tax; the principal exemption is anything which is inherited by his spouse or civil partner or is left to charity.[112]

Any potential settlor of a discretionary trust who is subject to United Kingdom taxation is virtually bound to be paying the highest possible rate of income tax of 40 per cent on any property which he is in a position to settle and, to the extent that that property has increased in value, it will potentially be subject to capital gains tax at 18 per cent; further, save to the extent that he intends to leave that property to his wife or civil partner, he is faced with the prospect that, on his death, 40 per cent inheritance tax will be payable on all of that property other than his nil rate sum. The simplest way of saving some or all of these taxes is to give property away outright to someone who pays income tax at a lower rate, although such a gift obliges the donor immediately to pay any capital gains tax to which the property is potentially subject; if the donor survives for more than three years after making the gift, the inheritance tax potentially payable thereon also starts to reduce and is completely eliminated if the donor survives for a total of seven years. But outright gifts are not necessarily as appropriate or desirable as the creation of a discretionary trust.

The incidence of taxation on discretionary trusts is considered in detail in the chapter on the taxation of trusts.[113] In brief outline, although the creation of a discretionary trust *inter vivos* gives rise to an immediate potential liability to inheritance tax of 20 per cent, no tax is actually payable to the extent that the value of the subject matter of the trust falls within the settlor's nil rate sum; the trust can be topped up every year as the nil rate sum rises and, after seven years, the whole of the then nil rate sum will be available again, less any intervening top-ups. Nor does it cost any more to create a discretionary trust by will than to dispose of its subject matter in any

6–048

---

[108] In 2008–09, the first £2,320 of unearned taxable income (taxable income is the income which exceeds a person's total allowances) was taxed at 10%, earned and further unearned taxable income up to £36,000 was taxed at 20%, and further earned and unearned taxable income in excess of that figure was taxed at 40%. The width of the different bands is also reviewed annually in each Budget and listed in each Finance Act.

[109] It was payable at the highest rate at which the taxpayer in question paid income tax.

[110] In 2008–09, £9,600. There are many other exemptions, including the taxpayer's main residence, chattels worth less than £6,000, and certain securities.

[111] In 2008–2009, £312,000.

[112] Further exemptions include gifts of agricultural property, business property, and woodlands, whether made *inter vivos* or on death, and small gifts made *inter vivos* of up to £3,000 per donor and £250 per donee per annum or in consideration of marriage (£5,000 by each parent, £2,500 by each grandparent, and £1,000 by anyone else)

[113] See *post*, Chapter 15, *passim*.

other way, other of course than to a surviving spouse or civil partner. If and to the extent that any inheritance tax is payable on the creation of a discretionary trust, a further charge to inheritance tax is made on every 10th anniversary of its creation at 30 per cent of whatever inheritance tax would have been payable had the property been settled at that time and the appropriate proportion of this 10-yearly charge is payable if any property is paid out to any of the beneficiaries during a 10-year period; however, these subsequent charges are not substantial and no inheritance tax will be payable at all in respect of a discretionary trust created *inter vivos* if the settlor settles no more than the total amount of his lifetime allowance in each seven-year period.

Further, while virtually the same capital gains tax is payable by the trustees of a discretionary trust as would be payable by its settlor,[114] there are also considerable potential income tax advantages. First, the terms of the trust instrument usually allow the trustees to decide whether to distribute or to withhold income. They can, therefore, distribute income to a beneficiary in a year when his total income is low, so that his total liability to income tax is kept down, and withhold income when the beneficiary's total income is high. Secondly, the trust instrument usually allows the trustees to accumulate income, so that it becomes converted into capital, although admittedly only after the payment of higher rate income tax on the income which is accumulated.[115] Thirdly, a discretionary trust allows income and capital to be spread among members of a family, rather than being bunched in the hands of one member. To take a simple example, suppose that Andrew, Basil and Colin are brothers whose top rate of income tax is respectively 40 per cent, 20 per cent and nil (because Colin is a student and has no earned income whatsoever). If each were to receive bank interest or rental income of £1,000, £400 income tax would be payable thereon by Andrew, £200 income tax would be payable by Basil and no income tax at all would be payable by Colin. If the £3,000 in question were instead earned by a discretionary trust, the trustees could in principle, ignoring the costs of administering the trust, pay the entire income to Colin free of income tax or at any rate divide it between the brothers in such a way that considerably less income tax was paid. However, the position is less favourable in the case of investment income; 10 per cent of this is withheld at source and cannot be recovered even if the income finishes up in the hands of someone who, like Colin, is not liable to income tax at all, while the remaining 90 per cent bears tax at rather more than the above rates if paid to someone who, like Basil or Andrew, pays income tax at the basic rate or at the higher rate.

Further, the legislature gives privileged treatment to discretionary trusts created by a will for the children of the deceased under the age of 25 provided that they become entitled to the subject matter of the trust either

---

[114] The only difference is that the discretionary trust will have its own annual exemption, which is generally half that enjoyed by a natural person.

[115] This is at present only possible for the first 21 years of the trust. However, when current proposals are enacted, the permissible periods will be increased to no less than 125 years; see *post*, para 7–053.

at the age of 18, in which case no inheritance tax is payable at all, or no later than the age of 25, in which case a maximum of 4.2 per cent inheritance tax is payable; nor is any capital gains tax payable on the subject matter of the trust (as would otherwise be the case) when the children reach the age in question. Until they attain that age, the income of the trust can either be accumulated or be applied for their maintenance, education or other benefit.[116]

Man will go to considerable lengths to preserve his wealth and the creation of discretionary trusts remains a popular and successful way of so doing, particularly if full advantage is taken of all the available exemptions and allowances. Further, settlors are not obliged to create their discretionary trusts in this jurisdiction. Consequently, where the property to be settled very greatly exceeds the settlor's lifetime allowance,[117] there has been an increasing tendency to use discretionary trusts set up not here but in other jurisdictions; the trust law of the majority of these jurisdictions was originally based on English law[118] but some of the others have enacted legislation specifically in order to adopt the English concept of a trust[119] while the remainder utilise quite different institutions including different concepts of trusts.[120] Since most of these jurisdictions do not tax discretionary trusts (or the equivalent institutions) at all, the fiscal advantages of such off-shore settlements are even greater. The legislature has, therefore, intervened with a view to discouraging the creation of such settlements. The increasingly stringent provisions which have been enacted in order to make the beneficial interests of those beneficiaries of off-shore trusts who are or are deemed to be domiciled and/or resident in some part of the United Kingdom liable to United Kingdom taxation are summarised in the chapter on taxation of trusts[121]; the manner in which a trust can be exported by the appointment of non-resident trustees is considered in the chapter on the appointment of trustees.[122]

6–049

---

[116] Until 2006, these advantages were instead enjoyed by what were known as accumulation and maintenance trusts, which had to be for the benefit of one or more persons under the age of 25, usually but not necessarily the children or grandchildren of the settlor; at least one beneficiary had to be alive at the outset and the beneficiaries had to become entitled to the trust property or to an immediate vested interest in its income on attaining an age not exceeding 25. Pre-existing trusts of this type continue subject, if the age which has to be attained is over 18, to the payment of inheritance tax in respect of any period between April 6, 2008 and the date when the beneficiary attains the age in question.

[117] In such circumstances, the available exemptions and allowances are much less relevant; further such settlors (and only such settlors) can afford the exorbitant fees normally charged in the off-shore jurisdictions for setting up and subsequently administering the trusts in question.

[118] Such as the Channel Islands, the Isle of Man, Gibraltar, Hong Kong, Bermuda, The Bahamas, The Cayman Islands, The British Virgin Islands and a number of other Caribbean and Pacific tax havens (the most notable, and notorious, example of the latter is The Cook Islands).

[119] Such as Nauru and Malta.

[120] Such as Liechtenstein, where bodies corporate such as foundations and establishments are the usual vehicles despite the existence of a concept of trust law which has now been held to be based primarily on contract.

[121] See *post*, Chapter 15, *passim*.

[122] See *post*, paras 13–50–13–62.

II. THE TYPES OF DISCRETIONS AND POWERS

1. *Generally*

6–050   Where it is up to the trustees, or for that matter to some other person, to decide either whether a particular individual will receive a benefit from a trust at all or the extent of the benefit of any particular beneficiary, the discretion or power vested in the trustees or other person will be one of two broad types, depending on whether or not there is any obligation to exercise it. If the trustees, or other persons, are under an obligation to exercise their discretion or power, then they are said to hold a trust power, also sometimes called a power in the nature of a trust. It is important to note that these terms have traditionally been used to denote two quite distinct situations. The first is where the person subject to the obligation has the property in question vested in him as a trustee; in this case the term trust power or power in the nature of a trust is virtually indistinguishable from the term discretionary trust—indeed in the leading case of *McPhail v. Doulton*,[123] the two terms were used interchangeably. The second is where the person subject to the obligation is not himself a trustee of the property in question so that his only role is that of exercising the discretion or power; in this case, although he may be described as the donee of a trust power or a power in the nature of a trust, he certainly cannot be described as a discretionary trustee since he is not a trustee of anything.

6–051   If a person is holding property on trust for such of the members of a defined class and in such proportions as he shall in his absolute discretion appoint, then he is likely to be held to hold a trust power or a power in the nature of a trust in the former sense; he is in effect a discretionary trustee. If, on the other hand, a person is holding property on trust for such of the members of a defined class and in such proportions as a third party shall in his absolute discretion appoint, the third party is likely to be held to have a trust power or a power in the nature of a trust in the latter sense; he is not a trustee of anything and no discretion whatever is vested in the person who is actually holding the property on trust. However, while it is necessary to remember that there is no requirement that the holder of a trust power should himself be a trustee of the property in question, there is no practical significance in this distinction. In each of the two cases, the holder of the trust power is under an obligation to exercise it and, in the event that he fails to do so, the court will exercise it instead. Traditionally, this was always done by dividing the property in question equally between all the objects of the power but, where this is not possible,[124] it will have to be done in one of the three ways envisaged by Lord Wilberforce in *McPhail v. Doulton*,[125] namely by either appointing new trustees, or directing persons representative of the donees of the power to prepare a scheme of distribution or,

---

[123] [1971] A.C. 424.
[124] As will be the case where the trust power in question is of the type validated by the decision of the House of Lords in *McPhail v. Doulton* [1971] A.C. 424 and a complete list of the objects of the power therefore cannot be drawn up.
[125] [1971] A.C. 424 at 457.

should the proper basis for distribution be apparent, directing the trustees how to proceed.

If, on the other hand, no obligation has been imposed on the trustees, or the other person in question, to exercise whatever discretion or power is vested in them or in him, then they or he are said to hold a mere power, also called a bare power or, less commonly, a power collateral.[126] Once again these terms cover two quite distinct situations, identified much more recently.[127] The first is where the donee of the mere power holds that power in his capacity as a trustee, either because he is actually trustee of the property which is to be appointed or where this is not the case but it is nevertheless apparent that the power has been given to him in a fiduciary capacity[128]; in this case, he is said to be a fiduciary donee. This is likely to be held to be the case where a person is holding property on trust for such of the members of a class and in such proportions as he may in his absolute discretion appoint and, in default of any such appointment, on trust for an identified beneficiary. The second is where the donee of the mere power is not a trustee in any sense, in which case he is said to be a non-fiduciary donee. This is likely to be held to be the case where a person is holding property on trust for such of the members of a class and in such proportions as a third party may in his absolute discretion appoint and, in default of any such appointment, on trust for an identified beneficiary.

6–052

This distinction between the two is extremely significant. Although a fiduciary donee of a mere power is under no obligation to exercise it, he does owe certain obligations towards the objects of the power (as well as a duty to those entitled in default of appointment not to misuse the power) and is "to some extent subject to the control of the courts in relation to its exercise".[129] In particular, he must consider periodically whether or not he should exercise the power (in default, the court may direct him to do so and, in the last resort, may remove or replace him), must consider the range of objects of the power, must consider the appropriateness of individual appointments and, above all, is not entitled to release the power so as to cause the property to pass to those entitled in default of appointment. On the other hand, a non-fiduciary donee of a mere power owes no obligations whatever to the objects of the power (his only duty, owed to those entitled in default of appointment, is not to misuse the power). In particular, he does not even have to consider whether to exercise the power and may release it at any time and consequently cause the property to pass to those entitled in default of appointment.

6–053

---

[126] See *Vestey v. I.R.C. (No.2)* [1979] Ch. 198, *per* Megarry J. at 206 (affirmed on other grounds in *Vestey v. I.R.C. (Nos. 1 & 2)* [1979] A.C. 1148) and *Re Hay's Settlement Trusts* [1982] 1 W.L.R. 202, *per* Megarry V.-C. at 210.

[127] In *Mettoy Pension Trustees v. Evans* [1990] 1 W.L.R. 1587 at 1614 (not the first enunciation of the distinction but the first fully developed statement of the remedies available against a fiduciary donee of a mere power). See generally Gardner 107 LQ.R. (1991) 214.

[128] In *Mettoy Pension Trustees v. Evans* [1990] 1 W.L.R. 1587, a company held a power to appoint any surplus in its pension fund, which was actually vested in a separate trustee company, in favour of the pensioners with a gift over in default of appointment to itself. The liquidators of the company wished to release this power and so enable the surplus in the pension fund to become available for its creditors. Warner J. held that the company held the power in a fiduciary capacity; consequently, it could not be released.

[129] *ibid.* at 1614.

6–054   Thus, the first and crucial question is whether or not there is any obligation to exercise the power in question. If the answer to that question is
affirmative, then the only remaining matter is in whose favour it should be
exercised, either by the donee of the power or, if he fails to do so, by the
court. If, on the other hand, the answer to that question is negative, it is
necessary to consider whether the donee of the power is a fiduciary or a
non-fiduciary; only in the former case is there any possibility of the court
intervening in the event that the donee himself fails to exercise his power
and even then the role of the court is almost certainly limited to ensuring
that the fiduciary has complied with his duty to consider periodically
whether or not to exercise the power.

2. The Distinction between Trust Powers and Mere Powers

6–055   The distinction between trust powers and mere powers must now be considered more closely. The question whether or not a trust or a power has
been created is essentially one of construction of the instrument. The distinction may be a fine one in any individual case, because what appears on the
face of the trust instrument to be a trust power may in fact be a mere power
and vice versa. Further, despite the fact that trust powers often appear in the
form of powers, they are nevertheless construed and take effect as trusts. It
is important to stress that, when what is in issue is whether a trust power or
a mere power has been created, it does not matter whether what has been
conferred on the donee of the power is a discretion or a power of appointment; although most of the discussion which follows refers to powers of
appointment, it is equally applicable to discretions.

The question of construction is best approached by reference to the following questions. An affirmative answer to either of the first two questions
is decisive and establishes that what has been created is a mere power. If
both the first two questions are answered in the negative, then the matter
generally has to be resolved by answering the third question; only if the
matter remains very evenly balanced after the third questions has been
answered can recourse ever be had to the fourth question.

(A)   Is the Discretion Power General or Intermediate, as distinct from Special?

6–056   A general power is by its nature incapable of being a trust power. A power
is described as general when it confers on its donee a power to exercise it in
favour of whoever he pleases, including the donee himself. Thus, the donee
of a general power of appointment can exercise it by appointing the property to himself beneficially. Since he is entitled to do this, the court cannot
compel him to appoint to any one else or indeed at all.

6–057   On the other hand, a special power is capable of taking effect as a trust
power. A power is described as special when it confers on its donee the
power to exercise it only in favour of one or more of a number of designated
persons or classes of persons. Thus the donee of a special power of appointment can only appoint the property in question to the persons or classes of
persons designated by the donor.

6–058   The position of the third type of power, the much more recently developed intermediate (or hybrid) power is not entirely clear. Such powers have

been described as a power "betwixt and between",[130] neither strictly general nor strictly special. The feature of such a power is that it confers on its donee the power to exercise it in favour of anyone other than one or more designated persons or classes of persons. The persons usually excluded are the settlor and his present and future spouses; this is generally done in order to forestall any argument that he has retained a beneficial interest under the trust in question, something which could have negative fiscal consequences.[131] It is also common to exclude the donee,[132] whether or not he is also the settlor. Thus the donee of an intermediate power of appointment can appoint the property in question to anyone other than the excluded person or persons. Another common type of intermediate power is the power to add persons to a class of beneficiaries; for the same reasons as above, it is usually crucial to ensure that the settlor and his present and future spouses cannot be so added. Intermediate powers are regarded as general powers for some purposes and as special powers for others.[133] It is, however, difficult to see how an intermediate power could possibly take effect as a trust power because, as in the case of a general power, there is no one in whose favour the court can compel appointment. It is, therefore, considered that such powers are, like general powers, necessarily mere powers.

(B) Is there a Gift Over in Default of Exercise?

If the settlor has provided for a gift over, an alternative gift in the event that the donee of the power fails to exercise it, then that power cannot be a trust power. The existence of a gift over is incompatible with the imperative nature of a trust and necessarily therefore operates as a denial of one's existence. Thus in *Re Mills*[134] a power was given to appoint among those children and remoter issue who in the opinion of the donee of the power should evidence a desire to maintain the family fortune. This limitation was followed by a gift elsewhere in default of appointment. The Court of Appeal held that because there was a gift over the power did not operate as a trust. It is not easy to think of any example of a gift over in default of exercise other than a gift which, like the gift in *Re Mills*, is a gift over in default of appointment. This second question therefore appears to relate exclusively to powers of appointment.

6–059

It is not always easy to decide whether any particular gift is indeed a gift over in default of exercise. Only if it actually is, will a trust power not be able to be upheld. Therefore, if the gift over is to take effect only in the event of a failure of the class in whose favour a power of appointment is to be

---

[130] *Re Gestetner Settlement* [1953] Ch. 672 at 685.

[131] As will be seen *post*, para 15–059, no inheritance tax is chargeable on the death of any person in respect of any property which he has transferred away more than seven years earlier. The retention of any benefit or potential benefit under the terms of any settlement to which the property has been transferred prevents the seven-year period from starting or continuing.

[132] As in *Re Park* [1932] 1 Ch. 580. See also *Re Jones* [1945] Ch. 105 (power to appoint to anybody being a person and not a corporation); *Blausten v. I.R.C.* [1972] Ch. 256; *Re Manisty's Settlement* [1974] Ch. 17; *Re Hay's Settlement Trusts* [1982] 1 W.L.R. 202.

[133] Such a power is a special power for the purposes of the Wills Act 1837, s.21 and the Perpetuities and Accumulations Act 1964, s.7.

[134] [1930] 1 Ch. 654.

exercised and/or their non-attainment of a specified age, it will operate only in those circumstances rather than as a result of any failure to make an appointment; consequently, such a power is capable of being held to be a trust power.[135] However, it is clear that a residuary gift (a gift of that part of the property of a testator which has not been specifically devised or bequeathed) is not a gift over for present purposes; consequently, the presence of a residuary gift will not necessarily deprive a prior power of the character of a trust power. Thus in *Re Brierley*[136] a testator gave his wife a life interest in £50,000 with the power to bequeath or appoint that sum among such of her relatives or next-of-kin as she thought proper. She was also given the residue of her husband's estate absolutely. The wife, having released and thereby purported to extinguish the power of appointment, claimed the whole £50,000 as her own beneficially by virtue of the gift of residue in her favour. The court held that this manoeuvre was not possible; a gift of residue was totally different from a gift over of specific property which is the subject of the power of appointment.

(C)   What was the Real Intention of the Settlor or Testator?

6–060   Where the matter has not been resolved by one of the first two questions, then whether or not there is a trust power is entirely a question of construction of the words used in the instrument[137] in order to establish the real intention of the settlor or testator. It must first be observed that, if the settlor or testator has specifically provided that the discretion or power in question is not a trust power, then it will not be even if the remaining words used point clearly and inescapably towards a trust power. The House of Lords held in *Gisborne v. Gisborne*[138] that this was the effect of a gift "upon further trust that my said trustees in their discretion, and of their uncontrollable authority, pay and apply the whole, or such portion only, of the annual income of my real and personal estate . . . as they shall think expedient, to or for" the testator's widow. This gift of course conferred a discretion but it has been recognised that the same principle applies to powers.[139]

6–061   In the absence of any such express provision, the question can be less straightforward. In *Burrough v. Philcox*,[140] the testator directed that, after certain contingencies had been fulfilled, property was to be held in trust for his two children for life, with remainder to their issue, and declared that, if they should both die without issue, the survivor should have power to dispose by will of the property among his nephews and nieces and their children as he should think fit. The testator's children did in fact die without issue and without any appointment having been made by the survivor of them. It was held that a trust had been created in favour of the testator's nephews and nieces and their children; the trust in their favour was simply

---

[135] *Re Llewellyn's Settlement* [1921] 2 Ch. 281.

[136] (1894) 43 W.R. 36.

[137] Extrinsic evidence, including evidence of the intentions of a testator, may in certain circumstances be admitted as an aid to the construction of a will; see Administration of Justice Act 1982, s.21 and see *ante*, para 3–007, n.8.

[138] (1877) 2 App.Cas. 300.

[139] See *Steele v. Paz* (1995) 1 *Butterworths Offshore Cases and Materials* 338 at 405 (Court of Appeal of the Isle of Man).

[140] (1840) 5 Myl. & Cr. 72.

subject to a power of selection vested in the surviving child. Lord Cottenham L.C. stated the principle in these words: "Where there appears a
general intention in favour of a class, and a particular intention in favour of
individuals of a class to be selected by another person, and the particular
intention fails from that selection not having been made, the court will carry
into effect the general intention in favour of the class".[141] It should also be
noted that, if the decision in *Burrough v. Philcox* is applied to a power in
favour of the donor's relations generally which is not exercised and a trust
is consequently deduced in their favour, the trust will take effect in favour
of the settlor's statutory next-of-kin.[142]

However, it must be emphasised that the fact that there is, as in *Burrough*   **6–062**
v. Philcox, no gift over in default of exercise of the power in question does
not automatically lead to the conclusion that a trust should be implied. It is
apparent from other decisions that a trust will not be implied unless there is,
on the true construction of the instrument in question, an indication of a
clear intention to benefit the designated person or class in any event with
only a mere power of selection conferred on the donee of the power. Thus in
Re Weekes' Settlement[143] there was a gift of land to the testatrix's husband for
life with "power to dispose of all such property by will amongst our
children" but without any gift over in default of appointment. When the
husband died without having exercised the power of appointment in favour
of the children, Romer J. held that what the husband had been given was a
mere power, not one coupled with a trust, and that accordingly no gift to the
children as a whole arose by implication. The judge pointed out that there
had been no express gift to such of the class as the husband might appoint
—as there had been, in effect, in *Burrough v. Philcox*—but only a mere power
to appoint among a class.

Similarly, in *Re Combe*[144] a life interest in property was given to the son of
the testator and, after his death, the property was to be held "in trust for
such person or persons as my said son shall appoint but such appointment
must be confined to any relation of mine of the whole blood"; there was
again no express gift over in default of appointment. It was held that the
words quoted had created a mere power and not a trust power; according to
Tomlin J., there was nothing in the words of the will to justify importing into
it something which was simply not there.

The principle laid down in both these decisions was applied in the
somewhat more recent decision in *Re Perowne*.[145] In this case the testatrix
gave all her estate to her husband for life, "knowing that he will make
arrangements for the disposal of my estate, according to my wishes, for the
benefit of my family". The husband did in fact purport to make an appointment but this turned out to be void; consequently, the question arose as to
whether, since the power had not been effectively exercised, what had been
created was a trust in favour of the family or a mere power to appoint in
their favour. Harman J. declined to spell a trust out of the words which had

---

[141] *ibid.* at 92.
[142] *Re Scarisbrick's Will Trusts* [1951] Ch. 622; *Re Baden's Deed Trusts (No.2)* [1973] Ch. 9 at 30,
per Stamp L.J.
[143] [1897]1 Ch. 289.
[144] [1925] Ch. 210.
[145] [1951] Ch. 785.

been used and held they had given the husband a mere power to distribute the testatrix's estate among the large and indefinite class in question.

6–063   These decisions illustrate a number of propositions: first, that the question is purely one of construction, namely whether or not the settlor has shown an intention to benefit the objects of the power; secondly, that the absence of a gift over in default of appointment does not raise any necessary inference that a trust is intended—it is an argument, and nothing more than an argument, that that was the intention of the settlor or testator; and, thirdly, that because the question is one of construction, the resolution of the problem may depend on "a few words" and "mere straws in the wind".[146] The fact that this is inevitable in relation to questions of construction is demonstrated by the leading case of *McPhail v. Doulton*.[147] The deed which had to be considered in this case provided that the trustees should apply the net income in making payments at their absolute discretion "to or for the benefit of any of the officers and employees or ex-officers or ex-employees of the company or to any relatives or dependants of any such persons in such amounts or on such conditions (if any) as they think fit". One of the questions which had to be decided was whether the clause had created a trust power or a mere power. At first instance, Goff J.[148] held that it had created a mere power; the Court of Appeal,[149] by a majority, reached the same conclusion; however, the House of Lords[150] unanimously held that it had created a trust power and, therefore, took effect as a trust—the clearly expressed scheme of the deed pointed to a mandatory construction. Lord Wilberforce, undoubtedly bearing in mind the differing judicial opinions expressed by the three different tribunals, said[151]:

"It is striking how narrow and in a sense artificial is the distinction, in cases such as the present, between trusts, or as the particular type of trust is called, trust powers, and powers. It is only necessary to read the learned judgments in the Court of Appeal to see that what to one mind may appear as a power of distribution coupled with a trust to dispose of the undistributed surplus, by accumulation or otherwise, may to another appear as a trust for distribution coupled with a power to withhold a portion and accumulate or otherwise dispose of it. A layman and, I suspect, also a logician would find it hard to understand what difference there is."

(D)   Will the Construction Adopted lead to that Real Intention being Put into Effected rather than being Frustrated?

6–064   It is only where the decision reached is as marginal as the Court of Appeal apparently thought that it was in *McPhail v. Doulton* that recourse is ever had to this fourth rule. In that case,[152] the majority of the Court of Appeal held

---

[146] *Re Baden's Deed Trusts* [1969] 2 Ch. 388 at 398, *per* Harman L.J. For a formulation of the relevant rules of construction, see *Re Leek* [1967] Ch. 1061 at 1073, *per* Buckley J.

[147] [1971] A.C. 424.

[148] [1967] 1 W.L.R. 1457.

[149] [1969] 2 Ch. 126. Russell L.J. dissented.

[150] [1971] A.C. 424.

[151] *ibid.* at 448

[152] [1969] 2 Ch. 126 (*sub nom. Re Baden's Deed Trusts*).

that, in cases where the considerations were very evenly balanced in arriving at one or other of the two possible constructions, the court was at liberty to lean towards the construction which would effectuate rather than frustrate the intentions of the settlor or testator.[153] In other words, the court could take account of the legal consequences of any given interpretation; in particular, the consequence that, if construed as a trust power, the gift would certainly be void for uncertainty of objects whereas, if construed as a mere power, it would be likely to be valid,[154] and might cause the court to lean in favour of construing it as a mere power.

The fourth question was relevant in the Court of Appeal because, as has **6–065** already been seen in a previous chapter,[155] at that time the test for certainty of objects was totally different for trust powers and for mere powers. But the House of Lords[156] subsequently held, by a bare majority, that the basic test for certainty of objects for trust powers and mere powers is in fact the same. Consequently, this fourth question did not arise in their Lordships' house. However, at least one[157] aspect of the test for certainty of objects may still differ depending on whether the limitation in question has created a trust power or a mere power. This is the question of whether the requirement of administrative workability, which clearly applies to trust powers, is or is not applicable to mere powers. Prior to the decision in *Mettoy Pension Trustees v. Evans*,[158] it seemed tolerably clear that this requirement did not apply to mere powers.[159] If this is indeed the case, then this fourth question may well be decisive in determining the validity of a limitation which does not satisfy this requirement.

But now that *Mettoy Pension Trustees v. Evans* has upheld the adaptation of **6–066** the remedies available for the enforcement of discretionary trusts, trust powers and powers in the nature of a trust to mere powers held by fiduciaries, it has been suggested[160] that this may cause the requirement of administrative workability also to be applied to at least this type of mere power. If this indeed turns out to be yet another consequence of this important decision, the applicability of the fourth question will be reduced still further and will only be capable of being decisive in respect of mere powers which are non-fiduciary or personal; indeed, if the decision in *Mettoy Pension Trustees v. Evans* is extended still further, this question may well[161] cease to have any relevance at all in relation to private trusts.[162] However, for the

---

[153] On the principle of *ut res magis valeat quam pereat*.

[154] As was indeed ultimately held by the Court of Appeal in *Re Baden's Deed Trusts (No.2)* [1973] Ch. 9; by then the test that the Court of Appeal had considered to be applicable to mere powers had been held by the House of Lords to apply to trust powers as well.

[155] See *ante*, para 3–040.

[156] [1971] A.C. 424.

[157] At least one commentator also thinks that the basic test is still different where what is in issue is an old fashioned power in the nature of a trust rather than a discretionary trust; see *ante*, para 3–046.

[158] [1990] 1 W.L.R. 1587.

[159] See *ante*, para 3–067.

[160] By Gardner, 107 L.Q.R. (1991) 214 at 218–219.

[161] This of course depends on whether the test for certainty of objects is indeed the same for all discretions and powers.

[162] It is clearly still applicable to public trusts; see *I.R.C. v. McMullen* [1981] A.C. 1 at 16, *I.R.C. v. Guild* [1992] A.C. 310; *post*, para 11–008.

moment it clearly remains relevant although the likelihood of it having to be considered is obviously extremely small.

3. *The Distinction between Fiduciary and Non-Fiduciary Donees of Mere Powers*

6–067   While the recently consolidated distinction between fiduciary and non-fiduciary donees of mere powers to which reference has already been made was certainly not new,[163] its initial enunciations did not receive universal judicial approval. As recently as 1969 Lord Upjohn, in *Re Gulbenkian's Settlement Trusts*,[164] felt able to deny that donees of mere powers of appointment ever owed any duties to the objects of those powers. However, in the following year, Lord Wilberforce, in *McPhail v. Doulton*,[165] foreshadowed the somewhat later decision in *Mettoy Pension Trustees v. Evans*[166] by remarking that a "trustee of an employees' benefit fund, whether given a power or a trust power, is still a trustee and he would surely consider in either case that he has a fiduciary duty"; he added that it would be "a complete misdescription of his position to say that, if what he has is a power unaccompanied by an imperative trust to distribute, he cannot be controlled by the court unless he exercised it capriciously, or outside the field permitted by the trust".

6–068   These remarks set the scene for the authoritative statement of the distinction made by Megarry V.-C. in *Re Hay's Settlement Trusts*.[167] Having stated that a trustee is not normally bound to exercise a mere power and that the court will not compel him to do so, he continued:

"That, however, does not mean that he can simply fold his hands and ignore it, for normally he must from time to time consider whether or not to exercise the power, and the court may direct him to do this. Whereas a person who is not in a fiduciary position is free to exercise the power in any way that he wishes, unhampered by fiduciary duties, a trustee to whom, as such, a power is given is bound by the duties of his office in exercising that power to do so in a responsible manner according to its purpose. It is not enough for him to refrain from acting capriciously; he must do more. He must 'make such a survey of the range of objects or possible beneficiaries' as will enable him to carry out his fiduciary duty. He must find out 'the permissible area of selection and then consider responsibly, in individual cases, whether a contemplated beneficiary was within the power and whether, in relation to the possible claimants, a particular grant was appropriate'."[168]

6–069   This statement established a clear distinction between a mere power held by the trustees of the property in question and a mere power held by a third

---

[163] See the authorities cited by Gardner, 107 L.Q.R. (1991) 214.
[164] [1970] A.C. 508 at 521, 524–525.
[165] [1971] A.C. 424 at 449.
[166] [1990] 1 W.L.R. 1587.
[167] [1982] 1 W.L.R. 202 at 209–210.
[168] The quotations come from the speech of Lord Wilberforce in *McPhail v. Doulton* [1971] A.C. 424 at 449, 457.

party and classified all mere powers held by trustees as fiduciary powers. However, this classification must be subject to at least one exception, namely where the settlor or testator has specifically provided that the power in question is a personal power. This qualification follows from the decision of the House of Lords in *Gisborne v. Gisborne*[169] considered above which was cited as authority for precisely this proposition by Hegarty J.A. in the Court of Appeal of the Isle of Man in *Steele v. Paz*.[170] Hegarty J.A. admittedly did go on to say that in such circumstances the donee might not necessarily be entirely free from the duties set out in *Re Hay's Settlement Trusts*, presumably envisaging the situation where the trustees had declined to give any consideration whatever to the exercise of their powers (*Gisborne v. Gisborne* was a case where the trustees had given proper thought to the exercise of their powers and were willing to exercise them but not in the same way as the court would have done). However, a decision of the House of Lords of this antiquity would not be easy to circumvent.

The decision in *Re Hay's Settlement Trusts* also showed that there was some significance in the distinction which it had established in that the court could direct the trustees to consider whether or not to exercise their power; this in turn led to the further conclusion, already enunciated in two earlier judgments,[171] that a refusal to follow such a direction from the court might well lead to the replacement of the existing trustees.   **6–070**

It has subsequently been established that a donee of a mere power may be classified as a fiduciary even if he is not a trustee of the property in question. In *Mettoy Pension Trustees v. Evans*,[172] a company held the following power in respect of any surplus in its pension fund, which was actually vested in a quite separate trust company: "any surplus of the trust fund remaining . . . may at the absolute discretion of the employer be applied to secure further benefits within the limits stated in the rules, and any further balance thereafter remaining . . . shall be paid to" the employer. The company became insolvent and its liquidators sought to release this power of appointment so that the gift over in default of appointment could take effect and immediately vest the surplus in the company for the benefit of its general creditors. Warner J. held that the company held this mere power as a fiduciary (he consequently held, as will be seen later in this chapter,[173] not only that the power could not be released but also that all the remedies available to the court for the purpose of enforcing discretionary trusts were also available to it in the case of mere powers held by fiduciary donees).   **6–071**

He adduced two main reasons for concluding that the company held this power as a fiduciary: first, that the inclusion of the power in the rules of the pension fund would have been quite pointless unless its donee were a fiduciary—since the company could have made such payments to its pensioners even if it had been absolutely entitled to the surplus, a non-fiduciary power would have added nothing; and, secondly, that the pensioners were not volunteers, in that it was unlikely that the surplus had arisen solely as   **6–072**

---

[169] (1877) 2 App.Cas. 300.
[170] (1995) 1 *Butterworths Offshore Cases and Materials* 338 at 405.
[171] *Re Gestetner* [1953] Ch. 672 at 688; *Re Manisty's Settlement* [1974] Ch. 17 at 25.
[172] [1990] 1 W.L.R. 1587.
[173] See *post*, para 6–121.

a result of over-contribution on the part of the company and, in any event, the existence of the power and the expectation that its utilisation in their favour would be the subject of proper consideration had undoubtedly formed part of the overall scheme which the employees had contracted to obtain. It is undoubtedly significant that this conclusion was reached in the context of a pension fund, a context in which, as will be seen in a later chapter,[174] a large number of the recent developments in the law of trusts have been enunciated. Thus, one commentator[175] has described the conclusion as "perhaps swayed by a deeper-lying consideration", namely that, if such powers are not held to be fiduciary powers, "the surpluses to which they apply will in practice fall to companies' creditors and successful take-over predators"; whether he is right also to describe the conclusion as "not overwhelming" is rather more questionable.

6–073   Whether or not the basis of the classification adopted in *Mettoy Pension Trustees v. Evans* was indeed the special nature of pension funds and the public concern about the security of pension schemes at the time, there seemed little doubt, particularly in the light of the wholly novel remedies which that decision had made available to the court, that there would be many future attempts to classify as fiduciaries donees of mere powers who are not trustees of the property in question.[176]

III. WHEN WILL THE EXERCISE OF DISCRETIONS AND POWERS BE IMPROPER?

6–074   It will be recalled that the donees of a trust power, in any of the meanings of that expression, are, whether or not they are also trustees, obliged to

---

[174] See *post*, Chapter 12.

[175] Gardner, 107 L.Q.R. [1991] 214 at 215–216. He cites in support of this proposition *Re Courage Group's Pension Schemes* [1987] 1 W.L.R. 495 and *Imperial Group Pension Trust v. Imperial Tobacco* [1991] 1 W.L.R. 589 and would now undoubtedly also cite *Re William Makin & Sons* [1993] B.C.C. 435. All these authorities are considered *post*, Chapter 12.

[176] Such an attempt was made in The Cayman Islands in *Re Z's Settlement Trusts* [1997] Cayman Islands L.R. 298, which concerned a provision that "this trust and any of its provisions may during the joint lives of the Grantor and E be altered or amended with the unanimous consent of the Grantor and the Management Committee, executed with the same formality as this trust and delivered to the Trustee". This power was exercised so as to confer an enhanced beneficial interest on one of the members of the Management Committee. Some of the beneficiaries contended that this power was a fiduciary power and that, consequently, the members of the Management Committee could not exercise it in such a way as to enhance the beneficial interests of any of them. It was held that the basic powers vested in the Management Committee were fiduciary powers, albeit of a qualified nature; however, the only natural and workable construction of the power to amend was that it conferred a personal or non-fiduciary power on the Management Committee and the Grantor together, subject only to the obligation to act in good faith. If viewed in any other way, the power would be potentially unenforceable since it would be impossible for the court to exercise such a fiduciary power on behalf of the Management Committee at the same time as complying with the Grantor's intentions. This decision appears to confirm that powers relating to pension funds of the type considered in *Mettoy Pension Trustees v. Evans* will come to be regarded as a special case and that the classification and the remedies adopted in that case will not be extended more generally. If this is the case, the traditional distinctions between trust powers and mere powers will not require any further reconsideration. However, confirmation that this is indeed the position must obviously await a decision to this effect in this jurisdiction.

exercise it, whereas the donees of a mere power are not obliged to exercise it, although if they are fiduciaries they must at the very least consider whether or not to do so. However, once a discretion or power has been exercised, the principles which determine whether or not its exercise was proper are the same whether the power in question was a trust power or a mere power and whether or not it was exercised by a trustee or other fiduciary.

1. *When will the Exercise of Discretions and Powers be Defective?*

The exercise of a discretion or power will be defective unless it is exercised **6–075** with whatever formalities are required by the trust instrument. In principle the exercise of neither a discretion nor a power requires any formality but in practice, while trust instruments do not normally prescribe any formality for the exercise of discretions, they almost always prescribe some formality for the exercise of powers of appointment.[177]

A discretion or power can also only be exercised within the limits pre- **6–076** scribed by law or by the trust instrument; consequently, if it can be exercised only with the consent of some person, that consent must be duly obtained. In *Breadner v. Granville-Grossman*,[178] a power of appointment was held to have been executed one day too late and its exercise was, therefore, ineffective; consequently, the interests of those entitled in default of exercise of the power took effect. The court rejected a somewhat optimistic argument that the trusts declared by the power nevertheless took effect in equity on the basis that it had no jurisdiction to deprive the default beneficiaries of their interests, even though no one had intended that they should ever obtain them. The court also rejected an argument that equity could relieve against the defective exercise of the power. As is shown by *Cooper v. Martin*,[179] there is indeed such a doctrine but Park J. held that it is confined to defects of form which are not of the essence of the power in question and to powers which are being exercised in discharge of some moral or natural obligation; further, and in any event, he held that, for this doctrine to apply, the power in question had to be in existence at the time of the defective exercise and the power in *Breadner v. Granville Grossman* no longer was, having expired the previous day.

Further, the person exercising the discretion or power must make a pos- **6–077** itive mental decision to do so rather than merely allowing a situation to arise as a result of his inaction. In *Turner v. Turner*,[180] the trustees left all the decisions to the settlor (who was not a trustee) and signed the necessary documents without actually reading them. A power of appointment which they signed in this manner was held to be defective. Similarly, in *Wilson v. Turner*,[181] the trustees had a power to pay or apply income arising from the trusts to or for the maintenance of an infant beneficiary. They did not make any conscious decision whether or not to do so but merely handed over the

---

[177] See *ante*, para 6–023.
[178] [2001] Ch. 523.
[179] (1867) L.R. 3 Ch.App. 47.
[180] [1984] Ch. 100.
[181] (1883) 22 Ch.D. 521.

income to the infant's father. The Court of Appeal held that their payments had been ineffective and that they had to reimburse to the trust fund out of their own assets the amount of the payments which they had improperly made. However, had the trustees actively considered the merits of the case and consciously decided to apply the income for the maintenance of the infant, their decision would have been valid and would have been upheld. The test is, therefore, not the consequences of the action or inaction of the holder of the discretion or power in question but the nature of his own mental processes.

2. *What is the Effect of a Mistake?*

6–078   Where a discretion or power has been exercised as a result of a mistake by the person exercising it, different considerations arise. This area of the law has been reviewed in a number of recent judgments, most notably by Lloyd L.J. in *Sieff v. Fox*[182] (this was a decision of the Chancery Division, Lloyd L.J. having been elevated to the Court of Appeal between hearing the case and delivering judgment). These reviews, particularly that of Lawrence Collins J. in *AMP (UK) v. Barker*,[183] demonstrate that such mistakes can be of a number of types, each of which leads to different consequences.

(A)   Rectifiable Mistakes
6–079   The first possibility is that the document by which the discretion or power was exercised may be able to be rectified as a result of the mistake. *AMP (UK) v. Barker*[184] concerned the power of amendment which is normally given to trustees of pension trusts (as will be seen in the chapter on pension trusts,[185] this power is the equivalent in a pension trust of the overriding power of appointment normally given to the trustees of a voluntary settlement; its exercise is usually subject to the consent of the employer in question). The trustees had exercised the power with the consent of the employer in order to enhance the benefits of employees who were forced to give up employment on the grounds of incapacity; no one had realised that, because their benefits were linked to the benefits of employees who left for any other reason, this would have the effect of enhancing the benefits of the latter as well. The trustees successfully sought rectification of the deed by which the amendment had been made.

6–080   There was no difficulty in establishing the convincing proof of what had been intended which is required for all rectification claims. Despite the fact that, in bilateral transactions, it is also necessary for all the relevant parties to have been under a common mistake as to the effect of the contract or document in question, it has long been established that a trust deed creating a voluntary settlement can be rectified where the mistaken belief of the settlor was not shared by some or all of the trustees who were, with the

---

[182] [2005] EWHC 1312 (Ch), [2005] 1 W.L.R. 3811. See also *AMP (UK) v. Barker* [2001] W.T.L.R. 1237, [2001] P.L.R. 79, (2000) 3 I.T.E.L.R., *Abacus Trust Co. (Isle of Man). v. Barr* [2003] EWHC 114 (Ch) 409, [2003] Ch. 409, and *Smithson v. Hamilton* [2007] EWHC (Ch) 2900, [2008] 1 W.L.R. 1463.

[183] [2001] W.T.L.R. 1237, [2001] P.L.R. 79, (2000) 3 I.T.E.L.R. 414.

[184] [2001] W.T.L.R. 1237, [2001] P.L.R. 79, (2000) 3 I.T.E.L.R. 414.

[185] See *post*, Chapter 12.

settlor, parties to it; the leading case is *Re Butlin's Settlement Trusts*.[186] However, in *AMP (UK) v. Barker* rectification was being sought not of an original trust deed but of a deed amending a valid original trust deed, which had obviously created proprietary rights. Lawrence Collins J. held that, in these circumstances, rectification would only be possible if the mistake was common both to the persons with the power to make the amendment and all the persons who had to consent to it. This was in fact the case so the deed by which the power of amendment had been exercised was duly rectified.

Rectification is, however, limited to amending the wording of the document in question where it can convincingly be proved that that wording has not achieved the intention of the relevant party or parties. In *Breakspear v. Ackland*,[187] by means of three documents executed one after another a new trustee had been appointed, all the trustees had then added that new trustee as a beneficiary, and all the trustees had then made an appointment in her favour. On the face of things the second and third documents were contrary to the self-dealing rule. It was contended that this result could be avoided by rectifying the second and third documents by deleting all reference to the new trustee and by inserting a provision into the first document so that it took effect only after the other two. This contention was rejected on the basis that rectification can only be used to rewrite a document, not rewrite the intended course of history.[188]

6–081

(B) Mistakes as to What has been Done

The second possibility is that the exercise of the discretion or power can be avoided because it was made as the result of a mistake as to what was being done. This principle is generally known as the Rule in *Gibbon v. Mitchell*[189] but its origin seems to be the decision of the House of Lords in *Ogilvie v. Allen*[190] where both Lord Halsbury L.C. and Lord Macnaghten agreed entirely with the judgment in the Court of Appeal of Lindley L.J.[191] who held: "In the absence of all such circumstances of suspicion a donor can only obtain back property which he has given away by showing that he was under some mistake of so serious a character as to render it unjust on the part of the donee to retain the property given to him." In *Gibbon v. Mitchell*[192] Millett J., to whom *Ogilvie v. Allen* had not been cited, stated that the mistake must be "as to the legal effect of the transaction itself and not merely as to its consequences or the advantages to be gained by entering into it". This approach was subsequently followed but it was specifically rejected by Lewison J. in *Ogden v. Griffiths*[193] in favour of the principle enunciated in *Ogilvie v. Allen*. Even before the general abrogation of the distinction between mistakes of fact and mistakes of law,[194] it was not in this respect

6–082

---

[186] [1976] Ch. 251.
[187] [2008] EWHC 220 (Ch), [2008] W.T.L.R. 777.
[188] *ibid.*, at [115, 129–130]. Briggs J. was however able to save the day by finding that the self-dealing was authorised by the terms of the settlement in question.
[189] [1990] 1 W.L.R. 1304.
[190] (1899) 15 T.L.R. 294.
[191] (1897) 13 T.L.R. 399 (*sub nom. Ogilvie v. Littleboy*) at 400.
[192] [1990] 1 W.L.R. 1304.
[193] [2008] EWHC 118 (Ch), so far only reported electronically.
[194] By the House of Lords in *Kleinworth Benson v. Lincoln City Council* [1999] 2 A.C. 349.

necessary to distinguish between them[195] and it is certainly not necessary to do so now.[196]

6–083   There is no doubt that this principle is applicable to a mistake as to the identity of the person in whose favour a discretion or power is being exercised. A mistaken belief that no previous appointment had been made in favour of the person to whom the appointment in question was being made led to the application of the principle in *Lady Hood of Avalon v. MacKinnon*.[197] It will also be applicable where there has been a mistake as to either the factual or the legal effect of the terms of what has been done. In *Anker-Peterson v. Christensen*[198] the tenants for life of a settlement which was to be varied under the Variation of Trusts Act 1958[199] were ignorant of the factual effect of the proposed variation, under which the settled property was to be assigned to off-shore trustees and re-settled. They gave the consent to this variation which was a pre-requisite of its approval by the court and subsequently assigned their interests to the new trustees in ignorance of the fact that their life interests under the new settlements would no longer be indefeasible. The deeds of assignment were set aside. So too, in *Gibbon v. Mitchell*,[200] was a deed assigning a beneficial interest under a protective trust[201] whose legal effect was not what had been intended; however, mistakes of law of this type will usually be as to the effect of some overriding rule of law, such as the various rules against perpetuities and accumulations.[202] Any mistake as to the factual or legal effect of the exercise of a discretion or power by the person exercising it would clearly lead to the same result. In *AMP (UK) v. Barker*,[203] Lawrence Collins J. stated that he would have invoked this principle to set aside the exercise of the power of amendment had he not already ordered rectification. Nor is the principle restricted to the exercise of some power or discretion pursuant to a pre-existing trust; it clearly extends to voluntary dispositions[204] and therefore necessarily to the creation of voluntary settlements.[205] In *Ogden v. Griffiths*[206] Lewison J. set aside an assignment of a reversionary interest to trustees of a pre-existing settlement because at the time of the assignment the assignor was mistaken about his state of health.

6–084   What is at present uncertain is whether a mistake merely as to the fiscal consequences of what has been done is within the scope of the principle. In *Anker-Peterson v. Christensen*[207] Davis J. referred to the distinction drawn by

---

[195] See *Gibbon v. Mitchell* [1990] 1 W.L.R. 1304.
[196] Lawrence Collins J. so stated in *AMP (UK) v. Barker* [2001] W.T.L.R. 1237, [2001] P.L.R. 79.
[197] [1909] 1 Ch. 476.
[198] [2002] W.T.L.R. 313.
[199] See *post*, para 21–018.
[200] [1990] 1 W.L.R. 1304.
[201] See *post*, para 8–003.
[202] See *post*, para 7–004.
[203] [2001] W.T.L.R. 1237, [2001] P.L.R. 79.
[204] *Ellis v. Ellis* (1909) 26 T.L.R. 166 (gift of pure personalty), *Wolff v. Wolff* [2004] W.T.L.R. 1349 (grant of a lease at a peppercorn rent).
[205] This would if necessary have been held in *Wolff v. Wolff* [2004] W.T.L.R. 1349, where the grantor of the lease had intended to settle it on a trust but had not in fact succeeded n doing so.
[206] [2008] EWHC 118 (Ch), [2008] W.T.L.R. 685.
[207] [2002] W.T.L.R. 313.

Millett J. between effects and consequences which has of course since been rejected in *Ogden v. Griffiths*[208]; he treated fiscal matters as consequences and so outside the scope of the principle. However, as Lloyd L.J. stated in *Sieff v. Fox*,[209] the more general test enunciated in *Ogilvie v. Allen*, which had not been cited to either Millett J. or Davis J., "might allow fiscal consequences to be taken into account if they were sufficiently serious" and, although Lewison J. did not have to resolve this issue in *Ogden v. Griffiths*,[210] his express rejection of the distinction drawn by Millett J. also points to that conclusion. It is also arguable, and has been held in the Isle of Man,[211] that the principle is applicable where it has simply not been realised that the creation of a trust will give rise to any tax liability at all. Such a situation is much more similar to the cases such as *Wolff v. Wolff*,[212] where the grantors of a lease which they intended to settle on trust were under the mistaken belief that they would nevertheless be able to continue indefinitely to occupy the leased property and the principle was applied.

It is also uncertain whether or not the principle is limited to voluntary dispositions and settlements. The judgments in both *Ogilvie v. Allen*[213] and *Gibbon v. Mitchell*[214] refer exclusively to voluntary transactions and to the mistaken conferring of bounty by one person on another. Nevertheless, in *AMP (UK) v. Barker*,[215] Lawrence Collins J. would have been prepared to invoke the principle in relation to a pension trust, which of course is neither a voluntary settlement nor confers any bounty on its members, in order to set aside the exercise of the power of amendment had he not already ordered rectification; there are similar dicta in two other cases.[216] However, in *Smithson v. Hamilton*,[217] Park J. declined to follow these dicta and specifically held that the principle extends only to voluntary dispositions and so is not applicable to pension trusts.   6–085

Where the principle is applicable, until recently the courts have consistently held that whatever has been done will be void *ab initio*. However, in *Ogden v. Griffiths*[218] Lewison J. instead held that the assignment in question was merely voidable at the discretion of the court, relying on the decision of the Court of Appeal in *Barrow v. Isaacs*,[219] where a relevant mistake was made and relief was nevertheless denied. There is, therefore, at present a conflict of authority in this respect. It is at least clear that, where the principle is applied but the effect of only part of what has been done is mistaken and that part can be severed from the remainder of what has been done, only the former will be void or voidable; the latter will take effect. This   6–086

---

[208] [2008] EWHC 118 (Ch), [2008] W.T.L.R. 685.
[209] [2005] EWHC 1312 (Ch), [2005] 1 W.L.R. 3811 at 3845.
[210] [2008] EWHC 118 (Ch), [2008] W.T.L.R. 685.
[211] In *Clarkson v. Barclays Private Bank & Trust (Isle of Man)* [2007] W.T.L.R. 1703.
[212] [2004] W.T.L.R. 1349.
[213] (1899) 15 T.L.R. 294.
[214] [1990] 1 W.L.R. 1304.
[215] [2001] W.T.L.R. 1237, [2001] P.L.R. 79.
[216] *Gallaher Ltd. v. Gallaher Pensions Ltd.* [2005] EWHC 42 (Ch), [2005] PLR 103; *Irish Pensions Trust v. Central Remedial Clinic* [2006] 22 PBLR (High Court of the Republic of Ireland).
[217] [2007] EWHC 2900 (Ch), [2008] 1 W.L.R. 1453, at [114]–[123].
[218] [2008] EWHC 118 (Ch), [2008] W.T.L.R. 685.
[219] [1891] 1 Q.B. 417 (CA).

happened in *Walker v. Armstrong*.[220] Where the principle is applied, any property transferred away will be recoverable by the donor or trustees from the transferee. If for any reason it cannot be recovered by trustees, they will be potentially liable for breach of trust; however, they may possibly be relieved from liability under section 61 of the Trustee Act 1925[221] and are highly likely to be so relieved if the mistaken exercise of the discretion or power was by a person other than themselves.

(C) Mistakes within the Rule in *Re Hastings-Bass (dec'd)*[222]

6–087 The third possibility is that the exercise of the discretion or power may be held to have been vitiated because of the failure of the persons who exercised it to take into account all the correct considerations. This principle has become known as the Rule in *Re Hastings-Bass (dec'd)*.[223] In that case, trustees exercised a power of advancement to resettle property on trust but misunderstood the effect of the rule against perpetuities with the result that, while a valid life interest was conferred on the person principally intended to benefit, all the remainders over were void for perpetuity. The question before the court was whether the entire transaction failed or whether the life interest nevertheless survived (a result which would produce the saving of estate duty which had been the objective of the advancement). The Court of Appeal said this:

"where a trustee is given a discretion as to some matter under which he acts in good faith, the court should not interfere with his action, notwithstanding that it does not have the full effect which he intended, unless (1) what he has achieved is unauthorised by the power conferred on him, or (2) it is clear that he would not have acted as he did (a) had he not taken into account considerations which he should not have taken into account or (b) had he not failed to take into account considerations which he ought to have taken into account."

It is the second of these two grounds for interference which constitutes the Rule.[224]

6–088 Subsequently, in *Mettoy Pension Trustees v. Evans*,[225] Warner J. reformulated the Rule in positive terms which were again reformulated by Lloyd L.J. in *Sieff v. Fox*[226]:

"The best formulation of the principle seems to me to be this. Where trustees act under a discretion given to them by the terms of the trust, in circumstances in which they are free to decide whether or not to exercise that discretion, but the effect of the exercise is different from that which they

---

[220] (1856) 8 De G.M. & G. 531. The deed in question carried out the wishes of the appointors by confirming their life interests but also contained gifts over which had not been intended. The life interests were upheld; the gifts over were held to be void.

[221] See *post*, para 22–088.

[222] [1975] Ch. 25. See Lord Walker [2002] P.C.B. 226; Hilliard [2002] T.L.I. 202.

[223] [1975] Ch. 25.

[224] The first ground is the subject matter of para 6–076 *ante*.

[225] [1990] 1 W.L.R. 1587.

[226] [2005] EWHC 1312 (Ch), [2005] 1 W.L.R. 3811 at 3848.

intended, the court will interfere with their action if it is clear that they would not have acted as they did had they not failed to take into account considerations which they ought to have taken into account, or taken into account considerations which they ought not to have taken into account."

Most recently of all, in *Smithson v. Hamilton*[227] Park J. suggested that the words "but the effect of the exercise is different from that which they intended" should instead be "whether or not the effect of the exercise is different from that which [they] intended".

In the interim, shortly after *Mettoy Pension Trustees v. Evans*,[228] the Court of Appeal held, in *Stannard v. Fisons Pension Trust*,[229] that the test is not whether the trustees *would* not have acted as they did but whether they *might* not have done so. In *AMP (UK) v. Barker*,[230] Lawrence Collins J., who would have set aside the defective exercise of the power of amendment under the Rule had he not already ordered rectification, regarded himself as bound[231] to hold that the test was "might" rather than "would", although he stated that this made no difference on the facts of that case. Lightman J. also stated that this made no difference on the facts in *Abacus Trust Co. (Isle of Man). v. Barr*[232] but instead expressed the view that the choice between the two criteria still remains open.[233] However, in *Sieff v. Fox*[234] Lloyd L.J. stated that the test is "might" only where the trustees are obliged to act and distinguished on that ground *Stannard v. Fisons Pension Trust*,[235] "which should not be treated as applying or endorsing the *Hastings-Bass* principle, but as being in the same line as" *Kerr v. British Leyland (Staff) Trustees*.[236]

6–089

It is not yet been established precisely what categories of mistakes will give rise to the application of the Rule. The facts of *Re Hastings-Bass (dec'd)* itself appear to have fallen within the Rule in *Gibbon v. Mitchell*[237] anyway in that there had been a mistake as to the effect of the exercise of the power in question; however, at that time, prior to *Gibbon v. Mitchell*, it was not generally appreciated that this possibility extended to mistakes of law. In any event, as was implicit in the negative formulation of the Rule which the Court of Appeal enunciated, the court declined to interfere in *Re Hastings-Bass (dec'd)* because what had been achieved was sufficient to bring about the saving of estate duty, in other words because, if the trustees had appreciated the true effect of the advancement, they would have acted broadly as they had done. Consequently, the advancement was held to take effect in so far as it could.

6–090

---

[227] [2007] EWHC (Ch) 2900, [2008] 1 W.L.R. 1453 at [53].
[228] [1990] 1 W.L.R. 1587.
[229] [1991] P.L.R. 224, [1992] I.R.L.R. 27.
[230] [2001] W.T.L.R. 1237, [2001] P.L.R. 79.
[231] By *Stannard v. Fisons Pension Trust* [1991] P.L.R. 224, [1992] I.R.L.R. 27 and by earlier, then unreported, statements of the Court of Appeal to the same effect in *Kerr v. British Leyland (Staff) Trustees* [2001] W.T.L.R. 1071 (CA).
[232] [2003] EWHC 114 (Ch) 409, [2003] Ch. 409.
[233] Relying on *Scott v. The National Trust* [1998] 2 All E.R. 705 at 718.
[234] [2005] EWHC 1312 (Ch), [2005] 1 W.L.R. 3811 at 3848.
[235] [1991] P.L.R. 224, [1992] I.R.L.R. 27.
[236] [2001] W.T.L.R. 1071 (CA).
[237] [1990] 1 W.L.R. 1304.

6–091   It has been contended that the Rule in *Re Hastings-Bass (dec'd)* should be confined to mistakes of this type,[238] in which case it would amount to little more than an alternative formulation of what was later decided in *Gibbon v. Mitchell*.[239] However, the Rule is clearly not so confined at present. It was specifically held in *Mettoy Pension Trustees v. Evans*[240] that the Rule extends to *any* taking into account of inappropriate considerations or failure to take into account appropriate considerations. In that case, it was contended that the grant by the trustees to the employer of the power to appoint the surplus in the pension scheme should be set aside because the trustees had not realised that they were depriving themselves of their pre-existing power so to do. However, Warner J. emphasised[241] that "it is not enough that it should be shown that the trustees did not have a proper understanding of the effect of their act. It must also be clear that, had they had a proper understanding of it, they would not have acted as they did." He therefore also declined to apply the Rule since, on the facts, he considered that the trustees would still have done the same thing anyway.

6–092   The Rule was purportedly applied in *Stannard v. Fisons Pension Trust*,[242] where the Court of Appeal set aside the deed by which the trustees of a pension trust had exercised a discretion on the basis of an out of date valuation of the pension fund.[243] It has to be admitted that, if the Rule is ever to be extended to mistakes which go beyond mistakes as to the effect of what has been done, this is an obvious case for its application; the discretion was exercised on the basis of a mistaken view of a factor which was clearly crucial to the decision taken by the trustees. However, in *Sieff v. Fox*[244] Lloyd L.J. stated that *Stannard v. Fisons Pension Trust*[245] "should not be treated as applying or endorsing the *Hastings-Bass* principle", although of course that does not actually dispose of the point under discussion. The question is whether it is possible to formulate a rule which will permit the application of the Rule in these circumstances without also permitting its application whenever a discretion or power has been exercised on the basis of a mistake as to or failure to take into account the possible consequences.

6–093   In *Breadner v. Granville-Grossman*[246] Park J. held that the decision in *Stannard v. Fisons Pension Trust* turned mainly on principles particularly applicable to pension trusts and not on what he described as the "general" Rule, a conclusion which has obviously been confirmed by *Sieff v. Fox*.[247] He said that, although the limits to the Rule had not yet been established, it must have some; it could not be right that, whenever trustees did something which they later regretted and thought that they ought not to have done, they could say that they never did it in the first place. He also emphasised

---

[238] This is in effect the contention of Lord Walker in [2002] P.C.B. 226.
[239] [1990] 1 W.L.R. 1304.
[240] [1990] 1 W.L.R. 1587.
[241] *ibid.* at 1624.
[242] [1991] P.L.R. 224, [1992] I.R.L.R. 27.
[243] Such valuations normally have to be produced every three years but tend to appear some considerable time after the end of the three-year period in question.
[244] [2005] EWHC 1312 (Ch), [2005] 1 W.L.R. 3811 at 3848.
[245] [1991] P.L.R. 224, [1992] I.R.L.R. 27.
[246] [2001] Ch. 523.
[247] [2005] EWHC 1312 (Ch), [2005] 1 W.L.R. 3811 at 3848.

that he knew of no decision in which the principle had been applied to take away the beneficial interests of those properly entitled under the trust instrument[248] (presumably meaning the beneficial interests of those already entitled to interests in possession since the exercise of any dispositive power is bound to take away any default interests which have not yet vested in possession, something which the exercise of the power of advancement under consideration in *Re Hastings-Bass (dec'd)* itself undoubtedly did). However, these remarks were no more than dicta because what Park J. actually held was that the Rule is limited to undoing something which has been done; it was, therefore, not applicable to the case before him, where it was being invoked in order to do something which the trustees had not done.[249] This restriction on the application of the Rule seems wholly appropriate.

By then the Rule had already been applied in *Green v. Cobham*,[250] where the mistake by the trustees amounted merely to a failure to take into account the possible fiscal consequences of what they had done, and the Rule was subsequently applied again in similar circumstances in *Abacus Trust Co. (Isle of Man) v. N.S.P.C.C.*.[251] In both these cases the exercise of the powers in question[252] had had exactly the intended effect but had the unforeseen consequences of imposing unintended substantial charges to capital gains tax,[253] which were saved as a result of the application of the Rule. In cases such as this, of course, it is in the interests of everyone involved with the settlement in question that the Rule is applied and the only serious opposition to its application is, therefore, likely to come from H.M. Revenue and Customs in the event that they are invited and agree to appear.[254]

6–094

Subsequently, in *Abacus Trust Co. (Isle of Man). v. Barr*[255] the categories of mistakes which will give rise to the application of the Rule were restricted. The trustees and the protector had exercised a power of appointment in respect of 60 per cent of the trust property with the intention of giving effect to the wishes of the settlor. However, the relevant intermediary had misinformed them as to the wishes of the settlor, who only wanted 40 per cent to be so appointed. On this occasion there was serious opposition to the application of the Rule,[256] as there had also been in *Breadner v. Granville-*

6–095

---

[248] This would have been the consequence of the application of the Rule in the case before him since what he had earlier held to have been the failure of the trustees to exercise the power of appointment in time had caused the interests of those entitled in default to vest indefeasibly.

[249] They had failed to exercise the power of appointment in time and as a result their purported exercise of it was ineffective.

[250] [2000] W.T.L.R. 1101.

[251] [2001] W.T.L.R. 953.

[252] A power to appoint additional trustees in *Green v. Cobham*; a straightforward power of appointment in *Abacus Trust Co. (Isle of Man) v. N.S.P.C.C.*

[253] In *Green v Cobham* because of a subsequent reduction in the number of non-resident trustees; in *Abacus Trust Co. (Isle of Man) v. N.S.P.C.C.* because the power of appointment had been executed three days too early.

[254] The Revenue was apparently not informed in advance about the proceedings in *Green v. Cobham* but was informed about the proceedings in *Abacus Trust Co. (Isle of Man) v. N.S.P.C.C.* and declined either to be joined to or to be bound by them.

[255] [2003] EWHC 114 (Ch) 409, [2003] Ch. 409.

[256] From the persons in whose favour the appointment had been made.

Grossman.[257] Lightman J. was, therefore, faced by competing contentions: on the one hand, that the Rule could be applied whenever there had been a mistake, no matter how that mistake arose; and, on the other hand, that the Rule could only be applied where the mistake in question was sufficiently fundamental (and that, on the facts, it was not). He rejected both contentions and instead held that the Rule was only applicable where the exercise of the discretion or power amounts to a breach of fiduciary duty by the person exercising it, in other words where the latter was under a duty to consider what he had failed to take into account or was under a duty not to consider what he had taken into account.

6–096   This conclusion enabled Lightman J. to apply the Rule on the basis that the intermediary had been acting as agent for the trustees when he misrepresented the wishes of the settlor to them. The view that this rendered the trustees' subsequent exercise of the power a breach of fiduciary duty is just about supportable on the basis that they had by then decided to act in accordance with the settlor's wishes and can therefore be regarded as having been under a duty to establish what those wishes actually were. However, Lightman J. made no reference to the fact that trustees are not as such under any duty whatever to act in accordance with the wishes of their settlor; indeed, any argument that they were in the case of any individual trust would point inevitably to the conclusion that the trust in question was a sham.[258] Nor does a failure effectively to exercise a discretion or power amount, without more, to a breach of fiduciary duty.

6–097   But if Lightman J. was correct to hold that the Rule can only be applied where there has been a breach of fiduciary duty, then it must follow that the Rule should not have been applied in *Stannard v. Fisons Pension Trust*[259]; it is not easy to see how the trustees could have been held to be in breach of fiduciary duty merely because they had acted on the basis of an out of date valuation for whose preparation they were not responsible (of course, in *Sieff v. Fox*[260] Lloyd L.J. stated that *Stannard v. Fisons Pension Trust*[261] "should not be treated as applying or endorsing the *Hastings-Bass* principle" anyway). It is also at least arguable that on this basis the Rule should not have been applied in *Green v. Cobham*[262] either; while trustees who fail to take fiscal consequences into account are at least arguably acting in breach of fiduciary duty, the negative fiscal consequences in that case arose out of events which could not possibly have been foreseen at the time when the powers were exercised.

6–098   However, in *Sieff v. Fox*[263] Lloyd L.J. did not consider that the *Hastings-Bass* principle "applies only in cases where there has been a breach of duty by the trustees, or by their advisers or agents, despite what Lightman J.

---

[257] [2001] Ch. 523. In that case, the opposition had been from the default beneficiaries who had taken as a result of the trustees' failure to exercise the power of appointment in time.
[258] See *ante*, para 3–127.
[259] [1991] P.L.R. 224, [1992] I.R.L.R. 27.
[260] [2005] EWHC 1312 (Ch), [2005] 1 W.L.R. 3811 at 3848.
[261] [1991] P.L.R. 224, [1992] I.R.L.R. 27.
[262] [2000] W.T.L.R. 1101.
[263] [2005] EWHC 1312 (Ch), [2005] 1 W.L.R. 3811 at 3848.

said". It seemed to him[264] that the main ways of controlling the application of the Rule are "(a) to insist on a stringent application of the tests as they have been laid down, (b) to take a reasonably and not over-exigent view of what it is that the trustees ought to have taken into account, and (c) to adopt a critical approach to contentions that the trustees would have acted differently if they had realised the true position, perhaps especially so in cases . . . where it is in the interests of all who are before the court that the appointment should be set aside".

The question of precisely what types of mistake will give rise to the application of the Rule requires urgent review at appellate level, preferably by the House of Lords (the Court of Appeal could conceivably be hampered by its own decision in *Stannard v. Fisons Pension Trust*[265] unless the view of Lloyd L.J. that *Stannard v. Fisons Pension Trust*[266] "should not be treated as applying or endorsing the *Hastings-Bass* principle" is adopted). The choice seems most likely to be between mistakes of any type whatever (the view adopted in *Green v. Cobham*[267] and *Abacus Trust Co. (Isle of Man) v. N.S.P.C.C.*[268]), possibly subject to some or all of the safeguards envisaged by Lloyd L.J. in *Sieff v. Fox*,[269] and mistakes which amount to a breach of fiduciary duty (the view adopted in *Abacus Trust Co. (Isle of Man). v. Barr*[270]).[271]   **6–099**

When the Rule can be and is applied, the effect of its application is also at present uncertain. In *AMP (UK) v. Barker*,[272] Lawrence Collins J. stated that its application makes the exercise of the discretion or power void rather than voidable. However, the exact opposite was held by Lightman J. in *Abacus Trust Co. (Isle of Man). v. Barr*.[273] His conclusion that the appointment, which had been made 10 years earlier, was voidable rather than void was significant because substantial distributions of income and capital had been made pursuant to its provisions in the interim; whether the appointment was in fact to be avoided and, if so, on what terms was adjourned for further argument. In this respect, the view of Lightman J. seems preferable and, since it formed part of his ratio, must constitute the law at present; it also answers many of the criticisms which have been made of the Rule.[274] In *Sieff v. Fox*[275] Lloyd L.J. found the view of Lightman J. "attractive but seems to me to require further consideration, in the light of earlier authority". The last has certainly not yet been heard of this particular point either, particularly   **6–100**

---

[264] *ibid.*, at 3838.
[265] [1991] P.L.R. 224, [1992] I.R.L.R. 27.
[266] [1991] P.L.R. 224, [1992] I.R.L.R. 27.
[267] [2000] W.T.L.R. 1101.
[268] [2001] W.T.L.R. 953.
[269] [2005] EWHC 1312 (Ch), [2005] 1 W.L.R. 3811 at 3848.
[270] [2003] EWHC 114 (Ch) 409, [2003] Ch. 409.
[271] The author of this edition has suggested the adoption of the former view, provided that the mistakes in question are both mistakes as to the *existing* consequences of what has been done and mistakes but for which the discretion or power in question *would* not have been exercised (T.E.L.J. (April 2003) 4).
[272] [2001] W.T.L.R. 1237, [2001] P.L.R. 79.
[273] [2003] EWHC 114 (Ch) 409, [2003] Ch. 409.
[274] Particularly by Lord Walker [2002] P.C.B. 226.
[275] [2005] EWHC 1312 (Ch), [2005] 1 W.L.R. 3811 at 3848.

given that in most, if not all,[276] of the other situations in which the exercise of discretions is set aside their exercise is wholly void, a point to which Lightman J. did not expressly advert.

6–101   Another analogous but less significant point which still awaits resolution is whether or not it is possible, as Warner J. stated in *Mettoy Pension Trustees v. Evans*,[277] for the court, where it concludes that the donee of the discretion or power would have acted in the same way but with the omission of one or more of the clauses of the deed in question, to uphold that deed with the deletion of the provisions in question. Since this is possible where there has been a mistake as to the effect of what has been done,[278] there is no obvious objection to this where the offending provisions are capable of being severed. However, it remains to be seen whether the flexible approach manifested by this statement is in fact carried into effect and, if so, exactly how.

3. When will the Exercise of a Discretion or Power be Dishonest?

(A)   The Doctrine of Fraud on a Power

6–102   Different considerations arise where the discretion or power has not been exercised honestly. In such cases, there is said to have been a "fraud on a power" (this expression is used in connection with the exercise of both a power and a discretion). In equity the word "fraud" denotes nothing more than an improper motive. Various attempts have been made to categorise the circumstances in which there is a fraud on a power, the classic statement being found in the decision of the House of Lords in *Vatcher v. Paull*.[279] A number of propositions emerge from the decided cases.

6–103   First, where the donee of the discretion or power has exercised it bona fide, the court will not interfere even if it would itself have acted differently. In *Gisborne v. Gisborne*,[280] the trustees of a will had discretion to apply the whole or such portion of the income as they should think expedient for the benefit of the testator's wife, who was a person of unsound mind. The trustees refused to apply the whole of the income for her support and proposed to apply only so much of it as would be necessary to maintain her in care when the income from her own property was also taken into account. The House of Lords acknowledged that they would have ordered the trust fund to have been applied primarily for the benefit of the wife; however, in the light of their specific decision that the trustees had acted bona fide, they could not interfere with the exercise of the trustees' discretion.

6–104   Secondly, the fact that a discretion or power is exercised in such a way as to defeat the intention of the donor does not automatically make its exercise

---

[276] The only exception is if Lewison J. was right to hold, in *Ogden v. Griffiths* [2008] EWHC 118 (Ch), [2008] W.T.L.R. 685, that the effect of the Rule in *Gibbons v. Mitchell* is to render the transaction in question not void *ab initio* but merely voidable at the discretion of the court.

[277] [1990] 1 W.L.R. 1587 at 1624–1625.

[278] See *Walker v. Armstrong* (1856) 8 De G.M. & G. 531; *ante*, para 6–086.

[279] [1915] A.C. 372.

[280] (1877) 2 App.Cas. 628. See also *R. v. Archbishop of Canterbury and Bishop of London* [1903] 1 K.B. 289.

void.[281] This rule is comparable to the rule which permits beneficiaries who between them are absolutely beneficially entitled to join together and bring a trust to an end even though the intention of the settlor was that it should continue.[282] Once a discretion or power has been conferred, or a trust has been created, the donor or settlor ceases to have any control as such unless he has provided at the time when the discretion, power or trust was created that his consent (or the consent of the protector of the settlement) is a necessary pre-condition of any exercise.

Thirdly, in every case it is necessary to identify who would be entitled in default of exercise of the discretion or power (these persons may be specified in the trust instrument; alternatively there may be a resulting trust in their favour). Since these are the persons who will lose as a result of any improper exercise of the discretion or power, in the event that they agree to that exercise with knowledge of all the relevant facts, the exercise will inevitably be valid.[283]

6–105

Fourthly, the essential feature which makes the exercise of a discretion or power improper is the intention of the person exercising it. If it is exercised with the intention of benefiting some non-object of the discretion or power, whether that person is the person exercising it or someone else, the exercise is void. Classic examples are where a discretion or power is exercised in favour of a beneficiary when he has already agreed that he will apply the property in question in whole or in part for the benefit of someone who is not one of its objects[284] and where, even though there has been no such prior agreement, the discretion or power is exercised with the intention of benefiting someone outside its scope.[285] So, in the case of a settlement to A for life, remainder to such of A's issue as A may appoint and, in default of appointment to A's children in equal shares, an appointment by A in favour of his children with a view to A and his children breaking the trust and dividing the capital between them (which they would be able to do once the issue of A other than his children had thus been excluded) will indirectly benefit A and so will unquestionably amount to a fraud on his power.[286]

6–106

If, on the other hand, there is no such intention, but the exercise does in fact benefit a non-object, it is valid. Thus, in the situation where a father has a discretion or power to appoint in favour of his child, an appointment in favour of that child is basically valid[287]; however, if it is made when the child is very ill, with the intention that the appointor will benefit by taking the child's estate on his or her death, the exercise will be invalid and will strictly be so even if the child subsequently recovers.[288] On the other hand, if a discretion or power is exercised with a view to bringing the trust to an end as part of a tax-saving scheme, and the appointment in question is made with the intention of benefiting its objects, the appointment is valid even

---

[281] *Lee v. Ferrie* (1839) 1 B. 483.
[282] See *post*, para 19–019.
[283] *Re Turner's Settled Estates* [1884] 28 Ch.D. 205; *Re Greaves* [1954] Ch. 434.
[284] *ibid.*
[285] *Portland v. Topham* (1867) 11 H.L.Cas. 32; *Vatcher v. Paull* [1915] A.C. 372.
[286] However, the same result can be achieved in a different way, by A releasing his power; see *post*, para 6–116.
[287] *Henty v. Wrey* (1882) 21 Ch.D. 332.
[288] *Lord Hinchinbroke v. Seymour* (1789) 1 Bro.C.C. 395.

though it confers an incidental benefit on the appointor or on other persons.[289] Further, it has been held[290] that it would not be a fraud on a power for trustees to add a father as a beneficiary of a settlement of which the principal beneficiaries were his infant children and then to appoint some of the trust property to him in order to enable him more easily to make the financial provision which he had been ordered to provide for the mother, not herself a beneficiary, in their divorce proceedings.

6–107   Fifthly, where a discretion or power is to be exercised in favour of one of its objects but in the hope that the recipient will benefit a non-object, the validity of the exercise will depend upon whether the recipient had legal and moral freedom of action.[291] Suppose a discretion or power is exercisable in favour of a person who makes it known that, if it is in fact exercised in his favour, he will give part of the fund to his parents, who are not objects. If the intention of the appointment is to benefit the parents, the exercise is invalid under the rule stated in the previous paragraph. If that is not the case but the recipient is under great pressure to benefit the parents, the exercise is also invalid.[292] However, if the recipient has genuine freedom of action but wishes to give his parents a benefit, the exercise of the power is good.[293]

(B)   The Reasons for Exercise

6–108   The donee of a discretion or power does not have to give the objects of that power or discretion the reasons for his decisions; however, as Robert Walker J. stated in *Scott v. The National Trust*,[294] if his decision is challenged in the courts he may be compelled to do so either through the process of disclosure if there are any relevant documents or, in practical terms, as the only way of avoiding an adverse inference being drawn.

6–109   In *Re Beloved Wilkes' Charity*,[295] trustees had a duty from time to time to select a candidate to be sent to the University of Oxford to be trained as a minister of the Church of England; they were obliged to select any suitable candidate who came forward from certain nominated parishes but in default had a more general discretion. They decided to nominate a candidate from outside those parishes rather than one from within them. Lord Truro L.C. declined to interfere with this decision, saying:

"It is to the discretion of the trustees that the execution of the trust is confided, that discretion being exercised with an entire absence of indirect motive, with honesty of intention, and with a fair consideration of the subject. The duty of supervision on the part of this court will thus be confined to the question of the honesty, integrity and fairness with which the deliberation has been conducted, and will not be extended to the accuracy of the conclusion arrived at."

---

[289] *Re Merton* [1953] 1 W.L.R. 1096; *Re Robertson's Will Trusts* [1960] 1 W.L.R. 1050.
[290] *Netherton v. Netherton* [2000] W.T.L.R. 1171.
[291] *Birley v. Birley* (1858) 25 B. 299.
[292] *Re Crawshay* [1948] Ch. 123; *Re Dick* [1953] Ch. 343.
[293] *Re Marsden's Trusts* (1859) 4 Drew. 594.
[294] [1998] 2 All E.R. 705 at 717–719.
[295] (1851) 3 Mac. & G. 440.

However, if the trustees do choose to state their reasons, the court will   6–110
examine them in order to ascertain whether or not the trustees have acted in
error. In *Klug v. Klug*,[296] a mother who was one of a number of trustees
declined to concur in the exercise of a power in favour of her daughter on
the grounds that she disapproved of the latter's marriage. The court held
that this was an impermissible reason; consequently she had acted dishonestly and her refusal to concur was set aside. Trustees of pensions trusts
also tend, quite understandably, to give reasons for their decisions. But, as
Robert Walker J. stated in *Scott v. The National Trust*,[297] the principles on
which the court must proceed are the same whether or not the trustees give
their reasons; it simply becomes easier for the court to examine a decision if
the reasons for it have been disclosed.

In *Edge v. Pensions Ombudsman*[298] a pension trust had a surplus which had   6–111
to be reduced in order to preserve the tax advantages given to pension
trusts. The trustees decided to use £20,000,000 of the surplus to credit
additional service to those members in employment on a particular date and
to reduce the contributions of both employers and employees from a date six
months earlier; no additional service was credited either to those already
receiving pensions or to a number of employees who were to be made
redundant during the six-month period. The trustees explained to one of the
latter that their decision had been taken in order to encourage all employees
to become and remain members of the pension scheme and to support the
employers in providing continued employment for their current employees.
The Pensions Ombudsman set aside the trustees' decision on the grounds
that the trustees had breached their duty of impartiality and had not acted
in the best interests of all the beneficiaries. His decision was reversed by the
Court of Appeal, who held that the duty to act impartially was no more than
the ordinary duty imposed on any holder of a discretionary power, namely
to exercise the power for the purposes for which it is given, giving proper
consideration to the matters which are relevant and excluding from consideration matters which are irrelevant. Provided the trustees complied with
that duty, they were entitled to reach a decision which appeared to prefer the
claims of some beneficiaries over others.

(C) The Effect of Fraud on a Power

In principle, where the exercise of a discretion or power is successfully   6–112
impugned on the grounds of fraud on a power, its exercise is totally invalid.[299] However, this can in some circumstances work harshly on the objects
of the discretion or power. If the person with the discretion or power reaches
an agreement with one of the objects that he will appoint £1,000 to the object
provided that the latter pays £500 to someone who is not an object, then in
principle the whole appointment is invalid and the object will receive
nothing. Accordingly, in an attempt to help objects, in some cases the court
will try to sever the improper element in the appointment from the remainder of that appointment.[300] If there is no intent to benefit the object of the

---

[296] [1918] 2 Ch. 67.
[297] [1998] 2 All E.R. 705 at 717–719.
[298] [2000] Ch. 602.
[299] *Daubeney v. Cockburn* (1816) 1 Mer. 626.
[300] *Topham v. Duke of Portland* (1858) 1 D.J. & S. 517.

power at all, the exercise is clearly wholly invalid.[301] If, however, there is an intent to benefit the object to some extent, and the improper element is in the form of a condition attached to the appointment, the court will delete the condition to leave the object free to take unconditionally.[302]

6–113   As has already been seen,[303] the latter possibility has been held[304] to be open to the court where the exercise of a discretion or power is set aside under the Rule in *Re Hastings-Bass (dec'd)*,[305] although this has not yet actually been done. Thus far, the effect of the application of that Rule and of fraud on a power are therefore the same. However if, as Lightman J. held in *Abacus Trust Co. (Isle of Man). v. Barr*,[306] the effect of the application of the Rule in *Re Hastings-Bass (dec'd)* is that the exercise of the discretion or power in question is voidable rather than void, the normal consequences of the application of the two doctrines will be completely different. It is arguable that Lightman J. should have considered this point when reaching his decision.

4. Can the Exercise of Powers and Discretions be Categorised as Unreasonable?

6–114   Quite apart from any of the possibilities which have been considered so far, beneficiaries of pension trusts appear to have the further possibility of being entitled to attack the exercise of a power or discretion on the grounds that it was in administrative law terms "unreasonable" in accordance with what is known as the *Wednesbury* test (laid down in *Associated Provincial Picture Houses v. Wednesbury Corporation*[307] in the context of judicial review of administrative action). This possibility emerges from *Harris v. Lord Shuttleworth*[308] and *Wild v. Pensions Ombudsman*.[309] The applicability of this test was also reviewed in *Edge v. Pensions Ombudsman*,[310] where the Court of Appeal held that pension trustees are chosen to exercise discretions for very much the same reasons as the local authority in the *Wednesbury* Case had been chosen to exercise a discretion, namely their knowledge and experience.

6–115   It is not generally thought that the *Wednesbury* test is in this jurisdiction applicable to voluntary settlements as such. However, it was applied to such a settlement in New Zealand in *Blair v. Vallely*,[311] where trustees were enjoined from carrying into effect what the court classified as an unreasonable decision as to how to attribute what the trustees described as intangible benefits to beneficiaries whom they wished to treat equally; however, this conclusion was undoubtedly facilitated by the fact that the trustees had explained their reasons to the court, something which they are not actually

---

[301] *Re Cohen* [1911] 1 Ch. 37.
[302] *Hay v. Watkins* (1850) 3 Dr. & War. 339.
[303] See *ante*, para 6–101.
[304] See *Mettoy Pension Trustees v. Evans* [1990] 1 W.L.R. 1587 at 1624–1625.
[305] [1975] Ch. 25.
[306] [2003] EWHC 114 (Ch) 409, [2003] Ch. 409.
[307] [1948] 1 K.B. 223).
[308] [1994] I.C.R. 991.
[309] [1996] P.L.R. 275.
[310] [2000] Ch. 602.
[311] [2000] W.T.L.R. 1101.

obliged to do. Whether a similar approach is one day adopted in this jurisdiction remains to be seen. However, it appears that what is known as "legitimate expectation", which has an enormously important part to play in judicial review of administrative action, may have some part to play in the context of voluntary settlements. In *Scott v. The National Trust*,[312] which concerned a challenge to the decision of the National Trust to ban the hunting of deer with hounds on some of its lands, the claimants applied to bring both charity proceedings[313] (the National Trust being a charity) and proceedings for judicial review. Robert Walker J. allowed the former and not the latter but commented that no reasonable body of trustees who had for the last 10 years paid £1,000 a quarter to an elderly impoverished beneficiary would discontinue the payment without any warning and without giving the beneficiary the opportunity of trying to persuade the trustees to continue the payment, at least temporarily. This is obviously a very extreme example and this comment was anyway no more than a dictum. However, it does indicate one route down which the law might one day go.

IV. When can Discretions and Powers be Released?

1. *Reasons for the Release of Discretions and Powers*

Those entitled to exercise discretions and powers sometimes have to con-   **6–116** sider the possibility of releasing them. There are two overlapping reasons for releasing a discretion or power: first, in order to prevent the trust from being, or from continuing to be being, subject to some form of taxation and, secondly, in order to ensure that some particular beneficiary or class of beneficiaries will inevitably either become entitled to the trust property or be prevented from becoming entitled to the trust property.

A release solely for the first reason may be induced by the effect of   **6–117** changes in taxation law such as the one which occurred in 1973. Until April 5, 1973, all the income of a trust was taxable in the hands of the trustees at the same rate; however, thereafter an additional charge to tax was imposed on income which could be accumulated. In the case of a pre-existing trust under which the trustees had a power to accumulate but, subject thereto, could pay the income to a named person, one possible way of avoiding the additional charge to tax was for the trustees to release their power to accumulate so that the named beneficiary became entitled to the whole of the income. Taxation may also be saved as the result of a release which irrevocably fixes beneficial entitlement. Thus in *Re Wills' Trust Deeds*,[314] the trustees wished to release a power to appoint the trust property between charitable and non-charitable objects in order to convert the trust into one which was entirely charitable; although no comments as to their motives appear in the report of the decision, the only obvious one can have been a

---

[312] [1998] 2 All E.R. 705.
[313] See *post*, para 11–170.
[314] [1964] Ch. 219.

desire to obtain the exemption from most forms of taxation which is granted to all charitable trusts.[315]

6–118   A release made solely for the second reason is potentially, but not necessarily, more conflictive. A straightforward and non-controversial example of this type is where a release is made in order to ensure that a beneficiary will inevitably be entitled and so can deal with his beneficial interest; thus where trustees hold a fund on trust for such of three nominated beneficiaries as they may appoint and, in default of appointment, for all three equally, release of the power will give each of them a fixed interest which he can sell or mortgage. More controversially, a person with a right to appoint an interest in remainder away from himself may try to release that right in order himself to become absolutely beneficially entitled.[316] Further and, even more controversially, a release may be made to prevent one or more beneficiaries from becoming entitled and thus indirectly enable the only other beneficiaries to take (this was of course the objective of the proposed release in *Mettoy Pension Trustees v. Evans*[317]; a release of the power to use the surplus in the pension fund to enhance the benefits of the employees would, if it had been held to have been possible, enabled that surplus to have passed to the employer company and therefore to the latter's creditors).

6–119   In many of the situations where a release is being considered for the second reason, the same result could on the face of things be achieved by exercising the discretion or power in question. However, this will in practice often be impeded by the doctrine of fraud on a power.[318] The conventional view is that the doctrine of fraud on a power does not apply to the release of powers,[319] permitting the release of a power in circumstances where its exercise could be set aside. Thus, in the example already referred to[320] of a settlement to A for life, remainder to such of A's issue as A may appoint and, in default of appointment to A's children in equal shares, the inability of A to enable him and his children to break the trust by making an appointment A in favour of his children can be circumvented by A releasing his power which would equally produce the necessary exclusion of the issue of A other than his children.

6–120   However, in *Mettoy Pension Trustees v. Evans*,[321] Warner J., having stated that, where there is a gift over in default of appointment, the donee of a mere power owes no duty to the objects of that power but merely a duty to those interested in default of appointment not to misuse the power, held that "[the donee] may therefore release the power but he may not enter into any transaction that would amount to a fraud on the power, a fraud on the power being a wrong committed against the beneficiaries under the trust in default of appointment". This statement may well have produced a modification of the pre-existing law by making releases subject to the doctrine of fraud on a power but only in respect of fraud on those entitled in default of appointment, not as against the objects. However, this novel proposition,

---

[315] See *post*, para 11–009.
[316] See *Re Brierley* (1894) 43 W.R. 36, where the manoeuvre actually failed.
[317] [1990] 1 W.L.R. 1587.
[318] See *ante*, para 6–102.
[319] *Re Somes* [1896] 1 Ch. 250.
[320] See *ante*, para 6–102.
[321] [1990] 1 W.L.R. 1587 at 1613.

which is clearly no more than a dictum, would not have prevented the power in *Mettoy Pension Trustees v. Evans* from being released had that power been held to be a mere power rather than a fiduciary power since the liquidator would have owed no duties to the objects of the power other than the company; nor would it be applicable to the example set out above because all the default beneficiaries, A's children, would necessarily benefit from the release of the power. It remains to be seen whether this proposition is ever applied.

2. *The Propriety of a Release*

The traditional exposition of the circumstances in which a discretion or 6–121 power can be effectively released is found in *Re Wills' Trust Deeds*,[322] where Buckley J. formulated five general propositions which have been set out in previous editions of this work.[323] However, these propositions are arguably defective in at least one respect and, although this is certainly not the fault of Buckley J., undoubtedly now require some modification in the light of the subsequent evolution of the distinction between fiduciary and non-fiduciary donees of mere powers and of the rather different formulation which was adopted by Warner J. in *Mettoy Pensions Trustees v. Evans*.[324] The present position seems to be as follows.

(A) Trust Powers of All Types
There is no possibility whatever of a trust power being released. The very 6–122 essence of such a power is that the person entitled to exercise it is under an obligation so to do and, if he fails to do so, it will be exercised by the court. This was stated in *Re Wills' Trust Deeds*[325]; however, that case was decided before *McPhail v. Doulton*[326] so Buckley J. must there have been using the expression "trust power" in its traditional sense, in other words as not including a discretionary trust. However, in *Mettoy Pensions Trustees v. Evans*[327] Warner J. applied the same rule both to discretionary trusts and to discretions which have to be exercised and there certainly seems little point in drawing any distinction between the different categories of trust powers now.

(B) Mere Discretions or Powers held by Fiduciary Donees
A mere discretion or power vested in a fiduciary donee which expressly 6–123 authorises release can be released. This was specifically held in *Muir v. I.R.C.*,[328] where the wording of the relevant clause was held to authorise such a release. This was in effect also the position in *Blausten v. I.R.C.*,[329] where the Court of Appeal came to the conclusion that a resettlement of the trust fund upon trusts identical with the existing trusts, but excluding a

---

[322] [1964] Ch. 219 at 236, 237.
[323] See the 7th edn (1998), pp.197–198.
[324] [1990] 1 W.L.R. 1587 at 1613–1614.
[325] [1964] Ch. 219.
[326] [1971] A.C. 424.
[327] [1990] 1 W.L.R. 1587 at 1613–1614.
[328] [1966] 1 W.L.R. 1269.
[329] [1972] Ch. 256.

particular power vested in the trustees, was a good exercise of the power of appointment (the immediate effect of the appointment was simply to exclude the wife of the settlor from the objects of the discretionary trusts of income and that was held to be within the terms of the power of appointment).

6–124   However, a mere discretion or power vested in a fiduciary donee which does not authorise release cannot be released. This has always been the law where the donees of the discretion or power are the trustees and it has been conferred upon them *virtute officii*; this is the case whether it is vested in the trustees as such or in named persons selected because they are the trustees. Despite the fact that the trustees cannot be obliged to exercise the discretion or power, they cannot ignore it since, as has already been seen,[330] they must consider periodically whether or not to exercise the discretion or power, its range and objects, and the appropriateness of individual appointments. Thus in *Re Courage Group's Pension Schemes*,[331] it was held that a committee which had been established to manage a pension scheme could not deprive their successors of the right to exercise their powers even if (which was not in fact decided) they were themselves entitled to release, fetter or agree not to exercise those powers.

6–125   This principle was subsequently extended to fiduciary donees of mere powers who are not trustees by the decision in *Mettoy Pension Trustees v. Evans*.[332] Although doubts have been expressed as to whether the donee of that particular power was correctly classified as a fiduciary (as has already been seen, this conclusion has been described as "not overwhelming"[333]), there cannot be the slightest doubt that the extension of the principle to all fiduciary donees will be upheld.

(C)   Mere Discretions or Powers held by Non-Fiduciary Donees
6–126   Mere discretions or powers vested in non-fiduciary donees can certainly be released where there is no express or implied trust in favour of the members of the class in default of appointment. This was the situation and the decision reached in *Re Wills' Trust Deeds*.[334] However, in that case Buckley J. went on to state that, where there is an express or implied trust in favour of the members of the class in default of appointment, such powers cannot be released. Although he did not actually say so, Buckley J. may well have been thinking principally of gifts in default of appointment which are in favour of all rather than only some of the objects of the power in question. However, even if so restricted, his proposition is contrary to the much earlier decision of the Court of Appeal in *Re Radcliffe*,[335] which was not cited to him. In that case a father, who was not a trustee, released a mere power in order to enable the shares of his sons, who were entitled in default, to become absolute and the release was upheld even though it also benefited the father,

---

[330] See *ante*, para 6–068.
[331] [1987] 1 W.L.R. 495.
[332] [1990] 1 W.L.R. 1587.
[333] See *ante*, para 6–072.
[334] [1964] Ch. 219.
[335] [1892] 1 Ch. 227.

in that he thereby received the share of a deceased son. Nor is the proposition of Buckley J., whether or not restricted in the way already mentioned, consistent with *Mettoy Pension Trustees v. Evans*.[336] Warner J. there specifically held that release was possible where the only person entitled in default was the donee of the power but also seemed prepared to permit such a release where persons other than the donee were entitled in default provided that the release did not amount to a fraud on them.[337] The mainstream of authority therefore seems to be in favour of permitting a release even where there is a gift over in default of appointment.

3. *The Effectiveness of a Release*

Some doubt has been cast on the effectiveness of releases by holders of discretions or powers who hold them not in their personal capacity but as the result of holding an office such as a trusteeship (no corresponding difficulty arises concerning releases by holders who are named as such, even if they happen also to be trustees). This is another possible adverse effect of the decision in *Re Wills' Trust Deeds*.[338] Buckley J. held that, although the current trustees had validly released the power in accordance with the authorisation given by the trust instrument and so had precluded themselves from exercising it, that release would not prevent their successor trustees from exercising the power. He said[339]:

6–127

"A power granted to successive holders of an office is unlike trust property, the entire ownership of which is vested in the trustees for the time being of the settlement and devolves on each change of trustee by succession. Where a power is granted to successive holders of an office all that is vested in the incumbent for the time being of the office is the capacity to exercise the power while he holds that office."

A similar view was taken in *Re Courage Group's Pension Scheme*,[340] although in that case it was not actually decided whether or not the existing donees were entitled to release their power anyway.

Whether this is indeed the law has been questioned. The remarks of Buckley J. certainly do not seem entirely consistent with the later decision of the Court of Appeal in *Muir v. I.R.C.*,[341] where the court implicitly treated the release of the fiduciary power which it held to have been authorised as both complete and binding. It is suggested that the better view is that, in the absence of provision to the contrary, office holders who can release should be able to bind their successors. However, until this point has been resolved,

6–128

---

[336] [1990] 1 W.L.R. 1587 at 1613–1614.
[337] This was the novel proposition to which reference has already been made (see *ante*, para 6–120); its adoption would not affect the outcome of a case such as *Re Radcliffe*.
[338] [1964] Ch. 219.
[339] *ibid.* at 238.
[340] [1987] 1 W.L.R. 495.
[341] [1966] 1 W.L.R. 1269.

there must clearly be some doubt about the validity of some of the types of releases which have already been considered (particularly those made to enable a beneficiary to deal with his interest) where the holders of the discretion or power in question hold it by virtue of their appointment as trustees; this is obviously because of the possibility of the released power being exercised by later trustees. More is likely to be heard of this particular question. However, even if *Re Wills' Trust Deeds* and *Re Courage Group's Pension Schemes* are correct in this respect, their effect could undoubtedly be avoided by sufficiently sophisticated drafting since it would certainly be open to a settlor to provide that discretions or powers could be released in such a way as to bind successors to the original holders; many modern precedents so provide.

4. *The Possibility of Surrender to the Court*

6–129   Unless and until a discretion or power can be and is effectively released, it remains with its holder who alone can exercise it. Are there any circumstances in which the discretion or power in question can be surrendered to the court?

6–130   In *Re Allen-Meyrick's Will Trusts*,[342] the trustees of a will held the trust fund upon trust to pay so much of the income as they thought fit to the husband of the testatrix and, subject to the exercise of their discretion in his favour, upon trust for her god-daughters. The husband was an undischarged bankrupt and the trustees had, in the exercise of their discretion, paid the rent of the house in which he lived; however, apart from this, they could not agree as to whether or not to make any further payments to him. They therefore asked the court to accept a surrender of their discretion but Buckley J. refused to do so.

6–131   As Buckley J. specifically held, it is of course open to the trustees of any trust to seek the directions of the court in any particular circumstances and the court was prepared to give directions as to what should be done with the income which had accrued; however, the court would not accept a surrender of the trustees' discretion for the future. This seems to have been largely due to difficulties as to how matters could proceed following surrender since, had the court accepted the surrender, there would have been no ready way in which it could have been informed of the actual circumstances of the beneficiaries each time that a decision had to be made. However, the decision actually reached opened up the possibility that, although this would certainly not have been welcomed by the court, the trustees could have sought the directions of the court on a new application each year or so.

6–132   It is also possible for the holders of a discretion or power to give the court the opportunity of deciding whether to abrogate or vary that discretion or power by making an application for this purpose under the Variation of Trusts Act 1958.[343]

---

[342] [1966] 1 W.L.R. 499.
[343] See *post*, para 21–018.

V. THE POSITION OF THE POTENTIAL BENEFICIARIES

1. *The Potential Beneficiaries Themselves*

(A) The Individual Rights of an Object of a Discretion or Power

(1) When can application be made to the court?

A person who is one of the objects of a discretion or power can require its **6–133** holder to consider exercising it in his favour, or in favour of any of the other objects.[344] Accordingly, if he can show that the holder has refused to consider him as a possible object, he can apply to the court. This is, however, subject to any contrary provision in the instrument by which the discretion or power was created (some modern deeds authorise the holders of discretions and powers to exercise them in favour of some of their objects without even considering their other objects).

A person who is one of the objects of a discretion or power can also apply **6–134** to the court if, despite giving due consideration to his own position, its holder has acted capriciously in other respects. In *Re Manisty's Settlement*,[345] Templeman J. stated that holders of a discretion or power would be acting capriciously if they acted "for reasons which I apprehend could be said to be irrational, perverse or irrelevant to any sensible expectation of the settlor for example, if they chose a beneficiary by height or complexion or by the irrelevant fact that he was a resident of Greater London".

In other respects, a person who is one of the objects of a discretion or **6–135** power is in a curious position. On the one hand, he may well not know that he is an object; only in the case of discretionary trusts in favour of relatively small groups of beneficiaries are the trustees obliged to inform those beneficiaries of the existence of their interests.[346] On the other hand, where he does know that he is an object of the discretion or power in question, it seems that he is entitled to apply to the court in the event that the trustees in whom the property subject to the power is vested are guilty of any acts of improper administration or in the event that the holder of the discretion or power improperly exercises it or purports to release it. However, whether he will ever realise that he is in a position to do so obviously depends on his rights to obtain information from his trustees. The position is discussed in detail in a later chapter.[347] The Privy Council has recently held, in *Schmidt v. Rosewood Trust*,[348] that in this respect there is no formal distinction between the beneficiaries of trusts and those who are merely a possible object of a discretion or power. It was held that "their right to seek disclosure of trust documents, although sometimes not inappropriately described as a proprietary right, is best approached as one aspect of the court's inherent jurisdiction to supervise (and where appropriate intervene in) the administration of trusts". However the Board went on to hold that "in many cases the court

---

[344] *Re Gestetner* [1953] Ch. 672, *per* Harman J. at 688; *Re Manisty's Settlement* [1974] Ch. 17, *per* Templeman J. at 25.
[345] [1974] Ch. 17 at 25.
[346] See *post*, para 14–029.
[347] See *post*, para 14–026.
[348] [2003] 2 A.C. 709.

may have no difficulty in concluding that an applicant with no more than a theoretical possibility of benefit ought not to be granted any relief". The Privy Council did not have to apply their decision, which is bound to be followed by the English courts, to the facts but information is clearly likely to be restricted to those who in practical terms have a reasonable chance of receiving some part of the trust property at some point.

6–136   The persons entitled to the property in default of the exercise of a discretion or power will necessarily be beneficiaries of fixed trusts and will therefore be entitled to know about the existence of their beneficial interests. They are similarly entitled to apply to the court in the event that of any improper conduct by the trustees in whom the property in question is vested or by the holder of a discretion or power. But their rights to information may well now in practice be considerably restricted by the fact that they are even less likely ever to receive any part of the trust property than some of the possible objects of a discretion or power.

(2) Remedies where the discretion or power is not exercised

6–137   (a) **Trust powers** In the case of trust powers in any of the senses in which this expression is used, where, in other words, a mandatory discretion or power is vested in the trustees or in third parties (in the latter case it will in effect be an old fashioned power in the nature of a trust), the holder of the discretion or power will be under an obligation to exercise it; therefore, he can be directed to do so by the court.

6–138   Where the power is vested in trustees, the court will additionally have all the powers enunciated by Lord Wilberforce in *McPhail v. Doulton*.[349] Prior to that decision, a trust power was only valid for certainty of objects if a complete list of all its objects could be drawn up; consequently, in the event that the power was not exercised, the court would invariably order that the property should be divided equally between all the objects of the power. However, the new test for certainty of objects established by *McPhail v. Doulton* inevitably means that, in the case of trust powers validated by that decision, not all the objects of the power will be known either to the trustees or to the court. Lord Wilberforce consequently held that, in such circumstances, the court can either appoint new trustees or direct persons representative of the classes of beneficiaries to prepare a scheme of distribution or, should the proper basis for distribution be apparent, direct the trustees how to distribute the fund (this does not, of course, mean that equal distribution will never again be ordered; in the case of a small class of beneficiaries whose entire membership is known, it is almost inevitable that equal distribution will still be ordered).

6–139   Where, on the other hand, the power is vested in third parties, there does not seem any obvious basis on which the court can replace those third parties. Consequently, the court can presumably only either direct persons representative of the classes of beneficiaries to prepare a scheme for distribution or, should the proper basis for distribution be apparent (normally the case in old fashioned powers in the nature of a trust, which tend to be in

---

[349] [1971] A.C. 424 at 457.

favour of reduced groups), direct the trustees how to distribute the fund (in the case of a reduced group, inevitably in equal shares).

(b) Mere discretions or powers In the case of mere discretions or pow-   **6–140**
ers, the court is unable to direct their exercise. Where such a discretion or power is held by a non-fiduciary donee, the court can do nothing at all. Where, on the other hand, the discretion or power is held by a fiduciary donee, the court can direct him to consider whether or not to exercise it. It has been stated on several occasions[350] that a refusal to follow such a direction from the court might well lead to the replacement of the fiduciary in question.

More controversially, it has now been held, in *Mettoy Pension Trustees v.*   **6–141**
Evans[351] that all the remedies available to the court to enforce trust powers are also available in the case of mere discretions and powers held by fiduciary donees. This was the case in which a company held a power to appoint any surplus in its pension fund, which was actually vested in a separate trustee company, in favour of the pensioners with a gift over in default of appointment to itself. Warner J. held that the company was unable to release the power and thus make the surplus available for its general creditors. It was obviously impossible to leave the liquidators of the company to exercise the power since their duty to the creditors would have conflicted with and presumably prevailed over their duty to consider the claims of the pensioners. No application had been made for the appointment of new fiduciaries (had there been, the obvious remedy would have been to vest the power in the trustee company, which had been the donee of the power at an earlier stage). Warner J. therefore held that he was entitled to approve or dictate a scheme himself and invited further argument as to what scheme was appropriate.[352] This decision has been criticised[353] on the grounds that judicial exercise of fiduciary discretions is inappropriate, even "as regards quasi-public trusts such as pension funds" and that the judge should have confined himself to appointing suitable new fiduciaries. It remains to be seen whether the novel remedies enunciated in *Mettoy Pension Trustees v. Evans* for the non-exercise of a mere discretion or power by a fiduciary donee are ever actually put into effect.

(3) Remedies where the power is exercised improperly
The general rule is that any improper exercise of any discretion or power   **6–142**
will be set aside, both where the donees "exceed their power, and possibly if they are proved to have exercised it capriciously".[354] To this basic rule there may be two exceptional: first, if Lewison J. was right to hold, in *Ogden v. Griffiths*,[355] that the effect of the application of Rule in *Gibbons v. Mitchell*

---

[350] *Re Gestetner* [1953] Ch. 672 at 688; *Re Manisty's Settlement* [1974] Ch. 17 at 25; *Rosewood Trust v. Schmidt* [2001] W.T.L.R. 1081 (Court of Appeal of the Isle of Man; the point was not mentioned in the subsequent judgment of the Privy Council ([2003] 2 A.C. 709)).
[351] [1990] 1 W.L.R. 1587.
[352] This part of the case was adjourned pending an appeal. Both the appeal and the outstanding part of the case were subsequently settled.
[353] By Gardner 107 L.Q.R. (1991) 214 at 217–218.
[354] *McPhail v. Doulton* [1971] A.C. 424, *per* Lord Wilberforce at 456.
[355] [2008] EWHC 118 (Ch), [2008] W.T.L.R. 685.

is to render the transaction in question not void *ab initio* but merely voidable at the discretion of the court; and, secondly, if Lightman J, was right to hold, in *Abacus Trust Co. (Isle of Man) v. Barr*,[356] that the effect of the application of the Rule in *Re Hastings-Bass (dec'd.)*[357] is that the transaction in question is voidable rather than void. In the light of earlier judicial statements adopting the opposite view,[358] the law in both respects must at present be uncertain.

6–143   An example of the general rule is *Turner v. Turner*,[359] where the trustees had left all the decisions to the settlor (who was not a trustee) and had made a series of appointments without reading the necessary documents before signing them; all the appointments were held to be null and void other than one concerning land which had been effective to transfer the legal title, which the appointee therefore held on trust for the settlement.

6–144   If the person to whom the property was improperly appointed under a disposition which is avoided has dealt with that property in favour of a third party, the latter will not be able to claim to have taken free of the interests of those otherwise entitled under the discretion or power and so will be bound by their interests[360] except in the relatively unlikely situation in which the third party has acquired the legal title to the property in question (in which case he may be able to claim to be a bona fide purchaser for value without notice or, in the case of registered land, the statutory equivalent). The only other exception to this is the limited defence provided by section 157 of the Law of Property Act 1925, which rather curiously is available only when the appointee was at least 25 years old at the time of the transaction and only to the extent that he was presumptively entitled in default of appointment.

(B)   The Collective Rights of the Objects of a Discretion or Power

6–145   There is one respect in which the objects of a power have a more direct interest in the property subject to the power. It will be seen later that, where a beneficiary of a trust is of full age and *sui juris* and he alone is entitled to the trust fund, he may bring the trust to an end.[361] Somewhat similarly, where all the possible objects of a discretion or power combine, then they together may deal with the beneficial interest in the property subject to it; however, if the discretion or power is limited to income, that is all that they will be able to deal with unless they also combine with whoever is entitled to the capital, including, if necessary, the default beneficiaries. In *Re Smith*[362] a fund was held on discretionary trust as to income and capital for Lilian and, after her death, for her children. Lilian and her three children, who were between them the only persons entitled to benefit under the trust, together assigned all their interest therein to an insurance company. The assignee was held entitled to demand the whole of the income. Romer J. said that in such a case "you treat all the people put together as though they

---

[356] [2003] EWHC 114 (Ch) 409, [2003] Ch. 409.
[357] [1975] Ch. 25; see *ante*, para 6–087.
[358] Particularly in *AMP (UK) v. Barker* [2001] W.T.L.R. 1237, [2001] P.L.R. 79.
[359] [1984] Ch. 100.
[360] *Cloutte v. Storey* [1911] 1 Ch. 18.
[361] See *post*, para 19–019.
[362] [1928] Ch. 915.

formed one person, for whose benefit the trustees were directed to apply the whole of a particular fund".[363]

(C)   The Right to Release Interests

Just as a man cannot be forced to accept a gift,[364] so a man cannot be forced   **6–146** to remain an object of a discretion or power and he can, if he so wishes, release his rights thereunder. In that event, the discretion or power is administered as if his name did not appear among the class of those entitled to be considered as objects of the exercise of the holder's discretion.[365]

2. *Assignees and Trustees in Bankruptcy*

An assignee or trustee in bankruptcy of a potential beneficiary is, in princi-   **6–147** ple, in the same position as the potential beneficiary himself. Thus in *Re Coleman*[366] the Court of Appeal held that, where a discretionary beneficiary had assigned his beneficial interest, the trustees were compelled to pay to the assignee the amount which they had allotted to the beneficiary. In principle, the position of a trustee in bankruptcy ought to be the same but this is subject to the general principle of bankruptcy law that a bankrupt is entitled to retain sufficient funds for his own support, the trustee in bankruptcy being entitled only to the balance. This principle was applied by Vaughan Williams J. in *Re Ashby*.[367] In that case a discretionary beneficiary became bankrupt and the trustees continued to make payments to him. The beneficiary was held to be entitled to retain what was necessary for his basic support and his trustee in bankruptcy was held to be able to claim the excess.

The terms of a trust instrument may require payment to be made to the   **6–148** beneficiary personally; alternatively, they may entitle the trustees either to pay the beneficiary directly or to make payments to third parties for his benefit. In *Re Bullock*,[368] which was concerned with a discretionary trust containing the latter type of provision, Kekewich J. held that, when a discretionary beneficiary had become bankrupt, the trustees could continue to pay income to third parties for his benefit. The precise scope of this decision is a matter of some doubt and it has been suggested that such a discretion is restricted so that the trustees can only provide the bankrupt with sufficient funds to cover his necessaries. However, this is probably not correct. It seems that, so far as the trustees are concerned, they may continue to apply funds for the benefit of the beneficiary in the same way as they could have done before the bankruptcy. If as a result assets come into the hands of the beneficiary which are not required for his necessaries, as where

---

[363] See also *Re Nelson* [1928] Ch. 920N.
[364] *Thompson v. Leach* (1690) 2 Vent. 198; *Re Stratton's Deed of Disclaimer* [1958] 2 Ch. 42.
[365] *Re Gulbenkian's Settlement Trusts (No.2)* [1970] Ch. 408.
[366] (1889) 39 Ch.D. 443. See also *Re Smith* [1928] Ch. 915.
[367] [1892] 1 Q.B. 872.
[368] [1891] 64 L.T. 736.

the trustees apply the money in providing a luxury holiday for the beneficiary, it seems that the trustee in bankruptcy is powerless to intervene. However, the trustees must of course exercise their discretion in good faith and
must make their decision with a view to benefiting the beneficiary rather
than in order to spite his trustee in bankruptcy and creditors.

CHAPTER 7

LEGALITY OF A TRUST

I. GENERALLY

It is an elementary principle that a trust which is wholly illegal or contrary   **7–001**
to public policy will not be enforced. Indeed the court will not only prevent
the illegal trust from taking effect but will also generally go so far as to
refuse the settlor its assistance in recovering the property in question;
"Those who violate the law must not apply to the law for protection".[1] The
principle will not, however, be stretched to its ultimate limit. A settlor is
nevertheless entitled to recover the property in question where the illegal
purpose is merely contemplated; in these circumstances, there is what is
described as a *locus poenitentiae*.[2]

The consequences of a trust being partially unlawful can be rather differ-   **7–002**
ent. Strictly speaking it appears that, if part of the trust funds is to be
devoted to an unlawful purpose and the remainder to a lawful purpose,
then, where the part of the funds to be devoted cannot be ascertained, the
whole trust will fail because it will be impossible to ascertain the residue.[3]
However, it must be truly impossible to ascertain the relevant part; it
appears that the court will, if practicable, endeavour to ascertain that part in
order to uphold the remainder of the gift.[4] Indeed there is some, admittedly
indecisive, authority[5] for the proposition that, if the lawful purpose is
charitable, the whole of the property will be devoted to that purpose and the
trust for the illegal purpose will be completely disregarded. But, in view of
the confused state of the case law, it is not by any means certain that this is
indeed the law, despite the fact that this would be extremely convenient.

This chapter deals principally with the circumstances in which a trust will   **7–003**
be void for perpetuity or will be set aside because of the bankruptcy of the
settlor; both of these topics are of the greatest importance in any discussion
of the legality of a trust. It is beyond the scope of this work to deal
exhaustively with the many other types of illegality known to the law which

---

[1] *Benyon v. Nettlefold* (1850) 3 Mac. & G. 94 at 102, *per* Lord Truro L.C. See also *Ayerst v. Jenkins*
(1873) L.R. 16 Eq. 275 but compare *Phillips v. Probyn* [1899] 1 Ch. 811.
[2] *Symes v. Hughes* (1870) L.R. 9 Eq. 475.
[3] See *Chapman v. Brown* (1801) 6 Ves. 404.
[4] See *Mitford v. Reynolds* (1842) 1 Ph. 185.
[5] See *Fisk v. A.-G.* (1867) L.R. 4 Eq. 521; *Hunter v. Bullock* (1872) L.R. 14 Eq. 45; *Dawson v. Small*
(1874) L.R. 18 Eq. 114; *Re Williams* (1877) 5 Ch.D. 735; *Re Birkett* (1878) 9 Ch.D. 576 (all trusts for
maintenance of tombs with surplus for a charitable purpose); see also *Re Rogerson* [1901] 1 Ch.
715.

are just as capable of vitiating a trust as of vitiating any other transaction; just three examples will be briefly considered.

(1) Restraints on alienation. A restraint on the alienation of property given to a beneficiary absolutely is contrary to public policy and void.[6]

(2) Restraints on marriage. If a condition and/or a gift over to take effect upon that condition is contained in a settlement and amounts to a total restraint on marriage, both condition and gifts over are wholly void.[7] However, this rule does not apply to conditions or gifts restraining second or subsequent marriages[8] nor does it apply to a partial restraint operating against designated persons or designated categories of persons such as the members of a particular religious faith or everyone other than the members of a particular religious faith.[9] On the other hand, however, a gift of property until marriage—as opposed to a gift to a person on condition that he does not marry—is perfectly good[10]; validity depends on whether the wording is construed as having given rise to a (valid) determinable interest or a (void) conditional interest; this distinction is perhaps an unnecessarily fine one (some would say unnecessarily perverse) but is well established. Curiously enough, the same difficulties do not attach to a condition requiring the consent of a particular person to marriage; it is clearly established that such a condition will be valid despite the apparent illogicality that the withholding of consent will bar a marriage just as effectively as the void conditions already referred to.[11]

(3) Trusts designed to separate parent and child. If a trust is designed to separate a parent (even if he or she has been divorced[12]) from his or her child, that trust will be void as contrary to public policy.[13] Similarly, a trust will fail if it tends to interfere with parental duties; such duties should be discharged solely with a view to the moral and spiritual welfare of the child and without being influenced by mercenary considerations.[14]

II. Perpetuities and Accumulations

7–004　Since medieval times, English law has been subjected to the tension between two conflicting influences. Owners of land and of other types of property have generally wished to tie up their property indefinitely, usually for the

---

[6] See, for example, *Floyer v. Bankes* (1869) L.R. 8 Eq. 115.
[7] *Lloyd v. Lloyd* (1852) 2 Sim.(N.S.) 255.
[8] *Allen v. Jackson* (1842) 1 Ch.D. 399.
[9] *Jenner v. Turner* (1880) 16 Ch.D. 188.
[10] *Re Lovell* [1920] 1 Ch. 122.
[11] *Re Whiting's Settlement* [1905] 1 Ch. 96.
[12] *Re Piper* [1946] 2 All E.R. 503.
[13] *Re Boulter* [1922] 1 Ch. 75; *Re Sandbrook* [1912] 2 Ch. 471.
[14] *Re Borwick* [1933] Ch. 657.

benefit of their family or for some institution or cause, while the courts and the legislature have always felt that it is in the interest of the nation as a whole that property should not be made inalienable and that money should circulate freely and be spent. The result has been a compromise.

Property may be tied up indefinitely for one particular type of purpose which the law wishes to advance, namely for charitable purposes.[15] Otherwise property may be tied up only for a comparatively short period. The rule which enforces this restriction is known as the rule against perpetuities. There are in fact two rules: the rule against remoteness, which is of general application and determines how far in the future the identity of a person entitled to a gift of property can be established; and the rule against inalienability, which applies only to non-charitable purpose trusts and determines how long such trusts can last.

On the other hand, income can at present only be accumulated for a comparatively short period. The rule which enforces this restriction, which applies to both charitable and non-charitable trusts, is known as the rule against accumulations.

1. *The Rule Against Remoteness*

The rule against remoteness basically provides that every gift of property   **7–005**
must vest in the recipient not later than the end of a finite, although not necessarily pre-established, period. At common law, the permissible period was that of a life or lives in being at the time when the gift in question took effect plus a further 21 years thereafter (with allowance being made, where appropriate, for up to two periods of gestation).[16] This was the only possible period until July 15, 1964 and still applies today in the event that the settlor or testator has not expressly elected to adopt an alternative period which has been available in respect of gifts contained in instruments coming into effect after July 15, 1964, namely any fixed period of up to 80 years.[17] Current proposals from the Law Commission[18], which are at long last scheduled to be enacted in 2009, now envisage the prospective total abolition of the common law period and its replacement by a universal fixed period of 125 years.

The rule has, however, been bedevilled by an excess of zeal on the part of   **7–006**
the judges. On the basis that under the rule property must vest, if at all, within the perpetuity period, the judges have striven to find some possibility, no matter how remote, whereby it might not do so. Whenever, looking at matters from the point of time at which the instrument creating the gift in question came into effect, they have managed to envisage any such possibility, the gift in question has been held to be void at common law. Thus at common law a gift by a testator to such of his issue as should be living when some gravel pits should become exhausted is necessarily void as it stands unless the pits have already been worked out by the time of his death; the

---

[15] See *post*, Chapter 11.
[16] *Cadell v. Palmer* (1833) 1 Cl. & Fin. 372; *Re Wilmer's Trusts* [1903] 2 Ch. 411.
[17] See *post*, para 7–012.
[18] Law Comm. No. 251 (1998); see Sparkes [1998] Trust Law International 48. Earlier and now abandoned proposals were made in Law Comm. No. 133 (1993).

decision in *Re Wood*[19] shows that this is the case not only if by then it is highly probable that the pits will be worked out in five or six years but also if they have actually been worked out by the time that the court has to rule on the matter. Although bizarre, this example is at least logically defensible. But the common law has produced other examples where common sense has gone straight out of the window and Alice has walked in the front door.

The almost unbelievable nonsense which has ensued in this respect is illustrated by *Re Dawson*.[20] There a testator gave property to trustees to hold upon trust for his daughter for life, with remainder to such of her children as should attain the age of 21, with a provision that if any of her children should die under the age of 21, but should themselves leave issue, such issue on attaining the age of 21 would take the share of their parent. When the will came into effect on the death of the testator, his daughter was aged over 60 and all her children were over 21. The court nevertheless managed to hold this gift to be void. With blithe disregard for the principles of biology, it was held that the daughter was still capable of giving birth to a child who might himself subsequently die before reaching the age of 21 leaving issue. Such a future child was obviously not alive at the time of the death of the testator so that the relevant life in being was the testator's daughter. In such circumstances the issue of the after-born child would not attain his vested interest within 21 years from the death of the daughter. Therefore, since it was thus possible that one of the persons entitled in remainder might not obtain a vested interest within the perpetuity period, the entire remainder was, therefore, void for perpetuity at common law. In the same sort of way, in *Re Gaite*[21] the court solemnly proceeded on the basis that a girl aged less than five could give birth to a child. In the apt expression of Morris and Leach,[22] at common law the judicial world would seem to be populated by fertile octogenarians, precocious toddlers and various other freaks.

7–007   To order to overcome some of the traps and generally to restore some semblance of sanity, Parliament has so far intervened on two occasions and is now about to do so in 2009 on a third occasion. Small and relatively insignificant amendments were made by the Law of Property Act 1925; large-scale alterations were made by the Perpetuities and Accumulations Act 1964 ("the 1964 Act"), which, with only a few exceptions,[23] applies only to instruments coming into effect after July 15, 1964[24]; and the new legislation proposed by the Law Commission, which will build on but simplify the reforms introduced by the 1964 Act, will, when it is enacted, generally[25] also apply only to instruments coming into effect after the legislation comes into force.

7–008   The modified rule may be stated in the following way: where a gift is made to take effect in the future, it must be seen from the instrument by

---

[19] [1894] 3 Ch. 381.

[20] (1888) 39 Ch.D. 155.

[21] [1949] 1 All E.R. 459.

[22] *The Rule Against Perpetuities* 2nd edn (1964), p.89.

[23] See s.8(2).

[24] The date of the Royal Assent (s.15(5)).

[25] Wills which are made before but come into effect after the legislation comes into force will continue to be governed by the previous rules.

which it is created that, if it is to vest at all, it must necessarily vest within the period prescribed by law; however, in the case of instruments governed by the 1964 Act or by the proposed new legislation, if it appears that the gift may or may not vest within the prescribed period, the gift is treated as if it does not offend the rule against remoteness until such time, if at all, as it becomes clear that it cannot vest within that period. The elements of this definition must now be examined and expanded.

(A) The Rule Concerns Vesting

The rule against remoteness requires only that gifts must *vest* within the **7–009** perpetuity period. This rule—as opposed to the rule against inalienability which will be considered later[26]—has no application to the length of time during which property may be enjoyed once it has vested. Accordingly, if an outright gift is made to a limited company so that the gift vests in the company immediately, that company may hold the property for more than a thousand years without ever infringing the rule against remoteness.[27]

It is, therefore, essential to know what is meant by "vesting". A future gift may be either vested or contingent. A gift is vested if:

(i) the person or persons entitled to the gift are in existence and are ascertained;

(ii) the size of the beneficiaries' interests is ascertained[28]; and

(iii) any conditions attached to the gift are satisfied.

If, therefore, property is left upon trust for Romeo for life, with remainder to Juliet, the interest of Juliet is vested even if Romeo is still alive. Juliet's interest is vested because she herself is alive and is an ascertained person; the extent of her interest, namely an interest in the whole fund, is ascertained and no conditions have to be satisfied before she becomes entitled. On the other hand, if the gift were to Romeo for life, with the remainder to Juliet provided she has danced on the moon, her gift does not become vested until that condition is fulfilled.

A vested interest therefore may or may not carry the right to present **7–010** enjoyment of the property in question.[29] To connote this distinction, vested interests are classified as being:

(i) vested in possession, in which case the interest does carry the right to present possession or enjoyment; or

(ii) vested in interest, where the interest carries only the right to future possession or enjoyment of the property in question.

---

[26] See *post*, para 7–046.

[27] See, however, *post*, para 7–044.

[28] *Pearks v. Moseley* (1880) 5 App. Cas. 714. This requirement for vesting applies only to the rule against perpetuities.

[29] It is a question of construction whether an interest is contingent or is vested liable to be divested: *Brotherton v. I.R.C.* [1978] 1 W.L.R. 610.

The relevance of this for the purpose of the rule against remoteness is that the rule is satisfied despite the fact that the gift is only vested in interest. Thus, it was held in *Re Hargreaves*[30] that a gift to a person for life, with remainder to any woman who might become his widow for life, with remainder to his children who attained the age of 21, was necessarily good at common law. It is true that the woman who may become that person's widow need not be alive at the date of the settlement; however, at the end of the common law perpetuity period (21 years after the death of the life tenant), it will be possible to say that his widow (if any) and his children, who must by then necessarily have attained the age of 21, are between them the absolute owners of the property.

(B)   The Scope of the Rule

7–011   The general principle is that the rule against remoteness applies to all future gifts. In particular, for the purposes of the law of trusts, it applies to all future gifts arising under an *inter vivos* settlement or trust and to all trusts created by will. To this general principle there are three exceptions:

> (i)   a gift to a charity is exempt from the rule against remoteness if the immediately prior interest was also in favour of a charity[31] (this exception is considered in greater detail in a later chapter[32]);
>
> (ii) rights of redemption under mortgages are not within the rule against remoteness, so that a mortgagor's right to redeem any mortgage which has been granted can be exercised outside the perpetuity period[33]; similarly, certain provisions of leases, such as options to renew the lease[34] and options to purchase the freehold or any leasehold reversion,[35] are not within the rule against remoteness either; and
>
> (iii) future personal obligations are not within the rule against remoteness so that a covenant to pay future mining royalties can also be enforced outside the perpetuity period.[36]

(C)   The Perpetuity Period

7–012   The maximum period for which vesting may be postponed is:

> (i)   at common law, the period of a life or lives in being and a further period of 21 years (together, where appropriate, with up to two periods of gestation);
>
> (ii) also at common law but where there are no lives in being, a period of 21 years;

---

[30] (1889) 43 Ch.D. 401.

[31] *Re Tyler* [1891] 3 Ch. 252. The normal provisions of the rule against remoteness do however apply in the case of a gift from a non-charity to a charity and a gift from a charity to a non-charity.

[32] See *post*, para 11–004.

[33] *Knightsbridge Estates Trust v. Byrne* [1939] Ch. 441.

[34] *Woodall v. Clifton* [1905] 2 Ch. 257 at 265, 268.

[35] Perpetuities and Accumulations Act 1964, s.9(1).

[36] *Witham v. Vane* (1883) Challis R.P. 440.

(iii) in gifts governed by the 1964 Act in this respect, a fixed period of up to but not exceeding 80 years provided that that period is specified as the relevant perpetuity period in the instrument creating the gift; but

(iv) under the proposed new legislation, a fixed universal period of 125 years, which will replace all three of the previous possibilities.

It should be noted that, in certain circumstances, the statutory period of 80 years may actually turn out to be shorter than the common law period although this is unlikely to be the case under the proposed new legislation when the statutory period becomes 125 years. Nevertheless, the use of any statutory period, whether that period is, as at present, the maximum period which can be chosen or is instead fixed, has the great advantage of both simplicity and certainty. Indeed, the principal reason and justification for the proposed abandonment of lives in being is the fact that it can no longer be guaranteed that children will be born no later than nine months after the death of their parents. The recent developments in genetics whereby peoples' sperm and eggs can be frozen enable their children to be born far in the future; in such circumstances, the link between lives in being and the next generation on which the rule against remoteness has so far been based simply no longer exists. This difficulty obviously does not arise with a fixed period of years since a child or grandchild either will or will not have been born by the end of it.   **7–013**

One of the more difficult questions affecting the current law governing perpetuities is how to identify the life or lives in being (this will of course cease to be necessary under the proposed new legislation). It is clear that the life or lives chosen do not need to take any benefit under the gift or to have any connection with the persons who can benefit thereunder. Consequently, the use of what is known as "royal lives clauses" is not uncommon; these are clauses which specify the perpetuity period by reference to the Royal Family. One of the forms of royal lives clauses which is in use at the present time is "the period ending the day before the day upon which will expire the period of 21 years from the death of the last survivor of all the lineal descendants of his late Majesty King George VI[37] who shall be living at the time when the gift comes into effect". There is in principle no reason why other persons should not be used instead provided that their lifespan and that of their children is sufficiently well documented; however, in practice,   **7–014**

---

[37] The father of the present Queen. Consequently, the royal lives in question are those of H.M. Queen Elizabeth II, her descendants, and the descendants of her deceased sister, H.R.H. Princess Margaret. It is also probably just about still possible to use King George V (the grandfather of the present Queen), although the number of his descendants is now quite considerable. It is certainly unsafe to specify the descendants of any previous sovereign (see the doubts cast, as early as 1901, on the validity of using the lives of descendants of Queen Victoria (then still alive) in *Re Moore* [1901] 1 Ch. 936). One potential difficulty about such clauses today is the fact that "descendants" now includes illegitimate descendants, who are not necessarily identifiable. But there seems no reason why future "royal lives clauses" should not be expressly restricted to legitimate descendants. The proposed new legislation will permit trustees to switch to its new 125-year fixed period where it is not reasonably practicable to establish whether or not a period specified by reference to lives in being has ended. This is one of only two provisions of that legislation which will affect gifts which have already come into effect.

this would only be likely to work if the person in question was still alive, something which would substantially shorten the period. Nor is there in principle any limit to the number of lives which may be selected, provided they can all be identified. Indeed in *Re Moore*[38] the settlor specified the lives in being as all persons then living; however, the gift was held to be void on the ground that it was impossible to identify which of them would be the survivor.

7–015   In the case of royal lives clauses and their like, it is apparent from the wording of the instrument in question that they are intended to be the lives in being for the purposes of the rule against perpetuities. However, in other cases it may be far more difficult to decide whether or not a person is to be taken as a life in being. The basic principle (or a basic principle) is that every person who is living at the date of the gift and is mentioned or whose existence is implied in the words by which it is created is a life in being. Thus, a gift by a testator to "my grandchildren" necessarily presupposes the existence of the testator's children; therefore those of his children who are alive at the date of his death will be taken to be lives in being in respect of this gift for the purpose of the rule against remoteness.

7–016   It should also be noted that a child *en ventre sa mère* is treated as a child who is alive if this is necessary to save a gift. Accordingly, a gift to the children of a child *en ventre sa mère* will necessarily be valid, for the unborn child will by implication be regarded as a life in being and his or her own children must necessarily be born within his or her own lifetime or within nine months thereafter.[39] So is a gift to the children of a child *en ventre sa mère* at the age of 21 because, even if the unborn child is male and he dies leaving a child *en ventre sa mère*, the latter child will reach the age of 21, if at all, within 21 years and nine months of the death of his father, who must himself be born, if at all, within nine months of the gift taking effect. Thus a perpetuity period based on lives in being can potentially include two periods of gestation; one before the life in being in question is born and the other after his death; so a perpetuity period based on lives in being can be up to nine months plus a life in being plus a further nine months plus 21 years. Similarly, the end of a fixed period may be extended in the case of a pregnancy. If a period of 80 years is prescribed and at the end of that time a woman is pregnant with a child who would, if alive, take the gift, then that child will in fact take provided he or she is born alive.[40]

7–017   The somewhat obvious but nevertheless amusing proposition that any life selected must be human should also be noted; it is apparently not permissible to choose either a specified animal (because some animals, such as tortoises, are extremely long-lived) or a specified long-lived tree such as a Californian pine. Only in an Irish case has this point actually been pronounced upon; this was in *Re Kelly*,[41] where it was stated by way of dictum that the life chosen must be that of a human and not of an animal. A similar pronouncement on the subject of trees is awaited.

---

[38] [1901] 1 Ch. 936.
[39] *Long v. Blackall* (1797) 7 T.R. 100.
[40] See *Cadell v. Palmer* (1833) 1 Cl. & F. 372, especially at 421, 422.
[41] [1932] I.R. 255 at 260, 261.

In the case of instruments governed by the 1964 Act in which advantage   **7–018**
has not been taken of the possibility of specifying a fixed period of up to 80
years, section 3(4) of the 1964 Act prescribes rules for identifying the lives in
being; however, as will be seen later,[42] these statutory lives in being only
operate for the purpose of determining whether or not a gift does in fact
satisfy the requirements of the rule against remoteness within the perpetuity
period; they do not determine whether or not a gift is valid at common law
and so whether or not it is necessary to wait and see in the way considered
below.[43] The 1964 Act provides that such of the following as are alive and
ascertainable at the date of the gift, and no other persons, shall constitute the
lives in being for this purpose:

  (i) the person who made the disposition (obviously only relevant in a
       gift *inter vivos* since a testator will necessarily be dead);

 (ii) in the case of a contingent gift to an individual or individuals, any
       person who may in time satisfy the conditions and that person's
       parents and grandparents;

(iii) in the case of a class gift, any member or potential member of the
       class and that person's parents and grandparents;

 (iv) any person who is given any power, option, or other right in
       connection with the gift; and

  (v) where the interest is to arise only in the event that the prior interest
       of some person determines, the person having that prior interest.

The principal addition to persons who will be lives in being at common law
are the parents and grandparents included within the second and third
categories (at common law, they are only included in the case of a gift to
someone who is necessarily their child or grandchild, not more generally).
The lives of persons in the second, third and fourth categories are disregarded if the number of those persons in any of those categories is so large
as to render it impossible to ascertain the date of death of the survivor.
Further provisions apply where there is a special power of appointment.[44]

(D) "Possibilities not Probabilities"

The general principle is that *any* possibility, no matter how remote, of the   **7–019**
gift not vesting within the perpetuity period will make it void. This principle can be expressed by saying that the rule is concerned with "possibilities
not probabilities", subject in the case of gifts governed by the 1964 Act and
by the proposed new legislation to the "wait and see" rule considered
below.[45] Illustrations of this principle are provided by the decisions in *Re
Wood*, *Re Dawson* and *Re Gaite* which have already been mentioned above.[46]
However, the advances in biological knowledge made during the twentieth

---

[42] See *post*, para 7–020.
[43] *ibid.*
[44] See *post*, para 7–036.
[45] See *post*, *infra*.
[46] See *ante*, para 7–006.

century now enable the court, when considering gifts governed by the 1964 Act, to make certain presumptions,[47] namely that a male cannot have a child at an age of less than 14 and that a female can have a child between the ages of 12 and 55 but not outside that age-span (these presumptions will obviously not be relevant under the proposed new legislation where lives in being will themselves become irrelevant).

(E) "Wait and See"

7–020   In relation to gifts which came into effect prior to the 1964 Act, it is necessary to construe the instrument creating the gift as at the date when it comes into operation and only at that date. Therefore, if a gift is made on or before July 15, 1964 to a person for life, with remainder to the first of his sons who goes to Canada, and at the date when the gift comes into effect that person has no children, the gift to the son will be void for perpetuity at common law; the life tenant is the only life in being and it is self-evident that it cannot be guaranteed that any son of his will go to Canada within 21 years of his death. In respect of gifts from this era (a large number of which are still operating despite the fact that well over 40 years have passed since 1964), it is simply not possible to wait and see whether the life tenant does in fact have a son who goes to Canada within 21 years of his death.

7–021   However, section 3 of the 1964 Act provides that, in relation to gifts which are subject to that section, the court may in some cases "wait and see" whether or not any particular gift does in the event offend against the rule. The first and most important case is where a gift may or may not become vested within whichever of the common law perpetuity period or the statutory perpetuity period of up to 80 years is relevant; in such circumstances, the gift is to be treated as if it does not offend against the rule until it can be definitely shown that the gift will necessarily vest, if at all, after the end of the appropriate period. Thus, if an instrument coming into operation after July 15, 1964 contains a gift to a person who does not as yet have any children for life, with remainder to the first of his sons who goes to Canada, then it is possible to wait and see: first whether he has any sons at all and, secondly, whether any of the sons which he does have goes to Canada within 21 years of the death of the survivor of him and his parents.[48] If any does, the gift is valid. Otherwise, the gift becomes void for perpetuity (and the gift which next follows that gift vests) as soon as it is clear that that gift cannot vest; this will be at the earliest of the following times: the life tenant's death without any sons, the death of all his sons, or the expiry of 21 years from the death of the last survivor of him and of his parents.

7–022   "Wait and see" will work in the same way under the proposed new legislation. If a gift which is void for perpetuity at common law does not vest by the end of the 125-year period, it will become void and the provisions of the settlement dependant on its not vesting will then take effect (of course, in practice it will generally become clear long before the end of the 125 years that a gift is never going to vest, as where a person whose children

---

[47] Perpetuities and Accumulations Act 1964, s.2.

[48] For the purposes of wait and see, the life tenant's parents are also lives in being (under s.3) so it is possible to wait and see until 21 years after the death of the survivor of him and his parents.

are the beneficiaries of the gift dies childless; in such cases, the provisions of the settlement dependant on the gift in question not vesting will take effect at that point).

(F) Age-Reducing Provisions

Prior to 1926, if a qualifying age was not certain to be attained within the perpetuity period, then of course necessarily the perpetuity period at common law, the gift was wholly void. However, section 163(1) of the Law of Property Act 1925 provided that, where the vesting of property was made to depend on the attainment by the beneficiary of an age greater than 21 and by virtue of that condition the gift was void for perpetuity, the age of 21 was to be substituted for the age stated in the instrument. The section applies only when the gift would otherwise have been void for perpetuity and only to instruments coming into effect between January 1, 1926 and July 15, 1964 (both inclusive). 7–023

This provision was replaced by section 4 of the 1964 Act for instruments coming into effect after July 15, 1964. By this section the age substituted is not 21 but the age nearest to the age which would have prevented the disposition from being void. Under the 1964 Act, therefore, the instrument is altered only to the extent necessary to save the disposition from offending against the rule. Further, before applying this section, it is first necessary to apply the "wait and see" rule. Suppose, therefore, that there is a gift by will to the first child of William to attain the age of 30 and that William has no children when the testator dies. This gift is obviously void for perpetuity at common law. It is first necessary to wait and see until the death of the survivor of William and his parents, who are the statutory lives in being for the purposes of wait and see, and assess the position then. At that point there will still be 21 years to go. All William's children will be born or *en ventre sa mère* by then; if they have all reached the age of 10, the gift will necessarily vest, if at all, within the perpetuity period. If, however, his only child is then five, the vesting age will have to be reduced to save the gift; it will, therefore, be reduced to 26 so that the vesting takes place at the last possible moment prior to the end of the 21 years which are still left.[49] 7–024

The proposed new legislation will contain no provisions for age reduction. Either the intended beneficiary will reach the specified age by the end of the 125-year period and take a vested interest or he will not do so and the gift will fail. 7–025

(G) Gifts after the Death of a Surviving Spouse

A provision of the 1964 Act which had no equivalent in the Law of Property Act 1925 enables gifts to children to be saved in other situations. Suppose that there is a gift to such of the children of Andrew as are living at the date of death of the survivor of Andrew and his spouse. This gift is void at 7–026

---

[49] It is not entirely clear what will happen if William has two children aged five and three; is the age first reduced to 26 to enable the five-year-old to take and, if he fails to do so, reduced again to 24 to enable the three-year-old to take or is the age immediately reduced to the age which will enable the younger child to take? The principal difficulty about proceeding in the former way is deciding what happens if the five-year-old dies at the age of 25 and the qualifying age is as a result reduced to 24, an age which the five-year-old obviously attained during his lifetime; does he or does he not take posthumously?

common law, because Andrew may subsequently marry a woman who was not born at the date of the gift. In this case, only Andrew, and not his wife, will be a life in being at common law; since she may survive him for more than 21 years, the interest of the children may vest outside the perpetuity period. Under the 1964 Act, the "wait and see" rule again has to be applied first. If Andrew has no surviving spouse or his surviving spouse turns out to have been alive at the date of the gift or survives him and his parents for less than 21 years, the gift will have been saved by "wait and see". If this does not save the gift, which will mean that a surviving spouse of Andrew who was not alive at the date of the gift survives him and his parents[50] for 21 years, then by virtue of section 5 of the Act the gift vests in interest immediately before the end of the perpetuity period; thus the children alive then qualify and the gift will have vested in interest exactly 21 years after the death of Andrew and his parents. However, it should be noted that this does not terminate any interest held in possession at that time; the effect of section 5 is to vest the gift in interest not in possession. So if, as is quite likely, the surviving spouse has a prior life interest (so that the original gift was to Andrew for life, remainder to any surviving spouse of Andrew for life, remainder to the children of Andrew living at the death of Andrew and his spouse), her interest will continue until her death and only then will the interest of the children vest in possession.

7–027   The proposed new legislation does not contain any similar provision because lives in being will cease to be relevant. In practice, there is anyway no realistic possibility that a surviving spouse of someone who is alive when a gift comes into effect will still be alive 125 years later.

(H) Class Gifts
7–028 Special provisions relate to gifts to the members of a class. For this purpose, a class is a number of persons who "come within a certain category or description defined by a general or collective formula, and who, if they take at all, are to take one divisible subject in certain proportionate shares".[51] The problem that such gifts pose is that it is possible that, at the moment when the gift vests in possession, some of the potential members may have qualified but others may not yet have been born or may not yet have satisfied some other qualifying condition.

7–029   Although for the purposes of the general law any member of the class who has fulfilled all the necessary conditions is regarded as having a vested interest while those who have not yet qualified obviously still have only contingent interests, for the purposes of the rule against remoteness the gift is not regarded as vesting in any member of the class until all the members of the class are definitely known. In other words, the rule against remoteness demands that all the members of the class must qualify if at all within the perpetuity period.[52] A gift to the children of Brian who attain the age of 21 is clearly valid for perpetuity at common law since all the members of the class will necessarily attain that age if at all within 21 years of Brian's death and therefore within the perpetuity period. On the other hand, a gift to the

---

[50] His parents are also lives in being for the purposes of wait and see.
[51] *Pearks v. Mosely* (1880) 5 App.Cas. 714 *per* Lord Selborne L.C. at 723.
[52] *Leake v. Robinson* (1817) 2 Mer. 363.

children of Brian who marry is potentially void for perpetuity since one or more of Brian's children may not marry within 21 years of Brian's death in which case that child or children will not have qualified by the end of the perpetuity period. This is also a problem where a fixed perpetuity period is used since some of the potential members of the class may not have qualified by the end of that period either.

Class gifts are further complicated by the existence of certain rules of construction known as the class-closing rules.[53] These rules, which can be excluded by contrary intention,[54] provide that a class whose size is not yet fixed will close when any member of the class becomes entitled to claim a vested interest in possession. The class so closed will include any potential members of the class who have been born by then but will exclude all potential members of the class who have not yet been born.[55] The fact that these rules reduce the size of classes means that they can operate to save a gift which would otherwise be void for perpetuity. Thus the gift to the children of Brian who marry will be saved from being void for perpetuity if any child of Brian has married when the gift takes effect since the class will immediately close on the children born by then, who can only marry in their own lifetimes and therefore will necessarily qualify if at all within the perpetuity period.[56] But the class-closing rules operate in exactly the same way in respect of gifts which are entirely valid for perpetuity. Thus in the case of the gift to the children of Brian who attain the age of 21, the class will close when the first child reaches 21 on the children born by then even though the presence of the excluded children would not cause the gift to be void for perpetuity.   **7–030**

For a class gift in a instrument which came into effect on or before July 15, 1964 to be valid, it had to be possible to establish at the moment when the gift took effect that every single member of the class would necessarily fulfil any necessary conditions, if at all, within the perpetuity period; the possibility that any member of the class would fail to do so rendered the entire gift void.[57] Thus a gift to the children of Brian who marry which was contained in such an instrument would be wholly void for perpetuity unless it was saved by the class-closing rules in the manner already described.   **7–031**

Where the 1964 Act applies, however, the vast majority of class gifts will be saved by the wait and see provisions. In the case of the gift to the children   **7–032**

[53] These rules are often also known, not wholly accurately, as the Rule in *Andrews v. Partington* (1791) 3 Bro.C.C. 401. Relatively recent illustrations of the working of these rules can be found in *Re Chapman's Settlement Trusts* [1977] 1 W.L.R. 1163 and *Re Clifford's Settlement Trusts* [1981] Ch. 63.

[54] However, the contrary intention must be extremely clear: a gift "to the children of Brian who attain the age of 21 whenever born" would certainly contain a contrary intention but a gift "to all the children of Brian who attain the age of 21" would not.

[55] However, where the only requirement for membership of the class is birth, the class will close only if any member of the class has qualified when the gift vests in possession; if no member of the class has been born by then, the class can never close thereafter for the somewhat obvious reason that otherwise the first member's birth would cause the class to close on him alone.

[56] If no child of Brian has married by then, the class will close whenever the first child of Brian marries thereafter but that will not necessarily save the gift from being void for perpetuity because someone included within the closed class may nevertheless not marry by the end of the perpetuity period.

[57] *Pearks v. Moseley* (1880) 5 App.Cas. 714; *Re Hooper's Settlement Trust* [1948] Ch. 586.

of Brian who marry, if any child marries during the wait and see period, the class-closing rules will operate to exclude any children born thereafter and by the end of that period all possible members of the class may either have married or died unmarried. The wait and see provisions will not, however, have saved the gift if at that point one or more members of the class have qualified but one or more other members of the closed class have not yet done so but are still capable of so doing so.

At that point, what happens depends on the reason for the failure to qualify. If the reason is an age requirement over 21, that age can be reduced to the extent necessary to save the gift under section 4(1) of the Act in the manner already described.[58] Where the reason is some failure to satisfy a requirement other than an age requirement, recourse can instead be had to section 4(4) of the Act to save the gift. Under this subsection, any members of the closed class who have not qualified by the end of the relevant perpetuity period are simply excluded. In the case of the gift to the children of Brian who marry, the wait and see period will end 21 years after the death of the last survivor of Brian, Brian's parents, and any wife or children of Brian who were ascertainable when the instrument in question took effect. If at that point any of the children of Brian who were alive when the first child married have not yet themselves married, they will simply be excluded from membership of the class.[59]

7–033   Under the proposed new legislation, as in the case of individual gifts age reduction will no longer be feasible but any potential members of the class who have neither been excluded by the class-closing rules nor have qualified by the end of the 125-year period will simply be excluded.

(J) Dependent Limitations

7–034 Prior to the 1964 Act, where a gift followed and was dependent upon prior limitations which were void, that gift was necessarily also void.[60] Vested gifts are of course not subject to the rule against remoteness at all and so could not possibly be affected by the fact that they followed a prior void gift. Contingent gifts were, however, void if they not only followed but were also dependent upon a prior void gift.[61] The distinction between gifts which merely followed and gifts which both followed and were dependent on a

---

[58] See *ante*, para 7–024, n.49. It is again not entirely clear whether the age is immediately reduced to the age which will enable the youngest potential member of the class to take or whether the age is reduced progressively as necessary to enable individual members of the class to take. As before, the difficulty which arises about the latter way of proceeding, much more starkly than in the case of individual gifts, is what will happen if a potential member of the class has died without qualifying but would have qualified had the qualifying age to which it is later reduced to accommodate a younger potential member of the class; does he or does he not qualify posthumously?

[59] Where two requirements have to be satisfied, one of which is an age requirement, such as a gift to the children of Brian who marry and attain the age of 40, then it is possible under s.4(3) of the Act both to age-reduce and to exclude if that will cause fewer members to be excluded. Thus, if at the end of the wait and see period, some members have married but are not yet 40, some members are 40 but have not yet married, and some are neither married nor 40, the members of the first group can be saved by age reduction but the other two groups will have to be excluded.

[60] *Re Buckton* [1964] Ch. 497; compare *Re Robinson* [1963] 1 W.L.R. 628.

[61] *Re Coleman* [1936] Ch. 528.

prior void gift was not particularly easy to draw in practice[62]; in broad terms, a gift had to have its own independent date of vesting if it was not to be regarded as dependent.[63] Thus a gift for life to the first child of Charles who marries but, if none does, to the first child of David who attains the age of 21 for life was wholly void unless a child of Charles had already married—the gift to David's child, although it would have been valid if it had stood alone, is wholly dependent on the prior void gift. On the other hand, in the case of a gift to the first child of Charles who marries for life and, subject to that, to the first child of David who attains the age of 21, the gift to David's child is in no sense dependent on the prior gift and so was valid at common law.

However, section 6 of the 1964 Act provides that no gift governed by that   **7–035** Act can fail merely because it is dependent upon a prior void gift. This means that, where the 1964 Act applies, both the gifts to David's child are now valid for perpetuity; both the gifts to Charles' child remain void at common law unless a child of his has already married but both are obviously now highly likely to be saved by the wait and see provisions. This will remain the position under the proposed new legislation.

(K) Powers of Appointment

(1) Classification of powers
The classification of powers has already been discussed.[64] It is doubtful   **7–036** whether, at common law, intermediate powers should for the purposes of the rule against remoteness be classified as general or special powers (intermediate powers were effectively unknown when the rules of the common law were formulated). However, it is suggested that the rules prescribed by the 1964 Act for instruments governed by that Act should also be followed for common law purposes. In any event, by virtue of section 7 of the 1964 Act, a general power for the purposes of that Act is a power exercisable by one person only which can be exercised by that person to transfer property to himself without the consent of any other person[65]; a power may be general for this purpose even if it is exercisable only by will and not also *inter vivos*.[66] For the purposes of the rule against remoteness, it therefore follows that an intermediate power may be either general or special, depending on its terms. Thus a power to appoint to anyone except Eric will for these purposes be a general power unless the donee of the power is Eric himself.

(2) Validity of powers
Two questions have to be considered: first, whether the power is itself valid   **7–037** and, secondly, whether the appointment made under the power is valid.

---

[62] *Re Backhouse* [1921] 2 Ch. 51.
[63] *Re Coleman* [1936] Ch. 528.
[64] See *ante*, para 6–056.
[65] Except where any consent is required as to the mode of exercise of the power.
[66] This is also the position at common law; see *Rous v. Jackson* (1885) 29 Ch.D. 521.

(a) Whether the power is itself valid

7-038   (i) Special powers A special power is void at common law if it is capable of being exercised outside the perpetuity period.[67] However, for instruments governed by the 1964 Act, the wait and see provisions may be applied in order to establish whether the power is in fact fully exercised during the perpetuity period. Where it is exercised only partially within the period, the power is only void to the extent that it was not exercised during the perpetuity period.[68] This will also be the case for instruments governed by the proposed new legislation.

7-039   (ii) General powers As the donee of the power may appoint to himself, property subject to a general power is regarded for most purposes as property belonging to the donee. Therefore, so far as the validity of the power is concerned, it is necessary only that the power should be acquired by the donee within the perpetuity period; it is not necessary for it to be exercised within that period.[69] However, where the general power in question is exercisable by will, it is governed by the same rules as special powers.[70] No legislative reform of these rules has ever been necessary.

(b) Whether the appointment is valid

7-040   (i) Special powers As the disposition of property subject to a special power is restricted, the perpetuity period has up until now commenced at the date when the power is created, not when it is exercised. In principle, therefore, at common law it is necessary to consider the position as at the date of creation of the power, assume that the appointment is then made, and then see whether the gift made by virtue of the appointment necessarily vests, if at all, within the perpetuity period. Even at common law, however, it is permissible to take into account the circumstances prevailing at the time when the power is exercised. Therefore, despite the fact that the terms of the appointment might theoretically enable the gift to vest outside the perpetuity period, if the circumstances existing at the time of the appointment establish that the gift must vest, if at all, within the period, the appointment will be valid.

This can be illustrated by considering a gift by will by Charles to Desmond for life giving Desmond a power to appoint the subject matter to his children, which Desmond subsequently exercises by making an appointment in favour of his son Fergus "as and when he attains the age of 30" at a time when Fergus, who was born after the death of Charles, has attained the age of 10. If this situation is examined only as at the time when the power was created, that is to say on the death of Charles, the gift and appointment have to be read together as if they provided: "to Desmond for life, with remainder to Fergus as and when he attains the age of 30"; since Fergus was not alive at that point, he could clearly take more than 21 years

---

[67] Re Abbot [1893] 1 Ch. 54.
[68] Perpetuities and Accumulations Act 1964, s.3.
[69] Re Fane [1913] 1 Ch. 404.
[70] Woolaston v. King (1868) L.R. 8 Eq. 165.

after the death of Desmond to attain the age of 30 and so the gift would prima facie be void at common law. However, since it is permissible to take into account the circumstances existing when the power is actually exercised, it can be seen that, since Fergus is already 10, the gift will necessarily vest, if at all, within 20 years of the death of Desmond and consequently the appointment is valid.

Quite apart from the limited form of wait and see which is therefore **7–041** permissible at common law, the general wait and see provisions of the 1964 Act also apply to powers which are both created and exercised after July 15, 1964.[71]

Under the proposed new legislation, all special powers, whenever created, will be permitted under the new 125-year fixed period measured from the date of the original creation of the power. This is one of only two provisions of that legislation which will affect gifts which have already come into effect.

(ii) General powers In the case of general powers, the perpetuity period **7–042** runs from the date of the exercise of the power, not from the date of its creation. Therefore, rules in respect of property comprised in a general power are the same as for property comprised in an absolute gift. It must, however, be remembered that, if a power is general in its terms but is only exercisable by more than one donee, it is treated as a special power for the purposes of the Rule against Perpetuities.[72]

(L) The Effect of Failure to Comply with the Rule against Remoteness
If a limitation in a trust instrument infringes the rule against remoteness, **7–043** then any subsequent limitation which is nevertheless valid will take effect; in default of any such limitation, the property in question will be held on resulting trust[73] for the settlor. Where the void limitation is contained in a will, that means that the property in question will fall into the testator's residuary estate or, if the void limitation is itself the residuary gift or there is no residuary gift, it will be distributed according to the intestacy rules.

2. *The Rule Against Inalienability*

The corollary to the rule that a gift must vest, if at all, within the perpetuity **7–044** period is the principle that property must not be rendered inalienable.[74] The basis of this principle is that land and, for that matter, all other property should be kept freely marketable and in circulation among the members of the community. A gift is inalienable if there is some provision which prevents the property being disposed of. This provision may be either a term of

---

[71] Perpetuities and Accumulations Act 1964, s.3 (compare s.8, which relates only to administrative powers of trustees).
[72] *Re the Earl of Coventry's Indentures* [1974] Ch. 77.
[73] See *post*, para 9–051.
[74] *Carne v. Long* (1860) 2 De G.F. & J. 75 at 80.

the gift itself,[75] or, in the case of a gift to a club or association, a rule of that club or association.[76]

To this general principle there are two exceptions: first, by analogy with the rule against remoteness, it seems that property may validly be made inalienable during the lifetime or lifetimes of persons in being at the time of the gift and for 21 years thereafter[77] or for any fixed statutory perpetuity period which has been substituted for that common law perpetuity period; and, secondly, property may be made inalienable in the hands of a charity.[78]

A gift to a body corporate which is not a charity is not in general capable of falling foul of the rule against inalienability. Even though the company may, if it so wishes, retain the property indefinitely for the benefit of its shareholders, it will not be under any obligation to retain the property if the gift is absolute. It is only where some condition is imposed on the gift prohibiting the company from disposing of the property that the gift will offend against the rule and be void.

7–045   The rule is principally applicable to non-charitable purpose trusts and to gifts to unincorporated associations.[79] These have already been considered.[80] It should be noted that section 15(4) of the 1964 Act provides that a donor of property for these purposes cannot opt to use for the purposes of the rule against inalienability the statutory period of up to 80 years which section 1 makes available for the purposes of the rule against remoteness; in this respect, therefore, the position remains the same as it was before that Act.[81] The proposed new legislation will not affect the rule against inalienability either.

As will be seen later on,[82] a gift to a charity is not void even if the property in question is made inalienable.

3. *The Rule Against Accumulations*

7–046   Another consequence of the principle that property and wealth should generally be free to circulate has been the statutory control of accumulations. When the income of a trust is accumulated rather than being paid out to any of the beneficiaries, the income so accumulated becomes additional capital of the trust, although trust deeds sometimes give the trustees a discretion or power to utilise income accumulated in earlier years as income in the current year. However, except when the person entitled to the income in

---

[75] *Re Patten* [1929] 2 Ch. 276.

[76] *Rickard v. Robson* (1862) 31 Beav. 244; *Re Nottage* [1895] 2 Ch. 649; *Re Drummond* [1914] 2 Ch. 90.

[77] *Carne v. Long* (1860) 2 De G.F. & J. 75; *Re Dean* (1889) 41 Ch.D. 552 at 557.

[78] *Chamberlayne v. Brockett* (1872) 8 Ch.App. 206 at 211.

[79] A further reason for such trusts and gifts being void was that there was no person capable of enforcing the trust: *Morice v. Bishop of Durham* (1805) 10 Ves. 521 at 539; *Bowman v. The Secular Society* [1917] A.C. 406 at 441; *Re Wood* [1949] Ch. 498.

[80] See *ante*, para 3–076 *et seq.*

[81] The provision appears to be clearly to this effect but see Maudsley, *The Modern Law of Perpetuities*, p.177, in which the opposite view is argued.

[82] See *post*, para 11–004.

question is a minor (when accumulation is in certain circumstances permitted under section 31 of the Trustee Act 1925[83]), income can only be accumulated when the trust deed contains an express provision to this effect. Such a provision may either direct the trustees to accumulate income or give them a discretion whether or not to do so (it will be recalled that the presence or absence of such a discretion determines whether a discretionary trust is, respectively, non-exhaustive or exhaustive).

(A) Accumulation at Common Law

At common law, the rule was that a direction to accumulate income was valid if it was confined to the perpetuity period applicable to the rule against remoteness.[84] This rule was applied in *Thellusson v. Woodford*.[85] Thellusson had by his will directed that the income of his property should be accumulated during the lives of his sons, grandsons and their issue who were living at his death, and that on the death of the survivor, the accumulated fund should be divided among certain of his descendants. This direction, being confined to lives in being, was held to be valid (at that time this was generally regarded as the perpetuity period applicable to the rule against remoteness, the additional period of 21 years not yet having been firmly established[86]). This principle would presumably also have been applied to discretions to accumulate income had any relevant case come before the courts but discretionary trusts were not common at that time.

7–047

(B) Statutory Restrictions on Accumulation

At the time of *Thellusson v. Woodford*,[87] it was calculated that the fund accumulated under Thellusson's will would by the end of the period in question amount to many millions of pounds. Many of the members of Parliament did not relish either the prospect of Thellusson's descendants potentially becoming as wealthy as the Crown or the fact that the decision entitled their own parents to deprive them for their entire lifetimes of the capital which they were expecting to inherit on their parents' deaths. Consequently, Parliament intervened to prevent further directions, or for that matter discretions, to accumulate of this nature by enacting the ill-drafted Accumulations Act 1800 (the Act is for this reason often known as "the Thellusson Act"). The position is at present governed by sections 164–166 of the Law of Property Act 1925, as amended by section 13 of the Perpetuities and Accumulations Act 1964,[88] although further reform is now imminent.

7–048

Section 164 of the Law of Property Act 1925 lays down the general rule that income may not be accumulated for longer than any one of the following periods:

7–049

---

[83] See *post*, para 17–035.

[84] *Wilson v. Wilson* (1851) 1 Sim. (n.s.) 288 at 298.

[85] (1799) 4 Ves. 227; (1805) 11 Ves. 112.

[86] This did not occur until the decision of the House of Lords in *Cadell v. Palmer* (1833) 1 Cl. & F. 372.

[87] (1799) 4 Ves. 227; (1805) 11 Ves. 112.

[88] As further amended by Family Law Reform Act 1969, Sch.3, para.7.

(i) the life of the settlor (this is the period which is adopted in the case of gifts *inter vivos* where there is a direction to accumulate and no other period is expressly specified);

(ii) 21 years from the death of the testator or settlor (this is the period which is adopted in the case of gifts by will where there is a direction to accumulate and no other period is expressly specified);

(iii) the duration of the minority or minorities of any persons living at the death of the testator or settlor (this period begins from the death of the testator or settlor); or

(iv) the duration of the minority or minorities of any persons entitled under the settlement (in this case the beneficiary need not be alive at the death of the testator or settlor and the accumulation period will commence at the birth of that beneficiary).

7–050   The 1964 Act added two further possible periods in respect of instruments coming into operation after July 15, 1964:

(i) the period of 21 years from the date of making the disposition; or

(ii) the duration of the minority or minorities of any person in being at the date of the making of an *inter vivos* disposition.

7–051   It must be re-emphasised that, if none of these six periods is selected, income cannot be accumulated at all (except during minorities, where accumulation is in certain circumstances permitted under section 31 of the Trustee Act 1925[89]). Where the trust deed or will in question simply contains a direction or discretion to accumulate without a specific reference to any of these periods, it is a question of construction which of the six has been selected[90]; however, as indicated above, if the court cannot decide, the relevant period will be the life of the settlor in the case of a gift inter vivos and 21 years from the death of the testator in the case of a gift by will.

7–052   Section 165 of the Law of Property Act 1925 expressly upholds the validity of successive periods of accumulation where a direction is given for income to be accumulated for one of the authorised periods and at the end of that period, or indeed at some time thereafter, the income has to be accumulated under the general law or under some other statutory provision. As will be seen later on,[91] when an infant is entitled to the income of property which is held on trust for him, any income which is not applied for his maintenance has, by virtue of section 31 of the Trustee Act 1925, to be accumulated until he reaches the age of majority. So if a testator gives property to a person for life, with remainder to his eldest son, the testator can direct that the income be accumulated for a period of 21 years from his death and, in the event that the eldest son is still an infant at the death of his father, the

---

[89] See *post*, para 17–035.
[90] *Jagger v. Jagger* (1883) 25 Ch.D. 729.
[91] See *post*, para 17–035.

income can further be accumulated during any later period in which the eldest son is entitled to an interest in possession in the property but is an infant.[92]

(C) Proposed Statutory Reversion to *Thelluson*

The proposed new legislation will restore the common law rule and permit **7–053**
accumulation throughout the perpetuity period; however, the perpetuity period in question will be not the common law period but the same 125-year period which has been proposed for the rule against remoteness. The maximum period during which accumulation is permitted will therefore become 125 years, although there will obviously be nothing to stop a lesser number of years from being specified instead. The only exception to the 125-year period will be in the case of charitable trusts, where accumulation will still be permitted for only 21 years; this has been proposed on the basis that it is not consistent with the public benefit which charitable trusts are supposed to produce for income to be withdrawn from a charitable purpose for longer than that.

The proposed new legislation is likely to contain a provision similar to section 165 of the Law of Property Act 1925. While it is obviously unlikely that a minority will be feasible after the end of the new 125-year period, such a minority is at least theoretically possible after the end of a gift of income to a charitable trust.

(D) Excessive Accumulations

If the trustees are specifically directed to accumulate income for a period **7–054**
which is potentially longer than the relevant perpetuity period, the direction to accumulate is wholly void.[93] This applies even to accumulations for the benefit of charities.[94] However, where the trustees are merely given a discretion to accumulate income for a period which is potentially longer than the relevant perpetuity period, the "wait and see" principle of the 1964 Act will apply and may well operate so as to validate the accumulations made (if it does not do so, income accumulated during "wait and see" will presumably at the end of the "wait and see period" have to be paid to the persons who would have been entitled to it had it not been accumulated).

If, on the other hand, the trustees are specifically directed to accumulate income only for the relevant perpetuity period, the direction is invalid only as to the excess over the longest authorised period.[95] This will also be the case if they are specifically given a discretion to accumulate throughout the relevant perpetuity period. Consequently, such a direction must be followed and such a discretion may be exercised until the end of the longest authorised accumulation period.

These rules will continue to apply to the proposed new legislation in the event of a direction or a discretion to accumulate for longer than the permitted 125-year (or, in the case of a charitable trust, 21-year) period.

---

[92] See also *Re Maber* [1928] Ch. 88.
[93] *Curtis v. Lukin* (1842) 5 Beav. 147.
[94] *Re Bradwell* [1952] Ch. 575.
[95] *Re Jefferies* [1936] 2 All E.R. 626.

(E)   Exceptions to the General Rules

7–055   There are certain exceptions from the general restrictions on accumulations and in these cases any period of accumulation may be specified. These are:

(i) accumulations for the payment of the debts of any person;

(ii) accumulations for the purpose of raising portions[96] for the children or more remote issue of the settlor, or any person entitled under the settlement; and

(iii) accumulations of the produce of timber or wood.[97]

It should also be noted that, where income is merely retained in order to guard against the possibility that in future years there will be insufficient income to pay annuities, that income will not be being accumulated.[98] It is, therefore, not subject to the relevant rule against accumulations and does not become capital. Consequently, in the event that the income so retained does not ultimately have to be used to pay the annuities, it will have to be paid to whoever would otherwise been entitled to it.

III. SAFEGUARDING PROPERTY FROM CREDITORS

7–056   Ever since uses, the forerunners of trusts, were first invented, attempts have repeatedly been made by those who contemplate the actual or potential threat of financial ruin to employ uses and trusts in order to put their property beyond the reach of their creditors. Prima facie a transfer of property by a settlor to trustees on trust for his wife or some other relative or friend has the effect of removing that property from his assets and consequently of preventing his trustee in bankruptcy from claiming it on behalf of his creditors. Where the beneficiary of the trust is the settlor's wife, the effect and usually the objective is that the settlor can continue to enjoy the benefit of the settled property indirectly by living with her in property belonging to the trust and having his living expenses provided by her out of the income to which she is entitled. And even where a settlor does not act so blatantly as to derive indirect benefit from the property himself, there is no doubt whatever that he will inevitably prefer his property to be enjoyed by his relatives and friends rather than by his creditors.

It is not surprising that both these results are looked on with disapproval by the legislature which has long placed statutory restrictions on the use of trusts for these purposes. These statutory restrictions are what will be considered in this section; where they do not apply, trusts remain an effective means of preventing creditors from laying their hands on a person's property.[99] It should also be added that one of the principal reasons for the utilisation of off-shore trusts is in order to put property beyond the reach of

---

[96] *Re Bourne* (1946) 115 L.J.Ch. 152.

[97] Law of Property Act, s.164(2).

[98] *Re Earl of Berkeley* [1968] Ch. 744.

[99] See *post*, Chapter 8.

these statutory restrictions,[100] something which is generally effective provided that the settlor is not already the subject of adverse claims at the time of the creation of the off-shore trusts[101] and provided that the settled assets are also outside the settlor's home jurisdiction.[102]

Until relatively recently this area of the law was governed by two distinct statutory provisions: section 172 of the Law of Property Act 1925, which enabled dispositions of property made with intent to defraud creditors to be set aside, whether or not the person who made the disposition was bankrupt, and section 42 of the Bankruptcy Act 1914, which enabled various dispositions to be set aside when the person who had made them had become bankrupt. Both provisions were, however, repealed by the Insolvency Act 1985. The present law is contained in the Insolvency Act 1986.

1. *Transactions Defrauding Creditors*

The provisions of the Insolvency Act 1986 relating to dispositions of property made with intent to defraud creditors do not require that the person entering into the transaction should be bankrupt or even that he should be in debt. Previous provisions of this type have not done so either. As Jessel M.R. said in *Re Butterworth*,[103] where a settlement made by a prosperous baker immediately before purchasing a different type of business (that of a grocer) of which he had no experience was set aside under the predecessor of section 172 of the Law of Property Act 1925: **7–057**

"a man is not entitled to go into a hazardous business, and immediately before doing so, settle all his property voluntarily, the object being this: 'If I succeed in business, I make a fortune for myself. If I fail, I leave my creditors unpaid. They will bear the loss.' That is the very thing which the Statute of Elizabeth was meant to prevent."

It is admittedly somewhat ironic that, at about the time when this observation was made, legislation was being introduced permitting for the first time the incorporation of companies with limited liability, which makes it entirely legitimate, subject to certain minimum requirements as to membership, for the shareholders to adopt exactly the policy so stringently condemned by Jessel M.R. But, despite the fact that the legislature has accepted that an appropriate way for an investor to limit his possible losses in hazardous ventures is to carry them out in the name of a limited company, it has continued to prohibit the use of trusts and settlements for the same purpose.

Section 423 of the Insolvency Act 1986 enables the court to intervene whenever it is satisfied that any person, whether a natural person or a body

---

[100] See O'Sullivan, *Asset Protection Trusts* (2000); Jones in *The International Trust* (ed. Glasson, 2002).

[101] Off-shore jurisdictions will normally enforce adverse claims which pre-exist the creation of such a trust, although usually only for a short time.

[102] Assets within the settlor's home jurisdiction will generally be susceptible to execution there despite the fact that they are technically vested in an off-shore trust.

[103] (1882) 19 Ch.D. 588 at 598; see *Stileman v. Ashdown* (1742) 2 Atk. 477; *Mackay v. Douglas* (1872) L.R. 14 Eq. 106.

corporate,[104] has entered into a transaction at an undervalue for the purpose of putting assets beyond the reach of anyone who is making or may at some time make a claim against him or of otherwise prejudicing the interests of such a person in relation to the claim which he is making or may make. There is no requirement that that person should have acted dishonestly[105] nor is it necessary for the purpose in question to be his sole purpose or even his dominant purpose. In *I.R.C. v. Hashmi*[106] Arden L.J. held:

"It is sufficient if the statutory purpose can properly be described as a purpose and not merely as a consequence . . . it will often be the case that the motive to defeat creditors and the motive to secure family protection will co-exist in such a way that even the transferor himself may be unable to say what was uppermost in his mind . . . for something to be a purpose it must be a real substantial purpose; it is not sufficient to quote something which is a by-product of the transaction under consideration, or to show that it was simply a result of it, . . . or an element which made no contribution of importance to the debtor's purpose in carrying out the transaction under consideration. . . . trivial purposes must be excluded."

The Court of Appeal therefore set aside a declaration of trust of a freehold property made on the occasion of its acquisition by its existing tenant in favour of his son. He had been under-declaring his profits to the Inland Revenue for many years and so was potentially liable for substantial arrears of tax, interest thereon and penalties; it was for this reason that he was held to have intended to put the property beyond the reach of his creditors. Section 423 was also successfully invoked in *Moon v. Franklin*[107] when a husband made substantial gifts to his wife at a time when he was threatened with legal proceedings which he knew might not be covered by sufficient insurance. Similarly, the Court of Appeal held in *Barclays Bank v. Eustice*[108] that there was a strong prima facie case for the applicability of the section when a transfer of assets by a debtor left him with insufficient assets to meet an expected action by the bank.

A transaction will be at an undervalue in the following circumstances: first, if it is a gift or entered into on terms which provide for the transferor to receive no consideration; secondly, if it is made in the absence of consideration other than marriage consideration; or, thirdly, if it is entered into by the transferor for a consideration the value of which, measured in money or money's worth, is significantly less than the value, also measured in money or money's worth, of the consideration provided by the transferor.[109]

---

[104] See also Insolvency Act 1986, s.207.

[105] Hence the section can apply even where the transferor's legal advisers considered it proper; see *Arbuthnot Leasing International v. Havalet Leasing (No.2)* [1990] B.C.C. 636.

[106] [2002] W.T.L.R. 1027 at 1035.

[107] (1990) *The Independent*, June 22, 1990.

[108] [1995] 1 W.L.R. 1238.

[109] The latter formulation was approved by Lord Scott of Foscote in *Phillips v. Brewin Dolphin Bell Lawrie* [2001] 1 All E.R. 673 at 681–682, although this case actually concerned the analogous provision for setting aside transactions entered into by companies at an undervalue in the two years prior to going into liquidation.

The creation of any trust other than for money or money's worth will obviously satisfy these requirements. This was the case in *I.R.C. v. Hashmi*[110] and would have been the case in *Midland Bank v. Wyatt*[111] had the trust in question not been held to be a sham, which of course meant that the property had at all times been vested in the settlor anyway. A less straightforward case was *Chohan v. Saggar*,[112] where a house was transferred into the name of its sitting tenant on the basis that she would declare a trust of it in favour of a specific creditor of the transferor; the trust so declared was set aside because his beneficial interest thereunder substantially exceeded the sum which he was owed by the transferor. An example of a transaction at an undervalue outside the trust context is *Barclays Bank v. Eustice*,[113] where a father granted an agricultural tenancy and sold agricultural assets to his sons on unusual terms as to payment[114]; however, in such circumstances whether a transaction is actually at an undervalue is sometimes not at all straightforward.[115] But when a transaction has been made for full value,[116] it cannot be impeached under this section even where there was a clear intention to prejudice creditors.[117]

Under section 424, an application to the court can be made by anyone prejudiced by a transaction; however, where the person entering into the transaction has become insolvent (bankrupt, in the case of a natural person, wound-up or the subject of an administration order[118] in the case of a body corporate), any such application requires the leave of the court—in such circumstances, it is the official receiver, the trustee in bankruptcy, or the

---

[110] [2002] W.T.L.R. 1027.

[111] [1995] 1 F.L.R. 696; see *ante*, para 3–129.

[112] [1992] B.C.C. 306.

[113] [1995] 1 W.L.R. 1238.

[114] The rent was payable substantially in arrears and the payment of the purchase price was deferred.

[115] In *Agricultural Mortgage Corporation v. Woodward* (1995) 70 P. & C.R. 53, a mortgagor who was a farmer granted an agricultural tenancy to his wife at the full market rent which, if binding on the mortgagee, would have more than halved the value of its security. The Court of Appeal held that the wife had acquired not just the tenancy but also a number of additional benefits, the safeguarding of the family home, the ability to acquire and carry on the family business and a substantial surrender value, all of which enabled her to hold the mortgagee to ransom and for none of which she had given any value at all. However, the courts' preparedness to look in this way at the practical rather than the legal effects of what has been done does have limits; in *Pinewood Joinery v. Starelm Properties* [1994] 2 B.C.L.C. 412 at 418–419, the court declined to engage in speculative assessments of how the value of the property in question might increase as a result of a possible grant of planning permission and held that the transaction had been at the full market value.

[116] This would have been the case in *Re M.C. Bacon* [1991] Ch. 127 (actually a decision on preferences; see *post*, para 7–060), where a company which created a floating charge over its assets in favour of a bank to secure its overdraft in consideration of the bank making further advances, continuing to honour cheques and, consequently, not calling in the overdraft was held not to have entered into a transaction at an undervalue. The assets of the company had not been reduced by the creation of the floating charge and so it had not provided any consideration in money or money's worth. Since no value in money or money's worth could be attributed to the consideration provided by the bank either, there was no imbalance between the consideration provided by the two parties. See also *Re Kumar (a Bankrupt)* [1993] 1 W.L.R. 224.

[117] This was not the case under Law of Property Act 1925, s.172; see *Lloyds Bank v. Marcan* [1973] 1 W.L.R. 1387.

[118] Under Pt II of the Insolvency Act 1986.

liquidator who has the primary right to apply. Where a voluntary arrangement has been approved,[119] the supervisor of the voluntary arrangement can also apply. Any application made by any of these persons is treated as having been made on behalf of everyone prejudiced by the transaction.

On application, the court can, under section 423(2), make such order as it thinks fit for restoring the position to what it would have been if the transaction had not been entered into and protecting the interests of the persons prejudiced by the transaction. More specifically, section 425(1) enables the court to require the vesting in whoever it may direct, for the benefit of everyone in respect of whom the application is treated to be made, of the following: any property transferred, any property representing the application of the proceeds of sale of the property transferred or of any money transferred, and any sum which the court decides should be payable in respect of any benefit received as a result of the transaction. However, in the case of trusts, it will normally be sufficient for the trust in question to be set aside. An order of any of these types is obviously capable of prejudicing third parties; however, section 425(2) provides that no such order shall prejudice any interest in property acquired from a person other than the original transferor in good faith for value without notice nor require any person who was not a party to the original transaction to pay any sum in respect of any benefit received in good faith for value without notice.

2. *Transactions Capable of being Impeached on Bankruptcy*

7–058   The Insolvency Act 1986 has replaced section 42 of the Bankruptcy Act 1914 with a series of provisions which enable transactions at an undervalue and by way of preference entered into by natural persons and by bodies corporate to be set aside in the event that those transactions occurred during stipulated periods of time prior to the bankruptcy.

(A) Transactions Entered into by Natural Persons

(1) Transactions at an undervalue
7–059   Section 339 enables the trustee in bankruptcy to apply to the court for an order where a natural person has entered into a transaction at an undervalue (which has the same meaning as in section 423)[120] within the periods of time set out in section 341. The court may make such order as it thinks fit to restore the position to what it would have been if the transaction had not been entered into. The available orders, set out in section 342, are similar to those which may be made under section 425[121]; no order may either prejudice any interest in property which was acquired from a person other than the bankrupt in good faith for value without notice of the relevant circumstances or require a person who was not a party to the transaction to make any payment in respect of any benefit which he received as a result of the

---

[119] Under Pt I of the Insolvency Act 1986 in the case of bodies corporate and under Pt VIII in the case of natural persons.
[120] See *ante*, para 7–057.
[121] See *ante*, para 7–057.

transaction in good faith for value without notice of the relevant circumstances.

A trustee in bankruptcy can, therefore, claim a spouse's share in the matrimonial home to the extent that the beneficial interest held exceeds the contributions made to its acquisition during the appropriate period. The fact that that beneficial interest has been acquired as the result of a property adjustment order on divorce makes no difference since the order can be set aside[122]; particular problems may arise where the matrimonial proceedings were compromised since, if the compromise reached cannot be assessed in terms of money or money's worth, the section will apply.[123]

Section 341 provides that the basic period is two years prior to the date of the presentation of the bankruptcy petition but this period is increased to five years if the person later to become bankrupt was insolvent at the time of the transaction or became insolvent as a result of carrying it out. A person is insolvent for this purpose if at the time of the transaction he was unable to pay his debts as they fell due or if the value of his assets was less than the value of his liabilities, taking into account both contingent and prospective liabilities. There is a rebuttable presumption that a person was insolvent in this sense in the event that the other party to the transaction was an associate of his, defined by section 435 as including relatives of the bankrupt or of his spouse, his partners, his employers, his employees and any companies with which he was at the time related.

The length of this period, the rebuttable presumption of insolvency in the case of transactions between associates, and the very wide definition of associate pose very considerable potential problems, not only because of the difficulty of rebutting the presumption of insolvency but also because of the difficulty of proving five years after the event that the transaction was not at an undervalue. Consequently, the only safe way to proceed when entering into a transaction between persons who fall within the definition of associates is to obtain affidavit evidence at the time from suitably qualified persons that the transaction was not at an undervalue and/or from the accountants of the parties that neither of them was insolvent at the time of or in consequence of the transaction. This will obviously involve a certain amount of expense but will avoid any possibility of future problems if any of the parties becomes bankrupt in the next five years.

At one time, even greater problems arose in the case of gifts of unregistered land. Since any subsequent purchaser would see the deed of gift in the course of his investigation of title, he would necessarily have notice of the relevant circumstance that the land was acquired at an undervalue. Thus, the enactment of section 339 had the effect of rendering the title of any donee of unregistered land bad for two years because of the possibility of the transferor becoming bankrupt during that period; the donee was thus effectively prevented from disposing of the land for value for that period. Matters were even worse in the highly likely event that the donor and donee fell within the definition of associates; in such circumstances, the period increased to five years unless the donee could affirmatively prove, presumably by affidavit evidence from the donor's accountants, that the donor

---

[122] Insolvency Act 1986, Sch.14.
[123] *Re Kumar (a Bankrupt)* [1993] 1 W.L.R. 224.

was not insolvent either at the time of or in consequence of the transaction. However, following the making of representations,[124] it was provided by the Insolvency (No.2) Act 1994 that a transaction can be set aside against a purchaser of unregistered land only if he has notice both of the surrounding circumstances and of relevant bankruptcy proceedings. Thus a purchaser who knows as he necessarily will of a transaction at an undervalue will be protected provided, first, that he makes the normal conveyancing searches and enquiries and, secondly, that these do not reveal any bankruptcy proceedings being brought against the donor.

(2) Transactions by way of preference

7–060   Section 340 enables the trustee in bankruptcy to apply to the court for an order where a natural person has given a preference to any person within the periods of time set out in section 341. The court may make such order as it thinks fit to restore the position to what it would have been if the preference had not been given—the available orders are set out in section 342.[125] Such a preference will have been given if the effect of the transaction is to improve the position of a creditor, surety or guarantor in the event of bankruptcy. An order can only be made if the transaction was influenced by a desire to bring about this result, although such a desire will be presumed where the other person is an associate. However, it has been held that, where the transaction has been entered into as a matter of commercial necessity, it was not influenced by any desire to give a preference.[126]

Section 341 provides that the basic period is six months prior to the date of presentation of the bankruptcy petition but this period is increased to two years if the person to whom the preference was given was an associate. However, if the transaction was not only by way of preference but also at an undervalue, the longer periods which apply to transactions at an undervalue will be applicable instead.

(B) Transactions Entered into by Bodies Corporate

7–061   The provisions of the Insolvency Act 1986 which govern transactions entered into by bodies corporate are broadly similar to those which apply to natural persons; only the differences will be mentioned here.

Section 238 deals with transactions at an undervalue (defined in the same way but without any reference to marriage consideration); no order will be made if the court is satisfied that the company entered into the transaction in good faith for the purpose of carrying on its business and there were at the time reasonable grounds for believing that the company would be benefited thereby. The period of time is two years prior to the onset of insolvency but a transaction will only be set aside if the company was unable to pay its debts at the time of the transaction or became unable to do so as a result of it.

Section 239 deals with transactions by way of preference. In *Re M.C. Bacon*,[127] a company which could not have continued trading without its

---

[124] See (1992) 89/5 L.S.Gaz., p.13.
[125] See *ante*, para 7–059.
[126] *Re M.C. Bacon* [1990] B.C.L.C. 324.
[127] [1990] B.C.L.C. 324.

bank's support created a floating charge over its assets in favour of the bank to secure its overdraft shortly before becoming insolvent; it was held that, since the granting of the floating charge had been made for reasons of commercial necessity and not with any desire to improve the position of the bank in the event of insolvency, no preference had been given. The basic period is this time six months prior to the onset of insolvency but this period is increased to two years if the transaction by way of preference is in favour of a person connected with the company or at an undervalue. Once again, a transaction will only be set aside if the company was unable to pay its debts at the time of the transaction or became unable to do so as a result of it.

IV. SAFEGUARDING PROPERTY FROM CLAIMS BY DEPENDANTS

The development of statutory obligations to maintain dependants has inevi- **7–062** tably led to attempts being made to avoid these obligations by the use of trusts and, equally inevitably, to the introduction of statutory restrictions on the use of trusts to defeat claims for maintenance and for financial provision out of estates.

1. Claims made in the Course of Matrimonial Proceedings

Section 37 of the Matrimonial Causes Act 1973 enables a spouse to apply to **7–063** the court for an order where the other spouse is about to make or has made some disposition of property with the intention of reducing the assets available for the provision of financial relief in matrimonial proceedings.[128] Such an intention is presumed if the disposition was made within the three-year period prior to the date of the application for financial relief; otherwise, intention must be proved affirmatively. If the disposition has not yet been made, the court may make such order as it thinks fit; if the disposition has already been made, it may be set aside.

2. Claims for Financial Provision out of Estates

English law does not contain any general restrictions on the ability of **7–064** testators freely to dispose of their assets.[129] However, under the Inheritance (Provision for Family and Dependants) Act 1975,[130] a surviving spouse, a

---

[128] Most of the recent reported cases have concerned surrenders by one spouse of jointly held tenancies which are prima facie effective to determine them; see *Newlon Housing Trust v. Alsulaimen* [1999] 1 A.C. 313 and *Bater v. Bater* [1999] 4 All E.R. 944.

[129] The civil law systems of continental Europe and the Muslim legal systems require testators to leave to their descendants a substantial percentage (generally about 75%) of their assets and sometimes, in default of descendants, a lower percentage to any ascendants. Settlors from these jurisdictions often create trusts in off-shore jurisdictions in order to vary or exclude the rights of these "forcible heirs"; this is generally effective provided that the settled assets are also outside the settlor's home jurisdiction or jurisdictions with similar rules. See Duckworth [1995] P.C.B. 270, 334, 408.

[130] As amended by Law Reform (Succession) Act 1995.

cohabitee,[131] children and other dependants are entitled to apply to the court for a share of the estate of any testator or intestate if reasonable financial provision for them has not been made. In order to prevent a testator from defeating such claims by disposing of all his property *inter vivos*, sections 10–13 of the Act provide that any person who, during the last six years of the deceased's life, has benefited from a disposition made other than for value "with the intention of defeating an application for financial provision under this Act" can be required to provide sums of money up to but not exceeding the value of the property received so that appropriate financial provision can be made. It should be noted that section 12 of the Act specifically provides that the necessary intention has to be determined on a balance of probabilities and does not have to constitute the only motive of the deceased for the making of the disposition.

---

[131] Cohabitees were added in respect of deaths on or after January 1, 1996.

CHAPTER 8

PROTECTIVE TRUSTS

It has already been seen that a trust which contravenes the policy of the   **8–001**
insolvency legislation can be set aside.[1] This chapter discusses some indirect
means by which this result can be avoided, having first emphasised two
overriding fundamental points.

(1) Any proviso or condition in a trust of property in favour of a third
party that that property is not to be subject to the claims of the
creditors of the settlor will be void.[2]

(2) A trust set up by a person in favour of himself until bankruptcy and,
subject to that, in favour of others will generally also be ineffective.
This is the well known Rule in *Re Burroughs-Fowler*[3] which, usually
but not always, prevents the type of trusts considered in this chapter
from being created by the potential bankrupt, as distinct from any
one else.[4] Where a trust is created in contravention of this rule and
the person in question does in the event become bankrupt, the
settled property will generally[5] vest in his trustee in bankruptcy as
if the settlement had never been created.

Nevertheless, a settlor who wishes protect the property which he is settling
on a spendthrift or reckless beneficiary from the risk of alienation or bankruptcy, will need to use more sophisticated machinery than that which has
already been described. Essentially he will instead have to create a determinable interest in favour of a third party coupled, if necessary, with protective and discretionary trusts.

---

[1] See *ante*, para 7–056.
[2] *Younghusband v. Gisborne* (1844) 1 Coll.C.C. 400, affirmed (1846) 15 L.J. Ch. 355; *Re Sanderson's Trust* (1857) 3 Kay & J. 497.
[3] [1916] 2 Ch. 251.
[4] The Rule in *Re Burroughs-Fowler* has been rejected by the legislature in certain off-shore
jurisdictions such as The Cook Islands, thereby enabling such trusts to be created there.
[5] However, this will not be the case if the interest which the potential bankrupt has conferred
upon himself in fact determines prior to his bankruptcy. In *Re Detmold* (1889) 40 Ch.D. 585, a
husband had settled his own property on trust for himself for life or until alienation, whether
voluntary or involuntary by operation of law in favour of a particular creditor, and subject to
that on trust for his wife and children. His interest was the subject of an involuntary alienation
as the result of a judicial charge created by a judgment. He subsequently became bankrupt and
his trustee in bankruptcy sought to set the settlement aside. North J. held that the gift over in
favour of the wife and children was in such circumstances valid and effective; consequently, his
trustee in bankruptcy could take nothing. This decision shows that a provision for determination will be effective if the determining event which first occurs is one other than the bankruptcy of the settlor. See also *Re Johnson* [1904] 1 K.B. 134.

I. DETERMINABLE INTERESTS

8–002 It has long been established that a settlor can validly grant an interest to any beneficiary (other, of course, than himself) which is determinable in the event of the beneficiary's bankruptcy.[6] At first sight, it appears somewhat surprising that such a grant is effective to whisk the property away from the beneficiary's creditors in the event of his bankruptcy when the same settlor cannot settle property on the same beneficiary subject to a condition or proviso that it will not be available to the latter's creditors in the event of his bankruptcy. The different result follows from the basic distinction between the nature of determinable interests and conditional interests, a distinction which, no matter how outmoded, is nevertheless fundamentally logical. A provision for a determining event does not deprive the beneficiary, or his creditors, of anything; it merely sets the limits of the interest which is being granted. On the other hand, a condition of this nature, like all other conditions, technically operates so as to cut down an interest which has already been granted. However, the existence of this admittedly fine distinction means that a draftsman must take special care not to create a conditional interest by accident and thereby defeat the intentions of the settlor.

II. PROTECTIVE TRUSTS[7]

8–003 Protective trusts provide a highly effective means of restraining spendthrift beneficiaries. They combine a determinable life interest with a series of discretionary trusts. The beneficiary's life interest is normally made determinable in the event of alienation or bankruptcy and, if either occurs, will be replaced by a discretionary trust in favour of the former life tenant and the members of his family.

1. Section 33 of the Trustee Act 1925

8–004 At one time the normal practice was to set out the provisions of trusts of this kind *in extenso*. However, with the objective of shortening the length of settlements, section 33 of the Trustee Act 1925 was enacted to provide that the mere reference in a settlement to the fact that property is held "on protective trusts" will be sufficient to bring into play the protective trusts specifically set out in that section.

8–005   Section 33[8] provides that, where income, including an annuity or other periodical payment, is directed to be held on protective trusts for the benefit of any person for his lifetime or for any less period[9] (such person being described in the section as "the principal beneficiary"), then during that period the income will be held on the following trusts (this is of course

---

[6] *Billson v. Crofts* (1873) L.R. 15 Eq. 314; *Re Aylwin's Trusts* (1873) L.R. 16 Eq. 585.

[7] See Sheridan (1957) 21 Conv. (N.S.) 110.

[8] The section applies only to trusts coming into operation on or after January 1, 1926.

[9] For an illustration of protective trusts designed to last until remarriage and the effect of a nullity decree on the second marriage, see *D'Altroy's Will Trusts* [1968] 1 W.L.R. 120. See also Matrimonial Causes Act 1973, ss.11, 12, 16.

necessarily without prejudice to any prior interests arising under the settlement in question):

(i) upon trust for the principal beneficiary during the trust period or until he does or attempts to do any act or thing, or any event happens (other than an advancement made under any statutory or express power) whereby, if the income were payable during the trust period to the principal beneficiary absolutely during that period, he would be deprived of the right to receive the same or any part thereof; and

(ii) in the event that the trust fails or determines during the trust period, then for the residue of that period the income is to be held upon trust to be applied as the trustees in their absolute discretion (without being liable to account for the exercise of such discretion) think fit for the maintenance or support or otherwise for the benefit of all or any of the following persons, either for the principal beneficiary and his or her wife or husband, if any, and his or her children or more remote issue[10] if any or, if there are no such persons other than the principal beneficiary, for him or her and the persons who would, if he or she were dead, be entitled to the trust property or to its income.[11]

Section 33 is subject to any variation of its provisions which may be made **8–006** in the trust instrument in question.[12] In respect of any such variations, a distinction has been drawn, for the purposes of inheritance tax, between "trusts to the like effect as those specified in" section 33 and other protective trusts.[13] The best examples of the latter are where the beneficiaries of the discretionary trusts are not as stated above because they include, for example, the brothers and sisters of the principal beneficiary[14] and where provision is made for the forfeited life interest to revive after the lapse of a period of time and/or in certain specified circumstances. Section 33 also provides that none of its contents operates to validate any trust which, if contained in the trust instrument, would be liable to be set aside.[15]

2. *"On Protective Trusts"*

The purpose of the section is merely to avoid any need for the trusts in **8–007** question to be set out expressly in the trust instrument. Quite apart from the provision just referred to whereby the statutory provisions can be modified to suit the circumstances of any individual settlement, protective trusts can

---

[10] Including children and more remote issue who are illegitimate: Family Law Reform Act 1969, s.15(3).
[11] s.33(1).
[12] s.33(2).
[13] Inheritance Tax Act 1984, s.88; see *post*, para 8–019.
[14] The Inland Revenue have stated that such a protective trust is not "to the like effect" as section 33 (S.P. E-9).
[15] s.33(3). Accordingly, a settlement made on the settlor himself until bankruptcy and then on discretionary trusts may be ineffective; *Re Burroughs-Fowler* [1916] 2 Ch. 251. See *ante*, para 8–001.

also be (and often still are) expressly created by being set out *in extenso*. Further, irrelevant of whether the statutory form is used or its essence is set out in terms, its effect is confined to engrafting the trusts in question on the life interest granted. For this reason, it was held by Vaisey J. in *Re Allsopp's Marriage Settlement*[16] that, if the life interest is ever totally extinguished, as it was in that case by an order made by the court in divorce proceedings, the engrafted protective trusts are also extinguished on the basis that they are incapable of any separate existence.

3. *Determining Events*

8–008   The question of what events will be sufficient to produce a forfeiture of a protected life interest (as the interest of the principal beneficiary is described) and bring the discretionary trusts into operation has been considered in a large number of cases. This point is of importance not only where the trusts contained in section 33 have been employed but also where there is an express protective trust. Indeed many of the cases which are about to be considered involved express protective trusts; however, the general view is that the principles laid down therein are equally applicable to the statutory trusts.

8–009   It is self-evident that the bankruptcy of or any alienation by the principal beneficiary will bring about the forfeiture of the protected life interest. But it is less obvious (although it was nevertheless held to be the case by Luxmoore L.J. in *Re Walker*[17]) that the protected life interest will also be forfeited if the principal beneficiary has already become bankrupt by the time the protective trust first comes into operation.

8–010   However, determining events have taken the most diverse forms. In *Re Balfour's Settlement*,[18] various sums had in breach of trust been advanced by the trustees to the principal beneficiary. The trustees then asserted their right to retain the income of the fund in order to make good their own breach of trust. The principal beneficiary subsequently went bankrupt. Farwell J. held that, since the trustees had asserted their right to the income before the date of bankruptcy, the life interest had determined and the discretionary trust in question had come into operation; nothing therefore passed to the trustee in bankruptcy. Similarly, in *Re Baring's Settlement Trusts*,[19] the principal beneficiary had failed to comply with a court order to bring her children within the jurisdiction and a writ of sequestration was therefore issued empowering the sequestrators to take possession of all her real and personal estate until she did so. The sequestrators gave the trustees notice not to pay any further money to the principal beneficiary and required that all future income should be paid to them. Morton J. held that, since the trusts were designed to confer continuous enjoyment of the income on the principal beneficiary, the sequestration was effective to determine her life interest and bring the discretionary trusts into operation; the payment of income was, therefore, at

---

[16] [1959] Ch. 81.
[17] [1939] Ch. 974.
[18] [1938] Ch. 928.
[19] [1940] Ch. 737.

the discretion of the trustees and could not be demanded by the sequestrators. Again, in *Re Dennis' Settlement Trusts*,[20] Farwell J. held that the
execution of a deed of variation of the protective trusts set out in the
principal deed of settlement, which had the effect of providing for the payment of part of the income to another person, equally brought the forfeiture
clause into operation.

On the other hand, a wide variety of other events have been held not to   **8–011**
have the effect of determining a protected life interest. In *Re Tancred's
Settlement*,[21] the principal beneficiary appointed the trustees of the settlement as his attorneys to receive the income of the settled funds; not surprisingly Buckley J. held that this did not cause his life interest to be forfeited.
The same conclusion was reached in *Re Oppenheim's Will Trusts*,[22] where a
receiver had been appointed to a principal beneficiary who had been certified as a person of unsound mind. Similarly, it was held by the Court of
Appeal in *Re Westby's Settlement*[23] that a statutory charge on the settled
property to secure the expenses incurred by a receiver appointed in such
circumstances was not the kind of charge at which forfeiture clauses were
intended to be directed. All these decisions show that, in the words of
Farwell J., "we must bear in mind that the courts do not construe gifts on
forfeitures so as to extend their limits beyond the fair meaning of the words
unless they are actually driven to it. Forfeitures are not regarded with
favour."[24]

Consideration has also had to be given as to the effect of a court order on   **8–012**
a forfeiture clause. In *Re Mair*[25] Farwell J. held that an order of the court
under section 57 of the Trustee Act 1925[26] giving the trustees power to raise
capital moneys for the benefit of life tenants would not cause a forfeiture of
the protected life interests of those tenants; he held that this was because
section 57 was an overriding provision which is deemed to be read into
every single settlement. This decision must, however, be contrasted with
that of Eve J. in *Re Salting*,[27] where the scheme sanctioned by the court under
section 57 involved an agreement by the life tenant to pay the premiums on
insurance policies on the basis of a promise that the trustees would pay
them out of income if he failed to do so; the conclusion reached was that any
failure by the life tenant to pay the premiums would produce a forfeiture. In
cases of this type it is clear that what has produced the forfeiture is an act or
omission of the life tenant, rather than the exercise by the court of its
overriding power. However, while the principles established by these two

---

[20] [1942] Ch. 283.
[21] [1903] 1 Ch. 715.
[22] [1950] Ch. 633.
[23] [1950] Ch. 296.
[24] *Re Greenwood* [1901] 1 Ch. 887, 891 (assignment of income accrued due in the hands of
trustees: no forfeiture). See also *Re Longman* [1955] 1 W.L.R. 197 (authority given by beneficiary
for payment of debts out of a future dividend where no dividend was ever declared: no
forfeiture). For other cases involving the application of the Trading with the Enemy Act 1939,
which may be relevant in the case of future wars, see *Re Gourju's Will Trusts* [1943] Ch. 24; *Re
Hall* [1944] Ch. 46; *Re Wittke* [1944] 1 All E.R. 383; *Re Furness* [1944] 1 All E.R. 575; *Re Harris*
[1945] Ch. 316; *Re Pozot's Settlement Trusts* [1952] Ch. 427.
[25] [1935] Ch. 562.
[26] See *post*, p.742.
[27] [1932] 2 Ch. 57.

decisions are perfectly clear, the position is otherwise by no means straightforward.

8–013   Particular difficulty arises from cases involving orders in matrimonial proceedings varying protective trusts. In *General Accident, Fire and Life Assurance Corporation v. I.R.C.*,[28] the Court of Appeal had no doubt that an order in matrimonial proceedings for the principal beneficiary to pay an annual sum of money to his wife during her lifetime had not brought about a forfeiture of the protected life interest which he had under section 33; accordingly, the discretionary trusts set out in that section did not come into operation. This conclusion was reached because the court order in question overrode the trusts of the settlement. Not only was this an event to which both the life tenant and the trustee had to bow; it was moreover not an event of the type contemplated by the section, whose provisions were instead intended to protect spendthrift, improvident or weak life tenants.[29]

8–014   However, if the principle thus enunciated by the Court of Appeal is of general application, it is by no means easy to reconcile their decision with the earlier decision of Danckwerts J. in *Re Richardson's Will Trusts*.[30] In that case, an order had been made in matrimonial proceedings for the payment of an annual sum to the wife of the protected life tenant to be charged on the principal beneficiary's life interest and it was also ordered that a deed be settled to give effect to the charge. Danckwerts J. held that, because the order for the execution of a deed had not been complied with, the effect of that order was to create an equitable charge over the interest of the principal beneficiary; this in turn involved the forfeiture of his protected life interest and so the discretionary trusts set out in section 33 came into operation. This was in some ways undoubtedly a highly convenient result; the life tenant had subsequently been adjudicated bankrupt and the decision that a prior forfeiture had occurred meant that the income of the settlement did not fall into the hands of his trustee in bankruptcy. However, it does seem rather strange that a failure by the principal beneficiary to comply with an order of the court to settle a deed of variation will result in a forfeiture of his protected life interest while compliance with such an order will not do so.

8–015   While the policy behind the decision of the Court of Appeal in *General Accident, Fire and Life Assurance Corporation v. I.R.C.*[31] is considered to have been desirable, it is somewhat doubtful whether the principle which the court applied was actually the correct one. The effect of an order of the Family Division—whether or not that order has to be implemented by a deed—is to deprive the life tenant of some or all of his income, an event which must surely constitute a forfeiture under section 33 and would probably also do so under the terms of most express protective trusts. On the other hand, quite different considerations may well be regarded as applying to an order of the court under section 57 of the Trustee Act 1925 simply because, as has already been seen, that provision is to be read into every settlement.

---

[28] [1963] 1 W.L.R. 1207.
[29] *ibid.*, per Donovan L.J. at 1218.
[30] [1958] Ch. 504.
[31] [1963] 1 W.L.R. 1207.

4. *Advances*

Section 33 expressly provides that advances under any express or statutory[32] **8–016**
power of advancement do not produce a forfeiture and bring the discretionary trusts set out in that section into play.[33] This leaves open the question
of whether the absence of a provision of this type in an express protective
trust will necessarily mean that the protected life interest granted thereby
will determine if any advancement is in fact made.

The relevant authorities are not unanimous; however, they are in only **8–017**
slight disarray and the general consensus of judicial opinion is that no
advancement made either under an express power or a statutory power will
bring about a forfeiture. In *Re Hodgson*[34] Neville J. specifically held that an
advancement made under an express power did not bring about a forfeiture.
His Lordship found to be attractive and decisive an argument that the
provision for forfeiture "should be read as though there had been inserted
at the end of the clause 'But this provision is not to affect any steps taken by
the husband to enable the advances by the trustees hereinafter provided for
to take effect'." In *Re Shaw's Settlement*[35] Harman J. came to exactly the same
conclusion on similar facts. Further, in *Re Rees*,[36] Upjohn J. held that this
conclusion also applied to the statutory power of advancement which is
contained in section 32 of the Trustee Act 1925. Only in *Re Stimpson's Trusts*,[37]
where once again there was no express advancement clause so that reliance
had to be put on the statutory power, has it been held that the principal
beneficiary had forfeited his interest by consenting to an advancement
under section 32.

However, the last two cases can be distinguished on their facts. In *Re* **8–018**
Stimpson's Trusts the will in question had actually been executed in 1906,
although it did not come into effect until 1929, and so its draftsman could
obviously not have had in mind a provision of the Trustee Act 1925 which
was not enacted until nearly 20 years later. In *Re Rees*, on the other hand, the
will in question had been made in 1935 and so its draftsman necessarily had
to be taken to have been aware of that provision. In the almost inconceivable
event that a case like *Re Stimpson's Trusts* came before the courts today, it is
therefore possible that the court would view in the same way a situation
where a will made before 1926 had contained no express advancement
clause but the life tenant had after 1925 consented to an advancement being
made under the statutory power. In any event, although the validity of the
decision in *Re Stimpson's Trusts* has been doubted,[38] it does appear to have
applied the correct principle. The statutory power of advancement can
undoubtedly be ousted by a contrary intention[39] and the fact that the will in
question had been made before 1926 might well be held to constitute a
sufficient contrary intention for this purpose.

---

[32] Under Trustee Act 1925, s.32; see *post*, para 18–006.
[33] s.33(1).
[34] [1913] 1 Ch. 34 at 40.
[35] [1951] Ch. 833.
[36] [1954] Ch. 202.
[37] [1931] 2 Ch. 77.
[38] See *Re Rees* [1954] Ch. 202, *per* Upjohn J. at 209.
[39] Trustee Act 1925, s.69.

5. *The Fiscal Consequences of Forfeiture*

8–019 The interest of the principal beneficiary of any protective trust created before March 22, 2007 was and, if it has not yet been forfeited, still is what is known as an interest in possession for the purposes of inheritance tax. The principal beneficiary of any protective trust created since that date only has such an interest where the protective trust was created by will[40] rather than *inter vivos*. Forfeiture obviously brings about the determination of the interest of the principal beneficiary and causes one of the two alternative discretionary trusts to take effect. The replacement of an interest in possession by a discretionary trust normally triggers an immediate charge to inheritance tax because the creation *inter vivos* of a discretionary trust is what is known as an initial chargeable transfer and gives rise to an immediate liability to pay inheritance tax on the value of the property subject to the protective trust at half the death rate[41]). However, the inheritance tax legislation contains specific provisions[42] dealing with protective trusts in this respect.

8–020 It is provided that the interest in possession held by the principal beneficiary prior to forfeiture continues for the purposes of inheritance tax despite forfeiture. This has the advantage that not only is there no initial chargeable transfer when the protected life interest is forfeited but capital can be advanced to the principal beneficiary once he has obtained his discharge without any inheritance tax consequences whatever[43] (any advance out of a discretionary trust would normally give rise to a potential liability to inheritance tax by way of exit charge[44]). However, this special regime does not also apply to income tax and capital gains tax and this has some potentially negative consequences. Following forfeiture, the trust constitutes a discretionary trust for the purposes of income tax and of capital gains tax while remaining in the interest in possession regime for the purposes of inheritance tax. Consequently, in the event that the principal beneficiary dies after forfeiture while the discretionary trust is still ongoing, the value of the trust property falls into his estate for inheritance tax purposes and inheritance tax may, therefore, be payable thereon; however, the trust does not obtain the usual capital gains tax uplift on his death because, for the purposes of capital gains tax, he does not have an interest in possession (this result is obviously quite contrary to normal principles but has arisen as the result of steps being taken to close an earlier loophole, which was abused).

---

[40] It will then be what is known as an immediate post-death interest. However, if it does not take effect immediately on death but only after the determination of a prior interest, it will not qualify as such an interest and the principal beneficiary will then not have an interest in possession for the purposes of inheritance tax; the position will then be as set out in para.8–22, *post*.

[41] See *post*, para 15–068. The rate of inheritance tax is half the death rate and therefore at present (2008–2009) 20% charged on the value of the subject matter of the trust after deduction of any available balance of the principal beneficiary's lifetime allowance of, in 2008–2009, £315,000.

[42] Inheritance Tax Act 1984, s.88.

[43] There will however be a potential liability to capital gains tax if the capital advanced is anything other than cash; see *post*, para 15–136.

[44] See *post*, para 15–097.

This special regime applies only to "trusts to the like effect as those **8–021** specified in" Section 33[45] and not to other protective trusts. The best examples of the latter are where the beneficiaries of the discretionary trusts are not as stated in section 33 because they include, for example, the brothers and sisters of the principal beneficiary[46] and where provision is made for the forfeited life interest to revive after the lapse of a period of time and/or in certain specified circumstances. Where the principal beneficiary has an interest in possession but the special regime does not apply, forfeiture will give rise to an initially chargeable transfer and to the consequential immediate liability to pay inheritance tax on the value of the property subject to the protective trust at half the death rate; however, the subject matter of the trust will not then fall into the estate of the principal beneficiary no matter when he dies unless, of course, that subject matter is appointed out to him once he has been discharged from bankruptcy.

The principal beneficiary of a protective trust created *inter vivos* on or after **8–022** March 22, 2007 does not have an interest in possession for the purposes of inheritance tax. This is because all trusts created *inter vivos* on or after that date other than trusts for disabled persons fall into the inheritance tax regime which was formerly applicable only to discretionary trusts (this regime is technically known as the relevant property regime).[47] Consequently, the creation *inter vivos* of the protective trust itself gives rise to an immediate liability to pay inheritance tax on the value of the property subject to the trust at half the death rate and to further liabilities to pay inheritance tax on each 10-year anniversary of the creation of the trust. Forfeiture and the consequential replacement of the protected life interest by a discretionary trust does not give rise to any liability to pay inheritance tax for the simple reason that the protective trust is already in the regime applicable to discretionary trusts. Nor does the subject matter of the protective trust fall into the estate of the principal beneficiary for the purpose of inheritance tax, no matter when he dies. However, in the event that any of the subject matter of the protective trust is appointed out to him, there will then be a charge to inheritance tax by way of exit charge.

---

[45] Inheritance Tax Act 1984, s.88.
[46] The Inland Revenue have stated that such a protective trust is not "to the like effect" as section 33 (S.P. E-9).
[47] See *post*, para.15–092.

CHAPTER 9

IMPLIED OR RESULTING TRUSTS

I. INTRODUCTION

9–001　The vast majority of commentators regard the terms "implied trust" and "resulting trust" as synonymous[1]; this is also the view adopted in this edition of this work.[2] Such trusts arise where a settlor or testator carries out some intentional act other than the creation of a relationship of trustee and beneficiary from which the court infers a relationship of trustee and beneficiary. They consequently arise from the unexpressed but presumed intention of the settlor or testator. The two alternative names appear to stem from the fact that such a trust is not only implied by the court but also often causes the beneficial interest arising thereunder to "result" to the settlor or his estate, or to the testator's residuary beneficiaries or intestate successors. Trusts of this type are described as resulting trusts in this work.

1. Recognised Categories of Resulting Trusts

9–002　There are two sets of circumstances in which resulting trusts are universally recognised as arising. The first is where one person either pays, wholly or in part, for the purchase of property which is vested in the name of another (or in the joint names of himself and another) or gratuitously transfers property into the name of another (or into the joint names of himself and another); there is then generally[3] a rebuttable[4] presumption that no gift was intended, in accordance with which the property in question is presumed to be held on

---

[1] Other views exist. Some commentators consider that there are distinct categories of implied trusts and resulting trusts (for example, this view was adopted in the first five editions of this work (see 5th edn, p.154) and the first seven editions of *Megarry's Manual of the Law of Real Property*, although not in the current (8th) edition at p.292). Such commentators generally classify the subject matter of this chapter as resulting trusts and classify as implied trusts some of the trusts which the majority of commentators classify as constructive trusts (for example, earlier editions of this work have suggested that the trust which arises under mutual wills (see *post*, para 10–313) should be classified as an "implied, though not a resulting" trust). Another variant is to use the term "implied trust" as a collective term for both resulting trusts and constructive trusts (see Lord Millett, 114 (1998) L.Q.R. 399, 406); this usage is more traditional than appropriate.

[2] As it has been in the three previous editions.

[3] It has now been established that this is not the case where land is the subject of such a transfer.

[4] The presumption can be rebutted in two ways: either by a counter-presumption known as the presumption of advancement when the parties are in one of a number of established relationships or by affirmative evidence that the payer or transferor intended to make an outright beneficial transfer.

trust for the payer or transferor (or, in the case of a joint purchase, on trust for the joint purchasers in proportion to their contributions). The second is where a settlor or testator who is creating an express trust fails to dispose of the whole of the beneficial interest in the property in question; the law then implies that so much of the beneficial interest as is undisposed of is held on trust for the settlor or his estate, or for the testator's residuary beneficiaries or intestate successors.[5]

It has been contended that these two recognised categories of resulting trusts should respectively be classified as "presumed" resulting trusts and "automatic" resulting trusts. According to this distinction, suggested by Megarry J. in *Re Vandervell's Trusts (No.2)*,[6] a presumed resulting trust arises when a purchase is made in or a transfer is made into the name of another person without any express trust being constituted; in these circumstances, there is a presumption that that other holds the property in question on resulting trust for the real purchaser or the transferor but this implied or presumed intention can be rebutted either by other legal presumptions or by evidence to the contrary.[7] An automatic resulting trust, on the other hand, arises where a transfer has been made on trusts which have left the whole or some part of the beneficial interest undisposed of (because, for example, those are in some way ineffective or incomplete); in this situation, the transferee of the property in question automatically holds it on resulting trust for the transferor to the extent that the beneficial interest has not been disposed of. In the latter case, according to Megarry J., the resulting trust "does not depend on any intentions or presumptions, but is the automatic consequence of [the transferor's] failure to dispose of what is vested in him".[8]

9–003

The distinction between "presumed" and "automatic" resulting trusts appears at first sight to accord with common sense; however, it is fair to say that, just as what Megarry J. described as a presumed resulting trust is said to be created by implication as the result of a purchase in or transfer into the name of another, so an intention can be said to be implied on the part of a settlor or testator that the settled property should result to him to the extent that he has failed to dispose of it. The implication of an intention in the second type of resulting trusts does not actually appear to be markedly more artificial than in the first type of resulting trusts. Precisely this argument was adopted in the House of Lords in *Westdeutsche Landesbank Girozentrale v. Islington L.B.C.*[9] by Lord Browne-Wilkinson. He reasserted the traditional view that both types of resulting trusts are examples of trusts giving effect to the common intention of the parties and said that he was not convinced that Megarry J. had been right to suggest that the second type of resulting trust does not depend on intention but operates automatically. He also pointed out that resulting trusts of the second type are not, as the formulation of Megarry J. would appear to suggest, necessarily irrebuttable; if the

9–004

---

[5] *Westdeustche Landesbank Girozentrale v. Islington L.B.C.* [1996] A.C. 669 at 708.

[6] [1974] Ch. 269 at 294, 295. The actual decision of Megarry J. was reversed by the Court of Appeal at [1974] Ch. 269 but the Court of Appeal made no comment on the judge's formulation.

[7] See *post*, para 9–020.

[8] [1974] Ch. 269 at 294.

[9] [1996] A.C. 669 at 708.

settlor or testator has, expressly or by necessary implication, abandoned any beneficial interest in the trust property, that property is held not on a resulting trust but for the Crown as *bona vacantia*. Lord Browne-Wilkinson's view is certainly preferable to the view of Megarry J.[10]

9–005   However, a further definition of resulting trusts has also been propounded,[11] namely that such trusts require nothing more and nothing less than a transfer of property in circumstances in which the provider of that property did not intend to benefit the recipient. This definition seems highly convincing,[12] at least so far as the two recognised categories of resulting trusts are concerned.[13] Its influence can be seen in the decision of the Privy Council in *Air Jamaica v. Charlton*,[14] where Lord Millett, while accepting that resulting trusts arise by operation of law and give effect to intention, emphasised that a resulting trust "arises whether or not the transferor intended to retain a beneficial interest—he almost always does not—since it responds to the absence of any intention on his part to pass a beneficial interest to the recipient". These observations seem successfully to blend the new definition into the view propounded by Lord Browne-Wilkinson, which of course unquestionably represents English law at present.

2. *Other Possible Categories of Resulting Trusts*

9–006   It has sometimes been contended[15] that resulting trusts can also arise as a result of a transfer of property which is either void *ab initio* or voidable. Such contentions have been made both in order to enhance the quantum of recovery[16] and in order to impose liabilities whose prerequisites include the existence of a trust.[17] While the House of Lords has now rejected the contention that a resulting trust can arise as a result of a transfer of property which is void *ab initio*,[18] Lord Millett has stated, both judicially[19] and extrajudicially,[20] that a resulting trust will arise when property is transferred pursuant to a transaction which is voidable if and when that transaction is effectively avoided. However, when this issue arose in the Commercial

---

[10] Birks [1996] R.L.R. 3 at 11 regards Lord Browne-Wilkinson's view as "correct", despite the fact that it led to the rejection of his own argument that a resulting trust should arise whenever money is paid under a mistake or under a condition which is not subsequently satisfied.

[11] By Chambers, *Resulting Trusts* (1997).

[12] His extrapolation of that definition dealing with the nature of *Quistclose* trusts was, however, reviewed and rejected by Lord Millett in *Twinsectra v. Yardley* [2002] UKHL 12, [2002] 2 A.C. 164; see *post*, para 9–071.

[13] Chambers, *op.cit.*, also classifies as resulting trusts a large number of other situations which most commentators regard as having nothing whatever to do with resulting trusts.

[14] [1999] 1 W.L.R. 1399 at 1412.

[15] See Chambers, *Resulting Trusts* (1997) *passim*.

[16] As a result of being able to obtain either priority over the general creditors of the transferee or an increase in the value of the property transferred or compound rather than simple interest.

[17] Such as liability for knowing receipt of property transferred as the result of a breach of trust or liability for dishonest assistance in a breach of trust; see *post*, para 10–153 *et seq*.

[18] *Westdeutsche Landesbank Girozentrale v. Islington L.B.C.* [1996] A.C. 669 at 715.

[19] In *El Ajou v. Dollar Land Holdings* [1993] 3 All E.R. 717 [1993] 3 All E.R. 717 at 734 (as Millett J.).

[20] 114 L.Q.R. (1998) 399.

Court in *Papamichael v. National Westminster Bank*,[21] the judge[22] held that the trusts which had arisen as a result of a transfer of property which was both mistaken and procured by fraud were constructive trusts rather than resulting trusts, relying on what Lord Browne-Wilkinson had held in the House of Lords in *Westdeutsche Landesbank Girozentale v. Islington L.B.C.*[23] rather than what Lord Millett had said in the Chancery Division in *El Ajou v. Dollar Land Holdings*[24] (all these authorities are considered at the end of this chapter[25]). While it is highly unlikely that the last has yet been heard of the views expressed by Lord Millett, it therefore seems, at least for the moment, more appropriate to regard any trusts which arise as a result of a voidable transfer of property as constructive trusts rather than as resulting trusts.

II. PURCHASE IN THE NAME OF ANOTHER

One of the most important and the most common situations in which the presumption of resulting trust arises is where real[26] or personal[27] property is purchased in the name of another or in the name of the purchaser and another. In such circumstances, a resulting trust will be presumed to arise in favour of the person who is proved to have paid the purchase money; in other words, the beneficial interest in the property "results" to the true purchaser. This general principle was established as long ago as 1788 by Eyre C.B. in *Dyer v. Dyer*.[28] Such a presumption was recently held to arise in *Abrahams v. The Trustee of the Property of Abrahams*[29] in favour of a wife who had purchased in the name of her estranged husband a 15th share of a winning national lottery ticket bought by a syndicate of which they were both[30] members[31]; she was therefore held to be entitled to that proportion of the winnings as against his trustee in bankruptcy. **9–007**

Until 1973 this principle was particularly significant in establishing the ownership of matrimonial property, particularly the matrimonial home, on the breakdown of marriage; however, since then the courts have had an unfettered discretion to reallocate property interests on divorce and so this is no longer the case. However, the principle remains relevant in establishing the ownership of matrimonial property during marriage and is particularly important in relation to joint enterprises by members of a family unit, **9–008**

---

[21] [2003] EWHC 164 (Comm), [2003] 1 Lloyd's Rep. 341.
[22] Judge Chambers Q.C., sitting as a Judge of the Commercial Court.
[23] [1996] A.C. 669 at 715.
[24] [1993] 3 All E.R. 717, affirmed by the Court of Appeal without discussion of this particular point at [1994] 2 All E.R. 685.
[25] *post*, para 9–097.
[26] *Dyer v. Dyer* (1788) 2 Cox Eq. 92.
[27] *Re Scottish Equitable Life Assurance Society* [1902] Ch. 282, in respect of personal property.
[28] (1788) 2 Cox Eq. 92 at 93.
[29] [2000] W.T.L.R. 593.
[30] She had also paid for her own 15th share of the ticket and had duly received that proportion of the winnings.
[31] The presumption of resulting trust was not rebutted by the presumption of advancement (see *post*, para 9–022) and there was clear evidence that she did not intend to benefit him by herself paying the share of the price basically payable by him.

especially residential property occupied by partners who are neither married nor members of a civil partnership. In this respect, the division between resulting and constructive trusts is somewhat blurred,[32] basically because in the leading judgment, the speech of Lord Bridge in *Lloyds Bank v. Rosset*,[33] trusts of two different types which most commentators would classify respectively as resulting and constructive trusts were both described as constructive trusts. In any event, since what Lord Bridge described as "the first and fundamental question which must always be resolved" in such cases is whether the prerequisites of the imposition of what is on any view a constructive trust have been satisfied, it seems more appropriate to deal with this specific area in the chapter on constructive trusts.[34]

9–009   That remains the area which has been most often before the courts in recent decades. But both in that area and in joint purchases of any other type, everyone who has contributed directly to the purchase price is presumed to have a beneficial interest in the property in question; in this respect the identity of the person in whose favour that property is actually vested is irrelevant. In such circumstances, a question which always arises is the nature of the beneficial ownership, in other words whether the contributors are beneficial joint tenants, in which case, in the absence of any subsequent severance, their survivor will take the property absolutely, or beneficial tenants in common, in which case the share of each will devolve in accordance with his will or intestacy; in the latter case, the size of their respective shares will also have to be established.

9–010   Where the purchase money has been contributed in unequal shares, the position is straightforward. Irrelevant of the identity of the person in whom the property is vested, the beneficial interests will be held in common and will devolve in accordance with the will or intestacy of each beneficial owner in accordance with his respective contributions.[35] This is simply because, in many cases, equity leans against a joint tenancy because of the potential unfairness of its attendant consequence that the survivor is entitled to the whole of the property. Inequality in contributions to the purchase price is the clearest possible example of a situation which equity considers to be incompatible with the right of survivorship; consequently, even if the person in whom the legal title is vested happens to be the survivor, he will continue to hold the property on trust for himself and for those entitled to the estate of his co-proprietor in the same proportions as before.

9–011   Where, on the other hand, the purchase money has been contributed equally, the prima facie position is that the purchasers will be deemed to have purchased with a view to taking as joint tenants with the consequential applicability of the principle of survivorship.[36] However, equity regards the existence of a business relationship between the contributors as inconsistent with the existence of a right of survivorship, even if the contributions have

---

[32] See *Drake v. Whipp* [1996] 1 F.L.R. 826; *Collings v. Lee* [2001] 2 All E.R. 332.

[33] [1991] A.C. 107 at 132–133; the relevant passage is set out *post*, para 10–296.

[34] See *post*, para 10–291.

[35] *Wray v. Steele* (1814) 2 V. & B. 388.

[36] *Lake v. Gibson* (1732) 1 Eq.Cas.Abr. 290; *Lake v. Craddock* (1732) 3 P.Wms. 158 (seemingly reports of the same case under different names).

been equal.[37] It is not enough that both parties happen to be in business with one another; the property must be acquired in the course of that business.[38] However, the matter is treated broadly. In *Malayan Credit v. Jack-Chia MPH*,[39] the parties had separate businesses and were not in any sense partners; they leased business premises as joint tenants on the basis that each would occupy a particular part of the premises and contribute towards the rent and outgoings in proportion to the area each occupied. The Privy Council held that the equitable presumptions should not be treated rigidly as closed categories; holding premises for separate business purposes was sufficient to give rise to a tenancy in common in equity.

The position with joint mortgages is, however, much more straightfor-   **9–012** ward. If two persons advance money on the security of a mortgage, then, quite irrelevant of the identity of the person in whom the mortgage is vested and of the proportions in which the money was advanced, there is no right of survivorship and the interest of each mortgagee will devolve according to his will or intestacy. This is because a mortgage advance cannot possibly be regarded as anything other than a commercial undertaking; there therefore cannot conceivably have been any intention that an interest in a mortgage should be subject to any right of survivorship.[40] This is the case even if the mortgage in question incorporates, as it will in the absence of contrary intention, a statutory term[41] that the money is lent on a joint account[42]; the courts take the view that the purpose of this clause is to permit repayment to a surviving mortgagee rather than to affect the rights of the mortgagees *inter se*.

However, it must be emphasised that the general principle laid down in   **9–013** *Dyer v. Dyer* will not be applied arbitrarily. It is essential that a purchase is actually made. So, if a payment is made at the request of and by way of loan to the person in whose name the property is vested, there will be no resulting trust simply because in such circumstances the lender will not have advanced the purchase money as purchaser but merely as lender.[43] Further, there will be never be a resulting trust if it would be contrary to the law or to public policy to allow the presumption to arise. So, in an early case, it was decided that, if a person purchased an estate in the name of another so as to give the latter a vote at a parliamentary election, the latter will take beneficially even if there was no intention whatever to give the estate to him.[44]

---

[37] *Lake v. Gibson* (1729) 1 Eq.Cas.Abr.290; *Lake v. Craddock* (1732) 3 P.Wms. 158; *Malayan Credit v. Jack Chia-MPH* [1986] A.C. 549.

[38] *Tan Chew Hoe Noe v. Chee Swee Cheng* (1928) L.R. 56 Ind.App. 112.

[39] [1986] A.C. 549.

[40] *Morley v. Bird* (1798) 3 Ves. 628.

[41] Implied by Law of Property Act 1925, s.111.

[42] (1887) 34 Ch.D. 732.

[43] *Aveling v. Knipe* (1815) 19 Ves. 441. The opinion of Phillimore L.J. in *Hussey v. Palmer* [1972] 1 W.L.R. 1286 at 1291, which appears to be to the opposite effect, appears erroneous. Of course, completely different considerations apply where money is lent for a particular purpose which fails; in such circumstances, the borrower holds the money on trust for the lender: see *Barclays Bank v. Quistclose Investments* [1970] A.C. 567; *post*, para 9–057.

[44] *Groves v. Groves* (1829) 3 Y. & J. 163 at 175; see also *Gascoigne v. Gascoigne* [1918] 1 K.B. 223; *Re Emery's Investment Trusts* [1959] Ch. 410; *Chettiar v. Chettiar (No.2)* [1962] A.C. 294.

9–014   Further, given that on any view this kind of resulting trust is based upon some form of presumed intention, no trust will arise where no such intention can be implied. Thus in *Savage v. Dunningham*[45] it was held that, where there had been an informal flat-sharing arrangement under which the occupiers made contributions to the rent, the purchase of the flat by one of the flat-sharers did not give rise to a resulting trust in favour of the others. Plowman J. held that an income payment such as rent did not indicate any intention whatever in respect of the subsequent acquisition of the capital asset. However, the opposite result was reached in *Dewar v. Dewar*,[46] where the facts were admittedly very different. The plaintiff and the defendant, who were brothers, bought a house with their mother. The plaintiff and the mother each provided £500 and the defendant raised the remaining £3,250 on mortgage. The house was conveyed into the name of the defendant, as it presumably had to be in order to secure the mortgage advance. Goff J. held that the plaintiff's £500 had not been a loan; the presumption of a resulting trust applied and he was therefore entitled to a proportional share in the house. However, the mother's £500 was held on the facts to have been a gift and so there was no resulting trust in her favour.

III. Voluntary Conveyance or Transfer

9–015   When there has been a gratuitous transfer of property into the name of another or into the joint names of the transferor and another, the question of whether there is a presumption of a resulting trust depends on the effect of section 60(3) of the Law of Property Act 1925. This subsection deals with transfers of this type taking effect after 1925 by providing that: "In a voluntary conveyance a resulting trust for the grantor shall not be implied merely by reason that the property is not expressed to be conveyed for the use or benefit of the grantee".

9–016   The first question which has to be considered is the scope of this provision. The definitions section of the Law of Property Act 1925, section 205, provides that, unless the context otherwise requires, "property" means "any interest in real or personal property". Is section 60(3) therefore applicable both to land and to pure personalty? The unanimous view of the commentators is that the context (and in particular the references to "conveyance" and "conveyed") does otherwise require and that, consequently, the effect of the subsection is confined to land. This appears to be confirmed by the fact that the subsection has never been referred to in any reported case concerning pure personalty.

9–017   Consequently, it appears that a gratuitous transfer of pure personalty is presumed to give rise to a resulting trust in favour of the transferor. This was certainly the case before 1926[47] and, if section 60(3) of the Law of Property Act 1925 does not apply to pure personalty, that must still be the position

---

[45] [1974] Ch. 181.
[46] [1975] 1 W.L.R. 1532.
[47] See also *Fowkes v. Pascoe* (1875) 10 Ch.App. 343 at 345–348.

today. In any event, in *Re Vinogradoff*,[48] where war loan stock was transferred into the joint names of the transferor and her granddaughter, who was then four years of age but to whom she was not *in loco parentis*, Farwell J. held that a resulting trust had arisen; no reference was made to section 60(3).

However, section 60(3) undoubtedly applies to gratuitous transfers of   **9–018** land. Its effect has long been controversial.[49] The majority view has always been that, "in the absence of evidence to the contrary, there will be no resulting trust on a voluntary conveyance to another, unless it has been expressly conveyed upon trusts which fail to dispose of the entire equitable interest".[50] It has to be said that, on the face of things, this view goes much farther than the subsection, which restricts itself to stating that no resulting trust will arise merely because of the absence of the words in question; it is also far from clear what words in the provision justify the existence of a resulting trust where there is evidence to the contrary and nowhere else.[51] But the majority view has now been accepted by the Court of Appeal. In *Khan v. Ali*,[52] Morritt V.-C. held that the earlier decision at first instance in *Lohia v. Lohia*[53] "establishes that the presumption of a resulting trust on a voluntary conveyance of land has been abolished by s.60(3) of the Law of Property Act 1925". The law therefore no longer presumes that a resulting trust arises as the result of a gratuitous transfer of land; consequently, in *Lohia v. Lohia* it was held that no such trust arose as a result of a voluntary conveyance by a son of his tenancy in common to the other joint tenant, his father. However, a resulting trust may nevertheless be inferred if the transferor is able to adduce evidence that he did not intend the transferee to take beneficially. The Court of Appeal upheld the existence of such a resulting trust in *Khan v. Ali* on the basis that the only purpose of the transfer on sale of a property worth £75,000 for £25,000 had been to enable the transferees to raise a mortgage advance of £25,000 on the strength of their incomes so that

---

[48] [1935] W.N. 68.

[49] This was largely because of uncertainty as to what the position was before 1926, when the effect of transfers was governed by the Statute of Uses 1536. Where a transfer of property was intended to be voluntary and pass both legal and beneficial title to the transferee, the transfer would usually be expressed to be made "to the use of" or "for the benefit of" the grantee. The presence of these words undoubtedly passed legal title to the transferee in just the same way as a transfer "unto and to the use of" an intended trustee vested legal title in him (see *ante*, para 1–006, n.29). Their presence was clearly also intended to pass the equitable title to him as well but, despite dicta that this was indeed their effect (in *Young v. Peachey* (1742) 2 Atk. 254 at 257; *Lloyd & Johnson v. Spillet* (1741) 2 Atk. 148 at 150; *Fowkes v. Pascoe* (1875) 10 Ch.App. 343, 348), some commentators thought that, as a matter of principle, the absence of any further express beneficial gift meant that the transferee held the property on resulting trust for the transferor (see Maitland, *Equity* (2nd edn), p.77; White and Tudor, *Leading Cases in Equity* (9th edn), Vol. II, p.762).

[50] Pettit, *Equity and the Law of Trusts* (8th edn, 1997), p.161, citing *Snell's Principles of Equity* (29th edn), p.183. See also Underhill & Hayton, *Law of Trusts and Trustees* (17th edn, 2007), p.455.

[51] Previous editions of this work have therefore consistently adopted the contrary view that there appears to be nothing in section 60(3) which prevents a resulting trust from being implied for reasons other than the absence of the words in question and, in particular, as a result of the operation of general equitable principles.

[52] (2002) 5 I.T.E.L.R. 232.

[53] [2001] W.T.L.R. 101 at 113.

this sum could be utilised by the transferor, their father, who had no other means of raising the money.[54]

9–019   In effect, therefore, section 60(3) of the Law of Property Act 1925 affects the burden of proof. In the case of gratuitous transfers of land, where the subsection applies, there is no presumption of resulting trust and it is for the transferor to prove that he did not intend the transferee to take beneficially. In the case of gratuitous transfers of pure personalty, where the subsection does not apply, there is a presumption of resulting trust and it is for the transferee to establish that he has taken beneficially.[55]

IV. The Rebuttable Nature of the Presumptions

9–020   The presumptions which arise on a purchase in or a transfer into the name of another are rebuttable by parol or, for that matter, any other evidence that the purchaser or transferor intended to confer a benefit on that other. Further, in certain circumstances, the presumption is actually reversed and it is instead presumed that there is no resulting trust. This is the case where the person in whom the property is vested is the lawful wife or child of the purchaser or transferor or is a person to whom the purchaser or transferor stood *in loco parentis* at the time of the purchase or transfer. In these cases, the donor is presumed to have intended to make an "advancement" to the person in whom the property is vested and the presumption of resulting trusts is therefore said to have been rebutted by the presumption of advancement. It should also be remembered in this connection that section 53(1)(b) of the Law of Property Act 1925 (which provides that a declaration of trust as to land must be manifested and proved by writing) does not apply to implied, resulting or constructive trusts; consequently, oral evidence is admissible to show what the true nature of the transaction actually was.[56]

(A) Intention to Confer a Benefit
9–021   Whether the purchaser or transferor intended to confer a benefit on the person in whom the property is vested is entirely a matter of evidence. If it can be shown that there was such an intention, no resulting trust can arise. In *Standing v. Bowring*[57] the plaintiff transferred £6,000 Consols into the joint names of herself and her godson. She did this with the express intention that the godson, in the event that he survived her, should take the Consols but also intended that she should retain the right to the dividends during her lifetime; she had been told that her act was irrevocable. The Court of Appeal held that the presumption of a resulting trust had been rebutted; there was ample evidence that, at the time of the transfer and for some time previously,

---

[54] The presumption of advancement between father and child which would normally have rebutted the presumption of resulting trust in favour of the father was held to have been rebutted by these facts.

[55] Either by virtue of the counter-presumption known as the presumption of advancement when the parties are in one of a number of established relationships or by affirmative evidence that the transferor intended to make an outright beneficial transfer.

[56] Law of Property Act 1925, s.53(2).

[57] (1885) 31 Ch.D. 282.

the plaintiff had intended to confer a benefit on her godson by making the transfer. Similarly, in *Dewar v. Dewar*[58] the presumption of a resulting trust in favour of a mother who had made a contribution to the purchase of property in the name of her son was rebutted by evidence that she had intended to make a gift. Further, while the contention that there is a resulting trust cannot be barred by the passage of time for so long as the subject matter of the trust remains in the hands of the alleged trustee,[59] the amount of time that has elapsed by the time that such a contention is raised is capable of helping to rebut the presumption.[60]

(B) The Presumption of Advancement

The second situation where the presumption of a resulting trust does not operate is where its effect is reversed by a counter-presumption, the presumption of advancement. This is, however, only the case where the purchaser or transferor is the husband or father of or a person standing *in loco parentis* to the person into whose name the property is put. In these cases the presumption is that the purchaser or transferor intended to advance the property to the person into whose name it is put, in other words to give it to him; consequently, there is no resulting trust. Once the presumption has arisen (it is of course capable of being rebutted by contrary evidence), it cannot be upset by any subsequent event unless evidence of that event is admissible under the rules which will be discussed in the next section. This can be illustrated by the old case of *Crabb v. Crabb*,[61] where a father transferred stock from his own name into the name of his son and a broker. He also told the broker to carry the dividends to the son's account. Later, by a subsequent codicil to his will, the father bequeathed the stock to another person. It was held that the son had taken an absolute beneficial interest in the stock at the time of the transfer and so the father had nothing left to bequeath.

9–022

(1) Husband and wife

The presumption of advancement by a husband in favour of his wife now has an extremely limited application, particularly when the marriage has broken down. This is a result of the following restatement of the law elaborated by Lord Diplock in *Pettitt v. Pettitt*.[62]

9–023

"The consensus of judicial opinion which gave rise to the presumptions of 'advancement' and 'resulting trust' in transactions between husband and wife is to be found in cases relating to the propertied classes of the nineteenth century and the first quarter of the twentieth century among whom marriage settlements were common, and it was unusual for the wife to contribute her earnings to the family income. It was not until after World

---

[58] [1975] 1 W.L.R. 1532.

[59] There is no limitation period in such circumstances because Limitation Act 1980, s.21(1) will necessarily apply; see *post*, [para.22–047]. Where a resulting trustee has parted with the subject matter of the trust, the six-year limitation period under *ibid.*, s.21(3) will be applicable.

[60] *Vajpeyi v. Yusaf* [2003] EWHC 2339 (Ch), [2004] W.T.L.R. 989.

[61] (1834) 1 Myl. & K. 511.

[62] [1970] A.C. 777 at 783.

War II that the courts were required to consider the proprietary rights in family assets of a different social class. The advent of legal aid, the wider employment of married women in industry, commerce and the professions, and the emergence of a property-owning, particularly a real-property-mortgaged-to-a-building-society-owning democracy has compelled the courts to direct their attention to this during the last 20 years. It would, in my view, be an abuse of the legal technique for ascertaining or imputing intention to apply to transactions between the post-war generations of married couples 'presumptions' which are based on inferences of fact which an earlier generation of judges drew as to the most likely intentions of earlier generations of spouses belonging to the propertied classes of a different social era."

Notwithstanding these remarks of Lord Diplock, the doctrine of advancement between husband and wife can still have some application where for some reason, such as death, the evidence of one or both of the parties is unavailable. Where, on the other hand, both parties are available to give evidence, the court much prefers to hear them and to form its own view of their intention. Where this is done, it is highly unlikely that the presumption of advancement will ever have any effect as between husband and wife.

9–024   In so far, if at all, as the presumption may still be operative, it is immaterial that the marriage is later dissolved or is the subject matter of a decree of nullity on the grounds that the marriage was voidable.[63] However, if a marriage is held to have been void *ab initio*, the presumption of advancement does not appear to apply—this is simply because the marriage is treated as never having existed at all.[64] The essential requirement of the presumption is for the property to be purchased in the name of the lawful wife of the purchaser. For this reason the presumption does not apply in favour of a purchaser's de facto wife or his mistress.[65]

9–025   Nor has the presumption of advancement ever applied where a wife purchases property in the name of her husband; in such circumstances, what is presumed to arise is a resulting trust in favour of the wife.[66] Thus, the presumption of advancement did not apply in *Abrahams v. The Trustee of the Property of Abrahams*[67] to rebut the presumption of resulting trust in favour of a wife who had purchased in the name of her estranged husband a one-fifteenth share of a winning national lottery ticket. At one time a resulting trust in favour of a wife only arose where the property in question had been purchased with her capital, not where it had been purchased with her income. However, in *Mercier v. Mercier*[68] the Court of Appeal held that there was no fundamental distinction between capital and income except in

---

[63] *Dunbar v. Dunbar* [1909] 2 Ch. 639. A nullity decree in respect of a voidable marriage now has a prospective, not a retrospective effect. Accordingly the marriage is to be treated as if it had existed until the decree; Matrimonial Causes Act 1973, s.16. For the grounds on which a marriage is regarded as void or voidable, see *ibid.*, ss.11, 12.

[64] See *Re Ames' Settlement* [1946] Ch. 217. See also *Re D'Altroy's Will Trusts* [1968] 1 W.L.R. 120.

[65] *Soar v. Foster* (1858) 4 K. & J. 152.

[66] Although if the property is part of the matrimonial assets the court may apply the maxim that equality is equity: see, for example, *Jones v. Maynard* [1951] Ch. 572; *Rimmer v. Rimmer* [1953] 1 Q.B. 63 and *post*, paras 9–031, 10–291.

[67] [2000] W.T.L.R. 593.

[68] [1903] 2 Ch. 98.

degree, although Romer L.J. made it clear that the fact could still nevertheless be of importance when he said[69]: "No doubt in certain cases, in considering whether a gift was intended, the fact of the money having been income received by him with her consent may be material in respect of the weight of evidence but there is no other distinction, so far as I am aware, between capital and income". This decision certainly changed the pre-existing law; consequently, the fact that the wife used her income rather than her capital will now only be relevant as a matter of evidence as to whether or not any intention which she may have had to benefit the husband is sufficient to rebut the presumption of resulting trust in her favour.

(2) Parent and child

"Child" here means "legitimate child". It is absolutely clear that the presumption of advancement will apply if a father purchases property in or transfers property into the name of his legitimate child.[70] 9–026

The traditional view is that if a mother does the same thing the presumption will not apply.[71] However, the authorities are not unanimous. In *Sayre v. Hughes*,[72] Stuart V.-C. appears to have held that what was most material was whether the mother's motivation was to confer a benefit on her child—a view which, if accepted, could clearly lead to the opposite conclusion and work an advancement in favour of the child, although Stuart V.-C. was specifically considering only the case of a widowed mother. Nor do the authorities in support of the traditional view agree as to the justification for it. In *Re De Visme*[73] it was held that the presumption of advancement would not arise as between mother and child because a married woman was under no obligation to maintain her children. On the other hand, in *Bennet v. Bennet*[74] Jessel M.R. held that the presumption of advancement essentially applied only to the father not because the mother was under no liability to maintain her children but because the father alone was under a moral obligation to make provision for his child, no such obligation being imposed on the mother. A quite different reason for rejecting *Re De Visme* in modern conditions is the fact that, since the enactment of the National Assistance Act 1948,[75] mothers have been under a statutory duty to care for their children. However, in *Sekhon v. Alissa*,[76] the most recent case in which the traditional view was adopted, Hoffmann J. chose simply to apply the older authorities without distinguishing between the different views expressed in them and therefore held that the presumption of resulting trust, and not the presumption of advancement, applied where a mother provided the majority of the price of a property purchased in the name of her daughter. 9–027

---

[69] *ibid.*, at 101.

[70] *Dyer v. Dyer* (1788) 2 Cox Eq. 92.

[71] *Re De Visme* (1863) 2 De G.J. & S. 17; *Bennet v. Bennet* (1879) 10 Ch.D. 474. The same view was adopted much more recently in *Sekhon v. Alissa* [1989] 2 F.L.R. 94.

[72] (1868) L.R. 5 Eq. 376. See also *Garrett v. Wilkinson* (1848) 2 De G. & Sm. 244 at 246. The High Court of Australia upheld the existence of a presumption of advancement between mother and child in *Nelson v. Nelson* (1995) 132 A.L.R. 133.

[73] (1863) 2 De G.J. & S. 17.

[74] (1879) 10 Ch.D. 474.

[75] Ss.42(1), 64(1).

[76] [1989] 2 F.L.R. 94.

9–028   The traditional position is, frankly, unsatisfactory. It is particularly difficult to see why a mother, especially if she has money, is not under the same
moral obligation to maintain her children as their father is said to be. Having
said that, however, it may not matter all that much in practice. If there is
indeed no presumption of advancement between mother and child, the
presumption of resulting trust in favour of the mother which consequently
arises can be rebutted by any evidence of an intention on her part to benefit
the child[77] and it is improbable that children will find this particularly
difficult to achieve. The failure of the daughter to do so in *Sekhon v. Alissa*[78]
admittedly shows that this cannot be assumed; however, that decision is
perhaps best explained on the grounds that the mother was anyway able to
rely on evidence in support of the presumption of resulting trust and in
rebuttal of any presumption of advancement; although the transaction
between the mother and the daughter had been entered into for an illegal
purpose, with a view to evading capital gains tax, this evidence was nevertheless admissible.[79]

(3) Person *in loco parentis* and child

9–029   A person *in loco parentis* is a person standing in the position of a parent, that
is to say in the situation of the lawful father of the child. According to Jessel
M.R. in *Bennet v. Bennet*,[80] such a person is one who takes upon himself the
duty of the father of a child to make provision for that child. For example,
an uncle or grandfather may, in the particular circumstances of the case, put
himself *in loco parentis* to a child after, for example, the death of the child's
father.[81] Again, a father of an illegitimate child may, in the circumstances, be
in loco parentis to that child.[82] However, in order for a person to be held to be
in loco parentis, he must actually place himself in the situation of the father;
simply to pay an illegitimate child's school fees would not of itself be
enough in itself to raise the presumption.[83]

(4) The rebuttable nature of the presumption

9–030   When a presumption of advancement does arise, it is just as capable of being
rebutted by evidence of actual intention as is a presumption of resulting
trust. Only "comparatively slight evidence" is necessary to rebut the presumption.[84] Thus in *McGrath v. Wallis*,[85] a father contributed about four-
fifths of the purchase price of a house which was acquired for the occupation
of father, mother, son and daughter but the property was put in the name of
the son so that the balance of price could be raised by way of mortgage (the
father was unemployed). A declaration of trust was indeed drawn up by

---

[77] See *Beecher v. Major* (1865) 2 Drew. & Sm. 431.
[78] [1989] 2 F.L.R. 94.
[79] Because the mother had withdrawn from the transaction in question before the purpose
has been carried out; see *post*, para 9–048.
[80] (1879) 10 Ch.D. 474 at 477.
[81] *Ebrand v. Dancer* (1680) 2 Ch. Cas. 26 (grandchild whose father was dead); *Currant v. Jago*
(1844) 1 Coll.C.C. 261 (nephew of wife maintained by her husband).
[82] *Beckford v. Beckford* (1774) Lofft 490.
[83] *Tucker v. Burrow* (1865) 2 Hem. & M. 515.
[84] *Lavelle v. Lavelle* [2004] EWCA Civ. 223, [2004] 2 F.C.R. 418 *per* Lord Phillips M.R. at [17].
[85] [1995] 2 F.L.R. 114.

means of which the beneficial interests were to be four-fifths to the father and one-fifth to the son but for some reason this was never executed. Following the death of his parents, the son claimed to be absolutely beneficially entitled. However, the need for an acceptable mortgagor, the absence of any evidence that the father had instructed the solicitors not to proceed with the declaration of trust, and the absence of any reason why the father should have wished to give the property to his son absolutely, were held sufficient to rebut any presumption of advancement. The presumption will also be rebutted if the mental state of the purchaser is such that he is incapable of any intention at all.[86]

(C) Joint Bank Accounts

Special considerations apply to joint bank accounts because of the fact that any of the holders of a joint bank account is normally[87] entitled to draw on the balance of that account on his sole authority. **9–031**

Where the subject matter of the joint bank account has been provided by only one of its holders, the principles already discussed apply so that there is a rebuttable presumption that the whole of the subject matter of the account is held on resulting trust for the person who provided it. This presumption may be rebutted in either of the usual ways. **9–032**

It was rebutted on the grounds that the person providing the funds intended to confer a benefit on the other holder of the account in *Young v. Sealey*[88] where an aunt transferred the balances of several bank accounts into the name of herself and her nephew with the expressed intention that only she should operate the accounts and receive the interest payable thereon during her lifetime but that he should take the entire beneficial interest on her death. It is thought that the presumption would also be rebutted on this ground if the other party made substantial and regular withdrawals from the joint account for his own benefit.

The presumption will also be rebutted by the presumption of advancement where the subject matter of a joint bank account in the name of a husband and wife or of a father and child is provided by the husband or father; in such circumstances the wife or child will take the entire beneficial interest in the event of survivorship.[89] However, the presumption of advancement can obviously also be rebutted by contrary evidence and will be so rebutted if the account has been put into joint names purely for the

---

[86] *Simpson v. Simpson* [1992] 1 F.L.R. 601.

[87] It is of course possible for the authority of both or all of the holders of the account to be required. This is what is usually done in the case of bank accounts held by express trustees because they are under an absolute obligation to have the trust property under their control (see *post*, para 13–067); however family, as distinct from professional trustees, are nevertheless often, for the sake of convenience, prepared to leave the management of an account which merely receives income and pays disbursements to one of their number although if the latter makes off with the money the remaining trustees will unquestionably be liable to the beneficiaries for breach of trust and will have to make up the deficit out of their own resources (see the authorities cited *post*, para 22–008, n.9).

[88] [1949] Ch. 278.

[89] *Re Figgis* [1969] 1 Ch. 123 (husband and wife); *McEvoy v. Belfast Banking Co.* [1935] A.C. 24 (father and son).

sake of convenience because, for example, the person who provided its subject matter is unwell and unable to attend to his affairs;[90] but it seems that the "convenience" principle is applicable only to current accounts and not to deposit accounts.[91]

9–033 Where there is no resulting trust, the beneficial interest of the person who has not provided the subject matter of the joint account is capable of being a full beneficial joint tenancy and presumably would be if the reason why the presumption of resulting trust was rebutted was that he made substantial and regular withdrawals from the account for his own benefit. However, in all the cases of this type which have reached the courts, that person has not made, and was not intended to have made, any substantial use of the joint account during the lifetime of the person who provided its subject matter. In such cases, the former clearly has no beneficial interest unless and until he survives the latter. This gives rise to the potential difficulty that the gift of the balance of the account which takes effect on survivorship appears to be in the nature of a testamentary provision and, since it has necessarily not been made in accordance with formalities required by the Wills Act 1837,[92] could be argued to be ineffective. This argument, which has been accepted in some[93] but not all[94] of the other jurisdictions in which it has been raised, appealed to Romer J. in *Young v. Sealey*[95]; however, he declined to apply it[96] because it was inconsistent with earlier decisions in which gifts of this type had been upheld and would, therefore, have had a disturbing effect on existing titles. The point nevertheless remains open for adjudication by the Court of Appeal.

9–034 Where, on the other hand, the joint bank account has more than one source in that it has been maintained by spouses for the purpose of pooling some or all of their mutual resources, both of them will clearly have an immediate beneficial interest. However, in such circumstances it will be at the very least difficult, and in many cases quite impossible, to divide up the balance by ascertaining how much was paid in by each spouse. It has, therefore, been held that, in the event of dissolution of the marriage, each former spouse will be entitled to one half. Where the marriage is ended by death, the survivor will obviously take the entire balance beneficially, although for the purposes of inheritance tax each spouse is equally treated as being entitled to one half. The same principles apply to investments

---

[90] *Marshal v. Crutwell* (1875) L.R. 20 Eq. 328 at 330, *per* Jessel M.R.. However, the "convenience" principle was not applied in *Re Pattinson* (1885) 1 T.L.R. 216 and *Marshall v. Crutwell* was distinguished on the facts in *Re Harrison* (1920) L.J.Ch. 186 and *Re Figgis* [1969] 1 Ch. 123.

[91] See *Re Harrison* (1920) L.J.Ch. 186 and *Re Figgis* [1969] 1 Ch. 123.

[92] s.9 (as substituted by Administration of Justice Act 1982, s.17).

[93] *Owens v. Greene* [1932] I.R. 225 (Irish Free State), *McKnight v. Titus* 55 D.L.R. 416 (Supreme Court of New Brunswick, Canada); see also the similar decisions in *Re Pfrimmer* [1936] 2 D.L.R. 460 (Court of Appeal of Manitoba, Canada) and in *Hiranand v. Harilela* (2000) 3 I.T.E.L.R. 297 (Court of Appeal of Singapore), neither of which actually concerned a joint bank account.

[94] It was rejected by the Court of Appeal of Ontario, Canada, in *Re Reid* (1921) 50 Ont. L.R. 595 and by the High Court of Australia in *Russell v. Scott* (1936) 55 C.L.R. 440.

[95] [1949] Ch. 278.

[96] Following *Re Reid* (1921) 50 Ont. L.R. 595 rather than *Owens v. Greene* [1932] I.R. 225 and *McKnight v. Titus* 55 D.L.R. 416 (*Russell v. Scott* (1936) 55 C.L.R. 440 was not cited to him).

which have been made by the husband in his sole name out of money held in such a joint bank account.[97] However, it should be noted that, where such investments are instead made in the sole name of the wife out of money held in such a joint bank account, the situation may well be governed by the presumption of advancement; if the presumption applies, the wife will prima facie take the investments beneficially.[98]

The position of joint accounts which contain some or all of the resources of two or more persons other than husband and wife has not had to be considered by the courts and so it has yet to be decided whether or not the same principles (other of course than the presumption of advancement which obviously could not operate in such circumstances) apply to such accounts.   9–035

3. *The Admissibility of Evidence to Rebut the Presumptions*

(A) What Sort of Evidence is Admissible?
It is obviously important to determine exactly what sort of evidence is admissible for the purpose of rebutting the presumptions of resulting trust and advancement. The leading case on admissibility is *Shephard v. Cartwright*.[99] The deceased had been a successful businessman. He had at various times formed a number of private companies which had been so successful that he had amalgamated them and turned them into a public company. At varying times he had shares in this company allotted to his three children but there was no evidence that any share certificates had been issued in their favour. In any case, the father continued to deal in these shares; at various times he sold them and received the proceeds of sale. However, at a later stage, he did place to the credit of the children in separate deposit accounts the exact amount of the cash consideration for the shares which he had sold. Later still, he obtained the children's signatures to documents (as to the contents of which they were wholly ignorant) authorising him to withdraw money from these deposit accounts and indeed in due course, unknown to them, his drawings exhausted those accounts. When he died, some 13 years after the accounts had been exhausted, his children brought an action against his executors claiming an account of money due to them. The executors contended that the presumption of advancement in favour of the children had been rebutted by the control which the father had continuously exercised over the shares. This argument succeeded in the Court of Appeal but the House of Lords held that the registration of the shares in the names of the children gave rise to a presumption of advancement and that nothing had happened which was capable of rebutting that presumption.   9–036

---

[97] *Jones v. Maynard* [1951] Ch. 572; *Rimmer v. Rimmer* [1953] 1 Q.B. 63. Compare *Re Cohen* [1953] Ch. 88, where a bundle of notes found hidden in the matrimonial home after the death of both spouses, who died within a few months of each other, was held to be the property of the wife to whom the residue belonged.
[98] See *post, infra.*
[99] [1955] A.C. 431.

9–037   The law on the admissibility of evidence for the purposes of rebuttal was stated explicitly by Viscount Simonds. He adopted[100] the following passage from *Snell's Principles of Equity*.[101]

"The acts and declarations of the parties before or at the time of the purchase, or so immediately after it as to constitute a part of the transaction, are admissible in evidence either for or against the party who did the act or made the declaration; subsequent acts and declarations are only admissible as evidence against the party who made them, and not in his favour."

As Viscount Simonds said, there are numerous cases of high authority[102] on which this passage is founded. Admittedly its references to admissibility are no longer technically appropriate due to the subsequent enactment of section 2 of the Civil Evidence Act 1968, under which hearsay evidence, including evidence of subsequent declarations, is now formally admissible. Although the Court of Appeal has stated that a "less rigid approach should . . . be adopted to the admissibility of evidence to rebut the presumption of advancement",[103] the principles stated by Viscount Simonds were recently affirmed by the Privy Council[104] and there is no doubt that they still govern what evidence will be regarded as effective for the purpose of rebutting at least the presumption of resulting trust, if not also the presumption of advancement.

9–038   It is not too difficult to state the relevant principles in the abstract. They establish, in the context of the presumption of advancement between father and child, first that a father's declaration at the date of the transaction will be effective to enable him to rebut the presumption; secondly, that a father's declaration made after that date will not be effective to enable him to rebut the presumption but will be effective as against him to enable his child to support the presumption of advancement[105]; and, thirdly, that subsequent acts and declarations by the child will be effective as against him to enable his father to rebut the presumption.[106] However, difficulties may nevertheless arise in applying these principles in practice.

9–039   First, the question of whether or not a subsequent act is part of the same transaction as the original purchase or transfer is a potential cause of considerable difficulty—there is no universal criterion by which a link can, for this purpose, be found between one event and another but it is nevertheless essential that a link is able to be found.[107] In *Shephard v. Cartwright* itself, Viscount Simonds pointed out that the events which happened after the allotment of shares to the children did not form part of the original

---

[100] *ibid.*, at 445.
[101] (28th edn) p.185.
[102] See, for example, the cases cited *post*, nn.104, 105.
[103] *Lavelle v. Lavelle* [2004] EWCA Civ. 223, [2004] 2 F.C.R. 418 *per* Lord Phillips M.R. at [17].
[104] *Antoni v. Antoni* [2007] UKPC 10, [2007] W.T.L.R. 1335 (on appeal from The Bahamas).
[105] *Stock v. McAvoy* (1872) L.R. 15 Eq. 55; *Redington v. Redington* (1794) 3 Ridg.P.R. 106 at 177; *Sidmouth v. Sidmouth* (1840) 2 Beav. 447.
[106] *Scawin v. Scawin* (1841) 1 Y. & C.C.C. 65.
[107] [1955] A.C. 431 at 448–449, *per* Viscount Simonds.

transaction, that is to say that allotment. All subsequent events were independent of that original transaction and, far from flowing inevitably from it, they would never have happened at all but for the phenomenal success of the testator's business.

Secondly, difficulties arise as to whether, and if so what, subsequent acts **9–040** and declarations will rebut the relevant presumption. An early case which shows the difficulties that there may be in rebutting the presumption on this basis is *Lord Grey v. Lady Grey*[108]; Lord Finch L.C., having considered the fact that the son had permitted his father to continue to receive the profits of the property in question, said that that fact was insufficient to rebut the presumption because it was an "act of reverence and good manners"![109] Of course, there are some circumstances which will obviously rebut the presumption. Thus, it was held in *Warren v. Gurney*[110] that the fact that the father had retained the title deeds was, although not in itself conclusive, of great significance when coupled with certain contemporaneous declarations by the father. Another circumstance which assists in rebutting the presumption is the fact that the son is the father's solicitor.[111]

Yet, as Viscount Simonds said in *Shephard v. Cartwright*,[112] any such evi- **9–041** dence of subsequent acts is regarded jealously. A question which arose in that case was whether, even though the events which happened after the allotments of the shares did not form part of the original transaction, they nevertheless amounted to an acknowledgment by the children that they had not in fact acquired any interest. However, for such an acknowledgment to be effective, it must have been made with full knowledge of the material facts. It was not disputed that the children had done whatever they had been told to do by their father without any inquiry of him or any knowledge of the consequences. This fact prevented their conduct from constituting an acknowledgment of anything which was contrary to their own interest and prevented evidence of that conduct from having any probative value.

(B) Illegal and Fraudulent Conduct
There is a further restriction on the evidence which can be adduced in order **9–042** to rebut the presumptions of resulting trust and advancement.[113] Neither presumption can be rebutted by evidence that the reason for the transfer or purchase in question was an illegal or fraudulent purpose and that the transferor or purchaser nevertheless really intended to retain a beneficial interest in the subject matter. This basic rule has never been doubted; however, at least for the moment, it is subject to two exceptions. The first arises where the beneficial interest in question can be established independently; the existence of an illegal or fraudulent purpose will not prevent a beneficial interest being claimed where this can be done without any reliance being placed on any evidence of that purpose. The second arises where

---

[108] (1677) 2 Swans. 594.
[109] *ibid.*, at 600.
[110] [1944] 2 All E.R. 472.
[111] *Garrett v. Wilkinson* (1848) 2 De G. & Sm. 244.
[112] [1955] A.C. 431 at 449.
[113] See Davies in *Trends in Contemporary Trust Law* (ed. Oakley, 1996), p.31; Virgo [1996] C.L.J. 23.

the illegal or fraudulent purpose has been abandoned; evidence of such a purpose is admissible if the person relying on that evidence withdrew from the purpose before it had been carried out in any way.[114]

(1)   The basic rule

9–043   The basic rule may be illustrated by *Gascoigne v. Gascoigne*[115] where a husband who had put property into the name of his wife was held unable to adduce evidence to show that he had done so for the purpose of defeating his creditors; consequently, she was held to be beneficially entitled to that property. A similar result occurred in *Tinker v. Tinker*,[116] although in that case the husband's intention was apparently honest. In the words of Lord Denning M.R., he simply found himself on the horns of a dilemma in that, as between himself and his wife, he wanted to say that the property belonged to him whereas, as between himself and his creditors, he wished to say that it belonged to her. In such circumstances, the effect of the presumption of advancement was decisive. This was also the case in *Chettiar v. Chettiar (No.2)*,[117] where a father sought to evade regulations governing the holding of rubber plantations in Malaya which differed depending on whether more or less than 100 acres were held (in the former but not the latter case, the permissible production was controlled by an assessment committee). He acquired 40 acres at a time when he already owned 99 acres and, in order to avoid having to disclose to the authorities that he thereafter held more than 100 acres, he had the 40 acres put into the name of his son. He had not the slightest intention of making a gift of them and therefore subsequently claimed that the son held them on resulting trust for him. The Privy Council, in an opinion delivered by Lord Denning, held that the father could only rebut the presumption of advancement by disclosing his intention to deceive the authorities. The court was bound to take notice of this illegality and therefore would not lend him its aid; the legal and beneficial estate consequently lay where it had fallen, in the hands of the son.

---

[114] In 1999 the Law Commission produced a Consultation Paper (Law Com. C.P. No. 154) as part of a general review of the effect of illegality on contracts and trusts. This criticised the existing law and tentatively proposed that illegality should be available only as a defence and then, unless any statute which rendered the conduct in question illegal made express provision as to the consequences, only at the discretion of the courts, who would, in exercising their discretion, have to consider a series of factors; these are the seriousness of the illegal conduct; the knowledge and intention of the party seeking the enforcement of the transaction or the recognition of property rights; and the extent to which any refusal to assist would either deter illegality, and/or further the purpose of the rule making the transaction illegal and/or be proportionate to the illegality. Nothing further has been heard of these proposals and so, given that any legislation would first require this Consultation Proposal to be consolidated into a Report, none can be anticipated for the moment.

[115] [1918] 1 K.B. 223; see also *Re Emery's Investment Trusts* [1959] Ch. 410 (avoiding payment of taxes).

[116] [1970] P. 136. *Gascoigne v. Gascoigne* and *Tinker v. Tinker* were distinguished in *Griffiths v. Griffiths* [1973] 1 W.L.R. 1454, where a husband's false representation as to ownership formed no part of the legal proceedings between him and his wife (this decision was varied by the Court of Appeal on other grounds at [1974] 1 All E.R. 932).

[117] [1962] A.C. 294. A similar decision was reached in *Collier v. Collier* [2003] W.T.L.R. 617 (CA), which is discussed *post*, para 9–049 and in *Barrett v. Barrett* [2008] EWHC 1061 (Ch).

(2)   Where the beneficial interest can be established independently
Prior to the decision of the House of Lords in *Tinsley v. Milligan*,[118] it was   **9–044**
thought that the court would decline to intervene in favour of a participant
in an illegal or fraudulent purpose whether or not evidence of the illegal or
fraudulent conduct in question was necessary to his claim.[119] However,
while this was indeed the view adopted by the minority in that case, the
majority instead held that the existence of an illegal or fraudulent purpose
will not prevent a property right from being claimed if that right can be
established without any reliance being placed on any evidence of that
purpose.[120]

In *Tinsley v. Milligan*, two female lovers had agreed to put a house which   **9–045**
they were purchasing into the sole name of the plaintiff in order to enable
the defendant to make fraudulent claims for housing benefit. After this
fraud had been practiced for a number of years, the two quarrelled and the
plaintiff left. Subsequently, at a time when the defendant had discontinued
her fraudulent claims and "made her peace" with the authorities, the plaintiff sought her eviction; the defendant counterclaimed for a declaration that
the property was held on trust for both of them in equal shares. The Court
of Appeal[121] held that a more flexible approach should be adopted in cases
of illegal or fraudulent conduct on the basis that "the underlying principle
is the so-called public conscience test. The court must weigh, or balance, the
adverse consequences of granting relief against the adverse consequences of
refusing relief. The ultimate decision calls for a value judgment."[122] This
novel principle was unanimously rejected by the House of Lords, who
confirmed the basic rule that evidence of an illegal or fraudulent purpose is
not admissible to rebut a presumption of resulting trust or of advancement.
However, the majority held[123] that the defendant did not need to rely on any
such evidence to assert her claim. On its face, the transaction between the
parties had given rise to a presumption of resulting trust in her favour. The
relationship between the parties did not give rise to any presumption of

---

[118] [1994] 1 A.C. 340.
[119] On the basis of the "clean hands" policy laid down by Lord Eldon L.C. in *Muckleston v. Brown* (1801) 6 Ves. 52.
[120] This has been the subject of considerable criticism; see Halliwell [1994] Conv. 62, Stowe 57 M.L.R. (1994) 441. Council in 143 N.L.J. (1993) 1577 says that the effect of the decision is that "he who comes to equity should keep unclean hands in his pockets", an amusing addition to the list of equitable maxims which will no doubt in due course prove to be as misleading as most of the others.
[121] [1992] Ch. 310.
[122] *ibid.*, at 319, *per* Nicholls L.J. A different flexible public policy approach was subsequently adopted by the High Court of Australia in *Nelson v. Nelson* (1995) 132 A.L.R. 133, in which *Tinsley v. Milligan* was rejected. A mother was held able to rebut the presumption of advance-ment in favour of her children (which would probably not have arisen here anyway) by adducing evidence that she had purchased the property in their name in order to obtain housing subsidies which would not have been available had she purchased in her own name; she was, therefore, entitled to the property under a resulting trust but the majority went on to hold that as a condition of relief she was herself obliged to do equity by reimbursing the housing subsidies.
[123] It had long been established that the legal owner of property can rely on his title despite the fact that it was acquired as a result of an illegal transaction (*Bowmakers v. Barnet Instruments* [1945] K.B. 65). The disagreement between the members of the House of Lords was as to whether the "clean hands" policy to which courts of equity have always subscribed prevented this principle from also being applicable to an equitable owner.

advancement so as to rebut the presumption of resulting trust (had it done so, the basic rule would have prevented the defendant from introducing evidence of the illegal purpose in order to rebut the presumption of advancement). The defendant therefore had to be presumed to have an equitable proprietary interest in the property unless the plaintiff could rebut that presumption by contrary evidence. Thus the defendant could assert her claim to that interest without having to produce any evidence as to why the property had been conveyed into the sole name of the plaintiff and was consequently entitled to her beneficial interest.

9–046   The Court of Appeal has duly applied the decision in *Tinsley v. Milligan* but not always uncritically. In *Silverwood v. Silverwood*,[124] Nourse L.J.[125] emphasised that, by virtue of *Tinsley v. Milligan*, a claimant is entitled to recover provided that he is not forced either to plead or to rely on any illegal or fraudulent conduct; however, he repeated his preference for the more flexible approach rejected by the House of Lords in *Tinsley v. Milligan*. In *Lowson v. Coombes*,[126] Robert Walker L.J. stated[127] that the importance which the decision in *Tinsley v. Milligan* attached to the presumption of advancement does "create difficulties because the presumption has been cogently criticised both as being out of date in modern social and economic conditions[128] . . . and as being uncertain in its scope[129]".[130] As in *Tinsley v. Milligan*, there was no presumption of advancement in either of these cases and the absence of that presumption was admittedly crucial to the outcome of all three cases. But, as is shown by the more recent decision of the Court of Appeal in *Khan v. Ali*,[131] the presence of a presumption of advancement can

---

[124] (1997) 74 P. & C.R. 453. The majority of the testatrix's assets were placed in the names of two of her grandchildren and not declared to the Department of Social Security when she subsequently applied for income support. Her executor was held to be entitled to recover them on the basis that there was a presumption of resulting trust in her favour. Even on the assumption that the testatrix had been party to the illegal purpose (which was not held), she did not need to rely on any evidence of it since there was no presumption of advancement between her and her grandchildren which she needed to rebut.

[125] *ibid.*, at 758–759.

[126] [1999] Ch. 373. A man and his mistress both contributed to the purchase price of a series of houses, all of which were transferred into the sole name of the mistress so as to prevent any claim to them being asserted by the man's estranged wife (this was an illegal purpose under Matrimonial Causes Act 1973, s.37; *ante*, para 7–063). There was again no presumption of advancement so the man was able to rely on the presumption of resulting trust rather than on any evidence of the illegal purpose.

[127] *ibid.*, at 385.

[128] Referring to the remarks of Lord Diplock in *Pettitt v. Pettitt* set out *ante*, para 9–023.

[129] Referring to purchases and transfers by wives and mothers.

[130] See also *Tribe v. Tribe* [1996] Ch. 107 at 118 per Nourse L.J.; *Silverwood v. Silverwood* (1997) 74 P. & C.R. 453 at 458, per Nourse L.J.; Hanbury & Martin, *Modern Equity* (17th edn, 2005), p.263.

[131] (2002) 5 I.T.E.L.R. 232. A father was asserting a beneficial interest in a house which he had transferred into the names of two of his daughters, on sale but only for about a third of its real value, to enable a mortgage for that amount to be raised on the strength of the daughters' income. At first instance, it was held that any presumption of resulting trust in favour of the father would have been rebutted by the presumption of advancement and that the father would not have been able to rely on evidence of what the judge regarded as a fraudulent purpose in order to rebut the presumption of advancement. The Court of Appeal cast no doubt on that analysis but held that on the facts the purpose had not involved any fraud. A resulting trust in favour of the father was upheld, subject to suitable arrangements being made in respect of the potential liability of the daughters under the mortgage.

be equally crucial in that it can similarly be relied on by a party to illegal or fraudulent conduct to rebut the presumption of resulting trust.

It is of course feasible to criticise the exception created by the majority in   **9–047**
Tinsley v. Milligan as such and many have done so.[132] However, it does seem somewhat unreasonable to criticise that exception merely because of the impact on its application of the presumption of advancement. Even if that presumption has "fallen into disfavour", it is still part of English law and the House of Lords could not have overruled it in *Tinsley v. Milligan* even if the members of the House had wanted to do so. But, given the distinction of the members of the Court of Appeal who have criticised *Tinsley v. Milligan*, three of whom subsequently became members of the House of Lords, it cannot be assumed that the exception created by that decision will survive a further review at the highest level.

(3) Where the illegal or fraudulent purpose has been abandoned

The second exception to the basic rule was analysed, very considerably   **9–048**
clarified, and applied by the Court of Appeal in *Tribe v. Tribe*[133] and as a result it is no longer necessary to consider any of the earlier authorities. A father transferred shares in a family company to his son for a consideration which was not in fact paid in order to be able to deceive his landlord, to whom he was potentially liable for the cost of substantial works to the leased premises, as to his assets and consequently to safeguard them. In the event, the issue of the repairs was resolved without recourse to any deception.[134] The son subsequently claimed to be absolutely entitled to the shares by virtue of the presumption of advancement. The Court of Appeal held that, since the father's illegal purpose had not been carried out in any way, he could introduce evidence of it in order to rebut the presumption of advancement. Earlier authorities had required "repentance" from the illegal or fraudulent purpose, although it was far from clear whether or not this "repentance" had to be genuine (which it would not have been in *Tribe v. Tribe* because the father had not "repented" until the danger to his assets was past). The Court of Appeal rejected that requirement completely and held that evidence of an illegal or fraudulent purpose can be introduced by anyone who has withdrawn from the transaction in question before the purpose has been carried out. Although this undoubtedly broadened the scope of this second exception, the Court of Appeal felt that it was not inconsistent with the policy underlining the basic rule: "if the policy which underlines the [basic] rule is to discourage fraud, the policy which underlines the [exception] must be taken to be to encourage withdrawal from fraud before it is implemented, an end which is no less desirable".[135]

Tribe v. Tribe was not applied in *Collier v. Collier*,[136] where a father had, at   **9–049**
a time when a company whose debts he had guaranteed had been held liable for various breaches of covenant, granted to his daughter leases of two

---

[132] See Halliwell [1994] Conv. 62; Stowe 57 M.L.R. (1994) 441; Council 143 N.L.J. (1993) 1577.

[133] [1996] Ch. 107.

[134] The landlord agreed to take a surrender of one of the two leases and sold the father the reversion on the other one.

[135] [1996] Ch. 107, *per* Millett L.J. at 133.

[136] [2003] W.T.L.R. 617 (CA).

properties which included options to purchase their freeholds. In the event, an appeal by the company succeeded but the father subsequently mortgaged both freeholds without mentioning the options with a view to defrauding the mortgagees. The daughter then exercised the options with funds largely provided by the father, thus restricting the rights of the mortgagees to the sums paid under the options. The father, who had remained in possession throughout, subsequently sought to resist an action by the daughter for possession on the basis that she had agreed to hold the properties on trust for him. At first instance he succeeded but on appeal it was held that such a contention involved him relying on his own illegal conduct[137]; under the basic rule, he was not able to do so and the second exception did not apply because, although he had not in the event needed to rely on his original illegal purpose, he had nevertheless deceived other creditors, the mortgagees. The Court of Appeal therefore held that the daughter was beneficially entitled to the properties.[138]

9–050   The decision actually reached in *Tribe v. Tribe* is certainly compatible with the decision in *Tinsley v. Milligan* and there is no doubt that the exceptions to the basic rule which the two decisions establish are mutually consistent. However, in *Tribe v. Tribe* Millett L.J. said that a transferee cannot be prevented from rebutting a presumption by leading evidence of the transferor's subsequent conduct to show that it was inconsistent with any intention to retain a beneficial interest, giving the example of a transfer of property from uncle to nephew in order to conceal it from his creditors, with whom he subsequently settles on the basis that he has no interest in that property.[139] How can the admission of evidence of this illegal purpose in order to rebut the presumption of resulting trust possibly be consistent with the principle laid down in *Tinsley v. Milligan*, by virtue of which the uncle would undoubtedly be able to rely on the presumption of resulting trust? It may, therefore, be that any further review of *Tinsley v. Milligan* at the highest level may also have some effect on the nature and/or continued existence of this second exception.

V. FAILURE OF A TRUST OR ITS BENEFICIAL INTERESTS

9–051   Where a settlor or testator who is creating an express trust fails to dispose of the whole of the beneficial interest in the property in question; the law implies that so much of the beneficial interest as is undisposed of is held on trust for the settlor or his estate, or for the testator's residuary beneficiaries or intestate successors. Although the presumption which arises in this second category of resulting trusts is not rebuttable in the ways just considered, in *Westdeutsche Landesbank Girozentrale v. Islington L.B.C.*[140] Lord Browne-

---

[137] Only Aldous and Mance L.JJ. held that there had been such an agreement but Chadwick L.J., who disagreed and allowed the daughter's appeal on that ground, agreed what the consequences of such an agreement would have been.

[138] This may well have turned out to be only a temporary victory since both majority judges indicated that her apparent ownership was subject to potential claims by the defrauded mortgagees.

[139] *ibid.*, at 130.

[140] [1996] A.C. 669 at 708.

Wilkinson pointed out that resulting trusts of the second type are not[141] necessarily irrebuttable; if the settlor or testator has, expressly or by necessary implication, abandoned any beneficial interest in the trust property, that property is held not on a resulting trust but for the Crown as *bona vacantia*. However, the law is very reluctant to find that any such abandonment was intended; "it is only where it is absolutely clear that in no circumstances is a resulting trust to arise that it will be excluded".[142]

Such a situation did however arise in *Environment Agency v. Hillridge*.[143]   **9–052** As a condition of issuing a waste management licence under the Environmental Protection Act 1990, the Environment Agency required the holder of the licence to settle on trust a sum by way of provision in respect of its duties and obligations under the licence and in particular those relating to the aftercare of the site once the tipping of waste has ceased; the sums in question were payable for the purpose of satisfying any expenses incurred by the Agency in satisfying any such obligations but were returnable to the licence holder once those obligations had been satisfied. Following the end of tipping, the licence holder was put into voluntary liquidation and its liquidators disclaimed the licence.[144] It was held that this disclaimer necessarily also amounted to a disclaimer of its interest under the trust.[145] Given that the disclaimer also prevented the Agency from having any further recourse to the trust, its subject matter therefore had no longer had any beneficial owner and vested in the Crown as *bona vacantia*.

1. *Total Failure of a Trust*

Whenever the trusts of a settlement fail, there is a resulting trust of the trust   **9–053** property for the settlor or his estate. Thus in *Re Ames' Settlement*,[146] the funds of a marriage settlement were held to be subject to a resulting trust for the settlor's estate once the marriage had been declared void by a decree of nullity made by a Kenyan court. The settlement for which the marriage had constituted the consideration failed completely because, in that case, the legal effect of the decree was that the parties not only were no longer married to one another but had never been married at all.[147] Similarly, if property is transferred to a person to hold as a trustee without that person

---

[141] As the formulation adopted by Megarry J. in *Re Vandervell's Trusts (No.2)* [1974] Ch. 269 at 294, 295 would appear to suggest.

[142] *Jones v. Williams* (1988) unreported *per* Knox J., quoted in *Davis v. Richards & Wallington Industries* [1990] 1 W.L.R. 1511 at 1541.

[143] See *Environment Agency v. Hillridge* [2003] EWHC 3023 (Ch).

[144] Under Insolvency Act 1986, s.178.

[145] On the basis that the licence holder could not both be freed from its liabilities under the licence and retain its rights to the fund established in order to secure those liabilities; this had been held to be the effect of Insolvency Act 1986, s.178 in *Hindcastle v. Barbara Attenborough* [1997] A.C. 70 at 87 *per* Lord Nicholls.

[146] [1946] Ch. 217.

[147] In this case the marriage was merely voidable but the effect of the nullity decree was that the marriage was void *ab initio*. Since the Nullity of Marriage Act 1971, s.5 (now Matrimonial Causes Act 1973, s.16), this is no longer the position under English law; this section provides that a nullity decree in respect of a voidable marriage has only a prospective and not any retrospective effect. However, if the marriage is "void", it is treated as never having taken place. For a list of the grounds on which a marriage will be void or voidable, see Matrimonial Causes Act 1973, ss.11, 12.

having any beneficial entitlement but no effective trusts are ever established, the property will also be held on a resulting trust for the transferor or his estate.[148]

2. *Failure of a Specified Purpose*

9–054   When a person pays money for a specified purpose on the basis it will be used only for that purpose, the recipient of the money will generally hold it on trust to use it only for that purpose. If the specified purpose fails, then, save in the wholly exceptional situation in which the parties have specifically provided for what is to happen in that event, there will be a resulting trust of the money for the person who paid it.

(A) The Basic Principle
9–055   Trusts of this type were first upheld by the House of Lords in *Barclays Bank v. Quistclose Investments*[149] and for that reason are generally known as *Quistclose* trusts. Money was advanced to a company for the purpose of paying a dividend on its shares. The advance was made on the basis that the money was to be used only for this purpose but the company became insolvent before the dividend had been paid. Lord Wilberforce analysed this situation by reference to primary and secondary trusts, holding that the fact that "arrangements for the payment of a [debtor's] creditors by a third person give rise to a relationship of a fiduciary character or trust, in favour, as a primary trust, of the creditors, and secondarily, if the primary trust fails, of the third person has been recognised in a series of cases over some 150 years".[150]

9–056   The precise nature of the primary and secondary trusts so identified subsequently caused considerable controversy. As a result *Quistclose* trusts were variously classified as express trusts, resulting trusts and constructive trusts.[151] However, in the later decision of the House of Lords in *Twinsectra v. Yardley*[152] a different analysis of the effect of such trusts was adopted. The claimant made a loan on the basis that the sum advanced was paid to the borrower's solicitors, who gave an undertaking to the claimant to utilise the loan money solely for the acquisition of property on behalf of the borrower and for no other purpose. The House of Lords held that this undertaking had given rise to a trust and Lord Millett classified this trust as a *Quistclose* trust.[153] He went on to reach the conclusion, from which none of the other members of the House of Lords dissented, that in a *Quistclose* trust the

---

[148] *Re Vandervell's Trusts (No.2)* [1974] Ch. 269.

[149] [1970] A.C. 567.

[150] [1970] A.C. 567 at 580.

[151] See Lord Millett (pre-judicially) 101 L.Q.R. (1985) 269; Rickett 107 L.Q.R. (1991) 608 and in *Equity, Fiduciaries and Trusts 1993* (ed. Waters), p.325; Chambers, *Resulting Trusts*, Chap. 3 and in *The Quistclose Trust: Critical Essays* (ed. Swadling), p.77; Ho and Smart (2001) 21 O.J.L.S. 267. Although Lord Millett subsequently changed his mind in *Twinsectra v. Yardley* [2002] UKHL 12, [2002] 2 A.C. 164, his earlier view is still maintained by Penner in *The Quistclose Trust: Critical Essays* (ed. Swadling), p.41.

[152] [2002] UKHL 12, [2002] 2 A.C. 164.

[153] Lord Hoffmann, the only other law lord who specifically discussed the question of whether or not there was a trust, did not mention *Barclays Bank v. Quistclose Investments* at all and seems to have regarded the trust in *Twinsectra v. Yardley* as a simple express trust.

person to whom the money is advanced holds it on trust for the person advancing it subject to a power to expend that money for the purpose designated by the latter and for no other purposes. This analysis has unquestionably superseded the view expressed in *Barclays Bank v. Quistclose Investments* and leads to the conclusion that, save in the exceptional situation already referred to, *Quistclose* trusts are resulting trusts.[154]

(B)   The Scope of *Quistclose* Trusts
The full facts of *Barclays Bank v. Quistclose Investments*[155] were that a com-   9–057
pany which was substantially indebted to its bankers needed money in order to pay a dividend on its shares. Quistclose Investments advanced the necessary money on the basis that it was only to be used for this purpose and it was paid into a separate account with the company's bankers, who were made aware of the arrangement. The company went into liquidation before the dividend had been paid. If Quistclose Investments was only an unsecured creditor of the company, it would enjoy no priority over any other creditors, the money in the bank would belong to the company, and the bank would be entitled to set off the credit balance of the account against the much larger amount owed to it by the company.[156] If, on the other hand, the money was held on trust for Quistclose Investments, its proprietary interest in that money would enjoy priority over the rights of the bank.[157] The House of Lords held that the common intention of Quistclose Investments and the company was such that the money had indeed been held on trust unless and until it was utilised for the purpose of paying the dividend. If that purpose had been fulfilled, Quistclose Investments would have become no more than an unsecured creditor of the company. However, that purpose had in fact failed.[158] Consequently, the money was, as between the company and Quistclose Investments, still held by the former on trust for the latter. Quistclose Investments was therefore able to recover from the bank the money which it had advanced.

There is no difficulty about upholding the existence of a *Quistclose* trust   9–058
where, as in *Barclays Bank v. Quistclose Investments* itself, the payer and the recipient are held to have intended that the money in question should be held on trust. Such an intention will obviously be clearest where the parties have expressly provided in terms that this should be the case. In *Re Lewis's of Leicester*[159] about half of the floor space of a department store was licensed to independent traders who were operating "shops within a shop". Some of these traders had agreements with the store whereby their takings, which had to pass through the store's till system, should be held by the store on

---

[154] See Rickett [2002] R.L.R. 112; Yeo and Tho 119 L.Q.R. (2003) 13. A contrary view is expressed by Penner in *The Quistclose Trust: Critical Essays* (ed. Swadling), p.41.

[155] [1970] A.C. 567.

[156] Banks have a statutory right to amalgamate the balances of the different accounts held with them.

[157] Its beneficial interest would bind the bank because its officers had been aware of the basis on which the funds had been transferred.

[158] Although for present purposes all that matters is that the House of Lords so held, it has never been immediately obvious why the dividend could not have been paid despite the company's insolvency; see Lord Millett (pre-judicially) 101 L.Q.R. (1985) 269.

[159] [1995] 1 B.C.L.C. 428.

trust for them subject to the deduction of the store's commission. When the store became insolvent, these traders were held able to recover such of their takings as were traceable into the store's bank accounts. But any intention that the money should be segregated is also likely to lead the court to infer that the parties intended to create a trust, even if that word was never actually used by anyone. In *Re Lewis's of Leicester*, other independent traders had agreements which merely provided for the segregation of their takings in a separate bank account and they were held to be entitled to such money as had actually been segregated.

9–059   However, *Quistclose* trusts have also been upheld where the payer and the recipient have merely agreed that there should be restrictions on the purposes for which the money advanced could be employed and, as a result, that money was not at the free disposal of the recipient. As has already been seen, in *Twinsectra v. Yardley*[160] the claimant was induced by fraudulent misrepresentations (which are not relevant for present purposes) to make a loan on the basis that the sum advanced was paid to the borrower's solicitors. Those solicitors made the following undertaking to the claimant: "1. The loan monies will be retained by us until such time as they are applied in the acquisition of property on behalf of [the borrower]. 2. The loan monies will be utilised solely for the acquisition of property on behalf of [the borrower] and for no other purpose." The claimant was not actually looking to the property acquired as security for repayment of the loan but rather to a further undertaking given by the solicitors personally to repay the sum advanced four months later together with interest at 24 per cent per annum. Nor had the claimant actually intended that the sum advanced should be held by the solicitors on any trust in its favour (solicitors hold funds in their client accounts on bare trust for the client in question but the client of the solicitors was the borrower not the claimant). But in the event the solicitors breached their undertaking by transferring most of the sum advanced to another solicitor; they also failed to repay the sum advanced. The other solicitor disbursed the funds transferred to him in accordance with the instructions of the borrower but not all of those funds were spent on the acquisition of property.

9–060   Unexpectedly, it then became important whether or not the arrangement between the claimant, the borrower and the solicitors to whom the money had originally been paid had given rise to a trust. This was because only if that arrangement had given rise to a trust would it be possible for the claimant either to recover the product of the disbursements made by the other solicitor[161] or to seek to impeach the conduct of that solicitor because of his involvement in what would then amount to a breach of trust.[162] The House of Lords held that the restrictions on the purposes for which the money could be employed meant that the sum advanced was not at the free disposal of the solicitors who had received it; consequently, independent of the subjective intention of the claimant, the only possible construction of the terms of the undertaking was that they had been holding the sum advanced

---

[160] [2002] UKHL 12, [2002] 2 A.C. 164.
[161] The claimant would have an equitable proprietary interest in that product by virtue of the trust; see *post*, para 22–133.
[162] This aspect of the case is discussed *post*, para 10–175.

on trust for the claimant with power to apply it in the acquisition of property by the borrower. Lord Millett[163] classified that trust as a *Quistclose* trust.

It should also be noted that the fact that part of the money advanced has   **9–061** indeed been used for the specific purpose in question does not prevent a *Quistclose* trust arising in respect of whatever is left, enabling the payer to recover that amount.[164] Such a trust has also been held to arise where the money in question, although advanced for a specific purpose, had been paid not by way of loan but rather in satisfaction of a contractual debt.[165] In that respect Peter Gibson J. stated that "the principle in all these cases is that equity fastens on the conscience of the person who receives from another property transferred for a specific purpose only and not therefore for the recipient's own purposes, so that such person will not be permitted to treat the property as his own or to use it for other than the stated purpose."[166]

Some common intention or agreed restriction of the type referred to above   **9–062** is necessary in order to prevent the general creditors of an insolvent recipient from successfully contending that the creation of the *Quistclose* trust has deprived them of assets which would otherwise have been divisible between them and so amounts to an unlawful preference.[167] In the absence of any such common intention or agreed restriction in the cases discussed above, the money would simply not have been paid over to the recipient at all; consequently, it could never possibly have become part of his general assets. This was specifically held in *Re Lewis's of Leicester*. Nor is such a contention feasible where, at the time when the payer remitted the money, he unilaterally specified that it was to remain his property in equity unless and until the recipient was able to carry out his side of the bargain by, for example, providing goods which were being ordered and paid for in advance; money paid in such circumstances could not have become part of the general assets of the recipient either. However, while a reservation of this latter type will clearly bind the recipient and his trustee in bankruptcy, it will only bind any bank in which the recipient has deposited the funds if they are clearly segregated in what the bank knows to be an account maintained for this particular purpose.

The position of the general creditors of the recipient does, however, cause   **9–063** difficulties when the trust in question has been created as the result of a unilateral act by the recipient. The courts have held that it is possible for a *Quistclose* trust to be created, and for the same priority to be conferred, as the result of such an act. In *Re Kayford*[168] a mail-order company in financial difficulties became concerned as to its ability to provide the goods for which its customers were paying in advance. It consequently opened a separate bank account called its "Customers' Trust Deposit Account" into which all purchase moneys subsequently received from customers were paid; they were withdrawn from this account only as and when the orders in question

---

[163] Lord Hoffmann, the only other law lord who specifically discussed this issue, did not mention *Barclays Bank v. Quistclose Investments* at all and seems to have regarded the trust as a simple express trust.

[164] *Re EVTR* [1987] B.C.L.C. 646.

[165] *Carreras Rothmans v. Freeman Matthews Treasure* [1985] Ch. 207.

[166] [1985] Ch. 207 at 222.

[167] See *ante*, para 7–060.

[168] [1975] 1 W.L.R. 279.

could be fulfilled. When the company went into liquidation shortly after-wards, Megarry J. held that the money in this account was held on trust for the customers; by paying the purchase moneys into a trust account, the company had prevented the customers from ever becoming its creditors and so no question of an unlawful preference arose.

9–064   *Re Kayford* was subsequently followed and applied by the Court of Appeal in *Re Chelsea Cloisters*,[169] where deposits paid to the landlord company by tenants which were to be credited to them at the end of their leases after making good any delapidations and damage caused had also been paid into a separate bank account. On the other hand, *Re Kayford* was distinguished in *Re Multi Guarantee Co.*[170] where, despite the fact that the money in question had been paid into a separate account in the joint names of the solicitors of the two parties who had been designated, the party to whom it had origi-nally been paid had continued to contemplate the possibility of making further drawings for his own benefit; nor was *Re Kayford* applied in *Re Challoner Club*,[171] where donations to a club were paid into a separate account so that they would not become available to the creditors of the club but the circumstances in which the donations would become unconditional payments to the club had not been adequately defined.[172] The decision in *Re Kayford* has also on occasions been completely overlooked in circumstances where it would have been highly relevant.[173]

9–065   It has to be admitted that it is not easy to justify the existence of a *Quistclose* trust in cases of this kind. Those paying the money in question never had any intention of becoming anything other than general creditors of the recipient. Consequently, it is not easy to see why the unilateral creation of proprietary rights in their favour does not amount to an unlawful preference if the only reason why they did became beneficiaries of a trust rather than general creditors of the recipient is that unilateral act.[174] In *Re Kayford* itself the mail-order company could undoubtedly have rejected the orders and returned their customers' cheques, something which could not conceivably have been contended to have amounted to a preference; conse-quently the company's acceptance of the orders and segregation of the purchase moneys did not actually make the situation of the general creditors

---

[169] (1981) 41 P. & C.R. 98.

[170] [1987] B.C.L.C. 257.

[171] (1997) *The Times*, November 4, 1997.

[172] The intended trust thus failed for uncertainty of objects (see *ante*, para 3–029).

[173] In *Customs and Excise Commissioners v. Richmond Theatre Management* [1995] S.T.C. 257, a theatre had sold tickets in advance on the basis of its standard conditions which expressly imposed a trust on the money in favour of the purchasers until the performance in question had taken place. On the face of things, such a trust should have been binding in accordance with *Re Kayford*, indeed possibly in accordance with *Barclays Bank v. Quistclose Investments* as well. However, Dyson J. unexpectedly held that there was no trust because the standard conditions also provided that the theatre was "not accountable for interest or otherwise in respect of the use of the ticket money after its receipt"! As Hanbury & Martin, *Modern Equity* 17th edn, (2005) 54 observes, it is also far from obvious how this conclusion can be reconciled with the decision of the Court of Appeal in *R. v. Clowes (No.2)* [1994] 2 All E.R. 316, where it was said, in the context of theft, "that the requirement to keep money separately normally indicates a trust, and the absence of such a requirement normally negatives it if there were no other indicators of a trust the fact that the transaction contemplates the mingling of money is not necessarily fatal to a trust".

[174] See Goodhart and Jones 43 M.L.R. (1980) 489.

any worse. However, the decision in *Re Chelsea Cloisters* cannot possibly be justified in this way; the company clearly had to go on letting flats and had no realistic option of letting without taking deposits. What is more (and this was a point which clearly troubled Oliver L.J.), sums which had already been received as deposits and paid into the company's normal bank account were drawn out and paid into the segregated fund; the subsequent repayment of these sums to the tenants in question undoubtedly amounted to a preference of their interests at the expense of those of the general creditors. There can be little doubt that more will be heard of this particular point; however, it is only relevant where a *Quistclose* trust is created by a unilateral act of the recipient of the funds in question and does not in any way affect the validity of the types of *Quistclose* trusts upheld by the House of Lords in *Barclays Bank v. Quistclose Investments* and *Twinsectra v. Yardley.*

(C) The Nature of *Quistclose* Trusts

It will be recalled that, in *Barclays Bank v. Quistclose Investments,*[175] Lord **9–066** Wilberforce analysed the nature of *Quistclose* trusts by reference to primary and secondary trusts, holding that arrangements for the payment of a debtor's creditors by a third party give rise to a relationship of a fiduciary character or trust, in favour, as a primary trust, of the creditors, and secondarily, if the primary trust fails, of the third party. The precise nature of the trusts so identified subsequently caused very considerable controversy and they were variously classified as express trusts, resulting trusts and constructive trusts.[176]

The only normal practical significance of whether a trust is, on the one **9–067** hand, express or, on the other hand, resulting or constructive is in relation to formal validity and then only in respect of trusts of land or subsisting equitable interests[177]; in this respect it is inconceivable that land could form the subject matter of a *Quistclose* Trust and it seems highly unlikely, although not actually impossible, that a subsisting equitable interest could do so either. However, in the case of a *Quistclose* trust, the classification may also be relevant in identifying the location of the beneficial interest while what Lord Wilberforce classified as the primary trust is in existence (there is of course no doubt that the beneficial interest under what he classified as the secondary trust is in the person who advanced the money).

It is of course clear that the beneficial interest under what Lord Wilber- **9–068** force classified as the primary trust cannot be in the recipient of the money advanced since this would defeat the whole object of the exercise by enabling that money to be claimed by his trustee in bankruptcy. The only other possibilities are that that beneficial interest is in the persons, if any, who will receive the benefit of any payments made pursuant to the specified purpose,

---

[175] [1970] A.C. 567 at 580.

[176] Lord Millett, pre-judicially, 101 L.Q.R. (1985) 269; Rickett 107 L.Q.R. (1991) 608 and in *Equity, Fiduciaries and Trusts 1993* (ed. Waters), p.325; Chambers, *Resulting Trusts*, Chap. 3 and in *The Quistclose Trust: Critical Essays* (ed. Swadling), p.77; Ho and Smart (2001) 21 O.J.L.S. 267. Although Lord Millett subsequently changed his mind in *Twinsectra v. Yardley* [2002] UKHL 12, [2002] 2 A.C. 164, his earlier view is still maintained by Penner in *The Quistclose Trust: Critical Essays* (ed. Swadling), p.41.

[177] See *ante*, para 4–008 *et seq.*

that it is in suspense, or that it at all times remains in the person who advanced the money in the first place.

9–069   If the primary trust is an express trust, then it would appear to follow that the persons, if any, in whose favour payments can be made pursuant to the specified purpose (in *Barclays Bank v. Quistclose Investments*, the shareholders entitled to the dividend) have the right to call for payment of the sums due to them. In *Re Northern Development Holdings*,[178] Megarry V.-C. regarded the primary trust as an express trust but avoided this conclusion by classifying it as a purpose trust of the type recognised in *Re Denley's Trust Deed*.[179] Even if the decision in the latter case is acceptable in the first place, which is somewhat questionable, this conclusion has the effect of placing the beneficial interest under the primary trust in suspense until payment is either made or becomes impossible. This was indeed recognised in *Carreras Rothmans v. Freeman Matthews Treasure*[180] by Peter Gibson J. who, although he reached the same conclusion, seems instead to have regarded the primary trust as a constructive trust. It is frankly, difficult to see how a trust which comes into existence because of the express or implied intentions of its settlor and/or trustee can be classified as a constructive trust, since such a trust is imposed by the court as a result of the conduct of the trustee and therefore arises quite independently of the intentions of any of the parties.[181] The conclusion that the beneficial interest was in suspense was also one of two alternative views adopted by the Court of Appeal in *Twinsectra v. Yardley*.[182]

9–070   The other alternative view adopted by the Court of Appeal in *Twinsectra v. Yardley*[183] was that there is no trust at all while what Lord Wilberforce classified as the primary trust is in existence; the recipient receives the entire beneficial ownership of the money advanced subject only to a contractual right vested in the person who has advanced it to prevent the recipient using it other than for the specified purpose. If that purpose fails, then, and only then, does a resulting trust in favour of the person who has advanced the money.[184]

9–071   When *Twinsectra v. Yardley* reached the House of Lords, Lord Millett[185] and held that the recipient of the money advanced holds it on trust for the person who has advanced it subject to a power vested in the recipient to expend that money for the specified purpose and for no other purposes. He said this[186]:

---

[178] (1978) unreported but see (1985) 101 L.Q.R. 269 at 276–279.

[179] [1969] 1 Ch. 373; *ante*, para 3–086.

[180] [1985] Ch. 207.

[181] See *post*, Chapter 10.

[182] [1999] Lloyd's Rep. Bank. 438 at 456.

[183] [1999] Lloyd's Rep. Bank. 438 at 456.

[184] This is the view of Chambers, *Resulting Trusts*, Chap. 3, based on *Re Drucker* [1902] 2 K.B. 53 at 57, where the property in question was said to be "impressed with a trust—not in the strict sense of the word—but in substance with a quasi-trust that it should be applied" only for the purpose agreed); see also *The Quistclose Trust: Critical Essays* (ed. Swadling), p.77. Compare Ho and Smart: (2001) 21 O.J.L.S. 267.

[185] Taking a view different from that which he had already advocated pre-judicially in 101 L.Q.R. (1985) 269.

[186] [2002] UKHL 12, [2002] 2 A.C. 164 at 192.

'I . . . hold the *Quistclose* trust to be an entirely orthodox example of the kind of default trust known as a resulting trust. The lender pays the money to the [recipient] by way of loan, but he does not part with the entire beneficial interest in the money, and insofar as he does not it is held on a resulting trust for the lender from the outset. Contrary to the opinion of the Court of Appeal, it is the [recipient] who has a very limited use of the money, being obliged to apply it for the stated purpose or return it. He has no beneficial interest in the money, which remains throughout in the lender subject only to the [recipient's] power or duty to apply the money in accordance with the lender's instructions. When the purpose fails, the money is returnable to the lender, not under some new trust in his favour which only comes into being on the failure of the purpose, but because the resulting trust in his favour is no longer subject to any power on the part of the [recipient] to make use of the money. Whether the [recipient] is obliged to apply the money for the stated purpose or merely at liberty to do so, and whether the lender can countermand the [recipient's] mandate while it is still capable of being carried out must depend on the circumstances of the particular case.'

It should be noted that Lord Millett envisaged that the power vested in the recipient could either be a trust power or a mere power (if the latter, it will clearly be a mere power of a fiduciary nature, given that the recipient is a trustee). The power in *Twinsectra v. Yardley* was, however, clearly a mere power and there is no obvious example among the earlier cases where the recipient would have been held to have had a trust power if this analysis had been adopted.

According to Lord Millett's analysis, successive primary and secondary   **9–072**
trusts therefore do not arise. There is one trust throughout, a trust in favour of the person who advanced the funds. It has been said that this analysis leads inescapably to the conclusion that *Quistclose* trusts are resulting trusts.[187] This will indeed almost always be the case. If the person advancing the money expressly transferred it to the recipient on the basis that the latter held it on trust for him subject to a power to expend that money for the specified purpose and for no other purposes, the trust so created would obviously be an express trust and there would be no need or room for any resulting trust. In practice, however, it is highly unlikely that there will have been an express agreement in such specific terms and so it is virtually inevitable that the adoption of Lord Millett's analysis will mean that every *Quistclose* trust gives rise to a resulting trust.

(D) Failure of the Specified Purpose
Almost all the examples of *Quistclose* trusts other than *Twinsectra v. Yardley*   **9–073**
concern arrangements made in circumstances in which the recipient of the money advanced was known by the person paying it to be in financial difficulties. In the majority of those cases, the underlying objective of the arrangement was to try to stave off the recipient's bankruptcy while at the same time preventing the money advanced from passing to his creditors in the event of any bankruptcy. For this reason, it seems to have been assumed,

---

[187] See Rickett [2002] R.L.R. 112; Yeo and Tho 119 L.Q.R. (2003) 13. For a contrary view, see Penner in *The Quistclose Trust: Critical Essays* (ed. Swadling), p.41.

without discussion, that in the event of the recipient's bankruptcy the specified purpose will necessarily have failed. However, bankruptcy does not actually prevent the recipient's pre-existing debts being paid with money which, because it is held on trust, does not form part of the bankrupt's assets and so is capable of being used for this purpose. The reason why this issue has never been raised may be that in the first case to come before the courts, *Barclays Bank v. Quistclose Investments*,[188] the money was in an account with the recipient's bankers, who had purported to exercise their right to set off the credit balance of that account against the much larger amount owed to the bank by the company.[189] The money was, therefore, simply not available for payment to the company's shareholders at any stage prior to the decision of the House of Lords.

9–074   Before *Twinsectra v. Yardley*, the only way of dealing with this issue would presumably have been to have contended that the specified purpose of the primary trust was not only the payment of the recipient's debts but also the prevention of the recipient's bankruptcy. On the alternative view that there was no trust at all until the specified purpose failed, the contractual right vested in the person who advanced the money presumably extended to prevent the recipient from using it after bankruptcy. Now, pursuant to Lord Millett's analysis, the recipient of the money advanced holds it on trust for the person who has advanced it subject to a power vested in the recipient to expend that money for the specified purpose and for no other purposes. It is, therefore, instead presumably necessary to say either that the intention of the parties was that the power should determine in the event of the recipient's bankruptcy or that, following his bankruptcy, as a power held by a fiduciary it cannot be either exercised or released by his trustee in bankruptcy.[190]

9–075   It should also be noted that, in the passage set out above, Lord Millett specifically envisaged the possibility of the person who advanced the money having the right to countermand the recipient's mandate, or more technically to revoke his power, in appropriate circumstances. Such an action, where permissible, will of course have exactly the same consequences as the failure of the specified purpose.

3. Unexhausted Beneficial Interests

(A) Failure Wholly to Dispose of the Beneficial Interest

9–076   The same principle will be applied where the beneficial interest has not been wholly disposed of. However, it is not applied in all cases.

9–077   *Re Gillingham Bus Disaster Fund*[191] concerned an appeal set up in 1951 as a result of the deaths of 24 Cadets in the Royal Marines when a motor vehicle ran into them. The mayors of several boroughs in the area wrote the

---

[188] [1970] A.C. 567 at 580.

[189] Banks have a statutory right to amalgamate the balances of the different accounts held with them.

[190] See *Mettoy Pension Trustees v. Evans* [1990] 1 W.L.R. 1587, *ante*, para 6–123.

[191] [1958] Ch. 300 (affirmed on points not affecting this aspect of the decision by the Court of Appeal at [1959] Ch. 62; see also *post*, para 11–118; Atiyah (1958) 74 L.Q.R. 190. For charitable gifts the position is otherwise; see *post*, para 11–109.

following letter to *The Daily Telegraph*: "The Mayors have decided to promote a Royal Marine Cadet Memorial Fund to be devoted to defraying funeral expenses, caring for the boys who may be disabled and then to such worthy cause or causes in memory of the boys who lost their lives as the Mayors may determine". This appeal resulted in subscriptions amounting to the then very substantial sum of nearly £9,000, contributed partly by identifiable persons but mainly anonymously as a result of street collections and the like. The trustees spent about £2,500 in fulfilling the objectives set out in the letter and then took out a summons for guidance as to what to do with the surplus.

Harman J. held that the trust could not be classified as charitable; consequently, the surplus had to be held on resulting trust for the donors, even though many of them were in fact anonymous. This conclusion followed naturally from the principle that where money was held upon trust and the trust declared did not exhaust the fund it would revert to the donor or settlor upon a resulting trust. The reasoning behind the application of the principle to these particular facts was that a donor did not part with the money out and out but only to a certain extent, namely with the intention that the wishes contained in his declaration of trust should be carried into effect. It must be emphasised, as Harman J. duly observed, that this doctrine does not rest on any evidence of the state of mind of the donor who in the vast majority of cases of this type will certainly not expect to get his money back under any circumstances. A resulting trust arises even where the donor's expectation has been cheated of fruition for some reason which was totally unknown to him or anyone else at the time of the gift; this was indeed the case in *Re Gillingham Bus Disaster Fund*, where the donors' expectations failed because of an inference of law drawn only in the light of the knowledge of events which occurred after they had made their contributions to the fund.

It must be emphasised that the basis of the decision in *Re Gillingham Bus Disaster Fund* was that there was no intention on the part of the donors to part with their money out and out when they contributed it; in particular, such an intention could no more be attributed to the anonymous contributor who had made his gift in response to a street collection than it could to a contributor who was identifiable. As Harman J. said,[192] "I see no reason myself to suppose that the small giver who is anonymous has any wider intention than the large giver who is named. They all give for the one object. If they can be found by inquiry the resulting trust can be executed in their favour. If they cannot I do not see how the money could then change its destination and become *bona vacantia*."[193] Such part of the surplus whose donors could not be identified therefore had to be paid into court to await claims by them under the consequential resulting trusts[194]; most of it is probably still there today!

9–078

---

[192] [1958] Ch. 300 at 314.
[193] In similar circumstances a resulting trust was held to arise in *Re Holbourn Aero Components Air Raid Distress Fund* [1946] Ch. 86 but in that case there was no argument about *bona vacantia*. Compare *Re Hillier's Trusts* [1954] 1 W.L.R. 9, where Upjohn J. held in these circumstances in favour of *bona vacantia* (when the Court of Appeal affirmed this decision at [1954] 1 W.L.R. 700, Denning L.J. approved the formulation of Upjohn J.).
[194] Under Trustee Act 1925, s.63.

9–079   On the other hand, as the remarks of Harman J. indicate, if it could have
been shown that each donor made his gift out and out with no intention of
reclaiming it whatever the fate of the appeal might be, the surplus would
have belonged to the Crown as *bona vacantia*. There is no doubt that this is
a more practicable solution so far as the proceeds of collecting boxes are
concerned because it is obviously likely to be a wholly fruitless exercise to
try to establish who in fact contributed how many pounds or pence to the
collection and is therefore entitled to have his contribution returned—this is
of course precisely why most of the surplus had to be paid into court.
Doubts have subsequently been expressed as to whether the decision of
Harman J. in this respect was correct as a matter of law. In *Re West Sussex
Constabulary's Benevolent Fund Trusts*[195] Goff J. declined to follow *Re Gillingham Bus Disaster Fund*, at any rate so far as concerned the proceeds of
collecting boxes. He held that persons who put money into collecting boxes
should be taken to have intended to part with the money out and out
absolutely in all circumstances; consequently, the Crown was entitled to that
money as *bona vacantia* on the later failure of the trusts.

9–080   There are admittedly some dicta in other cases which support this view[196]
but they are not particularly weighty because they concerned a rather
different question, namely whether the fact that contributions were made by
unidentifiable donors to an appeal for charitable purposes indicated an
intention to make the gifts outright so as to enable the funds to be applied
cy-près, that is to say to other analogous charitable purposes.[197] Neither *Re
Gillingham Bus Disaster Fund* nor *Re West Sussex Constabulary's Benevolent
Fund Trusts* can therefore be regarded as decisive in this respect and so the
question of whether the proceeds of collecting boxes for non-charitable
purposes which fail are held on resulting trust or are *bona vacantia* remains
to be settled; while, on the one hand, it seems highly artificial to make a
distinction between the intention of unidentified donors and that of identified donors, it is on the other hand equally true that the consequences of the
existence of a resulting trust are highly inconvenient.

9–081   There is, in any event, another essential distinction between the facts of
the two decisions. *Re Gillingham Bus Disaster Fund* concerned a fund raised
to deal with one particular tragedy, a fund in which none of the contributors
had any direct or indirect financial interest (other, of course, than the possibility of recovering any unspent surplus in the event that that surplus was
indeed held on resulting trust); the contributors therefore paid their money
on an outward looking basis. *Re West Sussex Constabulary's Benevolent Fund
Trusts*, on the other hand, concerned a fund for the benefit of the dependants
of the members of an unincorporated association and the contributors therefore largely paid their money on an inward looking basis. Further, the fund
included not only the proceeds of collecting boxes, the proceeds of entertainments, raffles and sweepstakes, and donations and legacies but also the
contributions of past and present members. Goff J. had to deal with many

---

[195] [1971] Ch. 1.
[196] *Re Hillier's Trusts* [1954] 1 W.L.R. 700 at 715, *per* Denning L.J.; *Re Welsh Hospital (Netley)
Fund* [1921] 1 Ch. 655 at 659, 660, *per* P.O. Lawrence J.; *Re North Devon and Somerset Relief Fund
Trusts* [1953] 1 W.L.R. 1260 at 1266, 1267, *per* Wynn-Parry J.
[197] See *post*, para 11–118.

types of contribution which were not present in *Re Gillingham Bus Disaster Fund*.

It has already been seen that he rejected the applicability of the doctrine   **9–082**
of resulting trusts to the proceeds of street collections. He took a similar view in respect of the proceeds of entertainments, raffles and sweepstakes, holding that it was not appropriate to apply the doctrine of resulting trusts for two reasons: first, because the relationship was one of contract, not of trust (a contributor paid his money as the price of being entertained or of having his ticket put into the draw and that was precisely what he received); and, secondly, because there was no direct contribution to the fund at all—only the profit, if any, made out of the entertainment or the draw was ultimately received. The distinction thus made between trust and contract certainly seems sound in respect of these sources of funds. Goff J. consequently held that, since it was not appropriate to apply the doctrine of resulting trusts, the proceeds of these sources of funds must also be held for the Crown as *bona vacantia*. However, he held that the donations and legacies were indeed held on resulting trust.

That left the question of the contributions of past and present members, a   **9–083**
question which arises whenever the funds of an unincorporated association contain a surplus on its dissolution. Such a surplus can clearly be dealt with in a number of ways.

First, the surplus can be regarded as being held on resulting trust for the   **9–084**
members of the association in proportion to their contributions to its funds. This was the view taken in *Re Printers' and Transferrers' Society*,[198] where the surplus of the funds of a society which had collected weekly contributions from its members to provide defence and support, and in particular strike and lock-out benefits, for them was divided between those who were members at the time of its dissolution in proportion to their contributions. Similarly, in *Re Holbourn Aero Components Air Raid Distress Fund*,[199] a fund established for employees who were on war service or who suffered loss in air raids which was financed by voluntary subscriptions from the employees was divided up between all contributors in proportion to the amount contributed.

Secondly, and alternatively, the funds can be regarded as being subject to   **9–085**
the contractual rights and liabilities of the members towards one another as members of the association. This was the view taken in *Cunnack v. Edwards*,[200] where it was held that the personal representatives of members of a society founded to provide funds for the widows of the members could not claim a share when the purposes of the society came to an end. The members, in making their contributions to the society, had received all that they had contracted for in the form of pensions for the widows. Consequently, the Crown took the surplus as *bona vacantia*. Goff J. followed and applied this decision in *Re West Sussex Constabulary's Benevolent Fund Trusts* and therefore concluded that the contributions of the past and present members were also held for the Crown as *bona vacantia*. However, it must be stressed that this approach can equally lead to the funds being divided

---

[198] [1899] 2 Ch. 184.
[199] [1946] Ch. 86 and 194.
[200] [1896] 2 Ch. 679.

between the members of the association if that is the effect of the contract between them which is provided by the rules of the association. This was the outcome both in *Re G.K.N. Bolts & Nuts (Automotive Division) Birmingham Works, Sports and Social Club*[201] and in *Re Horley Town Football Club*[202]; in both cases the clubs had a variety of classes of members and the court held that the surplus should, in the absence of any contrary provision in the rules, be divided between the effective, as distinct from honorary, associate or temporary, members in equal shares.

9–086   It is now generally accepted that the resulting trust approach is normally no longer appropriate in respect of surpluses of the funds of unincorporated associations on their dissolution. It has already been seen[203] that there is now a strong presumption that the funds of an unincorporated association should be regarded as being subject to the contractual rights and liabilities of the members towards one another as members of the association. It is now also generally accepted that only in extreme circumstances should this approach lead to the assets being held as *bona vacantia* and that, to this extent at least, the decision in *Re West Sussex Constabulary's Benevolent Fund Trusts* is no longer good law. In *Re Bucks Constabulary Fund Friendly Society (No.2)*,[204] Walton J. held that only where the association has become moribund, in that all or all but one of the members have resigned or died, will the assets of the association be held as *bona vacantia* and that in all other circumstances they will be divided equally between the existing members at the time of its dissolution, save where the rules of the association provide for division in some other way. He therefore divided equally between the members alive at the date of dissolution the surplus of a fund established to provide benefits for the members and the dependants of the members of a police force which had been amalgamated with other constabularies. Given that the association in question was a friendly society, this decision can technically be distinguished from that in *Re West Sussex Constabulary's Benevolent Fund Trusts*. However, Walton J. criticised that case and it is tolerably clear that he would have decided it differently, dividing all the funds held by Goff J. to be *bona vacantia* equally between the members of the association; indeed, it is possible that he might also have done the same with the donations and legacies which Goff J. had held to be subject to resulting trusts.

9–087   Ever since the decision in *Re Bucks Constabulary Fund Friendly Society (No.2)*, it has generally been thought that the view adopted by Walton J. is the most appropriate of the various possibilities which have been discussed, principally because it is the view which fits most easily with the modern attitude to unincorporated associations in general.[205] Doubt was, however, cast on the position by the decision in *Davis v. Richards & Wallington Industries*,[206] which concerned the hypothetical situation of a surplus arising in a pension fund whose rules contained no provision as to how that surplus

---

[201] [1982] 1 W.L.R. 774.
[202] [2006] W.T.L.R. 1817.
[203] See *ante*, para 3–107.
[204] [1979] 1 W.L.R. 936.
[205] See *ante*, para 3–107; see also Gardner [1992] Conv. 41.
[206] [1990] 1 W.L.R. 1511; see Gardner *op. cit.*

should be dealt with. Scott J. took a view different from that of Walton J., opining that such part of the surplus as represented the employer's contributions would be held on resulting trust for the employer while such part as represented the employees' contributions would be held as *bona vacantia*. He accepted that neither the contractual relationship between employer and employees nor the fact that the employees had obtained everything for which they had contracted necessarily prevented there being a resulting trust in their favour as well. However, for two reasons he held that there was no such trust: first, because no intention could be imputed to the employees that they should receive a surplus greater than they were entitled to receive under the relevant tax legislation; and, secondly, because a resulting trust of their contributions would have been unworkable due to the need to value the benefits received by each employee in order to ascertain his entitlement to the surplus.

But in *Air Jamaica v. Charlton*[207] the Privy Council regarded the approach of Scott J. to the imputation of intention as erroneous, saying that it was not obvious that employees should ever be regarded as having no expectation of obtaining a return of excess contributions in the event of a surplus. However, this was no more than a dictum because the Privy Council was actually considering what was to happen to the subject matter of some of the trusts of the pension scheme in question which were void for perpetuity and in such circumstances it was impossible to say that the employees had received everything for which they had contracted anyway. The Privy Council therefore held that the subject matter of the trusts which were void for perpetuity was held on resulting trust for both the employers and the employees in proportion to their respective contributions. These resulting trusts arose by operation of law outside the provisions of the pension scheme and consequently outside the scope of the Jamaican tax legislation, which was therefore irrelevant. Nor did the valuation difficulty which Scott J. had identified apply in the light of the way in which the Privy Council had construed the provisions of the scheme which was before it. **9–088**

As will be seen in the chapter on pensions trusts,[208] such trusts are subject to many special rules and the treatment of surplus has been and remains a particular problem whose resolution has increasingly been regulated by statute; in any event, only rarely will such trusts not expressly provide what is to happen to any surplus. No provision of any approved pension trust can be void for perpetuity under English law anyway so, while the Privy Council's remarks as to the imputation of intention are clearly relevant to English pension trusts, an English court could not hold that any rights to surplus arose outside the pension scheme; it is, therefore, not clear whether the relevant English tax legislation could similarly be disregarded. Further, and in any event, it is questionable to what extent statutorily regulated pensions trusts can really be regarded as unincorporated associations in the normal sense of that expression. It is therefore unlikely that the decisions in *Davis v. Richards & Wallington Industries* and *Air Jamaica v. Charlton* will have **9–089**

---

[207] [1999] 1 W.L.R. 1399.
[208] See *post*, Chapter 12.

a decisive impact on the earlier authorities. To the extent that they are regarded as relevant, the rejection of *bona vacantia* by the Privy Council is clearly preferable to its adoption by Scott J.. It is anyway clear that, however *Air Jamaica v. Charlton* is applied, the question of how surpluses in the funds of unincorporated associations should be treated is unlikely to be finally settled until the matter is considered by the Court of Appeal.

9–090 Two principal questions thus remain outstanding and both await review at appellate level. First, the question of whether surplus funds of the type considered in *Re Gillingham Bus Disaster Fund*, where no unincorporated association was involved, are held on resulting trust or as *bona vacantia* has still to be clarified in the light of the opposing attitudes adopted in that case and in *Re West Sussex Constabulary's Benevolent Fund Trusts* in this respect. Secondly, the question of how surpluses in the funds of unincorporated associations on their dissolution should be treated awaits a final decision as to whether or not the resulting trust analysis preferred in the earlier authorities has been finally discredited by the decision in *Re Bucks Constabulary Fund Friendly Society (No.2)*.

(B) Incomplete Trusts

9–091 A resulting trust solution will generally be adopted where the instrument is silent as to the way in which the beneficial interest is to be applied. Thus, if property is settled upon trust to pay the income to a life tenant and the instrument makes no provision for the destination of the property on the death of the life tenant, the trustee will prima facie hold the property on a resulting trust for the settlor or his estate. This occurred in *Re Cochrane*[209] where, apparently as a result of a blunder by the draftsman, a provision was left out of the instrument so that the funds were not effectively disposed of. In such situations, there is no doubt that the nominated trustee cannot take beneficially, moreover, it has been held that he cannot even adduce evidence to that effect.[210]

9–092 However, it must be emphasised that the implication of a resulting trust is merely the prima facie solution and may well be overridden as a matter of construction of the instrument; the court may be still able to construe the instrument in such a way that the trustee takes beneficially subject to the fulfilment of the trust in favour of the life tenant. So, in *Re Foord*[211] property was given by will to the testator's sister absolutely on trust to pay his wife an annuity. The income was more than sufficient to meet the annuity and, upon a true construction of the will, the sister was held to be entitled to the balance. A similar conclusion was arrived at in *Re Andrew's Trust*[212] where a fund had been subscribed for the education of the children of a distressed clergyman and "not for equal division between them". Kekewich J. held that there was no resulting trust; consequently, after their education had been completed, the children were entitled to the balance equally.

---

[209] [1955] Ch. 309.
[210] *Re Rees' Will Trusts* [1949] Ch. 541.
[211] [1922] 2 Ch. 519.
[212] [1905] 2 Ch. 48.

However, this latter decision is not particularly easy to reconcile with the   9–093
decision in *Re The Trusts of the Abbott Fund*.[213] There a fund had been
subscribed for the maintenance of two distressed ladies and Stirling J. held
that on the death of the survivor the balance was held on a resulting trust for
the donors. Kekewich J. justified his decision in *Re Andrew's Trust* on the
ground that the subscribers parted with their money once and for all when
they gave it, the education of the children being merely the motive for their
gifts. While the distinction between these two cases is a very fine one,
ultimately the question is one of construction in each case; it is, therefore,
certainly possible that both *Re Andrew's Trust* and *Re The Trusts of the Abbott
Fund* may have been right on their particular facts. Precisely this point was
made in *Re Osoba*,[214] where gifts had been made to the mother, wife, and
daughter of the testator for various purposes which had failed or become
exhausted. The Court of Appeal held, on a construction of the will, that these
created trusts for the benefit of the beneficiaries and the respective purposes
were to be disregarded as no more than expressions of the testator's motives
in making the gifts.

(C) Failure of a Common Purpose
In most cases the parties to a transaction have the same purpose but this is   9–094
not necessarily so. The question, therefore, arises as to whether, when two or
more persons acquire property each for a separate purpose and one of those
purposes, previously uncommunicated to the other person(s) fails, a resulting trust arises. The answer appears to be that it does not.

In *Burgess v. Rawnsley*[215] an elderly widowed couple met and became
friendly.[216] The man was the tenant of a house in which he lived in the
downstairs flat, the upstairs flat being vacant. Subsequently, they agreed to
purchase the house, each of them providing half of the purchase price, and
it was conveyed to them as joint tenants. The man bought the house as a
matrimonial home in contemplation of marriage, but the woman said that
she had intended to live in the upstairs flat and that he had never mentioned
marriage to her. They did not in fact marry and she never moved into the
house. Later she orally agreed to sell her share in the house to him but then
refused to do so. Following his death, his daughter, as administratrix of his
estate, claimed that there was a resulting trust of his share in favour of his
estate or, alternatively, that the joint tenancy had been severed by the oral
agreement to sell. The woman claimed that the house was hers by
survivorship.

The Court of Appeal unanimously held that the joint tenancy had been
severed. That was of course sufficient to dispose of the case but there was a
difference of opinion as to whether there was also a resulting trust.

---

[213] [1900] 2 Ch. 326. In *Re West Sussex Constabulary's Benevolent Fund Trusts* [1971] Ch. 1, it was
held that *Re The Trusts of the Abbott Fund* was indistinguishable with regard to funds derived
from donations and legacies from identified persons. For discussion of other aspects of *Re West
Sussex Constabulary's Benevolent Fund Trusts*, see *ante*, p.302.

[214] [1979] 1 W.L.R. 247.

[215] [1975] Ch. 429.

[216] Apparently despite the fact that, according to her evidence, "he looked like a tramp" and
"had been picking up fag-ends".

Browne L.J. and Sir John Pennycuick held that, since the man alone had entered into the conveyance in contemplation of marriage and he had not communicated that purpose to the woman, there was no common purpose which could fail so as to give rise to a resulting trust. On the other hand, Lord Denning M.R. considered that, where parties contemplate different objects both of which fail, the position is the same as where their common object fails; consequently, in such circumstances, the property is held on resulting trust for the parties in proportion to their payments. The view of the majority seems to be more logical.

(D) Termination

9–095　It has been seen that a resulting trust comes into existence whenever there is a gap in the beneficial ownership. Accordingly, as was held in *Re Vandervell's Trusts (No.2)*,[217] when that gap is filled by someone becoming beneficially entitled, or where a trust is expressly declared, the resulting trust comes to an end.[218]

4. Bona Vacantia *arising on Intestacy*

9–096　It has already been seen[219] that, where a beneficial interest has not been wholly disposed of, the property in question will in some circumstances be applied as *bona vacantia* rather than subject to a resulting trust. The doctrine of *bona vacantia* is also relevant where a beneficiary who is entitled to property dies wholly or partially intestate without any intestate successors. It now makes no difference whether the property is vested in trustees or in executors.

If property is vested in trustees upon trust absolutely for a beneficiary who is living when the interest takes effect and the beneficiary then dies intestate leaving no one entitled to take as his intestate successor, there cannot possibly be a resulting trust because the beneficial interest will have effectively vested in the beneficiary during his lifetime. Whether the property in question is realty or personalty, it is now[220] clearly established that in such circumstances the beneficial interest belongs to the Crown as *bona vacantia*; it has no owner and must devolve accordingly.

Where the property is vested in executors, the Administration of Estates Act 1925[221] provides that, in the absence of any persons entitled on intestacy, executors will hold all the undisposed of property of their testator as *bona*

---

[217] [1974] Ch. 269. The facts are stated *ante*, para 4–030.

[218] *ibid.*, at 320. No consideration was given as to the question of whether the equitable interest under the resulting trust should have been disposed of by writing in accordance with Law of Property Act 1925, s.53(1)(c); see *ante*, para 4–008.

[219] See *ante*, para 4–076 *et seq.*

[220] The position was at one time different where the property in question was realty. The law used to be that the trustee took it beneficially because the Court of Chancery did not apply the law of escheat to interests in real property. The law was changed first by the Intestates Estates Act 1884, ss.4, 7 and then by the Administration of Estates Act 1925, ss.45, 46.

[221] ss.46, 49.

vacantia; this rule will only be overridden if the will clearly shows that the executors are to take beneficially.[222]

VI. RESULTING TRUSTS ARISING AS A RESULT OF VOID OR VOIDABLE TRANSACTIONS

It was mentioned in the introduction to this chapter that it has sometimes   9–097
been contended[223] that resulting trusts can also arise as a result of a transfer
of property which is either void *ab initio* or voidable and effectively avoided.
Such contentions have been made in order to enable the transferor to assert
that he has retained a sufficient equitable proprietary interest in the property
transferred to be able to bring an equitable proprietary claim in respect of
that property against the transferee or anyone claiming that property
through him. A successful claim of this nature will enable the transferor to
obtain an enhanced measure of recovery in one or more of the following
ways: first, by obtaining priority over the general creditors of the transferee[224]; secondly, by recovering any increase in the value of the property
transferred[225]; and, thirdly, by recovering compound rather than simple
interest.[226] It will also enable the transferor to seek the imposition of personal liability on the transferee, his successors in title, or his agents by virtue
of the fact that one or more of them has knowingly received property which
has been transferred in breach of trust[227] or has dishonestly assisted in a
breach of trust.[228]

Where a transfer of property is void *ab initio* for some reason such as   9–098
illegality, mistake or lack of capacity of the transferor, no title will generally
have passed to the transferee; in that case the transferor will not need any
trust as a prerequisite of asserting his title. Only where title has nevertheless
passed to the transferee because the property in question was or has subsequently been turned into money is a trust necessary and in such circumstances the fact that title has passed will mean that any trust will need to be

---

[222] The position at law at one time was that, if a testator died without having disposed of his residuary estate, his executors were entitled to it if the residue was personal estate or to the extent to which it consisted of personalty. Further, equity followed the rule of common law unless it was shown, on a true construction of the will, that the testator intended to exclude the executors from taking a benefit; if such an intention could be shown, they would of course hold as trustees for the testator's statutory next-of-kin. However, the law was changed by the Executors Act 1830, which provided that executors should hold as trustees for the next-of-kin unless it could be shown from the will that it was intended they should take beneficially. This statute had the effect of shifting the burden of proof from the next-of-kin to the executors. However, the executors nevertheless remained entitled to the residuary personalty beneficially if there were no next-of-kin. This last loophole was eventually closed by the Administration of Estates Act 1925.

[223] See Chambers, *Resulting Trusts* (1997) *passim*. The authorities are discussed *infra*.

[224] As in *Chase Manhattan Bank v. Israel-British Bank (London)* [1981] Ch. 105.

[225] As in *Papamichael v. National Westminster Bank* [2003] EWHC 164 (Comm), [2003] 1 Lloyd's Rep. 341.

[226] As in *Westdeutsche Landesbank Girozentrale v. Islington L.B.C.* [1996] A.C. 669.

[227] As in *El Ajou v. Dollar Land Holdings* [1993] 3 All E.R. 717 (Ch.D.), [1994] 2 All E.R. 685 (C.A.).

[228] As in *Papamichael v. National Westminster Bank* [2003] EWHC 164 (Comm), [2003] 1 Lloyd's Rep. 341.

imposed rather than implied; consequently, any trust which arises in such circumstances will necessarily be a constructive trust rather than a resulting trust. Further, neither type of trust can arise where title has passed to the transferee under a transaction which is within the capacity of the transferor but beyond the capacity of the transferee. This was specifically held by the House of Lords in *Westdeutsche Landesbank Girozentrale v. Islington L.B.C.*,[229] reversing the earlier decision of the House in *Sinclair v. Brougham*[230] where the existence of such trusts in circumstances of this type had been upheld.[231]

9–099   Controversy therefore remains only in respect of transfers of property which are voidable. In *El Ajou v. Dollar Land Holdings*,[232] Millett J. held that persons who had been induced by fraudulent misrepresentations to purchase shares were "entitled to rescind the transaction and revest the equitable title to the purchase money in themselves, at least to the extent necessary to support an equitable tracing claim", stating that "the trust which is operating in these cases is not some new model remedial constructive trust, but an old fashioned institutional resulting trust".[233] The judge has confirmed this view extra-judicially,[234] stating that, "where the plaintiff pays away his money by a valid payment, fully intending to part with the beneficial interest to the recipient, but his intention is vitiated by some factor such as fraud, misrepresentation, mistake and so on . . . , the beneficial interest passes, but the plaintiff has the right to elect whether to affirm the transaction or rescind it. If he elects to rescind it, it is usually assumed that the beneficial title revests in the plaintiff, and the authorities suggest that it does so retrospectively."

9–100   Earlier, in *Chase Manhattan Bank v. Israel-British Bank (London)*[235] Goulding J. had held that a New York bank which had, as the result of a clerical error, made twice rather than once a payment of US$2,000,000 to a London bank had at all times retained a beneficial interest in the sum overpaid under a trust, presumably a resulting trust. This decision was expressly applied by Cooke P. in the Court of Appeal of New Zealand in *Liggett v. Kensington*,[236] where he held that the mistaken belief of the purchasers of "non-allocated" bullion that they were acquiring gold, not merely contractual rights, from their gold-dealer meant that they had throughout retained an equitable proprietary interest in their purchase moneys. This point did not arise when the case reached the Privy Council under the name of *Re Goldcorp Exchange*[237] but Lord Mustill declined to express an opinion as

---

[229] [1996] A.C. 669.

[230] [1914] A.C. 398.

[231] Viscount Haldane L.C. and Lord Atkinson held "a resulting trust, not of an active character" had arisen, while Lord Parker of Waddington instead held that a constructive trust had arisen. Lord Sumner held that there was a trust but did not specify its type. Lord Dunedin did not find a trust at all.

[232] [1993] 3 All E.R. 717, affirmed by the Court of Appeal without discussion of this particular point [1994] 2 All E.R. 685.

[233] [1993] 3 All E.R. 717 at 734.

[234] 114 L.Q.R. (1998) 399 at 416.

[235] [1981] Ch. 105.

[236] [1993] 1 N.Z.L.R. 257.

[237] [1995] 1 A.C. 74.

to whether or not *Chase Manhattan Bank v. Israel-British Bank* had been correctly decided.[238] His clear doubts in this respect were confirmed in *Westdeutsche Landesbank Girozentale v. Islington L.B.C.*[239] by Lord Browne-Wilkinson, who specifically stated that he did not accept the reasoning of Goulding J. He said that "the mere receipt of the moneys, in ignorance of the mistake, gives rise to no trust"; however, he went on to say that "the retention of the moneys after the recipient bank learned of the mistake may well have given rise to a constructive trust". Lord Millett has also stated, extra-judicially,[240] that he considers that *Chase Manhattan Bank v. Israel-British Bank* was wrongly decided.

All these issues arose in the Commercial Court in *Papamichael v. National Westminster Bank*.[241] The claimant's husband deposited two billion Greek drachmas of the claimant's money with the bank; it was, as intended by everyone involved, converted into dollars, producing about US$6.5 million. The claimant thought that the dollars had been placed on fixed term deposit with the bank. However, unknown to her, her husband had fraudulently arranged for the dollars to be used as security for the operation by the bank of a foreign exchange margin account for his benefit. This account traded unsuccessfully and most of the dollars were lost. It was held that the claimant was entitled to the recovery of the two billion drachmas from the bank on the basis that she had been under a mistake of fact as to what would happen to that sum once it had been paid to the bank. However, because the drachma had depreciated by about 20 per cent as against the dollar during what she thought was the term of the fixed deposit, she was interested in recovering the US$6.5 million instead. This was only possible if the bank held the dollars on some form of trust for her.   9–101

In this respect, the judge[242] held that such a trust arose for three different reasons, two of which are relevant for present purposes: first, because the bank had received the dollars with knowledge of the claimant's mistake (in this respect, he relied on the explanation given by Lord Browne-Wilkinson of the decision in *Chase Manhattan Bank v. Israel-British Bank* and therefore on a constructive trust); and, secondly, because the husband had obtained the dollars as a result of fraudulent conduct of which the bank was aware. In the latter respect, the judge held that Lord Millett's statement in *El Ajou v. Dollar Land Holdings*[243] that "the trust which is operating in these cases is . . . an old fashioned institutional resulting trust"[244] was "all very well, but Lord Browne-Wilkinson was specific in saying [in *Westdeutsche Landesbank Girozentale v. Islington L.B.C.*] that what was being imposed was an institutional constructive trust not a resulting trust". The judge therefore proceeded on the basis that both these trusts were constructive trusts rather than resulting trusts. He then went on to hold that the bank was liable to account to the   9–102

---

[238] *ibid.*, at 103.
[239] [1996] A.C. 669.
[240] 114 L.Q.R. [1998] 399 at 412–413.
[241] [2003] EWHC 164 (Comm), [2003] 1 Lloyd's Rep. 341.
[242] Judge Chambers Q.C., sitting as a Judge of the Commercial Court.
[243] [1993] 3 All E.R. 717, affirmed by the Court of Appeal without discussion of this particular point [1994] 2 All E.R. 685.
[244] [1993] 3 All E.R. 717 at 734.

claimant for the whole of the dollars because it had dishonestly assisted in a breach of those trusts.[245]

9–103   This decision is contrary to and therefore inconsistent with the view expressed by Lord Millett that, where a transfer of property is voidable and is effectively avoided, beneficial title to that property revests in the transferor under a resulting trust. While it is obviously somewhat unlikely that the last has yet been heard of Lord Millett's views, it therefore seems, at least for the moment, more appropriate to regard any trusts which arise as a result of a voidable transfer of property as constructive trusts rather than as resulting trusts.

---

[245] See *post*, para 10–161.

CHAPTER 10

CONSTRUCTIVE TRUSTS[1]

I. INTRODUCTION[2]

1. *The Nature of Constructive Trusts*

Constructive trusts arise by operation of law. Unlike all other trusts, a   **10–001**
constructive trust is imposed by the court as a result of the conduct of the
trustee and therefore arises quite independently of the intention of any of
the parties. Exactly which trusts fall within this definition cannot be stated
with the same precision. As Edmund Davies L.J. remarked in *Carl-Zeiss
Stiftung v. Herbert Smith (No.2)*,[3] "English law provides no clear and all-
embracing definition of a constructive trust. Its boundaries have been left
perhaps deliberately vague, so as not to restrict the court by technicalities in
deciding what the justice of a particular case may demand." Judges have
preferred to describe constructive trusts rather than to define them; thus
Deane J. in *Muschinski v. Dodds*[4] described the constructive trust as "a
remedial institution which equity imposes regardless of actual or presumed
agreement or intention (and subsequently protects) to preclude the retention
or assertion of beneficial ownership to property to the extent that such
retention or assertion would be contrary to equitable principle". Lord Millett
has stated that a constructive trust "arises by operation of law whenever the
circumstances are such that it would be unconscionable for the owner of
property (usually but not necessarily the legal estate) to assert his own
beneficial interest in the property and deny the beneficial interest of
another".[5]

The lack of a precise definition makes it difficult to determine precisely   **10–002**
what trusts may properly be classified as constructive trusts. The line of
distinction between express and constructive trusts has been blurred by the
fact that, until the enactment of the Limitation Act 1939, express trustees

---

[1] Oakley, *Constructive Trusts* (3rd edn, 1997; 4th edn, 2009, forthcoming) deals specifically
with this topic, as do Elias, *Explaining Constructive Trusts* (1990); Cope, *Constructive Trusts* (1992);
Wright, *The Remedial Constructive Trust* (1998).

[2] See, in addition to the introductory sections of the works cited above: Scott: (1955) 71 L.Q.R.
39; Waters in *Equity and Contemporary Legal Developments* (ed. Goldstein, 1992), p.457; Goff &
Jones, *The Law of Restitution* (7th edn, 2007), Chapter 2.

[3] [1969] 2 Ch. 276 at 300.

[4] (1985) 62 A.L.R. 429 at 451 (High Court of Australia).

[5] *Paragon Finance v. D.B. Thakerar & Co.* [1999] 1 All E.R. 400 at 408. Millett L.J., as he then was,
accepted that a constructive trust will arise outside the scope of this description where "the
defendant has assumed the duties of a trustee by a lawful transaction which was independent
of and preceded the breach of trust and is not impeached by the plaintiff".

were unable to rely on the Statutes of Limitation as against the beneficiaries whereas the limitation period ran in favour of potential constructive trustees; this encouraged the courts to classify as express trusts certain trusts which were clearly nothing of the sort.[6] There has also been, historically, some confusion between resulting trusts and constructive trusts and, as has already been seen,[7] some judges have continued to use the terms almost interchangeably when endeavouring to establish the existence and extent of beneficial ownership of residential family property.[8]

10–003   However, some classifications are well-established, long-settled, and generally agreed. All the commentators accept that the following three situations give rise to the imposition of a constructive trust: first, where advantages have been obtained by fiduciaries breaching their duty of loyalty[9]; secondly, where there has been a disposition of trust property in breach of trust[10]; and, thirdly, where advantages have been obtained by fraudulent or unconscionable conduct.[11] However, there are certain other types of trust whose classification is more controversial. Such trusts include secret trusts,[12] the trusts which arise as a result of the making of mutual wills,[13] as a result of the creation of contracts of sale which are specifically enforceable,[14] as a result of the exercise by mortgagees of their powers under their mortgage,[15] and in order to give effect in equity to transfers of property which are at law incomplete.[16] These types of trust are extremely difficult to classify and have been classified in many different ways by different commentators. It is, however, suggested that all these types of trusts other than secret trusts should properly be classified as constructive trusts.

10–004   The imposition of a constructive trust potentially produces liabilities both of a proprietary and of a personal nature for the constructive trustee. Given the inherent nature of a trust as a relationship in respect of property, the imposition of a constructive trust necessarily confers on the beneficiary proprietary rights in the subject matter of the constructive trust, while the constructive trustee is necessarily subject to the liability which is imposed on every trustee to account personally to his beneficiary for his actions as trustee. However, the court is able to specify the precise moment at which the constructive trust takes effect and, consequently, the moment at which these proprietary rights and fiduciary obligations come into existence. As Millett J. observed in *Lonhro Plc v. Fayed (No.2)*,[17] "it is a mistake to suppose that in every situation in which a constructive trust arises the legal owner is necessarily subject to all the fiduciary obligations and disabilities of an express trustee".

---

[6] See *Soar v. Ashwell* (1893) 2 Q.B. 390, *Paragon Finance v. D.B. Thakerar & Co.* [1999] 1 All E.R. 400.

[7] See *ante*, para 2–012.

[8] See *Hussey v. Palmer* [1972] 1 W.L.R. 1286 at 1289.

[9] See Section II of this chapter, *post*, para 10–046.

[10] See Section III of this chapter, *post*, para 10–153.

[11] See Section IV of this chapter, *post*, para 10–240.

[12] See *ante*, para 4–051.

[13] See Section V of this chapter, *post*, para 10–313.

[14] See Section VI of this chapter, *post*, para 10–333.

[15] See Section VII of this chapter, *post*, para 10–337.

[16] See *ante*, para 5–026 and Section VIII of this chapter, *post*, para 10–339.

[17] [1992] 1 W.L.R. 1 at 12.

It might be expected to follow from the inherent nature of a trust that a   **10–005**
constructive trust can only be imposed if there is some identifiable property
upon which to impose it, in other words that the property which is the
subject matter of the trust must be able to be identified in the hands of the
constructive trustee, either at the time when the matter is brought before the
courts or at some earlier stage. There has long been authority for this
proposition[18] and it does indeed now seem to be accepted that it is inappropriate to use the expressions "constructive trust" or "constructive trustee" except in relation to identifiable property.[19]

However, when liability is imposed upon a person who has in one way or   **10–006**
another dishonestly assisted in bringing about a disposition of trust property in breach of trust,[20] such a person is often said to be a constructive
trustee whether or not any of the property disposed of in breach of trust has
ever been in that person's hands. The existence of authorities in which this
has been said has led some commentators to contend that there is a second
type of constructive trust which can arise without any necessity for there to
be any identifiable trust property[21]; indeed, in *Westdeutsche Landesbank
Girozentrale v. Islington L.B.C.*,[22] Lord Browne-Wilkinson specifically said
that the "only apparent exception" to the rule that there must be identifiable
trust property "is a constructive trust imposed on a person who dishonestly
assists in a breach of trust". No proprietary rights can conceivably be
acquired by anyone beneficially entitled under a trust without identifiable
property. Consequently, the existence of "this apparent exception" does not
serve any obvious purpose; what is the point of creating an exception to the
general rule requiring identifiable trust property if the exception so created
does not enjoy the principal advantage conferred by the existence of a trust
in the first place? The best which can be said for this alleged second type of
constructive trust is that it is "a fiction which provides a useful remedy
where no remedy is available in contract or in tort".[23]

In any event, the opposing view, that the imposition of this kind of   **10–007**
liability does not give rise to the imposition of a constructive trust, is now
increasingly prevalent. In *Dubai Aluminium Co. v. Salaam*,[24] Lord Millett,
building on earlier observations which he had made both judicially[25] and
extra-judicially,[26] said:

"Equity gives relief against fraud by making any person sufficiently implicated in the fraud accountable in equity. In such a case he is traditionally
(and I have suggested unfortunately) described as a 'constructive trustee'
and is said to be 'liable to account as a constructive trustee'. But he is not in
fact a trustee at all, even though he may be liable to account as if he were.

---

[18] *Re Barney* [1892] 2 Ch. 265 at 273.
[19] See the remarks of Lord Millett in *Dubai Aluminium Co. v. Salaam* [2003] 2 A.C. 366.
[20] See Section III of this chapter, *post*, para 10–153.
[21] See Ford & Lee, *Principles of the Law of Trusts* (looseleaf) para.22020 and previous editions of Hayton & Marshall, *op.cit.* (e.g. the 9th edn, 1991, pp.440–441).
[22] [1996] A.C. 669 at 705.
[23] Hayton (1985) 27 Malaya Law Review 313, 314.
[24] [2002] UKHL 48, [2003] 2 A.C. 366 at 404.
[25] As Millett J. in *Agip (Africa) v. Jackson* [1990] Ch. 265 at 291.
[26] In, among other places, 114 L.Q.R. (1998) 399 at 399–400.

He never claims to assume the position of trustee on behalf of others, and he may be liable without ever receiving or handling the trust property. . . . In this second class of case the expressions 'constructive trust' and 'constructive trustee' create a trap. . . . The expressions are 'nothing more than a formula for equitable relief'[27] . . . I think that we should now discard the words 'accountable as constructive trustee' in this context and substitute the words 'accountable in equity'."

Lord Millett's terminology is clearly preferable and it is to be hoped that it is universally adopted. That does not alter the fact that it is convenient to deal with the liability imposed upon a person who has dishonestly assisted in bringing about a disposition of trust property in breach of trust at the same time as other liabilities which on any view give rise to the imposition of a constructive trust[28]; this is because virtually all the authorities concern attempts to impose both types of liabilities, although not necessarily on the same defendants. For that reason, both are considered in this chapter.[29]

2. The Effect of the Imposition of a Constructive Trust[30]

(A) When Does a Constructive Trust Take Effect?

10–008   For a number of reasons, it is important to know at precisely what moment a constructive trust takes effect. The moment at which the constructive trust takes effect will determine the extent to which the rights of the constructive beneficiary will be binding upon third parties, whether the general creditors of the constructive trustee or any person to whom the property which forms the subject matter of the constructive trust has been transferred. Further, as from the moment at which the constructive trust takes effect, the constructive beneficiary will be entitled to any income or other fruits produced by the property which forms the subject matter of the constructive trust.

10–009   It seems to be generally accepted that, in the absence of any judicial order to the contrary, a constructive trust will take effect from the moment at which the conduct which has given rise to its imposition occurs. This was specifically held by Browne-Wilkinson J. in Re Sharpe (a Bankrupt)[31] and has been assumed without discussion on many other occasions. It is for this reason that the interest of a beneficiary under a constructive trust is binding on the trustee in bankruptcy of the constructive trustee and takes priority over the claims of his general creditors[32]; such an interest is also capable of taking priority over third party purchasers of the property or interests in

---

[27] Referring to Selangor United Rubber Co. v. Cradock (No.3) [1968] 1 W.L.R. 1555, 1582 per Ungoed-Thomas J.

[28] In particular, liability for receiving trust property with knowledge that it was being transferred in breach of trust.

[29] See Section III of this Chapter, post, para 10–153.

[30] See Equity and Contemporary Legal Developments (ed. Goldstein, 1992), p.427.

[31] [1980] 1 W.L.R. 219 at 225.

[32] As was held in Re Sharpe (a Bankrupt) [1980] 1 W.L.R. 219 at 225. See particularly Re Polly Peck (No.2) [1998] 3 All E.R. 812 at 827, where the Court of Appeal specifically held that one particular type of constructive trust (a remedial constructive trust) cannot be imposed if the effect of its imposition is to modify the statutory scheme establishing the order in which the assets of a bankrupt or insolvent person are to be distributed to his creditors; see post, para 10–038.

that property[33] provided that the third party in question has not taken free
of the beneficial interest in question.[34] Further, any order that the constructive trustee should account for income or profits has effect as from the
date upon which the constructive trust took effect.[35] Since the vast majority
of constructive trusts are imposed because of the circumstances in which the
constructive trustee has acquired the property which forms the subject
matter of the constructive trust, that trust will, therefore, normally take
effect from the moment at which the constructive trustee acquires the property in question. However, this is not an absolute rule; there are circumstances in which the conduct which has given rise to the imposition of a
constructive trust occurs only some time after the acquisition of the property
by the constructive trustee.[36] In this case, consistent with the general rule,
the constructive trust will obviously only take effect from the moment at
which that conduct occurred.

It is anyway clear that the general rule is capable of being varied by the   **10–010**
court in any individual case. The court is free to specify the precise moment
at which the constructive trust takes effect and can therefore modify the
effect of its imposition both on third parties and on the constructive trustee
himself. Thus, in *Muschinski v. Dodds*[37] the High Court of Australia imposed
a constructive trust to give effect to a variation in the beneficial interests in
property purchased by an unmarried couple but expressly held that, in
order to avoid any possible prejudice to third parties, the constructive trust
imposed in that case would take effect only as from the date of the publication of the judgments. In the same sort of way, in *Lonhro v. Fayed (No.2)*[38]
Millett J. stated that, in the event that the victim of a fraudulent misrepresentation elects to avoid the contract, the representor thereafter holds
its subject matter on constructive[39] trust for that victim but is not retrospectively subject to all the fiduciary obligations of an express trustee in
respect of the period before the contract was avoided. These statements
merely re-emphasise the universality of the general rule.

(B) How Does a Constructive Trust Take Effect?

There is some doubt as to whether a constructive trust takes effect automat-   **10–011**
ically or whether it can only take effect as the result of a court order
providing for its imposition. The question has not as yet had to be decided

---

[33] As in *Belmont Finance Corporation v. Williams Furniture (No.2)* [1980] 1 All E.R. 393.

[34] As in *Thompson's Trustee v. Heaton* [1974] 1 W.L.R. 605.

[35] As in *Boardman v. Phipps* [1967] 2 A.C. 46.

[36] As in *Bannister v. Bannister* [1948] W.N. 261; *Lyus v. Prowsa Developments* [1982] 2 All E.R.
953; *Ungurian v. Lesnoff* [1989] Ch. 206.

[37] (1986) 160 C.L.R. 583.

[38] [1992] 1 W.L.R. 1 at 11–12.

[39] Millett J. subsequently stated in *El Ajou v. Dollar Land Holdings* [1993] 3 All E.R. 717 at 734,
post, p.393, that "the trust which is operating in these cases is . . . an old fashioned institutional
resulting trust". However, in the Commercial Court in *Papamichael v. National Westminster Bank*
[2003] EWHC 164 (Comm), [2003] 1 Lloyd's Rep. 341, it was held that this statement was "all
very well, but Lord Browne-Wilkinson was specific in saying [in *Westdeutsche Landesbank
Girozentrale v. Islington L.B.C.* [1996] A.C. 669] that what was being imposed was an institutional
constructive trust not a resulting trust" and the judge therefore proceeded on the basis that the
trust in question was a constructive trust rather than a resulting trust.

definitively in any English case and there is some disagreement between the commentators as to the effect of the decisions in other jurisdictions.[40]

10–012   This question was considered in *Chase Manhattan Bank v. Israel (British) Bank*[41] by Goulding J., who held that, at least under the law of the State of New York (with which the case was primarily concerned), a court order is not necessary. This view was also adopted by a bare majority of the Supreme Court of Canada in *Rawluk v. Rawluk*.[42] These decisions were unquestionably influenced by the fact that, as will be seen later in this section,[43] the common law jurisdictions of both the United States of America and Canada recognise the constructive trust as a general equitable remedy, something which English law has so far declined to do. Further, doubt has anyway now been cast on both these decisions by the subsequent highly controversial decision of the United States Federal Court of Appeals in *Re Omegas Group*,[44] also considered later in this section,[45] that the imposition of a constructive trust does not, as a matter of American bankruptcy law, give the beneficiary priority over the general creditors of a constructive trustee who is already bankrupt.

10–013   Consequently, it is suggested that, at least in this jurisdiction, the better view is that a constructive trust should be able to take effect only as the result of a court order. The manner in which this question is resolved does not in any way affect priorities as between the beneficiary and third parties but may affect the fiscal position of the beneficiary; if a constructive trust can take effect without any need for a court order, the beneficiary may find himself liable to income tax and capital gains tax on an interest arising under a constructive trust which he has never claimed and never enjoyed. It is, therefore, very much to the advantage of the beneficiary that a constructive trust should not be able to take effect without a court order.

(C)   The Position of the Constructive Beneficiary

10–014   As has already been seen,[46] the interest of a beneficiary under a constructive trust is binding on the trustee in bankruptcy of the constructive trustee and takes priority over the claims of his general creditors; this is the case whether the constructive trustee is already bankrupt at the relevant time or becomes bankrupt thereafter.[47]

(1)   The distinct proprietary and personal liabilities of the constructive trustee

10–015   The position of the constructive beneficiary who chooses to rely on his proprietary rights will obviously primarily depend on the precise nature of the constructive trust which has been imposed; he will clearly have the

---

[40] The principal disagreement is between the two principal American practitioners works, *Scott on Trusts* and *Bogert: Trusts and Trustees*.

[41] [1981] Ch. 105 *passim*.

[42] (1990) 65 D.L.R. (4th) 161.

[43] See *post*, paras 10–027, 10–032.

[44] (1994) 16 Fed. 3d. 1443.

[45] See *post*, para 10–031.

[46] See *ante*, para 10–009.

[47] This may no longer be the position in the common law jurisdictions of the United States of America; see *Re Omegas Group* (1994) 16 Fed. 3d. 1443, *supra* and *post*, para 10–031.

rights appropriate to the interest in the trust property to which he has been held to be entitled.

(1) In the event that the beneficiary is held to have an absolute interest in the property in question, he will obviously be entitled to call for the transfer of that property to him together with any income or other fruits which the property has produced since the moment at which the constructive trust took effect.[48]

(2) In the event that the beneficiary is held to have some lesser interest, his position, at least in relation to the property in question, will be exactly the same as if that interest had been expressly created. Thus, where the beneficiary of a constructive trust is held to have a concurrent interest in land,[49] his rights to enforce that interest against a third party or to obtain an order for sale of the property will be determined by exactly the same criteria as apply to a co-ownership which has arisen as the result of an express or statutory trust of land.[50] The position is similar where the beneficiary is held to have a limited interest in land; thus when a constructive trust is imposed to enforce lifetime occupancy rights, the life interest thus conferred on the beneficiary will equally take effect as if it had been expressly created.[51]

(3) It is also possible, although much less common in practice, for the beneficiary to be given an interest by way of lien or charge in order to secure his right to a payment; this has been done[52] to secure a profit made by agents of a trust who utilised confidential income acquired in the course of representing the trust to acquire with their own funds a majority shareholding in a private company of which the trust was a substantial minority shareholder—had the profit not been paid over, the beneficiary, like the holder of any other charge, could have forced a sale of the shares.

---

[48] See *Re Duke of Marlborough* [1894] 2 Ch. 133; *Re Macadam* [1946] Ch. 73, discussed *post*, para 20–051; *Williams v. Barton* [1927] 2 Ch. 9, discussed *post*, para 10–077; *Lyell v. Kennedy* (1889) 14 App.Cas. 437, discussed para 10–160; *Belmont Finance Corporation v. Williams Furniture (No.2)* [1980] 1 All E.R. 393, discussed *post*, para 10–215.

[49] By virtue of having made direct or indirect financial or other contributions towards its acquisition. See *Burns v. Burns* [1984] Ch. 317 and *Grant v. Edwards* [1986] Ch. 638, discussed *post*, para 10–291 *et seq. passim*.

[50] These criteria are now contained in the Trusts of Land and Appointment of Trustees Act 1996.

[51] Under a trust of land pursuant to the Trusts of Land and Appointment of Trustees Act 1996. Prior to this legislation, such a beneficiary would usually have become a tenant for life under the Settled Land Act 1925 which had the inconvenient result of conferring on him full administrative powers to deal with the property (see *Ungurian v. Lesnoff* [1990] Ch. 206 and *Costello v. Costello* [1996] 1 F.L.R. 805). However, under the Trusts of Land and Appointment of Trustees Act 1996 these powers remain vested in the constructive trustee.

[52] In *Phipps v. Boardman* [1964] 1 W.L.R 993 (Ch.D.)—this decision was subsequently affirmed by both appellate courts without any comments being made as to the nature of the constructive trust imposed.

10–016　　If the beneficiary chooses instead to rely on the personal liability of the constructive trustee to account, he will in effect be claiming equitable compensation for breach of trust from the constructive trustee. He will thus recover the value of whatever interest he is held to have in the subject matter of the constructive trust, valued as at the moment at which the constructive trust took effect, together with interest thereon. (This is also the remedy, and usually the only remedy, available where a person is accountable in equity for having dishonestly assisted in bringing about a disposition of trust property in breach of trust, a liability classified by some, it has already been suggested wrongly,[53] as arising under a constructive trust). Since such reliance on the personal liability of the constructive trustee to account is normally[54] alternative to reliance on the beneficiary's proprietary rights, payment by the constructive trustee of the appropriate sum will have the effect of discharging those proprietary rights; consequently, the constructive trustee will thereafter be absolutely beneficially entitled to the property upon which the constructive trust was imposed.[55]

(2) The choice of remedy when the property is still in the hands of the constructive trustee

10–017　When the property upon which the constructive trust is imposed is still identifiable in the hands of the constructive trustee, the beneficiary will be able to choose either to exercise his proprietary rights or to rely on the personal liability of the constructive trustee to account or, in rare circumstances, to exercise both of these remedies.

10–018　　Where the constructive trustee is solvent, the election between these two remedies will not normally have any particularly significant effects on the measure of the recovery of the beneficiary.

　　(1) As has already been seen, reliance on his proprietary rights will entitle the beneficiary to recover the appropriate interest in the property together with any income or other fruits which the property has produced since the moment at which the constructive trust took effect, while reliance on the personal liability of the constructive trustee to account will entitle the beneficiary to recover the value of the appropriate interest at the moment at which the constructive trust took effect together with interest thereon.

　　(2) Consequently, if any increase in the value of the property plus the value of any income or other fruits which it has produced is more or less the same as the interest payable on the value of the property since the moment at which the constructive trust took effect, there will be no financial advantage in the beneficiary electing for one

---

[53] See *ante*, para 10–006 and *post*, para 10–161.

[54] Save in the unusual situation where the beneficiary seeks to rely on both the remedies available to him. See the next paragraph.

[55] Thus, once the agents of the trust referred to in the previous paragraph of the text had paid their profit to the constructive beneficiary, they would have once again become absolute owners of the shares which they had purchased and could have retained them indefinitely. However, in such circumstances prudence would normally dictate an immediate sale of the shares at that point in order to forestall any possibility of the beneficiary coming back with a claim for future income or capital profits.

remedy rather than for the other. This is only likely not to be the case in the event of a substantial rise or a substantial fall in the value of the property, when it will obviously be to the advantage of the beneficiary to opt respectively for his proprietary rights or for the personal liability of the constructive trustee to account.

(3) The only exception to this will be where it can be shown that any fall in the value of the property was the responsibility of the constructive trustee. In this event, there seems no reason why the beneficiary should not alternatively seek to rely on both the remedies available to him; if this is indeed possible, he will be able both to claim the appropriate interest in the property in question and, by relying on the personal liability of the constructive trustee to account, to obtain damages for the fall in value of the property. While this will not of course increase the total measure of recovery, it will enable the beneficiary to recover the property itself. There seems no reason whatsoever why such a process should not be possible in an appropriate case.

Where, on the other hand, the constructive trustee is insolvent, the election between the two remedies will be immensely significant.　**10–019**

(1) If the beneficiary chooses to rely on his proprietary rights, he will take priority over the general creditors of the insolvent constructive trustee, whereas if he instead chooses to rely on the personal liability of the constructive trustee to account, he will rank with, rather than ahead of, the general creditors.

(2) Consequently, the only situation in which the beneficiary is likely to choose to rely on the personal liability of the constructive trustee to account will be where the property which is the subject matter of the constructive trust has fallen in value to a percentage of its original value smaller than the percentage which is likely to be paid out by the trustee in bankruptcy to the general creditors.

(3) In such circumstances, in the event that it can be shown that the constructive trustee was responsible for the fall in value of the property, it will always be in the interest of the beneficiary to take advantage of the possibility of relying on both the remedies available to him in order both to recover the appropriate interest in the property in question and to claim damages for the fall in its value; this is because such a double claim will give him both the property and the same percentage of the claim for damages as is paid out to the general creditors.

However, except in the extremely unlikely situation which has just been considered, the beneficiary will, in the event of the insolvency of the constructive trustee, inevitably choose to rely on his proprietary rights so as to obtain priority over the general creditors. This will in turn diminish the mass of general assets available for distribution among the general creditors of the insolvent trustee so that each general creditor will therefore obtain a smaller proportion of the sum owed to him. Thus, the imposition of a　**10–020** constructive trust upon a person who is, or subsequently becomes, bankrupt will almost inevitably prejudice the interests of his general creditors, who will *ex hypothesi* not be before the court to object to the imposition of the constructive trust in question. In such circumstances, the only possibility of avoiding the consequent prejudice to the interests of the general creditors will be for the trustee in bankruptcy of the constructive trustee to go to the court under section 340 of the Insolvency Act 1986[56] in order to seek an order setting aside the constructive trust on the grounds that its imposition has given a preference to the beneficiary. Such a claim was successfully made in *Re Densham (A Bankrupt)*[57] but, as that case demonstrates, it is often a matter of pure chance whether the legislation is applicable and so this possibility cannot be regarded as a substantial safeguard for the interests of the general creditors.

(3) The choice of remedy when the property is no longer in the hands of the constructive trustee

10–021   When the property upon which the constructive trust is imposed is no longer identifiable in the hands of the constructive trustee, the property may nevertheless still be identifiable in the hands of a third party. In such circumstances, it will be possible for the beneficiary to recover the property by following it in equity into the hands of that third party, unless the latter is able to establish one of the accepted defences to the beneficiary's equitable proprietary claims; these include the defence of bona fide purchase for value of a legal interest in the property without notice of the beneficiary's adverse claim (or, in the case of property not subject to the equitable doctrine of notice, the statutory equivalent) and the defence of change of position. Such an equitable proprietary claim is possible because the imposition of a constructive trust gives rise to the relationship of trustee and beneficiary which, on any view, is sufficient to satisfy the prerequisites of such a claim.[58]

10–022   Where the trust property can be followed in this way into the hands of a third party, the situation will differ very little from that which has already been discussed. The beneficiary will have a choice between, on the one hand, exercising his proprietary rights in the subject matter of the constructive trust by following that property into the hands of the third party and, on the other hand, relying on the personal liability of the constructive trustee to account. The election between the two remedies will be dependant on exactly the same factors as have already been discussed. Where both the third party and the constructive trustee are solvent, the only relevant factors will be any changes in the value of the property, the presence or absence of income and other fruits, and the amount of interest payable by the constructive trustee. Where, on the other hand, the constructive trustee is insolvent, the beneficiary will almost always choose to rely on his proprietary rights and pursue his equitable proprietary claim against the third party.

---

[56] See *ante*, para 7–056.
[57] [1975] 1 W.L.R. 1519 (this case concerned the previous statutory provision, Bankruptcy Act 1914, s.42).
[58] See *post*, para 22–133.

It may, on the other hand, not be possible to recover the property upon   **10–023**
which the constructive trust has been imposed. This will be the case where
the property either has disappeared as the result of casual expenditure or
dissipation by the constructive trustee or a third party, or has reached the
hands of a third party against whom it is not possible to maintain an
equitable proprietary claim because he is able to establish one of the
accepted defences to such claims. In such circumstances, the only remedy
available to the beneficiary will be to rely on the personal liability of the
constructive trustee to account. Where the constructive trustee is solvent,
this will not normally produce any particularly significant disadvantage.
Where, on the other hand, the constructive trustee is insolvent, the absence
of any proprietary rights will prevent the beneficiary from being able to
claim priority over the general creditors of the constructive trustee since the
liability of the constructive trustee to account will rank with, rather than
ahead of, the claims of the general creditors.[59]

(4)   The remedy where there has never been any identifiable property
It has already been seen[60] that some commentators have contended that   **10–024**
there is a second kind of constructive trust, which can arise without any
necessity for there to be any identifiable trust property, a view which has
received judicial support at the highest level.[61] Constructive trusts of this
type allegedly arise where liability is imposed for having dishonestly
assisted in a disposition of trust property in breach of trust. It has already
been suggested[62] that it is preferable to adopt an alternative view which has
also received judicial support at the highest level[63] and instead classify a
person upon whom liability is imposed for this reason as being merely
accountable in equity to the beneficiaries of the trust in question. However,
no matter how this liability is classified, there is no doubt at all about its
nature. The absence of any identifiable property prevents any proprietary
claim from being available. Consequently, the beneficiaries in question will
have no choice of remedy; all that they can do is to rely on the personal
liability to account which has been imposed. Their rights will, therefore,
enjoy no priority over the general creditors of the person on whom liability
has been imposed and will rank with, rather than ahead of, the claims of
those creditors in the event of his insolvency.

3. *When and on what Grounds will a Constructive Trust be Imposed?*

The most important single factor that will determine when, and on what   **10–025**
grounds, a constructive trust will be imposed is the role which the courts
consider that the constructive trust occupies in the legal system as a whole.
Their perception of this role must inevitably take into account the various

---

[59] See *Selangor United Rubber Estates v. Cradock (No.3)* [1968] 1 W.L.R. 1555.
[60] See *ante*, para 10–006.
[61] From Lord Browne-Wilkinson in *Westdeutsche Landesbank Girozentrale v. Islington L.B.C.*
[1996] A.C. 669 at 705.
[62] See *ante*, para 10–007.
[63] From Lord Millett in *Dubai Aluminium Co. v. Salaam* [2002] UKHL 48, [2003] 2 A.C. 366 at
404.

possible consequences of the imposition of a constructive trust which have just been considered. In this respect, the different common law jurisdictions adopt different approaches.

10–026   The crucial issue is whether or not the jurisdiction in question is prepared to impose what is known as a remedial constructive trust. In the Court of Appeal of New Zealand in *Fortex Group v. MacIntosh*[64] Tipping J. summarised the difference between remedial constructive trusts and other types of constructive trusts, which he described as institutional constructive trusts, as follows.

"An institutional constructive trust is one which arises by operation of the principles of equity and whose existence the court simply recognises in a declaratory way. A remedial constructive trust is one which is imposed by the court as a remedy in circumstances where, before the order of the court, no trust of any kind existed.

The difference between the two types of constructive trust, institutional and remedial, is that an institutional constructive trust arises upon the happening of the events which bring it into being. Its existence is not dependent on any order of the court. Such order simply recognises that it came into being at the earlier time and provides for its implementation in whatever way is appropriate. A remedial constructive trust depends for its very existence on the order of the court; such order being creative rather than simply confirmatory. This description should not be regarded as definitive or as precluding further developments in this area of the law when greater refinement may be necessary."

In stating that the existence of an institutional constructive trust is not dependent on any order of the court, Tipping J. was adopting the view taken by Goulding J. in *Chase Manhattan Bank v. Israel (British) Bank*[65] as to the law of the State of New York and the view of the Supreme Court of Canada, by a bare majority, in *Rawluk v. Rawluk*[66] rather than the view preferred by this work that, at least in this jurisdiction, a constructive trust should be able to take effect only as the result of an order of the court. [67] However, what is relevant for present purposes is the different bases of the two types of constructive trust rather than precisely what brings institutional constructive trusts into effect.

(A) The Approach Adopted in the United States of America

(1) When will a constructive trust be imposed?

10–027 The common law jurisdictions of the United States of America have long regarded the constructive trust as an instrument for remedying unjust

---

[64] [1998] 3 N.Z.L.R. 171 at 172–173.
[65] [1981] Ch. 105 *passim*.
[66] (1990) 65 D.L.R.(4th) 161.
[67] See *ante*, para.10–013.

enrichment. Thus a constructive trust may be imposed whenever the constructive trustee has been unjustly enriched by receiving some item of property at the expense of the constructive beneficiary. In other words, all that has to be shown is that the constructive trustee has received some item of property which, as against the beneficiary, he cannot justly retain. This does not mean that a constructive trust will be imposed whenever unjust enrichment is found to exist; a constructive trust is merely one of a number of remedies available to the court and will be imposed when the court feels that it is appropriate to give the victim of the unjust enrichment a proprietary remedy. For this reason, this type of constructive trust is generally known as a remedial constructive trust.

The origin of this view of the constructive trust was *The Restatement of the Law of Restitution* published by the American Law Institute in 1937; paragraph 160 provides: "Where a person holding title to property is subject to an equitable duty to convey it to another on the ground that he would be unjustly enriched if he were permitted to retain it, a constructive trust arises." This provision unquestionably represents the attitude of the judges. As Cardozo J. has remarked[68]: "A constructive trust is the formula through which the conscience of equity finds expression. When property has been acquired in such circumstances that the holder of the legal title may not in good conscience retain the beneficial interest, equity converts him into a trustee." The principle of unjust enrichment is the underlying basis of the "principal types of situations in which a constructive trust is imposed"[69]; whether a constructive trust is imposed therefore depends on the presence or absence of unjust enrichment, not on whether the case can be brought within one of the distinct situations which English law recognises as giving rise to the imposition of a constructive trust.   **10–028**

However, the principle of unjust enrichment is not an absolute prerequisite of the imposition of a remedial constructive trust. Such trusts will also be imposed where property is obtained by mistake or by fraud or other wrong, whether or not the constructive trustee has been unjustly enriched.[70] The extent to which such constructive trusts are indeed remedies[71] and the extent to which they are distinguished from both express and resulting trusts is demonstrated by the fact that the constructive trust is not even included within the definition of a trust in *The Restatement of Trusts*; this is of course why constructive trusts are considered in *The Restatement of Restitution* rather than in *The Restatement of Trusts*.   **10–029**

(2)   The effect of the imposition of a constructive trust

In principle, as in this jurisdiction,[72] the imposition of a constructive trust in the common law jurisdictions of the United States of America gives the   **10–030**

---

[68] In *Beatty v. Guggenheim Exploration Co.* (1919) 225 N.Y. 380 at 386, 122 N.E. 378 (New York Court of Appeals).
[69] Seavey and Scott (1938) 54 L.Q.R. 29, 42.
[70] *Scott on Trusts* (4th edn, 1989 with cumulative supplements), para.461.
[71] The remedial theory of the constructive trust is considered in Cope, *op.cit.*, pp.24–49; Wright, *op.cit. passim*; Rotherham, *Property and Proprietary Remedies* (2002) Chap.1. See also Birks and Gardner in *Frontiers of Liability* (ed. Birks, 1994), Vol. II, pp.214, 186.
[72] See *ante*, para 10–009.

beneficiary priority over the general creditors of the constructive trustee. The courts of these jurisdictions have for many decades been much more ready than the English courts to interfere with existing third party rights. A claimant is permitted to bring an equitable proprietary claim whenever he can show that that property has been wrongfully disposed of with knowledge of the wrongful nature of the disposition[73] (the existence of a pre-existing equitable proprietary interest is not, as in English law, a prerequisite of such a claim[74]) and, when he is permitted so to do, will inevitably obtain priority over the third party creditors of the other party. The fact that the imposition of a remedial constructive trust brings about a similar alteration of priorities has therefore not been, of itself, a particularly significant consideration.

10–031   However, in 1994 in *Re Omegas Group*,[75] the Federal Court of Appeals held that a mere entitlement to a beneficial interest under a constructive trust does not, as a matter of American bankruptcy law, give the person entitled to that interest priority over the general creditors of the constructive trustee; such priority only arises where the constructive trust in question has actually been imposed prior to his bankruptcy or insolvency. This decision has been criticised[76] as being contrary both to binding precedent[77] and to the intention of the Bankruptcy Code. However, unless and until it is reversed,[78] its effect is to prevent the general creditors of a bankrupt whom a state court declares to be a constructive trustee from being adversely affected by the imposition of that trust.[79] Consequently, at least for the moment, the imposition of a remedial constructive trust will only adversely affect the third party creditors of the constructive trustee if he is not yet bankrupt at the time; however, if that is the case, its imposition will adversely affect them even if he becomes bankrupt thereafter and even if his bankruptcy occurs as a direct result of the imposition of the constructive trust. This of course makes the effect of the imposition of a constructive trust in the United States of America even more random than it was before. It obviously remains to be seen whether what has been described[80] as the "unravelling" of the remedial constructive trust in the United States of America as a result of the decision in *Re Omegas Group* is upheld or whether the law reverts to what it was formerly thought to be. However, the imposition of a remedial constructive trust is on any view still clearly capable of affecting the interests of third party creditors.

---

[73] *American Restatement of the Law of Restitution*, para. 202. See also Scott (1955) 71 L.Q.R. 39, 48.

[74] See *post*, para 22–133.

[75] (1994) 16 Fed. 3d. 1443.

[76] Kull (1998) 72 American Bankruptcy L.J. 265.

[77] See the decision of the United States Supreme Court in *Cunningham v. Brown* (1923) 265 U.S. 1 at 11.

[78] In *Re Dow Corning Corp.* (1996) 192 B.R. 428, some of what were described as the "broad statements" in *Re Omegas Group* were said to be "clearly in error" but the bankruptcy judge held that he was bound by the decision in that case.

[79] Bankruptcy is a matter of federal law and will therefore prevail over state law in every bankruptcy court.

[80] By Rotherham, *op.cit.* p.60.

(B) The Modified Approach Adopted Elsewhere
Canada and New Zealand have also recognised the possibility of imposing 10–032
remedial constructive trusts. Some 20 years ago Canada recognised the
possibility of doing so on the grounds of unjust enrichment[81] and, although
this remains Canadian law, the stated prerequisites for the imposition of a
constructive trust on this ground[82] now seem closer to the stricter prerequisite of unconscionability which has been adopted much more recently
in New Zealand.[83] The difference is that these jurisdictions do not regard
remedial constructive trusts as all-embracing; instead they regard remedial
constructive trusts as existing side by side with the more traditional situations in which constructive trusts have been imposed.[84]

In none of the cases in which the courts of Canada and New Zealand have 10–033
imposed remedial constructive trusts have there been genuine third party
creditors, as distinct from persons claiming through the constructive trustee,
who have been adversely affected by the imposition of the trust. It therefore
remains to be seen how those jurisdictions will deal with the issue which the
United States Federal Court of Appeals had to decide in *Re Omegas
Group*.[85]

(C) The Approach Adopted in this Jurisdiction
This jurisdiction, like Australia,[86] has not yet accepted the remedial con- 10–034
structive trust as such. The present law is illustrated by the decision of the
Court of Appeal in *Halifax Building Society v. Thomas*.[87] The defendant
obtained a mortgage advance from the plaintiff by fraudulently misrep-
resenting his identity and earnings. The plaintiff, having satisfied all sums
due to it under the mortgage out of the proceeds of sale, sought to retain the
surplus on the basis, *inter alia*, that it was beneficially entitled under a
constructive trust imposed on the defendant in accordance with *The American Restatement of Restitution* to prevent what would otherwise be his unjust
enrichment. The Court of Appeal specifically held that "English law has not
followed other jurisdictions where the constructive trust has become a

---

[81] The Supreme Court of Canada recognized that remedial constructive trusts could be
imposed on the grounds of unjust enrichment in *Pettkus v. Becker* (1980) 117 D.L.R. (3d) 257.
However, the remedial constructive trust has been deployed principally in relation to joint
enterprises by members of a family unit (see *Sorochan v. Sorochan* (1986) 29 D.L.R. (4th) 1; *Peter
v. Beblow* (1993) 101 D.L.R. (4th) 621 (also decisions of the Supreme Court of Canada)) but not
exclusively so (see *Lac Minerals v. International Corona Resources* (1989) 61 D.L.R. (4th) 14
(Supreme Court of Canada)).
[82] Set out in *Korkontzilas v. Soulas* (1997) 146 D.L.R. (4th) 214 at 231.
[83] The Court of Appeal of New Zealand recognized the possibility of imposing remedial
constructive trusts on the grounds of unconscionability in *Fortex Group v. MacIntosh* [1998] 3
N.Z.L.R. 171 but this has so far seems only to have been done in one reported case, in
Commonwealth Reserves 1 v. Chodar [2001] 2 N.Z.L.R. 374 where such a trust was imposed in
order to frustrate attempts to prevent the enforcement of a judgment (see Richardson [2002]
T.L.I. 53).
[84] *Korkontzilas v. Soulos* (1997) 146 D.L.R. (4th) 214. The present Canadian law is considered by
Chambers in [2001] T.L.I. 214 & [2002] T.L.I. 2.
[85] (1994) 16 Fed. 3d. 1443.
[86] Although the possibility of remedial constructive trusts being accepted in Australia was
envisaged by Deane J. in the High Court of Australia in *Muschinski v. Dodds* (1985) 160 C.L.R.
583 at 614–616, this has not yet been done.
[87] [1996] Ch. 217.

remedy for unjust enrichment" and declined "to extend the law of constructive trusts in order to prevent a fraudster benefiting from his wrong".[88]

10–035 Attempts to introduce the remedial constructive trust into English law had however been made with more success in the years immediately before and after 1970, when it did appear that English law might be moving towards an approach similar to that which was some years later adopted in Canada and, later still, in New Zealand. At that time, a number of decisions emanating from the Court of Appeal suggested that a constructive trust "is a trust imposed by law whenever justice and good conscience require it . . . it is an equitable remedy by which the court can enable an aggrieved party to obtain restitution".[89] However, subsequent decisions[90] rejected the approach manifested in this series of cases and English law therefore reverted, at least for the moment, to the traditional attitude towards constructive trusts which has already been described, an attitude which has perhaps been most accurately described by the statement that in England "the constructive trust continues to be seen as an institutional obligation attaching to property in certain specified circumstances".[91]

10–036 However, this attitude has not been universally adopted. In *Metall und Rohstoff A.G. v. Donaldson Lufkin & Jenrette*[92] the Court of Appeal accepted that "there is a good arguable case" that circumstances may arise in which "the court will be prepared to impose a constructive trust *de novo* as a foundation for the grant of equitable remedy by way of account or otherwise", classifying such a trust as a "remedial constructive trust". This isolated remark was subsequently seized on by Lord Browne-Wilkinson in *Westdeutsche Landesbank Girozentrale v. Islington L.B.C.*[93] as a possible justification for a decision[94] that a bank which had received the same sum twice rather than once held the second payment on trust for the mistaken payer; he took the view that "the retention of the moneys after the recipient bank learned of the mistake may well have given rise to a constructive trust"[95] and opined that "the remedial constructive trust, if introduced into English

---

[88] At 229. The surplus had anyway been the subject of a confiscation order under Criminal Justice Act 1988, Pt. 6 in favour of the Crown Prosecution Service so the case was effectively between the plaintiff and the Crown Prosecution Service.

[89] *Hussey v. Palmer* [1972] 1 W.L.R. 1286 at 1290, *per* Lord Denning M.R., who was the principal advocate of this particular development.

[90] See *Burns v. Burns* [1984] Ch. 317; *Grant v. Edwards* [1986] Ch. 638; *Ashburn Anstalt v. Arnold* [1989] Ch. 1. This followed earlier rejections by the Court of Appeal of New South Wales in *Allen v. Snyder* [1977] 2 N.S.W.L.R. 685 and by the High Court of New Zealand in *Avondale Printers and Stationers v. Haggie* [1979] 2 N.Z.L.R. 124.

[91] Waters in *Equity and Contemporary Legal Developments* (ed. Goldstein, 1992), pp.457, 463.

[92] [1990] 1 Q.B. 391 at 479.

[93] [1996] A.C. 669 at 715.

[94] By Goulding J. in *Chase Manhattan Bank v. Israel-British Bank (London)* [1981] Ch. 105; see *ante,* para 10–012, *post,* para 22–152.

[95] [1996] A.C. 669 at 714. His Lordship doubted the conclusion of Goulding J. that a mistaken payment is of itself sufficient to make the recipient a trustee of its subject matter. These remarks were applied and a constructive trust was imposed on this ground in the Commercial Court in *Papamichael v. National Westminster Bank* [2003] 1 Lloyd's Rep. 341. However, this decision is, as a matter of precedent, clearly wrong because of the repeated statements in the Court of Appeal that the remedial constructive trust does not form part of English law and that only the House of Lords can approve such a trust.

law, may provide a more satisfactory road forward".[96] Similar sentiments have been voiced in Australia.[97]

However, Lord Browne-Wilkinson clearly stated that "whether English law should follow the United States and Canada in adopting the remedial constructive trust will have to be decided in some future case when the point is directly in issue".[98] It has been made abundantly clear by the Court of Appeal on a number of occasions[99] that the contention that English law should adopt the remedial constructive trust cannot be maintained other than in the House of Lords. In *Twinsectra v. Yardley*[100] counsel for the claimant[101] would have argued for its adoption, admittedly as an argument of last resort, had the House not accepted the existence of a *Quistclose* trust.[102] There can, therefore, be little doubt that the House of Lords, or its successor the new Supreme Court, will one day be called upon to decide whether to return to the trail blazed by the Court of Appeal immediately before and after 1970 or to retain the more traditional approach adopted before and after that period. However, it is impossible to predict the outcome. The apparent preparedness of Lord Browne-Wilkinson to consider the adoption of the remedial constructive trust is markedly different from the sentiments which have subsequently been expressed by other senior judges. Lord Millett, writing extra-judicially,[103] has described the remedial constructive trust as "a counsel of despair which too readily concedes the impossibility of propounding a general rationale for the availability of proprietary remedies". Which view will be adopted by whichever of their successors have to decide this issue obviously remains to be seen. **10–037**

However, there can be little doubt that the future deliberations of the House of Lords or the Supreme Court will be very heavily influenced by its members' perception of the effects of the imposition of a remedial constructive trust. All of the commentators have thus far assumed that the imposition of such a trust will automatically give the constructive beneficiary priority over the general creditors of the constructive trustee. This was also the assumption of the Court of Appeal in *Re Polly Peck (No.2)*,[104] when it was specifically held that a remedial constructive trust cannot be imposed if the effect of its imposition is to modify the statutory scheme establishing the order in which the assets of a bankrupt or insolvent person are to be distributed to his creditors. This was of course another way of achieving the result arrived at by the United States Federal Court of Appeals in *Re Omegas Group*[105] where it was actually held that the imposition of a constructive trust did not anyway give priority over the general creditors of a constructive trustee who was already bankrupt. However, Nourse L.J. also **10–038**

---

[96] [1996] A.C. 669 at 716.
[97] *Muschinski v. Dodds* (1985) 160 C.L.R. 583 at 615 (Deane J. in the High Court of Australia).
[98] [1996] A.C. 669 at 716.
[99] See, for example, *Twinsectra v. Yardley* [1999] Lloyd's Rep. Bank 438 and *Bank of Credit and Commerce International (Overseas) v. Akindele* [2001] Ch. 437.
[100] [2002] UKHL 12, [2002] 2 A.C. 164.
[101] Who included the author of this edition.
[102] See *ante*, para 9–059.
[103] (1995–96) 6 King's College L.J. 1.
[104] [1998] 3 All E.R. 812 at 827.
[105] (1994) 16 Fed. 3d. 1443.

stated in *Re Polly Peck (No.2)*[106] that it was not seriously arguable that property rights can be varied by the imposition of a remedial constructive trust even if the potential constructive trustee is solvent; this was on the basis that "[i]t is not that you need an Act of Parliament to prohibit a variation of proprietary rights. You need one to permit it."[107] This conclusion is precisely the opposite of what follows from the decision in *Re Omegas Group*.[108] As will be seen below, it is not suggested that English law should adopt the position that the effect of a constructive trust differs depending on whether or not the constructive trustee is already bankrupt; the remedial constructive trust should either be rejected or adopted with all the usual consequences. But this is another reason why the outcome of the future deliberations of the House of Lords or the Supreme Court is not a foregone conclusion.

10–039 For the moment, pending the outcome of those deliberations, it is clear that the English courts, like those in Australia, continue to see the constructive trust "as an institutional obligation attaching to property in certain specified circumstances"[109]; they have, generally speaking, only been prepared to impose a constructive trust when some cause of action against the constructive trustee has arisen independently. It is not enough to say, as in America, that a constructive trustee "is not compelled to convey the property because he is a constructive trustee; it is because he can be compelled to convey that he is a constructive trustee".[110] In order to obtain the imposition of a constructive trust, the beneficiary must be able to demonstrate some legal or equitable wrong by the constructive trustee, be it breach of fiduciary duty, participation in a breach of trust, or fraudulent or unconscionable conduct. Such developments in the law as have occurred have been brought about by the enlargement of the concepts of fiduciary relationship[111] and unconscionable conduct rather than by recourse to the principle of unjust enrichment.[112] For the moment, therefore, the unjust enrichment of the constructive trustee is still not in itself sufficient.

(D) What Should Be the Approach of English Law?

10–040 It has long been argued that the English courts should adopt the remedial constructive trust. "What English law needs", wrote Professor Donovan Waters in 1964, "is a practical, down to earth remedy, as vivid as specific performance and injunction, and within which the courts are brought immediately face to face with the policy decisions or the equities that the courts must and do already make or weigh".[113] The adoption of a remedial constructive trust based on the principle of unjust enrichment has, however,

---

[106] [1998] 3 All E.R. 812 at 831.
[107] Referring to the Variation of Trusts Act 1958 (*post*, para 21–018) and the Matrimonial Causes Act 1973 (*post*, para 10–292).
[108] (1994) 16 Fed. 3d. 1443.
[109] Waters in *Equity and Contemporary Legal Developments* (ed. Goldstein, 1992), pp.457, 463. See also *Re Polly Peck International (No.2)* [1998] 3 All E.R. 812.
[110] *Scott on Trusts* (4th edn, 1987 with cumulative supplements), para. 462.
[111] See section II of this chapter, *post*, para 10–046.
[112] See section IV of this chapter, *post*, para 10–153.
[113] *The Constructive Trust* (1964), p.73; also in *Frontiers of Liability II* (ed. Birks, 1994) Vol. II, p.165. See also Wright, *op.cit., passim*; Rotherham, *op.cit.,* Chap. 1

been rejected by other commentators.[114] As is implicit in some of the recent judicial observations already considered,[115] there is in principle no reason why the categories of situations in which English courts will impose a constructive trust should be regarded as closed. However, the liabilities which arise as the result of the imposition of a constructive trust provide a strong argument against its use as a general equitable remedy to do justice in the instant case in the way in which it is used in the United States of America.

The proprietary nature of the liabilities which arise as the result of the **10–041** imposition of a constructive trust affects the existing property rights both of the constructive trustee and, in the event of his bankruptcy, of his general creditors. As a matter of principle, such alterations of existing property rights should not be able to ensue merely from the desire of a court to do justice in the instant case. It has never been the practice of English courts to alter existing property rights merely in order to do justice inter partes. The House of Lords has repeatedly stated that rights of property are not to be determined according to what is reasonable and fair or just in all the circumstances,[116] a principle which is crucial for the maintenance of that certainty which should be the hallmark of every system of law. The imposition of a constructive trust in the way that the Court of Appeal did immediately before and immediately after 1970 in order to resolve a dispute in a manner which appears to be just and equitable is inevitably contrary to such a principle. The consequences of the imposition of a constructive trust thus constitute powerful arguments against the use of the constructive trust as a means of doing justice *inter partes*.

It has already been seen[117] that in the United States of America these **10–042** important considerations have until recently borne no weight because the courts of its common law jurisdictions have for many decades been much more ready than the English courts to interfere with existing third party rights. Since the rights of third party creditors are generally susceptible to random alteration by the courts, the fact that the imposition of a constructive trust brings about such an alteration of priorities has not been a particularly significant consideration; there has, therefore, been no reason why this should have been specifically taken into account in deciding whether or not a constructive trust should be imposed. However, the decision of the Federal Court of Appeals in *Re Omegas Group*[118] means that, at least for the moment, the imposition of a remedial constructive trust will only adversely affect the third party creditors of the constructive trustee if he has not yet become bankrupt at that time, thus making the effect of the imposition of a remedial constructive trust in the United States of America even more random than it was before.

---

[114] See Cope, *op.cit.*, (1992), p.48 who is, however, prepared to accept that the constructive trust is remedial in nature; Birks in *Frontiers of Liability* (ed. Birks, 1994), Vol. II, pp.214, 223 who rejects the remedial constructive trust outright as "an object of suspicion" and in [1998] T.L.I. 202 writes of its "end" (compare Wright [1999] R.L.R. 128).

[115] See *ante*, para 10–001.

[116] *Pettitt v. Pettitt* [1970] A.C. 777; *Gissing v. Gissing* [1971] A.C. 886; *Lloyds Bank v. Rosset* [1991] 1 A.C. 107.

[117] *ante*, para 10–027.

[118] (1994) 16 Fed. 3d. 1443.

10–043   Whether what has been described[119] as the "unravelling" of the remedial constructive trust in the United States of America as a result of this decision is upheld or whether the law reverts to what it was formerly thought to be, it is at any rate clear both that the English courts are reluctant to interfere with existing property rights whether or not their holder is bankrupt and that the imposition of a constructive trust here adversely affects the interests of the general creditors of the constructive trustee whether or not he is already bankrupt. On any view, therefore, the position is totally different in England. Consequently, the fact that the imposition of a constructive trust has these effects should be a much more significant consideration in England than it is in the United States of America. Its far-reaching ramifications not only for the person upon whom it is imposed but also for third parties mean that its indiscriminate invocation and imposition is, at least in England, therefore highly undesirable.

10–044   Remedial constructive trusts should, therefore, not be invoked and imposed in the way that the Court of Appeal did immediately before and immediately after 1970 as some sort of instant remedy to prevent what the court regards as an unjust result in an individual case. In this sense at least, constructive trusts should not be imposed merely in order to prevent unjust enrichment. This does not mean that the present process whereby the principle of unjust enrichment is gradually being incorporated into English law[120] should not continue, merely that the constructive trust is not an appropriate instrument for dealing out justice inter partes. It would not become an appropriate instrument even if it were to be held that its imposition did not affect the interests of third party creditors; the random alteration of the property interests of the parties which would be produced by its imposition in order to deal out justice as between them would not be satisfactory either.

10–045   Although the categories of situations in which English courts will impose constructive trusts should not be regarded as closed, these categories should be extended only where the courts are prepared to lay down some new principle which will apply generally, as the House of Lords has done on occasions in the past[121]; the principle of unconscionability, so far applicable only in an admittedly increasing number of specific circumstances, could conceivably be converted into a general principle of this type. In any event, no such general principle should be established without the fullest consideration of its probable effects on the interests of third parties and of the possibility of reducing these effects by varying the normal consequences of the imposition of a constructive trust in the way which was done in *Muschinski v. Dodds*[122] and envisaged in *Lonhro v. Fayed (No.2)*[123]; in these respects, different types of constructive trusts should not be held to have

---

[119] By Rotherham, *op.cit.*, p.60.
[120] Most recently in *Lipkin Gorman v. Karpnale* [1991] 2 A.C. 548 (in relation to the defence of change of position); see *post*, p.833 and in *Woolwich Equitable Building Society v. I.R.C.* [1993] A.C. 70 (in relation to the recovery of overpayments of taxes made under statutory instruments subsequently held to be *ultra vires*).
[121] As in *Pettitt v. Pettitt* [1970] A.C. 777; *Gissing v. Gissing* [1971] A.C. 886 and *Lloyds Bank v. Rosset* [1991] 1 A.C. 107.
[122] (1985) 160 C.L.R. 583; see *ante*, para 10–010.
[123] [1992] 1 W.L.R. 1.

different effects on the interests of third parties either generally or just where the constructive trustee happens to be already bankrupt. Finally, any principle laid down must above all be capable of being applied with sufficient certainty to enable litigants to be safely advised as to the probable outcome of legal proceedings.

II. ADVANTAGES OBTAINED BY FIDUCIARIES BREACHING THEIR DUTY OF LOYALTY

One of the best known situations in which constructive trusts are imposed is where a fiduciary has obtained a benefit as a result of a breach of the duty of loyalty which he owes to his principal.[124]

10–046

1. What Relationships will be Classified as Fiduciary?

In *White v. Jones*[125] Lord Browne-Wilkinson said that "the paradigm of the circumstances in which equity will find a fiduciary relationship is where one party, A, has assumed to act in relation to the property or affairs of another, B", while in *Bristol and West Building Society v. Mothew*[126] Millett L.J. said:

10–047

"A fiduciary is someone who has undertaken to act for or on behalf of another in a particular matter in circumstances which give rise to a relationship of trust and confidence. The distinguishing obligation of a fiduciary is the obligation of loyalty. The principal is entitled to the single-minded loyalty of his fiduciary. The core liability has several facets. A fiduciary must act in good faith; he must not make a profit out of his trust; he must not place himself in a position where his duty and his interest may conflict; he may not act for his own benefit or the benefit of a third person without the informed consent of his principal. This is not intended to be an exhaustive list, but it is sufficient to indicate the nature of fiduciary obligations. They are the defining characteristics of the fiduciary."

---

[124] Of the vast literature on this subject, the most relevant work for present purposes is Goff & Jones, *op.cit.* pp.719–764. Books include: Finn, *Fiduciary Obligations* (1977), supplemented by his articles in *Equity, Fiduciaries and Trusts* (ed. Youdan, 1989), p.1, in *Commercial Aspects of Trusts and Fiduciary Obligations* (ed. McKendrick, 1992), p.9, in (ed. Cope, 1995), p.131, and in *Trends in Contemporary Trust Law* (ed. Oakley, 1996) 211; Shepherd, *The Law of Fiduciaries* (1981) (also in 97 L.Q.R. (1981) 51); Glover, *Commercial Equity: Fiduciary Relationships* (1995). Other materials include: Austin 6 O.J.L.S. (1986) 444, in *Equity and Commercial Relationships* (ed. Finn, 1987) 177, and in *Trends in Contemporary Trust Law* (ed. Oakley, 1996) 153; Birks, *An Introduction to the Law of Restitution* (1989) 338 and *passim* and [2002] T.L.I. 34; DeMott, 30 Osgoode Hall L.J. (1992) 472; Flannigan, 9 O.J.L.S. (1989) 285 and 54 Sask.L.R. (1990) 45; Frankel 71 Calif.L.Rev. 795 (1983) and in *Equity, Fiduciaries and Trusts 1993* (ed. Waters, 1993) 173; Maddaugh & McCamus, *The Law of Restitution* (1990) 575–621; Sealy [1962] C.L.J. 69, [1963] C.L.J. 83, [1967] C.L.J. 83, and 9 Journal of Contract Law (1995) 37; Weinrib, 25 Univ.Toronto L.J. (1975) 1.

[125] [1995] 2 A.C. 706 at 728.

[126] [1998] Ch. 1 at 18.

Finn, on whose "classic work"[127] these statements were based, has emphasised that the fiduciary's undertaking "may be of a general character. It may be specific and limited. It is immaterial whether the undertaking is gratuitous. And the undertaking may be officiously assumed without request."[128] A fiduciary is expected "to act in the interests of the other—to act selflessly and with undivided loyalty".[129] This obligation to act selflessly is what distinguishes a person who owes fiduciary obligations from a person who owes merely contractual obligations; the latter is permitted to act in his own self interest, provided that he does not engage in conduct which the courts are prepared to classify as unconscionable.[130]

10–048   The "category of cases in which fiduciary obligations and duties arise from the circumstances of the case and the relationship of the parties is no more closed than the categories of negligence at common law".[131]

(1) Certain relationships are always classified as fiduciary. Traditionally there have been four: trustee and beneficiary; agent and principal; director and company[132]; and partner and co-partner—the relationship in question may either have been expressly created or have arisen as a result of the officious conduct of the alleged fiduciary.[133]

(2) It has also long been clear that the relationship between solicitor and client is fiduciary.[134] However, the solicitor's fiduciary duty is not necessarily to be found in or confined to the terms of his contractual retainer with his client.[135] Thus while, save for a continuing obligation to preserve confidentiality, the fiduciary duty will generally last

---

[127] *Fiduciary Obligations* (1977), so described in *Hooper v. Gorvin* [2001] W.T.L.R. 575 at 590.
[128] *ibid.*, p.201.
[129] Finn in *Equity, Fiduciaries and Trusts* (ed. Youdan, 1989), pp.1, 4.
[130] *ibid.*
[131] *ibid.*
[132] A director does not normally owe fiduciary duties to his shareholders; see *Peskin v. Anderson* [2001] B.C.L.C. 372, *Percival v. Wright* [1902] 2 Ch. 421. However, in *Peskin v. Anderson* Morritt L.J. accepted at 379 that this does not preclude, in special circumstances, the co-existence of additional duties owed by the directors to individual shareholders, citing *Stein v. Blake (No.2)* [1998] 1 All E.R. 727 where Millett L.J. recognised that there may be special circumstances in which a fiduciary duty is owed by a director to a shareholder personally and in which breach of such duty has caused loss to him directly (for example, by being induced by a director to part with his shares at an undervalue), as distinct from loss sustained by him by a diminution in the value of his shares. Morritt L.J. also referred at 380 to *Coleman v. Myers* [1977] 2 N.Z.L.R. 225 (Court of Appeal of New Zealand) and *Brunninghausen v. Glavinics* (1999) 46 N.S.W.L.R. 538 (Court of Appeal of New South Wales), in both of which "fiduciary duties of directors to shareholders were established in the specially strong context of the familial relationships of the directors and shareholders and their relative personal positions of influence in the company concerned".
[133] Thus, a de facto director owes fiduciary duties to the company in question; *Ultraframe (UK) v. Fielding* [2005] EWHC 1638 (Ch), [2007] W.T.L.R. 835 at [1257]. However, a shadow director, a person who directs or instructs those who themselves owe a fiduciary duty to a company, will not usually owe fiduciary duties to that company; *ibid.* [1289].
[134] This was implicit in *Nocton v. Lord Ashburton* [1914] A.C. 14 and was specifically held in *Brown v. I.R.C.* [1965] A.C. 244.
[135] *Hilton v. Barker Booth & Eastwood* [2005] UKHL 8, [2005] 1 W.L.R. 567 at [28–30].

only for as long as his retainer,[136] a relationship of trust and confidence created during the retainer is capable of continuing thereafter.[137]

(3) In the relatively recent past the existence of two further fiduciary relationships, between senior management employee and employer[138] and between member of the Security Services and the Crown,[139] has been confirmed and other additions are possible.[140]

The full range of fiduciary obligations and prohibitions is normally imposed on fiduciaries within these categories, although this does not mean that the position of each is actually the same.[141]

The relationships between accountant and client, broker and client, promoter and company, and guardian and ward have also been held, in certain circumstances and in respect of specific transactions, to be fiduciary and a member of the armed forces of the Crown has even been held to be a fiduciary in respect of his uniform and the opportunities and facilities attached to it.[142] On the other hand, as has already been seen,[143] it has been held that a duty imposed by statute to perform certain functions does not, as a general rule, impose fiduciary obligations and that the presumption is, in the absence of indications to the contrary in the statute, that no such obligations are imposed[144]; it has also been held that the Crown will not become a fiduciary unless it deliberately chooses so to do.[145]

10–049

To what extent should fiduciary obligations be imposed outside the traditional categories? This question is relevant because such obligations are capable of giving rise to the imposition of a constructive trust. Such a trust was indeed imposed in *Hooper v. Gorvin*,[146] where one of a number of

10–050

---

[136] In *Bolkiah (Prince Jefri) v. KPMG* [1999] 2 A.C. 222, Lord Millett said: "The fiduciary relationship which subsists between solicitor and client comes to an end with the termination of the retainer. . . . The only duty to the former client which survives the termination of the client relationship is a continuing duty to preserve the confidentiality of information imparted during its subsistence."

[137] *Longstaff v. Birtles* [2001] EWCA Civ. 1219, [2002] 1 W.L.R. 470.

[138] *Sybron Corporation v. Rochem* [1984] Ch. 112 at 127. But an employment relationship as such is not a fiduciary relationship: *Nottingham University v. Fishel* [2000] I.R.L.R. 471 where three differences between the two were identified.

[139] *Att.-Gen. v. Guardian Newspapers (No.2)* [1990] 1 A.C. 109; *Att.-Gen. v. Blake* [1997] Ch. 84 (Ch.D.), [1998] Ch. 439 (C.A.), [2001] 1 A.C. 268 (H.L.).

[140] Other jurisdictions have added the relationships between doctor and patient (*McInerney v. MacDonald* (1992) 93 D.L.R. (4th) 415 (Supreme Court of Canada); *S.E.C. v. Willis* (1992) 787 Fed.Supp. 58 (U.S. District Court, New York) and the other authorities cited by Frankel in *Equity, Fiduciaries and Trusts 1993* (ed. Waters, 1993), p.173) and between child-abuser and victim when the parties are parent and child (*M.(K.) v. M.(H.)* (1993) 96 D.L.R. (4th) 449 (Supreme Court of Canada)) but not otherwise (*H. v. R.* [1996] 1 N.Z.L.R. 299 (New Zealand High Court)). The relationship between priest and parishioner is another potential addition (see Frankel *op.cit.*).

[141] *Henderson v. Merrett Syndicates* [1995] 2 A.C. 145 at 205.

[142] *Reading v. Att.-Gen.* [1951] A.C. 507.

[143] See *ante*, para 1–038.

[144] *Tito v. Waddell (No.2)* [1977] Ch. 106 at 235. See also *Swain v. The Law Society* [1983] A.C. 598, where The Law Society was held not to be in a fiduciary relationship with the members of the solicitors' profession; *Duggan v. Governor of Full Sutton Prison* [2003] 2 All E.R. 678.

[145] *Tito v. Waddell (No.2)* [1977] Ch. 106 at 212.

[146] [2001] W.T.L.R. 575 at 589–590.

leasehold tenants of a site had been nominated to act on their behalf in negotiations for the acquisition of the freehold. The statements of Lord Browne-Wilkinson, Millett L.J. and Finn set out above were relied on in support of the conclusion that, although the nominated person was not the agent of the other tenants, he had assumed fiduciary obligations towards them; he was, therefore, held to hold the freehold, which he had purchased in his sole name, on constructive trust for all of them. Similarly, in *Sinclair Investment Holdings v. Versailles Trade Finance*,[147] the Court of Appeal held that a *de facto* director was capable of owing fiduciary duties to an investor in the company in question whose investment the director had undertaken personally to monitor when the investor had chosen to continue rather than to withdraw the investment in reliance on that undertaking[148]; in this case the claimant was seeking to recover a profit which the *de facto* director had made by selling shares in an associated company whose value had been artificially enhanced as a result of the wrongful utilisation by the company of the claimant's investment.[149]

10–051   These decisions are both examples of the court deciding whether or not a relationship is classified as fiduciary by determining the extent to which it has satisfied the characteristics of a fiduciary relationship (statements of the type which were set out at the beginning of this section only purport to describe, rather than to define, a fiduciary relationship and none of the few comprehensive definitions which have been suggested has ever received any general approval). A number of different characteristics have been identified: the existence of an undertaking by the alleged fiduciary to the other party to the relationship; reliance placed on the alleged fiduciary by the other party to the relationship; property of the other party under the control of the alleged fiduciary; and vulnerability of the other party to the alleged fiduciary in that some power or discretion is vested in the latter which is capable of being used to affect the legal or practical interests of the former. None of these four characteristics is accepted to be of universal application (although the existence of an undertaking and, in particular, the existence of vulnerability are undoubtedly the most significant); however, each of them has, at one time or another, been held to be sufficient for fiduciary obligations the imposition of fiduciary obligations. Detailed consideration of these characteristics and the way in which they have been applied by the courts is, however, outside the scope of a book on the law of trusts.

10–052   It is, however, necessary to consider in detail the extent, if at all, to which fiduciary obligations should be upheld as between the parties to commercial transactions (in *Hooper v. Gorvin* and *Sinclair Investment Holdings v. Versailles Trade Finance*, the alleged fiduciary was not the other party to the transaction in question). Proceedings instituted in order to establish the existence of

---

[147] [2005] EWCA Civ. 722, [2006] W.T.L.R 1655.

[148] In the event, at trial, on the facts no such fiduciary duty was held to have arisen; see [2007] EWHC 915 (Ch).

[149] Rather than investing the investment in the agreed manner, the company used it (and the investments of all other investors) to make a series of circular payments which enabled the associated company to appear to have a very much higher turnover than was in fact the case; this in turn produced an enormous rise in its share price, of which the *de facto* director had taken advantage.

such obligations generally have the same primary objective, namely the imposition on one of the parties to the commercial transaction in favour of the other party of a constructive trust of some benefit obtained by the alleged fiduciary.[150] The proprietary claim which such a trust automatically makes available to the other party is obviously capable of stripping away a substantial proportion of the assets of the party held to be a fiduciary, particularly if the constructive trust is imposed in such a way as to deprive him of both the past and future profits of the transaction in question. These will be profits to which the fiduciary will have appeared to have been entitled and whose disappearance is capable of reducing very considerably the assets available for his general creditors,[151] who will necessarily not be before the court to defend their interests; the recovery sought by such a claimant will therefore more often than not be at the expense of the general creditors of the fiduciary rather than the fiduciary himself. This is why the extent to which commercial relationships entered into at arm's length and on an equal footing should be held to give rise to fiduciary obligations has been the subject of so much discussion in recent years.

No difficulties of this type arise where the commercial transaction in question has expressly created a fiduciary relationship by, for example, expressly providing that one or more of the parties is subject to fiduciary obligations in certain respects or by expressly creating a relationship which is always classified as fiduciary, such as a partnership. Where this is not the case, the English courts have, generally speaking, preferred to protect the interests of general creditors and have been "mindful of the stern warnings uttered by Lindley L.J.[152] and Atkin L.J.[153] of the dangers of applying equitable doctrines to commercial transactions. To do so would paralyse the trade of the country and fundamentally affect the security of business transactions."[154] **10–053**

Further, there "has been a natural reluctance to impose upon parties in a commercial relationship who are in a relatively equal position of strength the higher standards of conduct which equity prescribes. One manifestation of this reluctance is the disinclination of judges to find a fiduciary relationship when the arrangement between the parties is of a purely commercial kind and they have dealt with each other at arm's length and on an equal footing."[155] This was undoubtedly the attitude adopted by the Privy Council on an appeal from Bermuda in *Kelly v. Cooper*[156] in relation to an estate agency contract. The Privy Council held that, despite the fact that it is normally a breach of an agent's duty to act for competing principals, it is the business of estate agents to act for numerous principals and to acquire **10–054**

---

[150] This is the principal motive but not the only one. Others include more favourable limitation periods and more favourable rules governing the assessment of financial compensation.

[151] Indeed in *Re Goldcorp Exchange* [1995] 1 A.C. 74 (discussed *post*, para 10–056), the objective was to obtain priority not only over the general creditors but also over a secured creditor, the holder of a floating charge (a charge over whatever assets a company may have at any one time).

[152] In *Manchester Trust v. Furness* [1895] 2 Q.B. 539 at 545.

[153] In *Re Wait* [1927] 1 Ch. 606 at 634 *et seq.*, especially at 639–640.

[154] Sir Anthony Mason (when Chief Justice of Australia) extra-judicially 110 L.Q.R. (1994) 238, p.245.

[155] Mason, *op.cit.*, p.245.

[156] [1993] A.C. 205.

information which is confidential to each principal[157]; that being so, the fiduciary duties owed by them to each principal were to be defined by the terms of the contract of agency.[158/159]

10–055   While this attitude has also persisted in other jurisdictions,[160] their courts now appear to be much more ready to hold that the parties have not been dealing on an equal footing. In such cases, the "fiduciary relationship has been the spearhead of equity's incursions into the area of commerce".[161] In Australia and in New Zealand, joint venture arrangements have very readily been held to give rise to fiduciary obligations[162] and in 1994 the then Chief Justice of Australia stated, extra-judicially, that "a fiduciary relationship will arise out of a commercial arrangement when one party undertakes to act in the interests of the other party rather than in his or her own interests in relation to a particular matter or aspect of their arrangement and that other party, being unable to look after his or her interests in that matter or aspect of the arrangement, is basically dependent upon the first party acting in conformity with his or her undertaking".[163] However, his views have yet to be carried into effect by the Australian courts. In Canada, the courts have expressed a willingness to impose fiduciary obligations in favour of any party to a commercial transaction who is vulnerable to the other, even where the vulnerability has arisen only by virtue of the relative sizes and resources of the two commercial enterprises involved, but have emphasised that it is only rarely that such vulnerability will be found to exist.[164]

10–056   What are the possibilities of English law adopting similar attitudes? The consequences of the imposition of fiduciary obligations both for the fiduciary himself and for his general creditors constitute strong arguments against the adoption in England of the approach advocated in the Commonwealth and any thoughts that English law might have been about to develop along those lines were rapidly disabused by the opinion of the Privy Council in *Re Goldcorp Exchange* in 1994.[165] This, curiously enough, was an appeal from the decision which constituted the principal authority cited by the Chief Justice

---

[157] This is also the case for auditors. See *Bolkiah (Prince Jefri) v. KPMG* [1999] 2 A.C. 222, where *Kelly v. Cooper* was explained; this case was an attempt to restrain alleged potential breaches of confidence—the auditors in question could not thereby have committed a breach of fiduciary duty after they had ceased to act as such (see *ante*, para 10–048, n.136)

[158] However, an estate agent who had advised his principal to accept a price lower than that for which he knew that a similar adjoining property had already been sold was held liable to him in tort for having given negligent advice in *John D. Wood v. Knatchbull* [2003] T.L.R. 12.

[159] See also *Re Stapylton Fletcher* [1994] 1 W.L.R. 1181.

[160] *Jirna v. Master Donut of Canada* (1973) 40 D.L.R. (3d) 303 (Supreme Court of Canada); *United States Surgical Corporation v. Hospital Products International* (1984) 156 C.L.R. 41 (High Court of Australia).

[161] Mason, *op.cit.*, p.245.

[162] *United Dominion Corporation v. Brian* (1985) 157 C.L.R. 1 (High Court of Australia).

[163] Mason C.J. *op.cit.*, pp.245–246, citing *Liggett v. Kensington* [1993] 3 N.Z.L.R. 257, where the Court of Appeal of New Zealand imposed fiduciary obligations upon a gold trader who had offered purchasers the option of leaving their bullion in the custody of the trader on the purchasers' behalf as "non-allocated bullion". This decision was subsequently reversed by the Privy Council *sub. nom. Re Goldcorp Exchange* [1995] 1 A.C. 74; see *post*, para 10–056.

[164] *Lac Minerals v. International Corona Resources* (1989) 61 D.L.R.(4th) 14; *Hodgkinson v. Simms* (1994) 117 D.L.R.(4th) 161 (both Supreme Court of Canada).

[165] [1995] 1 A.C. 74.

of Australia in support of the proposition set out in the previous paragraph. The Court of Appeal of New Zealand[166] had imposed fiduciary obligations on a gold-dealer which had offered its purchasers the option of leaving their bullion in its custody on the purchasers' behalf as "non-allocated bullion". Purchasers who did so were issued with a certificate of ownership and were entitled to take physical possession of their bullion on seven days' notice. The Court of Appeal's conclusion that the company was a fiduciary was based on two propositions: first, that it was bound to protect the interests of the purchasers; and, secondly, that it was, for all practical purposes, free from control and supervision by them.[167] The Privy Council, however, heeded the warnings of Lindley L.J. and Atkin L.J. to which reference has already been made. Lord Mustill said this:

"But what kind of fiduciary duties did the company owe to the customer? None have been suggested beyond those which the company assumed under the contracts of sale read with the collateral promises; ... No doubt the fact that one person is placed in a particular position *vis-à-vis* another through the medium of a contract does not necessarily mean that he does not also owe fiduciary duties to that other by virtue of being in that position. But the essence of a fiduciary relationship is that it creates obligations of a different character from those deriving from the contract itself. ... Many commercial relationships involve just such a reliance by one party on the other, and to introduce the whole new dimension into such relationships which would flow from giving them a fiduciary character would (as it seems to their Lordships) have adverse consequences far exceeding those foreseen by Atkin L.J. in *Re Wait*.[168] It is possible without misuse of language to say that the customers put faith in the company, and that their trust has not been repaid. But the vocabulary is misleading; high expectations do not necessarily lead to equitable remedies."

These observations seem to rule out, at least for the present, any possibility of English law developing along the lines of the Australian and New Zealand decisions even in respect of joint venture arrangements, never mind in accordance with the wider principles enunciated in those jurisdictions and in Canada. The attitude manifested by the Privy Council does have the great advantage that the interests of third parties cannot be prejudiced by the conversion of a general creditor into a preferential creditor as the result of the imposition of fiduciary obligations on a bankrupt. For this reason, it is hoped that, in the event that English law does one day develop along the lines advocated in the Commonwealth, the courts will not lose sight of the interests of third parties but will take them into account in the manner envisaged in the introductory section of this chapter.

---

[166] [1993] 1 N.Z.L.R. 257.

[167] *ibid.*, at 583, 584, *per* Cooke P. at 596, 597, *per* Gault J. Compare the view of the dissentient, McKay J. at pp.604, 605.

[168] [1927] 1 Ch. 606 at 634 *et seq.*, especially at 639–640.

2. The Nature of the Liability of Fiduciaries

10–057   In *Bray v. Ford*[169] Lord Herschell laid down two overlapping principles: a fiduciary cannot be permitted to profit from his fiduciary position (sometimes known as "the no profit rule") and a fiduciary must not allow his personal interest to prevail over his duty of loyalty to his principal (sometimes known as "the no conflict rule"). The precise relationship between these two rules has been expressed in a number of ways. In *Swain v. The Law Society*,[170] Stephenson L.J. regarded the first of these principles as merely one of the many examples of the second principle. However, it is clear that a fiduciary cannot profit from his fiduciary position even when there is no real conflict of interest and duty. Consequently, it is perhaps preferable to adopt the view of Deane J. in *Chan v. Zacharia*[171] that the two principles "while overlapping, are distinct".

10–058   Within these principles, the attitude of English law towards fiduciaries is relatively consistent.[172] Of course, as is only to be expected, the law differs from fiduciary relationship to fiduciary relationship.[173] This is the case even as between the traditional categories of fiduciary relationships; thus a director is in a more favourable position with regard to property transactions with his company than is a trustee with regard to property transactions with his trust. This apart, the attitude of English law towards fiduciaries is, generally speaking, a harsh one. As James L.J. remarked in *Parker v. McKenna*,[174] the rule that a fiduciary may not profit from his position without the knowledge and consent of his principal "is an inexorable rule, and must be applied inexorably by this court, which is not entitled, in my judgment, to receive evidence, or suggestion, or argument as to whether the principal did or did not suffer any injury in fact by reason of the dealing of the [fiduciary]". Not only is it thus irrelevant that the principal has suffered no loss; it is also irrelevant that the fiduciary acted in the utmost good faith and that his actions in fact benefited his principal. This attitude was recently reaffirmed by the Court of Appeal in *Murad v. Al-Saraj*,[175] where it was held, by a majority, that a fiduciary was liable to account for the whole of profit notwithstanding the fact that, had he disclosed the true facts, his principal would have gone ahead on the transaction on the basis that the fiduciary obtained part of that profit. The majority acknowledged "the possibility that at some time in the future the House of Lords may consider that the time has come to relax the severity of the 'no conflict' rule to some extent in appropriate cases" but "that day has not yet arrived".[176]

10–059   This inexorable rule exists for reasons of policy, namely to avoid the remotest risk of a fiduciary being swayed from his duty of loyalty to his principal by his own self interest. However, the decided cases provide innumerable examples of courts penalising fiduciaries (particularly trustees)

---

[169] [1896] A.C. 44 at 51–52.
[170] [1982] 1 W.L.R. 17 at 29.
[171] (1984) 53 A.L.R. 417 at 433 (High Court of Australia).
[172] See generally Conaglen, 121 L.Q.R. (2005) 452.
[173] See Millett J. in *Lonrho v. Fayed (No.2)* [1992] 1 W.L.R. 1 at 11–12.
[174] (1874) L.R. 10 Ch. 96.
[175] [2005] EWCA Civ. 589, [2005] W.T.L.R. 1573.
[176] *ibid.*, *per* Jonathan Parker L.J. at [121–122]; see also *per* Arden L.J. at 82.

totally irrespective of whether there was any serious conflict between their duty of loyalty and their self interest. A fiduciary is only allowed to retain a profit in very limited circumstances: first, when the conflict of interest which produced the profit must necessarily have been envisaged at the time when the fiduciary relationship was created[177]; secondly, when the making of the profit was specifically authorised in advance in the instrument by which the fiduciary relationship was created[178]; and, thirdly, when the fully informed prior consent or subsequent ratification of the principal to the making of the profit has been given.[179]

Lord Herschell remarked in *Bray v. Ford*[180] that this harsh rule "might be departed from in many cases, without any breach of morality, without any wrong being inflicted, and without any consciousness of wrongdoing". However, English law has never given much indication of being disposed to relax its strict penal rule in favour of a more flexible rule that fiduciaries should only be penalised where there has been a serious conflict of interest and duty. A rare example of flexibility some 40 years ago were the remarks of Danckwerts and Sachs L.JJ. in *Holder v. Holder*[181] to the effect that whether or not a transaction should be set aside because of an alleged conflict of interest and duty was a matter for the discretion of the judge. However, this approach was not subsequently adopted as a general principle and the majority of the Court of Appeal has recently emphasised that this will only be able to be done by the House of Lords[182] or, now, the future Supreme Court. **10–060**

Greater signs of flexibility have been shown in relation to pension trusts. In *Re Drexel Lambert UK Pension Plan*,[183] Lindsay J., while acknowledging that the remarks of Lord Herschell were "not a licence for the rule to departed from when it can be seen that no breach of morality or wrongdoing would ensue", did hold that "the rule does not apply with such force as to deny the court even the jurisdiction to give directions"[184]; he therefore approved an application made by the trustees of a pension scheme, all of whom were by virtue of being members of the scheme also beneficiaries and therefore had a conflict of duty and interest, for the distribution of the actuarial surplus of the pension fund in question. Scott V.-C. subsequently went even further in *Edge v. Pensions Ombudsman*,[185] where the trustees had had to make an amendment to the rules of a pension scheme in order to eliminate an excessive surplus. The effect of the amendment was to reduce employee contributions and to enhance pensions in payment, as a result of which some of the trustees benefited. Scott V.-C. held that, given that **10–061**

---

[177] In cases where the fiduciary relationship has been created by the parties to it, the person who will have to have envisaged the conflict of interest in question is the principal; in the case of a voluntary settlement, it will instead be the settlor or testator.

[178] *Sergeant v. National Westminster Bank* (1990) 61 P. & C.R. 518.

[179] *Holder v. Holder* [1968] Ch. 353.

[180] [1896] A.C. 44 at 51.

[181] [1968] Ch. 353; see *post*, para 10–090.

[182] *Murad v. Al-Saraj* [2005] EWCA Civ. 589, [2005] W.T.L.R. 1573 *per* Arden L.J. at 82, *per* Jonathan Parker L.J. at [121–122].

[183] [1995] 1 W.L.R. 32.

[184] *ibid.*, at 41.

[185] [1998] Ch. 512 at 539.

statute[186] now requires pension schemes to have member-nominated trustees, it was "quite simply ridiculous" to contend that any trustees who were members had to be excluded from any new or enhanced benefits obtained by the exercise of their powers. His remarks were subsequently approved by the Court of Appeal.[187] It remains to be seen whether this understandable, but nevertheless highly desirable, relaxation of the traditional position in the area of pension trusts is also applied outside that area.

10–062   One important restriction on the potential liability of fiduciaries has admittedly now been made clear as a result of the decision of the Court of Appeal in *Bristol and West Building Society v. Mothew*.[188] This was one of a number of cases brought by banks and building societies as a result of the crash in residential property values at the beginning of the 1990s. These institutional lenders were endeavouring to recover shortfalls in the proceeds of their mortgage securities by imposing liability on the solicitors who had acted both for them and for the borrower at the time when the mortgage in question was created; in such circumstances the solicitors of course owe fiduciary duties both to the borrower and to the mortgagee. The Court of Appeal held that breaches of contract and acts of negligence committed by fiduciaries of this type will only give rise to the normal contractual and tortious remedies; such acts with therefore not give rise to the enhanced measures of compensation which can be recovered from fiduciaries[189] without the presence of some additional factor such as a clear conflict between the interests of the borrower and the interests of the mortgagee of which the solicitor has chosen not to inform the mortgagee.[190]

10–063   If English law ever does relax the strict rule which has traditionally been applied in the way that other jurisdictions have done, it will have to be decided whether the conflict of interest and duty is to be measured prospectively or retrospectively, whether, in other words, the question of whether there was a real sensible possibility of conflict has to be considered in the light of the facts existing at the time when the course of conduct complained of commenced or in the light of the facts existing at the time when that course of conduct ended. No clear answer to this question has been given in any of the decided cases, perhaps because the adoption of the strict penal rule has rendered it irrelevant. It is, however, suggested that the retrospective approach is preferable.

3. *Remedies for Breach of Fiduciary Duty*

10–064   The first and most significant remedy for breach of fiduciary duty, the one which is most favourable to the principal, and also the one with which this chapter is obviously mainly concerned, is the imposition of a constructive

---

[186] Pensions Act 1995, ss.16–21.

[187] [2000] Ch. 602.

[188] [1998] Ch. 1.

[189] See *post*, para 22–009.

[190] A number of conflicts of this type were identified in *Nationwide Building Society v. Balmer Radmore* [1999] Lloyd's P.N. 241 and the mortgagee duly recovered the measure of compensation appropriate to a breach of fiduciary duty.

trust. It has already been seen[191] that this requires the identification of some specific property which either is or has been in the hands of the fiduciary on which the trust can be imposed and that the precise position of the principal depends on the nature of the constructive trust which has been imposed. When a constructive trust is not available, the principal can have recourse only to some form of personal remedy.

The second possible remedy is for the principal to seek an account. This remedy will be sought where the principal wishes to recover assets which have passed through the hands of a fiduciary who has committed a breach of fiduciary duty but cannot identify any specific property which either is or has been in the hands of the fiduciary which represents those assets or their product. In these circumstances, he will seek an account of whatever assets have reached the hands of the fiduciary. This involves the fiduciary rendering an account of what he has done with the property which has been in his hands. If the principal is dissatisfied with what the fiduciary has done, then he has the right to "surcharge" or "falsify" the account rendered. The effect of him opting to take either of these courses of action is considered in a later chapter.[192] Any compensation which the principal recovers will be equitable compensation of the type which courts of equity have always been able to award; its continued availability was confirmed by the decision of the House of Lords in *Nocton v. Lord Ashburton*.[193] However, such an award will give him no priority over the fiduciary's general creditors—an account remains a personal remedy despite the fact that the person against whom it is sought is a fiduciary. A fiduciary is liable to account only for assets actually received by him or by a company which is wholly owned and controlled by him.[194] A fiduciary is not otherwise liable to account for a benefit received by someone else; in particular, the better view is that he is not liable to account for assets received by a company of which he is merely a substantial shareholder.[195]

10–065

The third possible remedy, which is available only as an alternative and not in addition to the first two,[196] is for the principal to seek equitable compensation for breach of fiduciary duty; the availability of this type of compensation was established by the decision of the House of Lords in *Nocton v. Lord Ashburton*.[197] The purpose of such an award is, basically, to restore the principal to the position which he occupied prior to the breach of fiduciary duty in question. A number of examples of awards of equitable compensation of this type will be seen later on: first, where the principal is the victim of a conflict of interest and duty in that the fiduciary has, without

10–066

---

[191] See *ante*, para 10–005.

[192] See *post*, para 22–010.

[193] [1914] A.C. 932.

[194] *Trustor AB v.Smallbone (No.2)* [2001] 1 W.L.R. 1177 at [22–23].

[195] *Ultraframe (UK) v. Fielding* [2005] EWHC 1638 (Civ), [2007] W.T.L.R. 835 at [1576], not following *CMS Dolphin v. Simonet* [2001] 2 B.C.L.C. 704, where such a fiduciary was held to be jointly and severally liable with such a company on the basis of joint participation.

[196] *Tang Man Sit v. Capacious Investments* [1996] 1 A.C. 514 (Privy Council on appeal from Hong Kong).

[197] [1914] A.C. 932.

adequate disclosure, entered into some form of transaction with his principal[198]; secondly, where the principal is the victim of a conflict of interest and interest in that a fiduciary who owes fiduciary duties to two or more principals has preferred the interests of the other(s)[199]; thirdly, where there has been a breach of an equitable obligation of confidence[200]; and, fourthly, where a fiduciary has disposed of trust property in breach of trust[201] (this situation is unconnected with the subject matter of this chapter). The precise measure of recovery is a matter of some controversy but the general view seems to be that common law principles of remoteness of damages should be applied to the assessment of equitable compensation.[202]

10–067   The fourth possible remedy, which is available only where the fiduciary has, without adequate disclosure, entered into some form of transaction with his principal, is for that transaction to be rescinded *ab initio*.[203] However, this is only possible for so long as *restitutio in integrum* is still possible, in other words while both fiduciary and principal are still able to restore the other to his initial position. This remedy is available only as an alternative to the three remedies already discussed.

10–068   Finally, there is obviously nothing to prevent the principal from seeking injunctive relief as a supplement to any of the remedies already discussed (usually in order to prevent a fiduciary from disposing of property which is claimed to be subject to a constructive trust or susceptible of *restitutio in integrum*); injunctive relief is also often sought independently in cases involving a breach of the equitable obligation of confidence. In theory, it is also possible for the principal to seek damages in lieu or in addition to an injunction under Lord Cairns' Act[204] but in practice it is now almost inevitable that any monetary award for breach of fiduciary duty will instead be made pursuant to *Nocton v. Lord Ashburton*.

4. The Classification of the Authorities

10–069 The many authorities have been classified in a number of different ways. It is proposed to consider them in this order: first, cases where a fiduciary has as a result of his position obtained unauthorised remuneration; secondly, cases where a fiduciary has entered into a transaction in a double capacity in that he has purported to represent either the interests of two principals to both of whom he owes fiduciary duties or the interests of both his principal and himself; and, thirdly, cases where a fiduciary has as a result of his position obtained a benefit to the exclusion of his principal.

---

[198] See *post*, para 10–081.

[199] See *post*, ibid.

[200] See *post*, para 10–147.

[201] See *post*, para 22–029.

[202] See *Constructive Trusts* (3rd edn, 1997), pp.117–121 and the authorities there cited (the 4th edn is in preparation).

[203] See *post*, para 10–081.

[204] The name usually given to the Chancery Amendment Act 1858. This Act has long since been repealed but the jurisdiction conferred thereby is now contained in the Supreme Court Act 1981, s.50.

5. *Unauthorised Remuneration Obtained by a Fiduciary as a Result of his Position*

(A) When is a Fiduciary Entitled to Claim Remuneration?

The detailed rules governing the extent to which a trustee is entitled to claim and retain remuneration and benefits are discussed in a later chapter.[205] For present purposes, it is merely necessary to state that trustees have, historically, been under a duty to act without remuneration, even when they devote a considerable amount of time and trouble to managing the trust business, save to the extent that remuneration is permitted by the trust deed or the will in question. This remains the position save to the extent that the Trustee Act 2000[206] provides the contrary in the case of trust corporations and trustees who are acting in a professional capacity.[207] This legislation has given both enhanced rights to charge whatever remuneration has been authorised and provides that, where no remuneration has been authorised at all, trust corporations and, if any other trustees agree, trustees who are acting in a professional capacity can charge such remuneration as is reasonable in the circumstances. The same rules apply to any remuneration received by a trustee by virtue of holding, as a result of his position as trustee, an office of profit such as a directorship in a company in which the trust has a shareholding.

10–070

The position of other express fiduciaries is more favourable. While they are in principle, like trustees, expected to act without remuneration,[208] it is in practice highly unlikely that they will have agreed to act without first having made provision for the payment of the appropriate remuneration. Thus the Articles of Association of a company generally provide for the payment of remuneration to its directors[209]; a Partnership Deed will normally provide for the payment of remuneration to the partners; and a contract of agency will normally make provision for the payment of the appropriate remuneration to the agent. Thus, in normal circumstances, a director of a company who is appointed by the board to a directorship of a subsidiary may undoubtedly retain both sets of directors' fees and a partner who is appointed by his partners to a directorship in a company in which the partnership holds shares may similarly retain his director's fees. However, in the event that the payment of remuneration has not been authorised, or the formula by which authorisation has to be obtained has not been complied with,[210] the fiduciary will not be entitled either to remuneration or to the benefits of any other office to which he has been appointed by virtue of his fiduciary position and will be liable to account to his principal for any

10–071

---

[205] See *post*, Chapter 20.

[206] ss.28, 29.

[207] Defined as acting in the course of a profession or business which consists of or includes the provisions of services in connection with the management or administration of trusts generally or in some respect. See *post*, para 20–021.

[208] *Guinness v. Saunders* [1990] 2 A.C. 663 at 689–690.

[209] The Table A Articles of Association recommended by statute reserve to the company in general meeting the right to determine the remuneration of the directors of the company.

[210] In *Guinness v. Saunders* [1990] 2 A.C. 663, the remuneration of the director in question had not, as required by the Articles of Association, been approved by the board of directors.

sums received.[211] Further, the House of Lords has held that, where the formula by which authorisation has to be obtained has not been complied with, the court has no inherent jurisdiction to award remuneration to the fiduciary in question.[212]

(B) Liability in respect of Unauthorised Remuneration

10–072   Where a fiduciary is liable to account for remuneration received as such, he will in principle clearly be liable as a constructive trustee in respect of the remuneration so obtained. However, only where the remuneration in question is still identifiable at the date of action (as will be the case where the remuneration takes the form of shares or, as is very common today in the case of directors, of share options) will there be any purpose in imposing such a trust. Where the remuneration has already passed into the general funds of the fiduciary (as will obviously be more usual), then the fiduciary will be liable merely to account to his principal for its value. In this situation there will obviously be no need for the imposition of a constructive trust since any fiduciary liable to account for remuneration of this kind will inevitably be an express fiduciary.

(C) Liability in respect of Illicit Profits

10–073   A fiduciary will also be liable to account for any other payments which he may receive as a result of his position. Such payments are generally described as secret profits. However, not infrequently there is nothing whatever about the making the profit which is secret itself; what is secret is instead the circumstances in which it was made. Thus in *Sinclair Investment Holdings v. Versailles Trade Finance,*[213] the fact that the *de facto* director had been making profits by selling shares in an associated company was not of itself the basis of any claim and the claimant must unquestionably have been aware of that fact or, at any rate, would have been if any thought had been given to the matter; the complaint was rather that that profit had been made as the result of the wrongful utilisation by the company of the claimant's investment. Consequently, it seems more appropriate to describe such profits as "illicit profits". But, however, they are described, it is clearly established that no fiduciary who receives such a profit may retain it as against his principal unless its retention was either authorised in advance or subsequently ratified by the principal with full knowledge of all relevant facts.

(1) Who is regarded as a fiduciary for these purposes?

10–074   For the purposes of the recovery of illicit profits, the courts take a particularly broad view of what constitutes a fiduciary relationship. In *Attorney-General v. Goddard*[214] the principle was applied to a police officer who had been bribed not to report brothel keepers; in *Reading v. Attorney-General*[215] it was applied to an ex-R.A.M.C Sergeant who had obtained large sums from smugglers for riding in his uniform through Cairo in lorries in which

---

[211] *ibid.*

[212] *ibid.*, at 693–694, 700–702.

[213] [2005] EWCA Civ. 722, [2006] W.T.L.R 1655.

[214] [1929] L.J.(K.B.) 743.

[215] [1951] A.C. 507.

smuggled goods were being transported, thus enabling the lorries to pass the civil police without search; and, in modern conditions, it would presumably be applied to a security guard who was bribed to switch off the alarm system, thus facilitating the entrance of thieves.[216]

It is in fact arguable whether it is really appropriate for relationships of this kind to be classified as fiduciary. In *Reading v. Attorney-General*, the sergeant was claiming by petition of right that the Crown return to him some £19,000 which had been found in his possession and confiscated when he was eventually apprehended. For this action to fail, some basis for the Crown's right to confiscate the money had to be found. At first instance[217] Denning J. held that there was no fiduciary relationship between the sergeant and the Crown but also held that no such relationship was in fact necessary. However, in the Court of Appeal,[218] Asquith L.J. took a different view, holding that, assuming a fiduciary relationship to be necessary, such a relationship arose from the use by the sergeant of his uniform and of the opportunities attached to it. He admitted that this was using the concept of fiduciary relationship "in a very loose sense" but this did not stop the House of Lords from confirming his view. It is possible to criticise this reasoning on the grounds that the relationship between Sergeant Reading and the Crown does not appear to satisfy any of the criteria for the existence of a fiduciary relationship other than (possibly) the existence of property of the other party under the control of the alleged fiduciary property; in particular, it is not easy to see how the Crown was in any way vulnerable by virtue of some power or discretion vested in the sergeant which was capable of being used to affect its legal or practical interests. That is not to say that *Reading v. Attorney-General* was wrongly decided since its result can certainly be justified on other grounds.[219] However, the decision undoubtedly demonstrates how widely the courts are prepared to construe the concept of fiduciary relationship in order to permit the recovery of illicit profits.[220] It is questionable whether the concept should be construed so widely for other purposes.[221]

(2) For what profits will a fiduciary be liable?
It has already been stated that a fiduciary will be liable for any payments which he may receive as a result of his position. The vast majority of the reported cases have concerned bribes and commissions received by the fiduciary in order either to induce him to take a particular course of action

10–075

10–076

---

[216] This illustration was provided by Lord Millett extra-judicially in [1993] R.L.R. 7. In *Brinks v. Abu-Saleh (No.3)* [1996] C.L.C. 133, a security guard who provided both a key to and information about the security of a Heathrow warehouse was held to be a fiduciary but this was not for the purpose of imposing any liability on him but for the rather more questionable purpose of imposing liability on third parties (see *post*, para 10–169).

[217] [1948] 2 K.B. 268.

[218] [1949] 2 K.B. 232.

[219] By virtue of the principle that no criminal may benefit from his crime. See section IV of this Chapter, *post*, para 10–241.

[220] *Reading v. Att.-Gen.* was approved and applied in the equally extreme case of *Jersey City v. Hague* (1955) 155 At.(2d) 8, which concerned a successful attempt to recover from the Mayor of Jersey City the percentages of the salaries of each employee of the city which he had extorted over a period of 30 years in consideration of continued employment.

[221] See *post*, para 10–169.

or to reward him for having done so. A bribe may be defined as an undisclosed payment made to a person known by the payer to be a fiduciary in circumstances in which it could induce the fiduciary to favour the payer in some way in his dealings with the fiduciary or with the fiduciary's principal.[222] In such circumstances, the principal has a choice of remedies. He can rescind any transaction entered into as a result of the bribe,[223] provided of course that he is still in a position to make *restitutio in integrum*, and, additionally or alternatively, he can sue either the briber[224] or the fiduciary[225] for the amount of the bribe.

10–077　　It is the last of these remedies which is relevant for present purposes. In the two leading cases, *Lister & Co. v. Stubbs*[226] and *Attorney-General for Hong Kong v. Reid*,[227] liability of this type was imposed on the recipients of bribes. Such persons necessarily act in bad faith but liability is imposed on the recipients of commissions even if they are in good faith, something which is wholly inconsistent with normal commercial practices. In *Williams v. Barton*[228] a trustee used a firm of which he was a member to value trust securities. His action was completely bona fide but he was nevertheless held liable to account to the trust as a constructive trustee for the commission which he had made out of the introduction of the trust business. This decision means that a solicitor who receives a commission for introducing a client to a broker will be liable to account to the client for this commission unless the latter has expressly authorised the retention of the payment in question.

10–078　　In normal circumstances, it will be virtually impossible for a fiduciary successfully to contend that any particular payment by way of illicit profit was not in fact received as a result of his position. However, it has recently been held that the law will not go so far as to impose unreasonable restraints either on the freedom of speech of a former fiduciary or on his ability to earn his living by exploiting expertise acquired during the fiduciary relationship. This was in *Attorney-General v. Blake*,[229] which concerned an attempt by the Crown to intercept the royalties payable in respect of the autobiography of George Blake, a former member of the Secret Intelligence Service who had become a spy for the Soviet Union, to which he managed to escape after having been imprisoned. The Attorney-General contended that Blake owed the Crown a fiduciary duty: first, not to use his position as a former member of the Security Intelligence Service so as to make himself a profit; and, secondly, not to use the Crown's property, including intangible property such as originally confidential information, for his profit. Only the first of these alleged duties is relevant for present purposes. Scott V.-C. held that

---

[222] *Hovenden and Sons v. Milhoff* (1900) 83 L.T. 41 at 43; *Industries and General Mortgage Co. v. Lewis* [1949] 2 All E.R. 573 at 575.

[223] *Logicrose v. Southend United F.C.* [1988] 1 W.L.R. 1256.

[224] *Hovenden and Sons v. Milhoff* (1900) 83 L.T. 41; *Mahesan v. Malaysian Government Officers' Co-operative Housing Society* [1979] A.C. 374 at 383.

[225] These claims were held to be alternative rather than cumulative in *Mahesan v. Malaysian Government Officers' Co-operative Housing Society* [1979] A.C. 374.

[226] (1890) 45 Ch.D. 1.

[227] [1994] 1 A.C. 324 (Privy Council on appeal from New Zealand).

[228] [1927] 2 Ch. 9.

[229] [1997] Ch. 84.

both were formulated in terms too wide to be acceptable and went on to dismiss the Crown's claim for the reasons stated above, both of which appear to relate principally to the second duty. No doubt was cast on this reasoning on appeal[230]; the Court of Appeal specifically held that Blake was not in breach of fiduciary duty but both there and in the House of Lords the Crown instead succeeded on public law and contractual arguments not raised at first instance. However, there seems little likelihood that the arguments which commended themselves to Scott V.-C. will often be invoked successfully; it is hardly likely that the courts would look very charitably on a trustee who deferred the receipt of bribes and commissions until after his retirement and then sought to retain them on that ground.

(3) The nature of the liability

In principle, a fiduciary who is liable to account for illicit profits will be   **10–079**
liable as a constructive trustee in respect of the profit in question. This remedy was imposed in *Williams v. Barton*,[231] which of course meant that the principal was, therefore, entitled to follow the payment made to the fiduciary into its product in the admittedly unlikely event that it could be shown to have been invested in assets which had appreciated in value. However, until the decision of the Privy Council in *Attorney-General for Hong Kong v. Reid*,[232] the decided cases appeared in this respect to draw a distinction between bribes and other illicit profits. In *Lister & Co. v. Stubbs*[233] the Court of Appeal had held that the only obligation of a bribed fiduciary was to pay over the sums received to his principal, the relationship between them being debtor-creditor rather than trustee-beneficiary. Although this decision was consistently followed,[234] it seemed quite extraordinary that the defendant in *Williams v. Barton* should have been held to have been a constructive trustee of a commission which he had earned in good faith if the defendant in *Lister & Co. v. Stubbs* was held not to have been a constructive trustee of an illicitly earned bribe.[235]

Attorney-General for Hong Kong v. Reid[236] concerned a Hong Kong Public   **10–080**
Prosecutor who had been convicted of having accepted bribes as an inducement to him to exploit his official position to obstruct the prosecution of certain criminals. He was ordered to pay the Crown the sum of HK$12,400,000, the value of assets then controlled by him which could only

---

[230] [1998] Ch. 439 (CA), [2001] 1 A.C. 268.
[231] [1927] 2 Ch. 9.
[232] [1994] 1 A.C. 324.
[233] (1890) 45 Ch.D. 1.
[234] In, *inter alia*, *Att.-Gen. Ref. (No.1 of 1985)* [1986] 2 All E.R. 219 and in *Islamic Republic of Iran Shipping Line v. Denby* [1987] 1 F.T.L.R. 30.
[235] All the commentators agreed that both cases should have been decided in the same way. Birks in *An Introduction to the Law of Restitution* (1989) 388 and Goode in (1987) 103 L.Q.R. 433, 422–445 thought that a constructive trust should not have been imposed in either case on the grounds that proprietary remedies should be limited to situations where the claimant can show that he has lost property which, but for the conduct of the fiduciary, he would have obtained. Lord Millett, extra-judicially in [1993] Restitution L.R. 7, and various other commentators whom he cited thought that a constructive trust should have been imposed in both cases on the grounds that a fiduciary should never be allowed to retain any advantage from the violation of his fiduciary obligations, something which can only be achieved by the imposition of a proprietary remedy.
[236] [1994] 1 A.C. 324.

have been derived from the bribes. No payments having been made, the Attorney-General for Hong Kong brought proceedings in New Zealand claiming that three freehold houses which the bribes had been used to purchase were held on constructive trust for the Crown. The Court of Appeal of New Zealand applied *Lister & Co v. Stubbs* and dismissed this claim.[237] The Privy Council reversed this decision, holding that *Lister & Co. v. Stubbs* had been wrongly decided.[238] Although the decision in *Attorney-General for Hong Kong v. Reid* was not, of course, formally binding on English courts, it has now been held that that decision will be followed.[239] Thus the liability of a fiduciary who receives a bribe is now exactly the same as that of a fiduciary who receives any other type of illicit profit.

6. *Transactions into which a Fiduciary has Entered in a Double Capacity*

10–081 This second group of cases concerns transactions in which a fiduciary has purported to represent the interests of more than one person at the same time. The persons in question may be the principal and the fiduciary himself, in which case there is said to be a conflict of duty and interest, namely between the fiduciary's duty of loyalty towards his principal and his personal interest in the transaction. Alternatively, the persons in question may be two or more principals to each of whom the fiduciary owes a duty of loyalty, in which case there is said to be a conflict of interest and interest. In both situations, no matter how fair the transaction, any principal has the right to have the transaction set aside unless he was fully aware of the facts.

(A) Acquisitions of Property from a Principal

10–082 Acquisitions by a fiduciary of the property of his principal are regulated by two rules, which Megarry V.-C. in *Tito v. Waddell (No.2)*[240] described as the self-dealing rule and the fair-dealing rule, names which have been in general use ever since. The self-dealing rule applies to purchases by trustees of property belonging to their trust and also to appointments by trustees of trust property or beneficial interests therein to themselves as beneficiaries; the self-dealing rule also applies, at least in theory, to purchases by directors of property belonging to their companies (although in practice the Articles of Association of virtually all companies expressly permit such purchases

---

[237] [1992] 2 N.Z.L.R. 385.

[238] Lord Templeman's opinion did not directly consider the important issue of policy on which the commentators were divided. He held that, as soon as any bribe is received, the fiduciary becomes in equity the debtor of his principal for the amount of the bribe, which should immediately be transferred to his principal. Because equity considers as done that which ought to have been done, the bribe therefore becomes subject to a constructive trust in favour of the principal as soon as it is received. Although this analysis is questionable in a number of respects (see [1994] C.L.J. 31), it provided a basis for an examination of the case law, from which Lord Templeman concluded (at p.336) that *Lister & Co. v. Stubbs* was consistent neither with prior authority nor "with the principles that a fiduciary must not be allowed to benefit from his own breach of duty, that the fiduciary should account for the bribe as soon as he receives it and that equity regards as done that which ought to be done".

[239] This was held in *Daraydan Holdings v. Solland International* [2004] EWHC 622 (Ch), [2005] Ch. 119.

[240] [1977] Ch. 106 at 224–225.

provided that appropriate disclosure is made). The fair-dealing rule applies to purchases by trustees of the beneficial interests of their beneficiaries and to purchases by other fiduciaries (such as agents) of property belonging to their principals. The fair-dealing rule also applies where a fiduciary who owes fiduciary duties to more than one principal purchases the property of one of his principals from another of his principals except in the case of a purchase on behalf of one trust from another trust where the trustees of the two trusts are absolutely identical, in which case the self-dealing rule appears to apply.

(1) The self-dealing rule

In *Tito v. Waddell (No.2)*,[241] Megarry V.-C. said that "if a trustee purchases **10–083** trust property from himself, any beneficiary may have the sale set aside *ex debito justitiae*, however fair the transaction". The rationale of the self-dealing rule was laid down by Lord Eldon L.C. in *Ex parte Lacey*.[242] He applied the principle that a trustee must not place himself in a position where his interest and duty conflict, holding that, since in a purchase by a trustee of property belonging to his trust he is both vendor and purchaser, the sale is necessarily bad. In such circumstances it is impossible to determine from the evidence whether or not the purchase has been made on advantageous terms and so the court has no option but to set aside the purchase at the instance of any beneficiary. In principle, this rule ought also to apply to a purchase on behalf of one trust from another trust where the trustees of the two trusts are absolutely identical; formerly the rule also applied where any trustee of the two trusts was identical[243] but this seems no longer to be, or at any rate should not be, the case where any trustee of either trust is not a trustee of the other one.[244]

Most purchases which fall foul of these authorities are, as Megarry V.-C. **10–084** said, not wholly void but only voidable at the instance of any beneficiary. However, this is not always the case since his formulation overlooks the fact that it is impossible for a person to contract with himself or for a trustee to exercise his power of sale in favour of himself.[245] Any transaction which falls foul of either of these rules is not merely voidable but wholly void. Since 1925,[246] this will admittedly only be the case when the same person is, or the same persons are, both vendor and purchaser. Therefore, a sole trustee cannot sell to himself and a plurality of trustees cannot sell to themselves (validity depends on there being at least one party who is not both vendor and purchaser) unless such a transaction is authorised by the trust instrument. These rules apply whether the purchaser is the trustee or trustees in

---

[241] [1977] Ch. 106 at 224–225.

[242] (1802) 6 Ves. 625.

[243] *Re Bell's Indenture* [1980] 1 W.L.R. 1217 at 1231; *Re Thompson's Settlement* [1986] Ch. 99 at 115.

[244] *Hillsdown Holdings v. Pensions Ombudsman* [1997] 1 All E.R. 862 at 895–896; see also *Public Trustee v. Cooper* [2001] W.T.L.R. 901.

[245] See McPherson J., extra-judicially, in *Trends in Contemporary Trust Law* (ed. Oakley, 1996), p.135.

[246] Until 1926, prior to the enactment of Law of Property Act 1925, s.82, the rule applied if anyone either contracted with or conveyed to himself, even if someone else was also a party on one side or the other.

question in his or their personal capacities or in his or their capacities as trustee or trustees of another trust. These rules are readily avoidable by the simple expedient of the appointment of a nominee on one side or the other (either of an additional trustee vendor or purchaser or of a nominee purchaser). However, if these rules are breached, both contract and conveyance will be wholly void.[247] If this has actually happened, there are only two ways out: first, for the purchaser to try to acquire the beneficial interests of the beneficiaries of the trust which is selling, either as well[248] or instead (such a transaction will be governed by the fair-dealing rule); or, secondly, for the trustee to seek permission to purchase from the court.

10–085   Where, on the other hand, there is one party to the transaction who is not both vendor and purchaser, even if that party is a specially appointed nominee, that transaction will indeed not be void but only voidable at the instance of any beneficiary. The many cases in which this rule has been applied have illustrated that it is quite irrelevant that the fiduciary was honest, the sale open and the price fair. In *Wright v. Morgan*[249] property was devised to two trustees on trust for sale for one of them. The will stated that the trustees were required to offer the trustee-beneficiary the land at a price to be fixed by independent valuers. The trustee-beneficiary assigned his beneficial interest to the other trustee, who bought the property at the price fixed by the independent valuers in accordance with the terms of the will. The Privy Council held that, since only a sale to the trustee-beneficiary had been authorised by the will, this sale had to be set aside. The fact that the price was to be fixed independently was not sufficient, for the trustees could themselves fix the time at which the property was to be sold and this could clearly have had a substantial effect on the price ultimately received. This seems to be a somewhat artificial conflict of interest. However, a similar attitude was taken in an eighteenth-century case,[250] in which it was held that a trustee must not purchase trust property which is put up for auction since he is in a position to discourage bidders.

10–086   The self-dealing rule also applies to appointments by trustees of trust property or beneficial interests therein to themselves as beneficiaries. In *Breakspear v. Ackland*[251] by means of three documents executed one after another a new trustee had been appointed, all the trustees had then added that new trustee as a beneficiary, and all the trustees had then made an appointment in her favour. On the face of things the second and third documents were contrary to the self-dealing rule and were therefore voidable at the instance of the other beneficiaries, who indeed sought to avoid them. They would indeed have been avoided had Briggs J. not been able to save the day by finding that the self-dealing in question was authorised by the terms of the settlement. However, the self-dealing rule no longer applies to pension trusts. In *Edge v. Pensions Ombudsman*,[252] the trustees had had to

---

[247] Hence the decision in *Franks v. Bollans* (1868) 3 Ch.App. 717, where a trustee sold to himself, would still be the same today.

[248] This would have worked in *Williams v. Scott* [1900] A.C. 499 (Privy Council on appeal from New South Wales) had there been sufficient disclosure by the trustees to the beneficiaries.

[249] [1926] A.C. 788.

[250] *Whelpdale v. Cookson* (1747) 1 Ves.Sen. 9.

[251] [2008] EWHC 220 (Ch), [2008] W.T.L.R. 777.

[252] [1998] Ch. 512 at 539.

make an amendment to the rules of a pension scheme in order to eliminate an excessive surplus. The effect of the amendment was to reduce employee contributions and to enhance pensions in payment, as a result of which some of the trustees benefited. Scott V.-C. held that, given that statute[253] now requires pension schemes to have member-nominated trustees, it was "quite simply ridiculous" to contend that any trustees who were members had to be excluded from any new or enhanced benefits obtained by the exercise of their powers. His remarks were subsequently approved by the Court of Appeal.[254]

Both *Wright v. Morgan* and *Breakspear v. Ackland* demonstrate that, just as **10–087** in the case of potentially void transactions, the trust instrument can specifically authorise a transaction which is potentially voidable. Indeed, where a settlor has made the same person an original trustee and a beneficiary or has granted an original trustee a power of appointment which he can exercise in his own favour, the self-dealing rule will not apply to him at all.[255] Specific authorisation was also held to have been given, in the context of director and company, in *Sargeant v. National Westminster Bank*.[256] As has already been mentioned, the Articles of Association of virtually all companies also expressly permit purchases by directors provided that disclosure of their interest is made in whatever way is required by the provision in question.[257]

Where the self-dealing rule does nevertheless apply, the only option for a **10–088** purchaser will be to do the same as in the case of a potentially void transaction, either to try to acquire the beneficial interests of the beneficiaries of the trust which is selling or to seek permission to purchase from the court. Such permission will only be granted on the basis of very clear evidence that the sale is in the interests of all the beneficiaries. Such leave is obviously necessary in cases where some of the beneficiaries are either unborn, unascertained or not *sui juris*. Where the beneficiaries are all *sui juris* and are between them absolutely entitled to the whole of the beneficial interest in the property in question, there seems in principle to be no reason why a trustee should not purchase property belonging to his trust without the permission of the court if all the beneficiaries do in fact agree; there is no reason for the court to upset a sale where the beneficiaries have genuinely agreed to it, although such an agreement would obviously only be effective if the trustees had disclosed to the beneficiaries all the information which the trustees possessed relating to the property.

---

[253] Pensions Act 1995, ss.16–21.
[254] [2000] Ch. 602.
[255] *Breakspear v. Ackland* [2008] EWHC 220 (Ch), [2008] W.T.L.R. 777 at [114].
[256] (1990) 61 P. & C.R. 518.
[257] The Companies Acts have long contained a provision requiring directors who are in any way, whether directly or indirectly, interested in a contract or proposed contract with the company to declare the nature of their interest at a meeting of the directors of the company. The present provision is Companies Act 2006, s.177. The Table A Articles of Association recommended by statute provide that directors will not be liable to account for benefits resulting from transactions with the company which have been duly disclosed in accordance with the section. Many Articles of Association additionally provide that such directors should neither vote nor be counted in the quorum on any matter in which they are interested; see *Movitex v. Bullfield* [1988] B.C.L.C. 625.

10–089   Nevertheless, despite the theoretical possibility of an unimpeachable sale taking place in this way, there are in practice two serious objections: first, the onus on the trustee-purchaser of demonstrating that the beneficiaries were indeed given all the relevant information and that they all freely gave their consent is an extremely difficult burden of proof to discharge; and, secondly, even when the trustee-purchaser does acquire a valid title, the property will thereafter often be as unmarketable as if his purchase had been potentially voidable. A right to avoid a transaction is enforceable against successors in title with notice; consequently, if a purchaser becomes aware that his vendor acquired title from a trust of which he was a trustee, it will be most unlikely that he will complete the sale. Even where the former trustee of the property is able to produce a written agreement showing that all the beneficiaries did indeed consent, his purchaser will never be able to be sure that those beneficiaries received all the information in the possession of their trustee before they entered into the agreement with him; consequently, it is only in quite exceptional circumstances that a subsequent purchaser will complete his purchase. For these reasons, a trustee-purchaser will be wise to obtain the permission of the court in every case.

10–090   Where a potentially voidable transaction has been entered into without any appropriate authorisation, it is only in most extraordinary circumstances that the court will refuse to set aside an acquisition of trust property by a trustee at the instance of the beneficiary save where the trustee can successfully raise the defence of delay, usually known as "laches".[258] Exceptionally, however, the court did refuse to upset a transaction in *Holder v. Holder*.[259] One of the executors of a will renounced his executorship after carrying out certain acts which, it was conceded, amounted to intermeddling. He was the tenant of certain farms which the remaining executors offered for sale by auction subject to his tenancy. At the auction he purchased the farms at a good price, probably higher than would have been paid by anyone other than a sitting tenant and well above the reserve price, which had been fixed by an independent valuer. One of the beneficiaries subsequently sought to have the sale set aside. The Court of Appeal refused to do so.

Two of the members of the court declined to accept what Lord Eldon L.C. had said in *Ex parte Lacey*[260] as to the impossibility of determining from the evidence whether or not the purchase has been made on advantageous terms;[261] they instead regarded the rule in *Ex parte Lacey* as no more than a rule of practice. This was originally though to be an indication that the courts might be about to move away from the automatic application of the self-dealing rule and instead apply the fair-dealing rule to purchases by a

---

[258] See *Tito v. Waddell (No.2)* [1977] Ch. 106 at 249–250.

[259] [1968] Ch. 353.

[260] (1802) 6 Ves. 625.

[261] Danckwerts L.J. said that Chancery judges were daily engaged in ascertaining the knowledge and intentions of parties to proceedings; the court could unquestionably sanction such a purchase and so the rule in *Ex parte Lacey* could be no more than a rule of practice. He therefore held that this type of issue was a matter for the discretion of the judge. Sachs L.J. took very much the same view.

trustee of the property belonging to his trust.[262] However, *Holder v. Holder* has not in fact been interpreted in this way. It was subsequently held in *Re Thompson's Settlement*[263] that that decision had instead been reached for the reasons enunciated by the third member of the court, Harman L.J. He held that the purchaser had played no real part in the administration of the estate and had renounced his executorship long before the sale; all the beneficiaries were aware of this and so could not have been looking to him to protect their interests. Thus the mischief which the rule in *Ex parte Lacey* was intended to prevent, the risks associated with one man being both vendor and purchaser, did not arise and there was no reason to set aside the sale.[264] Such an attitude, while quite different from that adopted in *Wright v. Morgan*, does not in any way affect the rule itself. It must also be emphasised that all three members of the court then went on to hold that, in any event, the beneficiaries had acquiesced in the purchase and could not now seek to set it aside; this is obviously another basis on which the decision in *Holder v. Holder* can be explained.

(2) The fair-dealing rule

This rule, which is less stringent, applies to purchases by trustees of the beneficial interests of their beneficiaries and to purchases by other fiduciaries (such as agents) of property belonging to their principals. It also applies where a fiduciary who owes fiduciary duties to more than one principal purchases the property of one of his principals from another of his principals except, as has already been seen, in the case of a purchase on behalf of one trust from another trust where the trustees of the two trusts are absolutely identical, in which case the self-dealing rule appears to apply.   **10–091**

Where a trustee purchases the beneficial interest of one of the beneficiaries under the trust, the mischief which the rule in *Ex parte Lacey* was intended to solve does not arise since the trustee is not both vendor and purchaser. Hence the courts have always been prepared to uphold such purchases provided that the trustee is able to establish that he obtained no advantage by reason of his position[265]; in particular, he must be able to show that he did not abuse his position as trustee, that he concealed no material facts, that the price was fair, and that the beneficiary did not rely solely on his advice.[266] This will be an almost impossible burden of proof to discharge when the beneficiary is a minor[267]; in such circumstances, the trustee will again need to seek the permission of the court to purchase.   **10–092**

Similarly, where a fiduciary such as an agent purchases property belonging to his principal, he is again in practice unlikely to be both sole vendor   **10–093**

---

[262] See Jones, 84 L.Q.R. (1968) 472, the first three editions of *Constructive Trusts* and earlier editions of this work.

[263] [1986] Ch. 99.

[264] In *Re Thompson's Settlement* [1986] Ch. 99 at 115, Vinelott J. therefore held that the self-dealing rule "is applied stringently in cases where a trustee concurs in a transaction which cannot be carried into effect without his concurrence and who also has an interest in or holds a fiduciary duty to another in relation to the same transaction". He held that two leases in favour of a company and a partnership of which the two trustees were respectively a shareholder and a partner were not valid.

[265] *Chalmer v. Bradley* (1819) 1 J. & W. 51.

[266] *Coles v. Trescothick* (1804) 9 Ves. 234.

[267] See *Sanderson v. Walker* (1807) 13 Ves. 601.

and purchaser; even if he is, in comparison with the position of a trustee or a director who is purchasing property belonging to his principal, he will have far fewer possibilities of taking any unfair advantage. Consequently, such purchases will similarly be upheld provided that the fiduciary is able to show that he did not abuse his position in any way, that he paid a fair price, and that he has made full disclosure of his interest and of any information which he possesses about the property.[268]

10–094   Further, where a fiduciary who owes fiduciary duties to more than one principal purchases the property of one of his principals from to another of his principals, then, except in the case of a purchase on behalf of one trust from another trust where the trustees of the two trusts are absolutely identical in which case the self-dealing rule appears to apply anyway, the fiduciary will also have far fewer possibilities of taking any unfair advantage. Consequently, such purchases will similarly be upheld provided that the fiduciary is able to show that he did not abuse his position in any way, that he paid a fair price, and that he has made full disclosure of his interest and of any information which he possesses about the property.[269]Consequently, such purchases will similarly be upheld provided that the fiduciary is able to show that he did not abuse his position in any way, that he paid a fair price, and that he has made full disclosure of his interest and of any information which he possesses about the property.

(3)   The precise limits of the rules
10–095   The self-dealing rule and the fair-dealing rule cannot be evaded by selling to an associate of the purchaser rather than to the purchaser himself; the rules have proved strong enough to prevent evasion. Most of the decided cases concern purchases by associates of trustees. In the first place, although a sale to a relative of the trustee is not necessarily bad,[270] a purchase taken in the name of the trustee's children will usually be upset[271] and it is very risky to take a purchase in the name of the trustee's spouse,[272] at least if at the time the two "were living in perfect amity" rather than "separate and in enmity for a dozen years".[273] Nor can the rules be overcome by selling to a limited company of which the trustee is the majority shareholder[274] or of which he has control.[275] It seems that a sale by a trustee to a company of which he is a member, but which he does not control, which is necessarily not void, is not *ipso facto* voidable either; however, if the beneficiaries seek to upset the transaction, the company may have to show that the trustee had taken all reasonable steps to find a purchaser and that the price paid by the company was at the time adequate.[276]

---

[268] *Edwards v. Meyrick* (1842) 2 Hare 60.
[269] See *Hillsdown Holdings v. Pensions Ombudsman* [1997] 1 All E.R. 862 at 895–896.
[270] *Coles v. Trescothick* (1804) 9 Ves. 234.
[271] *Gregory v. Gregory* (1821) Jac. 631.
[272] *Ferraby v. Hobson* (1847) 2 Ph. 255; *Burrell v. Burrell's Trustee* 1915 S.C. 333.
[273] *Tito v. Waddell (No.2)* [1977] Ch. 106 at 240.
[274] *Silkstone and Haigh Moor Coal Co. v. Edey* [1900] 1 Ch. 167; *Movitex v. Bullfield* [1988] B.C.L.C. 104.
[275] *Re Thompson's Settlement* [1986] Ch. 99; *Movitex v. Bullfield* [1988] B.C.L.C. 104.
[276] *Farrar v. Farrar's* (1888) 40 Ch.D. 395.

Similar rules presumably apply to partnerships; certainly, a sale by a **10–096** trustee to a partnership comprising the trustee and his family will not be valid.[277] It is equally offensive to the rules to sell the property to a third person, with an agreement or understanding for its repurchase.[278] However, it has been held that, where there was no agreement or understanding for repurchase at the time of the sale to the third person, the fact that the trustee had sold the property to that person with the hope of being able to repurchase was not a sufficient ground for setting the sale aside.[279] Finally, a sale may be upset if a trustee retires with the intention that the property will be conveyed to him after his retirement.[280] If, however, a sufficient length of time has elapsed between the retirement and the sale for the court to be satisfied that the ex-trustee has not taken any advantage of knowledge about the property gained while he was a trustee, the sale will be upheld. Such a transaction was upheld where there had been an interval of 12 years between the trustee's retirement and his purchase.[281]

(4) The consequences of liability

When a transaction is void under the principles discussed above, it will **10–097** simply have no effect. Thus in *Franks v. Bollans*,[282] a trustee contrived, by means of an extremely intricate deed, to sell to himself part of the land which he was holding on trust. One of the beneficiaries was subsequently held still to be beneficially entitled to it on the grounds that both contract and conveyance were wholly void. She was, however, fortunate that the purchaser still held the property which he had purchased. Where this is not the case, the property will only be able to be recovered from a third party if the latter has not taken free of the beneficiary's interest.[283] If the third party has done so, then the only recourse of the beneficiary will be to attempt to follow the property into its product in the way which will be discussed in a later chapter[284] or to attempt to obtain compensation for the breach of fiduciary duty.[285]

On the other hand, when a transaction is not void but only voidable at the **10–098** instance of the principal, the latter must avoid it within a reasonable time, otherwise his failure to do so will entitle the purchaser to invoke the defence of laches.[286] If the sale is so avoided, the consequences will be as follows.

---

[277] *Re Thompson's Settlement* [1986] Ch. 99.

[278] *Williams v. Scott* [1900] A.C. 499.

[279] *Re Postlethwaite* (1888) 37 W.R. 200, 60 L.T. 514.

[280] *Wright v. Morgan* [1926] A.C. 788; *Re Mullholland's Will Trusts* [1949] 1 All E.R. 460.

[281] *Re Boles and the British Land Company's Contract* [1902] 1 Ch. 244.

[282] (1868) 3 Ch.App. 717.

[283] Only likely if the third party has not purchased for value or if the property is unregistered land. A purchaser for value of registered land or pure personalty will almost inevitably have taken free.

[284] See *post*, para 22–133 *et seq.*

[285] Contrary to earlier indications in *Tito v. Waddell (No.2)* [1977] Ch. 106 at 246–249, the Court of Appeal held in *Gwembe Valley Development Co. v. Koshy* [2003] EWCA Civ. 1478, [2004] W.T.L.R. 97 that a breach of the self-dealing rule or the fair-dealing rule is a breach of fiduciary duty.

[286] See *Tito v. Waddell (No.2)* [1977] Ch. 106 at 249–250.

10–099   If the subject matter of the purchase is still in the hands of the purchaser, then the principal will have a choice.

> (1) He will be able to recover the property together with any income produced in the meantime provided that he is in a position to make *restitutio in integrum* by returning to the purchaser the price which the latter paid for it. In the case of beneficiaries under a trust, this option will require the consent of all of them because of the risk that the property may not be able subsequently to be resold at a higher value, in which case "the beneficiaries would be worse off than if the claim had never been made".[287]

> (2) Alternatively, the principal can require the property to be put up for sale again under the direction of the court[288]; the fiduciary will not be allowed to bid at this resale if any of his principals objects to him so doing.[289] The reserve price will normally be the price originally paid by the purchaser together with interest in respect of the time during which he has held the property, plus the value of any improvements which he has made to the property and interest on that amount, minus any income produced by the property or, if the purchaser has himself been in occupation, the appropriate occupation rent.[290] If the sale "realises more than the reserve fixed by the court, the surplus belongs to the [principal], whereas if it realises less [the fiduciary] will be held to his bargain"[291] and so will lose the difference.

It will only be in the interests of the principal to use either of these remedies where the property is worth at least as much as the fiduciary paid for it. If it has fallen in value, avoiding the transaction will give the principal a property worth less than the sum which he has to return to the fiduciary; consequently, it will be in his interests to affirm the transaction.

10–100   If, on the other hand, the property is no longer in the hands of the principal, any third party to whom it has been transferred will have acquired legal title to that property because of the fact that the transaction was voidable rather than void. If the third party has not taken free of the right of the principal to have the purchase set aside (which is of course a mere equity), the third party will be in exactly the same position as the fiduciary. If, however, he has taken free of this mere equity because he is a bona fide purchaser for value without notice or a statutory equivalent, then the property will not be able to be recovered by the principal, whose position will be as follows.

---

[287] *Holder v. Holder* [1968] Ch. 353 at 370–371 (Cross J.).

[288] This was what was ordered at first instance in *Holder v. Holder, ibid.*, where the purchase was set aside.

[289] *Tennant v. Trenchard* (1869) 4 Ch.App. 537.

[290] This was the form of order made in *Holder v. Holder* at first instance; although the right to add to the reserve price the value of any improvements was conceded in that case, the existence of the right to do so emerges clearly from *O'Sullivan v. Management Agency and Music* [1985] Q.B. 428 at 466.

[291] *Holder v. Holder* [1968] Ch. 353 at 371 (Cross J.).

(1) He will be entitled to recover any profit made by the fiduciary on the resale[292] with interest on that profit.[293]

(2) In the event of a resale at less than the true value, he will also be able to claim the difference between the price paid and the true value with interest thereon[294]; this will be recoverable by way of compensation for breach of fiduciary duty under *Nocton v. Lord Ashburton*[295] (such compensation is also available as an alternative to an account of profits[296]).

(3) If, on the other hand, the price paid by the third party was less than the price paid by the fiduciary because the property had fallen in value, the fiduciary will have made no profit and the principal will have suffered no loss; consequently, in such circumstances, the principal will neither have nor be entitled to any remedy.

(B) Sales of Property to a Principal

A sale by a fiduciary to his principal of property belonging to himself, or belonging to another principal to whom he also owes fiduciary duties, will be set aside at the instance of the purchasing principal unless the fiduciary has fully disclosed the nature of his interest in the transaction; this is the case no matter how honest the fiduciary or fair the price.[297] Such a sale may be set aside even where the property in question was purchased before the entered into the fiduciary relationship with the purchasing principal. Thus, in *Armstrong v. Jackson*[298] a stockbroker did not disclose to his client that he had owned the shares which he was encouraging the client to buy ever since the company in question had originally been formed. Five years later, by which time the shares had fallen in value to less than a fifth of the purchase price which the client had paid, he discovered the true facts and successfully sought rescission of the sale. However, where the property has instead increased in value, it will not be in the interests of the purchasing principal to set aside the transaction. In the event that, for this or any other reason, he seeks not to set aside the sale but to recover the profit made out of the transaction, his right to do so will depend on when the property was originally purchased.

In *Bentley v. Craven*[299] the defendant was responsible for the purchase of sugar for a partnership of sugar refiners of which he was a member but also

10–101

10–102

---

[292] *Hall v. Hallett* (1784) 1 Cox 134; *Ex parte James* (1803) 8 Ves. 337 at 351; *Silkstone and Haigh Moor Coal Co. v. Edey* [1900] 1 Ch. 167.

[293] Formerly 4% but, following *Bartlett v. Barclays Bank Trust Co.* [1980] Ch. 515 at 547, it seems that the rate will now be that of the court's short-term investment account (established under the Administration of Justice Act 1965, s.6 (1)).

[294] *Lord Hardwicke v. Vernon* (1800) 4 Ves. 411.

[295] [1914] A.C. 932. See Davidson (1982) 13 Melbourne U.L.R. 349.

[296] *McKenzie v. McDonald* [1927] V.L.R. 134 (Court of Appeal of Victoria). This is one of the possible explanations of *Coleman v. Myers* [1977] 2 N.Z.L.R. 225 (Court of Appeal of New Zealand), where minority shareholders recovered compensation from the directors of the company (held, unusually, to owe them fiduciary duties because of the family nature of the company) who had recommended the acceptance of an under-valued takeover bid without disclosing that the offeror was a company controlled by one of them.

[297] *Gillett v. Peppercone* (1840) 3 Beav. 78.

[298] [1917] 2 K.B. 822.

[299] (1853) 18 Beav. 75.

carried on an independent business as a sugar dealer. He purchased a quantity of sugar which he later resold to the partnership at a price which, although resulting in a profit to him, was the fair market price of the day. He was held liable to account for his profit to the partnership since he had been a fiduciary at the date of purchase and so should have purchased for the partnership rather than for himself. A similar decision was reached where an investment adviser purchased a property of a type which he knew that his client wished to purchase and subsequently sold it on to her at a substantial profit.[300]

10–103   On the other hand, in *Re Cape Breton Co.*[301] a director acquiesced in the sale to his company of certain mining claims in which he had a beneficial interest. After discovering the facts, the company elected not to set aside the sale. Subsequently, after the property had been sold on at a loss, the company tried to claim the profit which the director had made on the original sale. This action failed because the director had acquired the property more than two years before the company in question had been formed. This conclusion is clearly correct when the fiduciary sold the property to his principal at the market value. The Court of Appeal actually held, by a majority, that it made no difference that the director had sold above the market value. However, the House of Lords[302] held that there was no evidence that the sale price was above market value. This point, therefore, did not have to be decided but Lord Herschell considered that an agent employed to purchase non-specific goods in the market would be liable for the excess if he sold his own goods to the company above market value.[303] Therefore, although the decision of the Court of Appeal clearly constitutes the law at present, this particular point cannot be regarded as finally settled.

10–104   These authorities show that, when the principal does not seek to rescind the sale or cannot do so because rescission is barred on the grounds of affirmation, laches or bona fide purchase, he will only have a remedy where the fiduciary acquired the property after he entered into the fiduciary relationship in question or, possibly, where the sale price was above the market value. All the authorities discussed deal with fiduciary relationships other than that of trustee and beneficiary. There appears to be no English authority dealing with a purchase by a trustee of his own property for his trust; however, an American decision[304] and dicta in *Bentley v. Craven* suggest that the same rules will also apply to such transactions.

(C) Regular Trading

10–105 Where a fiduciary engages in regular trading between a business which he is managing in a fiduciary capacity and his own business, or another business which he is also managing in a fiduciary capacity, the situation will be

---

[300] *Cook v. Evatt (No.2)* [1992] 1 N.Z.L.R. 676 (High Court of New Zealand).

[301] (1885) 29 Ch.D. 795.

[302] *Sub nom. Cavendish Bentinck v. Fenn* (1887) 12 App.Cas. 652.

[303] *ibid.*, at 659. The remedy would presumably have been either an account of profits or compensation under *Nocton v. Lord Ashburton*.

[304] *Cornet v. Cornet* (1916) 269 No. 298.

governed by exactly the same principles as in the case of a sale of property by a fiduciary to his principal.[305]

(D) Loans

This situation only seems to have arisen in one reported case, *Swindle v.* **10–106**
Harrison.[306] A solicitor made a loan to his client to enable her to complete the purchase of a property and avoid the loss of the 20 per cent deposit which she had already paid. No other source of finance was available to her. The transaction did not ultimately prove profitable and she was unable to repay the advance, which was secured on the property. She had obviously been aware of the source of the funds but sought to prevent the solicitor from realising his security on the grounds that he had not explained to her exactly how much interest he would be making. The Court of Appeal accepted that his failure fully to explain this amounted to a breach of fiduciary duty. However, since *restitutio in integrum* was obviously impossible because of her inability to repay the sum advanced to the solicitor, her only conceivable remedy for his breach of fiduciary duty was equitable compensation under *Nocton v. Lord Ashburton.*[307] In the event the Court of Appeal denied her any equitable compensation because her position would have been even worse if the loan had never been made.[308]

It is not easy to envisage a fiduciary such as a trustee making a loan to his **10–107**
principal other than on a short-term basis in order to deal with some temporary shortage of liquidity. Further, the making of a loan will normally be to the advantage of the borrower anyway unless the rate of interest is excessive. Consequently, even if the making of such a loan were to be regarded as a breach of fiduciary duty, the only obvious sanction would be to deprive the fiduciary of any right to any interest on the sum advanced.

7. Benefits obtained by a Fiduciary as a result of his Position to the Exclusion of his Principal

This third group of cases has emerged as the result of the rigorous applica- **10–108**
tion by the courts of a decision in 1726[309] which established what was, in the light of the prevailing legal rules and financial circumstances, a wholly understandable prohibition on trustees renewing for their own benefit leases formerly held by their trusts. This decision has had two quite distinct effects. First, it has produced a line of authority concerning the extent to which this prohibition also applies to other fiduciaries and the associated question of whether a fiduciary may purchase for his own benefit the freehold reversion in property of which his principal is lessee. Secondly, and totally unconnected with any question of the renewal of leases or the purchase of reversions, the decision has also had a profound effect on the general question of what opportunities a fiduciary is entitled to utilise for his own benefit.

---

[305] This situation is discussed by Finn, *Fiduciary Obligations* (1977), pp.228–231.
[306] [1997] 4 All E.R. 705.
[307] [1914] A.C. 932.
[308] See *post*, para 22–009 *et seq.*
[309] *Keech v. Sandford* (1726) Sel.Cas.Ch. 61.

(A)   Speculation by a Fiduciary with the Property of his Principal

10–109   This is almost the only situation within this third group of cases which is wholly uncontroversial. Where a fiduciary engages in speculation with the property of his principal, the latter will be entitled to all the profits made by the fiduciary under a constructive trust.[310] A somewhat extreme example of the operation of this principle is *Reid-Newfoundland Co. v. Anglo-American Telegraph Co.*[311] Under the terms of a contract, a telegraph company had erected a special telegraph wire for use in the operation of a railway. The contract provided that no commercial messages should be passed over this wire except for the account of the telegraph company. When this prohibition was directly contravened, the telegraph company successfully claimed that the profits made thereby were held subject to a constructive trust in its favour. The Privy Council appear to have regarded the company operating the railway as the agent of the telegraph company in respect of its use of the latter's telegraph wire. Thus, the former had in breach of fiduciary duty made a profit out of the use of the latter's property and so was clearly bound to account for that profit under a constructive trust.

10–110   However, a similar claim failed in *Attorney-General v. Blake*.[312] It has already been seen[313] that the Attorney-General contended that the Soviet spy Blake owed the Crown a fiduciary duty, *inter alia*, not to use the Crown's property, including intangible property such as originally confidential information, for his profit. Scott V.-C. held that this duty was formulated in terms too wide to be acceptable and went on to dismiss the Crown's claim on the grounds that the law will not go so far as to impose unreasonable restraints either on the freedom of speech of a former fiduciary or on his ability to earn his living by exploiting expertise acquired during the fiduciary relationship. No doubt was cast on this reasoning on appeal[314]; the Court of Appeal specifically held that Blake was not in breach of fiduciary duty but both there and in the House of Lords the Crown instead succeeded on public law and contractual arguments not raised at first instance. However, there seems little likelihood that the arguments which commended themselves to Scott V.-C. will often be invoked successfully; it is hardly likely that the courts would look very charitably on a fiduciary who speculated with what had to be regarded as the property of his principal and then sought to retain his profit on that ground.

10–111   When liability is imposed in this type of case, the situation will be as follows. Where the principal has been owner of the property throughout, and also in cases where the fiduciary is already holding the property in question on trust for his principal, the constructive trust will be imposed merely on the profit. But if the property has instead reached the hands of the fiduciary in some other way, both the property and the fiduciary's profit will be subject to a constructive trust. If there is no profit, because the speculation has resulted in a loss, a constructive trust may still be imposed, if necessary, upon any of the property remaining in the hands of the fiduciary and, in the

---

[310] *Brown v. I.R.C.* [1965] A.C. 264.
[311] [1912] A.C. 555.
[312] [1997] Ch. 84.
[313] See *ante*, para 10–078.
[314] [1998] Ch. 439 (CA), [2001] 1 A.C. 268.

event that the value of the property has fallen as a result of the breach by the fiduciary of his duty of loyalty, the principal will be able to recover compensation for that loss under *Nocton v. Lord Ashburton*.[315] The latter actually occurred in *Tang Man Sit v. Capacious Investments*.[316] The defendant had made secret profits from letting certain houses on his land which he had agreed to assign to the plaintiff, who had financed their construction pursuant to a joint venture agreement. The plaintiff recovered not only those profits but also compensation for the diminution in value of the houses caused by their wrongful occupation.

(B) Competition between a Fiduciary and the Business of his Principal
There are certain circumstances in which a fiduciary will not be able to compete with the business of his principal. Different rules apply to the different fiduciary relationships. **10–112**

(1) Trustees
Where the trust property includes a business, or the trustees carry on any income earning activity, a trustee must not commence a business or activity on his own account which will compete with that of the trust. Thus, in *Re Thomson*[317] one of the assets of a trust was a yachtbroker's business, which was being carried on by the trustees. One of them sought to set up on his own a similar business in the same town, which would have competed with the trust business, but the court granted an injunction restraining him from doing so. The decision in *Re Thomson* appears to be at variance with that in *Moore v. M'Glynn*,[318] to which the court was not referred. There an injunction was refused although it was thought that the setting up of a competing business would be a good ground for removing the trustee from his trusteeship. It was said that a breach of trust would only be committed if, in carrying on the new business, the trustee practised deception or solicited the customers from the old shop. It is sometimes suggested that this decision can be reconciled with that in *Re Thomson* on the basis that the yachtbroker's business was so specialised that any other yachtbroking business in the town was bound to compete with the trust business, even if the customers were not solicited. This is a possible solution but it does not actually appear to have been the basis of the decision in *Re Thomson*. **10–113**

The decision in *Re Thomson* seems clearly right in principle and it may well be that *Moore v. M'Glynn* would not now be followed. As has been shown, in other circumstances the court has been so astute to find a conflict of interest that it is doubtful if the court would stop itself from finding a conflict where the same business was being carried on, at least if that business were serving the same locality. Where, however, a person who is carrying on a business is then appointed to be a trustee, the position seems to depend on whether the person making the appointment knew of that business. If he did, the trustee will be entitled to continue his business but, **10–114**

---

[315] [1914] A.C. 932.
[316] [1996] 1 A.C. 514 (Privy Council on appeal from Hong Kong).
[317] [1930] 1 Ch. 203.
[318] [1894] 1 Ir.R. 74.

if it then appears that there is an actual conflict of interest, he may be
required to resign or may be removed.[319]

(2) Other fiduciaries

10–115   It might be expected that, if an unpaid trustee may thus in appropriate
circumstances be prevented from competing, the paid director and partner
would necessarily be prohibited from so doing. Partners are indeed under a
statutory duty not to compete with the partnership business[320] but the
position of directors is both obscure and anomalous. At common law, a
director is not under any obligation not to compete with his company; this
emerges from *London and Mashonaland Exploration Co. v. New Mashonaland
Exploration Co.*,[321] where it was held that a director cannot be restrained from
acting as a director of a rival company, a decision which was approved in
Bell v. Lever Bros[322] by Lord Blanesburgh, who added that "[w]hat he could
do for a rival company he could, of course, do for himself". Merely to accept
directorships in competing companies still does not constitute a breach of
the duty of loyalty owed by the director to the first company. Further, these
decisions were applied by the Court of Appeal in *In Plus Group v. Pyke* [323] to
deny a claim for an account of profits against a director who had started a
competing company after he had been wholly excluded from all participation in the original company and was being denied either any repayment of
a very substantial loan or any salary. However, Sedley L.J. regarded the
principle of the previous decisions as "very limited" and certainly would
not have applied it to a situation where the two companies in question had
been preparing to tender for the same contract.[324]

10–116   Further and in any event, it is now clear that, just as an employee may not
compete with the business of his employer,[325] an executive director is under
a similar duty not to compete with his company. This seems to have been
recognised by Lord Denning in *Scottish Co-operative Wholesale Society v.
Meyer*,[326] which concerned an application under what is now section 994 of
the Companies Act 2006 to wind a company up on the grounds that the
manner in which its affairs were being conducted was unfairly prejudicial to
the applicant. In practice, the matter must often be dealt with in the Articles
of Association or in the service contract of any individual director. Thus, in
Thomas Marshall Exports v. Guinle,[327] a managing director had specifically
agreed in his service contract not to engage in any other business without
the company's consent or to disclose confidential information. It was alleged
that he had done both these things as a means of diverting the company's
business to himself and that, subsequently, he had repudiated his service

---

[319] See, by analogy, *Peyton v. Robinson* (1823) 1 L.J.(O.S.)Ch. 191; *Moore v. M'Glynn* [1894] 1 Ir.R.
74.
[320] By virtue of the Partnership Act 1890, s.30.
[321] [1891] 1 W.N. 165.
[322] [1932] A.C. 161 at 165.
[323] [2002] EWCA Civ. 370, [2002] 2 B.C.L.C. 201.
[324] *ibid.*, at [84].
[325] *Hivac v. Park Royal Scientific Instruments* [1946] Ch. 169.
[326] [1959] A.C. 324 at 366–367.
[327] [1979] Ch. 227.

contract by resigning half way through a fixed 10-year contract. Interim injunctions were granted restraining him from dealing with the company's customers and from disclosing any confidential information. This decision was based primarily on the express contractual stipulation but also, to a lesser extent, on his fiduciary obligations as a director. Subsequently in *Coleman Taymar v. Oakes*,[328] a company decided to cease the operations in which a particular executive director was engaged. He wished to continue these operations on his own account and so, during the subsequent period until the termination of his employment and without informing the company, he made arrangements to obtain new leases of the company's premises and to acquire some of its equipment and he also used the company's employees to carry out preliminary work for his own business. It was held that, as a result, he had been able to start up his own business only two months after the termination of his employment with the company rather than up to a year later. He was held to have acted in breach of his contract of employment and in breach of his fiduciary duty to the company. The company had suffered no loss whatsoever and so were awarded merely £2 damages for breach of contract; however, the company was awarded an account of the benefits which the director had obtained as a result of his conduct.

The authorities discussed establish that, where a fiduciary has breached his duty of loyalty by competing with the business of his principal, the latter can obtain an injunction restraining such competition. Further, it is now clear from *Coleman Taymar v. Oakes*[329] that a fiduciary who has engaged in unlawful competition is liable to account to his principal for any profits which he has made thereby; this will usually take the form of equitable compensation for breach of fiduciary duty but, in principle, could in appropriate circumstances also be by way of the imposition of a constructive trust. **10–117**

(C) Renewal by a Fiduciary for his own Benefit of a Lease Formerly Held by his Principal

In *Keech v. Sandford*[330] a lease of a market was held on trust for an infant. The trustee sought, unsuccessfully, to renew the lease for the benefit of the trust. However, the landlord, although not prepared to renew the lease to the trust, was prepared to grant a renewal to the trustee in his personal capacity and the trustee duly took up the lease in his own right. Lord King L.C. held that any trustee who abuses his position by entering into a transaction with a third party must account for the benefit of the transaction as a constructive trustee. Consequently the trustee held the benefit of the lease on constructive trust for the infant. The rationale of the rule was stated both simply and cynically: if a trustee on the refusal of a lessor to renew a lease to the **10–118**

---

[328] [2001] 2 B.C.L.C. 749.
[329] [2001] 2 B.C.L.C. 749. Such claims had previously been made, unsuccessfully, in *Moore v. M'Glynn* [1894] 1 Ir.R. 74 and in *In Plus Group v. Pyke* [2002] 2 B.C.L.C. 201, where the fiduciary was held to have been entitled to compete with his principal.
[330] (1726) Sel.Cas.Ch. 61.

trust were permitted to take a lease himself, few leases would ever be renewed in favour of trusts.

10–119　　This prohibition was wholly understandable at that time. Many ecclesiastical, charitable and public bodies were by law restricted as to the length of leases which they were able to grant and leases were therefore renewed more or less as a matter of right. By taking a renewal of a lease for himself, a trustee was therefore in practice depriving the trust of a grant which it had a right to expect. This was also the time of the South Sea Bubble, a period of extravagant financial speculation and even more extravagant financial collapses, when the existence of stringent controls on the activities of fiduciaries was unquestionably necessary. However, the rule laid down in *Keech v. Sandford* has continued to be applied despite the relaxation of the rules as to the length of leases and the greater financial stability of the nineteenth and twentieth centuries; indeed it has been extended so as to apply also to other fiduciaries.

10–120　　The precise limits of the rule were discussed very fully in *Re Biss.*[331] The Court of Appeal held that the rule applies with all its stringency to persons clearly occupying a fiduciary position such as trustees or agents; there is an irrebuttable presumption that such persons cannot retain the benefit of transactions entered into in their personal capacity. On the other hand, persons owing a special but non-fiduciary duty are subject only to a rebuttable presumption. Thus if such a person can show that he did not abuse his position, he can retain the benefit of the transaction. The court considered mortgagees, tenants for life, joint tenants, tenants in common and (rather unexpectedly) partners to be in this category. There seems no good reason why partners, who are quite clearly fiduciaries for all other purposes, should be in the latter rather than the former category and *Thompson's Trustee v. Heaton*[332] and *Popat v. Shonchintra*[333] (both of which actually concerned purchases of freehold reversions) may well have changed the law in this respect, although this question cannot yet be regarded as finally settled. On the other hand, it is clear that the rule in *Keech v. Sandford* does not apply to a person who owes neither fiduciary obligations nor a special non-fiduciary duty. Thus in *Savage v. Dunningham*,[334] where three persons were sharing an unfurnished flat and the rack rent payable for that flat, it was held that one of them was perfectly entitled to purchase a long leasehold interest in that flat for his own benefit.

10–121　　While the rule in *Keech v. Sandford* is certainly a stringent penal rule which it is impossible to justify in modern conditions, there is absolutely no doubt that it remains English law. Where the rule applies, the principal will be entitled to take over the lease but will obviously have to pay the rent due thereunder. There has never been a reported case where the fiduciary has paid a capital sum for the lease in question. In this event, the result would presumably be the same as where a fiduciary has purchased the reversion on a lease held by his principal, discussed below.

---

[331] [1903] 2 Ch. 40.
[332] [1974] 1 W.L.R. 605. See *post*, para 10–124.
[333] [1995] 1 W.L.R. 908. See *post*, para 10–125, n.345.
[334] [1974] Ch. 181.

(D) Purchase by a Fiduciary of the Reversion on a Lease Held by his Principal

The rule in *Keech v. Sandford* has been extended to cases where the fiduciary **10–122** has acquired the reversion, normally but obviously not necessarily the freehold reversion, in property of which his principal is lessee.

When the fiduciary has acquired the reversion by means of an abuse of his **10–123** fiduciary position, it is clearly in accordance with principle for a constructive trust to be imposed. A trust was imposed on this ground in *Hooper v. Gorvin*,[335] where one of a number of leasehold tenants of a site had been nominated to act on their behalf in negotiations for the acquisition of the freehold. As has already been seen,[336] he was held to have assumed fiduciary obligations towards them and therefore held the freehold, which he had purchased in his sole name, on constructive trust for all of them. This will also be the case where the fiduciary has only obtained the opportunity to purchase because, as fiduciary, he was the nominal lessee.[337] Similarly, when leases were renewable by custom, a fiduciary who purchased the reversion would also be held to hold the reversion on constructive trust for his principal since, otherwise, he would be able to prejudice the interests of his principal by declining to renew the lease.[338]

On the other hand, where the lease in question is not renewable by custom **10–124** or by right, the acquisition of the reversion by the fiduciary can hardly be said to prejudice his principal and until relatively recently it was held that in such circumstances a fiduciary who had not abused his position was entitled to retain the reversion for his own benefit.[339] This seemed wholly in accordance with principle. However, more recent cases have raised some doubt as to whether a fiduciary can ever purchase a reversion for his own benefit. In *Protheroe v. Protheroe*[340] a husband held a leasehold on trust for himself and his wife in equal shares. After they had separated, he acquired the freehold reversion. The Court of Appeal, in a short extempore judgment which did not refer to any of the authorities just discussed, held that a trustee of leasehold property can never acquire the freehold for himself and imposed a constructive trust. It seems highly likely that the husband only obtained the opportunity to acquire the reversion because he was, as trustee, the nominal lessee. If this was the case, discussion and application of the earlier authorities would have made no difference. However, the broad principle thus enunciated was subsequently applied in *Thompson's Trustee v. Heaton*.[341] After the dissolution of a partnership, one of the partners remained in possession of land of which the partners had been and remained joint lessees. After that partner's death 14 years later, his executors acquired the freehold reversion and subsequently resold the land. The trustee in bankruptcy of the other partner successfully claimed to be entitled to one half of the profit so obtained, Pennycuick V.-C. holding that on the

---

[335] [2001] W.T.L.R. 575 at 589–590.
[336] *ante*, para 10–050.
[337] *Griffith v. Owen* [1907] 1 Ch. 105.
[338] *Phillips v. Phillips* (1885) 29 Ch.D. 673.
[339] *Randall v. Russell* (1817) 3 Mer. 190; *Bevan v. Webb* [1905] 1 Ch. 620.
[340] [1968] 1 W.L.R. 519.
[341] [1974] 1 W.L.R. 605.

facts the leasehold interest remained an undistributed asset of the partner-ship and thus, by virtue of *Protheroe v. Protheroe*, neither partner could acquire the reversion for his sole benefit.

10–125   *Thompson's Trustee v. Heaton*[342] obviously casts doubt on the statement by the Court of Appeal in *Re Biss*[343] that partners were only to be caught by the rule in *Keech v. Sandford* if it could be shown that an advantage had actually been obtained by virtue of their position (this dictum has admittedly already been criticised[344] but should surely at the very least have been discussed). More significantly, the broad statement in *Protheroe v. Protheroe* was applied without reference to the earlier authorities, the application of which might well have led to a different result.[345] Subsequently, in *Don King Productions Inc. v. Warren*,[346] the Court of Appeal did not accept that it was an open question whether the rule in *Keech v. Sandford* applies to the acquisition of reversions. It may therefore well be that *Protheroe v. Protheroe* has swept away all the earlier distinctions and has established that a fiduciary may never purchase for his own benefit a reversion in property of which his principal is lessee. If this is indeed the case, then only where, as in *Savage v. Dunningham*,[347] a purchaser of a reversion is not a fiduciary at all will he be able to acquire it for his own benefit. The principle enunciated in *Protheroe v. Protheroe* seems unnecessarily harsh and it is therefore suggested that the approach of the earlier authorities was preferable.

10–126   Where the purchase of a reversion by a fiduciary is successfully impugned, the imposition of a constructive trust does not mean that he will lose the money which he has paid for it. His principal is entitled to purchase the reversion from him for the price which he originally paid, so that he is only deprived of his profit. Where, as in *Hooper v. Gorvin*,[348] it was always intended that the fiduciary would acquire a share in the reversion, he will nevertheless be entitled to retain that share. In such circumstances, *Popat v. Shonchintra*[349] establishes that the beneficial interests in such reversions are divided in proportion to each person's capital injections—an entirely justifi-able extrapolation of the rule in *Keech v. Sandford*. However, the principal may well be unable or unwilling to purchase the reversion; it is not unlikely that this will be the position of a trust, at least when the trust was not the only tenant. In that event, the principal can nevertheless insist on the reversion being resold and he will then take any profit made on the resale; this was also held in *Hooper v. Gorvin*.

---

[342] [1974] 1 W.L.R. 605.

[343] [1903] 2 Ch. 40.

[344] See *ante*, para 10–120.

[345] This would not, however, have been the case in *Popat v. Shonchintra* [1995] 1 W.L.R. 908, in which *Thompson's Trustee v. Heaton* was subsequently applied, where another former partner had only acquired the opportunity to purchase the freehold because he had continued to run the business and so was clearly a trustee of it (on appeal ([1997] 1 W.L.R 1367), this case was decided on the basis of technical partnership rules).

[346] [2000] Ch. 291 at 340 (CA).

[347] [1974] Ch. 181.

[348] [2001] W.T.L.R. 575 at 589–590.

[349] [1995] 1 W.L.R. 908. On appeal ([1997] 1 W.L.R 1367), the case was decided on the basis of technical partnership rules.

(E) Renewals of Other Contracts by a Partner for his own Benefit

The principles established by the authorities which have just been discussed **10–127** were, in *Don King Productions Inc. v. Warren*,[350] applied to the renewal by a partner for his own benefit of management and promotion agreements entered into between himself and a number of professional boxers for the benefit of a partnership. The principal issue in the case was whether, despite the non-assignable nature of such contracts, their benefit was held by the English manager and promoter in question on trust for a partnership which he had formed with an American promoter. This question having been answered in the affirmative, it then became necessary to decide whether the benefit of any such contract which was renewed between the dissolution of the partnership and the conclusion of its winding-up was also held on trust for the partnership.

The English partner contended that the rule in *Keech v. Sandford* is confined to the renewal of leases (and possibly also to the acquisition of reversions) but does not apply to the renewal of ordinary commercial contracts. However, the Court of Appeal specifically agreed with the statement of principle enunciated by Pennycuick V.-C. in *Thompson's Trustee v. Heaton*[351] and declined to accept that the principle which underlies the rule in *Keech v. Sandford* does not apply to a partner in respect of all property owned by the partnership at the time of dissolution. It was held that both of what Deane J. had identified in *Chan v. Zacharia*[352] as overlapping principles were satisfied; the contracts were renewed in circumstances where a significant conflict of interest existed between the partner's duty of good faith and his personal interest and any renewal was by use or by reason of the partners' fiduciary position. However, it is obviously likely that this extension of the rule in *Keech v. Sandford* to the renewal of ordinary commercial contracts is limited to partnerships.

(F) Utilisation by a Fiduciary for his own Benefit of an Opportunity of Profit

A fiduciary is obviously entitled to utilise opportunities for his own benefit **10–128** which have nothing whatever to do with the fiduciary relationship in question. The mere fact that a person is a trustee of an investment fund does not prevent him from purchasing shares in his private capacity—were this not the case, it would be impossible to find any natural person who was prepared to accept a trusteeship. Equally obviously, if such a trustee obtains the opportunity to take up a rights issue by virtue of the fact that the trust is a shareholder in the company in question, then he is not entitled to take up that rights issue in his personal capacity and, if he does so, the shares in question will be subject to a constructive trust in favour of the fund. A fiduciary will only be in breach of his duty of loyalty to his principal if the transactions into which he enters in his personal capacity fall within the scope of his fiduciary obligations. As Oliver L.J. stated in *Swain v. The Law Society*[353]:

---

[350] [2000] Ch. 291 at 340 (CA).
[351] [1974] 1 W.L.R. 605.
[352] (1984) 53 A.L.R. 417 at 433 (High Court of Australia).
[353] [1982] 1 W.L.R. 17 at 37. This approach was approved by Lord Brightman in the House of Lords at [1983] 1 A.C. 598 at 619.

"What one has to do is ascertain first of all whether there was a fiduciary relationship and, if there was, from what it arose and what, if there was any, was the trust property and then to inquire whether that of which an account is claimed either arose, directly or indirectly, from the trust property itself or was acquired not only in the course of, but by reason of, the fiduciary relationship."

10–129   The question of whether a transaction falls within the scope of a fiduciary relationship will sometimes be capable of being resolved by reference to the terms of the agreement between the fiduciary and principal. Thus in *Aas v. Benham*[354] a member of a ship-broking partnership utilised information which he had received in his capacity as partner to help form a ship-building company of which he became a director. An action by his partners for an account of the benefits received from the company failed on the grounds that the business of the company was quite different from the business of the partnership, the Court of Appeal held that there was nothing to prevent a partner utilising information obtained in his fiduciary capacity provided that he was not competing with the partnership business.[355] However, the scope of a fiduciary obligation is not often closely defined by the parties to it and, when it is not, rather more difficulties can be encountered.

(1) Clear misconduct by the fiduciary

10–130   Cases of clear misconduct by a fiduciary are of course quite straightforward. In *Cook v. Deeks*[356] three of the four directors and shareholders of a company, with the intention of excluding the fourth member, arranged for a contract which they had negotiated on behalf of the company to be made with them in their private capacities. The excluded member claimed successfully that the company was entitled to the benefit of this contract. The Privy Council held that the whole reputation of the three had been obtained with the company; they could have excluded the plaintiff quite legitimately by using their majority shareholding to wind up the company but instead had used their position as directors to deprive the company of any chance of obtaining the contract. This was a clear case of abuse of fiduciary position. However, an identical attitude has been adopted where the misconduct of the fiduciary has been much more questionable. The decided cases of this type have generally arisen when the principal in question has been unable or unwilling to utilise an opportunity and the fiduciary has subsequently utilised that opportunity for his own benefit.

(2) Opportunities unutilised by the principal

10–131   **(a) The basic approach of the English authorities** In *Regal (Hastings) v. Gulliver*[357] the plaintiff company owned a cinema in Hastings and wished to

---

[354] [1891] 2 Ch. 244.

[355] See also *British American Oil Producing Co. v. Midway Oil Company* (1938) 82 P. (2d) 1049 (Supreme Court of Oklahoma).

[356] [1916] A.C. 554.

[357] [1942] 1 All E.R. 378 [1967] 2 A.C. 134N.

acquire two other local cinemas with the intention of selling the whole enterprise as a package. A subsidiary, with a capital of 5,000 £1 shares, was formed to take leases of these two cinemas. The original scheme was for only 2,000 of these shares to be paid up but the owner of the cinemas declined to grant the leases on this basis. Since the company could not afford to put more than £2,000 into the subsidiary, four of the directors and the company solicitor each subscribed for 500 shares and the fifth director found some outsiders to take up the remaining 500. The combined concern was then sold not as a whole but by way of takeover and each holder of shares in the subsidiary obviously made a profit. The purchasers then brought an action against all five directors and the company solicitor claiming that this profit had been made out of a breach of their fiduciary duty and therefore had to be accounted for to the company (this claim was wholly unmeritorious; its only objective was to recover part of the price which the purchasers had freely agreed to pay).

The action against the director who had not subscribed for any shares   **10–132**
obviously failed, for he had made no profit.[358] So too did the action against the company solicitor, for he had subscribed for his shares with the consent of the board of directors as then constituted. But the actions against the other four directors succeeded in the House of Lords, whose decision was based fairly and squarely on *Keech v. Sandford*. Lord Russell of Killowen stated that the directors had unquestionably acquired their shares by virtue of their fiduciary position. It made no difference that the company could not itself have subscribed for the shares—the trust in *Keech v. Sandford* could not itself have obtained a new lease and that had made no difference. Thus the four directors had to surrender a profit which they would have been able to retain had the transaction been carried out in a different way and so were deprived of any return on their investment, while the purchasers finished up paying less for the cinemas than they had originally bargained to pay.

Given that the company could not afford to put more than £2,000 into the   **10–133**
subsidiary, what alternative did the directors have? Lord Russell of Killowen thought that they should have obtained a resolution of the shareholders in general meeting approving the transaction.[359] This view seems to conflict with the decision in *Cook v. Deeks*,[360] where such a resolution had been obtained and was held to be ineffective. It was suggested in *Prudential Assurance Co. v. Newman Industries (No.2)*[361] that a ratification by a company in general meeting will only be effective if the directors in question do not control the majority of the votes. It is not clear whether or not the directors of Regal (Hastings) did in fact control the majority[362]; only if they did not is this a valid distinction between *Cook v. Deeks* and *Regal (Hastings) v. Gulliver*.

---

[358] No claim was brought against the outsiders for their profit. Any such claim would have been governed by the principles to be discussed in the next section of this chapter (see *post*, para 10–153).

[359] [1942] 1 All E.R. 378 at 389; [1967] 2 A.C. 134N at 150.

[360] [1916] A.C. 554.

[361] [1981] Ch. 257 at 308 (Vinelott J.).

[362] The Editorial Note in [1942] 1 All E.R. 378 at 379 assumed that they did; Vinelott J. in *Prudential Assurance Co. v. Newman Industries (No.2)* [1981] Ch. 257 at 308 disagreed.

10–134   However, a very much more generous attitude to ratification was subsequently demonstrated by the Privy Council in *Queensland Mines v. Hudson*.[363] The board of the plaintiff company, having been fully informed of all relevant facts, decided to renounce all interest in the exploitation of certain mining exploration licences which it had obtained and assented to the venture being taken over by the defendant; he was still a director of the company and had earlier been its managing director until a shortage of finance had prevented the plaintiff from exploiting the licences itself. The plaintiff subsequently claimed to be entitled to the profit obtained by the defendant. The Privy Council held that the defendant had obtained the opportunity to make this profit by virtue of his position as managing director of the plaintiff and was therefore in principle liable under *Regal (Hastings) v. Gulliver* to account for his profit; however, the fully-informed decision of the board amounted to sufficient consent to enable him to retain his profit.

10–135   This conclusion is clearly inconsistent with the decision in *Regal (Hastings) v. Gulliver*, where all the members of the board had taken part in the impeached transaction and so must necessarily have consented to it. The approach taken by the Privy Council may be able to be justified on the grounds that the plaintiff had only two shareholders, both of whom were represented on the board, and the shareholder represented by the defendant held only 49 per cent of the shares; the decision of the board can thus be regarded as a decision of the shareholders where the majority was not controlled by the defendant, which satisfies the test suggested in *Prudential Assurance Co. v. Newman Industries (No.2)*. Until recently, the only option thus seemed to be a decision of the shareholders in general meeting and even that could only be guaranteed to work if the directors in question did not control the majority of the shares. However, statute has now intervened to permit, as an alternative, approval by the uninvolved members on the board for the "exploitation of any property, information or opportunity of the company",[364] although it has been questioned "whether this is a wise innovation" on the basis that "although the approving directors may have no interest in a particular case, they may have an underlying interest in a culture of easy conflict approvals".[365] But this would not have worked in *Regal (Hastings) v. Gulliver* because there were no independent directors.

10–136   However, there is no doubt at all that the decisions in *Regal (Hastings) v. Gulliver* and *Queensland Mines v. Hudson* are entirely consistent on the question of the basic liability of the directors in question to account and certainly represent English law at present. In both cases it was assumed that, in the absence of the appropriate consent, any director who obtained an opportunity by virtue of his fiduciary position was liable to account to the company for this profit. Thus it is clear that the courts are not prepared to countenance a fiduciary exploiting an opportunity for his own benefit and are more concerned to penalise him for having taken up an opportunity of entering into a profitable transaction on his own behalf than to ascertain whether or

---

[363] (1977) 18 A.L.R. 1.
[364] Companies Act, s.175; the quoted words are from s.175(2).
[365] *Gower and Davies' Principles of Modern Company Law* 8th edn (London, Sweet & Maxwell, 2008), para 16–69.

not there has been a conflict between his duty of loyalty to his principal and his own self-interest.

(b) The approach of other jurisdictions Other jurisdictions have felt   10–137
able to adopt a more flexible approach and have permitted directors to take
up opportunities for their own benefit without the prior consent or subsequent ratification of their companies where there was no serious conflict of
duty and interest.

In *Peso Silvermines v. Cropper*,[366] the defendant was on the board of the   10–138
plaintiff company at a time when the company geologist invited and
advised that board to purchase certain mining claims, some of which were
contiguous to claims already owned by the company. The board rejected this
offer, partly for financial reasons and partly because some of the directors
considered the claims to be an uninviting business risk. Subsequently, the
geologist, with the defendant and two other directors of the plaintiff, formed
a company to purchase and exploit these claims. In due course, the plaintiff
was taken over and its new board claimed that the defendant held his shares
in the new company on constructive trust for the plaintiff. The Court of
Appeal of British Columbia rejected *Regal (Hastings) v. Gulliver* and held, by
a majority, that the strict penal rules of equity had been carried far enough
and were not appropriate for a modern country in a modern era. The
Supreme Court of Canada took a rather narrower view and merely distinguished *Regal (Hastings) v. Gulliver* on the grounds that the defendant had
acted entirely in good faith in participating in the initial decision of the
board not to purchase the claims. He had not obtained any advantage at all
as a result of participating in this decision and was therefore entitled to take
up a subsequent offer in his private capacity without being liable to account
for his profit. Even this narrower view seems preferable in every way to the
approach adopted in *Regal (Hastings) v. Gulliver*. It is undoubtedly possible
to criticise *Peso Silvermines v. Cropper* on the grounds that to allow directors
to decide that the company shall not accept the opportunity and then to
accept the opportunity themselves might impose too great a strain on their
impartiality.[367] However, the sort of attitude adopted by the House of Lords
in *Regal (Hastings) v. Gulliver* prevents such matters of policy being raised at
all; this in itself is an argument for the adoption of a more flexible attitude,
even if its adoption does not alter the conclusion actually reached by the
courts in the end.

In *Consul Development v. D.P.C. Estates*[368] the High Court of Australia   10–139
adopted an attitude similar to that of the Supreme Court of Canada. The
plaintiff was one of a group of property companies which employed a
manager to find properties for purchase. He was under an express duty of
confidentiality in respect of all group business and had undertaken not to
engage in real estate business other than for the group. However, in breach
of these obligations, he collaborated with another employee of the group,

---

[366] (1966) 56 D.L.R.(2d) 1 (British Columbia Court of Appeal); 58 D.L.R.(2d) 1 (Supreme Court
of Canada).

[367] This was stated by Gower and Davies, *op.cit.*, in an earlier edition, by Prentice in (1967) 30
M.L.R. 450 and by Swan J. in *Irving Trust Co. v. Deutsch* (1934) 73 Fed. (2d) 121, 124 (United
States Circuit Court of Appeals).

[368] (1975) 132 C.L.R. 373.

who was also the managing director of the defendant, by providing him with information about a number of properties which the defendant then acquired, telling him, for reasons which were entirely plausible, that the group was not interested in their acquisition. The plaintiff succeeded in recovering the manager's own profit on the grounds that he had breached his duty of loyalty but failed in its claim that the properties were subject to a constructive trust. A majority of the High Court held that the manager would have been entitled to purchase the properties for himself if the group had really declined to buy them. The defendant was entitled to believe that this was in fact the case and so was clearly entitled to purchase them for its own benefit and retain its entire profit. This approach also seems preferable to that adopted in *Regal (Hastings) v. Gulliver.*

10–140   **(c) The two approaches contrasted in** *Phipps v. Boardman*[369] The contrast between the two approaches emerges extremely clearly from the majority and minority speeches handed down in the controversial decision of the House of Lords in *Phipps v. Boardman.* A testator established a trust for the benefit of his widow and children. Some 12 years after his death, the trust solicitor, Boardman, became concerned about one of the principal assets of the fund—a 27 per cent holding in a private company. After an unsuccessful attempt to bring about the election of one of the testator's sons to the board of the company, Boardman reached the conclusion that the only way of protecting the trust investment was to acquire a majority holding in the company. He suggested this to the managing trustee, who said that it was entirely out of the question for the trust to acquire such a holding. Boardman and the son then decided to purchase the outstanding shares themselves. They duly obtained control of the company and by capitalising some of the assets, were able to make a distribution of capital without reducing the value of the shares. The trust benefited by this distribution to the tune of £47,000 and Boardman and his colleague made a profit of about £75,000.

10–141   However, in the course of the extremely lengthy negotiations which had preceded the takeover, Boardman had purported to represent the trust and thereby had incontrovertibly obtained information which would not have been made available to the general public. On this basis, one of the other sons of the testator, who had admittedly not been particularly fully consulted, claimed that this profit of £75,000 had been made by the utilisation of information which had reached Boardman while acting on behalf of the trust and so in a fiduciary capacity. All the members of the House of Lords agreed that (as was clearly the case) the defendants had placed themselves in a fiduciary relationship by acting as representatives of the trust for a number of years and that out of this fiduciary relationship they had obtained the opportunity to make a profit and the knowledge that a profit was there to be made. A bare majority of the House went on to hold that the shares which had been acquired were subject to a constructive trust in favour of the trust. Thus the trust potentially[370] obtained the whole of the

---

[369] [1967] 2 A.C. 46.

[370] In fact the defendants only lost one-third of their profit since the son who brought the proceedings only had a one third beneficial interest, the remaining two thirds being held by his brother, Boardman's associate, and their sister, who made no claim.

profit made on the takeover; the defendants in effect had a choice between paying this over to the trust and retaining their shares or having the shares sold and the profit deducted from the proceeds of sale. However, the House awarded an allowance to Boardman under its inherent jurisdiction by way of remuneration for the work which he had done.[371]

The majority adduced two inter-connected reasons for going on to hold   **10–142** that the defendants were therefore liable as constructive trustees to account for their profit to the trust. Lord Hodson and Lord Guest both held that, since the only basis on which the defendants had obtained their information was the fact that they had been purporting to represent the trust, this information was trust property. Therefore, the defendants had, in effect, made a profit out of speculating with trust property and thus were clearly liable. If the information was indeed properly classifiable as trust property, then the defendants had of course made a profit out of speculating with property of the trust and were therefore clearly liable as constructive trustees under the principle laid down in *Reid-Newfoundland Co. v. Anglo-American Telegraph Co.*,[372] which was discussed at the beginning of this section.[373] However, if information is trust property in any normal sense, it could presumably be followed into the hands of the whole world other than a bona fide purchaser thereof for value without notice. Given the essential nature of information, which can be divulged in its entirety to any number of persons, such a conclusion could lead to quite absurd results.[374] None of the three remaining Law Lords agreed with this classification. The third member of the majority, Lord Cohen, held that information was not property in the strict sense of the word and that it did not necessarily follow that a fiduciary must account for any profit obtained by the use of information acquired in his fiduciary capacity. Lord Upjohn, dissenting with Viscount Dilhorne, said that information was not property in any sense; equity would merely restrain its transmission to another in breach of confidence and this was not a case of that type.

However, what is important for present purposes is the fact that the   **10–143** majority also followed and applied *Regal (Hastings) v. Gulliver*. Lord Cohen held that on the facts that decision was applicable because the information in question had been acquired while the defendants had been purporting to represent the trust. All three members of the majority also felt that Boardman had placed himself in a position where his duty and interest might conflict (they said that such a conflict would have arisen had the trustees sought his advice as to the merits of the trust acquiring a majority holding in the company). No matter how remote the possibility of such a conflict arising, a fiduciary who placed himself in this position was bound to account to his principal for any profit he had made. Since the defendants had accepted that their positions were the same, both were thus liable to account for their profit. In the opinion of the majority, it was quite immaterial that the defendants had acted honestly and openly in a manner highly

---

[371] This aspect of the decision will be discussed *post*, paras 10–180, 20–038.
[372] [1891] 2 Ch. 244.
[373] See *ante*, para 10–109.
[374] See Jones (1968) 84 L.Q.R. 472.

beneficial to the trust in a situation where the trust itself could not have utilised the information which they had received.

10–144 The dissentients took the view that the remoteness of the possibility of any conflict of interest arising and the various factors just referred to which the majority had found irrelevant led inescapably to the conclusion that the defendants had not breached their duty of loyalty to the trust. Lord Upjohn said that a conflict of interest only arose where the reasonable man looking at all the relevant circumstances would think that there was a real sensible possibility of conflict and not where the only possibility of conflict arose from events not contemplated as real sensible probabilities by any reasonable person. Boardman knew when he decided to proceed on his own behalf that there was no possibility of the trustees seeking his advice as to the merits of a purchase by the trust—the managing trustee had already told him that this was quite out of the question. This view seems preferable in every way, particularly since the commentators[375] have demonstrated that the conflict of interest found to exist by the House of Lords is in fact wholly illusory; given that it arose out of the mere possibility that Boardman might in the future have been asked to advise the trustees, in this eventuality he could, like any other solicitor, have declined to advise them or, if they insisted, have declared his interest.[376] There is also much to be said for the preferences which have been expressed for the more flexible approach which has been adopted in other jurisdictions.[377]

10–145 However, it must be stressed that, apart from the controversial classification, by only two of the majority, of the information as trust property, the members of the House of Lords were in agreement as to the principles which are applicable to a fiduciary who has utilised an opportunity of profit for his own benefit. As the Court of Appeal specifically held much more recently in *Re Bhullar Brothers*,[378] the disagreement between the majority and the minority was over the application of those principles to the facts of *Phipps v. Boardman*. No one contends that a fiduciary should automatically be entitled to utilise for his own benefit information which has come to him in his fiduciary capacity; a fiduciary who by the utilisation of such information abuses his fiduciary position should clearly be liable as a constructive trustee.

10–146 Such a case was *Industrial Development Consultants v. Cooley*.[379] The defendant, who was managing director of the plaintiff company, had been attempting, on behalf of the plaintiff, to obtain a contract to design certain depots for the Eastern Gas Board. These attempts failed because the Gas

---

[375] See particularly Jones (1968) 84 L.Q.R. 472 and Finn, *Fiduciary Obligations*, pp.244–246.

[376] If it is indeed the law that a person cannot benefit himself in any matter in which he might in the future be asked to advise, it is difficult to see how any professional person can ever safely enter into a transaction on his own behalf in any area in which he habitually advises.

[377] In the authorities discussed *ante*, para 10–137 and also in *Manufacturers Trust Co. v. Becker* (1949) 338 U.S. 304, where the Supreme Court of the United States of America held that directors of a company had been entitled to encourage their associates to purchase its debentures at a time when their market value was a fraction of their face value; not only had the directors acted in the best interests of the company, their associates' profits had been made at the expense not of the company but of the selling bond-holders, who had in no way been misled or deceived.

[378] [2003] EWCA Civ. 424, [2003] 2 B.C.L.C. 241.

[379] [1972] 1 W.L.R. 443.

Board did not like the plaintiff's organisation and were not prepared to deal with the plaintiff in any capacity. The following year, a representative of the Gas Board sought a meeting with the defendant in his private capacity and intimated to him that if he could free himself from his ties with the plaintiff he had a very good chance of obtaining the contract for himself. The defendant therefore secured his release from his contract with the plaintiff by a totally false representation that he was on the verge of a nervous breakdown and accepted an offer from the Gas Board to do substantially the same work which he had unsuccessfully attempted to obtain for the plaintiff the year before. The plaintiff claimed that the defendant was a trustee of that contract for the benefit of the plaintiff and successfully sought an account of the defendant's profits. At the time when the defendant first realised that he had an opportunity of obtaining the contract for himself, the only capacity in which he was carrying on business was as managing director of the plaintiff and as such he was under a fiduciary duty to pass on to the plaintiff any information which reached him while carrying on business in that capacity. His failure to do so and subsequent utilisation of the information for his own benefit was a clear breach of fiduciary duty which made him a trustee of the contract for the plaintiff, who was entitled to all the profit arising from that contract.[380]

The facts were somewhat more marginal in the much more recent decision **10–147** of the Court of Appeal in *Re Bhullar Brothers*.[381] Two brothers, together subsequently with their respective sons, were the equal shareholders of a company which held their chain of grocery stores and also some investment property. At a time when the two branches of the family had fallen out and were in the process of dividing up the assets, the sons of one of the brothers became aware, entirely fortuitously, that land adjoining one of the investment properties was for sale.[382] They acquired it in their own names and, when the purchase was challenged by the other brother's side of the family, relied both on the admitted fact that the latter had stated that they were not prepared to engage in any further joint investment and on the entirely fortuitous nature of the acquisition of the information. The Court of Appeal held that they were obliged to sell the adjoining land to the company for the price which they had paid for it and to account for the appropriate proportion of any intervening income. Considerable reliance seems to have been placed on the fact that the sons had asked their solicitor whether there was any potential conflict of interest. Because of the source of the information, this is the type of case which the critics of *Phipps v. Boardman* would be likely also to criticise.

That does not alter the fact that the approach adopted by the majority of **10–148** the House of Lords and, much more recently, by the Court of Appeal in relation to the rights of fiduciaries to utilise for their own benefit opportunities of profit is entirely consistent with the earlier authorities such as *Regal*

---

[380] Similar decisions have been reached in other jurisdictions. See *Pre-Cam Exploration Co. v. McTavish* [1966] S.C.R. 551; *Canadian Aero Services v. O'Malley* (1973) 40 D.L.R.(3d) 371 (both decisions of the Supreme Court of Canada); *Consul Development v. D.P.C. Estates* (1975) 49 A.L.J.R. 74 (High Court of Australia).

[381] [2003] EWCA Civ. 424, [2003] 2 B.C.L.C. 241.

[382] The investment property was leased for the purposes of a ten pin bowling operation and the sons saw a "for sale" sign on the adjoining land when going bowling.

(Hastings) v. Gulliver and undoubtedly constitutes English law at present. Admittedly, in *Murad v. Al-Saraj*,[383] the majority of the Court of Appeal acknowledged "the possibility that at some time in the future the House of Lords may consider that the time has come to relax the severity of the 'no conflict' rule to some extent in appropriate cases" but "that day has not yet arrived".[384] Cases such as *Regal (Hastings) v. Gulliver* and *Phipps v. Boardman*, "where the fiduciaries acted out of the best of motives", were clearly regarded as potential candidates for any such relaxation but not cases[385] in which the fiduciary in question acted in bad faith. It remains whether any relaxation ever occurs and, if so, what form that takes.

10–149   The House of Lords, or the future Supreme Court, could conceivably also derive some encouragement to review the present law from the statement by Lord Browne-Wilkinson, admittedly made in an entirely different context,[386] in *Target Holdings v. Redferns*[387] that it is "wrong to lift wholesale the detailed rules developed in the context of traditional trusts and then seek to apply them to trusts of quite a different kind". No better example of this practice can be found than the utilisation by Lord Russell of Killowen in *Regal (Hastings) v. Gulliver* of the decision in *Keech v. Sandford* more than two centuries earlier: it made no difference in *Regal (Hastings) v. Gulliver* that the company could not itself have subscribed for the shares—the trust in *Keech v. Sandford* could not itself have obtained a new lease and that had made no difference there. These remarks suggest that judges should think twice before automatically applying conclusions reached in totally different legal and economic contexts to modern conditions and might therefore also lead to some relaxation of "the no conflict rule".

10–150   **(d) Potentially alleviating factors** It has already been seen that the effects of what its critics regard as the harsh attitude at present adopted under English law were alleviated in *Phipps v. Boardman* by the House of Lords awarding an allowance to Boardman under its inherent jurisdiction by way of remuneration for the work which he had done. This jurisdiction, which will be discussed in detail later on,[388] was considerably extended in *Badfinger Music v. Evans*[389] where a former member of a rock group which had broken up in very acrimonious circumstances had retained some tapes of a live concert which, after a considerable amount of essential remixing and remastering, he succeeded in releasing in a form which achieved a commercial success. He did not dispute that he was in a fiduciary relationship with the other members of the group or that they were entitled to share in the profit. The question was whether he was entitled to remuneration for the work which he had done. This was not a case where a fiduciary had, as in *Boardman v. Phipps*, acted honestly and openly in the best interests of his

---

[383] [2005] EWCA Civ. 589, [2005] W.T.L.R. 1573.
[384] *ibid.*, *per* Jonathan Parker L.J. at [121–122]; see also *per* Arden L.J. at 82.
[385] Like *Murad v. Al-Saraj* itself.
[386] That of the liability of trustees who have paid away trust property in breach of trust to reconstitute the trust fund.
[387] [1996] 1 A.C. 421, see *post*, para 22–012.
[388] See *post*, para 20–037.
[389] [2001] W.T.L.R. 1.

principal, although there was no doubt that his work had ultimately bene-fited the others. However, the judge[390] held that he could award remunera-tion despite a lack of honesty and openness[391] and did so because the work done was not only of a special character calling for the exercise of a partic-ular kind of professional skill but also could realistically only have been done by the fiduciary. He added that, in appropriate circumstances, the court's jurisdiction might extend to an award of a share of the profits. Such awards of remuneration, and possibly shares of profits, are available even where, as in all the decisions adverse to fiduciaries which have been dis-cussed in this section, a constructive trust has been imposed.

The High Court of Australia has provided a further potentially alleviating factor by holding in *Warman International v. Dwyer*[392] that the other remedies available for breach of fiduciary duty which have already been discussed[393] can also be utilised in cases of this type. The plaintiffs had declined an opportunity to participate in a joint venture with a manufacturer whose products they distributed. The manufacturer therefore terminated the dis-tributorship, as it was entitled to do at any time, and instead carried out the joint venture with the defendant, the employee of the plaintiffs most closely connected with the distributorship. He had clearly committed a technical breach of fiduciary duty[394] but the court declined to hold that the goodwill of the joint venture was held on constructive trust for the plaintiffs, award-ing instead an account of the first two years' profits of the joint venture less an appropriate allowance for the expenses, skill expertise, effort and resources contributed by the joint venturers. The High Court specifically distinguished between cases in which a fiduciary acquires an asset which was within the scope and ambit of his fiduciary responsibilities, where it will be appropriate to impose a constructive trust, and cases in which a business is acquired and operated, where it may well not be. A similar approach was adopted in Hong Kong in *Kao Lee & Yip v. Koo Hoi Yan*,[395] which concerned a claim by the partners of a law firm to the profits made by a new law firm which had set up by a former partner.

10–151

However, in *Murad v. Al-Saraj*,[396] the Court of Appeal did not regard *Warman v. Dyer* "as sanctioning any departure from, or as recognising any qualification to, the 'no conflict' rule" but rather as recognising that a time could come when it could safely be recognised that future profits were no longer attributable to the breach of fiduciary duty. Further, it also has to be said that the adoption of this approach by the English courts would anyway not necessarily alter the result of either *Regal (Hastings) v. Gulliver* or *Phipps v. Boardman*. This would only be the case if the shares acquired in those cases

10–152

---

[390] Lord Goldsmith Q.C., sitting as a Deputy Judge of the Chancery Division.

[391] He relied heavily on *O'Sullivan v. Managment Agency and Music* [1985] 1 Q.B. 428, where remuneration had been awarded to an agent who had exercised actual undue influence over his principal, the singer Gilbert O'Sullivan.

[392] (1995) 128 A.L.R. 201.

[393] See *ante*, para 10–064.

[394] Although he had not participated in the plaintiffs' decision to reject the manufacturer's proposal, his conduct had probably caused the manufacturer to terminate its agency earlier than it might otherwise have done.

[395] [2003] W.T.L.R. 1283.

[396] [2005] EWCA Civ. 589, [2005] W.T.L.R. 1573 *per* Jonathan Parker L.J. at [115].

by the respective fiduciaries could be held not to fall within the scope and ambit of their fiduciary responsibilities. It is somewhat improbable that such a conclusion would ever be reached on the facts of *Regal (Hastings) v. Gulliver* although the critics of *Phipps v. Boardman* would certainly argue that such a conclusion should have been in that case and, possibly, also in *Re Bhullar Brothers*. Nevertheless, the adoption of this approach would have a profound effect on the liability of fiduciaries who acquire and operate businesses as a result of a purely technical breach of fiduciary duty.

III. DISPOSITIONS OF TRUST PROPERTY IN BREACH OF TRUST

1. *The Different Types of Liability*

10–153   When trust property has been disposed of in breach of trust, the courts will, in certain circumstances, impose equitable obligations on those responsible for the wrongful disposition. Equity has always been prepared to impose on any person who has officiously chosen to act as a fiduciary the appropriate fiduciary obligations, by virtue of which he will hold any property which he has received in his assumed capacity on constructive trust for the person on whose behalf he has chosen to act. Such a person has obviously intermeddled with property which is subject to a trust but this is merely the most obvious example of equity imposing obligations as a result of a disposition of trust property in breach of trust. Equity is also prepared to do so in three other situations: first, on anyone who has dishonestly been accessory to, or assisted in, a disposition of property in breach of trust (this type of liability is now generally known as "liability for dishonest assistance"[397]); secondly, on anyone who, with the requisite level of knowledge, has received for this own benefit property which has been disposed of in breach of trust (this type of liability is generally known as "liability for knowing receipt"); and, thirdly, on anyone who has received lawfully and not for his own benefit property subject to a trust but who has subsequently either misappropriated it or dealt with it in some other manner which is inconsistent with the trust (this type of liability is generally known as "liability for inconsistent dealing"). It is important to distinguish between these different types of liability.

10–154   If solicitors or accountants invest trust funds in their hands without any instructions from the trustees, they will be potentially liable to be treated as trustees of the investments because of their officious conduct. If, in accordance with directions from the trustees, they transfer trust funds to a third party in breach of trust, they will be potentially liable for dishonest assistance. If, in accordance with directions from the trustees, they use trust funds to settle their professional fees, they will be potentially liable for knowing receipt. Finally, if they themselves debit the trust funds to settle their professional fees, they will be potentially liable for "inconsistent dealing".

---

[397] Until a change in the law in 1995 it was instead generally known as "liability for knowing assistance".

Similarly, if a bank deals with funds in an account which it knows to be **10–155** a trust account without any instructions from the trustees, it will be potentially liable to be treated as a trustee of those funds because of its officious conduct. If it permits a cheque drawn on that account to be credited in breach of trust to the account of a third party but acts merely as the conduit by means of which the funds are transferred from one account to the other, it will be potentially liable for dishonest assistance, although in this respect a distinction has unjustifiably been drawn between transfers of sterling and transfers of foreign currency which have instead been held potentially to impose liability for knowing receipt[398]; however, there is no doubt that, if the account of the third party is overdrawn at the time of the transfer, the bank may be potentially liable for knowing receipt to the extent that it has utilised the funds in reduction of the overdraft. Finally, if the bank itself debits the balance of the account to cover an overdraft created in another account held by the same person, it will potentially be liable for inconsistent dealing. Debiting the fees and commissions which banks commonly charge for carrying out certain types of transactions to such an account ought also potentially to give rise to liability for dishonest assistance but this potential liability has generally been ignored.[399]

The growth of discovered corporate fraud in recent years has ensured that **10–156** the courts have had to consider the availability and scope of these remedies on an ever-increasing number of occasions. The proceedings which have been brought have, however, generally involved not only one or more of the types of liability listed above but also a considerable number of other claims arising out of the same disposition of property in breach of trust; the possibilities include proprietary claims, both at law and in equity, to follow the property into the hands of its recipients, personal claims at law for money had and received, and personal claims in equity against whoever

---

[398] In *Polly Peck International v. Nadir (No.2)* [1992] 4 All E.R. 769, a bank effectively controlled by the plaintiff company made a number of transfers of the plaintiff's funds totaling about £45,000,000 to the London branch of the Central Bank of Northern Cyprus in exchange for a corresponding amount of either sterling or Turkish lire being credited to its account with the Central Bank in Northern Cyprus. Scott L.J. held at 777 that the potential liability of the Central Bank to the liquidators of the plaintiff company in respect of the sterling transfers was for dishonest assistance since it had "received the funds transferred not in its own right but as banker and, as a banker, credited the funds . . . in Northern Cyprus" but that its potential liability in respect of the Turkish lire transfers was for knowing receipt because "it was exchanging Turkish lire for sterling and became entitled to the sterling not as banker . . . but in its own right". Apart from any fees or commissions which the Central Bank may have charged, to which no reference was made, the bank became no more beneficially entitled to the Turkish lire than it did to the sterling. It is, therefore, difficult to justify the distinction made by Scott L.J. and it is suggested that it should not be followed (it was not followed in New Zealand in *Nimmo v. Westpac Banking Corporation* [1993] 3 N.Z.L.R. 218 and *Cigna Life Insurance New Zealand v. Westpac Securities* [1996] 1 N.Z.L.R. 80).

[399] The amount of the fixed fees sometimes charged for keeping accounts open and for paying cheques would be unlikely to be sufficient to justify proceedings but charges whose amount is related to the value of the transaction, such as the fees normally charged for transactions such as issuing banker's drafts and the commissions normally charged for bank transfers, particularly those to other jurisdictions, might well be. In the event that such a transaction amounts to a breach of trust, the potential liability of the bank in respect of the value of the banker's draft or the sum transferred will clearly be for dishonest assistance; however, in principle, the bank should also be potentially liable for knowing receipt in respect of any fees or commissions which it has charged.

was responsible for initiating the disposition in question. However, there is no doubt at all that by far the most effective way to proceed is to seek the imposition of one or more the equitable obligations at present under discussion, particularly if anyone can be found who is potentially liable for dishonest assistance; potential defendants of the latter type tend to be either members of the professions with insurance against liability for professional negligence or financial institutions of virtually guaranteed solvency.[400] Such persons are far more likely to be able to satisfy any unfavourable judgment than the other potential defendants—the initiators of the offending disposition and the recipients of the property in question. Indeed the presumed solvency of persons who have been accessory to or dishonestly assisted in a disposition of property in breach of trust is the basic reason why this particular area of the law has become so important in recent years.

2. *Officiously Acting as a Fiduciary*

10–157   Any person who takes it upon himself to act as a fiduciary without having been appointed as such will in every respect be treated as if he had been expressly appointed to the office in question and will be held to be a constructive trustee of any property acquired by him in the course of his intervention. In *Mara v. Browne*[401] A.L. Smith L.J. stated that "if one, not being a trustee and not having authority from a trustee, takes upon himself to intermeddle with trust matters or to do acts characteristic of the office of trustee, he may therefore make himself what is called in law a trustee of his own wrong—i.e. a trustee de son tort, or, as it is also termed, a constructive trustee". In *Dubai Aluminium Co. v. Salaam*,[402] Lord Millett expressed a preference for alternative terminology, saying that "[s]ubstituting dog Latin for bastard French, we would do better today to describe such persons as de facto trustees". He went on to say: "In their relations with the beneficiaries they are treated in every respect as if they had been duly appointed. They are true trustees and are fully subject to fiduciary obligations. Their liability is strict; it does not depend on dishonesty." However, it is classified, control of the property is a prerequisite of this type of liability, to which Kekewich J. was specifically referring when, in *Re Barney*,[403] he stated particularly clearly that "it is essential to the character of a trustee that he should have trust property actually vested in him or so far under his control that he has

---

[400] Liability for dishonest assistance is potentially much more onerous than liability for knowing receipt or inconsistent dealing. The latter will generally merely restore the status quo; any order for repayment of the trust funds utilised will normally simply reconstitute the original potential loss in respect of the professional fees or overdraft in question. The only situation in which the position will be any worse than it was at the outset will be if the use of the trust funds to discharge the fees or overdraft has given a false impression of the financial position of the client and thus caused further fees to be run up or further advances to be made. The imposition of liability for dishonest assistance will, on the other hand, necessarily involve the payment of funds which have never been beneficially received by the member of the professions or advanced by the financial institution in question; what is more, the quantum of potential liability is not in any way restricted to the value of the fees and commissions which the services rendered could reasonably have been expected to bring in.

[401] [1896] 1 Ch. 199 at 209.

[402] [2002] UKHL 48, [2003] 2 A.C. 366 at [138].

[403] [1892] 2 Ch. 265 at 273.

nothing to do but require that, perhaps by one process, perhaps by another, it should be vested in him".

A good illustration of the imposition of this type of liability is provided by **10–158** *Blyth v. Fladgate*.[404] Trust funds were, by direction of the sole trustee, paid to a firm of solicitors and invested in Exchequer Bills, which were deposited in the name of the firm. Subsequently, following the death of the sole trustee and before any new trustees had been appointed, the Exchequer Bills were sold and the proceeds of the sale invested in a mortgage, the security for which proved to be insufficient. The partners of the firm were held liable to account to the trust for the sums so lost on the basis that they themselves had been carrying out the functions of the trustees; they were clearly constructive trustees of the proceeds of sale and, as such, were responsible for any improper investment. It is entirely proper that the law should impose the office of trustee upon a person who purports to act as such without authority and that such a person should be burdened with all the same responsibilities and liabilities as an express trustee.[405] Thus, in addition to being a constructive trustee of any property which he receives, he will also be responsible for any diminution in its value and will be subject to all the rules discussed in the previous section of this chapter; if an intermeddler obtains a secret profit, he will be in exactly the same position as if he had been an express trustee.

The position of a person who acts as a personal representative of a **10–159** deceased person without having obtained any grant of representation is the same. Such a person is known as an executor *de son tort*, although Lord Millett would presumably prefer the expression de facto executor. In *James v. Williams*[406] a son of an intestate remained in possession of a cottage following her death for longer than the statutory limitation period of 12 years; on this ground his niece, on whom the cottage had devolved from him, subsequently sought to resist the claim of his sister to be entitled to a share in the cottage under the intestacy rules. The Court of Appeal held that in such circumstances an executor *de son tort* is also a constructive trustee for the beneficiaries of the estate of the deceased because it would be inequitable to allow him to assert full beneficial ownership of the property; that was sufficient to prevent time running as against the sister. However, the court emphasised that such a constructive trust cannot be imposed on a complete stranger who takes possession of the land of a deceased person; that would undermine the objectives of the doctrine of adverse possession.

Similar principles apply to fiduciaries other than trustees. Most of the **10–160** cases have concerned persons who have taken it upon themselves to act as agents. In *Lyell v. Kennedy*,[407] during the 22 years which it took to determine the identity of the heir at law of a landowner, his manager continued to collect the rents from the tenants without telling them of the death of their landlord. The House of Lords held that, since he had taken it upon himself to receive the rents of property which he knew to belong to another, he held

---

[404] [1891] 1 Ch. 337. The explanation of the decision given in the text is that adopted by Vinelott J. in *Re Bell's Indenture* [1980] 1 W.L.R. 1217.
[405] See *Soar v. Ashwell* [1893] 2 Q.B. 390 at 394, *per* Lord Esher M.R.
[406] [2000] Ch. 1.
[407] (1889) 14 App.Cas. 437.

these sums (which had been placed in a separate bank account) on constructive trust for the heir. Lord Selborne emphasised that the motives which induce a person to intermeddle in the administration of a trust or other fiduciary relationship are totally irrelevant to the imposition of a constructive trust; thus it made no difference whether the manager had intervened with the intention of protecting the interests of the heir at law or with the intention of taking the benefit for himself. The latter was clearly the intention of the prospective purchaser in *English v. Dedham Vale Properties*[408] who, purporting without authority to act as agent for the prospective vendors, submitted an application for planning permission in respect of part of the subject matter of the proposed sale; he was held liable to account to the vendors for the profits made thereby.[409]

3. *Dishonestly Assisting in a Disposition of Property in Breach of Trust*

(A) Terminology

10–161 The type of liability imposed upon a person who has in one way or another dishonestly assisted in bringing about a disposition of trust property in breach of trust is now generally known as "liability for dishonest assistance".[410] Until recently the vast majority of the relevant judgments have described persons held liable for what is now known as dishonest assistance as constructive trustees. However, it has already been seen that the essential feature of this type of liability is the fact that property subject to a trust has by virtue of the assistance provided reached the hands of a third party who may or may not himself be under some proprietary or personal obligation to restore it. What is more, it is only ever necessary to attempt to impose liability for dishonest assistance on persons who have not beneficially received the property in question (anyone who has actually taken the property beneficially will be subject to the different, and probably more stringent, heads of liability for knowing receipt or inconsistent dealing which will be discussed later on in this section). The classification of such persons as constructive trustees is as a matter of principle somewhat difficult to reconcile with the inherent nature of a trust—given that a trust is a relationship in respect of property, it might be expected to follow that a constructive trust can only be imposed if there is some identifiable property upon which to impose it. Yet liability for dishonest assistance has often been imposed when there has been no obviously identifiable property subject to the trust.

10–162 Where a person held liable for dishonest assistance has played an active part in the disposition of the property in question, as in the case of a solicitor or bank who, following the instructions of trustees, has actually made the disposition in question, it is just about possible to identify property subject to the alleged constructive trust. This is because the fact that the property in question passed through the hands of the person upon whom liability is imposed makes it possible to argue that a constructive trust in fact arose at

---

[408] [1978] 1 W.L.R. 93.

[409] Had he waited until after exchange of contracts, the equitable interest thereby acquired would have entitled him to make the application for his own benefit.

[410] Until a change in the law in 1995 it was instead generally known as "liability for knowing assistance".

the moment when the property was actually in his hands. However, quite apart from the fact that none of the judges has ever seemed to have regarded as important the question of what property was subject to the constructive trust said to be being imposed, there are other decisions in which it is, on any view, totally impossible to identify any such property. This is because in these cases liability for dishonest assistance was imposed on persons who had never received or in any way controlled the property in question. Thus in *Eaves v. Hickson*[411] what is now known as liability for dishonest assistance was imposed on a father who produced a forged marriage certificate to the trustees of a settlement in order to convince them that his children were legitimate and so entitled to the trust property, which was duly distributed to them. Liability was imposed on the basis that he had dishonestly induced the trustees to make the distribution in question and so was accessory to it.

The existence of authorities of this type has led some commentators to contend that there is a second type of constructive trust which can arise without any necessity for there to be any identifiable trust property[412]; indeed, in *Westdeutsche Landesbank Girozentrale v. Islington L.B.C.*,[413] Lord Browne-Wilkinson specifically said that the "only apparent exception" to the rule that there must be identifiable trust property "is a constructive trust imposed on a person who dishonestly assists in a breach of trust". No proprietary rights can conceivably be acquired by anyone beneficially entitled under a trust without identifiable property. Consequently, the existence of "this apparent exception" does not serve any obvious purpose; what is the point of creating an exception to the general rule requiring identifiable trust property if the exception so created does not enjoy the principal advantage conferred by the existence of a trust in the first place? The best which can be said for this alleged second type of constructive trust is that it is "a fiction which provides a useful remedy where no remedy is available in contract or in tort".[414] **10–163**

In any event, the opposing view, that the explanation for the existence of authorities of this type is that the imposition of this kind of liability does not give rise to the imposition of a constructive trust anyway, is now increasingly prevalent. In *Dubai Aluminium Co. v. Salaam*,[415] Lord Millett, building on earlier observations which he had made both judicially[416] and extra-judicially,[417] said: **10–164**

"Equity gives relief against fraud by making any person sufficiently implicated in the fraud accountable in equity. In such a case he is traditionally (and I have suggested unfortunately) described as a 'constructive trustee' and is said to be 'liable to account as a constructive trustee'. But he is not in fact a trustee at all, even though he may be liable to account as if he were.

---

[411] (1861) 30 Beav. 136.
[412] See Ford & Lee: *op.cit.*, para.22020 and previous editions of Hayton & Marshall: *op.cit.* (e.g. the 9th edn, 1991, pp.440–441).
[413] [1996] A.C. 669 at 705.
[414] Hayton (1985) 27 Malaya Law Review 313, 314.
[415] [2002] UKHL 48, [2003] 2 A.C. 366 at 404.
[416] As Millett J. in *Agip (Africa) v. Jackson* [1990] Ch. 265 at 291.
[417] In, among other places, 114 L.Q.R. (1998) 399 at 399–400.

He never claims to assume the position of trustee on behalf of others, and he may be liable without ever receiving or handling the trust property. . . . In this second class of case the expressions 'constructive trust' and 'constructive trustee' create a trap. . . . The expressions are 'nothing more than a formula for equitable relief'[418] . . . I think that we should now discard the words "accountable as constructive trustee" in this context and substitute the words 'accountable in equity'."

Lord Millett's terminology is clearly preferable. Although its adoption entails a recognition that the imposition of liability for dishonest assistance does not give rise to a constructive trust, that type of liability is nevertheless best dealt with in this chapter; this is because virtually all the relevant authorities also concern attempts to impose liability for knowing receipt or liability for inconsistent dealing, which on any view give rise to the imposition of a constructive trust.

(B) The Elements of Liability for Dishonest Assistance

10–165   For some 120 years the starting point for every discussion of what is now known as liability for dishonest assistance was the statement of Lord Selbourne L.C. in *Barnes v. Addy*[419] in 1874 that "strangers are not to be made constructive trustees merely because they act as the agents of trustees in transactions within their legal powers, transactions, perhaps, of which a Court of Equity may disapprove, unless . . . they assist with knowledge in a dishonest and fraudulent design on the part of the trustees". Peter Gibson J. subsequently[420] identified four distinct elements of this type of liability: the existence of a trust; the existence of a dishonest and fraudulent design on the part of the trustee of the trust; the assistance by the stranger in that design; and the knowledge of the person potentially liable.

Neither formulation has survived the decision of the Privy Council in *Royal Brunei Airlines v. Tan*[421] in 1994. This decision was subsequently definitively accepted as representing English law by the House of Lords in *Twinsectra v. Yardley*[422] and the latter decision was in turn clarified by the further decision of the Privy Council in *Barlow Clowes International v. Eurotrust International*.[423] Lord Selborne's statement[424] remains important only because of its manifestation of a continuing policy, the need to protect from liability agents of trustees who are guilty only of following instructions which have given to them. The current requirements for the imposition of liability for dishonest assistance were instead identified by Mance L.J., sitting in the Commercial Court, in *Grupo Torras v. Al-Sabah*[425] as "(i) a breach

---

[418] Referring to *Selangor United Rubber Co. v. Cradock (No.3)* [1968] 1 W.L.R. 1555, 1582 *per* Ungoed-Thomas J.
[419] (1874) 9 Ch. App. 244 at 251–252.
[420] In *Baden v. Société Générale* (1983) [1993] 1 W.L.R. 509N at 573 (the full name of this case is *Baden v. Société Générale pour Favoriser le Developpement du Commerce et de l'Industrie en France S.A.*).
[421] [1995] 2 A.C. 378.
[422] [2002] UKHL 12, [2002] 2 A.C. 164.
[423] [2005] UKPC 37, [2006] 1 W.L.R. 1476.
[424] Which was anyway not wholly consistent with the pre-existing authorities; see Harpum (1986) 102 L.Q.R. 114, 267.
[425] [1999] C.L.C. 1469.

of trust or fiduciary duty by someone other than the defendant, (ii) in which the defendant assisted (iii) dishonestly, together with (iv) resulting loss".

(1) "A breach of trust or fiduciary duty by someone other than the defendant"

Most of the older cases concerned the situation expressly envisaged by Lord **10–166** Selborne, where agents of trustees have assisted in bringing about a misapplication of the trust property by following the instructions of the trustees.[426] Many modern cases have equally concerned express trusts, frequently the situation where a failure to segregate funds held on trust from the other funds of the trustee has permitted the funds to be taken in discharge of the trustee's overdraft.[427]

However, it is clear that "the trust need not be a formal trust. It is **10–167** sufficient that there should be a fiduciary relationship between the 'trustee' and the property of another person."[428] Consequently, this first requirement is equally satisfied where the misapplication of property occurs as a result of agents following the instructions of any other express fiduciary. The "directors of a company are treated as if they were the trustees of the company's property under their control"[429] and many modern cases have concerned illegal or unauthorised transactions carried out in accordance with the instructions of company directors, sometimes for their own personal benefit.[430]

It is also sufficient if the trust in question is a resulting trust[431] or a **10–168** constructive trust,[432] even if the latter only arose as a result of the misapplication of the property itself. Millett J. emphasised in *Agip (Africa) v. Jackson*[433] that "the embezzlement of a company's funds almost inevitably involves a breach of fiduciary duty on the part of one of the company's employees or agents" and he went on to hold that "there is a receipt of trust property when a company's funds are misapplied by a director and, in my judgment, this is equally the case where a company's funds are misapplied by any person whose fiduciary position gave him control of them or enabled him to misapply them". This principle is not of course confined to funds but applies to property of any type.[434] A glance at the authorities cited in the footnotes will emphasise the substantial sums which were at stake in some

---

[426] As in *Barnes v. Addy* (1874) 9 Ch.App. 214 itself; *Williams v. Williams* (1881) 17 Ch.D. 437; *Williams-Ashman v. Price & Williams* [1942] 1 Ch. 219.

[427] As in *Royal Brunei Airlines v. Tan* [1995] 2 A.C. 378.

[428] *Baden v. Société Générale* (1983) [1993] 1 W.L.R. 509N at 573.

[429] *ibid.*

[430] In some while a number of cases have resulted from directors misapplying a company's funds for their own personal benefit; see, for example, *Polly Peck International v. Nadir (No.2)* [1992] 4 All E.R. 769. There was also a series of cases resulting from successful attempts to use the funds of a company to finance its own acquisition; see, for example, *Belmont Finance Corporation v. Williams Furniture* [1979] Ch. 250, *(No.2)* [1980] 1 All E.R. 393.

[431] *Twinsectra v. Yardley* [2002] UKHL 12, [2002] 2 A.C. 164.

[432] *Competitive Insurance Company v. Davies Investments* [1975] 1 W.L.R. 1240.

[433] [1990] Ch. 265 at 290.

[434] Information in respect of which a manager owed a fiduciary duty to his company would have sufficed in *Consul Development v. D.P.C. Estates* (1975) 132 C.L.R. 373 (High Court of Australia).

of them and the extent to which the victims of corporate fraud are increasingly looking towards members of the professions and financial institutions to compensate them for their losses.

10–169   Only rarely has there been any dispute as to whether or not this first requirement has been satisfied. However the unusual facts of *Brinks v. Abu-Saleh (No.3)*[435] did produce a contention that the claim brought in that case failed because of the lack of any trust. The theft of over £26,000,000 from the plaintiff's Heathrow warehouse had been facilitated by one of the plaintiff's employees, a security guard who had provided both a key to the premises and information about its security arrangements to the other persons involved in the robbery. In proceedings seeking the imposition of liability for dishonest assistance, the plaintiff contended that, because the robbery had taken place as a result of the actions of a dishonest fiduciary (the security guard), it "had an equity to trace into [the proceeds of the robbery], which were in the nature of trust moneys". It was conceded that the security guard was a fiduciary but it was argued that he did not owe a fiduciary duty which was sufficient to impress the proceeds of the robbery with a trust. Rimer J. predictably rejected this argument so the claim satisfied this first requirement. The defendant might have been better advised to have argued that, even though the security guard was a trustee of any property which reached his hands, that did not make him a trustee of the entire £26,000,000 at all, or at any rate not a sufficient trustee to lead to the imposition of liability for dishonest assistance on a third party; however, it is now clear from subsequent authority[436] that this first requirement was satisfied by virtue of the fact that the thieves were constructive trustees of the stolen property. In any event, Rimer J. went on to hold that the claim satisfied neither the second nor the third requirements.

(2)   "In which the defendant assisted"

10–170   It is "a simple question of fact"[437] whether someone has been accessory to, or assisted in, the misfeasance or breach of trust in question. It makes no difference whether the agent has previously advised against the course of conduct in question,[438] whether he has made the appropriate enquiries and reasonably come to what was in fact an incorrect conclusion,[439] or whether he has simply relied on the instructions given without checking relevant documents in his possession.[440] All that matters is the fact of having been accessory to or assisted in a misfeasance or breach of trust in a significant way.

10–171   In this connection, it should be noted that, although the vast majority of cases of this type inevitably involve agents of trustees or other fiduciaries, liability also extends to persons who have been in some other way an accessory to a disposition of property in breach of trust. Thus, in *Eaves v. Hickson*[441] liability was imposed on a person who had merely induced the

---

[435] [1996] C.L.C. 133.
[436] *Westdeutsche Landesbank Girozentrale v. Islington L.B.C.* [1996] A.C. 669 at 705.
[437] *Baden v. Société Générale* (1983) [1993] 1 W.L.R. 509N at 574–575.
[438] As in *Barnes v. Addy* (1874) 9 Ch.App. 214.
[439] As in *Williams v. Williams* (1881) 17 Ch.D. 437.
[440] As in *Williams-Ashman v. Price & Williams* [1942] 1 Ch. 219.
[441] (1861) 30 Beav. 136.

disposition in question; he had produced a forged marriage certificate to the trustees of a settlement in order to convince them that his children were legitimate and so entitled to the trust property, which was duly paid to them. In *Royal Brunei Airlines v. Tan*[442] liability was imposed on the managing director and therefore the person who was in physical control of a company which had misapplied money which was held on trust. Persons with such control are not "strangers" to the defaulting trustee in the way that its solicitors and bankers are but they are nevertheless its agents. They have immunity from direct liability as insiders (directors owe fiduciary duties only to their company, not to either its shareholders or beneficiaries) and it would be absurd if they could also claim immunity from liability for dishonest assistance on the grounds that they were not "outsiders". The possibility of imposing liability for dishonest assistance on the directors of a company which was acting as a corporate trustee has since been expressly confirmed by Lindsay J. in *H.R. v. J.A.P.T.*,[443] which concerned a claim against the corporate trustee of a pension scheme which had invested a high proportion of the assets of the scheme in purchases of property from the employer company at excessively high prices. However, liability for dishonest assistance will only actually be imposed if there is held to have been sufficient dishonesty to satisfy the third requirement discussed below.[444]

It is rare for the significance of the conduct of a person potentially liable **10–172** for dishonest assistance to be challenged as a matter of fact but this was done successfully in *Brinks v. Abu-Saleh (No.3)*.[445] As has already been seen,[446] £26,000,000 had been stolen from the Heathrow warehouse of the plaintiff who, in these particular proceedings,[447] was seeking the imposition of liability for dishonest assistance on a defendant who had accompanied her husband on various trips by car in the course of which he had transported to Zurich over £3,000,000 of the proceeds of the robbery for one of the convicted robbers, thereby enabling this sum to be laundered. Rimer J. held that she had accompanied him merely in her spousal capacity; so her presence therefore had not constituted relevant "assistance" in furtherance of the breach of trust complained of. Therefore, although the plaintiff's claim satisfied the first requirement considered above, this rather generous finding

---

[442] [1995] 2 A.C. 378.

[443] [1997] P.L.R. 99.

[444] *H.R. v. J.A.P.T.* also threw up a possible alternative means of imposing liability on the directors of a corporate trustee without any need to show dishonesty on their part. If their activities amount to breach of the fiduciary duty which they owe to the corporate trustee as its directors, a duty of strict liability not dependant on them having been dishonest or even negligent, Lindsay J. accepted that it was arguable that the members of the scheme were entitled to argue that such rights of action as the corporate trustee had against its directors were themselves part of the property of the pension trust, thus enabling the members of the scheme to force the trustee company to sue the directors and hold the fruits of that action on trust for them (by analogy with the decision in *Fletcher v. Fletcher* (1844) 4 Hare 67; see *ante*, para 5–111). But such a claim (described by Lindsay J. as a "dog-leg claim") was subsequently expressly rejected in *Gregson v. HAE Trustees* [2008] EWHC 1006 (Ch), which has clearly restricted its possible scope to situations where the corporate trustees' only role is the trusteeship of the trust in question, in which case the beneficiaries will be only general creditors.

[445] [1996] C.L.C. 133.

[446] See *ante*, para 10–169.

[447] Proceedings had been brought against no fewer that 57 defendants.

of fact meant that the plaintiff's claim failed to satisfy this second requirement (as will be seen later on,[448] Rimer J. then went on to state that the third
requirement was not satisfied either). However, the facts of this case were
extremely unusual and it is unlikely that the presence or absence of this
requirement will often be the subject of dispute.

(3) "Dishonestly"

10–173   This is the aspect of liability for dishonest assistance which has produced
most judicial disagreement. In *Barnes v. Addy*[449] Lord Selborne held that
liability would only be imposed on persons who assisted "with knowledge". This caused Peter Gibson J. in *Baden v. Société Générale*[450] both to
regard knowledge as the last of his four distinct elements and to identify five
different categories of knowledge.[451] However, in *Royal Brunei Airlines v.
Tan*[452] the Privy Council specifically rejected knowledge as a prerequisite of
the imposition of liability and replaced it by a requirement for dishonesty by
the accessory or person assisting.[453]

10–174   In that case the airline was seeking to impose liability on the managing
director and principal shareholder of an insolvent travel agency which had
paid into its ordinary current account the ticket moneys which, according to
I.A.T.A. regulations, it held on trust for the airline. This claim had failed in
the court below because it had not been established that the travel agent had
been guilty of any fraudulent and dishonest design, which was then a
requirement for the imposition of liability. However, the Privy Council held
that there was no such requirement and that in this respect it was only
necessary to satisfy the requirement which it substituted for there to have
been a breach of trust or fiduciary duty by someone other than the defendant. This conclusion would in itself have enabled the Privy Council to
allow the appeal; since it had been conceded that there had been a breach of
trust in which the managing director had assisted with actual knowledge, all
the requirements for the imposition of liability were clearly satisfied. But the
Board also held that "[a] conclusion cannot be reached on the nature of the
breach of trust which may trigger accessory liability without at the same
time considering the other ingredients including, in particular, the state of
mind of the third party".[454] Lord Nicholls considered and rejected the two
extreme possibilities of imposing either no liability at all or strict liability on
accessories to breaches of trust. Having thus necessarily opted for the

---

[448] See *post*, para 10–183.
[449] (1874) 9 Ch.App. 214.
[450] (1983) [1993] 1 W.L.R. 509N at 575–576.
[451] These were "(i) actual knowledge; (ii) wilfully shutting one's eyes to the obvious; (iii)
wilfully and recklessly failing to make such inquiries as an honest and reasonable man would
make; (iv) knowledge of circumstances which would indicate the facts to an honest and
reasonable man; (v) knowledge of circumstances which would put an honest and reasonable
man on inquiry". Eventually it became generally accepted that liability would only be imposed
on persons whose knowledge fell within the first three categories.
[452] [1995] 2 A.C. 378 (on appeal from Brunei Darussalam).
[453] Hence the change of name from liability for knowing assistance to liability for dishonest
assistance.
[454] [1995] 2 A.C. 378 at 386.

imposition of some form of fault-based liability, he reviewed the existing authorities and the opinions of the commentators and concluded[455]:

"Drawing the threads together, their Lordships' overall conclusion is that dishonesty is a necessary ingredient of accessory liability. It is also a sufficient ingredient. A liability in equity to make good resulting loss attaches to a person who dishonestly procures or assists in a breach of trust or fiduciary obligation. It is not necessary that, in addition, the trustee or fiduciary was acting dishonestly, although this will usually be so where the third party who is assisting him is acting dishonestly. 'Knowingly' is better avoided as a defining ingredient of the principle, and in the context of this principle the *Baden* scale of knowledge is best forgotten."

Although there was never any real doubt[456] that these observations of the Board constituted English law, considerable doubts were expressed as to whether the courts would adopt a wholly objective standard when considering whether or not any particular third party had been dishonest or would also take into account more subjective factors applicable only to the specific third party so as to impose either a higher or a lower standard of behaviour on him.[457]

This issue was reconsidered by the House of Lords in *Twinsectra v. Yardley*.[458] The claimant had made a loan on the basis that the sum advanced was paid to the borrower's solicitors who gave an undertaking to the claimant to utilise the loan money solely for the acquisition of property on behalf of the borrower and for no other purpose. The solicitors breached their undertaking by transferring most of the sum advanced to another solicitor, Leach; he disbursed the funds transferred to him in accordance with the instructions of the borrower but not all of those funds were spent on the acquisition of property; some of the funds were used on behalf of the borrower for other purposes, including the payment of Leach's own fees. The claimant contended that the arrangement between himself, the borrower and the original solicitors had given rise to a trust. If there was such a trust, the transfer by the original solicitors in breach of their undertaking would amount to a breach of trust; consequently, Leach would be potentially liable for dishonest assistance in that he had been an accessory to the disposition in breach of trust and had subsequently disbursed the funds transferred to him in ways which were inconsistent with the undertaking.[459]

10–175

---

[455] *ibid.* at 392.

[456] Despite one unsuccessful challenge in the Commercial Court in *Dubai Aluminium Company v. Salaam* [1999] 1 Lloyd's Rep. 387 at 452 and the occasional contrary statement such as that of Nourse L.J. in *Heinl v. Jyske Bank (Gibraltar)* [1999] Lloyd's Rep. Bank. 511.

[457] Despite the fact that Lord Nicholls had clearly warned against over-categorisation, the members of the Court of Appeal were unable to resist developing in subsequent cases, particularly in *Grupo Torras v. Al-Sabah* [2001] Lloyd's Rep. Bank. 36, no fewer than five categories of dishonesty.

[458] [2002] UKHL 12, [2002] 2 A.C. 162.

[459] The existence of such a trust would also make Leach potentially liable for knowing receipt of the sums used to pay his own fees and, further, would enable the claimant to recover all the property which had been purchased on behalf of the borrower from the companies into whose names that property had been put (this would be by virtue of the equitable proprietary interest in that property which the claimant would then have under the trust; see *post*, para 22–133).

10–176   At first instance, Carnwath J. held that the arrangement had not given rise to any trust; that in itself was enough to prevent Leach from being liable for dishonest assistance[460] but Carnwath J. held that, although Leach had not been dishonest, he had wilfully shut his eyes. The Court of Appeal held[461] that the arrangement had given rise to a trust and that Leach had been dishonest; he was consequently held liable for dishonest assistance.[462] Leach appealed to the House of Lords,[463] who confirmed the existence of a trust.[464] Was Leach liable for dishonest assistance?

10–177   Lord Hutton, with whose speech three of the other members of the House of Lords agreed, held that there were three possible interpretations of what Lord Nicholls had meant by "dishonesty"[465]: first, "a purely subjective standard, whereby a person is only regarded as dishonest if he transgresses his own standard of honesty, even if that standard is contrary to that of reasonable and honest people"; secondly, "a purely objective standard whereby a person acts dishonestly if his conduct is dishonest by the ordinary standards of reasonable and honest people, even if he does not himself realise this"; and, thirdly, "a standard which combines an objective test and a subjective test, and which requires that before there can be a finding of dishonesty it must be established that the defendant's conduct was dishonest by the ordinary standards of reasonable and honest people and that he himself realised that by those standards his conduct was dishonest". His Lordship opted for the third of these interpretations, which he described as "the combined test".[466]

10–178   However, the majority had considerable difficulty in applying these statements of law to the facts because of the apparent mutual inconsistency of the statements of Carnwath J. that Leach, on the one hand, had not been dishonest but, on the other hand, had wilfully shut his eyes; the difficulty arose because everyone else has always regarded a wilful shutting of eyes as amounting to dishonesty. However, the majority felt unable to do what the

---

[460] Because the first requirement above was not satisfied.

[461] [1999] Lloyd's Rep. Bank. 438.

[462] He was also held liable for knowing receipt of the sums used to pay his own fees and the claimant also recovered all the property which had been purchased on behalf of the borrower from the companies into whose names that property had been put.

[463] The companies into whose names the property purchased had been put also obtained leave to appeal to the House of Lords but withdrew their appeal at the last minute for financial reasons. They would in fact have lost because the House of Lords confirmed the existence of a trust. Consequently, the claimant did finish up with all the property which had been purchased in their names.

[464] See *ante*, para 9–059.

[465] [2002] UKHL 12, [2002] A.C. 164 at 171–172.

[466] The dissentient, Lord Millett, held at 200–201 that Lord Nicholls had been adopting a purely objective standard of dishonesty. However, he held that the issue before the House was not what Lord Nicholls had meant by dishonesty but whether it was necessary "to establish that an accessory to a breach of trust had a dishonest state of mind (so that he was subjectively dishonest . . . .); or whether it should be sufficient to establish that he acted with the requisite knowledge (so that his conduct was objectively dishonest)". He preferred the latter view, holding that "it should not be necessary that the accessory realised that his conduct was dishonest; it should be sufficient that it constituted intentional wrongdoing". He went on to comment that "the introduction of the criterion of dishonesty is an unnecessary distraction, and conducive to error" and advocated a return to the "traditional description of this head of equitable liability as arising from 'knowing assistance' ". However, he did not go further into precisely what he meant by knowledge of intentional wrongdoing.

Court of Appeal had done and go behind the statement that Leach had not been dishonest. Faced with the consequential choice between ordering a new trial and allowing Leach's appeal, they opted for the latter.[467]

Lord Hutton's combined test was not devoid of problems either. Later in **10–179** his speech,[468] he emphasised that an accessory "should not escape a finding of dishonesty because he sets his own standards of honesty and does not regard as dishonest what he knows would offend the normally accepted standards of honest conduct". This statement was wholly consistent with his combined test but overlooked the possibility that the accessory might fail to realise that his conduct was dishonest by the ordinary standards of reasonable and honest people because of the fact that he wrongly but genuinely regarded his own standards of dishonesty as the ordinary standards of reasonable and honest people. If such an accessory were to be regarded as liable (and it is highly unlikely that he would not have been), then it necessarily followed that there were limits beyond which a subjective belief that conduct was honest would not be accepted by the court. On this basis, subjectivity clearly had to be subdivided in some way, possibly into reasonable subjectivity and unreasonable subjectivity.

However, what Lord Hutton said in *Twinsectra v. Yardley* has now been **10–180** reinterpreted and restated by the Privy Council in *Barlow Clowes International v. Eurotrust International*.[469] Some of the funds invested in a fraudulent offshore investment scheme run through a Gibraltar company had been dissipated by being paid through bank accounts maintained by companies administered from the Isle of Man by the defendants. The liquidators of the Gibraltar company brought proceedings in the Isle of Man claiming that the defendants were liable for dishonest assistance. At first instance, the judge had found that, although one of the defendants had strongly suspected what the source of the funds actually was, he had seen nothing wrong in what he was doing, having thought that the carrying out of his clients' instructions was all important and that that attitude was honest. However, at that point *Twinsectra v. Yardley* had not yet been decided so she nevertheless held him liable on the basis of *Royal Brunei Airlines v. Tan*. Her decision was reversed on appeal on the grounds that it was not a necessary inference that the defendant would have concluded that the funds of which he was disposing were held on trust. On the further appeal of the liquidators to the Privy Council, the defendant also relied on what Lord Hutton had held in *Twinsectra v. Yardley*.

The Privy Council included both Lord Nicholls and two of the Law Lords **10–181** who had heard the appeal in *Twinsectra v. Yardley*, one of whom, Lord Hoffmann, delivered the opinion of the Board. He acknowledged[470] that

---

[467] Lord Millett would, on the other hand, have held Leach liable because he had known every detail of the undertaking which the payment to him had breached (not only had he himself at an earlier stage been asked by the claimant and had refused to give a similar undertaking but the solicitor who had agreed to give the undertaking had, before doing so, faxed a copy of it to him for his comments); presumably it was due to the fact that Leach's knowledge of the breach of the undertaking was so clear cut that Lord Millett did not define what he meant by knowledge of intentional wrongdoing.

[468] *ibid.* at 174.

[469] [2005] UKPC 37, [2006] 1 W.L.R. 1476 (on appeal from the Isle of Man).

[470] *ibid.*, at [15] and [16].

there was "an element of ambiguity" in what Lord Hutton had said and continued:

"The reference to 'what he knows would offend normally acceptable standards of honest conduct' meant only that his knowledge of the transaction had to be such as to render his participation contrary to normally acceptable standards of honest conduct. It did not require that he should have had reflections about what those normally acceptable standards were.
Similarly in the speech of Lord Hoffmann, the statement . . . that a dishonest state of mind meant 'consciousness that one is transgressing ordinary standards of honest behaviour' was in their Lordships' view intended to require consciousness of the elements of the transaction which make participation transgress ordinary standards of honest behaviour. It did not also require him to have thought about what those standards were."

10–182   It is extremely difficult to believe that this is really what Lord Hutton can have meant since this restated test does not seem to contain any element of subjectivity whatsoever, unless that element is provided by the requirement which the court below had held to be lacking, namely that the accessory be aware or shut his eyes as to the existence of a trust in the first place.[471] However, the Privy Council has at least made clear that there is no need for the accessory either to realise that his conduct was dishonest by the normally accepted standards of honest conduct or to be conscious that he is transgressing those standards. Further, the inevitable debate as to whether it is open to the lower English courts to adopt this new test laid down by the Privy Council in place of what Lord Hutton actually held in the House of Lords in *Twinsectra v. Yardley*[472] has been rapidly and mercifully truncated by the repeated application of the new test at first instance[473] and its clear acceptance by one member of the Court of Appeal.[474]

10–183   Given the way in which the Privy Council had reinterpreted what Lord Hutton had said, the accessory was obviously not protected by the fact that he had believed that he was acting honestly The appeal therefore turned on whether it is necessary for the imposition of liability for dishonest assistance that the accessory was actually aware of the existence of a trust. This is in fact a potential difficulty to which any test based on dishonesty inevitably gives rise. This question had not arisen in *Twinsectra v. Yardley* because Leach knew every detail of the facts which were held to have given rise to the trust of the funds lent by the claimant. But it had arisen in *Brinks v. Abu-Saleh (No.3)*[475] where a further ground on which Rimer J. had dismissed the attempt to impose liability for dishonest assistance on the defendant in question for having accompanied her husband on various trips by car to Zurich was because she had clearly been unaware of the source of the funds

---

[471] See *post*, para 10–177.
[472] See Yeo, 122 L.Q.R. (2006) 171, Conaglen and Goymoor [2006] C.L.J. 18.
[473] In *Abou-Rahman v. Aboucha* [2005] EWHC 2662 (Q.B.) [2006] 1 All E.R. (Comm) 247 at [43], *Barnes v. Tomlinson* [2006] EWHC 3115 (Ch), [2007] W.T.L.R. 377 at [78], *Att-Gen of Zambia v. Meer Care & Desai* [2007] EWHC 952 (Ch), [2007] All E.R. (D) 97 (May) at [368–369].
[474] In *Abou-Rahman v. Aboucha* [2006] EWCA Civ. 1492, [2007] 1 All E.R. (Comm) 827 *per* Arden L.J. at [66–70], clearly *ratio* but in the absence of any decision on the point by her brethren.
[475] [1996] C.L.C. 133.

being transported and so was necessarily also unaware of the existence of any trust; he held that liability could not be imposed unless the accessory knows of the existence of the trust or at least of the facts which give rise to the trust. But the Privy Council did not agree, holding that "someone can know, and can certainly suspect, that he is assisting in a misappropriation of money without knowing that the money is held on trust or what a trust means".[476] The appeal of the liquidators was therefore allowed.

This conclusion was consistent with the very much earlier decision of **10–184** Millett J. in *Agip (Africa) v. Jackson*,[477] where he held that: "it is no answer for a man charged with having knowingly assisted in a fraudulent and dishonest scheme to say that he thought that it was 'only' a breach of exchange control or 'only' a case of tax evasion. . . . A man who consciously assists others by making arrangements which he knows are calculated to conceal what is happening from a third party, takes the risk that they are part of a fraud practised on that party."[478] However, where someone who has assisted in a disposition of trust property in breach of trust neither actually knows nor objectively has any reason to suspect that the property in question is held on trust, he clearly cannot be held to be dishonest and so cannot be liable for dishonest assistance. Thus in *Ultraframe (UK) v. Fielding*[479] it was held that, for a wife to be held liable for dishonest assistance, it was not necessary that she had known every detail of what her husband had been doing; however, liability depended on her having known that what he had been doing was dishonest and she had not known or suspected this. To this extent, the imposition of liability for dishonest assistance is still dependant on the accessory having knowledge or shutting his eyes as to the existence of facts giving rise to a trust.

(4) Resulting loss

Until the decision in *Grupo Torras v. Al-Sabah*,[480] it was generally thought that **10–185** the quantum of recovery for dishonest assistance was the loss suffered as a result of the dishonest assistance in question and that it was for the claimant to prove what that loss actually was. However, in that case, the claimant submitted that a defendant who is guilty of dishonest assistance is liable for the whole loss resulting from the breach of trust in question, whether or not causally linked to his acts of specific assistance. At first instance, Mance L.J. said this:

"The starting point in my view is that the requirement of dishonest assistance relates not to any loss which may be suffered, but to the breach of trust or fiduciary duty. The relevant enquiry is in my view what loss or damage has resulted from the breach of trust or fiduciary duty which has been

---

[476] [2005] UKPC 37, [2006] 1 W.L.R. 1476 at [28], relying on what had been said by both Lord Hoffmann and Lord Millett in *Twinsectra v. Yardley* [2002] UKHL 12, [2002] A.C. 164 at [19] and [135].

[477] [1990] Ch. 265 at 295.

[478] A slightly different view was adopted by Mance L.J. at first instance in *Grupo Torras v. Al-Sabah* [1999] C.L.C. 1469 but this has necessarily been superseded by the decision of the Privy Council.

[479] [2005] EWHC 1638 (Ch), [2007] W.T.L.R. 835.

[480] [1999] C.L.C. 1469 (the point did not arise on appeal).

dishonestly assisted. In this context, as in conspiracy, it is inappropriate to become involved in attempts to assess the precise causative significance of the dishonest assistance in respect of either the breach of trust or fiduciary duty or the resulting loss. . . . But it is necessary to identify what breach of trust or duty was assisted and what loss may be said to have resulted from that breach of trust or duty. An allegation of a single and continuing conspiracy to commit and cover up a misappropriation is one thing. But it may involve a series of breaches of trust and fiduciary duty. The actual loss may have resulted at the early stage of misappropriation, rather than from the cover up. Dishonest assistance confined to the cover up stage may or may not necessarily attract liability for such previous loss."

This proposition unquestionably formed part of the ratio of Mance L.J. (the point did not arise on appeal). This effective acceptance of the claimant's contention, subject only to the exclusion of losses which occurred before the dishonest assister first became involved, obviously increases still further the potential burden of liability for dishonest assistance.

10–186   The possibility of recovering profits, as distinct from compensation for losses, was considered in *Fyffes Group v. Templeman*.[481] The shipping manager of the claimant had received secret commissions of 1.25 per cent on the lump sum freight paid by the defendant shipping company for transporting the claimant's bananas. The claimant now sought, among other heads of recovery, an account of the profits which the shipping company had made on the voyages as part of the compensation for its dishonest assistance in the breach of fiduciary duty by the shipping manager. Toulson J. held that in principle such relief should be available in appropriate circumstances. However, he held that it should not be granted to the claimant in these circumstances so as to deprive the shipping company of the ordinary profit element of the freight charged; the extent to which the claimant had paid more than it would otherwise have done had already been compensated in damages and there was no justification for awarding any further relief.

10–187   In *Crown Dilmun v. Sutton*,[482] a director of the claimant had diverted a conditional contract for the purchase of Fulham Football Ground to a company of which he and his wife were, indirectly, 49 per cent shareholders. The question arose as to whether the company, as distinct from the director, was potentially liable to account for any profit which it made out of the contract. Peter Smith J. held that the company had participated in the breach of duty by the director with actual knowledge of his dishonesty. It was, therefore, liable both for dishonest assistance and for having received property of the claimant with notice that it was being acquired in breach of fiduciary duty. On both grounds, the company was liable to account for any profit. A similar conclusion was reached in *Ultraframe (UK) v. Fielding*,[483] although in the event no liability for dishonest assistance was in fact imposed in that case. However, there is now no doubt that that the potential remedies for dishonest assistance include an account of profits.

---

[481] [2000] 2 Lloyd's Rep. 643.
[482] [2004] EWHC 52 (Ch), [2004] W.T.L.R 497.
[483] [2005] EWHC 1638 (Ch), [2007] W.T.L.R. 835.

Where a number of persons are liable in respect of the same act of dishonest **10–188** assistance, it was held in *Ultraframe (UK) v. Fielding*[484] that they are jointly and severally liable to compensate the victim of the dishonest assistance for his loss and that each is therefore potentially liable for the whole of the loss; however, insofar as they are obliged to account for their profit, it was held, in accordance with *Crown Dilmun v. Sutton*,[485] that each is only obliged to account for the profit actually made by him and not for the profit which has been made by anyone else who was guilty of dishonest assistance.

(C) The Liability of Agents of Invalidly Appointed Trustees

The primary concern of Lord Selborne when he gave his judgment in *Barnes* **10–189** *v. Addy* was to protect agents of a trust who act in accordance with the instructions of the trustees. Is this protection available to an agent even if the trustee by whom he is instructed has not himself been validly appointed? This issue arose in *Mara v. Browne*[486] where it was argued that an agent appointed by such a trustee must act as a principal and so would be deprived of the protection of *Barnes v. Addy*—this would of course mean that the agent in question would be treated as if he were officiously acting as a fiduciary and so, under the principles which have already been discussed,[487] would inevitably be liable no matter what his motives and his honesty. This argument succeeded at first instance before North J.[488] but the Court of Appeal found that the trustee in question had been validly appointed and so the issue did not have to be decided. However, Lord Herschell stated that the protection of *Barnes v. Addy* would be available to such an agent. It is suggested that this latter view, although not clearly established, is preferable since it is unreasonable to expect an agent to carry out a detailed investigation into the status of his principal.

(D) The Liability of Partners and Employers of Dishonest Assisters

When liability for dishonest assistance is imposed on a person as a result of **10–190** something which he has done or failed to do while engaged in his habitual occupation, the question arises as to whether his partners or his employers are also liable for dishonest assistance.

(1) The liability of partners

The answer to the question of whether the partners of a person who is held **10–191** liable for dishonest assistance are vicariously liable for the acts or omissions which have caused this type of liability to be imposed upon him was far from clear prior to the decision of the House of Lords in *Dubai Aluminium Co. v. Salaam*.[489] However, as a result of that decision, the earlier authorities[490] can now, at least for the moment, be disregarded. The House of Lords

---

[484] [2005] EWHC 1638 (Ch), [2007] W.T.L.R. 835.
[485] [2004] EWHC 52 (Ch), [2004] W.T.L.R 497.
[486] [1896] 1 Ch. 199.
[487] See *ante*, para 10–157.
[488] [1895] 2 Ch. 69.
[489] [2002] UKHL 48, [2003] 2 A.C. 366.
[490] *Blythe v. Fladgate* [1891] 1 Q.B. 337; *Mara v. Browne* [1895] 2 Ch. 69 (North J.), [1896] 1 Ch. 199 (C.A.); *Re Bell's Indenture* [1980] 3 All E.R. 425; *Agip (Africa) v. Jackson* [1990] Ch. 265 (Millett J.), [1991] Ch. 547 (C.A.).

held unanimously that liability for dishonest assistance fell within the scope of section 10 of the Partnership Act 1890 and that, consequently, the partners of a person held liable for dishonest assistance were vicariously liable for the wrongful acts or omissions which had led to the imposition of liability if "he was acting in the ordinary course of the business of the firm, or with the authority of his co-partners". The latter situation is self-evident; the former requires further consideration.

10–192   In *Dubai Aluminium Co. v. Salaam*, the senior partner of a firm of solicitors had to be assumed[491] to be liable for dishonest assistance by virtue of the fact that he had prepared the documentation by means of which the other defendants had succeeded in defrauding the claimant of some US$50,000,000; this sum had been paid out pursuant to a bogus consultancy agreement which was nothing more or less than a sham device for abstracting money from the claimant. The senior partner had purported to act for the other defendants as a member of his firm, which had charged and had been paid relatively modest fees for the work which he had done. The House of Lords held that, for liability to arise, the wrongful conduct of the partner in question had to be so closely connected with acts which he was authorised to do that, for the purpose of the liability of the firm to third parties, the wrongful conduct could fairly and properly be regarded as done while he had been acting in the ordinary course of the firm's business. This involved a factual conclusion based on primary facts rather than a simple question of fact. It was held that drafting the necessary agreements would have been within the ordinary course of the firm's business even though the documents were being drafted for a dishonest purpose. Consequently, on the facts as pleaded by the claimant, the senior partner would have been liable for dishonest assistance and so his partners would have been vicariously liable for his conduct.

10–193   In normal circumstances, this conclusion would have prejudiced the partners who would have been potentially liable for the entire US$50,000,000, in the same way as a partner of an accountancy firm was held, by Millett J. and the Court of Appeal in *Agip (Africa) v. Jackson*,[492] to be potentially liable for the whole of the money which his partner had, by acting as a director of a series of dummy companies, enabled a fraudster to launder. However, in *Dubai Aluminium Co. v. Salaam* the conclusion in fact benefited the partners because it entitled them to claim contribution from the other defendants, the persons who had actually benefited from the fraud. This result was not in itself objectionable but, controversially and probably wrongly,[493] the House of Lords went on to allow the firm of solicitors to recover the whole of the sum for which they had settled the proceedings brought against them[494] by way of contribution, thus enabling them to escape the entire liability imposed on them by the Partnership Act 1890.

---

[491] His partners had settled the claim against him for US$10,000,000 on the basis that all allegations of dishonesty against him were withdrawn but, for the purpose of their claim for contribution against the defendants who had actually benefited from the fraud, it had to be assumed that he was liable.
[492] [1990] Ch. 265 (Millett J.), [1991] Ch. 547 (C.A.).
[493] See *post*, para 22–040.
[494] £10,000,000.

Dubai Aluminium Co. v. Salaam does at least make clear the criteria for the   **10–194**
imposition of vicarious liability on the partners of a person held liable for
dishonest assistance; the latter at least now have the comfort of knowing
that they cannot be held liable for the acts or omissions of one of their
partners who goes off on a frolic of his own or, as Lord Millett specifically
held, of one of their partners who is held to be a constructive trustee as a
result of having decided officiously to act as a fiduciary or, as Lord Millett
would prefer to describe him, as a "de facto trustee".[495] However, it will not
be often that the partners who are vicariously liable for dishonest assistance
will find anyone from whom to claim contribution (most fraudsters will
have either disappeared or have become bankrupt); further, even if they do
manage to find a solvent potential contributory, they are unlikely often to
encounter such judicial generosity in respect of their contribution claim.
Their position is undoubtedly much more likely to be as in *Agip (Africa) v.
Jackson*, where there was no one from whom either the accountant or his
partner had the slightest chance of being able to obtain any contribution.

(2) The liability of employers

The question of when the employers of a person who is held liable for   **10–195**
dishonest assistance will be vicariously liable for the acts or omissions which
have caused this type of liability to be imposed upon him was considered in
Balfron Trustees v. Petersen.[496] A firm of solicitors was one of a number of
defendants on whom it was sought to impose liability for dishonest assistance as a result of a misappropriation of funds from a pension trust. The
basis of its alleged liability was the fact that it had been the employer of a
solicitor who had allegedly assisted in the misappropriation. On an application by the firm of solicitors to strike out the claim against it, Laddie J.
referred to the decision of the House of Lords in *Lister v. Hesley Hall*[497] and
held that an employer would only be vicariously liable for the conduct of his
employee where he owed some duty or responsibility to the victim. Where
this was the case, the employer would be liable even where the employee's
acts were so heinous that they could not reasonably be said to form part of
his obligations to the employer; this was because the employee had been
employed to discharge the employer's duty or responsibility to the victim.
The liability of the firm of solicitors thus depended on the identity of the
person to whom it owed its duty of care. Since it was arguable that this duty
was owed to the members of the pension scheme, the claim therefore could
not be struck out. It was subsequently settled before the claim against the
other defendants went to trial.

(E) What Should a Suspicious Agent Do?

If an agent suspects that he may be assisting in a misapplication of property   **10–196**
subject to a trust and it is too late for him to withdraw from the transaction
(this would be the position of a solicitor or a bank who became suspicious
about the provenance of funds being held to the order of a client), he is
entitled to make an application to the High Court under Part 64 of the Civil

---

[495] That was held not to be conduct within the ordinary course of the business of anyone.
[496] [2002] W.T.L.R. 157.
[497] [2001] UKHL 22, [2002] 1 A.C. 215.

Procedure Rules 1998[498] for administration directions. In the event that there are sufficient grounds for his suspicions, it was held in *Finers v. Miro*[499] that any directions given by the court can, if necessary, override any legal or other professional privilege of confidentiality to which the client would normally have been entitled.

10–197   However, *Finers v. Miro* was distinguished in *Moss v. Integro Trust B.V.I ,*[500] where the beneficiaries were ascertainable, of full age, and between them absolutely beneficially entitled to the trust property and brought an action successfully claiming the trust property under the rule in *Saunders v. Vautier.*[501] Nor can an agent safely refuse to comply with his client's instructions merely because he has become suspicious; this can only safely be done where he has positive evidence of a misfeasance or breach of trust on the part of the client. In *T.T.S. International v. Cantrade Private Bank,*[502] the Royal Court of Jersey went so far as to enter summary judgment against a bank who had refused to comply with instructions to transfer the balance of an account out of the jurisdiction; the court found, first, that at the relevant time there was no evidence of a dishonest and fraudulent design (still necessary at that time); secondly, that there was no evidence that the funds would be paid to anyone other than their true owners; and, thirdly, that the bank had taken an overly cautious view of its duties, appearing more concerned to protect itself against possible claims than to look after the interests of its account holders. Refusing to comply with the instructions of clients therefore appears only to be feasible in very extreme cases.

10–198   However, if the funds do have to be paid out for one of the reasons set out above, it has been held in Hong Kong[503] that this fact will constitute a defence to any subsequent attempt to impose liability for dishonest assistance on the agent who has been obliged to pay them out. It was held in that case that this followed from the fact that a bank, in that case the Bank of China, is normally liable to comply with the instructions of its client. This decision suggests that a suspicious agent will be best advised to apply for administration directions in any event because, even if he is unsuccessful, his liability will be limited to the costs of that application since it is likely that he will thereafter be protected from being held liable to the principal of his client for dishonest assistance.

4. *Receiving Property Disposed of in Breach of Trust*

(A)   The Different Remedies Available Against the Recipient

10–199   The imposition of the obligations of trusteeship on the recipient of property disposed of in breach of trust is generally known as "liability for knowing receipt". The imposition of such liability is, however, only one of a number

---

[498] Part 64 replaced Order 85 of the Rules of the Supreme Court in December 2002.

[499] *Finers v. Miro* [1991] 1 All E.R. 182.

[500] (1997) 2 Butterworths Offshore Service 173 (British Virgin Islands High Court).

[501] (1841) Cr. & Ph. 240; *post*, p.637. It is of course not particularly likely that all the beneficiaries of an offshore trust will satisfy these requirements—this caused a similar action to fail in Barbados in *Bank of Nova Scotia Trust Company (Caribbean) v. Tremblay* (1998) 2 B.O.S. 89.

[502] (1995), unreported but see (1995) 4 J.Int.Tr. 60.

[503] In *Bardissy v. D'Souza* (1999) [2003] W.T.L.R. 929.

of claims which may be available to the person from whom the property has been abstracted. If the property or its product is still identifiable in the hands of the recipient or of any third party to whom it has been subsequently transferred, he will also have the possibility of bringing a proprietary claim, either at law or in equity, to enable him to follow the property into the hands of its present holder.[504] Additionally he may be able to bring a personal action at law for money had and received against the recipient, a personal action in equity against whoever was responsible for initiating the misapplication, and a claim to make accountable in equity anyone who has been guilty of dishonest assistance.[505]

For example, in *Agip (Africa) v. Jackson*,[506] an employee of the plaintiff   **10–200** company fraudulently altered the names of the payees on a number of payment orders to make them payable to one of a series of dummy companies operated by the defendant firm of accountants who, as soon as the funds were received, transferred the funds on to third parties and wound-up the company in question. The plaintiff, having already obtained an unsatisfied judgment against the dummy company in question, sought the following relief against the defendants: at law, a proprietary claim to follow the funds into the hands of the defendants and a personal claim for money had and received and, in equity, a proprietary claim to follow the funds into the hands of the defendants and the imposition of liability for knowing receipt and dishonest assistance. In *Lipkin Gorman v. Karpnale*,[507] a member of a firm of solicitors had drawn from the firm's client accounts funds which he subsequently gambled away at a casino. The solicitors claimed that its bank was liable for conversion of cheques, for conversion of a draft, for breach of contract and for dishonest assistance; they also claimed that the casino was liable for money had and received, for negligence, for conversion of cheques, for conversion of a draft, and for knowing receipt and, additionally, was liable in equity to both proprietary and personal claims as a result of its receipt of the solicitors' funds.

It is hardly necessary to state[508] that the interrelation of these different   **10–201** claims makes proceedings of this type extremely complex. The principal difficulty arises from the fact that both the prerequisites for the imposition of liability and the available defences are different at law and in equity. It is perhaps inevitable that, as will be seen in a later chapter,[509] the prerequisites of and defences to proprietary claims differ depending on whether the claim is being brought at law or in equity. But there are also distinctions between the different personal claims. An action at law for money had and received will succeed quite irrelevant of the state of mind of the recipient of the money; liability is strict subject only to the defences of bona fide purchase for value without notice and of change of position.[510] On the other hand,

---

[504] See *post*, para 22–133.
[505] See *ante*, para 10–161.
[506] [1990] Ch. 265 (Millett J.) [1991] Ch. 547 (Court of Appeal).
[507] [1987] 1 W.L.R. 987 (Alliott J.); [1989] 1 W.L.R. 1340 (CA); [1991] 2 A.C. 548 (HL).
[508] See *ante*, para 10–156.
[509] See *post*, paras 22–114, 22–133.
[510] *Lipkin Gorman v. Karpnale* [1989] 1 W.L.R. 1340 (C.A.) [1991] 2 A.C. 548. See Birks [1991] L.M.C.L.Q. 473.

although there is some uncertainty as to precisely what mental element will lead to the imposition of liability for knowing receipt, that liability is certainly not at present strict (nor, as has already been seen, is liability for dishonest assistance).

10–202　　For present purposes, it is important only to distinguish between, on the one hand, the possibility of following the property disposed of in breach of trust into the hands of its recipient by means of an equitable proprietary claim and, on the other hand, the imposition of liability for knowing receipt. Where property has been disposed of in breach of trust, the interests of the beneficiaries in that property are, in accordance with the basic principles of property law, enforceable against the whole world unless and until the property in question reaches the hands of someone who takes it free of their equitable proprietary interests therein.[511] Any recipient of property disposed of in breach of trust who is liable to an equitable proprietary claim will of course be a trustee of such property as is in his hands—this is simply because the equitable interests of the beneficiaries in that property must necessarily take effect behind a trust of the legal interest. However, the fact that it is possible to bring an equitable proprietary claim against the recipient does not necessarily mean that he will also be held liable for knowing receipt. This was stated particularly clearly by Megarry V.-C. in *Re Montagu's Settlement*.[512]

10–203　　An often overlooked point is that it is in fact only in three situations that it is actually necessary to seek the imposition of liability for knowing receipt: first, where the recipient has dealt with some or all of the property in such a way that it can no longer be the subject of an equitable proprietary claim; secondly, where the property has depreciated in value while in the hands of the recipient; and, thirdly, where the recipient has obtained some incidental profit from the property.[513] In these circumstances, the equitable proprietary claim will enable the beneficiaries to recover only such property, if any, as remains in the hands of the recipient; the loss caused by any dealing with or reduction in the value of the property and any incidental profit obtained will only be recoverable if the recipient is held to have been a constructive trustee of the whole of the property originally transferred to him. In the overwhelming majority of the cases in which the imposition of liability for knowing receipt has been sought, the recipient has dealt with some or all of the property in such a way that it can no longer be the subject of an equitable proprietary claim.

---

[511] When the property or its product is pure personalty or unregistered land, the interests of the beneficiaries will be enforceable against the whole world other than a bona fide purchaser for value of a legal interest therein without notice of those interests. When it is registered land, their interests will be enforceable against the whole world if they either override registration or have been protected by an entry on the Land Register but otherwise will not be enforceable against any bona fide purchaser for value claiming under a registered disposition. Further, whatever the nature of the property, any claim of the beneficiaries to enforce their interests will additionally be subject to the established defences to equitable proprietary claims considered *post*, para 22–191 *et seq.*

[512] [1987] Ch. 264 at 272–273.

[513] Such as one of the types of secret profits discussed in the previous section of this chapter.

(B)   The Elements of Liability for Knowing Receipt

Liability for knowing receipt has never been dependent on the existence of   **10–204**
any dishonest or fraudulent design on the part of the person who disposed
of the property in breach of trust.[514] In *El Ajou v. Dollar Land Holdings*,[515]
Hoffmann L.J. isolated three distinct elements of this type of liability: a
disposition of property in breach of trust, beneficial receipt of the property
disposed of in breach of trust or of its traceable product, and knowledge by
the recipient.

(1)   A disposition of property in breach of trust

This first requirement is exactly the same as the first requirement for the   **10–205**
imposition of liability for dishonest assistance. Thus, "the trust need not be
a formal trust. It is sufficient that there should be a fiduciary relationship
between the 'trustee' and the property of another person",[516] which can be
either express or constructive, and that there should have been a disposition
of property in breach of the appropriate fiduciary duty. In practice this
requirement is likely to cause as few problems as the equivalent requirement
for the imposition of liability for dishonest assistance. But it was because of
the absence of such a disposition that the House of Lords did not impose
any liability for knowing receipt in *Twinsectra v. Yardley.*[517]

(2)   Beneficial receipt of the property disposed of in breach of trust or of its traceable product

Whether the property disposed of in breach of trust or its traceable product   **10–206**
has been beneficially received by the person on whom it is sought to impose
liability for knowing receipt is merely a question of fact. There are in fact
two distinct elements of this second requirement: first, that the property
should actually have reached the hands of that person; and, secondly, that
he should have received that property beneficially.

As for the first element, the conventional view is that actual receipt is   **10–207**
determined in the same way as in legal and equitable proprietary claims.
However, some doubts were cast on this by the judgment of Millett J. at first
instance in *El Ajou v Dollar Land Holdings*,[518] which seems to indicate that the

---

[514] Consequently the decision of the Privy Council in *Royal Brunei Airlines v. Tan* [1995] 2 A.C.
378 to replace this requirement for the imposition of liability for what is now known as
dishonest assistance did not in any way affect liability for knowing receipt, which had never
required more than the misfeasance or breach of trust preferred by the Privy Council

[515] [1994] 2 All E.R. 685.

[516] Peter Gibson J. in *Baden v. Société Générale* (1983) [1993] 1 W.L.R. 509N at 573, referring to
what is now known as liability for dishonest assistance.

[517] [2002] UKHL 12, [2002] 2 A.C. 164. In the Court of Appeal liability for knowing receipt had
been imposed on Leach, the solicitor to whom the majority of the funds had been transferred
in breach of the undertaking given to the claimant, in respect of the funds which, in accordance
with the instructions of the borrower, he had used to pay the fees which he had charged for
carrying out a conveyancing transaction. Contrary to what Lord Millett said in his speech, the
claim in respect of those fees was never withdrawn. However, in the course of argument in the
House of Lords, the Appellate Committee decided that the expenditure on these conveyancing
fees had been within the spirit of the undertaking on the strength of which the funds had been
advanced. This meant that Leach had not disbursed the sums in question in breach of trust and
so could not be liable for knowing receipt; for this reason, no argument was called for in respect
of liability for knowing receipt.

[518] [1993] 3 All E.R. 717.

rules for following property from one person to another are less strict in the case of liability for knowing receipt than in the case of equitable proprietary claims.

10–208   In this case,[519] a claim for the imposition of liability for knowing receipt was brought by and on behalf of the victims of a fraudulent share dealing operation carried out from Amsterdam on behalf of three Canadians. The latter had subsequently, through a Panamanian company, entered into a joint venture for the development of property in England with an English company which had not been involved in the fraud. They subsequently decided to withdraw from the joint venture and sold their interest in it to the English company. The plaintiff claimed that the Canadians' investment in the joint venture had been made with the funds of which he and the other victims had been defrauded. That in itself would not have made the English company liable in any way; at that stage the plaintiff's only conceivable claim would have been to attempt to attach the 50 per cent interest in the joint venture held by the Canadians' Panamanian company. But the plaintiff claimed that, as a result of the subsequent purchase of the Canadians' interest by the English company, that company had in effect received the funds of which he and the other victims had been defrauded and was therefore liable for knowing receipt.

10–209   The problem about this claim which is relevant for present purposes was the fact that the victims' funds had, prior to their investment in the joint venture, been moved through several civil law jurisdictions which do not recognise the existence of trusts and that at one point a substantial sum had been sent from Geneva to Panama, where it had disappeared for a short time prior to the reappearance of a roughly similar sum in Geneva. Millett J. held that the property could be followed despite the passage of the funds through the civil law jurisdictions and that, notwithstanding their brief disappearance in Panama, there was sufficient evidence to conclude that the victims' funds had indeed been used to make this investment. Although Millett J. indicated the contrary, no equitable proprietary claim could possibly have survived the disappearance of the funds in Panama and it is not easy to see how such a claim could have survived the passage of the funds through the civil law jurisdictions either. If, for the purposes of knowing receipt, actual receipt is indeed determined in the same way as in legal and equitable proprietary claims, then this case was wrongly decided. Nor does it seem appropriate that actual receipt should be determined in any different way for the purposes of knowing receipt; only if it is can the decision of Millett J. in this respect be supported.

10–210   His decision that the funds of the victims had indeed been received by the English company as a result of the purchase of the Canadians' share was not of course in itself sufficient for the imposition of liability for knowing receipt. It was also necessary to satisfy the third requirement, knowledge by the recipient. The chairman of the English company, who had originally brought the joint venturers together, had had dealings with the Canadians prior to the joint venture and was unquestionably aware of the manner in which they had acquired their funds. The Court of Appeal held, reversing

---

[519] [1993] 3 All E.R. 717 (Millett J.); [1994] 2 All E.R. 685 (C.A.).

Millett J. in this respect, that knowledge of the fraud acquired by the chairman in a quite different capacity prior to any involvement with the English company could be attributed to that company once he became its chairman. The English company, was therefore, obliged to pay a second time for the Canadians' 50 per cent interest. To make matters worse still, they were held liable in subsequent proceedings[520] to account not for the sum which they had actually paid to the Canadians but for 50 per cent of the substantially higher amount for which the joint venture property had eventually been sold on.

As for the second element of this requirement, it is (or at least ought to be) **10–211** merely a question of fact whether the property disposed of in breach of trust or its traceable product has been beneficially received by the person on whom it is sought to impose liability for knowing receipt. When property disposed of in breach of trust is received by persons for them to hold on trust, the recipient trustees are for these purposes regarded as receiving it beneficially. A solicitor certainly receives his fees beneficially[521] and, in principle, a banker receives beneficially the fees normally charged for transactions such as issuing banker's drafts[522] and the commissions normally charged for bank transfers, particularly those to other jurisdictions. However, while the potential liability of banks for knowing receipt in respect of any fees or commissions which it has charged has generally been ignored by the courts, in *Polly Peck International v. Nadir (No.2)*[523] Scott L.J. held that the potential liability of the Central Bank of Northern Cyprus in respect of Turkish lire which it had exchanged for sterling and transferred to Northern Cyprus was for knowing receipt because it "became entitled to the sterling not as banker... but in its own right". Apart from any fees or commissions which the Central Bank may have charged, to which no reference was made, the bank became no more beneficially entitled to the Turkish lire than it did to the sterling which it had also sent to Northern Cyprus (in respect of which its potential liability was held to be only for dishonest assistance). It is suggested that this potential liability for knowing receipt cannot be justified and that the decision of Scott L.J.[524] should not in this respect be followed.

(3) Knowledge by the recipient

Where a recipient of property has no knowledge whatever that it has been **10–212** disposed of in breach of trust, this third requirement will obviously not be satisfied and he will not be liable for knowing receipt (it is for the claimant to prove knowledge, not for the recipient to disprove it[525]). This is the case

---

[520] *El Ajou v. Dollar Land Holdings (No.2)* [1995] 2 All E.R. 213.

[521] This was the basis of the unsuccessful claim for knowing receipt in *Twinsectra v. Yardley* [2002] UKHL 12, [2002] 2 A.C. 162.

[522] Fees are also often charged simply for keeping accounts open and for each cheque but it is hardly likely that the amounts involved would be sufficient to justify proceedings.

[523] [1992] 4 All E.R. 769 at 777.

[524] It has not been followed in New Zealand; see *Nimmo v. Westpac Banking Corporation* [1993] 3 N.Z.L.R. 218 and *Cigna Life Insurance New Zealand v. Westpac Securities* [1996] 1 N.Z.L.R. 80.

[525] *Polly Peck International v. Nadir (No.2)* [1992] 4 All E.R. 769 at 777.

whether or not the recipient gave value for the property which he received.[526]

10–213 In *Carl-Zeiss Stiftung v. Herbert Smith (No.2)*[527] an East German Company sought to impose liability for knowing receipt on the firm of solicitors who were representing a West Germany Company in proceedings in which the East German Company was claiming that the property and the assets of the West German Company either belonged to or were held on trust for them (both claimed to be the original Zeiss Foundation and hence to be entitled to use the Zeiss trademark—the company had become divided due to the division of Germany after the Second World War). The basis of the claim against the solicitors was that they had actual notice that the East German Company claimed to be entitled to all the assets of the West German Company including, obviously enough, any legal fees which they had paid out. The Court of Appeal dismissed this claim on the somewhat controversial ground[528] that notice of an adverse claim to the property of the West German Company had not amounted to notice of a trust since difficult questions both of fact and law were involved in the claim; the solicitors, therefore, had had no effective knowledge whatever of any adverse claim to the funds which they had received and were, in effect, bona fide purchasers for value without notice of the fees which they had received.[529] A more straightforward illustration is *Cowan de Groot Properties v. Eagle Trust*,[530] where an attempt was made to impose liability for knowing receipt on the purchaser of five properties sold at a gross undervalue by a company in urgent need of liquid funds in order to make an urgent payment needed to keep an important company project in existence. Knox J. held that the purchaser did not actually have any knowledge whatsoever that the transaction was at an undervalue and so was consequently not liable.

10–214 The courts have also declined to impose "the heavy obligations of trusteeship"[531] upon recipients of property disposed of in breach of trust who received that property in good faith without any knowledge of the breach of trust in question. In *Re Diplock*,[532] under the provisions of a will subsequently declared to be void for uncertainty, executors distributed large sums of money to various charities who received the property in good faith without the slightest idea that the House of Lords would at a later stage hold that the will was void.[533] The next of kin of the testator (who were entitled under the resulting intestacy) brought an action against the charities to

---

[526] On the other hand, whether or not he gave value will of course be highly relevant in relation to an equitable proprietary claim, since only if he did will he be able to make out the defence of bona fide purchase for value without notice.

[527] [1969] 2 Ch. 276.

[528] See Gordon (1970) 44 A.L.J. 261.

[529] Although the Court of Appeal did not specifically say so, it is thought by practitioners that this restrictive view of notice can be relied on only by solicitors and possibly only by solicitors engaged in litigation. Further, the courts will generally not make orders validating in advance the payment in any event of the costs of solicitors who are defending clients who are accused of involvement in dishonest breaches of trust (see *United Mizrahi Bank v. Docherty* [1998] Ch. 435).

[530] [1992] 4 All E.R. 700.

[531] This was the description utilised by Lord Greene M.R. in *Re Diplock* [1948] Ch. 465.

[532] [1948] Ch. 465.

[533] In *Chichester Diocesan Fund v. Simpson* [1944] A.C. 341.

recover the money. They were obviously entitled to bring an equitable proprietary claim in order to follow the sums so paid into their product.[534] But the Court of Appeal held that the charities were not liable for knowing receipt and so the sums which could not be recovered by means of the equitable proprietary claim could not be recovered by the imposition of a constructive trust. This decision was expressly approved by the House of Lords in *Westdeutsche Landesbank Girozentrale v. Islington L.B.C.*[535]

Where the situation is not so clear cut, the authorities conflict. Discussion   **10–215** of the position formerly focused principally around the five categories of knowledge identified by Peter Gibson J. in *Baden v. Société Générale*[536]: "(i) actual knowledge; (ii) wilfully shutting one's eyes to the obvious; (iii) wilfully and recklessly failing to make such inquiries as an honest and reasonable man would make; (iv) knowledge of circumstances which would indicate the facts to an honest and reasonable man; (v) knowledge of circumstances which would put an honest and reasonable man on inquiry". However, the most recent pronouncement by the Court of Appeal, which therefore presumably at present constitutes English law, makes the criterion for the imposition of liability whether or not the state of the recipient's knowledge make receipt by him unconscionable.[537] However, there is still authority for the following conflicting propositions as to what will lead to the imposition of liability: first, that any of the five categories of knowledge identified in *Baden v. Société Générale* will suffice; secondly, that only the first three of these categories will suffice; thirdly, that the question of whether the fourth and fifth of these categories will suffice only arises in non-commercial transactions, only the first three of those categories being relevant in commercial transactions; and, fourthly, that the state of the recipient's knowledge must make it unconscionable for him to retain the benefit of the receipt. It was hoped that the conflict between these lines of authority would be resolved by the House of Lords in *Twinsectra v. Yardley* but this did not occur

---

[534] See *post*, p.807.

[535] [1996] A.C. 669.

[536] (1983) [1993] 1 W.L.R. 509N at 575–576

[537] Prior to the enunciation of this principle by the Court of Appeal in *B.C.C.I. v. Akindele* [2000] Lloyd's Rep. Bank 292, both Rix J. and the Court of Appeal had held, in *Dubai Aluminium Co. v. Salaam* [1999] 1 Lloyd's Rep. 415 at 453 (Rix J.), [2000] 2 Lloyd's Rep. 168 at 172 (CA) that liability for knowing receipt will only be imposed if the defendant has been dishonest in the sense necessary for the imposition of liability for dishonest assistance, in other words that the test for knowledge in knowing receipt was the same as that for dishonesty in dishonest assistance. Subsequently, in *Bank of America v. Arnell* [1999] Lloyd's Rep. Bank 399 at 406, Aikens J. held both that this was the test and that it had been established as such by the Court of Appeal in *Twinsectra v. Yardley* [1999] Lloyd's Rep. Bank. 438, although this was not in fact the basis on which liability for knowing receipt was imposed by the Court of Appeal in that case (liability was imposed on some of the recipients of the funds which had been transferred to Leach in breach of trust on the basis that the borrower's knowledge of what was going on had to be attributed to them and liability was imposed on Leach himself on the grounds that he had notice of the breach of trust). Admittedly, prior to *Royal Brunei Airlines v Tan* [1995] 2 A.C. 378, many commentators had thought that the better view was that the basis of liability for what was then called knowing assistance and for knowing receipt should be the same. However, there seems no obvious reason why the wholly justifiable restricting of accessory liability to persons who are dishonest should also apply to those who have actually received the property in question. In any event, the dishonesty test enunciated in *Dubai Aluminium Co. v. Salaam* was specifically rejected by the Court of Appeal in *B.C.C.I. v. Akindele* [2000] Lloyd's Rep. Bank 292 and it is therefore considered that this possible test can now be ignored.

because, as has already been seen, the claim for knowing receipt before the House failed to satisfy the first requirement.

10–216   No matter what the current law is, a recipient of property disposed of in breach of trust who has actual knowledge of the breach of trust will obviously be liable for knowing receipt. In *Belmont Finance Corporation v. Williams Furniture (No.2)*,[538] the directors of a company had had actual knowledge of a transaction whereby that company had permitted its wholly owned subsidiary to be purchased with its own money, a transaction which amounted to a breach of trust by the directors of the subsidiary. The purchase price for the subsidiary had of course been paid to the parent company which had, therefore, received property with actual knowledge that it had been disposed of in breach of trust. The Court of Appeal held that the parent company was liable for knowing receipt and so was a constructive trustee of the purchase moneys received. Similarly, in *El Ajou v. Dollar Land Holdings*,[539] the Court of Appeal imposed liability for knowing receipt on a company because it had acquired the interest of a co-venturer at a time when, through its chairman, it was aware that the co-venturer had originally acquired its interest in the joint venture with the proceeds of fraud.

10–217   It is also self-evident that liability for knowing receipt should not be confined to cases of actual knowledge. In *Nelson v. Larholt*[540] one of the executors of a will drew eight cheques on the estate's bank account, all of which were signed by him as executor of the testator, in favour of the defendant who cashed the cheques in good faith. The other executor and the beneficiaries claimed that the defendant held the proceeds of the cheques on constructive trust for the estate. Denning J. held that the defendant must be taken to know what any reasonable man would have known. Eight successive requests to cash cheques clearly drawn on the bank account of an estate would have placed a reasonable man on enquiry. Thus the defendant must be taken to have known of the executor's breach of trust and so, although he had obtained the cheques for value in good faith, he was held to be liable for knowing receipt and was a constructive trustee of their proceeds. The category of knowledge relied on by Denning J. as the basis for the imposition of this constructive trust appears to fall within the fifth category of knowledge which would later be identified by Peter Gibson J. (knowledge of circumstances which would put an honest and reasonable man on inquiry). Consequently, *Nelson v. Larholt*, together with dicta of the Court of Appeal in *Belmont Finance Corporation v. Williams Furniture (No.2)*[541] and in a number of first instance decisions,[542] was subsequently cited in *Cowan de Groot Properties v. Eagle Trust*[543] as authority for the proposition that liability for knowing receipt will be imposed if the recipient has any of the five categories of knowledge identified by Peter Gibson J.; and, much more recently, Lord

---

[538] [1980] 1 All E.R. 393.
[539] [1994] 2 All E.R. 685.
[540] [1948] 1 K.B. 339.
[541] [1980] 1 All E.R. 393.
[542] *International Sales and Agencies v. Marcus* [1982] 3 All E.R. 551 at 558; *Agip (Africa) v. Jackson* [1990] Ch. 265 at 290; *Westpac Banking Corp v. Savin* [1985] 2 N.Z.L.R. 41 at 71 (High Court of New Zealand).
[543] [1992] 4 All E.R. 700.

Millett[544] stated in *Twinsectra v Yardley*[545] that "constructive notice is sufficient".[546]

However, *Nelson v. Larholt* was explained in a different way in *Carl-Zeiss*   **10–218**
Stiftung v. Herbert Smith (No.2),[547] where Sachs L.J. described *Nelson v. Larholt*
as a case where there had been an obvious shutting of eyes as opposed to a
mere lack of prudence and suggested that a negligent, if innocent, failure to
make inquiry was not sufficient to attract liability for knowing receipt. This
interpretation of the decision appears to place the defendant in *Nelson v.
Larholt* within the second category of knowledge which would later be
identified by Peter Gibson J. (knowledge that he would have obtained but
for wilfully shutting his eyes to the obvious).

This narrower interpretation of *Nelson v. Larholt* was adopted by Megarry   **10–219**
V.-C. in *Re Montagu's Settlement*,[548] where he held that liability would be
imposed only on a recipient who had had one of first three of the five
categories of knowledge identified by Peter Gibson J., namely actual knowledge, wilfully shutting one's eyes to the obvious, and wilfully and recklessly
failing to make such inquiries as an honest and reasonable man would
make. This case concerned a settlement made in 1923 under one of the
clauses of which certain chattels, largely comprising the furniture, plate,
pictures and other heirlooms of the Montagu family, were assigned to the
trustees who, in the events which happened, were under a fiduciary duty,
after the death in 1947 of the ninth Duke of Manchester, to select and make
an inventory of such of the chattels as they considered suitable for inclusion
in the settlement and to hold the residue of the chattels on trust for the tenth
Duke of Manchester absolutely. However, the trustees in fact made no such
selection or inventory but instead treated all the chattels as being the absolute property of the tenth Duke. Many of the chattels were therefore sold by
him in 1949 and the remainder were taken by him to Kenya where he was
then living. Following his death in 1977, the eleventh Duke of Manchester
sought to recover the chattels or their value from his step-mother, the tenth
Duke's executrix. Megarry V.-C. ordered an inquiry in order to establish
which of the chattels would have been selected had the trustees complied
with their obligations in 1947. Such of the selected chattels as were still in the
hands of the executrix could be recovered from her by means of an equitable
proprietary claim but recovery of the value of those which had been sold
required the imposition of liability for knowing receipt.

Megarry V.-C. held that the 10th Duke did not fall into any of the first   **10–220**
three categories of knowledge identified by Peter Gibson J. and so his
executrix was not liable for knowing receipt. He held that the mistake as to
the interpretation of the settlement had occurred as a result of what his
Lordship described as "an honest muddle". Admittedly the 10th Duke's

---

[544] Repeating what he had said in *Agip (Africa) v. Jackson* [1990] Ch. 265 at 290.

[545] [2002] UKHL 12, [2002] 2 AC 164 at 194.

[546] As already indicated, these categories are: (i) actual knowledge; (ii) wilfully shutting one's
eyes to the obvious; (iii) wilfully and recklessly failing to make such inquiries as an honest and
reasonable man would make; (iv) knowledge of circumstances which would indicate the facts
to an honest and reasonable man; and (v) knowledge of circumstances which would put an
honest and reasonable man on inquiry.

[547] [1969] 2 Ch. 276 at 298.

[548] [1987] Ch. 264.

solicitor, and possibly also the 10th Duke himself as one of the settlers of the 1923 settlement, had at one stage been aware of the true position. However, his Lordship held that "a person is not to be taken to have knowledge of a fact that he once knew but has genuinely forgotten: the test (or a test) is whether the knowledge continues to operate on that person's mind at the time in question".[549] He also held that, where a person has received property as a result of a disposition in breach of trust, any knowledge which may be possessed by his solicitor will not be imputed to him, "at all events if the donee or beneficiary has not employed the solicitor to investigate his right to the bounty, and has done nothing else that can be treated as accepting that the solicitor's knowledge should be treated as his own". This narrower view of liability for knowing receipt was subsequently applied by Alliott J. at first instance in *Lipkin Gorman v. Karpnale*[550] and by Steyn J. in *Barclays Bank v. Quincecare.*[551]

10–221   At this stage there were consequently two conflicting lines of authority based on the two different interpretations of the decision in *Nelson v. Larholt*. A further refinement was subsequently introduced by Vinelott J. in *Eagle Trust v. S.B.C. Securities.*[552] He held that the question of whether the fourth and fifth categories of knowledge identified by Peter Gibson J. suffice for the imposition of liability for knowing receipt only arises in non-commercial transactions[553]; "these categories are knowledge of circumstances which would indicate the facts to an honest and reasonable man and knowledge of circumstances which would put an honest and reasonable man on inquiry". In commercial transactions, on the other hand, "if, in the ordinary course of business, a payment is made in discharge of a liability to the [recipient], the [recipient] cannot be made liable as a constructive trustee merely upon the ground that he knew or had reason to suspect that there had been a breach of trust disentitling the trustee to make the payment. It must be shown that the circumstances are such that knowledge that the payment was improper can be imputed to him".[554] Thus in commercial transactions, liability for knowing receipt will be imposed if the recipient has any of the first three categories of knowledge identified by Peter Gibson J. or "if the circumstances are such that, in the absence of any evidence or explanation by the [recipient], that knowledge can be inferred"—it being inferred "if the circumstances are such that an honest and reasonable man would have

---

[549] *ibid.* at 285. In *El Ajou v. Dollar Land Holdings* [1993] 3 All E.R. 717 at 739–740. Millett J. held that, in the same way, "where the knowledge of a director is attributed to a company, but is not actually imparted to it, the company should not be treated as continuing to possess that knowledge after the director in question has died or left its service. In such circumstances, the company can properly be said to have 'lost its memory'." Although the Court of Appeal reversed Millett J., Nourse L.J. stated ([1994] 2 All E.R. 685) that, while this proposition did not assist the defendant, he "might agree" with it.

[550] [1987] 1 W.L.R. 987 (the question did not have to be decided in the Court of Appeal ([1989] 1 W.L.R. 1340) and did not arise in the House of Lords ([1991] 2 A.C. 548).

[551] (1988) [1992] 4 All E.R. 363.

[552] (1991) [1993] 1 W.L.R. 484.

[553] For such transactions, Vinelott J. appeared to favour the broader view of liability for knowing receipt rather than the view expressed in *Re Montagu's Settlement*.

[554] (1991) [1993] 1 W.L.R. 484 at 506.

inferred that the moneys were probably trust moneys and were being misapplied".[555]

This case concerned an attempt to impose liability for knowing receipt on the underwriter of a rights issue made by the plaintiff company in connection with a share exchange takeover; the underwriter had received in discharge of the sub-underwriting obligations of the plaintiff's chief executive what turned out to be the plaintiff's own funds. Because these funds had been received in a commercial context to discharge a debt, Vinelott J. struck out a claim alleging only knowledge within the fourth and fifth categories identified by Peter Gibson J. The Court of Appeal subsequently granted the plaintiff leave to amend the pleadings so as to allege knowledge within the first three categories as well. When the case came on for trial,[556] Arden J. followed and applied the statement of principle enunciated by Vinelott J. She held that, in a knowing receipt case "where the receipt occurs in the discharge of a lawful debt (at least one arising out of a transaction which does not itself constitute a breach of trust[557]), actual knowledge within categories (i), (ii) and (iii) in the *Baden* case is required". The underwriter was held to have had no such knowledge so the action failed. The principle enunciated by Vinelott J. had in the meantime also been applied with exactly the same consequences by Knox J. in *Cowan de Groot Properties v. Eagle Trust*.[558] While the further refinement introduced by these authorities is certainly consistent with the traditional reluctance of equity to extend the doctrine of constructive notice to commercial transactions,[559] to have distinct tests for different types of transactions may well only succeed in confusing the situation even further.   **10–222**

However, in *B.C.C.I. (Overseas) v. Akindele*,[560] the Court of Appeal rejected all of the pre-existing lines of authority and established a wholly new test, holding that liability for knowing receipt will only be imposed if the state of the recipient's knowledge makes it unconscionable for him to retain the benefit of the receipt. The case concerned an agreement into which the defendant had entered for the investment of US$10,000,000 in the shares of the holding company of a Cayman Islands bank; the other contracting party, a company associated with the group, was to provide the shares and to arrange for their repurchase between two and five years later if the defendant so wished at a price which would give him a profit of 15 per cent per annum, compounded annually. The agreement had been entered into at a time when no one had any reason to doubt the integrity of the management of the bank; in fact, however, the transaction enabled the other contracting party to conceal a number of dummy loans it had made to enable the holding company to acquire its own shares and thus boost its capital in the   **10–223**

---

[555] *ibid*.

[556] *Eagle Trust v. S.B.C. Securities (No.2)* (1994) [1996] 1 B.C.L.C. 121 at 152.

[557] Such as the transaction in *Belmont Finance Corporation v. Williams Furniture (No.2)* [1980] 1 All E.R. 393; this was the ground on which Arden J. distinguished this decision.

[558] (1991) [1992] 4 All E.R. 700. However, both Arden J. and Knox J. went on to state that, in the event that they were wrong as to the law, the respective recipients had had no knowledge within the fourth or fifth categories either, so both claims would actually have failed on any view of the law.

[559] See *Manchester Trust v. Furness* [1895] 2 Q.B. 539 at 545.

[560] [2000] Lloyd's Rep. Bank 292.

eyes of the world. But the defendant did have some suspicions about the way in which the bank was operating by the time that he realised his investment and recovered his capital and the guaranteed profit. Since the relevant sum was in fact paid to him by the Cayman Islands bank in breach of a fiduciary duty, that bank's liquidators subsequently sought to hold him liable for his profit on the grounds of dishonest assistance and knowing receipt. Carnwath J. held that the defendant had not been dishonest (which was enough to dispose of the claim for dishonest assistance) and that he would have had no reason to question the form of the transaction and so was not liable for knowing receipt either.

10–224   In the Court of Appeal Nourse L.J., after a full review of all the earlier authorities[561] held[562]:

"I have come to the view that, just as there is now a single test of dishonesty for knowing assistance, so ought there to be a single test of knowledge for knowing receipt. The recipient's state of knowledge must be such as to make it unconscionable for him to retain the benefit of the receipt. A test in that form, though it cannot, any more than any other, avoid difficulties of application, ought to avoid those of definition and allocation to which the previous categorisations have led. Moreover, it should better enable the courts to give common-sense decisions in the commercial context in which claims in knowing receipt are now frequently made."

Nourse L.J. then went on to apply this test by holding that the defendant's state of knowledge was not such that it was unconscionable either for him to have entered into the transaction or for him to be entitled to retain the benefit of the profit which he received when he had enforced it; consequently, he was not liable for knowing receipt.

10–225   The decision in *B.C.C.I. (Overseas) v. Akindele*, which was subsequently considered by the Court of Appeal in *Criterion Properties v. Stratford UK Properties*,[563] constitutes both the most recent statement of principle and the only occasion on which this third requirement for the imposition of liability for knowing receipt has received detailed consideration at Court of Appeal level; consequently, this new test must, at least as a matter of precedent, constitute the law at present. However, apart from reciting the findings of Carnwath J. and saying that the defendant would not have had actual or constructive knowledge of the breach of fiduciary duty, Nourse L.J. gave no specific indications as to why he was holding that there had been no unconscionability. It is, therefore, at present difficult to predict precisely when a recipient's state of knowledge will be held to be such as to make it unconscionable for him to retain the benefit of the receipt (there has as yet been no reported case in which liability for knowing receipt has been imposed on this somewhat amorphous basis). The application of the new

---

[561] Having specifically rejected dishonesty as the criterion for the imposition of liability for knowing receipt.

[562] [2000] Lloyd's Rep. Bank 292. at 301.

[563] [2002] EWCA Civ. 1783, [2003] 1 W.L.R. 2108 at [28–40] (the decision was affirmed on other grounds at [2004] UKHL 28, [2004] 1 W.L.R. 1846).

test is bound, and was clearly intended to be, much more "broad brush" than the pre-existing law with its reliance on different categories of knowledge. Further, as the final sentence of the passage cited indicates, this test is going to require virtually every claim to impose liability for knowing receipt to be litigated, something which is far from an ideal state of affairs for potential litigants. What is, however, clear is that, as a result of the adoption of this test, it has for the first time been clearly established that a person may have sufficient knowledge to be liable for knowing receipt while being insufficiently dishonest to be liable for dishonest assistance.

(C) Quantum
A person on whom liability for knowing receipt is imposed will be liable to return the value of the property which he has received together with compound interest thereon; in addition, the claimant can recover any fruits produced by the property while it has been in the hands of the recipient and any secret profits made by the recipient by virtue of his position as constructive trustee. These remedies are restitutionary and there can be no double recovery from successive recipients of the same property.[564] Nor is a knowing recipient liable to account for a benefit received by someone else.[565]   **10–226**

(D) Defences
It follows from the fact that the constituents of liability for knowing receipt include a requirement of knowledge that neither a bona fide purchaser of a legal estate for value without notice (or the statutory equivalent) nor an innocent volunteer will be liable for knowing receipt. This is shown by the authorities which have already been discussed.[566] In principle, the defence of change of position established by the House of Lords in *Lipkin Gorman v Karpnale*[567] should also be available as a defence to a claim in knowing receipt. However, there seems to be no scope for its operation under the present law since there is no obvious way in which anyone found liable for knowing receipt under any of the present views of the law could successfully show a change of position in good faith; that person will necessarily have some form of knowledge, either of the disposition of property in breach of trust itself or of something else, which either in itself suffices for the imposition of liability or makes it unconscionable for him to retain the benefit of the receipt. However, this defence will become extremely relevant if the law is ever reformed in the way envisaged below.   **10–227**

(E) Possible Law Reform
The availability of all the different claims to which reference was made at the beginning of this section has led commentators to question whether so many   **10–228**

[564] *Trustor AB v. Smallbone (No.2)* [2001] 1 W.L.R. 1177 at [63–64].
[565] *Ultraframe (UK) v. Fielding* [2005] EWHC 1638 (Civ), [2007] W.T.L.R. 835 at [1577–1578].
[566] See *ante*, paras 10–213, 10–214.
[567] See *post*, para 22–144.

different remedies should continue to be available for the same misapplication of property.[568] Indeed Millett J. once commented[569] that he did not see "how it would be possible to develop any logical and coherent system of restitution if there were different requirements in respect of knowledge for the common law claim for money had and received, the personal claim for an account in equity against a knowing recipient and the equitable proprietary claim"; the reform of liability for knowing receipt has also been canvassed by a large number of commentators. As a result, the Law Commission at one stage considered reviewing this whole area of the law with a view to rationalising all the available remedies but no review has in fact taken place. Among a number of other suggestions made by commentators,[570] an ever-increasing majority, including three Lords of Appeal in Ordinary writing extra-judicially, have expressed the view that the best way forward is to sweep the existing law away completely and replace it by the introduction of a universal principle of strict liability subject only to specified defences, namely the defence of bona fide purchase for value without notice (or statutory equivalent) and the defence of change of position. The principal loser under such a reform would of course be an innocent volunteer, such as the charities in *Re Diplock*,[571] who was not able to show a change of position; such a person would for the first time become liable for knowing receipt.

10–229   The most significant advocate of this view has been Lord Nicholls of Birkenhead, writing extra-judicially.[572] Specific reference to his views was made by the Court of Appeal in *BCCI (Overseas) v. Akindele*,[573] although no argument was based on this suggestion and the court said that "at this level of decision, it would have been a fruitless exercise". The Court of Appeal then went on to doubt whether any such change in the law would be appropriate anyway. However, Lord Nicholls' views had been envisaged by

---

[568] See particularly Lord Millett extra-judicially (1991) 107 L.Q.R. 71; Lord Hoffmann extra-judicially in *Frontiers of Liability* (ed. Birks, 1994), p.27; Harpum *ibid.*, at p.9; Finn in *Equity, Fiduciaries and Trusts 1993* (ed. Waters), p.195; Lord Nicholls of Birkenhead extra-judicially in *Restitution—Past, Present and Future* (ed. Cornish, 1998), p.231, Lord Walker extra-judicially 27 Sydney L.R. (2005) 187. See also Birks, who over time changed his mind as to what reform should be made: compare [1989] L.M.C.L.Q. 296 with *Breach of Trust* (ed. Birks and Pretto, 2002), p.223.

[569] In *El Ajou v. Dollar Land Holdings* [1993] 3 All E.R. 717 at 739–740.

[570] Two other views deserve attention: Lord Hoffmann extra-judicially in *Frontiers of Liability* (ed. Birks, 1994), p.27, has advocated that liability for knowing receipt should arise, if at all, under the law of tort and in particular the torts of negligence and deceit, and that all the forms of equitable liability should be abolished; Finn pre-judicially in *Equity, Fiduciaries and Trusts 1993* (ed. Waters, 1993), p.195, has argued for the abandonment of much, if not all, of the existing law and its replacement by the following three questions, all of which need to be answered in the affirmative before what he denominates "participatory liability" can be imposed: (1) Has a fiduciary committed a breach of fiduciary duty or breach of trust? (2) Has the third party participated in the manner in which the breach has occurred? (3) In so doing, did that party know or have reason to know that a wrong was being committed by the fiduciary on his or her beneficiaries?

[571] [1948] Ch. 465, *ante*, para 10–214.

[572] In *Restitution—Past, Present and Future* (ed. Cornish, 1998) 231. See also Birks [1993] L.M.C.L.Q. 218; Harpum in *Frontiers of Liability* (ed. Birks, 1993) 9.

[573] [2000] Lloyd's Rep. Bank. 399.

Millett J. some years earlier in *El Ajou v Dollar Land Holdings*[574] and were subsequently referred to by the same judge in the House of Lords in *Twinsectra v. Yardley*.[575] In that case Lord Millett, who had observed in the course of the argument that: "[i]f Leach succeeds on dishonest assistance, the House will have to consider knowing receipt in the light of his honesty, on which there are a number of irreconcilable authorities at first instance including some statements of my own", enunciated the following dictum. Having commenced by saying, uncontroversially, that a claim to impose liability for knowing receipt is a receipt based restitutionary claim, he continued:

"There is no basis for requiring actual knowledge of the breach of trust, let alone dishonesty, as a condition of liability. Constructive notice is sufficient, and may not even be necessary. There is powerful academic support for the proposition that the liability of the recipient is the same as in other cases of restitution, that is to say strict but subject to a change of position defence."

Lord Millett's reference to constructive notice being sufficient was, of course, consistent with the earlier statements of his own to which he had referred in argument[576] but completely overlooked *B.C.C.I. (Overseas) v. Akindele*,[577] a decision of the Court of Appeal which, although obviously not binding on the House of Lords, nevertheless as a matter of precedent must then have constituted (and, for that matter, must still constitute) English law. But, quite irrespective of this point, Lord Millett's apparent support for Lord Nicholls' proposal showed that a future reform of the law in accordance with that proposal certainly could not be discounted, particularly since that proposal was also subsequently supported by Lord Walker. But two of these three Law Lords have now retired and, in the light of the subsequent direct rejection of this argument by the High Court of Australia,[578] this reform now appears less likely, unless of course the Law Commission does eventually make proposals which are implemented by the legislature. If any such reform is ever effected, the scope of the defence of change of position will obviously become extremely important in relation to liability for knowing receipt, in particular the question of precisely what constitutes a change of position in good faith. It will then become significant that, in *Niru Battery Manufacturing Co. v Milestone Trading*,[579] Moore-Bick J. held that lack of good faith is not confined to dishonesty in the sense identified in *Twinsectra v. Yardley* "but is capable of embracing a failure to act in a commercially acceptable way and sharp practice of a kind that falls short of outright dishonesty as well as dishonesty itself".

10–230

---

[574] [1993] 3 All E.R. 717 at 739–740.
[575] [2002] 2 A.C. 164 at 194.
[576] In *Agip (Africa) v. Jackson* [1990] Ch. 265 at 290 and *El Ajou v. Dollar Land Holdings* [1993] 3 All E.R. 717 at 739–740.
[577] [2000] Lloyd's Rep. Bank 292.
[578] In *Farah Construction Pty v. Say-Dee Pty* [2007] HCA 22, (2007) 81 A.L.J.R. 1107 at [148].
[579] [2002] 2 All E.R. (Comm.) 705.

10–231   The introduction of strict liability is not the preferred option of this work because of the impact which its introduction would have on innocent volunteers by potentially subjecting them to the burdens of constructive trusteeship. The only effective choice[580] therefore remains between, on the one hand, some or all of the categories of knowledge identified by Peter Gibson J. in *Baden v. Société Générale* and, on the other hand, the test substituted for them by the Court of Appeal in *B.C.C.I. (Overseas) v. Akindele*.

10–232   At the time when liability for both dishonest assistance and knowing receipt were governed by the categories of knowledge identified by Peter Gibson J., the principal justification for preferring the view expressed by Megarry V.-C. in *Re Montagu's Settlement*[581] was that it achieved a much needed consistency between the circumstances in which liability to account would be imposed upon a person who had assisted in bringing about a disposition of trust property in breach of trust and the circumstances in which a constructive trust would be imposed on a person who had received property disposed of in breach of trust; on this basis this work used to contend that only the first three of these categories of knowledge should give rise to the imposition of liability for knowing receipt. This justification ceased to exist when the Privy Council specifically rejected these categories of knowledge in relation to liability for dishonest assistance in *Royal Brunei Airlines v. Tan*, a rejection which was of course subsequently confirmed by the House of Lords in *Twinsectra v. Yardley*.

10–233   In the light of the similar rejection of these categories of knowledge in relation to liability for knowing receipt in *B.C.C.I. (Overseas) v. Akindele*, it might be thought to be both perverse and pointless to continue to advocate that the imposition of liability for knowing receipt should require the presence of one of these three categories of knowledge or, possibly, of some more felicitously worded equivalents. However, the application of these three categories of knowledge still seems considerably more predictable than the substitute based on unconscionability preferred by the Court of Appeal. For this reason, these categories of knowledge, or some equivalent, remain the preferred option of this work, although it is recognised that it can no longer realistically be contended that they constitute the present English law.

5. Inconsistent Dealing with Property Subject to a Trust

10–234   Any person who has received lawfully and not for his own benefit property subject to a trust will be liable to account for that property as a constructive trustee if he subsequently either misappropriates it or deals with it in some other manner which is inconsistent with the trust. The decided cases on what is generally known as "liability for inconsistent dealing" fall into two groups.

10–235   The first group of cases concerns agents. It has already been seen[582] that banks enjoy a right of set-off between different accounts held by the same

---

[580] Leaving on one side the option of a test based on dishonesty, which has not been advocated by a single commentator and has been specifically rejected both by the Court of Appeal and by Lord Millett.

[581] [1987] Ch. 264.

[582] See *ante*, para 1–058, n.145.

customer. If a bank manager has been duly notified that an account held at his branch in the name of an individual is in fact a trust account, the bank will be holding the credit balance of that account wholly lawfully and in no sense for its own benefit. If, however, the bank seeks to debit the credit balance of the trust account by way of set-off against an overdraft created in another account held in the name of the same individual, it will potentially be liable for inconsistent dealing.

In *Barclays Bank v. Quistclose Investments*,[583] Quistclose Investments made   **10–236** a loan to a company for the specific purpose of paying a dividend and the funds were paid into a new account at Barclays Bank opened by the company specifically for the purpose. When the company went into liquidation prior to the date on which the dividend was due to be paid, Barclays Bank claimed to offset the balance of this new account against the indebtedness of the company in other accounts. As has already been seen,[584] the House of Lords held that the company had been holding the funds in question on trust to pay the dividend and, subject to that for Quistclose Investments; since the bank had been made aware of the situation but had failed to draw the appropriate inference from facts known to it, it held the funds which it had sought to misapply on trust for Quistclose Investments.

Similarly in *Neste Oy v. Lloyds Bank*[585] the plaintiff shipowner was accus-   **10–237** tomed whenever one of its vessels entered a United Kingdom port to transfer to the bank account of its agent at Lloyds Bank sufficient funds to enable the agent to discharge all liabilities incurred by the vessel. A number of such payments were made immediately before and immediately after the agent appointed a receiver and therefore could not longer trade. Lloyds Bank set off all the payments so made against the agent's indebtedness to that bank. Bingham J. held that there was no express trust of any of the payments and that, even if there had been a trust in respect of any of the payments made before the appointment of the receiver, the bank would have taken free of that trust on the grounds that it did not fall within any of the categories of knowledge identified by Peter Gibson J. in *Baden v. Société Générale*. However, he held that the agent had become a trustee of the payment received after the appointment of the receiver; at the time of its arrival, the bank had already known of the appointment of the receiver and had therefore been placed upon enquiry. The bank was consequently bound by this trust and was not subsequently entitled to set-off the payment.

An agent will thus clearly be liable for inconsistent dealing if he know-   **10–238** ingly misapplies property subject to a trust; the criterion which in this respect suffices for the imposition of liability for knowing receipt, whether that criterion be knowledge or, as the law presumably stands at present, unconscionability, should also apply to the imposition of liability for incon-sistent dealing.

The second group of cases concerns strangers who receive property sub-   **10–239** ject to a trust which has been misapplied without fulfilling whatever crite-rion is in this respect sufficient for the imposition of liability for knowing

---

[583] [1970] A.C. 567.
[584] *ante*, para 9–057.
[585] [1983] 2 Lloyd's Rep. 658.

receipt. If such a stranger subsequently comes to fulfil that criterion, typically by acquiring the necessary knowledge of the misapplication of the property in breach of trust, that will not of itself render him liable as a constructive trustee. However, he will become so liable if he subsequently deals with the property in a manner inconsistent with the trust which has been breached. In *Sheridan v. Joyce*[586] a trustee lent out trust funds in breach of trust. The borrower originally had no knowledge whatever of this breach of trust and so was clearly not liable for knowing receipt. He subsequently discovered the true facts and thereafter made all the payments of interest to the beneficiary rather than to the trustee. Nevertheless, when the trustee subsequently sought repayment of part of the principal, the borrower made the repayment to him despite the contrary requests of the beneficiary and the money so repaid was lost. The borrower was held liable to repay the sum a second time on the grounds that he had dealt inconsistently with property which he knew to be subject to a trust. Once again, the criterion which in this respect suffices for the imposition of liability for knowing receipt, whether that criterion be knowledge or, as the law presently stands, unconscionability, should also apply to the imposition of liability for inconsistent dealing.

IV. ADVANTAGES OBTAINED BY FRAUDULENT OR UNCONSCIONABLE CONDUCT

10–240   From its earliest days, equity has always been prepared to grant relief against fraudulent and unconscionable conduct and one aspect of this relief is the imposition of a constructive trust on any person who has obtained an advantage as the result of such conduct. The different situations which fall under this heading will be considered in descending order of moral turpitude.

1. *Obtaining Property as a Result of Crime*[587]

10–241   It has long[588] been clear that "no system of jurisprudence can with reason include among the rights which it enforces rights directly resulting to the person asserting them from the crime of that person".[589] There are two obvious areas where this principle might be expected to operate, where property has been acquired as a result of an unlawful killing and where property has been acquired by means of theft.

(A) As a Result of an Unlawful Killing
10–242   The classic illustration of the operation of the principle as a result of an unlawful killing is *In the Estate of Crippen*.[590] Dr. Crippen was convicted of

---

[586] [1844] 1 Jo. & Lat. 41 (Court of Chancery of Ireland).
[587] See Goff & Jones, *op.cit.*, Chap. 37; Youdan (1973) 89 L.Q.R. 235; Earnshaw & Pace (1974) 37 M.L.R. 481.
[588] At least since *Bridgman v. Green* (1755) 2 Ves.Sen. 627.
[589] *Cleaver v. Mutual Reserve Fund Life Association* [1892] 1 Q.B. 147 at 156.
[590] [1911] P. 108.

murdering his wife and was duly hanged. His residuary legatee, who was his mistress, was held not to be entitled to the property which Crippen would normally have received as the intestate successor of the wife whom he had murdered.

Some difficulties have arisen as to the precise scope of the operation of the **10–243** principle. It clearly applies to anyone found to have committed murder, even unsuccessfully[591]; it is not necessary for a conviction to have been secured in criminal proceedings[592] nor are the results of any criminal proceedings decisive.[593] On the other hand, the principle does not apply to an insane killer (a person found not guilty of murder by reason of insanity or subsequently held by a civil court to have been insane[594]), since a finding of insanity constitutes an acquittal.[595] The extent to which the principle should operate between these two extremes is a matter of some controversy. It has been contended[596] that its operation should be limited to intentional killing and should, therefore, not apply to a person convicted either of unintentional manslaughter (involuntary manslaughter or voluntary manslaughter on the ground of diminished responsibility) or of causing death by dangerous or careless driving.[597] However, although it has been stated that there may be some types of unlawful killing to which the principle does not apply,[598] the courts have so far taken the view that it is not appropriate to draw any distinction between voluntary and involuntary manslaughter and have applied the principle to both[599]; it seems to follow from this approach that the principle would also be applied to the offence of causing death by dangerous or careless driving. It has now been held[600] that the principle also applies to the survivor of a suicide pact in the event that it is found that she aided and abetted the suicide.[601]

When applicable, the principle will deprive the unlawful killer of benefits **10–244** received under his victim's will,[602] his victim's intestacy,[603] the proceeds of

---

[591] In *Evans v. Evans* [1989] 1 F.L.R. 351, a wife convicted of inciting others to murder her former husband, who survived, was deprived of benefits payable under the divorce settlement.

[592] In *Re Sigsworth* [1935] 1 Ch. 89, the murderer committed suicide and so no criminal proceedings could be brought.

[593] *Gray v. Barr* [1971] 2 Q.B. 554 (principle applied where the defendant was acquitted of both murder and manslaughter); this is possible because of the different standards of proof, although according to *Halford v. Brookes* (1991) *The Times*, October 10, 1991 a finding of murder in civil proceedings requires the criminal standard of proof.

[594] *Re Holgate* (1971) (discussed by Earnshaw & Pace *op.cit.*).

[595] Criminal Procedure (Insanity) Act 1964, s.1.

[596] By Youdan *op.cit.*, pp.237–238; Earnshaw & Pace *op.cit.*, pp.492–496.

[597] A death in a motor accident can give rise to three distinct offences (see *R. v. Cooksley* [2003] 3 All E.R. 40): causing death by dangerous driving; causing death by careless driving when under the influence of drink or drugs; and motor manslaughter (the first two have a maximum sentence of 10 years imprisonment, while motor manslaughter has a maximum sentence of life imprisonment).

[598] In *Gray v. Barr* [1971] 2 Q.B. 554 at 581.

[599] *Re Giles* [1972] Ch. 544; *R. v. Chief National Insurance Commissioner, ex parte Connor* [1981] 1 Q.B. 758; *Re Royse (deceased)* [1985] Fam. 22; *Re K. (deceased)* [1986] Fam. 180; *Re Murphy* [2003] W.T.L.R. 687.

[600] In *Dunbar v. Plant* [1998] Ch. 412.

[601] An offence under Suicide Act 1961, s.2(1).

[602] *Re Sigsworth* [1935] 1 Ch. 89.

[603] *In the Estate of Crippen* [1911] P. 108; *Re Sigsworth* [1935] 1 Ch. 89.

a life insurance policy maintained on the life of his victim,[604] and enhanced social security benefits arising out of the death of his victim.[605] In the unlikely event that the property has already reached the unlawful killer's hands (it will normally be intercepted), a constructive trust will be imposed for the benefit of those otherwise entitled. In *Re Sigsworth*[606] a murderer was absolutely entitled under the will of his victim, his mother, and was also, together with his brother, her intestate successor; her entire estate went to the brother, who was undoubtedly otherwise entitled under her intestacy.

10–245   A specific difficulty which has arisen in determining precisely who is otherwise entitled is whether someone who would have taken by substitution in the event that the unlawful killer had predeceased his victim is also disqualified or whether the unlawful killer is instead treated for this purpose as having predeceased his victim. This question would have arisen in *Re Sigsworth* if the murderer had had any issue. It did arise in *Re DWS*,[607] where an only child murdered both his parents, both of whom died intestate. Their only grandchild, the murderer's son, claimed to be entitled under the intestacy rules as the issue of a child who had predeceased the intestates.[608] The alternative claimants were the parents' more remote intestate successors,[609] on the basis that none of the issue of the intestates had obtained a vested interest, or, if those claimants could not take either, the Crown. The Court of Appeal held unanimously that the grandchild could only take under the intestacy rules if his father had predeceased the intestates and that this was simply not the case. The court went on to hold, by a majority, that the fact that the grandchild could not take did indeed mean that none of the issue of the intestates had obtained a vested interest and so the more remote intestate successors had taken. Although it is virtually inconceivable that this decision can have coincided with the wishes of the murdered parents, or for that matter of the murderer, it cannot possibly be faulted as a matter of statutory interpretation. Where, on the other hand, a victim has died testate, the result will be determined by the provisions of his will; it seems likely that the type of substitutionary provisions which are in general use will produce the same result.[610] However, the Law Commission has issued a Consultation Paper[611] proposing that these results should be reversed by statute so that, when a person by virtue of the forfeiture rule loses any rights as intestate successor, the intestacy rules are applied as if he had died immediately before the intestate; it has also been proposed that, when the loss is instead of rights under a will, any gift contingent on that

---

[604] *Cleaver v. Mutual Reserve Fund Life Association* [1892] 1 Q.B. 147; *Davitt v. Titcumb* [1990] Ch. 110.

[605] *R. v. Chief National Insurance Commissioner, ex parte Connor* [1981] 1 Q.B. 758 (murderess of husband deprived of widow's pension).

[606] [1935] 1 Ch. 89.

[607] [2001] W.T.L.R. 445.

[608] This view had consistently been advocated in Goff & Jones, *op.cit.* (see 7th edn, para 38–008) but contrast Ryder, 40 Conv. (1976) 86.

[609] The sister of the father and the nephews and nieces of the mother.

[610] It may well be that, in the light of *Re DWS*, the form of such substitutionary gifts may require reconsideration so as to envisage the possibility of a primary beneficiary being disqualified from taking for this or any other reason. However, this will not be necessary if the proposals of the Law Commission referred to below in the text are duly enacted.

[611] Law Commission Consultation Paper No.172 (2003).

person having died before the testator should be given effect as if he had in fact so died. Both proposals are most welcome and they are now scheduled to be enacted in 2009.

A similar difficulty arises where the unlawful killer and his victim hold   **10–246**
joint or successive interests? Where one of two joint tenants unlawfully kills the other, it has been held that the killer acquires the entire legal title to the property by virtue of the principle of survivorship but holds that legal title on constructive trust for himself and the representatives of his victim in equal shares as tenants in common.[612] Where a person entitled to property in remainder unlawfully kills the life tenant,[613] it has been suggested[614] that the killer's enjoyment should be postponed for as long as mortality tables predict that the victim would have lived, the latter's representatives receiving the income in the meantime under a constructive trust.

In any event, the court now has a discretion under the Forfeiture Act 1982   **10–247**
to grant relief against forfeiture to a person guilty of unlawful killing other than murder.[615] Where a court has determined that the principle has operated to bring about a forfeiture, it can modify the effect of the principle where it "is satisfied that, having regard to the conduct of the offender and of the deceased and to such other circumstances as appear to the court to be material, the justice of the case requires the effect of the rule to be so modified in that case".[616] Such an order was made in *Re K (deceased)*[617] wholly relieving from forfeiture a wife convicted of the manslaughter of her husband, who had for years been violently attacking her; during one such attack, with the intention of frightening him and deterring him from following her out of the room, she picked up a loaded shot gun which went off and killed him. The survivor of a suicide pact was similarly wholly relieved in *Dunbar v. Plant*[618] but no relief whatever was given in *Re Murphy*[619] to a companion convicted of the voluntary manslaughter (on the grounds of diminished responsibility) of a person suffering from senile dementia.

(B) By Means of Theft

There is relatively little scope for the operation of the principle that no man   **10–248**
may benefit from crime in relation to thefts since a thief acquires no title to the property which he steals and so is normally[620] unable to pass any title to any third party.[621] However, where a thief has sold the property which he

---

[612] *Re K. (deceased)* [1986] Fam. 180. This conclusion, supported by Commonwealth authority, is consistent with the view that the unlawful killer is not treated as having predeceased his victim (were he so treated, the representatives of the victim would of course be entitled to the property absolutely).

[613] The problem has not as yet arisen, although it was postulated in *Re Callaway* [1956] Ch. 559.

[614] By Youdan *op.cit.*, pp.250–251.

[615] Excluded by Forfeiture Act 1982, s.5.

[616] Forfeiture Act 1982, s.2(2).

[617] [1985] 1 W.L.R. 262 (Vinelott J.); [1986] Ch. 180 (C.A.).

[618] [1998] Ch. 412.

[619] [2003] W.T.L.R. 687.

[620] Except where the purchaser is protected by the Sale of Goods Act 1979 or the Consumer Credit Act 1974.

[621] Although the principle might have been a preferable ground for the conclusion reached in *Reading v. Att.-Gen.* [1951] A.C. 507, see *ante*, para 10–075.

has stolen, the question sometimes arises as to whether his victim can trace the stolen property into the proceeds of that sale. When the stolen property or its product have ceased to be identifiable as a result, for example, of being mixed with other money in a bank account, such a process requires the existence of a trust.[622] In this respect, Lord Browne-Wilkinson indicated in *Westdeutsche Landesbank Girozentrale v. Islington L.B.C.*,[623] that a constructive trust can be imposed on a thief as a result of his fraudulent conduct (this principle will be considered below). An alternative possibility is to regard a thief as holding stolen property on resulting trust for his victim; such a conclusion was reached by the High Court of Australia in *Black v. S. Freeman & Co.*,[624] a decision which was cited with approval by Lord Templeman in *Lipkin Gorman v. Karpnale.*[625] The difficulty about either of these views is, however, to work out what the thief would actually be holding on trust, given that he does not acquire title to the stolen property. The only other possibility is to argue that the constructive trust envisaged by Lord Browne-Wilkinson arises not when the thief steals the property but only if and when he turns it into money; that money, being the universal medium of exchange, does become his property and so can become the subject matter of a trust. However, in practice a court would inevitably find some sort of trust in order to prevent a thief from profiting at the expense of its victim and is obviously unlikely to be unduly fussy about the technical justification for that trust's existence.

2. *Obtaining Property as a Result of Fraud*

10–249   It is now clear that a victim of fraud, including theft, may treat any property obtained by whoever has practised the fraud on him as being subject to a constructive trust in his favour. In *Westdeutsche Landesbank Girozentrale v. Islington L.B.C.*[626] Lord Browne-Wilkinson said:

"Although it is difficult to find clear authority for the proposition, when property is obtained by fraud equity imposes a constructive trust on the recipient: the property is recoverable and traceable in equity. Thus, an infant who has obtained property by fraud is bound in equity to restore it: . . . Moneys stolen from a bank account can be traced in equity: . . . "

10–250   This was no more than a dictum because in that case no argument had been founded on the existence of a constructive trust. Lord Browne-Wilkinson's proposition has subsequently been applied on at least two occasions. In *Twinsectra v. Yardley*[627] the Court of Appeal[628] held that such a constructive trust would arise in respect of the funds which like the loan in that case, had been transferred pursuant to a contract which had been induced by a fraudulent misrepresentation, although the court indicated

---

[622] See *post*, para 22–133.
[623] [1996] A.C. 669 at 715–716.
[624] [1910] 12 C.L.R. 105.
[625] [1992] 2 A.C. 548.
[626] [1996] A.C. 667 at 716.
[627] [1999] Lloyd's Rep. Bank 438 at [96–100].
[628] The issue did not have to be considered in the House of Lords.

that this might be dependant on the plaintiff's continuing ability to rescind that contract. The court approved the summary of the position in *Underhill & Hayton: Law of Trusts and Trustees*[629] to the effect that "equity imposes a constructive trust on property where a transferor's legal and equitable title to his property has passed to the transferee according to basic principles of property law but in circumstances (e.g. involving fraud and misrepresentation) where the transferor has an equitable right (i.e. mere equity) to recover the property by having the transfer set aside".[630] In *Niru Battery Manufacturing Co. v. Milestone Trading Co.*[631] Moore-Bick J. held that such a constructive trust would arise in respect of funds whose transfer had been procured by means of the issue of a bill of lading which fraudulently stated that the issuer had taken charge of the cargo which was being purchased by the transferor.

However, on at least two other occasions doubts have been expressed about the scope of the dictum of Lord Browne-Wilkinson. In *Box, Brown and Jacobs v. Barclays Bank*[632] Ferris J. would not have applied the dictum had he been prepared to hold, which he was not, that money which had been deposited in an account with the defendant bank had been obtained from the plaintiffs by fraud. He briefly stated,[633] obviously also by way of dictum, that in his view "it would be wrong" to treat the dictum of Lord Browne-Wilkinson "as a general statement of the law applicable to all cases of fraud". In *Shalson v. Russo*[634] Rimer J. held[635] that the authorities cited by Lord Browne-Wilkinson did not support the proposition that sums transferred pursuant to a voidable contract induced by fraud will be held on trust prior to the rescission of that contract; however, in the event he was able to hold that the contract had been impliedly rescinded and that a trust had therefore then arisen.[636] More generally,[637] he regarded those authorities as providing "less than full support" for the proposition that property obtained by fraud is automatically held by the recipient on a constructive trust for the person defrauded.

10–251

It was accepted in all four of these authorities that, as Millett J. stated in *Lonrho v Fayed (No.2)*,[638] unless and until the transferor elects to avoid the transfer, the transferee will not be a constructive trustee of the property transferred to him and no fiduciary relationship will exist between him and the transferor. Further, if and when it becomes impossible for the transferor

10–252

---

[629] (15th edn) p.372.

[630] The Court of Appeal then went on to state that "nowadays it seems better to regard a restitutionary resulting trust as arising", echoing Lord Millett's earlier statement in *El Ajou v. Dollar Land Holdings* [1993] 3 All E.R. 717 at 734 that "the trust which is operating in these cases is ... an old fashioned institutional resulting trust". However, this view was rejected in *Papamichael v. National Westminster Bank* [2003] 1 Lloyd's Rep. 341, where it was held that Lord Millett's statement was "all very well, but Lord Browne-Wilkinson was specific in saying that what was being imposed was an institutional constructive trust not a resulting trust".

[631] [2002] EWHC 1425 (Com), [2002] All E.R. (Comm.) 705.

[632] [1998] Lloyd's Rep. Bank 185 at 199–201.

[633] *ibid.*, at 201.

[634] [2003] EWHC 1637 (Ch), [2005] Ch. 281 at [106–119].

[635] *ibid.*, at [111].

[636] *ibid.*, at [124, 127].

[637] *ibid.*, at [111].

[638] [1992] 1 W.L.R. 1 at 11–12.

to avoid the transfer, no constructive trust will ever be capable of arising on this ground. It may become impossible to avoid the transfer because the transferor has instead elected to pursue an alternative remedy which is inconsistent with subsequently setting the transfer aside[639]; alternatively, the property in question may have reached the hands of a third party who has taken that property free of any right of the transferor to avoid the transfer.

10–253   In all these cases the potential constructive trustee was the recipient of funds which had been transferred to him by the constructive beneficiary. However, in *Sinclair Investment Holdings v. Versailles Trade Finance*,[640] it was contended that an analogous principle applies to permit the imposition of a constructive trust whenever profits, whatever their source, have been made as the result of fraud. In this case funds which the claimant had invested in a company had not been used in the way which had been agreed; instead the company had expended these funds (and the investments of all the other investors) in making a series of circular payments which enabled an associated company to appear to have a very much higher turnover than was in fact the case. This in turn produced an enormous rise in that company's share price, of which its majority shareholder had taken advantage to make very substantial profits on sales of shares. There was no doubt that the majority shareholder had procured the claimant's investment by making fraudulent misrepresentations as a result of which that investment had been lost. But none of the claimant's funds had actually been transferred to him and he had really made his profit at the expense of the purchasers of the shares which he had sold.

10–254   In the Court of Appeal, the claimant accepted, and was held by the Court of Appeal to have been right to accept that there was no authority which specifically supported this contention[641] and that a dictum of Peter Gibson L.J. in *Halifax Building Society v. Thomas*[642] was against it. In that case the Court of Appeal held that a mortgagee who had made an advance on the basis of a fraudulent misrepresentation could not recover the entire proceeds of sale of the mortgaged property, not merely sufficient to discharge principal, interest and costs, in priority to the Crown Prosecution Service which had obtained a confiscation order against the fraudster. Peter Gibson L.J. stated that one of the authorities later relied on by Lord Browne-Wilkinson[643] could not "be elevated into a universal principle that wherever

---

[639] See *Twinsectra v. Yardley* [2000] W.T.L.R. 527 at 569 (C.A.), where the issue was whether the claimant's decision to sue the borrower to judgment both on the loan and in the tort of deceit was inconsistent with a later attempt to avoid the loan. If this issue had arisen in the House of Lords, the claimant would have contended that it was nevertheless still able to avoid the loan because it had made no financial recovery under either judgment; such a flexible approach to election would have been consistent with the earlier decisions of the House of Lords in *Foskett v. McKeown* [2001] 1 A.C. 102 and of the Court of Appeal in *Heinl v Jyske Bank (Gibraltar)* [1999] Lloyd's Rep. Bank. 511, in both of which recourse to a proprietary remedy was held not to bar subsequent attempts to impose personal liability.

[640] [2005] EWCA Civ. 722, [2006] W.T.L.R 1655.

[641] In the courts below (this was a second appeal), the claimant had relied on Lord Browne-Wilkinson's proposition and the decisions in which it had been applied.

[642] [1996] Ch. 217.

[643] *McCormick v. Grogan* (1869) L.R. 4 H.L. 82, actually a case on secret trusts; see *ante*, para. 4–XX.

there is personal fraud the fraudster will become a trustee for the party injured by the fraud". The Court of Appeal accepted that this was no more than a dictum and that a case where the claimant mortgagee had already recovered in full (and had, therefore, been the victim of fraud only in a semantic sense) was very different from a claim by an investor which had lost its entire investment as a result of fraud. The claim was, therefore, allowed to proceed to trial where it was presented in a different way by different counsel and failed. It is not inconceivable that this analogous principle could be upheld in an appropriate case.

3. *Obtaining Property as a Result of Undue Influence*[644]

Since the eighteenth century, it has been a rule of equity that a person who obtains a manifest and unfair disadvantage as a result of undue influence will be unable to retain the benefit of the transaction in question. The equitable doctrine of undue influence which has been developed in the subsequent centuries applies only to inter vivos transactions.[645] The specific situations in which the doctrine is applicable have been recently reviewed on a number of occasions by the House of Lords.

10–255

(A) The Scope of the Doctrine
In *Barclays Bank v. O'Brien*,[646] Lord Browne-Wilkinson said: "A person who has been induced to enter into a transaction by the undue influence of another ('the wrongdoer') is entitled to set that transaction aside as against the wrongdoer. Such undue influence is either actual or presumed." His Lordship went on to adopt the following classification.[647]

10–256

He stated that what he described as cases of "actual" undue influence fall into Class 1. A claimant who alleges this type of undue influence has "to prove affirmatively that the wrongdoer exerted undue influence on the complainant to enter into the particular transaction which is impugned".[648] If he can discharge this burden of proof, the wrongdoer will be unable to retain the benefit of the transaction in question whether or not it was to the manifest disadvantage of the claimant. This was held by the House of Lords in *C.I.B.C. Mortgages v. Pitt*.[649] A husband exerted actual undue influence on his wife in order to induce her to join with him in mortgaging their matrimonial home, ostensibly to raise funds for the purchase of a holiday home but in fact to enable the husband to raise funds for the purchase of shares. Although the transaction was not manifestly disadvantageous to her, she was held entitled to set aside the transaction as against him, although not as against the mortgagee. "Actual undue influence is a species of fraud. Like any other victim of fraud, a person who has been induced by undue

10–257

---

[644] See generally Goff & Jones, *op.cit.*, Chap. 10; Hedley & Halliwell, *op.cit.*, Chap. 10.
[645] The analogous probate doctrine is much more rigid.
[646] [1994] 1 A.C. 180 at 196–197.
[647] Originally laid down by the Court of Appeal in *Bank of Credit and Commerce International v. Aboody* [1990] 1 Q.B. 923 at 953.
[648] [1994] 1 A.C. 180 at 196–197.
[649] [1994] 1 A.C. 200, overruling on this point the decision of the Court of Appeal in *Bank of Credit and Commerce International v. Aboody* [1990] 1 Q.B. 923 at 953.

influence to carry out a transaction which he did not freely and knowingly enter into is entitled to have that transaction set aside as of right."[650]

10–258   Lord Browne-Wilkinson went on to state that cases of what he described as "presumed" undue influence fall into Class 2[651]:

"In these cases the complainant only has to show, in the first instance, that there was a relationship of trust and confidence between the complainant and the wrongdoer of such a nature that it is fair to presume that the wrongdoer abused that relationship in procuring the complainant to enter into the impugned transaction. In Class 2 cases therefore there is no need to procure evidence that actual undue influence was exerted in relation to the particular transaction impugned: once a confidential relationship has been proved, the burden then shifts to the wrongdoer to prove that the complainant entered into the impugned transaction freely, for example by showing that the complainant had independent advice."[652]

He went on to hold that such a confidential relationship can be established in two ways, which he described as Class 2(A) and Class 2(B) cases.

10–259   Class 2(A) comprises "[c]ertain relationships (for example solicitor and client, medical advisor and patient) [which] as a matter of law raise the presumption that undue influence has been exercised". Other relationships of this kind include parent-child, trustee-beneficiary and, particularly, spiritual adviser-religious devotee.[653] However, he specifically held that the relationship between husband and wife and between cohabitees does not fall within Class 2(A).

10–260   He then went on to define Class 2(B) cases as follows:

"Even if there is no relationship falling within Class 2(A), if the complainant proves the de facto existence of a relationship under which the complainant generally reposed trust and confidence in the wrongdoer, the existence of such relationship raises the presumption of undue influence. In a Class 2(B) case therefore, in the absence of evidence disproving undue influence, the complainant will succeed in setting aside the impugned transaction merely by proof that the complainant reposed trust and confidence in the wrongdoer without having to prove that the wrongdoer exerted actual undue influence or otherwise abused such trust and confidence in relation to the particular transaction impugned."

The many cases in recent years in which the doctrine of undue influence has been relied on by spouses, or de facto partners, in order to challenge the validity of mortgages of their homes made in order to secure financial support for the business of the other spouse or partner are all examples of conduct falling within Lord Browne-Wilkinson's definition of Class 2(B). So

---

[650] *ibid.* at 808.

[651] [1994] 1 A.C. 180 at 189.

[652] This was done in *Inche Noriah v. Shaik Allie Bin Omar* [1929] A.C. 127 at 135 (P.C.). See also *Banco Exterior Internacional v. Thomas* [1997] 1 W.L.R. 221.

[653] In *Allcard v. Skinner* (1887) 36 Ch.D. 145 at 183 Lindley L.J. stated that "the influence of one mind over another is very subtle, and of all influences religious influence is the most dangerous and the most powerful".

was a relationship between son-in-law and trusting father-in-law in *Mahoney v. Purnell*[654] and between a frail widow and her cleaner in *Re Morris*.[655]

However, in the more recent decision of the House of Lords in *Royal Bank of Scotland (No.2) v. Etridge*,[656] it was concluded that this sort of categorisation was not a useful tool. Lord Clyde said this: **10–261**

"the attempt to build up classes or categories may lead to confusion. The confusion is aggravated if the names used to identify the classes do not bear their actual meaning. Thus on the face of it a division into cases of 'actual' and 'presumed' undue influence appears illogical. It appears to confuse definition and proof. There is also room for uncertainty whether the presumption is of the existence of an influence or of its quality as being undue. I would also dispute the utility of the further sophistication of subdividing 'presumed undue influence' into further categories. All these classifications to my mind add mystery rather than illumination."

But this does not in any way detract from the utility of the descriptions of the different categories of undue influence made by Lord Browne-Wilkinson, irrelevant of the disputed question of how, if at all, they should have been described or labelled. Further, at least for the moment, some distinction between what Lord Browne-Wilkinson described as "actual" and "presumed" undue influence is undoubtedly necessary. This is because in the latter, but not in the former, case the person who exerted the undue influence will nevertheless be able to retain the benefit of the transaction unless it can be shown to have been wrongful in that, as the House of Lords held in *National Westminster Bank v. Morgan*,[657] it constituted "a disadvantage sufficiently serious to require evidence to rebut the presumption that in the circumstances of the relationship between the parties it was procured by the exercise of undue influence".

The existence of this restriction on the ability of the courts to set aside   **10–262**
transactions on the grounds of undue influence has been consistently criticised. Its extension to "actual" undue influence was specifically rejected in *C.I.B.C. Mortgages v. Pitt*[658] but in *Royal Bank of Scotland (No.2) v. Etridge*[659] the House of Lords equally specifically declined to remove its effect in the case of "presumed" undue influence. Lord Nicholls instead advocated that the "manifest disadvantage" label should be removed and be replaced by a more direct adherence to the test outlined in *Allcard v. Skinner*.[660] In that case, Lindley L.J. had said: "But if the gift is so large as not to be reasonably accounted for on the ground of friendship, relationship, charity or other ordinary motives on which ordinary men act, the burden is upon the donee to support the gift." This is obviously the way in which the requirement will

---

[654] [1996] 3 All E.R. 61.
[655] [2001] W.T.L.R. 1137.
[656] [2001] UKHL 44, [2002] 2 A.C. 773.
[657] [1985] A.C. 686 at 704.
[658] [1994] 1 A.C. 200, overruling on this point the decision of the Court of Appeal in *Bank of Credit and Commerce International v. Aboody* [1990] 1 Q.B. 923 at 953.
[659] [2001] UKHL 44, [2002] 2 A.C. 773.
[660] (1887) 36 Ch.D. 145 at 185.

be satisfied in the case of a gift. In the case of a bilateral transaction, it will be satisfied by any inadequacy of consideration in favour of the person who has exerted the undue influence; a sale at an undervalue will satisfy this requirement[661] but the transaction which was challenged in *National Westminster Bank v. Morgan*,[662] a short-term loan made at a commercial rate of interest to enable the borrower to prevent a mortgagee from going into possession of her home, did not do so.

(B) The Effect of the Application of the Doctrine

10–263   Where the doctrine of undue influence applies, it is normally sufficient for the courts simply to set aside the transaction. If property has actually been transferred to the person who exerted the undue influence, the court will order its return; if, on the other hand, as is usually the case in bilateral transactions of the type which have been before the courts so often in recent years, the person who exerted the undue influence has obtained some mortgage or charge by way of security for the liabilities of himself, the chargor (if different) or a third party, that security will be unenforceable. However, where the property in question has reached the hands of third parties who have taken it free of the right of the victim of the undue influence to set the transaction aside, it will obviously no longer be able to be set aside; in this situation the courts have power to award the victim fair compensation in equity[663] under *Nocton v. Lord Ashburton*.[664] In none of these circumstances is it necessary to classify the nature of the interest retained by the person upon whom the undue influence was exerted in any property which he has transferred away.

10–264   However, such a classification does become necessary as soon as any third party becomes involved. It is clear that the right to have a transaction set aside on the grounds of undue influence is capable of being assigned both *inter vivos*[665] and upon death[666] and so may be enforced by the successors of the person upon whom the undue influence was exerted. It also seems clear that, in the event of the death or insolvency of the person who exerted the undue influence, the interest of the person whom he influenced is regarded as analogous to an interest arising under a trust; thus in effect the person who exerted the undue influence holds any property transferred to him as a result of that undue influence on constructive trust. His personal representatives or trustee in bankruptcy will, therefore, obviously be bound by this constructive trust so that the person who transferred the property will be able to trace it in equity into their hands and, if necessary, claim priority over the general creditors of the transferee. But where, on the other hand, the person exerting the undue influence transfers property which he has received on to a third party or causes property to be transferred directly to

---

[661] *Possathurai v. Kannappa Chettiar* (1919) L.R. 47 I.A. 1 at 3–4 (P.C.).
[662] [1985] A.C. 686 at 703.
[663] *Mahoney v. Purnell* [1996] 3 All E.R. 61.
[664] [1914] A.C. 932; see *ante*, paras 10–065, 10–066.
[665] *Dickinson v. Burrell* (1866) L.R. 1 Eq. 337.
[666] *Stump v. Gaby* (1852) 2 De G.M. & G. 623.

a third party in the first place, the interest of the transferor seems to be regarded as a mere equity rather than a full equitable interest. Such a mere equity clearly binds a volunteer[667] and any third party who has notice of the undue influence, even if he has purchased the property for value.[668] Further, it seems to follow from the authorities that the transferor will be able to trace the property in equity into the hands of persons who are so bound by his interest.[669] However, it will not bind any bona fide purchaser for value of a legal or equitable interest in the property who has no notice of the undue influence.

(C) Mortgages of Homes in order to Secure Business Debts

In the last 20 years the doctrine of undue influence has been invoked on many occasions in relation to mortgages granted by married couples or de facto partners over their homes in order to secure financial support for the business of one of the mortgagors; the other mortgagor subsequently attempts to resist the mortgagee's action for possession by claiming that the mortgage was obtained by undue influence. Most of the examples of mortgages allegedly being obtained as a result of undue influence occurred at the beginning of this period in the late 1980s at a time when general financial difficulties had produced a considerable fall in land values coupled with a substantial rise in interest rates. Many small businesses had fallen into financial difficulties and their owners came under pressure from their banks to secure their existing overdrafts and future facilities by guarantees secured on their matrimonial homes.   **10–265**

The facts of the first of a number of leading cases, *Barclays Bank v. O'Brien*,[670] were typical. The husband's company's bank manager agreed to an increased overdraft facility on the basis that the husband would guarantee the company's indebtedness and that this guarantee would be secured by a charge on the matrimonial home. The documents were sent by the bank to a branch near the matrimonial home with instructions fully to explain the transaction and the nature of the documentation and to advise the couple that if they were "in any doubt they should contact their solicitors before signing". The wife was told by the husband that liability under the charge was limited to £60,000 when it was in fact unlimited, the bank gave her neither explanation nor advice and she signed the documents without reading them. The mortgage was set aside as against her beneficial interest.   **10–266**

A much less typical variant was for an advance actually to be obtained on the security of the residential property ostensibly for the benefit of both husband and wife when it was in fact to be used for the purposes of only one of them. Thus in another leading case, *C.I.B.C. Mortgages v. Pitt*,[671] a couple obtained an advance on the security of their matrimonial home on the basis   **10–267**

---

[667] *Goddard v. Carlisle* (1821) 9 Price 169.
[668] *Lancashire Loans v. Black* [1934] 1 K.B. 380.
[669] *ibid.* at 417, *per* Lawrence L.J.
[670] [1994] 1 A.C. 180.
[671] [1994] 1 A.C. 200.

that its proceeds were to be used for the purchase of a holiday home. In fact the husband wished to purchase shares and had pressured his wife into signing the application and the charge, neither of which she read. Given that the mortgagee had no reason to think that both co-owners were not to benefit from the transaction, it was not placed on inquiry as to the possibility of any undue influence; the mortgage was consequently binding on the wife.

10–268   Precisely when will a mortgagee be affected by any undue influence which is found to have been exerted by the debtor? The mortgagee will clearly be affected by any such conduct by the debtor where the latter has been used as the agent of the former for the purposes of obtaining the signature of the surety. However, reliance on this agency argument is highly artificial since, in obtaining the signature of the surety, the debtor is acting for himself not for the mortgagee.[672] Therefore, it is only in very unusual circumstances[673] that mortgagees will be adversely affected by this argument. It is also theoretically possible, where mortgagee and surety have used the same solicitor, for information communicated by the surety to the solicitor to be imputed to the mortgagee; however, because any information is likely to have been communicated to the solicitor before he was instructed by the mortgagee[674] and, even if it was communicated to him thereafter, probably could not be revealed by him to the mortgagee anyway,[675] this is highly unlikely in practice. Consequently, in the normal case, a mortgagee will only be affected by any undue influence if he is held to have notice of it.

10–269   The effect of *Barclays Bank v. O'Brien*[676] was only to put a mortgagee on inquiry as to the possibility of undue influence where the relationship between the debtor and surety was an emotional relationship between cohabitees[677] or where the mortgagee was aware that the surety reposed trust and confidence in the debtor in relation to his or her financial affairs or was actually under the debtor's influence in other respects.[678] However, as a result of the later decision of the House of Lords in *Royal Bank of Scotland Plc v. Etridge (No.2)*,[679] a mortgagee is now put on inquiry in every case where the relationship between the debtor and the surety is non-commercial. In such circumstances, the mortgagee must always take reasonable steps to bring home to the individual surety the risks which he or more usually she is running by acting as such. A mortgagee who fails to take those steps will be deemed to have notice of any claim which the surety may have that the transaction was procured by undue influence on the part

---

[672] *Barclays Bank v. O'Brien* [1994] 1 A.C. 180.
[673] An example was where the employees of the bank, its debtor and the guarantor were all members of the same religious sect; see *Shams v. United Bank* (May 24, 1994) on Lexis.
[674] *Halifax Mortgage Services v. Stepsky* [1996] Ch. 207 (C.A.).
[675] *Halifax Mortgage Services v. Stepsky* [1996] Ch. 1 (Ch.D.).
[676] [1994] 1 A.C. 180.
[677] The requirement for cohabitation was not rigid; see *Massey v. Midland Bank* [1995] 1 All E.R. 929.
[678] *Crédit Lyonnais Bank Nederland v. Burch* [1997] 1 All E.R. 144.
[679] [2001] UKHL 44, [2002] 2 A.C. 773.

of the debtor.[680] This principle applies not only to co-owners who act as sureties but also to absolute owners of property who do so.[681]

A mortgagee who is put on inquiry need do no more than take reasonable **10–270** steps to ensure that the practical implications of the proposed transaction have been brought home to the surety in a meaningful way, so that he or she enters into the transaction with her eyes open so far as its basic elements are concerned. After *Barclays Bank v. O'Brien*, any duty of inquiry could be satisfied by representatives of the mortgagees holding a private meeting with the surety in the absence of the debtor, informing him or her as to potential liability and risk, and urging him or her to take independent legal advice. Only in exceptional cases where the mortgagee knew further facts which made undue influence not only possible but probable was it necessary for the mortgagee to insist on independent advice. However, mortgagees came increasingly to rely on the confirmation of solicitors that such advice had been given and it was held in *Royal Bank of Scotland Plc v. Etridge (No.2)*[682] that such confirmation will ordinarily suffice in respect of past transactions.

For transactions after the decision in *Royal Bank of Scotland Plc v. Etridge* **10–271** *(No.2)* in 2001,[683] the mortgagee is not required to satisfy any duty of inquiry by means of a personal meeting with the surety. Ordinarily it will be reasonable for the mortgagee to rely upon confirmation from a solicitor, acting for the surety, that he has advised him or her appropriately. Such a solicitor acts for the surety, not as the agent of the mortgagee, and any deficiencies in his advice are a matter between solicitor and surety. However, if the mortgagee knows that the solicitor has not duly advised the surety or knows facts from which it ought to have been realised that the surety has not received appropriate advice, the mortgage will be at risk if the mortgagee proceeds. The process of obtaining confirmation from the solicitor has been formalised as a series of requirements and detailed guidelines have also been provided for the solicitor advising the surety.

Although transactions entered into before the process was formalised in **10–272** this way are likely to come before the courts for some years yet, the existence of all these guidelines makes it unlikely that any mortgagees will be adversely affected by any undue influence by the debtor in respect of future transactions; any remedy by the surety will instead be sought from the solicitor who advised him or her. The only remaining area of controversy relates to the precise nature of the right of the surety to have the transaction set aside when the mortgagee has in some way failed to comply with the requirements; is it a right to have the transaction set aside *in toto* or only subject to such of the terms of the transaction as the surety was aware of at the time it was entered into? The situation at present seems to be that the surety is entitled to have the transaction set aside *in toto*[684] unless he or she

---

[680] *ibid*; see also *Crédit Lyonnais Bank Nederland v. Burch* [1997] 1 All E.R. 144.

[681] As in *Crédit Lyonnais Bank Nederland v. Burch* [1997] 1 All E.R. 144 (the surety was the debtor's employee).

[682] [2001] UKHL 44, [2002] 2 A.C. 773.

[683] [2001] UKHL 44, [2002] 2 A.C. 773.

[684] *TSB Bank v. Camfield* [1995] 1 W.L.R. 430.

received a direct financial benefit from it.[685] However, this question still requires definitive resolution.

4. *Relying on the Absence of Statutory Formalities*

10–273   The courts have always been prepared to impose a constructive trust in order to prevent a transferee of property from going back on an undertaking or agreement made at the time of acquisition to respect an interest therein which has not been created or protected in the manner required by the law. Such cases are manifestations of the principle that equity will not permit the provisions of a statute to be used as an instrument of fraud.[686]

10–274   Of course it is not always fraudulent to rely on a failure to comply with the requirements of the law. Equity will not prevent a party to an oral contract for the sale of land from repudiating it on the grounds that it does not comply with the Law of Property (Miscellaneous Provisions) Act 1989[687] nor prevent a settlor who has made an oral declaration of trust respecting land from raising the absence of the writing required by the Law of Property Act 1925.[688] Similarly, if an incumbrancer has neglected to protect his interest in land by the appropriate registration, equity will not prevent a subsequent third party purchaser for value of the land from relying on a statutory right to take free of the interest in question.[689] Equity will only intervene in the event of an attempt to renege on an undertaking or agreement.

10–275   Sometimes the imposition of a constructive trust may prevent the relevant statutory provision from applying at all. This was controversially held to be the case in *Yaxley v. Gotts*,[690] where a person who had renovated a property in reliance on an oral agreement that he would become entitled to its ground floor was held to be entitled to rely on an equitable proprietary estoppel which, because of the unconscionable conduct of the other party, gave rise to a constructive trust. As a matter of statutory interpretation, this trust was held to be sufficient to prevent the relevant provision of the Law of Property (Miscellaneous Provisions) Act 1989[691] from applying at all.

10–276   Where the relevant statutory provision is prima facie applicable, equity can nevertheless impose a constructive trust on the grounds that that provision cannot be used as an instrument of fraud. In *Bannister v. Bannister*[692] the defendant sold and conveyed two adjoining cottages to the plaintiff on the basis that she could continue to occupy one of them rent free for as long as she wished. When he subsequently sought to evict her on the basis that the conveyance did not mention her right of occupation, she successfully counterclaimed for a declaration that the plaintiff held the cottage on trust for her

---

[685] *Midland Bank v. Greene* [1994] 2 F.L.R. 827.
[686] *Rochefoucauld v. Boustead* [1897] 1 Ch. 196 at 206.
[687] s.2 requires that all the terms of such a contract must be in writing and signed by all the parties.
[688] s.53(1)(b). See *ante*, para 4–008.
[689] *Midland Bank Trust Company v. Green* [1981] A.C. 513.
[690] [2000] Ch. 162.
[691] s.2 did not apply because of s.2(5) which excludes resulting, implied and constructive trusts from its scope.
[692] [1948] W.N. 261.

for her lifetime. The Court of Appeal classified as fraudulent the conduct of the plaintiff in attempting to rely on the absence of the writing which the Law of Property Act 1925 then required for the creation of the interest claimed by the defendant and imposed a constructive trust under which he held the property on trust for her for her lifetime.[693] This was of course a case where the informal agreement in question was being enforced by the person in whose favour it had originally been made.

However, equity is equally prepared to enforce agreements made for the benefit of third parties. In *Binions v. Evans*[694] a cottage was sold at a reduced price on the basis that the purchasers would honour the right of a widow of a former employee of the vendor to occupy the property rent-free for the rest of her life. When they sought to evict her, the majority of the Court of Appeal classified the conduct of the purchasers as unconscionable, applied *Bannister v. Bannister* and imposed a constructive trust on the purchasers to give effect to the interest of the widow.[695] Similarly, in *Lyus v. Prowsa Developments*[696] a building plot was sold by mortgagees subject to and with the benefit of a building contract between the mortgagor and the plaintiffs. The purchaser subsequently claimed to have taken the land free of this contract because the plaintiffs had failed to protect it in the manner required by the Land Registration Act 1925. It was held that the provision in the contract of sale relating to the building contract had conferred new rights on the plaintiffs, which the purchaser had expressly agreed to honour. Consequently, because of the subsequent attempt to renege on this agreement, the purchaser held the plot on constructive trust to complete the house on the plot and convey the plot to the plaintiffs for the price agreed in the original contract. **10–277**

5. Informal Agreements for the Joint Acquisition of Property

In *Holiday Inns v. Broadhead*,[697] Megarry J. stated that "if A and B agree that A shall acquire some specific property for the joint benefit of A and B on terms yet to be agreed, and B, in reliance on A's agreement, is thereby induced to refrain from attempting to acquire the property, equity ought not to permit A, when he acquires the property, to insist on retaining the whole benefit for himself to the exclusion of B." **10–278**

Until recently, the principal reported authority in support of this proposition was the decision of Harman J. in *Pallant v. Morgan*.[698] In that case, an **10–279**

---

[693] This caused the imposition of a settlement under the Settled Land Act 1925 and thus potentially involved the reconveyance of the cottage to the defendant, an admittedly odd result but one of which the plaintiff could hardly complain. However, this would no longer be the case today since no more settlements of this type can be created following the Trusts of Land and Appointment of Trustees Act 1996; the plaintiff would now simply hold the cottage in question on trust for the defendant.

[694] [1972] Ch. 359. See also *Neale v. Willis* (1968) 19 P. & C.R. 839.

[695] Lord Denning M.R. reached the same conclusion by a different route: see *post*, para 10–289.

[696] [1982] 1 W.L.R. 1044. This decision has been criticised on the grounds that it casts doubt on the ability of a purchaser to rely on his statutory right to take free of incumbrances of which he is aware but which have not been protected in the appropriate way. However, the statements of the Court of Appeal in *IDC Group v. Clark* [1992] 1 E.G.L.R. 187 at 190 confirmed that the decision is explicable for the reasons stated in the text.

[697] (1969) Unreported but quoted in *Banner Homes v. Luff Developments* [2000] Ch. 372.

[698] [1953] Ch. 43.

agreement was made by the agents of two neighbouring landowners immediately prior to a land auction that the plaintiff's agent should refrain from bidding and that the defendant, if his agent was successful, would divide the land according to a formula agreed between the agents. Unfortunately, some details of the formula were left to be agreed later on and, although the defendant duly acquired the land at the auction, the parties were unable to agree those details. Harman J. held that, although the agreement for division was too uncertain to be specifically enforceable, the defendant was nevertheless not entitled to retain the whole of the property in the light of the agreement between the agents. He therefore held that the land was subject to a trust for the parties jointly and, in the event that they could not agree on a division, would have to be auctioned a second time.

10–280   The principle so established was applied by Oliver J. in *Time Products v. Combined English Stores Group*[699] on the following basis:

"It is a fraud in the defendant to retain for himself the benefit of the bargain obtained with the plaintiff's assistance whether that assistance was obtained by the defendant through the plaintiff's erroneous belief in a given state of facts or through a promise, contractual or otherwise, given by the defendant. It is, in my judgment, equally unconscionable for the defendant, having reaped the benefit of the transaction, now to seek to retain the property and to disregard the rights which, under the agreement the plaintiff stipulated even though the agreement may lack certainty or be a mere gentlemen's agreement not enforceable as a contract."

In such circumstances, as Browne-Wilkinson V.-C. expressly held in *Frogmore Estates v. Berger*,[700] whichever person has acquired the property in question holds it on constructive trust to give effect to the agreement between the parties in so far as this is possible.[701]

10–281   The Court of Appeal considered this principle for the first time in *Banner Homes v. Luff Developments*.[702] The parties agreed that a site whose purchase and development neither felt able to finance alone would be purchased through a new single purpose company which they would own in equal shares. The purchase, which both parties realised would precede any formal agreement, was duly made by a company acquired for the purpose by the defendant at a point when the plaintiff believed that the defendant had every intention of proceeding with the agreement; however, the defendant was by then having second thoughts and, shortly thereafter, withdrew from the agreement. Before the Court of Appeal it was accepted that the defendant was affected neither by any binding contract nor by any estoppel.

10–282   Chadwick L.J., who gave the only reasoned judgment, held that the following series of rather repetitive propositions will determine whether or not what he described as "The *Pallant v. Morgan* Equity" will arise, although he eschewed any attempt at an exhaustive classification: first, there must be

---

[699] (1974) Unreported but quoted in *Banner Homes v. Luff Developments* [2000] Ch. 372.
[700] (1989) 139 N.L.J. 1560.
[701] He also reiterated that if, as in *Pallant v. Morgan*, it is not possible to establish what benefit each was intended to take, they will take the property jointly.
[702] [2000] Ch. 372.

an arrangement or understanding ("the deal") between A and B preceding the acquisition of property by A which colours that acquisition and leads to A being treated as a trustee if he acts inconsistently with the deal; secondly, the deal need not necessarily be contractually enforceable; thirdly, not only must the deal contemplate that A will take steps to acquire the property and that, if A does acquire it, B will obtain some interest in it but also A must not have informed B that A no longer intends to honour the deal before it is too late to restore both of them to a position in which there is neither advantage nor detriment; fourthly, in reliance on the deal, B must do or omit to do something which confers an advantage on A in relation to the acquisition of the property or is detrimental to B's ability to acquire the property on equal terms; and, fifthly, it is not necessary either that B agrees to keep out of the market or that there is both advantage to A and detriment to B.

At first instance the plaintiff was denied relief: first, because the fact that **10–283** both parties had at all times had an implicit right to withdraw from the deal was inconsistent with the intervention of equity, which could not turn a deal which was qualified by a right to withdraw into an unqualified deal which denied any such right; and, secondly, because the plaintiff had failed to show that it had acted to its detriment in reliance on the deal. However, Chadwick L.J. disposed of the first ground by stating, very briefly, that what was required for equity to intervene was not a fully enforceable bargain but an acquisition of property in circumstances where it would be inequitable for the acquirer to treat the property as his own and rejected the second ground on the basis that detriment and advantage were alternative, not cumulative, requirements.[703] He therefore applied *Pallant v. Morgan* and held that the defendant held half the shares in the single purpose company on trust for the plaintiff.

While the reasoning of Chadwick L.J. is undoubtedly consistent with the **10–284** relevant parts of the propositions which he had already enunciated, those propositions all required reliance on the deal by the plaintiff. It is extremely difficult to see how the plaintiff could conceivably have relied on the deal if, as Chadwick L.J. necessarily had to accept, the defendant had at all times had the right to withdraw. Therefore, while the propositions enunciated by Chadwick L.J. are both sound and workable and will undoubtedly be repeatedly applied, it has to be said that their application in *Banner Homes v. Luff Developments* is somewhat questionable; the plaintiff in that case must therefore be regarded as having been extremely fortunate.

6. Damages paid in respect of Services of Third Parties

In *Hunt v. Severs*[704] the House of Lords held that, when a tortiously injured **10–285** claimant recovers, as part of the damages paid by his tortfeasor, the value of care, past and anticipated, provided voluntarily by a third party, typically a spouse or sibling or adult child, who has no cause of action of his or her own against the tortfeasor, the claimant holds those damages on trust for the

---

[703] *ibid.*, p.400.
[704] [1994] 2 A.C. 350.

carer.[705] It has subsequently been held, clearly correctly, that this trust is a constructive trust.[706] In the case of whatever sums are due to the carer for services which have been provided by the time that the damages are paid, there is no difficulty; the trust in question will be a bare trust and those sums will presumably be paid out to him or her. However, it is hard to see how sums provided in respect of future services can be subject to a valid trust.[707] No particular carer has any obvious right to insist on continuing to provide the care and thus to receive any future payments. Further, the care will of course only have to be performed for as long as the injured person needs it. If he dies prematurely or recovers more speedily than anticipated, then, unless the surplus sums are held on resulting trust for the tortfeasor, which is hardly likely, they presumably pass to the injured person or to his estate. Any continuing trust would, therefore, in effect be for the injured person, the trustee, save to the extent that he chose to make payments to anyone else; any such trust would, therefore, appear to be illusory.

10–286   A related question arose in *Hughes v. Lloyd*.[708] Part of the damages awarded in 2002 to someone who had suffered brain damage in the 1989 Hillsborough Football Stadium disaster were in respect of the voluntary care which had been provided to him by his mother, who had died in 2000 and so before the damages had actually been awarded. The rival claimants to the relevant sum were the mother's estate and the injured person. The judge[709] held, relying on the definition of constructive trust enunciated by Millett L.J. in *Paragon Finance v. D.B. Thakerar & Co.*,[710] that "it would be unconscionable for the claimant, who has recovered damages in respect of past care voluntarily provided by another, to retain for himself those damages which are referable to care provided by a third party, such as the mother". He therefore held that, although the trust established by *Hunt v. Severs* only became completely constituted when the damages were actually recovered, it then became constituted in favour of the mother's estate. This decision appears to be supportable, if only because a decision in favour of the injured person would have conferred an entirely fortuitous benefit on him and there was certainly no reason why the tortfeasor should have benefited from the mother's death pursuant to any resulting trust.

7. *Contractual Licences*

10–287   Contractual licences have traditionally been regarded more as creatures of the law of contract than of the law of property. While it has long[711] been recognised that a contractual licensee may, in appropriate circumstances, be able to obtain the assistance of equity to force the licensor to perform his

---

[705] See also *H v. S* [2003] Q.B. 965.
[706] *Hughes v. Lloyd* [2007] EWHC 3133 (Ch), [2008] W.T.L.R. 473.
[707] See Matthews [1994] Civil Justice Quarterly 302.
[708] [2007] EWHC 3133 (Ch), [2008] W.T.L.R. 473.
[709] HH Judge Hodge Q.C., sitting as a Judge of the High Court.
[710] [1999] 1 All E.R. 400 at 408J; see *ante*, [para.10–1].
[711] Since *Winter Garden Theatre (London) v. Millenium Productions* [1948] A.C. 173.

contract,[712] until 1952 it had never been suggested that he had any proprietary right in the subject matter of his licence capable of binding a third party, unless the latter had in some way estopped himself from revoking the licence.[713] However, in *Errington v. Errington and Woods*,[714] despite the existence of clear House of Lords authority to the contrary,[715] the Court of Appeal held that a contractual licence which could be enforced in this way against the licensor created an interest in land capable of binding third parties.

It has already been seen that, in the years immediately before and after **10–288** 1970, a series of decisions emanating from the Court of Appeal imposed constructive trusts not only as a result of fraudulent or unconscionable conduct of the types which have just been considered but also as a result of conduct which the individual judges were prepared to classify merely as inequitable. The underlying and indeed often expressed objective of the judges in question was to prevent results which would otherwise have been inequitable. If application of the basic principles of property law led to a result which, in the view of the court in question, was contrary to good conscience, that court acted upon the conscience of the party who would otherwise have obtained this unjust benefit and imposed a constructive trust upon him to bring the result into line with the requirements of justice.

As part of this development, and despite the subsequent doubts[716] which **10–289** had been expressed about the decision of the Court of Appeal in *Errington v. Errington and Woods*,[717] Lord Denning M.R. carried the novel proposition enunciated in that case a stage further in *Binions v. Evans*.[718] He there held that a contractual licence which was capable of binding a third party could be enforced by the imposition of a constructive trust if it was just and equitable so to do. This view was subsequently ratified by the whole of the Court of Appeal in *D.H.N. Food Distributors v. Tower Hamlets L.B.C.*[719]

However, the Court of Appeal subsequently "put the quietus to the heresy **10–290** that a mere licence creates an interest in land"[720] in *Ashburn Anstalt v. Arnold*.[721] The court accepted that a third party who attempted to renege on an agreement or undertaking to honour a contractual licence would be liable as a constructive trustee in the manner which has already been discussed.[722] However, in the absence of any such agreement or undertaking, the court

---

[712] *Foster v. Robinson* [1951] 1 K.B. 149 (injunction); *Verrall v. Great Yarmouth Borough Council* [1981] Q.B. 202 (specific performance).

[713] *Inwards v. Baker* [1965] 2 Q.B. 29; *Greasley v. Cooke* [1980] 1 W.L.R. 1306; *Hopgood v. Brown* [1955] 1 All E.R. 550; *E.R. Ives Investment v. High* [1967] 2 Q.B. 379. In *Re Basham* [1986] 1 W.L.R. 1498, the existence of a proprietary estoppel was held to give rise to the existence of a "floating" constructive trust similar to that which arises in the case of Mutual Wills (see *post*, p.430) but this view is generally held to be misconceived.

[714] [1952] 1 K.B. 290.

[715] *King v. David Allen and Sons, Billposting* [1916] 2 A.C. 54.

[716] As a result of *National Provincial Bank v. Hastings Car Mart* [1965] A.C. 1175 at 1239, 1251 (matter left open for future discussion) and *Re Solomon (A Bankrupt)* [1967] Ch. 573 at 583 (contrary view preferred).

[717] [1952] 1 K.B. 290.

[718] [1972] Ch. 359; see *ante*, para 10–227.

[719] [1976] 1 W.L.R. 852.

[720] *I.D.C. Group v. Clark* [1992] 1 E.G.L.R. 187 at 190.

[721] [1988] Ch. 1.

[722] See *ante*, para 10–227.

held that a contractual licence could bind no third party and that in such circumstances it would not be appropriate for a constructive trust to be imposed. Although the court obviously could not overrule *Errington v. Errington and Woods*, it stated that that decision had been made *per incuriam*, which makes it unlikely that anything further will be heard either of the principle enunciated therein or of its subsequent extension in *Binions v. Evans*. This legacy of the series of decisions emanating from the Court of Appeal in the years immediately before and after 1970 thus appears to have been nullified.

8. *Joint Enterprises in a Non-Commercial Context*

10–291   It has already been seen[723] that, where property has been purchased in the name of another, it will be presumed to result to whoever actually provided the purchase moneys, including if appropriate the person into whose name the property has been put, in proportion to their respective contributions. Such resulting trusts are, at least in principle, just as applicable to joint enterprises entered into in a non-commercial or family context as to any other situation. However, during the last 50 years, the courts have had to grapple with an increasing variety of less direct contributions to the acquisition of property, usually contributions to the acquisition or improvement of residential property made by one of its occupiers; the interests of such contributors have often been protected by what have been described[724] as "common intention constructive trusts" and, rather more recently, also by the principle of equitable proprietary estoppel.

10–292   The first cases of this type concerned the devolution of matrimonial property on the breakdown of marriage. The law contained in these cases no longer applies where the marriage has been terminated since the courts have now acquired an absolute discretion to vary matrimonial property rights at the termination of marriage[725]; this is now also the case for civil partnerships. That law is, however, still applicable to disputes that arise during marriage concerning the property rights of the spouses, to analogous situations involving unmarried couples and to other types of joint enterprises. It is important to emphasise that such disputes will not necessarily be between the persons who have, or claim to have, the property rights in question; such disputes may well arise as the result of a creditor of one of those persons wishing to enforce his rights against that person's share of the property.

10–293   It is now clear from the recent decision of the House of Lords in *Stack v. Dowden*[726] that a distinction must be drawn between the situation where the legal title to the property is held by only one of the persons in question and the situation where that legal title is held in the joint names of both of them. Unlike the three previous decisions of the House of Lords to which reference

---

[723] See *ante*, para 9–007.
[724] See, particularly, Hayton [1990] Conv. 370.
[725] Under what is now Matrimonial Causes Act 1973, s.23.
[726] [2007] UKHL 17, [2007] 2 W.L.R. 831.

is made below, *Stack v. Dowden* concerned the second of these two situations.[727] The House of Lords also held in *Stack v. Dowden*[728] that:

"Just as the starting point where there is sole legal ownership is sole beneficial ownership, the starting point where there is joint legal ownership is joint beneficial ownership. The onus is upon the person seeking to show that the beneficial ownership is different from the legal ownership. So in sole ownership cases it is upon the non-owner to show that he has any interest at all. In joint ownership cases, it is upon the joint owner who claims to have other than a joint beneficial interest."

The authorities discussed below, all of which pre-dated *Stack v. Dowden*, now have to be considered in the light of this statement.

(A) Cases where the legal title is in one name only
The underlying principle applicable to cases of this type was originally laid down by the House of Lords in *Pettitt v. Pettitt*[729] and *Gissing v. Gissing*,[730] namely that property rights have to be determined in the light of the intentions of the parties at the time of acquisition of the property. However, in *Gissing v. Gissing* Lord Diplock said this[731]:   **10–294**

"A resulting, implied or constructive trust—and it is unnecessary for present purposes to distinguish between these three classes of trust—is created by a transaction between the trustee and the cestui que trust in connection with the acquisition by the trustee of a legal estate in land, whenever the trustee has so conducted himself that it would be inequitable to deny to the cestui que trust a beneficial interest in the land acquired. And he will be held so to have conducted himself if by his words or conduct he has induced the cestui que trust to act to his own detriment in the reasonable belief that by so acting he was acquiring a beneficial interest in the land."

It should be noted that, although this fact is no longer relevant to the present law in this area, it was the first sentence of this passage which, when isolated from the qualification subsequently placed upon it, was cited in the series of decisions emanating from the Court of Appeal in the years immediately before and after 1970 as authority for the proposition that the courts may impose a constructive trust to do justice inter partes whenever the result would, otherwise, be inequitable.[732] Hence, in one of these cases[733] Lord Denning M.R. stated that "whenever two parties by their joint efforts acquire property to be used for their joint benefit, the courts may impose or impute a constructive or resulting trust". But subsequent authorities instead   **10–295**

---

[727] See *ibid.*, *per* Lord Walker at [15].
[728] *ibid.*, *per* Lady Hale at [56]; see also *per* Lord Hope at [4], *per* Lord Walker at [14].
[729] [1970] A.C. 777.
[730] [1971] A.C. 886.
[731] *ibid.*, at 905.
[732] *Heseltine v. Heseltine* [1971] 1 W.L.R. 342 (dispute during marriage concerning the property rights of the spouses); *Cooke v. Head* [1972] 1 W.L.R. 518 (unmarried couple); *Hussey v. Palmer* [1972] 1 W.L.R. 1286 (joint enterprise between married couple and parent).
[733] *Cooke v. Head* [1972] 1 W.L.R. 518 at 520.

applied *Pettitt v. Pettitt* and *Gissing v. Gissing* correctly,[734] requiring an inference from the circumstances that there had been an arrangement between the parties whereby each was to acquire a beneficial interest in the house as a pre-condition of the imposition of what was described as "a common intention constructive trust". Thus in *Grant v. Edwards*[735] the Court of Appeal held that a property purchased as a home for an unmarried couple, which had been conveyed into the name of the man alone on a pretext, was held to be subject to a constructive trust for the two of them in one half shares because there had clearly been a common intention that the woman was to have a beneficial interest in the property on which she had acted to her detriment by making substantial financial contributions.[736]

10–296 The scope of the "common intention constructive trust" was restated, if anything more narrowly, by the House of Lords in *Lloyds Bank v. Rosset*.[737] In this case Lord Bridge, with whose speech the remaining members of the House of Lords agreed, said this[738]:

"The first and fundamental question which must always be resolved is whether, independently of any inference to be drawn from the conduct of the parties in the course of sharing the house as their home and managing their joint affairs, there has at any time prior to acquisition, or exceptionally at some later date, been any agreement, arrangement or understanding reached between them that the property is to be shared beneficially. The finding of an agreement or arrangement to share in this sense can only, I think, be based on evidence of express discussions between the partners, however, imperfectly remembered and however imprecise their terms may have been."

Both the House of Lords[739] and the Law Commission[740] have classified this statement as obiter dicta which have arguably "set that hurdle rather too high in certain respects".

---

[734] The two different approaches can be seen side by side in *Eves v. Eves* [1975] 1 W.L.R. 1338. The parties, who were living together as man and wife, purchased a delapidated house as a home for themselves and their children, which was conveyed into the sole name of the man because he pretended to the woman that she was too young to acquire the legal title. All the purchase price was found by the man but the woman did a very considerable amount of work on the house. In the Court of Appeal she was granted a one-quarter share therein under a constructive trust. Lord Denning M.R. imposed a constructive trust on the strength of the first sentence of the passage from *Gissing v. Gissing* cited above in the text. The majority instead held that it could be inferred from the circumstances that there had been an arrangement between the parties whereby the woman was to acquire a beneficial interest in the house in return for her labour in contributing to its repair and improvement; this entitled her to an interest under a constructive trust.
[735] *Grant v. Edwards* [1986] Ch. 638.
[736] Other contemporaneous decisions were *Midland Bank v. Dobson* [1986] 1 F.L.R. 171 (dispute during marriage concerning the property rights of the spouses), *Burns v. Burns* [1984] Ch. 317, (unmarried couple) and *Re Sharpe (a Bankrupt)* [1980] 1 W.L.R. 219 (joint enterprise between nephew and aunt).
[737] [1991] 1 A.C. 107.
[738] *ibid.*, at 132–133.
[739] In *Stack v. Dowden* [2007] UKHL 17, [2007] 2 W.L.R. 831 *per* Lady Hale at [63].
[740] In "Sharing Homes—a Discussion Paper" Law.Com. No. 278 (2002) para.4–23.

Lord Bridge then considered the consequences of the two possible   **10–297**
answers to this question.

"Once a finding to this effect is made it will only be necessary for the partner
asserting a claim to a beneficial interest against the partner entitled to the
legal estate to show that he or she has acted to his or her detriment or
significantly altered his or her position in reliance on the agreement in order
to give rise to a constructive trust or a proprietary estoppel.

In sharp contrast with this situation is the very different one where there
is no evidence to support a finding of an agreement or an arrangement to
share, however reasonable it might have been for the parties to reach such
an agreement if they had applied their minds to the question, and where the
court must rely entirely on the conduct of the parties both as the basis from
which to infer a common intention to share the property beneficially and as
the conduct relied on to give rise to a constructive trust. In this situation
direct contributions to the purchase price by the partner who is not the legal
owner, whether initially or by payment of mortgage instalments, will readily
justify the inference necessary to the creation of a constructive trust. But, as
I read the authorities, it is at least extremely doubtful whether anything less
will do."

This statement of the law established that, provided that there had been
some express agreement, arrangement or understanding that the property
was to be shared beneficially, then any act of detriment would be sufficient
to give rise to a constructive trust; on the other hand, where an agreement
between the parties could only be inferred, only direct financial contributions to the purchase price[741] would justify the inference necessary to give
rise to a constructive trust.

(1) Lord Bridge's first situation
Lord Bridge's conclusion as to the effect of evidence of express discussions   **10–298**
between the partners was analysed by the Court of Appeal in *Oxley v.
Hiscock*,[742] in a passage with which the majority of the House of Lords
agreed in *Stack v. Dowden*.[743] Chadwick L.J. stated that "Lord Bridge was
addressing only the primary question—'was there a common intention that
each should have a beneficial interest in the property?' He was not addressing the secondary question—'what was the common intention of the parties
as to the extent of their respective beneficial interests?' "[744] Consequently,

---

[741] The payment of mortgage installments will give the payer the proportion of the value of
the property secured by the mortgage in question whether or not he ultimately pays it off; the
amount of the outstanding mortgage debt will be deducted from the value of his proportion of
the overall value (*Huntingford v. Hobbs* [1993] 1 F.L.R. 736). On the other hand, someone who
does not make any mortgage repayments at all and became a co-mortgagor merely so that
sufficient income could be shown to justify the making of the mortgage advance will not
thereby become entitled to any, or to any additional, beneficial interest (see *Carlton v. Goodman*
[2002] 2 F.L.R. 259).

[742] [2005] EWCA Civ. 546, [2005] Fam. 211 *per* Chadwick L.J. at [47–48].

[743] [2007] UKHL 17, [2007] 2 W.L.R. 831 *per* Lady Hale at [65], with whom the remaining
members of the majority agreed.

[744] Chadwick L.J. accepted that this was not the basis on which the members of the Court of
Appeal had proceeded in *Springette v. Defoe* [1992] 2 F.L.R. 388.

when evidence of express discussions between the parties enables the primary question to be answered in the affirmative, "the court may well have to supply the answer to that secondary question by inference from their subsequent conduct"; this will clearly be the case whenever the evidence of express discussions between the parties does not provide any answer to the secondary question.

10–299   It is of course apparent that, where there actually is evidence of the common intention of the parties as to the extent of their respective beneficial interests, that will determine the outcome. It is also apparent, and was even before *Oxley v. Hiscock*, that the existence of evidence of express discussions between the parties could give rise to the non-owing party obtaining a larger beneficial interest than under the pre-existing law; not only the contribution envisaged in the express discussions but also any other act of detriment, even if not envisaged in those discussions, would be taken into account in calculating that beneficial interest. That is not to say that acts done behind the back of the legal owner would be taken into account for this purpose but any act of detriment in which he had acquiesced would be taken into account whether or not envisaged in the initial express discussions. However, on the face of things, there was no possibility of the non-owing partner being given a share larger than that which corresponded to the relevant acts of detriment.

10–300   This no longer appears to be the law. In *Oxley v. Hiscock*, the property in question had been conveyed into the name of the man who had provided just under 50 per cent of the purchase price; the woman had provided just under 30 per cent and the remainder had been raised on a mortgage, necessarily taken out by the man; the mortgage had subsequently been discharged but there was no finding as to who had paid it off (this was presumably because the trial judge had taken the view that the existence of express discussions between the partners coupled with financial contributions by each of them necessarily led to the conclusion that they had equal shares, a conclusion which was on any view clearly wrong). On appeal the man contended that, in the absence of any evidence of the common intention of the parties as to the extent of their respective beneficial interests, the woman was limited to a beneficial interest equivalent to her contribution, a conclusion which accorded with what was then generally understood to be the law. But the Court of Appeal held[745] that in such circumstances "each is entitled to the share which the court considers fair having regard to the whole course of dealing between them in relation to the property" which "includes the arrangements which they make from time to time in order to meet the outgoings (for example, mortgage contributions, council tax and utilities, repairs, insurance and housekeeping) which have to be met if they are to live in the property as their home". This statement was approved by the majority of the House of Lords in *Stack v. Dowden*[746] (that case actually concerned a property which had been transferred into joint names); their

---

[745] [2005] EWCA Civ. 546, [2005] Fam. 211 *per* Chadwick L.J. at [69].
[746] [2007] UKHL 17, [2007] 2 W.L.R. 831 *per* Lady Hale at [61], with whom the remaining members of the majority agreed (see *per* Lord Hope at [12], *per* Lord Walker at [36]).

Lordships added that contributions in the form of manual labour on improvements were also included.[747]

In contrast the dissentient in *Stack v. Dowden*, Lord Neuberger, was unhappy with the formulation of Chadwick L.J. stating[748] that: "First, fairness is not the appropriate yardstick". Secondly, the formulation appears to contemplate an imputed intention. Thirdly "the whole course of dealing . . . in relation to the property" is too imprecise, as it gives insufficient guidance as to what is primarily relevant, namely dealings which cast light on the beneficial ownership of the property, and too limited, as all aspects of the relationship could be relevant in providing the context, by reference to which any alleged discussion, statement and actions must be assessed." He also disagreed that outgoings, which are income expenses, are likely to be relevant to the question of ownership. This view is clearly preferable. Chadwick L.J. seems to have made the law in this area nothing more than a judicial lottery and, in effect although not in form, to have returned the law to the situation which it briefly occupied in the years immediately before and after 1970 when the courts felt able to impose a constructive trust to do justice inter partes whenever the result would, otherwise, be inequitable. Thus, in *Oxley v. Hiscock* itself, the Court of Appeal relied on the findings by the judge that there had been "a classic pooling of resources" and conduct consistent with an intention to share the burden of the property and therefore awarded the woman a 40 per cent interest[749]; this in effect assumed that she had made half the mortgage repayments, an issue on which there had been no finding. This appears to indicate that, at least for the moment, every case will have to be litigated because of the impossibility of being able to predict the outcome in advance. Future decisions will obviously show whether or not these criticisms are justified.

10–301

(2) Lord Bridge's second situation

In contrast, Lord Bridge's conclusion as to the effect of the absence of any evidence of express discussions between the partners was, on the face of things, considerably more restrictive than the pre-existing law. In such circumstances, only a direct financial contribution to the purchase price by the non-owing party would entitle him or her to a beneficial interest, no matter how many indirect financial contributions he or she had made or how much work he or she had done. In *Lloyds Bank v. Rosset* itself, the wife had supervised builders who were renovating a delapidated building and had herself done a certain amount of preparatory cleaning and some painting and decorating but had made no direct financial contribution to the purchase price; this was held to be insufficient to justify the inference of any common intention that she should have a beneficial interest. While it was and is highly desirable that unsolicited work on the property of another should not, in the absence of express subsequent ratification, lead to the creation of an interest therein, the requirement for a direct financial contribution to the purchase price may cause difficulties when substantial indirect

10–302

---

[747] *ibid.*, in particular *per* Lord Walker at [36].
[748] *ibid.*, at [144].
[749] [2005] EWCA Civ. 546, [2005] Fam. 211 *per* Chadwick L.J.

financial contributions to, for example, household expenses have been necessary to enable the holder of the legal title to repay the mortgage. Prior to
Lloyds Bank v. Rosset, such contributions would have caused a common
intention that the contributor is to have a beneficial interest to be inferred
but, after that decision, it appeared that this would no longer be the case and
that the contributor was, therefore, limited to claiming what was likely to be
a much smaller beneficial interest proportional to any direct contributions
actually made. This aspect of the decision in *Lloyds Bank v. Rosset* was clearly
less than satisfactory.

10–303   Subsequently, the position in this respect was to some extent ameliorated
by the decision of the Court of Appeal in *Midland Bank v. Cooke*,[750] although
this decision did somewhat obscure the clear distinctions established by
Lloyds Bank v. Rosset. The matrimonial home had been purchased, in part,
with a sum provided by the husband's parents. This was held to have been
a gift to both spouses so the wife had to this extent made a direct contribution to the purchase price and therefore had a beneficial interest of at least
6.47 per cent (half of the percentage provided by the parents). She had
subsequently discharged household outgoings out of her earnings and contributed both physically and financially to the improvement of the house
and garden. However, both spouses testified that there had been no discussion or agreement at the time of acquisition as to the beneficial ownership of
the property. According to *Lloyds Bank v. Rosset*, the absence of any common
intention meant that the wife's subsequent contributions could not be taken
into account and that was what was held at first instance. Unexpectedly,
however, the Court of Appeal took a wholly different view. Waite L.J.
referred to the speech of Lord Diplock in *Gissing v. Gissing*[751] and held[752]:

"When the court is proceeding, in cases like the present where the partner
without legal title has successfully asserted an equitable interest through
direct contribution, to determine (in the absence of express evidence of
intention) what proportions the parties must be assumed to have intended
for their beneficial ownership, the duty of the judge is to undertake a survey
of the whole course of dealing between the parties relevant to their ownership and occupation of the property and their sharing of its burdens and
advantages. That scrutiny will not confine itself to the limited range of acts
of direct contribution of the sort that are needed to found a beneficial
interest in the first place. It will take into consideration all conduct which
throws light on the question what shares were intended. Only if that search
proves inconclusive does the court fall back on the maxim that 'equality is
equity'."

He then assessed the wife's beneficial interest at 50 per cent on the basis that
"[o]ne could hardly have a clearer example of a couple who had agreed to

---

[750] [1995] 2 F.L.R. 915.
[751] [1971] A.C. 886 at 908: set out *ante*, p.362.
[752] [1995] 2 F.L.R. 915 at 926.

share everything",[753] a conclusion which it is not particularly easy to square with the spouses' own evidence that they had never considered the beneficial ownership of the house at all!

The speech of Lord Diplock in *Gissing v. Gissing* did indeed provide **10–304** support for the propositions enunciated by Waite L.J. in the passage cited. The difficulty is that this was precisely the respect in which *Lloyds Bank v. Rosset* had narrowed the pre-existing law, a point which Waite L.J. does not appear to have taken into account. Consequently, it appeared that, whenever some direct contribution to the purchase price could be shown, no matter how small provided, presumably, that it is not *de minimis*, the court could infer from the conduct of the parties not only a common intention that indirect contributions were to enhance that interest but also the amount by which that interest was to be enhanced. In contrast, the position of the indirect contributor who could not show any direct contribution to the purchase price at all was still wholly governed by *Lloyds Bank v. Rosset* and such a person was consequently be unable to establish any beneficial interest whatever. This revival, for some but not for all purposes, of those aspects of *Gissing v. Gissing* which were thought to have been abrogated by *Lloyds Bank v. Rosset* was scarcely satisfactory either.

On the face of things, the decision in *Midland Bank v. Cooke* provided some **10–305** support for the conclusion which the trial judge had reached in *Oxley v. Hiscock*. Consequently, when that case reached the Court of Appeal, the man contended that *Midland Bank v. Cooke* had been wrongly decided. In fact, the trial judge's finding that there had been express discussions between the partners meant that *Midland Bank v. Cooke*, a case where there had been no such discussions, was not strictly speaking relevant at all. However, the Court of Appeal ignored that point completely and simply stated that the law had moved on since that decision.[754] The court held[755] that, in Lord Bridge's second situation—"where the evidence is that the matter was not discussed at all—an affirmative answer [to the question of whether there is evidence from which to infer a common intention] will necessarily be inferred from the fact that each has made a financial contribution". This is of course consistent with what was held in *Midland Bank v. Cooke*. The court then went on to hold that in such circumstances the beneficial interests of the parties would be worked out neither in the way in which this had been done in *Midland Bank v. Cooke* nor in the manner suggested in *Gissing v. Gissing*. Instead they would be worked out in the same way as in Lord Bridge's first situation and so "each is entitled to the share which the court considers fair having regard to the whole course of dealing between them in relation to the property". This was also approved by the majority of the House of Lords in *Stack v. Dowden*. The criticisms already made of this conclusion are obviously equally applicable here.

---

[753] *ibid.*, at 928. A similar "broad brush" approach to the quantification of beneficial interests was subsequently taken by the Court of Appeal in *Drake v. Whipp* [1996] 1 F.L.R. 826 although, in the light of concessions made by counsel at first instance, it might be a mistake to read too much into this decision.

[754] [2005] EWCA Civ. 546, [2005] Fam. 211 *per* Chadwick L.J. at [60].

[755] *ibid.*, at [69–71].

(B)   Cases where the legal title is in joint names

10–306   The situation where the legal title is in joint names is what had to be considered by the House of Lords in *Stack v. Dowden*.[756] It has never been doubted that in this situation any express statement of the beneficial interests in the conveyance or transfer is decisive unless varied by subsequent agreement or affected by proprietary estoppel.[757] The Transfer Form whose use the Land Registry has required since 1998 provides a box with three alternatives for the transferees to select: beneficial joint tenancy, tenancy in common in equal shares, or some other stated trusts. If utilised, this will therefore be decisive. However, the form in use at the time of the acquisition of the property whose beneficial ownership was in issue in *Stack v. Dowden* merely required the purchasers to indicate whether their survivor could give a valid receipt for capital money, which has long been held not to be decisive.[758]

10–307   Having held, as has already been seen, that the starting point where there is joint legal ownership is joint beneficial ownership and that the onus is open the person seeking to show that the beneficial ownership is different from the legal ownership,[759] the House of Lords asked[760] whether the contrary is to be proved by recourse to the presumption of resulting trust or in the manner envisaged by Chadwick L.J. in *Oxley v. Hiscock* and resolved. It was emphasised[761] that the questions are different in a joint names case, namely "did the parties intend their beneficial interests to be different from their legal interests?" and "if they did, in what way and to what extent?" and that, in a joint names case, unlike a sole name case, a beneficial joint tenancy is a realistic option. Nevertheless, the House of Lords held, by the same majority,[762] that the contrary is to be proved in the manner envisaged by Chadwick L.J. in *Oxley v. Hiscock*. The criticisms already made of this conclusion are again applicable here, but the House of Lords did emphasise[763] that in a joint names case this is "unlikely to lead to a different result unless the facts are very unusual". They were held to be in *Stack v. Dowden* because, save for the acquisition of the property, the parties had kept their finances rigidly separate; consequently, the proceeds of sale of the property were divided in the proportions 65 per cent to 35 per cent.

(C)   Overlap with equitable proprietary estoppel

10–308   Under the law as it stood prior to *Oxley v. Hiscock*, further difficulties[764] potentially arose in quantifying the beneficial interests. Where the express

---

[756] [2007] UKHL 17, [2007] 2 W.L.R. 831.
[757] *Goodman v. Gallant* [1986] Fam. 106 (CA). This was specifically stated in *Stack v. Dowden* [2007] UKHL 17, [2007] 2 W.L.R. 831 *per* Lady Hale at [49].
[758] *Harwood v. Harwood* [1991] 2 F.L.R. 274 (CA), *Huntingford v. Hobbs* [1993] 1 F.L.R. 736 (CA).
[759] *Stack v. Dowden* [2007] UKHL 17, [2007] 2 W.L.R. 831 *per* Lady Hale at [56]; see also *per* Lord Hope at [4], *per* Lord Walker at [14].
[760] *ibid., per* Lady Hale at [59].
[761] *ibid., per* Lady Hale at [66].
[762] *ibid., per* Lady Hale at [69–70], with whom the remainder of the majority agreed.
[763] *ibid., per* Lady Hale at [68].
[764] Highlighted by Hayton [1990] Conv. 370.

common intention of the parties envisaged that the beneficial interest should be held in specific proportions, then this common intention clearly had to be upheld provided that the parties had duly made whatever contribution was envisaged. But what was to happen where one of the parties had failed to provide the whole of the contribution which was envisaged?[765] The difficulties were even greater where a common intention envisaging a beneficial interest but no contribution was followed by acts of detriment in reliance on the existence of the beneficial interest. Were the beneficial interests to be quantified in the proportions envisaged quite irrelevant of the scale of the acts of detrimental reliance? These questions never had to be considered by the courts but it was suggested[766] that the courts should adopt the flexible approach already utilised in the area of equitable proprietary estoppel and provide a remedy appropriate to the circumstances of each individual case.[767] Prior to *Stack v. Dowden*, it had been repeatedly stated that in this area of the law there was an increasing overlap between the constructive trust and the doctrine of equitable proprietary estoppel[768]; indeed in *Oxley v. Hiscock* Chadwick L.J. said "I think that the time has come to accept that there is no difference in outcome, in cases of this nature, whether the true analysis lies in constructive trust or in proprietary estoppel".[769] However, in *Stack v. Dowden*, the House of Lords was "rather less enthusiastic about this"[770]; further, in the light of the majority decision, these quantification difficulties are now likely to be resolved in the manner envisaged by Chadwick L.J. anyway. The extent to which this potential overlap is still of any particular relevance is therefore questionable.

(D) The Future

There is not the slightest doubt that, rightly or wrongly, the beneficial **10–309** ownership of residential property acquired for occupation by its owners is for the moment to be determined in the manner envisaged by Chadwick L.J. in *Oxley v. Hiscock* and that this is the case whether the legal title to the property in question is held by only one of the persons in question or is held in the joint names of both of them, even though different questions arise in the two situations and, in a joint names case, this is unlikely to lead to any result other than joint beneficial ownership unless the facts are very unusual. Admittedly, the Law Commission had already issued a Report and a Consultation Paper dealing with this area of the law[771] and a further Report

---

[765] Hayton, *ibid.* envisages the situation where half of the potential contribution is withheld.

[766] *ibid.*

[767] Following suggestions made by Browne-Wilkinson V.-C. in *Grant v. Edwards* [1986] Ch. 638 at 656.

[768] See particularly *per* Browne-Wilkinson V.-C. in *Grant v. Edwards* [1986] Ch. 638 at 656 and *per* Lord Bridge in *Lloyds Bank v. Rosset* [1991] 1 A.C. 107 at 132.

[769] [2005] EWCA Civ. 546, [2005] Fam. 211 at [70] summarising the earlier discussion at [60].

[770] [2007] UKHL 17, [2007] 2 W.L.R. 831 *per* Lord Walker at [37]; see also *per* Lord Neuberger at [128].

[771] Law.Com. No. 278 (2002), Consultation Paper No.179 (2006),

had been promised. However, in March 2008 the Government announced that no action was to be taken for the present, although campaigners have since indicated that they will seek the reversal of this decision.

9. *Possible Future Developments*

10–310   The approach manifested in the series of decisions emanating from the Court of Appeal in the years immediately before and after 1970, to which reference has already been made, was of course much closer to the American attitude to the constructive trust[772] and was thought to be symptomatic of a general change of attitude towards the constructive trust. Even though, as has also been seen, subsequent decisions rejected the approach manifested in this series of cases and English law consequently appeared to have reverted to its traditional position, indications of a more remedial approach have continued to make their appearance.

10–311   In particular, in *Westdeutsche Landesbank Girozentrale v. Islington L.B.C.*[773] Lord Browne-Wilkinson seized on an isolated remark of this kind by the Court of Appeal in *Metall und Rohstoff A.G. v. Donaldson Lufkin & Jenrette*[774] as a possible justification for the decision of Goulding J. in *Chase Manhattan Bank v. Israel-British Bank (London)*[775] that a bank which had received the same sum twice rather than once held the second payment on trust for the mistaken payer. Lord Browne-Wilkinson took the view that "the retention of the moneys after the recipient bank learned of the mistake may well have given rise to a constructive trust"[776] and opined that "the remedial constructive trust, if introduced into English law, may provide a more satisfactory road forward".[777] These remarks were applied and a constructive trust was imposed on this ground in the Commercial Court in *Papamichael v. National Westminster Bank.*[778] However, this decision is, as a matter of precedent, clearly wrong because of the repeated statements in the Court of Appeal[779] that the remedial constructive trust does not form part of English law and that the contention that it should be adopted by English law can only be maintained in the House of Lords or the future Supreme Court. For the moment, therefore, it is inappropriate to regard this possible justification for the decision in *Chase Manhattan Bank v. Israel-British Bank (London)* as part of English law.

---

[772] See *ante*, para 10–027.

[773] [1996] A.C. 669 at 715.

[774] [1990] 1 Q.B. 391 at 479. The Court of Appeal accepted that "there is a good arguable case" that circumstances may arise in which "the court will be prepared to impose a constructive trust *de novo* as a foundation for the grant of equitable remedy by way of account or otherwise", classifying such a trust as a "remedial constructive trust".

[775] [1981] Ch. 105; see *post*, para 22–152.

[776] [1996] A.C. 669 at 714. His Lordship doubted the conclusion of Goulding J. that a mistaken payment is of itself sufficient to make the recipient a trustee of its subject matter.

[777] [1996] A.C. 669 at 716.

[778] [2003] 1 Lloyd's Rep. 341.

[779] Most significantly in *Twinsectra v. Yardley* [1999] Lloyd's Rep. Bank 438 and *Bank of Credit and Commerce International (Overseas) v. Akindele* [2001] Ch. 437.

That does not alter the fact that the House of Lords or the future Supreme 10–312
Court will undoubtedly one day soon be called upon to decide "whether
English law should follow the United States and Canada by adopting the
remedial constructive trust"[780]; however, as has already been seen,[781] the
outcome of their future deliberations is certainly not a foregone conclusion,
either in the context of mistaken payments or more generally.

V. MUTUAL WILLS

Mutual wills arise where two or more persons enter into a legally binding 10–313
agreement to make wills in a particular form with the intention that the
provisions of such wills will be irrevocably binding. As soon as the first of
the parties dies leaving a will made in accordance with the agreement,
equity regards that agreement as irrevocable so far as the survivor is concerned and gives effect to it by the imposition of a trust. Thus if the survivor
ultimately leaves his property other than in accordance with the agreement,
his personal representatives will be deemed to hold it on trust for the agreed
beneficiary.

This intervention of equity is, on the face of things, directly contrary to the 10–314
Wills Act 1837 in that the agreement between the parties will normally[782]
have to be proved by evidence which does not comply with the formal
requirements for wills contained in section 9 of that Act. This provision was
enacted for an obvious and important reason of policy—to ensure that false
claims cannot be generated after the death of a testator when he is in no
position to refute them. However, it has long been accepted that the intervention of equity can be justified by the fact that the survivor would
otherwise be enabled to benefit by his own fraud.[783] As soon as one of the
parties dies leaving a will made in accordance with the agreement, he will
irrevocably have disposed of his property in reliance upon the agreement.
Therefore, any revocation of the mutual will at this stage will be a blatant
fraud in that it will enable the survivor to take the benefit for which he
contracted—the disposition by the other party of his property in accordance
with that agreement—without the corresponding burden. This will be the
case not only where the survivor takes some material benefit under the will
but also where he disclaims any such benefit and where the agreement gave
him no such benefit; this is because in all three situations he will have
obtained the benefit which he sought—the disposition of the property under
the will. Consequently, equity imposes a trust to prevent the survivor from
benefiting by his own fraud.

---

[780] [1996] A.C. 669 at 716.

[781] See *ante*, para 10–038.

[782] The agreement between the parties may be recited in one or both of the wills in question
although this is not usually the case. It will certainly not be mentioned in any will executed in
breach of the agreement.

[783] *Dufour v. Pereira* (1769) Dick 419, 421 (better reported in 2 Hargrave, *Jurisconsult Exercita-
tions* 100, 104).

1. *The Prerequisites of Mutual Wills*

(A) A Legally Binding Agreement Between the Parties

10–315   Evidence must be adduced that the parties intended that the provisions of their wills should be irrevocably binding.[784] The best conceivable evidence is obviously recitals in the wills themselves. In *Re Hagger*[785] a husband and wife made a joint will[786] which expressly stated that the parties had agreed to dispose of their property by that will and that there was to be no alteration or revocation except by agreement. Although the mere fact that the parties had made a joint will did not necessarily make it a mutual will, this recital clearly showed that the parties had agreed to bind themselves to make a mutual will. Equally convincing proof will be recitals of this type in the separate wills of the parties to the agreement.[787] However, cases normally only reach the courts where the survivor has revoked his mutual will in breach of the agreement and in such a situation there will obviously be no such recital in his later will. A recital in the sole will of the first party to die will be no more than prima facie evidence of an agreement.[788] In such a case, and also in situations where there is no mention of any agreement in either will, the agreement will have to be proved by some other form of evidence.

10–316   No agreement will be inferred merely because two parties make wills in substantially similar form. In *Re Oldham*[789] a husband and wife both made wills leaving their property to the other absolutely with the same alternative provisions in the event of the other's predecease. Although it was clear that they had agreed to make substantially identical wills, no evidence could be adduced of any agreement not to revoke and so the judge declined to infer such an agreement, particularly since both had left their property to the other absolutely (although this will clearly be a factor against the implication of such an agreement, there is nothing to prevent parties expressly agreeing to make mutual wills in this form, something which occurred both in *Re Green*[790] and in *Re Cleaver*[791]). Even the fact that both parties clearly intended that their assets should eventually go to the same third party in any event will not be enough, unless it can also be shown that they intended to enter into a legally binding obligation. Thus in *Re Goodchild (deceased)*,[792] a husband and wife, as part of a wider scheme dealing with the disposal of their business, each made wills in favour of the other absolutely and, subject to that, in favour of their son. Evidence from their solicitor as to the advice

---

[784] Writing signed by both parties is in principle necessary where land is included but in practice it will be unconscionable for the survivor to rely on its absence; see *Healey v. Brown* [2002] W.T.L.R. 849.

[785] [1930] 2 Ch. 190.

[786] Such a document takes effect not as one will but as the separate wills of each party and is admitted to probate successively as the will of each testator.

[787] As in *Healey v. Brown* [2002] W.T.L.R. 849.

[788] If it is finally found that there is insufficient evidence to prove the existence of mutual wills, it is possible that the equitable doctrine of election may apply.

[789] [1925] Ch. 75.

[790] [1951] Ch. 148.

[791] [1981] 1 W.L.R. 939.

[792] [1996] 1 W.L.R. 694 (Carnwath J.); [1998] 1 W.L.R. 1216 (C.A.).

which he habitually gave[793] led the court to conclude that the fact that the wife had understood that her intentions would be binding on the husband after her death, something which he would at that stage have taken for granted, did not mean that he had thought it necessary to bind himself to comply with those intentions; the wills were therefore not mutual.[794]

(B) A Disposition of Property in Accordance with the Agreement

Equity will only intervene once one of the parties has died leaving a will **10–317** made in accordance with the agreement. The vast majority of mutual wills involve the parties making a disposition in favour of the other with the same ultimate or substitutionary beneficiary; thus each party may leave property to the other for life and subject thereto to the same third party[795] or to the other absolutely with the same substitutionary provisions in the event of predecease.[796] The property in question is most commonly the residuary estate of each but there is no reason why the agreement should not be for each to leave a specific sum of money or specific assets in this way with no restriction whatever on the disposition of the residue. Even where the agreement in question is for each party to dispose of his residue in this manner, it is common for each to make individual specific bequests or pecuniary legacies.[797]

It was long unclear whether or not it is a prerequisite of the doctrine of **10–318** mutual wills that the will of the first to die should, as in all the examples discussed so far, contain some disposition in favour of the survivor; however, it has now been established that this is not actually necessary. In *Re Dale*[798] spouses both made wills, which they had agreed should be irrevocable, in favour of their two children in equal shares. It was contended that the doctrine of mutual wills could only operate where the survivor obtained a personal financial benefit under the will of the first to die. Morritt J. rejected this argument, holding that it would be no less a fraud on the first to die if the agreement was that each party should leave his property to third parties rather than to the other; in both cases, the survivor would have obtained the benefit for which he had contracted—the agreed disposition of property in the will of the first to die. It must follow from this decision that the survivor will be equally bound to dispose of his property in accordance with the agreement if he disclaims any benefit to which he is entitled under the will of the first to die; in this case also, he will have obtained the benefit for which he has contracted but will have freely chosen to renounce it.[799]

All the examples discussed so far have related to agreements for the **10–319** making of wills in substantially similar form. However, there seems to be no

---

[793] He had never advised any of his clients to make mutual wills and had never had occasion to look into how such wills were drafted.

[794] However, the son was held entitled to make a claim under the Inheritance (Provision for Family and Dependants) Act 1975 in respect of the will of the wife (who had died first) on the grounds that it did not make reasonable provision for him; however, this claim could obviously only reach her property, not the property of the husband.

[795] As in *Re Haggar* [1930] 2 Ch. 190.

[796] As in *Re Green* [1951] Ch. 148 and *Re Cleaver* [1981] 1 W.L.R. 939.

[797] As in *Re Cleaver* [1981] 1 W.L.R. 939.

[798] [1994] Ch. 31.

[799] This was stated obiter in *Re Haggar* [1930] 2 Ch. 190 and must now clearly have been confirmed by *Re Dale* [1994] Ch. 31.

reason in principle why the doctrine of mutual wills should be limited to agreements of this type and should not also extend to an agreement that, if A leaves property to B, B will leave that property and other property of his own[800] on to C. Such an agreement is obviously subject to two pre-conditions: A must both die before B and leave the property in question to B; equally obviously, if either of these pre-conditions is not fulfilled, B will clearly be under no obligation to leave his own property to C. In *Birch v. Curtis*[801] a husband and wife agreed that the wife, who was terminally ill, should leave her interest in their matrimonial home to the husband and that he should leave the whole of his property to their respective children in equal shares. Both made wills in the form envisaged and the wife duly died first; however, the husband, having remarried, made a new will from which his former wife's children were excluded. The latter relied on the doctrine of mutual wills.[802] Rimer J. held that the nature of the agreement was not "a relevant difference" but did not find the necessary evidence that the husband had been legally bound. It is therefore clear that an agreement of this type is capable of falling within the doctrine of mutual wills; when it does so, once A has predeceased B having by his will made the appropriate disposition of property in B's favour, equity will intervene to prevent B from going back on the agreement.

2. *The Effect of Mutual Wills*

(A) Before Either Party has Died

10–320   Equity will not intervene until one of the parties has died leaving a will made in accordance with the agreement. Consequently the position before either party has died will be governed by contractual principles. Like any other contract, the agreement between the parties can of course be revoked at any time by mutual agreement. On the other hand, any change made by one of the parties to the provisions of his or her mutual will without the knowledge and approval of the other party amounts to a breach of the agreement and, therefore, to a breach of contract; it has been held that any such unapproved change, no matter how minor, also amounts to revocation of the agreement.[803]

10–321   If the other party discovers such a unilateral revocation before either party has died, he is entitled to recover damages for breach of contract. However, since the only possible loss is the loss of the right to receive an unascertained amount at an unascertained time in the future and since the other party still

---

[800] If the agreement relates only to A's own property, C will not actually need to rely on the doctrine of mutual wills but will instead be able to claim, as in *Ottaway v. Norman* [1972] Ch. 698 (*ante*, para 4–084), that B held that property on secret trust for C. Such a trust of course requires only an affirmative response from or the silent acquiescence of B to A's request that B should act in that way rather than the legally binding agreement between A and B which is necessary for there to be mutual wills. There is no obvious reason why an agreement of the type referred to in the text which is held not to be legally binding should not, insofar as it concerns A's property, nevertheless take effect as a secret trust.

[801] [2002] W.T.L.R. 965.

[802] No claim was made that the husband held the wife's share of the matrimonial home on what would have been a fully secret trust; on the evidence such a claim might well have been successful.

[803] *Re Hobley (deceased)* (1997) [2006] W.T.L.R. 467.

has unrestricted powers to dispose of his own property, it is relatively unlikely that any substantial damages could be recovered. A further bar to any successful action for damages in these circumstances is the fact that it seems that no such action will be available if the mutual will was revoked not by the act of the party but by operation of law (for example by his marriage, divorce or remarriage[804]); it appears that only intentional revocation will ground an action for damages.[805] Thus no effective remedy is likely to result to the other party.

However, it is clear that any revocation of the mutual will during the joint **10–322** lives of the parties will determine the agreement and release the other party from his obligations under that agreement.[806] He may, therefore, then dispose of his property in any way which he pleases free from the restrictions imposed by the agreement. This appears to be the case even if the other party was unaware of the revocation. In *Re Hobley (deceased)*[807] a husband and wife made mutual wills but the husband subsequently made a relatively minor amendment to his will by codicil; there was no evidence that the wife had either known or approved this amendment but, following the husband's death, she executed a similar codicil. She later made a number of further wills which did not comply with the agreement in much more substantial respects. After her death, the question arose as to whether her property devolved according to her mutual will or according to her last will; it was held that the alteration made by the husband had released the wife from her agreement and her property therefore devolved in accordance with her last will.

(B) Where the First Party to Die Does Not Leave a Will Made in Accordance with the Agreement

If the other party does not discover that the first party to die has revoked his **10–323** will until after the latter has died without leaving a will in accordance with the agreement, he will be able to claim damages from the latter's estate. However, although the loss suffered will certainly be able to be quantified in such a case, the other party will not have relinquished his powers over his own property and so may still find difficulty in obtaining substantial damages. The only exception to this seems to be the situation where he himself dies so soon after the first party to die that he does not have any opportunity of changing his own will and so dies leaving a will made in accordance with the agreement; in these circumstances, there seems no reason why his estate should not successfully bring an action for damages for breach of contract against the estate of the first to die for the value of the property which, according to the agreement, should have been disposed of in the will of the first to die. However, save in this exceptional situation, where the first party to die does not leave a will made in accordance with the agreement, the survivor is unlikely to have any effective remedy against the estate of the

---

[804] Wills Act 1837, ss.18, 18A.

[805] *Robinson v. Ommanney* (1883) 23 Ch.D. 285. See also *Re Marsland* [1939] Ch. 820, where the Court of Appeal reached a similar conclusion in respect of a covenant not to revoke a will contained in a deed of separation.

[806] *Stone v. Hoskins* [1905] P. 194.

[807] (1997) [2006] W.T.L.R. 467.

first to die; but, as has already been seen,[808] he will of course be released from his own obligations under the agreement.

(C) Where the First Party to Die Leaves a Will Made in Accordance with the Agreement[809]

10–324   Once the first party to die has made the disposition of property envisaged by the agreement, a trust is immediately imposed upon the survivor for the benefit of those entitled under the agreement. This emerges most clearly from *Re Hagger*[810] where one of the ultimate beneficiaries under the joint mutual will of a husband and wife survived the wife but predeceased the husband. Clauson J. held that her interest under the trust imposed by equity arose on the death of the first to die, the wife, and therefore did not lapse when she predeceased the husband.

10–325   The purpose of the imposition of the trust is to prevent the survivor from revoking his will in breach of the agreement. However, equity does not interfere with the fundamental probate principle that no will is irrevocable. If the survivor revokes his mutual will in breach of the agreement, his property will pass under his new will or his intestacy to his personal representatives, who will hold it on trust to give effect to the agreement.[811] This will be the case even if the survivor's mutual will is revoked by operation of law upon a subsequent marriage, divorce or remarriage.[812]

10–326   However, whether or not the survivor revokes his will, difficulties arise in determining precisely what property is subject to the trust. Of course this will primarily be determined by the agreement. In *Re Green*[813] the agreement specifically provided that each party would leave his property to the other absolutely and, on the death of the survivor, half his residuary estate was to be treated as the survivor's property and the other half was to be treated as property received by the survivor under the will of the first to die. Vaisey J. held that only the property which was to be treated as the property of the first to die was subject to the trust. This decision is justifiable as a matter of construction of the agreement in question but certainly cannot apply where an agreement contains no such provision. In such a case, there is absolutely no doubt that all the property received by the survivor under the mutual will is subject to a trust. If the survivor receives a limited interest, such as a life interest, that property will already be held on an express trust and so there is no scope for the trust imposed by equity. If, on the other hand, he receives an absolute interest, a trust will clearly be imposed but its precise nature is far from clear. In one sense, the survivor will be holding the property on trust for himself for his lifetime and then for the benefit of the ultimate beneficiary of the mutual will. But it is most unclear whether the interest of the survivor is a life interest in the technical sense (in which case he will have no right to resort to the capital) or whether the survivor has the right to dispose of the capital for his own benefit. This problem becomes

---

[808] *supra*; see *Stone v. Hoskins* [1905] P. 194; *Re Hobley (deceased)* (1997) [2006] W.T.L.R. 467.
[809] See Mitchell (1951) 14 M.L.R. 137.
[810] [1930] 2 Ch. 190.
[811] *In the Estate of Heys* [1914] P. 192.
[812] *Re Green* [1951] Ch. 148.
[813] [1951] Ch. 148.

even more acute when the survivor's own property is considered. Is this property subject to a trust from the time the first party dies and, if so, what is the nature of this trust?

It seems fairly clear from the decision in Re Hagger[814] that the survivor's own property is also subject to a trust from the death of the first party to die since in that case the beneficiary was held to have an interest in property which was quite clearly vested in the survivor until his death. But if all the property owned by the survivor at the death of the first party becomes subject to a trust in favour of himself for life and thereafter for the ultimate beneficiary of the mutual will, the survivor will not be able to dispose of his own property for his own benefit without committing a breach of trust. Further, what happens to any property acquired by the survivor after the death of the first party? Does it immediately become subject to the same trust? If so, the effect of the death of the first party will be to make the survivor a life tenant not only of the property which he receives under the will but also of his own property, whether then existing or after acquired. The survivor will, therefore, have no power during the rest of his life to apply any capital for his own benefit. It could of course on the other hand be argued that the intention of the parties could reasonably be assumed to be that the survivor has the right to deal as he wishes with his own property and perhaps also with the property left to him absolutely under the terms of the agreement. The difficulty about this view is that the trust imposed by equity then becomes so uncertain as to be virtually useless since the survivor can destroy the subject matter of the agreement by alienation or dissipation.

10–327

This problem has only rarely had to be considered by the courts because most litigation involving mutual wills does not commence until after the death of the survivor—only then will the ultimate beneficiary discover whether or not the survivor has honoured his agreement. Where the subject matter of the agreement is a specific property,[815] the beneficiaries of the mutual will can clearly recover it or, if the survivor has in breach of trust sold it during his lifetime, its proceeds of sale and their product. But where the subject matter is, as is more usual, each party's residuary estate, litigation commenced after the death of the survivor can in practice only be concerned with the property owned by the survivor at his death; consequently, the English courts have generally been content to apply the terms of the agreement to this property. However, in the Australian case of Birmingham v. Renfrew,[816] Dixon J. considered the nature of the trust imposed during the life of the survivor and said this:

10–328

"The purpose of an arrangement for corresponding wills must often be, as in this case, to enable the survivor during his life to deal as absolute owner with the property passing under the will of the party first dying. That is to say, the object of the transaction is to put the survivor in a position to enjoy for his own benefit the full ownership so that, for instance, he may convert it and expend the proceeds if he choose. But when he dies he is to bequeath

---

[814] [1930] 2 Ch. 190.
[815] As it was in Re Newey (deceased) [1994] 2 N.Z.L.R. 590 (High Court of New Zealand).
[816] (1937) 57 C.L.R. 666 at 689 (High Court of Australia).

what is left in the manner agreed upon. It is only by the special doctrines of equity that such a floating obligation, suspended, so to speak, during the lifetime of the survivor can descend upon the assets at his death and crystallise into a trust. No doubt gifts and settlements, inter vivos, if calculated to defeat the intention of the compact, could not be made by the survivor and his right of disposition, inter vivos, is, therefore, not unqualified. But, substantially, the purpose of the arrangement will often be to allow full enjoyment for the survivor's own benefit and advantage upon condition that at his death the residue shall pass as arranged."

10–329   This decision was cited with approval by Carnwath J. in *Re Goodchild (deceased)*,[817] where he held that: "the trust which is held binding in equity . . . is an unusual form of trust, since it does not prevent the surviving testator using the assets during his lifetime. It is 'a kind of floating trust which finally attaches to such property as he leaves upon his death'[818]". A somewhat similar view was expressed by Brightman J. in *Ottaway v. Norman*,[819] a case concerning secret trusts, where he said: "I am content to assume for present purposes but without so deciding that if property is given to the primary donee on the understanding that the primary donee will dispose by will of such assets, if any, as he may have at his command at his death in favour of the secondary donee, a valid trust is created in favour of the secondary donee which is in suspense during the lifetime of the primary donee, but attaches to the estate of the primary donee at the moment of the latter's death."

10–330   These views undoubtedly recognise what actually happens in most mutual will cases. However, the passages from *Birmingham v. Renfrew* cited with approval by Carnwath J. seem to envisage the possibility of the ultimate beneficiary restraining an *inter vivos* disposition by the survivor (this would certainly be possible where the subject matter of the mutual will is a specific property and the beneficiaries of the will discover that the survivor intends to sell it). On the other hand, Brightman J. instead limits the scope of the trust to the property available to the survivor at this death (this difference may be because Brightman J. was actually dealing with a secret trust rather than with mutual wills).

10–331   It would be extremely interesting to see how, where the subject matter of mutual wills was each party's residue, a court reacted to an attempt to restrain an *inter vivos* disposition by the survivor and, in particular, whether any relief given was limited to the property received under the will of the first to die or also extended to the survivor's own property. It would also have been extremely interesting to see how the court dealt with the attempt which was made by the unsuccessful claimants in *Birch v. Curtis*[820] to recover part of the property subject to the alleged mutual will from someone to whom the survivor had given it during his lifetime—in this case the subject matter of the agreement had been the survivor's entire estate, although he

---

[817] [1996] 1 W.L.R. 694 at 700.
[818] Citing *Birmingham v. Renfrew* (1937) 57 C.L.R. 666, *per* Latham C.J. at 675 (High Court of Australia).
[819] [1972] Ch. 698 at 713.
[820] [2002] W.T.L.R. 965.

only received a specific property under the will of the first to die, and he subsequently sold that property and purchased a property in the joint names of himself and a new wife. No matter how the courts resolve difficulties of this type if and when the occasion arises, it must in any event be said that it seems hardly satisfactory to describe the suspended obligation referred to by the judges in the passages set out above as a trust; such an obligation clearly lacks the element of certainty of subject matter which is one of the principal requirements of a valid trust. The only answer to this conceptual difficulty may well be to regard the trust imposed to give effect to mutual wills as an entrenched historical anomaly.

3. *The Nature of the Trust Imposed by Equity*

It is quite clear that the trust imposed to give effect to mutual wills is not an   **10–332**
express trust. However, there is a difference of opinion as to whether this trust is an implied or resulting trust or a constructive trust. Nothing turns on the classification adopted. Earlier editions of this work have suggested that it should be classified as an "implied, though not a resulting" trust.[821] However, in *Re Cleaver*[822] Nourse J. took the view that it should be classified as a constructive trust. Both views are referred to with apparent approval in different sections of the judgment in *Re Dale*.[823] However, since the trust imposed to give effect to mutual wills is imposed to prevent the survivor obtaining a benefit by his own fraudulent conduct, it seems to the author of the present edition of this work that that trust is akin to the types of constructive trust described in the previous section of this chapter and should, therefore, be classified as a constructive trust.

VI. THE VENDOR AS CONSTRUCTIVE TRUSTEE

When a vendor has entered into a contract of sale which is capable of being   **10–333**
specifically enforced, equity regards as done that which ought to be done; this in accordance with one of its earliest maxims of equity. This is one of the situations in which the equitable doctrine of conversion still operates[824]; equity therefore regards the purchaser as owner of the subject matter of the contract and the vendor as owner of the purchase money. The operation of this equitable doctrine does not, of course, affect the legal title to the subject matter of the contract, which remains in the vendor pending performance of the contract. Thus the effect of the operation of the doctrine is to separate the legal and beneficial ownership of the property; it is, therefore, only to be expected that equity regards the vendor as a constructive trustee of the property pending performance of the contract. No corresponding trust of the purchase money will arise simply because such a trust would lack the

---

[821] (5th edn), p.154.

[822] [1981] 1 W.L.R. 939. See also *Healey v. Brown* [2002] W.T.L.R. 849.

[823] [1994] Ch. 31.

[824] Since 1996, the doctrine has not operated when land is held on trust for sale (Trusts of Land and Appointment of Trustees Act 1996, s.3); until then this was the most significant example of the operation of the doctrine.

necessary certainty of subject matter; however, the vendor acquires a lien or charge on the property for the unpaid purchase money.

10–334   The operation of the equitable doctrine of conversion and the consequential existence of a constructive trust are important because of the effect that can be produced both on the devolution of property and on the liabilities of the parties. Where a party to a contract dies after the equitable doctrine has operated, his property will devolve as if the contract has been performed. Thus, if a vendor or purchaser of freehold land dies after the doctrine of conversion has operated, the interest of the vendor devolves with his personalty and the interest of the purchaser devolves with his realty. However today[825] this is important only in the relatively unlikely case of a testator leaving his realty and his personalty (or his land and his pure personalty) to different persons. But the effect of the operation of the doctrine of conversion on the liabilities of the parties remains as important today as it has ever been; this is precisely because of the fact that the vendor becomes a trustee of the subject matter of the contract. His liability to deal with the property as a trustee can be relied on by the purchaser not only in the event that the vendor fails to take reasonable care to preserve the property in a reasonable state of preservation[826] but also to recover secret profits[827] and to follow the subject matter of the trust into its product[828]; the corollary of this, however, is that the purchaser becomes liable for all the risks attendant upon ownership, in particular that of accidental destruction.[829] Of course, this trusteeship of the vendor is of an extremely unusual nature; the vendor himself retains a substantial interest in the property for the simple reason that, in the event that the contract is not in the end completed, he will once again become absolute legal and beneficial owner; further, he is entitled to receive and retain any income produced by the property until the completion of the sale.[830] However, as soon as the purchase price has been paid in full, the qualified nature of the vendor's trusteeship will disappear since he no longer has any interest to protect; from that moment onwards he will be a bare trustee of the property for the purchaser.

10–335   Since the doctrine of conversion will only operate when a contract of sale is capable of being specifically enforced, it is a prerequisite of its operation that the failure of the vendor to transfer the subject matter of the contract to the purchaser is incapable of being adequately compensated by an award of damages. Little or no difficulties have been encountered in applying the equitable doctrine to the relatively few contracts for the sale of chattels

---

[825] Before 1926, when real and personal property devolved in different ways on intestacy, this effect was of much greater importance.

[826] *Clarke v. Ramuz* [1891] 2 Q.B. 456 at 459–460; see also *Michaels v. Harley House (Marylebone)* [2000] Ch. 104.

[827] *English v. Dedham Vale Properties* [1978] 1 W.L.R. 95.

[828] *Lake v. Bayliss* [1974] 1 W.L.R. 1075.

[829] The Law Commission has proposed that this risk should pass only on completion (Law Commission No.191 (1990), para.2.25); although this proposal has not been enacted, it has been accepted by the draftsmen of standard form conveyancing contracts; see, for example, the provision to this effect which has been inserted in the Standard Conditions of Sale as Condition 5.1.1.

[830] *Cuddon v. Tite* (1858) 1 Giff. 395.

which satisfy this requirement[831]; such contracts are capable of being specifically enforced from the moment at which they are entered into and so the vendor under such a contract will hold its subject matter on trust for the purchaser from the moment of contract. However, the vast majority of contracts which are capable of being specifically enforced are contracts for the sale of land; the application of the equitable doctrine to contracts of this type has encountered difficulties caused by the nature of title to land and, in particular, by the fact that a contract for the sale of land is not specifically enforceable until the vendor has made title in accordance with the contract or the purchaser has agreed to accept such other title as the vendor actually has. The constructive trusteeship of the vendor does not therefore arise until title has been so made or accepted,[832] when it is generally thought to have retrospective effect to the date of the contract. This is not an appropriate place to consider the various ways in which this basic principle has been developed in the light of the many different situations which can arise under the various types of contracts for the sale of land; these matters are fully discussed elsewhere.[833]

It has to be admitted that the inevitable self-interest of the vendor in the **10–336** successful conclusion of the transaction does not sit very easily with his classification as a trustee. For this reason, many doubts have been expressed[834] as to whether it is appropriate for the relationship of vendor and purchaser to be classified as that of trustee and beneficiary. There is no doubt that the classification has led to the development of some anomalous rules but it is by no means certain that different anomalies would not have resulted from basing the relationship entirely on the law of contract. In any event, for the moment there seems little justification for or likelihood of any attempt to recast the relationship between the vendor and the purchaser under a specifically enforceable contract on any basis other than that of constructive trustee and beneficiary.

VII. THE MORTGAGEE AS CONSTRUCTIVE TRUSTEE

At one time[835] the majority of mortgages of land were effected by means of **10–337** transfer of the subject matter of the mortgage to the mortgagee subject to a proviso for retransfer to the mortgagor upon discharge of the mortgage debt; many judges then saw fit to describe the mortgagee as a constructive trustee of the mortgaged property. Even when the courts came to recognise that the mortgagee, as such, was not a trustee at all,[836] it was still clearly established that he might nevertheless become a constructive trustee; first, he might be held to have become a constructive trustee as a result of the exercise of his powers under the mortgage; and, secondly, once the mortgage debt had been fully repaid, he did become a constructive trustee of the

---

[831] Such as contracts to sell a rare antique, a rare book, or shares in a private company.

[832] *Lysaght v. Edwards* (1876) 2 Ch.D. 499 at 506–507, 510, 518.

[833] See *Constructive Trusts* (3rd edn, 1997), pp.282–292 (4th edn in preparation) and Farrand, *Contract & Conveyance* (4th edn, 1983), pp.167–173.

[834] Notably by Waters, *The Constructive Trust* (1964), pp.141–142.

[835] Prior to the enactment of the Property Legislation of 1925.

[836] See *Marquis Cholmondeley v. Lord Clinton* (1820) 2 Jac. & W. 1.

mortgaged property pending its retransfer to the mortgagor. But now[837] that mortgages of land cannot be created by the transfer of its subject matter to the mortgagee, the latter cannot possibly become a constructive trustee of the mortgaged property for the simple reason that it cannot now be vested in him; he can, therefore, only become a constructive trustee of property which reaches his hands as a result of the exercise of his powers under the mortgage.

10–338   After some initial uncertainty, it became clear that the mortgagee was not a trustee of his power of sale and therefore could exercise his express or implied contractual right of sale quite irrespective of the interests of the mortgagor[838]; but it became equally clear that any surplus produced by the exercise of this power of sale was held by the mortgagee on a constructive trust for the mortgagor.[839] However, this old constructive trust of the proceeds of sale seems now to have been totally superseded by the creation of a statutory trust.[840] Further, the better view is that a mortgagee in possession is not a constructive trustee of any rents and profits which he has or should have received but is merely under an obligation to account for them to the mortgagor.[841] It consequently seems that, so far as the mortgagee is concerned, the constructive trust no longer has any role to play.

VIII. TRANSFERS OF PROPERTY WHICH ARE AT LAW INCOMPLETE

10–339   As has already been seen,[842] the formalities necessary for the transfer of the legal title to certain kinds of property cannot all be carried out by the parties themselves. A transfer of registered land is not effective to pass the legal title to that land until the duly executed transfer form is presented to the Land Registry and registered in the Register of Title. Similarly, a transfer of shares is not effective to pass the legal title to those shares until the transferor has complied with the procedure required by the Articles of Association of the company in question and the transfer is duly registered in the Register of Shareholders. In both these cases, the intervention of a third party is necessary to enable legal title to pass; consequently the transfer will not be effective at law until the third party in question acts. However, it has been held that once the parties have complied with all the formal requirements capable of being carried out by themselves, the transfer will become effective in equity and the transferor will hold the property in question on trust for the transferee pending the intervention of the third party. This rule was established in two unconnected cases both named *Re Rose*[843] and for this reason is generally known as the Rule in *Re Rose*.

10–340   The precise scope of this Rule, which is clearly English law at the present time, has already been considered.[844] It is also clear that the trust which

---

[837] Law of Property Act 1925, s.85.
[838] *Warner v. Jacob* (1882) 20 Ch.D. 220.
[839] *Banner v. Berridge* (1881) 18 Ch.D. 254.
[840] Law of Property Act 1925, s.105 (originally Conveyancing Act 1881, s.21(3)).
[841] *Kirkwood v. Thompson* (1865) 2 De G.J. & S. 613.
[842] See *ante*, para 5–007.
[843] [1949] Ch. 78; [1952] Ch. 499.
[844] See *ante*, para 5–026.

arises as a result of the operation of the Rule in *Re Rose* does not arise out of any intention of the parties to that trust; it must, therefore, necessarily be brought into existence by operation of law and should, therefore, be classified as a constructive trust.

CHAPTER 11

CHARITABLE TRUSTS

I. Introduction

11–001 After many decades of debate, the Charities Act 2006[1] finally introduced a statutory definition of charity[2] to replace the longstanding fourfold classification of charitable trusts which was enunciated by Lord Macnaghten in *Commissioners for Special Purposes of Income Tax v. Pemsel* ("*Pemsel's* Case").[3] The case law from which his classification was derived had at least originally been based on the preamble to a statute dating from the reign of Elizabeth I,[4] which is generally known as the Charitable Uses Act 1601.[5] The statute itself had long since been repealed[6] but its preamble remained alive, arguably as a matter of statutory interpretation[7] and certainly as a result of the practice of the courts in continuing to ask whether or not a particular purpose was within the "spirit and intendment" or the "equity" or the "mischief", a practice which sometimes remained necessary in borderline

---

[1] See Maclennan, *Blackstone's Guide to The Charities Act 2006*.

[2] This had earlier been suggested by the Report of the Nathan Committee in 1925 (Cmd. 9538), by the Expenditure Committee of the House of Commons in 1975 (10th Report Session 1974–75) and in the 1989 White Paper "Charities: A Framework for the Future" (Cmd. 694).

[3] [1891] A.C. 531 at 583. His classification, which was based on the argument of Sir Samuel Romilly in *Morice v. Bishop of Durham* (1805) 10 Ves. 522 at 532, was: first, trusts for the relief of poverty; secondly, trusts for the advancement of education; thirdly, trusts for the advancement of religion; and, fourthly, trusts for other purposes beneficial to the community which do not fall under any of the other three heads.

[4] 43 Eliz. I (1601), c.4.

[5] In the preamble of this statute, the following charitable objects are listed: "The relief of aged, impotent and poor people, the maintenance of sick and maimed soldiers and mariners, schools of learning, free schools and schools in universities, the repair of bridges, ports, havens, causeways, churches, sea-banks and highways, the education and preferment of orphans, the relief, stock or maintenance for houses of correction, the marriage of poor maids, the supportation, aid and help of young tradesmen, handicraftsmen and persons decayed, the relief or redemption of prisoners or captives and the aid or ease of any poor inhabitants concerning payment of fifteens, setting out of soldiers and other taxes."

[6] By Mortmain and Charitable Uses Act 1888, s.13(2).

[7] The repealing provision, Mortmain and Charitable Uses Act 1888, s.13(2), itself expressly preserved the preamble, although not specifically for all purposes, and, when that provision was itself repealed by the Charities Act 1960, both that Act and subsequent statutes provided that a reference in any enactment or document to a charitable purpose within the scope of the preamble should be construed as a reference to charity in the meaning which that expression bore as a legal term according to the law of England and Wales. Such a provision is also found in the Charities Act 2006.

cases even in modern times.[8] The new legislation was enacted because the government review on which it was based[9] took the view that Lord Macnaghten's four heads and the preamble had produced uncertainty and confusion and did not accurately represent the full range of different types of organisation which enjoy charitable status in the twenty-first Century; it was hoped that the new statutory definition of charity as an organisation which provides public benefit and which has one or more of the listed 11 specific purposes and one general purpose would provide a clearer framework while retaining existing case law and the flexibility to evolve as society changes.

The law and practice of charitable trusts, but not the definition of charity, **11–002** had already been reformed by a series of statutes commencing with the Charities Act 1960.[10] This Act, which implemented, wholly or in part, many of the recommendations of the Report of the Nathan Committee on charitable trusts published in 1952,[11] renovated what had by then become an appalling mass of statute law relating to charitable trusts by clearing a great deal of dead wood from the statute book. What was not obsolete was extracted from those statutes and reenacted in the new statute, which therefore contained the whole of the statute law relating to charitable trusts from the sixteenth century onwards and added new provisions in keeping with the twentieth Century. Subsequently, as a result of the Woodfield Report,[12] further reforms were enacted in the Charities Act 1992 with the intention of increasing the powers of what is now known as the Charity Commission, a statutory governmental organisation which regulates charities subject to the supervision of the courts, and of controlling abuse and maladministration by the trustees of charitable trusts. The Charities Act 1960 and much of the Charities Act 1992 were subsequently consolidated in the Charities Act 1993, which has in turn been substantially amended by the Charities Act 2006, both by amendments of pre-existing provisions and by the insertion of new provisions into that Act. The final section of this chapter contains a summary

---

[8] Thus in *Scottish Burial Reform and Cremation Society v. Glasgow City Corporation* [1968] A.C. 138, the House of Lords had to decide the novel question of whether or not cremation was a charitable purpose. In the course of deciding that it was, the House acknowledged that recourse to the preamble was undoubtedly the accepted practice, although "in only a very wide and broad sense" (see at 151); this meant, in the words of Lord Wilberforce (at 154), "that what must be regarded is not the wording of the preamble, but the effect of decisions given by the courts as to its scope, decisions which have endeavoured to keep the law as to charities moving according as new social needs arise or old ones become obsolete or satisfied". Similarly, in *Incorporated Council of Law Reporting for England and Wales v. Attorney-General* [1972] Ch. 73, when the Court of Appeal had to decide the equally novel question of whether law reporting was a charitable purpose, its decision that the publication or dissemination of law reports was a purpose beneficial to the community and therefore charitable was specifically based on the conclusion that that purpose was within the spirit and intendment of the preamble to the Charitable Uses Act 1601.

[9] A Report published by the Government's Strategy Unit in 2002 entitled "Private Action, Public Benefit.

[10] For accounts of the Charities Act 1960, see Nathan, *Charities Act 1960*; Maurice, *Charities Act 1960*.

[11] Cmd. 9538 (its full title is the "Committee on the Law and Practice relating to Charitable Trusts").

[12] "Efficiency Scrutiny of the Supervision of Charities" (1987 National Audit Office Report); House of Commons Paper 380, 1986–87.

of the present law governing the administration of charitable trusts as laid down in this legislation.[13]

II. DISTINCTIONS FROM PRIVATE TRUSTS

11–003　A charitable trust is intended to benefit society as a whole or an appreciable part of society whereas a private trust is intended to benefit defined persons or defined classes of persons. In general, charitable trusts are subject to the same rules as private trusts but, because of their public nature, they enjoy a number of advantages which are not shared by private trusts.

1. *Perpetuity*[14]

11–004　Charitable trusts are not subject to that aspect of the Rule against Perpetuities generally known as the Rule against Inalienability. Despite the fact that the objects of a charity may last for ever, a gift for such purposes will nevertheless be valid.[15]

11–005　However, charitable trusts are, generally, subject to that aspect of the Rule against Perpetuities generally known as the Rule against Remoteness in that the charity's interest in the property in question must vest in the charity within the perpetuity period. Thus, in *Re Lord Stratheden and Campbell*[16] an annuity of £100 was bequeathed for provision "for the Central London Rangers on the appointment of the next lieutenant-colonel". Since the next lieutenant-colonel might not be appointed within the perpetuity period, the limitation transgressed the rule and the gift was held by Romer J. to be invalid. However, provided that a trust in favour of one charity vests within the perpetuity period, a gift over from that charity to another charity on the happening of an event which may occur outside the perpetuity period will nevertheless be valid.[17] However, this exception does not apply to a gift over to a charity which follows a gift to a non-charity[18]; in such a case, the normal rules as to vesting within the perpetuity period must be observed. It is as if for this purpose the law regards "charity" as a unity—thus a gift from one charity to another charity is from or to this "unity" so that there is no scope for the operation of the perpetuity rule, while a gift from or to this unity is subject to that rule in the usual way.

---

[13] This is discussed in greater detail in Maclennan, *Blackstone's Guide to The Charities Act 2006.*

[14] See *ante*, para 7–004.

[15] *Chamberlayne v. Brockett* (1872) L.R. 8 Ch.App. 206.

[16] [1894] 3 Ch. 265, applying *Chamberlayne v. Brockett* (1872) L.R. 8 Ch.App. 206. It is now possible to take advantage of the "wait and see" rule introduced by Perpetuities and Accumulations Act 1964, s.3 in respect of instruments which take effect after July 15, 1964. This will continue to be possible under the proposed new legislation governing perpetuities.

[17] *Re Tyler* [1891] 3 Ch. 252 but compare *Re Dalziel* [1943] Ch. 277; these cases are discussed *ante*, para 3–106.

[18] *Re Bowen* [1893] 2 Ch. 491 at 494; *Re Peel's Release* [1921] 2 Ch. 218; *Re Wightwick's Will Trusts* [1950] Ch. 260; *Re Spensley's Will Trusts* [1954] Ch. 233.

At present, the Rule against Accumulations[19] applies to charitable trusts **11–006** in the same way as it applies to private trusts. However, the proposed new legislation on perpetuities and accumulations, which will introduce a 125-year accumulation period, will for the first time treat private trusts and charitable trusts differently in this respect. The proposed 125-year period will not apply to charitable trusts, where accumulation will only be permitted for 21 years; this has been proposed on the basis that it is not consistent with the public benefit which charitable trusts are supposed to produce for income to be withdrawn from a charitable purpose for any longer than that.

2. *Certainty*

A charitable trust will not fail for uncertainty of objects provided that the **11–007** settlor clearly intended the fund to go exclusively to charity.[20] If this requirement is satisfied, the trust will not fail if the settlor omits sufficiently to particularise the objects.[21] If this occurs, a *cy-près* scheme[22] will be made to make the objects more precise. For this purpose too it seems that the law regards charity as a unity so that, once a gift to this unity is established, that gift cannot fail.

3. *Construction*

In construing instruments in circumstances where the settlor or testator **11–008** intended to set up a charitable trust but did so ambiguously, it is established that a "benignant" construction should be given if possible.[23] This was confirmed by the House of Lords in *I.R.C. v. McMullen*[24] (although it was not in the event necessary to resort to such a construction in that case) and such a construction was subsequently adopted by the House of Lords in *Guild v. I.R.C.*[25]

4. *Taxation*

For taxation purposes, the distinction between a charitable trust and a **11–009** private trust is seen both in the special taxation privileges which are afforded to a charitable trust and in the taxation inducements which are offered to individuals for them to confer benefits on charitable trusts.

---

[19] See *ante*, para 7–046.
[20] See *Moggridge v. Thackwell* (1803) 7 Ves. 36, affirmed (1807) 13 Ves. 416. Provided that the gift has a charitable object, it does not matter that the precise purposes specified are too vague and uncertain to be charitable themselves; *Re Koeppler's Will Trusts* [1986] Ch. 423.
[21] *Harris v. Sharp* (1986) [2003] T.L.I. 41, where the principle of executory trusts, *ante* para 5–073, was relied on in this connection.
[22] See *post*, para 11–118.
[23] See *ante*, para 3–011 in relation to construction of private trusts.
[24] [1981] A.C. 1 at 16. The facts are stated *post*, para 11–084. See also *Re Hetherington (deceased)* [1990] Ch. 1.
[25] [1992] 2 A.C. 310.

(A)   Income Tax and Corporation Tax

(1)   A Charity's Liability to Income Tax and Corporation Tax
11–010   In this respect, it is necessary to distinguish between the investment income and the trading income of a charity. The investment income of an unincorporated charity is exempt from income tax provided that that income is applied for charitable purposes only.[26] However, if that charity carries on a trade, its profits from the trade are exempt from income tax only if, first, they are applied solely for its charitable purpose and, secondly, if either the purpose (or one of the primary purposes) of the charity is to carry on that particular trade or the work carried out in connection with the trade is mainly done by the beneficiaries of the charity.[27] In the case of an incorporated charity, the same principles apply to corporation tax.[28]

11–011   Whether or not a body is established for charitable purposes is a question of law to be decided in accordance with the usual principles but the question of whether or to what extent income is applied to charitable purposes is a question of fact.[29] However, in *I.R.C. v. Helen Slater Charitable Trust*[30] the Court of Appeal held that one charity "applies" its income for charitable purposes if it pays that income to another charity, even if the terms of the instrument governing the second charity are almost identical to those of the instrument governing the first charity.

(2)   The Treatment of Donations
11–012   Donations by an individual to charity can, in appropriate circumstances, be treated as donations of the amount in question after the deduction by the donor of income tax at the basic rate, in which case the charity is entitled to claim a refund of the income tax paid. In 2008/09 the basic rate of income tax is 20 per cent. Accordingly, where an individual is liable to income tax at this rate, he can enable the charity to receive a donation of £5,000 by making a net payment to it of £4,000.[31] If the donor is a higher rate taxpayer, his threshold for the payment of higher rate tax at 40 per cent will also be increased by the gross cost of his donation, thereby effectively saving him a further 20 per cent of his donation. Consequently, where an individual who is liable to income tax at the higher rate has paid £4,000 to charity, he can save a further £800 which he would otherwise have had to pay in higher rate income tax; the net cost to him after income tax of paying £5,000 per annum to charity is therefore reduced still further to £3,200. This system now[32] operates   only   under   what   is   known   as   Gift   Aid;   which   requires

---

[26] Income Tax Act 2007, ss.529–537.

[27] *ibid.*, ss.524–528.

[28] Income and Corporation Taxees Act 1988, ss.505(1), 506(1).

[29] See *Williams' Trustees v. I.R.C.* [1947] A.C. 447.

[30] [1982] Ch. 49.

[31] Because until 2008–2009 the basic rate of Income Tax was 22% and the reduction to 20% would have deprived charities of a 25th of their anticipated income from donations, charities have been allowed to continue to recover 22% on a transitional basis for 2008–2009, 2009–2010 and 2010–2011.

[32] Since April 6, 2000 (until then, the donor had to execute a deed by which he covenanted to pay a part of his income to a charity for a period which was capable of lasting for more than three years (four-year periods were habitually employed); this enabled the charity to recover the basic rate tax paid thereon but did not enable the donor to recover higher rate tax.

merely a written or electronic declaration by the donor (in the case of gifts made other than in writing, the charity has to send the donor a written notification).[33] In contrast, corporate donors can now[34] deduct the amount of charitable donations from their profits; consequently, charities no longer need to reclaim any tax and the full amount of the donation can, therefore, be paid directly to the charity by the corporate donor.[35]

(B) Capital Gains Tax

A capital gain accruing to a charity will not attract capital gains tax provided **11–013** that the gain in question is both applicable and is in fact applied to the charitable purposes.[36] If the charity is incorporated, then it is entitled to exemption from corporation tax on its capital gains on the same basis.[37]

An inducement to make gifts of capital assets to charities is provided by **11–014** the fact that the capital gains tax is not payable on such a gift; in contrast, when an individual makes a gift to another individual, he potentially has to pay capital gains (basically the difference between the value of the asset at the time of the gift and its value at the time of its acquisition,[38] which is at present, after any available exemptions, taxed at 18 per cent). No such relief is necessary in the case of corporate donors because capital gains made by corporations are subject to corporation tax rather than to capital gains tax.

(C) Inheritance Tax

In comparison with private individuals or corporations, charities enjoy **11–015** important privileges with regard to inheritance tax:

    (i) gifts made to charities, whether *inter vivos* or by will, are wholly exempt from inheritance tax[39];

    (ii) gifts made to a charity by way of a payment from a discretionary trust are also wholly exempt from inheritance tax[40];

    (iii) heritage property which is lent to nationally important institutions, such as the National Gallery, the British Museum or the National Trust, is wholly exempt from inheritance tax, whether lent *inter vivos* or following a death; and

    (iv) the Treasury is empowered to accept in lieu of inheritance tax a gift of land of outstanding scenic or historical or scientific interest, gifts of buildings of outstanding historical or architectural or aesthetic interest, property given as a source of income for the upkeep of

---

[33] Income Tax Act 2007, ss.413–418, 520–521.

[34] Until April 5, 2000, the position of corporate donors was the same as that of individual donors.

[35] Income and Corporation Taxes Act 1988, s.339 (as amended by Finance Act 2000, s.40).

[36] Taxation of Chargeable Gains Act 1992, s.256.

[37] Capital gains tax applies only to individuals (and to trusts which are taxed as individuals). Capital gains made by corporations are potentially subject to corporation tax.

[38] Taxation of Chargeable Gains Act 1992, s.35.

[39] Inheritance Tax Act 1984, s.23.

[40] *ibid.*, s.76.

such land or buildings, and pictures, books, manuscripts, works of art, and so forth, of national or historic or scientific interest.[41]

It is, however, important to emphasise that, as a general rule, the exemptions apply only to gifts to charities which are immediate and absolute. To this general rule, there is the qualification that, if the donor wishes a charity to benefit only after the death of himself and his spouse, he can leave a life interest in the property to the spouse, and on the latter's death, to the charity absolutely. Inheritance tax will not be payable on the death either of the donor or of his spouse.

(D)   Stamp Duty Land Tax and Stamp Duty

11–016   Charities are exempt from stamp duty land tax in relation to any conveyance, transfer or letting of land made or agreed to be made to them[42] and are also exempt from stamp duty on any transfer of stocks and shares.[43]

(E)   Value Added Tax

11–017   Although there is no general exemption for charities from value added tax, a considerable number of supplies by charities are zero-rated which means that no value added tax is charged on the supply.[44] The construction of buildings intended for use solely for charitable purposes are also zero-rated although this exemption can be and often is waived to enable the charity to recover the value added tax it itself has to pay.[45]

(F)   Council Tax

11–018   All of the successive regimes which have governed the different taxes which have from time to time been payable by landowners to local authorities have provided for relief (both mandatory and discretionary) to be given to charities. Mandatory relief to the extent of 80 per cent[46] of the non-domestic rates which would otherwise be chargeable is available in respect of land occupied by or used by trustees for a charity and wholly or mainly used for charitable purposes.

With regard to occupation, it will generally be clear that the charity or the trustees of the charity are in occupation but difficulties may arise where the charity has provided a house or accommodation for its staff, in which case it appears that mandatory relief can only be claimed if the occupation is necessary for the more efficient performance of their duties and for that reason constitutes occupation by the charity.[47]

---

[41] ibid., s.27.
[42] Finance Act 2003, s.68 and Sch.8.
[43] Finance Act 1982, s.129.
[44] Value Added Tax Act 1994, s.30 and Sch.8, Group 16.
[45] ibid., s.30 and Sch.8, Group 5; s.51 and Sch.10.
[46] Special mandatory relief in the form of total exemption from rates is available in respect of places of public religious worship and buildings ancillary to them; Local Government Finance Act 1988, Sch.5, para.11 and see *Broxtowe Borough Council v. Birch* [1983] 1 W.L.R. 314 for the meaning of "public religious worship".
[47] *Glasgow Corporation v. Johnstone* [1965] A.C. 609; *Northern Ireland Valuation Court v. Fermanagh Protestant Board of Education* [1969] 1 W.L.R. 1708.

With regard to the requirement that the land be wholly or mainly used for charitable purposes, it appears to be required that the charity's use of the property be wholly "ancillary to" or "directly facilitates" the carrying out of its main charitable purposes.[48] The meaning of these expressions was considered by the House of Lords in *Oxfam v. Birmingham City District Council*,[49] where Oxfam claimed relief from rates in respect of gift shops which it used for the sale of articles, mostly clothing, which had been donated to it, the profits being applied to the sale of objects brought from Oxfam. It was held that the charity gift shops did not "directly facilitate" the main object of the charity and that rating relief could not be claimed. Lord Cross held[50] that there was a distinction between user for the purpose of getting in, raising or earning money for the charity, as opposed to user for purposes directly related to the achievement of the objects of the charity. The charity gift shops simply raised money for Oxfam and were accordingly excluded from relief. The decision has been reversed by statute in respect of such shops so as to make them eligible for relief; however, it remains intact in relation to property of other types which is owned by charities.

In addition to this mandatory relief, which is obviously obtainable as of right, any local authority has a discretion to reduce further, or to remit entirely, the tax which would otherwise be payable by a charity.

III. THE DEFINITION OF CHARITY

Section 1 of the Charities Act 2006 provides: **11–019**

"(1) For the purposes of the law of England and Wales, "charity" means an institution which—

(a) is established for charitable purposes only, and
(b) falls to be subject to the control of the High Court in the exercise of its jurisdiction with respect to charities.

(2) The definition of 'charity' in subsection (1) does not apply for the purposes of an enactment if a different definition of that term applies for those purposes by virtue of that or any other enactment.

(3) A reference in any enactment or document to a charity within the meaning of the Charitable Uses Act 1601 (c.4) or the preamble to it is to be construed as a reference to charity as defined by subsection (1)."

The definition in subsection 1 parallels a definition in the Charities Act   **11–020**
1993 but that definition only concerned the question of whether the Charity Commission and the High Court had jurisdiction to register and regulate the charity in question. Now the issue is whether the purpose is or is not

---

[48] *Glasgow Corporation v. Johnstone* [1965] A.C. 609 at 622, *per* Lord Reid.
[49] [1976] A.C. 126. Compare *Aldous v. Southwark L.B.C.* [1968] 1 W.L.R. 1671.
[50] *ibid.* at 146.

charitable although the trust in question will still only be a charity for the purposes of English law if it is subject to the control of the High Court; this will in practice be determined by whether or not any of the trustees is within the jurisdiction.[51]

11–021   Subsection 2 acknowledges that charitable status can also be conferred by any other legislation which contains a different definition for its own purposes; a typical example would be an Education Act. Such a charity would inevitably be regulated by some body other than the Charity Commission and the High Court, typically by a body established by the legislation in question. The Charities Act 2006 also recognises that even a charity which falls within the definition in subsection 1 can be primarily regulated by some body other than the than the Charity Commission and the High Court. Section 13 obliges any body or Minister of the Crown who is the principal regulator in relation to an exempt charity (certain charities listed in the Charities Act 1993[52]) to "do all that it or he reasonably can to meet the compliance objective[53] in relation to the charity".

11–022   Subsection 3 is, in effect, a reenactment of a provision in the Charities Acts 1960, 1992 and 1993. Those provisions made it clear that the law of England and Wales, which had been based on the preamble to the Charitable Uses Act 1601 for a period approaching 400 years, should remain intact. Subsection 3, by referring to subsection 1, has a more limited function, merely ensuring that trusts which were charitable under the pre-existing law retain that status; unlike its predecessors, it does not permit recourse to the preamble for the purpose of deciding whether new trusts are or are not charitable.

11–023   Section 2 of the Charities Act 2006 contains the new statutory definition of charitable purpose which must, according to subsection (1)(a), fall within the list of 11 specific purposes and one general purpose in subsection (2) and, according to subsection (1)(b), be for the public benefit. The latter requirement will be considered first.

1. *Public Benefit*

11–024   Section 3(3) of the Charities Act 2006 provides that the requirement in section 2(1)(b) is a reference "to the public benefit as that term is understood for the purposes of the law relating to charities in England and Wales". Thus there is no new statutory definition of public benefit and so the pre-existing law as to what constitutes public benefit has been preserved. However, it is no longer to be presumed that a purpose of a particular description is for the

---

[51] *Gaudiya Mission v. Bramachary* [1998] Ch. 341; thus in *Re Carapiet's Trusts* [2002] EWHC 1304 (Ch), [2002] W.T.L.R. 989 the trust in question was subject to the jurisdiction of the High Court because the trust property was held by a bank in England.

[52] Sch.2, as amended by Charities Act 2006, s.11 (*ibid.*, s.12 increases the extent to which such charities are subject to regulated under the Charities Act 1993).

[53] One of a number of statutory objectives imposed on the Charity Commission by s.7; this one is "to promote compliance by charity trustees with their legal obligations in exercising control and management of the administration of their charities".

public benefit.[54] The removal of this presumption is probably the most radical change made by the Charities Act 2006.

This is because trusts which fell within the first three of the four heads of **11–025** charity identified by Lord Macnaghten in *Pemsel's* Case,[55] trusts for the relief of poverty, trusts for the advancement of education and trusts for the advancement of religion, enjoyed the benefit of a presumption that they were established for the benefit of the public. The strength of the presumption varied across the three categories. In the case of trusts for the relief of poverty, it was virtually impossible for the presumption to be rebutted save where the trust was for the benefit of an extremely small number of persons all connected with the settlor. In the case of trusts for the advancement of religion, the presumption was not rebutted merely by reason of the fact that the trust was for the benefit of a relatively small number of persons restricted both by their beliefs and by where they worshipped; thus what was known as "a class within a class" was compatible with public benefit. In contrast, in the case of trusts for the advancement of education, the presumption was rebutted whenever the trust was for the benefit of a group of persons who were ascertained by reference to some personal tie, such as the relations of a particular individual, the members of a particular family, the members of a particular association, or the employees of a common employer.

On the other hand, in the case of trusts which fell within Lord Macnaght- **11–026** en's fourth head, trusts for other purposes beneficial to be public, there was no such presumption and the existence of public benefit had to be positively demonstrated. In particular, as will also be seen below, any class within a class or double restriction of the type permitted in trusts for the advancement of religion was absolutely fatal.

Now all charitable trusts need positively to demonstrate the provision of **11–027** public benefit. Nor, as was the case under the pre-existing law, does the public benefit requirement have to be satisfied only at the time of their creation. They are now obliged to demonstrate that they satisfy this requirement on an annual basis by means of reports to the Charity Commission,[56] which in turn must issue guidance in pursuant of its public benefit objective of promoting awareness and understanding of the operation of the requirement.[57] It has been clear from the outset that a particular target of the Charity Commission will be charities such as private schools and private hospitals which charge relatively high fees for the services which they provide; it will become increasingly necessary for such charities to be able to demonstrate that they are providing benefits to the public as a whole. It will certainly no longer be enough that the services which they provide to those who pay for them save the Exchequer the public funds which would otherwise have to be expended on providing those services to their recipients free of charge; there is no doubt that it is positive benefit to the public rather than non-recourse to public services which must now be demonstrated.

---

[54] By virtue of section 3(2), to which, by virtue of section 3(4), section 3(3) is expressly subject.

[55] [1891] A.C. 531 at 583.

[56] See the guidelines to the Charity Commission's Approach to Public Benefit which are published on its website at *http://www.charity-commission.gov.uk/spr/pubben.asp*.

[57] Charities Act 2006, s.4(1), (2).

(A) The Basic Public Benefit Rule

11–028 A straightforward illustration of the basic public benefit rule was *Re Compton*,[58] where a trust for the education of the descendants of three named persons was held not to be a valid charitable trust, because the beneficiaries were defined by reference to a personal relationship and the trust therefore lacked the quality of a public trust; the trust was in reality a family trust and not one for the benefit of a section of the public. Similarly, in *Re Holbourn Aero Components Air Raid Distress Fund*,[59] an emergency fund which had been built up during the Second World War had been used partly for comforts for ex-employees serving in the Forces and, subsequently, for employees who had suffered distress from air-raids. It was held that, because of the absence of any public element, no charitable trust had been created and the surplus funds, in respect of which the application had been made to the court, should be returned to the contributors.[60]

11–029 However, the most important illustration is to be found in the decision of the House of Lords in *Oppenheim v. Tobacco Securities Trust Co.*,[61] where the decision in *Re Compton* was applied to a trust for a much more extensive class of beneficiaries. The trustees were directed to apply funds in providing for the education of children of employees or ex-employees of British American Tobacco or any of its subsidiary or allied companies. The employees numbered over 110,000. A majority of the House of Lords held that, although the group of persons indicated was numerous, the nexus between them was employment by a particular employer and it therefore followed that the trust did not satisfy the test of public benefit which was required to establish it as charitable. The argument that the court should take into account the number of employees was rejected. As Lord Normand said,[62] if there is no public element to be found in the bare nexus of common employment, all attempts to build up the public element out of circumstances which had no necessary relation with it but were adventitious, accidental or variable must be unavailing where the settlor had chosen to define the selected class solely by the attribute of common employment. Putting this more generally, an aggregate of individuals ascertained by reference to some personal tie, for example, blood or contract, such as the relations of a particular individual, the members of a particular family or the members of a particular association, does not amount to the public or a section of the public for the purpose of the general rule; a trust for that aggregate of individuals will not, accordingly, rank as legally charitable.[63]

11–030 Lord MacDermott dissented, saying[64] that he saw "much difficulty in dividing the qualities or attributes, which may serve to bind human beings

---

[58] [1945] Ch. 123.

[59] [1946] Ch. 194.

[60] On the basis that they were the members of an unincorporated association (see *ante*, para 9–084).

[61] [1951] A.C. 297, in turn applied in *I.R.C. v. Educational Grants Association* [1967] Ch. 993 (up to 85% of the income of an educational trust was paid to children of employees of Metal Box Ltd.; income tax was not recoverable because the income was not being applied only for charitable purposes).

[62] *ibid.* at 310–311.

[63] *Re Scarisbrick* [1951] Ch. 622 at 649, *per* Jenkins L.J.

[64] [1951] A.C. 297 at 317.

into classes, into two mutually exclusive groups, the one involving individual status and purely personal, the other disregarding such status and quite
impersonal. As a task this seems to me no less baffling and elusive than the
problem to which it is directed, namely the determination of what is and
what is not a section of the public for the purposes of this branch of the law."
Subsequently in *Dingle v. Turner*[65] Lord Cross was of the same opinion.
Moreover, he felt that whether or not the potential beneficiaries of a trust
could fairly be said to constitute a section of the public was "a question of
degree" and depended on the purpose of the trust. This sort of formulation,
however, seems to be no more helpful, perhaps less helpful, in the present
state of the law than the old formulation based on the distinction between
personal and impersonal relationship.

On the other hand, if the trust is construed in such a way as merely to   **11–031**
grant a preference to a limited class, such as employees or relations, the trust
will succeed as a charity. This was the case, for example, in *Re Koettgen's Will
Trusts*,[66] where a trust was established for the furtherance of the commercial
education of British-born persons, with a direction that preference be given
to employees of a particular firm. The essential question is whether or not
there is anything more than an expression of preference. If the terms of the
trust go beyond that and amount to a positive obligation, the trust will not
be regarded as charitable because the obligation will vitiate the public
character of the trust. Indeed on this basis it is certainly possible to argue,
and it has been argued,[67] that *Re Koettgen's Will Trusts* was wrongly decided.
Its validity was doubted both by Lord Radcliffe in *Caffoor v. Commission of
Income Tax, Colombo*,[68] where the Privy Council held that the trust in question
was no more than a family trust, and by Walton J. in *Re Martin*[69] where a
trust to establish a home for old people, with a right for either or both of the
testator's daughters to reside there, was held not to be charitable. But in
essence, the question will always come down to one of construction.

A number of major charities carry on part of their activities in foreign   **11–032**
countries. In *Re Carapiet's Trusts*[70] Jacob J. settled a long-standing controversy by holding that the correct approach to institutions operating
abroad was as the Charity Commission had stated in 1993[71]: it should first
be considered whether they would be regarded as charities if their operations were confined to the United Kingdom; if they would, then they should
be presumed also to be charitable even though operating abroad unless it
would be contrary to public policy to recognise them. Jacob J. held that the
most important authority was *Camille and Henry Dreyfus Foundation v.
I.R.C.*,[72] where the Court of Appeal had been invited to overrule the earlier
decision in *Re Robinson*[73] that the purpose of benefiting German soldiers

---

[65] [1972] A.C. 601 at 621.
[66] [1954] Ch. 252.
[67] See, for example, *I.R.C. v. Educational Grants Association* [1967] Ch. 123.
[68] [1961] A.C. 584 at 604. Compare *Re George Drexler Ofrex Foundation Trustees v. I.R.C.* [1966]
Ch. 675.
[69] (1977) *The Times*, November 16, 1977.
[70] [2002] W.T.L.R. 989.
[71] In (1993) 1 C.Comm.Dec. 17
[72] [1954] Ch. 672.
[73] [1932] 2 Ch. 122.

injured in the First World War was charitable and had declined to do so, indicating that the key factor was not where the purpose was carried out but the public policy of the United Kingdom. Jacob J. also held that in this respect there was no distinction between the different heads mentioned in *Pemsel's* Case[74] and so there is presumably now no distinction between the different heads listed in section 2(2) of the Charities Act 2006.

11–033   The normal requirements of public benefit, which of course then did and probably still do differ from head to head, therefore apply to activities carried out abroad. This of course means that, where what is being provided abroad are public works or development projects such as roads and irrigation, these will only be charitable "if they are a reasonably direct means to the end of relieving poverty in observable cases". Nor will the courts ignore the probable results of the trust on the community of the country in question, which may of course have a wholly distinct history and social structure. One of the reasons why a trust to bring about the abolition of torture and other inhuman punishments was held not to be charitable in *McGovern v. Attorney-General*[75] was that the court could not judge the probable effects of the necessary legislation on the local community in question.

11–034   On the other hand, foreign charities cannot acquire charitable status in the United Kingdom for the simple reason that the law of charity in the foreign country may be different from the equivalent English law and also, now, because, unless one of the trustees is in the United Kingdom, they will be outside the control of the High Court and, consequently, outside the definition of charity in section 1 of the Charities Act 2006.

(B)   The Former Position of Trusts for the Relief of Poverty

11–035   It has already been seen that, in the case of trusts for the relief of poverty, it was virtually impossible for the presumption that they were established for the benefit of the public to be rebutted. Another way of expressing this proposition was to say that such trusts constituted an exception to the requirement for public benefit. Certainly such trusts have been upheld when the only possible beneficiaries were linked either by contract or by blood; an example of the former was the so-called "poor relations" cases, while an example of the latter was a trust for the relief of poverty amongst employees of a particular firm or company. This so-called exception could not be accounted for by reference to any principle,[76] but it was established by authorities of long standing which have long since been binding on the Court of Appeal and which were reaffirmed by the House of Lords in *Dingle*

---

[74] [1891] A.C. 531 at 583. It had previously been thought that, while the first three heads mentioned in *Pemsel's* Case (the relief of poverty, the advancement of education and the advancement of religion) would be charitable purposes in whatever part of the world they were carried out, purposes within the fourth head of that classification (the advancement of other purposes beneficial to the community) would only be charitable if they were of benefit to the community of the United Kingdom.

[75] [1982] Ch. 321.

[76] It has been tentatively suggested that "the relief of poverty is of so altruistic a character that the public benefit may necessarily be inferred"; see *Re Scarisbrick* [1951] Ch. 622 at 639, *per* Evershed M.R. But this is not the basis of the case law and in any event seems highly debatable. In *Dingle v. Turner* [1972] A.C. 601 it was assumed that the law was anomalous.

v. Turner.[77] In that case there was a trust to apply income in paying pensions to poor employees of a company; it was held that the trust was charitable.

Having said that, the more recent decisions manifested a change of atti-   **11–036**
tude towards "poor relations" cases. While the older cases of this type[78] seem to have been approved more or less as a matter of course, in the more recent cases some consideration was given to the nature of the relief granted and the size of the class in question. Trusts for such of the testator's relatives as shall be "in needy circumstances" and "in special need" were upheld in, respectively, *Re Scarisbrick*[79] and *Re Cohen*,[80] while in *Re Segelman*[81] a gift to "poor and needy" members of a class of six named relatives and their issue, totalling 26 persons at the date of the testator's death and likely to increase substantially in the future, was also upheld.

The contractual tie was illustrated by cases such as *Dingle v. Turner* and   **11–037**
Gibson v. South American Stores (Gath & Chaves),[82] where a gift to employees of a particular company to whom a poverty qualification was attached was upheld as a valid charitable gift, in both cases. The principle was also applied in *Re Young*[83] to members of a club and in *Spiller v. Maude*[84] to members of a society.

It was argued in *Dingle v. Turner* that the tests postulated in *Re Compton*[85]   **11–038**
and *Oppenheim v. Tobacco Securities Trust*[86] ought, in principle, to apply to all charitable trusts and that the "poor relations" cases, the "poor members" cases and the "poor employees" cases were all anomalous and should be overruled; alternatively, that if it was not practicable to overrule the "poor relations" cases because of their antiquity, the same could not be said of the "poor employees" cases which dated only from 1900.[87] However, it was held that the "poor members" and "poor employees" decisions were a natural development of the "poor relations" cases and to draw a distinction between them would be quite illogical; moreover, although not as old as "poor relations" trusts, "poor employees" trusts had been recognised for many years and there would be a large number of such trusts in operation today. However, the so-called exception would not have been extended to other classes of trusts even before the enactment of the Charities Act 2006[88] and it certainly will not be extended now.

---

[77] [1972] A.C. 601.
[78] See, for example, *Isaac v. Defriez* (1754) Amb. 595; *White v. White* (1802) 7 Ves. 423; *Att.-Gen. v. Price* (1810) 17 Ves. 371.
[79] [1951] Ch. 622. It was also held in this case that it does not matter that the trust fund can be distributed to the "poor relations" in such a way as to exhaust the capital.
[80] [1973] 1 W.L.R. 415.
[81] [1996] Ch. 171.
[82] [1950] Ch. 177. See also *Re Coulthurst* [1951] Ch. 661 (officers and ex-officers of bank).
[83] [1955] 1 W.L.R. 1269.
[84] (1881) 32 Ch.D. 158N.
[85] [1945] Ch. 123.
[86] [1951] A.C. 297.
[87] *Re Gosling* [1900] 2 W.R. 300.
[88] *Re Compton* [1945] Ch. 123 (education); *Oppenheim v. Tobacco Securities Trust* [1951] A.C. 297 (education); *Davies v. Perpetual Trustee Co.* [1959] A.C. 439 (religion).

11–039   It was also decided by the Court of Appeal in *Re Scarisbrick*[89]—and this
did not appear to have been expressly decided before—that the exception
was not restricted to perpetual or continuing trusts (to which it will normally apply) but even covered a trust for immediate distribution. Here a gift
for poor members of the class of relations of three children of the testatrix
was upheld as a valid charitable trust, even though the distribution of the
property had to be made within the perpetuity period.

11–040   Since the enactment of the Charities Act 2006 it can certainly no longer be
said that trusts for the relief of poverty constitute an exception to the
requirement for public benefit. Existing trusts will, however, clearly continue to be valid under sections 2(2)(m) and 4(a) of the Charities Act 2006,
which include in the definition of charitable purposes "any purposes recognised as charitable purposes under existing charitable law".[90] Trusts of the
types which have previously been accepted to be charitable are also likely to
be upheld if they are created by wills executed before the Charities Act 2006
came into force. However, it does not necessarily follow that a trust created
by a document executed today which, like the trust in *Re Segelman*,[91] is for
the "poor and needy" members of a class of six named relatives and their
issue will now be accepted to be charitable, even if, as in that case, the class
totalled 26 persons by the date of the testator's death and was likely to
increase substantially in the future; further, even if such a trust were initially
accepted, each annual report would clearly be scrutinised extremely closely.
Consequently, no testator would now be well advised to take the chance. A
trust for the relief of poverty in general with an expressed preference for the
relatives and issue in question would certainly be a much safer way in
which to proceed.

(C) The Limits of Public Benefit

11–041   It is important to note that, although the general rule is that every charitable
trust should have a public element, it is not essential that every member of
the public should be able to avail himself of its benefits. As Viscount
Simonds said in *I.R.C. v. Baddeley*,[92] there is a distinction "between a form of
relief extended to the whole community, yet by its very nature advantageous
only to the few, and a form of relief accorded to a selected few out of a larger
number equally willing and able to take advantage of it". Illustrations of the
first class of trusts referred to by Viscount Simonds, trusts which will be
charitable, include a gift for the benefit of New South Wales soldiers returning after the First World War was held by the Privy Council in *Verge v.
Somerville*[93] to be valid and trusts for the erection of a sea wall even though
such trusts are likely primarily, if not exclusively, to benefit persons whose
houses front the sea. On the other hand, illustrations of Viscount Simonds'
second class, trusts which will fail as a charity, include a gift to Presbyterians
who could claim a particular descent which was held by the Privy Council

---

[89] [1951] Ch. 622.
[90] See *post*, para 11–094.
[91] [1996] Ch. 171.
[92] [1955] A.C. 572 at 592. The case is considered *post*, para 11–082.
[93] [1924] A.C. 496.

to fail for this reason in *Davies v. Perpetual Trustee Co.*[94] and the trust in *I.R.C. v. Baddeley*[95] itself, which was in favour of the Methodists in West Ham and Leyton and was held by the House of Lords to fail.

2. *The List of Charitable Purposes*

Eleven specific charitable purposes are listed in section 2(2) of the Charities Act 2006 and six of these 11 are either explained or qualified in section 2(3). The 11 include variants of the first three heads of charitable trusts identified by Lord Macnaghten in *Pemsel's* Case, a number of purposes which formerly were clearly within his fourth head, a number of purposes which formerly were squeezed into one of his four heads, and a few purposes which are wholly new.   **11–042**

Most of the trusts which have previously been held to be charitable can be allocated to one or more of the new purposes and, as that statement makes clear, it is clearly possible for a charitable trust to fall within more than one of the 11 purposes. But not all the trusts which have previously been held to be charitable can be allocated to one or more of the new purposes and so section 2(4) contains a general charitable purpose to sweep up and render charitable any trusts which are in this position. Section 2(5) provides that any of the expressions used in relation to the 11 specific statutory purposes which has hitherto had a particular meaning under charity law is to be taken to have retained that meaning. Finally, sections 2(6) and 2(7) provide that any references to charitable purposes or to institutions having charitable purposes in documents and enactments, whether prior or subsequent to the Charities Act 2006, are now to be construed in accordance with the meaning of charity set out in section 2(1).   **11–043**

Before the listed 11 specific charitable purposes and the one general charitable purpose are reviewed, two restrictions which are imposed on all potentially charitable trusts must be noted (these will be considered later on): first, no trust whose purposes include the attainment of political objects can be charitable[96]; and, secondly, no trust can be charitable unless its trustees are bound to devote its subject matter exclusively to charitable purposes.[97]   **11–044**

(A) The Prevention or Relief of Poverty
This purpose is found in section 2(1)(a). A slightly differently worded purpose, trusts for the relief of poverty, was the first of the four heads of charitable trusts identified by Lord Macnaghten in *Pemsel's* Case.[98] Strictly speaking, the formulation in the Charitable Uses Act 1601 had been trusts for the relief of "the aged, impotent and poor" but, despite the presence of the word "and", it had long been well-settled that the expression should be   **11–045**

---

[94] [1959] A.C. 439.
[95] [1955] A.C. 572.
[96] See *post*, para 11–095.
[97] See *post*, para 11–101.
[98] 1891] A.C. 531 at 583.

read disjunctively.[99] Given that section 2(2)(a) refers to poverty alone, this is no longer relevant but trusts for the aged and impotent anyway now fall within section 2(2)(j), which contains a list of six alternative "disadvantages" which will necessarily be read disjunctively.

11–046   A person can be in a state of "poverty" without being totally destitute. Consequently, gifts for such objects as "ladies of limited means",[100] "decayed actors"[101] and similar purposes are recognised to be charitable. All that seems to be required is that the individuals in question are in straitened circumstances and are unable to maintain a modest standard of living.[102] But it is essential that all the objects fall within the designation "poor" if a trust for the relief of poverty is to be upheld. If someone who is not poor is able to benefit, the gift will not qualify as a gift for the relief of poverty. Thus, in *Re Gwyon*[103] a fund was directed to be set aside to provide "knickers" (by which was meant a type of short trouser) for the boys of Farnham. The garments were unusual not only in their name but also because there were to be embroidered on the waistband the words "Gwyon's Present". Successful applicants were to be entitled to a new pair of knickers each year provided that on the subsequent application the legend "Gwyon's Present" was still decipherable on the old ones. Whatever may have been the testator's intention, none of these conditions necessarily imported poverty and the trust failed as a charity. Similarly, it was held in *Re Sanders' Will Trusts*[104] that a gift for the "working classes" was not a gift for the relief of poverty because this expression did not necessarily indicate poor persons. It is possible, as Harman J. said, and as it has indeed been held,[105] that, if the gift had been made to members of the "working classes" who were aged or widows, then the object of relieving poverty might have been implied. But, as Harman J. made plain, in *Re Sanders Will Trusts* there was nothing of this kind. The members of the working class were not old persons, they were not widows, they were simply men working in the docks and their families; it was, therefore, impossible to infer any element of poverty. However, *Re Sanders Will Trusts* was distinguished in *Re Niyazi's Will Trusts*,[106] where a trust for a working men's hostel in Famagusta, Cyprus, which provided

---

[99] Earlier decisions to this effect were confirmed in *Re Robinson* [1951] Ch. 198, where there was a gift to the old over 65 years of a certain district, and in *Re Lewis* [1955] Ch. 104, where there was a gift for 20 blind children of another district; both gifts were upheld. The question was most recently considered in *Joseph Rowntree Memorial Trust Housing Association v. Attorney-General* [1983] Ch. 159; Peter Gibson J. confirmed the disjunctive reading but added a significant rider, which had not emerged from the cases previously cited, that in order to be charitable the gift to the aged or the impotent had to have as its purpose the relief of a need attributable to their condition. This finally scotched the theory that a trust for the relief of "aged peers" or "impotent millionaires" will be charitable (see 71 L.Q.R. (1975) 16); a gift of money to such persons would not relieve a need of theirs as aged or impotent persons.

[100] *Re Gardom* [1914] 1 Ch. 662.

[101] *Spiller v. Maude* (1881) 32 Ch.D. 158N.

[102] See *Re Mary Clark Homes* [1904] 2 K.B. 645; *Re Gardom* [1914] 1 Ch. 662; *Shaw v. Halifax Corporation* [1915] 2 K.B. 170; *Re Clarke* [1923] 2 Ch. 407; *Re De Carteret* [1933] Ch. 103. See also Cross (1956) 72 L.Q.R. 182 at 206.

[103] [1930] 1 Ch. 225.

[104] [1954] Ch. 265 (appeal settled; *The Times*, July 22, 1954).

[105] *Re Glyn* (1950) 66 T.L.R. (Pt 2) 510; see also *Re Cottam* [1955] 1 W.L.R. 1299 (provision of flats for aged).

[106] [1978] 1 W.L.R. 910.

modest accommodation for persons of the lower income group was upheld as charitable, although, in the words of Megarry V.-C., the case was "desperately near the border-line".[107]

A trust for poor persons may of course take effect as a private trust rather than as a charitable trust; the distinction is, as a matter of construction, whether the gift is for the relief of poverty amongst poor people of a particular description or merely a gift to particular poor persons for the purpose of relieving poverty among them. In the former case the trust will be charitable, in the latter it will be private.[108] Difficulties have arisen in this connection in the case of housing associations which provide housing for the poor (hitherto, of course, for the "aged, impotent and poor") and which enjoy charitable status for that reason. It is, or at any rate has been, common to find such associations feeling the need to adopt a particular policy of tenant selection, for example, selecting tenants who earn less than the national average wage, so as to preserve their charitable status. Such a policy may not only be inconvenient; it may actually fail if one of the residents is in fact not poor.[109] However, such difficulties now appear to have been alleviated to some extent by the decision in *Joseph Rowntree Memorial Trust Housing Association v. Attorney-General*.[110] A charitable housing association wished to build small self-contained dwellings for sale to elderly people on long leases in consideration of a capital payment. It was held that, since the provision of special accommodation relieved a particular need of the elderly, whether poor or not, attributable to their aged condition, the proposed housing schemes were charitable. It was also held that it was not essential that a charitable gift was made solely by way of bounty and so, accordingly, the beneficiaries could be required to contribute to its cost. In reaching that conclusion, Peter Gibson J. applied the reasoning of Lord Wilberforce in *Re Resch's Will Trusts* [1969] 1 A.C. 514, where the House of Lords held charitable a gift to a private hospital which charged substantial fees but was not run for the profit of individuals. Consequently, the fact that the housing schemes concerned made provision for special housing for the elderly on a contractual basis did not therefore prevent the schemes from being charitable. It was also held that the possibility that a beneficiary might profit by an increase in value of the property on a subsequent sale by him did not alter the fact that the trusts were charitable.

Finally, it should be noted that section 2(2)(a) also includes the prevention of poverty. Save to the extent that poverty is obviously prevented by providing accommodation for poor people at affordable rents, which has hitherto been regarded as relieving against rather than preventing poverty, this appears to be an innovation. In one sense, the best form of prevention of poverty is necessarily the education of the poor, or at any rate of the children of the poor, but that clearly cannot be what is meant since education is a separate listed purpose. It may be that issues such as the reduction of unemployment, which has hitherto been regarded as falling under Lord

11–047

11–048

---

[107] *ibid.* at 915.
[108] *Re Scarisbrick* [1951] Ch. 622 at 650, 651 *per* Jenkins L.J.; *Dingle v. Turner* [1972] A.C. 601 at 617, *per* Lord Cross; *Re Cohen* [1973] 1 W.L.R. 415 at 423, *per* Templeman J.
[109] *Over-Seventies Housing Association v. Westminster L.B.C.* (1974) 230 E.G. 1593.
[110] [1983] Ch. 159.

Macnaghten's fourth head of other purposes beneficial to the community, will from now on instead be addressed under this head.

(B) The Advancement of Education

11–049   This purpose, which was the second of the four heads of charitable trusts identified by Lord Macnaghten in *Pemsel's* Case,[111] is found in section 2(2)(b). Conventionally, the general rule is that, in order for a trust to be charitable on the grounds of the advancement of education, its provisions must manifest an intention that learning should be imparted, not simply that it should be accumulated. But this may now have become a somewhat misleading yardstick, because the tendency in many of the cases has been to widen the field of "education" in this context. However, the addition as separate purposes of the advancement of the arts, culture, heritage or science and the advancement of amateur sport may mean that such widening of the field of "education" is now no longer necessary.

11–050   The conventional meaning does appear to have been adopted by Harman J. in *Re Shaw*.[112] George Bernard Shaw directed the trustees of his will to use his residuary estate for a number of designated purposes. These included: first, an inquiry into how much time per individual scribe would be saved by substituting for the established English alphabet one containing at least 40 letters; secondly, an inquiry into how many persons were speaking and writing English in the usual form at any moment in the world; thirdly, the ascertainment of the time and labour wasted by the lack of at least 14 unequivocal syllables and an estimate of the loss of income in British and American currency caused thereby; and, fourthly, the employment of a phonetic expert to transliterate the testator's play *Androcles and the Lion* into the proposed new English alphabet. Harman J. held that the trusts were not charitable; they were merely intended to increase public knowledge in the advantages of the proposed alternative alphabet. Consequently, the research and propaganda directed by the testator would merely increase public knowledge in a particular respect, the saving of time and money achievable by the use of the proposed new alphabet; "no element of teaching or education" was combined with this.[113]

11–051   It is unlikely that *Re Shaw* would be decided any differently following the enactment of the Charities Act 2006. But the subsequent cases in which the question of the ambit of "education" was given fresh consideration would now be considered as possible trusts for the advancement of the arts, culture, heritage or science.[114] In *Re Hopkins' Will Trusts*,[115] the testatrix had given part of her residuary estate to "the Francis Bacon Society" to be applied towards finding the "Bacon-Shakespeare Manuscripts". One of the main objects of the society was "to encourage the general study of the evidence of Francis Bacon's authorship of plays commonly ascribed to

---

[111] [1891] A.C. 531 at 583.

[112] [1957] 1 W.L.R. 729 (appeal dismissed by consent on terms that a sum of money should be devoted to these inquiries; [1958] 1 All E.R. 245N).

[113] Harman J. also rejected an argument that the trusts were charitable as being in some way beneficial to the community (within the fourth head of Lord Macnaghten's classification) because it was highly controversial whether the proposals were in fact beneficial.

[114] See *post*, para 11–072.

[115] [1965] Ch. 669.

Shakespeare". The terms of the will were, therefore, held to mean that the money was to be used to search for manuscripts of plays commonly ascribed to Shakespeare but believed by the testatrix and the society to have been written by Bacon. Wilberforce J. held that this was both a trust for the advancement of education and a trust for other purposes beneficial to the community, within the fourth head of Lord Macnaghten's classification, as a gift for the improvement of this country's literary heritage (both grounds would now instead cause the trust to fall within section 2(2)(f) as a trust for the advancement of the arts, culture, heritage or science). However, his consideration of the dictum of Harman J. in *Re Shaw* that the increase of knowledge was not in itself a charitable object unless it was combined with teaching or education remains relevant for this head. He was unwilling to regard this as meaning that the promotion of academic research was not a charitable purpose unless the researchers were engaged in teaching or education in the conventional sense. He concluded (and many would agree) that the term "education" should be used in a wide sense and certainly extended beyond teaching.[116] He valuably also spelt out the requirements that "research" must satisfy in order to be charitable, although he did not regard this formulation as exhaustive: first, it must be of educational value to the researcher; secondly, it must be so directed so as to produce something which will pass into the store of educational material; or, thirdly, it must improve the sum of communicable knowledge in an area which may be covered by education, which in this last context extends to the formation of literary taste and appreciation.[117]

Many other cases demonstrate how widely the idea of education has been **11–052** extended[118] and most of these would still be classified as trusts for the advancement of education.[119] So would *Re South Place Ethical Society*[120] where it was held that the cultivation of a rational religious sentiment was for the advancement of education because a rational sentiment could only be cultivated by educational methods. But precisely how one of the most striking, if not startling, cases in which education was given an extremely and perhaps unjustifiably wide connotation would now be classified is hard to say. This was *Re Shaw's Will Trusts*[121] where the testatrix, who was the wife of George Bernard Shaw and (it is necessary to add) herself of Irish origin, bequeathed the residue of her estate upon trusts for, among other things, the teaching, promotion and encouragement in Ireland of self-control, elocution,

---

[116] *ibid.* at 680.

[117] *ibid.*

[118] *Re Dupree's Deed Trusts* [1945] Ch. 16 (the playing of chess); *Re Delius* (appreciation of music) [1957] Ch. 299; *Re The Town and Country Planning Act 1947* [1951] Ch. 132 (the promotion of art); *Re Mellody* [1918] 1 Ch. 228 (annual school treat); *Re Cranstoun* [1932] 1 Ch. 537 (preservation of ancient buildings); *Re Spence* [1938] Ch. 96 (collection of arms and antiques); *Re Webber* [1954] 1 W.L.R. 1500 (Boy Scouts); *Re Levien* [1955] 1 W.L.R. 964 (raising musical standards); *Re Koettgen's Will Trusts* [1954] Ch. 252 (commercial education); *Royal Choral Society v. I.R.C.* (1943) 112 L.J.K.B. 648 (choral society); *Re Royce* [1940] Ch. 514 (church choir).

[119] All except *Re Delius* (appreciation of music) [1957] Ch. 299, *Re The Town and Country Planning Act 1947* [1951] Ch. 132 (the promotion of art), *Re Cranstoun* [1932] 1 Ch. 537 (preservation of ancient buildings) and, probably, *Re Spence* [1938] Ch. 96 (collection of arms and antiques) and *Re Dupree's Deed Trusts* [1945] Ch. 16 (the playing of chess).

[120] [1980] 1 W.L.R. 1565. For other aspects of the case see *post*, paras 11–060, 11–115.

[121] [1952] Ch. 163.

oratory, deportment, the arts of personal contact, of social intercourse and the other arts of public and private life. It was held that these somewhat eccentric trusts were wholly educational in character and constituted valid charitable trusts. The only other obvious possible classification for this trust is to regard it as falling with section 2(2)(j) as a trust for the relief of those in need by reason of youth!

11–053   As might be expected, trusts for the establishment and support of professorships and lectureships are educational in character[122] but it should also be noticed that satellite purposes such as increasing the stipends of university teachers and fellows of colleges will also be upheld.[123] The same principles apply to schools,[124] colleges and universities,[125] and learned societies and institutions.[126]

11–054   It was also held in *Incorporated Council of Law Reporting for England and Wales v. Attorney-General*[127] that the Council was an educational charity[128]; the preparation of law reports was for the advancement of education because their purpose was to record accurately the development and application of judge-made law and thereby disseminate knowledge of that law. The law, it was held by the Court of Appeal, was properly to be regarded as a science and therefore books which were produced for the purpose of enabling it to be studied were published for the advancement of education. It was also held that the fact that the reports were used by the legal profession for the purpose of earning fees did not make the purposes non-charitable. It may be observed that, despite the fact that the Council was carrying on a business, its profits could only be applied in the pursuit of the Council's objects; if the profits could have enured for the benefit of its individual members, it would not have achieved charitable status.[129]

11–055   Another case which may be thought to have given an equally robust interpretation to educational charity is *London Hospital Medical College v. I.R.C.*,[130] which involved the students' union of the London Hospital. The union was under the control of the medical college, an educational charity, and its objects were to "promote social, cultural and athletic activities amongst the members and to add to the comfort and enjoyment of the students". The question was whether the predominant object of the union

---

[122] *Att.-Gen. v. Margaret and Regius Professors at Cambridge* (1682) 1 Vern. 55.

[123] *Case of Christ's College, Cambridge* (1751) 1 W.B.I. 90.

[124] See *The Abbey Malvern Wells v. Ministry of Local Government and Planning* [1951] Ch. 728, where a girls' school was carried on by a private company but under a trust deed all dividends were applied for school purposes. The school was held charitable. Danckwerts J. said (at 737) that all schools of learning are treated as charitable unless they exist purely as profit-making ventures. Compare *Re Girls Public Day School Trust* [1951] Ch. 400 where the school in question was not charitable because shareholders were beneficially interested.

[125] *Case of Christ's College, Cambridge* (1751) 1 W.B.I. 90.

[126] For example, the Royal College of Surgeons: see *Royal College of Surgeons v. National Provincial Bank* [1952] A.C. 631.

[127] [1972] Ch. 73.

[128] Russell L.J. dissented, so far as the educational aspect was concerned, but all the members of the Court of Appeal agreed that it was also charitable as being for the benefit of the community within the fourth head of Lord Macnaghten's classification.

[129] Compare the cases cited *ante*, n.124.

[130] [1976] 1 W.L.R. 613; compare *Re Bushnell* [1975] 1 W.L.R. 1596 in which a trust for the advancement of "socialised medicine" was held not to be educational; see *post*, para 11–098.

was the furtherance of the purposes of the medical college as a school of learning (in which case it was charitable) or whether its objects were the private and personal benefit of those students who were members of the union (in which case it would not be).[131] Brightman J. held that it had no *raison d'être* except to further the educational purposes of the medical college and it was accordingly charitable. He said that what it did and was intended to do was to assist the teaching of medicine by providing those physical, cultural and social outlets which were needed, or at any rate highly desirable, if the art of teaching was to be efficiently performed at the College.[132]

It might be thought to be an elementary proposition that, if an institution is devoted to educational purposes (or indeed any other specific charitable purposes), its funds can only be applied to those purposes. Nevertheless the question arose for decision in *Baldry v. Feintuck*.[133] In this case the University of Sussex Students Union, which was conceded in argument[134] to be an educational charity, voted to authorise payments to "War on Want", a charitable but non-educational organisation, and to a campaign of protest against the Government's policy of ending the supply of free milk to school-children, a political and therefore non-charitable purpose.[135] Brightman J. held that the moneys could not be applied for such purposes. A similar decision was reached in *Webb v. O'Doherty*,[136] where expenditure of student union funds on a campaign to end the First Gulf War was restrained.

11–056

One of the current more controversial questions in the field of education concerns the charitable status of independent schools[137]; there is no doubt whatever that many of them are registered charities. In practice, the vast majority of them have long endeavoured to deflect attacks, or potential attacks, on their charitable status by utilising their income to provide a certain number of free places and by enabling facilities such as playing fields to be utilised by their local community (usually as little as possible). However, they are now obliged to demonstrate on an annual basis by means of reports to the Charity Commission[138] that they satisfy the requirement for public benefit. It is becoming increasingly apparent that they are likely to have to do very much more than at present. Indeed some private schools have now formed associations with state schools in underprivileged areas to whom they provide tuition, coaching and other assistance. This is certainly the type of public benefit for which the Charity Commission will be looking. It is equally certain that private schools are no longer likely to be able to demonstrate that their facilities are accessible to the public as a whole

11–057

---

[131] This was the result in *I.R.C. v. City of Glasgow Police Athletic Association* [1953] A.C. 380, discussed *post*, para 11–077.

[132] *London Hospital Medical College v. I.R.C.* [1976] 1 W.L.R. 613 at 623, 624. It was apparently thought relevant that the London Hospital is on a site adjoining the Whitechapel and Commercial Roads in the East End of London; this was described as a "somewhat remote part of London" *ibid.* at 621.

[133] [1972] 1 W.L.R. 552.

[134] On the basis of *London Hospital Medical College v. I.R.C.* [1976] 1 W.L.R. 613 at 624.

[135] See *post*, para 11–095.

[136] (1991) *The Times*, February 11, 1991.

[137] See *ante*, para 11–027.

[138] See the guidelines to the Charity Commission's Approach to Public Benefit which are published on its website at *http://www.charity-commission.gov.uk/spr/pubben.asp*.

merely by permitting access to those facilities during school holidays. Precisely what the minimum requirements will turn out to be remains to be seen.

(C) Trusts for the Advancement of Religion

11–058 This purpose, which was the third of the four heads of charitable trusts identified by Lord Macnaghten in *Pemsel's* Case,[139] is found in section 2(2)(c). In its statutory form, its breadth is explained by section 3(a), which provides that "religion" includes "a religion which involves belief in more than one god" and "a religion which does not involve belief in a god".

11–059   This explanation emphasises that, in the area of religion, the law has always manifested a considerable measure of tolerance. This was recognised over almost 150 years ago in *Thornton v. Howe*,[140] where Romilly M.R. recognised as charitable a trust for the publication of the work of Joanna Southcott even though he evidently thought her doctrines to be ridiculous. This decision indicates that the advancement of all religions which are "not subversive of all morality"[141] will be held to be charitable. There is not actually a great deal of authority on non-Christian religions[142] but there has never seemed to be any reason why all of them should not be recognised. The Report from the Strategy Unit confirmed the general view of the commentators that the time has come to recognise formally all the major religions of the world, whatever their forms; this was why section 3(a) was enacted to provide that "religion" includes "a religion which involves belief in more than one god" and so confirm that there is no longer any restriction to monotheistic religions. That does not necessarily mean that the decision in *Yeap Cheah Neo v. Ong Cheng Neo*,[143] where the Privy Council held that a trust requiring ancestor worship was not charitable, is no longer good law; this decision could certainly be distinguished on the grounds that the required religious observances were not for the public benefit, merely for the alleged advantage of the deceased and his family. Further, some of the "fringe" religious organisations which have increasingly been coming into

---

[139] [1891] A.C. 531 at 583.

[140] (1862) 31 Beav. 14.

[141] *ibid.* at 20. This principle was applied by Plowman J. in *Re Watson* [1973] 1 W.L.R. 1472 in upholding a trust for the publication and distribution of religious writings of no intrinsic merit but which displayed a religious tendency, and by Walton J. in *Holmes v. Att.-Gen.* [1981] Ch.Com.Rep. 10 in upholding a trust for the Exclusive Brethren. However, the correctness of the statement of principle of Romilly M.R. in *Thornton v. Howe* remains open to review by the court. See also *Bowman v. Secular Society* [1917] A.C. 406.

[142] Among the few examples are: *Straus v. Goldsmid* (1837) 8 Sim. 614 (trust for practice of Jewish religion valid); *Neville Estates v. Madden* [1962] Ch. 832 (trust for Catford synagogue valid); *Dawkins v. Gown Suppliers (PSA)* (1993) *The Times,* February 4, 1993 (Rastafarians).

[143] (1875) L.R. 6 P.C. 381 (appeal from the Straits Settlements). See also *Re Hummeltenberg* [1923] 1 Ch. 237 (gift to college for training spiritualistic mediums); *Re Price* [1943] Ch. 422 (gift to the "Anthroposophical Society"). Neither of the cases fell within trusts for the advancement of religion and could only be considered under the fourth head of Lord Macnaghten's classification. The former was held invalid, the latter valid. On the other hand, in *Funnell v. Stewart* [1996] 1 W.L.R. 288, a gift to a group which engaged in faith healing but also held religious services some of which were open to the public was held to be charitable on the basis that the religious element contained sufficient public benefit.

existence[144] are so fanciful or freakish that charitable status can justifiably be denied to them on the basis that are they lacking public benefit.

However, the provision in section 3(a) that "religion" includes "a religion   **11–060** which does not involve belief in a god" has certainly changed the pre-existing law. Previously, gifts for ethical or moral societies not founded on belief in a deity were held not to be for the advancement of religion, although they could nevertheless be held to be charitable on other grounds. Thus in *Re South Place Ethical Society*,[145] which was established for the study and dissemination of "ethical principles" and for the cultivation of a rational religious sentiment eschewing all supernatural belief, Dillon J. described "ethical principles" as belief in the excellence of truth, love and beauty, but not belief in anything supernatural, and held that the Society was not founded for the advancement of religion because "religion is concerned with man's relations with God, and ethics are concerned with man's relations with man"[146]; however, the objects of the Society were upheld as charitable on other grounds.[147] The Society would now necessarily be held to be for the advancement of religion, as would Buddhism[148] and other previously rejected gifts, such as those to the "Anthroposophical Society"[149] and to a college for training spiritualistic mediums,[150] although even under the pre-existing law a gift to a group which engaged in faith healing but also held religious services open to the public was held to be charitable on the basis that the religious element contained sufficient public benefit.[151]

Quite apart from gifts for the advancement of a religion or a religious sect   **11–061** as such, a number of satellite purposes have been recognised as charitable under this head and still will be. Thus in *Re Moon's Will Trusts*[152] a bequest was made for "mission work". This expression was held on the evidence to connote "Christian mission work" which was held to be charitable; arguably "mission work" on behalf of other religions should now also suffice, provided that the work contained no political element.[153] Trusts for the maintenance and repair of a church, of a stained glass window,[154] or of a vault[155] within a church have also been held to be charitable; this will also apply to a churchyard and a burial ground even if restricted to a particular religious sect[156] and also to the graves in it, provided that the object of the gift is the

---

[144] The Unification Church (The "Moonies") has been registered as a Charity (Annual Report 1982, paras 36–38).

[145] [1981] 1 W.L.R. 1565.

[146] *ibid.* at 571.

[147] First, because they were for the mental and moral improvement of man and were therefore beneficial to the community within the fourth head of Lord Macnaghten's classification; and, secondly, because they were for the advancement of education.

[148] Dillon J. noted (at 573) that Buddhism was accepted as a religion although there was no belief in a god, but that question was not explored further.

[149] *Re Hummeltenberg* [1923] 1 Ch. 237.

[150] *Re Price* [1943] Ch. 422.

[151] *Funnell v. Stewart* [1996] 1 W.L.R. 288.

[152] [1948] 1 All E.R. 300.

[153] While overt politicisation would clearly prevent charitable status (see *post*, para 11–095), it is questionable how "mission work" whose objective was to assert the superiority of the religion in question over Christianity would be treated.

[154] *Re King* [1923] 1 Ch. 243. See also *Re Royce* [1940] Ch. 514.

[155] *Hoare v. Osborne* (1886) L.R. 1 Eq. 585.

[156] *Re Manser* [1905] 1 Ch. 68 (Society of Friends).

maintenance of all the graves.[157] Indeed, even cremation has also been held to be a charitable purpose.[158]

11–062   The general rule, considered in detail later on,[159] that, subject to the Charitable Trusts (Validation) Act 1954,[160] the purposes of a charitable trust must be exclusively charitable causes particular problems in the case of trusts for the advancement of religion. A draftsman may easily quite unwittingly say far too much, or just a word or two too much, in the trust instrument. At any rate the cases on the question of whether a trust is exclusively religious are certainly difficult and present several fine distinctions. This is because gifts are normally made to a person holding a religious office, such as a bishop; the additional words that may permissibly be used to create a valid charitable trust appear to fall into two groups. However, despite the attempts which have been made to rationalise the case law, the cases are not at all easy to reconcile and depend on an extremely close reading of the gift or trust in question; indeed at times recognising the distinction between any two cases decided differently requires hair-splitting to an extent which seems, frankly, to be quite excessive.

11–063   First, the words may confer an absolute discretion on the donee. In *Re Garrard*,[161] a gift was made "to the vicar and churchwardens of Kingston to be applied by them in such manner as they shall in their sole discretion think fit". Similarly, in *Re Rumball*[162] a gift was made "to the bishop for the time being of the Windward Islands to be applied by him as he thinks fit in his diocese". In both cases, as in several others[163] where an absolute discretion was conferred, the gift was upheld as charitable. The reason was that the gift was made to a person by his official name whose official status required charitable duties to be performed. Accordingly, the gift was assumed to be made for the charitable purposes inherent in that official status (it should be noted that this principle, which arises *virtute officii*, applies not only to religious office holders but also to the holders of other offices).

11–064   Secondly, the words used may confine the object of the gift within the ambit of the donee's religious function. For example, in *Re Eastes*[164] a gift "to the vicar and churchwardens, to be used by them for any purpose in connection with the Church which they shall select" was held to be charitable. But if the donor goes on to invite the donee to take into account the

---

[157] *Re Pardoe* [1906] 2 Ch. 184; in this case a gift for a peal of bells on the anniversary of the restoration of the monarchy also held to be charitable but this is questionable. Compare Brunyate (1946) 61 L.Q.R. 268, 274; *Re Eighmie* [1935] Ch. 524 (keeping in repair burial ground and monument to testator's late husband) and see *ante*, para 3–106.

[158] *Scottish Burial Reform and Cremation Society v. Glasgow Corporation* [1968] A.C. 138.

[159] See *post*, para 11–101.

[160] See *post*, para 11–109.

[161] [1907] 1 Ch. 382.

[162] [1956] Ch. 105. The judgment of Jenkins L.J. is a notable exposition of the law.

[163] See *Re Simson* [1946] Ch. 299 ("to the Vicar of St. Luke's Ramsgate, to be used for work in the parish"; valid). Compare *Farley v. Westminster Bank* [1939] A.C. 430 ("for parish work"; bad) *Re Flinn* [1948] Ch. 241 (to the Archbishop of Westminster Cathedral to be used by him "for such purposes as he shall in his absolute discretion think fit"; valid). See also *Re Norman* [1947] Ch. 349 (to the editors of a missionary periodical who were also trustees of a missionary church, to be applied "for such objects as they may think fit"; valid).

[164] [1948] Ch. 257. See also *Re Bain* [1930] 1 Ch. 224 (to a vicar "for such objects connected with the church as he shall think fit") *Re Norton's Will Trusts* [1948] 2 All E.R. 842 ("for the benefit of the parish"). Compare *Farley v. Westminster Bank* [1939] A.C. 430.

social as well as the religious functions of his office, the gift will fail; this is a respect in which the donor may unconsciously say too much. This apparent principle is illustrated by the leading case of *Dunne v. Byrne*[165] where a gift was made to the Roman Catholic Archbishop of Brisbane and his successors to be used as they "may judge most conducive to the good of religion in the diocese". The words in inverted commas were held by the Privy Council to be too wide and the gift failed. Perhaps the most notorious words to induce fatality are "parish work"; a gift was held by the House of Lords to fail for this reason in *Farley v. Westminster Bank*.[166]

Trusts for the advancement of religion are not exempt from the requirement for public benefit. Even though it is obviously sometimes difficult to see much, if any, public benefit in a religious trust, the test nevertheless has to be satisfied. Thus, in the controversial decision in *Gilmour v. Coats*,[167] the trust fund was to be applied for the purposes of a Carmelite convent occupied by a group of strictly cloistered and purely contemplative nuns who did not engage in any activities for the benefit of anyone outside the convent. The House of Lords held, first, that the benefit of intercessory prayer could not be proved in law and, secondly, that the element of edification was too vague and intangible. It is possible that too stringent a test of public benefit was applied in this case. However, whether or not this is the case, *Gilmour v. Coats* is readily distinguishable from cases such as *Neville Estates v. Madden*,[168] which concerned a synagogue in Catford which was not open to the public as of right. Cross J. held that a trust in favour of the synagogue was charitable; the distinction was that the enclosed nuns lived apart from the world whereas the members of the synagogue lived in the world and a public benefit accrued as a result of their attendance at a place of religious worship.

11–065

Rather different considerations have been applied to trusts for the saying of masses for the dead.[169] In *Re Caus*[170] Luxmoore J. held that a gift for such purposes was charitable. There was no provision in the testator's will that the masses should be said in public and the judge did not distinguish between masses said in public and those said in private; indeed he appeared to indicate that a gift for masses was in all cases charitable. This appeared

11–066

---

[165] [1912] A.C. 407 (appeal from Australia).

[166] [1939] A.C. 430. The words "parochial institutions or purposes" were also fatal in *Re Stratton* [1931] 1 Ch. 197. On the other hand, a gift "to the Vicar of St. Luke's Ramsgate, to be used for work in the parish" was held to be valid in *Re Simson* [1946] Ch. 299.

[167] [1949] A.C. 426. Likewise see *Cocks v. Manners* (1871) L.R. 12 Eq. 574 (enclosed Roman Catholic convent); *Hoare v. Hoare* (1886) 56 L.T. 147 (private chapel); *Re Joy* (1889) 60 L.T. 175 (to suppress cruelty to animals by prayer); *Re Warre's Will Trusts* [1953] 1 W.L.R. 725 (retreat house but this case seems to have been wrongly decided; retreatants do mix in the world since they go into retreat only for a few days' contemplation and prayer). Compare *Neville Estates v. Madden* [1962] Ch. 832 discussed in the text and *Re Banfield* [1968] 1 W.L.R. 846, where the gift was to a religious community ("Pilsdon Community House") which was held to be a charitable trust because of its primarily religious character and also because it was for the general public benefit in providing a temporary home of rest for those who needed it.

[168] [1962] Ch. 832 and see *Holmes v. Att.-Gen.* (1981) Ch. Com. Rep. 10 (Exclusive Brethren).

[169] It is established that a gift for masses is not void as being for superstitious uses; *Bourne v. Keane* [1919] A.C. 815. The question remains however whether it is charitable.

[170] [1934] Ch. 162.

erroneous in the light of the subsequent decision in *Gilmour v. Coats*, something which was duly confirmed in *Re Hetherington (deceased)*,[171] where a gift of £2,000 to the Roman Catholic Bishop of Westminster for "masses for the repose of the souls of my husband and my parents and my sisters and also myself when I die" was held to be charitable only on the grounds that sufficient public benefit was conferred by the public celebration of a religious rite and that the provision of stipends for the celebrants endowed the priesthood. It does not, however, seem likely that the latter reason would be sufficient to cause a gift for masses to be said in private to be charitable. Such trusts can, however, take effect as non-charitable purpose trusts.[172]

(D) The Advancement of Health or the Saving of Lives

11–067   This purpose is found in section 2(2)(d), while section 3(b) defines "the advancement of health" as "including the prevention or relief of sickness, disease or human suffering". Trusts for the relief of the sick, the endowment of hospitals, and other similar purposes are obviously well-established charitable purposes under Lord Macnaughten's fourth head, trusts for other purposes beneficial to the community.[173] However, as section 3(b) makes clear, this new head is considerably wider in that it clearly includes the prevention of disease, whether by preventative medicine or by means of the education of the public; in this respect, the creation of the wholly new head of the advancement of amateur sport[174] is also relevant. The saving of lives has also long since been recognised as charitable under the same fourth head, as is indicated by the charitable status of the Royal National Lifeboat Association. Its specific inclusion in this head will also enable other voluntary organisations such as mountain rescue services to obtain charitable status to the extent that they have not already done so.

(E) The Advancement of Citizenship or Community Development

11–068   This purpose is found in section 2(2)(e), while section 3(c) provides that this paragraph includes rural or urban regeneration and the promotion of civic responsibility, volunteering, the voluntary sector or efficiency of charities. Prior to the legislation, the Charity Commission had argued for the recognition of these purposes as a charitable purpose; the acceptance of this argument has not of course provided any body of case law to assist in the interpretation of the legislation. There is no doubt that encouraging participation in socially or economically deprived areas produces public benefit, but this may be less self-evident for organisations operating in well-off communities so it cannot be assumed that they will be able to show the necessary public benefit.

11–069   Also within this head is the promotion of urban and rural development and the building of community relations. This seems an appropriate place to observe that, so far as trusts for ethnic or national groups are concerned, there is a limited exception in favour of charities in the Race Relations Act

---

[171] [1990] Ch. 1.

[172] See *ante*, para 3–101.

[173] See *Re Dean's Will Trusts* [1950] 1 All E.R. 882; *Re White's Will Trusts* [1951] 1 All E.R. 528; *Re Smith's Will Trusts* [1962] 2 All E.R. 563; *Re Adams* [1967] 1 W.L.R. 162; *Le Cras v. Perpetual Trustee Co.* [1967] 1 All E.R. 915; *Re Resch's Will Trusts* [1969] A.C. 514.

[174] See *post*, para 11–077.

1976; section 34 provides that any discrimination necessary to comply with the terms of the governing instrument of a charity which is established to confer a benefit on persons of a particular racial group shall not be unlawful, but it specifically excludes from the exception any provision which restricts the benefits by reference to race or colour. Accordingly, a school for the education of Pakistanis or Spaniards could lawfully be confined to such persons but any provision excepting persons on racial grounds would be in breach of the Act. There is also an exception in favour of charity under the Sex Discrimination Act 1975; section 43 provides that where the trusts contain a provision for conferring benefits on one sex only, anything done by the charity trustees to comply with that provision is not unlawful. This safeguards the position of single sex charities, like the Y.M.C.A., the Y.W.C.A., the Boy Scouts and the Girl Guides and many small parochial charities restricted to one sex (such as a trust for the benefit of elderly widows).

Trusts which are designed for the provision of a village hall, community **11–070** centre, or other similar institutional purposes have been held to be valid charitable trusts if their provisions are drawn so as to fall within the Recreational Charities Act 1958, whose effect will be considered below.[175] It may well be that this is where trusts of this kind fit into the new statutory framework.

It is more questionable whether gifts to a locality, such as a town or **11–071** village, which have been held to be charitable even if no charitable purposes have been specified,[176] fit into the new statutory framework at all, other than into the general charitable purpose in section 2(2)(m); however, if such gifts do fit in anywhere else, it can only be here. Such gifts will be dealt with by means of a scheme made by the Charity Commission[177] so that the funds can be devoted to such purposes within the locality as are charitable. It has also been decided that the same principle applies to a gift to "my country, England".[178] That such trusts should be valid as charities seems curious[179] but is now established beyond all possible doubt. But if a locality trust is to be upheld, it is most important to ensure either that exclusively charitable purposes within the locality are specified in the trust instrument, or, alternatively, that no purposes whatsoever are specified. If the settlor uses words which demonstrate in terms that the subject-matter of the gift may be used for non-charitable purposes, it will fail. This was the case in *Houston v. Burns*,[180] where the trust was for "public, benevolent or charitable purposes" in a Scottish parish. If the purposes are not charitable *per se*, the localisation

---

[175] See *ante*, para 11–081.

[176] See *Goodman v. Saltash Corpn* (1882) 7 App.Cas. 633; *Re Allen* [1905] 2 Ch. 400; *Re Norton's Will Trusts* [1948] 2 All E.R. 842.

[177] See *post*, para 11–118.

[178] *Re Smith* [1932] 1 Ch. 153. See also *Nightingale v. Goulbourne* (1847) 5 Hare 484 (gift to "the Queen's Chancellor of the Exchequer for the time being" to be used by him for the benefit of "my beloved country, Great Britain" valid. The case can also be justified on the ground that it was made *virtute officii*, see *ante*, para 11–063).

[179] See Albery 21 L.Q.R. (1940) 49; *Williams' Trustees v. I.R.C.* [1947] A.C. 447 at 459, *per* Lord Simonds.

[180] [1918] A.C. 337; see also *Att.-Gen. v. National Provincial and Union Bank of England* [1924] A.C. 262 (patriotic purposes in the British Empire); *Re Strakosch* [1949] Ch. 529. The matter is discussed generally *post*, para 11–101.

of them will not of itself make them charitable.[181] Nor can gifts to "organisations or institutions operating for the public good" be held charitable by analogy with the locality cases by being limited to those organisations operated for the public good by charitable means; this was specifically held by the Privy Council in *Attorney-General of the Cayman Islands v. Wahr-Hansen*.[182]

(F)   The Advancement of the Arts, Culture, Heritage or Science

11–072   This purpose is found in section 2(2)(f). Many of the charitable trusts which now fall within this head were previously classified as trusts for the advancement of education. Thus in *Re Shakespeare Memorial Trust*[183] a trust for the erection and endowment of a Shakespeare Memorial National Theatre with the object of performing Shakespeare's plays, reviving English classical drama and stimulating the art of acting was held to be a trust for the advancement of education and so a valid charitable trust. However, theatres such as the Royal Opera House which charge substantial sums for access to performances may, like private schools, find the demonstration of public benefit increasingly difficult given the financial impossibility of the immense majority of the public being able to purchase tickets. The Charity Commission may not indefinitely continue to consider that the provision on the day of each performance of a limited number of cheap seats in unattractive locations in the theatre satisfies this requirement.

11–073   Also within this head now fall the trusts which were upheld in a number of cases in which the question of the ambit of "education" was given a wider consideration than Harman J. had done in *Re Shaw*.[184] In *Re Hopkins' Will Trusts*,[185] the testatrix had given part of her residuary estate to "the Francis Bacon Society" to be applied towards finding the "Bacon-Shakespeare Manuscripts". One of the main objects of the society was "to encourage the general study of the evidence of Francis Bacon's authorship of plays commonly ascribed to Shakespeare". The terms of the will were therefore held to mean that the money was to be used to search for manuscripts of plays commonly ascribed to Shakespeare but believed by the testatrix and the society to have been written by Bacon. The judge held that the purposes of search or research for original manuscripts of England's greatest dramatist were within the law's conception of a charitable purpose on two grounds: first, as being for education; and, secondly, as being for other purposes beneficial to the community, within the fourth head of Lord Macnaghten's classification, as a gift for the improvement of this country's literary heritage. Both these grounds would now cause the trust instead to fall within this head.

---

[181] *Williams' Trustees v. I.R.C.* [1947] A.C. 447 at 459–460, *per* Lord Simonds. This case involved an Institute of Welshmen in London which was not charitable because they were not an identifiable section of the community.

[182] [2001] 1 A.C. 75 (appeal from the Cayman Islands).

[183] [1923] 2 Ch. 398.

[184] [1957] 1 W.L.R. 729; see *ante*, para 11–050.

[185] [1965] Ch. 669.

Another example is *Re Delius*,[186] where the wife of the composer Delius   **11–074**
had given her residuary estate for the advancement of her late husband's
musical work by means of gramophone recordings, publication of his works
and financing of public performances of his work; it was held that the
purpose of the trust was to spread the knowledge and appreciation of
Delius' work throughout the world and constituted an effective educational
charity.[187] Similarly in *Re The Town and Country Planning Act 1947*, the
promotion of "art" was held to be charitable.[188] It is also arguable that *Re
Dupree's Deed Trusts*,[189] one of the many cases which demonstrate how
widely the idea of education has been extended,[190] which concerned a trust
for the encouragement of chess playing among the boys and youths of
Portsmouth, would now also be held to fall within this head as a trust for the
advancement of heritage and science.

Further, a trust which was at the time rejected as a potential trust for the   **11–075**
advancement of education would clearly now equally be rejected from this
head. In *Re Pinion*,[191] a testator gave his studio and pictures, one of which he
attributed to Lely and some of which were painted by himself, his antique
furniture, silver, china and other things to be offered to the National Trust to
be kept intact in the studio and maintained as a collection. In the event that
the National Trust declined the trust, as in fact it did, he authorised the
appointment of trustees to carry it out instead. It was acknowledged that a
gift to found a public museum may be assumed to be charitable if no one
questions that fact. But if the utility of the gift was brought into question, as
it was here, it was essential to know something of the quality of the exhibits
and for this purpose expert evidence was admissible to assist the court in
judging the educational value of the gift.[192] The evidence was to the effect
that the collection was of low quality; the Lely was bogus and the testator's
own paintings were bad. Among the furniture, there were some genuine
English and Continental pieces of the seventeenth and eighteenth centuries
which might have been acceptable as a gift to a minor provincial museum.
But, according to the terms of the will, everything had to be exhibited

---

[186] [1957] Ch. 299.
[187] It seems rather curious that it was found necessary to point out that the fact that pleasure
was an incident of that appreciation or that the effect of the trust was to enhance the reputation
of Delius did not prevent this result.
[188] [1951] Ch. 132. But "artistic" is too vague to be charitable; see *Associated Artists v. I.R.C.*
[1956] 1 W.L.R. 752.
[189] [1945] Ch. 16.
[190] Others are *Re Mellody* [1918] 1 Ch. 228 (annual school treat); *Re Cranstoun* [1932] 1 Ch. 537
(preservation of ancient buildings); *Re Spence* [1938] Ch. 96 (collection of arms and antiques); *Re
Webber* [1954] 1 W.L.R. 1500 (Boy Scouts); *Re Levien* [1955] 1 W.L.R. 964 (raising musical
standards); *Re Koettgen's Will Trusts* [1954] Ch. 252 (commercial education); *Royal Choral Society
v. I.R.C.* (1943) 112 L.J.K.B. 648 (choral society); *Re Royce* [1940] Ch. 514 (church choir). Of these,
Re Cranstoun [1932] 1 Ch. 537 (preservation of ancient buildings) would certainly and *Re Spence*
[1938] Ch. 96 (collection of arms and antiques) would probably be regarded as falling within
this head but the others would clearly still be regarded as trusts for the advancement of
education.
[191] [1965] Ch. 85.
[192] For another example of expert evidence being admitted, see *Gilmour v. Coats* [1949] A.C.
426.

together with the result that the good things would be stifled by the large number of absolutely valueless pictures and objects. Harman L.J. could conceive of no useful purpose in "foisting on the public this mass of junk"[193] and so the Court of Appeal, reversing Wilberforce J., held that the trust had neither public utility nor educational value and therefore failed as a charity.

11–076   The trusts considered so far all fall within the advancement of the arts and culture. Heritage property has long been regarded as a valid charitable purposes, as is typified by the bodies such as the National Trust. As for science, this term is not defined but is most unlikely to be restricted to natural science and is presumably wide enough to include other analogous purposes which have previously been recognised as charitable such as the trust for the advancement of horticulture recognised in *Re Pleasants*.[194]

(G)   The Advancement of Amateur Sport
11–077   This purpose is found in section 2(2)(g), while section 2(3)(g) defines "sport" as sports or games which promote health by involving physical or mental skill or exercise. This reflects a fundamental change of the law to the extent that hitherto a gift for the promotion of a specific sport was not as such charitable. Accordingly, in *Re Nottage*,[195] where a trust was established to provide annually a cup for the most successful yacht of the season, with the expressed object of encouraging the sport of yacht racing, the Court of Appeal held that this was a gift for the encouragement of a mere sport which, although it might be beneficial to the public, was not charitable because the private benefit of the participants outweighed the public benefit.[196] Equally, in *I.R.C. v. City of Glasgow Police Athletic Association*[197] the police athletic association was held not to be charitable because it was simply a sports club for the benefit of its members. Both trust and association would now necessarily be held to be charitable. Further, even before the change in the law, the provision of prizes for sport in a school was held in *Re Mariette*[198] to be valid as advancing that part of the education of students which had to do with their bodily and physical development.[199] In *I.R.C. v. McMullen*[200] the House of Lords reached a similar decision as to the legal status of the Football Association Youth Trust. Both trusts were held to be valid charitable trusts for the advancement of education but such a finding is obviously no longer necessary and so the controversy in this respect in

---

[193] [1965] Ch. 85 at 107.
[194] (1923) 39 T.L.R. 675.
[195] [1895] 2 Ch. 649.
[196] See also to the same effect *Re Clifford* (1911) 106 L.T. 14 (angling); *Re Patten* [1929] 2 Ch. 276 at 289, 290 (cricket); *Re King* [1931] W.N. 232 (general sport).
[197] [1953] A.C. 380 at 391.
[198] [1915] 2 Ch. 284. See also *Re Dupree's Deed Trusts* [1945] Ch. 16 (chess; see *ante* para 11–074).
[199] The similar decision in *Re Gray* [1925] Ch. 362, whose validity was doubted in *I.R.C. v. McMullen* [1981] A.C. 1, that a gift for the promotion of a sport in an army regiment was charitable because it increased the army's efficiency would now certainly be upheld as falling within Section 2(2)(l); see *post*, para 11–093.
[200] [1981] A.C. 1.

I.R.C. v. McMullen is no longer of any relevance.[201] Trusts for purely recreational purposes instead fall within section 2(2)(j).[202]

(H) The Advancement of Human Rights, Conflict Resolution or Reconciliation or the Promotion of Religious or Racial Harmony or Equality and Diversity

This purpose is found in section 2(2)(h) and is wholly new. Prior to the   **11–078** legislation, the Charity Commission had already recognised the promotion of human rights as a charitable purpose but there is no body of case law to assist in the interpretation of the legislation.

(I) The Advancement of Environmental Protection or Improvement

This purpose is found in section 2(2)(i). Trusts for the protection of the   **11–079** environment and the conservation of the national heritage have become increasingly common. Their existence and the legislation reflect the growing concern for the protection and the improvement of the environment. While such trusts often appear to be involved in the political arena,[203] they will be capable of taking effect as charitable trusts provided that the political activity carried on by the trustees is ancillary to and is not their main objective.

(J) The Relief of Those in Need by reason of Youth, Age, Ill-Health, Disability, Financial Hardship or Other Disadvantage

This purpose is found in section 2(2)(j), while section 2(3)(e) provides that   **11–080** this purpose includes relief given by the provision of accommodation or care to the mentioned persons.

The vast majority of the trusts which fall under this head are trusts which   **11–081** fall within the Recreational Charities Act 1958, which section 5 has amended in such a way as to make apparent that all trusts which now fall within that Act must necessarily fall under this head.[204] That Act, which came into force on March 3, 1958, regulates all recreational trusts. It was passed because of the highly inconvenient decision of the House of Lords in *I.R.C. v. Baddeley*[205] which concerned certain trusts "for the promotion of the moral, social and physical well-being of persons resident in West Ham and Leyton who for the time being are members or likely to become members of the Methodist

---

[201] The House of Lords held, unanimously reversing Walton J. and the Court of Appeal, that the purpose of the deed was not merely to organise the playing of Association Football in schools and universities but also to promote the physical education and development of students as an addition to their formal education; therefore, it created a valid charitable trust for the advancement of education, the sporting activities contributing to a balanced education. Lord Hailsham of St Marylebone L.C. was at pains to reject any idea which would confine the education of the young to schools or university campuses, limit that education to formal instruction or render it devoid of pleasure in the exercise of skill.

[202] See *post*, para 11–080.

[203] See *post*, para 11–095.

[204] This is because, as a result of section 5, the Recreational Charities Act 1958 now applies if the recreational facilities in question either are provided primarily with the object of improving conditions of life for persons who have need of the facilities by virtue of falling within this head or are to be available to the members of the public at large or to male, or to female, members of the public at large.

[205] [1955] A.C. 572.

Church by the provision of facilities for moral, social and physical training and recreation". It was held, by a majority, that the trusts failed because they were expressed in language so vague as to permit the property to be used for purposes which the law did not recognise as charitable and also because they did not satisfy the necessary test of public benefit. This case produced a situation where legislation of some kind was essential because, as a result of the decision, it appeared that there might be grave doubts as to the charitable status of many organisations and trusts, including women's institutes, boys' clubs, miners' welfare trusts and village halls, which had for a very long time been assumed to enjoy charitable status. The Recreational Charities Act 1958 was therefore enacted extremely promptly.

11–082   The Recreational Charities Act 1958 provides that it shall be and shall be deemed always to have been charitable to provide, or assist in providing, facilities for recreation or other leisure-time occupations if the facilities are provided in the interest of social welfare.[206] This is subject to the overriding proviso that the trust will not be charitable unless it is for the public benefit.[207] Further, the requirement that facilities must be provided in the interest of social welfare is not satisfied unless: first, they are provided with the object of improving the conditions of life for the persons for whom the facilities are primarily intended[208]; and,[209] secondly, either those persons have need of such facilities because they fall within the categories of persons listed under this head[210] or the facilities are to be available to the members of the public at large or to the male or to the female members of the public at large.[211]

11–083   The composition of this part of the Recreational Charities Act 1958 has always been and remains somewhat curious. In particular, the two final ingredients are alternative to one another. Accordingly, it appears that a recreational trust in favour of a limited class of the public will be within the Act if the beneficiaries are within the appropriate categories of persons, now the persons who have need of the facilities by virtue of falling within one of the categories listed in section 2(2)(j) of the Charities Act 2006. But, if the beneficiaries do not have need of the facilities by falling into these categories, the facilities must be available to members of the public at large (or members of the public at large of one or the other sex) and a trust in favour of a more limited class will fail. Whether or not there was a case for confining the objectives of the Act in this way, the position has obviously been confirmed by the Charities Act 2006. But it remains unfortunate that the position was not formulated with more precision.

11–084   The effect of these provisions, in particular the terms "social welfare" and "conditions of life", was considered by the Court of Appeal in *I.R.C. v. McMullen*,[212] which concerned the Football Association Youth Trust. The majority held, among other things, that the recreational facilities provided

---

[206] s.1.(1). The expression "social welfare" is also used in the Local Government Finance Act 1988.
[207] s.1(1) proviso.
[208] s.1(2)(a).
[209] As amended by Charities Act 2006, s.5.
[210] s.1(2)(b)(i).
[211] s.1(2)(b)(ii).
[212] [1979] 1 W.L.R. 130; see Warburton [1980] Conv. 173.

were primarily intended for pupils in schools and universities but that they were not provided with the object of improving the conditions of life of such pupils; they were instead provided for those of them who were persuaded to, or did, play football or some other game or sport irrespective of their conditions of life. Consequently, the trusts did not fall within the Recreational Charities Act 1958. Bridge L.J. dissented on the ground that the provision of recreational facilities for pupils unquestionably improved the pupils' conditions of life and met a social need of youth. This decision was reversed by the House of Lords on other grounds which have already been considered,[213] so the question of the effect of the Act did not fall to be considered. However, as a matter of statutory interpretation, the view of Bridge L.J. appeared highly persuasive and has now duly been approved by the House of Lords in *Guild v. I.R.C.*[214] This case concerned a gift of residue "to the town council of North Berwick for the use in connection with the sports centre in North Berwick or some similar purpose in connection with sport". This gift was held to fall within the Act on the grounds that "persons in all walks of life and all kinds of social circumstances may have their condition of life improved by the provision of recreational facilities of suitable character" and the facilities of the centre would have this effect.

Subject to the facilities being provided in the interests of social welfare, the Recreational Charities Act 1958 is specifically applied, in particular, to the "provision of facilities at village halls, community centres and women's institutes and to the provision and maintenance of grounds and buildings to be used for purposes of recreation or leisure-time occupation and extends to the provision of facilities for those purposes by the organising of any activity".[215] It is not apparent how these purposes fall within this head or, for that matter, within the Recreational Charities Act 1958 as amended by the Charities Act 2006. These purposes instead now fall within section 2(2)(m).[216] **11–085**

The Recreational Charities Act 1958 left untouched the general law as to the meaning of charity,[217] now of course anyway amended by the Charities Act 2006. That Act also seemed to have left untouched the principle that charitable trusts must be for the public benefit which also came under consideration in *I.R.C. v. Baddeley.* Judging from the speech of Viscount Simonds,[218] it certainly seemed that the membership, whether actual or potential, of the Methodist Church, at least in a defined area, did not amount to a class sufficient to satisfy the test of public benefit.[219] If the view of Viscount Simonds continues to prevail, trusts such as those which the House **11–086**

---

[213] [1981] A.C. 1; see *ante*, para 11–076.

[214] [1992] 2 A.C. 310 (a Scottish Appeal but the English definition of charity is incorporated into Scots law for tax purposes).

[215] s.1(3).

[216] See *post*, para 11–094. Recreational Charities Act 1925, s.2 made specific provision for miners' welfare trusts; those which had been declared before December 17, 1957 were validated retrospectively, although there were certain savings as to past transactions. Miners' welfare trusts created on or after that date were governed by the general provisions of the Act. Charities Act 2006, s.5(3) has now abolished these special conditions completely.

[217] s.3(1).

[218] [1955] A.C. 572 at 589–593.

[219] Lord Somervell seemed to agree with Lord Simonds; Lord Reid, who dissented, took a different view. Lord Porter and Lord Tucker expressed no opinion on this point.

of Lords was actually considering in *I.R.C. v. Baddeley* would still fail. It was anyway the other aspect of the decision, that the trusts were too uncertain, which aroused apprehension among the women's institutes and other bodies which the Recreational Charities Act 1958 was designed to cure. This limited objective was probably successfully achieved, even though the material provisions are somewhat clumsily and ambiguously expressed. It was thought at the time that the Act would be difficult to apply and probably create more difficulties than it solved[220]; however, it has only occasionally had to be considered in decisions which have been reported.[221]

11–087   This new statutory purpose enacted in section 2(2)(j) of the Charities Act 2006 must now necessarily also include the trusts formerly held to be for the relief of the aged and/or impotent. There has never been any decisive definition of either of these terms. It has in the past been held that people who are not under the age of 50 are "aged".[222] But, in view of advances in medical science, this conclusion now seems very doubtful; a settlor who wished to specify an age today might well be taking a risk if the age specified were lower than 65, which has long since been the official retirement age for men and will in 2020 also become the official retirement age for women.[223] In contrast "impotent", although generously construed, has never been precisely defined; it does however include persons with a permanent disability[224] and the seriously ill or wounded.[225]

11–088   However, the enactment of section 2(2)(j) does at least seem to have reversed the controversial and unfortunate decision of the Court of Appeal in *Re Cole*,[226] where the majority held that a gift for "the general benefit and general welfare" of the children for the time being in a children's home maintained by a local authority was not charitable. Romer L.J. in particular based his decision to this effect on a close reading of the preamble to the Charitable Uses Act 1601 and concluded that the conceivable provision of benefits, which could include such "new-fangled devices" as television sets, for the children in question, who might well be juvenile delinquents, were not within the express terms of the preamble or within its spirit and intendment. The decision was followed by Danckwerts J. in *Re Sahal's Will Trusts*[227] on similar facts. But the dissenting view of Lord Evershed M.R. in *Re Cole* seems the more commendable because of its wider outlook "that the inference to be drawn from the preamble is that the care and upbringing of children who for any reason have not got the advantage or opportunity of being looked after and brought up by responsible and competent persons, or

---

[220] See Maurice (1959) 23 Conv. (N.S.) 15.

[221] See *Wynn v. Skegness U.D.C.* [1967] 1 W.L.R. 52 where a seaside holiday home for Derbyshire miners was assumed to fall within the 1958 Act as a recreational charity; *I.R.C. v. McMullen* [1979] 1 W.L.R. 130, reversed on other grounds [1981] A.C. 1, see *ante*, para 11–084.

[222] *Re Wall* (1889) 42 Ch.D. 510. See also *Re Payling's Will Trusts* [1969] 1 W.L.R. 1595; *Re Armitage* [1972] Ch. 438.

[223] Women both before April 6, 1950 retire at the age of 60, whereas women born on or after April 6, 1955 retire at the age of 65 (the retirement date of women born between those two dates increases progressively in accordance with Pensions Act 1995, Sch.4, para.1).

[224] *Re Fraser* (1883) 22 Ch.D. 827; *Re Lewis* [1955] Ch. 104.

[225] *Re Hillier* [1944] 1 All E.R. 486.

[226] [1958] Ch. 877.

[227] [1958] 1 W.L.R. 1243.

who could by these or other reasons, properly be regarded as defenceless or 'deprived' are matters which prima facie qualify as charitable purposes".[228] Section 2(2)(j) clearly confirms this view.

Section 2(2)(j) may also just about justify one of the most striking, if not   **11–089** startling, cases in which education was given an extremely and perhaps unjustifiably wide connotation. This was *Re Shaw's Will Trusts*[229] where the testatrix, who was the wife of George Bernard Shaw and (it is necessary to add) herself of Irish origin, bequeathed the residue of her estate upon trusts for, among other things, the teaching, promotion and encouragement in Ireland of self-control, elocution, oratory, deportment, the arts of personal contact, of social intercourse and the other arts of public and private life. It was held that these somewhat eccentric trusts were wholly educational in character and constituted valid charitable trusts. The only other obvious possible classification for this trust is as a trust for the relief of those in need by reason of youth!

(K) The Advancement of Animal Welfare
This new purpose is found in section 2(2)(k). It is not clear whether its   **11–090** introduction has changed the pre-existing law. It has long been clearly established that a trust for the protection of animals in general is a valid charitable trust.[230] It has been held that this is the case because such trusts benefit humanity by promoting morality and curbing an inborn tendency to cruelty,[231] a somewhat surprising process of reasoning even in a supposedly animal-loving country. But, however surprising, this indicates that the reason for the recognition of these trusts is that they promote the moral or spiritual welfare of the community. It should, however, be noted that, although an animal hospital is, according to the general principle, prima facie charitable,[232] it will not be charitable if it is carried on for private profit as a profession, occupation or trade.[233]

In contrast, the decision in *Re Grove-Grady*[234] established that, if a donor   **11–091** sets up a trust to provide a sanctuary for all kinds of animals from human molestation with no safeguards against the destruction of the weaker animals by the stronger, that trust is not charitable. As Lord Hanworth M.R. pointed out,[235] the only characteristic of the trust was that the sanctuary was to be free from molestation by man, while all the fauna within it were to be free to molest and harry one another. Such a purpose did not afford any

---

[228] [1958] Ch. 877 at 892.
[229] [1952] Ch. 163.
[230] *Re Wedgwood* [1915] 1 Ch. 113 (secret trust for protection and benefit of animals).
[231] *Re Wedgwood* [1915] 1 Ch. 113 at 117, *per* Lord Cozens-Hardy M.R.; *Re Moss* [1949] 1 All E.R. 415 at 497–498, *per* Romer J. (cats and kittens). Compare earlier cases: *London University v. Yarrow* (1857) 1 De G. & J. 72 (animal hospital) and *Re Douglas* (1887) 35 Ch.D. 472 (Home for Lost Dogs), where the court emphasised public utility but this is not the modern trend. See *ante*, para 3–102.
[232] *London University v. Yarrow* (1857) 1 De G. & J. 72.
[233] See *Re Satterthwaite's Will Trusts* [1966] 1 W.L.R. 277 at 284, *per* Russell L.J.
[234] [1929] 1 Ch. 557, compromised on appeal *sub nom. Att.-Gen. v. Plowden* [1931] W.N. 89.
[235] [1929] 1 Ch. 557 at 573–574.

advantage to animals or any protection from cruelty to animals nor did it afford any elevating lesson to mankind.[236]

11–092   What is unclear is whether the fact that this head is entitled "the advancement of animal welfare" rather than the protection of animals generally has had any impact on the decision of the House of Lords in *National Anti-Vivisection Society v. I.R.C.*[237] It was held that a trust to abolish vivisection was not charitable for two reasons: first, that the advantages accruing from the abolition of vivisection did not equal those derived from its retention; and, secondly,[238] that anti-vivisection could not be achieved except by legislation and so the law could not stultify itself by holding that it was for the public benefit that the law itself should be changed. While it would obviously advance the welfare of animals if they could not be the subject of vivisection, on balance the reasons enunciated by the House of Lords, particularly the second one which is obviously associated with the general ban on political activities,[239] nevertheless appear to hold good. However, it is not unlikely that the appearance of the statutory definition will cause this question to be relitigated sooner rather than later.

(L)   The Promotion of the Efficiency of the Armed Forces of the Crown, or of the Efficiency of the Police, Fire and Rescue Services or Ambulance Services

11–093   This purpose is found in section 2(2)(l), while section 2(3)(f) defines "fire and rescue services" as services provided by fire and rescue authorities under the relevant legislation,[240] thus excluding voluntary mountain rescue services and so forth (which are anyway with section 2(2)(d)[241]). The restriction to the promotion of the efficiency of the listed bodies is on the face of things in some respects more limited than the existing law. All trusts which promote the armed forces of the Crown have been held to be charitable[242] and this rule has been held to apply even if the means of promotion are indirect.[243] Similarly, a trust for the benefit of the Mercantile Marine, which is not strictly part of the armed forces of the Crown at all, has been held to be charitable.[244] Further it certainly cannot be said that a more general purpose which has been held to be charitable, that of promoting the defence of the

---

[236] This decision of course re-emphasises the importance of careful drafting of the trust instrument so that the "public benefit" requirement is satisfied. There is no doubt that a competently drawn trust for the preservation of wild life, taking due account of public benefit, will be charitable.

[237] [1948] A.C. 31, reversing *Re Foveaux* [1895] 2 Ch. 501. See also *Re Jenkins's Will Trusts* [1966] Ch. 249 (gift to the British Union for the Abolition of Vivisection).

[238] Adopting *Tyssen on Charitable Bequests*, 1st edn (1898), p.176. See also *Bowman v. Secular Society* [1917] A.C. 406 at 442, *per* Lord Parker (political purposes) and see *post*, para 11–095.

[239] See *post*, para 11–095.

[240] Fire and Rescue Services Act 2004, Part 2.

[241] See *ante*, para 11–067.

[242] *Re Stratheden and Campbell* [1894] 3 Ch. 265 (benefit of volunteer corps); *Re Stephens* (1892) 8 T.L.R. 792 (for teaching shooting); *Re Barker* (1909) 25 T.L.R. 753 (for prizes to be competed for by cadets).

[243] *Re Good* [1905] 2 Ch. 60 (providing a library for the officers' mess and providing plates for the mess); *Re Donald* [1909] 2 Ch. 410 (for the mess of the regiment and the poor of the regiment); *Re Gray* [1925] Ch. 362 (regimental fund for the promotion of sport).

[244] *Re Corbyn* [1941] Ch. 400.

United Kingdom from the attack of hostile aircraft,[245] was promoting the efficiency of any of the listed bodies. However, the statutory purpose is consistent with *Re Wokingham Fire Brigade Trusts*,[246] where Danckwerts J. held that the provision and maintenance of a public fire brigade was a charitable purpose because it was designed to prevent damage to property and loss of life, and with the statement in *I.R.C. v. City of Glasgow Police Athletic Association*[247] that the promotion of the efficiency of the police is self-evidently charitable (the actual decision in that case, that the athletic association in question was not charitable because it was simply a sports club for the benefit of its members, has in effect been reversed by the enactment of section 2(2)(g)[248]).

(M) Any Other Purpose Within Subsection (4)
This purpose is found within section 2(2)(m), defined as "any other pur-   **11–094**
poses within subsection (4)". Subsection 4 in turn defines these purposes as: (a), any other purposes "recognised as charitable purposes under existing law or by virtue of section 1 of the Recreational Charities Act 1958"[249]; (b), any purposes which may reasonably be regarded as analogous to, or within the spirit of, purposes within section 2(2)(a) to (l) or section 2(4)(a) and (c), any purposes which may reasonably be regarded as analogous to, or within the spirit of, purposes within section 2(4)(b) or (c). Section 2(4)(c) simply emphasises that any purpose which has been recognised as charitable as being for the public benefit will still be charitable under the Charities Act 2006 despite the fact that it is not within any of the listed statutory purposes or the Recreational Charities Act 1958. This head sweeps up and renders charitable any trusts which have previously been held to be charitable which cannot be allocated to one or more of the 11 specific purposes. However, future settlors of charitable trusts should not assume that wholly new trusts for purposes which do not fall within any of the 11 specific purposes will automatically be held to be charitable just because their purposes are similar to those of trusts which have previously been held to be charitable; the purposes of such new trusts may well be able to be distinguished from the purposes of the former trusts on which they have been modelled. A well advised settlor should, therefore, take care to ensure that his charitable purposes fall fairly and squarely within one of the 11 specific purposes.

3. *Political Purposes*

It has long been established, and remains the law, that a trust whose objects   **11–095**
are, or include, political purposes cannot be a charitable trust. In *Bowman v.*

---

[245] *Re Driffill* [1950] Ch. 92.
[246] [1951] Ch. 373.
[247] [1953] A.C. 380 at 391.
[248] See *ante*, para 11–077.
[249] Thus they include "provision of facilities at village halls, community centres and women's institutes and to the provision and maintenance of grounds and buildings to be used for purposes of recreation or leisure-time occupation and extends to the provision of facilities for those purposes by the organising of any activity", purposes which do not fall within section 2(2)(j) or, for that matter, within the Recreational Charities Act 1958 as amended by the Charities Act 2006.

The Secular Society[250] Lord Parker of Waddington stated the general position as follows:

"A trust for the attainment of political objects has always been held invalid, not because it is illegal, for everyone is at liberty to advocate or promote by any lawful means a change in the law, but because the court has no means of judging whether a proposed change in the law will or will not be for the public benefit, and therefore cannot say that a gift to secure the change is a charitable gift."

11–096   This most straightforward application of this principle is to trusts in favour of political parties, which are obviously not charitable. Trusts in favour respectively of the Conservative Party and the Labour Party failed for this reason in *Bonar Law Memorial Trust v. I.R.C.*[251] and in *Re Hopkinson.*[252] Trusts whose objects necessarily involve a change in the law are also not charitable for this reason. As has been already seen,[253] the principle in *Bowman v. The Secular Society* was applied by the House of Lords in *National Anti-Vivisection Society v. I.R.C.*[254] when rejecting as charitable a trust to abolish vivisection on the grounds that its purposes would involve the promotion of legislation in bring about a change the law. However, most of the more recent cases have involved trusts which have purported to be trusts for the advancement of education (now of course they might instead purport to be trusts under one or more of the new statutory heads) but are really intended to educate the public into the adoption of a particular political viewpoint aimed at bringing about an alteration in the law or governmental policy of the United Kingdom and/or of a foreign country.

11–097   *McGovern v. Attorney-General*[255] concerned the legal status of Amnesty International. The general object of this unincorporated non-profit making body was expressed to be to secure throughout the world the observance of the provisions of the Universal Declaration of Human Rights in regard to various categories of persons referred to in its constitution as "prisoners of conscience", namely persons who were imprisoned, detained or restricted because of their political, religious or conscientiously held beliefs or because of their ethnic origin, sex, colour or language. The association also had various specific objects whose legal effect had to be considered: first, the release of prisoners of conscience, which was held to be a clear political purpose because it involved putting pressure on foreign governments to change their policies; secondly, the abolition of torture or inhumane treatment or punishment, which was similarly held not to be charitable because it would involve legislation requiring the abolition of corporal or capital punishment; and, thirdly, providing research into the observance of human rights and the dissemination of that research, which would have been charitable had it had stood alone but, because it did not, also failed because

---

[250] [1917] A.C. 406.
[251] (1933) 49 T.L.R. 220.
[252] [1949] 1 All E.R. 346.
[253] See *ante*, para 11–092.
[254] [1948] A.C. 31.
[255] [1982] Ch. 321.

of the requirement that charitable trusts must be exclusively charitable. Slade J. therefore held that Amnesty International was not a charity.

McGovern v. Attorney-General was applied in *Re Bushnell*,[256] where a testa-   **11–098**
tor had directed a fund to be used "for the advancement and propagation of the teaching of socialised medicine", with directions as to how the managers of the fund should carry out and foster this purpose. Goulding J. held that the trust could not be supported as an educational trust since the directions with regard to the principles of "socialised medicine" dominated the whole of the trust. Nor was the trust beneficial to the community since its validity had to be tested at the date of the testator's death in 1941, when the court could not have decided the question because it would have involved considering what would then have been a political question, the desirability or otherwise of legislation to bring into being a state health service.[257] Both decisions were confirmed and applied by the Court of Appeal in *Southwood v. Attorney-General*,[258] where it was held that the court could not determine whether or not it promoted the public benefit for the public to be educated into an acceptance of the belief that world peace would be best secured by "demilitarisation"; this belief was a political objective and the trust which had been set up to propagate it was therefore not charitable. The court rejected the contention of the settlors that their objective was instead to educate the public as to the differing means of securing a state of peace and avoiding a state of war, an objective which the court would have held to be charitable.

As that dictum in *Southwood v. Attorney-General* demonstrates, the mere   **11–099**
existence of some political motive is not necessarily fatal to the existence of a charitable trust. Thus in *Re Koeppler's Will Trust*[259] the organisation of conferences with political themes but without any intention of furthering the interests of any particular political party was held to be an educational charitable purpose. The question is whether a trust's leading purpose is political, by for example promoting legislation with a view to changing the law, in which case it will fail, or whether that purpose is subsidiary. This may also be a way of justifying the much earlier decision of Stirling J. in *Re Scowcroft*[260] which concerned a gift for the maintenance of a village club and reading-room "to be used for the furtherance of Conservative principles and religious and mental improvement, and to be kept free from intoxicants and dancing". This was held to be charitable, apparently on the grounds that all the prescribed purposes were to be carried out simultaneously so that the clearly political purpose was not, in the event, predominant.

There is no doubt about the increasing desire of charities to become   **11–100**
"'involved" in the causes with which their work is connected, not just in the international arena as in *McGovern v. Attorney-General* but in areas such as the provision of housing and other services for the under-privileged in society. The desire of organisations whose objectives are otherwise clearly charitable to draw to the attention of the public as forcefully as possible the

---

[256] [1975] 1 W.L.R. 1596.
[257] The fact that a state health service had subsequently been introduced was irrelevant; the trust had to stand or fall by the character of its objects as at the date of the testator's death.
[258] [2000] W.T.L.R. 1199.
[259] [1986] Ch. 423.
[260] [1898] 2 Ch. 638.

need for action to remedy certain social conditions has led them to form pressure groups, action groups and lobbies for this purpose whose "political" nature is potentially capable of affecting their charitable status. In 1981, the Charity Commissioners suggested fairly detailed guidelines for charity trustees in these circumstances, which included the following[261]: first, a charity should undertake only those activities which can reasonably be said to be directed to achieving its purposes and which are within the powers conferred by its governing instrument; secondly, the governing instrument should not include powers to exert political pressure except in a way that is merely ancillary to a charitable purpose; thirdly, the powers and purposes of a charity should not include a power to bring pressure to bear on the Government to adopt, alter or maintain a particular line of action; fourthly, the charity should spend its money on the promotion of public general legislation only if in doing so it is exercising a power which is ancillary to and in furtherance of its charitable purposes; fifthly, if the objects include the advancement of education, care should be taken not to overstep the boundary between education and propaganda; sixthly, if the objects include research, the charity must aim for objectivity and balance; and, seventhly, charities, whether operating in this country or overseas, must neither seek to influence or remedy those causes of poverty which lie in the social, economic and political structures of countries or communities nor bring pressure to bear on a government to procure a change in policies or administrative practices, nor seek to eliminate social, economic, political or other injustice.

4. The Exclusive Nature Of Charity

11–101   It is essential, subject to the effect of the Charitable Trusts (Validation) Act 1954 when it applies, that the trustees of a charitable trust are bound to devote the funds to exclusively charitable purposes. This is the case whether those purposes are expressed specifically or in a general way. Where the purposes of a trust include both charitable and non-charitable purposes, then if it is possible for the whole of the trust property to be devoted to the non-charitable purposes the entire trust will be void.

11–102   A case where the purposes in question were expressed specifically was *Hunter v. Attorney-General*,[262] where the testator left his personal estate to trustees for three alternative purposes: first, the purchase of advowsons (rights to present clergymen to parishes); secondly, the erection, improvement or endowment of churches, chapels or schools; and, thirdly, the payment of clergymen or teachers. The latter two purposes were unquestionably charitable but the first purpose was held by the House of Lords not to be charitable because the testator had not specified the trusts on which the advowsons were to be held. The entire gift was, therefore, held to be void and the testator's personal estate went to his intestate successors. The Earl of Halsbury L.C. said[263]:

---

[261] For further details, see the Report for 1981, pp.19–22 and the Annual Report 1986, App. A.

[262] [1899] A.C. 309.

[263] At 315.

"It is undoubtedly the law that, where a bequest is made for charitable purposes and also for an indefinite purpose not charitable and no apportionment is made by the will, so that the whole might be applied for either purpose, the whole bequest is void."

However, the majority of the cases of this type have instead concerned trusts for non-specific purposes, where the decision as to the destination of the funds in question is to be made by the trustees. In these cases what is crucial is how those purposes are described; typically the donor joins the word "charitable" with another adjective, such as "benevolent", "patriotic", "philanthropic" or "public"; all the latter adjectives include purposes which are not charitable. In such circumstances, if the testator has used the expressions conjunctively, for example, by saying "charitable and benevolent purposes", then the trust property will only be able to be used for such benevolent purposes as are also charitable and the trust will therefore be a valid charitable trust. But if, on the other hand, the testator has used the expressions disjunctively, for example by saying "charitable or benevolent purposes", then the trust property will be able to be utilised for benevolent purposes which are not charitable and the trust will therefore be void.   **11–103**

The expression "charitable and benevolent institutions" was construed conjunctively in *Re Best*[264] and the gift in question was upheld. On the other hand, the expression "charitable or benevolent purposes" was construed disjunctively by the House of Lords in *Chichester Diocesan Fund and Board of Finance (Incorporated) v. Simpson*[265] and the gift in question therefore failed; in this respect, the House echoed its earlier decisions in *Houston v. Burns*,[266] where a gift was made for "public benevolent or charitable purposes" in a Scottish parish, and in *Blair v. Duncan*,[267] where the relevant expression was "charitable or public purposes". However, it must be emphasised that the test is not whether the word "and" or the word "or" has been used, although this is generally decisive, but whether the phrase used is as a whole conjunctive or disjunctive, something which is entirely a question of construction. It is therefore possible for the word "and" to have been used disjunctively and for the word "or" to have been used conjunctively[268]; the expression "and/or" can obviously be construed either way.[269]   **11–104**

As the facts of *Chichester Diocesan Fund and Board of Finance (Incorporated) v. Simpson*[270] emphasise, the consequences of a trust being held void for this   **11–105**

---

[264] [1904] 2 Ch. 354 (see also *Blair v. Duncan* [1902] A.C. 37 at 44 where Lord Davey considered that a gift for "charitable and public purposes" would be valid.
[265] [1944] A.C. 341.
[266] [1918] A.C. 337.
[267] [1902] A.C. 37.
[268] See *Re Sutton* (1885) 28 Ch.D. 464; *Re Best* [1904] 2 Ch. 354 ("charitable and deserving" and "charitable and benevolent" objects respectively were upheld). Contrast *Att.-Gen. of the Bahamas v. Royal Trust Co.* [1986] 1 W.L.R. 1001, where a gift for "education and welfare" was interpreted disjunctively and was held void.
[269] See, in addition to the cases mentioned in the text, *Morice v. Bishop of Durham* (1805) 10 Ves. 522; *Re Davidson* [1909] 1 Ch. 567; *Re Da Costa* [1912] 1 Ch. 337; *Att.-Gen. for New Zealand v. Brown* [1917] A.C. 393; *Re Chapman* [1922] 2 Ch. 479; *Re Davis* [1923] 1 Ch. 225; *Att.-Gen. v. National Provincial and Union Bank of England* [1924] A.C. 262; *Att.-Gen. for New Zealand v. New Zealand Insurance Co.* [1936] 3 All E.R. 888; *Re Atkinson's Will Trusts* [1978] 1 W.L.R. 586 (evidence inadmissible to show that by "worthy" the testator meant "charitable").
[270] [1944] A.C. 341.

reason can be very striking. The executors of the estate in question had paid the whole of the very substantial sum which constituted the testator's residuary estate to some 139 charities before his intestate successors, his next-of-kin, successfully challenged the validity of the gift. The executors had, therefore, unwittingly committed what was in effect a breach of trust.[271] The next-of-kin not only issued proceedings against the executors, which were eventually compromised,[272] but also made both personal and proprietary claims against the charities to recover the sums paid to them. The personal claim went all the way to the House of Lords (*Ministry of Health v. Simpson*[273]) where it succeeded and where no appeal was made against the equal success of the proprietary claim in the Court of Appeal (under the name *Re Diplock*[274]). Both of these claims will have to be considered in detail in a later chapter.[275]

(A) Apportionment

11–106   It should, however, be remembered that a donor may direct an apportionment of his funds between charitable and non-charitable purposes. This class of gift will not fail, even if the trustees fail to make the apportionment, because in the last resort the courts will apportion the funds equally between the objects. Consequently, if the non-charitable purposes are void for, for example, uncertainty, only the trust of the part of the funds devoted to those purposes will fail.[276]

(B) Incidental Non-Charitable Purposes

11–107   It is also important to note that the fact that a non-charitable purpose is incidental or ancillary to the achievement of a purpose which is, in fact, charitable will not destroy the gift. Thus, in *Royal College of Surgeons v. National Provincial Bank*[277] the House of Lords held that the College was in law a charity since its object, as recited in the Charter, was "the due promotion and encouragement of the study and practice of surgery", the professional protection of its members provided for in its bye-laws being merely ancillary to that object. Similarly, in *Incorporated Council of Law Reporting for England and Wales v. Attorney-General*,[278] it was held that the fact that legal practitioners used law reports in order to earn their professional fees did not have the result that the objects of the Council were not charitable. The same result occurred in *Re Coxen*,[279] where Jenkins J. held that the provision made by the testator for a dinner to be held for the Aldermen of the City of London after their annual meeting to consider the management of a trust in favour of orthopaedic hospitals which he had also set up was purely ancillary to the primary charitable trust and procured its better

---

[271] Technically, because they were administering an estate rather than a trust, they had committed what is known as *devastavit*.
[272] But not before one of the executors had committed suicide.
[273] [1951] A.C. 251.
[274] [1948] Ch. 465.
[275] See *post*, para 22–102 *et seq.*, para 22–133 *et seq.*
[276] *Salusbury v. Denton* (1857) 3 K. & J. 529; *Re Clarke* [1923] 2 Ch. 407.
[277] [1952] A.C. 631.
[278] [1972] Ch. 73.
[279] [1948] Ch. 747.

administration. Further, in *London Hospital Medical College v. I.R.C.*,[280] once it had been held that the students' union in question existed to further the educational purposes of the College,[281] it was held to be immaterial that the union also provided personal benefits for the individual students who were elected members and chose to make use of its facilities.[282]

(C) Subsidiary Purposes

Incidental purposes such as those just mentioned must be carefully distin-   **11–108** guished from purposes which are subsidiary but not merely incidental. In *Oxford Group v. I.R.C.*[283] the Court of Appeal held that one of the objects set out in the Group's memorandum of association, the support of "any charitable or benevolent" associations, actually conferred powers which were so wide that they could not be regarded as charitable; they were not merely ancillary to the main, admittedly charitable, objects set out elsewhere in the memorandum. The Group did not therefore constitute a charity.

(D) The Charitable Trusts (Validation) Act 1954

The decision in *Oxford Group v. I.R.C.* was thought to affect a large number   **11–109** of charities and the Nathan Committee therefore recommended some amendment of the law but not, however, the complete reversal of the decision.[284] The result was the Charitable Trusts (Validation) Act 1954, a short statute which has turned out to be exceptionally difficult to interpret.

Section 1(1) of the Act defines as an "imperfect trust provision" any   **11–110** provision declaring the objects and so describing them that, consistently with the terms of the provision of the property, they could be used exclusively for charitable purposes but could nevertheless be used for purposes which are not charitable. The instrument in which the "imperfect trust provision" is contained must have taken effect before December 16, 1952,[285] the date of the publication of the Nathan Report. The Act is to apply, by virtue of section 2(1), to any disposition or covenant to make such a disposition where, apart from the Act, the disposition or covenant would have been invalid[286] under the law of England and Wales, but would have been valid if the objects had been exclusively charitable.[287] Finally, in respect of the period before the Act came into force on July 30, 1954, the imperfect trust provision takes effect as if the whole of the declared objects had been charitable but, in respect of the period after the Act came into force, as if that

---

[280] [1976] 1 W.L.R. 613.

[281] See *ante*, para 11–055.

[282] See also, to a similar effect, *Neville Estates v. Madden* [1962] Ch. 852, in which it was held that the social activities of a synagogue were merely ancillary to the strictly religious activities of the synagogue; see *ante*, para 11–065.

[283] [1949] 2 All E.R. 537. See also *Ellis v. I.R.C.* (1949) 31 Tax Cas. 178.

[284] 1952 Cmd. 8710, Ch.12.

[285] s.1(2).

[286] For example, for perpetuity, uncertainty or other similar reason: *Vernon v. I.R.C.* [1956] 1 W.L.R. 1169.

[287] The Act will not however apply where the property or income from the trust has been paid or distributed on the basis that the imperfect trust provision was void (s.2(2)).

provision required the property to be applied for the declared objects only in so far as they are charitable.[288]

11–111   Very real difficulty has been found in the interpretation of these provisions; indeed one judge confessed on two occasions[289] that he was "floored" by them. Particular difficulty has been found in reconciling section 1(1) and section 2(1). The definition of an imperfect trust provision in section 1(1) is limited to a provision declaring the objects for which the property is held, "objects" being synonymous with purposes. How then should section 2(1) be interpreted? It can be convincingly argued that the definition in section 1(1) includes certain gifts which are already valid, for example, a gift for not longer than the perpetuity period for certain named purposes, some of which are charitable and some of which (e.g. a gift "for my dog Winston") are not charitable but nevertheless valid. According to this line of argument, section 2(1) then takes this class of gift outside the mischief of the Act into which section 1 has put it. It is hard to disagree with the observation that it is "an odd state of things if Acts of Parliament are passed in such a form that it is necessary to amend the effect of the first section by putting in a second".[290]

11–112   Other difficulties have also arisen. One of them which arose in *Re Gillingham Bus Disaster Fund*[291] was whether the Act had validated an appeal launched in *The Daily Telegraph* by the mayors of several boroughs, after a number of cadets had been killed and injured in a road accident. The purpose of the appeal was "to promote a Royal Marine Cadet Memorial Fund to be devoted to defraying funeral expenses, caring for the boys who may be disabled and then to such worthy cause or causes in memory of the boys who lost their lives as the Mayors may determine". The majority of the Court of Appeal held that an imperfect trust provision was not validated unless the contributions to the fund were dispositions to which the Act applied, namely dispositions creating more than one interest in the same property.[292] A contribution was admittedly a disposition but, in view of the terms of the appeal, it did not create separate interests in the same property for funeral expenses, for the care of the disabled, and for worthy causes; accordingly, it was held not to have been validated by the Act.[293]

11–113   This is also what Harman J. had held at first instance and, despite a dissent, seems to be correct. However, Harman J. also stated that section 1(1) should be construed as applying only to trusts framed in such terms that the objects referred to included some express reference to charitable purposes as well as to other non-charitable purposes; on this basis, the Act therefore did not apply to a gift stating purposes in a general way, whose terms were capable of embracing charitable purposes but contained no express reference either to charity in general or to any specific charitable purpose. The majority of the Court of Appeal, having held that the Act was not applicable for the reasons already mentioned, did not have to decided this point and,

---

[288] s.1(2)(a), (b).

[289] *Re Harpur's Will Trusts* [1962] Ch. 78 at 95 (Harman L.J.); *Re Gillingham Bus Disaster Fund* [1958] 1 Ch. 300 (Harman J.).

[290] *Re Harpur's Will Trusts* [1962] Ch. 78 at 96, *per* Harman L.J.

[291] [1959] Ch. 62.

[292] s.2(3).

[293] Compare *Re Chitty's Will Trusts* [1970] Ch. 254.

while they expressed some sympathy with the view of Harman J., abstained from expressing any opinion on it. The point did however have to be decided by the dissentient, Ormerod L.J., who decided that section 1(1) should not be construed in the restricted manner favoured by Harman J. but more broadly in accordance with what he regarded as its unambiguous language.

In these circumstances, in *Re Wykes' Will Trusts*[294] Buckley J. felt able to adopt the view favoured by Ormerod L.J. and declared that a trust for "benevolent or welfare" purposes was an imperfect trust provision to which the Act did indeed apply. Shortly afterwards, this decision was on two occasions reviewed by Cross J. In *Re Mead's Trust Deed*[295] he said that a benevolent or welfare fund "is closely akin to a trust for the relief of poverty".[296] He therefore held that a trust to provide a convalescent home for members of a trade union and a home for its poor retired members was validated by the Act and that, as from the date of the Act, the property should be held for those members of the union who were poor persons and, in the case of the home for the aged, for its poor retired members. In *Re Saxone Shoe Co.'s Trust Deed*[297] he actually held that the trust in question was essentially a private trust and therefore incapable of being validated. However, he nevertheless assumed *Re Wykes' Will Trusts* to have been correctly decided, while at the same time setting some limits on to the doctrine enunciated by Buckley J. Cross J. said[298]:

"In such a phrase as 'welfare purposes' there is at least some flavour of charity which may justify one in saying that the testator was seeking to benefit the public through the relief of a limited class. Here there is nothing of that kind, and if such a trust as this is validated by the Act, I do not see why one should stop short of turning any such invalid private trust into a trust for the relief of such beneficiaries as may from time to time be poor."

Nevertheless this problem, which is essentially one of construction of the Act, is still open for adjudication by the Court of Appeal. There seems no overwhelming reason why the restrictive application favoured by Harman J. should be adopted; all that seems to be essential is that the expression used has a charitable connotation. Indeed, in *Re South Place Ethical Society*[299] Dillon J. held that the words "for such purposes either religious or civil" as the trustees might appoint did constitute an imperfect trust provision within the meaning of the Act; they were to be construed as "such purposes, either religious or civil, being charitable" and the provision was accordingly held to have been validated.

Another aspect of the effect of the Act had to be decided in *Re Harpur's Will Trusts*.[300] The Court of Appeal had to consider the question of whether

11–114

11–115

11–116

---

[294] [1961] Ch. 229.
[295] [1961] 1 W.L.R. 1244.
[296] *ibid.* at 1251.
[297] [1962] 1 W.L.R. 943.
[298] *ibid.* at 958–959.
[299] [1980] 1 W.L.R. 1565.
[300] [1962] Ch. 78.

the Act had validated a trust to divide a trust fund "between such institutions and associations having for their main objects the assistance and care of soldiers, sailors, airmen and other members of HM Forces who have been wounded or incapacitated during the recent [second] world war" as the trustees thought fit. It was held that this provision was not within the scope of section 1(1) because that was limited to provisions which declare the objects and describe them in such a ways as to enable effect to be given to them by an application for purposes which are exclusively charitable. This decision has the somewhat surprising result that a gift to an institution whose objects are not described in the trust instrument will not fall within the scope of the subsection.

11–117   The Act can only apply to instruments taking effect before December 16, 1952 and its importance is necessarily by now considerably reduced. However, it cannot yet be regarded as merely of academic interest; the validity of a provision may still arise for consideration on the determination of a life or other limited interest created before that date[301] and the charitable status of a trust which has been in existence since before that date may even today still be challenged.[302]

IV. THE CY-PRÈS DOCTRINE

11–118   It is possible that it may either from the outset be impossible or may subsequently become impossible for a designated charitable purpose to be carried out. In these circumstances, the charitable purpose will not necessarily fail because of what is known as the *cy-près* doctrine[303] which, if it applies, will enable the funds to be applied for whatever charitable purposes are closest to the charitable purpose which was intended.

11–119   This issue only arises if the gift to charity is absolute. Such a gift will have been made where an absolute and perpetual gift which has been made to charity remains intact following the failure of a gift over for remoteness or for some other reason. It will not have been where a gift to charity is only for a limited period, in which case any interest which is undisposed of will result to the grantor. Which has occurred is a question of construction.[304]

11–120   The *cy-près* doctrine is obviously only applicable where it is actually "impossible" for the designated charitable purpose to be carried out; whether or not this is the case is sometimes by no means straightforward. Where it is, then the doctrine is generally, but not always, only applicable

---

[301] If a person has a future interest in property the subject of the provision, he may challenge its validity within one year of the interest vesting in possession: s.3. *Re Chitty's Will Trusts* [1970] Ch. 254.

[302] In 2002 the author of this edition had to advise on a challenge made by the Charity Commissioners to the charitable status of a trust which had been in existence for over 70 years on grounds which might have been capable of being cured by the Act.

[303] For a full survey of the subject, see Sheridan and Delaney, *The Cy-près Doctrine*.

[304] See *Re Cooper's Conveyance Trusts* [1956] 1 W.L.R. 1096 at 1102, *per* Upjohn J. Compare *Re Peel's Release* [1921] Ch. 218; *Re Bawden's Settlement* [1954] 1 W.L.R. 33N. The Rule in *Hancock v. Watson* [1902] A.C. 14, which was formerly known as the Rule in *Lassence v. Tierney* (1849) 1 Mac. & G., whereby a gift to donee with further directions which do not exhaust the funds is taken by the donee absolutely, also applies to charitable gifts: *Re Monk* [1927] 2 Ch. 197 at 211.

where what is known as a general charitable intention can be shown to exist. The jurisdiction to apply property *cy-près* is exercisable by the courts or, in practice almost invariably, by the Charity Commission.[305]

1. *"Impossibility"*

It may be impossible to carry out a designated charitable purpose from the outset, either because it has never been possible at any stage or because it ceases to be possible during the interval between the making of a will and the death of the testator. It may be or become impossible because the specific charitable purpose has never existed or because a specific or general charitable purpose has become impracticable. It is also possible for a charitable trust which has initially taken effect to become impossible or impracticable,[306] or to become illegal,[307] or to fail, or to be satisfied without exhausting the whole of the trust fund.[308] Two specific situations require discussion: first, where the designated charitable object is an institution which does not exist, because it has either never existed or no longer exists in the form in which the donor described it; and, secondly, where section 13 of the Charities Act 1993 applies.

11–121

(A) Where the charitable object is an institution which does not exist

(1) Institutions which have never existed
It is possible for a donor to specify as his intended charitable object an institution which has never existed, either because the deed or will in question has described the intended institution by the wrong name or because he has simply invented one. In the former case, if there is convincing evidence of what the settlor or testator intended, the deed or will in question can be rectified to bring its provisions into line with that intention.[309] Even if there is insufficiently convincing evidence for rectification to be possible, the court can still decide as a matter of construction that the intended object was an existing institution; thus in *Re Spence*[310] a gift to a particular Blind Home was held by Megarry V.-C. to be identifiable with a home for the blind of a different name and address and so was valid. In these cases, no "impossibility" will occur in the first place. If the gift cannot be saved in either of these two ways, the purpose will fail; this will necessarily also occur where an institution has simply been invented. However, in such circumstances, provided that the designated institution would have

11–122

---

[305] See *post*, para 11–153.

[306] See the cases cited in the text and also *Att.-Gen. v. City of London* (1790) 3 Bro.C.C. 171 (promotion of Christianity among the infidels of Virginia); *Ironmongers Co. v. Att.-Gen.* (1844) 10 Cl. & F. 908 (redemption of British slaves in Turkey or Barbary).

[307] For example, where income is settled for a period which exceeds the permissible accumulation period; see *Re Monk* [1927] 2 Ch. 197; *Re Bradwell* [1952] Ch. 575.

[308] *Re King* [1923] 1 Ch. 243; *Re North Devon and West Somerset Relief Fund* [1953] 1 W.L.R. 1260; *Re Raine* [1956] Ch. 417.

[309] This has always been possible in the case of deeds; see *ante*, para 6–079. Wills have only been able to be rectified since the enactment of Administration of Justice Act 1982, s.21.

[310] [1979] Ch. 483 at 491.

been charitable had it existed, the property will in practice almost always be applied *cy-près* because, as will be seen below, it appears to be relatively easy to infer the necessary general charitable intention.[311]

(2) Institutions which formerly existed

11–123   Where the donor has specified as his intended charitable object an institution which formerly existed but no longer does in the form in which he described it, the question which arises is whether any continuing institution can be identified with the previous one. If this is possible, once again no "impossibility" will occur.

11–124   Institutions continue to exist where they have been amalgamated with others as a result of a scheme made by the court or by the Charity Commission. In *Re Faraker*[312] a scheme had been made by the Commissioners consolidating the endowments of a number of charities with the general purpose of relief of the poor of Rotherhithe. A gift was subsequently made to one of these charities, "Hannah Bayley's Charity", whose original object was rather more limited; it was held that the gift took effect in favour of the amalgamated charity. Alterations to the constitution or objects of an institution may also be made by statute,[313] or improperly by the trustees under the terms of the trust deed without the necessary sanction of the court or the Charity Commissioners.[314] Subsequent gifts to the institution will similarly take effect. However, if an institution has the power to dissolve itself and formally does so, Plowman J. held in *Re Stemson's Will Trusts*[315] that a subsequent gift in its favour will not take effect; consequently, the gift will fail unless it can be applied *cy-près* as a result of the existence of a general charitable intention.

11–125   The effect of changes of these and other types was reviewed relatively recently by the Court of Appeal in *Re Broadbent's Will*[316] The resulting decision appears to have considerably simplified the law governing the question of whether or not there is "impossibility". The testatrix had left one-third of her residuary estate to the Vicar and Church Wardens of a Mission Church "for the general purposes of such Church but with the request that the money be used primarily for the upkeep of the fabric of the Church". There had never been a Vicar and Churchwardens. The Church was held pursuant to a deed of trust of 1913 of which the testatrix's deceased husband had been a trustee. This deed both envisaged the sale of the church and provided that the proceeds of sale, if not invested in another church, were to be held for "such other religious or charitable purpose as the Trustees shall in their absolute discretion think proper". Between the date of

---

[311] *Re Harwood* [1936] Ch. 285. See *post*, para 11–148.
[312] [1912] 2 Ch. 488.
[313] Many of the cases involved re-organisation of hospitals nationalised and re-organised under the National Health Schemes Act 1946; see *Re Morgan's Will Trusts* [1950] Ch. 137; *Re Glass* [1950] Ch. 643N; *Re Hutchinson's Will Trusts* [1953] Ch. 387.
[314] See *Re Bagshawe* [1954] 1 W.L.R. 238, where a scheme was made simply in accordance with the trust machinery, not by an outside body.
[315] [1970] Ch. 16.
[316] [2001] W.T.L.R. 967.

the will and the testatrix's death, the trustees did sell the Church and it was demolished; no new church was purchased. Mummery L.J. said:

"It appears . . . that the court must ascertain whether the intention of the testator was to benefit a charitable purpose promoted in the work of the named institution, as distinct from an intention to benefit only the named institution in the carrying out of its charitable purpose at or in connection with particular premises. This problem commonly arises in the case of bequests to a named college, school, hospital, or Home which, prior to the death of the testator, has closed down, moved, amalgamated, expanded or undergone some other potentially significant change, such as a scheme altering its objects. If, on examination of all the relevant material, the court is satisfied that the gift is for a charitable purpose which the institution existed to promote and there are existing funds dedicated to that purpose (to which the bequest can be added), the gift will not be allowed to fail simply because the particular institution used as a means of attaining the charitable end has ceased to exist."

The Court of Appeal held that "the general purposes of the Church" included the trusts on which the proceeds of sale were to be held if not reinvested in another church. Consequently, the one-third was held on the trusts of the deed of 1913. A contrary decision would not have given rise to any issue of *cy-près* because the will provided that in that event there would be cross-accruer to the remaining gifts of residue.[317] However, that does not affect the value of this decision as an authority on when there is "impossibility".

(B) Section 13 of the Charities Act 1993[318]
This section applies only where circumstances change after a charitable trust **11–126** has come into existence and render some alteration of its original terms desirable. The problem which it was enacted to resolve arose out of the fact that the wishes of a donor could not be, and for that matter still cannot be, disregarded simply because they are unpopular or because the funds in question could be applied for a more beneficial purpose. However, in *Re Dominion Students Hall Trust*,[319] the charity in question was restricted to Dominion students[320] of European origin, yet the objects were stated to be the promotion of community interest in the Empire. An application was made to the court to delete the words "of European origin". Evershed J. held that the retention of these words amounted to a "colour bar" which would defeat the object of the charity; the word "impossibility" should be construed widely and therefore enabled the deletion to be made. In view of this dilution of "impossibility", it became desirable to provide a new test to

---

[317] These were in favour of other charities, who contended that the gift to the Church had failed.
[318] Formerly Charities Act 1960, s.13.
[319] [1947] Ch. 183.
[320] "Dominion" broadly meant the states which were the original members of the Commonwealth, such as Australia, Canada, New Zealand and South Africa.

clarify its nature. This was originally provided by section 13 of the Charities Act 1960. This section was re-enacted as section 13 of the Charities Act 1993 which has in turn been amended by the Charities Act 2006. Under the section, *cy-près* is feasible, subject to the requirement for a general charitable intention, if the matter can be brought under one of the following heads.

11–127   (1) Under paragraph (a), where the original purposes,[321] in whole or in part, have as far as may be been fulfilled, or cannot be carried out, or not according to the directions given and to the spirit of the gift.[322] This expression "spirit of the gift" is relevant to four of the five paragraphs. It is not a new phrase, being apparently borrowed from the Education (Scotland) Act 1946.[323] Although doubts about its meaning have been expressed,[324] it should not create any real difficulties. It has been said that "it is equivalent in meaning to the basic intention underlying the gift, as ascertained from its terms in the light of the admissible evidence".[325]

The working of paragraph (a) is illustrated by *Re Lepton's Charity*.[326] This case concerned a gift by will in 1715 of land to be held on trust to pay out of the rents a sum of £3 a year to the minister of a chapel and the net surplus to the poor and aged of the town. The evidence was to the effect that at the date of the will the total income was £5 a year. The land had been sold and was represented by investments yielding £791 a year. Pennycuick V.-C. held that the basic intention had plainly been defeated when, in modern conditions, the minister took a derisory £3 out of the total of £791; he therefore made an order by way of a *cy-près* scheme to provide for the payment to the minister to be raised from £3 to £100 per annum.

11–128   (2) Under paragraph (b), where the original purposes provide a use for only part of the property.[327] This paragraph can be illustrated by the facts of *Re North Devon and West Somerset Relief Fund*,[328] where a surplus remained out of funds subscribed for the relief of a flood disaster at Lynmouth.

(3) Under paragraph (c), where the property given and other property applicable for similar purposes can be more effectively used in conjunction and to that end can suitably be made applicable for

---

[321] The words "original purposes" appear in all five paragraphs. They are applicable to the trusts of the disposition as a whole, and not severally in relation to its respective parts; *Re Lepton's Charity* [1972] Ch. 276 at 285.
[322] Charities Act 1993, s.13(1)(a).
[323] s.116(2).
[324] By Viscount Simonds, 221 HL Official Report 601 (March 1, 1960).
[325] *Re Lepton's Charity* [1972] 276 at 285, *per* Pennycuick V.-C. See also *Re Lysaght* [1966] Ch. 191; see *post*, para 11–145.
[326] [1972] Ch. 276. See also *post*, para 11–133.
[327] s.13(1)(b).
[328] [1953] 1 W.L.R. 1260; see also *Re King* [1923] 1 Ch. 243; *Re Raine* [1956] Ch. 417.

common purposes, regard being had to the appropriate considerations.[329] The expression "appropriate considerations" was inserted by the Charities Act 2006 in place of "the spirit of the gift" and is defined[330] as meaning "(a) (on the one hand), the spirit of the gift concerned, and (b) (on the other) the social and economic circumstances prevailing at the time of the proposed alteration of the original purposes". Strictly speaking, this Paragraph does not involve a *cy-près* scheme at all since it has never been necessary to show "impossibility" to order to effect a consolidation of a number of charities.[331]

(4) Under paragraph (d), where the original purposes were laid down **11–129** by reference to an area which was then, but has since ceased to be, a unit for some other purpose or by reference to a class of persons or to an area which has for any reason since ceased to be suitable, regard being had to the appropriate considerations, or to be practical for the purposes of administering the gift.[332] Common examples of the application of this paragraph are where the area in which the charity was originally to operate is, because of changes in local government boundaries or the class of beneficiaries, hard to identify or where the area or class of beneficiaries has dwindled or is otherwise provided for, so that no substantial public benefit is being conferred by the fulfilment of the original purposes. Thus in *Peggs v. Lamb*[333] this paragraph was applied to a gift for the benefit of the freemen of the borough of Huntingdon, whose numbers had become substantially reduced; a scheme was directed so as to enlarge the class to cover the inhabitants of the borough as a whole.

(5) Under paragraph (e), where the original purposes have, in whole or **11–130** in part, in the period since they were originally laid down either (i) been adequately provided for by other means, (ii) ceased as being useless or harmful to the community or, for other reasons, to be in law charitable, or (iii) ceased in any other way to provide a suitable and effective method of using the property given, regard being had

---

[329] s.13(1)(c), as amended by Charities Act 2006, s.15. Formerly the reference was to the spirit of the gift alone rather than to appropriate considerations which, as indicated in the text, are the spirit of gift and the social and economic circumstances prevailing at the time of the proposed alteration of the original purposes. This change, made in paragraphs (c), (d) and (e)(iii), but not in paragraph (a), seems to constitute a formal recognition of what actually occurs in the process of application *cy-près* rather than a requirement for change of the current practice; the decision in *Peggs v. Lamb* [1994] Ch. 172, discussed below in the text, is a clear recognition of the social and economic circumstances prevailing at the time of the proposed alteration of the original purposes, even though at the time of this decision this was not technically a relevant consideration.

[330] By s.13(1A), which was inserted by Charities Act 2006, s.15(3).

[331] See *Re Faraker* [1912] 2 Ch. 488.

[332] s.13(1)(d), as amended by Charities Act 2006, s.15. Formerly the reference was to the spirit of the gift alone rather than to appropriate considerations, which are the spirit of gift and the social and economic circumstances prevailing at the time of the proposed alteration of the original purposes; see *ante*, n.329.

[333] [1994] Ch. 172.

to the spirit of the gift.[334] The jurisdiction created by this paragraph, and in particular by sub-paragraphs (i) and (iii), affords the most important relaxation of the old *cy-près* rule and will probably be of the most practical use in enabling funds to be utilised for the maximum benefit of the public.

11–131   Sub-paragraph (i) may be illustrated by the situation where the original benefits of the charity are now provided for by the statutory services of public or local authorities. This would apply, for example, to a charity for the upkeep of a road or bridge; if the original purpose were kept on foot, its only real purpose would be to relieve the rates or the exchequer and it is, therefore, now possible to apply the funds *cy-près*.

11–132   Sub-paragraph (ii) will not often arise; indeed, there does not seem to have been a single reported case where a valid charitable trust has ceased to be charitable. But the principle may well in the future be applied more often than has hitherto been thought. This is because an institution registered by the Charity Commission is conclusively presumed to be a charity while on the register for all purposes other than rectification of the register.[335] This sub-paragraph will clearly be applicable if a charity is removed[336] from the register on the ground that its purposes have never been or are no longer charitable; the latter possibility was somewhat improbable prior to the enactment of the Charities Act 2006 but may well now become not uncommon in the light of the requirement for existing charities to demonstrate their continuing compliance with the public benefit requirement. This sub-paragraph will therefore be applicable to the endowments of charities such as independent schools or private hospitals if their charitable status is ever withdrawn.[337]

11–133   Sub-paragraph (iii) provides the widest relaxation of all but, despite the generality of its wording, it does not have a completely unlimited effect because it is still necessary to take into account the appropriate considerations,[338] something which will prevent a *cy-près* scheme being made simply because the original purpose selected by the donor is less effective than some other application of the funds. It is still essential to establish that the mode of application which the donor selected has ceased to be suitable or effective. In *Re Lepton's Charity*,[339] it was held that the court had jurisdiction under this sub-paragraph (as well as under the wider terms of paragraph (a), where the original purposes, in whole or in part cannot be carried out, or not according to the directions given and to the spirit of the gift[340]) to direct an application of the property *cy-près*. More significantly, in *Varsani v. Jesani*,[341] the Court of Appeal held that the sub-paragraph applied where a

---

[334] s.13(1)(e).

[335] Charities Act 1993, s.4(1).

[336] s.4(2).

[337] See Jaconelli [1996] Conv. 24.

[338] "The appropriate considerations" were substituted for "the spirit of the gift" by Charities Act 2006, s.15; see *ante*, n.327.

[339] [1972] Ch. 276.

[340] See *ante*, p.485. Pennycuick V.-C. was of opinion that this sub-paragraph was no more than "a final writing out at large" of paragraph (a); *ibid.* at 285.

[341] [1999] Ch. 219.

religious sect whose beliefs the charity had been set up to promote had split into two groups over a dispute as to whether its leader still had divine status. The need to consider the original purposes did not oblige the court to order an enquiry as to which of the groups was right; it was clear that the original purposes had ceased to be a suitable and effective means of using the available property. The court upheld the making of a scheme *cy-près* dividing the property between the two groups.

It must be emphasised that these provisions of section 13 of the Charities **11–134** Act 1993 alter the law only so far as it previously required a failure of the original purposes of a charity before a *cy-près* application could be ordered.[342] *Cy-près* is therefore only possible if the requirement for a general charitable intention, which is discussed below, is satisfied.

2. *A General Charitable Intention*

Where it is indeed impossible for the designated charitable purpose to be **11–135** carried out, the *cy-près* doctrine is generally, but not always, only applicable where it can also be shown that there was a general charitable intention. The two situations where this is not necessary will be considered first.

(A) Subsequent Impossibility
A general charitable intention is only necessary where the charitable pur- **11–136** pose of the donor has failed *ab initio*. Where a charitable trust has initially taken effect but at a later stage it becomes impossible for its purpose to continue to be carried out, the property subject to the charitable trust will always be applicable *cy-près*. Once property has been effectively and abso-lutely dedicated to charity, whether in pursuance of a general or a particular charitable intent, the donor and those claiming through him such as his residuary legatees or next-of-kin are excluded forever. It was held in *Re Wright*[343] that this is the case even if the failure occurs during the existence of a prior life interest before the charity is entitled in possession to the funds. The material date for the purpose of deciding whether the *cy-pres* doctrine is applicable is, therefore, the date when the trust came into existence (the date of the relevant deed or, in the case of a will, the death of the testator). It is only if the trust has failed by then that the question of whether a general charitable intention has been shown becomes relevant.

This is also the case where an institution which is to carry out the **11–137** charitable purpose in question ceases to exist after the charitable trust has come into effect. The Court of Appeal held in *Re Slevin*[344] that in such circumstances it is also unnecessary to show any general charitable intention in order for the gift to be upheld. The subject-matter of the gift will already have vested in the institution and, since the latter has ceased to exist, it will devolve on the Crown with the rest of the institution's property. The Crown will in practice allow the subject matter of the gift to be disposed of in favour of charity.

---

[342] s.13(2).
[343] *Re Wright* [1954] Ch. 347 at 363, *per* Romer L.J. See also *Re Wokingham Fire Brigade* [1951] Ch. 373.
[344] [1891] 2 Ch. 236.

(B) Unidentifiable Donors

11–138   A general charitable purpose is also not necessary even when it has from the outset been impossible for the designated charitable purpose to be carried out insofar as the donors of the property subscribed for that purpose cannot be identified. In this respect, section 14 of the Charities Act 1960, now section 14 of the Charities Act 1993, introduced reforms which were long overdue (until then, unless a general charitable intention could be shown in the usual way, the trustees were bound to refund the property and, if the donors could not be found, it had to be paid into court to await the usually remote possibility that they would reclaim it[345]; however, since the reform was retrospective,[346] any property which had not been reclaimed by the commencement of the Charities Act 1960 was able to be applied *cy-près* thereafter).

11–139   Section 14 provides that property given for specific charitable purposes which fail is to be applicable *cy-près* as though it had been given for charitable purposes generally, provided that it belongs, first, to any donors who, after such advertisements and inquiries as are prescribed by regulations made by the Charity Commission,[347] cannot be identified or found or, secondly, to any donor who has executed a written disclaimer of his right to have the property returned.[348] It is further provided that, for these purposes, property is to be conclusively presumed, without the necessity for advertisements or inquiries, to belong to donors who cannot be identified if it consists either of the proceeds of cash collections made by means of collecting boxes or other means not adapted for distinguishing one gift from another or of the proceeds of any lottery, competition, entertainment, sale or other such money-raising activity, although, as regards the latter, allowance must be made for prizes or articles for sale to enable the activity to be undertaken.[349] Donors who can be identified or who apply within six months of the making of a scheme are entitled to the return of their property or its proceeds of sale.[350] The court or the Charity Commission[351] may, by order, direct that property be treated, without advertisement or inquiry, as belonging to donors who cannot be identified whenever it appears to the court either that it would be unreasonable, having regard to the amounts likely to be returned to the donor, to incur expense with a view to returning the property, or that it would be unreasonable, having regard to the nature, circumstances and amount of the gifts, and to the lapse of time since they were made, for the donors to expect the property to be returned.[352]

11–140   Section 14A of the Charities Act 1993, which was inserted by the Charities Act 2006,[353] deals with the situation which arises where the particular purpose for which funds have been raised, usually as the result of an appeal

---

[345] This was the result in *Re Ulverston* [1956] Ch. 622.

[346] Charities Act 1993, s.14(10); Charities Act 1960, s.14(7).

[347] Charities Act 1993, s.14(8).

[348] s.14(1).

[349] s.14(3).

[350] s.14(5),(6), (10).

[351] The Charity Commission acquired this power for the first time as a result of Charities Act 2006, s.16(2).

[352] Charities Act 1993, s.14(4) as amended by Charities Act 2006, s.16.

[353] Charities Act 2006, s.17.

for the purpose of ameliorating the effect of some natural disaster or accident, are in the event not all needed in order to fulfil the purpose. Prior to the enactment of this section, the only two alternatives were for the trustees to apply for a *cy-près* scheme in order to allow the surplus funds to be used for an associated or a similar purposes or for the surplus donations to be returned to the original donors, something which was in practice not always possible since such donors could not always be traced. The new section envisages that any such appeal will be accompanied by a statement that, in the event that the funds subscribed are not all used for the specified purposes, they will be applicable *cy-près* as if given for charitable purposes generally unless the donor makes a declaration that in that event he wishes the trustees to give him the opportunity of requesting the return of his donation.[354] If he makes such a declaration, the trustees must take certain prescribed steps for the purpose of endeavouring to find him.[355] The donation of any such donor whom the trustees fail to find, or who does not respond to their communications, is treated in the same way as the donation of any donor who has not made a declaration in the first place. All such donations are treated as belonging to donors within section 14(1)(b) and as given for charitable purposes generally; they can therefore be applied *cy-près*.[356]

(C) Where a General Charitable Intention is Necessary

Where a general charitable intention is necessary, a distinction has to be drawn between gifts for charitable purposes and gifts to charitable institutions. Gifts to a mixture of charitable and non-charitable purposes also require separate consideration. **11–141**

(1) Gifts for charitable purposes

The question of whether or not a general charitable intention has been shown is entirely one of construction of the instrument in question. It is necessary to consider, as in all matters of construction, the whole scope and intent of that instrument. The essential question which has to be decided in this process is whether the paramount object of the settlor was to benefit a particular object *simpliciter* or whether it was instead to effect a particular mode of charity independently of the given object even though an object was specifically indicated.[357] Bearing in mind the fact that the cases do not by any means present a consistent picture, the authorities may perhaps be divided into two classes. **11–142**

The first class of case is where the gift is in form made for a particular charitable purpose but it is possible, taking the instrument as a whole, to say that, notwithstanding the form of the gift, the paramount intention is to give the property in the first instance for a general charitable purpose rather than a specified purpose; in such cases, a direction has in effect been engrafted onto the general gift as to the intention of the settlor which relates to the manner in which the general gift is to be carried into effect. In these **11–143**

---

[354] Charities Act 1993, s.14A (2), (3).
[355] s.14A (4), (5).
[356] s.14A (6), (7).
[357] See *Re Taylor* (1888) 58 L.T. 538 at 543.

circumstances, even though it may be impossible to carry out the specified directions, the gift for the general charitable purpose will remain perfectly good and the court or the Charity Commissioners will direct a scheme as to how it is to be carried out *cy-près*.

11–144 The second class of case is where, on the true construction of the instrument, the gift is not only in form but also in substance one for a particular purpose only; in such circumstances, if it proves impossible to carry out that particular purpose, the whole gift will fail and there is no room for the application of *cy-près*.[358]

11–145 The question as to the class in which a gift falls often raises serious problems of construction. The way in which the court sets about its task may be illustrated by the following cases. In *Biscoe v. Jackson*[359] money was to be applied towards the establishment of a soup kitchen in Shoreditch and a cottage hospital there. It was not in fact possible to apply the fund in the manner indicated. The Court of Appeal held that there was a sufficient general intention of charity for the benefit of the poor of Shoreditch to entitle the court to execute the trust *cy-près*. It was in effect therefore decided that the direction to establish a soup kitchen and a cottage hospital manifested only two ways of benefiting the poor of Shoreditch whom there was a general intention to benefit. A more difficult example is *Re Lysaght*.[360] The testatrix gave a fund to the Royal College of Surgeons, for the establishment of studentships but provided that Jews and Roman Catholics should be excluded from them; the College would not accept the fund subject to these restrictions. Buckley J. held, first, that these discriminatory provisions did not form an essential part of the testatrix's intention; secondly, that her paramount intention was that the College should be the trustee of the fund; and, thirdly, that the impracticability of giving effect to this inessential part of her intention by virtue of the fact that the College had refused to accept her gift subject to the restrictions would not be allowed to defeat her paramount intention. Accordingly a scheme was directed under which the offending provision was deleted. Although the principle behind the decision is entirely clear, it is not at all easy, as a matter of construction of the will, to accept the judge's conclusion that the discriminatory provisions did not form part of the testatrix's paramount intention. Another illustration, which is probably more straightforward from the point of view of construction, is *Re Woodhams*,[361] where the testator gave the residue of his estate to two colleges of music to found scholarships which were to be restricted to boys who were orphans from named children's homes. The colleges refused to accept the gift on these conditions, partly because of the decrease in the number of orphans and partly because of the adequacy of public grants for education, but was prepared to accept it if the restrictions were deleted. Vinelott J. held that the testator had chosen orphans from these homes on the basis that they were the persons most likely to need assistance but that it was not an essential part of the scheme that the scholarships should be so

---

[358] The substance of this formulation is borrowed from *Re Wilson* [1913] 1 Ch. 314 at 320. For another formulation, see *Re Lysaght* [1966] Ch. 191 at 201, 202, *per* Buckley J.

[359] (1887) 35 Ch.D. 460.

[360] [1966] Ch. 191, applying *Re Robinson* [1923] 2 Ch. 332 (requirement of wearing a black gown in church held impracticable).

[361] [1981] 1 W.L.R. 493.

restricted; accordingly, the trusts could be modified without frustrating his intention.

A case on the other side of the line is *Re Good*,[362] where there was a trust **11–146** to provide rest homes in Hull. The testator had drawn up a detailed scheme of the types of home to be provided, the types of inmates to be admitted, and the management powers of the trustees. The scheme was in fact impracticable because the funds were insufficient. Wynn-Parry J. held that the language of the will and in particular the detailed instructions which had been given were inconsistent with the implication of a general charitable intention; therefore the *cy-près* doctrine did not apply. Similarly in *Re Spence*,[363] Megarry V.-C. held that, as a matter of the construction of the will, a gift to a specified old folk's home was one for a specific charitable purpose which, although possible when the will was made, had become impossible; it was not a gift to the old people of a particular district. Accordingly there was no general charitable intention and the gift failed.

(2) Gifts to charitable institutions

Gifts to charitable institutions need to be dealt with separately since the **11–147** circumstances of such institutions may vary considerably.

(a) Institutions which have never existed It appears to be relatively **11–148** easy to infer a general charitable intention where the charity named by the testator has never existed. In *Re Harwood*[364] it was held that a gift to a "peace society" which had never existed indicated a general charitable intention; thus the fund could be applied *cy-près* to other existing similar organisations. Such a construction may, however, be rebutted by the circumstances of the gift. Thus, in *Re Goldschmidt*[365] Harman J. held that the presence in the will of a residuary gift in favour of other charitable purposes into which lapsed funds would fall was a factor against deducing a general charitable intention.

(b) Institutions which formerly existed Where the institution specified **11–149** by the donor as his intended charitable object formerly existed but no longer does in the form in which he described it, it has already been seen that it is possible that no "impossibility" will have occurred. But the fact that "impossibility" has occurred does not prevent a general charitable intention being found.

None was found in *Re Rymer*,[366] where there was a gift by will to the **11–150** Rector for the time being of St Thomas' Seminary for the education of priests

---

[362] [1950] 2 All E.R. 653. See also to the same effect *Re Packe* [1918] 1 Ch. 437 (holiday home for clergymen of Church of England and their wives); *Re White's Trusts* (1886) 33 Ch.D. 449 (almshouses); *Re Wilson* [1913] 1 Ch. 314 (school); *Re Harwood* [1936] Ch. 285. Compare *Re Finger's Will Trusts* [1972] Ch. 286.

[363] [1979] Ch. 483; another gift in the same will to a Blind Home was held to be identifiable with a home for the blind of a different name and address and so was valid.

[364] [1936] Ch. 285. See also *Re Davis* [1902] 1 Ch. 876 ("Homes for the Homeless"). See also *Re Satterthwaite's Will Trusts* [1966] 1 W.L.R. 277.

[365] [1957] 1 W.L.R. 524 (gift to "Fund for Relief of Distressed German Jews" and no fund of that name existed; failed).

[366] [1895] 1 Ch. 19. See, for a similar result, *Re Goldney* (1946) 115 L.J.Ch. 337.

in the diocese of Westminster for the purposes of such a seminary. The seminary ceased to exist during the testator's lifetime. It was held that the gift had been made to a particular institution; this meant that not only was there "impossibility" but there could be no general charitable intention either. It is of course much less likely that this question will arise when the institution in question is unincorporated than when it is incorporated. In the case of an unincorporated body, the gift is in itself a purpose trust; provided that the work is still being carried on, it is unlikely that the disappearance of the donee during the lifetime of the testator will amount to "impossibility" in the first place unless there is something positive to show that the continued existence of the donee was essential to the gift. In the case of a corporation, on the other hand, the position is different, since there has to be something positive in the will to create a purpose trust at all[367]; this is because a gift to a corporate body prima facie takes effect as a gift to that body beneficially.[368] The distinction is illustrated by Re Finger's Will Trusts.[369] There were gifts by will both to an unincorporated association, the National Radium Commission, and to an incorporated body, the National Council for Maternity and Child Welfare. Both had been dissolved before the testator's death. The gift to the Commission was held to be a purpose trust for the work of the Commission which was not dependent on its continuing existence; consequently, there was no "impossibility". There was, however, "impossibility" in respect of the gift to the Council because the testator could not be taken to have intended that the gift could be applied for its purposes. Goff J. however held that the share of the fund which had been intended for the Council could nevertheless be applied cy-près because the will as a whole showed a general charitable intention. A similar conclusion was reached in Re Stemson's Will Trusts.[370]

(3)   Gifts to a mixture of charitable and non-charitable purposes or institutions

11–151   The fact that one gift for a non-charitable purpose is found among a number of gifts for charitable purposes does not permit the inference that the testator intended the non-charitable gift to take effect as a charitable gift when in terms it is not charitable. This is so even though the non-charitable gift may have a close relation to the purposes for which the charitable gifts were made. This was held to be the position in Re Jenkins's Will Trusts[371] where a gift made to an non-charitable anti-vivisection association was coupled with gifts for the charitable purpose of preventing cruelty to animals. As Buckley J. said, in rejecting a cy-près application: "If you meet seven men with black hair and one with red hair you are not entitled to say that there are eight men with black hair".[372] It is not entirely clear whether the previous case of Re Satterthwaite''s Will Trusts[373] is consistent with this decision. In this case a human-hating testatrix gave money to the "London Animal Hospital". No

---

[367] [1972] Ch. 286 at 295.
[368] See Re Stemson's Will Trusts [1970] Ch. 16.
[369] [1972] Ch. 423.
[370] [1970] Ch. 16.
[371] [1966] Ch. 249.
[372] [1966] Ch. 249 at 256.
[373] [1966] 1 W.L.R. 277.

hospital of this name could be identified but, because of other gifts in favour of established animal charities, the gift was held by the Court of Appeal to be applicable *cy-près*. The case is, however, probably distinguishable on the ground that a gift to an admittedly unidentified animal hospital had a sufficient charitable "flavour" about it to justify this result.

V. THE ADMINISTRATION OF CHARITIES[374]

1. *Central Authorities*

Since 1974 there has been only one central authority exercising jurisdiction over charities[375]; this was formerly the Charity Commissioners for England and Wales but, since the enactment of the Charities Act 2006, is a body corporate known as the Charity Commission for England and Wales.[376] Formerly, the Secretary of State for Education and Science and the Secretary of State for Wales had concurrent jurisdiction with the Charity Commissioners and exercised it in relation to charities of an educational nature.[377] The reason for conferring the exercise of functions under the Charities Act 1993 exclusively upon the Charity Commissioners and, now, on the Charity Commission is that these functions are primarily judicial and not, therefore, appropriately to be exercised by Ministers of the Crown. The objectives, general functions and duties of the Charity Commission are set out in the Charities Act 2006[378] and are as follows: the public confidence objective to increase public confidence and trust in charities; the public benefit objective to promote awareness and understanding of the public benefit requirement; the compliance objective to promote compliance by charity trustees with their legal obligations in exercising control and management of the administration of charities; the charitable resources objective to promote the effective use of charitable resources; and the accountability objective to increase the accountability of charities to donors, beneficiaries, and the public. These five objectives and whether the Charity Commission has met them are matters which are to be included in an annual report to Parliament which then has to be considered at a public meeting organised for the purpose.

11–152

2. *The Charities Tribunal*

The Charities Act 2006[379] introduced the Charities Tribunal, which has been given two different jurisdictions. What is likely in practice to be its principal

11–153

---

[374] See generally Maclennan, *Blackstone's Guide to The Charities Act 2006*.

[375] This has been the case since the Education Act 1973, s.1(1)(a), which came into force on February 4, 1974.

[376] Charities Act 2006, s.6, inserting into the Charities Act 1993 a new section, s.1A, and Sch.1A (Charities Act 1993, s.1 and Sch.1, which provided for the existence of the Charity Commissioners, cease to have effect.

[377] Charities Act 1960, s.2(1), repealed by Education Act 1973, s.1(1)(a).

[378] Charities Act 2006, s.7, inserting into the Charities Act 1993 four new sections, ss.1B, 1C, 1D and 1E.

[379] Charities Act 2006, s.8, inserting into the Charities Act 1993 four new sections, ss.2A, 2B, 2C and 2D.

jurisdiction is to hear appeals from and conduct reviews of decisions of the Charity Commission. The Charity Commission enjoys more freedom than any other public body in deciding what a person or a charitable trustee should do and in regulating the persons and the institutions which it advises. The Charities Tribunal has been created in order to address what appeared to be a lack of accountability for decisions made and actions taken and to give trustees who consider that they have been treated unfairly a means of redress. Appeals may be brought against any decision of the Charity Commission other than what are known as reviewable matters; the latter matters are entirely administrative in nature and may instead be the subject matter of a review conducted in the manner of an application for judicial review of administrative action. A table appended to Schedule 1C of the Charities Act 2006 sets out the decisions which may be appealed or reviewed, the persons entitled to seek the relevant appeal or review, and the powers which the Charities Tribunal has in each case. The other jurisdiction of the Charities Tribunal is to hear matters which are referred to it by the Charity Commission with the consent of the Attorney-General or by the Attorney-General himself in his historic role as representative of the public interest in ensuring the proper application of charitable funds; although trustees of any charitable trust affected or any other affected persons cannot therefore initiate such a reference, they are nevertheless entitled to be represented at the hearings. This jurisdiction is confined to questions relating to the functions of the Charity Commission, the operation of charity law in any respect or its application to a particular state of affairs; thus references are limited to matters where the underlying issue is one of law. The Charity Tribunal had not yet commenced operations at the time when this edition had to go to press. At present any appeal from its decisions is scheduled to be to the High Court but this may be modified as a result of the ongoing review which is being conducted into tribunals in general with a view to producing a unified and more coherent system.

3. The Official Custodian for Charities

11–154   The Official Custodian for Charities is a custodian trustee in whom property which is held on charitable trusts can be vested.[380] There are advantages in vesting property in such a custodian trustee: first, it may make the title to that property more straightforward and, secondly and more importantly, it makes the appointment of new trustees on deaths or retirements unnecessary, thus saving the expense of new appointments. The Official Custodian for Charities is an officer of the Charity Commission and ranks as a corporation sole, having perpetual succession and an official seal. Because he is simply a custodian trustee, the actual management and control of the property in question remains in the charity trustees, who can in their own name commence or defend proceedings relating to the property without seeking his permission or joining him as a party.[381] Since the coming into force of the Charities Act 1992, the ability of charitable trustees to vest property in the

---

[380] Charities Act 1993, s.2(1). See also Charities Act 1993, ss.21–22 for the vesting of property in the Official Custodian.
[381] *Muman v. Nagasena* [2000] 1 W.L.R. 299.

Official Custodian has been limited to land.[382] But the Charity Commission can still make, under Section 18 of the Charities Act 1993, an order for the vesting in the Official Custodian of both land and moveable property when the Charity Commission considers that this is necessary for the protection of the charity in question.[383]

4. *Registration*

Sections 3, 3A, 3B and 4 of the Charities Act 1993[384] provide for a central register of charities. There is now a positive duty on all charity trustees to apply for registration enforceable by order of the Charity Commission. All charities are registrable[385] unless they are expressly relieved from the requirement.[386] One example of the latter is to be found in the so-called "exempt charities"; these are not subject to any of the supervisory powers of the Commissioners because satisfactory arrangements have already been made for carrying out the objects of such trusts and safeguarding the trust property. Examples of exempt charities are certain universities and colleges, the Church Commissioners, industrial and provident societies and friendly societies.[387] Charities whose gross income does not exceed £5,000 a year are also not required to be registered.[388] Furthermore, any charity excepted by order or regulation is not required to be registered[389]; a number of regulations to this effect covering, for example, voluntary schools,[390] and boy scouts and girl guides[391] have been made. A further exemption operates in favour of registered places of worship.[392]

11–155

Registration raises a conclusive presumption that the institution is a charity at any time while it is on the register.[393] This accordingly removes a

11–156

---

[382] The Official Custodian then had progressively to divest himself of holdings of moveable property with a value in excess of £1.25 billion by transferring those holdings to the trustees, or to such other persons as they nominated; this reform was carried out in order to increase the responsibility of the trustees.

[383] See (1992) 142 N.L.J. 541.

[384] s.3 was substituted and ss.3A, 3B were added by Charities Act 2006, s.9. The first effective obligation to register was imposed by the Charities Act 1960, since when its scope has been substantially broadened.

[385] It is necessary that, in order to be a charity, the organisation in question be subject to control by the High Court in the exercise of the court's jurisdiction with respect to charities. If that jurisdiction is wholly ousted by statute in relation to the organisation, then the organisation is not a charity and cannot be registered; see *Construction Training Board v. Att.-Gen.* [1973] Ch. 173 (where, however, the Board was held to be a charity because the provisions of the Industrial Training Act 1964 did not oust the jurisdiction of the court; the court still had control over the Board's functions).

[386] Charities Act 1993, s.3, as substituted by Charities Act 2006, s.9.

[387] See Charities Act 1993, s.3A(2)(a), added by Charities Act 2006, s.9, and Charities Act 1993, Sch.2.

[388] Charities Act 1993, s.3A(2)(d), added by Charities Act 2006, s.9.

[389] Charities Act 1993, s.3A(2)(c), added by Charities Act 2006, s.9.

[390] The Charities (Exception of Voluntary Schools from Registration) Regulations 1960 (S.I. 1960 No. 2366).

[391] The Charities (Exception of Certain Charities for Boy Scouts and Girl Guides from Registration) Regulations 1961 (SI 1961/1044).

[392] Places of Worship Registration Act 1855, s.9.

[393] Charities Act 1993, s.4(1).

great deal of uncertainty about the status of certain institutions. But provision is necessarily made for a person who is or may be affected by the registration of an institution or trust as a charity to object to its entry on the register or apply for its removal on the ground that it is not in fact a charity, something which is of course a question for the general law.[394] This provision is intended for the benefit of anyone, especially a donor's residuary legatees or next-of-kin, whose interests will be affected by the answer to the question of whether the institutions or trusts should be classified as charities. An appeal against any decision of the Charity Commission on registration matters will be able to be made to the Charity Tribunal once it has commenced operations (until then the appeal is to the High Court).[395] The Charity Commission also has a positive duty to remove from the register any institution which no longer appears to be a charity and also to remove any charity because it has ceased to exist or is not operating.[396]

11–157   Any registered charity with a gross income of over £5,000 in its last financial year must state the fact of its registration in all documents soliciting donations and on all bills, invoices and receipts.

5. Accounts

11–158   The Charities Act 1993[397] also imposed much more rigorous duties on the trustees of unincorporated charities (the duties in this respect of incorporated charities are the usual ones imposed on all companies by the Companies Act 2006) to keep proper accounts and to prepare annual accounts. These must be audited if income exceeds £100,000; on the other hand, if income is less than £25,000, all that is required is statements of income and expenditure and a balance sheet. The trustees must also send to the Charity Commission annual reports of their activities, enclosing the accounts and, where appropriate, their auditors' report.

6. Co-ordination of Charitable Activities

11–159   Sections 76 to 78 of the 1993 Act have as their aim the formation of a basis for co-operation between charities and the statutory welfare services. They authorise local authorities to review the working of those charities with that of the statutory services.[398] However, no obligation is put on a charity actually to co-operate; the Act requires mutual agreement between the local authority and the charity.[399] It was obviously hoped that this would lead to rationalisation of charitable activities over the country as a whole but few reviews seem yet to have been put in hand. Moreover, the review powers

---

[394] s.4(2).
[395] s.4(3), (4).
[396] s.3(4), as substituted by Charities Act 2006, s.9. A charitable company incorporated under the Companies Acts may also be wound up on an application made by the Attorney-General under Charities Act 1993, s.63(1); see *Liverpool and District Hospital for Diseases of the Heart v. Att.-Gen.* [1981] Ch. 193.
[397] Charities Act 1993, s.5(1).
[398] ss.41–49 and Charities (Accounts and Reports) Regulations (SI 1995/2724).
[399] s.78(2).

relate only to local charities; there are no powers to ensure reviews or co-ordination of national charities.

7. Scheme-Making and Other Powers

Section 16 of the 1993 Act empowers the Charity Commission to exercise a **11–160** jurisdiction concurrent with that of the High Court to make schemes relating to the administration of the charity, or orders for the appointment and removal of trustees and with regard to the vesting or transfer of property.[400] Although the court has a scheme-making power, it should be emphasised that in practice the vast majority of such schemes will be made by the Charity Commission.[401] A scheme can obviously take a wide variety of forms; it may, for example, take the drastic form of rewriting the original user trusts or management trusts of the charity or both. Appointments and removals of trustees will not normally require a scheme; they will be made simply by order of the Charity Commission. The same applies to any vesting of the property of a charity in the Official Custodian for Charities.[402] Jurisdiction to make a scheme can only be exercised by the Charity Commission on an application made by the charity or on a reference by the court[403] or, save in the case of an exempt charity, on the application of the Attorney-General. However, in the case of a non-exempt charity with an annual income of less than £500, the Charity Commission may exercise their jurisdiction on the application of any trustee, of any person interested in the charity, or of any two inhabitants in the locality where it operates.[404]

Power is also specifically given to the Charity Commission to act for the **11–161** protection of charities where there has been misconduct or mismanagement and where the property of the charity needs to be protected and properly applied[405] and these powers have been substantially increased by the Charities Act 2006.[406] In these circumstances they are empowered to remove or appoint trustees, remove them from membership of the charity, and to prevent the operation of any banking account.

A number of miscellaneous powers are also conferred on the Charity **11–162** Commission. Perhaps most important of all is the power to make an order where it appears that the proposed action is in the interests of the charity, authorising dealings or other action to be made or taken, whether or not it is within the administrative powers of the trustees.[407] This power, which is primarily administrative, is akin to the powers conferred by section 57 of the Trustee Act 1925[408] and by section 64 of the Settled Land Act 1925.[409] It may, for example, authorise any given transaction, compromise or application of property or may, more specifically, authorise a charity to use common

---

[400] s.16(1).
[401] s.16(1), (4).
[402] s.18.
[403] s.16(4).
[404] s.16(5).
[405] s.18(1).
[406] s.18A, added by Charities Act 2006, s.19.
[407] s.26(1).
[408] See post, paras 14–142, 21–004.
[409] See post, para 21–008.

premises, or employ a common staff or otherwise combine, for any administrative purposes, with any other charity, although these are purely examples and do not limit the generality of the statutory power.[410] Other powers include that of advising charity trustees if the latter apply for advice,[411] which is in practice a particularly convenient facility, and powers to preserve charity documents.[412]

8. Investment

11–163 The powers and duties of trustees of a charity in relation to the investment of the trust funds are generally governed, in the same way as in the case of non-charitable trusts, by the terms of the trust instrument, if any, and by the general law of trusts relating to investments.[413] Since the enactment of the Trustee Act 2000,[414] trustees, including the trustees of charitable trusts, have had what section 3 of that Act describes as "the general power of investment", enabling them to make any kind of investment that they could make if they were absolutely entitled to the assets of the trust, subject to having regard to standard investment criteria and to obtaining and considering proper advice.[415] But in order to make effective use of this general power of investment, and the more restricted power in the Trustee Investment Act 1961 which it replaced, a relatively substantial fund is necessary so that risk can be spread and management expenses assimilated without difficulty. Many charities have extremely small trust funds and, if special provision were not made, they would not always be able to invest those funds efficiently. At the time of the passing of the Charities Act 1960, it was therefore thought desirable to make general provision, by way of common investment schemes, for the joint administration of a number of charitable trust funds for the purposes of investment. Common investment schemes had been made before, but only in particular cases, by statute[416] and by the court[417] and the Charity Commission has always had the power to make schemes of a similar nature; but the Charities Act 1960 contained the first general provisions of this type. These provisions are now contained in sections 24 and 25 of the Charities Act 1993, to which the provisions of the Trustee Act 2000 expressly do not apply.[418]

---

[410] Charities Act 1993, s.26(2).

[411] s.29.

[412] s.30.

[413] See *post*, para 14–055 and see also *Soldiers', Sailors' and Airmen's Families Association v. Att.-Gen.* [1968] 1 W.L.R. 313, where it was held that a corporation incorporated by royal charter cannot, by the making of rules, confer upon itself powers wider than those conferred upon it by the general law or the royal charter.

[414] See *post*, para 14–002.

[415] Trustee Act 2000, ss.3–5.

[416] See Universities and Colleges (Trusts) Act 1943, which enabled the Universities of Oxford and Cambridge and the Colleges in those universities and also Winchester College to make schemes providing for funds to be administered as a single fund. (See *Re Freeston's Charity* [1978] 1 W.L.R. 741.) Private Acts have established common investment schemes for other universities; see, e.g. Liverpool University Act 1931; Birmingham University Act 1948.

[417] See *Royal Society's Charitable Trusts* [1956] Ch. 87; *Re University of London Charitable Trusts* [1964] Ch. 282.

[418] Trustee Act 2000, s.38.

Section 24 of the Charities Act 1993 enables the court and the Charity   **11–164**
Commission to make schemes, known as "common investment schemes",
for the establishment of common investment funds. These provide for property transferred to the fund by or on behalf of a charity participating in the
scheme to be invested under the control of trustees appointed to manage the
fund; they also provide for the participating charities to be entitled, subject
to the provisions of the scheme, to the capital and income of the fund in
shares determined by reference to the amount or value of the property
transferred to it by or on behalf of each of them and to the value of the fund
at the time of the transfers.[419] The first common investment scheme, known
as the Charities Official Investment Fund, in which all charities may participate, was made by the Charity Commissioners in 1962 and in 1976 two
further schemes were made.[420] Section 24 also provides that the court or the
Charity Commission may make a common investment scheme on the application of any two or more charities.[421] In *Re University of London Charitable
Trusts*[422] Wilberforce J. held that this provision enabled an application to be
made by the trustees of any two or more charitable trusts, notwithstanding
the fact that, as in this case, the trustees of the trusts in question are the same.
More recently, the creation of common deposit funds was also authorised so
as to still any doubts as to whether, under the earlier schemes, it was only
possible to deposit funds at interest. These common deposit funds are what
are now governed by section 25 of the Charities Act 1993.

9. *Dealings with Property Belonging to Charities*

The modern law governing dealings with property belonging to charities is   **11–165**
contained in section 36 of the Charities Act 1993. No land may be sold,
leased or otherwise disposed of without an order of the court or of the
Charity Commission unless the trustees have obtained and considered a
written report on the proposed disposition from a qualified surveyor, adver-
tised the proposed disposition for such period and in such manner as the
surveyor has advised, and are satisfied that the terms are the best reasonably
obtainable. Leases for seven years are subject to less stringent requirements.[423] Where the land in question is expressly held on trust for the
purposes of the charity, it is also required that public notice be given and any
representations received within one month duly considered, unless the
purpose of the transaction is to acquire replacement property. The instrument by which any disposition is effected must certify that these provisions
have been complied with; the certificate is conclusive in favour of a purchaser for money or money's worth.[424] However, this does not help a

---

[419] Charities Act 1993, s.24(1).
[420] Charinco Charities Narrower-Range Common Investment Fund, and Charibond Charities
Narrower-Range Common Investment Fund; see the Report of the Charity Commissioners for
1976. s.18(1).
[421] Charities Act 1993, s.24(2).
[422] [1964] Ch. 282.
[423] Comparable provisions apply to mortgages; see s.38.
[424] s.37.

purchaser under an uncompleted contract, since entering into a contract is not within section 36 in the first place.[425]

10. *The Making of Ex Gratia Payments*

11–166 The court and the Attorney-General have the power to authorise charity trustees to make *ex gratia* payments out of funds held on charitable trusts,[426] for example in pursuance of a moral obligation to relatives of the deceased. But this jurisdiction is not exercised lightly; it is necessary to show that, if the charity were an individual, it would be morally wrong of him not to make the payment.[427]

11. *The Appointment of Trustees of Charities*[428]

11–167 Generally, the rules which apply to private trusts also govern the appointment of trustees of charities.[429] A major exception is that the restriction on the number of trustees imposed by section 34 of the Trustee Act 1925,[430] does not apply to charities. But there were and still are certain other specific provisions.

11–168 The Charities Act 1960 provided in what is now section 83 of the Charities Act 1993 that new trustees may be appointed at a meeting, if a memorandum of the appointment is signed at the meeting by the person presiding or in some other manner prescribed by the meeting, and attested by two witnesses; that is then "sufficient" evidence of the appointment. This provision applies to all charities but it can be made use of only when the trusts permit it and, most importantly, it is only "sufficient" evidence of appointment, thus enabling its sufficiency to be checked on investigation of title by a purchaser.

11–169 The Charities Act 1992 in what is now section 73 of the Charities Act 1993 provided for the disqualification from holding the office of charitable trustee of anyone convicted of an offence involving dishonesty or deception, of undischarged bankrupts, and of those previously removed from such an office on the grounds of misconduct or mismanagement. Any one who acts while so disqualified is guilty of an offence carrying a maximum sentence of two years imprisonment and/or a fine. The Charity Commission may remove any trustee[431]: first, if they are satisfied that there has been misconduct or mismanagement and that this is necessary or desirable for the purpose of protecting the property of the charity; and, secondly, if a trustee has been discharged from bankruptcy during the last five years, is a corporation in liquidation, is mentally incapable, has not acted, is outside England and Wales, or cannot be found. An appeal against any decision of the

---

[425] *Bayoumi v. Women's Total Abstinence Educational Union* [2003] EWCA Civ. 1548, [2004] Ch. 46.

[426] *Re Snowden* [1970] Ch. 700.

[427] *ibid.* at 710.

[428] For the powers of a receiver and manager appointed for a charity, see *Att.-Gen. v. Schonfeld* [1980] 1 W.L.R. 1182.

[429] See *post*, Chapter 13.

[430] See *post*, para 13–049.

[431] Charities Act 1993, s.18.

Charity Commission to remove a trustee will be able to be made to the Charity Tribunal once it has commenced operations (until then the appeal is to the High Court).[432]

12. *Enforcement of Charitable Trusts*[433]

The Crown has the function of enforcing charitable trusts as *parens patriae* **11–170** and the Attorney-General, on behalf of the Crown, will be joined as a party to any proceedings involving a charity. Where there is a bona fide dispute as to the existence of a charitable trust, the Attorney-General should bring the proceedings or, where the existence of the charitable trust is being challenged by those who would otherwise be entitled to the property in question, defend them[434]; in the latter circumstances, it is therefore necessary for the person challenging the existence of the charitable trust to write to the Treasury Solicitor to enquire whether the Attorney-General wishes to make any representations on behalf of charity. Proceedings for the enforcement of charitable trusts which do not challenge the existence of the charitable trust in question can be brought not only by the Attorney-General, but also by the charity itself, by any of the trustees of the charity or by any persons interested in the charity or, if the charity in question is a local charity, by any two or more inhabitants from the area of the charity.[435] However, anyone who brings such proceedings other than the Attorney-General must first obtain an order from the Charity Commission or from a judge of the Chancery Division of the High Court authorising the institution of proceedings.[436] But this requirement does not apply where the trustees of a charity are bringing proceedings against an outsider, such as an action for possession against a commercial tenant of property owned by the charity; such proceedings are not for the enforcement of the charitable trusts.[437]

---

[432] s.4(3), (4).

[433] For personal liability of charity trustees, see Hawkins (1979) 75 L.Q.R. 99.

[434] *Re Belling* [1967] Ch. 425; *Hauxwell v. Barton-upon-Humber U.D.C.* [1974] Ch. 432; *Childs v. Att.-Gen.* [1973] 1 W.L.R. 497.

[435] Charities Act 1993, s.33(1).

[436] Charities Act 1993, s.33(2).

[437] See *Muman v. Nagasena* [2000] 1 W.L.R. 299, where permission was held to be necessary where the trustees' action for possession was against an insider, the patron or resident monk of the Buddhist charity in question.

CHAPTER 12

PENSION TRUSTS[1]

12–001   One of the most important purposes for which trusts are employed today is to provide pensions for retired persons and their dependants. Since the Second World War, pension schemes have become increasingly important and are now regarded as an essential part of virtually every contract of employment and an important factor for the self-employed. About half the national work force are, by virtue of their employment, members of what are known as occupational pensions schemes; what are known as personal pension schemes have been taken out by about a quarter of the work force, either the self-employed or employees who are "topping-up" the pension provision made by their occupational pension scheme. However, these figures also meant that, at least until 2001, considerably more than a quarter of the work force had no pension other than their state pension; however, since April 6, 2001, every employer with more than five employees has had to offer those employees the right to join what is known as a stakeholder pension scheme (the terms of these schemes determine whether they take effect as occupational pension schemes or as personal pensions schemes).

12–002   Pension provision is of enormous social significance, which is likely to become even more important in the light of the declared policy of the present government to move towards an increasing dependence on private rather than state pensions, a policy of which the introduction of stakeholder pension schemes was intended to form merely the first stage (since 2001 the government has instead concentrated on encouraging savings through what are at present known as ISAs and which produce tax free income for as long as those savings are maintained). Pension schemes are also important because the net value of their investment assets constitutes a very substantial proportion of the available investment capital of the country.

12–003   This chapter is principally concerned with pension schemes whose assets are held by trustees. This is the case for the vast majority of pension funds which are provided for employees, the objective, usually but sadly not always[2] achieved, being to assure the employee that his pension will in fact

---

[1] Pensions law is considered in detail in the regularly updated *Pensions Law Handbook* published by Tottel Publishing, 8th edn (2008). More detailed are the two loose-leaf practitioner works: Ellison, *Pensions Law & Practice* and Sweet & Maxwell, *The Law of Pension Schemes*. The immense quantity of Statutes, Statutory Instruments, and announcements by the Inland Revenue and the Occupational Pensions Regulatory Authority may be found in the loose-leaf *NAPF Pensions Legislation Service.*

[2] The systematic looting by the late Robert Maxwell of about £450 million from the pension fund established to provide pensions for ex-employees of *The Daily Mirror* caused great concern among employees in general. Pension fund administration then became the subject of a Committee of Inquiry, the Pensions Law Reform Committee, which reported in the autumn of 1993 (*Pension Law Reform*: [1993] Cmd. 2342, generally known as "the Goode Report") and came

be forthcoming on his retirement and that in the meantime his employer cannot in any way dispose of the pension contributions which have been made. This objective has been considerably enhanced by the requirement that one-third of the trustees (or, where the trustee is a trust company, of its directors) must be nominated by the employees.[3] The funds contributed to personal pension schemes by both the self-employed and by employees can also be held by trustees, in such cases usually trust corporations, in the form of investments; however, such funds are more typically paid to insurance companies for investment in insurance policies.

A basic knowledge of the working of pension trusts is now essential for every trust lawyer simply because many of the leading decisions in the last 15 years or so relating to the basic principles of the law of trusts have involved a pension scheme in one way or another. However, such litigation invariably involves pension funds which are held on trust for employees; even when the funds invested in a personal pension scheme are held by trustees, there is no real likelihood of any litigation of this type simply because the membership of the scheme is confined to the contributor and his dependants. **12–004**

I. THE NATURE OF PENSION SCHEMES

While this chapter is largely concerned with those occupational pension schemes in which payments are made to trustees to be invested and in due course used for the provision of benefits for the employees, all pension schemes are, of course, superimposed on the basic old age pension provided by the State. The way in which the State pension is calculated is relevant to the way in which occupational pension schemes work (and in particular the terminology employed in its calculation is often utilised in judgments); some consideration of the scope of the State pension is therefore necessary and, for the sake of completeness, personal pension schemes and stake-holder pension schemes will also briefly be considered. **12–005**

1. *The State Pension*

The provision made by the State pension scheme for employees (Category A pensions) comprises a basic pension[4] and an additional element, related to the employee's earnings. The State also provides the same two elements by way of pension to the widow or widower of a deceased employee (Category B pensions) if the former's own State pension entitlement is lower. The State also used to provide non-contributory pensions to persons who retired **12–006**

---

down on the side of continuing to utilise the trust vehicle. However, the Committee proposed a substantial number of reforms, some of which were enacted in the Pensions Act 1995 (see Nobles (1996) 59 M.L.R. 241).

[3] Pensions Act 1995, ss.16–21. As a result of Pensions Act 2004, ss.241, 243, since April 6, 2006 it has no longer been possible for the employer to persuade the members to accept alternative arrangements more favourable to himself.

[4] In the year 2008–2009, £90.70 per week for each person who qualifies, £54.35 extra per week for a non-qualifying spouse of a person who qualifies (after the death of the person who qualifies, the non-qualifier receives the higher amount).

before the State scheme started (Category C pensions) but there cannot possibly now be any one still alive in that category; the State still provides non-contributory pensions to persons who are over 80, satisfy certain residence conditions, and have no other category of State pension (Category D pensions).[5] All these pensions are increased annually in line with the Retail Prices Index. To qualify for the basic pension, anyone who reaches state retirement age before April 6, 2010 must have paid, or been credited with, National Insurance Contributions for approximately 90 per cent of his working life[6] but anyone who reaches state pension age on or after that date must have paid or been credited with them for not less than 30 years of his working life[7] (a considerably shorter period).

12–007   The additional element which is related to the employee's earnings between April 6, 1978 (when entitlement to this element commenced) and April 5, 2002 came from the State earnings-related pension scheme, generally described by reference to the acronym "SERPS"; since April 6, 2002, SERPS has been replaced by the State Second Pension or "S2P". Both apply only to earnings between the lower and upper limits in respect of which basic[8] National Insurance Contributions are payable[9] and a percentage of those earnings, revalued each year to take account of inflation during the period prior to retirement, is what constitutes the additional element. The value of the SERPS element has been progressively reduced. Earnings during the first 10 years during which the system operated (until April 5, 1988) are averaged and multiplied by 25 per cent. Earnings thereafter are averaged during throughout a person's entire working life and multiplied by a figure which is being reduced from the former figure of 25 per cent[10] by $\frac{1}{2}$ per cent each year until it reaches 20 per cent.[11] The value of the S2P element varies from 40 per cent to 10 per cent depending on which of three bands between the lower and upper limits is relevant. The principal change is that for the first time credits are being given to those caring for children under six years of age and for sick and disabled persons and to sick and disabled persons themselves; they will be treated as if they had earned an interim figure known as the low earnings threshold. The pension payable is of one-eightieth of the total amount of the relevant earnings for each of the years during which SERPS or SUP has been earned or credited up to a maximum of forty-eightieths.

12–008   The two elements of the State pension are payable whether or not the person in question is a member of a private pension scheme. However, it is

---

[5] This pension is now the same as the pension for a non-qualifying spouse of a person who qualifies (formerly, it was two-thirds of the above rates).

[6] 49 years for a man and for a woman born on or after April 6, 1955, both of whom retire at 65; 44 for a woman born before April 6, 1950 who retires at 60 (the working life and retirement age of women born between these two dates increases progressively in accordance with Pensions Act 1995, Sch.4, para.1). Persons born on or after April 6, 1959 will be subject to a progressive increase in the retirement age to 68 over a period of 22 years beginning on April 6, 2024.

[7] Pursuant to Pensions Act 2007.

[8] Since April 6, 2003, a further 1% has been payable on all earnings above the upper limit.

[9] In the year 2008–2009, the lower limit was £5,436 and the upper limit was £40,040.

[10] Which applied up to April 5, 1999.

[11] For persons who reached retirement age before April 6, 1999, the average is instead the average of their best 20 years.

possible for an occupational pension scheme to contract out of SERPS and S2P. This means that its members agree not to take the additional element of their pension from the State and the private pension scheme then has to meet that liability instead. Financial incentives are provided to encourage contracting out in the form of reduced National Insurance Contributions by both employers and employees. Where the members of a scheme have elected to contract out, it is obviously essential that the pension provided to each member on retirement is at least as much as he would have obtained by way of the SERPS element. For service prior to April 6, 1997 this amount was known as the guaranteed minimum pension ("GMP") and was calculated by a formula similar, but not actually identical, to that by which the SERPS element itself is calculated. During this period, it was possible for schemes to cease to be contracted out, in which case its members had to be bought back into the SERPS scheme by the payment of what were known as "state scheme premiums".[12] Schemes which contracted out on or after April 6, 1997 (schemes which had already done so were obliged to re-elect so to do) have instead to meet a statutory standard (accumulated GMPs survive) and it is no longer possible to contract back into the SERPS scheme. The statutory benefits in respect of each year worked are basically one-eightieth of 90 per cent of the average earnings between the lower and upper limits in respect of which National Insurance Contributions are payable during the three years prior to termination of service, together with a spouse's pension of one-half, revaluation of the pension payable during any further period up to actual retirement, and limited indexation of pensions in payment. Obviously, if a person ceases to be employed by an employer with a contracted out scheme, he accrues entitlement to SERPS or, now, S2P in respect of non-contracted out earnings.

2. *Personal Pension Schemes*

Personal pension schemes are taken out either by the self-employed or by employees who are either unable or unwilling to join an occupational pension scheme or by employees who want to "top-up" the pension provision made for them by their occupational pension scheme. Personal pension schemes first became available on July 1, 1988. Initially the member of the scheme had to leave the investment of his contributions entirely to the

12–009

---

[12] Where a member leaves a contracted out scheme prior to retirement, the pension to which he remains entitled to obtain on his retirement will include his GMP element, which will continue to grow by virtue of the process of revaluation. Originally only the GMP element of his pension was revalued (thereby gradually consuming any additional pension to which he was entitled) but by what is known as "anti-franking legislation", any excess in his pension over his GMP element was first preserved and eventually made subject to revaluation itself (see Pension Schemes Act 1993, ss.87–92, 83–86 respectively). However, a member who leaves an occupational pension scheme is now entitled to transfer his pension rights to any other approved pension scheme which he joins (Pension Schemes Act 1993, Pt IV Pensions Act 1995, s.95); if he chooses to do so, the sum transferred to his new scheme in respect of his accrued pension entitlements must include the GMP (or current equivalent) element of that entitlement.

provider of the scheme. However, in 1989 the concept of the self-invested personal pension scheme was introduced to enable the member to become involved in decisions about the investment of his contributions; however, the complexity of such arrangements tends to result in higher costs of membership and administration.

12–010   Since April 6, 2007, personal pension schemes have only been able to be established, operated and administered by persons who have permission so to do from the Financial Services Authority. The person who establishes the scheme may or may not be the same person as the operator of the scheme, who is responsible to its members for administering the assets and income of the scheme and the benefits payable under it; in a trust-based scheme, the operator will be the trustee. The operator will also normally be the scheme administrator, who is responsible for reporting matters to H.M. Revenue & Customs and for paying certain tax charges. However, in the case of self-invested personal pension schemes, which will invariably be trust-based, a separate scheme administrator is normally appointed alongside the operator-trustee.

12–011   Before April 6, 2006 there were no restrictions on the total amount of assets that a person could have invested in private pension schemes but there was an annual limit on contributions which in 2005–2006 was £105,600; this annual limit was also the maximum amount of earnings on which the member could obtain relief from income tax. From April 6, 2006 the Pensions Act 2004, as amended by subsequent Finance Acts, imposed a new fiscal regime which applies to all "registered pension schemes" and therefore to all private pensions schemes. A lifetime allowance was imposed on the total amount of assets that a person can have in any pension scheme. This was £1,500,000 in 2006–2007 and is increased each year; in 2008–2009 it was £1,650,000 (transitional relief is available to anyone who already had more than £1,500,000 in pension schemes on April 6, 2006). There is nothing to stop tax relievable contributions being made to enable an individual to build up benefits with a value in excess of the lifetime allowance but, if the lifetime allowance is exceeded, there is an additional tax charge on any excess that exists when the benefits come into payment; this is 25 per cent if the excess funds are taken in the form of annuity or of 55 per cent if the excess funds are taken out as a lump sum. In contrast, there is now no limit on the amount of contributions to personal pension schemes, merely a much higher annual limit on the amount of earnings in respect of which the member can obtain relief from income tax which, in 2008–2009, was £235,000; contributions to personal pension schemes in excess of the limit will, therefore, have been taxed at 40 per cent.

12–012   Initially the only benefits which could be provided to the member of a personal pension scheme were an annuity payable to the member on his retirement (or, on his death, to his spouse and/or dependants) and/or a lump sum payable on his retirement or his earlier death. Retirement could not, and still cannot, normally occur earlier than the age of 50 (55 from 2010) or later than the age of 75. However, since May 1995, it has also been possible for a member to defer the purchase of an annuity from the date of his actual retirement until his 75th birthday and in the meantime to make income withdrawals from his scheme.

3. *Stakeholder Pension Schemes*

Stakeholder pension schemes straddle the normal division between per-   **12–013**
sonal pension schemes and occupational pension schemes. Since 2001, every
employer with more than five employees has had to offer those employees
the right to take out a stakeholder pension. Such pensions, which were
introduced by the Welfare Reform and Pensions Act 1999, came into effect
on April 6, 2001 and employers were obliged to have schemes in place by
October 8, 2001. There are at present exemptions for employers who offer
membership of an occupational pension scheme to all employees within a
year of the commencement of their employment, to employers who offer a
group personal pension to which they contribute at least 3 per cent per
annum of their employees' earnings, and to employers whose employees all
earn less than the National Insurance Contributions lower earning limit.

The obligations of an employer who is obliged to offer his employees the   **12–014**
right to take out a stakeholder pension are confined, first, to providing the
scheme, either directly or through a pension provider, and, secondly, to
enabling each employee's desired contributions to be deducted from his
remuneration. It must be emphasised that employers are not obliged to
make any contributions whatsoever. Employees cannot make contributions
of less than £20 net of basic rate tax. Otherwise, they can contribute as much
as they like,[13] subject to the fiscal limits which apply to all pension contributions,[14] as often as they like; there is no obligation to make regular contributions. No fees can be charged by the employer or anyone else for setting up
the scheme and administration charges were originally limited to 1 per cent
per annum of the value of the fund built up; however, for members who
joined on or after April 6, 2005, the limit has been raised to 1.5 per cent but
only for the first 10 years.

Stakeholder pension schemes can either be established on a contract basis,   **12–015**
in which case they take effect as personal pension schemes, or on a trust
basis, in which case they take effect as occupational pension schemes and
are governed by the vast majority of the rules considered in the remainder
of this chapter. The choice is in principle that of the employer, although
"industry-wide" schemes (schemes in which the definition of membership
is by reference to employment in the industry, rather than by any particular
employer[15]) must be established on a trust basis. Any existing occupational
pension schemes which are converted to stakeholder pension schemes will
also in practice have to be established on a trust basis, although such
conversions are highly unlikely because of the low level of fees able to be
charged under a stakeholder pension scheme. However, all stakeholder
pensions which have been offered by pension providers have been offered
on a contract basis. Consequently, apart from industry-wide schemes and
any conversions, the only stakeholder pension schemes which are likely to
have been set up on a trust basis are those schemes set up by employers
alongside their existing occupational pension schemes; it was thought that

---

[13] There is an annual maximum figure for contributions by non-employees which for many
years been £3,600.
[14] See *ante*, para 12–011, *post* para 12–037.
[15] An example is the Merchant Navy Pension Scheme.

such schemes would particularly assist employees who have an irregular working pattern or who have not been members of an occupational pension scheme throughout their working lives but there is no evidence that this practice is at all widespread. The response so far to the offer of stakeholder pension schemes of both types seems to have been fairly poor.[16]

4. *Occupational Pension Schemes*

12–016 It should first be re-emphasised that no employer is under any legal obligation whatever to make any provision for his employees by way of pension; this remains the case despite the introduction of stakeholder pensions, since employers are obliged merely to provide such schemes, not to contribute to them. Employers who make no contributions to any pension scheme for their employees simply pay National Insurance Contributions at the higher contracted in rate so that the employees will receive both the basic and the additional elements of the State pension when they retire. Given the low level of pension provided by the State, most employees in this position need to give serious consideration to taking out a personal pension scheme or joining a stakeholder pension scheme.

(A) Types of Schemes
12–017 Of the various types of occupational pension schemes which exist, this chapter is principally concerned with those occupational pension schemes in which employees and/or employers make payments to trustees to be invested in assets which will provide the payment of the benefits for which the scheme provides as they fall due. Brief mention should, however, be made of some of the other types of schemes.

12–018 The majority of schemes for employees in the public sector (the best example is the civil service) are established by legislation and are, therefore, backed by the revenue of the Government rather than by a segregated trust fund; in such circumstances, the employees have to rely on the certainty of the continuity of Government revenue to meet its statutory obligations rather than the performance of any fund.

12–019 Some non-statutory schemes are also, in the same sense, unfunded in that the employer does not segregate any assets for the purpose of providing for the payment of the benefits as they fall due; such schemes are known as "pay-as-you-go" schemes and are necessarily non-contributory. Employer

---

[16] The principal target of stakeholder pension schemes was obviously employees who had no existing pension provision, for whom the restriction on the level of administration costs is extremely beneficial since their only alternative, personal pension schemes, invariably have very much higher initial charges. The Government also hoped that holders of personal pension schemes who are "topping-up" their occupational pension schemes would convert to stakeholder pension schemes and that all such schemes would opt out of SERPS or S2P, thus saving the State a considerable amount of money. Neither objective was particularly realistic: the holders of existing personal pensions who converted would be prejudiced in that the charges under their personal pension schemes would in later years be likely to be considerably less than the 1% which stakeholder pension schemes will inevitably charge; nor is it in the interest of employees for their stakeholder pension schemes to opt out of SERPS or S2P except in the unlikely event that their employer is contributing. Further, because non-employees can also join a stakeholder pension scheme, these schemes have also become a means of enabling the adult children of the wealthy to build up pension provision at the expense of taxpayers.

and employees have to rely on the employer still having sufficient assets to fund the appropriate benefits at the appropriate time. The employees would certainly be most ill-advised so to rely in the case of a trading company, which could simply become insolvent or sell its business to a third party who was not bound by the contracts of employment in question, and the employer could find himself with the need to make a substantial payment before he expected to have to do so if any employee who left before retirement exercised his statutory right to an immediate cash transfer of the value of his accrued benefits to another pension scheme. Further, such schemes do not enjoy any of the taxation benefits of funded schemes so the employer will need to be satisfied that the net return which he can receive by leaving in his business the funds which would otherwise have provided the pension contributions will be at least as much as the gross returns which would be obtained by investing them in a funded scheme. However, employers such as the owners of large historic landed estates which they are in practice incapable of selling could certainly run "pay-as-you-go" schemes; their employees would presumably be content to rely on the underlying value of the estates in question while the benefits payable by way of pensions and lump sums in any one year could be charged by the employer as trading expenses against the income of the estate.

Even within the vast majority of private pension schemes which are **12–020** funded by the segregation of assets in the hands of trustees, many of the smaller schemes operate as insured schemes, under which the trustees take out a contract with an insurance company in respect of each employee to provide the benefits which he has contracted to receive and use the pension contributions merely to pay the premiums on the policy. In such schemes, assuming that the policies in question provide whatever cover is appropriate from time to time, the only question which the trustees ever have to consider is whether the contributions are sufficient to pay the premiums.

(B) Funded Schemes

The remaining schemes, where the trustees place the contributions paid to **12–021** them in a fund which they then invest in order to provide in advance for the payment of pensions as they fall due, are known as funded schemes. They pose rather more problems.

Most schemes of this type are associated with groups of trading com- **12–022** panies or a single trading company, where membership is dependent on being an employee of a company within the scheme. However, there are also what are known as "industry-wide" schemes, in which the definition of membership is by reference to employment in the industry, rather than by any particular employer.[17] One of the many ways in which schemes are classified is into "defined benefit schemes" and "defined contribution schemes". Both may be either contributory or non-contributory.

(1) The difference and the choice between the two types of scheme

The essential difference between a defined benefit scheme and a defined **12–023** contribution scheme is as follows: a defined benefit scheme provides benefits in accordance with length of service and the salary being earned at or

---

[17] An example is the Merchant Navy Pension Scheme.

shortly before retirement and those benefits are not in any way affected by
the total contributions which have been made by employer and employee or
the value at the date of retirement of the investments in which those
contributions have been invested by the trustees; in contrast, a defined
contribution scheme provides benefits which are entirely conditioned by the
value at the date of retirement of the investments in which the contributions
made by employer and employee have been invested by the trustees. In
other words, a fall in the value of the assets held by a pension trust does not,
in principle, affect the benefits payable to the members of a defined benefit
scheme; the employer has to come up with any additional funding which
may be necessary in order to provide those benefits so it is the employer
rather than the employee who runs the risk of a poor investment performance. In contrast, the value of the benefits of a member of a defined contribution scheme depends entirely on his share of the net return made by the
investments in which the trustees invest the fund; thus it is the employee,
not the employer, who assumes the risk of a poor investment
performance.

12–024   It is self-evident that, if the choice were that of the employee, a defined
benefit scheme would always be chosen in preference to a defined contribution scheme. However, given that no employer is under any legal obligation
to make any provision whatever for his employees by way of pension, the
choice of whether to implement a defined benefit or a defined contribution
scheme and, for that matter, of whether whatever scheme is selected should
be contributory or non-contributory is inevitably that of the employer.
Nevertheless, defined benefit schemes predominated until 1995, when the
Pensions Act 1995 introduced, with effect from 1997, a minimum funding
requirement, since replaced from December 30, 2005, pursuant to the Pensions Act 2004, by the obligation to have a scheme-specific funding standard.
Once the Pensions Act 1995 had been enacted, employers introducing new
occupational pension schemes tended instead to opt for defined contribution schemes, to which the minimum funding requirement did not apply, in
order to be able to cap, and more importantly to be able to predict the
amount of, their own contributions. However, this did not initially have any
impact on existing defined benefit schemes, other of course than potentially
raising the level of employer's contributions to them.

12–025   From 1999, however, many defined benefit schemes became faced with
actual or potential deficits as a result of the combination of the minimum
funding requirement, of the withdrawal from 1998, originally announced in
1997, of the tax credit previously given to pension schemes in respect of their
income from company distributions, and of a substantial fall in the value of
shares which commenced in 1999; a further drain on defined benefit
schemes was, and is, the increasing longevity of their members. As early as
2000, the Government announced proposals for the eventual, but not
immediate, abolition of the minimum funding requirement and, with effect
from 2002, lengthened the periods for compliance with it. However, this
interim reform and the subsequent replacement with effect from December
30, 2005 of the minimum funding requirement by a scheme-specific funding
standard proved to be too little too late.

12–026   From 2001 onwards, an ever-increasing number of major companies
closed their defined benefit schemes to new employees, offering the latter

only membership of defined contribution schemes. Admittedly, no one could justifiably complain about this but some companies went further and closed their defined benefit schemes completely so that future service by both existing and new employees could only generate benefits under defined contribution schemes. This did not of course affect benefits already earned but nevertheless altered the overall employment package of existing employees, producing some threats of industrial action. A few companies have provoked much more vociferous threats of this type by deciding to wind-up their defined benefit schemes completely; this process tends also to reduce benefits already earned unless the scheme in question is extremely well funded.[18] It must, however, be emphasised that none of these courses of conduct is actually prohibited, or even frowned on, by the present law.

What is, therefore, self-evident is that defined contribution schemes now **12–027** predominate, at any rate for employees who have commenced their employment in the last 10 years because, even if they are employed by an employer who still has a defined benefit scheme, it is increasingly likely that that scheme will have been closed to new employees.

(2) Defined benefit schemes
Because a defined benefit scheme provides benefits in accordance with **12–028** length of service and the salary being earned at or shortly before retirement, such schemes are more commonly known as "final salary schemes". Such schemes are normally now contributory (except in the case of relatively low paid employment) and are usually on a "balance of cost" basis; the employee makes a fixed contribution of an established percentage of his salary and the employer has to make whatever contributions are from time to time actuarially necessary to provide the benefits for which the scheme is potentially liable as they fall due. As indicated above, in this type of scheme it is the employer rather than the employee who runs the risk of a poor investment performance. Since December 30, 2005, there has been an obligation on trustees of a defined benefit scheme to have a scheme-specific funding standard requiring each scheme to have sufficient and appropriate assets to cover its liabilities or to have a recovery plan in place to achieve that within a stated period.[19] On the other hand, a good investment performance may enable the employer to take what is known as a "contributions holiday" by ceasing to pay any contributions whatever until an established surplus in the fund has been used up.

In its simplest form, "defined benefit" relates to the salary being earned by **12–029** the employee at the date of his retirement but this is usually varied; the most common variants are the highest salary in the last three (or five) years of employment prior to retirement or the average salary during one of those periods (however, not all the payments received by the employee will necessarily qualify for this purpose; allowances and bonuses are generally not pensionable, which means that they are excluded). The benefits provided by the scheme are determined, subject to limits imposed by H.M Revenue & Customs as a condition of approval of the scheme, by length of

---

[18] See *post*, para 12–101.
[19] Pensions Act 2004, Part 3. This replaced the "minimum funding requirement" introduced by Pensions Act 1995.

service; a fairly standard percentage is one-sixtieth for each year of service up to a maximum of 40 years service, thus potentially providing a pension of two-thirds of the final salary; however, many quasi-public employees, such as university lecturers, who have their own separately funded schemes, only receive a much more miserly one-eightieth for each year of service also up to a maximum of 40 years service, thus potentially providing a smaller pension of only one-half of the final salary.

12–030   The benefits provided always include an annuity of the appropriate percentage of the relevant salary, usually guaranteed for five years (which means that the balance is payable to the pensioner's estate if he dies during this period). They also have to include, since April 6, 1973,[20] preservation rights, that is to say the right to what is known as a "deferred pension" by means of which the accumulated pension rights of any employee who leaves prior to retirement age are preserved and enhanced by revaluation and, since April 6, 1978[21] in the case of contracted-out schemes, provision for the payment in priority to all other liabilities of the scheme of the additional element of the State pension. The package of benefits usually also includes some or all of the following: an option to commute part of the annuity for the immediate payment of a lump sum—the annuity is then reduced by reference to a formula; an annuity, usually between a half and two-thirds of the pensioner's annuity, for a surviving widow (sometimes also extended to widowers) and/or any dependent children; and a death in service benefit, a lump sum which the trustees have the discretion to distribute, sometimes with a right of nomination for the member.[22] All pensions which were in payment before April 6, 2005 or which relate entirely to pensionable service before that date are subject to "limited price indexation" ("LPI"), in that they are required to increase in line with the retail prices index or, if less, by 5 per cent per annum in respect of service on and after April 6, 1997.[23] Pensions which come into payment after that date must be increased only by the lesser of 2.5 per cent per annum or the increase in the retail prices index.[24]

12–031   Because of the factors already referred to, namely the withdrawal from 1998, of the tax credit previously given to pension schemes in respect of their income from company distributions, the substantial fall in the value of shares which commenced in 1999, and the increasing longevity of the members of pension schemes, the obligation of employer to come up with any additional funding which may be necessary in order to provide the benefits payable to the members of a defined benefit scheme has become increasingly burdensome. Indeed, the potential liability so to do has become an increasingly important factor when companies are being taken over. The

---

[20] By virtue of Social Security Act 1973, now Pension Schemes Act 1993, ss.93–101.

[21] Social Security Pensions Act 1975, introducing SERPS and (for "defined benefit" schemes) contracting-out of SERPS with effect from April 1978, now Pensions Schemes Act 1993, s.14.

[22] See Inheritance Tax Act 1984, s.151(5); in *Wild v. Smith* [1996] O.P.L.R. 129, Carnwath J. upheld the ruling of the Pensions Ombudsman that the member in question had not validly nominated his mistress as a dependant.

[23] Pensions Act 1995, s.51.

[24] Pensions Act 1995, s.51, as amended with effect from April 6, 2005 by Pensions Act 2004.

nightmare scenario for the members of a defined benefit scheme is that the employer will become insolvent and will, therefore, be unable to provide the additional funds, thus leading to the winding-up of the scheme. In these circumstances, payments to existing pensioners enjoy priority over future payments to existing employees and it has not been uncommon in such circumstances for the latter to lose their pension rights completely, something which for them is a total disaster, particularly for those relatively near to retirement.

The political fall out from disasters of this kind caused the creation, by the **12–032** Pensions Act 2004, of the Pensions Protection Fund, which became operational on April 6, 2005 (the Board of the Pension Protection Fund also manages the Fraud Compensation Fund which provides compensation where the assets of a scheme whose employer has become insolvent have been reduced as the result of an action of dishonesty). The idea is that the Pensions Protection Fund will assume responsibility for any defined benefit scheme which, as a result of the insolvency of the employer in question, is insufficiently funded; it will supplement the assets of the scheme by an amount sufficient to provide pensioners with 100 per cent of their entitlement and members who have yet to reach normal pension age with 90 per cent of their entitlement subject, in each case, to a cap of, in 2007–2008, just under £27,000. The subject matter of the fund is provided by two annual levies on all defined benefit schemes: first, a risk-based levy, which is assessed by reference to the difference between the value of the scheme's assets and the amount of its protected liabilities, and the likelihood of an employer becoming insolvent; and, secondly, a scheme-based levy, which is assessed by reference to various factors which include the amount of a scheme's liabilities, the number of members, and the total amount of pensionable earnings of active members of the scheme.

The introduction of the Pensions Protection Fund did nothing for mem- **12–033** bers of a defined benefit scheme who had already lost some or all of their benefits as the result of the winding-up of a scheme which commenced before the fund became operational. Consequently, the Pensions Act 2004 also envisaged the introduction of a Financial Assistance Scheme. As subsequently amended by the Pensions Act 2007, this scheme requires the Secretary of State to provide for all the members of a defined benefit scheme which commenced winding-up between January 1, 1997 and April 5, 2005 to receive 80 per cent of their expected benefits subject to a fixed cap of £26,000. This scheme has been provided by the Government rather than by levies largely because of even more sustained political pressure and the fact that the European Court of Justice found that the Government had failed properly to protect pensions on the insolvency of an employer.[25] The introduction of the Pensions Protection Fund and the Financial Assistance Scheme obviously provides a substantial, although, because of the incidence of caps and percentages, not absolute, safeguard for members of defined benefits schemes.

---

[25] In *Robins v. Secretary of State for Work and Pensions* (Case C-278/05) [2007] All E.R. (EC) 895.

(3) Defined contribution schemes

12–034   Defined contribution schemes are commonly also known as "money purchase schemes". Such schemes are usually, but not necessarily, contributory; where they are, the employer and the employee tend to contribute equal amounts, which for the employer will almost inevitably be less than he would have had to contribute to a defined benefit scheme.[26] The contributions made to the scheme are invested by the trustees and held by them for each member of the scheme and his dependants. Each member has in effect his own notional sub-fund comprising the contributions made by or on his behalf and the value of his benefits depends entirely on his share of the net return made by the investments in which the trustees invest the fund; his position is not unlike that of the holder of units in a unit trust. In such schemes, it is consequently the employee, not the employer, who assumes the risk of a poor investment performance. For this reason, the minimum funding requirement introduced by the Pensions Act 1995 did not and the replacement scheme-specific funding standard introduced by the Pensions Act 2004 does not apply to defined contribution schemes. Because of the fact that employers do not have to contribute to stakeholder pension schemes, such schemes are necessarily defined contribution schemes.

12–035   On retirement, or death in service, the notional sub-fund is realised and used to purchase an annuity, usually index linked, for the benefit of the member and his dependants and to provide whatever other benefits are envisaged by the scheme (such as the right to commutation of part of the annuity for the payment of an immediate lump sum). The payments of the annuity were subject to limited price indexation in respect of service on or after April 7, 1997 where the pension came into payment before April 6, 2005 (in which case it had to increase in line with the retail prices index or (if less) by 5 per cent per annum); the difference, of course, was that the employer was not obliged to pay for these increases which, therefore, had to be borne in mind when the annuity was being purchased. There is no obligation to increase payments when pensions come into payment on or after April 6, 2005.

12–036   Although the Fraud Compensation Fund provides compensation where the assets of a defined contribution scheme whose employer has become insolvent have been reduced as the result of an action of dishonesty, neither the Pensions Protection Fund nor the Financial Assistance Scheme applies to defined contribution schemes for the somewhat obvious reason that employers' contributions to such schemes are fixed from the outset and so there is no scope for more than very limited sums, by way of arrears, to be due to such schemes by employers who become insolvent.

(C) Fiscal Regulation

12–037   Part 4 of the Finance Act 2004, as amended by subsequent Finance Acts, replaced the previous eight fiscal regimes which applied to different types of

---

[26] Because few employees would be enthusiastic about contributing as much of their emoluments as employers have to contribute to a final salary scheme.

pensions schemes with a single integrated fiscal regime which, with effect from April 6, 2006 applies to all "registered pension schemes" (the equivalent of what were previously known as "approved pension schemes"). A lifetime allowance was imposed on the total amount of assets that a person can have in any pension scheme. This was £1,500,000 in 2006–2007 and is increased each year; in 2008–2009 it was £1,650,000 (transitional relief is available to anyone who already had more than £1,500,000 in pension schemes on April 6, 2006). For this purpose, the payment of an occupational pension is valued at 20 times its amount so that the payment of a pension of £25,000 per annum uses up £500,000 of the lifetime allowance. There is nothing to stop tax relievable contributions being made to enable an individual to build up benefits with a value in excess of the lifetime allowance but, if the lifetime allowance is exceeded, there is an additional tax charge on any excess that exists when the benefits come into payment; this is 25 per cent if the excess funds are taken in the form of annuity or of 55 per cent if the excess funds are taken out as a lump sum. In contrast, there is now no limit on the amount of contributions to personal pension schemes, merely a much higher annual limit on the amount of earnings in respect of which the member can obtain relief from income tax which, in 2008–2009, was £235,000; contributions to occupational pensions schemes in excess of the limit are taxed at 40 per cent in the hands of the employee whether those contributions are provided by him or by his employer.

The new regime governing the form in which pensions have to be paid is **12–038** broadly as follows. Retirement cannot normally occur earlier than the age of 50 save in the case of incapacity and that age will rise to 55 from 2010.[27] Defined benefit schemes can only pay "scheme pensions", pensions out of their own resources or by an insurance company selected by the scheme's administrator, and scheme pensions must, generally speaking, be payable until the date of the member's death or the later of the member's death and a fixed period of 10 years.[28] Defined contributions schemes may pay either a scheme pension, or a lifetime annuity, or an unsecured annuity which is in effect either a short-term annuity or income withdrawal.[29] In all cases, on commencement of the payment of any pension, on the winding-up of any occupational pension scheme, a tax free lump sum of up to one quarter of the value of the relevant pension entitlement as calculated for the purpose of the lifetime allowance may be paid.[30] Payments of pensions and of lump sums to dependants in the event of the death of are limited to payments to spouses or civil partners of the member, to children of the member under 23 or dependant on the deceased because of physical or mental impairment, and to anyone else who was financially dependant on the member and was either in a financial relationship with the member of mutual dependence or was dependant on him because of physical or mental impairment.[31]

---

[27] Finance Act 2004, s.165; Rule 1.
[28] Finance Act 2004, s.165; Rule 3.
[29] Finance Act 2004, s.165; Rule 4.
[30] Finance Act 2004, s.166.
[31] Finance Act 2004, s.167.

12–039   However, pursuant to transitional provisions, unless occupational pension schemes take steps to disapply those provisions, they will not be able to pay out benefits in excess of the limits which existed prior to April 6, 2006 for at least five years after that date. These limits restricted payments by way of pension to two-thirds of "final salary" and, in the case of employees joining after March 1987, only after 20 years' service (with the appropriate number of thirtieths until then).[32] Lump sum payments were restricted to 150 per cent of "final salary" and only then after 20 years' service (with the appropriate number of three-eightieths until then) with further restrictions to 225 per cent of the initial annuity for those joining after May 1989. Death in service lump sum benefits were restricted to four times the amount of remuneration at the time of death plus the return of all contributions paid with interest. A widow's (or, where relevant, widower's or civil partner's) pension was restricted to two-thirds of the maximum pension payable. The total permissible benefits and contributions were the appropriate percentages of a figure known as "the pension cap", which was increased each year in line with inflation (it was £105,600 in 2005–2006). This figure formerly also constituted the maximum amount of tax free contributions[33] but, although this is no longer the case, it continues to restrict total permissible benefits and contributions during the transitional period and for that purpose alone is still increased each year.

12–040   In other respects, the fiscal position of what was until April 6, 2006 known as an exempt approved scheme remains the position of a registered pension scheme. The contributions of the employer are treated as trading expenses and thus are exempt from both income and corporation tax, while the employee is exempt from income tax both on his own contributions and on those of the employer. Lump sum payments are tax free in the hands of a pensioner, although his pension payments will be subject to income tax at his marginal rate. A registered pension scheme is liable neither to income tax nor to capital gains tax on its investments; as has already been seen, the benefit of the income tax exemption was substantially reduced in 1998 when the exemption from what was then the 20 per cent tax retained by companies on their dividends was abolished (admittedly, the retention was subsequently reduced to 10 per cent anyway but, as has already been mentioned, the abolition of the exemption had the effect of placing many defined benefit schemes in actual or potential deficit and was a contributory factor in their closure). An approved or registered insured scheme (a scheme which operates by purchasing insurance policies for each member) is entitled to equivalent benefits.

12–041   Approval was and registration is available both to all types of funded schemes and to insured schemes. There seems no reason why "pay-as-you-go" schemes should not also be approved at the discretion of H.M. Revenue

---

[32] Employees who joined before March 1987 reached the two-thirds limit after 10 years service but until then could have only the appropriate number of sixtieths.

[33] Not more than 15% of an employee's pensionable earnings from any employment could be contributed to the relevant occupational pension scheme but he could make additional contributions to personal pension schemes up to a higher percentage, which increases in line with his age (a total of 17.5% at the age of 35 or below, increasing to 40% at the age of 61 or more).

& Customs if satisfied with the level of their underlying assets and with their limits on benefits; this would enable lump sum payments made under such schemes to be tax free in the hands of their beneficiaries.

(D) Non-Fiscal Regulation

A considerable quantity of non-fiscal regulation is provided by the statutory provisions which have already been considered relating to preservation values, transfer values, contracting out, limited price indexation, and the minimum funding requirement. Further regulation has been provided by the decisions of the European Court of Justice relating to aspects of sex discrimination, where it has been held to be discriminatory to confer pension entitlements on women at any earlier age than on men[34] and to part-time employees.[35] A number of other legislative provisions which are discussed in the course of this chapter have also provided such regulation.   **12–042**

A quite different form of non-fiscal regulation is provided by tribunals.   **12–043**
There are two tribunals specifically dealing with pension schemes: first, the Pensions Regulator, set up by the Pensions Act 2004 with effect from April 6, 2005 in substitution for the Occupational Pensions Regulatory Authority; and, secondly, the Pensions Ombudsman, a two-man tribunal originally created in 1990 which is now regulated by the Pension Schemes Act 1993 as amended by the Pensions Act 1995 and the Pensions Act 2004. Additionally, there are a number of investment and financial regulatory bodies which are the appropriate tribunals for the investigation of matters such as complaints about the selling of personal pension schemes, which have been very frequent in recent years.

The Pensions Regulator is charged with the objectives of protecting the   **12–044**
benefits of scheme members under occupational pension schemes and personal pension schemes, of reducing the risk of situations arising which may lead to compensation being paid from the Pension Protection Fund, and of promoting, and improving understanding of, the good administration of "work-based" pension schemes. Anyone involved with a pension scheme is under a duty to report to the Pensions Regulator any non-compliance with the statutory rules relating to the requirement for member-nominated trustees, the payment of surplus or excess assets to the employer, the restrictions on employer related investments, the requirements to appoint professional advisers and to keep books and records, the scheme-specific funding requirement and schedules of contributions made pursuant to that requirement, and the requirement for defined contribution schemes to keep schedules of payment. Once a matter is reported, the Pensions Regulator is charged with the investigation of the matter in question and has very considerable powers, including the powers to remove trustees from office, to impose fines and civil penalties for breach of statutory duty, to direct the winding-up of a scheme where it feels that this is in the interests of the

---

[34] *Barber v. Royal Exchange Assurance Group* [1991] 1 Q.B. 344; *Coloroll Pension Trustees v. Russell* [1995] I.C.R. 179.
[35] *Preston v. Wolverhampton NHS Trust* [2001] 2 A.C. 415.

members as a whole, to authorise modifications, to issue and extend freezing orders, to issue contribution notices, and to issue restoration orders where there has been a transaction at an undervalue. Its decisions are subject to an appeal to the Pensions Regulator Tribunal. However, the Pensions Regulator cannot otherwise order the payment of compensation for the benefit of the members of the scheme. Nor is it authorised to investigate breaches of the equal treatment or indexation provisions or breaches of the general law of trusts. These excluded matters can only be dealt with by a complaint to the Pensions Ombudsman or by proceedings in the High Court.

12–045   The Pensions Ombudsman has no jurisdiction to deal with any of the matters with whose investigation the Pensions Regulator is primarily charged. His jurisdiction is instead to investigate complaints made against past or present trustees, managers and employers about the way in which pensions schemes are. It extends to: complaints of maladministration, whether of an occupational or a personal pension scheme, made by or on behalf of any actual or potential beneficiary and any employer, manager or trustee about any employer, manager or trustee and, in the case of a trustee, also about the trustees of another pension scheme; ancillary disputes of fact or law, whether relating to an occupational or a personal pension scheme, raised by any of the same persons about the same persons; and ancillary complaints and disputes relating to an occupational pension scheme raised by at least half its trustees, a sole trustee or the independent trustee against any other trustees. Maladministration for this purpose has been said to involve "bias, neglect, inattention, delay, incompetence, ineptitude, perversity, turpitude, arbitrariness and so on".[36] The jurisdiction does not extend to breaches of trust unless they fall within one of these heads; this was held in *Hillsdown Holdings v. Pensions Ombudsman*.[37] Appeals from the determinations of the Pensions Ombudsman now lie to the Chancery Division of the High Court.[38]

12–046   There have been a number of doubts about the jurisdiction of the Pensions Ombudsman. In procedural terms, he is an automatic party to appeals against his own adjudications and his right to appear if he so chooses to defend his own adjudication as a kind of *amicus curiae* is now accepted.[39] However, the Court of Appeal has now held[40] that leave should not be given to him to appeal to the Court of Appeal against a decision of the High Court adverse to his original adjudication on the grounds that it is inappropriate for him to appeal from the decisions of the tribunal authorised to review his own decisions except, perhaps, when he wishes to query an award of costs made against him by the High Court. As for his remedial powers, he can clearly direct apologies, order the holding of another meeting or election,

---

[36] This is the famous "[Richard] Crossman Catalogue" of what constitutes maladministration.
[37] [1997] 1 All E.R. 862 at 884.
[38] Formerly it was to the Crown Office List of the Queen's Bench Division.
[39] *Dolphin Packaging Materials v. Pensions Ombudsman* (1993) unreported.
[40] *Edge v. The Pensions Ombudsman* [2000] Ch. 602.

and award compensation for financial loss. However, the Court of Appeal has held[41] that, where the act of maladministration consists of a breach of trust, he cannot order any remedy which could not have been ordered by the High Court. Whether he can order compensation of types which could not have been ordered by the High Court is less clear.[42] Doubts have also been expressed[43] as to whether his jurisdiction extends to claims in tort. These and other aspects of the jurisdiction of the Pensions Ombudsman will doubtless be clarified in due course.

II. SPECIAL FEATURES OF PENSION TRUSTS[44]

A pension trust has all the characteristics of a private trust, the employer being the settlor, the trustees being the trustees, and the members of the scheme and their dependants being the beneficiaries. There are further parallels with private trusts in that the remedies of a member are those of a beneficiary enforceable in equity against the trustees—there is no need for privity of contract—and in that the trustees have duties in relation to matters such as investment and discretionary powers which they can exercise. In particular, they normally have a power of amendment similar to the over-riding powers of appointment given to the trustees of private trusts. However, these similarities with private trusts are in many ways less important than the differences; there is almost invariably an underlying contract of employment whose existence affects the construction of the trust documents and almost every aspect of the parallels between employer as settlor and member as beneficiary needs qualification. These differences are revealed, above all, when any question arises as to the destination of surplus.

12–047

1. *The Position of the Employer*

Because of the absence of any obligation on employers to make any financial provision for their employees by way of pension, the decision to set up a pension scheme other than a stakeholder pension scheme is necessarily that of the employer. In the case of stakeholder pension schemes to which the employer is not contributing, as the overwhelming majority are likely to be, the employer will merely provide the scheme by giving instructions for

12–048

---

[41] *ibid.*

[42] This was in issue but was not finally decided in *Westminster City Council v. Hayward* [1998] Ch. 377. A jurisdiction to award compensation for distress was upheld in the High Court by Robert Walker J. (his decision was subsequently followed by Carnwath J. in *Wild v. Smith* [1996] O.P.L.R. 129 contrary to the latter's own earlier decision in *Miller v. Stapleton* [1996] 2 All E.R. 449). However, this specific issue was not considered by the Court of Appeal. Also in issue is the Pension Ombudsman's jurisdiction to award compensation for delay and for inconvenience.

[43] In *NHS Pensions Agency v. Beechier* [1997] P.L.R. 95.

[44] See Lord Walker, writing extra-judicially, in *Trends in Contemporary Trust Law* (ed. Oakley, 1996), p.123.

and financing the preparation of the necessary documentation.[45] In other cases, the employer will additionally need to initiate the necessary discussions with its employees and provide the (usually nominal) initial trust property. In all cases this clearly makes the employer the settlor. However, save in the case of stakeholder pension schemes to which the employer is not contributing, the employer will, unlike the settlor of a private trust, inevitably have a continuing obligation to make financial contributions to the scheme for so long as it continues to have employees who are members.

12–049   The employer may well also be the trustee of the scheme or appoint the members of its board of directors as the trustees or, in the not infrequent case where the trustee is a separate company, appoint its own directors as directors of the trustee company—small schemes almost invariably follow one of these practices, although it is now necessary for at least one-third of the trustees, or the directors of a trustee company, to be nominated by the members of the scheme.[46] In any event the scheme will unquestionably vest powers in the employer. Some of these powers will clearly be fiduciary in the full sense of the term—an example is powers of the type considered in *Mettoy Pension Trustees v. Evans*[47] to appoint any surplus in the pension fund, which in that case was vested in a separate trustee company. Even where such powers are not actually fiduciary, the employer will nevertheless be subject to what has become known as the *"Imperial"* obligation of good faith,[48] by virtue of which a power cannot be exercised in such a way that it seriously damages the relationship of good faith between the employer and its employees and ex-employees.

12–050   Further, save in the case of stakeholder pension schemes to which the employer is not contributing, the employer will almost certainly also be a beneficiary of the scheme in that it is virtually bound to have a claim to at least some part of any surplus which arises while the scheme is still ongoing or as a result of its being wound-up.

---

[45] Pension scheme documentation tends to be bulky. Because of the need for Inland Revenue approval, schemes tend to be created by an Interim Deed, which identifies the employer(s), the trustees, and the criteria for membership and also deals with contracting-out and priorities on the winding-up of the scheme. Following approval, this Interim Deed is replaced by a Definitive Deed, often containing little more than the appointment of the trustees and a power of amendment, to which extremely detailed Rules are appended; these set out the nature of the benefits provided, the rules as to contributions and transfers into and out of the scheme, and provisions relating to contracting-out, administrative powers, and the events which will trigger and the priorities on winding-up. The Deed and the Rules tend to be the subject of frequent amendment, usually in the form of an updated version of both incorporating all the amendments to date. An important role can also be played by the announcements and booklets issued to the members by the employer or the trustees; these have been known to give rise to an estoppel by convention even when they are not actually consistent with the Deed and Rules —see *Icarus (Hertford) v. Driscoll* [1990] P.L.R. 1; *ITN v. Ward* [1997] P.L.R. 131; *Steria v. Hutchinson* [2006] EWCA Civ. 1551 (Ch). Other scheme documentation includes the scheme accounts and the actuarial reports and three-yearly valuations.

[46] Pensions Act 1995, ss.16–21. As a result of Pensions Act 2004, ss.241, 243, since April 6, 2006 it has no longer been possible for the employer to persuade the members to accept alternative arrangements more favourable to himself.

[47] [1990] 1 W.L.R. 1587; see *ante*, para 6–071.

[48] Because it was laid down in *Imperial Group Pension Trust v. Imperial Tobacco* [1991] 1 W.L.R. 589.

2. *The Position of the Trustees*

(A) The Composition of the Trustees

As has already been seen, the employer may well also be the trustee of the schemes or appoint the members of its board of directors as the trustees or, in the not infrequent case where the trustee is a separate company, appoint its own directors as directors of the trustee company—small schemes almost invariably follow one of these practices. However, it is now necessary for at least one-third of the trustees, or the directors of a trustee company, to be nominated by the members of the scheme.[49] Under the Pensions Act 2004, all trustees must be "conversant" with key documents and also must have knowledge of certain prescribed areas of law.[50]

12–051

If the employer becomes insolvent, it is the responsibility of its liquidator to ensure that there is at least one "independent trustee", someone nominated neither by the employer nor by the members, and, if there is not, to appoint one[51]; this is in order to deal with conflicts of interest which can become particularly acute on insolvency.[52] The appointment of an independent trustee does not displace the other trustees but all the discretionary powers conferred on the trustees, and all fiduciary powers conferred on the employer, become exercisable only by the independent trustee.[53]

12–052

(B) Duties and Powers

The duties of the trustees are in principle the same as those of the trustees of any other private trust, namely to protect the trust funds and to administer them in accordance with the trusts on which they are held. In the pension trust context, the former duty is straightforward, merely obliging the trustees to ensure that the employer pays whatever contributions it is obliged to make and to inform the Pensions Regulator and the members in the event of any failure to comply with the relevant funding requirement. The latter duty is complicated by a number of special factors.

12–053

The most important of these is the endemic conflicts of interest arising out of the fact that a majority of the trustees are likely to be representatives of the employer and that at least one third of the remainder must be members (or at the very least representatives of the members) of the scheme. These conflicts of interest become particularly acute whenever it is necessary to deal with surplus, whether on the winding-up of the scheme or while it is on-going. Indeed, it has been held that no member trustee can take any benefit under any augmentation of benefits arising out of the exercise of a discretion vested in him or which he has helped to negotiate.[54] However, it

12–054

---

[49] Pensions Act 1995, ss.16–21. As a result of Pensions Act 2004, ss.241, 243, since April 6, 2006 it has no longer been possible for the employer to persuade the members to accept alternative arrangements more favourable to himself.

[50] Pensions Act 2004, ss.247–249.

[51] Pensions Act 1995, ss.22–26.

[52] See *Icarus (Hertford) v. Driscoll* [1990] P.L.R. 1 and *Mettoy Pensions Trustees v. Evans* [1990] 1 W.L.R. 1587, *ante*, para 6–071.

[53] An independent trustee can automatically lose his independence, in which case, unless he is the sole trustee, he equally automatically ceases to be a trustee even if he is unaware of the fact. See *Clark v. Hicks* [1992] P.L.R. 213.

[54] By Vinelott J. in *Re William Makin & Sons* [1993] O.P.L.R. 171 at 179 and in *British Coal Corporation v. British Coal Staff Superannuation Scheme Trustees* [1994] O.P.L.R. 51 at 62.

does not seem that this view can possibly survive the remarks of Scott V.-C. at first instance in *Edge v. Pensions Ombudsman*,[55] which were subsequently approved by the Court of Appeal,[56] where he held that it was "quite simply ridiculous" to contend that the member trustees had to be excluded from an augmentation of benefits made as the result of the exercise of their discretion as to how to deal with a surplus.

12–055   Other special factors include the fact that pension trusts are very long lasting—registered pension schemes (and some others) are specifically exempted from the rule against perpetuities[57]—and the fact that pensions trusts are often extremely flexible and confer on the trustees considerable powers of amendment and augmentation of benefits. In exercising these powers, which are often exercisable by the trustees only with the prior consent of the employer, it appears that the trustees are not under any obligation to be impartial as between the different classes of beneficiaries or to adopt a starkly confrontational role with the employer or to ignore the latter's interests; all this was specifically held by the Court of Appeal in *Edge v. Pensions Ombudsman*.[58] However, the way in which the powers are exercised must be consistent with the purposes for which they were conferred and must of course not infringe any express or implied restrictions in the trust deed or affect any accrued rights of any class of beneficiaries.[59] Further, their exercise must be in the interests of the beneficiaries when all relevant considerations, including any corresponding benefits validly demanded by the employer as a condition of its consent,[60] are taken into account.

12–056   Other standard powers of trustees are also considerably modified in the case of pension trustees. In particular, the Pensions Act 1995[61] modifies the normal investment powers of trustees.[62] The Act both confers on the trustees unrestricted powers of investment and entitles them to delegate those powers to fund managers. It requires them to have a formal statement of investment principles and puts on a statutory basis their duties to diversify, to take advice, to select suitable investments, and to consider whether to retain them. Employer-related investments are limited by statute to 5 per cent of the assets of the scheme and loans to the employer are totally prohibited.[63] Liability for any breach of the trustees' duty of care or skill in the performance of any investment function cannot be excluded. Finally, the trustees are now required themselves to appoint their advisers, such as auditors and solicitors, in writing.[64]

---

[55] [1998] Ch. 512 at 539.

[56] [2000] Ch. 602.

[57] Pension Schemes Act 1993, s.163.

[58] [2000] Ch. 602.

[59] If it does, Pensions Act 1995, s.67 will have to be complied with.

[60] Some threats by employers not to consent other than on certain terms are quite legitimate; others fall foul of the *"Imperial"* duty of good faith; see *ante*, n.48.

[61] Pensions Act 1995, ss.33–36.

[62] See *post*, para 14–055 *et seq.*

[63] Pensions Act 1995, s.40.

[64] Pensions Act 1995, s.47. Previously actuaries and solicitors were generally appointed by the employer prior to the scheme being set up. Trustees now at the very least have to confirm these appointments however.

(C) Recovery of Lost Funds

Where pension funds have been lost, the trustees also have a duty to seek to   **12–057**
recover them. This is sometimes necessary because of some fairly blatant
intentional breach of trust, such as over-investment in the employer or the
excessive augmentation of the benefits of its directors but this is now
relatively unlikely given the requirement for one-third of the trustees to be
nominated by the members. This is now more likely to be necessary when
a scheme is being wound-up because at this point the liabilities of the
scheme will for the first and only time be able to be assessed exactly. In any
of these circumstances, recovery can potentially be sought from three groups
of defendants: first, from past trustees; secondly, from those who have
already received benefits under or from the scheme; and, thirdly, from
professional advisers such as solicitors and actuaries. A case where recovery
was sought from members of all three of these groups as a result of substantial purchases by the pension fund of assets from the employer at what
were alleged to have been highly excessive prices and because of excessive
augmentation of benefits for its chairman was *H.R. v. J.A.P.T.*,[65] although
only some interlocutory proceedings were reported.

There are a number of difficulties about seeking recovery from past   **12–058**
trustees. First, in the absence of fraud they are, like any other trustee,[66] likely
to be protected by the trustee exemption clauses which are absolutely
standard in pension trusts deeds (although, as has just been seen, these
cannot cover any breach in their duty of care or skill in the performance of
any investment function). Secondly, save in the case of small pension
schemes, there is little likelihood that any individual trustee will be able to
make up a sufficient amount of any loss to be worth suing. And, thirdly,
where (as is more often than not the case) the trustee is a £100 company
without a single asset, its own directors will not owe direct fiduciary duties
to the members of the scheme[67] and so cannot be sued directly unless they
have actually acted dishonestly and so can be held liable for dishonest
assistance.[68] However, a possibility has now been found of suing them
indirectly where the conduct complained of is not dishonest but is nevertheless a breach of the fiduciary duty which as directors they owe to the
corporate trustee. In *H.R. v. J.A.P.T.*[69] it was contended, and Lindsay J.
accepted as arguable and so declined to strike out a claim, that in such
circumstances the members of the scheme were entitled to argue that such
rights of action as the corporate trustee had against its directors were
themselves part of the property of the pension trust, thus enabling the
members of the scheme to force the trustee company to sue the directors and
hold the fruits of that action on trust for them. However the possibility of
this type of claim has now been restricted to the situation where the corporate trustee's only role is the trusteeship of the trust in question.

---

[65] [1997] P.L.R. 99 (an appeal was compromised).
[66] See *Armitage v. Nurse* [1998] 1 Ch. 241; see *post*, para 22–079.
[67] *Bath v. Standard Land Co.* [1911] 1 Ch. 618.
[68] See *ante*, para 10–161 *et seq.*
[69] [1997] P.L.R. 99. But see now *Gregson v. H.A.E. Trustees* [2008] EWHC 1006 (Ch), *ante*
para 10–172, n.446.

12–059   Seeking recovery from a pensioner who has simply received an over-
payment of his pension is in principle relatively straightforward; the over-
payment can either simply be recouped out of future payments or be the
subject of an action for money paid under a mistake (it no longer matters
whether the mistake was one of fact or one of law). However, the payment
of a pension must amount to at least some form of representation that the
recipient is entitled to it and a series of overpayments may well therefore
give rise to an estoppel. Sums paid away to anyone else in breach of trust are
potentially recoverable by means of either an equitable proprietary claim[70]
or a claim for knowing receipt.[71] Neither type of claim is likely to be
particularly straightforward. Equitable proprietary claims depend on the
ability to identify the sums paid and, quite apart from the continuing
uncertainty as to precisely what knowledge will actually lead to the imposition of liability for knowing receipt, it is doubtful whether anyone other than
a former trustee or the employer or their associates could be held to have
any knowledge of any breach of trust at all. However, in *Hillsdown Holdings
v. Pensions Ombudsman*[72] liability for knowing receipt was imposed on an
employer in respect of the part of a surplus of £18 million[73] which it had
received as the result of an improper use of a power.

12–060   Finally, the difficulties of successfully maintaining proceedings for professional negligence against solicitors and actuaries are well known. Where
pension funds have been lost, the principal problem is usually that of
showing that the advice which the scheme's professional advisers either
gave or failed to give actually caused the breach of trust complained
of—paradoxically, the more blatant the breach of trust, the more difficult it
becomes to demonstrate a causal connection with whatever professional
advice was given.

12–061   Because of these difficulties, before bringing any such proceedings the
trustees will inevitably make an application seeking the approval of the
court in advance for their expenditure of the trust funds on the costs
involved; this is in order to avoid any risk of them having to pay the costs
themselves if they lose. Representative beneficiaries will be joined to any
such application, which is generally known as an application for a *Beddoe*
Order,[74] so that they can express their view as to whether the likelihood of
success in the proceedings justifies the expenditure of part of what is left of
the trust fund on an attempt to recover what has been lost. The decision
of the court in this respect is further complicated by the fact that the costs of
these beneficiaries, both in the application for the *Beddoe* Order and in the
main proceedings, generally also have to be paid out of the trust fund.

---

[70] See *post*, para 22–133 *et seq.*

[71] See *ante*, para 10–199 *et seq.*

[72] [1997] 1 All E.R. 862. An equitable proprietary claim was also held to lie against the
employer as a matter of principle but no findings of fact had been made below as to what assets
were still identifiable when it acquired notice of the members' adverse claim.

[73] The employer had only actually received 60% of the surplus because the remaining 40% of
the surplus was payable and had been paid in tax. However, the pension fund also recovered
the tax from the Inland Revenue (*Hillsdown Holdings v. I.R.C.* [1999] S.T.C. 566).

[74] After the decision in *Re Beddoe* [1893] 1 Ch. 547; see *post*, para 14–131. Such proceedings
were considered in *McDonald v. Horn* [1995] 1 All E.R. 961 and *Alsop Wilkinson v. Neary* [1996]
1 W.L.R. 1220 (which did not involve a pension trust).

3. *The Position of the Beneficiaries*

While a pension trust is on-going, its beneficiaries always include at least **12–062** three classes: those persons at present in pensionable employment with the employer ("members"); those persons who have been but are no longer in pensionable employment with the employer but are not yet in receipt of pensions from the scheme ("deferred members"); and those persons who have retired and are in receipt of pensions from the scheme ("pensioners"). However, once the winding-up of a pension scheme has commenced, its trusts will have no beneficiaries of any of these types[75]; the assets will instead be held for whoever is entitled to them under the provisions for winding-up; as will be seen later on,[76] in this respect the relevant rules of the deed of trust now only operate to the extent that they are not overridden by statute.

The interests of the members, the deferred members and the pensioners **12–063** are often quite different, particularly on a winding-up where there is a shortfall in assets since in such circumstances the pensioners will be paid in full before the members and deferred members receive anything.[77] Further, the employer is likely also to be a beneficiary in that, save in the case of stakeholder pension schemes to which the employer is not contributing, it is virtually bound to have a claim to at least some part of any surplus which arises while the scheme is still on-going or as a result of its being wound-up.

The essential difference[78] between the beneficiaries of a pension scheme **12–064** and the beneficiaries of a family trust is that the former will inevitably have provided consideration for their beneficial interests by virtue of the contributions paid to the scheme on their behalf. This is as much the case in a non-contributory scheme as a contributory scheme since either way the payment of the contributions will be a term of their contract of employment. Thus, in the unlikely event that the pension trust does not become completely constituted, its beneficiaries will have a contractual remedy against the employer.[79] This is also the reason for the existence of the *"Imperial"* obligation of good faith to which reference has already been made,[80] by virtue of which the employer cannot exercise a power in such a way that it seriously damages the relationship of good faith between the employer and its employees and ex-employees.

However, this does not mean that the beneficiaries of a pension trust have **12–065** any more rights than the beneficiaries of a family trust to be informed about the reasons for decisions made by the trustees as to the exercise of the

---

[75] *Bus Employees Pension Trustees v. Harrod* [2000] Ch. 258.

[76] See *post*, para 12–101.

[77] See *post*, para 12–101.

[78] See *Imperial Group Pension Trust v. Imperial Tobacco* [1991] 1 W.L.R. 589; *Thrells v. Lomas* [1993] 1 W.L.R. 456; *McDonald v. Horn* [1995] 1 All E.R. 961.

[79] See *ante*, para 5–084 *et seq.* Such a claim was made in *Davis v. Richards & Wallington Industries* [1990] 1 W.L.R. 1511 but the trust was in fact held to be a valid executory trust (see *ante*, para 5–081).

[80] Because it was laid down in *Imperial Group Pension Trust v. Imperial Tobacco* [1991] 1 W.L.R. 589.

discretions vested in them; this was specifically held in *Wilson v. Law Debenture Corporation*.[81] However, the beneficiaries (and prospective beneficiaries such as their spouses and dependants) do have a statutory right to see all the scheme documentation, including in particular accounts, actuarial reports and valuations, and documents relating to the minimum funding requirement.[82]

12–066   The remedies available to the beneficiaries of a pension trust against the trustees are also exactly the same as those available to the beneficiaries of a family trust. Where the only dispute is as to the proper construction of the trust deed, this will normally be resolved by the trustees taking out a construction summons, effectively "friendly" litigation in which all parties' costs will be paid out of the trust fund in any event.[83] "Hostile" litigation, on the other hand, is likely to be one of two kinds of dispute: either an individual dispute, where a particular beneficiary claims not to have been properly treated, or a collective dispute, where a complaint is made on behalf of the beneficiaries as a whole or of one of the classes of beneficiaries. In the event that an individual dispute of this type comes to court (as distinct from being dealt with by whatever internal dispute resolution procedure the pension scheme in question has[84] or as a result of the intervention of the Pensions Advisory Service[85] or, where appropriate, of the Pensions Ombudsman), costs will follow the event and do not come out of the assets of the pension trust.[86] Collective disputes pose rather greater problems of costs in the event that they come to court; this is because it is likely that the employer, the trustees, and the beneficiaries, either as a whole or in distinct classes where their interests are different, will need to be separately represented and expert evidence may well be necessary as well. In such circumstances, a representative beneficiary will be appointed to represent each class of beneficiaries which has a distinct interest; such representative beneficiaries will generally be able to obtain a what is now known as a prospective costs order,[87] whereby their own costs, and any costs which they may eventually be ordered to pay to any other party, will be paid out of the trust fund in any event.[88]

4. *The Power of Amendment*

12–067 The power of amendment is the equivalent in pension trusts of the overriding powers of appointment which are now invariably inserted in all private trusts whose provisions include some form of discretionary trust.[89]

---

[81] [1995] 2 All E.R. 337. These rights are discussed *post*, para 14–026.

[82] Pensions Act 1995, s.41.

[83] *Re Buckton* [1907] 2 Ch. 406.

[84] Some such procedure is now obligatory under Pensions Act 1995, s.50(1).

[85] Formerly known as the Occupational Pensions Advisory Service, this is an independent voluntary organisation giving free help and advice to members of the public; since 1991, it has been a company limited by guarantee and is funded entirely by grants.

[86] *McDonald v. Horn* [1995] 1 All E.R. 961 (followed in *Alsop Wilkinson v. Neary* [1996] 1 W.L.R. 1220, which did not involve a pension trust).

[87] See the Practice Direction in [2001] 1 W.L.R. 1082.

[88] Orders of this type were made in *McDonald v. Horn* [1995] 1 All E.R. 961.

[89] See *ante*, para 6–013.

Like overriding powers of appointment, a power of amendment is not necessarily vested in the trustees; it is frequently vested in the employer, although the trustees' consent to its exercise may nevertheless be necessary.[90] A power of amendment is even more essential than overriding powers of appointment because occupational pension schemes usually continue for many decades, during which their provisions are likely to need to be modified in the light of changes in circumstances which could not possibly have been foreseen at the outset.[91]

The exercise of an express power of amendment of this type is not the only   **12–068** way in which a pension scheme may be amended. An application can be made to the court for the rectification[92] or the variation[93] of a pension trust in exactly the same way as in the case of a private trust. It is also possible for a pension trust to become amended as a result of a contract entered into between the employer and some of its employees, under which those employees agree, for example, to accept lower pension benefits than those to which they are entitled under the provisions of their pension trust.[94] Conversely, the employer or the trustees may estop themselves from denying that the employees are entitled to higher pension benefits than those to which they are entitled under the provisions of their pension trust as a result of the making of announcements and the issuing of booklets to the members in which those higher benefits are set out.[95] The Pensions Regulator has power[96] to order the amendment of a pension trust in three specified circumstances.[97]

Finally, the trustees of a pension trust have a statutory power of amend-   **12–069** ment for a number of specific purposes,[98] principally[99] in order to bring the provisions of the trust into line with new statutory requirements, adoption of which is necessary in order to preserve the trust's status as an exempt approved scheme (recent examples are the requirement for equal treatment of men and women,[100] the requirement for the appointment of member

---

[90] Either as a result of express provision or because this is required by Pensions Act 1995, s.67 (see *infra*).

[91] If no power of amendment is included in the interim deed, it may still be possible to include one in the definitive deed (*Re Imperial Foods Ltd. Pension Scheme* [1986] 2 All E.R. 802); in default, the only possibility is to apply to the court for rectification (see the next footnote).

[92] See *ante*, para 6–079 and *Re Butlin's Settlement Trusts* [1976] Ch. 251. Cases involving pension trusts will generally concern applications to rectify a deed exercising the power of amendment rather than the original trust deed; see *AMP (UK) v. Barker* [2001] W.T.L.R. 1237, [2001] P.L.R. 79, *ante* para 6–079.

[93] See *post*, para 21–018.

[94] *South West Trains v. Wightman* [1998] P.L.R. 113. In such circumstances, the employer is able to restrain the employees from claiming from the trustees the additional pension provision to which they are entitled under the trust deed.

[95] *Icarus (Hertford) v. Driscoll* [1990] P.L.R. 1; *ITN v. Ward* [1997] P.L.R. 131.

[96] Under Pensions Act 1995, ss.69–71.

[97] In connection with a necessary reduction of surplus (see *post*, para 12–075), a distribution of assets to the employer when a scheme is being wound-up (see *post*, para 12–101), and the contracting-out of a relevant employment between April 6, 1997 and April 5, 1999.

[98] Pensions Act 1995, s.68 as amended by Pensions Act 2004.

[99] A purpose quite distinct from that mentioned in the text is to extend, with the consent of the employer, the class of persons who may receive death in service benefits.

[100] See *ante*, para 12–042.

nominated trustees,[101] and the requirement to permit pension sharing on divorce[102]).

12–070   Where an express power of amendment is utilised, that power, like a power of appointment, has to be exercised in the manner envisaged by its terms[103]; in particular, when the consent of the employer is necessary, it must be obtained in the prescribed way. The employer must always act in accordance with the *"Imperial"* duty of good faith which has already been considered.[104] The trustees must exercise their own discretion rather than simply following the suggestions of the employer[105]; they cannot validly make an amendment which reduces rights to present or future pensions which have already accrued and cannot generally make one which reduces the future accrual of benefits. Further, both employer and trustees must use the power of amendment for the purpose for which it was conferred; in the absence of contrary indication, this is to promote the purposes of the scheme, whether those purposes are expressly stated in the trust deed or not. However, it is accepted that these purposes are not immutable and may change over time as the pension scheme itself evolves.[106]

12–071   Amendments were successfully challenged on the ground that they did not promote the purposes of the scheme in *Re Courage Group's Pension Schemes*.[107] The employer was part of a group which had been taken over by a purchaser who intended in due course to sell off the different parts of the group but wanted in the meantime to extract a part of the substantial surplus in the three relevant pension schemes. The amendments made for this purpose, which involved making the purchaser the employer under the schemes, were held to conflict with the purpose for which the schemes had been established, the provision of retirement benefits. This conclusion was undoubtedly assisted by a finding that the purchaser was not recognisably the successor either to the employer's business or to its workforce.[108]

12–072   Amendments must also comply with the provisions of section 67 of the Pensions Act 1995.[109] Both the original section, which applied to amendments prior to April 6, 2006, and the substituted section,[110] which applies to amendments on or after that date, prevent a power "to modify the scheme"[111] being exercised in a manner which would or might affect any entitlement, or accrued right, of any member of the scheme acquired before the power is exercised except on certain elaborately drafted conditions;

---

[101] See *ante*, para 12–051.

[102] See *post*, para 12–094.

[103] This was specifically held in *Sovereign Trustees v. Glover* [2007] EWHC 1750 (Ch); see also *ante*, para 6–074.

[104] See *ante*, para 12–049. This is also the case when, rarely, the employer can require the trustees to exercise the power.

[105] Save, rarely, when the employer can require them to exercise the power; his ability to do so is now further restricted by Pensions Act 1995, s.67, discussed *infra* in the text.

[106] *Re Courage Group's Pension Schemes* [1987] 1 W.L.R. 495.

[107] [1987] 1 W.L.R. 495.

[108] See also *Harwood-Smart v. Caws* [2000] P.L.R. 101; *BEST v. Stuart* [2001] P.L.R. 283,

[109] Pensions Act 1995, s.67; see Schaffer [1999] British Pensions Lawyer 3.

[110] Substituted by Pensions Act 2004, s.262.

[111] This expression may not actually be limited to formal amendments of the trust deed, although this is not relevant for present purposes.

broadly speaking, the trustees must have satisfied themselves, before deciding to amend, either that every affected member has given his fully informed consent in writing or that the actuary has certified that the amendment will not affect the entitlements or acquired rights of those members. The substituted section also applies to modifications which would or might result in the reduction of any pension in payment and/or convert defined benefit rights into defined contribution rights; in this case, the trustees can only validly decide to amend if they have satisfied themselves of the fully informed written consent of each affected member. For both purposes, a member includes anyone entitled or prospectively entitled to a payment under the scheme in question.

An amendment can also be successfully challenged if its terms fail to comply with any restrictions written into the power of amendment by the trust deed; these tend to be substantial. Whether or not the terms fail to comply is entirely a matter of construction of the provisions of the power of amendment in question.[112] The following principles apply irrelevant of the construction adopted.   **12–073**

(1) It has been held[113] that, unless a power of amendment is specifically included in the provisions of the trust deed governing winding-up, that power cannot be exercised after the winding-up has commenced, although this is apparently possible during the period of any notice given by the employer to the trustees to wind-up the scheme.[114]

(2) A provision permitting retrospective amendments is valid but, in the absence of any such provision, an amendment would be unlikely to be permitted to have retrospective effect[115] unless that effect was entirely uncontroversial, such as to enable retrospective compliance with some new statutory requirement.

(3) A provision permitting the amendment of the power of amendment itself is valid, although an increase in the restrictions on that power could never be justified[116] and the removal of existing restrictions on it will not be easy to justify either unless they are purely formal. In the absence of any such provision, such an amendment will not be possible.

(4) Where the power of amendment requires the consent of the members to any or to specific types of amendments, this can be treated as having been given one month after the second of two notifications at least two months apart sent to a member's last known

---

[112] For the extent to which the courts do or should adopt particular principles of construction and, in particular the question of whether they should be pro-employer or pro-beneficiary, see Nobles, *Pensions, Employment and the Law* (1993) Chap. 2; McAllister 11 Superannuation (2000) 73.

[113] *Thrells Ltd. (1974) Pension Scheme v. Lomas* [1992] P.L.R. 149, confirming the earlier unreported decision in *Re ABC Television* (1973), in Ellison, *op.cit.*, sources p.28.

[114] *Municipal Mutual v. Harrop* [1998] P.L.R. 149.

[115] An amendment retrospectively taking away vested rights was disallowed in *Municipal Mutual v. Harrop* [1998] P.L.R. 149.

[116] Because the trustees would thereby be fettering their own discretion.

address.[117] This rule does not apply to the types of amendments which must comply with either form of section 67 of the Pensions Act 1995 where, depending on the nature of the amendment, either the only substitute for the written consent of the members is the actuary's certification or there is no substitute for the written consent of the members at all.

12–074   The types of difficulties of construction with which the courts have to grapple are well illustrated by the facts of *National Grid Co. v. Mayes*,[118] the only case concerning powers of amendment which has so far reached the House of Lords. Since the case also concerns the treatment of surplus, it is best considered in the discussion of that topic which immediately follows.

5. *The Treatment of Surplus*[119]

12–075   Until April 6, 2006, the question of what had to be done about a surplus in a pension scheme could arise in three situations. However, one of these, whenever an obligatory three-yearly actuarial valuation showed that an exempt approved scheme had a surplus of assets over liabilities which exceeded the then statutory limit of 105 per cent under the relevant pre-scribed actuarial assumptions,[120] can no longer arise.[121] One of the remaining two situations is where an actuarial valuation shows a surplus which is substantially in excess of what is needed fully to fund the scheme, in which case the trustees or the employer will generally have a power under the trust deed to dispose of some or all of this surplus (in the unlikely event that there is neither any such power nor any possibility of adding one by means of the power of amendment, nothing will be able to be done at all). The other situation is where a surplus arises as a result of the winding-up of a pension scheme.

12–076   In the first of these two situations, there are potentially four different ways of proceeding: first, paying the whole or part of the surplus to the employer; secondly, permitting the employer and/or the employee to stop or to reduce their contributions to the scheme until the surplus has been used up (this is known as a "contributions holiday"); thirdly, enhancing the existing benefits provided by the scheme or creating new ones (this can of course potentially benefit both past and present employees); and, fourthly, leaving the surplus

---

[117] Pensions Act 1995, s.67(6).

[118] [2001] 1 W.L.R. 864.

[119] See Pollard 17 T.L.I. (2003) 2.

[120] This situation was always improbable because the actuarial assumptions in question were generally regarded as rather "conservative" and it was, therefore, possible for there to be a very substantial surplus in the fund when it was valued in accordance with the actuary's normal assumptions and criteria without there being any statutory surplus at all; for a scheme to have an excessive statutory surplus, it would have to have had a valuation of around 200% of the minimum funding requirement. However, if this situation arose, then by virtue of Income and Corporation Taxes Act 1988, Sch.22 immediate steps had to be taken to eradicate the resulting excessive statutory surplus or the fiscal authority's approval of the scheme would be withdrawn with extremely adverse retrospective fiscal consequences. In these circumstances, one of the first three ways listed below in the text had to be used since there was obviously no possibility of leaving the surplus in the scheme to constitute a reserve.

[121] Because the relevant provisions were repealed by Finance Act 2004.

in the scheme to constitute a reserve, although this will only be possible if the trustees are not under a mandatory obligation to proceed in one of the other three ways. In the second of these two situations, which will be dealt with separately at the end of this chapter,[122] the only two of the possibilities mentioned so far which are feasible are the second and third ones set out above.

Concentrating, therefore, on the situation where an actuarial valuation shows a surplus which is substantially in excess of what is needed fully to fund the scheme, it is immediately apparent that in such circumstances the interests of the employer and of the past and present employees will almost inevitably be diametrically opposed, as will the interests of the past employees and the present employees *inter se* if both are not treated equally (something which is not only unlikely but will of course also be an indirect consequence of any reduction of employee contributions). Further, if leaving the surplus in the scheme to constitute a reserve is a possibility, the trustees will have an obvious interest in this rather than anything else being done, thus adding a further element to the potential conflicts of interest.   **12–077**

During the 1980s the surpluses produced in pension schemes were often so substantial that they became an important element in takeovers, leading to subsequent disputes as to what was to happen to the surpluses between the employees and whoever took over the employer. In present financial conditions, a purchaser of a business is more likely to be concerned about inheriting a deficit in its pension scheme than about having the opportunity of extracting a surplus. However, even today, enough pension schemes are still in surplus for disputes of this kind between employers, employees and, where appropriate, trustees to remain a possibility. In theory such a dispute can arise both in defined benefit schemes and defined contribution scheme.[123] In practice, however, surpluses in the latter have always been less likely than in the former because of the lower level of employer contributions and, even if such a surplus had to be eradicated while a scheme was still on-going, there would be little or no potential for the sort of conflicts of interest referred to above. All the pensioners would already have their annuities and so would effectively be out of the picture and the fact that the employer and the employees tend to contribute equal amounts to money purchase schemes would remove any conceivable justification for any payment being made to the employer. Consequently, in practice, the trustees would have no option but to give both employer and employees a contributions holiday until the desired amount of surplus had been used up.   **12–078**

On the other hand, when there is an available surplus in a defined benefit scheme, both the employer and its past and present employees are likely to take the view that the surplus belongs to them; the employer will do so on the basis that the pension fund is a security provided for the protection of those employees and that it is, therefore, entitled to any surplus over and above the security which is necessary, while the employees will do so on the basis that the fund constitutes part of their emoluments. Neither of these views constitutes the whole truth but each has a point in relation to a defined benefit scheme: on the one hand, the open-ended commitment   **12–079**

---

[122] *Post*, para 12–101.
[123] See Pollard 17 T.L.I. (2003) 2.

under which the employer has to make up any deficit while the scheme is on-going must give it at least some rights to any surplus in such a scheme; on the other hand, the beneficiaries are entitled not only to their fixed rights under the scheme but also to unquantifiable expectations of enhanced benefits. Further, as indicated above, in the absence of any mandatory obligation to do anything else, the trustees may well adopt the view that nothing should be done at all on the basis that the surplus is a necessary reserve against the results of over-optimism by the scheme's actuary or under-performance by the scheme's investments. In reality, as Vinelott J. said in *Taylor v. Lucas Pensions Trust*,[124] the surplus of an occupational pension trust "does not in any intelligible sense belong to anyone".

12–080   The disputes which have been litigated have usually been between the employees and employers who have just taken over the business. The latter of course want the whole of the available surplus paid to them but the past and present employees understandably want at least part of it to be utilised for their own benefit. The employees' challenge to such an employer succeeded in *Re Courage Pension Schemes*[125] for the reasons discussed in the previous part of this section.[126] However, Millett J. drew a clear distinction between the two possible methods of enabling the employer to benefit from a surplus. He rejected a contention that the employees were entitled as of right to a contributions holiday when the available surplus permitted this, taking the view that any surplus in a defined benefit scheme arose primarily from the employer and so it was the latter who should be primarily entitled to any contributions holiday. On the other hand, he stated that, where the employer was instead seeking a payment out of the scheme, it could be anticipated that the employer would be influenced by the desire to maintain good industrial relations with its workforce while the trustees could and should press for enhanced benefits for both present and past employees.

12–081   Section 37 of the Pensions Act 1995 subsequently provided that any power to return assets to the employer had to be exercised by the trustees, even if the trust deed confers it on someone else, and could be exercised only if there had been maximum limited price indexation of all pensions payable under the scheme and if the trustees were satisfied that this is in the interests of the beneficiaries. The requirement for maximum limited price indexation has been removed from the version which was substituted with effect from April 6, 2006[127] but the trustees must now obtain a written valuation from the actuary. The circumstances and form in which the trustees are obliged to serve a notice on all the members have also been modified but it remains the case that no payment can still be made until at least three months after the notice. Any member, or anyone else, can make representations to the Pensions Regulator and, if the latter considers that there is sufficient doubt as to whether all these requirements have been met, the trustees will be notified that no payment should be made until the Pensions Regulator is satisfied that this is indeed the case. The trustees must notify the Pensions Regulator

---

[124] [1994] O.P.L.R. 29.
[125] [1987] 1 W.L.R. 498.
[126] An amendment which was necessary in order to make the purchaser of the group the new employer under the schemes was held to be impermissible.
[127] By Pensions Act 2004, s.250.

within one week of making any payment anyway and the Pensions Regulator has power to order the return of the payment in appropriate circumstances.

This statutory intervention has, however, done little to resolve the outcome of disputes as to the destination of surplus, which still primarily depend on the terms of the pension trust in question. As Knox J. said in *L.R.T. Pension Fund Trustee Co. v. Hatt*,[128] quoting the words of Cooke P. in a New Zealand decision,[129] "Considerations of the merits are of little importance. What must be decisive are the terms of the trusts constituted by the particular scheme." This is what has also emerged from *National Grid Co. v. Mayes*[130]; although this case went to the House of Lords, the best summary of the current law in this respect was made by the Court of Appeal[131]: "The solution lies within the terms of the scheme itself, and not within a world populated by competing philosophies as to the true nature and ownership of actuarial surplus."

12–082

Consequently, in any individual case, what is necessary is to establish which of the possible methods of dealing with a surplus is permitted by the deed of trust and, in so far as the desired method is not, whether the necessary permission can be inserted be the use of the power of amendment. Everything therefore depends on the terms of the scheme, properly construed, and on any statutory provisions which override them. In the latter respect, in addition to the provisions of the Pensions Act 1995 which have already been mentioned, the Pensions Regulator has a statutory power to override the prohibitions on the return of any surplus to the employer which are found in many older schemes because the Inland Revenue at one time required such prohibitions as a condition of approval.[132]

12–083

The principal issues of construction are usually whether or not the method which has been or is to be used to deal with the surplus is permitted by the provisions of the trust deed governing the treatment of surplus and/ or whether or not that method is prohibited by any other provision of the trust deed. Given the nature of issues of this type,[133] it is appropriate only to state the following general propositions:

12–084

(1) Giving the employer a contributions holiday does not amount to a payment of surplus to the employer and so neither breaches a provision of the trust prohibiting the payment of surplus to the employer nor, more significantly, triggers the provisions of the Pensions Act 1995.[134]

---

[128] [1993] P.L.R. 227.

[129] *U.E.B. Industries v. Brabant* [1991] P.L.R. 109 (Court of Appeal of New Zealand).

[130] [2001] 1 W.L.R. 864.

[131] [1999] P.L.R. 37.

[132] Now in Pensions Act 1995, s.69 (first introduced in 1973).

[133] For the extent to which the courts do or should adopt particular principles of construction and, in particular the question of whether they should be pro-employer or pro-beneficiary, see Pollard 17 T.L.I. (2003) 2.

[134] Pension Act 1995, s.37; a new version of this provision was substituted by Pensions Act 2004, s.250.

(2) Where the trust deed permits the payment of surplus to the employer, that is not outside the purposes of the pension scheme.[135] However, where the treatment of surplus requires the consent of the employer, it is appropriate for the trustees not simply to do what the employer wants but to bargain with the employer on behalf of the past and present employees for benefit improvements.[136]

(3) Leaving a surplus in a pension scheme is a permitted use of that surplus unless the trust deed specifically mandates or requires surplus to be used for something else, such as the enhancement of benefits.

12–085   The types of difficulties of construction with which the courts have to grapple are well illustrated by the facts of *National Grid Co. v. Mayes*,[137] the only case concerning either powers of amendment or the treatment of surplus which has so far reached the House of Lords. The two employers each had both a power to deal with surplus, which simply stated that the employers "shall make arrangements, certified by the actuary as reasonable, to deal with the surplus", and a power of amendment, which prohibited amendments "making any moneys . . . payable to" the employers. Both employers used about one-third of the surpluses to enhance benefits[138] and the remainder to extinguish debts which they owed to their respective pension schemes in respect of the sums necessary in order to fund additional pension payments to employees who had been made redundant or had retired early. The questions which arose were, first, whether this cancellation of debts was permitted by the power to deal with the surplus and, secondly, whether it amounted to the making of payments to the employers.

12–086   The Pensions Ombudsman held, first, that cancellation of debts did amount to payments to the employers and, secondly, that the wording of the power of amendment led to the conclusion that the power to deal with the surplus did not permit payments to the employers; the debts could not therefore be cancelled. Robert Walker J.[139] disagreed with the second conclusion and held that the debts could be cancelled because the power to deal with the surplus was wholly unrestricted and was not in any way affected by the other provisions of the trust deed such as the power of amendment; he therefore did not have to consider the first conclusion. The Court of Appeal[140] agreed with the Pensions Ombudsman, and not with Robert Walker J., as to the second conclusion and so held that the debts could not be cancelled. But they disagreed with the first conclusion of the Pensions Ombudsman and stated that the cancellation of debts did not amount to

---

[135] *National Grid Co. v. Mayes* [2001] 1 W.L.R. 864.

[136] *Re Courage Group's Pension Schemes* [1987] 1 W.L.R. 495.

[137] [2001] 1 W.L.R. 864.

[138] In both cases by increasing death in service benefits and spouses' pensions and, in one case, by also reducing employee contributions by 50% for three years and increasing by 10% the lump sum benefits of deferred members. Since employer contributions were twice employee contributions, this reflected the proportion of the surplus produced by the employees' contributions.

[139] [1997] P.L.R. 157.

[140] [2002] I.C.R. 174.

payments to the employers. Consequently, the power of amendment could be used to amend the power to deal with the surplus retrospectively[141] and the employers duly used their respective powers to do so before the hearing of their appeal to the House of Lords.

The House of Lords held that, taking into account the fiscal origin of prohibitions of the type found in the power of amendment, the cancellation of debts did not amount to payments to the employers; an amendment to permit such a process would therefore not be prohibited by the power of amendment. This meant that the debts could be cancelled whether or not this was permitted by the power to deal with the surplus since, if it was not, that power could be amended anyway.[142] But the House went on to consider whether or not this was in fact permitted by that power and concluded that it was; no amendment was therefore actually necessary and it was up to the employers as to whether or not they chose to embody the arrangements which they had made into a formal amendment.

12–087

When a power of this kind is being exercised by the employer, it can have regard to its own financial and other interests but only to the extent that it can do so without breaching the *"Imperial"* obligation of good faith to its employees[143] which has already been considered.[144] When, on the other hand, the power is being exercised by the trustees, as will now always be the case if any payment is to be made to the employer,[145] they are under no obligation to act impartially as between the different categories of members, deferred members and pensioners. In *Edge v. Pensions Ombudsman*,[146] the trustees decided to use surplus to credit additional service to those members in employment on a particular date and to reduce the contributions of both employers and employees from a date six months earlier; no additional service was credited either to the pensioners or to the deferred members or to a number of employees who were to be made redundant during the six month period. The trustees explained to one of the latter that their decision had been taken in order to encourage all employees to become and remain members of the pension scheme and to support the employers in providing continued employment for their current employees. The Pensions Ombudsman set aside the trustees' decision on the grounds that the trustees had breached their duty of impartiality and had not acted in the best interests of all the beneficiaries. His decision was reversed by the Court of Appeal, who held that the duty to act impartially was no more than the ordinary duty imposed on any holder of a discretionary power, namely to exercise the power for the purposes for which it is given, giving proper consideration to the matters which are relevant and excluding from consideration matters

12–088

---

[141] This was permitted by the wording of the power of amendment.

[142] The House of Lords also rejected an argument by the employees that, if an amendment was needed, it would under Pensions Act 1995, s.37 (*supra*) have to make the power exercisable by the trustees and not by the employers because cancellation of debts would amount to payment to the employees for the purposes of that provision. The House held that the provision only applies to funds which have actually been paid into a pension trust, not sums owing to that trust.

[143] The obligation laid down in *Imperial Group Pension Trust v. Imperial Tobacco* [1991] 1 W.L.R. 589.

[144] See *ante*, para 12–049.

[145] By virtue of Pension Act 1995, s.37, *supra*.

[146] [2000] Ch. 602.

which are irrelevant. Provided the trustees complied with that duty, they were entitled to reach a decision which appeared to prefer the claims of some beneficiaries over others.

III. INTERESTS UNDER PENSION TRUSTS AND THIRD PARTIES

12–089   Because the purpose of a pension scheme is to provide an income on retirement, the Pensions Act 1995 provided that accrued rights thereunder cannot, generally speaking, be dealt with by the beneficiary by way of assignment, surrender or charge[147]; this does not of course affect assignments or surrenders in favour of the beneficiary's surviving spouse and dependants after his death. However, in two situations, on bankruptcy and on divorce, third parties may wish to assert a claim to the interest of a beneficiary under a pension trust.[148]

1. *The Position on Bankruptcy*

12–090   It is not the policy of the insolvency legislation to deprive a bankrupt beneficiary of a pension scheme of the provision which he has made for his retirement and consequently the basic rule has generally been that his accrued rights are not available to his creditors.[149] Whether that necessarily meant that he would nevertheless be entitled to his present or future benefits under any occupational pension scheme of which he was a member used to depend on the rules of the scheme in question; many schemes contain provisions forfeiting a beneficiary's rights in the event of his bankruptcy to which the courts used to give effect,[150] a possibility which the Pensions Act 1995[151] expressly confirmed. Further, the basic rule did not anyway apply to benefits to which the bankrupt beneficiary of a personal pension scheme or a retirement annuity policy was entitled and these benefits vested directly in his trustee in bankruptcy.[152]

12–091   However, the Welfare Reform and Pensions Act 1999 now expressly provides[153] that any rights which a bankrupt may have under any exempt approved pension scheme, whether occupational, personal or stakeholder, are excluded from the bankrupt's estate when a bankruptcy order is made on or after May 29, 2000. Any provision in a pension trust deed providing for forfeiture in the event of bankruptcy will therefore be ineffective in respect of bankruptcies on or after that date. Only the benefits to which a

---

[147] Pensions Act 1995, s.91(1).
[148] See Miller [2001] P.C.B. 46.
[149] Pensions Act 1995, s.91(3).
[150] Thus in *Re Scientific Investment Pension Plan Trust* [1999] Ch. 53 Rattee J. upheld a rule which provided that, in the event of any assignment or anything happening which would vest the beneficiary's property in someone else, his benefits would be forfeited but the trustees should have power in the event of hardship to apply them for the benefit of his dependants. Although this case concerned a bankruptcy in 1992, the result would still have been the same under Pensions Act 1995, s.92.
[151] Pensions Act 1995, s.92.
[152] *Re Landau* [1997] 3 All E.R. 322.
[153] Welfare Reform and Pensions Act 1999, s.11.

bankrupt is entitled under an unauthorised pension scheme will now vest in his trustee in bankruptcy and even in that respect the Secretary of State has been given power to make regulations to govern certain situations.[154]

The Welfare Reform and Pensions Act 1999 has not affected other provi-   **12–092** sions of the Pensions Act 1995, which permit pension schemes to contain provisions for outright forfeitures of benefits in a number of other situations: first, where prior to the pension becoming payable, a beneficiary is convicted of treason or of offences under the Official Secrets Acts; and secondly, where a beneficiary has failed to claim a pension within the appropriate limitation period or within six years.[155] Pensions schemes may also contain provisions permitting a lien or a charge to be made against an individual's benefits in respect of any monetary obligations incurred by him to the employer or to the scheme arising out of any criminal, negligent or fraudulent act or omission, or, in the case of the scheme only, any breach of trust.[156] Provisions of this type will clearly continue to be upheld.

Nevertheless, despite these general rules, it would be wholly inappropri-   **12–093** ate if a beneficiary who anticipated that he was in some danger of becoming bankrupt was allowed to deprive his creditors of assets by making additional voluntary contributions to an existing occupational pension scheme. The Pensions Act 1995[157] has, therefore, inserted into the Insolvency Act 1986 provisions relating to the setting aside of such contributions made within the five years immediately prior to the bankruptcy similar to the provisions relating to the setting aside of settlements made during the same period which have already been considered[158]; the criterion is whether the contributions were excessive and unfairly prejudicial to the creditors, a question to which the intentions of the beneficiary in making them will clearly be particularly relevant.

2. *The Position on Divorce*

The two most valuable assets of most married couples are likely to be their   **12–094** matrimonial home and their pension rights. The courts have long had[159] an absolute discretion to vary matrimonial property rights at the termination of marriage and among the matters to which they must have regard are the value to either party of any pension which he or she will lose the chance of acquiring as a result of the divorce. The discretion of the courts includes the ability to make what are known as deferred lump sum orders and such orders have been made requiring one spouse to pay to the other one half of whatever lump sum he becomes entitled to receive from a pension trust on

---

[154] *ibid.*, s.12(2). The situations envisaged are where the bankrupt either makes an agreement with his trustee in bankruptcy or applies to the court.

[155] Pensions Act 1995, ss.92, 93.

[156] Pensions Act 1995, s.91; Pensions Act 2004, s.266 has inserted a new provision entitling payments to be suspended in order to recoup for this purpose overpayments of benefits already made.

[157] Pensions Act 1995, s.95.

[158] See *ante*, para 7–056.

[159] Under what is now section 25 of the Matrimonial Causes Act 1973.

his retirement.[160] However, the courts generally considered pension entitlements as being too far in the future or too speculative to be the subject of specific orders and, in so far as they took pension rights into account at all, they generally limited themselves to offsetting likely pension rights against the other property of the former spouses.

12–095   The courts nevertheless could, and still can, order the payment of pensions as well as lump sums, in the relatively rare situation where the pension trust in question can be held to constitute a marriage settlement. This is only likely where a private pension scheme has been set up for both spouses by one of them or by a company of which the latter is the alter ego. This was indeed what had happened in *Brooks v. Brooks*,[161] where such a settlement was found to have been created by virtue of the fact that the husband had power under a pension scheme set up for him by his company to elect to provide a pension for a spouse out of the fund; the House of Lords therefore varied the pension trust to provide his wife with both an immediate pension and a deferred pension payable from the husband's death. But Lord Nicholls emphasised in his speech that this procedure would not work where persons other than the spouses were beneficiaries of the pension trust in question and specifically stated that legislation would be necessary to enable the courts "to split pension rights on divorce in the more usual case of a multi-member scheme where the wife has no earnings of her own from the same employer".[162]

12–096   This was the only basis on which the courts could order the payment of pensions, as distinct from lump sums, until the Pensions Act 1995[163] inserted new provisions into the Matrimonial Causes Act 1973[164] to enable the court, when making a financial provision order, to divert all or part of the benefits (whether lump sum or periodical payments) payable to one of the former spouses under an occupational or a private pension scheme to the other former spouse as and when they become payable under the scheme. This process was originally known as earmarking; since the coming into force of the Welfare Reform and Pensions Act 1999, it has instead been known as attachment, by which name it will be referred to here.

12–097   The legislation does not appear to be proving easy to apply.[165] The matter is complicated by the court's statutory obligation to consider whether it would be appropriate to make what is known as a clean break and its power to bring one about; attaching of future, as distinct from present, pension rights is clearly inconsistent with a clean break. Further, even in non-clean break cases, orders attaching future pension payments have been refused on the basis[166] that the courts would be in just as effective a position jurisdictionally to deal with the matter at the time of retirement and would then be far better informed. This suggests that attaching pension payments is only

[160] See the authorities referred to in *SRJ v. DWJ (Financial Provision)* [1999] 2 F.L.R. 176, although no such order was made in that case.
[161] [1996] A.C. 375.
[162] [1996] A.C. 375 at 396.
[163] Pensions Act 1995, s.166.
[164] Matrimonial Causes Act 1975, ss.25B, 25C and 25D.
[165] See the judgments in two of the few reported decisions on attachment: *T v. T (Financial Relief: Pensions)* [1998] 1 F.L.R. 1072; *Burrow v. Burrow* [1999] 1 F.L.R. 508.
[166] By Singer J. in *T v. T (Financial Relief: Pensions)* [1998] 1 F.L.R. 1072.

likely even in non-clean break cases when a divorce occurs very close to retirement age. On the other hand, it is obviously possible to attach any lump sum payable on retirement,[167] since this could be done, although not formally by way of attachment, even before the Pensions Act 1995. If this is done, it will generally be necessary also to attach the quite different death in service benefits which will be paid if the beneficiary dies before reaching retirement age,[168] usually a lump sum which the trustees have discretion as to how to distribute with, sometimes, a power of nomination given to the deceased beneficiary.

The Family Law Act 1996 subsequently enacted provisions envisaging a rather different process, the splitting of pensions, on divorce but these provisions have never been brought into force. Instead the Finance Act 1999 and the Welfare Reform and Pensions Act 1999 inserted further provisions into the Matrimonial Causes Act 1973, introducing what is effectively the same thing but which is instead known as pension sharing on divorce; these provisions affected divorce proceedings commenced after December 1, 2000. All existing approved pension were then obliged, as a condition of continued approval, to amend their rules so as to enable pension sharing to be introduced; this has applied to all schemes seeking approval or continued approval since May 10, 2000 or, since the enactment of the Pensions Act 2004, registration.　　　　　　　　　　　　　　　　　　　　　　　　**12–098**

Under the new provisions inserted into the Matrimonial Causes Act 1973,[169] a pension sharing order can provide that a specific percentage of one party's pension rights, including SERPS or S2P rights but not the basic State pension, is subject to pension sharing. The former spouse acquiring the rights has a choice between becoming a member of the other spouse's pension scheme (although this is necessarily the only option in the case of unfunded schemes) and taking a transfer out into a personal pension scheme or stakeholder scheme of his or her own choice. Statutory instruments have laid down how benefits under pension schemes are to be valued and provide for a uniform measure of valuation for all types of pensions, which is known as the Cash Equivalent Transfer Value ("the CETV"). The pension provider or the State is obliged to provide information to enable this to be done. It is the appropriate percentage of the CETV which is awarded. Death benefits, discretionary benefits, future expectations and non-United Kingdom pensions are excluded from the CETV, which values the pension on the assumption that the service of the member of any relevant schemes terminates at the valuation date, thus also excluding future service. However, that does not prevent the court from taking into account likely future service when assessing what percentage of the CETV to award.　　**12–099**

Attachment continues alongside pension sharing and is brought into line with it by having to be expressed as a percentage of the CETV but it is not possible to make an attachment and a pension sharing order in respect of the same pension scheme. It is not considered likely that this will increase the　　**12–100**

---

[167] This was done in *Burrow v. Burrow* [1999] 1 F.L.R. 508.

[168] The court was prepared to do this in both *T v. T (Financial Relief: Pensions)* [1998] 1 F.L.R. 1072 and *Burrow v. Burrow* [1999] 1 F.L.R. 508 but in the event did not regard this as actually necessary.

[169] Matrimonial Causes Act 1975, s.24B.

overall number of attachment orders made; pension sharing is clearly likely to predominate. The courts will obviously also at least consider continuing to offset pension benefits against the other assets of the former spouses rather than making pension sharing orders. It must now follow from the recent decisions of the House of Lords on the assets which are and are not relevant to the process of reallocation of property[170] on divorce that pension sharing orders will be considerably restricted in their scope where a significant part of the pension in question has been "earned" prior to the marriage in question. This had indeed been foreshadowed many years earlier in a pre-attachment case,[171] which concerned a doctor of 41 who had belonged to the National Health Service Pension Scheme for 13 years, it was said that, "in deciding what weight to give to pension rights it is more important . . . to look at the value of what has been earned during cohabitation than to look at the prospective value of what may be earned over the course of the 25 or 30 years between separation and retirement age".

IV. WINDING-UP PENSION SCHEMES

1. How are Pension Schemes Wound-Up?

12–101   It is often necessary for pension schemes to be wound-up. The two most common situations are where the employer becomes insolvent or decides to stop making contributions to the Scheme but the Rules of the Scheme can provide for winding-up in a number of further situations. Since 1997 it has also been possible for what is now the Pensions Regulator to order that a scheme should be wound-up.[172] Where the employer becomes insolvent, it is the responsibility of its liquidator to ensure that there is at least one "independent trustee" and, if there is not, to appoint one[173]; although this does not displace the other trustees, all the discretionary powers conferred on the trustees (and all fiduciary powers conferred on the employer) become exercisable only by the independent trustee so he will have the conduct of the winding-up. In all other cases, the trustees will have the conduct of the winding-up.

12–102   On winding-up the trustees have to realise the assets of the Scheme and purchase annuities for everyone who is beneficially entitled unless any members or deferred members instead opt for a transfer into another approved pension scheme or a personal pension fund within three months of being notified what their benefits are (after that point the trustees can buy annuities without any need for their consent).[174] In the case of a defined contribution scheme, the sub-fund of each member and deferred member

---

[170] See in particular *McFarlane v. McFarlane* [2006] UKHL 24, [2006] 2 A.C. 618, also *Miller v. Miller* (reported with *McFarlane v. McFarlane*), both of which developed the earlier decision in *White v. White* [2001] 1 A.C. 596.

[171] *H v. H* [1993] 2 F.L.R. 335.

[172] Pensions Act 1995, s.11.

[173] *ibid*. ss.22–26; see *Icarus (Hertford) v. Driscoll* [1990] P.L.R. 1 and *Mettoy Pensions Trustees v. Evans* [1990] 1 W.L.R. 1587, *ante*, p.182.

[174] *ibid.*, s.24.

will simply be used to purchase the necessary annuity or make the appropriate transfer (pensioners will of course already have annuities because that is the way that defined contribution schemes work). In the case of a defined benefit scheme, annuities will have to be purchased for each pensioner and for any member or deferred member who does not opt for a transfer.

Trustees are often given an express power and now have a statutory power[175] to defer the commencement of the winding-up and instead operate the scheme as a paid up scheme for a period. However, in the case of a defined benefit scheme, this runs the risk of favouring the interests of some members (those close to retirement who retire in the interim) at the expense of the other members because they will go into a higher priority group in the event of any shortfall; further, operating the scheme as a paid up scheme will in the event of a shortfall favour both members and pensioners at the expense of the deferred members because it will use up assets which would otherwise be available for them (in the interim the members will acquire more pensionable service, thus increasing their final benefits, and the pensioners will receive their pensions in full). It is therefore generally felt to be unwise for trustees to exercise this power, although they must at least consider whether or not to do so.

It has been held that, once winding-up has commenced, the trustees no longer have the powers and discretions conferred on them by the provisions of the scheme except in so far as such powers and discretions are specifically included in the provisions governing winding-up.[176] The specific decision was that a power of amendment could not be exercised after the winding-up had commenced, although such a power can apparently be exercised during the period of any notice given by the employer to the trustees to wind-up the scheme.[177] Any necessary amendments to powers or to the order of priorities therefore will not normally be able to be made after winding-up has commenced. Further, the trustees will be at risk of being impugned for fraud on a power if they make amendments immediately before that point which prejudice the interests of some particular group of beneficiaries (however in practice, because of the statutory order of priorities considered below, the trustees can at present only effectively make amendments in respect of benefits other than SERPS equivalents which accrued to members and deferred members before April 6, 1997 and any guaranteed increases to those benefits).

12–103

2. *The Effect of a Shortfall*

This is only an issue in defined benefit schemes since in defined contribution schemes each person has his own sub-fund and that is the beginning and end of his rights unless the sub-fund has been reduced by criminal conduct, in which case the employer has to make up the amount lost or, if this is not possible, recourse can be had to the Fraud Compensation Fund. Shortfalls in

12–104

---

[175] *ibid.*, s.38.
[176] *Thrells Ltd (1974) Pension Scheme v. Lomas* [1992] P.L.R. 149, confirming the earlier unreported decision in *Re ABC Television* (1973), in Ellison, *op.cit.*, sources p.28.
[177] *Municipal Mutual v. Harrop* [1998] P.L.R. 149.

defined benefit schemes are very common because the minimum funding requirement proceeded and the scheme-specific funding requirement which replaced it proceeds on the basis that the scheme will continue; the costs of providing annuities is often as much as 20 per cent more than the funding notionally held for each pensioner, member and deferred member. Further, the costs of winding-up a final salary scheme are very considerable because of the need to calculate the benefits of every single person; most actuaries make provision of about 4 per cent of the fund for this and include that within the relevant funding requirement but in difficult cases and, in particular where there are a large number of deferred pensioners with relatively short periods of pensionable service, the costs can be considerably higher.

12–105   Unless the Scheme is in substantial surplus, shortfalls are a problem even where the employer is solvent because, although any shortfall constitutes a statutory debt[178] payable by the employer to the trustees, the employer only has to satisfy the relevant funding requirement shortfall, taking into account also all the likely costs of winding-up the scheme, rather than the cost of funding the annuities. Further, in such circumstances the absence of any insolvency means that no recourse can be had to the Pension Protection Fund or to the Financial Assistance Scheme. In such circumstances, the benefits of some of the beneficiaries of the scheme will clearly have to be reduced in the light of the shortfall and exactly who suffers will be determined by the order of priorities which is considered below.

12–106   On the other hand, when the employer is insolvent, even that statutory debt will not be paid in full because, since it is not a preferred debt, the scheme will only receive the same number of pence in the pound as all the other general creditors of the employer. However, in such circumstances recourse will admittedly be able to be had to the Pension Protection Fund or to the Financial Assistance Scheme but that does not enable benefits to be funded in full. The Pension Protection Fund, which applies to winding-ups commenced on or after April 6, 2005, will ensure that pensioners receive 100 per cent of their entitlement and members who have yet to reach normal pension age are credited with 90 per cent of their entitlement but in each case this is subject to a cap which increases in line with the Retail Prices Index depending on when the winding-up commences; the order of priorities has been changed so that it does not affect priorities as between these entitlements but is still capable of adversely affecting the benefits not covered by the Pension Protection Fund. The Financial Assistance Scheme, which applies to winding-ups commenced between January 1, 1997 and April 6, 2005 restricts both pensioners and members who have yet to reach normal retirement age to 80 per cent of their entitlements, this time subject to a fixed cap of £26,000; however, where the insolvency is only marginal, the order of priorities may enable pensioners to do better than members who have yet to reach normal retirement age.

12–107   The provisions of the trust deed invariably provide a list of the order in which benefits are to be funded but since 1997 this has been subject to a

---

[178] Pensions Act 1995, s.75(1).

statutory list.[179] The following list applied to winding-ups which commenced between April 6, 1997 and April 5, 2004 (all such winding-ups are potentially covered by the Financial Assistance Scheme):

(i) the benefits purchased by members or deferred members who had made additional voluntary contributions[180];

(ii) insurance policies taken out prior to April 6, 1997 in respect of any particular member whose entitlement to some payment had arisen if either the policies could not be surrendered or the proceeds of their surrender would not exceed the potential pension liability;

(iii) pensions in payment or whose payment had been deferred because a member had continued to work after normal retirement age[181];

(iv) ranking equally,

(a) refunds of contributions to members with less than two years' pensionable service;

(b) whatever constituted the SERPS equivalent prior to April 6, 1997; and

(c) benefits accruing after April 5, 1997 including any pension share of those benefits given to a divorced spouse (the priority thus given to this and to category (iv)(a) was very unfair since it favoured short term employees at the potential expense of long term employees and deferred members);

(v) (because the amounts necessary to fund future increases in pensions were excluded from all the categories so far except, obviously, additional voluntary contributions) the amounts necessary to fund future increases in pensions payable under (ii) and (iii) above, ranking equally as between them;

(vi) (for the same reason) the amounts necessary to fund future increases in SERPS equivalents and benefits accruing after April 5, 1997; and lastly

(vii) everything else, which was basically all remaining benefits (other than SERPS equivalents which accrued before April 6, 1997) and any guaranteed increases to those benefits (thus all the benefits of

---

[179] Contained in Pensions Act 1995, s.73 (the original form of this section has been substantially altered by the Occupational Pension Schemes (Winding Up) Regulations 1996 (SI 1996/3126).

[180] Payments made by members who will not have completed enough years of service to obtain the maximum pension on their retirement in order to acquire additional years of service. Although such contributions were very common in the years when final salary schemes were in substantial surplus in order to acquire an additional proportion of any enhancement of benefits subsequently given, there is less point in making them in present circumstances; however, because of their position in the list, they are not actually at any risk.

[181] Where a normal retirement age has been increased as the result of *Barber v. Royal Exchange Assurance Group* [1991] 1 Q.B. 344 (see *ante*, para 12–043), it was held in *Cripps v. Trustee Solutions* [2007] EWCA Civ. 771 that the benefits which anyone who as a result was still working would already have had on earlier retirement fall into this category; any further benefits still being acquired fall into category (vii).

members who had yet to reach normal retirement age, other than SERPS equivalents which accrued before April 6, 1997, were last in the queue).

12–108   Other than additional voluntary contributions and pensions in payment or whose payment has been deferred, benefits were not funded in full at each level but were limited to the minimum funding requirement valuation. This worked in respect of members and deferred members if they took transfers, assuming that there were enough assets to cover the minimum funding requirement; however, there might well not have been in the light of the amount it was likely to have cost to purchase the annuities for the pensioners (this was likely to cost up to 20 per cent more than the minimum funding requirement earmarked for them and so could eat into the minimum funding requirement earmarked for the members and deferred members, particularly if the scheme has a substantial proportion of pensioners). The situation could become catastrophic for members and deferred members if annuities had to be purchased for some or all of them as well, leading to substantial reductions even if the employer had been able to comply with the minimum funding requirement at all times; in such circumstances, winding-up the scheme could cause inroads to be made into benefits other than SERPS equivalents which accrued before April 6, 1997 and the Financial Assistance Scheme obviously did not apply. In contrast, where the fund was not brought up to the minimum funding requirement because of the insolvency of the employee, then pensioners would do better than members who had yet to reach normal retirement age where there were sufficient funds to provide the pensioners' benefits in full. Only where there were insufficient funds to provide 80 per cent of those benefits, would the Financial Assistance Scheme equalise the benefits of the two classes subject to the cap.

12–109   The above order of priorities was varied in the case of winding-ups which commenced between April 6, 1997 and April 5, 2004 (all of which are also potentially covered by the Financial Assistance Scheme) so that the benefits of members who had yet to reach normal retirement age, other than the amounts necessary to fund further increases in those benefits, were moved up to category (iv). This meant that all amounts necessary to fund further increases came after the existing benefit of members who had yet to reach retirement age which produced a measurable improvement for the latter.

12–110   The current order of priorities, which applies to winding-ups commencing on or after April 6, 2005 (all of which are potentially covered by the Pension Protection Fund) is as follows:

(i)   insurance policies taken out prior to April 6, 1997 in respect of any particular member whose entitlement to some payment had arisen if either the policies could not be surrendered or the proceeds of their surrender would not exceed the potential pension liability (category (ii) above);

(ii) the cost of securing the benefits which would be provided by the Pension Protection Fund in the event that it assumed responsibility for the scheme;

(iii) the benefits purchased by members or deferred members who had made additional voluntary contributions (category (i) above); and

(iv) everything else.

Although the relegation of additional voluntary contributions is undoubt- **12–111**
edly unfair to persons who had made those contributions prior to the enactment of the Pensions Act 2004, this is consistent with the fact that the Pension Protection Fund does not cover such contributions. What is significant is that, even where the Pension Protection Fund does not apply, either because there has not been an insolvency or because, despite an insolvency, the fund has sufficient assets to provide the benefits which the Pension Protection Fund would potentially have provided, the rights of pensioners and of members who have yet to reach normal retirement age are initially limited to the benefits which would be provided by the Pension Protection Fund (which are of course 100 per cent and 90 per cent respectively subject to the cap) and then thereafter, after payment of the additional voluntary contributions, the remaining benefits of pensioners and of members who have yet to reach normal retirement age rank equally.

Windings-up tend to take a considerable time, usually at least a year, and **12–112**
the trustees can face very considerable difficulties in deciding what to do in the interim in respect of early requests to refund contributions, early requests to make transfers, applications for early retirement or retirement on the grounds of incapacity, normal retirements, deaths and increases to pensions. In all cases, they will simply not know how much they can afford to pay until it is clear how many of the members and deferred members will have to be bought annuities; on the other hand, failure to comply with such requests or to commence payments of pensions and death benefits will produce a tremendous amount of aggravation so they clearly have to pay something, presumably initially only what would be payable on a worst case scenario with a further reduction to cover the possibility of the fund falling in value during winding-up (it has as yet not been decided whether or not in these circumstances the statutory debt[182] can be reviewed enabling the trustees to go back to the employer and ask for a further payment).

3. *The Effect of a Surplus*

In present conditions, a surplus on a winding-up is unlikely; in practice it is **12–113**
only feasible if, first, the pension scheme was in substantial surplus or, secondly, most of the members and deferred members take transfers rather than annuities and the proportion of pensioners is not substantial. However, a surplus can nevertheless arise both in a defined benefit scheme and in a defined contribution scheme; if it does, what then happens to it? There are three possible situations.

First, the trustees may have a power under the provisions of the trust deed **12–114**
to return the surplus to the employer. In this event, the trustees must[183] first

---

[182] Under Pensions Act 1995, s.75(1).
[183] *ibid.*, s.76.

provide for any annual increases which have not yet been funded and then consider whether to augment benefits up to the maximum permissible fiscal limits. They must then notify all the beneficiaries on two occasions of their decision in this respect and of their decision to return the surplus to the employer. If no one objects to the Pensions Regulator within a specified period of at least three months from the second notice, they can then pay the surplus to the employer; if anyone objects, they can only do so after the Pensions Regulator has reached the conclusion that all the requirements of the section have been satisfied, something which will in practice also involve the Pensions Regulator in deciding whether the trustees have been guilty of fraud on a power in making any of the relevant decisions.

12–115   Secondly, the provisions of the trust deed may prohibit the trustees from returning the surplus to the employer. In this event, the trustees must[184] provide for any annual increases which have not yet been funded and then augment benefits up to the maximum possible fiscal limits; only then may they pay the surplus to the employer.

12–116   Thirdly, the provisions of the trust deed may contain no provisions as to what is to happen to any surplus. This is obviously a relatively unlikely situation, particularly given the possibility of inserting a provision by use of the power of amendment before winding-up commences.

12–117   This situation was, however, considered by Scott J. in *Davis v. Richards & Wallington Industries*.[185] The benefits of the employees had been augmented up to the permitted maximum fiscal limits, which in practice will be inevitable in this situation. Scott J. opined that such part of the remaining surplus as represented the employer's contributions would be held on resulting trust for the employer while such part as represented the employees' contributions would be held as *bona vacantia*. He accepted that neither the contractual relationship between employer and employees nor the fact that the employees had obtained everything for which they had contracted necessarily prevented there being a resulting trust in their favour as well. However, for two reasons he held that there was no such trust: first, because no intention could be imputed to the employees that they should receive a surplus greater than there were entitled to receive under the relevant tax legislation; and, secondly, because a resulting trust of their contributions would have been unworkable due to the need to value the benefits received by each employee in order to ascertain his entitlement to the surplus.

12–118   Subsequently, in *Air Jamaica v. Charlton*,[186] the Privy Council regarded the approach of Scott J. to the imputation of intention as erroneous, saying that it was not obvious that employees should ever be regarded as having no expectation of obtaining a return of excess contributions in the event of a surplus. But this was no more than a dictum because the Privy Council was actually considering what was to happen to the subject matter of some of the trusts of the pension scheme in question which were void for perpetuity and in such circumstances it was impossible to say that the employees had received everything for which they had contracted anyway. Nor did the valuation difficulty which Scott J. had identified apply in the light of the way

---

[184] *ibid.*, s.77.
[185] [1990] 1 W.L.R. 1511.
[186] [1999] 1 W.L.R. 1399.

in which the Privy Council had construed the provisions of the scheme which was before it.

However, the rejection of *bona vacantia* by the Privy Council is clearly   **12–119** preferable to its adoption by Scott J., at least where a resulting trust of the employees' contributions is workable. If this is the case then, in the unlikely event that this situation recurs, it is to be hoped that there would be held to be resulting trusts of both the part of the remaining surplus which represents the employer's contributions and that part which represents the employees' contributions.

CHAPTER 13

THE APPOINTMENT, RETIREMENT AND REMOVAL OF TRUSTEES

13–001 Once a trust has been set up, the settlor will have handed to his chosen trustees complete control over the property subject to the trust, save to the extent that he has specifically reserved powers to himself. Those trustees will be the persons to whom the beneficiaries look for the protection of their interests and those interests will only be adequately protected if the trustees are scrupulously honest, are prepared to give adequate time to the administration of the trust, have enough common sense and business acumen to manage the trust property efficiently and are able to treat fairly beneficiaries whose interests potentially conflict, such as a tenant for life and his remainderman.[1] As for each individual trustee, his position cannot be taken lightly. Unless there is a provision in the trust instrument to the contrary or the trustee is either a trust corporation or is acting as trustee in a professional capacity,[2] he will have to devote his time to the administration of the trust entirely without payment or other benefit.[3] In return for his efforts, he may well receive from the beneficiaries not gratitude but bitterness[4] and, if he is not as careful as he might have been and consequently makes a mistake, he may find himself liable to make good any loss out of his own pocket.[5] For all these reasons, it is crucial to be able to identify who are the trustees at any one time and consequently the rules governing the appointment, retirement and removal of trustees are a matter of prime concern for everyone who is connected with a trust.

I. TYPES OF TRUSTEE

1. *Ordinary Trustees*

13–002 In general, any individual, limited company or other corporation may be appointed as a trustee and a limited company may act as a trustee jointly

---

[1] The conflict of interest between tenant for life and remainderman is explained in connection with investments, see *post*, para 14–057 *et seq*.

[2] This will be the case if he acts in the course of a profession or business which consists of or includes the provision of services in connection with the management or administration of trusts generally or in any particular respect. See Trustee Act 2000, ss.28, 29.

[3] See *post*, Chapter 20.

[4] In *Re Londonderry's Settlement* [1965] Ch. 918, a discretionary beneficiary to whom and to whose family a total of £165,000 had been paid showed anything but gratitude to the trustees.

[5] See *post*, Chapter 22.

with an individual,[6] as well as with another limited company or other corporation.[7] Except in the case of minors,[8] there is no statutory prohibition upon the appointment of any person as a trustee; however, there are some persons who, while they have the legal capacity to be trustees, may nevertheless be regarded as so undesirable as trustees that the court will remove them if they are ever appointed. A person may be regarded as undesirable in this sense either because a past history of financial irresponsibility, manifested by a past bankruptcy or near bankruptcy, some circumstances leading to bankruptcy,[9] because he has been convicted of a crime involving dishonesty,[10] or because he would, if appointed a trustee, be placed in a position where his interest as a beneficiary under the trust would conflict with his duty as a trustee. However in the latter respect, while the appointment of a beneficiary as a sole trustee may well be undesirable, the appointment of a beneficiary as one of two or more trustees will often be advantageous, because the beneficiary will then be induced to do the best he can for the trust because of his own financial interest in the trust property as well as by his duty as trustee.

Minors are in a curious position. It is clear that a minor may be a trustee. **13–003** In *Re Vinogradoff*[11] a woman transferred a holding of War Stock into the joint names of herself and of her granddaughter, then aged four. There was no presumption of advancement[12] and the court decided that the granddaughter held that stock as a trustee on resulting trust.[13] But although a minor may thus become a trustee by implication and may also do so by operation of law, he cannot be expressly appointed as a trustee; section 20 of the Law of Property Act 1925 declares void the appointment of a minor as a trustee. If a minor is to be a trustee, he will, therefore, have to become one other than by express appointment.

An ordinary trustee is not normally entitled to remuneration for his **13–004** services unless this is authorised by a provision in the trust instrument, the trustee is either a trust corporation or is acting as trustee in a professional capacity.[14] Remuneration is considered in detail in a later chapter.[15]

---

[6] The Bodies Corporate (Joint Tenancy) Act 1889. See *Re Thompson's Settlement Trusts* [1905] 1 Ch. 229.

[7] While it has always been possible for all the original trustees to be limited companies or other corporations and for a trust corporation to be sole trustee, in recent times it is only since January 1, 1997 that it has been possible for individual trustees to retire leaving as trustees only limited companies and/or other corporations (Trusts of Land and Appointment of Trustees Act 1996, Sch.3, para.3(12), (13) amending Trustee Act 1925, ss.37(1)(c), 39(1)).

[8] See Law of Property Act 1925, s.20, *infra*.

[9] *Re Barker's Trusts* (1875) 1 Ch.D. 43.

[10] *Coombe v. Brookes* (1871) L.R. 12 Eq. 61; *Re Forster* (1886) 55 L.T. 479; *Re Henderson* [1940] Ch. 764.

[11] [1935] W.N. 68.

[12] Such a presumption would only have arisen if the woman had been *in loco parentis* to her granddaughter and this was not the case.

[13] See *ante*, para 9–017.

[14] This will be the case if he acts in the course of a profession or business which consists of or includes the provision of services in connection with the management or administration of trusts generally or in any particular respect. See Trustee Act 2000, ss.28, 29.

[15] See *post*, Chapter 20.

2. *Judicial Trustees*

13–005   A judicial trustee is a person or corporation appointed by the court to act as a trustee where the administration of the trust is intended to be subject to close supervision by the court. Such an appointment is made under the provisions of the Judicial Trustees Act 1896; it is not to be confused with the appointment of an ordinary trustee by the court. The appointment of a judicial trustee is generally made on the application of an existing trustee or beneficiary but the appointment can also be made at the instance of a person who is intending to create a trust.[16] It is also possible to appoint a judicial trustee in order to administer an estate. At one time, when there was no machinery by means of which a personal representative could retire, this provided a means of replacing one who was no longer able to act. However, the court can now appoint a replacement personal representative under section 50 of the Administration of Justice Act 1985. In an application under the 1985 Act, the court may proceed as if there had instead been an application under the 1896 Act and vice versa.[17]

13–006   The distinctive feature of a judicial trustee is that the beneficiaries are protected in the event of his default by virtue of the fact that he is usually required to give security to the court for the proper performance of his duties.[18] He is subject to close supervision by the court and special provisions govern the auditing of his accounts.[19] As a result, a judicial trustee becomes an officer of the court, so that he is able to obtain the directions of the court informally at any time. However, in practice it is rare for a judicial trustee to be appointed save where complex litigation is in prospect,[20] where there has been gross mismanagement of the trust in question in the past, or where the admininstration of a trust involves problems of extraordinary complexity or difficulty.[21] When a judicial trustee is appointed, he may always charge for his services[22] and is necessarily paid out of the trust property.

3. *Trust Corporations*

(A)   Definition

13–007   It has already been seen[23] that, in principle, any company as well as any individual can be appointed as a trustee. However, a company which is appointed a trustee is not by virtue of that fact alone a trust corporation. That term is applied only to a body corporate which is engaged in the business of acting as a trustee, usually of many different trusts, and which

---

[16] Judicial Trustees Act 1896, s.1(1).

[17] Administration of Justice Act 1985, s.50(4); Judicial Trustees Act 1896, s.1(7).

[18] Judicial Trustees Act 1896, s.4(1); Judicial Trustee Rules 1983, r.6.

[19] Judicial Trustees Act 1896, ss.1(6), 4(1); Administration of Justice Act 1982, s.57; *Re Ridsdel* [1947] Ch. 597.

[20] See *Re Diplock* [1948] Ch. 465, affirmed *sub nom. Minister of Health v. Simpson* [1951] A.C. 251.

[21] *Re Chisholm* (1898) 43 S.J. 43.

[22] Judicial Trustees Act, ss.1(5), 4(1); Judicial Trustee Rules 1983, r.11.

[23] See *ante*, para 13–002.

fulfils certain conditions; such companies are generally associated with banks or insurance companies.[24] The basic conditions are[25]:

(i) its constitution must authorise it to undertake the business of acting as a trustee and of acting as a personal representative;

(ii) it must have an issued capital of not less than £250,000, of which not less than £100,000 must have been paid up in cash;

(iii) the company must be incorporated either in the United Kingdom or in some other European Union country; and

(iv) the company must have a place of business in the United Kingdom, no matter where it is incorporated.

The second of these conditions, which at the time when it was originally imposed was intended to afford a considerable measure of protection to beneficiaries, is now totally inadequate for this purpose. The value of the assets in any one trust may exceed by many times the amount of the minimum required paid up capital. Further, the test relates to the amount of the issued share capital of the company, not to the value of its assets. Thus, provided that a company has actually issued shares to the extent of £250,000, it is still eligible to be a trust corporation even if it has by some act of imprudence managed to lose all its shareholders' funds.

In addition to commercial companies which carry on the business of **13–008** acting as trustees, a number of other bodies also rank as trust corporations. They are given this status so that they can take advantage of the privileges given to trust corporations.[26] The following persons and bodies are included in the definition of trust corporation:

(i) any body corporate which is appointed by the court to be a trustee in any particular case[27];

(ii) certain bodies which are incorporated to act as trustees of charitable trusts[28];

(iii) certain public officers, such as the Public Trustee,[29] the Treasury Solicitor, and the Official Solicitor[30]; and

---

[24] The path to the definition is tortuous: first, certain bodies are entitled to act as custodian trustee (see *post*, para 13–014) by virtue of the Public Trustee Rules 1912, as amended; secondly, the Public Trustee Rules 1912 were made under the power conferred by the Public Trustee Act 1906; and, thirdly, s.68(18) of the Trustee Act 1925, provides that the definition of a "trust corporation" for the purposes of the Act includes any corporation entitled to act as a custodian trustee under the rules made under the Public Trustee Act 1906.

[25] The Public Trustee (Custodian Trustee) Rules 1975 (SI 1975/1189). The rules were made to implement the EEC Council Directive 73/183/EEC.

[26] See *post*, para 13–010.

[27] Trustee Act 1925, s.68(18).

[28] The incorporation must be by Special Act, or Royal Charter, or under the Charitable Trustees Incorporation Act 1872; Public Trustee Rules 1912, r.30(c), (d), as substituted.

[29] Trustee Act 1925, s.68(18). See also the Public Trustee and Administration of Funds Act 1986, which confers on the Public Trustee all the functions of the Judge of the Court of Protection under the Mental Health Act 1983, Part VII.

[30] Law of Property (Amendment) Act 1926, s.3(1).

(iv) major local authorities[31] and certain public authorities such as the Gas Council and Regional Hospital Boards.[32]

(B) Ability to Act

13–009   A trust corporation can act in the administration of any trust[33] unless the trust instrument forbids its employment.

(C) Privileges

13–010   The general principle is that, whenever statutory provisions require an act to be done by two private trustees, that act can be done by a sole trustee where that trustee is a trust corporation. It follows that the main privileges of a trust corporation are as follows:

(i) a trust corporation can by itself give a good receipt for capital money under a trust of land[34] or a settlement under the Settled Land Act 1925[35];

(ii) a trust corporation can by itself exercise various powers of management, such as the apportionment of blended funds, accepting compositions and effecting compromises[36];

(iii) where a private trustee acts jointly with a trust corporation and the private trustee wishes to delegate the performance of his duties, he may delegate them to the trust corporation[37]; and

(iv) a private trustee may be discharged without a fresh trustee being appointed in his place where a trust corporation will be left to perform the trusts.[38]

As a result of these provisions, it is common to find a trust corporation acting as the sole trustee of a trust, despite the fact that it can act jointly with a private trustee.

(D) Remuneration

13–011   Since the enactment of the Trustee Act 2000 a trust corporation has been able to charge "reasonable remuneration" out of the trust funds for any services which it provides to or on behalf of a private trust[39]; this is defined as "such remuneration as is reasonable in the circumstances for the provision of those services to or on behalf of that trust by that trustee".[40] Prior to this legislation, a trust corporation was in the same position as an ordinary trustee and

---

[31] The Public Trustee Rules 1912, r.30(g); Local Government Act 1972, s.241.
[32] The Public Trustee Rules 1912, r.30(e), (f).
[33] *Re Cherry's Trusts* [1914] 1 Ch. 83.
[34] Trustee Act 1925, s.14(2), as amended by Trusts of Land and Appointment of Trustees Act 1996, Sch.3, para.3(3).
[35] Settled Land Act 1925, ss.94, 95.
[36] Trustee Act 1925, s.19.
[37] s.25(1)(2), substituted by the Powers of Attorney Act 1971. In contrast, he cannot permanently delegate his powers to his co-trustee if the co-trustee is a private trustee unless he is a trustee-beneficiary of a trust of land See *post*, pp.566, 570
[38] See *post*, para 13–075.
[39] Trustee Act 2000, s.29(1); this provision does not apply to charitable trusts.
[40] s.29(3).

was only entitled to remuneration where there was a provision to that effect in the trust instrument; this meant that in practice a trust corporation would not agree to act as an original trustee until express arrangements had been made for its remuneration. It is obviously likely that trust corporations will continue to insist on such express arrangements in order to avoid any dispute as to what constitutes "reasonable remuneration".[41] It remains to be seen what attitude the courts will now adopt when appointing a trust corporation to be a trustee, usually of course as a replacement trustee; the courts remain entitled to fix its remuneration[42] but may instead now prefer to leave the trust corporation to claim the reasonable remuneration to which it is entitled under the Trustee Act 2000.

4. *The Public Trustee*

The Public Trustee is a corporation sole which was established by the Public Trustee Act 1906. His main function is to administer private trusts, particularly small trusts, although he may be appointed as a judicial[43] a or custodian trustee[44] and may be appointed to administer the property of a convicted criminal.[45] His functions were extended by the Public Trustee and Administration of Funds Act 1986, which confers on him all the functions of the Judge of the Court of Protection in relation to the property and affairs of mental patients under what is now the Mental Capacity Act 2005.[46] He may not act as the trustee of a religious or a charitable trust[47] and may only carry on a business owned by a trust for the purpose of winding it up.[48] Although the Public Trustee is a public officer, he can only act in the administration of any trust if he has been appointed to do so in the same way as a private individual. He may also refuse to accept any trust for any reason other than the smallness of the trust property and the present policy of the Public Trustee is to refuse to act except as a last resort, namely when there is no one else suitable, able or willing to act and a refusal to act would result in injustice. When he does act, he may act either alone or jointly with other trustees but is able to act alone notwithstanding any normal requirement for a plurality of trustees to act in, for example, the case of an overreaching conveyance.[49]

13–012

Because he is a corporation sole, the Public Trustee never dies. This means that, whenever he is the sole trustee, it is never necessary for a new trustee to be appointed. A further advantage is that, if he acts improperly and loss occurs, the State makes good that loss.[50] The other side of the coin is that the

13–013

---

[41] Express provisions in a trust instrument oust the provisions relating to reasonable remuneration; s.29(5).
[42] Trustee Act 1925, s.42.
[43] See *ante*, para 13–005.
[44] See *post, infra*.
[45] Public Trustee Act 1906, s.5.
[46] s.3.
[47] *Re Hampton* (1918) 88 L.J.Ch. 103.
[48] Public Trustee Rules 1912, r.7(1),(2).
[49] *Re Duxbury* [1995] 1 W.L.R. 425.
[50] Public Trustee Act 1906, s.7.

Public Trustee may always charge for his services[51] and that his fees are calculated by reference to the amount of work which he actually does but to the value of the property which he is administering and so can be very substantial.[52]

5. *Custodian Trustees*

13–014   The function of a custodian trustee, who may be the Public Trustee or any other trust corporation, is merely to hold the property of a trust, leaving the administration of the trust in the hands of managing trustees. A custodian trustee is usually appointed so that, once the trust property is vested in his name, it will not be necessary to have any further appointment of new trustees and so that he may have custody of the trust deeds and securities. A custodian trustee may always charge for the services which he performs in that capacity.[53]

II. THE APPOINTMENT OF TRUSTEES

13–015   Trustees are obviously appointed either on the creation of a new trust or during the continuance of an existing trust, either in substitution for a trustee who is retiring or who has died or in addition to the existing trustees. In both cases, the appointment is almost always made by deed without the court becoming involved in any way but, in exceptional cases, when there is no one else able to do so, the court can make the appointment itself. Thus both appointments made extra-judicially and appointments made by the court itself have to be considered. In some circumstances there are restrictions on the maximum number of trustees. It is also possible for a trustee to assume office as a result of his own officious conduct.

1. *Appointing the Original Trustees*

13–016   When a settlor creates a trust inter vivos, he will usually appoint the first trustees of the settlement himself. If he wishes to appoint only people other than himself to be the trustees, he will include a clause appointing them in the original trust instrument. If, on the other hand, he wishes to appoint himself, he may make a declaration of trust to the effect that from then on he will be holding specified property on certain trusts, in which case he will immediately become sole trustee of the trust; alternatively, he may appoint himself and one or more other persons to be the first trustees. However, as soon as the trust has come into existence, the settlor loses his right as settlor to appoint the trustees of the settlement. It is common for a settlor to include in the trust instrument a provision giving himself (or, for that matter, someone else) the power to appoint new trustees in the future[54]; however, if he makes any future appointment under that power, he will be doing so

---

[51] *ibid.*, s.9, as amended by the Public Trustee (Fees) Act 1957.
[52] See *post*, para 20–013.
[53] Public Trustee Act 1906, s.2.
[54] See *post*, para 13–023.

because he has given himself that power in the trust instrument, not because he was the settlor.

Occasionally there may turn out to be no trustees of a new trust. The **13–017** trustees named in the trust instrument by the settlor may turn out to be dead, may refuse to act or the settlor may simply have forgotten to name any. If the trust instrument has given anyone a power to appoint new trustees, that power can then be used; otherwise, an appointment will have to be made by the court.[55] By so appointing, the court will be giving effect to the equitable maxim that "the court will not allow a trust to fail for want of a trustee".

In practice, trusts arise most frequently as the result of a death. Where the **13–018** deceased has left a will, he may thereby have expressly set up a trust. Alternatively, a trust may arise by operation of law. Thus, if the deceased has left a legacy to a child, the money cannot actually be paid to that child until he reaches the age of 18 because a minor cannot give a good receipt for capital money. Until then the money will have to be held on trust for the minor. If, on the other hand, the deceased died intestate, the devolution of his property will be governed by the Administration of Estates Act 1925, as varied by subsequent statutes and statutory instruments.[56] In some circumstances, the intestate's property will have to be held on statutory trusts.[57] For example, if the deceased was worth £200,000 and left a wife and children, the wife will at present be entitled to the first £125,000[58] and the remaining £75,000[59] will be divided into two halves, one half going to the children outright and the other half being held on trust for the wife for life, remainder to the children.[60]

It is possible where a trust is created by will to designate different persons **13–019** as executors and as trustees but normally the same persons are appointed to fulfil both functions. In the absence of the appointment of any different person to be the trustee, the executor may in due course automatically become the trustee. Whether and when he will in fact do so depends on the function which he is discharging at the point in time being considered. The functions of an executor (or, where there is no executor, an administrator) are:

(i) in the case of an executor, obtaining probate of the deceased's will or, in the case of an administrator, obtaining letters of administration of the deceased's estate;

(ii) getting in the deceased's property, including any debts owed to him;

---

[55] *Dodkin v. Brunt* (1868) L.R. 6 Eq. 580.

[56] Such as the Intestates Estates Act 1952, the Family Provision Act 1966, and the Inheritance (Provision for Family and Dependents) Act 1975.

[57] Administration of Estates Act 1925, s.46(1).

[58] This is the fixed net sum payable under Administration of Estates Act 1925, s.55(1)(x), which is raised periodically by statutory instrument (Family Provision Act 1966, s.1; Administration of Justice Act 1977, s.28.; the current statutory instrument is Family Provision (Intestate Succession) Order 1993 (SI 1993/2906)).

[59] Under Administration of Estates Act 1925, s.46(1), the wife would in addition receive the personal chattels of the deceased.

[60] Administration of Estates Act 1925, s.46(1).

    (iii) paying any inheritance tax and the debts owed by the deceased;

    (iv) paying any legacies;

    (v) agreeing the distribution account with the beneficiaries; and

    (vi) distributing all the property which can be immediately distributed, that is to say all the property remaining after the payment of debts and legacies other than any which is governed by a trust or which is not immediately payable to a beneficiary because he is still under 18.

When all this has been done, in general the executor or administrator will cease to be a personal representative; if any of the deceased's property is still in his name, from then on he will hold it as trustee, not as personal representative. In the case of land, however, an executor or administrator will continue to hold the property as personal representative until he assents to its vesting in himself as trustee; in the case of legal interests in land, the assent must be in writing.[61] In this last case, therefore, the test is not one of function, but whether or not there has been an assent.

2. *Assumption of Office by Conduct*

13–020   Acceptance of the office of trustee of an *inter vivos* trust is usually signified by the trustee executing the trust deed. But where a trustee does any act which amounts to performance of the trust, in that event he will be presumed to have accepted the office of trustee as a result of his conduct. Any act, however slight, by way of performance of the terms of the trust is sufficient.[62]

3. *Appointing New Trustees*

13–021   It is necessary to distinguish, on the one hand, the persons who are able to appoint new trustees from, on the other hand, the occasions on which they are able to do so.

(A)   The Persons who can Appoint New Trustees
13–022   The rules relating to the appointment of new trustees are the same whether the trust was set up *inter vivos* or arose as the result of a death.

(1)   The order in which the rules are applied
13–023   Where the trust instrument makes provision for the appointment of new trustees, either generally or in the specific situation which has arisen, the person or persons nominated clearly have the primary right to make any appointment. However, if reliance is placed on that power, then its terms must be strictly followed.

---

[61] *Re King's Will Trusts* [1964] Ch. 542; see *ante*, para 1–066.
[62] *Lord Montfort v. Lord Cadogan* (1816) 19 Ves. 635; *James v. Frearson* (1842) 1 Y. & C.C.C. 370. Thus a person designated a trustee should expressly announce if he does not wish to act.

Where, on the other hand, the trust instrument does not make any provision for whatever situation has arisen, then new trustees may be appointed in two distinct ways which exist alongside one another: first, by virtue of the statutory power in section 36 of the Trustee Act 1925 (if there is a conflict between the provisions of the trust instrument and the statutory power, the statutory power prevails), the following persons in the following order have the right to appoint new trustees: the person or persons nominated in the trust instrument[63]; if there is no such person or no such person able or willing to act, the surviving or continuing trustees[64]; and, if there is no surviving or continuing trustee, the personal representatives of the last or only surviving trustee[65] (only if there is no person in any one group or if the persons in that group refuse to appoint can an appointment be made by a person in the subsequent group); and, secondly, by virtue of section 19 of the Trusts of Land and Appointment of Trustees Act 1996, which only applies where the trust instrument has made no provision for the appointment of new trustees, where all the beneficiaries are of full age and capacity and between them absolutely entitled to the trust property; in such circumstances, they can direct the appointment of new trustees. **13–024**

Additionally, in one particular situation, where a trustee is incapable by reason of mental disorder of exercising his functions as such and there is no one able and willing to exercise the statutory power contained in section 36 of the Trustee Act 1925, then by virtue of section 20 of the Trusts of Land and Appointment of Trustees Act 1996, where all the beneficiaries are of full age and capacity and between them absolutely entitled to the trust property, they can direct his replacement. **13–025**

Finally, failing all else, new trustees can be appointed by the court. **13–026**

(2) Observations about the rules

The rules are applied strictly in the order set out above; thus in *Re Higginbottom*[66] the existing trustee had the power to appoint new trustees and her right to do so was held to prevail against the wishes of a large majority of the beneficiaries who sought to appoint others.[67] Where an appointment is made in good faith by the person entitled, the court will not interfere with the appointment even if it would have preferred someone else to have been appointed.[68] **13–027**

Where two or more persons have the power of appointing new trustees, they must exercise the power jointly unless there is a provision in the trust instrument to the contrary. If they cannot agree who the new trustee should be, they are treated as having refused to exercise their power and so the power to appoint becomes exercisable by the persons in the next category. Thus in *Re Sheppard's Settlement Trusts*[69] the trust instrument gave the power of appointing trustees to two persons. When they could not agree on the appointee, it was held that the power could be exercised by the continuing **13–028**

---

[63] s.36(1)(a).
[64] s.36(1)(b).
[65] *ibid.*
[66] [1892] 3 Ch. 132.
[67] See also Re *Brockbank* [1948] Ch. 206.
[68] *Re Gadd* (1883) 23 Ch.D. 134; *Re Norris* (1884) 27 Ch.D. 333; *Re Sales* (1911) 55 S.J. 838.
[69] [1888] W.N. 234.

trustees. The position is the same if the person having the power to appoint cannot be found[70] or is incapable of making the appointment.[71]

13–029   The person who has the power of appointing new trustees may appoint a separate set of trustees for any part of the trust property which is held on trusts distinct from those on which the remainder of the trust property is held.[72] If, therefore, trustees hold three quarters of the trust fund upon trust for Andrew and his family, and one quarter for Bernard and his family, separate trustees can be appointed for the quarter held for Bernard. While, however, the appointment is valid for all purposes connected with the administration of the trust, for certain fiscal purposes the original trustees will continue to be regarded as trustees of the whole.[73]

(B) The Occasions on which Trustees may be Appointed

(1) By the exercise of an express power in the trust instrument

13–030   Where a person is nominated in the trust instrument,[74] whether it is the settlor, the protector of the settlement (if there is one), or anyone else, he is usually given the power to appoint new trustees in all circumstances; he may even be given power at any time to replace all the existing trustees without having to show cause. Such a power was conferred on a protector in *Von Knieriem v. Bermuda Trust Co.*[75] and his exercise of it was held to have been valid even though he had apparently acted more in the interests of the settlor than of the beneficiaries.

13–031   Where, however, a power is able to be exercised only in limited circumstances, that power is strictly construed. In *Re Wheeler*,[76] a person was nominated to appoint a new trustee in the place of any trustee who was "incapable" of acting. One trustee became bankrupt and so became "unfit" to act[77] but not "incapable" of acting. It was held that the nominated person did not have a power to appoint in those circumstances because the condition was not fulfilled.[78] Further, where a power to appoint is given jointly to two or more persons, it can only be exercised by those persons. Unless, therefore, there is evidence of a contrary intention, the power will not be exercisable at all where one of the donees of the power dies, or becomes incapable of making the appointment.[79] On the other hand, where a beneficiary is nominated in the trust instrument as having power to appoint new trustees, the power of appointment is generally treated as being detached from the beneficial interest. Thus, if the beneficiary disposes of his beneficial

---

[70] *Craddock v. Witham* [1895] W.N. 75.

[71] *Re Blake* [1887] W.N. 75.

[72] Trustee Act 1925, s.37(1)(b).

[73] *Roome v. Edwards* [1982] A.C. 279.

[74] See *Re Walker and Hughes* (1883) 24 Ch.D. 698 and *Re Sheppard's Settlement Trusts* [1888] W.N. 234.

[75] (1994) 1 Butterworths Offshore Service 116. See *ante*, para 6–035.

[76] [1896] 1 Ch. 315 (a case on Trustee Act 1893, s.10(1), re-enacted in Trustee Act 1925, s.36(1)).

[77] As to the distinction, see *post*, para 13–039 (v).

[78] See also *Turner v. Maule* (1850) 15 Jur. 761; *Re Watts' Settlement* (1851) 9 Hare 106; *Re May's Will Trusts* [1941] Ch. 109.

[79] *Re Harding* [1923] 1 Ch. 182.

interest, he will still, unless there is a provision in the trust instrument to the contrary, be entitled to appoint new trustees.[80]

An illogical difference exists between the position where a new trustee is being appointed to replace an existing trustee who is retiring and where a new trustee is being appointed as an additional trustee without any of the existing trustees retiring. If a person who is nominated in the trust instrument to appoint new trustees has been given only the statutory power[81] rather than some broader power, he may appoint himself to be a new trustee in the place of a retiring trustee but not as an additional trustee. This results from a difference of wording between the different provisions of the Trustee Act 1925. Section 36(1), which applies where a new trustee is being appointed in the place of a retiring trustee, gives to the nominated person power to appoint "one or more other persons (whether or not being the persons exercising the power) to be a trustee", while section 36(6), which confers the power to appoint additional trustees, gives the nominated person power to appoint "another person or other persons to be the trustee". It is difficult to imagine that this difference was actually intended by the legislature.

13–032

(2) By exercise of the statutory power

Section 36(1) of the Trustee Act 1925 sets out a number of circumstances in which new trustees can be appointed. As has already been seen,[82] the following persons in the following order have the right to appoint new trustees: the person or persons nominated in the trust instrument[83]; if there is no such person or no such person able or willing to act, the surviving or continuing trustees[84]; and, if there is no surviving or continuing trustee, the personal representatives of the last or only surviving trustee[85] (only if there is no person in any one group or if the persons in that group refuse to appoint can an appointment be made by a person in the subsequent group). However, it must be emphasised that this provision gives rise only to a power to appoint a new trustee; it does not impose any duty so to do.

13–033

The right of a surviving or continuing trustee so to appoint under section 36(1) is, rather surprisingly, extended by virtue of section 36(8) to a trustee who has refused to act or wishes to retire in the event that he is willing to act in exercising the powers granted by the section. The curious result of this is that, despite the fact that a trustee refuses to act as a trustee or that he wishes to retire, he must be allowed to join in the appointment of a new trustee if he wishes to do so. However, for the purposes of this provision, the expression "refusing or retiring trustee" is narrowly construed. In *Re Stoneham's Settlement Trusts*[86] a new trustee was appointed in the place of another trustee who had remained out of the United Kingdom for longer than 12

13–034

---

[80] *Hardaker v. Moorhouse* (1884) 26 Ch.D. 417.
[81] *Re Power's Settlement Trust* [1951] Ch. 1074.
[82] See *ante*, para 13–024.
[83] s.36(1)(a); such a person will not need to rely on the statutory power where he has been given express power to appoint in the situation which has arisen but only in other situations not expressly envisaged by his power.
[84] s.36(1)(b).
[85] *ibid.*; *Re Shafto's Trusts* (1885) 29 Ch.D. 247.
[86] [1953] Ch. 59.

months, something which justifies compulsory removal from office. When the displaced trustee returned, he applied to the court to upset the appointment on the ground that he had not participated in it. However, Danckwerts J. held that a trustee who is removed compulsorily from the trust is not a "refusing or retiring" trustee but a "removed" trustee; consequently, his participation is not necessary. Trustees who are unfit to act and who are incapable of acting are also "removed" trustees. It is sufficient for the relevant facts to be recited in the document appointing the new trustee although, if the trustee purportedly "removed" challenges those facts, he can of course apply to the court in the way in which the displaced trustee did, in the event unsuccessfully, in *Re Stoneham's Settlement Trusts*.

13–035   Where there are no surviving or continuing trustees and the appointment can instead be made by the personal representative of the last surviving trustee, it is necessary to distinguish between, on the one hand, the power of appointment itself and, on the other hand, the method of proving entitlement to exercise that power. The executor of the last surviving trustee has the power to appoint new trustees as soon as that last trustee dies. Accordingly, it is not necessary for him to obtain a grant of probate before exercising his power to do so.[87] However, a personal representative can only actually prove his entitlement to exercise the power by producing a grant of probate or letters of administration in respect of the estate in question.

13–036   This can cause problems in respect of overseas grants. It is the general practice of the English courts only to recognise grants of probate or letters of administration which have been issued in the United Kingdom or, if issued by a court overseas, have been re-sealed by a court in the United Kingdom. The point arose in *Re Crowhurst Park*.[88] The deceased was the sole trustee of various tenancies of land in England. His widow obtained a grant of probate of his will in Jersey, but she did not obtain a grant in the United Kingdom. The widow executed a deed by which, in her capacity as the personal representative of the deceased, she purported to appoint herself as the new trustee of the trust on which the land was held. It was held that, while she was entitled to exercise the power of appointment, she could only prove that entitlement by a grant of probate or letters of administration granted in the United Kingdom. Accordingly, the widow could not bring proceedings in respect of the tenancies until she had obtained a United Kingdom grant.

13–037   Although the personal representatives of the last surviving trustee may therefore appoint new trustees, this is a mere power and they cannot be compelled to do so.[89] They are, however, given statutory encouragement to exercise their power; even if they intend to renounce their office as personal representatives, they are still entitled to appoint new trustees before they renounce.[90] Without the express statutory provision, the exercise of the power would be sufficient to show an acceptance of the office of personal representative.

13–038   The statutory power makes provision for the appointment of new trustees both in place of an outgoing trustee and as an additional trustee, where all

---

[87] *Re Parker's Trusts* [1894] 1 Ch. 707; *Re Crowhurst Park* [1974] 1 All E.R. 991 at 1001.
[88] [1974] 1 All E.R. 991.
[89] *Re Knight's Will* (1883) 26 Ch.D. 82.
[90] Trustee Act 1925, s.36(5).

the existing trustees are remaining. In both cases the appointment must be made *inter vivos*; it cannot be made by will.[91] The only formal requirement is that it should be made in writing; however, it is in most cases desirable that it should be made by deed.[92]

(a) Using the statutory power to appointing a replacement for an outgoing trustee Where an appointment is being made of a replacement for an outgoing trustee, the section applies in the case of any outgoing trustee, whether or not he was the original trustee of the trust and whether or not he was appointed by the court. The statutory power applies in the following situations: **13–039**

    (i) *Where a trustee is dead.* This includes the situation where a person nominated as a trustee dies without ever having taken up his office. This would be the case, for example, where a person who is nominated as the trustee of a will dies before the death of the testator.

    (ii) *Where a trustee remains out of the United Kingdom for more than 12 months.* The period abroad must be a continuous period and a break for even a very short time, such as a week, will prevent this provision operating.[93] The motive for the absence is irrelevant,[94] so that even if the trustee has been absent because he has been imprisoned abroad, he can still be removed from his trusteeship. In some circumstances, the trust instrument modifies this statutory provision and seeks to achieve the same broad effect by different wording. Where this is done, the provision must be carefully construed but the courts lean towards an interpretation that the period abroad must have an element of permanence. This was satisfied in *Re Earl of Stamford*,[95] where the power arose if a trustee should "be abroad" and a trustee lived in France, making only occasional visits to England.[96] It should also be noted that this the provision is often totally inappropriate where a foreign trust is to be established or where an English trust is to be "exported"[97]; in such cases, it is prudent to provide expressly that a trustee shall not be capable of being replaced merely because he is resident abroad.

    (iii) *Where a trustee desires to be discharged.* This statutory provision is wide enough to include the position where the trustee desires to be discharged from only part of the trust.[98] Thus a trustee might wish to remain a trustee of part of a trust fund which was being set aside

---

[91] See *Re Parker's Trust* [1894] 1 Ch. 707.
[92] So that Trustee Act 1925, s.40 may operate; see *post*, para 13–068.
[93] *Re Walker* [1910] 1 Ch. 259.
[94] *Re Stoneham* [1953] Ch. 59.
[95] [1896] 1 Ch. 288.
[96] See also *Re Moravian Society* (1858) 26 Beav. 101.
[97] See *post*, para 13–050.
[98] If this statutory power is excluded, a trustee cannot be discharged from part only of the fund without the intervention of the court; *Savile v. Couper* (1887) 36 Ch.D. 520; *Re Moss's Trusts* (1888) 37 Ch.D. 513.

to provide a life interest for a beneficiary, while wishing to retire as a trustee of the main fund.

(iv) *Where a trustee refuses to act.* Logically, this provision should apply only to a person who has accepted the trusteeship and refuses to act after accepting office. Until that time, it is difficult to see how he can be said to be a "trustee". However, there is old authority on the predecessor of the section to the effect that its scope also includes a trustee who disclaims.[99]

(v) *Where a trustee is unfit to act.* There is little authority as to the meaning of "unfitness" for the purposes of this provision but it seems clear that "unfitness" here refers not to medical infirmity but to defects of character. In the absence of authority, it is only possible to deduce the meaning of the expression from some of the circumstances in which the court will remove trustees.[100] These cases include conviction of a crime involving dishonesty[101] and, in certain circumstances, bankruptcy. In the case of bankruptcy, the court will generally remove a trustee who has become bankrupt,[102] particularly if the beneficiaries request this to be done, if only on the ground that a person who has lost all his own money ought not to be in charge of other people's money. But as an exception to this, the court has refused to remove a trustee whose bankruptcy was due to misfortune and who was entirely free of moral blame.[103]

(vi) *Where a trustee is incapable of acting.* Incapacity here refers to physical or mental incapacity to attend, or to attend properly, to the administration of the trust.[104] Mental incapacity is defined in the Mental Capacity Act 2005; a person lacks capacity in relation to a matter if it is determined on a balance of probabilities that at the material time he is unable to make a decision for himself in relation to the matter because of an impairment of, or a disturbance in the functioning of his brain, whether permanent or temporary. However, where the trustee in question also has a beneficial interest in possession in the property, no appointment of a new trustee in his place by a surviving or continuing trustee[105] may be made without the consent of the authority having jurisdiction over him under the Mental Capacity Act 2005.[106] A person is also incapable of acting if

---

[99] *Noble v. Meymott* (1841) 14 Beav. 471; *Re Hadley* (1851) 5 De G. & Sm. 67; *Viscountess D'Adhemar v. Bertrand* (1865) 35 Beav. 19; *Re Birchall* (1889) 40 Ch.D. 436.

[100] See *post*, parar 13–084.

[101] *Turner v. Maule* (1850) 15 Jur. 761; *Re Wheeler and De Rochow* [1896] 1 Ch. 315; *Re Sichel's Settlements* [1916] 1 Ch. 358.

[102] *Re Barker's Trusts* (1875) 1 Ch.D. 43.

[103] *Re Bridgman* (1860) 1 Drew. & Sm. 164.

[104] *Re Moravian Society* (1858) 26 Beav. 101; *Re Watt's Settlement* (1872) L.R. 7 Ch. 223; *Turner v. Maule* (1850) 15 Jur. 761; *Re East* (1873) 8 Ch.App. 735; *Re Lemann's Trusts* (1883) 22 Ch.D. 633; *Re Blake* [1887] W.N. 173; *Re Weston's Trusts* [1898] W.N. 151.

[105] Under s.36(1)(b); a person nominated in the trust instrument to do so can still rely on s.36(1)(a).

[106] The current Trustee Act 1925, s.36(9) was substituted by Mental Health Act 1959, ss.149(1), 153 and Sch.VII, which has been subsequently reenacted in Mental Health Act 1983 and Mental Capacity Act 2005.

there is any legislation in force which expressly prohibits persons in specified circumstances from holding property or acting as trustees. Such a prohibition has applied to enemy aliens in time of war.[107]

(vii) *Where a trustee is a minor.* As has been seen,[108] a minor cannot validly be expressly appointed a trustee and the provisions will only apply where the minor is a trustee under a resulting or constructive trust.

(viii) *Where section 36(3) applies.* The statutory power can also be utilised where a corporation which has been acting as a trustee is dissolved.

(b) Using the statutory power to appoint an additional trustee The **13–040** statutory power to appoint additional trustees is contained in section 36(6). This provision only permits the appointment of an additional trustee where there are not more than three existing trustees. Although more than one additional trustee may be appointed at the same time, the section provides that the total number of trustees must not be increased beyond four (this restriction applies to all trusts, not only to trusts affecting land where there is always a limit of four[109]). However, the trust instrument can provide for a higher number,[110] although such a provision is ineffective when the trust affects land. The former rule that additional trustees could not be appointed under this section if any existing trustee was a trust corporation has now been abrogated.[111]

(3) By the beneficiaries

Where the trust instrument does not make any provision for the appoint- **13–041** ment of new trustees,[112] then in two situations the beneficiaries of the trust will have a power of appointment unless it is excluded by the settlor.[113]

The first situation exists alongside the statutory power of appointment **13–042** conferred by section 36 of the Trustee Act 1925. Where all the beneficiaries of the trust are of full age and capacity and between them absolutely entitled

---

[107] *Re Sichel's Settlements* [1916] 1 Ch. 358.

[108] See *ante*, para 13–003.

[109] See *post*, para 13–049.

[110] s.36(6), like all the provisions of the Trustee Act 1925, can be ousted by contrary intention by virtue of s.69(2).

[111] Trusts of Land and Appointment of Trustees Act 1996, Sch.3, para.3(11).

[112] The relevant legislation (Trusts of Land and Appointment of Trustees Act 1996) refers throughout to "trusts created by a disposition" and, although this must presumably include trusts created orally because of the incorporation (by virtue of s.23(2)) of the non-inclusive definition of "disposition" in the Law of Property Act 1925, s.205(1)(ii), the wording of the 1996 legislation does not always fit very easily with trusts so created.

[113] Trusts of Land and Appointment of Trustees Act 1996, s.21(5) provides that the two provisions conferring this power on the beneficiaries (ss.19 and 20) can be excluded by the trust instrument and in practice they generally are so excluded. In respect of trusts created before January 1, 1997, the provisions can be excluded by a deed executed by the settlor (or the survivor of joint settlors) but if this is not done the provisions apply to such trusts (which of course means that they necessarily apply to all trusts created by will before that date).

to the trust property,[114] they have at any time and in any circumstances the power to give a written direction to the existing trustee(s) or, if there are none to the personal representatives of the last surviving trustee, to appoint as trustee(s) whatever person or persons they specify. This is a new power contained in section 19 of the Trusts of Land and Appointment of Trustees Act 1996. It can be coupled with a direction to some or all of the existing trustees to retire[115] and will have to be so coupled if its effect is that the permissible number of trustees[116] is exceeded. It is important to stress that, whereas the power given by section 36 of the Trustee Act 1925 is limited to the circumstances listed in that section, the power given by section 19 of the Trusts of Land and Appointment of Trustees Act 1996 can be exercised whenever the beneficiaries fulfil its sole precondition and as often as they like; where this provision applies, they can therefore completely frustrate the power conferred by the Trustee Act 1925.

13–043   The second situation, however, has not one but a number of preconditions. The beneficiaries must still all be of full age and capacity and between them absolutely entitled to the trust property. But they only have a power of appointment where a trustee is incapable by reason of mental disorder of exercising his functions as such and where, in addition, neither anyone with a power of appointment under the trust instrument nor the surviving trustees nor any personal representative of the last surviving trustee is able and willing to appoint a trustee in his place. If all three of these preconditions are satisfied, then, by virtue of section 20 of the Trusts of Land and the Appointment of Trustees Act 1996, the beneficiaries may give a written direction to an appropriate representative of the incapable trustee (a deputy appointed for the trustee by the Court of Protection, the holder of his enduring power of attorney or lasting power of attorney registered under the Mental Capacity Act 2005 or a person authorised for the purpose by the Court of Protection) to appoint whoever they specify in his place.

(4)   By the court

13–044   If all else fails, new trustees may be appointed by the court. Whenever it is desirable that a new trustee should be appointed and it is "inexpedient, difficult or impracticable so to do without the assistance of the court", the court may appoint a new trustee either as an additional trustee, or in substitution for an existing trustee.[117] The court will not, in the absence of exceptional circumstances, exercise its power if advantage can be taken of a

---

[114] "Absolutely entitled to the trust property" would normally include the beneficiaries of a discretionary trust as a whole. However, "beneficiary" is defined in s.22(1) of the Act as "a person who under the trust has an interest in property subject to the trust". Barraclough & Matthews, *The Trusts of Land and Appointment of Trustees Act 1996* (1997) take the view that, because the House of Lords held, in *Gartside v. I.R.C.* [1968] A.C. 553 that, at least for tax purposes, an object of a discretionary trust has no interest in any part of the property, discretionary beneficiaries may not be able to utilise these powers. However, this decision does not necessarily have any effect other than for tax purposes and so the author of this edition of this work does not agree with this view; the matter obviously awaits judicial resolution.

[115] See *post*, para 13–072.

[116] See *post*, para 13–049.

[117] Trustee Act 1925, s.41. See also *Re Hodson's Settlement* (1851) 9 Hare 118; *Finlay v. Howard* (1842) 2 Dru. & War. 490.

provision in the trust instrument or of the statutory power.[118] Further, there appears to be no reported decision in which the court has appointed a trustee against the wishes of a person who has the power to appoint and who is prepared to exercise it in good faith. This is so even if the court would prefer to see someone else appointed.[119] Where the court proposes to appoint a new trustee in substitution for an existing trustee, it may do so even against the wishes of the existing trustee.[120]

In practice, this power is used mainly in the following circumstances: first, where there is doubt as to whether the statutory power can be exercised, for example, whether a trustee is in fact "unfit" to act; secondly, where there is no person capable of making an appointment; and, thirdly, where it is wished to increase the number of trustees and the statutory power under section 36 of the Trustee Act 1925 does not apply. However, occasionally an application is made to the court for the appointment of a new trustee simply because, if a new trustee is so appointed, it cannot afterwards be alleged that the trustee was appointed in circumstances which were improper or in order to facilitate a breach of trust.[121] The court will, therefore, only exercise its power where it is clearly in the interest of the beneficiaries for it to make the appointment. An example of a case where the court refused to exercise its power is *Re Weston's Settlement*,[122] which is discussed below.[123]   **13–045**

The court has a discretion as to whom it will appoint as a trustee, but the principles upon which this discretion will be exercised are as follows: **13–046**

(i) If the settlor has expressly or by clear implication made known his wishes, the court will have regard to his wishes. This is particularly so if the settlor has indicated whom he does not wish to be appointed.

(ii) A trustee will not be appointed to promote the interest of some of the beneficiaries in opposition to the interest of other beneficiaries.[124] The attitude of the courts has, however, changed over the last century or so in two important respects. First, the courts have gone back on their former practice of not appointing a beneficiary to be a trustee[125]; it has been realised that in some circumstances a person who has a beneficial interest may put a greater effort and enthusiasm into the administration of the trust than someone who does not and that the appointment of such a person as a trustee may be appropriate, particularly where there is also an independent trustee. Secondly, the courts are now much more ready than

---

[118] *Re Gibbon* (1882) 45 L.T. 756, 30 W.R. 287.
[119] *Re Higginbottom* [1892] 3 Ch. 132, see *ante*, p.552; *Re Brockbank* [1948] Ch. 206.
[120] *Re Henderson* [1940] Ch. 764.
[121] See *post*, Chapter 22.
[122] [1969] 1 Ch. 223.
[123] See *post*, para 13–055.
[124] *Re Parsons* [1940] Ch. 973.
[125] For fear that the trustee-beneficiary would be tempted to act more in his own interest than that of the other beneficiaries; see *Re Harrop's Trusts* (1883) 24 Ch.D. 717; *Re Knowles' Settled Estates* (1884) 27 Ch.D. 707.

they formerly were[126] to appoint professional advisers such as a family solicitor as trustees, particularly where this is desired by the beneficiaries; this is in the light of their greater confidence in the integrity of professional advisers and the realisation of the advantage which detailed knowledge of the family circumstances brings, such persons may now be appointed.

(iii) The court will have regard to whether the proposed appointment will promote the execution of the trust, or whether it will impede it.[127]

13–047   An interesting situation arises when the existing trustees have made it known that they will refuse to act with the person whom the court proposes to appoint. On the one hand, the court's dignity is involved. In *Re Tempest*[128] Turner L.J. said:

"I think it would be going too far to say that the court ought, on that ground alone, to refuse to appoint the proposed trustee: for this would, as suggested in the argument, be to give the continuing or surviving trustee a veto upon the appointment of the new trustee. In such a case I think it must be the duty of the court to inquire and ascertain whether the objection of the surviving or continuing trustee is well founded or not, and to act or refuse to act upon it accordingly."

On the other hand, the basic object of the court's power is to promote the interests of the beneficiaries and these interests will not be protected by the existence of serious friction between the trustees. Indeed, on this ground alone the court will sometimes remove a trustee.[129]

13–048   Unless, presumably, a trustee has been guilty of serious malpractice, so that his removal is a matter of urgency, the court is reluctant to appoint new trustees in the place of existing trustees if to do so would place the existing trustees in a worse financial position. In *Re Pauling's Settlement (No.2)*,[130] it was sought to remove trustees against whom an action had been brought for breach of trust.[131] But this was resisted because they might have been able to have impounded the beneficiaries' interests[132] in the event that they were successful in an appeal in the other action. Wilberforce J. held that, even if the existing trustees were removed, they could still exercise their right to impound. As it happened, the court refused to appoint new trustees in the place of the existing trustees, *inter alia* because to have done so would have deprived them of security for the costs which would be payable to them if the appeal were successful.

---

[126] See *Re Kemp's Settled Estates* (1883) 24 Ch.D. 485; *Re Earl of Stamford* [1896] 1 Ch. 288; *Re Spencer's Settled Estates* [1903] 1 Ch. 75.

[127] *Re Tempest* (1866) 1 Ch.App. 485.

[128] (1866) L.R. 1 Ch.App. 485 at 490.

[129] *Re Henderson* [1940] Ch. 764.

[130] [1963] Ch. 576.

[131] This case is discussed at paras 18–016, 22–096.

[132] As to the circumstances in which a beneficiary's interest can be impounded, see *post*, para 22–099.

4. *Restrictions on the Numbers of Trustees*

The general principle is that any number of persons may be trustees; the **13–049** determining factor as to how many there should be is not a legal one but the practical one of having, on the one hand, enough trustees to be able to take advantage of various skills and experience but, on the other hand, not too many to make the working of the trust unwieldy. Nevertheless, there are certain restrictions on the numbers of trustees:

(i) The maximum number of trustees of a trust of land or of a settlement subject to the Settled Land Act 1925 is four, and if more than four persons are named, the first four named who are able and willing to act are the trustees; this is provided by section 34 of the Trustee Act 1925. This limitation does not apply in the case of land held upon trust for charitable, ecclesiastical or public purposes.[133]

(ii) There need only be one trustee to hold land but, unless that trustee is a trust corporation two or more trustees are needed to give a valid receipt for capital money,[134] so that two or more trustees are in fact needed to sell land.

(iii) Where, under a will or an intestacy, property is to be held for an infant and no trustees are appointed by any will, the personal representatives of the deceased may appoint trustees to hold that property on trust for the infant but the number of those trustees must not exceed four.[135] This applies whatever the nature of the property.

(iv) Where an additional trustee is being appointed under the power in section 36 of the Trustee Act 1925 (referred to above) and all the existing trustees are remaining, the section provides that the number of trustees must not be increased to more than four in any case. However, the trust instrument can provide for a higher number,[136] although such a provision is ineffective when the trust affects land.

(v) Where a trustee wishes to retire but it is not proposed to appoint a new trustee in his place, he can only do so if a minimum of two persons or a trust corporation will remain as trustees thereafter; this is provided by section 39 of the Trustee Act 1925.[137]

In any event, a minimum of two trustees is usually desirable, in order to give the beneficiaries adequate protection. One of the basic safeguards for beneficiaries is that property must usually be under the control of at least two

---

[133] Trustee Act 1925, s.34(3).

[134] Trustee Act 1925, s.14(2).

[135] Administration of Estates Act 1925, s.42.

[136] s.36(6), like all the provisions of the Trustee Act 1925, can be ousted by contrary intention by virtue of s.69(2).

[137] As amended by Trusts of Land and Appointment of Trustees Act 1996, Sch.3, para.3(13). See *post*, para 13–075

persons, so that it is very much more difficult for one to misappropriate the money.

5. When may Non-Resident Trustees be Appointed?

13–050 There are a number of jurisdictions where trusts are not taxed at all (these are all off-shore jurisdictions) or are subject to a lower rate of tax than in the United Kingdom. Sometimes, in order to pay less tax and/or for other reasons,[138] trustees or more usually the settlor or the beneficiaries, wish to export a trust whose applicable law[139] is English law from England and Wales.[140] As will be seen in the chapter on the taxation of trusts, a pre-condition of the avoidance of United Kingdom tax is for the majority of the trustees of the trust in question to become resident outside the United Kingdom. In principle, and very much in theory, the existing trustees (or one or more of them) could themselves simply emigrate. This is obviously possible where the existing trustees include the settlor and/or the bene-ficiaries but is almost inconceivable in the case of professional trustees and corporate trustees could not emigrate even if they wanted to. In practice, therefore, it is almost inevitable that it will be necessary to replace at least some of the existing resident trustees by non-resident trustees. Superficially, this process appears quite straightforward. Whoever has the power to appoint new trustees to the trust in question can simply appoint new non-resident trustees in place of the existing trustees, who can then retire, with the trust property being simultaneously transferred to the new trustees or being left to vest in them automatically. Unfortunately, however, this appar-ently straightforward process is not always as simple as it seems.

---

[138] They may also wish to do so in order to take advantage of what are perceived as the more favourable provisions of the trust law of some other jurisdiction, such as a longer accumulation period,, or simply a wish to have the trust property administered in accordance with the trust law of the jurisdiction where it or the administration of the trust is to be situated. However, in these cases, the exporting of the trust will also have to be accompanied by a change in its applicable law to the law of the new jurisdiction. will require either the existence of a provision in the trust instrument expressly permitting this, or the agreement of all the beneficiaries which, if any of the beneficiaries is not *sui juris*, will require an order of the court under the Variation of Trusts Act 1958 (see *post*, para 21–018).

[139] See *post*, para.23–039.

[140] There is nothing to stop a trust whose applicable law and/or place of administration is already that of an off-shore jurisdiction from being exported to another off-shore jurisdiction. This is unlikely to have any fiscal consequences so there are only likely to be two possible reasons for this, either in order to take advantage of new or more favourable rules of trust law created in that other jurisdiction or because of anxieties about the stability of the existing off-shore jurisdiction. Trusts in some off-shore jurisdictions habitually contain what are known as "flee clauses", change of applicable law clauses which are drafted in such a way that they operate automatically, that is to say, without the trustees needing to take any action, in the event of certain things happening. When such a clause is triggered, the applicable law and also the site where the trust is being administered, if different, are automatically changed to that of another jurisdiction and trustees from that jurisdiction are automatically appointed in place of the pre-existing trustees. Some of the triggering events are of a political nature, such as the election of an unfriendly government (which obviously has to be defined) or a *coup d'état*. Other types of flee clauses attempt to oust the jurisdiction of the courts of the applicable law by providing for any attempt by the courts of that jurisdiction to assert control over the affairs of the trust to be a triggering event. It is questionable whether the latter type of flee clauses work and whether any type of flee clause is valid; see McCall [1995] P.C.B. 419.

There are no statutory provisions referring specifically to the appointment   **13–051**
of non-resident, as distinct from resident, trustees, probably because the
possibility would not even have occurred to anyone until the middle of the
nineteenth century and certainly did not become at all common until long
after the Trustee Act 1925 was enacted. Such rules as have been developed
have therefore had to be developed by the courts. However, the courts
undoubtedly have power to appoint non-resident trustees of a settlement
which is to be exported from England and Wales[141] and also have power to
approve an arrangement under the Variation of Trusts Act 1958 by which
non-resident trustees are appointed and the trust is consequently
exported.[142] These powers will be exercised if the court considers that such
an appointment is in the interest of the beneficiaries.

It will usually be in the interest of the beneficiaries for the trust to be   **13–052**
administered and for the trustees to be resident in the same territory as that
in which the beneficiaries, or a majority of them, reside. *Re Seale's Marriage
Settlement*[143] was concerned with a marriage settlement made in 1931 at a
time when the husband and wife were domiciled in England. The husband
and wife subsequently emigrated to Canada with their children and at the
date of the hearing in 1961 had been living in Canada for some years and
were domiciled there. Buckley J. found as a fact that they intended to
continue to reside there. They wanted to export the trust to Quebec in two
stages: first, by the appointment of a Canadian trust corporation as trustee
of the marriage settlement with the consequential discharge of the English
trustees; and, secondly, by the property subject to the marriage settlement
being transferred to the Canadian corporation as trustee of a new Quebec
settlement. The new settlement followed as closely as possible the terms of
the English settlement but could not include certain protective life interests
which were not recognised by the law of Quebec. Buckley J. was satisfied
that it was to the advantage of all the beneficiaries for the settlement to be
exported and he approved the arrangements. This decision was followed in
Re Windeatt's Will Trusts.[144] The testator, who died domiciled in England,
created a will trust for the benefit principally of his daughter and her
children. The daughter and her children had lived in Jersey for 19 years
prior to the application and were held to be permanently resident there.
Pennycuick J. approved an arrangement for two Jersey residents to be
appointed as trustees and for the trust assets to be transferred to them.

In certain circumstances it will also be in the interests of the beneficiaries   **13–053**
for non-resident trustees to be appointed even if the beneficiaries are resident in a jurisdiction different from that in which the trustees are resident.
It may be in the interests of the beneficiaries for the trust to be exported from
the United Kingdom so that it may cease to be liable to United Kingdom
taxation but not appropriate for the trust to be exported to the jurisdiction
in which the beneficiaries are resident if that jurisdiction does not recognise,
or is not fully acquainted with, the concept of a trust; in such circumstances,

---

[141] *Meinertzhagen v. Davis* (1844) 1 Coll.N.C. 355; *Re Long's Settlement* (1869) 17 W.R. 218; *Re Seale's Marriage Settlement* [1961] Ch. 574; *Re Whitehead's Will Trusts* [1971] 1 W.L.R. 833.
[142] *Re Seale's Marriage Settlement* [1961] Ch. 574; *Re Windeatt's Will Trusts* [1969] 1 W.L.R. 692; *Re Whitehead's Will Trusts* [1971] 1 W.L.R. 833.
[143] [1961] Ch. 574.
[144] [1969] 1 W.L.R. 692.

it may clearly be appropriate for the trust to be exported to a territory which does recognise trusts. In *Re Chamberlain*[145] some of the beneficiaries of a trust subject to English law were resident in France and the others were resident in Indonesia; neither of these jurisdictions recognised trusts and so the court approved an arrangement to export the trust to Guernsey by the appointment of trustees resident there.

13–054   On the other hand, the court will not approve the appointment of non-resident trustees if they are resident in a territory which may be reluctant to enforce the trust. If all the trustees are non-resident and the assets are situated abroad, the court will be incapable of protecting the beneficiaries and it will, therefore, wish to be satisfied that, in the case of any maladministration, the beneficiaries will be given protection by the local law. This was a factor which influenced the Court of Appeal in *Re Weston's Settlement*[146] to refuse to appoint non-resident trustees, although, as will be seen later on, this was not the principal reason for their decision. The basis of this conclusion was the fact that at that time there was no equivalent of the Trustee Act 1925 in Jersey and no inter vivos settlement had ever had to be enforced by the courts of Jersey. While this general principle is unquestionably sound, the particular objection to Jersey appears to have been misconceived and Pennycuick J. subsequently approved the exportation of trusts to Jersey in both *Re Windeatt's Will Trusts*[147] and *Re Whitehead's Will Trusts*.[148] It should be added that comprehensive trust legislation was enacted in Jersey in 1984.[149]

13–055   Whether the court will approve exportation where the beneficiaries are all resident in England and the principal purpose is the mitigation of fiscal liabilities is much less clear. In principle, in view of the attitude which the court has taken in the case of applications to mitigate such liabilities in other circumstances,[150] there should be no insuperable objection to the export of a trust in these circumstances. However, some doubts were cast on this conclusion by the decision in *Re Weston's Settlements*,[151] where there were admittedly three different grounds on which approval was denied.

13–056   The settlor had in 1964 transferred a total of 500,000 shares in The Stanley Weston Group to the trustees of two settlements for the benefit of his two sons. In the very next year, the legislature introduced, for the first time, a capital gains tax, something which neither the settlor nor his advisers had anticipated. The shares rose in value and, by the time of the hearing at first instance in 1968, they were pregnant with a liability to capital gains tax of £163,000. The settlor lived in England until 1967. Having in the first half of that year made three visits of a few days each to Jersey, he then purchased a house there, in which he lived from August 1967. In November 1967 an application was made to the court for the appointment as trustees of the two settlements of two professional men in Jersey of impeccable standing and

---

[145] [1976] N.L.J. 1934.
[146] [1969] 1 Ch. 223, discussed in detail *post, infra*.
[147] [1969] 1 W.L.R. 692; see *ante*, para 13–052.
[148] [1971] 1 W.L.R. 833; see *post*, para 13–059.
[149] Trusts (Jersey) Law 1984.
[150] See for example, *Pilkington v. I.R.C.* [1964] A.C. 612, *ante*, p.703 and decisions on the Variation of Trusts Act 1958, *post*, para 21–018.
[151] [1969] 1 Ch. 223; see also *post*, para 21–018.

the approval of an arrangement under which the property subject to the settlements could be transferred to settlements in identical terms subject to the law of Jersey. It was hoped that the property subject to the settlements would thereby avoid capital gains tax[152] and also estate duty.[153]

Both Stamp J. and the Court of Appeal refused to sanction the arrangement. They were influenced by two main factors.[154] First, there was clearly some doubt whether the settlor and his children, the main beneficiaries, would live in Jersey permanently, particularly as they had only been there for a few months prior to the date of the hearing; that was insufficient to show any settled intention to remain and the court was clearly worried about the possibility that, following the approval of the arrangement and a sale of the shares free of capital gains tax, the beneficiaries would return to England.[155] Secondly, as has already been mentioned in a previous chapter,[156] this was, according to Stamp J., "a cheap exercise in tax avoidance" which ought not to be sanctioned,[157] a view also taken in the Court of Appeal by Harman L.J., who described it as "an essay in tax avoidance naked and unashamed".[158]

13–057

It is, frankly, somewhat surprising that this seems to have disturbed the court in the light of the fact that numerous applications under the Variation of Trusts Act 1958 have had as their main, if not their only, motive the minimisation of fiscal liabilities.[159] It is impossible to avoid wondering whether the court was influenced by the feeling that the settlor, who was the son of a Russian immigrant who had built up his fortune in England during the 1939–45 war, should not be permitted to escape the tax liabilities to which he would normally have been subject. With the benefit of hindsight, it seems that the trustees were unfortunately advised and that the arrangement would have been approved if it had been made a few years later, when it could have been shown that the beneficiaries had genuinely settled in Jersey. However, in Re Windeatt's Will Trusts[160] Pennycuick J. expressed himself to be "in the most complete agreement" with the decision in Re Weston's Settlements and in Richard v. MacKay[161] Millett J. said that the court was unlikely to appoint non-resident trustees "where the scheme is nothing more than a device to avoid tax and has no advantages of any kind". However, since neither of these decisions involved any tax avoidance whatever, it remains to be seen what view is adopted when the question actually has to be decided; facts such as those in Re Weston's Settlements are obviously unlikely to recur. Provided that the scheme is not entirely motivated by tax avoidance, the practical answer for trustees in this position is probably to make the appointment themselves, assuming of course that they have

13–058

---

[152] Today the exportation of the trust would give rise to a liability to capital gains tax anyway; see post, para 15–160.

[153] Now replaced by inheritance tax.

[154] A third one, whether the courts of Jersey would enforce the trust, has already been considered; see ante, para 13–054.

[155] [1969] 1 Ch. 223 at 245, 246, per Lord Denning M.R.

[156] See ante, para 21–018.

[157] [1969] 1 Ch. 223 at 234.

[158] ibid., at 246.

[159] See post, para 21–018.

[160] [1969] 1 W.L.R. 692 at 696.

[161] (1987) unreported; see (1997) 11 Trust Law International 22 and post, para 13–061.

power to do so, in the way envisaged in *Re Beatty (deceased) (No.2)*,[162] which is discussed below.[163]

13–059   The authorities considered so far have concerned the question of when the courts will appoint non-resident trustees. It is now necessary to consider whether, and if so when, resident trustees who have adequate powers for the purpose under the trust instrument or the Trustee Act 1925 can themselves do so. It has long been clear that, where the court would itself be prepared to appoint non-resident trustees, resident trustees with the power to do so can make an effective appointment without the intervention of the court. In *Re Whitehead's Will Trusts*,[164] the main beneficiary had emigrated to Jersey in 1959 and was found to be permanently resident there.[165] In 1969 the trustees, who were resident in the United Kingdom, executed a deed under section 36 of the Trustee Act 1925 appointing persons resident in Jersey as new trustees and retiring from the trusts. But since the resident trustees wished to be fully protected, the deed of retirement and appointment was made conditional upon the principal beneficiary obtaining from the court a declaration that the resident trustees were effectively discharged. Pennycuick V.-C. duly made the declaration sought.

13–060   However, two further questions arise: first, are the trustees only protected if a declaration of this sort is obtained; and, secondly, can the trustees also exercise their own powers in circumstances where the courts would not themselves appoint non-resident trustees? In *Re Whitehead's Will Trusts*,[166] where a declaration was of course obtained, Pennycuick V.-C. said[167]:

"the law has been quite well established for upwards of a century that there is no absolute bar to the appointment of persons resident abroad as trustees of an English trust. I say 'no absolute bar', in the sense that such an appointment would be prohibited by law and would consequently be invalid. On the other hand, apart from exceptional circumstances, it is not proper to make such an appointment, that is to say, the court would not, apart from exceptional circumstances, make such an appointment, nor would it be right for the donees of the power to make such an appointment out of court. If they did, presumably the court would be likely to interfere at the instance of the beneficiaries. There do, however, exist exceptional circumstances in which such an appointment can properly be made. The most obvious exceptional circumstances are those [which actually occurred in that case] in which the beneficiaries have settled permanently in some country outside the United Kingdom and what is proposed to be done is to appoint new trustees in that country."

13–061   However, this view has subsequently been rejected in two unreported decisions. In *Richard v. MacKay*,[168] trustees sought a declaration that they were entitled to exercise a power undoubtedly vested in them to transfer

---

[162] (1991) unreported; see (1997) 11 Trust Law International 7.
[163] See *post*, para 13–061.
[164] [1971] 1 W.L.R. 833.
[165] *ibid.*, at 838.
[166] [1971] 1 W.L.R. 833.
[167] *ibid.*, at 837.
[168] (1987) unreported; see (1997) 11 Trust Law International 22.

about a quarter of the assets of a trust for the benefit of the settlor's children to a new trust which the settlor proposed to create in Bermuda. The settlor, his Malaysian wife, and the children were all resident in the United Kingdom but they had substantial contacts with the Far East both of a financial and of a family nature and there was a real possibility that the children, and indeed their mother in the event of early widowhood, would decide to settle in the Far East. The trust's assets were invested all over the world and the principal motive was flexibility and diversification rather than any immediate tax advantage. Millett J. referred to the observations of Pennycuick V.-C. set out above and said:

"In my judgment, the language of Sir John Pennycuick, which is narrowly drawn, is too restrictive for the circumstances of the present day if, at least, it is intended to lay down any rule of practice. Nor, in my view, is it accurate to equate the approach that the court adopts in the exercise of its own discretion with the approach which it adopts when asked to authorise the trustees to exercise theirs.

Where the court is invited to exercise an original discretion of its own, . . . the court will require to be satisfied that the discretion should be exercised in the manner proposed. The applicants must make out a positive case for the exercise of the discretion, and the court is unlikely to assist them where the scheme is nothing more than a device to avoid tax and has no advantages of any kind.

Where, however, the transaction is proposed to be carried out by the trustees in exercise of their own discretion, entirely out of court, the trustees retaining their discretion and merely seeking the authorisation of the court for their own protection, then, in my judgment, the question that the court asks itself is quite different. It is concerned to ensure that the proposed exercise of the trustees' power is lawful and within the power and that it does not infringe the trustees' duty to act as ordinary, reasonable and prudent trustees might act, but it requires only to be satisfied that the trustees can properly form the view that the proposed transaction is for the benefit of beneficiaries or the trust estate.

. . . In my judgment, where the trustees retain their discretion, as they do in the present case, the court should need to be satisfied only that the proposed transaction is not so inappropriate that no reasonable trustee could entertain it."

He therefore made the declaration sought. His views were subsequently approved and applied by Vinelott J. in another unreported case, *Re Beatty (deceased) (No.2)*,[169] where a similar declaration was sought by the trustees of the will of a testatrix who had died domiciled and resident in the United Kingdom; they wished to appoint replacement trustees resident in Jersey and transfer to them an absolutely enormous residuary estate, held in more or less equal shares for one resident beneficiary, one non-resident beneficiary, and one beneficiary who was about to become non-resident, in order to

---

[169] (1991) unreported; see (1997) 11 Trust Law International 7.

avoid a liability to capital gains tax which would arise when the latter two obtained interests in possession.[170]

13–062   Trustees can, therefore, certainly exercise their own powers to appoint non-resident trustees in circumstances where the courts would not themselves do so provided that the proposed transaction is not so inappropriate that no reasonable trustee could entertain it. Given that this is now clearly the law, there cannot possibly be any formal need for the trustees to go to the court for a declaration in every case, although they might well feel that it was prudent for them to do so in a case with facts as extreme as those in *Re Weston's Settlements!*[171] However, where they do not seek a declaration, they may be well-advised to seek adequate indemnities from the non-resident trustees or the beneficiaries, particularly if only part rather than the whole of the trust in question is being exported.[172]

6. *Actions which Trustees should Carry Out on their Appointment*

(A)   Disclosure Prior to Appointment

13–063   It has already been seen in that a trustee should not, except with the express consent of the person setting up the trust or of all the beneficiaries, put himself in a position in which his own interests might conflict with his duties of impartiality as a trustee. As a result of this rule, it has been decided that a person who is asked to become a trustee ought before being appointed to disclose any circumstances unknown to the persons appointing him which might bring his interest and duty into conflict. In *Peyton v. Robinson,*[173] a beneficiary under a trust was indebted to the trustee personally but this fact was not known to the settlor. The terms of the trust instrument gave the trustee a discretion to make payments to this beneficiary. In exercise of this discretion, the trustee made payments; however, it was held that he could not accept repayment of his debt from the amount paid to the beneficiary. The trustee was placed in a position where his interest, to pay trust money to the beneficiary with a view to being repaid his debt, conflicted with his duty, to exercise his discretion entirely without thought for his own personal advantage.

(B)   Following Appointment

13–064   When a person accepts a trusteeship, he should do four things: first, acquaint himself with the terms of the trust; secondly, inspect the trust instrument and any other trust deeds; thirdly, procure that all the property subject to the trust is vested in the joint names of himself and his co-trustees and that all title deeds are placed under their joint control; and, fourthly, in

---

[170] Fortunately for the beneficiaries, judgment in this case was given just 19 days before the law was changed to make the exportation itself give rise to a liability to capital gains tax.

[171] [1969] 1 Ch. 223.

[172] In certain circumstances the tax legislation will treat the trustees of both the exported and the non-exported parts of the trustee as together constituting and acting on behalf of a single body of trustees, in which case the trustees who remain resident may find themselves liable to pay tax which is due on the assets which have been exported; see *Roome v. Edwards* [1981] 1 All E.R. 736.

[173] (1823) 1 L.J. (O.S.) Ch. 191.

the case of an appointment as a new trustee of an existing trust, to investigate any suspicious circumstances which indicate a prior breach of trust, and to take action to recoup the trust fund if any breach has in fact taken place. If he fails to do these things, he may make himself liable to the beneficiaries in an action for breach of trust.

(1) Acquainting himself with the terms of the trust

The first duty of a trustee on appointment is to ensure that he knows and understands the terms of the trust instrument because, as is explained elsewhere,[174] if a trustee pays money to a wrong beneficiary, or pays the right beneficiary too little money, or departs in any other way without authority from the terms of the trust instrument, he thereby commits a breach of trust, however honestly he may act. Admittedly, in certain circumstances he may apply to the court for relief from liability[175]; however, even if the court grants total or partial relief, that will not alter the fact that he has committed a breach of trust. In *Nestlé v. National Westminster Bank*[176] the trustee bank had doubts as to the precise nature of its investment powers. The Court of Appeal described these doubts as "understandable" but held that it was "inexcusable that the bank took no step at any time to obtain legal advice as to the scope of its powers"[177] (in fact, however, the plaintiff beneficiary was unable to show that she had suffered any loss thereby so no liability was actually imposed.)

13–065

(2) Inspection of the trust documents

The second duty of a trustee on appointment is to inspect the trust instrument in order to ascertain whether any notices have previously been given to the trustees of dealings by beneficiaries with their interests in the trust fund. A beneficiary who has a fixed beneficial interest under a trust is usually entitled to sell, mortgage, give away or in some other manner deal with his interest in the trust fund, just as he may deal with any other property. As far as the trustees are concerned, this disposition is complete when the assignee gives notice of the disposition to the trustees.[178] Once such notice has been given, the trustees must pay to the assignee the trust money to which the beneficiary named in the trust instrument would otherwise have been entitled. If a memorandum of the transaction is endorsed on the trust instrument, this is sufficient to give the persons who are the trustees for the time being notice of the dealing by the beneficiary with his equitable interest.[179] Furthermore, if a beneficiary should attempt to assign or charge his interest more than once, the assignee or chargee who is the first to give notice of the dealing to the trustees takes priority.[180] If, therefore, a newly appointed trustee finds on inspection of the trust instrument more than one notice of assignment, he must ascertain carefully the order in which such notices were received.

13–066

---

[174] See *post*, para 22–015.
[175] Under Trustee Act 1925, s.61, discussed *post*, para 22–088.
[176] [1993] 1 W.L.R. 1260.
[177] *ibid.*, at 1265, per Dillon L.J.
[178] By virtue of the rule in *Dearle v. Hall* (1828) 3 Russ. 1.
[179] Law of Property Act 1925, s.137.
[180] *Dearle v. Hall* (1828) 3 Russ. 1.

(3) Placing the trust property under joint control

13–067   The third duty of a trustee on appointment is to ensure that all the trust property is placed in the joint names of himself and his co-trustees. As soon as he is appointed he becomes responsible with his co-trustees for what happens to the trust property, and if he negligently allows property to remain in the names of others and loss occurs, he may be liable to make good the loss to the beneficiaries out of his own pocket.[181] The property may be placed in the name of the new trustee, jointly with the continuing trustees, by the mode of transfer appropriate to the type of property.[182] The appropriate mode of transfer in respect of the major types of property is:

(a)	unregistered freehold land	conveyance
(b)	unregistered leasehold land	assignment
(c)	registered freehold or leasehold land	transfer and subsequent registration of the transfer at the Land Registry
(d)	bearer stocks and shares	delivery (these will generally already be held by a custodian[183] in which case no action will be necessary)
(e)	other stocks and shares	transfer and subsequent registration of the transfer by the company or authority concerned
(f)	debts and other choses in action	assignment (plus notice to the other party in order to secure priority)
(g)	indorsable negotiable instruments payable to bearer	delivery and indorsement
(h)	personal chattels	either assignment or physical delivery

13–068   However, these formalities can sometimes be avoided by virtue of section 40 of the Trustee Act 1925, when a person is appointed a new trustee, or retires from trusteeship, and the appointment or retirement, as the case may be, is effected by deed (the section does not, however, apply where property is held by a personal representative[184] because, in this case, there is not an existing trust). Section 40 provides that, unless the deed contains a provision to the contrary, it automatically vests the trust property in the new or remaining trustees as joint tenants. The section applies to all types of trust property with the following exceptions: first, mortgages of land, when a

---

[181] See *post*, para 22–015.

[182] The use of the appropriate mode of transfer is also discussed in connection with whether a trust is completely constituted; see *ante*, para 5–007.

[183] Where the trust property includes bearer securities, the trustees are obliged by Trustee Act 2000, s.18 to appoint a custodian to hold them unless the trust already has a custodian or they are exempted from complying with this requirement by the trust instrument or by any statutory provision.

[184] See *ante*, para 1–060.

formal transfer of mortgage is required; secondly, leasehold land where the lease provides that before any assignment the permission of the landlord must be obtained and the landlord's permission has not been obtained before the deed of appointment or retirement has been executed (the reason for this exception is to prevent an unwitting breach of covenant under the lease, so giving rise to a possible claim for forfeiture); thirdly, stocks and shares, where a formal transfer has to be registered by the company; and fourthly, registered land, in respect of which, although no transfer is actually necessary,[185] the deed of appointment or retirement has to be registered so that the proprietorship register is brought up to date. The first three of these exceptions arise by virtue of section 40(4) of the Trustee Act 1925 and the fourth arises by virtue of section 27 of the Land Registration Act 2002.

Further, section 40 of the Trustee Act 1925 obviously cannot apply to **13–069** "bearer" securities, in respect of which difficulties sometimes arise. "Bearer" securities are issued securities which are not registered in the name of anyone. The issuing company pays dividends to whoever at the time when the dividend is payable is able to produce to the company the bearer certificate, or any coupons attached to it. By definition bearer securities cannot be placed in the names of the trustees. However, section 18 of the Trustee Act 2000 provides that the trustees must appoint a custodian of any bearer securities unless the trust already has a custodian or they are exempted from complying with this requirement by the trust instrument or by any statutory provision. Prior to this Act, trustees were obliged to deposit bearer securities with a bank[186] and, in *Lewis v. Nobbs*,[187] where one trustee allowed bearer securities to remain in the hands of his co-trustee, who misappropriated them, it was held that the trustee was guilty of a breach of trust for having allowed the securities to remain under the control of the other so that they could be so misappropriated. Even today, all title deeds to trust property should be deposited with a bank or agent to be held to the order of all trustees.

Finally, where a trustee has been removed and replaced under section **13–070** 36(1) of the Trustee Act 1925,[188] he does not need and will not normally be able to join in the document by which his replacement is appointed. In these circumstances, where section 40 of the Trustee Act 1925 does not operate to vest the trust property in his replacement, there will be no document of transfer or assignment signed by the removed trustee either. In such circumstances, it will be necessary for the trustees to apply to the court for a vesting order under sections 44–56 of the Trustee Act 1925; the most relevant sections are section 44, which applies to land, and section 51 which applies to stock and choses in action. The court can also, and when necessary will, make such orders itself when appointing new trustees.

---

[185] Although this is formally the case, for practical purposes a transfer is desirable since, if one is not executed, the Land Registry may insist on retaining the deed of appointment or retirement, or at the very least on being supplied with a certified copy of it.

[186] Trustee Act 1925, s.7.

[187] (1878) 8 Ch.D. 591.

[188] See *post*, para 13–083.

(4) Investigating previous breaches of trust

13–071   The final duty of a trustee on appointment is to consider the possibility that there may have been previous breaches of trust. A new trustee is not expected to act like a bloodhound straining to sniff out some breach of trust; in the absence of suspicious circumstances he may assume that the previous trustees have properly discharged their duties.[189] But the new trustee must inquire into any circumstances which might suggest that a breach of trust has been committed; if, as a result of the fact that he has not inquired into such circumstances, and the trust fund suffers loss, he may find himself liable. In such circumstances, he will be liable not because he participated in the original breach of trust but because he himself has committed a breach of trust in not making sufficient inquiry.[190] The most obvious circumstances which would put a new trustee on inquiry is if the trust fund is materially less at the time of his appointment than it was at some previous point of time. There may be many bona fide explanations of this but the new trustee must inquire and, if appropriate, take action.

III. THE RETIREMENT OF TRUSTEES

1. *The Circumstances in which Trustees Must Retire*

13–072   A trustee must retire from his office if the beneficiaries are able to give him and do give him a direction so to do under section 19 of the Trusts of Land and Appointment 1996. Where a trust instrument does not make any provision for the appointment of new trustees and all the beneficiaries of the trust are of full age and capacity and between them absolutely entitled to the trust property,[191] then, unless their power so to do has been excluded by the settlor,[192] the beneficiaries have at any time and in any circumstances the power to give a written direction to any existing trustee requiring him to retire. However, he is only obliged to execute the necessary deed of retirement if three further conditions are satisfied: first, there will be a sufficient number of trustees left thereafter[193]; secondly, either a replacement is to be appointed[194] or the continuing trustees consent; and, thirdly, "reasonable arrangements have been made for the protection of any rights of his in connection with the trust".[195]

---

[189] *Re Straham* (1856) 8 De G.M. & G. 291.

[190] *Harvey v. Olliver* (1887) 57 L.T. 239.

[191] See *ante*, n.114.

[192] See *ante*, n.113.

[193] Two persons or a trust corporation.

[194] Such a trustee will obviously normally be appointed by the beneficiaries, also pursuant to Trusts of Land and Appointment of Trustees Act 1996, s.19; see *ante*, para 13–041. However, this is not actually necessary so the replacement trustee could equally be appointed by whoever has the statutory power of appointment under Trustee Act 1925, s.36.

[195] It is not entirely clear what this means. The "reasonable arrangements" can hardly be intended to replace the indemnity and the lien on the trust property which Trustee Act 1925, s.30(2) confers on any retiring trustee (see *post*, para 14–118); therefore this presumably enables a trustee who is forced to retire to claim more security than he would otherwise have been able to.

2. *The Circumstances in Which Trustees May Retire*

A trustee may retire from his office in any of four ways: **13–073**

    (i) by taking advantage of any power in the trust instrument;

    (ii) by taking advantage of the powers in the Trustee Act 1925, namely

        (a) section 36, where a new trustee is being appointed in his place[196]; or

        (b) section 39, where no new trustee is being appointed;

    (iii) by obtaining the consent of the beneficiaries, all of whom must be *sui juris* and between them absolutely entitled to the whole beneficial interest; or

    (iv) by obtaining the consent of the court.

If the trust instrument makes provision for a trustee to retire, then a   **13–074**
trustee can take advantage of this power, even though it is wider than the statutory power. In fact, however, the statutory power in sections 36 and 39 of the Trustee Act 1925 is so wide that specific provisions are not now normally included in trust instruments. Retirement under section 36 when this is coupled with the appointment of a new trustee has already been considered but under section 39 a trustee can retire even where no new trustee is being appointed in his place. There are two important differences between the two sections: first, as indicated above, a valid retirement under section 36 requires the appointment of a new trustee in place of each retiring trustee[197] but is not necessary when a trustee retires under section 39; and, secondly, under section 36 a trustee can retire from part only of the trusts whereas under section 39 the trustee can retire only from the whole of the trusts.

Under section 39,[198] a trustee may retire if: **13–075**

    (i) after his retirement there will remain as trustees a minimum of two persons[199] or a trust corporation (this requirement applies to all trusts and has nothing whatever to do with the rule is independent of the fact that at least two trustees or a trust corporation are necessary in order for a valid receipt to be given for capital payments arising under a trust of land or a settlement under the Settled Land Act 1925[200]);

---

[196] For a valid retirement under s.36, one new trustee must be appointed in place of each trustee who retires; however, this is not necessary when a trustee retires under s.39.

[197] *Adam & Co. International Trustees v. Theodore Goddard* [2000] W.T.L.R. 349, criticized by Barlow [2003] Conv. 15.

[198] As amended by Trusts of Land and Appointment of Trustees Act 1996, Sch.3, para.3(13).

[199] Since 1996, it no longer matters whether these trustees are natural persons or corporations. Until 1997, they had to be natural persons, a provision whose impact was frequently overlooked with potentially disastrous consequences for the trustee who thought that he had retired.

[200] See *ante*, para 13–010.

(ii) the trustee obtains the consent to his retirement of the remaining trustees;

(iii) the trustee obtains the consent of anyone named in the trust instrument as having the power to appoint new trustees;

(iv) the retirement is formalised by deed; but

(v) none of these conditions applies if one of the remaining trustees is the Public Trustee.[201]

Provided the conditions of section 39 are fulfilled, the retirement will be effective; however, if the trustee has retired in order to procure or facilitate a breach of trust, he may nevertheless remain liable for any such breach.[202]

13–076   In the last resort, if none of these situations applies, a trustee may apply to the court to be discharged as a trustee. The court will usually discharge a trustee provided that there is at least one other trustee who continues or some suitable new trustee can be found; however, the trustee who wishes to retire will usually be ordered to pay the costs of the application unless he can show that the circumstances have materially altered since he accepted the trusteeship.[203]

13–077   Whether these conditions can be overridden by the express provisions of the settlement is not entirely clear. It is questionable as a matter of principle whether a statutory power of this type should be able to be ousted, a view which appeared to be confirmed by Warner J. in *Mettoy Pension Trustees v. Evans*[204] when he stated that there was a doubt as to whether the purported retirement of two individual trustees had left the remaining trustee company as sole trustee of the scheme. However, in *L.R.T. Pension Trust Co. v. Hatt*[205] Knox J. in effect decided that it was possible to exclude the now abrogated requirement for either two individuals or a trust corporation to continue as trustees[206]; although his specific decision is no longer of any relevance, his approach must constitute the law at present. It remains to be seen which of the two approaches will be adopted in future decisions.

13–078   There is, however, no doubt at all that a retirement which does not comply with these requirements is invalid and that the trustee in question will consequently remain in office.[207] Any decisions to make appointments and exercise discretions made by the other trustees following the supposed retirement will be ineffective because the trustee who was wrongly thought to have retired will not have joined in those decisions. This is capable of

---

[201] Public Trustee Act 1906, s.6.

[202] See *post*, para 22–006.

[203] The court has expressed its disapproval of applications being made to the court for the appointment of a new trustee where advantage could be taken of the statutory power, and doubtless it would be equally disapproving if applications were made to it for retirement when advantage could be taken of the statutory power.

[204] [1990] 1 W.L.R. 1587 at 1607; see Jacobs (1986) 1 Trust Law & Practice 95.

[205] [1993] P.L.R. 227.

[206] As a result of Trusts of Land and Appointment of Trustees Act 1996, Sch.3, para.3(13), the requirement is now only for two "persons" or a trust corporation.

[207] *Mettoy Pension Trustees v. Evans* [1990] 1 W.L.R. 1587; *Adam & Co. International Trustees v. Theodore Goddard* [2000] W.T.L.R. 349.

causing total havoc because the transfer of any property pursuant to the decisions will have been ineffective and therefore a potential breach of trust, while actions which were intended to be tax efficient will not have had the desired effect.[208] Further, the trustee who has not in fact retired will remain jointly and severally liable for any breaches of trust committed by the other trustees.

3. *Release of Retiring Trustees*

When trustees retire, they sometimes request a formal release from any liability which may have arisen during their trusteeship. If trustees retire in favour of new trustees, they are not entitled to such a release from their successors unless the trust instrument contains a provision which enables this to be granted, something which trusts instruments prepared in most off-shore jurisdictions habitually do. However, it seems that, when a trust is being wound-up at the request of the beneficiaries, its retiring trustees are entitled to such a release.[209] Either way, however, a release is only effective to the extent that the beneficiaries are in possession of all the relevant facts at the time when it is executed.   **13–079**

IV. THE REMOVAL OF TRUSTEES

1. *When may a Trustee be Removed from Office*

A trustee may be removed from his office: **13–080**

    (i) in effect, as a result of the beneficiaries directing him to retire under section 19 of the Trusts of Land and Appointment of Trustees Act 1996;

    (ii) under a power contained in the trust instrument;

    (ii) under the statutory power contained in section 36 of the Trustee Act 1925; or

    (iv) by the court.

The circumstances in which the beneficiaries can direct a trustee to retire under section 19 of the Trusts of Land and Appointment of Trustees Act 1996 have already been considered; although such a direction will have the effect of removing the trustee in question, he will technically have retired rather than been removed.   **13–081**

Powers of removing trustees contained in the trust instrument are strictly construed; consequently, if it is desired to take advantage of any such power, it must be clear that the circumstances envisaged by such power have actually arisen.[210]   **13–082**

---

[208] *Jasmine Trustees v. Wells & Hind* [2007] 1 All E.R. 1142 at [52–57].
[209] *Tiger v. Barclays Bank* [1951] 2 K.B. 556.
[210] *London and County Banking Co. v. Goddard* [1897] 1 Ch. 642. Such a power was of course exercised in *Von Knieriem v. Bermuda Trust Co.* (1994) 1 B.O.S. 116; see *ante*, para 6–035.

13–083   The power of removal of trustees under section 36 of the Trustee Act 1925 when a new trustee is being appointed has been dealt with above. It will be recalled that the circumstances are:

> (i) where the trustee remains out of the United Kingdom for more than 12 months consecutively;
>
> (ii) where he refuses to act;
>
> (iii) where he is unfit to act; or
>
> (iv) where he is incapable of acting.[211]

13–084   The final method, removal by the court, presents rather more difficulty. The court's primary concern is to protect and enhance the interests of the beneficiaries. Thus where the trustee is convicted of dishonesty or, by becoming bankrupt or otherwise,[212] shows that he is not fit to be in charge of other people's property, the court will remove him.[213] Nevertheless, removal by the court does involve, at least to the outside world, some degree of moral stigma and difficulties arise where an application is made to remove a trustee, not because he has done anything wrong, but because he cannot agree with or work with his co-trustees.

13–085   The position was considered by the Privy Council in *Letterstedt v. Broers*,[214] where Lord Blackburn observed:

"In exercising so delicate a jurisdiction as that of removing trustees, their Lordships do not venture to lay down any general rule beyond the very broad principle that their main guide must be the welfare of the beneficiaries. Probably it is not possible to lay down any more definite rule in a matter so essentially dependent on details often of great nicety."

Mere friction between trustee and beneficiary is not an adequate ground but if there were a permanent condition of hostility between one trustee and the other trustees, the court would probably remove him. In *Re Wrightson*[215] Warrington J. said: "You must find something which induces the court to think either that the trust property will not be safe or that the trust will not be properly executed in the interests of the beneficiaries." A permanent condition of hostility between trustees would probably be a sufficient deterrent to efficient administration of the trust for the court to exercise its powers. It is difficult to appeal successfully against an order by an inferior court ordering the removal of a trustee. Thus, in *Re Edwards' Will Trusts*,[216] where Megarry V.-C. had removed a trustee without giving any reasons for so doing, the Court of Appeal refused to interfere with his decision.

---

[211] *Re Lemann's Trust* (1883) 22 Ch.D. 633.
[212] *Re Lemann's Trust* (1883) 22 Ch.D. 633; *Re Phelps' Settlement Trust* (1885) 55 L.J.Ch. 465 (intellectual decay).
[213] See the cases discussed *ante*, para 13–039.
[214] (1884) 9 App.Cas. 371 at 382. See also *Earl of Portsmouth v. Fellows* (1820) 5 Madd. 450.
[215] [1908] 1 Ch. 789 at 803.
[216] [1981] 2 All E.R. 941.

2. *Protection of Purchasers where a Trustee has been Removed*

Some of the grounds for the removal of a trustee under section 36 of the   **13–086**
Trustee Act 1925 and his replacement by a new trustee are that the trustee
has remained out of the United Kingdom for more than 12 months, or that
he refuses to act, or that he is unfit to act. These grounds can give rise to
dispute. Thus a displaced trustee could argue that he was not in fact unfit to
act so that his purported removal was ineffective. In the absence of a
provision to the contrary, a purchaser from the new trustees would not
obtain a good title in the event that the purported removal was ineffective.
However, purchasers of land in this position will be protected by section 38
of the Trustee Act 1925, which provides that a statement in a deed of
appointment that a trustee:

    (i) has remained out of the United Kingdom for more than 12
       months;

    (ii) refuses to act;

    (iii) is incapable of acting; or

    (iv) is unfit to act

"shall, in favour of a purchaser of a legal estate, be conclusive evidence of
the matter stated". Because it is "conclusive" evidence, a purchaser need not
look behind the statement.[217] Further, in favour of a purchaser, an appointment of trustees which depends on such a statement being true and any
express or implied vesting declaration are also valid.[218] However, section 38
only applies in the case of land and no protection is conferred by the
inclusion of such a statement in other circumstances.

But although this section gives protection to purchasers, it does not affect   **13–087**
the position of a person who has not in fact ceased to be a trustee. If,
therefore, a person is purportedly removed as a trustee on the ground that
he is unfit to act and another person is purportedly appointed in his stead,
the person purportedly removed could apply to the court for a declaration
that he continues to be a trustee. However, even if such a declaration were
to be made, that would not prejudice a purchaser of land who had relied on
the statement in the instrument of appointment that the trustee had been
removed on that ground.

V. THE DELEGATION OF TRUSTEESHIP

In limited circumstances, a trustee can delegate his powers as such without   **13–088**
himself ceasing to be a trustee. This is generally only possible for periods of

---

[217] Contrast the position where enactments provide only for "sufficient" evidence. See, for
example, Administration of Estates Act 1925, s.36(7) and *Re Duce and Boots Cash Chemists
(Southern) Ltd.'s Contract* [1937] Ch. 642.
[218] Trustee Act 1925, s.38(2).

up to 12 months at a time but a trustee of a trust of land who is also a beneficiary of that trust can delegate his powers as such indefinitely.

13–089   Under section 25 of the Trustee Act 1925,[219] a trustee can, by power of attorney, delegate all or any of the trusts, powers and discretions vested in him as a trustee, whether he is a sole trustee or one of a number of trustees.[220] The delegation cannot be for a period of more than 12 months, although that period does not have to start on the date on which the power of attorney is executed[221]; there appears to be no restriction on the number of times on which a delegation can be made. It is now possible for the delegation to be in favour of anyone, even the only other trustee.[222] Before or within seven days of granting the power of attorney, the donor must[223] give written notice of the delegation to each of the other trustees and to any other person who has a power of appointing new trustees. This notice must specify the date when the power comes into operation, its duration, the donee, the reason why the power is being given, and which of the trusts, powers and discretions are being delegated. However, even if this notice is not given, a person dealing with the donee of the power is not prejudiced. The donor remains liable for the acts or defaults of the donee as if they were his own.[224] The donee is in the same position as the donor, except that he cannot himself exercise any power of delegation under the section.

13–090   This provision is in practice rarely used. While it is useful in enabling discretions and powers to be delegated, the fact that the donor remains liable for every act or default of the donee is potentially disadvantageous to him. Trustees can collectively appoint agents to carry out their functions in the manner which will be discussed in the next chapter,[225] although such agents admittedly cannot exercise functions relating to the manner in which the assets of the trust are distributed. Trustees who have so appointed an agent are only liable for his acts or defaults if they fail to exercise the statutory duty of care imposed by section 1 of the Trustee Act 2000.[226] Consequently, when the donee of a power of attorney does something which could have been done by an agent, the donor of the power is potentially liable for an act or default of the donee when he would not have been liable for the same act or default of an agent. Section 25 is therefore capable of working in a completely unjust way, particularly since the donor is likely to have no more control over the donee than he would have over an agent. However, where only one of a number of trustees wishes to appoint someone to act on his behalf, he will have no option but to use one of the two provisions at present under discussion.

13–091   The other possibility of delegating trusteeship is under section 1 of the Trustee Delegation Act 1999. This is limited to the situation where the delegating trustee has a beneficial interest in land held by the trust and was

---

[219] As substituted by Trustee Delegation Act 1999, s.5.
[220] Trustee Act 1925, s.25(1).
[221] ibid., s.25(2).
[222] ibid., s.25(3). Until the substitution by the Trustee Delegation Act 1999, delegation could not be in favour of the only other trustee.
[223] Trustee Act 1925, s.25(4).
[224] ibid., s.25(7).
[225] See post, para 14–101.
[226] See post, para 14–002.

intended principally to be utilised in cases of co-ownership of land, where all the trustees are normally also beneficiaries and, when the co-ownership is expressly created and there are no more than four co-owners, all the beneficiaries are also trustees. Such co-owners are not only able to delegate without being restricted by the provisions of section 25 of the Trustee Act 1925; they can also make provision for the disposal of the land if they become mentally incapable.[227] Section 1 provides:

"(1) The donee of a power of attorney is not prevented from doing an act in relation to—

    (a) land,
    (b) the capital proceeds of a conveyance of land, or
    (c) income from land

by reason only that the act involves the exercise of a trustee function of the donor if, at the time when the act is done, the donor has a beneficial interest in the land, proceeds or income."

A trustee function of the donor is a function which the donor has as trustee (either alone or jointly with any other person or persons).[228] Section 1(1) only applies in the absence of a contrary intention in the instrument creating the power of attorney or in the trust instrument[229] and where the donee of the power is not authorised to exercise the trustee function in question in some other way, such as under a provision of the trust instrument or by virtue of a power of attorney granted under section 25 of the Trustee Act 1925[230] (thus keeping the two types of powers of attorney separate). A statement by the donee of the power that the donor had the requisite beneficial interest is "conclusive evidence" in favour of a purchaser whose interest depends on the donee having had power under section 1(1) if the statement was made at the time of the act in question or within three months thereafter.[231]

Both the provisions which have been discussed enable one of two trustees to grant a power of attorney to the other and each of two or more trustees to grant powers of attorney to the same donee. The obvious risk that this poses in relation to overreaching conveyances, where a purchaser will only take free of overreachable interests if any capital money arising is paid to not less than two trustees or to a trust corporation, has been addressed by section 7 of the Trustee Delegation Act 1999, which provides that this requirement for the payment of capital money is not satisfied by a receipt being given by a person other than a trust corporation who is acting either both as a trustee and as attorney for one or more trustees or as attorney for two or more trustees. This simply means that a person who is in either of these two situations will have to exercise the power which he will normally have by virtue of being able to exercise the discretions of all the relevant

13–092

---

[227] Because the power of attorney can be made in the form of an enduring power of attorney; see *infra*.
[228] Trustee Delegation Act 1999, s.1(2).
[229] *ibid*., s.1(3), (5).
[230] *ibid*., s.1(8).
[231] *ibid*., s.2.

trustees[232] to appoint a further trustee to join with him in receiving the capital money.

13–093   New provisions have also been inserted[233] into section 36 of the Trustee Act 1925[234] to enable the donees of these types of power of attorney to exercise the statutory power of appointment of new or additional trustees conferred by that section.[235]

13–094   Both the types of powers of attorney considered were, until September 30, 2007, able to be made in the form of and take effect as enduring powers of attorney.[236] Such powers of attorney would (and those created until then still will) survive the incapacity of the donor provided that they are registered once the donor has become incapable; unless and until he does so, such powers can be exercised in the same manner as any other power of attorney. On October 1, 2007 enduring powers of attorney were replaced by lasting powers of attorney.[237] Such powers similarly survive the incapacity of the donor provided that they are duly registered (although in a different manner) once the donor has become incapable. Consequently, the change has neither increased nor reduced the scope for delegation by trustees who subsequently cease to have mental capacity.

---

[232] See *ante*, para 13–021. He will only not have this power if the power of appointment of new trustees is vested in someone else, which is highly unlikely in the case of co-ownership trusts, which are the only circumstances in which these situations are likely to arise.

[233] By Trustee Delegation Act 1999, s.8(1).

[234] s.36(6A), (6B), (6C), (6D).

[235] See *ante*, para 13–033.

[236] This is implicit in the wording of Trustee Delegation Act 1999, s.1 in the case of the type of power created by that Act, s.6 of which also specifically so provided in the case of powers under Trustee Act 1925, s.25 (this was therefore only possible with effect from March 1, 2000 when the Trustee Delegation Act 1999 came into force). The Trustee Delegation Act 1999 also removed an anomaly created by the Enduring Powers of Attorney Act 1985, s.3(3) of which seemed to have given trustees a quite separate right to delegate their powers as such by enduring power of attorney which was not only not subject either to any time limit or to any obligation to notify anyone but which would also arise whether or not the donor trustee had considered the matter and so intended; this subsection has now been repealed by Trustee Delegation Act 1999, s.4, subject to elaborate transitional provisions.

[237] Mental Capacity Act 2005, ss.9–15 and Sch.1, which came into force on that date.

CHAPTER 14

THE ADMINISTRATION OF TRUSTS

This Chapter is concerned with the general obligations of the trustees with regard to the trust property and various specific powers which they are given in order to facilitate its administration. Several aspects of the law governing the administration of trusts were substantially amended by The Trustee Act 2000, which enacted a number of recommendations of the Law Commission,[1] produced only after extensive consultation, and came into force on February 1, 2001. Given that the time which generally elapses before any maladministration of a trust is even detected, never mind made the subject of litigation, it is not surprisingly that, seven years later, none of the provisions of this legislation has yet had to be considered by the courts. However, such litigation will become increasingly likely during the life of this edition.   **14–001**

I. THE TRUSTEES' DUTY OF CARE

Section 1 of the Trustee Act 2000 imposed on trustees the following new statutory duty of care: **14–002**

"(1) Whenever the duty under this subsection applies to a trustee, he must exercise such care and skill as is reasonable in the circumstances, having regard in particular—

(a) to any special knowledge or experience that he has or holds himself out as having, and
(b) if he acts as trustee in the course of a business or profession, to any special knowledge or experience that it is reasonable to expect of a person acting in the course of that kind of business or profession."

Under the pre-existing common law rule, unpaid trustees were bound to use only such due diligence and care in the management of the trust as an ordinary prudent man of business would use in the management of his own affairs.[2] This rule had been incorporated into a number of statutory provisions, all of which were duly repealed by the Trustee Act 2000. However, because the statutory duty of care only applies in the situations specifically   **14–003**

---

[1] Law Com. No. 260 (1999), *Report on Trustees' Powers and Duties*.
[2] *Speight v. Gaunt* (1883) 9 App.Cas. 1.

listed in the Trustee Act 2000,[3] it is possible, depending on what attitude is adopted to statutory interpretation, that the common law rule may have survived, presumably unintentionally, in some of the situations not specifically included in the list.

14–004   The common law rule provided an objective standard of reference, admittedly not at all easy to apply to particular circumstances. It was however clear that that standard was not measured by the standard actually adopted by the trustee in question in the management of his own affairs.[4] In contrast, the criterion of the new statutory duty of care is what is "reasonable in the circumstances"; two of these circumstances are specified, relating to specialist knowledge or experience which the particular trustee has, holds himself out as having or, if he is acting as trustee in the course of a business or profession, can be reasonably expected to have. Here there is clearly room for the personal characteristics of the particular trustee to be relevant since one of the specified circumstances is itself such a characteristic. So it may be that a trustee who is unintelligent or unworldly owes a lower statutory duty of care, not just than that of a trustee who is neither but also than that of the prudent man of business under the pre-existing law. The Law Commission appears to have thought that the introduction of the statutory duty of care could only increase the requisite level of care and skill[5] but it is not obvious that this is in fact the case.

14–005   On the other hand, the two specified characteristics are undoubtedly meant to impose a higher standard of care and skill. The first, in section 1(1)(a), gives the beneficiaries the benefit not only of any special knowledge or experience that the trustee actually has but also of any which he has held himself out as having (the advantage of judging him by his own professed standards is, however, somewhat undermined by the fact that the provision does not say to whom he has to have held himself out[6]). The second, in section 1(1)(b), adds special knowledge or experience which it is reasonable to expect of a trustee acting in the course of a business or profession, whether or not he actually has it or professes it. The pre-existing law did tend to expect higher standards of trust corporations[7] but the inclusion of professional trustees as such in this category is new; however, it is unclear whether it is reasonable to expect a solicitor acting as a trustee as part of his general practice to have the special knowledge and experience of solicitors in general or that of a solicitor specialising in trusts and estates.

14–006   The statutory duty of care applies only to the situations listed in the Trustee Act 2000, principally in Schedule 1. This Schedule also provides[8] that the statutory duty of care may be excluded "in so far as it appears from the trust instrument that the duty was not meant to apply". The intention of this

---

[3] Principally in Sch.1, to which s.2 specifically refers.

[4] *Rae v. Meek* (1889) 14 App. Cas. 558 at 569; *Re Lord de Clifford's Estate* [1900] 2 Ch. 707 at 716.

[5] Law Com. No. 260 (1999), para.3.24(2).

[6] It is hardly likely that he will so have held himself out to the beneficiaries, although this would clearly suffice, so presumably a holding out to the settlor or testator must be meant also to suffice.

[7] See *Bartlett v. Barclays Bank Trust Co.* [1980] Ch. 515; *Australian Securities Commission v. AS Nominees* [1996] P.L.R. 297 (Federal Court of Australia).

[8] Trustee Act 2000, Sch.1, para.7.

provision must have been to confirm beyond any doubt that the statutory duty of care can be varied or excluded by what are known as trustee exemption clauses,[9] obviously subject to any restrictions which from time to time may exist as to the permissible scope of such clauses[10]; this is wholly satisfactory but the way in which the provision has been formulated is, frankly, asking for trouble.[11] The situations listed in the Trustee Act 2000 are as follows:

(i) exercising any power of investment, including carrying out the new duties imposed by the Trustee Act 2000[12] to review investments and to obtain advice[13];

(ii) exercising any power to acquire land and any power in relation to land so acquired[14];

(iii) "entering into arrangements" to appoint agents, nominees and custodians (this peculiar formulation was intended to exclude from the scope of the statutory duty of care the decision as to whether or not to utilise such persons at all[15] and leave subject to it only the decision as to exactly who to utilise)[16];

(iv) exercising powers of compromise "and so on"[17];

(v) exercising a power of insurance[18]; and

(vi) exercising any power to agree the value of reversionary interests, to fix the value of trust property for the purpose of giving effect to the trust, and to do associated things.[19]

On the other hand, the following situations appear to be excluded from the application of the statutory duty of care.

14–007

---

[9] See *post*, para 22–079.

[10] See *ibid*. At present, trustee exemption clauses cannot validly exclude liability for dishonest and fraudulent breaches of trust and cannot generally oust the fundamental obligation of a trustee to account to his beneficiary; however, the exclusion of liability for everything else up to and including wilful default is still permissible. At one time legislative intervention to impose further restrictions on the ability of professional trustees to exclude liability for breach of trust seemed inevitable; however, this now seems to have been abandoned, at least for the moment, on the basis that professional trustees will, at most, only exclude liability for negligence.

[11] It clearly goes well beyond express exclusions. Does the not uncommon provision that the trustees are to have "wholly uncontrolled discretion" in respect of, say, the exercise of a power of appointment therefore also oust the statutory duty of care in respect of administrative powers like the power of investment? Hopefully not but someone is bound to litigate this.

[12] Trustee Act 2000, ss.4, 5.

[13] *ibid*., Sch.1, para.1.

[14] *ibid*., para.2.

[15] Law Com. No. 260 (1999), para.3.12; para.3.e suggests that "perverse" decisions of this type can be attacked but it is not obvious how.

[16] Trustee Act 2002, Sch.1, para.3.

[17] *ibid*., para.4.

[18] *ibid*., para.5.

[19] *ibid*., para.6. This refers to the powers in Trustee Act 1925, s.22(1) and (3) which confer power to do the things mentioned in the text and to "any corresponding power". The heading of the paragraph also refers to "audit" but this seems to be an error unless a power to conduct an audit can somehow be regarded as a corresponding power.

14–008   1. The obligation of the trustees to get in the trust property has always been absolute[20]; it was unaffected by the common law rule and is now unaffected by the statutory duty of care. This was clearly intentional and is sound as a matter of principle.

14–009   2. The custody and management of the trust property is not specifically referred to anywhere in the list of situations subject to the statutory duty of care except in the case of land. While the Trustee Act 2000 expressly confers on trustees the powers to appoint nominees and custodians[21] to hold the trust property, no provision is made as to the nature of their liability to take care of the trust property if they choose not to do so. While all matters relating to the management of land seem within the statutory duty of care, the management of chattels is not, although that is admittedly unlikely to be particularly significant. However, the important obligation to inquire into or intervene in the affairs of any company in which the trust has a controlling or majority interest also seems to have been omitted unless it can somehow be squeezed into the obligation "from time to time to review the investments of the trust and consider whether . . . they should be varied". Admittedly, this was a respect in which the common law duty was more stringent anyway, at least so far as corporate trustees were concerned.[22] It will, therefore, not be the end of the world if this obligation is held still to be governed by this duty rather than by the statutory duty of care but this can hardly be what was intended.

14–010   3. The issuing and defending of proceedings on behalf of the trust does not seem to be subject to the statutory duty of care either except, possibly, in the case of proceedings involving land held by the trust. There is no difficulty in respect of the costs of such proceedings since, in the types of proceedings where there is any risk of the trustees being personally liable for those costs, they can protect themselves against any such liability by making an application seeking the advance approval of the court for the potential expenditure of the trust funds on the costs of the litigation[23]; if they do not do so, their liability depends on whether approval would have been given if it had been sought. But this does not cover the duty of the trustees to consider whether or not to bring proceedings of this type. It would clearly be appropriate for this to be governed by the statutory duty of care; to the extent that it is not, it must presumably still be governed by the common law rule, which again cannot possibly be what was intended

14–011   Trustees will be well advised to bear in mind constantly that at some time in the future some disgruntled beneficiary may well seek to question their actions. Thus where, for example, trustees wish to sell or lease property, they

---

[20] See *ante*, para 13–067.
[21] Trustee Act 2000, ss.16, 17; see *post*, para 14–110.
[22] See *Bartlett v. Barclays Bank Trust Co.* [1980] Ch. 515.
[23] See *post*, para 14–131; this is generally known as an application for a *"Beddoe* Order".

should normally take the precaution of employing a valuer and sell or lease with regard to his figures.[24] While the numerous authorities on the common law rule are obviously no longer good law, the absence as yet of any authorities on the Trustee Act 2000 means that the facts of some of the older authorities are still worth consideration. In *Ward v. Ward*[25] the House of Lords held that a trustee had acted reasonably in not immediately issuing proceedings in the way in which he would normally have been obliged to do[26] against a beneficiary who was also a debtor to the trust; had proceedings been issued, that beneficiary would have been ruined and his children, who were also beneficiaries, would have been placed in difficult circumstances. On the other hand, in *Re Lucking's Will Trusts*,[27] a trustee was a director of a private company, in which the trust held a majority shareholding. The trustee-director allowed another director to overdraw heavily from the company by signing and returning blank cheques sent to him by the other director. When these drawings proved to be irrecoverable, the trustee-director was held liable to the trust for the consequential reduction in the value of the trust shares. Much more straightforward examples of the imposition of liability, this time for failure to take action, have been on trustees who have allowed rent to fall into arrears[28] or have failed to register a transaction which needs to be registered, such as a transfer of registered land or of shares, and as a result someone else obtains priority.[29]

Occasionally, the common law rule has conflicted with the rule that a trustee must do the best he can for his beneficiaries and it is apparent that the statutory duty of care is capable of doing so also. Suppose, for example, that trustees who have put a property up for sale have received and provisionally accepted an offer for £500,000 but subsequently receive an offer for £550,000. They are under a clear obligation to consider the second offer, even if, had they been dealing with their own property, they would not have entertained that offer out of considerations of ordinary commercial morality. They still of course retain their discretion and, if there is some reason which genuinely leads them to conclude that the first offer should be accepted (if, for example, the sale to the first proposed purchaser would be completed materially earlier), they may conclude that the first offer should be accepted. But their discretion must be exercised generally in the interests of the beneficiaries[30] and, in the example given, they should accept the second offer unless there is some good reason for accepting the first.

14–012

II. JOINT ACTS

Although in some circumstances, the decision of the majority of trustees of a charitable trust can bind all its trustees,[31] in the case of private trusts an act

14–013

[24] *Oliver v. Court* (1820) 8 Pr. 127.
[25] (1843) 2 H.L.Cas. 777.
[26] See *Re Brogden* (1888) 38 Ch.D. 546.
[27] [1968] 1 W.L.R. 866.
[28] *Tebbs v. Carpenter* (1816) 1 Madd. 290.
[29] *Macnamara v. Carey* (1867) Ir.R. 1 Eq. 9.
[30] *Buttle v. Saunders* [1950] 2 All E.R. 193.
[31] *Re Whiteley* [1910] 1 Ch. 600.

or decision will generally only be effective if it is the act or decision of all the trustees. There is no question of a decision of the majority binding all the trustees[32] in the absence of an express provision to the contrary. The settlor or testator has reposed his trust in all the trustees, not just some of them; the liabilities and responsibilities are consequently those of all the trustees. Actions taken and decisions made in the administration of the trust must therefore be those of all the trustees. It may often happen that one trustee who is more enthusiastic in his duties than his co-trustee will come to be spoken of as the "acting trustee", whose decisions are merely endorsed by his co-trustee(s). But in this context, "acting trustee" is not a concept recognised by law. Each of the trustees must exercise his discretion and each is equally liable.[33]

14–014   Should a dispute arise, a trustee may be justified in concurring in an action of his co-trustee with which he is not in favour, either because he considers his co-trustee to be more experienced in, or to be more knowledgeable about, the type of transaction in hand[34] or in order to prevent a complete deadlock in the administration of the trust. Whether he is being reasonable in deferring to his co-trustee, or whether he should have stood firm and if necessary made an application to the court, will depend on the circumstances of the particular case.

14–015   To this general rule that all the trustees must act jointly there are certain exceptions. First, the trust instrument can of course authorise individual action. Secondly, one trustee alone often has power to give a receipt for income, whether rent or dividends from shares (the latter is a necessary provision, because the articles of association of most companies provide that dividends are to be paid to the first-named registered holder of those shares). Thirdly, just as some acts can be delegated to an agent, so most of those acts can be delegated by all the trustees to one of their number. Lastly, in the case of trustees of a private trust, a majority of trustees can pay money into court[35] even if the minority objects.

14–016   Although it is not an exception to the basic principle, it is possible to achieve the practical result that not all the trustees need agree on a certain course of action if a provision to this effect is contained in the trust instrument. This can be done by imposing a primary duty on the trustees to follow a particular course of conduct but also giving them a secondary power not to do so, or to follow some other course, if they all agree. This method is adopted by the Trusts of Land and Appointment of Trustees Act 1996 in respect of land which is subject to an express trust for sale; despite the primary duty imposed on the trustees to sell the land, section 4 of that Act gives the trustees an express power to exercise a discretion to postpone sale indefinitely without being responsible for so doing. However, the trustees can only exercise their power to postpone sale if they all agree so to do; consequently, if only one of them wishes to sell, all the trustees have to comply with their duty so to do.[36] Prior to the enactment of the 1996 Act, the

---

[32] *Boardman v. Phipps* [1967] 2 A.C. 46.
[33] *Munch v. Cockerell* (1840) 5 Myl. & Cr. 178.
[34] *Re Schneider* (1906) 22 T.L.R. 223.
[35] Trustee Act 1925, s.63.
[36] *Re Mayo* [1943] Ch. 302.

Law of Property Act 1925 both imposed such a duty and conferred such a power on the trustees of all jointly owned land.[37] However, such land is now instead subject to a trust of land[38]; that trust, while equally conferring on the trustees the same power to postpone sale,[39] imposes no specific duty to sell.

III. The Trustees' Discretions and Powers

It is an inherent part of the position of every trustee that he give due consideration to the exercise of any discretions and powers vested in him[40]; there are a wide variety of circumstances in which he will need to do so.   **14–017**

Trustees can of course only exercise the discretions and powers vested in them within the limits prescribed by law or by the trust instrument. Their exercise will be defective unless it is exercised with whatever formalities are required by the trust instrument. In principle the exercise of neither a discretion nor a power requires any formality but in practice, while trust instruments do not normally prescribe any formality for the exercise of discretions, they almost always prescribe some formality for the exercise of powers of appointment.[41] A discretion or power can also only be exercised within the limits prescribed by law or by the trust instrument; consequently, it must be exercised within any time limit fixed by the trust instrument and, if it can be exercised only with the consent of some person, that consent must be duly obtained. In *Breadner v. Granville-Grossman*,[42] a power of appointment was held to have been executed one day too late and its exercise was, therefore, ineffective; consequently, the interests of those entitled in default of exercise of the power took effect. In *Re Massingberd's Settlement*[43] trustees were given power to vary investments with the consent of the tenant for life. They sold an authorised security and, with the consent of the tenant for life, invested the proceeds in an unauthorised one. Subsequently they realised that unauthorised investment and reinvested in an authorised one; however, this time they did not obtain the consent of the tenant for life and as a result they were held to have committed a breach of trust.   **14–018**

Assuming that all such limits on the trustee's discretion are observed, it is of paramount importance that the trustees should exercise their discretion as the result of an active mental process and not allow a situation to arise merely as a result of their inaction. In *Turner v. Turner*,[44] the trustees left all the decisions to the settlor (who was not a trustee) and signed the necessary documents without actually reading them. A power of appointment which   **14–019**

---

[37] By virtue of ss.34–36 and s.25 respectively.
[38] ss.25 and 35 were repealed by Trusts of Land and Appointment of Trustees Act 1996, Sch.4 and the effect of ss.34 and 36 was amended by Trusts of Land and Appointment of Trustees Act 1996, s.1.
[39] Trusts of Land and Appointment of Trustees Act 1996, s.4.
[40] Generally with regard to the trustee's discretion, see *ante*, Chapter 6.
[41] See *ante*, para 6–023.
[42] [2001] Ch. 523.
[43] (1890) 63 L.T. 296.
[44] [1984] Ch. 100.

they signed in this manner was held to be defective. Similarly, in *Wilson v. Turner*,[45] the trustees had a power to pay or apply income arising from the trusts to or for the maintenance of an infant beneficiary. They did not make any conscious decision whether or not to do so but merely handed over the income to the infant's father. The Court of Appeal held that their payments had been ineffective and that they had to repay the money to the trust fund. However, had the trustees actively considered the merits of the case and consciously decided to apply the income for the maintenance of the infant, their decision would have been valid and would have been upheld. The test is, therefore, not the consequences of the action or inaction of the holder of the discretion or power in question but the nature of his own mental processes.

14–020	However, where the trustees do consciously exercise their discretion, they derive a large measure of support from the courts. When they exercise a discretion or power, they do not have to give the objects of that power or discretion the reasons for their decisions; however, as Robert Walker J. stated in *Scott v. The National Trust*,[46] if their decision is challenged in the courts they may be compelled to do so either through the process of disclosure if there are any relevant documents or, in practical terms, as the only way of avoiding an adverse inference being drawn.

14–021	In *Re Beloved Wilkes' Charity*,[47] trustees had a duty from time to time to select a candidate to be sent to the University of Oxford to be trained as a minister of the Church of England; they were obliged to select any suitable candidate who came forward from certain nominated parishes but in default had a more general discretion. They decided to nominate a candidate from outside those parishes rather than one from within them. Lord Truro L.C. declined to interfere with this decision, saying:

"It is to the discretion of the trustees that the execution of the trust is confided, that discretion being exercised with an entire absence of indirect motive, with honesty of intention, and with a fair consideration of the subject. The duty of supervision on the part of this court will thus be confined to the question of the honesty, integrity and fairness with which the deliberation has been conducted, and will not be extended to the accuracy of the conclusion arrived at."

14–022	However, if the trustees do choose to state their reasons, the court will examine them in order to ascertain whether or not the trustees have acted in error. In *Klug v. Klug*,[48] a mother who was one of a number of trustees declined to concur in the exercise of a power in favour of her daughter on the grounds that she disapproved of the latter's marriage. The court held that this was an impermissible reason; consequently she had acted dishonestly and her refusal to concur was set aside. Trustees of pensions trusts also tend, quite understandably, to give reasons for their decisions. But, as

---

[45] (1883) 22 Ch.D. 521.
[46] [1998] 2 All E.R. 705 at 717–719.
[47] (1851) 3 Mac. & G. 440.
[48] [1918] 2 Ch. 67.

Robert Walker J. stated in *Scott v. The National Trust*,[49] the principles on which the court must proceed are the same whether or not the trustees give their reasons; it simply becomes easier for the court to examine a decision if the reasons for it have been disclosed.

In *Edge v. Pensions Ombudsman*[50] the trustees of a pension trust had to **14–023** decide how to utilise a surplus which was not needed for the provision of the benefits payable under the pension scheme. They decided to use it to credit additional service to those members in employment on a particular date and to reduce the contributions of both employers and employees from a date six months earlier; no additional service was credited either to those already receiving pensions or to a number of employees who were to be made redundant during the six-month period. The trustees explained to one of the latter that their decision had been taken in order to encourage all employees to become and remain members of the pension scheme and to support the employers in providing continued employment for their current employees. The Pensions Ombudsman set aside the trustees' decision on the grounds that the trustees had breached their duty of impartiality and had not acted in the best interests of all the beneficiaries. His decision was reversed by the Court of Appeal, who held that the duty to act impartially was no more than the ordinary duty imposed on any holder of a discretionary power, namely to exercise the power for the purposes for which it is given, giving proper consideration to the matters which are relevant and excluding from consideration matters which are irrelevant. Provided the trustees complied with that duty, they were entitled to reach a decision which appeared to prefer the claims of some beneficiaries over others.

Decisions can also be reviewed if trustees have exercised a discretion or **14–024** power as a result of a mistake.[51] If there is convincing proof that they did not do what they had really intended to do, their decision will be rectifiable. If they acted on the basis of a serious mistake, their decision may be set aside, as it also may if they merely fail to take into account all the correct considerations, although in the latter case it is at present unclear both what types of mistake will produce this effect; in both these situations, it has yet to be definitively established whether their decision is void *ab initio* or merely voidable at the discretion of the court. It is also possible successfully to impugn their exercise of a discretion or power on the grounds that the trustees have not acted honestly and so are guilty of what is known as "fraud on a power" (this expression is used in connection with the exercise of both a power and a discretion)[52]; thus far fraud on a power has always been held to render a decision void *ab initio*. All the relevant authorities were considered in the chapter on discretionary trusts.[53]

Where trustees who have a discretion or power fail to exercise it, the **14–025** position depends on whether or not they were under any obligation to exercise it. If they were not, their ability to do so will lapse after a reasonable

---

[49] [1998] 2 All E.R. 705 at 717–719.
[50] [2000] Ch. 602.
[51] See *ante*, para 6–078.
[52] See *ante*, para 6–102.
[53] See *ante*, paras 6–074–6–115.

period and cannot later be revived.[54] If, on the other hand, they were under an obligation to exercise it, their ability to do so will never lapse, but will instead be enforced. In *Re Locker's Settlement Trusts*[55] the trustees of a discretionary trust held income subject to a positive obligation to distribute the income among such of the beneficiaries as they should determine. They failed to distribute income which had arisen during a three-year period but some years later wished to distribute it then. On their application to the court for a declaration as to whether the discretion was still exercisable, the court held that it was because it was of an obligatory nature.

IV. THE DUTY TO PROVIDE INFORMATION

14–026 Trustees must be prepared at all times to provide information as to the state of the trust property and as to any dealings with it; they must therefore be in a position to provide any relevant accounts and, within certain limits, documents relating to actions taken in the administration of a trust.[56] Precisely who is entitled to require such trust documents has been a matter of some controversy; while there has never been any doubt about the right of beneficiaries of both fixed and discretionary trusts to do so, the position of persons who are merely potential beneficiaries of a trust by virtue of being potential objects of the exercise of a discretion or power has been more uncertain. However, the Privy Council has recently held[57] that the right to require trust documents is best approached as one aspect of the court's inherent jurisdiction to supervise (and where appropriate intervene in) the administration of trusts and that there is no reason to distinguish either between the holders of fixed and discretionary interests or between the rights of an object of a discretionary trust and those of the object of a fiduciary power. This view is clearly likely to become generally accepted. But beneficiaries and potential beneficiaries can anyway only ask for trust documents if they are actually aware of their rights or potential rights in the first place. It is, therefore, necessary to commence with a consideration of the extent to which trustees must provide beneficiaries with information as to the existence of a trust in their favour.

1. *The Duty to Provide Information as to the Existence of a Trust*

14–027 A settlor of an *inter vivos* trust is not obliged to notify either the trustees or the beneficiaries of its existence. Thus in *Fletcher v. Fletcher*[58] a settlor entered into a covenant with trustees that, if either or both of his two illegitimate sons survived him, his executors should, within 12 months of his death, pay to the trustees £60,000 which was to be held on trust for such of the two as reached the age of 21. He never revealed the existence of the deed either to

---

[54] *Re Allen-Meyrick's Will Trusts* [1966] 1 W.L.R. 499; *Re Gulbenkian's Settlement Trusts (No.2)* [1970] Ch. 408.
[55] [1978] 1 All E.R. 216.
[56] *Tiger v. Barclays Bank* [1952] 1 All E.R. 85.
[57] In *Schmidt v. Rosewood Trust* [2003] UKPC 26, [2003] 2 A.C. 709.
[58] (1844) 4 Hare 67.

the trustees or to his sons; he retained the deed in his possession until his death and it was only discovered some years later among his papers. As has already been seen,[59] this did not prevent the one son who survived him and reached the age of 21 from enforcing what was held to be a completely constituted trust of the benefit of that covenant. This was of course a most unusual case and in such circumstances the trustees are under no obligation to act. However, save where an *inter vivos* trust is created by declaration, it will only be validly constituted once the trust property has been vested in the trustees[60]; this will in practice normally require the trustees to be parties to the trust instrument, in which case they will necessarily be aware of the trust's existence.

It is much more common for testamentary trusts to be created without   **14–028**
either trustees or beneficiaries being aware of their existence. A testator is under no obligation whatever to inform his executors and testamentary trustees that he has nominated them to act as such and there is certainly no reason to suppose that he will inform the beneficiaries of his will of their possible future interests thereunder. Executors and testamentary trustees are under no obligation to act even if they have been informed of their appointment, never mind if they have not. If an executor agrees to act, in practice one of the first things which he will do is to send a copy of the will to each beneficiary who has rights thereunder. But it has been held that executors are under no duty to do so.[61]

However, the position of executors will clearly change once the admini-   **14–029**
stration of the estate is concluded if they continue to hold assets of the estate as trustees. This is because it is clear that trustees who have agreed to act are under a duty to inform the beneficiaries of the existence and nature of their interests under the trust. This was held in *Hawkesley v. May*,[62] where the plaintiff was jointly entitled with his sister to the income and capital of the trust fund at 21. When he reached that age, the trustees failed to inform him of his rights and continued accumulating the income until his sister also reached that age. Havers J. held that they had been under a duty to inform him of his interest and of his immediate entitlement to call for his share of the income. This was a fixed trust but the same principle presumably applies to discretionary trusts in favour of relatively small groups of beneficiaries. However, the position of potential members of the enormous classes of beneficiaries in favour of whom many modern discretionary trusts are created is more problematical. It is clearly impracticable to oblige or to expect trustees of this type of discretionary trust to notify every single potential member of his potential rights thereunder[63]; the most that they could conceivably be expected to do would be to advertise for potential

---

[59] See *ante*, para 5–113.

[60] See *ante*, para 5–001.

[61] *Re Lewis* (1868) 5 L.R. Eq. 545. This was a particularly strong case since the executor was entitled to the subject matter of a legacy in the event that the beneficiary in question failed to claim it and the failure to inform the latter of the existence of the legacy meant that he failed to do so prior to his death.

[62] [1956] 1 Q.B. 304.

[63] See Davies (1995) 7 Bond Law Review 5, referring to the remarks of Mahoney J.A. in *Hartigan Nominees v. Rydge* (1992) 29 N.S.W.L.R. 405 at 425 & 432 (Court of Appeal of New South Wales).

beneficiaries to present themselves so that the trustees can comply with the duty to survey the field which, as has already been seen,[64] is imposed on them by *McPhail v. Doulton*[65] and *Re Hay's Settlement Trusts*.[66] However, it cannot seriously be doubted that the need to compel the proper administration of trusts dictates that trustees should be obliged to give a truthful answer to any potential beneficiary who actually enquires.[67]

14–030   Similar considerations obviously also apply to persons who are not beneficiaries at all but are simply potential objects of a power to add beneficiaries. The fact that it is possible for such a power to be intermediate, and therefore in favour of anyone in the world, clearly indicates the impossibility of the trustees notifying all the potential objects. This was recognised by Templeman J. in *Re Manisty's Settlement Trust*,[68] the case in which the validity of intermediate powers was finally upheld; he stated that in such circumstances the trustees were not even obliged to advertise. However, he went on to say that, where an object of the power is aware of its existence, he can ask the trustees to consider exercising it in his favour and in that case they must do so on pain of being removed from office if they do not. It has not yet had to be considered whether the same principles apply to the trustees of a *Quistclose* trust[69] who have of course now been held[70] to hold its subject matter for the whoever advanced it to them subject to a power to apply it for the specified purpose; it therefore remains to be seen whether or not they will be held to be under an obligation to notify the persons who in whose favour the power can be exercised of its existence—there does not seem to be any case of a *Quistclose* trust other than the controversial decision in *Re Northern Development (Holdings)*[71] in which the trustees have actually done so.

14–031   A rather different aspect of the right of a beneficiary to know of the existence of his interest had to be considered in *Murphy v. Murphy*.[72] Most if not all the shares in a family company were settled on discretionary offshore trusts by their respective owners. The plaintiff was aware that he had been specifically named as a beneficiary of two discretionary trusts, one set up by his father, who had reserved the power to appoint its trustees, and one set up by his deceased mother, who had not reserved any such power but whose estate had been administered by the father; he also thought that he was a potential beneficiary of other discretionary trusts set up by them and

---

[64] See *ante*, para 3–074.
[65] [1971] A.C. 424.
[66] [1982] 1 W.L.R. 202, *per* Megarry V.-C. at 209–210.
[67] The Bahamas has legislated in this respect. (The Bahamas) Trustee Act 1998, s.83 provides that trustees are only obliged to inform beneficiaries of the trust's existence if they have a vested interest under the trusts although, at any time when there is no such beneficiary, they must inform at least one person who is in a position to enforce the trust. Although some of the consequences are rather absurd (default beneficiaries will have to be informed even though there is little or no likelihood that they will ever become entitled to anything), this clarification is nevertheless extremely helpful and the provision is likely to be copied widely.
[68] [1974] Ch. 17 at 25.
[69] See *ante*, para 9–071.
[70] In *Twinsectra v. Yardley* [2002] UKHL 12, [2002] 2 A.C. 164.
[71] (October 6, 1978) unreported but see *Twinsectra v. Yardley* [2002] UKHL 12, [2002] 2 A.C. 164 at 188–189 *per* Lord Millett; also Lord Millett, pre-judicially, in 101 L.Q.R. (1985) 269.
[72] [1999] 1 W.L.R. 282.

his brother. He therefore issued a summons to compel his father to disclose to him the names and addresses of the current trustees of all these trusts so that he could find out what had happened to the trust property and make out a case that he should receive some of the property. Neuberger J. held that no principle of equity had been invoked to suggest that the court had no power to grant such relief and ordered the father to make discovery of the information sought in respect of the trusts of which the plaintiff was an actual beneficiary, on the basis that the father must know this information.[73] However, he denied this relief in respect of all the other trusts, saying that it would be most undesirable to make orders which would be likely to result in trustees being badgered with claims by large numbers of potential beneficiaries, particularly when the plaintiff, as someone who was at best only entitled to be considered as a possible additional member, was in reality in no better position than anyone else in the world who had not been specifically excluded.

2. The Right to Require Trust Documents

Prior to the recent decision in *Schmidt v. Rosewood Trust*,[74] there had never been any doubt about the right of beneficiaries of both fixed trusts and small discretionary trusts to require information as to the state of the trust property and to any dealings with it and the corresponding trust documents; nor was any distinction drawn between beneficiaries with interests in possession and those whose interests had either not yet vested or had not yet vested in possession. It had been clear since the decision in *Re Londonderry's Settlement*[75] that this right was not confined to beneficiaries of fixed trusts since the Court of Appeal there regarded the right as basically applicable to a discretionary trust whose beneficiaries were the members of a family,[76] although different considerations there determined the non-availability of the documents which the beneficiary wanted to see. But doubts had been expressed both as to whether the right was or should be available to every single potential member of the enormous classes of beneficiaries which many modern discretionary trusts now have[77] and as to the position of persons who are not among the actual beneficiaries of a discretionary trust but are merely among the possible objects of a power of appointment.[78]

14–032

---

[73] But he gave the father the right to adduce evidence as to any possible inconvenience and cost and to be reimbursed for the latter.

[74] [2003] UKPC 26, [2003] 2 A.C. 709.

[75] [1965] Ch. 918.

[76] This was subsequently confirmed in *Chaine-Nickson v. Bank of Ireland* [1976] Irish Reports 393 (Supreme Court of Ireland); *Spellson v. George* (1987) 11 N.S.W.L.R. 300, 315–316 (Supreme Court of New South Wales).

[77] *Hartigan Nominees v. Rydge* (1992) 29 N.S.W.L.R. 405 (Court of Appeal of New South Wales).

[78] It had been suggested in *Chaine-Nickson v. Bank of Ireland* [1976] Irish Reports 393 (Supreme Court of Ireland) and in *Spellson v. George* (1987) 11 N.S.W.L.R. 300, 315–316 (Supreme Court of New South Wales) that there was no distinction between such persons and persons who are actually beneficiaries but this view was decisively rejected in *Rosewood Trust v. Schmidt* in the Court of Appeal of the Isle of Man ([2001] W.T.L.R. 1081).

According to the Privy Council in *Schmidt v. Rosewood Trust*,[79] these distinctions no longer have any formal significance; the right to require information is instead now to be approached as merely one aspect of the court's inherent jurisdiction to supervise (and where appropriate intervene in) the administration of trusts; in practice, however, these distinctions will obviously remain highly relevant in the court's exercise of that inherent jurisdiction.

14–033   In *Schmidt v. Rosewood Trust*, the effective objects of two discretionary trusts set up in the Isle of Man were Russian businessmen associated with one of the largest privatised oil companies in Russia. They and the Royal National Lifeboat Institution were beneficiaries of both trusts, under each of which the trustees had a power to accumulate income and an overriding power of appointment in favour of the beneficiaries exercisable with the prior written consent of the protector. In the first trust, there was a provision for each beneficiary's "portion" of the trust fund to be held on his death for the persons notified by him to the trustees and in default for his closest relatives. In the second trust, there was instead a power to add beneficiaries and a discretionary trust of income in favour of the beneficiaries in default of accumulation or appointment. The claimant was the son and personal representative of one of the beneficiaries, who had also been protector of the first trust. Some $US27,000,000 had been appointed out to nominee companies which were regarded as his but no beneficial interest in either trust had ever actually been appointed to him. He had, however, written to the trustees notifying them that the claimant was to be his successor under the first trust on his death and expressing the wish that the claimant should be given his share of the second trust.

14–034   The claimant, who had been paid the funds actually held by the nominee companies, wanted to find out whether these comprised the whole of the funds actually allocated to those companies and whether, but for possible breaches of fiduciary duty, including over-charging, more funds would have been available for allocation to his father. He therefore sought full disclosure of documents which, had he or his father been a beneficiary of the trusts, he would undoubtedly have been allowed to see under the authorities discussed above. But the trustees claimed that he was not entitled to that disclosure since he was not himself a beneficiary of either trust and his father, whose personal representative he was, had been no more than an object of the overriding powers of appointment under both trusts (in fact he himself was undoubtedly also a possible object of the power to add beneficiaries to the second trust who, in the light of his father's letter, had "exceptionally strong claims to be considered" but this added nothing).[80] This claim succeeded before the Court of Appeal of the Isle of Man,[81] who held that there is a distinction between a beneficiary of a discretionary trust and an object of a mere power of appointment, the latter being entitled only

---

[79] [2003] UKPC 26, [2003] 2 A.C. 709.

[80] In the Privy Council, the claimant himself claimed to be a beneficiary of the first trust as a result of the combined effect of the notification provision and the notification; however, the Privy Council held that he could not be treated as such pending resolution of the proper construction of the documents. At no stage was any point taken that his father had been a default discretionary beneficiary of income under the second trust, possibly because relatively little of the funds allocated to his father's companies had come from that trust.

[81] Technically known as "The Staff of Government Division".

to have his case considered from time to time by the trustees, in default to seek directions from the court that they should consider his case and, if they still refused, to seek their replacement.[82] This of course meant (as the court accepted) that, towards the end of a trust period, there might be no one with both the legal standing and the economic interest to hold the trustee to account.[83]

However, the Privy Council held that there was for this purpose no formal **14–035** distinction between the different types of beneficiaries and potential beneficiaries of a trust and allowed the claimant's appeal. Lord Walker stated that[84]:

"a beneficiary's right to seek disclosure of trust documents, although sometimes not inappropriately described as a proprietary right, is best approached as one aspect of the court's inherent jurisdiction to supervise (and where appropriate intervene in) the administration of trusts. There is therefore in their Lordships' view no reason to draw any bright dividing-line either between transmissible and non-transmissible (that is, discretionary) interests, or between the rights of an object of a discretionary trust and those of the object of a mere power (of a fiduciary character) . . . . However, the recent cases also confirm that no beneficiary (and least of all a discretionary object) has any entitlement as of right to disclosure of anything which can plausibly be described as a trust document . . . . Evaluation of the claims of a beneficiary (and especially of a discretionary object) may be an important part of the balancing exercise which the court ahs to perform on the materials placed before it. In many cases the court may have no difficulty in concluding that an applicant with no more than a theoretical possibility of benefit ought not to be granted any relief."

The case was sent back to the Isle of Man for this decision to be applied but Lord Walker indicated that, on the face of things, the claimant as the personal representative had a powerful case for the fullest disclosure in respect of the funds actually allocated to his father's companies and in respect of his claims for breach of fiduciary duties; Lord Walker also emphasised that he personally had "exceptionally strong claims" to be considered as an object of the power to add beneficiaries to the second trust.

Although *Schmidt v. Rosewood Trust* is, as a decision of the Privy Council, **14–036** not technically binding on the English courts, it is bound to be followed. However, trustees would be unwise to take too literally Lord Walker's remark that "no beneficiary (and least of all a discretionary object) has any entitlement as of right to disclosure of anything which can plausibly be described as a trust document". The immediate beneficiaries of fixed trusts and of small discretionary trusts are bound in practice to be given exactly

---

[82] This is admittedly the effect of *Re Manisty's Settlement* [1974] Ch. 17 and *Re Hay's Settlement Trusts* [1982] 1 W.L.R. 202; see *ante*, paras 6–017, 6–067.

[83] (The Bahamas) Trustee Act 1998, s.83(5) confines the rights to information to those beneficiaries who have to be informed of the existence of the trusts (*ante*, n.67) and thus has the same effect as the decision of the Manx court; it therefore also excludes beneficiaries with contingent or other non-vested interests.

[84] [2003] UKPC 26, [2003] 2 A.C. 709 at [66].

the same trust documents as at present. Room for manoeuvre for the trustees continues to exist in relation to the beneficiaries of large discretionary trusts and potential beneficiaries of all types of trusts; in respect of the latter categories, the criteria laid down by Lord Walker are likely to restrict disclosure to those who in practical terms have a reasonable chance of receiving some part of the trust property at some point. However, the rights of default beneficiaries, the ultimate beneficiaries of discretionary trusts who, although they are necessarily beneficiaries of fixed trusts, are only likely to take in the event of the death of all the other beneficiaries, may well now in practice be considerably restricted by these criteria.

3. *The Nature of Trust Documents*

14–037   A person who is entitled to require the trustees to show him the trust documents will be entitled to see documents of a number of different types.

(A) Accounts and Investments
14–038   A trustee must maintain accurate accounts of the trust property. He must allow a person entitled to see trust documents, or that person's solicitor, to inspect those accounts and the vouchers supporting them and he must be prepared to give full information as to the amount of the trust fund. He is not obliged to supply copies of the accounts, or settlements of account, to the beneficiaries unless the beneficiaries themselves pay for those copies. Under the modern law, trustees will be entitled to employ agents to keep the accounts whether or not they are capable of doing so themselves.[85]

14–039   Where trust money is invested, the trustees must on request supply a person entitled to see trust documents with details of the investments, and even produce the stock or share certificates, or other deeds and documents, representing that investment. Where, however, such a person requires information as to his position under a trust, and this information cannot be supplied by the trustees without incurring expense, the trustees can pass on the expense to him. Trustees who do not keep proper accounts may be ordered to do so by the court, and may be forced to bear personally the costs of the application to the court.[86] As the trustees may at any time be called upon to give information as to the administration of a trust, it is advisable for them to keep in addition to the trust accounts a trust diary. This is a type of minute book in which decisions taken in the administration of a trust are recorded. However, in view of the fact that access is usually given to the trust diary, trustees may, in the light of the authorities discussed in the previous section of this chapter, choose to record their decisions but not the reasons for them.

---

[85] See *post*, para 14–101. At one time this was not the case; but in *Wroe v. Seed* (1863) 4 Giff. 425 it was held that a trustee who was illiterate, and so could not keep accounts, was justified in employing an agent simply for the purpose of keeping them.
[86] See (1936) 52 L.Q.R. 365.

It seems that the court has a discretion to withhold even documents of this   **14–040**
kind "if the probative value is minimal and is outweighed by prejudice to
the other beneficiaries or to the proper administration of the trust".[87]

(B) Counsel's Opinions

Where the trustees instruct and take the opinion of Counsel on behalf of   **14–041**
their trust and at the expense of the trust funds, the beneficiaries have an
absolute right to see a copy of any written advice provided by Counsel and
of any note of advice given by Counsel in conference. This was specifically
stated by Harman L.J. in *Re Londonderry's Settlement*.[88] This is not the case
where the trustees instruct Counsel on their own behalf, whether in order to
obtain advice as to their own potential liability or in their capacity as
beneficiaries, and themselves pay his fees; however, in such circumstances
Counsel will be well-advised to protect himself against any possible claims
by the beneficiaries by obtaining specific written confirmation of the
capacity in which he is being instructed. Further, advice obtained by trustees
when proceedings against them by the beneficiaries have been intimated or
have commenced is of course protected by legal professional privilege in the
normal way.

(C) Other Documents

A person entitled to see trust documents is also entitled to inspect most   **14–042**
other documents relating to the trust.[89] However, this right will not be
allowed to impinge on the rule that trustees are not obliged to give reasons
for their decisions. This was the issue which *Re Londonderry's Settlement*[90]
actually had to resolve. The trustees of a settlement were to distribute the
trust fund in such proportions as they, in consultation with nominated
"appointors", thought fit among certain named persons. One of the latter
considered that she had received too little[91] and, in order to launch an attack
upon the trustees, sought to inspect numerous trust documents which
would probably have indicated the reasons which had led the trustees to
make the distributions which they had made. The disgruntled beneficiary
claimed that she had a right to inspect the documents. The trustees claimed
that she had not; they could not to be compelled to give reasons for their
decisions and, if the court ordered that the beneficiary was able to see the
documents which she wished to see, the rule which enabled the trustees to
keep their reasons to themselves would be defeated. The Court of Appeal
held, in effect, that the rule enabling a beneficiary to inspect trust documents
did not extend to documents which gave reasons for the trustees' decisions;

---

[87] *Lemos v. Coutts & Co. (Cayman)* (1993) 1 Butterworths Offshore Service 171 at 216; *Re Rabaiotti 1989 Settlement* 2000 J.L.R. 173, [2000] W.T.L.R. 953.

[88] [1965] Ch. 918.

[89] The older authorities, such as *O'Rourke v. Darbishire* [1920] A.C. 581, stated that this was because, just as the beneficiaries were the equitable owners of the trust property, they were also the equitable owners of the documents which had arisen in the course of the trust administration, and often at the expense of the trust. However, this view was rejected in *Schmidt v. Rosewood Trust*.

[90] [1965] Ch. 918.

[91] She and her family had in fact received £165,000. The total amount of the trust fund is not recorded.

indeed the court went so far as to order that, where a document is basically
in the category of those which the beneficiary is entitled to see but also
contains details of the trustees' reasons, the latter passages should be
redacted, that is to say covered up, when the document is produced to the
beneficiary.

14–043   Although this decision was unquestionably welcome, the reasons given
by the court are far from clear. The court clearly had sympathy with the
trustees' contention that family strife would result if the beneficiary were
given access to documents which gave their reasons for their dealings with
the trust property. It may well be that the court first decided what conclusions they wanted to reach and then tried to find some reasons with which
to support it. Harman L.J. considered, but did not decide, whether the
documents were trust documents at all, presumably on the basis that, if they
were not, the beneficiary would not have a right of access to them at all. He
said[92]:

"I would hold that, even if documents of this type ought properly to be
described as trust documents, they are protected for the special reason
which protects the trustees' deliberations on a discretionary matter from
disclosure. If necessary, I hold that this principle overrides the ordinary
rule."

Danckwerts L.J. based his decision firmly on the practical ground that, if the
trustees' reasons were not protected from disclosure, it would be impossible
for them to do their job. The third member of the Court of Appeal,
Salmon L.J., also toyed with the idea of declaring that the documents were
not trust documents but had to admit defeat.[93]

14–044   There are thus several possible reasons for the conclusion reached; however, the decision does at least clearly establish that beneficiaries do not have
a right of access to documents which the trustees intend to be private and
which record the reasons for their decisions. The order of the Court of
Appeal in Re Londonderry's Settlement[94] exempted from disclosure: the
agenda of the meetings of the trustees; correspondence between the trustees
and the appointors; correspondence between, on the one hand, the trustees
and appointors and, on the other hand, the beneficiaries; and minutes of the
meetings of trustees or appointors and other documents disclosing their
deliberations as to the manner of exercise of or their reasons for exercising
their powers and/or the materials on which such reasons were or might
have been based.

14–045   The conclusions reached in Re Londonderry's Settlement were reviewed in
Wilson v. The Law Debenture Trust Corp.[95] in the context of the discretions
vested in the trustees of a pension trust, specifically in respect of a decision
not to transfer a surplus in the fund to another pension scheme to which its
member employees had been transferred. Despite the fact that, as has

---

[92] [1965] Ch. 918 at 933.
[93] ibid. at 938.
[94] This order is set out in Breakspear v. Ackland [2008] EWHC 220 (Ch), [2008] W.T.L.R. 777 at
[23].
[95] [1995] 2 All E.R. 337.

already been seen,[96] the beneficiaries of a pension fund are not volunteers. Rattee J. affirmed the applicability of the decision in *Re Londonderry's Settlement* and refused to order the trustees to reveal their reasons.[97] In *Breakspear v. Ackland*[98] Briggs J., after an extensive review of authorities from a number of jurisdictions, held that the principles enunciated in *Re Londonderry's Settlement* remain good law and, in any event, law binding on a judge at first instance.

The question which actually had to be decided in *Breakspear v. Ackland*[99]   **14–046** was whether beneficiaries are entitled to see letters of wishes. As has already been seen,[100] letters of wishes are documents which exist outside the formal trust documents; they set out the wishes of the settlor but are not binding on the trustees. This question had not previously had to be considered in this jurisdiction although Briggs J. considered a number of decisions from other jurisdictions.[101] He held that, in principle, letters of wishes[102] are a further category of documents additional to those identified in *Re Londonderry's Settlement* which are exempt from disclosure; he placed particular reliance on the fact that the exempt categories in *Re Londonderry's Settlement* had included the materials on which the trustees' reasons for exercising their powers were or might have been based. But he emphasised that the view of the settlor as to whether or not his wishes should be disclosed was irrelevant; it was for the trustees to decide whether or not to disclose letters of wishes and the reasons for their decision in this respect were equally exempt from disclosure unless they chose to disclose those reasons, in which case the court could obviously review them. On the other hand, the court had, as part of its jurisdiction in the administration of trusts, a discretion to order

---

[96] See *ante*, para 12–062.

[97] The decision has been criticised by Schaffer (1994) 8 Trust Law International 118. It may anyway in practice be indirectly undermined by the fact that the Pensions Act 1995 now requires that every pension trust must have member trustees; see *ante*, para 12–051.

[98] [2008] EWHC 220 (Ch), [2008] W.T.L.R. 777 at [53].

[99] [2008] EWHC 220 (Ch), [2008] W.T.L.R. 777 at [23].

[100] See *ante*, para 6–041.

[101] In particular, *Hartigan Nominees v. Rydge* (1992) 29 N.S.W.L.R. 405, where the Court of Appeal of New South Wales, by a majority, denied access but each of the three members of court took a different view: one of the members of the majority held that letters of wishes are not trust documents and so do not fall within the basic right of access; the other member of the majority held that letters of wishes are trust documents but do not have to be disclosed because they provide insight into the trustees' reasons; and the dissentient held that letters of wishes are trust documents but should be disclosed even if they do provide insight into the trustees' reasons (in effect, therefore, rejecting *Re Londonderry's Settlement*). Different majorities therefore held that letters of wishes are trust documents and that they do not have to be disclosed on the grounds of confidentiality. The view that letters of wishes are not trust documents and for that reason do not have to be disclosed was followed and applied by the Royal Court of Jersey in *Re Rabaiotti 1989 Settlement* 2000 J.L.R. 173, [2000] W.T.L.R. 953 in relation to two settlements subject to the law of Jersey, which contains a specific statutory provision to this effect (Trusts (Jersey) Law 1984, Art.25) and two subject to the law of the British Virgin Islands, which does not. However, the court went on to hold that it did, in all four cases, have discretion to order disclosure in appropriate circumstances and duly did so on the basis that disclosure was in the interests of both the adult beneficiaries, who supported it (one of them had been ordered by an English court to produce the documents for the purposes of his divorce; it was clearly in the interests of all the beneficiaries for the true position to be known).

[102] For some reason, Briggs J. preferred to use the ungrammatical expression "wish letters" ("wish" is not an adjective).

disclosure. In the event, the trustees had not remained entirely silent as to their reasons for refusing disclosure, thus entitling the court to review those reasons; further the trustees had indicated that they proposed, as soon as they were in a position to distribute the trust property, to seek the approval of the court for their proposed distribution in the manner which is discussed later in this chapter.[103] Since the court would necessarily have to see the letter of wishes in order to be able to decide whether or not to give its approval, Briggs J. decided that it would be an unpardonable waste of time and money if the question of disclosure had to be relitigated then. Consequently, for those reasons and only for those reasons, he ordered disclosure. But it is absolutely clear that, if the trustees had declined to give any reasons for their refusal to disclose and had given no indication of any intention of seeking the approval of the court in any respect, disclosure would not have been ordered.

14–047   The fact that documents which are, like those in *Re Londonderry's Settlement*, held to be trust documents do not have to be disclosed for the reasons stated in that case is, however, not necessarily the end of the matter. In that case, the beneficiary had made a direct application to inspect the documents in question. The Court of Appeal made it clear that their decision did not govern the question of whether such documents were disclosable in pending proceedings brought upon some other ground. If, for example, a beneficiary brings proceedings against the trustees for breaches of trust which involve an allegation of improper motive on the part of the trustees, it may well be that in the course of disclosure the beneficiary will be entitled to see all the trustees' documents, including those which reveal the reasons for their decisions. Robert Walker J. stated this expressly in *Scott v. National Trust*[104] and added that the trustees may in practical terms be compelled to reveal their reasons in order to avoid any adverse inference being drawn.

14–048   However, in *Murphy v. Murphy*[105] Neuberger J. emphasised the traditional judicial reluctance to sanction proceedings brought mainly in order to try to flush out the documents[106] in question; he stated that trustees who have done nothing wrong should not be identified for the purpose of enabling a party to consider whether or not to bring proceedings of a highly speculative nature. This clearly shows that, if disclosure of documents showing reasons is some day sought in proceedings brought on some other ground, the courts will have to try to decide whether there is a genuine need for disclosure in the other proceedings or whether the latter have been brought mainly in order to try to flush out the documents in question. But dicta in *Hartigan Nominees v. Rydge*[107] suggest that the principle that reasons should not be revealed is paramount and may not be circumvented even by the process of disclosure.[108]

---

[103] See *post*, para 14–124.
[104] *Scott v. National Trust* [1998] 2 All E.R. 705.
[105] [1999] 1 W.L.R. 282.
[106] An impermissible tactic which is generally known as a "fishing expedition".
[107] (1992) 29 N.S.W.L.R. 405, per Mahoney J.A. at 437.
[108] (The Bahamas) Trustee Act 1998, s.83(8) specifically so provides.

V. Administrative Powers Relating to Trust Property

Part II of the Trustee Act 1925 confers general powers on trustees, particularly with regard to the administration of property. Like all the provisions of that Act, they can be increased, reduced or completely ousted by any contrary provision in the trust deed in question.[109] Under these powers, trustees may where appropriate raise money by sale or mortgage, sell trust property at auction, and insure the property. Further, although this is not actually mentioned in the statute, trustees are bound to see that trust property does not fall into decay through want of repair.[110] The following provisions require consideration.   **14–049**

Section 15 of the Trustee Act 1925 governs the trustees' power to compound liabilities by giving them the power to   **14–050**

"(a) accept any property, real or personal, before the time at which it is made transferable or payable; or

(b) sever and apportion any blended trust funds or property; or

(c) pay or allow any debt or claim on any evidence that he or they think sufficient; or

(d) accept any composition or any security, real or personal, for any debt or for any property, real or personal, claimed; or

(e) allow any time for payment of any debt; or

(f) compromise, compound, abandon, submit to arbitration, or otherwise settle any debt, account, claim, or thing whatever relating to the testator's or intestate's estate or to the trust."

The section goes on to provide that the trustees will not be liable for any loss which occurs from the exercise of any of these powers, provided that they have discharged the statutory duty of care.[111] The consent of the beneficiaries has never been necessary; it is for the trustees to decide whether they consider the compromise to be in the interest of all beneficiaries taken together and that, if they do, they have power to accept it despite the opposition of one of the beneficiaries.[112]

Section 16 of the Trustee Act 1925 governs the trustees' power to mortgage the trust property. This applies where trustees are authorised either by the general law or by the trust instrument "to pay or apply capital money subject to the trust for any purpose or in any manner". In these circumstances, the section gives the trustees power to raise the necessary money either by mortgaging or selling the trust assets. However, the section is construed narrowly and is confined to the cases where money is required either to preserve assets or to advance capital. In *Re Suenson-Taylor's Settlement*[113] the trustees, who had very wide powers of investment and who, in   **14–051**

---

[109] Trustee Act 1925, s.69(2).
[110] *Re Hotchkys* (1886) 32 Ch.D. 408.
[111] Trustee Act 1925, s.15; Trustee Act 2000, s.1 and Sch.1, para.4.
[112] *Re Earl of Strafford* [1979] 1 All E.R. 513.
[113] *Re Suenson-Taylor's Settlement* [1974] 3 All E.R. 397.

accordance with these powers, properly held a large area of land for investment purposes, wished to borrow upon the security of that land in order to buy further land. It was held that this would be outside the power conferred by section 16. The court however observed that there could be cases where it was necessary to purchase further land in order to protect existing investments. For example, if trustees own a house, it may be appropriate to buy land which the house overlooks in order to prevent anyone else building upon it. Such a purchase is now clearly permissible under the Trusts of Land and Appointment of Trustees Act 1996 since trustees of land now have all the powers of an absolute owner.[114] However, that does not necessarily mean that the purchase price can be raised on mortgage.

14–052   Section 19 of the Trustee Act 1925 governs the trustees' power to insure the trust property. This provision used to be less than wholly satisfactory in that trustees had power to insure the trust property only for an amount not exceeding three-quarters of its full value. However, this was remedied by the Trustee Act 2000,[115] which substituted a new provision under which the power of the trustees to insure trust property against risks of loss or damage is unrestricted both as to the risks insured and the level of cover obtained.[116] The Trustee Act 2000 also makes the power to insure subject to the statutory duty of care,[117] which trustees will inevitably breach if they do not insure adequately. The new section 19 also specifically provides that the premiums can be paid out of the trust funds, which for this purpose means any income or capital of the trust[118]; it is not stated on which premiums are primarily chargeable. If the insured assets are income producing, the premiums will obviously be primarily chargeable on that income as an expense of obtaining it. If, on the other hand, land is not income producing because it is occupied by a beneficiary, the trustees should in principle make the payment of insurance premiums a condition of occupation; they are entitled to impose such conditions under the Trusts of Land and Appointment of Trustees Act 1996[119] where land is occupied by a beneficiary with an interest in possession; it is not clear whether they can do so when land is occupied by a beneficiary without an interest in possession. However, where trust property is not income producing for some other reason or the premiums cannot be paid in the ways envisaged above,[120] then, in the event that there is no specific provision in the trust deed (which there usually will be), the trustees will be entitled to pay insurance premiums out of capital; this is obviously preferable to leaving the property uninsured.

14–053   It should be noted that there is no statutory power to insure the life of any beneficiary. This will sometimes in practice be desirable since any of the trust property in which a beneficiary holds an interest which, for the purposes of inheritance tax, is an interest in possession will be subject on his or

---

[114] Trusts of Land and Appointment of Trustees Act 1996, s.6(1).
[115] Trustee Act 2000, s.34(1).
[116] The power of bare trustees to insure is subject to any direction given by the beneficiaries; Trustee Act 1925, s.19(2)–(4).
[117] Trustee Act 2000, Sch.1, para.5.
[118] Trustee Act 1925, s.19(1), (5).
[119] Trusts of Land and Appointment of Trustees Act 1996, s.13(1)(3), (5).
[120] Such as the fact that a beneficiary occupying land is doing so pursuant to an express provision of the trust deed which does not permit him to be charged insurance premiums.

her death to inheritance tax which the trust will be primarily liable to pay; however, the reforms to the taxation of trusts made in 2006 have to all intents and purposes restricted such interests in possession to immediate life interests arising under a will or intestacy.[121] Anyway modern trust deeds generally expressly confer on the trustees a power to ensure the lives of beneficiaries.[122]

In addition to the powers already referred to, the trustees have all the powers of a legal owner of the property in question and powers which can only be exercised on proof of legal ownership can only be exercised by them. In *Schalit v. Nadler*[123] a beneficiary who was solely entitled to trust property which was leased levied distress for arrears of rent. It was held that only the trustee as legal owner could levy distress; consequently, the distress actually levied was wrongful. Similarly, only the legal owner can serve a notice to quit on a tenant.

14–054

VI. INVESTING THE TRUST PROPERTY

1. *The Duty of Care*

(A) The Statutory Duty of Care
The statutory duty of a care[124] applies to trustees exercising any power of investment.[125] Formerly the normal common law duty, to use only such due diligence and care in the management of the trust as an ordinary prudent man of business would use in the management of his own affairs,[126] was modified in the case of powers of investment so that trustees investing trust funds were to take such care as an ordinary prudent man of business would take if he were under a duty to make the investment for the benefit of other persons for whom he felt morally bound to provide.[127] This was because "business men of prudence may, and frequently do, select investments which are more or less of a speculative character but it is the duty of a trustee to confine himself to the class of investments which are permitted by the trust and likewise to avoid all investments of that class which are attended with hazard".[128] Some of the extended elements of this test are likely to be considered relevant in deciding whether a trustee has satisfied the statutory duty of care by exercising such care and skill as is reasonable in the circumstances.

14–055

The relevant principles of course apply not just to the initial investment of the trust property but also to the variation and continuation of investments. In their consideration of the investments of the trust as a whole, Hoffmann J.

14–056

---

[121] See *post*, para 15–084.

[122] See the different sets of administrative provisions set out and discussed in J. Kessler, *Drafting Trusts and Will Trusts: A Modern Approach* 8th edn (London, Sweet & Maxwell, 2007).

[123] [1933] 2 K.B. 79 and see *ante*, para 1–036.

[124] See *ante*, para 14–002.

[125] Trustee Act 2000, s.1 and Sch.1, para.1.

[126] *Speight v. Gaunt* (1883) 9 App. Cas. 1.

[127] *Re Whiteley* (1886) 33 Ch.D. 347 at 355, affirmed *sub nom. Learoyd v. Whiteley* (1887) 12 App. Cas. 727.

[128] *Learoyd v. Whiteley* (1887) 12 App. Cas. 727 at 733.

made clear in *Nestlé v. National Westminster Bank*[129] that "modern trustees acting within their investment powers are entitled to be judged by the standards of current portfolio theory, which emphasises the risk level of the entire portfolio rather than the risk attaching to each investment taken in isolation". This view was subsequently adopted by the Treasury in a Consultation Paper on the Investment Powers of Trustees published in May 1996 and must therefore now be regarded as part of the general law.

(B) Trusts for Persons by way of Succession

14–057   As part of the modified common law duty, trustees were also bound to make their investments in such a way that those entitled in possession obtain a reasonable income and the capital is nevertheless preserved for those entitled to it in remainder[130] and this will undoubtedly continue to be the case under the statutory duty of care. High income investments are likely to produce little, if any, capital appreciation and thus will generally benefit the tenant for life at the expense of the remaindermen, while low income investments are likely to produce more substantial capital appreciation and thus will generally benefit the remaindermen at the expense of the tenant for life. A balance must be secured so that all beneficiaries are treated equally and fairly.

14–058   In *Nestlé v. National Westminster Bank*,[131] the remainderman complained that the fund to which she became entitled when her interest vested in possession would have been worth almost four times as much had it been properly invested. The trustees had erroneously regarded their investment powers as more limited than they actually were and, as a result, had invested in a more restricted range of investments than they were actually obliged to. Further, they had failed to make sufficiently regular reviews of the fund. However, since the remainderman was unable to prove that any loss had been suffered thereby, the Court of Appeal held that she was not entitled to any compensation. The Court also emphasised that trustees are entitled to take into account the taxation position of the beneficiaries. Consequently, they had been entitled, where the tenant for life was non-resident, to purchase investments which would not be subject to deduction of income tax at source or to what is now inheritance tax on his death; further, they could take into account the relative wealth of the tenant for life and the remainderman in deciding whether to purchase high income or low income investments. However, the Court did hold that at least half of a trust fund held for persons by way of succession should be invested in "equities", ordinary shares issued by commercial companies which tend to keep pace with inflation.[132]

14–059   It therefore follows that, even if the trustees invest entirely in accordance with the powers conferred on them by statute[133] and the trust instrument[134] itself, they will not necessarily be protected from attack by the beneficiaries. Even an authorised investment may in the particular circumstances of the

---

[129] (1988) unreported but transcribed in (1996) 10 Trust Law International 112.
[130] *Re Whiteley* (1886) 33 Ch.D. 347 at 350.
[131] [1993] 1 W.L.R. 1260.
[132] See *post*, para 14–086.
[133] See *post*, para 14–055.
[134] See *post*, para 14–083.

case be unjustified and amount to a breach of the trustees' general duties of care and impartiality. But in circumstances such as these, the onus would be on the beneficiaries to establish that the investment was imprudent and not for the trustees to show the converse.[135] As Hoffmann J. said at first instance in *Nestlé v. National Westminster Bank*[136]:

"Trustees like the Bank act for reward and therefore owe duties of professional skill, but the engagement into which they enter is not one of insurance. They do not guarantee results. Possibly for a suitable premium such a guarantee could be obtained, but I very much doubt it and the transaction would be very different from that which the Bank undertook for modest reward."

(C) Non-Financial Considerations

Relatively recent authorities have also considered whether trustees, in reaching their decisions as to the selection and retention of particular investments, are entitled to take into account non-financial considerations. In *Cowan v. Scargill*,[137] five of the 10 trustees of a mineworkers' pension fund were appointed by the National Union of Miners. They refused to accept an investment plan submitted to the trustees by an advisory panel of experts in so far as it envisaged new or continuing investment overseas and in energies which were in direct competition with coal. Such investments were contrary to the policy of the National Union of Miners, which was understandably primarily interested in preserving the prosperity and, consequently, in ensuring the continued existence of the British coal mining industry. Their arguments were thus ideological in nature. There can be little doubt that most pension funds would indeed be benefited by the maintenance of the prosperity of the industry in question but, as Megarry V.-C. commented, the mineworkers' pension fund was in this respect unusual because of the declining nature of the coal mining industry, there being substantially more pensioners than miners so that the assets of the fund far exceeded the value of the industry. Further, overseas investments can be substantially more risky than home investments because of the possibility of exchange rate variations.

14–060

However, Megarry V.-C. held that the trustees would be in breach of trust unless they accepted the submitted investment plan. Their duty was to act in the best interests of their beneficiaries[138] and, if the purpose of the trust was the provision of financial benefits, a power of investment had to be exercised so that the funds yielded the best return by way of income and capital appreciation.

14–061

"Trustees may have strongly held social or political views. They may be firmly opposed to any investment in South Africa or other countries, or they

---

[135] *Shaw v. Cates* [1909] 1 Ch. 389 at 395.

[136] (1988), unreported except in (1996) 10 Trust Law International 112.

[137] [1985] Ch. 270. See generally Ellison (1991) 5 Trust Law International 157; Irish & Kent (1994) 8 Trust Law International 10; Lord Nicholls of Birkenhead, extra-judicially, (1995) 9 Trust Law International 10.

[138] The Uniform Prudent Investor Act 1994, s.5 (United States of America) now similarly requires investment solely in the interest of the beneficiaries.

may object to any form of investment in companies concerned with alcohol, tobacco, armaments or many other things. In the conduct of their own affairs, of course, they are free to abstain from making any such investments. Yet under a trust, if investments of this type would be more beneficial to the beneficiaries than other investments, the trustees must not refrain from making the investments by reason of the views that they hold."[139]

In exceptional cases, account could be taken of the particular inclinations of the beneficiaries but this was not relevant in the case in hand since many of the beneficiaries no longer had any financial interest in the welfare of the coal industry. The trustees were therefore pursuing union policy at the potential expense of the beneficiaries and, in the last resort, would have to be removed from office.

14–062   It is possible that the fact that the trustees so overtly based their case on ideological grounds did not favour their case. There seems no reason why trustees should not limit themselves to investments which they regard as politically and ethically "sound" provided that they have satisfied themselves that these investments are no less financially sound than those which they have rejected. What *Cowan v. Scargill* decides is that they must not fetter their discretion by deciding to exclude any particular class of investments irrelevant of their financial merits. This is confirmed by *Martin v. City of Edinburgh District Council*,[140] where a Scottish court held that a breach of duty had been committed by a local authority which, in order to oppose the regime in the then apartheid-ridden South Africa, had adopted a policy of disinvesting in companies which had interests in that country without considering whether this was in the best financial interests of the beneficiaries. It is therefore clear that no investment policy, whether to prefer or whether to avoid particular classes of investments, can be adopted unless the trustees have paid the necessary attention to the financial interests of the beneficiaries.

14–063   It has also been contended that trusts for charitable purposes should not make investments in undertakings whose operations are incompatible with those purposes. In *Harries v. Church Commissioners*,[141] the Bishop of Oxford sought a declaration that in the management of their assets the Church Commissioners were obliged to have regard to the object of promoting the Christian faith through the established Church of England and were not entitled to act in a manner which would be incompatible with that object. This declaration was denied. Nicholls V.-C. held that, where charitable trustees held assets as investments, the discharge of their duty of furthering the purposes of the trust would normally require them to seek the maximum return which was consistent with commercial prudence and they could not properly use such assets for non-investment purposes. The Commissioners already had a policy of excluding investments in certain business activities which might be offensive to the Church of England, such as in armaments, gambling, tobacco and newspapers and in South Africa (then still subject to apartheid). This was entirely proper but it would not be right for them to

---

[139] [1985] Ch. 270 at 287–288.
[140] [1988] S.L.T. 329.
[141] [1992] 1 W.L.R. 1241.

adopt a still more restrictive policy which would entail taking into account non-financial considerations to an extent which would give rise to a risk of significant financial detriment to the proper object of the trusts.

The cases just discussed all concerned trusts which had some public **14–064** element. While the considerations expressed in the judgments clearly also apply to wholly private trusts, there is of course nothing to stop any settlor, or indeed the totality of the beneficiaries if they are all *sui juris*, from prescribing that the trustees either must make or must refrain from making investments of any particular type.

(D) Continuing Supervision

In addition to making investments, the duties of the trustees inevitably **14–065** extend to keeping their investments under review. In the case of holdings in large quoted public companies, a periodic review will usually be sufficient. However, where the trustees have a majority holding or a controlling interest in a company or some other special position of influence, they will be expected to take advantage of it. If an individual shareholder in this position would require information about the company's affairs which is not generally available, the trustees will also need to obtain it. If an individual would insist on board representation, or board control, the trustees will themselves need to insist on it.

In *Bartlett v. Barclays Bank Trust Co.*,[142] the settlor settled almost the whole **14–066** of the shares in a company which he had incorporated to manage his properties on trust for his wife and issue. Initially the board of the company included members of the settlor's family but that gradually changed. However, the trustees, while sending a representative to statutory meetings of the company, did not seek representation on the board. The company purchased a property opposite the Old Bailey in the City of London at a price well in excess of its investment value, in the hope that permission would be obtained for its development. Permission was not forthcoming and the company later disposed of the property at a loss. Brightman J. held that the trustees were in breach of their duty to obtain the information which, as they were majority shareholders, was available to them.

Information is not, however, an end in itself[143] and must be used to protect **14–067** the interests of the beneficiaries. If necessary, a trustee must intervene to remove directors and procure the appointment of his own nominees. [144]

Some professional trustees and trust corporations are reluctant to assume **14–068** this responsibility and therefore include in their standard trust deeds a provision which negatives what would otherwise be their duty to interfere in the management of companies in which they are shareholders. These provisions are not necessarily effective at all unless they also negative any power so to interfere, since the trustees could be held liable for failure to exercise what would necessarily be a fiduciary power. It remains to be seen whether they are upheld by the courts.

---

[142] [1980] Ch. 515.
[143] See *Re Lucking's Will Trust* [1968] 1 W.L.R. 866, discussed *ante*, para 14–011, where the trustees had information but did not use it.
[144] [1980] Ch. 515 at 530.

2. *The Statutory Powers of Investment*

(A)   The General Power of Investment

14–069   Section 3(1) of the Trustee Act 2000 confers on a trustee the power to "make any kind of investment that he could make if he were absolutely entitled to the assets of the trust"; this power is described as "the general power of investment".[145] The general power of investment is additional to any powers conferred on trustees in any other way,[146] obviously in particular by the trust instrument, but is subject to the following restrictions:

   (i)   the word "investment" is restricted to investment in assets from which a profit or some income is expected;

   (ii)   the phrase "investments which he could make" is not in the form habitually used by express powers of investment, which confer the powers of an absolute beneficial owner on the trustees in question, and this may affect the position of corporate trustees, whose powers of investments of their own corporate assets are limited in some way;

   (iii)   investments in land are not permitted other than by way of loans secured on land[147];

   (iv)   a trust instrument made on or after August 3, 1961[148] may restrict the general power of investment in any way; and

   (v)   the general power of investment does not apply to pension trusts,[149] to unit trusts,[150] or to common investment schemes or common deposit schemes made for charitable trusts.[151]

(B)   Investment in Mortgages of Land

14–070   The Trustee Act 2000 makes it clear that investments "by way of loans secured on land" are within the general power of investment by excluding

---

[145] Trustee Act 2000, s.3(2). Prior to this legislation, the statutory powers of investment of trustees, contained in the Trustee Investment Act 1961, depended on the nature of the investment and only a specified proportion of the trust property could be invested in "equities", ordinary shares issued by commercial companies. However, since the general power of investment applies to all trusts whenever created, the pre-existing law is only relevant to alleged breaches of trust committed before the Trustee Act 2000 came into force on February 1, 2001; any claims in respect of such breaches are now likely to be statute barred.

[146] Trustee Act 2000, s.6(1)(a).

[147] Trustee Act 2000, s.3(3) which does however refer to s.8; see *post*, para 14–073.

[148] The date on which the Trustee Investment Act 1961 came into force (the reason for this exclusion is that until then there were no general statutory powers of investment, merely a statutory list of permitted investments, to which trust instruments simply tended to add; this approach was incompatible with the Trustee Investment Act 1961 and remains incompatible with the Trustee Act 2000).

[149] Trustee Act 2000, s.36(3). Pension trusts are governed by Pensions Act 1995, s.34(1) which enables the trustees to invest "as if they were absolutely entitled", does not exclude investment in land, but requires the preparation of written statements of the principles governing investment decisions and the obtaining of advice and is subject to rigid restrictions on the making of employer-related investments.

[150] Trustee Act 2000, s.37. Unit trusts often invest exclusively in shares of companies engaged in particular types of business or in particular jurisdictions and so such trusts necessarily have to be governed by express investment clauses.

[151] Trustee Act 2000, s.38; see *ante*, para 11–163.

them from the prohibition on investments in land. However, trustees are not always justified in investing the trust funds in mortgages of land. They must comply with the statutory duty of care and act with impartiality. They should not, therefore, make this sort of investment simply for the benefit of one of the beneficiaries and certainly not for the benefit of a person who is not even a beneficiary.[152] The rule that trustees are not necessarily free from responsibility because they invest in accordance with the powers conferred on them by statute and the trust instrument[153] applies with considerable force to investments in mortgages of land and this is clearly shown by the limitations on the trustees' powers imposed by the decided cases; these are obviously likely to be applied to investments in mortgages of land made pursuant to the general power of investment.

According to these authorities, trustees should, in the absence of express **14–071** authority to do otherwise, invest only in first mortgages of freehold or leasehold land. The security should be a first mortgage because it is desirable that the mortgage should enjoy priority. While the Trustee Act 2000 does not prohibit investments in second mortgages, it seems consistent with the statutory duty of care for these generally to be avoided since the first mortgagee will be able to exercise his power of sale irrelevant of the fact that this will leave nothing for the second mortgagee.[154] It used also to be said that trustees should obtain a legal mortgage rather than an equitable mortgage because otherwise their mortgage might be postponed to a subsequent legal mortgage but in practice the possibility of protecting equitable mortgages under the provisions of the Land Registration Act 2002 and the Land Charges Act 1972 will prevent this happening and this seems to constitute sufficient protection. Trustees should, however, avoid what is called a contributory mortgage (that is to say, a joint loan by the trustee and other persons) because in such a case the trustee would not possess complete control.[155] On the other hand, a sub-mortgage may be quite proper,[156] for here the mortgagee will mortgage to the trustee and the latter will obtain either a legal mortgage or an equitable mortgage which is capable of protection.

The Trustee Act 1925 (and its predecessors) expressly imposed various **14–072** conditions, which were not affected by the Trustee Investments Act 1961, which in effect required the trustees first to have been acting upon a report as to the value of the property made by a person whom they reasonably believed to be an able practical surveyor or valuer instructed and employed independently of any owner of the property and, secondly, not to lend more than two-thirds of the value of the property as stated in that report[157]; in the event of failure to comply, they were liable only in respect of any excess over the sum properly advanced.[158] These provisions have been repealed by the Trustee Act 2000 but their general tenor must necessarily remain relevant in

---

[152] See *Whitney v. Smith* (1869) L.R. 4 Ch. 513 at 521; *Re Walker* (1890) 62 L.T. 449.
[153] See *ante*, para 14–055.
[154] *Norris v. Wright* (1851) 14 Beav. 291; *Lockhart v. Reilly* (1857) 1 De G. & J. 464.
[155] *Webb v. Jonas* (1888) 39 Ch.D. 660.
[156] *Smethurst v. Hastings* (1885) 30 Ch.D. 490.
[157] Trustee Act 1925, s.8.
[158] Trustee Act 1925, s.9.

assessing whether or not trustees have satisfied the statutory duty of care. The trustees should therefore certainly still obtain a report as to the value of the property from an able practical surveyor or valuer instructed and employed independently of any owner of the property. Further it is likely that the trustees will still have to exercise their own judgment in deciding whether the surveyor or valuer is competent and will not be safe to trust blindly even in a nomination from their own solicitor, never mind one from the mortgagor's solicitor.[159] But there is no reason why the trustees should continue to restrict themselves rigidly to advances of two-thirds of the value of the security although an advance of more than the amount which institutional lenders are at the time prepared to consider or without the additional security which such institutional lenders would require is likely to be held to be a breach of the statutory duty of care. Nor is there any reason why the former restriction on the level of the trustees' liability for an excessive advance should be continued; if the trustees are held to have breached their statutory duty of care, their liability is therefore likely potentially to extend to the entire loss suffered by the trust.

(C)   The Acquisition of Land

14–073   Although trustees have long been able to invest in mortgages of land, until the enactment of the Trustee Act 2000 they had no general power to purchase land by way of investment and, even when the purchase of land was authorised (by statute or by the trust instrument), the authorisation did not necessarily include the purchase of land for residential purposes. The latter restriction was removed by the enactment of the Trusts of Land and Appointment of Trustees Act 1996. This legislation applies to any trust of land as defined in that Act,[160] namely any trust of property which consists of or includes land[161] and any trust of the proceeds of sale of land.[162] In its original form, section 6(3) conferred on the trustees of any such trust the power to purchase a legal estate in any land in England and Wales, whether for investment, for occupation by a beneficiary or for any other reason (this subsection has now been amended in form, although not in substance, by the Trustee Act 2000). Further, section 12(1) conferred (and confers) on any beneficiary who is entitled to an interest in possession in land subject to a trust of land the right to occupy it at any time if either the purposes of the trust include making the land available for his occupation or the land is held

---

[159] *Shaw v. Cates* [1909] 1 Ch. 389 at 404. Nor should they rely on the former statutory provision that the surveyor or valuer need not necessarily be a local man or have specialised local knowledge.

[160] This excludes settlements under the Settled Land Act 1925, which continue to be governed by s.73(1)(xi) of that Act, although such settlements irrevocably cease to be governed by that Act once all land and heirlooms held under the settlement in question have been sold (Trusts of Land and Appointment of Trustees Act 1996, s.2(4))

[161] Trusts of Land and Appointment of Trustees Act 1996, s.1(1)(a).

[162] *ibid.*, s.17(1), referring to s.17(3) under which "trust of proceeds of sale of land" means any trust of property which consists of or includes any proceeds of a disposition of land held in trust (which includes a settlement formerly subject to the Settled Land Act 1925) or any property representing such proceeds.

by the trustees so as to be so available,[163] subject to the trustees' right[164] to impose reasonable conditions on him in relation to that occupation.[165]

Section 8(1) of the Trustee Act 2000 has extended to all trusts a slightly **14–074** modified form of the power of investment enacted for trusts of land in the Trusts of Land and Appointment of Trustees Act 1996 (which, presumably in the interests of consistency, has been amended to provide that trustees of land can instead acquire land under the power conferred by section 8 of the Trustee Act 2000[166]). This provision[167] enables trustees to acquire freehold or leasehold land in the United Kingdom (defined for the purposes of England and Wales as a legal estate in land[168]) as an investment, for occupation by a beneficiary, or for any other reason. Trustees can also now acquire such land with mortgage finance whether or not the trust already holds any land (under the Trusts of Land and Appointment of Trustees Act 1996, this was only possible where the trust already held land). Trustees who acquire land by virtue of section 8 have all the powers of an absolute owner of the land in question.[169]

Once trustees have exercised their power under section 8, they will be **14–075** trustees of land and so they will additionally have all the powers and duties conferred by the Trusts of Land and Appointment of Trustees Act 1996. Thus the trustees,[170] when considering exercising any of their functions relating to land held by them, will have, so far as practicable, to consult the beneficiaries of full age who are entitled to an interest in possession in the land and give effect to their wishes[171] in so far as this is consistent with the general interest of the trust. Further, any beneficiary who is entitled to an interest in possession will have the right to occupy the land at any time if either the purposes of the trust include making the land available for his occupation or the land is held by the trustees so as to be so available,[172] subject to the trustees' right to impose reasonable conditions on him in relation to that occupation.[173]

---

[163] This right does not extend to any land which is unavailable or unsuitable for his occupation (*ibid.*, s.12(2)). Detailed provisions (*ibid.*, s.13) govern the trustees' rights to exclude and restrict beneficiaries' rights of occupation.

[164] *ibid.*, s.13(3). By s.13(5), these include the payment of outgoings and expenses and the assumption of any other obligation in relation to the land or to any activity which is or is proposed to be conducted there.

[165] However, where a trust was not a trust of land, which was the case where the property settled was entirely pure personalty, the basic prohibition on the purchase of land in the absence of an express power in the trust instrument continued to apply.

[166] Trustee Act 2000, s.40(1), Sch.2, Part II, para.45(1). This adds nothing to Trustee Act 2000, s.8.

[167] Which does not apply to settlements under the Settled Land Act 1925 or to certain types of charitable trusts (*ibid.*, s.10).

[168] *ibid.*, s.8(2)(a).

[169] *ibid.*, s.8(3), paralleling Trusts of Land and Appointment of Trustees Act 1996, s.6(1).

[170] Trusts of Land and Appointment of Trustees Act 1996, s.11.

[171] Or in the event of dispute to the wishes of the majority by value.

[172] Trusts of Land and Appointment of Trustees Act 1996, s.12(1); this right does not extend to any land which is unavailable or unsuitable for his occupation (*ibid.*, s.12(2)). Detailed provisions (*ibid.*, s.13) govern the trustees' rights to exclude and restrict beneficiaries' rights of occupation.

[173] *ibid.*, s.13(3). By s.13(5), these include the payment of outgoings and expenses and the assumption of any other obligation in relation to the land or to any activity which is or is proposed to be conducted there.

14–076   Section 8 of the Trustee Act 2000 permits the purchase of land for occupation by "a beneficiary", not merely a beneficiary with an interest in possession. The provision must therefore implicitly enable trustees to purchase land for occupation of land by beneficiaries who do not have an interest in possession and, for that matter, permit land already held to be occupied by such beneficiaries, even though they are not within the scope of the provisions of the Trusts of Land and Appointment of Trustee Act 1996. However, trustees who did so would have to be careful not to prejudice the interests of other beneficiaries since this could breach their duty of impartiality. There is, therefore, no obvious reason why the trustees should not permit land to be occupied by a beneficiary of a discretionary trust where that trust is the current interest in possession, provided that, as would usually be the case, the trustees had a discretion to pay the whole of the income of the trust to that beneficiary anyway. However, trustees could not permit occupation by a remainderman without prejudicing the interests of the beneficiaries with prior interests, whether those interests (and for that matter the interest of the remaindermen) arose under a fixed or a discretionary trust, although they could obviously do so if those beneficiaries consented. Further, the Trustee Act 2000 does not in terms enable trustees to impose reasonable conditions in relation to occupation by a beneficiary who does not have an interest in possession. This is presumably an oversight and might be able to be remedied by regarding the imposition of such conditions as implicit in the power to purchase for occupation, although such an argument is hardly consistent with the fact that an express power to impose such conditions was included in the Trusts of Land and Appointment of Trustees Act 1996.

14–077   It is not entirely clear what reason other than investment or occupation by a beneficiary there could be for trustees to exercise their power under section 8. They could presumably acquire premises in the relatively unlikely event that these were necessary for the administration of the trust and, possibly, for the use of a company wholly owned by a beneficiary who had an interest in possession. However, it is unlikely that the trustees would be able to acquire land for the purposes of a business carried on by the trust itself, unless the carrying on of that business was itself specifically authorised by the trust instrument. This is of course a specific manifestation of the general rule that the provisions of section 8 are not only additional to any other powers conferred on the trustees but are also subject to any restrictions imposed by the trust instrument.[174] Any such restrictions are likely to be strictly construed and will be particularly relevant in relation to the ability to purchase land with mortgage finance and the right to permit occupation by beneficiaries.

(D)   Standard Investment Criteria

14–078   Section 4 of the Trustee Act 2000 lays down what it describes as standard investment criteria. Trustees must have regard to these criteria both when exercising the general power of investment or any other investment power, and when carrying out the obligation which that section also imposes on them from time to time to review the investments of the trust and consider

---

[174] Trustee Act 2000, s.9.

whether they should be varied (annual reviews will generally be sufficient[175] unless the investments are of a particularly volatile type). The criteria are:

"(a) the suitability to the trust of investments of the same kind as any particular investment proposed to be made or retained and of that particular investment as an investment of that kind; and

"(b) the need for diversification of investments of the trust, in so far as is appropriate to the circumstances of the trust."

The sort of problem with which the trustees will be faced in relation to the first criterion is whether, and to what extent, present income should be sacrificed in the interests of future growth; in this respect, much will depend on arriving at a decision on the actual needs of the beneficiaries, the expected duration of the trust and, today, the beneficiaries' tax position. The way in which these factors have to be considered is shown by taking three examples: **14–079**

1. If trustees are holding property on trust for a minor beneficiary at the age of 18 in, say, 2013, they might invest in a government stock maturing in that year and therefore redeemable then at its highest value, just in time for the proceeds to be paid to the beneficiary with the additional advantage that the increase in its capital value will be exempt from capital gains tax[176] (increases in the capital value of most other investments will be subject to capital gains tax when the beneficiary reaches the age of 18 and becomes absolutely entitled to the trust property as against the trustees).

2. If a very small sum is to be held for a fairly short period of, for example, between five and 10 years but the beneficiary has adequate income from other sources, National Savings Certificates might be a suitable investment; although the rate of interest is small, this interest is free of tax[177] and the capital is also exempt from capital gains tax.[178]

3. If the beneficiary to whom the trustees are obliged to pay or in whose favour the trustees intend to exercise a discretion to pay the income of the trust has only a small total income,[179] the trustees might endeavour to invest at least part of the fund in a security which produces a high income, so far as they consider that this is consistent with their duties to the remainderman. But they should not select just any security which produces a high income, or even just any security

---

[175] The trustees will need to review the trust's investments towards the end of every tax year in order to utilise the trust's annual capital gains tax exemption and will also often need to take decisions on individual investments between reviews, particularly in the event of company reorganisations, mergers or takeovers.

[176] Taxation of Chargeable Gains Act 1992, s.115.

[177] Income and Corporation Taxes Act 1988, s.326.

[178] Taxation of Chargeable Gains Act 1992, s.121.

[179] Of £7,755 or less (in 2008–2009, he paid income tax at 10% on the first £2,320 of unearned income after his personal allowance of £5,435 (and at 20% thereafter until the higher rate kicked in at £36,000).

which produces a high income and is considered particularly safe. A beneficiary with a small total income will only have to pay income tax of 10 per cent on this income (even if the trust is a discretionary trust, the balance of the overall income tax which is payable will be recoverable by him). However, the tax liability may well be higher in respect of income from foreign companies and there will certainly be no possibility of any foreign tax being recovered. Consequently, in these circumstances the trustees must look for a company which has virtually the whole of its activities in England so that the minimum amount of tax will ultimately be payable.

It is in the light of considerations of this type that the full significance of this first criterion becomes apparent.

14–080 So far as the need for diversification is concerned, diversification is not actually defined but obviously means maintaining a spread of investments. The need referred to is the reduction of risk by spreading the trust's funds across a diversified portfolio of investments. But it is in this respect particularly that "modern trustees acting within their investment powers are entitled to be judged by the standards of current portfolio theory, which emphasises the risk level of the entire portfolio rather than the risk attaching to each investment taken in isolation".[180] Circumstances of the trust which could legitimately be taken into account to reduce or remove any need for diversification would undoubtedly include the smallness of the fund or the life tenant's paramount need of income.

(E) Advice

14–081 As for advice, section 5 of the Trustee Act 2000 provides that, before exercising the general power of investment or any other investment power and before each review of the investments, the trustees "must (unless the exception applies) obtain and consider proper advice about the way in which, having regard to the standard investment criteria, the power should be exercised". The exception[181] is that the trustees need not obtain such advice if they "reasonably conclude that in all the circumstances it is unnecessary or inappropriate so to do"; this would apply where the fund was small and any investment proposed was a comparatively safe one or where one or more of the trustees was competent to give the necessary advice.

14–082 The operative words of the basic rule are "obtain and consider"; the trustees are not therefore bound to follow the advice. Proper advice is defined[182] as "the advice of a person who is reasonably believed by the trustee to be qualified to give it by his ability in and practical experience of financial and other maters relating to the proposed investment". Since the enactment of the Financial Services Act 1986 (now the Financial Services and Markets Act 2000), the adviser must now be licensed anyway although the trustees must bear in mind that not everyone licensed under that legislation will necessarily be qualified to advise as to the particular circumstances of

---

[180] *Nestlé v. National Westminster Bank* (1988) unreported but transcribed in (1996) 10 Trust Law International 112.

[181] Trustee Act 2000, s.5(3).

[182] *ibid.*, s.5(4).

their trust. Although written advice is not actually required, trustees will be well advised to require any advice to be put into writing and also to minute whatever decisions they take as a result of receiving it.

3. *Express Investment Clauses*

When statutory powers of investment were restricted, as they were until the enactment of the Trustee Act 2000, clauses in trust deeds expressly enlarging the trustee's powers of investment beyond the scope authorised by law were extremely common. Historically such clauses tended to be construed strictly.[183] It is debateable to what extent this attitude to construction was adopted in practice in the decades immediately prior to the enactment of the Trustee Act 2000 anyway but, since the enactment of that legislation, it is certainly arguable that express investment clauses should be given a liberal interpretation.

14–083

The following illustrations from the case law manifest the different approaches, one from the late nineteenth century and the others from the present day. In *Bethell v. Abraham*[184] trustees were given power to "continue or change securities from time to time as to the majority shall seem meet". This clause was strictly construed by Jessel M.R., who held that the words related merely to determining the time at which a change of securities was to be made; they did not authorise a substantive change of investment outside the range of investments which were authorised. This case may be compared with the more recent decision in *Re Harari's Settlement Trusts*[185] where the clause empowered the trustees to invest "in or upon such investments as to them may seem fit"; Jenkins J. held that there was no justification for implying any restriction on these words and that the trustees were consequently able to make investments outside the range of investments which were authorised. A similarly liberal result was arrived at in *Re Peczenic's Settlement Trusts*,[186] where the trustees were authorised to make such investments in "any shares stocks property or property holding company as the trustees in their discretion shall consider to be in the best interest of" the beneficiary. Buckley J. held that the trustees were authorised to invest in anything of these types which was properly able to be treated as an investment but not to invest merely on personal security, which was clearly not within the list. These illustrations appear to manifest different attitudes to investment clauses in the modern law; however, the true position seems to be that it is entirely a question of construction of the particular investment clause before the court and that, although previous cases may be helpful, they will not necessarily be decisive.[187]

14–084

In the light of the present statutory powers of investment, use of express investment clauses is no longer as necessary. However, there is little doubt

14–085

---

[183] *Re Peczenic's Settlement Trusts* [1964] 1 W.L.R. 720 at 722.
[184] (1873) L.R. 17 Eq. 24.
[185] [1949] 1 All E.R. 430.
[186] [1964] 1 W.L.R. 720.
[187] See also, in addition to the cases cited in the text, *Re Maryon-Wilson's Estate* [1912] 1 Ch. 55; *Re McEacharn's Settlement Trusts* [1939] Ch. 858; *Re Hart's Will Trusts* [1943] 2 All E.R. 557; *Re Douglas' Will Trusts* [1959] 1 W.L.R. 744 (affirmed on another point [1959] 1 W.L.R. 1212); *Re Kolb's Will Trusts* [1962] Ch. 531 (interpretation of various investment clauses).

that trusts *inter vivos,* as distinct form wills, will continue to utilise one of the well-known model clauses giving the trustees even more unrestricted investment powers than the statutory powers. In particular such powers are necessary for investment in non-income producing investments and, probably, on personal credit; they are also advisable if a settlor wishes trustees to be able to retain particular investments, such as shares in his own or his family companies, without having to be concerned about their obligation under the second of the standard investment criteria to diversify investments. The Society of Trusts and Estate Practitioners has produced a set of standard administrative provisions which can be incorporated by reference[188]; these are particularly useful for wills, where tailor-made provisions are not generally necessary. However, it must be emphasised that the statutory duty of care applies just as much to the exercise of express powers of investment as it does to the statutory powers of investment.

4. *Types of Investment*

14–086   It has already been seen that, when any investment is contemplated, the trustees will have to give due consideration to the interest of all the beneficiaries and will have to hold the balance equally between them; the trustees will also have to consider advice and comply with the standard investment criteria, particularly the need for diversification of investments. Before the trustees can adequately do any of these things, they must have some knowledge of the characteristics of the different types of investment.

(A)   Securities

14–087   Investments in stocks, shares and bonds are colloquially termed "securities" but that term is somewhat dangerous; a "security" in this sense is not necessarily "secure".) The points to consider with any investment are, *inter alia*:

> (i) whether or not that investment is a "fixed-interest" security;
>
> (ii) whether or not the capital value will fluctuate; and
>
> (ii) if the capital value will fluctuate, in what way such fluctuation is likely.

14–088   If a security is a "fixed-interest" security, the amount of interest or dividend which is produced will never alter. Trustees who buy £10,000 Treasury 5.5 per cent Stock 2012 know that, whatever happens to the economic state of the nation, they will receive £550 per annum income. On the other hand, if they invest in ordinary shares of commercial companies, known as "equities", they do not know what they will receive, for this will depend entirely on the amount of the dividend which the companies in each year decide to

---

[188] These can be found in Kessler, *Drafting Trusts and Will Trusts* 8th edn (London, Sweet & Maxwell, 2007), which also contains, among the administrative provisions of the precedents of different types of trusts, a rather more detailed model investment clause.

pay. In bad years the companies may pay nothing, but in other years they may pay a larger amount than any fixed-interest security.

As regards capital value, there are only a few types of security where there will be no fluctuation. This will only occur where such securities are purchasable solely from the Government or other persons issuing them and are not bought and sold among private individuals. The best known examples are National Savings Certificates, which may be bought over the counter of the Post Office or Trustee Savings Bank, and some bonds issued by local authorities. **14–089**

By contrast, the capital value of all other securities, whether of the Government, local authorities, or commercial undertakings dealt with on a stock exchange, will fluctuate. To understand the terminology used in connection with this fluctuation, it is necessary to distinguish between the nominal price of an investment and its market price. The nominal price is the value of the investment as named on its face and at which, usually, it was originally issued. The market price is the price at which that security can for the time being be purchased. Suppose that the Government issued in 2005 a new stock which carries interest at £8 per cent and that a person then purchased from the Government a holding of £100 of the stock for £100 cash. Suppose also that in 2008 someone buys that holding on the Stock Exchange for £120 cash. The purchaser would be described as buying that holding of £100 nominal stock for a market price of £120. The interest, of course, is always calculated on the nominal value and so, however much the market price alters, the amount of interest will always be the same. When a security is bought for the same amount of cash as its nominal value, as in the example just given of the purchase in 2005 of £100 nominal stock for £100, that security is said to be bought at "par". **14–090**

The other term which is used in this context is "yield". This is the amount of income from a security expressed as a percentage of the market price paid for it and not of its nominal price. So if £120 cash is paid for £100 nominal £8 per cent stock, as the interest is fixed at £8 per annum the yield is: **14–091**

$$\frac{£8}{200} \times 100 = £6.67 \text{ per annum}$$

More precisely, the "yield" as just described is the "interest only" or "flat" yield. Where an investment is purchased at less than its nominal value but will be redeemed at its nominal value, its "redemption yield" may also be calculated. Very broadly, the redemption yield measures the gain to be expected on the redemption of the security together with the income which will be derived.[189]

It must be stressed that there are many factors which will govern fluctuations of market price but, in the case of Government securities, there are two in particular. First, there is the general level of interest rates obtainable elsewhere. If the normal yield at any time is £10 per cent from investments which are considered "safe", the market price of Government securities is **14–092**

---

[189] The redemption yield is, strictly, the amount by which the eventual capital sum which will be obtained on the redemption of the security, together with the income which will arise until redemption, has to be discounted to reduce the security to its present value.

likely to be adjusted so that that security will produce a yield of about £10 per cent. If the market price were substantially higher, no one would buy the Government securities since a safe £10 per cent yield could be obtained elsewhere. The second factor is whether and at what pace inflation (and so, depreciation in the purchasing power of money) is likely to occur. If a period of rapid inflation is forecast, most investors will not favour fixed-interest securities but will choose investments from which the return is likely to increase as inflation occurs; thus lack of demand will force down the market value of the fixed-interest securities. An example is the undated 3.5 per cent War Loan stock, which during the last period at which inflation was relatively high (during 1993) had a market value in the region of £38 for each £100 nominal of stock. By 1994, inflation had fallen and so the market value had risen to £58. It was thereafter remained relatively constant (for example, its market value during 1998 fluctuated between a low of £55 and a high of £60) until the substantial fall in the prices of equities which took place in 2002, as a result of which in the year to May 2003 its value fluctuated between a low of £65 and a high of £80 (at the time of writing in July 2008 its market value was £75, producing a yield of £4.67 per annum).

14–093   In the case of ordinary shares in commercial companies, the yield will also be important and this may be expected to be rather higher than from Government securities A commercial undertaking cannot give the capital guarantee which the Government does and the yield is greater to compensate for this; even companies of national standing can become insolvent. But there are two other important factors which influence the capital value of ordinary shares: first, the anticipated ability of the company to pay dividends in the future at least at the rate which it has paid for them in the past; and, secondly, the company's prospects for any increased profits and growth in the future.

(B) Land

14–094   The possible range of investments in land has already been considered.[190] Trustees can both invest in mortgages of land and acquire a legal estate in freehold or leasehold land in the United Kingdom as an investment, for occupation by a beneficiary, or for any other reason.

(C) Bank Deposits

14–095   Bank deposits of course produce no capital appreciation, merely income, and as such are the clearest possible example of an investment which favours the tenant for life at the expense of the remaindermen; nor is the rate of interest paid usually much in excess of inflation save in the case of long fixed-term deposits. Where property is held for persons by way of succession, trustees will generally be unwise to leave any more of the trust property on deposit than is likely to be necessary to cover the next few years' anticipated regular payments, such as income tax and professional fees (it is not usually desirable for a trust to have no liquid funds at all since securities may then have to be sold at disadvantageous times in order to fund regular payments of this type). In other types of trusts, such as immediate discretionary trusts, trustees will have a freer hand in this respect

---

[190] See *ante*, paras 14–070, 14–073.

but bank deposits should nevertheless still be restricted to a relatively small percentage of the total trust property.

(D) Non-Income Producing Investments

Non-income producing assets are the exact converse of bank deposits since **14–096** they can produce only capital appreciation and are the clearest possible example of an investment which favours the remaindermen at the expense of the tenant for life. Such investments are not within any of the statutory powers of investment; this is because the legal meaning of "investment" is still its traditional meaning, namely an asset which produces income with the connotation that it is likely to produce a surplus on revenue account over the anticipated period of holding of the asset.[191] This means that such investments can only be purchased pursuant to an express investment clause.[192] When property is held for persons by way of succession, trustees will generally be unwise to invest any of the trust property in non-income producing assets except to the extent that the part of the property in question is sufficiently balanced by investments which produce a high rate of income at the expense of capital appreciation. In other types of trust, however, as a result of fiscal legislation it has become more and more prudent in many situations to reduce or eliminate income and instead to seek capital appreciation. Consequently, in general and financial usage, the word "investment" now implies any asset which will produce a good return even if that is entirely in the form of capital appreciation.

The fiscal legislation has produced the following results[193]:   **14–097**

(i) Income, when paid to a beneficiary, is taxable in his hands at the same rate as that at which he pays income tax[194] up to a maximum effective rate of 40 per cent[195] although the trust's administration expenses will always bear tax at the rate at which the sums in question are taxed in the hands of the trustees, which varies according to their source and the nature of the trust.

(ii) Where trustees instead accumulate income, that income will be subject to income tax of 34 per cent (25 per cent in the case of company distributions).

(iii) Capital gains realised by anyone are now taxable at the rate of 18 per cent.

(iv) If the trustees instead hold an asset which never produces income, their liability is to capital gains tax only.

---

[191] See the reasoning in *Cooke v. Haddock* (1960) 39 T.C. 64; *Johnston v. Heath* [1970] 1 W.L.R. 1567.

[192] *Re Power* [1947] Ch. 572.

[193] See *post*, Chapter 15.

[194] Save that income from company distributions will suffer income tax of 10% (the amount retained by the company) even if the beneficiary himself is not taxable at this rate and so is not basically taxable at all.

[195] Although income from company distributions paid out to a beneficiary of a discretionary trust who pays income tax at 40% will in fact bear a total of 37% income tax.

As a result, trustees have increasingly sought to lay out trust funds in the acquisition of non-income, or low-income, producing assets. It must be repeated that this can only be done where there is an express power to this effect in the trust instrument but, where there is such a power, the following are some of the possibilities which have recently found favour.

(1) Non-Income-Bearing Securities

14–098 A number of securities have been developed particularly to meet this need. Under split-level shares and units, one of the two classes carries the entitlement to all income but no capital appreciation and the other class, which is what is acquired by the trust, carries entitlement to all capital appreciation but no income. Under single-premium bonds, a policy of assurance is effected with an insurance company for the payment of one premium only at the outset; on maturity (after a fixed period of years or the earlier death of the assured), the payee receives a sum equivalent to the original premium paid, together with a profit which depends on the success which the insurance company has had in the investment of its funds. In principle, the total proceeds of both securities are received as capital.

(2) Chattels

14–099 A wide variety of chattels have been purchased by trustees as growth investments. Over the last few years trustees have invested in works of art, antique furniture, silver, silver bullion and oriental carpets. Almost invariably these are unsuitable as investments unless the trustees have considerable freedom of choice as to the time of disposal; due to the volatility of the various markets, a period of some years may have to elapse before it becomes a good time to sell.

(3) Loans to Beneficiaries

14–100 In some circumstances, it may be thought desirable that capital appreciation should accrue to a beneficiary rather than to the trustees. In such circumstances, the trustees may choose to lend trust funds to the beneficiary, interest free, perhaps securing the loan by taking a charge over the assets which the beneficiary purchases with them. On the death of the beneficiary, the loan is repaid from his estate. However, where this is done, the whole of the capital appreciation accrues to the beneficiary and not to the fund as a whole, so that this will only be proper where it is specifically authorised by the trust instrument or where all the other beneficiaries affected agree.

VII. THE EMPLOYMENT OF AGENTS

14–101 Trustees often wish to engage other persons to assist them in the execution of their trust or the administration of the trust property. Examples are where the trustees consider it appropriate for the trust accounts and records to be kept by a solicitor or an accountant; where particular action requires special skills, such as the type of advice in relation to the investments of the trust which has already been considered; or where particular difficulties arise in the course of the administration of the trust property, as may happen when trust property is situated abroad. Any person appointed by trustees to act on their behalf in the execution of their trust is known as their "agent", although two types of agents with specific functions, nominees and custodians, are generally known by the latter names.

1. *The Trustees' Powers to Appoint Agents*

It is possible that the trust instrument itself may confer on the trustees an   **14–102** effective power for the appointment of agents. However, this is not actually necessary and so is in practice uncommon because of the existence of general statutory powers now contained in the Trustee Act 2000. These powers are additional to any other powers to appoint agents conferred on the trustees and are subject to any restrictions or exclusions imposed by the trust instrument;[196] they comprise both a general power to appoint agents and specific powers to appoint nominees and custodians.

The statutory powers enable appointment to be made on such terms as to   **14–103** remuneration and other matters as the trustees may determine but these terms cannot, unless it is reasonably necessary, include either a provision permitting the agent to appoint a substitute, or any exemption clause restricting the agent's liability, or any term permitting the agent to act in circumstances which give rise to potential conflicts of interest.[197] For so long as the agent in question continues to act, the trustees must[198] keep under review the arrangements and the way in which they are working and consider in appropriate circumstances whether there is a need to exercise any power of intervention which they may have; such a power is defined[199] as including a power to give directions as well as a power to revoke the agent's appointment. If the trustees consider that there is a need to intervene, they must do so. Trustees must exercise their powers of appointment, particularly in relation to the selection of the agent and the terms on which he is to act, and also their duty of review in accordance with the statutory duty of care.[200]

(A) The General Power to Appoint Agents

Section 11 of the Trustee Act 2000 confers a general authority for trustees   **14–104** collectively[201] to delegate their delegable functions to agents. Trustees have, as they had under the provision which this replaced,[202] the power to appoint an agent to do an act even if they could readily have done that act themselves.[203] The agent may be one of the trustees,[204] provided that he is not also a beneficiary, but may not be one of the beneficiaries, whether or not he is

---

[196] Trustee Act 2000, s.26.
[197] *ibid.*, ss.14, 20.
[198] *ibid.*, s.22(1).
[199] *ibid.*, s.22(4).
[200] *ibid.*, s.1 and Sch.1, para.3; see *ante*, para 14–002.
[201] The Trustee Act 2000 is not concerned with individual delegation, delegation by individual trustees of their functions as such. This is the subject of the Trustee Delegation Act 1999; see *ante*, para 13–088.
[202] Trustee Act 1925, s.23(1).
[203] But see *ante*, para 13–090.
[204] Trustee Act 2000, s.12(1).

also a trustee.[205] Two or more persons may not be authorised to exercise the same function unless they are to do so jointly[206] but it does not matter if the agent is also the nominee and/or the custodian of the trustees.[207]

14–105   The Law Commission[208] originally proposed that a distinction should be drawn between administrative powers, which would be delegable even if they involved considerably more than merely ministerial acts, and distributive powers, which would not be delegable. However, it was wisely concluded that such a broad distinction would cause difficulties, particularly in the case of powers to appoint and replace trustees which the Law Commission considered should not be delegable in the absence of express authority in the trust instrument. Section 11 therefore contains a general power to delegate under which "the trustees of a trust may authorise any person to exercise any or all of their delegable functions as their agent".[209] This is followed by a list of delegable functions which differs depending on whether or not the trust in question is charitable.

14–106   Section 11(2) provides that, in the case of a trust which is not a charitable trust, any function is a delegable function except the following four types:

(i) "any function relating to whether or in what way any assets of the trust should be distributed" (these functions are of course true dispositive discretions or powers);

(ii) "any power to decide whether any fees or other payment due to made out of the trust funds should be made out of income or capital";

(iii) "any power to appoint a person to be a trustee of the trust" (it was presumably concluded that any power to remove trustees would not be likely to be vested in any or all of the existing trustees); or

(iv) "any power conferred by any other enactment or the trust instrument which permits the trustees to delegate any of their functions or to appoint a person to act as a nominee or custodian".

14–107   On the other hand, Section 11(3) provides that, in the case of a charitable trust, only the following functions are delegable:

(i) "any function consisting of carrying out a decision that the trustees have taken" (purely ministerial functions);

(ii) "any function relating to the investment of assets subject to the trust (including, in the case of land held as an investment, managing the land and creating or disposing of an interest in the land)";

---

[205] *ibid.*, s.12(3).
[206] *ibid.*, s.12(2).
[207] *ibid.*, s.12(4).
[208] Law Com. No. 260 (1999), *Report on Trustees' Powers and Duties*, Part IV.
[209] Trustee Act 2000, s.11(1).

(iii) "any function relating to the raising of funds for the trust otherwise than by means of profits of a trade which is an integral part of carrying out the trust's charitable purpose" (defined[210] as a trade[211] whose profits are applied solely for the purposes of the trust where either "the trade is exercised in the course of the actual carrying out of a primary purpose of the trust" or the relevant work is mainly carried out by its beneficiaries); and

(iv) "any other function prescribed by an order made by the Secretary of State" exercisable by statutory instrument subject to parliamentary review.[212]

Where an agent is authorised to exercise a function which is itself subject to specific duties or restrictions, such as the requirement to have regard to the standard investment criteria when exercising any power of investment,[213] he is subject to those duties or restrictions[214] unless the latter relate to the obtaining of advice and he is a person from whom it would be proper for that advice to have been obtained.[215] However, an agent is not obliged to carry out the consultations with beneficiaries of full age with interests in possession in land held by the trust which are envisaged by the Trusts of Land and Appointments of Land Act 1996[216]; on the other hand, the terms of any delegation of functions relating to land held by the trust must not prevent the trustees from themselves complying with their duty to carry out such consultations.[217]   **14–108**

Special provisions[218] apply to agents who are to exercise asset management functions, which are defined[219] as the investment of trust assets, the acquisition of trust property, the management of trust property, and the disposal of, or the creation or disposal of an interest in, trust property (this broad definition goes well beyond pure investment management). The agreement with the agent must be in, or be evidenced in, writing[220] and must include a term to the effect that the agent will secure compliance with a written policy statement, or any revisions to it, prepared in advance by the trustees giving guidance as to how the agent's functions should be exercised; the guidance must be formulated with a view to ensuring that the agent will exercise his functions in the best interests of the trust.[221] The trustees' general obligation[222] to keep under review the arrangements and the way in which they are working specifically includes[223] a duty to consider   **14–109**

---

[210] *ibid.* s.11(4).
[211] Whether or not it is carried on in the United Kingdom.
[212] Trustee Act 2000, s.11(4).
[213] See *ante*, para 14–078.
[214] Trustee Act 2000, s.13(1).
[215] *ibid.*, s.13(2).
[216] *ibid.*, s.13(5). Such consultations are discussed *ante*, para 14–075.
[217] *ibid.*, s.13(4).
[218] *ibid.*, s.15.
[219] *ibid.*, s.15(5).
[220] *ibid.*, s.15(1).
[221] *ibid.*, s.15(2)–(4).
[222] *ibid.*, s.22(1).
[223] *ibid.*, s.22(2).

whether there is any need to revise or replace the policy statement, a duty to revise or replace it if they consider that this is necessary, and a duty to assess whether the policy statement is being complied with.

(B) Nominees and Custodians

14–110 Until the enactment of the Trustee Act 2000, trustees had no statutory power to appoint nominees and custodians. The lack of any such power, in the absence of any provision to this effect in the trust instrument, was extremely inconvenient in the light of modern investment practices whereby securities are almost invariably held by nominees in order to facilitate rapid sales. The Trustee Act 2000 has now conferred on trustees:

(i) a power to appoint a nominee in relation to such of the assets of the trust other than settled land as they determine and take such steps as are necessary to secure that those assets are vested in him[224];

(ii) a power to appoint a custodian, defined as someone who undertakes the safe custody of assets or of any documents or records concerning them, in relation to such of the assets of the trust as they determine[225]; and,

(iii) where the trust property includes bearer securities, a duty to appoint a custodian of those securities, unless the trust already has a custodian or the trustees are exempted from complying with this requirement by the trust instrument or by any statutory provision.[226]

In all three cases, the appointment must be made in, or be evidenced in writing. The person appointed must[227] either carry on a business which consists of or includes acting as a nominee or custodian, or be a body corporate controlled by the trustees, or be an incorporated solicitors practice[228] (charitable trustees must additionally act in accordance with any guidance given by the Charity Commission). The nominee or custodian may be any trustee who is a trust corporation or two or more trustees acting jointly (contrary to the position for agents, there is no prohibition on them also being beneficiaries). It does not matter if the person appointed is both nominee and custodian and/or also an agent of the trustees.

2. *The Liability of Trustees for the Acts or Defaults of Agents*

14–111 Prior to the enactment of the Trustee Act 2000, the law governing the liability of trustees for the acts or defaults of their agents was a matter of some controversy.[229] However, that Act simply provides[230] that a trustee is not

---

[224] *ibid.*, s.16.

[225] *ibid.*, s.17.

[226] *ibid.*, s.18.

[227] *ibid.*, s.19.

[228] Under Administration of Justice Act 1985, s.9.

[229] This was due to doubts as to the correct interpretation of the now repealed section 30 of the Trustee Act 1925 and due to the existence of inconsistencies between that section, no matter how it was interpreted, and the equally repealed section 23(1) of the Trustee Act 1925.

[230] Trustee Act 2000, s.23(1).

liable for any act or default of any agent, nominee or custodian unless he has
failed to comply with the statutory duty of care applicable to him[231] "when
entering into the arrangements under which the person acts as agent, nominee or custodian" or when carrying out the duties to keep under review
those arrangements and the way in which they are working which have
already been considered.[232] Where, unusually,[233] the trustee has agreed a
term under which the agent, nominee or custodian can appoint a substitute,
the trustee will similarly not be liable for any act or default of the substitute
unless he has failed to comply with the statutory duty of care applicable to
him[234] "when agreeing that term" or when carrying out his duties of
review.[235]

There are as yet no reported cases on these provisions but an authority on   **14–112**
the pre-existing common law duty to use the diligence and care of an
ordinary prudent man of business whose facts remain relevant is *Fry v.
Tapson*.[236] Trustees were prepared to lend trust money on mortgage, as they
were entitled to do; however, instead of exercising their own judgment as to
the valuer to be appointed, they relied on the advice of their solicitors. The
surveyor chosen in fact was the agent of the potential mortgagor and had a
financial interest in the transaction being completed. The money was lent
and, when loss occurred, it was held that the trustees were bound to make
it good. They would not have been made liable if they had made an
independent choice of the agent themselves. This is an example of a decision
which the trustees ought themselves to have made, an act which could not
properly be delegated, and it is inevitable that trustees who acted in this
way today would be held to have breached their statutory duty of care.

VIII. PAYMENTS TO BENEFICIARIES

The general principle is that a trustee is absolutely responsible for ensuring   **14–113**
that the right amount is paid to the right beneficiary. In *Eaves v. Hickson*[237]
trustees were provided with a forged marriage certificate which led them to
believe that certain children were legitimate and consequently beneficiaries;
they therefore paid the trust funds out to them. The trustees were nevertheless held liable to make good to the rightful beneficiary so much of these
funds as could not be recovered either from the children or from their father,
who had provided the forged certificate. Similarly, where trustees pay trust
money to the wrong beneficiary, on an erroneous but bona fide construction
of the trust instrument[238] or simply because they assumed that its provisions
were valid when they were in fact void for uncertainty,[239] they will be held
liable to make good the loss. Where the trustees have in the particular

---

[231] Under *ibid.*, s.1 and Sch.I, para.3.
[232] See *ante*, para 14–002.
[233] This is only possible where it is reasonably necessary; Trustee Act 2000, ss.14(2), 20(2).
[234] *ibid.*, s.1 & Sch.I, para.3.
[235] *ibid.*, s.23(2).
[236] (1884) 28 Ch.D. 268.
[237] (1861) 30 Beav. 136.
[238] *Hilliard v. Fulford* (1876) 4 Ch.D. 389.
[239] See the facts which gave rise to *Re Diplock* [1948] Ch. 465.

circumstances acted honestly and reasonably and ought fairly to be excused, the court has a discretion to grant them relief,[240] but this does not alter the trustees' primary obligation of ensuring payment to the right beneficiary.

14–114   Where there is any doubt as to who is entitled to trust property, the trustees should apply to the court for directions in the manner discussed later in this chapter. They will then be protected if they comply with whatever directions the court gives. If the beneficiary entitled cannot be traced, the trustees may pay the money into court, and so obtain a good discharge for it. And where one of several beneficiaries cannot be traced, the court may authorise the trustees to distribute the trust fund as if the beneficiary who cannot be traced were dead.[241] Nevertheless, the court is keen to discourage trustees from making payment into court of trust money where there is no good reason for doing so; the trustees can therefore be made personally liable for the costs of the application for payment in. The power of payment into court is one of the exceptional cases in which the wishes of the majority of the trustees binds them all. The court equally discourages applications by trustees for protection where they incur no practical risk at all. Thus, in Re Pettifor[242] Pennycuick J. said that, in normal circumstances, the court would consider it an unnecessary waste of money for trustees to come to court and ask for permission to distribute a trust fund on the basis that a woman of 70 would not have a further child.

14–115   When making distributions, trustees must remember that beneficial interests under the trust can be assigned or charged. Where an assignee makes a claim to trust property, the trustees will, before making payment, have to investigate his title to the interest assigned; however, they will be obliged to give effect to effective assignments.

14–116   Before finally distributing the trust property, the trustees must take care to discharge all the trust's debts. In most cases of long-standing trusts, there cannot be any debts due from the trust of which the trustees are unaware. However, where there is a possibility of outstanding debts, advantage should be taken of section 27 of the Trustee Act 1925. Under this section, the trustees may advertise in the London Gazette, and usually also in another newspaper, their intention of distributing the trust fund to the beneficiaries and requiring persons interested in the trust fund to send them notice of their claim. Any such claims must be sent in within the time fixed by the notice, which must not be less than two months after it is published. At the expiration of that time, the trustees can safely distribute the trust fund after discharging only those claims of which they have notice. If a creditor subsequently comes forward, he may in appropriate circumstances be able to follow the trust property into the hands of the beneficiaries to whom it has been distributed; however, he will have no remedy against the trustees themselves.

14–117   Finally, when a trusteeship comes to an end, the trustees are entitled to put themselves into the position in which no further disputes can be raised

---

[240] Trustee Act 1925, s.61; see post, para 22–088.
[241] The so-called "Benjamin Order"; see Re Benjamin [1902] 1 Ch. 723, Re Taylor's Estate [1969] 2 Ch. 245; Re Lowe's Will Trust [1973] 1 W.L.R. 882 at 887; Re Green's Will Trust [1985] 3 All E.R. 455; Re Evans (deceased) [1999] 2 All E.R. 777.
[242] [1966] Ch. 257.

about payments to the beneficiaries. To achieve this, they are entitled to present their final accounts to the beneficiaries and to require them to give a formal discharge from the trusteeship. If the beneficiaries refuse, the trustees may have the accounts taken in court, that is, examined by an official of the Chancery Division, at the expense of the trust fund and in that way obtain confirmation that those accounts are in order.

IX. Payment of Trustees' Expenses

It will be seen in a later chapter[243] that, in the absence of a provision in the trust instrument permitting a trustee to be paid for his services, only trust corporations and trustees who act in the course of a profession or business which consists of or includes the management or administration of trusts are entitled to be paid for their services. Trustees are, however, entitled to be reimbursed all expenses which have been properly incurred (however, they are not normally entitled to interest thereon). This right of reimbursement is in respect both of money actually spent by the trustee and of liabilities which he has incurred. Thus in *Benett v. Wyndham*[244] a trustee of an estate directed woodcutters employed on the estate to fell some trees. The woodcutters were negligent and allowed a bough to fall on a passer-by who was injured. The trustee, as legal owner of the estate, was sued and he was allowed to reimburse himself the damages out of the trust fund. However, it does not follow that a trustee will be allowed all his expenses; they must be reasonable and proper in all the circumstances. In *Malcolm v. O'Callaghan*[245] an ingenious trustee made a number of journeys to Paris to be present at the hearing of a case in the French courts which concerned the trust, but which turned solely on a question of French law and for which the trustee's presence was in no way necessary. He was not allowed his expenses against the trust.

14–118

Trustees are obviously entitled to be reimbursed the expenses of properly taking or defending legal proceedings on behalf of the trust in the same way as other expenses. However, it is generally prudent for trustees, before taking or defending proceedings, to apply to the court for its approval in the manner discussed below. If they do not do so and the proceedings are unsuccessful, it will be up to them to prove that they had reasonable grounds for taking or defending proceedings; if they cannot prove this, they will be deprived of their costs (and for that matter may well finish up paying the costs of the other side as well).

14–119

The trustees' right of indemnity is generally against the trust property,[246] not against the beneficiaries. If, therefore, the trustees' right of indemnity exceeds the value of the trust property, they will not normally be able to claim the balance from the beneficiaries personally. The right of indemnity can, however, be enforced against a beneficiary personally in three circumstances: first, where the beneficiary in question was the creator of the

14–120

---

[243] See *post*, Chapter 20.
[244] (1862) 4 De G. 7. & J. 259.
[245] (1835) 3 Myl. & Cr. 52.
[246] Trustee Act 2000, s.31(1).

trust[247]; secondly, where the trustees accepted the trust at the request of a beneficiary[248]; and, thirdly, where the trustees are nominees.[249]

X. APPLICATIONS TO THE COURT

14–121　There are a number of circumstances in which it is appropriate for trustees to seek the guidance of the court. Such applications to the court used to be made by way of originating summons but, since the introduction of the Civil Procedure Rules 1998, they are instead made by application under Part 23 of those Rules.

1. *Applications by way of Construction Summons*

14–122　One of the most common grounds on which trustees apply to the court is in order to determine the proper construction of words in a will or settlement whose meaning is uncertain; the words in question may be those which determine the beneficial interests or those which determine the powers of the trustees. An application of this type has traditionally been known as a "construction summons" and this expression has survived despite the fact that what is now made is an application rather than a summons. In principle, all the beneficiaries have to be joined as defendants; where what is in issue is the beneficial interests, this involves joining all those persons who could conceivably be beneficiaries according to any of the possible constructions of the documents in question. In practice, however, where a trust has more than a small number of beneficiaries, the trustees will generally, before the construction summons is actually heard, make an application to the court for directions with a view to the appointment of a number of representative beneficiaries[250] to argue in favour of the different possible constructions of the relevant documents; on such an application the court can, if necessary, also be asked to specify the particular issues which are to be determined.[251] Whether or not this is done, all the beneficiaries who have been joined as defendants and have been duly served with notice of the proceedings will be bound by the judgment of the court whether or not they enter an appearance and, in the event that they do, whether or not they choose to attend and take part in the proceedings.[252] All the costs of a construction summons and of any necessary preliminary applications, both those incurred by the trustees and those incurred by any beneficiaries who do take part, are invariably paid out of the trust property.

14–123　Alternatively trustees (and personal representative) can rely on section 48 of the Administration of Justice Act 1985 and apply to the court for an order, made without hearing argument, which authorises them to adopt and to act

---

[247] *Matthews v. Ruggles-Brise* [1911] 1 Ch. 194.
[248] *Jervis v. Wolferstan* (1874) L.R. 18 Eq. 18 at 24.
[249] *Hardoon v. Belilios* [1901] A.C. 118.
[250] Under Civil Procedure Rules 1998, Part 19.
[251] The court did both in *Russell-Cooke Trust Co. v. Prentis* [2003] 2 All E.R. 478; see at 482–483.
[252] See *Russell-Cooke Trust Co. v. Prentis* [2003] 2 All E.R. 478 at 482–483.

on the basis of the conclusion as to the correct construction of a document in an opinion given by a barrister or solicitor-advocate who has a 10-year High Court qualification (this basically means that the lawyer in question has had the right to appear in the High Court as an advocate for more than 10 years). The court must be satisfied that no dispute exists which makes it inappropriate for the court to make the order without hearing argument. In practice this procedure can only be adopted where there is either no dispute at all or one of two conflicting views as to the correct construction is obviously wrong. In any case in which conflicting opinions are provided by well-qualified legal advisers, the procedure is not appropriate. While the making of an order under this section will inevitably protect the trustees from any liability for breach of trust to beneficiaries who are adversely affected by the order, there does not appear to be anything to prevent those beneficiaries from issuing proceedings against the beneficiaries who are advantaged by the order with a view to establishing a different construction and recovering the property distributed to them. Perhaps for this reason, in more than 10 years practice at the Chancery Bar, the author of this edition has yet to encounter a case in which this procedure has been employed.

2. *Applications for Directions*

Where trustees are in doubt as to the manner in which they should act, they **14–124** may make an application to the court for directions. Provided that the trustees place before the court all the relevant facts and subsequently act in accordance with the court's directions, it is an established principle that they will be absolutely protected. The most straightforward example is the type of application for the appointment of representative beneficiaries made prior to a construction summons in the manner explained above. However, trustees may also by application ask the court to adjudicate on some course of action on which they propose to embark.

In this context, a distinction has to be drawn between four types of **14–125** proceedings[253]: first, a construction summons, where the trustees are in effect asking the court whether they have power to carry out the course of action in question; secondly, an application in circumstances where there is no doubt about the powers of the trustees to carry out the course of action in question but where, because the decision is particularly momentous, the trustees wish to obtain the blessing of the court in advance[254]; thirdly, an application where, although there is again no doubt about the powers of the trustees to carry out the course of action in question, the trustees are unable or unwilling to take the decision themselves and therefore ask the court to take the decision for them, thus in effect surrendering their own discretion to the court; and, fourthly, where the beneficiaries are challenging a course

---

[253] See *The Public Trustee v. Cooper* [2001] W.T.L.R. 901 at 922–924.
[254] Such a case was *X v. A* [2005] EWHC 2706 (Ch), [2006] 1 W.L.R. 741, where the trustees wished the court to bless the exercise of a power of advancement by, at the request of the life tenant, advancing the bulk of the trust assets to her so that she could apply them for charitable purposes. The application was not supported by the remaindermen and was denied.

of action which has already been taken by the trustees on the grounds that it is outside their powers or amounted to an improper exercise of those powers (such proceedings are of course hostile litigation between beneficiaries and trustees and are therefore outside the scope of the present discussion). Where there are doubts both about the scope of the powers of the trustees and whether, if they have the necessary powers, those powers should be or should have been exercised, it will in effect be necessary to combine a construction summons with one of the other three types of proceedings.

14–126   The distinction between the second and third types of proceedings has not always been easy to draw. However, it is now clear that the court will only accept a surrender by the trustees of their own discretion where there is a good reason, the most obvious reasons being that the trustees are honestly deadlocked, in other words where there is a disagreement over a proposed course of action which cannot be resolved simply by the removal of a recalcitrant trustee, or that they are unable to decide because all, or nearly all, of them are disqualified from doing so as the result of a conflict of interest. Only in such circumstances will the court take the decision for the trustees. Otherwise it is inevitably the case that the trustees are in a much better position than the court to know what is in the best interests of the beneficiaries and so the court will instead make a scrupulous examination of the evidence put before them by the trustees and by any of the beneficiaries who objects to the proposed course of action.[255] In such circumstances, provided that the trustees have in fact reached a decision at which a reasonable body of trustees properly instructed could properly have arrived and provided that that decision is not vitiated by any conflict of interest under which any of the trustees had or might have been labouring, the court will give its blessing to the course of action in question.

14–127   Thus, where the trustees of a trust for, primarily, the employees of a company but, subject to that, for charity were obliged not to sell or otherwise dispose of the trust's only asset, an 18 per cent shareholding in the employer company, "unless in the opinion of the Trustees there are special circumstances which make it desirable to do so", the court gave its blessing to a sale against the wishes of a representative employee beneficiary when the trustees had, in the absence of any effective conflict of interest, taken their decision to sell in the light of the impact of changes in the economic conditions of the industry in question on the future prospects of the company and in the light of the decision of a 30 per cent shareholder, a charitable trust created by the same settlor, to refuse to support the only other feasible means of securing the future of the company and to sell come what may.[256] In contrast, where trustees wished the court to bless the exercise of a power of advancement by, at the request of the life tenant, advancing the bulk of the trust assets to her so that she could apply them for charitable purposes, the court, having actually denied the application on the grounds that the advancement would not be for the benefit of the life tenant, went to state

---

[255] ibid., at 925.
[256] ibid., at 925–936.

that the application would also have been denied because there was insufficient evidence that the trustees had looked in sufficient detail into the individual circumstances of the remaindermen and the potential remaindermen, some of whom had not supported the application.[257]

It has already been indicated that, where trustees act in accordance with a decision of the court before whom all the relevant facts have been placed, they are completely protected from any subsequent claim by the beneficiaries that, by so doing, they have committed a breach of trust. This was specifically held by Harman L.J. in *Re Londonderry's Settlement*.[258] What then is the position if the trustees consider the decision of the court to have been erroneous? **14–128**

In *Re Londonderry's Settlement*[259] the trustees had sought directions as to whether certain documents sought by a beneficiary ought to be disclosed. At first instance Plowman J. decided that they ought to be disclosed. The trustees appealed, successfully in the event, but the Court of Appeal nearly refused to hear the appeal. Harman L.J. observed that it seemed to him that the appeal was "an irregularity" on the basis that "trustees seeking the protection of the court are protected by the court's order and it is not for them to appeal".[260] Although the trustees would certainly have been protected had they acted in accordance with what turned out to be the erroneous decision of Plowman J., why should they not have been entitled to appeal if they considered the decision both wrong and adverse to the interests of the other beneficiaries?[261] Fortunately Salmon L.J. took a different view, saying[262] that in his view the trustees were "fully justified in bringing this appeal" and that "it was their duty to bring it since they believed, rightly, that an appeal was essential for the protection of the general body of beneficiaries". What is remarkable is not that Salmon L.J. made this statement but that he had to make it in the first place. **14–129**

Unfortunately, however, these remarks of Salmon L.J. have introduced a further difficulty. It might have been thought that permitting the trustees to appeal in *Re Londonderry's Settlement*[263] would simply have established the principle that, in the event that trustees apply to the court and are given a decision which is wrong, they may appeal. But, according to Salmon L.J., they have a duty to do so. As a result it may one day have to be decided to what extent trustees are protected if they act in accordance with a decision of the court which they believe to be clearly wrong. The general view, encapsulated by the remarks of Harman L.J., is that they would be protected; however, this does not square with the enunciation by Salmon L.J. of a duty to appeal in such circumstances. **14–130**

---

[257] *X v. A* [2005] EWHC 2706 (Ch), [2006] 1 W.L.R. 741.

[258] [1965] Ch. 918 at 930.

[259] [1965] Ch. 918 at 930.

[260] *ibid.*, at 930.

[261] It is particularly ironic that this statement by Harman L.J. should have been made in a case where, because the trustees did appeal, the law was patently improved for the benefit of all trustees.

[262] *ibid.*, at 936.

[263] [1965] Ch. 918.

3. Applications for a "Beddoe Order"

14–131   A further, and from the point of view of the trustees probably the most important, situation in which it will be necessary for them to apply to the court is in relation to taking and defending legal proceedings on behalf of the trust. This is because of the risk that, in the event that the proceedings are unsuccessful, a challenge may be made to the propriety of their conduct with the consequential risk that they may have to pay out of their own pockets not only the costs incurred by the trust but also any costs awarded by the court to the other party. Trustees will be at risk if they act without either the consent of all the beneficiaries, which is only feasible if all are ascertainable and *sui juris*, or pursuant to the directions of the Chancery Division of the High Court. An application of this type is known as an application for a "*Beddoe* Order".[264]

14–132   Such an application is made in separate proceedings, to which all the beneficiaries, or representative beneficiaries appointed in the way which has already been considered, have to be joined; full disclosure must be made in order to enable the court to form a view on the prospects of success of the claim or defence and therefore to determine what ought to be done in the best interests of the trust.[265] Where a *Beddoe* Order is obtained, the trustee "is entitled to take his costs out of the trust fund on an indemnity basis unless the court otherwise orders and the court can otherwise order only on the ground that he has acted unreasonably in the prosecution or defence of the action or that he failed to make full and proper disclosure at the time when the court's directions were sought".[266] However, a trustee who does not apply for such an order will not necessarily incur personal liability for costs; "he will normally be entitled to his costs out of the trust fund if the court is satisfied that if he had applied for directions he would have been directed to prosecute or defend the proceedings".[267]

14–133   In *Alsop Wilkinson v. Neary*[268] Lightman J. classified the different types of proceedings in which trustees are likely to be involved in the following way[269]:

> (i) what Lightman J. called "a trust dispute", a dispute as to the trusts on which they hold the subject matter of the settlement, which may be

---

[264] After the case of *Re Beddoe* [1893] 1 Ch. 547, in which the Court of Appeal deprived a trustee of the costs of an action for detinue which he had unsuccessfully defended in the Queen's Bench Division and in which an adverse order for costs had been made against him; he was allowed only what it would have cost for him to make what is now known as an Application to the Chancery Division for directions.

[265] *Weth v. The Attorney-General* [2001] W.T.L.R. 155 at 175. The court obviously does not determine the rights of anyone since the other party will not normally be either before the court or indeed aware of the application.

[266] *McDonald v. Horn* [1994] P.L.R. 33 at 40.

[267] *ibid.*; see also *Weth v. The Attorney-General* [2001] W.T.L.R. 155 at 175.

[268] [1996] 1 W.L.R. 1220.

[269] These categories were a development of the categories enunciated by Kekewich J. in *Re Buckton* [1907] 2 Ch. 406 at 413–415, which had been approved by the Court of Appeal in *McDonald v. Horn* [1995] 1 All E.R. 961, a case which actually concerned costs incurred by beneficiaries in such proceedings.

(a) "friendly" litigation involving either the true construction of the trust instrument (and so in effect a construction summons[270]) or some other question arising in the course of the administration of the trust, such as the appointment of a replacement trustee[271] or the making of an investment which is not permitted by the trustees' investment powers[272]; or

(b) "hostile" litigation involving a challenge in whole or in part to the validity of the settlement by a person who is not formally a beneficiary of the trust but has a potentially valid claim to a proprietary interest in its subject matter;

(ii) what Lightman J. called "a beneficiaries dispute", a dispute with one or more of the beneficiaries as to the propriety of any action which the trustees have taken or omitted to take or which they may or may not take in the future; and

(iii) what Lightman J. called "a third party dispute", a dispute with persons who are neither beneficiaries of the trust nor have a potentially valid claim to a proprietary interest in its subject matter in respect of rights and liabilities assumed by the trustees as such in the course of the administration of the trust—this category also includes non-proprietary claims against the settlor which could, in the event of a successful outcome, be enforced against the subject matter of the trust by virtue of the fact that his disposition of the trust property to the trustees would, by virtue of the successful judgment against the settlor, be converted into a disposition in fraud of the other party to that litigation, who would thus become one of his creditors.

The nature of these different disputes determines whether or not it is appropriate for the trustees to consider protecting themselves by applying for a *Beddoe* Order. The present position appears to be as follows.   **14–134**

(1) In the case of a trust dispute, Lightman J. stated that the primary duty of the trustees is to remain neutral and to offer to submit to the order of the court, leaving it to the rival contenders to fight their battles, in which case the trustees will be entitled to the costs necessarily and properly incurred in so doing out of the trust property[273]; consequently, he stated that no application for a *Beddoe* Order is appropriate in the case of a trust dispute. Where this principle is applicable (as will be seen below, it has since been held not to apply in certain circumstances), the position differs depending on whether the litigation is friendly or hostile.   **14–135**

In the case of friendly litigation, the trustees will invariably appear in the proceedings, they or their legal representatives will present the issues in dispute to the court, and they will then leave   **14–136**

---

[270] See *ante*, para 14–125.

[271] See *ante*, para 13–044, *post*, para 14–144.

[272] Such an application is made under Trustee Act 1925, s.57; see *post*, para 14–142.

[273] This is what occurred in *Merry v. Pownall* [1895] 1 Ch. 306.

14–137

the rival contenders (in practice, the different beneficiaries or groups of beneficiaries) to dispute the outcome if the latter choose to do so. In such circumstances, the costs of both trustees and beneficiaries will invariably be paid out of the trust property.

In the case of hostile litigation, the trustees will have to appear but will not necessarily be represented at the relevant hearing; often they will simply state that they will respect the eventual order of the court. In such circumstances, as Lightman J. stated, they will be entitled to the costs which they have necessarily and properly incurred out of the trust property. However, Lightman J. went on to state that, in the event that the trustees instead choose to take an active part in hostile litigation and win, then they may be entitled to their costs out of the trust property. This actually happened in *In re Holder, ex parte Official Receiver*[274]—of course, although Lightman J. did not actually say so, in such circumstances the trustees will normally obtain an order for at least some of their costs against the losing party. But if the trustees choose to take an active part in hostile litigation and lose, they will not be entitled to their costs[275] save in very exceptional circumstances.[276] Consequently, trustees who do choose to take an active part in hostile litigation will need to consider protecting themselves by seeking a *Beddoe* Order.

14–138

Further, the basic principle enunciated by Lightman J., has since been qualified. In *Evans v. Evans*.[277] Nourse L.J. stated that the remarks of Lightman J. had been "directed only to cases where all the beneficiaries are adult and sui juris. The position might be entirely different if, for example, one of the beneficiaries was under age". This dictum was later amplified in a case of hostile litigation in the Isle of Man involving a potential challenge to the validity of a settlement as a whole[278]; it was stated that the scope of the dictum is not limited to the situation where the under age beneficiary has an interest distinct from that of the adult beneficiaries but also applies where he or she has the same interest as the adult beneficiaries by virtue, for example, of being, as in that case, one of the members of a class of immediate discretionary beneficiaries of a trust. The judge[279] went on to state that trustees nevertheless have a duty, and

---

[274] (1887) 20 Q.B.D. 43).

[275] Lightman J. cited *National Anti-Vivisection Society v. Duddington* (1989) *The Times*, November 23, 1989, disagreeing with what had been said by Kekewich J. in *Ideal Bedding Co. v. Holland* [1907] 2 Ch. 157 as to trustees having a duty to defend the trust and a right to their costs if the court so decides.

[276] Such as those which arose in *Bullock v. Lloyd's Bank* [1955] 1 Ch. 317.

[277] [1985] 3 All E.R. 289 at 292.

[278] *Attorney-General for the Isle of Man v. Poyiadjis* [2001–03] M.L.R. 478 (High Court of the Isle of Man). It was alleged that the subject matter of the settlements in question was the profits made on the sales of shares whose price had been artificially inflated by fraudulent misrepresentations as to the income of the company in question and was therefore susceptible to forfeiture by the Government of the U.S.A. and/or to an adverse claim by the defrauded investors (the judgment referred to was given in the forfeiture proceedings but the principles enunciated were also applied in the separate proceedings brought by the defrauded investors).

[279] Deputy Deemster Hazel Williamson Q.C. (now H.H. Judge Marshall Q.C.).

therefore a power, to act to protect the interests of the beneficiaries of the settlement not only where there are beneficiaries under disability but also where all the beneficiaries are adult and sui juris but do not themselves have the resources to take the necessary steps to defend the settlement (the latter proposition was novel but an appeal against this decision was subsequently abandoned[280]). It was stated that in both these circumstances (both of which applied in this case) it would, in the case of a trust dispute of a hostile nature,[281] be appropriate for the trustees to seek a *Beddoe* Order.

2. In the case of a beneficiaries dispute, Lightman J. stated that, given that such a dispute is ordinary hostile litigation, costs follow the event and do not come out of the trust property; no application for a *Beddoe* Order is therefore appropriate.   **14–139**

3. In the case of a third party dispute, Lightman J. stated, and it is anyway self-evident, that the trustees will always need to consider protecting themselves by applying for a *Beddoe* Order. This was what actually happened in the Isle of Man proceedings to which reference was made above.[282] The effective plaintiff[283] was held to have not a proprietary claim against the assets of the trusts in question (in which case the claim would have been a trust dispute) but merely a potential right to enforce its judgment against the assets of those trusts in the event that it was successful; this was a third party dispute rather than a trust dispute and so the trustees could apply for a *Beddoe* Order on this basis.[284]   **14–140**

Where trustees have been authorised to issue or to defend proceedings and the circumstances which existed at the time when they originally sought their *Beddoe* Order subsequently change before or during the course of those proceedings, there is in principle no obvious reason why they should not return to the court and ask whether, in the new circumstances, they are still authorised to proceed. Indeed such a further application was made in the Isle of Man proceedings referred to above, although in that case what the trustees wanted was for the court to authorise them not to proceed. Trustees may also need to return to the court in the event that they lose the proceedings which they have been authorised to bring or defend and the question   **14–141**

---

[280] On July 4, 2003 in the course of the hearing before the Staff of Government Division (the name by which the appellate court of the Isle of Man is known).

[281] It was actually held that, because the plaintiff's claim did not amount to a claim to a proprietary interest in the subject matter of the trusts in question but merely to enforce a claim to damages against its subject matter, this dispute was properly classifiable as a third party dispute.

[282] *Attorney-General for the Isle of Man v. Poyiadjis* [2001–03] M.L.R. 478 (High Court of the Isle of Man).

[283] The United States of America, on whose behalf the Attorney-General for the Isle of Man was acting.

[284] It was stated that, on the facts, they would also have been entitled to apply for a *Beddoe* Order had the dispute been a trust dispute of a hostile kind both because of the presence of under age beneficiaries and because the adult beneficiaries did not have any resources with which to defend themselves.

then arises as to whether or not they should appeal (this in practice must often be rendered essential by the confusion under present English law, as a result of the differing views expressed by the Court of Appeal in *Re Londonderry's Settlement*,[285] as to whether trustees can actually appeal a decision which they regard as manifestly wrong given that, if they do not appeal, it appears that they will be fully protected by that decision; it is also unclear whether, if they can appeal, they are actually obliged to do so in appropriate circumstances[286]). However, when the trustees have won authorised proceedings and subsequently have to decide whether or not to defend an appeal, they will presumably generally be protected by the original *Beddoe* Order if they decide to defend it.

4. *Applications under Section 57 of the Trustee Act 1925*

14–142   When trustees wish to effect any sale, letting, charge, or any other disposition of trust property, or wish to purchase property or make an investment with trust money and have no power to do so either under the trust instrument or under the general law, they can make an application asking the court to sanction the transaction in question under section 57 of the Trustee Act 1925.[287] The court has jurisdiction to impose any conditions which it thinks fit when approving such a transaction but can only authorise a transaction which is made "in the management or administration" of the trust property. The court has power to give authority under this section only where:

(i) the trustees propose to do an act not authorised by the general law or by the trust instrument;

(ii) that act is in the management or administration of the trust property; and

(ii) the court thinks that it is expedient to sanction it.

---

[285] [1965] Ch. 918.

[286] As seen *ante*, paras 14–042, 14–128, this was an application by trustees for directions as to whether documents sought by one of the beneficiaries ought to be disclosed. At first instance Plowman J. decided that they ought to be. The trustees appealed, successfully in the event, but the Court of Appeal nearly refused to hear the appeal. Harman L.J. observed (at 930) that it seemed to him that the appeal was "an irregularity" on the basis that "trustees seeking the protection of the court are protected by the court's order and it is not for them to appeal". There is little doubt that, had the trustees acted under what turned out to be the erroneous decision of Plowman J., they would have been protected. But if they considered the decision both wrong and adverse to the interests of the beneficiaries, as they did, why should they not have been entitled to appeal? However, Salmon L.J. took a different view, saying (at 936) that in his view the trustees were "fully justified in bringing this appeal" and that "it was their duty to bring it since they believed, rightly, that an appeal was essential for the protection of the general body of beneficiaries"; this of course suggests that the trustees were not only able to appeal but were obliged to do so. Since the appeal in *Re Londonderry's Settlement* was heard, trustees must certainly at present be able to appeal but the difference of opinion certainly provides a strong incentive for trustees who have lost proceedings at first instance in respect of which they sought and obtained a *Beddoe* Order (not the case in *Re Londonderry's Settlement* since that was a beneficiaries dispute) to return to the Court for guidance as to whether or not they should appeal.

[287] See also *post*, para 21–004.

Section 57 is designed to ensure that the property is administered as advantageously as possible in the interests of the beneficiaries. However, the provision must be considered in conjunction with the general principle that the court will not rewrite a trust. For this reason it does not appear that section 57 can be utilised in order to permit trustees to act thereafter in accordance with the view of only a majority of them. For the same reason the power of the court will only be exercised in order to authorise specific dealings with trust property. In *Phipps v. Boardman*[288] the trustees held shares in a private company and had the opportunity to acquire further shares, although such acquisition was not authorised by the trust instrument. In litigation in which one of the beneficiaries successfully impugned the subsequent purchase of the same shares by another beneficiary and the trust solicitor, Lord Denning M.R. said in the Court of Appeal[289] that the acquisition of these shares was so clearly in the interest of the beneficiaries that the proper course would have been for the trustees to have applied to the court under section 57 for power to make the purchase. However, only the briefest reference was made to this point in the subsequent appeal to the House of Lords[290] because it had formed no part of the pleaded case and had not been mentioned in the argument at any stage.

Section 57 does not authorise the rearrangement of beneficial interests but   **14–143**
this can be effected in other ways, principally under the Variation of Trusts Act 1958; this possibility is considered in a later chapter.[291]

5. *Applications as to Trusteeship*

Where the intervention of the court is being sought in relation to the   **14–144**
appointment or removal of a trustee in the manner discussed in the previous chapter,[292] that will also be done by way of application. This can be made either by one or more of the existing trustees, or by the beneficiaries, or by a statutory regulator who wishes a member of the body which it is responsible for regulating to be replaced as trustee. For example, following an intervention by The Law Society into the practice of a solicitor on the grounds of professional misconduct, an application sometimes has to be made by The Law Society for the removal and replacement of that solicitor as trustee of assets held by him on trust for his clients.[293]

Where a trustee has been removed and replaced under section 36(1) of the   **14–145**
Trustee Act 1925,[294] he does not need and will not normally be able to join

---

[288] [1967] 2 A.C. 46.

[289] [1965] Ch. 992 at 1020.

[290] [1967] 2 A.C. 46. Their controversial decision is analysed in detail *ante*, para 10–140.

[291] See *post*, para 21–018.

[292] See *ante*, paras 13–044, 13–084.

[293] On the basis that the trusts constitute "controlled trusts" as defined by Solicitors Act 1974, s.87; see *Russell-Cooke Trust Co. v. Prentis* [2003] 2 All E.R. 478 at 482–483. However, no such application is necessary in respect of funds held by the solicitor in his client account on trust for his clients since on an intervention the balance of such accounts vests directly in The Law Society under Solicitors Act 1974, Sch.1, Part I, para.6 (this Schedule contains the provisions governing such interventions).

[294] See *ante*, para 13–033.

in the document by which his replacement is appointed. In these circumstances, where section 40 of the Trustee Act 1925 does not operate to vest the trust property in his replacement,[295] there will be no document of transfer or assignment signed by the removed trustee either. In such circumstances, it will also be necessary for an application to be made to the court, this time by the continuing and the new trustees for a vesting order under sections 44–56 of the Trustee Act 1925; the most relevant sections are section 44, which applies to land, and section 51 which applies to stock and choses in action. The court can also, and when necessary will, make such orders when appointing new trustees itself.

14–146   A more unusual application relating to trusteeship, outside the statutory framework discussed in the previous chapter, was made to the court in *Barker v. Peile*.[296] Several actions had arisen as a result of uncertainty as to who were proper beneficiaries and the court acceded to the wish of the trustee to be relieved of the liability and annoyance of being a trustee. Special circumstances must, however, exist before the court will release a trustee from his obligations in this way.

---

[295] See *ante*, para 13–068.
[296] (1865) 2 Dr. & Sm. 340.

CHAPTER 15

THE TAXATION OF A TRUST

In order to appreciate the contemporary significance of a trust, it is neces- **15–001**
sary to understand the basic principles of taxation which affect trusts. On
rthe one hand, the prime motive for the creation of the trust may be the
mitigation of a family's taxation liabilities.[1] On the other hand, when a trust
is already in existence, taxation considerations will weigh heavily with the
trustees. These considerations may influence the way in which the trust
fund is invested,[2] how the trustees deal with income,[3] and the manner in
which they exercise their discretion in respect of capital in favour of beneficiaries.[4] Trustees are primarily concerned with the following taxes[5]:

(i) Stamp Duty and Stamp Duty Land Tax;

(ii) Income Tax;

(iii) Inheritance Tax; and

(iv) Capital Gains Tax.

In particular circumstances, trustees are also concerned with other types of
taxation (for example, if they own land, they may be subject to council tax)
but these other types of taxation are not considered in this chapter.

All taxes discussed in this chapter have been the subject of recent statu- **15–002**
tory reform: Stamp Duty has been partially replaced by the introduction of
Stamp Duty Land Tax; the burden of Income Tax on discretionary trusts has
been greatly increased; the incidence of Inheritance Tax on the creation and
operation of trusts has been substantially increased, which in turn has had
an effect on the incidence of Capital Gains Tax in these circumstances; and
the nature of the charge to Capital Gains Tax has been completely altered.
Given that this chapter is intended to enable the reader to understand the
impact of taxation on current trusts, the author of this edition has decided to
discuss only the present incidence of these taxes and will, therefore, completely ignore both the previous tax regimes and any transitional provisions
save to the extent that references to such matters are necessary in order to
understand the present law. A discussion of all previous regimes can of
course be found in the earlier editions of this work.

---

[1] See *ante*, para 1–084.
[2] See, generally, *ante*, para 14–055.
[3] See *post*, Chapter 17.
[4] See *post*, Chapter 18.
[5] For charitable trusts, see *ante*, para 11–009.

15–003   Stamp duty and stamp duty land tax are once-and-for-all taxes payable on a variety of different transactions and in this respect trustees are treated in exactly the same way as private individuals. However, for the purposes of income tax, capital gains tax and inheritance tax, trustees are treated as a separate and continuing body of persons.[6] Because trustees constitute a separate body, the liability of the trust to tax is computed without taking into account the trustees' personal tax position. Because trustees constitute a continuing body, the tax liability of the trust is unaffected by any changes in the persons who are from time to time the trustees. For most taxation purposes, therefore, a trust is treated almost as if it had its own separate legal personality.

15–004   However, it should be noted that the position of most unincorporated associations is different. All unincorporated associations are taxed as if they were bodies corporate.[7] It has already been seen[8] that the property of the vast majority of unincorporated associations is held by trustees on trust to be applied in accordance with the contract between the members contained in the rules of the association. When trustees of this type are bare trustees, which will almost always be the case,[9] neither income tax nor capital gains tax will be payable; instead the income and capital gains of the unincorporated association will be subject to corporation tax and the tax will be payable by the association rather than by the trustees (no liability to inheritance tax can arise in respect of this type of unincorporated association once the property in question has vested in it).

I. STAMP DUTY AND STAMP DUTY LAND TAX

15–005 As already mentioned, stamp duty and stamp duty land law are once-and-for-all taxes payable on a variety of different transactions. Stamp duty now only applies to transfers of shares and securities. Land transactions, which comprise both transfers of land and interests in land and contracts to enter into such transfers, now give rise to a liability to stamp duty land tax. Both duties are payable to H.M. Revenue & Customs.

15–006   In the case of stamp duty, a stamp is impressed on the document in question showing the amount of the duty paid. It therefore follows that, if a transaction can be effected without any document, such as a purely oral declaration of trust,[10] no question of stamp duty can arise. The main inducement to pay stamp duty at present is that a document which ought to have been stamped but has not been cannot be admitted in evidence in any legal proceedings.[11] Further no registrar will register a stampable document

---

[6] The principle is assumed but not expressly enacted for the purposes of income tax.

[7] Income and Corporation Taxes Act 1988, s.832(1).

[8] See *ante*, para 3–107.

[9] *Booth v. Ellard* (1980) 53 S.T.C. 393, *Frampton v. I.R.C.* [1985] S.T.C. 186. Only where the property is settled property, as would be the case where trustees held property on trust for an unincorporated association for a limited time and subject to that for someone else, would the trust in question not be a bare trust and the trustees consequently be liable for income tax and capital gains tax.

[10] See, however, *ante*, paras 4–008 *et seq.*

[11] Stamp Act 1891, s.14(4). *Ram Rattam v. Parma Nand* (1945) L.R. 73 Ind.App. 28.

which is unstamped because, if he does so, he renders himself liable to a fine.[12] Trustees must therefore insist that a trust deed is properly stamped, because they may at any time have to justify their position, or their acts as trustees, by production in court of that deed; however, stamping is not now normally necessary of documents which actually create trusts.

There is no general principle that every document by which every transac-   **15–007** tion involving shares is effected attracts stamp duty; a document is only stampable if it comes within one of the classes of documents specifically mentioned in the Stamp Act 1891. The amount of stamp duty to be paid depends on the class of document in question; the sum payable will be either a fixed duty (usually £5[13]) or an *ad valorem* duty. In the case of shares and securities (now of course the only property liable to stamp duty), stamp duty has for many years been charged at the rate of 0.5 per cent where they are registered in the name of their holder; the duty on bearer shares is 1.5 per cent. In some cases, even though no duty is actually payable, the legislation nevertheless requires the document to be presented for adjudication and in these cases the document is deemed not to have been properly stamped unless it contains a stamp to the effect that it has been adjudicated.[14] Technically an instrument should be stamped before execution but in prac- tice stamping is permitted within 30 days of execution without the imposi- tion of any penalty.[15] Where it is not stamped within that period, H.M. Revenue & Customs are entitled to charge, as a condition for stamping the document out of time, the amount of the stamp duty, interest on that duty from the end of the 30-day period,[16] and a penalty, which for the first year is limited to £300 but thereafter can be for the whole of the amount of the unpaid stamp duty.[17]

In the case of stamp duty land tax, no stamp is impressed on any docu-   **15–008** ment; indeed, one of the principal reasons which led to the introduction of stamp duty land tax was the fact that the Land Registration Act 2002 envisaged the introduction of a system of electronic conveyancing and, when that system is introduced, there will be no physical documents capa- ble of being stamped anyway. Instead, where stamp duty land law is payable, it is paid by sending a land transaction return to H.M. Revenue & Customs with a self-assessment of the liability and payment of the tax due.[18] No document evidencing or effecting a land transaction can be registered at any Land Registry without a certificate of compliance in respect of stamp duty land tax[19]; either H.M. Revenue & Customs will issue a certificate stating that a land transaction return has been delivered or the purchaser will confirm, by self-certification, that no Land Transaction Return is required.

The amount of stamp duty land tax to be paid also depends on the class   **15–009** of document in question within which it falls; the sum payable will always

---

[12] Stamp Act 1891, s.17.
[13] *ibid.*, s.62.
[14] *ibid.*, s.12.
[15] *ibid.*, s.15.
[16] *ibid.*, s.15A.
[17] *ibid.*, s.15B.
[18] Finance Act 2003, s.76.
[19] *ibid.*, s.79.

be an *ad valorem* duty which is charged at variable rates. In 2008–2009, transactions involving residential freehold land up to and including £125,000 and non-residential freehold land up to and including £150,000 were exempt; transactions up to and including £250,000 were charged at 1 per cent; transactions up to and including £500,000 were charged at 2 per cent; and transactions over £500,000 were charged at 4 per cent. In the case of transactions involving leasehold land, what is charged is the net present value of the rent which is the total of any premium paid and the net present value of the rent paid over the entire term of the lease; in 2008–2009, the same exemptions applied and thereafter transactions were charged at 1 per cent. The appropriate percentage is charged on the entire value of the transaction. The land transaction return has to be made and the tax paid within 30 days of the effective date of the land transaction in question. Failure to do so gives rise to a liability to interest from the end of the 30-day period[20] and a penalty, which for two months thereafter is limited to £100, for the first year is limited to £200, but thereafter can be for the whole of the amount of the unpaid stamp duty land tax.[21]

15–010   It is appropriate to consider the incidence of stamp duty and stamp duty land tax on the inception of a trust, during the continuance of a trust, and upon its termination.

1. On the Inception of a Trust

15–011   Since March 26, 1985, a transfer of property to trustees on trust as such has not attracted *ad valorem* stamp duty[22] and since 1987 has not attracted stamp duty of any kind[23]; nor does such a transfer now attract stamp duty land tax. The only exception is in the relatively unlikely case that consideration in money or money's worth is furnished for the transfer to the trustees, in which case the transaction will be a transfer on sale and will be subject to the appropriate *ad valorem* stamp duty or stamp duty land tax. A declaration in writing by a settlor that he is himself holding shares or securities on trust is subject to the fixed stamp duty of, now, £5; there is no similar liability to stamp duty land tax on a declaration by a settlor that he is himself holding land on trust. Neither stamp duty nor stamp duty land tax is payable in the cases of transfers inter vivos of shares or of conveyances, transfers or leases

---

[20] Finance Act 2003, s.88.
[21] *ibid.*, Sch.10.
[22] A voluntary disposition executed before March 26, 1985 was subject to *ad valorem* duty "as if" it were a conveyance or transfer on sale so that both a declaration of trust which, while not voluntary, was not for full consideration and a voluntary declaration of trust was held to do so (a declaration of trust in consideration of marriage was, however, exempt). Consequently, the creation *inter vivos* in writing of a trust of property which could only be transferred by a document, such as land, shares, and securities, was subject to *ad valorem* stamp duty, although a transfer of cash was subject only to the fixed duty of (then) 50p. This charge to *ad valorem* duty was abolished by Finance Act 1985, s.82. Various devices were employed in attempts to create trusts orally since there would then be no documents to stamp; it was one of these devices which gave rise to the litigation in *Grey v. I.R.C.* [1960] A.C. 1 (see *ante*, para 4–027). A description of these devices can be found in all earlier editions of this work.
[23] Between March 26, 1985 and 1987, the fixed duty (then of 50p) and an adjudication stamp were required until 1987 when these requirements were also removed.

of land to a charity.[24] As for testamentary trusts, no stamp duty or stamp duty land tax has ever been payable on either a will or a grant of representation and so neither has ever been payable in respect of the creation of a testamentary trust.

2. *During the Administration of a Trust*

Where a transfer of property subject to a trust is made without causing any   **15–012**
change in the beneficial interests, there is no liability either to stamp duty or to stamp duty land tax. Thus a deed of retirement of trustees or of appointment of new trustees and other document executed in connection with such retirement or appointment, such as a transfer of shares or of land from an old to a new trustee gives rise to no liability. However, where trust property includes shares and securities, in principle the fixed duty of £5 ought to be payable; although an exemption is given by Stamp Duty (Exempt) Regulations 1987, it is nevertheless necessary for a certificate to be included in, endorsed on, or attached to the document to the effect that the instrument falls within the appropriate category of the Schedule to the Regulations. Nothing similar is necessary where the trust property comprises only cash and/or land.

If the trustees in the course of administration of the trust sell some of the   **15–013**
trust property and purchase shares or securities or land with the proceeds of sale, they will be liable to stamp duty or stamp duty land tax, as the case may be, on the purchase of those assets at the same rate as on a purchase by any individual. This is so notwithstanding that the value of the trust fund is not increased, for these taxes are payable on each transaction. Stamp duty and stamp duty land tax paid on such purchases rank as part of the cost of the asset in question for the purposes of capital gains tax.[25]

One apparent anomaly is that, by virtue of a Practice Direction,[26] when an   **15–014**
order is made under the Variation of Trusts Act 1958,[27] an undertaking is given to submit a duplicate of the order for adjudication for the purposes of stamp duty. At the time when the Practice Direction was made, voluntary dispositions were subject to *ad valorem* stamp duty. Now that this is no longer the case, there seems no good reason for the continuing requirement of adjudication, which should be declared to be redundant. However, it continues to exist if the trust property includes any shares or securities. It does not apply if the trust property comprises only cash and/or land.

3. *On the Termination of a Trust*

In normal circumstances no *ad valorem* stamp duty or stamp duty land tax is   **15–015**
payable on the termination of a trust, for by that time the beneficiary has become absolutely entitled beneficially to the trust property and so the termination of the trust produces no change in the beneficial interests. Where the trust property includes shares and securities, in principle the

---

[24] See *ante*, para 11–016.
[25] See *post*, para 15–125.
[26] [1966] 1 W.L.R. 345.
[27] See *post*, para 21–018.

fixed duty of £5 ought again to be payable; however, an exemption is again given by Stamp Duty (Exempt) Regulations 1987 and this time there is no need for any certificate.[28]

II. INCOME TAX

15–016   Income tax is payable only in respect of the income of natural persons (corporation tax is payable in respect of the income of bodies corporate and, as has already been explained,[29] the income of the vast majority of unincorporated associations is also subject to corporation tax[30] payable by the association rather than to income tax payable by the trustees). The income tax treatment of the income of trusts is in many ways more simple than that of the income of private individuals, because the various allowances and reliefs which affect the computation of an individual's liability do not apply. In the case of a private individual, the effect of personal allowances is to exempt from income tax the first "slice" of his income.[31] The next "slice" is taxable at what is known as "the starting rate" of, at present, 10 per cent, although since April 6, 2008 this rate has only been applicable to unearned income and not to earned income; the next "slice" is taxable at what is known as "the basic rate" of, at present, 20 per cent; and the residue is taxable at what is known as "the higher rate" of, at present, 40 per cent.[32] Trust income, on the other hand, is chargeable at the same rate whether it is £1 per annum or £100,000 per annum although again, as will be seen below, the rates payable in respect of bank interest and company distributions differ from those payable in respect of other income.

15–017   The principles which govern the taxation of the income of trusts are as follows:

> (1) The whole of the income of a trust is taxable at the appropriate rate, irrespective of its ultimate destination. This is the case whether the income is absorbed in administration expenses, which are not deductible for the purposes of income tax and so have to be paid out of the income after it has been taxed, whether the income is paid to

---

[28] The position was formerly different if the termination came about as the result of a rearrangement of beneficial interests; this constituted (and constitutes) a voluntary disposition of a beneficial interest and so was subject to *ad valorem* duty for so long as this was payable on voluntary dispositions.

[29] See *ante*, para 15–004.

[30] Corporation tax is payable on the net income of the association; the rate of tax payable depends on the amount of profits made.

[31] In 2008–09, each person under 65 was entitled to a personal allowance of £5,435. Additional allowances are available to pensioners, which vary depending on their age and marital status, and also in certain other circumstances. The size of these allowances is reviewed annually in each Budget and listed in the Finance Act by means of which each Budget is brought into effect

[32] In 2008–09, the first £2,320 of unearned taxable income (taxable income is the income which exceeds a person's total allowances) was taxed at 10%, earned and further unearned taxable income up to £36,000 was taxed at 20%, and further earned and unearned taxable income in excess of that figure was taxed at 40%. The width of the different bands is also reviewed annually in each Budget and listed in each Finance Act.

one or more of the beneficiaries, or whether the income is accumulated.

(2) Where the income of the trust is taxable only in the hands of the trustees,[33] the rate at which tax is payable depends on whether or not any beneficiary has a right to the income in question. When this is the case, the income is taxed at the basic rate of taxation. Where this is not the case, either because the income has to be accumulated or because the trustees have a discretion as to its payment,[34] then the income is taxed at what is known as the rate applicable to trusts. It should be noted that the test is not whether the trust in question is fixed or discretionary since, although the income of all discretionary trusts is taxed at the rate applicable to trusts, the income of a fixed trust will also be taxed at this rate where the immediate beneficiary is an infant and the trustees have either a statutory[35] or an express[36] discretion as to whether to use the income for his maintenance or to accumulate it.

(3) In some circumstances income is treated as the income of the settlor if he is still alive. This is the case where the settlor or his spouse or his civil partner is treated as having retained an interest under the trust in question and where more than nominal income is paid to an unmarried infant child or stepchild of the settlor. Further, where the settlor or his spouse or his civil partner or an infant child of the settlor has received a capital payment from the trust or from a body corporate connected with the trust, that payment will be taxed as the income of the settlor to the extent that the trust has undistributed net income. The settlor himself has to pay the income tax at his highest marginal rate, although he is given credit for any income tax which has already been paid by the trustees.

(4) It follows from these principles that all payments of income from the trust to the beneficiaries are paid from a fund which has already been taxed. Accordingly, with each payment of income, the trustees, or the settlor, are bound to issue to the beneficiary a certificate of the tax notionally deducted from that payment. The gross equivalent of the net payment made to the beneficiary (in other words, the net payment plus the tax already paid) is then regarded as part of the beneficiary's total income and he is in turn liable to income tax on that amount. Although he will have to pay the same tax on that gross equivalent as he would have had to have paid had there not been a trust, he too will be given credit for whatever tax has already been paid. Further, if more tax has been paid by the trustees than the beneficiary would himself have been liable to pay, he can recover

---

[33] There are some circumstances where the income of the trust is instead taxable in the hands of the settlor; see (3) below.

[34] The discretion may be as to whether it is paid out or accumulated and/or as to whom it is paid.

[35] Under Trustee Act 1925, s.31 (*post*, para 17–035); this statutory power of maintenance can be excluded by the trust instrument.

[36] It is common to modify the statutory discretion in some respects.

the balance; however, he cannot recover any of the tax which has been paid by the settlor.

15–018 The discussion which follows assumes that the trustees are obliged to make an income tax return in the year in question which they would be if their income was as set out in the examples. However, the first £1,000 of the income of a trust after deduction of expenses is now necessarily taxable only at the basic rate even in the case of a trust whose income is all prima facie taxable at the rate applicable to trusts.[37] Consequently, the trustees of a trust whose gross income is less than £1,000 and is made up of company distributions and bank interest (both of which are taxed at source at the basic rate) will normally only need to make a tax return periodically.[38] However, this does not affect the obligation of the settlor to include the trust income in his own tax return which it is taxable in his hands.

1. *Income taxed in the hands of the Settlor*

15–019 It has just been seen that in some circumstances the income of a trust is treated as the income of the settlor if he is still alive. Any income so treated is taxed at the settlor's highest marginal rate of income tax,[39] in practice inevitably at 40 per cent, and he himself has to pay the tax[40]; however, he is given credit for any tax which has already been paid by the trustees. Further, where the settlor has been taxed on the basis that he or his spouse or his civil partner have retained an interest under the trust in question or the income in question has been paid to an unmarried infant child or stepchild of the settlor, he can seek to recover the tax which he has paid from the trustees or from any other person to whom the income is payable under the provisions of the trust.[41]

15–020 Where the settlor or his spouse or his civil partner is treated as having retained an interest in a trust, all the income of that trust will be treated as that of the settlor.[42] The most obvious example of this is where his wife or his civil partner has an express beneficial interest under the settlement such as a life interest. However, this will also be the case where at some future date the capital is to revert to the settlor or to pass to his wife or to his civil partner. However, he will not be treated as having retained an interest merely because of the possibility that the property may devolve on him as the result of a disposition by or the bankruptcy of or the death of a beneficiary or on the death of a child of his over the age of 25; this will also be the case where there is a living beneficiary under the age of 25 during whose life the income cannot be applied for the benefit of the settlor save in the event of a disposition by or the bankruptcy of or the death of that beneficiary.

15–021 If more than £100 of the income of a trust is paid in any tax year to an unmarried infant child or stepchild of the settlor, the income is treated as the

---

[37] Income Tax Act 2007, s.491.
[38] Finance Act 2005, s.14 as amended by Finance Act 2006.
[39] Income Tax (Trading and Other Income) Act 2005, s.619A.
[40] *ibid.*, s.622.
[41] *ibid.*, s.646.
[42] *ibid.*, ss.624, 625.

income of the settlor.[43] It does not matter whether the income is paid to the child because he has a fixed beneficial interest or as the result of the exercise of a discretion by the trustees and income for this purpose includes income which has previously been accumulated.[44] The only exception is where the child or stepchild is a vulnerable person for the purposes of Finance Act 2005, in that he is disabled or has lost his other parent, and the trustees have made a successful claim under Finance Act 2005, s.25 for special income tax treatment.[45]

The remaining situation in which income is taxed as the income of the settlor are where the settlor or his spouse or his civil partner or an infant child or stepchild of the settlor has received a capital payment, which includes a loan or the repayment of a loan, from the trust or from a body corporate connected with the trust to whom the trustees have directly or indirectly made a payment. If the trust has undistributed net income in the year in which the capital payment is made, the capital payment is taxed as the income of the settlor to the extent that that income matches that payment. If that income does not match that payment in full, then the remainder of the payment will be taxed as the income of the settlor in any of the next 11 years in which the trust has further undistributed net income until such time as the whole of the payment has been matched by the income.[46] In this case, unlike the other two, the settlor cannot seek to recover the tax which he has paid. **15–022**

2. *Income taxed at the Basic Rate of Taxation*

Where a trust has a beneficiary who is entitled for the time being to its income, (the most obvious example is the holder of a life interest), the income of the trust is taxed only at the basic rate of taxation. In principle this rate is 20 per cent.[47] However, it is regarded as satisfied by the 10 per cent which is retained at source out of income arising from company distributions and by the 20 per cent which is retained at source out of bank interest (in the latter case, even when the basic rate of taxation is more than 20 per cent). This means that the trustees only actually have to pay any income tax, at 20 per cent, on income from sources other than company distributions and bank interest; the most obvious example is rental income. **15–023**

Whatever income remains after payment of tax and of any expenses incurred by the trustees in administering the trust and is paid to the beneficiary who is for the time being entitled to it is also potentially taxable in his hands. If he is a non-taxpayer or a starting rate taxpayer (this is of course unearned income so the starting rate remains relevant), his liability to income tax will be less than the tax which has already been paid. Consequently, he will be entitled to recover the excess, other than the 10 per cent withheld from company distributions, which can never be recovered by anyone. If he is a basic rate taxpayer, his liability to income tax will be **15–024**

---

[43] *ibid.*, s.629.
[44] *ibid.*, s.631.
[45] See *post*, paras 15–045—15–046.
[46] *ibid.*, ss.633–643.
[47] In 2008–2009.

exactly the same as the tax already paid so he will have to pay nothing more. If he is a higher rate taxpayer, he will have to pay such further tax as is necessary to bring the overall tax paid in respect of each source up to the appropriate rate, 32.5 per cent in respect of company distributions and 40 per cent in respect of all other income, including bank interest.

15–025   The following example illustrates these principles. Suppose that a trust fund has an income of £8,000 per annum gross, £4,000 of which proceeds from company distributions, £1,000 from bank interest, and £3,000 from other sources (such as rent); the administration expenses are £900 and the trustees are obliged by the trust instrument to distribute the whole of the income to a beneficiary who has a fixed interest. It should be noted that the administration expenses are deducted first from company distributions, then from bank interest, and then from other income,[48] in each case after basic rate income tax; on these facts this will mean that they are all deducted from the company distributions.

15–026   The 10 per cent tax retained at source out of company dividends will be the subject of a tax credit from the companies in question; the trustees will not need to take any action in respect of this income. The 20 per cent tax retained at source out of the bank interest will be the subject of a tax credit from the bank in question; the trustees will not need to take any action in respect of this income either. However, they will be responsible for all the tax payable in respect of the income from other sources, which will be taxable at the basic rate of 20 per cent. The gross figures determine the tax liability of the beneficiary to whom the income is distributed. The calculation is as follows.

Gross income		£8,000
Less: Tax @ 10% retained out of company distributions (£4,000)	£400	
Net administration expenses (charged against above)	£900 +	
Tax @ 20% retained out of on bank interest (£1,000)	£200 +	
Tax @ 20% payable on other income (£3,000)	£600 +	
	£2,100	£2,100 –
Income available for distribution to beneficiary		£5,900

15–027   The beneficiary will therefore actually receive £5,900. However, he is treated as having received £7,010 from which tax of £1,110 is treated as

---

[48] Income Tax Act 2007, s.503.

having been deducted (the administration expenses are all deducted from the income from the company distributions so that income is treated as only £3,100, producing a tax credit of £310; the tax credit in respect of the other two sources of income is the whole of the income tax of £800 which has been paid). If £7,010 had been less than the beneficiary's personal allowance and he had had no other income whatever, he would have been able to recover the £800 (tax withheld on company distributions can never be recovered); a certificate of deduction of tax issued by the trustees is necessary for this purpose. The net benefit to him would then be £6,700 (£5,900 plus £800).[49] In fact £7,010 is more than the beneficiary's personal allowance, at any rate in 2008–2009[50] so, even if he has no other income whatever, he will be potentially liable to pay a small amount of income tax himself at the starting rate of 10 per cent; however, this will be much less than the tax credit so he will be able to recover the difference between whatever income tax he has to pay himself and the £800. None of the tax paid will be able to be recovered by a beneficiary paying tax at the basic rate. If, finally, the beneficiary is already paying income tax at the higher rate of 40 per cent, he will equally have received £5,900 net and will be treated as having received £7,010 from which tax of £1,110 has been deducted. However, he will have to pay income tax at the higher rate of 40 per cent. Therefore, his overall tax liability will be £2,804 (40 per cent of £7,010) and he will consequently have to pay a further £1,694 (£2,804 less the £1,110 treated as having been paid by the trust). The net benefit to him will therefore only be £4,206 (£5,900 less £1,694).

3. Income taxed at the Rate Applicable to Trusts[51]

Discretionary trusts have historically been used as devices to take income away from taxpayers who are liable to pay income tax at the higher rate. It was in order to reduce this advantage that the rate applicable to trusts was introduced in the first place and that rate was progressively raised until the advantages was totally eliminated in 2004 when that rate was finally raised to the rate of tax payable by higher rate taxpayers, 40 per cent on income arising from all sources other than company distributions (credit being given for the 20 per cent retained at source out of bank interest) and 32.5 per cent on income from company distributions (22.5 per cent in addition to the 10 per cent retained at source). Expenses incurred by the trustees in administering the trust are taxed only at the basic rate, not at the rate applicable to trusts, but have to be grossed up for the purposes of calculating the tax payable at the rate applicable to trusts.[52] Further, the first £1,000 of the income of a trust after deduction of expenses is now necessarily taxable only at the basic rate even in the case of a trust whose income is all prima facie

15–028

---

[49] This figure does not equal the total income of £6,000 because the tax on the company dividends and the tax payable on the administration expenses (in this example set entirely against the company dividends anyway) cannot be recovered.

[50] The personal allowance was £5,435 in 2008–2009.

[51] The relevant legislation is Income Tax Act 2007, ss.479–483.

[52] Income Tax Act 2007, s.486, confirming what had always been accepted practice.

taxable at the rate applicable to trusts.[53] Nothing further is payable in the event that the income is accumulated, although the trustees can only do so if they have the appropriate power.

15–029   The income tax which has been retained or paid, other than the 10 per cent retained at source out of company distributions, notionally goes into what is known as the tax pool. In the event that the trustees can and do accumulate the income, the contents of the tax pool can be set against the income tax which is charged on distributions made in future years under the rules set out below. In the event that some or all of the income is not accumulated but is immediately distributed, the contents of the tax pool are immediately set against the income tax which is charged on that distribution under those rules. It is self-evident from the above that trustees who have a power to accumulate can decide to accumulate only some of the income and to distribute the rest.

15–030   Any income which is distributed is treated as if it were made after deduction of tax at the rate applicable to trusts[54] (the effect of this provision is to treat the distributed income as a further source of income for the trust). This further round of tax is charged[55] but the trustees do not actually have to pay the tax to the extent that it is covered by tax which has already been retained or paid, although the irrecoverable 10 per cent withheld on company distributions is not available for this purpose; the tax already retained or paid is said to "frank" (wipe out) the further tax payable. But, to the extent that the tax is not so "franked", the trustees have to pay the tax on the distribution, thus reducing the amount of income which can actually be distributed. Each beneficiary to whom a distribution is made then receives that distribution with a credit for the further round of tax which has either been "franked" or paid.

15–031   If income distributed is from a source other than company distributions, then the whole of the tax of 40 per cent which that income has already borne will be able to frank the further tax payable so nothing further will in fact be payable by the trustees (in fact, not all the 40 per cent already paid will be needed anyway if there are any administration expenses). That in turn means that the beneficiaries will receive their distributions with a credit for the 40 per cent tax already paid by the trustees thereon. So beneficiaries who are higher rate taxpayers will not have to pay any further income tax thereon and beneficiaries who are not higher rate taxpayers will be able to recover the tax paid by the trustees to the extent that it exceeds the amount of income tax actually payable by those beneficiaries.[56]

15–032   If, on the other hand, the income is from company distributions, then it will have borne tax of 32.5 per cent of which credit is given only for the 22.5 per cent paid by the trustees (because the 10 per cent retained at source is

---

[53] Income Tax Act 2007, s.491.
[54] Income Tax Act 2007, s.494.
[55] Income Tax Act 2007, s.496.
[56] This will not necessarily enable the recovery of all the income tax paid by the trust because any income expended on administration expenses will not be able to be distributed and so the tax paid in respect of these expenses will not be able to be recovered.

never recoverable). So the trustees will have 67.5 per cent of the original dividend left and will have to pay a further 40 per cent tax on that 67.5 per cent, that is 27 per cent overall when they have a credit for only 22.5 per cent overall, and so they will have to pay a further 4.5 per cent overall. Consequently, the percentage of the original dividend which the beneficiaries actually receive will be 63 per cent (67.5 per cent less 4.5 per cent) together with a tax credit for the 27 per cent overall tax paid by the trustees. Of course these percentage figures ignore both the incidence of administration expenses and the fact that the first £1,000 of income is not subject to the rate applicable to trusts.

Continuing to ignore the administration expenses and the £1,000 exemption, a beneficiary who is a non-taxpayer will be able to recover the whole of the 27 per cent overall tax paid by the trustees. He will, therefore, finish up with a total of 90 per cent of the original dividend and so the income paid to him will have suffered only the 10 per cent tax retained at source; he will therefore not be prejudiced in any way. But all beneficiaries who are taxpayers will be prejudiced: a beneficiary who is a starting rate taxpayer will be able to recover only 90 per cent, or 24.3 per cent, of the 27 per cent tax paid by the trustees (because he has to pay 10 per cent of that tax himself) and so will finish up with a total of 87.3 per cent of the original dividend; a beneficiary who is a basic rate taxpayer will recover only 50 per cent, or 23.5 per cent, out of 27 per cent tax paid by the trustees (because he has to pay 50 per cent of that tax himself) and so will finish up with 76.5 per cent of the original dividend; and a beneficiary who is a higher rate taxpayer will recover none of the 27 per cent tax paid by the trustees (because he has to pay all of that tax himself) and so will finish up with 63 per cent of the original dividend. Since income arising from company distributions which is received directly by starting rate taxpayers, basic rate taxpayers and higher rate taxpayers bears only total tax of 10 per cent, 10 per cent and 32.5 per cent respectively, this means that, when such taxpayers receive out of a discretionary trust income from company distributions, that income bears more income tax than would have been the case had the assets in question not been subject to a discretionary trust in the first place. **15–033**

Taking the same example as before (a trust fund having an income of £8,000 per annum gross, £4,000 of which proceeds from company dividends, £1,000 from bank interest, and £3,000 from other sources (such as rent) with administration expenses of £900) but with the trustees this time being obliged by the trust instrument either to accumulate or to distribute all the income pursuant to a discretionary trust, it will be recalled that the administration expense have to be grossed up and that the first £1,000 of the income of a trust after deduction of expenses is taxable only at the basic rate even in the case of a trust whose income is, as in the present example, all prima facie taxable at the rate applicable to trusts.[57] It will be assumed for the purposes of this example that this is the trust's first year and so the tax pool was empty at the start of the year. **15–034**

---

[57] Income Tax Act 2007, s.491.

15–035　　The income tax at the rate applicable to trusts is calculated as follows:

Gross income		£8,000
Less: Tax @ 10% retained on company distributions (£4,000)	£400	
Net administration expenses (charged against above)	£900 +	
Tax @ 20% retained on bank interest (£1,000)	£200 +	
Tax @ 20% payable on other income (£3,000)	£600 +	
	£2,100	£2,100 –
Income net of basic rate tax and administration expenses		£5,900
Less: Tax at rate applicable to trusts on company distributions:		
Company distributions liable to rate applicable to trusts	£4,000	
Less: Grossed-up administration expenses (£900 × 100/90)	£1,000 –	
£1,000 income not liable to rate applicable to trusts	£1,000 –	
	£2,000	
Tax payable at rate applicable to trusts @ 22.5%	£450	£450 –
Less: Tax at rate applicable to trusts on bank interest and other income:		
Bank interest liable to rate applicable to trusts	£1,000	
Other income liable to rate applicable to trusts	£3,000 +	
	£4,000	
Tax payable at rate applicable to trusts @ 20%	£800	£800 –
Income available for accumulation		£4,650

15–036　　If the trustees instead want to pay the income to one or more of the beneficiaries, the amount which they can actually pay has to be calculated in the light of the fact that any payment is treated as if it were made after deduction of tax at the rate applicable to trusts and that the trustees will actually have to pay that tax to the extent that it is not "franked" (wiped out) by the tax which they have already paid (other than the irrecoverable 10 per cent retention on company distributions).

If they were to pay out the whole of the income of £4,650, the grossed up **15–037** income tax payable thereon would be £3,100. This tax can be "franked" only in respect of the total of £2,050 which has been retained or paid (a total of £1,600 on the bank interest and other income, plus £450 on the company distributions—the £400 retained out of the company distributions does not count for this purpose); so the trustees would have to pay a further £1,050 income tax and would have nothing with which to pay it. So they will have to pay out less than the whole of the income. The maximum which they can pay out is in fact £4,020. The grossed up income tax on that sum will be £2,680; the difference between that and the £2,050 tax which they have already paid is £630, while is exactly the same as the difference between £4,650 and £4,020. So they can pay out £4,020 and use the remaining £630 to pay the further tax.

If instead the trustees choose to pay out less than £4,020, they will **15–038** accumulate the balance after paying any further tax which is necessary; any already paid tax which is not needed to "frank" the distribution will remain in the tax pool to "frank" distributions in future years. Thus, if they choose to pay out £3,600, the grossed up income tax on that sum will be £2,400 so they will have to pay £250 further tax and the £800 balance of the income (£4,650 − £3,600 − £250) will be accumulated; if instead they choose to pay out £3,000, the grossed up income tax on that sum will be £2,000 so £50 will remain in the tax pool and the £2,650 balance of the income (£4,650 − £2,000) will be accumulated.

On the assumption that the trustees distribute the maximum income **15–039** possible, the beneficiary in question will therefore actually receive £4,020. However, he is treated as having received £6,700 from which tax of £2,680 is treated as having been deducted. If £6,700 had been less than the beneficiary's personal allowance and he had had no other income whatever, he would have been able to recover the £2,680. The net benefit to him would then be £6,700.[58] In fact £6,700 is more than the beneficiary's personal allowance, at any rate in 2008–2009[59] so, even if he has no other income whatever, he will be potentially liable to pay a small amount of income tax himself at the starting rate of 10 per cent; however, this will be much less than the tax credit so he will be able to recover the difference between whatever income tax he has to pay himself and the £2,680. If the beneficiary pays income tax at the basic rate, he only has to pay 20 per cent so he will be able to recover half the £2,680 and the benefit to him will be £5,360 (£4,020 + £1,340). If, finally, the beneficiary is already paying income tax at the higher rate of 40 per cent, he pays tax at the same rate as was paid on the distribution and so cannot recover anything; the benefit to him will therefore be £4,020.

If the figures in the previous paragraph are contrasted with the figures in **15–040** paragraph 15.27 above, it will be seen that the position of a non-taxpayer is

---

[58] This figure does not equal the total income of £6,000 because the tax on the company dividends and the tax payable on the administration expenses (in this example set entirely against the company dividends anyway) cannot be recovered.

[59] The personal allowance was £5,435 in 2008–2009.

exactly the same whether there is a fixed trust or a discretionary trust since the non-taxpayer will receive £6,700 either way; in contrast, a basic rate taxpayer will receive £5,900 under a fixed trust but only £5,360 under a discretionary trust, while a higher rate taxpayer will receive £4,206 under a fixed trust but only £4,020 under a discretionary trust. The disadvantageous position of basic rate taxpayers and higher rate taxpayers (the position of the former is actually worse than that of the latter) is entirely due to the non-recoverability of the 10 per cent retained out of income from company distributions. It is also notable that the amount which the trustees could have accumulated, £4,690, is higher than the net benefit to a higher rate taxpayer; consequently, trustees of discretionary trusts are still best advised to make distributions to beneficiaries who are not higher rate taxpayers.

4. *General Considerations*

15–041 The principles which have been discussed produce three general results which trustees need to bear in mind.

15–042   As the whole income of the trust is taxable, liability to tax can only be avoided if non-income-producing assets are held by the trust. An example would be for a trust to purchase pieces of silver or works of art.[60] A more prosaic example is the purchase of National Savings Certificates, which produce no income but are repayable on maturity with a capital bonus. However, such increments will be of a capital nature for all purposes, so that a life tenant will not, in general, be entitled to any part of the bonus.[61] While a trustee must keep tax considerations in mind, he must also keep in mind his general obligation to balance the interests of tenant for life and remainderman.[62]

15–043   Where trustees have a discretion to accumulate income, they can only accumulate out of taxed income. Accordingly, accumulation is not a method of avoiding income tax completely but, as is shown in a later chapter,[63] in some circumstances it may be appropriate to accumulate income as capital and then to make an advancement of capital.

15–044   Trustees will wish to consider the likely taxation result of a distribution of income on the tax position of the beneficiary. If, as in the examples given above, the personal tax position of the beneficiary is such that he can make a repayment claim, a distribution of income to him will be clearly advantageous. If, however, the beneficiary is already paying income tax at the higher rate of 40 per cent, the trustees will know that any income paid to him will finish up by being taxed at as least as high a rate, and sometimes a higher rate, than that it which it has been taxed in the hands of the trustees.

---

[60] Provided that the pieces of silver are sold for a figure not in excess of £6,000, no capital gains tax is payable. Trustees hope, therefore, to dispose of the silver at a profit which will attract liability neither to income tax, because the profit is not of an income nature, nor to capital gains tax.

[61] *Re Holder* (1953) Ch. 468. See however *post*, para 16–056.

[62] In *Nestlé v. National Westminster Bank* [1993] 1 W.L.R. 1260, the remainderman accused the trustees of allowing the tax interests of the tenant for life to influence unduly their choice of investments. The judgments contain an important discussion of the criteria which trustees should follow (see *ante*, para 14–057).

[63] See *post*, Chapter 18.

Consequently, as has already been seen,[64] most tax will be recoverable if the trustees pay as much as possible of the income to the beneficiaries with the lowest personal rate of taxation since they will be able to reclaim at least some of the tax paid by the trust on the sum actually distributed to them.[65] If, on the other hand, all the beneficiaries are paying tax at the higher rate of 40 per cent, then no tax will be able to be recovered but less income tax will be paid overall if the income is accumulated than if it is distributed to a higher rate taxpayer.

5. *Trusts for Vulnerable Beneficiaries*

Vulnerable beneficiaries are a disabled person, defined as a person who is incapable by reason of mental disorder of administering his property or managing his affairs or a person in receipt of attendance allowance or disability living allowance, and a minor who has lost at least one parent. It is relatively unlikely and usually undesirable that the whole of the income produced by a trust for such a person will be distributed; yet it is equally undesirable that that income should have to bear tax at the rate applicable to trusts if it is accumulated. Consequently, with effect from April 6, 2004, it has been possible for an election to be made in the case of a qualifying trust for a vulnerable beneficiary that the income of that trust to be deemed to be the income of the vulnerable beneficiary and to be taxed on that basis.[66] Thus, even some or all of the income is in fact accumulated, all of it will be taxed taking into account the vulnerable beneficiary's personal allowance and at the rates of tax payable by him rather than at the rate applicable to trusts. Substantial income tax will obviously be saved unless the vulnerable beneficiary is a higher rate tax payer and even then there will be some savings in respect of income which is paid to the vulnerable beneficiary which is derived from company distributions.

15–045

A trust for a disabled person will be a qualifying trust if during the disabled person's lifetime or the earlier termination of the trust, any property applied for the benefit of a beneficiary must be applied for the benefit of the disabled person and either the disabled person is entitled to all the income or it cannot be applied for the benefit of any other person. A trust for a minor who has lost at least one parent will be a qualifying trust if it falls within the definition of a trust for a bereaved minor. Such a trust can arise pursuant to the will or intestacy of a parent of the minor in question or be established under the Criminal Injuries Compensation Scheme but in no other ways; the bereaved minor must be given an absolute beneficial interest in both income and capital either outright or not later than the age of 18; until he reaches that age, any income must either be accumulated or used for his benefit and so must any capital payment. The necessary election must be irrevocable and must be made jointly by the trustees and by, or on behalf of,

15–046

---

[64] See *ante*, para 15–040.

[65] As has already been seen, the tax paid on any administration expenses will not be able to be recovered since the right of recovery is limited to the income actually received by the beneficiary; nor will the 10% tax which is withheld out of income from company distributions.

[66] Finance Act 2005, ss.23–45.

the vulnerable person. All trusts which are qualifying trusts also receive inheritance tax and capital gains tax advantages.[67]

6. *Non-Resident Trusts*

15–047   In order to determine the taxation position of a trust which is for the time being non-resident[68] and, consequently, the advantages of having a trust which is non-resident, it is necessary to consider the potential liability to income tax of both the settlor, the trustees and the beneficiaries.

(A)   The Settlor
15–048   A non-resident settlor of a non-resident trust is obviously beyond the reach of H.M. Revenue & Customs. The position of a resident settlor of a non-resident trust is exactly the same as the position of the settlor of a resident trust. However, it is hardly likely that he would make himself a beneficiary of that trust but, in the event that he were to do so his position would be the same as that of any other beneficiary. But if, as is obviously more likely, his unmarried infant children are beneficiaries, then, in the highly unlikely event that any income is actually paid to and applied for their benefit, that income will, as in the case of a resident trust, be treated as the settlor's income for the purposes of income tax.[69]

(B)   The Trustees
15–049   An underlying principle of United Kingdom income tax law is that a person is liable to income tax on his total world-wide income if he is resident here but, if he is not resident here, is liable to income tax only on income which is derived from a source in the United Kingdom.

15–050   It therefore follows that non-resident trustees will not be liable to income tax in respect of income derived from sources outside the United Kingdom; consequently, they will be wholly free of United Kingdom income tax if all the investments are made abroad. However, they will be liable to income tax in respect of income derived from sources within the United Kingdom to the same extent as trustees who are resident here. It has already been seen[70] that, in the case of fixed trusts, this liability will be 10 per cent (withheld) in the case of company distributions, 20 per cent (also withheld) in the case of bank interest) and the basic rate of income tax, at present also 20 per cent, on all other income; in the case of discretionary trusts, this liability will be 40 per cent except in the case of company distributions, on which 32 per cent is payable, which are accumulated[71]

(C)   The Beneficiaries

(1)   Actual income
15–051   Where a beneficiary is entitled to receive income from a foreign trust, he is liable to income tax on that income whether or not he actually physically

---

[67] See *post*, paras 15–086, 15–133.
[68] For the sake of simplicity, in this section the expression "non-resident" is used to mean both non-resident in the strict sense and non-ordinarily resident.
[69] Income Tax (Trading and Other Income) Act 2005, s.629.
[70] See *ante*, para 15–023.
[71] See *ante*, para 15–028.

receives it.[72] This is so irrespective of the jurisdiction in which the trust assets are situated. No income tax saving is effected, therefore, where the beneficiary is actually entitled to the income.

(2) Other benefits from income

Were there no other provision, the beneficiaries would therefore escape 15–052 liability if income were accumulated abroad and either retained abroad or subsequently paid to them as capital. To counter this, there are two far-reaching anti-avoidance provisions.

(a) **Section 720 of the Income Tax Act 2007** This provision applies 15–053 where all the following requirements are satisfied:

(1) An asset[73] is transferred to a person abroad.[74] This requirement is satisfied even if the asset has not been transferred from the United Kingdom. So, if Andrew, a resident of, say, South Africa, offers to make a gift of R20,000 to Bertram, who is a United Kingdom resident, but Bertram directs Andrew to pay that sum to trustees on his behalf in Guernsey,[75] the payment of that sum will constitute a transfer of an asset for this purpose. In *I.R.C. v. Brackett*,[76] the taxpayer entered into a contract of employment with a Jersey company and was held to be caught by the section because the rights created by the contract were assets transferred to a person abroad.

(2) By virtue of, or as a consequence of, that transfer, the income is either directly or indirectly[77] payable to a person or company resident abroad.[78] There is no requirement that that person should have been non-resident at the time of the transfer.[79]

(3) Either the transferor or his spouse or his civil partner[80] is a United Kingdom resident and enjoys, or has power to enjoy, that income (it no longer[81] matters where the transferor or his spouse or his civil

---

[72] Liability is deferred if it is impossible to remit the income to the UK. If the person entitled to the income is resident but not domiciled in the UK, foreign income is only liable to UK income tax if remitted to the UK.

[73] The expression includes money and property or rights of any kind.

[74] That is to say out of Great Britain and Northern Ireland.

[75] Which is "abroad" for this purpose.

[76] [1986] S.T.C. 521.

[77] This follows from the application of the general principle to a transfer by "an associated operation". Section 719 defines "associated operation" in relation to any transfer as "an operation of any kind effected by any person in relation to any of the assets transferred or any assets representing, whether directly or indirectly, any of the assets transferred, or to the income arising from any such assets, or to any assets representing, whether directly or indirectly, the accumulations of income arising from any such assets".

[78] For this purpose, "income" does not include a director's remuneration.

[79] *Congreve v. I.R.C.* [1948] 1 All E.R. 948.

[80] *Vestey v. I.R.C.* [1980] A.C. 1148.

[81] In respect of income arising on or before November 25, 1996, either the transferor or his spouse had to have been a United Kingdom resident at the time of the transfer or his civil partner was at the time of the transfer a United Kingdom resident (*I.R.C. v. Willoughby* [1997] 1 W.L.R. 1071, the result of which was reversed by Finance Act 1997, s.81).

partner were resident at the time of the transfer); the definition of "power to enjoy" is very wide indeed.[82]

Where the section applies, the income arising abroad is treated for income tax purposes as the income of the United Kingdom resident with the power to enjoy it to the extent that the foreign resident does not actually distribute it to anyone else.

15–054   Section 737 establishes two exceptions to section 720:

(1) Where the individual satisfies an officer of H.M. Revenue & Customs that it would not be reasonable to draw the conclusion that the purposes of avoiding liability to taxation was the purpose, or one of the purposes, for which the relevant transactions or any of them were effected. The House of Lords has held that taking advantage of an offer of freedom from tax which the legislation has specifically made does not constitute tax avoidance for the purpose of this exception, stating that "tax avoidance within the meaning of section [720] is a course of action designed to conflict with or defeat the evident intention of Parliament".[83] This exception is therefore likely to prove much more useful than was previously thought.[84]

(2) Where the individual satisfies an officer of H.M. Revenue & Customs that all the relevant transactions were genuine commercial transactions and that it would not be reasonable to draw the conclusion, from all the circumstances of the case, that anyone or more of those transactions was more than incidentally designed for the

---

[82] s.722 provides that for the purposes of the section an individual is deemed to have power to enjoy the income of a person abroad if any the conditions set out in s.723 are met:

"Condition A is that the income is in fact so dealt with by any person as to be calculated at some time to enure for the benefit of the individual, whether in the form of income or not.

"Condition B is that the receipt or accrual of the income operates to increase the value to the individual—(a) of any assets the individual holds; or (b) of any assets held for the individual's benefit.

"Condition C is that the individual receives or is entitled to receive at any time any benefit provided or to be provided out of that income or out of related money, which means money which is or will be available for the purpose of providing the benefit as a result of the effect or successive effects—(a) on the income, and (b) on any assets which directly or indirectly represent the income.

"Condition D is that the individual may become entitled to the beneficial enjoyment of the income if one or more powers are exercised or successively exercised [and] it does not matter (a) who may exercise the powers, or (b) whether they are exercisable with or without the consent of another person.

"Condition E is that the individual is able in any manner to control directly or indirectly the application of the income.

Even this is extended by s.722(3), (4), which provide that regard must be had to be substantial result and effect of all the relevant transactions and all benefits accruing to the individual as a result of the transfer and any associated operations must be taken into account irrelevant of their nature and whether the individual has any legal or equitable rights to them.

[83] I.R.C. v. Willoughby [1997] 1 W.L.R. 1071 at 1079, per Lord Nolan.

[84] Earlier editions of this work described this exception, clearly wrongly, as "more apparent than real" (5th edn, p.431; 6th edn, p.564). Precisely how the "evident intention" of Parliament will be established of course remains to be seen.

purpose of avoiding liability to taxation. Section 738 provides that a transaction is a genuine commercial transaction only if effected in the course of a trade or business and for its purposes, or with a view to setting up and commencing a trade or business and not be on terms other than those that would have been made between persons not connected with each other dealing at arm's length or not be a transaction that would not have been entered into between such persons so dealing. The definition has resolved, adversely to the individual, doubts which had been expressed about the scope of the expression in the previous legislation, which was "bona fide commercial transaction".[85]

Nevertheless in most cases where someone who is, or later becomes, a United Kingdom resident forms a trust abroad and places money or other assets in that trust under which he or his spouse is a beneficiary, section 720 will apply and there will be no saving of income tax. Indeed, the liability incurred can be greater than if the income had arisen within the United Kingdom. In *Lord Chetwode v. I.R.C.*,[86] Lord Chetwode created a settlement in the Bahamas, which owned the entire share capital of a Bahamian investment company. It was held that he was assessable on the whole[87] of the income of the investment company and that he could not even deduct the expenses of the management of that company in computing the amount of income to be brought into account for tax.   **15–055**

(b) Section 731 of the Income Tax Act 2007 The provision just considered, section 720, applies only where the transfer of assets was made by the taxpayer or his spouse or his civil partner. Section 731 applies where an individual who is resident in the United Kingdom can benefit under a foreign trust but was not a settlor in relation to it. If, therefore, Edward creates a non-resident discretionary settlement under which he and his son Frank are discretionary beneficiaries and both are residents, during Edward's lifetime section 720 will apply. Frank will be liable on general principles to income tax on any income which he actually receives but, provided he took no part in setting up the arrangements, he will only be liable, if at all, under section 731 in respect of income which he does not actually receive. During Edward's lifetime, Frank will not be taxed under section 731 in respect of income on which Edward is taxed under section 720. But, after Edward's death, Frank is clearly potentially liable under section 731.   **15–056**

Under section 731, it is necessary to calculate all the income of a foreign trust which arose after March 9, 1981 directly or indirectly from a transfer of assets and which can be used for providing a benefit for an individual who is resident in the United Kingdom. Thus, in the example, income which is accumulated on which Edward is not taxed under section 720 is relevant   **15–057**

---

[85] The point was specifically left open in *I.R.C. v. Willoughby* [1997] 1 W.L.R. 1071 at 1081, *per* Lord Nolan.

[86] [1977] 1 All E.R. 638.

[87] In practice, the Revenue do allow a very limited deduction from the gross income in respect of the costs of collecting that income.

income for this purpose because it is capable of providing a benefit for Frank at some time in the future. A running notional record is kept of this income but no liability arises at that stage. When, however, the individual receives a benefit from the trust which is not taxable as ordinary income, the value of that benefit is treated as forming part of his income for the year in which he actually receives it. Thus, if the trustees made a discretionary capital payment to Frank, he will be subject to income tax on it to the extent that it is covered by income which has already arisen to the trustees on which tax has not yet been paid.

15–058   In summary, therefore, the general position is that:

(i) a beneficiary resident in the United Kingdom will be liable to income tax on the actual income which he receives or to which he is entitled;

(ii) the settlor and his spouse and his civil partner[88] will, if resident in the United Kingdom, be liable to income tax on income retained within the trust unless it cannot be applied for his or her benefit, this liability being to tax when the income arises; and

(iii) other beneficiaries resident in the United Kingdom will only be liable to income tax on income retained within the trust when they actually receive benefit from it.

Non-resident trusts are, therefore, a useful means by which the liability to income tax can be deferred.

III. INHERITANCE TAX

15–059   Inheritance tax is governed by what is now known as the Inheritance Tax Act 1984,[89] which has since been substantially modified, first in 1986 and, so far as concerns trusts, again in 2006. It is imposed on such part of a person's estate, which for this purpose includes any property disposed of by him other than for value during the seven years immediately prior to his death, as, after deduction of any exemptions to which his estate is entitled, exceeds his lifetime allowance of, at present,[90] £312,000; the relevant figure, which is raised periodically in line with inflation is generally known as "the nil rate sum" and as comprising what is known as "the nil rate band". The rate of inheritance tax payable on property outside the nil rate band has been 40 per cent for many years.[91]

---

[88] Which for this purpose includes his widow and former civil partner.

[89] It was originally called the Capital Transfer Tax Act 1984 (the tax was re-christened in 1986) and the Act may be cited in either form; in this work it will be cited as the Inheritance Tax Act 1984.

[90] In 2008–2009.

[91] This has been the case since March 15, 1988; before that there were a number of different rates of inheritance tax ranging from 30% to 60% which applied progressively after deduction of the nil rate sum.

Certain property is excluded from a deceased's estate for the purposes of **15–060** inheritance tax.[92] On the other hand, for these purposes, his estate includes any property in which he has, or within seven years of his death has had, an interest in possession for the purposes of inheritance tax. However, the circumstances in which this will be the case have been greatly reduced by the reforms made to the Inheritance Tax Act 1984 with effect from March 22, 2006; ignoring transitional provisions, this will now only be the case where the interest in possession took immediate effect pursuant to the provisions of a will or to the intestacy rules, or in the case of a trust for a disabled person, however created. Thus, for example, where the deceased is the life tenant of a *post mortem* settlement, the whole of the capital value of the settled property will be potentially liable to inheritance tax on his death. But, again ignoring transitional provisions, this will not now[93] be the case for any other type of trust.

1. *Exempt, Potentially Exempt, and Chargeable Transfers*

Inheritance tax focuses around transfers of value, which occur whenever a **15–061** person makes a disposition as a result of which the value of his estate immediately after the disposition is less than it would have been but for that disposition. The value transferred by the transfer of value is the amount by which his estate is reduced; it is irrelevant that this amount is either less or more than the increase in the value of the estate of the person in whose favour the disposition is made.[94] A transfer of value may be exempt, potentially exempt, or chargeable.

The principal example of an exempt transfer is any transfer of any amount **15–062** between spouses, whether *inter vivos* or *mortis causa*.[95] There are a number of further exemptions. Some are personal, such as are lifetime gifts of up to £3,000 per annum, any unused part of which can be carried forward to the following year but only to that year, any number of small gifts of up to £250 per donee per annum, gifts in consideration of marriage of varying amounts up to £5,000,[96] and payments for the maintenance of dependants. Some arise from the nature of the property, namely if it is agricultural property, business property, or woodlands. Others are institutional, including gifts to charities, gifts to certain bodies concerned with the preservation of the national heritage or of a public nature, gifts to political parties, and gifts of works of art.

A potentially exempt transfer[97] is any transfer made *inter vivos* by a **15–063** private individual after March 17, 1986 which is not an exempt transfer; consequently, if the transferor has not made used his gift allowance of £3,000 per annum in the year in question (and in the previous year) the amount(s)

---

[92] Overseas property held by a person who is not domiciled in the United Kingdom for the purposes of inheritance tax (there is a special definition); reversionary interests; and certain government securities.

[93] See *post*, para 15–084.

[94] Inheritance Tax Act 1984, s.3.

[95] *ibid.*, s.18.

[96] Depending on the relationship of the donor to the spouses (£5,000 by each parent, £2,500 by each grandparent, and £1,000 by anyone else).

[97] Inheritance Tax Act 1984, s.3A (introduced by Finance Act 1986, s.101).

in question are deducted from the amount of the potentially exempt transfer. The transfer may be in favour of one or more private individuals absolutely, in which case it must be either directly to the recipient(s) or increase his or their estate (paying school fees or for a holiday does not suffice). Alternatively, the transfer may be to trustees but, since March 22, 2006, only if it is on trust for a disabled person or into what is known as a trust for a bereaved minor following the termination of an interest in possession.[98]

15–064   If the transferor dies within three years of making the transfer, the rate of inheritance tax payable is the same as that chargeable on death; the tax is payable on the value of the property at the time of transfer or the value of the property at the date of death, whichever is the lower; if the value of the property increases, there can therefore be an advantage even if the transferor does not survive for three years. If the transferor dies more than three years but less than seven years after making the transfer, the rate of inheritance tax payable is a proportion of that chargeable on death as a result of the availability of what is known as "taper relief", under which there is a reduction of 20 per cent of the tax for each year or part of a year after the first three that the transferor has survived. As before, the tax is payable on the value of the property at the time of transfer or the value of the property at the date of death, whichever is the lower. If the transferor survives for seven years after making the transfer, it then becomes an exempt transfer.

15–065   A potentially exempt transfer will not take effect as a transfer of that type in the event that the transferor continues to derive some benefit from the property which he has transferred; this is for the somewhat obvious reason that he cannot be permitted to enjoy the advantages of making a potentially exempt transfer if he has retained enjoyment of the property in question. In the meantime, the subject matter of the transfer is described as property subject to a reservation and is regarded as continuing to form part of the estate of the transferor unless and until such time as the benefit in question ceases (from which time the seven-year period will start to run) and will be taxed accordingly on his death. Property is treated as being subject to a reservation in two cases[99]: first, where the transferee has not, prior to the seven-year period preceding the transferor's death (or, if the transferor has died within seven years of the gift, at the date of the gift), bona fide assumed the possession and enjoyment of the property; and, secondly, where, at any time during the seven years prior to the transferor's death (or, if he dies within seven years of the gift, at any time after the gift), the property is not enjoyed "to the entire exclusion, or virtually to the entire exclusion, of the [transferor] and of any benefit to him by contract or otherwise".

15–066   However, property can never be subject to a reservation as a result of a gift between spouses[100] but this exemption now only applies for so long as the spouse to whom the property has been transferred retains an interest in possession therein; any enjoyment of that property by the transferor spouse thereafter will render that property subject to a reservation in his favour

---

[98] See *post*, para 15–089.
[99] Finance Act 1986, s.102(1).
[100] *ibid.*, s.102(5).

from then on.[101] Nor is property subject to a reservation when what the potentially exempt transfer has transferred is an undivided share of a property which both transferor and transferee continue to occupy and when the transferor continues to bear his own living expenses and at least his proportionate share of the property expenses (it does not in fact matter if the transferor continues to pay all the property expenses but the property will be subject to a reservation if the transferee pays any substantial part of the transferor's share of those expenses).[102]

There are two types of chargeable transfer: first, a transfer of value made **15–067** by a private individual *inter vivos* which is neither an exempt transfer nor a potentially exempt transfer (the best example of such transfers, which are known as initially chargeable transfers, is any transfer of property to trustees other than on trust for a disabled person or into what is known as a trust for a bereaved minor following the termination of an interest in possession[103]); and, secondly, the transfer of value which every private individual is deemed to make on his death to the extent that it is not an exempt transfer (this deemed transfer includes the amounts of all potentially exempt transfers and chargeable transfers made by him during the seven years immediately prior to his death).

An initially chargeable transfer is immediately liable to inheritance tax, at **15–068** half the rate applicable on death and therefore at present stands at 20 per cent, although the tax only actually has to be paid to the extent that the value of the transfer exceeds whatever is left the balance of the transferor's lifetime allowance of, at present, £312,000.[104] The tax so paid forms part of the property transferred; consequently, if the transferor pays the tax himself, the transfer must be "grossed up" for this purpose.[105] If the transferor survives seven years, no further inheritance tax is payable but, if he fails to do so, there is an additional liability to inheritance tax on his death.

The deemed transfer of value which arises on death gives rise to a liability **15–069** to inheritance tax, again only to the extent that the value of the deemed transfer exceeds whatever is left the balance of the transferor's lifetime allowance of, at present, £312,000. Inheritance tax is, therefore, payable on the remaining value of the assets transferred on death or in the three years before death at, at present, 40 per cent,[106] at the appropriate proportion of that rate in respect of potentially exempt transfers made within seven years of but more than three years before death,[107] credit being given for the tax already paid in respect of any initially chargeable lifetime transfers.[108]

---

[101] Finance Act 2003, s.185, reversing the effect of the decision in *I.R.C. v. Eversden* [2003] S.T.C. 822 (CA).

[102] Finance Act 1986, s.102B(1), (2), (4).

[103] Until March 22, 2006, the exceptions included a transfer to trustees on trusts which created an immediate interest in possession or what is known as an accumulation and maintenance trust but this is no longer the case.

[104] In 2008–2009.

[105] Inheritance Tax Act 1984, s.7. Where tax is payable on an immediately chargeable transfer of £100,000 (it may be absorbed by the transferor's nil rate band) and is paid by the transferor in addition to rather than out of the property transferred, the "grossed up" figure will be £125,000 (because 80% of this amount is £100,000), thus producing a tax liability of £25,000.

[106] Inheritance Tax Act 1984, s.7(1) and Sch.1.

[107] *ibid.*, s.7(4).

[108] *ibid.*, s.7(2).

15–070   It is, therefore, necessary to keep a lifetime record of all transfers *inter vivos*: first, because, if any potentially exempt transfer becomes chargeable, any transfers made during the seven-year period preceding that transfer will have to be aggregated with it in order to decide the inheritance tax ultimately payable on that potentially exempt transfer; and, secondly, because any transfers made within the seven years preceding death will have to be aggregated with the estate of the transferor in order to determine the amount of inheritance tax payable in respect of his estate (the total of chargeable transfers during any seven-year period is known as the transferor's "cumulative total"). The presence of potentially exempt transfers makes the calculation of the inheritance tax payable far from straightforward.

2. *How Inheritance Tax is Calculated*

15–071 Suppose that a person who has died in 2007–2008, when the nil rate band was £300,000, leaving an estate, other than that part which he has left to his spouse and which is therefore exempt from inheritance tax, of £50,000, made the following *inter vivos* transfers: eight years before his death, a transfer of £100,000 to his son (a potentially exempt transfer); five and a half years before his death, when the nil rate band was £250,000, a transfer of £200,000 to his son (another potentially exempt transfer) and, a few days later, a transfer of £300,000 to trustees on discretionary trust for all his descendants (an initially chargeable transfer); and, in the year of his death, a transfer of £200,000 to his daughter (a potentially exempt transfer). At all times throughout this period, the only rate of inheritance tax was 40 per cent (as it has been since March 15, 1988). It is necessary to calculate the inheritance tax payable twice: first, transfer by transfer during the deceased's lifetime; and, secondly, on his death.

15–072   Calculating transfer by transfer, both the transfers to the son were potentially exempt so no inheritance tax was payable on either occasion. The transfer of £300,000 was, however, initially chargeable so inheritance tax was payable. At that time, the deceased had not used up any of his then lifetime allowance of £250,000 (the potentially exempt transfers were assumed not to be chargeable and therefore did not have to be aggregated for that purpose); consequently, the first £250,000 of the £300,000 used up that allowance so that inheritance tax was payable at 20 per cent (half the death rate) on the remaining £50,000, thus requiring the immediate payment of £10,000 (it will be presumed that the tax was paid by the trustees of the settlement out of the £300,000 settled—had it been paid by the deceased, the total amount of the transfer would have had to be "grossed up" to take account of the tax). The transfer of £200,000 was also potentially exempt so no inheritance tax was payable then either. Thus the total inheritance tax payable during the deceased's lifetime was £10,000.

15–073   Calculating on death, by then the potentially exempt transfer of £100,000 made eight years earlier had become exempt. However, all the other three transfers and the deceased's estate give rise to inheritance tax liabilities which need to be calculated individually in chronological order. The value of these transfers at the date when they were made is deducted from the nil rate band in full, without giving any credit for any taper relief, before the liability to inheritance tax of the deceased's remaining assets is established.

His personal representatives are liable to pay any inheritance tax due in respect of the property which devolves as a result of the deceased's death; any liability in respect of the inter vivos transfers falls primarily on the individual transferees but in default also passes to the deceased's personal representatives.

(1) The potentially exempt transfer of £200,000 made five and a half **15–074** years before his death is not in fact exempt. During the seven years preceding that transfer, the deceased had made one transfer, that of £100,000. That transfer used up £100,000 of his then lifetime allowance of £250,000. Thus, £150,000 of that allowance remained at that time to offset against the transfer of £200,000. The £50,000 balance is thus liable to inheritance tax. The death rate is 40 per cent but because the deceased survived for five further years, there is a reduction of 60 per cent (20 per cent for each year or part of a year after the first three). Consequently, the inheritance tax payable is 40 per cent of 40 per cent of £50,000, thus £8,000.

(2) The initially chargeable transfer of £300,000 made five and a half **15–075** years before the testator's death has already suffered inheritance tax of £10,000. This was on the basis that the transfers of £100,000 and £200,000 were both potentially exempt. In the event only the transfer of £100,000 turned out to be potentially exempt; consequently £200,000 of the deceased's lifetime allowance of £250,000 had already been used up. Thus, £250,000 of the £300,000 was then liable to inheritance tax of 20 per cent so a further £40,000 (£50,000 minus the £10,000 already paid) is payable in this respect. This £250,000 is also liable to further inheritance tax on the testator's death. The death rate is a further 20 per cent but because the deceased survived for five and a half further years, there is again a reduction of 60 per cent (20 per cent for each year or part of a year after the first three). Consequently, the further inheritance tax payable is 40 per cent of 20 per cent of £250,000, thus £20,000.

(3) The potentially exempt transfer of £200,000 made in the year of the **15–076** testator's death is not in fact exempt. During the seven years preceding that transfer, the deceased had made two transfers, those of £200,000 and £300,000. These used up all his then lifetime allowance of £250,000. Thus, the whole of the £200,000 is liable to inheritance tax. The death rate is 40 per cent and there is no reduction because the deceased did not survive for three years. Consequently, the inheritance tax payable is 40 per cent of £200,000, thus £80,000.

(4) The deceased's estate of £50,000, other than the part which he left to **15–077** his spouse, which is exempt from inheritance tax, is liable to inheritance tax. During the seven years preceding his death, the deceased made three previous transfers, those of £200,000, £300,000, and £200,000. These used up all the lifetime allowance of £300,000 which he had at the time of his death. Thus, the whole of the £50,000 is liable to inheritance tax. The death rate is 40 per cent. Consequently, the inheritance tax payable is 40 per cent of £50,000, thus £12,500.

15–078　As the amount of inheritance tax payable illustrates, this is of course a splendid illustration of how not to do it! In general, the potentially exempt transfers and, preferably, also the initially chargeable transfers during any seven-year period should be restricted to the amount of the current lifetime allowance because of the risk that the transferor may die before they have become exempt, thus producing the sort of count-back and the level of inheritance tax liability evidenced in the example.

15–079　On the testator's death any potential exempt transfers and initially chargeable transfers which have not by then become exempt are the first charge on his nil rate band; they are charged in full even if the tax actually paid in respect of them is reduced by taper relief. The rate of tax actually paid on each of the relevant assets (subject where appropriate to taper relief) is known as the estate rate. Thus, if the nil rate band is £300,000 and the deceased made a potentially exempt transfer of £100,000 two years before his death, that failed potentially exempt transfer will absorb the first £100,000 of the £300,000,[109] leaving £200,000 to be set against the deceased's other assets. If he had taxable assets of £400,000 on his death, inheritance tax of £80,000 will be payable (40 per cent of the £200,000 which remains after the first £100,000 of the nil rate band has been used up on the potentially exempt transfer). Since a total of £80,000 is payable on assets totalling £500,000 (including the value of the failed potentially exempt transfer), the estate rate is 16 per cent. This is the percentage of tax which will have to be borne by the subject matter of the failed potentially exempt transfer and, in the absence of any contrary provision in the will in question,[110] by each of the assets in the estate.

3. The Liability to Inheritance Tax of Settlements

(A)　On the Creation of a Settlement

15–080　A settlement may be created post mortem in four ways: first, pursuant to the provisions of a will; secondly, pursuant to the intestacy rules; thirdly, as the result of a variation of the effect of a will and/or an intestacy in one of the two ways permitted by the Inheritance Tax Act 1984[111]; and, fourthly, as the result of a successful application under the Inheritance (Provision for Family and Dependants) Act 1975 for reasonable financial provision out of the estate of the deceased. The only possible settlement which can arise pursuant to the intestacy rules is one in favour of the surviving spouse or civil

---

[109] This will be the case even if the testator had survived for more than three years but less than seven years; while the taper relief available will reduce the tax eventually payable and therefore the estate rate, its availability does not reduce the attribution of the potentially exempt transfer to the nil rate band.

[110] It is in fact extremely common for testators to provide that all the inheritance tax payable in respect of their deaths should be paid out of their residuary estate, thus enabling all specific gifts and pecuniary legacies to take effect free of inheritance tax (assuming of course that there is enough residuary estate to cover the tax in question).

[111] By a deed of variation executed pursuant to Inheritance Tax Act 1984, s.142 by any beneficiary who is giving up a right conferred on him by the will and/or intestacy or by an appointment by the trustees of a will out of a discretionary trust created by its provisions pursuant to Inheritance Tax Act 1984, s.143. Such variations have to be carried out within two years of the death of the deceased, who is deemed to have disposed of his assets in the manner provided by the deed of variation or the appointment.

partner of the intestate for life, remainder to the children of the intestate; any type of trust can arise in any of the other ways. But in all cases, the liability of its subject matter to inheritance tax will be determined by the liability to that tax of the estate of the testator or intestate rather than by the nature of the trust which has been created.

When a settlement is created *inter vivos*, the settlor will necessarily have made either a potentially exempt transfer or a chargeable transfer. Prior to March 22, 2006, transfers of property to the trustees both of settlements in which there was an immediate beneficial interest in possession and of accumulation and maintenance trusts could take effect as potentially exempt transfers. But since that date this has only been possible in the case of transfers to trustees on trust for a disabled person or into what is known as a trust for a bereaved minor following the termination of what is known as an immediate post-death interest. The creation of any other type of trust inter vivos is an initially chargeable transfer and will give rise to an immediate charge to inheritance tax, at half the rate applicable on death and therefore at present at 20 per cent, although the tax only actually has to be paid to the extent that the value of the transfer exceeds whatever is left the balance of the transferor's lifetime allowance of, at present, £312,000.[112] **15–081**

A disabled person is defined as a person who is incapable by reason of mental disorder of administering his property or managing his affairs or a person in receipt of attendance allowance or disability living allowance. The creation of a trust in favour of such a person will be a potentially exempt transfer whether it confers on him a fixed interest in possession in respect of the trust property or makes him one of the beneficiaries of a discretionary trust, in which case at least half of the capital of the trust must be applied for his benefit during his lifetime but there are no restrictions on the use of the income.[113] However, if a trust for a disabled person is to qualify as a trust for a vulnerable person and the possibility of an election to have its income and capital gains taxed as the income and capital gains of the disabled person, any property applied for the benefit of a beneficiary must be applied for the benefit of the disabled person and either the disabled person must be entitled to all the income or it must not be able to be applied for the benefit of any other person.[114] Such trusts are subject to the interest in possession regime whether they are fixed or discretionary. **15–082**

A trust for a bereaved minor can arise pursuant to the will or intestacy of a parent of the minor in question, either immediately on death or following the termination of an immediate post-death interest (in practice likely to be in favour of the parent's surviving spouse); such a trust can also be established under the Criminal Injuries Compensation Scheme but in no other ways. The bereaved minor must be given an absolute beneficial interest in both income and capital either outright or not later than the age of 18 and enjoys very considerable fiscal advantages.[115] Such trusts necessarily cannot take effect subject to the interest in possession regime. An immediate post-death interest is a life or lesser interest arising immediately upon death in **15–083**

---

[112] In 2008–2009.
[113] Inheritance Tax Act 1984, ss.89–89B.
[114] See *ante*, paras 15–045—15–046, *post*, para 15–133.
[115] Inheritance Tax Act 1984, ss.71A–71C.

one of the four ways set out above; if its holder renounces his interest in favour of a trust for a bereaved minor, he will be making a potentially exempt transfer. Examples are where a parent leaves his estate to his surviving spouse for life and subject to that on trust for the children or where a parent dies intestate and under the intestacy rules, property is held on trust for his spouse for life, and the remainder to his children; if the spouse renounces his or her interest before a child reached the age of 18, he or she will be making a potentially exempt transfer and therefore saving the inheritance tax on the subject matter of the trust which would otherwise arise on his or her death.

(B) Under a Settlement subject to the Interest in Possession Regime

15–084   The categories of settlements in which there will be an interest in possession for the purposes of inheritance tax have been greatly reduced with effect from March 22, 2006. Ignoring transitional provisions, the interest in possession inheritance tax regime now only applies in the case of what is known as an immediate post-death interest, namely where an interest in possession under a trust takes immediate effect as the result of a death, or in the case of a trust for a disabled person whether created *inter vivos* or by will. The effect of the interest in possession regime is that the holder of the immediate post-death interest or the disabled person in question is regarded as being beneficially entitled to the property which forms the subject matter of the trust in his favour—the fact that he may have no more than a life interest in that property is irrelevant for this purpose.[116]

15–085   An immediate post-death interest can be created in any of the four ways set out above: first, pursuant to the provisions of a will; secondly, pursuant to the intestacy rules; thirdly, as the result of a variation of the effect of a will and/or an intestacy in one of the two ways permitted by the Inheritance Tax Act 1984[117]; and, fourthly, as the result of a successful application under the Inheritance (Provision for Family and Dependants) Act 1975 for reasonable financial provision out of the estate of the deceased. The obvious example of such an interest is an immediate life tenancy, in which case the whole of the capital value of the settled property will be treated as the property of the life tenant for the purposes of inheritance tax.[118] Other examples are where a beneficiary has an immediate right to receive any income produced by the trust, or by some specific asset of that trust, or has the right to occupy a residential property owned by the trust (although in the latter two cases only the asset or property in question will be treated as his property for the

---

[116] Inheritance Tax Act 1984, s.49.

[117] By a deed of variation executed pursuant to Inheritance Tax Act 1984, s.142 by any beneficiary who is giving up a right conferred on him by the will and/or intestacy or by an appointment by the trustees of a will out of a discretionary trust created by its provisions pursuant to Inheritance Tax Act 1984, s.143. Such variations have to be carried out within two years of the death of the deceased, who is deemed to have disposed of his assets in the manner provided by the deed of variation or the appointment.

[118] While the tax is computed on the basis that the settled property forms part of his estate, any tax payable has to be paid by the trustees of the settlement, not by the personal representatives of the life tenant.

purposes of inheritance tax).[119] It is irrelevant that any of these rights is revocable or is capable of being overridden by the exercise of an overriding power of appointment.[120]

A trust for a disabled person[121] may either confer on him a fixed interest **15–086** in possession in respect of the trust property or make him one of the beneficiaries of a discretionary trust, in which case at least half of the capital of the trust must be applied for his benefit during his lifetime but there are no restrictions on the use of the income.[122] However, if a trust for a disabled person is to qualify as a trust for a vulnerable person and the possibility of an election to have its income and capital gains taxed as the income and capital gains of the disabled person, any property applied for the benefit of a beneficiary must be applied for the benefit of the disabled person and either the disabled person must be entitled to all the income or it must not be able to be applied for the benefit of any other person.[123] The fact that such trusts are subject to the interest in possession regime whether they are fixed or discretionary means that none of the inheritance tax charges which normally apply to discretionary trusts arises, either periodical 10-yearly charges or exit charges; as a result no inheritance tax is payable when capital is appointed to the disabled person. However, a charge to inheritance tax will arise on his death and so the subject matter of the disabled trust will be aggregated with his other property for the purpose of calculating the incidence of inheritance tax on his death.

Whenever an interest within the interest in possession regime comes to an **15–087** end, its holder is regarded as having made a transfer of the value of his interest, no matter why it has ended; this may be as the result of a positive act by him, such as a disposal or surrender, or as the result of a positive act by the trustees, such as the exercise of an overriding power of appointment, or as the result of the interest reaching its natural limit because of a determining event or the death of a life tenant.[124] The deemed transfer may be exempt, potentially exempt, or chargeable.

(1) The transfer will be exempt if it falls within any of the general **15–088** exemptions already mentioned (other than the small gifts exemption of £250, which does not apply to settlements)[125]; consequently,

---

[119] Further, although this is nothing to do with the taxation of trusts as such, where a trust owns an undivided share of a residential property and its trustees permit that property to be occupied by the owner of the other undivided share, who is also a beneficiary of the trust, H.M. Revenue & Customs have argued that the owner of the other undivided share has an interest in possession in the whole of the property, not merely in his or her undivided share; this argument, which is based on Trusts of Land and Appointment of Trustees Act 1996, s.12, is bound to be litigated at some point.

[120] The authorities all concern capital transfer tax, where the same criteria applied. See particularly *Pearson v. I.R.C.* [1981] A.C. 753.

[121] Defined as a person who is incapable by reason of mental disorder of administering his property or managing his affairs or a person in receipt of attendance allowance or disability living allowance.

[122] Inheritance Tax Acct 1984, ss.89–89B.

[123] See *ante*, paras 15–045—15–046, *post*, para 15–133.

[124] *ibid.*, ss.51, 52.

[125] *ibid.*, s.57.

if a husband has an immediate post-death interest under a settlement for his lifetime and, subject to that, his wife or his civil partner is absolutely beneficially entitled,[126] no inheritance tax will be payable whether his interest passes as the result of a surrender inter vivos or as the result of his death.

15–089   (2) The transfer will now be potentially exempt only when it is in favour of one or more private individuals absolutely or to trustees to hold on trust for a disabled person or to the trustees of a bereaved minor's trust. Consequently, while an outright disposal of the interest in possession itself will always be a potentially exempt transfer, the effect of a surrender of the interest *inter vivos* or its determination *inter vivos* as a result of the exercise of an overriding power of appointment or of the interest reaching its natural limit is determined by the nature of the interest which then takes effect. Where there is a potentially exempt transfer, then as usual the transfer will become exempt if the former holder of the interest survives for a further seven years and, if he does not do so, the transfer will become chargeable.

15–090   (3) The transfer will be chargeable: first, when a transfer which is neither exempt nor potentially exempt occurs *inter vivos*; secondly, when a transfer which is not exempt occurs on death; and, thirdly, when a potentially exempt transfer fails as a result of the failure of the former holder of the interest to survive for the necessary seven years. In all these cases, the inheritance tax payable is assessed on the basis of the lifetime transfers made by the former holder of the interest, not those made by the settlor.[127] However, any tax due is actually payable out of the settled property since it is the trustees of the settlement, any person with an interest in possession in the settled property, and any person for whose benefit any of the property or income from the settlement is applied who are jointly responsible for its payment.[128]

15–091   There are certain special reliefs from the inheritance tax otherwise payable as a result of an interest in possession coming to an end.

(i) Where the settled property then reverts to the settlor or his spouse or civil partner, there is, subject to certain qualifications, total relief.[129]

(ii) Where, as a result of the transfer in question, the beneficiary becomes entitled to some other interest in the settled property,

---

[126] Where the next interest is not an absolute interest, the trust will then leave the interest in possession regime and there will accordingly be a chargeable transfer (in order to avoid any possible confusion, it should be pointed out that a transitional provision prevents this result where the previous interest existed before March 22, 2006 and terminated before April 5, 2008 or terminates in favour of a spouse or civil partner after that date; *ibid.*, ss.49C, 49D, 49E).

[127] *ibid.*, s.52.

[128] *ibid.*, s.200(1)(b), (c), (d) (transfers on death), s.201 (1) (transfers *inter vivos*; in the latter case, the settlor is also liable if he is still alive and the trustees are non-resident).

[129] *ibid.*, s.54.

there will be partial relief if and to the extent to which his new interest is worth less than his previous interest (there being a potentially exempt transfer to this extent); if, on the other hand, he becomes entitled to the settled property absolutely, there will be a potentially exempt transfer of the amount of any purchase moneys which he has paid for the interests in the settled property to which he was not previously entitled in possession.[130]

(iii) In the case of a protective trust whose trusts are "to the like effect as those specified in" section 33 of the Trustee Act 1925,[131] the forfeiture of the protected life interest and its replacement by the appropriate discretionary trust does not amount to an initially chargeable transfer because the protected life tenant's interest in possession is deemed to continue.[132]

(iv) Where tax is payable within five years of a previous chargeable transfer, quick succession relief reduces the rate of tax.[133]

(C) Under a Settlement subject to the Relevant Property Regime

Any settlement which is not subject to the interest in possession regime is subject to the relevant property regime (this peculiar name derives from the wording of section 58(1) of the Inheritance Tax Act 1984) except for certain trusts within the relevant property regime which are given certain privileges, such as a trust for a bereaved minor and an 18–25 trust, both of which will be considered in the next part of this section, and certain other trusts which are given special treatment, including charitable trusts, pension trusts, newspaper trusts, maintenance funds for historic buildings, trusts for the benefit of employees and protective trusts[134] (these are not considered further in this work).   **15–092**

As has already been seen, the creation *inter vivos* of any trust which is subject to the relevant property regime is an initially chargeable transfer and consequently is subject to an immediate payment of inheritance tax, charged at half the death rate; thus at present[135] it will be charged at 20 per cent if and to the extent that the total of transfers which are neither exempt nor potentially exempt during the seven years preceding the transfer exceed the   **15–093**

---

[130] *ibid.*, s.53(2).

[131] See *ante*, para 8–004.

[132] *ibid.*, s.88. The advantages and disadvantages of this special regime are as follows. As well as the advantage that there is no initial chargeable transfer when the protected life interest is forfeited, capital can be advanced to the principal beneficiary once he has obtained his discharge without any inheritance tax consequences whatever (although there may be a liability to an exit charge to capital gains tax). However, because this special regime does not also apply to income tax and capital gains tax, following forfeiture the trust is in the discretionary trust regime for the purposes of income tax and of capital gains tax while remaining in the interest in possession regime for the purposes of inheritance tax. Consequently, in the event that the principal beneficiary dies after forfeiture while the discretionary trust is still ongoing, the trust property falls into his estate for inheritance tax purposes but the trust does not obtain the usual capital gains tax uplift because, for the purposes of capital gains tax, he does not have an interest in possession. This peculiar result is quite contrary to normal principles but has arisen as the result of an earlier loophole being closed.

[133] *ibid.*, s.141.

[134] *ibid.*, ss.58, 86, 87, 88 and 89.

[135] In 2008–2009.

settlor's lifetime allowance. Further, in the event that the settlor dies within seven years of the transfer, the amount of inheritance tax payable may have to be reassessed if any transfer which was potentially exempt at the time of the original assessment turns out in the end not to be exempt from inheritance tax (see the example discussed in the previous part of this section). This total of transfers is deemed to be the discretionary trust's own total of transfers which will never be lost throughout its existence.

15–094   It has also already been seen that the liability of a settlement *post mortem* to inheritance tax will be determined by the liability to that tax of the estate of the testator or intestate rather than by the nature of the trust which has been created; in other words, the creation *post mortem* of any trust which is subject to the relevant property regime will similarly give rise to an immediate charge to inheritance tax to the extent that its subject matter is not absorbed within whatever remains of the deceased's lifetime allowance at the time of his death. However, many, in fact probably the vast majority, of the discretionary trusts in existence today were created precisely in order to ensure that that allowance was utilised in full. These are the so-called "nil rate band discretionary trusts", which were until October 16, 2007 habitually contained in the wills of spouses in order to ensure that none of the lifetime allowance of the first spouse to die was wasted, as it would have been if the whole of his or her property was left to the surviving spouse. Under such a trust, whatever remains of the lifetime allowance was left to trustees to hold on discretionary trust for, usually, the surviving spouse and children; the idea was that the surviving spouse could, if necessary, receive the income of that trust without its capital becoming potentially liable to inheritance tax on his or her death. But difficulties did arise in this respect when it was necessary for the trust to include some or all of the value of the deceased's share of the former matrimonial home.[136]

15–095   However, this is no longer actually necessary because, on the death of a surviving spouse or surviving civil partner, his estate can now utilise any of the nil rate band of the first to die which was not utilised on his death. Existing trusts of this type obviously continue and such trusts contained in the wills of those yet to die which are not amended will duly come into effect. Further, there are also still some advantages in using such trusts, in order to protect the assets in question from the ravages of care home fees incurred by the survivor and also from any risk that the survivor will leave those assets away from the children to a new spouse or companion. However, because of the publicity given by the Government to the change in the

---

[136] At one time, pursuant to a much utilised tax avoidance scheme, the interest of the first spouse to die in the former matrimonial home, usually a one half share of that property, was commonly appropriated to the nil rate band discretionary trust and the surviving spouse, who would obviously still be entitled to the remaining share of that property, was then permitted to occupy the deceased's share under the discretionary trust. However, in the light of a decision that this occupation could in some circumstances give the surviving spouse an interest in possession in the deceased spouse's share of the property (*I.R.C. v. Lloyds Private Banking* [1999] S.T.C. 559), this was subsequently no longer generally done. Instead the surviving spouse commonly purchased the deceased's share of the former matrimonial home from his or her personal representatives, if necessary by giving them an I.O.U. which was sometimes also secured on the property by a charge; it was the purchase money or the I.O.U. rather than any share of the property which was then appropriated to the nil rate band discretionary trust.

law, few testators can now be convinced to pay the fees involved in the creation of such trusts.

The inheritance tax potentially payable in respect of the initially chargea- **15–096** ble transfer is not the only liability to inheritance tax which may be incurred by a settlement which is subject to the relevant property regime since all such trusts other than trusts for bereaved minors are potentially subject to further charges. The incidence and amount of these charges depend on how long the discretionary trust in question has been in operation; the crucial dates occur at 10-year intervals from the date on which the settlement in question was originally created (not from the date on which the discretionary trust itself came into effect[137]). In chronological order, these potential further charges are as follows.

The first possibility of a further charge to inheritance tax arising is if any **15–097** of the settled property ceases to be subject to the discretionary trust during the first 10-year period.[138] Property now ceases to be subject to a discretionary trust only where a capital payment is made to a beneficiary absolutely (since March 22, 2006, it now longer does so when the trustees, pursuant to an overriding power of appointment, appoint some or all of the property subject to the discretionary trust on an interest in possession trust because the latter trust is still subject to the relevant property regime[139]). The intention of this charge is to produce the appropriate proportion of the inheritance tax which would otherwise have been payable at the end of the first 10-year period in the manner explained below. The rate of tax payable is the appropriate fraction, taking into account the number of quarters which have passed since the discretionary trust came into effect, of 30 per cent of the rate of tax which would have been payable on a hypothetical chargeable transfer of the property originally settled, taking into account the state of the settlor's lifetime allowance at the time when the settlement was originally created[140] (the 30 per cent figure is utilised because that is what is utilised at the end of the first 10-year period); consequently, if two years have passed since the discretionary trust came into effect, the appropriate fraction is eight-fortieths so the rate of tax payable is eight-fortieths of 30 per cent of the rate of tax payable on the hypothetical chargeable transfer).

The second possibility of a further charge to inheritance tax arising is on **15–098** the first (and, for that matter, every subsequent) 10th anniversary of the date on which the settlement containing the discretionary trust was created. The rate of tax payable on the value of the property subject to the settlement on the day before the 10th anniversary in question is 30 per cent of the rate of inheritance tax which would have been payable if that property had been

---

[137] Thus if property is settled by will on a person for life and, subject to that, on discretionary trusts, the 10-year periods will run from the date of the settlement, not from the date of the death of the life tenant, although none of the further charges to inheritance tax will actually become payable until after the life tenant's death.

[138] Inheritance Tax Act 1984, s.65.

[139] This was not the case before then because such an interest in possession would have been subject to the interest in possession regime.

[140] *ibid.*, s.68. The value of other property, such as property settled by the same settlor on the same day or property which has been added to the settlement, is sometimes also relevant but these complexities are outside the scope of this work.

transferred to the settlement at that time.[141] The tax notionally payable in respect of that hypothetical transfer is assessed by reference both to the state of the settlor's cumulative total at the time when the settlement was originally created (this remains relevant no matter how much time has since passed) and to the amount of any settled property which has ceased to be subject to the discretionary trust during the preceding 10 years (inheritance tax will already have been potentially payable at the time when that property ceased to be subject to the trust). The tax actually payable is assessed in the light of the nil rate band as it exists at the time of the hypothetical transfer.

15–099   The third possibility of a further charge to inheritance tax arising is if any of the settled property ceases to be subject to the discretionary trust at any time after the first 10-year period. This charge arises in the same circumstances as during the first 10-year period and the intention of this charge is also similar, namely to produce the appropriate proportion of the inheritance tax which would have been payable at the end of the next 10-year period. This time the rate of tax payable is the appropriate fraction of the rate of tax paid on the last 10-year anniversary, as before taking into account the number of quarters which have passed in the current 10-year period[142] (if two years have passed since the last 10-year anniversary, the appropriate fraction is again eight-fortieths so the tax payable on the value of the property which ceases to be subject to the settlement is eight-fortieths of the rate of tax payable on the last 10-year anniversary, which was of course itself 30 per cent of the rate of inheritance tax which would have been payable had the property then subject to the settlement been settled then).

15–100   The following two relatively simple examples illustrate how these formulae work (more complex illustrations are provided in specialist works on taxation). Suppose in each case that £150,000 was settled on discretionary trusts in 1992–1993, when the lifetime allowance was £150,000; that, exactly five years after the creation of the settlement, the trustees appoint an interest in possession in £100,000 to one of the beneficiaries; that, 10 years after the creation of the settlement, the lifetime allowance is £250,000; and that, exactly 16 years after the creation of the settlement, the trustees make a similar appointment of £100,000 to another beneficiary.

15–101   In the first example, suppose that the discretionary trust was a nil-rate band discretionary trust created by the will of a testator whose entire lifetime allowance of £150,000 was available to form the subject matter of the trust.

15–102   (1) No inheritance tax will be payable on the creation of the discretionary trusts settlement since its subject matter comprised the testator's lifetime allowance.

15–103   (2) Nor will any inheritance tax be payable on the appointment of £100,000 to one of the beneficiaries exactly five years after the creation of the settlement either. This is because, since the rate of tax payable on the creation of the settlement was 0 per cent, the fraction

---

[141] ibid., ss.64, 66. The value of other property is again sometimes also relevant.
[142] Inheritance Tax Act 1984, s.69.

of that rate which is appropriate will inevitably also be 0 per cent. In fact, for this reason, during the first 10-year period, no inheritance tax will be payable no matter how much of the £150,000 ceases to be subject to the discretionary trust during that period or at what point during that period it does so.

(3) On the 10th anniversary of the creation of the settlement in 2002–2003, inheritance tax will only be payable if the value of the property then subject to the discretionary trust, plus the value of any property which has by then ceased to be subject to the discretionary trust, exceeds the then lifetime allowance of £250,000. All that lifetime allowance is available because the whole of the testator's lifetime allowance was available on the creation of the settlement; in other words, his cumulative total was then nil. So inheritance tax will only be payable then to the extent that the property subject to the discretionary trust has outperformed the rate of inflation, which is what is supposed to determine the annual increases to the lifetime allowance.
15–104

If the value of the property subject to the settlement is £300,000 in 2002–2003,[143] the notional transfer will be of that amount. The tax notionally payable in respect of that notional transfer is assessed by reference to the state of the testator's cumulative total at the time when the settlement was originally created (which was nil) and of the £100,000 appointed out during the preceding 10 years. The tax notionally payable is thus 20 per cent of that part of £300,000 which exceeds what is left of the then nil rate band of £250,000, namely £150,000 (£250,000 less the £100,000 appointed out); this is 20 per cent of £150,000 (£300,000 minus £150,000), thus £30,000. The rate of tax payable on the 10th anniversary is thus 10 per cent (£30,000 divided by £300,000). The rate of inheritance tax actually payable will therefore be 30 per cent of 10 per cent, or 3 per cent. Therefore, the tax payable is 3 per cent of £150,000, thus £4,500 (this will have to be paid out of the settled property).

(4) If no inheritance tax is payable on the 10th anniversary of the creation of the settlement in 2002–2003, none will be payable on the appointment of £100,000 to one of the beneficiaries exactly 16 years after the creation of the settlement either. Only if any inheritance tax is payable on that 10th anniversary is any inheritance tax payable during the next 10-year period. If tax was then payable on the 10th anniversary, then a further 24 quarters will have passed when £100,000 ceases to be subject to the settlement exactly 12 years after its creation. Consequently, the inheritance tax payable in respect of this £100,000 is 24 fortieths (60 per cent) of the rate of tax paid on the 10th anniversary, which was 10 per cent. Therefore, the tax payable is 60 per cent of 10 per cent, that is 6 per cent, of £100,000, thus £6,000.
15–105

---

[143] Due to capital appreciation and the accumulation of some income.

15–106   All this means that a discretionary trust which is limited to the lifetime allowance of the settlor will give rise to no liability to inheritance tax whatever during the first 10-year period, even if the whole of the property ceases to be subject to the discretionary trust during that period, and will only give rise to any inheritance tax thereafter to the extent that the value of the property subject to it outperforms the rate of inflation.

15–107   Secondly, suppose the discretionary trust of £150,000 was created *inter vivos* by a settlor who had already used up all his then lifetime allowance of £150,000 in the preceding seven years and whose cumulative total stood at that £150,000 (in this event, depending on how long he survived, further inheritance tax may also have been payable on his death; this possibility is illustrated by the example which has already been discussed[144] but it will be assumed for the purposes of the present example that this was not the case).

15–108   (1) On the creation of the settlement, inheritance tax is payable at half the death rate. Since the settlor had at the date of the settlement already used up all his then lifetime allowance of £150,000 in the preceding seven years, this tax is payable in full. Consequently, £30,000 tax (20 per cent of £150,000) is payable. It will be assumed that this is paid by the trustees out of the sum settled (were it to be paid by the settlor, the sum settled would have to be "grossed up"). Thus only £120,000 is actually held on discretionary trust initially.

15–109   (2) On the appointment of £100,000 exactly five years after the creation of the settlement, 20 quarters have passed. Consequently, the inheritance tax payable is twenty-fortieths (50 per cent) of 30 per cent of the rate of tax payable on a hypothetical chargeable transfer of the property originally settled taking into account the state of the settlor's lifetime allowance at the date of the creation of the settlement. The latter rate is once again 20 per cent, since the settlor had already used up all his then lifetime allowance at the date of the creation of the settlement. Consequently, the overall rate of tax is 50 per cent of 30 per cent of 20 per cent, which is 3 per cent. Therefore, the tax payable is 3 per cent of £100,000, thus £3,000. It will be assumed that this is paid by the beneficiary out of the £100,000 appointed to him (were it to be paid by the trustees, the sum appointed would equally have to be "grossed up").

15–110   (3) On the 10th anniversary of the creation of the settlement, if the value of the property subject to the settlement is, as before, £300,000, the notional transfer will be of that amount. The tax notionally payable in respect of that notional transfer is assessed by reference to the state of the testator's cumulative total at the time when the settlement was originally created (when it stood at £150,000) and of the £100,000 appointed out during the preceding 10 years. The tax notionally payable is thus 20 per cent of that part of £300,000 which exceeds what is left of the then nil rate band of £250,000, which is in fact nothing (£250,000 less the original cumulative total of £150,000

---

[144] See *ante*, pp.642–644.

and the £100,000 appointed out); this is 20 per cent of £300,000 (£300,000 minus nothing), thus £60,000. The rate of tax payable on the tenth anniversary is thus 20 per cent (£60,000 divided by £300,000), which is the maximum possible. The rate of inheritance tax actually payable will therefore be 30 per cent of 20 per cent, or 6 per cent, also the maximum possible. Therefore, the tax payable is 6 per cent of £300,000, thus £18,000 (this will have to be paid out of the settled property).

(4) On the appointment of £100,000 exactly 16 years after the creation of the settlement, 24 quarters have passed since the 10th anniversary of the creation of the settlement. Consequently, the inheritance tax payable is 24 fortieths (60 per cent) of the rate of tax paid on the 10th anniversary of the creation of the settlement, which was 6 per cent. Therefore, the tax payable is 60 per cent of 6 per cent, that is 1.2 per cent, of £100,000, thus £3,600. It will once again be assumed that this is paid by the beneficiary out of the £100,000 appointed to him (were it to be paid by the trustees, the sum appointed would again have to be "grossed up"). **15–111**

It will be seen from these examples that, apart from the inheritance tax payable on the creation of the settlement, which will be avoided if the property settled falls within the settlor's lifetime allowance and still remains within it at the date of his death, that the incidence of inheritance tax is not substantial. This type of trust therefore retains some attraction for a settlor, particularly if it is limited to the settlor's lifetime allowance. **15–112**

(C) Privileged Settlements under the Relevant Property Regime
Until March 22, 2006, the only privileged type of settlement under the relevant property regime was an accumulation and maintenance trust, which had to be for the benefit of one or more persons under 25, usually but not necessarily the children or grandchildren of the settlor, who had to become entitled to the trust property or to an immediate vested interest in possession in its income upon reaching an age not exceeding 25; in the meantime, the income was either accumulated or applied for the maintenance, education or benefit of the beneficiaries.[145] Such trusts can no longer be created although existing ones continue.[146] **15–113**

The privileged settlement which was intended to replace the accumulation and maintenance trust from March 22, 2006 is the trust for a bereaved minor. Such a trust can arise pursuant to the will or intestacy of a parent of the minor in question, either immediately on death or following the termination of an immediate post-death interest (in practice likely to be in favour of the parent's surviving spouse); such a trust can also be established under the Criminal Injuries Compensation Scheme but in no other ways. The bereaved minor must be given an absolute beneficial interest in both income and capital either outright or not later than the age of 18; until he reaches **15–114**

---

[145] Inheritance Tax Act 1984, s.71.
[146] The existing fiscal privileges continue provided that the qualifying age was reduced to 18 by April 5, 2008. If it was not, the trusts became liable to 10-year charges and exit charges in respect of the share of any beneficiary who is over 18.

that age, any income must either be accumulated or used for his benefit and so must any capital payment.[147] Although the inheritance tax fiscal privileges are similar to those of an accumulation and maintenance trust, the scope of trusts for bereaved minors is much more limited in two respects: first, they can normally only be created pursuant to the will or intestacy of a deceased parent (the typical settlor of an accumulation and maintenance trust was a grandparent and such a trust could be created both *inter vivos* and by will); secondly, the qualifying age has been reduced to 18 (although this restriction can be avoided, at some fiscal cost, if an 18–25 trust is used instead).

15–115   The creation of a trust for a bereaved minor is an initially chargeable transfer unless it arises as a result of the determination *inter vivos* of an immediate post-death interest, which constitutes a potentially exempt transfer. The privileged position of such a trust is that there are no 10-year charges nor is there any exit charge either when the beneficiary reaches the age of 18 or if he dies under that age (there is, however, an exit charge if property leaves the trust in any other way such as, for example, a resettlement on different trusts). A further fiscal privilege is that the charge to capital gains tax which would normally arise when a beneficiary becomes absolutely entitled to trust property against the trustees is not levied when the bereaved minor reaches the age of 18, any capital gain being held over.[148] Such a trust will also necessarily be a qualifying trust for a vulnerable beneficiary[149] and so it will be possible for an election to be made for its income to be taxed as the income of the beneficiary rather than as the income of the trust.

15–116   The other type of privileged settlement is what is known as an 18–25 trust. Such trusts are similar to trusts for bereaved minors in that that they can only be created on the death of a parent of the beneficiary (because of their terms necessarily only pursuant to his will) or under the Criminal Injuries Compensation Scheme.[150] This time the beneficiary, who despite the name of the trust can be any age under 25, must be given an absolute beneficial interest in both income and capital not later than the age of 25 (and in practice, of course, after the age of 18); until he reaches that age, any income must either be accumulated or used for his benefit and so must any capital payment.[151] The inheritance tax position of an 18–25 trust is exactly the same as that of a trust for a bereaved minor save that there is an exit charge when the beneficiary becomes absolutely entitled or dies at any age over 18. This charge is calculated in the same way as any other charge but only in respect of the period between the age of 18 and the age at which the beneficiary dies or becomes entitled; consequently, the maximum charge cannot be more than 4.2 per cent (reflecting the fact that, if the maximum period that can be taken into account, which applies if the age is 25, is seven years). The potential capital gains tax charge when the beneficiary reaches the age in

---

[147] Inheritance Tax Act 1984, ss.71A–71C.
[148] Taxation of Chargeable Gains Act 1992, s.260(2)(da), added by Finance Act 2006.
[149] See *ante*, paras 15–045—15–046.
[150] Such a trust can also arise under the transitional provisions governing accumulation and maintenance trusts.
[151] Inheritance Tax Act 1984, ss.71D.

question is also held over.[152] However, an 18–25 trust is not a qualifying trust for a vulnerable beneficiary[153] and so there will be no possiblity of an election to be made for its income to be taxed as the income of the beneficiary rather than as the income of the trust.

Because these two types of privileged settlements depend on the death of **15–117** a parent of the beneficiary, they will clearly arise considerably less frequently than accumulation and maintenance trusts did. As between the two, a trust for a bereaved minor has the potential fiscal advantage that it will be a qualifying trust for a vulnerable beneficiary (the only other adverse fiscal consequence of an 18–25 trust, the potential presence of an exit charge, will always be able to be avoided by appointing out at 18); on the other hand, an 18–25 trust enables both vesting to be delayed to what many regard as a preferable age and the decision whether or not to delay it at the cost of the exit charge to be deferred until the beneficiary is approaching the age of 18. It is obviously far too early to say to what extent either type of trust will be expressly created (a trust for a bereaved minor will arise by operation of law both under the intestacy rules and as the result of an absolute gift to a bereaved minor).

4. *Non-Resident Trusts*

In order to determine the taxation position of a trust which is for the time **15–118** being non-resident[154] and, consequently, the advantages of having a trust which is non-resident, it is necessary to consider the potential liability to inheritance tax of both the settlor, the trustees and the beneficiaries.

Where property which forms the subject matter of a non-resident trust is **15–119** situated in the United Kingdom, inheritance tax will in any event be payable by the settlor, the trustees and the beneficiaries according to the rules which have already been discussed.

Where property which forms the subject matter of a non-resident trust is **15–120** situated outside the United Kingdom, that property is "excluded property" for inheritance tax purposes if, but only if, the settlor was domiciled outside the United Kingdom at the time when the settlement was made.[155] If property is excluded property, there will be no liability upon the coming to an end of an interest in possession, or upon any of the occasions on which inheritance tax is normally payable in the case of a discretionary trust, such as on the 10th anniversary of the creation of the settlement or on an appointment of capital out of the settled property.

The settlor will be treated as being domiciled in some part of the United **15–121** Kingdom at the time when the settlement was created if:

---

[152] The charge to capital gains tax which would normally arise when a beneficiary becomes absolutely entitled to trust property against the trustees is also not levied when the age at which the beneficiary takes is 18 or less; Taxation of Chargeable Gains Act 1992, s.260(2)(db), added by Finance Act 2006. There is no need for this section to apply when the beneficiary takes over the age of 18 because the existence of the exit charge permits holdover anyway.

[153] Because the beneficiary will not become absolutely entitled both to capital and income at 18. See *ante*, paras 15–045–15–046.

[154] For the sake of simplicity, in this section the expression "non-resident" is used to mean both non-resident in the strict sense and non-ordinarily resident.

[155] Inheritance Tax Act 1984, s.6(1).

(i) he would have been treated as so domiciled according to the general law;

(ii) he would have been treated as so domiciled according to the general law at any time within three years prior to the creation of the settlement[156]; or

(iii) he had been resident in the United Kingdom for at least 17 out of the 20 years ending with that in which the settlement was made.[157]

The last two categories only have full application where the property became settled after December 9, 1974.

15–122   Where, at the time when a settlement was made, the settlor was domiciled, or is treated as having been domiciled, in some part of the United Kingdom, that settlement will, in principle, be permanently within the purview of inheritance tax. Strictly speaking, inheritance tax will be payable even if the settlor subsequently ceases to be domiciled in the United Kingdom, the trustees and all possible beneficiaries are resident outside the United Kingdom and all the settled property is situated outside the United Kingdom. Realistically, however, H.M. Revenue & Customs will only have any chance of collecting any inheritance tax due if on his death the settlor left assets in the United Kingdom in respect of which a grant of representation is necessary; otherwise, the H.M. Revenue & Customs are unlikely even to discover that he has died, never mind have any assets against which to charge the tax. This is one of a number of examples of circumstances in which, following the export of a settlement, the parties are content to rely on the rule that one state will not enforce the tax laws of another; in other words, although inheritance tax may be payable, the parties will so conduct themselves that the tax cannot in practice be recovered. However, where any of the beneficiaries is resident in the United Kingdom, H.M. Revenue & Customs will inevitably find about the existence of the settlement as soon as any of its income or capital shows up as part of the beneficiaries' assets, in which case all due inheritance tax will unquestionably be claimed, if necessary against the assets in the hands of the beneficiaries.

15–123   In some circumstances, it may anyway be possible to rely on a specific exemption which applies to Government securities. Most United Kingdom Government securities issued before April 6, 1998[158] are exempt from all United Kingdom taxation, including inheritance tax,[159] while they are in the beneficial ownership of persons who are neither domiciled,[160] nor ordinarily resident in the United Kingdom. This exemption applies to settled property

---

[156] *ibid.*, s.267(1)(a).

[157] *ibid.*, s.267(1)(b); for this purpose, domicile has its normal meaning and s.267 does not apply to treat the person in question as domiciled (s.267(2)).

[158] *ibid.*, s.6(2).

[159] But the specific requirements for obtaining the exemption which are set out in the inheritance tax legislation must be satisfied; *Van Ernst & Cie S.A. v. I.R.C.* [1980] 1 All E.R. 677.

[160] "Domiciled" here has its ordinary, and not its extended, meaning.

where a person who is neither domiciled nor resident in the United Kingdom has an interest in possession in the securities.[161] If there is no interest in possession in the securities, the exemption only applies if it can be shown that all known persons for whose benefit the settled property or its income has been or might be applied are neither domiciled nor ordinarily resident in the United Kingdom.[162] Anti-avoidance provisions prevent exempt securities from being channelled from a trust with resident discretionary beneficiaries to one without any.[163] It follows that where, for example, a fund is held upon trust for Andrew for life, with remainder to Hamish, inheritance tax will be avoided if, at the death of Andrew, he is neither domiciled nor resident in the United Kingdom and the fund is invested in exempt Government securities.

However, liability to inheritance tax does not generally depend on the **15–124** residential status of the trust. If the settlement was created by a non-domiciled settlor and the property is situated abroad, the excluded property rules apply whether the trust is resident or non-resident. If the trust property consists of exempt British Government securities and the beneficiaries are non-domiciled and non-resident, the exemption will also apply whether the trust is resident or non-resident. Therefore, creating a non-resident trust or exporting a trust which was initially resident will neither mitigate nor exacerbate the liability to inheritance tax.

IV. CAPITAL GAINS TAX

Capital gains tax is payable only in respect of the capital gains of natural **15–125** persons; corporation tax is payable in respect of the capital gains of bodies corporate and, as has already been explained,[164] the capital gains of the vast majority of unincorporated associations are also subject to corporation tax[165] payable by the association, rather than to capital gains tax payable by the trustees. In either case, the object is to make a charge on capital gains made as a result of any actual or deemed disposal of an asset *inter vivos*, whether by way of sale, exchange or gift; no charge is made on disposals *mortis causa*.[166] Capital gains tax (or, where relevant, corporation tax) is imposed on any increase in the value of an asset between the date of its acquisition and the date of its disposal; any decrease in the value of an asset can be set off against future capital gains.

---

[161] Inheritance Tax Act 1984, s.48(4).

[162] *ibid.*

[163] *ibid.*, s.48(5).

[164] See *ante*, para 15–004.

[165] The net capital gains are added to the net profits of the association; the rate of tax depends on the total amount in respect of which corporation tax is payable.

[166] The property of a deceased person is deemed to be acquired by his personal representatives for its market value on the date of his death, thus giving the beneficiaries a "tax-free uplift" in the event that this value is superior to its acquisition value. However, the property of the deceased will of course be potentially liable to inheritance tax and any inheritance tax payable in respect of the settled assets will, in the event that it is chargeable on those assets, have the effect of reducing the "tax-free uplift".

15–126   Until April 5, 2008, the value of the asset at the date of its acquisition was adjusted in two ways: first, to take account of whatever inflation occurred prior to April 6, 1998 and, secondly, by reducing the capital gains made after April 5, 1998 by a percentage, which differed depending on whether or not the property was business assets and which rose in accordance with the period after that date during which the asset in question had been owned. Also until April 5, 2008, capital gains tax was payable, after deducting any capital gains which were the subject of exemptions, by private individuals at the highest rate at which they paid income tax[167] and by trusts at 40 per cent.[168] However, the only aspect of this system which now survives is the exemptions. A private individual has an annual exemption which, in 2008–2009, was £9,600 and other exemptions which include his principal private residence,[169] chattels worth less than £6,000,[170] and certain securities.[171] A trust has an annual exemption of half that of a private individual (so £4,800 in 2008–2009) and the same other exemptions; any principal private residence must be that of a beneficiary who is occupying it pursuant to the provisions of the trust. The capital gains tax payable is now simply 18 per cent of the difference between its value at the date on which it was acquired and its value at the date on which it was disposed of.[172]

15–127   The basic principle of the trust provisions of the capital gains tax legislation is that property is regarded as "settled property" for the purposes of the capital gains tax legislation whenever it is held on trust.[173] However, there are three situations in which trust property is instead treated as if any capital gains had been realised by the beneficiaries[174]: first, where a beneficiary is absolutely entitled to the property in question as against the trustees; secondly, where a beneficiary would be absolutely entitled to the property as against the trustees were he not a minor[175] or under some other disability; and, thirdly, where two or more persons jointly are or would be, if one or more of them were not minors or under some other disability, absolutely entitled to the property as against the trustees. These exceptions are interpreted narrowly. In *Tomlinson v. Glyns Executor and Trustee Company*[176] trustees held property in trust for such of four minor beneficiaries as attained the age of 21 or married under that age. When the trustees disposed of certain investments at a profit, they claimed that the infant beneficiaries

---

[167] Taxation of Chargeable Gains Act 1992, s.4. Hence the rate was either 10%, 22% or 40%.

[168] *ibid.*, s.4 (1AA), originally inserted by Finance Act 1998, s.120 and subsequently amended by Finance Act 1999, s.26. This provided that all trusts had to pay capital gains tax at the rate of income tax rate applicable to discretionary trusts (34% in 1998, raised to 40% in 2004). Until 1998, trusts other than discretionary trusts paid capital gains tax at the basic rate of income tax (then 23 per cent).

[169] *ibid.*, s.222.

[170] *ibid.*, s.262.

[171] *ibid.*, s.115.

[172] Finance Act 2008. The Act had not yet been passed when this edition had to go to press but will substitute the relevant new provisions into Taxation of Chargeable Gains Act 1992.

[173] *ibid.*, s.68.

[174] *ibid.*, s.60.

[175] This means 18 even for a settlement created when the age of majority was 21; see *Begg-MacBrearty v. Stilwell* [1996] S.T.C. 413.

[176] [1970] Ch. 112.

were together absolutely entitled to the investments as against the trustees.[177] The Court of Appeal held that their minorities were not the only
reason which, at the time of the disposal of the investments, prevented the
beneficiaries from being absolutely entitled; their interests were also contingent until they reached the age of 21 or married under that age.

There is also one situation in which trust property is treated as if any   **15–128**
capital gains had been realised by the settlor. This is where the settlor or his
spouse or his civil partner has retained an interest under the trust, which
will be the case where any of the trust property or its income is, will, or may
become applicable for the benefit of or payable to the settlor or his spouse
or his civil partner or where one of them enjoys a benefit deriving directly
or indirectly from any of the trust property or its income.[178] This provision
of course parallels the equivalent provision where income as taxed as if it
were the income of the settlor.[179]

1. *Capital Gains on the Creation of a Settlement*

The creation of a settlement by will has never given rise to a chargeable   **15–129**
capital gain because of the tax free uplift which is automatically given on
death. However, the creation of a settlement *inter vivos* does constitute a
disposal of the trust property by the settlor at its market value, even if the
settlement is revocable, and whether or not he or his spouse or his civil
partner is a beneficiary.[180] If chargeable assets are settled, any chargeable
gain will be made by the settlor and capital gains tax will be payable by him
in respect of that gain at the same rate as that at which he pays income tax;
any chargeable loss will also be made by the settlor but, because he and the
trustees are connected persons,[181] that loss will be deductible only from
future chargeable gains arising out of subsequent disposals by the settlor to
the same settlement. It used to be possible always to elect to postpone
(technically, "hold over") the payment of the capital gains tax until the
settled property was eventually sold.[182] This then ceased to be possible
unless the assets settled comprise business property[183] or if the creation of
the trust involves a chargeable transfer for the purposes of inheritance tax.[184]
However, as the result of the changes made, with effect from March 22, 2006,
to the inheritance tax regime for trusts, the creation of any trust *inter vivos*
except for a trust for a disabled person now involves a chargeable transfer
for the purposes of inheritance tax anyway. Consequently, with the sole

---

[177] If the trustees had succeeded in their contention, there would still have been a capital
gains tax liability. However, it would have been calculated according to a special basis then in
force which was open only to private individuals; see Finance Act 1965, s.21.
[178] Taxation of Chargeable Gains Act 1992, ss.77–78.
[179] See *ante*, para 15–019.
[180] *ibid.*, s.70.
[181] By virtue of Taxation of Chargeable Gains Act 1992, s.18(3).
[182] Under Finance Act 1980, s.79 (repealed in 1989).
[183] Taxation of Chargeable Gains Act 1992, s.165.
[184] *ibid.*, s.260; see *ante*, para 15–067. It is possible to create a settlement in such a way as to
give rise to a very small chargeable transfer and thus enable hold over of the capital gains tax
otherwise payable (see *Melville v. I.R.C.* [2001] S.T.C. 1271); however, this will now only work
where the settled property is ultimately to be given to someone absolutely rather than, as in
Melville v. I.R.C., held on discretionary trusts (this is the effect of Finance Act 2002, s.119).

exception of a trust for a disabled person, it is now once again possible for an election for holdover relief to be made in the case of every trust created *inter vivos*.

2. *Capital Gains on the Disposal of Assets by the Trustees*

15–130   When a trust is created, the trustees are deemed to acquire the trust property at its market value. When an asset is purchased in a transaction at arm's length, the consideration, together with the expenses associated with the purchase, constitute the acquisition value. As has already been seen, certain assets are exempt from capital gains tax but the only one of those which is likely to be held by trustees is a residential property occupied by a beneficiary as his principal private residence; in this event, the principal private residence exemption is available to the trustees whether or not the beneficiary in question has an interest in possession under the trust.[185] Any disposition by the trustees of an asset which is not exempt for a consideration in excess of its acquisition value gives rise to a chargeable gain in respect of the difference. Where the trustees incur expense such as stamp duty, legal costs and registration fees in acquiring an asset and in arranging for its disposal, the total of these costs is added to the acquisition value and only the difference is chargeable. As has also already been seen, all capital gains made by trusts (and for that matter by anyone else) are now taxable at 18 per cent.

15–131   A simple transaction would be as follows:

Proceeds of sale of shares		£10,100
Less: purchase price	£8,000	
broker's commission on purchase	£100	
stamp duty on purchase	£40	
	£8,140	£8,140
		£1,960
Less: expenses of sale		£160
Chargeable gain		£1,800
Capital gains tax payable: 18% of £1,800:		£324

Of course, if this were the only chargeable gain made by the trust during the year in question, it would be within the annual exemption of, at present, £3,950. The tax shown above would therefore only be payable in full if the annual exemption had already been completely used up.

---

[185] *Sansom v. Peay* [1976] 3 All E.R. 375 decided that the exemption is available even where the beneficiary in question is merely one of a number of beneficiaries of a discretionary trust who has been permitted to occupy the property as a result of the exercise of the trustees' discretion.

Clearly, the most usual situation in which trustees will incur this type of **15–132** liability is where they switch assets in the course of the administration of the trust. Equally clearly, the incidence of capital gains tax is likely to encourage trustees to limit their capital gains to the amount necessary to use up the trust's annual exemption. However, all other matters being equal, they should certainly use that exemption in full each year in order to avoid unnecessary capital gains tax in the future.

In the case of qualifying trusts for vulnerable beneficiaries,[186] where an **15–133** election has been made for the income of the trust to be treated as the income of the vulnerable beneficiary and to be subject to income tax only on that basis, the capital gains of the trust will similarly be treated as the capital gains of the vulnerable beneficiary and will be subject to capital gains tax only on that basis.[187]

3. *Capital Gains on the Disposal of Interests by the Beneficiaries*

The basic rule is that a disposal by a beneficiary of his beneficial interest **15–134** under a settlement, whether or not for value, does not amount to a disposal for the purposes of capital gains tax.[188] A disposal other than for value does however constitute a transfer of value for the purposes of inheritance tax. However, the disposal other than for value of future interests in settled property is often crucial for inheritance tax planning precisely because it has no inheritance tax consequences; it is, therefore, important that such a disposal has no capital gains tax consequences either.

The protection provided by this rule is given to the original beneficiaries **15–135** of the settlement and to anyone else who acquired the beneficial interest in question other than for money or money's worth (which for this purpose does not include another interest under the same settlement). However, since March 6, 1998, the rule has not applied to any settlement which has ever been non-resident,[189] nor, since March 21, 2000, has it applied to sales by beneficiaries of interests under settlements in which the settlor or the settlor's spouse has, or at any time during the previous two tax years has had, an interest under the settlement or under settlements whose assets were derived from such a settlor-interested settlement during the previous two tax years.[190] Where the rule does not apply, the disposal of the beneficial interest does amount to a disposal for the purposes of capital gains tax.[191]

4. *The Exit Charge*

When a beneficiary becomes absolutely entitled to an interest in possession **15–136** in the whole or any part of the trust property, the trustees are deemed to have disposed of the assets in question to him at their market value at that

---

[186] See *ante*, paras 15–045—15–046.
[187] Finance Act 2005, s.30.
[188] Taxation of Chargeable Gains Act 1992, s.76(1).
[189] *ibid.*, s.76(1B).
[190] *ibid.*, s.76A and Sch.4A.
[191] The trustees are deemed to dispose of and reacquire the relevant proportion of the trust property.

date and he is deemed to have acquired them for their market value at that date.[192] A beneficiary will become absolutely entitled in this sense on fulfilling some contingency, such as attaining the age of 18, or on the determination of a prior interest, or when in other circumstances the trustees make a decision to pay or to transfer the asset to him. The effect of the acquisition of the beneficial interest under a settlement, which is not normally a disposal for the purposes of capital gains tax, may also, when that interest merges with some other interest under the settlement which the acquirer already has, make him absolutely entitled in this sense.[193] An immediate liability to capital gains tax will arise which is, in principle, payable by the trustees. If the trustees thereafter continue to hold the assets in their name, they will do so as nominees for the beneficiary. In this case, the trust will no longer be a settlement for the purposes of the capital gains tax legislation and the property will be deemed to be held by the beneficiary so that any future liability for capital gains tax will fall on the beneficiary and not on the trustees; this is of course advantageous because each beneficiary will have double the annual exemption of the trust.

15–137   However, as before, payment of the capital gains tax by the trustees can be held over if the assets settled comprise business property[194] or if the creation of the trust involves a chargeable transfer for the purposes of inheritance tax.[195] Where a trust is within the inheritance tax relevant property regime, a beneficiary cannot become absolutely entitled to an interest in possession in the whole or any part of the trust property without triggering an exit charge to inheritance tax; this is a chargeable transfer and so the payment of capital gains tax can be held over. Prior to the changes made, with effect from March 22, 2006, to the inheritance tax regime for trusts, this applied only to discretionary trusts. But it now applies to all trusts other than an immediate post-death interest, namely where an interest in possession under a trust takes immediate effect as the result of a death, or in the case of a trust for a disabled person whether created *inter vivos* or by will. Thus, in the case of trusts created on or after March 22, 2006, holdover will always be available except in these two cases. But it is still important to know whether or not there is a liability to capital gains tax so that it can be decided whether or not to make an election and, if so, so that it can be made.

15–138   Thus if shares worth £100,000 were by will settled on trust for the testator's niece contingent on her reaching the age of 25, a deemed disposal will take place when she attains that age.[196] If the shares are then worth £120,000, capital gains tax of £3,600 (18 per cent of £20,000) will be payable by the trustees, although this liability may be absorbed by any unused part of the trust's annual exemption. If the shares are subsequently sold for £130,000,

---

[192] Taxation of Chargeable Gains Act 1992, s.71(1).

[193] *ibid.*, s.76(2).

[194] Taxation of Chargeable Gains Act 1992, s.165.

[195] *ibid.*, s.260; see *ante*, para 15–067. It is possible to create a settlement in such a way as to give rise to a very small chargeable transfer and thus enable hold over of the capital gains tax otherwise payable (see *Melville v. I.R.C.* [2001] S.T.C. 1271); however, this will now only work where the settled property is ultimately to be given to someone absolutely rather than, as in *Melville v. I.R.C.*, held on discretionary trusts (this is the effect of Finance Act 2002, s.119).

[196] Unless the trust was created by the will of one of her parents, in which case the capital gain can be held over until she herself disposes of the property.

then, whether they have in the meantime been retained by the trustees or transferred to the niece, the further capital gain of £10,000 will be attributable to the niece and she will pay capital gains tax on that gain, also at 18 per cent to the extent that the liability of £1,800 is not absorbed by her own annual exemption.[197]

In principle, one beneficiary can become absolutely entitled as against the   **15–139** trustees even though there are other beneficiaries who do not do so. If property is held on trust for such of the testator's nephews and nieces as attain the age of 25 and, if more than one of them does so, in equal shares, the membership of the class will become fixed when the eldest nephew or niece attains the age of 25.[198] If there are then three members of the class, the eldest one will immediately become absolutely entitled to a one third share in the property even though the younger ones are still under 25. If the second one dies under the age of 25, the eldest one will then become absolutely entitled to a further one sixth share (one half of the deceased second one's presumptive share) and, when the youngest child attains the age of 25, the latter will become absolutely entitled to the remaining half share of the property.[199] However, where the settled property consists of land, it seems that one beneficiary cannot become absolutely entitled if the other beneficiaries do not also do so.[200]

When a beneficiary becomes absolutely entitled as the result of the deter-   **15–140** mination of a prior life interest because of the death of the life tenant, then special rules apply if that life interest is, for the purposes of inheritance tax, treated as an interest in possession; this will now only be the case if it was an immediate post-death interest. Although there is still a deemed disposal by the trust and a deemed acquisition by the beneficiary, no capital gains tax will be payable because, for inheritance tax purposes, the subject matter of the life interest is treated as the property of the life tenant, it is therefore he who is deemed to have disposed of it and no charge to capital gains tax is made on disposals *mortis causa*.[201] The absolutely entitled beneficiary will therefore acquire the trust property at its market value on the date of the death of the life tenant, thereby obtaining the benefit of a tax free uplift. This uplift is available because of the fact that the trustees will be potentially liable to pay inheritance tax in respect of the settled property, whose capital value is deemed to fall into the estate of the life tenant for this purpose. Capital gains tax will only be payable where the settlor held over the payment of the capital gains tax payable on the creation of the settlement; in that case and only in that case, the relevant capital gains tax becomes payable on the death of the life tenant.[202]

In contrast, when a beneficiary becomes absolutely entitled as the result of   **15–141** the determination of a prior life interest because of the death of a life tenant whose interest is not, for the purposes of inheritance tax, treated as an

---

[197] In the situation envisaged in the previous footnote, she would then have to pay capital gains tax of £5,400, all of which is capable of being absorbed by her annual exemption.

[198] Under the class closing rules mentioned *ante*, para 7–030 and n.55.

[199] *Stephenson v. Barclays Bank Trust Company* [1975] S.T.C. 151; *Pexton v. Bell* [1976] 1 W.L.R. 885.

[200] *Crowe v. Appleby* [1976] 1 W.L.R. 885.

[201] Taxation of Chargeable Gains Act 1992, s.73.

[202] Taxation of Chargeable Gains Act 1992, s.74.

interest in possession, the deemed disposal by the trust and the deemed acquisition by the beneficiary will give rise to a potential liability to capital gains tax. But there will necessarily be an exit charge to inheritance tax and therefore the capital gains tax will be able to be held over.

5. *Where a Settlement Continues*

15–142   Where on the determination of a prior interest a settlement continues without any beneficiary becoming absolutely entitled, there are no capital gains tax consequences unless the prior interest has determined because of the death of a life tenant who had an interest in possession for the purposes of inheritance tax, in which case the rules discussed immediately above also apply. In this situation the trustees are deemed both to dispose and to reacquire the trust property at its market value on the date of the death of the life tenant and so the trust obtains the benefit of the tax free uplift[203]; however, the trustees will again be potentially liable to pay inheritance tax. Capital gains tax will again be payable if, and only if, the settlor held over the payment of his own capital gains tax.

6. *Resettlements*

15–143   The almost inevitable existence of overriding powers of appointment in settlements today means that the trust property can at any time be resettled by the exercise of these powers. However, while the original settlement continues, there will be no deemed disposal for the purposes of capital gains tax unless, as a result of the exercise of the powers, a beneficiary becomes absolutely beneficially entitled as against the trustees to an interest in possession, in which case the exit charge will arise in the manner already discussed.

15–144   When, on the other hand, trust property is resettled by being transferred from one settlement to another, the trustees of the second settlement (even if they are the same persons as the trustees of the original settlement) become absolutely entitled as against the original trustees and a deemed disposal for the purposes of capital gains tax will normally occur.[204] However, if a resettlement of this type occurs only as the result of the exercise by the trustees of their overriding powers of appointment under the original settlement, it seems that the exercise of such a special power of appointment will not in itself amount to a resettlement and so there will be no automatic deemed disposal of the property in question[205]; on the other hand, while the exercise of a wider power, such as a power of advancement, will not necessarily amount to a resettlement either, it will have this effect if the new settlement is complete in itself and is sufficiently separate to require no further reference back for any purpose to the original settlement.[206]

---

[203] *ibid.*, s.72.
[204] *Hoare Trustees v. Gardner* [1979] Ch. 1.
[205] *Roome v. Edwards* [1981] S.T.C. 96; *Bond v. Pickford* [1983] S.T.C. 517.
[206] *Swires v. Renton* [1991] S.T.C. 490.

It should be noted that, since April 6, 2006, when trust property has been **15–145** the subject of a resettlement, the settlor of the resettled property is treated from the time of the disposal as the settlor of the new settlement.[207]

7. Non-Resident Trusts

In order to determine the taxation position of a trust which is for the time **15–146** being non-resident[208] and, consequently, the advantages of having a trust which is non-resident, it is necessary to consider the potential liability to capital gains tax of both the settlor, the trustees and the beneficiaries.

For capital gains tax purposes, a trust will, in principle, only be regarded **15–147** as non-resident if both the following conditions are fulfilled:

    (i) the general administration of the trust is ordinarily carried on outside the United Kingdom (there is no definition of precisely what this means but the general administration of the trust is probably regarded as ordinarily carried on in the place where the trustees habitually meet or, if the trust is large enough to have its own secretariat, in the place where that secretariat is situated); and

    (ii) the majority of the trustees are not resident or ordinarily resident in the United Kingdom.[209]

These requirements can be satisfied despite the fact that the settlor was resident in the United Kingdom at the time when the trust was created.

However, a trust will also be regarded as non-resident if all the following **15–148** three conditions are satisfied:

    (i) all the trust property is derived from a person who is not domiciled or resident in the United Kingdom;

    (ii) some or all of the trustees are individuals or companies whose business consists of or includes the management of trusts or of acting as trustees; and

    (iii) a majority of the trustees are either such persons, or persons who are actually non-resident.[210]

Trusts who satisfy these three requirements are regarded as being non-resident even if their general administration is actually carried on in the United Kingdom.

(A) The Settlor

A settlor of any non-resident trust who in any year is both domiciled and **15–149** resident in the United Kingdom will be personally liable to capital gains tax

---

[207] Taxation of Chargeable Gains Act 1994, s.68B, added in 2006.

[208] For the sake of simplicity, in this section the expression "non-resident" is used to mean both non-resident in the strict sense and non-ordinarily resident.

[209] Taxation of Chargeable Gains Act 1992, s.69(1).

[210] *ibid.*, s.69(2).

on all gains realised by the trust which would have been taxable if the trust had been resident where a "defined person" benefits or will or may become entitled to a benefit in either the income or the capital of the trust.[211] A "defined person" is the settlor, the settlor's spouse, the settlor's civil partner, any child or the spouse of any child of either the settlor or the settlor's spouse, and companies controlled by any such person.[212] In the case of trusts which are created or receive further property or go "off-shore" on or after March 17, 1998, the list also includes any grandchild or the spouse of any grandchild of either the settlor or the settlor's spouse.[213] From the same date, these liabilities also apply to the settlors of trusts created before March 19, 1991,[214] which were formerly exempt.[215]

15–150   This is an absolutely lethal provision, particularly because it includes children and step-children (and now grandchildren and step-grandchildren) of any age. However, some alleviation is provided by the fact that it only applies where the settlor is both domiciled and resident in the year in question. A settlor of an off-shore trust can therefore avoid liability either by leaving the trust property in the form of assets such as cash which are not liable to capital gains tax in the first place or by becoming non-resident himself before substantial capital gains are realised, although he will have to be non-resident for five years if he was resident for four of the seven years prior to his departure.[216] Further, many trusts which are created, as distinct from transferred, off-shore are purportedly created by non-resident settlors who, for a consideration, settle a nominal amount of their own money; the real trust property then reaches the hands of the trustees by a route which can best be described as circuitous (this was admittedly easier to achieve when it was still easy to deposit large amounts of cash with a bank and considerably more difficult to follow bank transfers than it has now become).[217] Settlements with genuine off-shore settlors are of course outside the scope of this provision altogether.

(B) The Trustees
15–151   In common with non-resident individuals, non-resident trustees are not chargeable to capital gains tax in respect of gains arising on the disposal of assets, even if the assets are situated in the United Kingdom.[218]

(C) The Beneficiaries
15–152   The liability of the beneficiaries of non-resident trusts to capital gains tax depended until March 16, 1998 on whether the trust in question was what

---

[211] *ibid.*, s.86.
[212] *ibid.*, Sch.5, para.2(3).
[213] Finance Act 1998, s.130.
[214] *ibid.*, s.132.
[215] Taxation of Chargeable Gains Act 1992, Sch.5, para.9. The subsequent addition of property or of a "defined person" as a beneficiary destroyed the exemption.
[216] Taxation of Chargeable Gains Act 1992, ss.10A, 86A.
[217] For this reason the extension to non-resident trusts created before March 19, 1991 (which were formerly exempt trusts) is unlikely to have had much impact.
[218] Taxation of Chargeable Gains Act 1992, s.2(1). There is, however, a liability if a non-resident, whether an individual or a trustee, carries on a trade in the U.K. and disposes of trading assets (*ibid.*, s.10(1))

was known[219] as a section 87 trust[220] and or a fully foreign trust.[221] However, in respect of capital gains arising on or after March 17, 1998 all non-resident trusts are subject to the regime which formerly applied only to section 87 trusts.

The provisions of section 87 of the Taxation of Chargeable Gains Act 1992, **15–153** which now apply to all capital gains realised by non-resident trusts, are similar to those of section 731 of the Income Tax Act 2007.[222] A notional record is maintained of all gains which accrue to the trustees after March 9, 1981. These are known as "trust gains". When the trustees make a capital payment to a beneficiary,[223] that payment is treated as representing a capital gain to the extent of the available trust gains.

Suppose, therefore, that the trustees realise the following gains, and make **15–154** the following capital payments:

Year of assessment	Gains	Capital Payment
2005–2006	nil	£8,000 to Andrew
2006–2007	£20,000	nil
2008–2009	£20,000	£15,000 to Brian
2009–2010	£20,000	£50,000 to Charles
2010–2011	£20,000	nil

The trust gains for 2005–2006 are nil. Of the gains realised in 2006–2007, £8,000 is attributed to Andrew for 2006–2007 because of the capital payment made to him the previous year and the balance of £12,000 is carried forward to 2007–2008. The trust gains for 2007–2008 are the balance brought forward

---

[219] Colloquially, not by statute.

[220] "Section 87" trusts, that is trusts which were within section 87 of the Taxation of Chargeable Gains Act 1992, were trusts in which, during the year of assessment being considered:
  (i) the trustees were non-resident;
  (ii) if the trust was created *inter vivos*, and the settlor was still alive, the settlor
    (a) was domiciled and resident in the United Kingdom at the time when the settlement was created; or
    (b) was domiciled and resident in the United Kingdom in the year of assessment being considered; or
  (iii) if the settlement was created *inter vivos* and the settlor was dead, he was domiciled and resident in the United Kingdom when the settlement was created; or
  (iv) if the settlement was created by will, the testator was domiciled and resident in the United Kingdom at the date of his death.

[221] A "fully foreign trust" was one which was non-resident and which was outside the scope of s.87. No liability attached to beneficiaries, even if resident in the UK, in respect of gains realised by the trustees of a fully non-resident trust. This was so whether or not the trustees made capital payments to the beneficiaries. However, where a beneficiary became absolutely entitled to assets as against the trustees of a fully foreign trust, he would in general be treated as acquiring those assets at a nil base cost and so he would be taxable on the whole of the proceeds of sale when he disposed of them. This regime does not apply to any capital gains realised by a non-resident trust on or after March 17, 1998. However, beneficiaries who became absolutely entitled to assets as against the trustees of a fully foreign trust before that date will still be taxable on the whole of the proceeds of sale when they dispose of them.

[222] See *ante*, para 15–056.

[223] Whether resident or non-resident.

from 2006–2007 of £12,000, plus the gains arising in the year of £20,000, minus £15,000 which is attributed to Brian; the balance of £17,000 is carried forward. In 2008–2009 the trust gains total £37,000[224] so that £37,000 is attributed to Charles for 2008–2009. The remaining £13,000 which Charles has received in that year will have the gains for 2010–2011 attributed to it.

15–155   If any of Andrew, Brian or Charles is domiciled and resident in the United Kingdom in the year in which any of these gains is attributed to a capital payment made to him (as distinct from the year in which the capital payment was made to him, if different), he will have to pay the appropriate capital gains tax on the gain in question in accordance with the normal rules; thus, he can deduct from the attributed gain any losses and his annual exemption and he will be taxed on the balance at 18 per cent. However, no capital gains tax will be payable by any beneficiary who is not domiciled and resident in the United Kingdom in the year in which the gain is so attributed.

15–156   Further, in addition to the basic capital gains tax payable in the manner illustrated in this example, beneficiaries who receive capital payments after April 5, 1992 and are liable to pay capital gains tax because they are domiciled and resident in the United Kingdom also have to pay a supplementary interest charge of 10 per cent per annum of the tax actually payable in respect of any period up to six years during which payment of capital gains tax has been deferred.[225] In the example above, the capital payment to Andrew is not liable to this interest charge because no capital gains tax was actually deferred. However, the capital payments made to Brian and Charles will be liable to this payment. Of the £15,000 attributed to Brian in 2007–2008, £12,000 was brought forward from 2006–2007; if he is domiciled and resident in the United Kingdom in 2007–2008, he will, therefore, have to pay an extra 10 per cent of the tax due in respect of that £12,000 by way of interest (no interest will be payable in respect of the other £3,000 since that gain arose in the year in which he received the capital payment). In the same way, Charles will, if domiciled and resident in the United Kingdom in 2009–2010, have to pay an extra 10 per cent of the tax due in respect of £17,000 of the £37,000 attributed to him in 2008–2009 by way of interest.

15–157   The provisions seem complicated but their effect is that no liability can attach to a resident beneficiary until he actually receives a capital payment. Accordingly, deferment of capital gains tax can be achieved merely by retaining all capital within the trust, although such deferment will of course now be liable to an interest payment of 10 per cent per annum of the tax due in respect of any gains during the six years prior to the receipt of a capital payment by a resident beneficiary.

15–158   It is obviously possible for the same capital payment to be capable of being treated both as the income of the beneficiary under section 731 of the Income Tax Act 2007 for the purposes of income tax and as representing a capital gain by that beneficiary to the extent of the available trust gains under section 87 of the Taxation of Chargeable Gains Act 1992 for the purpose of capital gains tax. In such circumstances, the treatment of the

---

[224] That is to say, £17,000 brought forward from 2007/2008 and the £20,000 which arises in 2009/2010.
[225] Taxation of Chargeable Gains Act 1992, ss.91–97.

payment as income enjoys priority over its treatment as representing a capital gain.

Finally, it should be noted that dispositions of beneficial interests by the **15–159** beneficiaries of non-resident trusts give rise to a chargeable gain and, therefore, to a potential liability to capital gains tax. The exemption given to resident trusts by section 76 of the Taxation of Chargeable Gains Act 1992[226] does not apply to non-resident trusts.[227]

(D) Exporting Trusts

Since March 19, 1991, the process of exporting a resident trust so that it **15–160** becomes non-resident has constituted a deemed disposal by the trustees[228] similar to that which occurs when a beneficiary becomes absolutely entitled to the whole or any part of the trust property.[229] The deemed disposal is said to take place immediately before the trustees cease to become resident in the United Kingdom. Consequently, it is the retiring United Kingdom trustees who make the disposal and become primarily liable for the tax. This obviously means that exporting a trust involves the payment of capital gains tax on all gains made prior to export. Subsequent capital gains realised before March 17, 1998 escaped tax to the extent that the trust when exported did not become a section 87 trust (which it usually would have anyway).[230] Otherwise capital gains tax will be payable if any capital payments are made to beneficiaries who are domiciled and resident in the United Kingdom. The introduction of this exit charge has made exporting trusts considerably less attractive than hitherto. Nevertheless, provided that the settlor does not himself become liable to tax on the capital gains realised by the trust, there is still some merit in hiving off and exporting those assets in a trust which are likely to make substantial capital gains in the future and there is everything to be said for hiving off and exporting those assets in a trust which are actually showing a capital loss.

---

[226] See *ante*, para 15–135.
[227] *ibid.*, s.76(1A), (1B).
[228] *ibid.*, s.80(2).
[229] See *ante*, para 15–136.
[230] Because of the domiciliary and residential status of the settlor; see *ante*, n.220.

CHAPTER 16

APPORTIONMENTS

16–001 It has already been seen[1] that a fundamental rule is that a trustee must not allow a conflict of interest to arise between his own personal position and his duties to the beneficiaries. The sister rule is that, where there is a conflict between the interests of different beneficiaries, a trustee must hold a balance between them. This is not so much because this is what the settlor actually did intend, for he may well never have given the matter any thought at all, but rather because equity presumes that this is what the settlor would have intended had he directed his mind to the point. It is, therefore, not necessary to find any actual evidence of intention on the part of the settlor for this principle to apply, yet on the other hand he is able to provide expressly or by implication that the principle shall not operate. Avoidance of a conflict of interest is of particular importance in relation to investments; this principle also underlies the rules governing apportionments.[2] These formal rules apply as between tenants for life and remaindermen. However, other conflicts of interest can arise. In *Lloyds Bank v. Duker*,[3] the conflict of interest was between majority and minority beneficiaries. The testator who owned 999 of the 1,000 shares of a private company, left 46/80ths of the 999 shares to his wife. It was held that the 574 shares which represented this proportion could not be transferred to her because such a majority holding would give her the control of the company and, in relation to the remaining minority shares, would be worth more than her due proportion. Consequently, the trustees were directed to sell all 999 shares and distribute the proceeds of sale in the appropriate proportions.

I. APPORTIONMENTS BETWEEN CAPITAL AND INCOME

1. *The Principle*

16–002 Suppose that Basil settles property upon trust for Clare for life, remainder to Priscilla absolutely, and the trust property consists of: £5,000 of some Governmental War Stock; the cow Buttercup; and the right under Basil's grandfather's will to receive £15,000 on the death of his father, Fred, who is still alive (this right is known as a reversionary interest).

---

[1] See *ante*, para 10–047.

[2] There have been a number of recommendations made for the reform of the subject matter of this chapter, most recently by the Trust Law Committee. However, since there is no indication that any of these recommendations is to be enacted, no further reference to them seems appropriate.

[3] [1987] 1 W.L.R. 1324.

If these assets are retained in their present form, the holding of War Stock **16–003** will produce a steady income, and a capital sum will be available to Priscilla on the death of Clare. Buttercup, a fine milk-yielding cow, may produce at first a high income but, as she grows old and her milk production decreases, she will become less and less valuable. She may well die before Clare and, if this is the case, Clare will have derived the whole of the benefit from her and Priscilla will have had none. The case of the reversionary interest is precisely the opposite. Until Fred dies, income is paid to neither Clare nor Priscilla and, if Clare dies before Fred, she will have received no benefit at all from this asset. Equity presumes that it was not Basil's intention that the beneficiaries should be treated so haphazardly and their fortunes left so much to chance. The basic solution is, therefore, for Buttercup and the reversionary interest to be sold and the proceeds invested in authorised securities so that the income may be paid to Clare and a capital sum preserved intact for Priscilla. The rules which follow prescribe how this is to be done. However, once any necessary apportionment between capital and income according to these rules has been made, the trustees are apparently entitled to make investments which produce either high or low income depending on the relative wealth of the tenant for life and the remainder-man.[4]

The rules governing the necessary sale are not, however, always easy to **16–004** apply. There are three questions to consider:

(i) Is there a duty to convert a particular asset into an authorised investment?

(ii) If so, does the income have to be apportioned between the date when the duty arises and the date when the conversion actually takes place?

(iii) If so, how is such apportionment calculated?

These questions are progressive so that, if the answer to any one is "no", there is no need to consider the remaining questions.

2. *Is There a Duty to Convert?*

The duty to convert the trust property into authorised investments may **16–005** arise in two circumstances.

- First, if the trust instrument so directs. The most frequent case of an express direction to convert occurs when there is an express trust for sale but any direction to convert is for this purpose equally adequate.

- Secondly, as a result of the operation of the rule in *Howe v. Lord Dartmouth*,[5] which directs that the conversion of an asset should

---

[4] *Nestlé v. National Westminster Bank* [1993] 1 W.L.R. 1260.
[5] (1802) 7 Ves. 137. For a relatively up-to-date account of the rule, see L. A. Sheridan "*Howe v. Lord Dartmouth* Re-examined" (1952) 16 Conv. (N.S.) 349.

take place where there is no express direction to this effect in the trust instrument, but only where all the following conditions are satisfied:

(i) the trust was created by will;

(ii) there are at least two beneficiaries, and they are entitled in succession;

(iii) the property consists of residuary personalty;

(iv) the asset is wasting, reversionary or of an unauthorised character; and

(v) there is no contrary intention in the will.

The rule does not apply to a settlement *inter vivos*; the terms of such settlements must be observed strictly because, so it is said, the settlor knew exactly the state of the assets when the settlement was created.[6]

16–006   The only one of the five conditions listed which is likely to cause any difficulty is the question of whether or not there is a contrary intention. In *Re Sewell's Estate*[7] the trustees were given a discretion as to what part of the testator's estate should be converted. This was held to have excluded the rule in *Howe v. Lord Dartmouth* because a discretion to convert was inconsistent with the duty to convert which the rule would impose. However, in order to exclude the rule, the power must be consciously exercised.[8] In *Alcock v. Sloper*[9] property was left on trust for a life tenant and, after his death, on trust to be sold and the proceeds divided between various named beneficiaries. Here too it was held that the Rule in *Howe v. Lord Dartmouth* had been excluded, because the express duty to convert on the death of the life tenant was inconsistent with an implied duty to convert on the death of the testator, which is what the rule would have imposed.

16–007   The decision in *Alcock v. Sloper*[10] must be contrasted with that in *Re Evans*,[11] where property was given to trustees on trust for a life tenant and, after her death, on trust to be divided into three equal shares and distributed to three other members of the family. It was held that *Howe v. Lord Dartmouth* did apply, because the division on the death of the life tenant could be of property in either its converted or unconverted form; consequently, the directions in the will were not inconsistent with a duty to convert implied by *Howe v. Lord Dartmouth*.

16–008   Where the settlor shows an intention that the property should be enjoyed *in specie*, this clearly negatives the rule.[12] Bennett J. took this proposition a stage further in *Re Fisher*[13] by saying that, where there is a trust for conversion with a power to postpone, the settlor thereby shows that he intends that

---

[6] *Re Van Straubenzee* [1901] 2 Ch. 779, *per* Cozens-Hardy J. and see *Milford v. Peile* (1854) 2 W.N. 181; *Hope v. Hope* (1855) 1 Jur. (N.S.) 770.

[7] (1870) L.R. 11 Eq. 80; see also *Simpson v. Earles* (1847) 11 Jur. 921.

[8] *Re Guinness* [1966] 1 W.L.R. 1355.

[9] (1833) 2 My. & K. 699; *Daniel v. Warren* (1843) 2 Y. & Coll. C.C. 290

[10] (1833) 2 My. & K. 699.

[11] [1920] 2 Ch. 309.

[12] *Macdonald v. Irvine* (1878) 8 Ch.D. 101.

[13] [1943] Ch. 377.

the property may be enjoyed in specie, and that this also is inconsistent with the duty to convert which would be imposed by *Howe v. Lord Dartmouth*. However, in the later case of *Re Berry*,[14] Pennycuick J. refused to follow *Re Fisher*. Although the logical basis of the latter decision is clear, Pennycuick J. commented that that decision was "contrary to the whole current of authority"; it was an attempt to extend the scope of the exceptions from *Howe v. Lord Dartmouth* too far.

The cases turn on fine differences in wording and, while it may be very   **16–009** difficult to say on any particular set of facts whether *Howe v. Lord Dartmouth* is excluded, the rule itself is clear: has the testator made any provision which is expressly or impliedly inconsistent with a duty to convert at the date of death? If he has not done so and the other conditions listed above are fulfilled, *Howe v. Lord Dartmouth* will apply.

3. *Whether There is a Need to Apportion Income*

If there is a duty to convert, it will be seen below that conversion should take   **16–010** place either at the date of death, or as at one year from the date of death.[15] It will be obvious that in the former case there is no conceivable way of effecting actual conversion at that date while, even in the latter case, actual conversion will often be delayed. The question therefore arises whether, in the event of conversion being delayed, the tenant for life is entitled to the actual income produced by the asset until it is converted or whether he is entitled only to an apportioned part of it. The primary rule is that, if the testator has provided, expressly or by implication, that the tenant for life is to enjoy the actual income which the property produces, then that intention will prevail. Where it cannot be shown that the testator expressed any such intention, then the following rules apply.

First, where the trustees improperly postpone conversion, an apportion-   **16–011** ment will be ordered. Thus in *Wentworth v. Wentworth*[16] the trustees had a power to postpone conversion until a certain date. The trustees improperly postponed conversion beyond that date and the Privy Council held that apportionment should be made as from that date.

Secondly, where the property in question is real property, the tenant for   **16–012** life is entitled to the actual income which the property produces. It will be remembered that *Howe v. Lord Dartmouth* never operates to impose a duty to convert realty so that such a duty in respect of realty can only have come into existence as the result of an express trust for conversion.

Thirdly, in the case of personalty, the tenant for life is entitled only to an   **16–013** apportioned part of the income, unless there is an intention that he shall enjoy the asset *in specie*.[17] Thus the presumption is in favour of the enjoyment of actual income in the case of realty and of only an apportioned part of the income in the case of personalty.

---

[14] [1962] Ch. 97.
[15] See *post, infra*.
[16] [1900] A.C. 163.
[17] *Re Chaytor* [1965] 1 Ch. 233. Where there is a trust for conversion with a power to postpone, the beneficiary will only receive an apportioned part of the income; *Re Berry* [1962] Ch. 97.

4. How is the Apportionment Calculated?

16–014 If there is a duty to convert and if, because the property has not been converted by the due date, the income has to be apportioned until conversion takes place, how is such apportionment calculated? Where the asset concerned is a reversionary interest, the rule in *Re Earl of Chesterfield's Trusts*[18] applies; this is dealt with below. As regards other property which has to be converted, it is necessary first to ascertain the valuation date. At common law there was a presumption that the executor's functions in administering the estate ought to be completed within one year from the death of the testator. From this the rule evolved that, where there is no power to postpone sale, conversion ought to be effected within one year from the date of death; in this case, in order to be able to calculate the apportionment, the asset has to be valued as at one year from the date of death.[19] If, however, there is a power to postpone sale, this negatives the intention that the property should be valued as at one year from the date of death and, because a better date could not be thought of, in this case the property is valued at the date of death.[20] Thus, if there is no power to postpone sale, the valuation date is one year from the date of death but, if there is a power to postpone sale, the valuation date is the date of death.

16–015 Whichever the valuation date, the tenant for life is entitled to interest on the value of the asset as at the valuation date from the date of death until the date of actual conversion. Traditionally, the rate of interest applied has been 4 per cent,[21] but, as this has sometimes been unrealistically low, it may be that the court would now adopt the rate which is equivalent to that paid on the court's short-term investment account.[22] If the actual income is larger than the apportioned figure, the balance is added to capital. If the actual income is smaller than the appropriate rate, the tenant for life receives that actual income, and is entitled to have it made up from future surpluses of income or, if there are none, from capital when the asset is sold. The deficiency cannot be made good from previous surpluses of income because these have already been notionally added to capital.

16–016 An example may help. Suppose that the copyright to a book is left upon trust for Angela for life, remainder to Mary and that the copyright is worth £1,200 at the date of death and £1,000 one year from the date of death. The copyright is eventually sold three years after the date of death and during the intervening three years the royalties actually received are: Year 1: £70; Year 2: £32; and Year 3: £48. It is necessary first to ascertain the valuation date. Where there is a power to postpone, this will be the date of death. At this date the copyright is worth £1,200 so that, if the appropriate rate of interest is 4 per cent, Angela is entitled to 4 per cent × £1,200 = £48 per

---

[18] (1883) 24 Ch.D. 643.

[19] *Re Eaton* (1894) 70 L.T. 761.

[20] *Re Owen* [1912] 1 Ch. 519; *Re Parry* [1947] Ch. 23.

[21] The actual rate of interest is in the discretion of the court, but 4% is usually taken as the appropriate figure; see *Re Lucas* [1947] Ch. 558; *Re Parry* [1947] Ch. 23; *Re Berry* [1962] Ch. 97.

[22] See *Bartlett v. Barclays Bank Trust Co. (No.2)* [1980] Ch. 515 and *Jaffray v. Marshall* [1993] 1 W.L.R. 1285 (overruled on other grounds by the House of Lords in *Target Holdings v. Redferns* [1996] 1 A.C. 421); see *post*, p.774. See also *Re Fawcett* [1940] Ch. 402; *Re Parry* [1947] Ch. 23.

annum. In Year 1 she will receive £48, the balance of £22 being added to capital. In Year 2 she will receive £32, with the right to make good the deficiency of £16 in the future. In Year 3 she will receive £48, and will be entitled to a further £16 from the proceeds of the sale of the copyright to make good the deficiency in Year 2. If, however, there is no power to postpone, the valuation date will be one year from the date of death. Angela is therefore entitled to receive 4 per cent × £1,000 = £40 per annum. In Year 1 she will receive £40, with £30 being added to capital. In Year 2 she will receive £32. In Year 3 she will receive £40, plus £8 to make good the shortfall in Year 2, thus using up all the income for that year. She will therefore need to receive no part of the proceeds of sale of the copyright.

At this point it must again be stressed that the questions posed at the beginning of this discussion (is there a duty to convert; if so, does the income have to be apportioned; if so, how is such apportionment calculated) are progressive. Therefore, it is only if there is a duty to convert that it is necessary to consider whether the income has to be apportioned and it is only if there is a duty to convert and if the income does have to be apportioned that it is necessary to make the type of calculation just considered.   **16–017**

5. Re Earl of Chesterfield's Trusts[23]

A special method is necessary for calculating the apportionment of reversionary interests because these do not actually produce any income until they fall into possession. At the outset it should be noted that reversionary interests are saleable. Thus, going back to the original example,[24] one of the assets which Basil left upon trust for Clare for life, remainder to Priscilla absolutely, was the right to receive £15,000 on the death of his father, Fred, who was still alive. At Basil's death the trustees could have sold that reversionary interest. The price which would be obtained would be largely governed by Fred's age at the date of Basil's death but whatever was obtained would have been invested in authorised securities, the income paid to Clare for life, and the capital held for Priscilla. However, it is usually economically better not to sell but rather to retain the reversionary interest until it falls into possession. If this is done, it is clearly equitable, before the money that is eventually received is invested, to pay part of the amount received to Clare as compensation for the fact that she has had no income from the asset since the trust came into operation. The rule in *Re Earl of Chesterfield's Trusts* provides that, where a reversionary interest which ought to be converted is retained until it falls into possession, part of it is to be treated as arrears of income and paid to the tenant for life and only the balance is to be regarded as capital.   **16–018**

The rule itself says that the proportion of the amount actually received which is to be regarded as capital is that which, if invested at 4 per cent compound interest with yearly rests, would, after allowing for the deduction of income tax at the basic rate for the time being in force, have produced   **16–019**

---

[23] (1883) 24 Ch.D. 643.
[24] See *ante*, para 16–002.

the sum actually received. It remains to be decided whether 4 per cent is still the appropriate rate of interest to be applied.[25] "Yearly rests" are the intervals at which the interest is compounded.[26]

16–020   Returning to the example, suppose that Fred lived for three-and-a-quarter years after the trust came into operation and assume that the basic rate of income tax throughout that period was 20 per cent (although in recent years the basic rate has been higher, utilising the current basic rate of 20 per cent makes the mathematical calculations considerably easier and therefore more comprehensible); the trustees would find that £13,539.13 invested when the trust came into operation at 4 per cent compound interest with yearly rests would, after allowing for the deduction of income tax at 20 per cent, have produced £15,000 at the date when this sum was actually received.[27] The £13,539.13 would therefore be invested by the trustees as capital, and the remaining £1,460.87 would be paid to Clare as income for the preceding three-and-a-quarter years.

---

[25] See *ante*, para 16–015.

[26] The calculation can be complicated, but, for those who do not have super mathematical skills, the most straightforward method of making the calculation will be to follow these steps:
   (1) Determine the gross rate of interest to be applied. Traditionally this has been 4% but, as has been noted, a higher rate may be appropriate.
   (2) Deduct the basic rate of income tax, to give a net rate of interest.
   (3) Calculate the amount which £100 would produce if invested for the period between the date of death and the date when the reversionary interest falls in at the net rate of interest compounded annually.
   (4) Multiply the amount received when the reversionary interest falls in by the following fraction:

$$\frac{100}{\text{the sum calculated in 3 above}}$$

   (5) The product is the capital element.
   (6) The balance is the income element.

[27] Following the steps outlined in n.26, the calculation is as follows (as indicated in the text, although in recent years the basic rate has been higher (22% until 2008–2009), utilising a basic rate of 20% makes the mathematical calculations considerably easier and therefore more comprehensible):
   (1) Gross rate: taken as 4%
   (2) Basic rate of income tax: taken as 20%. The net rate is, therefore,

$$4\% \times \frac{80}{100} = 3.2 \text{ per cent}$$

   (3) The compounded amount £110.09 is calculated as follows:

Period	Amount on which calculated	Rate	Interest for period	Total at end of period
Year 1	£100.00	3.2%	£3.20	£103.20
Year 2	£103.20	3.2%	£3.30	£106.50
Year 3	£106.50	3.2%	£3.41	£109.91
Last 3 months	£109.91	0.8%	£0.88	£110.79

   (4) The capital element of the amount received, £15,000, is:

$$£15,000 \times \frac{100}{110.79} = £13,539.13$$

   (5) The income element is £15,000 − £13,539.13) = £1,460.87.

The same rule applies to any other property which does not produce any   **16–021**
income. Thus it applied in *Re Duke of Cleveland's Equity*[28] to a debt which
bore no interest and was not receivable immediately. And in *Re Chance*[29]
compensation for the refusal of planning permission under Part I of the
Town and Country Planning Act 1954[30] was held to be apportionable.

6. *Leaseholds*

It used to be necessary to give special consideration to leaseholds.[31] How-   **16–022**
ever, since 1997 all leaseholds have been authorised investments by virtue of
section 6(3) of the Trusts of Land and Appointment of Trustees Act 1996.[32]
Consequently, there is now no question of any apportionment in respect of
any leasehold.

II. OTHER APPORTIONMENTS

1. *The Rule in* Allhusen v. Whittell[33]

There will always be an interval of time between the date of death and the   **16–023**
date when an asset is realised. Where a person creates a trust by will in
favour of persons in succession and there are debts and liabilities to be paid,
it would appear that the tenant for life will gain increasingly as that delay
increases. Suppose that the gross assets of an estate held on trust for persons
by way of succession amount to £20,000 and that the debts amount to £5,000.

---

[28] [1895] 2 Ch. 542.

[29] [1962] Ch. 593.

[30] The Town and Country Planning Act 1947 provided, in general terms, that an owner of
land could not carry out any building or other works on his land without obtaining the
permission of the local authority, and without paying a "development charge". The value of
land was often less after the passing of this Act than before it, and in an effort to give to the
landowner compensation, it was proposed that a £300 million fund would be established, on
which landowners could make a claim for the depreciation in the value of their land. The fund
was, in fact, never set up and the system was changed under the Town and Country Planning
Act 1954, whereby the amount of the landowner's claim, plus 1/7th of it for interest (less
payments for certain events made before the 1954 Act came into force), formed what is known
as an "unexpended balance of established development value". Where such a balance exists, in
certain cases compensation is payable up to the amount of that balance where an application
for planning permission is refused. This was the situation in *Re Chance* [1962] Ch. 593. Part of
the interest of the decision lies in the fact that an unexpended balance of established development value and so of money paid under the system represents interest and the amount of that
interest could be determined. Wilberforce J. however, took the whole amount of the compensation received and apportioned that.

[31] Before 1926, a residuary gift of leaseholds was treated in the same way as any other gift of
residuary personalty. From 1926 to 1996, leases with over 60 years to run were authorised
investments so there was no question of any apportionment in respect of them. So far as leases
with less than 60 years to run, which were not authorised investments, were concerned, it was
clear that, by virtue of the now repealed section 28(2) of the Law of Property Act 1925, the
tenant for life was entitled to the actual income where there was an express trust for the
conversion of leaseholds, but it was thought in some quarters that the pre-1926 position still
applied where the duty to convert the leaseholds in question arose only by virtue of the Rule
in *Howe v. Lord Dartmouth*.

[32] See *ante*, para 14–073.

[33] (1867) L.R. 4 Eq. 295.

If the debts are paid forthwith then the tenant for life will have the income from the remaining £15,000. If, however, the debts are not paid for a year, the tenant for life will receive the income for that year on £20,000. The essence of the rule of apportionment laid down in *Allhusen v. Whittell* is to charge the tenant for life with interest on the amount subsequently used for the payment of debts so that, broadly, the tenant for life is placed in the same position as if the debts had been paid on death.

16–024   In its modern form[34] the rule requires a calculation of the average income of the estate from the date of death to the date of payment, taken net after deduction of income tax at the basic rate.[35] The tenant for life is charged with interest at the rate of the net average income, so that the debt once paid is regarded as being paid partly from income and partly from capital. Suppose that a debt of £500 is paid one year from the date of death, that the average income of the estate taken throughout that period is 4 per cent and that the basic rate of income tax during that year is 20 per cent. The calculation is therefore:

Take a basic unit of		£100.00
Add		
Average income for one year at £4 per cent	£4.00	
Less tax	£0.80	
	£3.20	£3.20
		£103.20

16–025   Each debt paid one year from death is therefore regarded as being paid in the proportion:

$$\frac{100.00}{103.20} \quad \text{from capital and}$$

$$\frac{3.20}{103.20} \quad \text{from income.}$$

Thus, the debt of £500 will be paid:

$$\frac{100.00}{£103.20} \times £500 = £484.50 \quad \text{from capital; and}$$

$$\frac{3.20}{£103.20} \times £500 = £15.50 \quad \text{from income.}$$

This £15.50 will be charged to the tenant for life.

16–026   It is easy to appreciate the theoretical justification for this rule and it is also easy to see its practical defects. In particular, a separate calculation is

---

[34] *Re McEwen* [1913] 2 Ch. 704; *Re Wills* [1915] 1 Ch. 769; *Corbett v. C.I.R.* [1938] 1 K.B. 567.
[35] *Re Oldham* (1927) 71 S.J. 491.

necessary for each debt paid at a different time. Further, where payments are to be made a considerable time after death, as where the testator in his lifetime entered into a covenant to pay an annuity and the annuity was charged on the residue of his estate, the proportion borne by income steadily increases.[36] Except where very large debts are involved or where a very long delay occurs in payment, the trouble of making the calculation does not justify the small adjustment between tenant for life and remainderman; consequently it is now very common to exclude the operation of the rule.

2. *The Rule in* Re Atkinson[37]

Where an authorised mortgage forms part of the estate and, upon realisation   **16–027**
of the security by sale, the proceeds of sale are insufficient to pay the outstanding principal and interest in full, the proceeds of sale are apportioned between the tenant for life and remainderman in the proportion which the amount due for arrears bears to the amount due in respect of principal. This is the rule in *Re Atkinson*[38] and it applies to any mortgage which forms part of the assets derived from the testator or settlor and also to any authorised mortgage taken by the trustee himself.

Suppose that during his lifetime a testator made a mortgage advance of   **16–028**
£25,000 upon the security of a house at £12 per cent interest. Suppose also that the mortgagor pays a total of only £1,200 interest in respect of the period after the death of the testator and that the property is sold for £23,000 three years after death, no part of the capital secured by the mortgage having been repaid at any point. The apportionment of the £23,000 is as follows:

Capital outstanding		£25,000
Interest outstanding:		
3 Years at £12 per cent on £25,000	£9,000	
less: actually paid	£1,200	
	£7,800	£7,800
Total capital and interest due		£32,800
Capital element of proceeds of sale	$\dfrac{£25,000}{£32,800}$	× £23,000 = £17,530
Income element of proceeds of sale	$\dfrac{£7,800}{£32,800}$	× £23,000 = £5,470
Total proceeds of sale		£23,000

---

[36] *Re Dawson* [1906] 2 Ch. 211; *Re Perkins* [1907] 2 Ch. 596; *Re Poyser* [1910] 2 Ch. 444.
[37] [1904] 2 Ch. 160.
[38] [1904] 2 Ch. 160.

16–029   The scope of the rule is in doubt. In principle it ought to apply whenever an asset carrying both capital and interest at a fixed rate is realised at a loss and it has been held to apply to an amount received in a liquidation on account of principal and arrears of interest due under a holding of debenture stock.[39] However, the rule is not applied where preference dividends are in arrears.[40]

16–030   The rule in *Re Atkinson* is applied only to a capital sum realised on the sale of a security and not to income received from the asset. Thus, if under a power contained in a mortgage the trustees take possession of the property and let it, the net rents are applied entirely in the discharge of arrears of interest and only when those arrears have been paid in full is the surplus applied as capital.[41] If there are arrears of interest outstanding at the date of death, those are paid in full in priority to the interest due to the estate from the period from the date of death to the date of extinction of the mortgage.[42]

16–031   Where trustees foreclose under a mortgage, the mortgagor then loses all title to the property and the property itself becomes an asset of the estate. Accordingly, from the date of foreclosure the tenant for life is entitled to the whole of the net rents and profits until sale[43]; but, if there are arrears of interest before foreclosure, it seems that a *Re Atkinson* apportionment will be made when the property is ultimately sold.[44]

16–032   There is no authority as to whether income tax should be deducted in making a calculation for the purposes of the rule in *Re Atkinson*. It is suggested that the appropriate method of applying the rule is first to ascertain the arrears of interest and the proportion due to income without taking into account income tax. When that proportion has been calculated, the tenant for life's entitlement should be reduced by an amount equal to income tax at the basic rate on that sum.

III. APPORTIONMENTS RELATING TO STOCKS AND SHARES

16–033   In contrast to the Rule in *Howe v. Lord Dartmouth*, which applies to unauthorised investments, apportionments of a different type are sometimes necessary in the case of authorised investments.

1. *Dividends*

16–034   The first case is of apportionment of dividends received for shares. Thus, if shares are left on trust for Peter for life, with remainder to Paul for life, it may be necessary, on the death of Peter, to apportion dividends between Peter's estate and Paul. The Apportionment Act 1870 applies to most types of periodical payment and deems them to accrue from day to day. If,

---

[39] *Re Walker* [1936] Ch. 280; compare *Re Taylor* [1905] 1 Ch. 734.
[40] *Re Sale* [1913] 2 Ch. 697; *Re Wakley* [1920] 2 Ch. 205.
[41] *Re Coaks* [1911] 1 Ch. 171.
[42] *ibid.*
[43] Law of Property Act 1925, s.31; *Re Horn* [1924] 2 Ch. 222.
[44] *Re Horn* [1924] 2 Ch. 222 at 226.

therefore, Peter dies on the 59th day of a year, and the company declares a dividend amounting to £150 for that calendar year, 59/365ths of £150 will belong to Peter's estate and the balance will be payable to Paul. The period in respect of which the company in question states that it is paying the dividend necessarily governs the rights of all the beneficiaries. This can produce superficially rather strange results. If a company pays no dividend in 2008 and 2009 but pays a dividend in 2010 which is three times as large as normal but which is stated by the company to be in respect of 2010. If Peter as before dies on the 59th day of 2010, he will only be entitled to 59/365ths. It might have been thought more equitable in these circumstances for Peter to have received 789/1096ths (being the fraction of days for the period 2008, 2009 and 2010 for which Peter has lived) but this is not the rule.[45]

It is also necessary to make a time apportionment when there is an **16–035** alteration in the class of income beneficiaries. In *Re Joel*[46] a fund was held upon trust for the testator's grandchildren contingently on attaining the age of 21. The gift carried the intermediate income, which could accordingly be utilised for the benefit of the grandchildren.[47] Goff J. held that, each time a member of the class died under 21 or a new grandchild was born, the income of the trust ought to be apportioned; that way each member of the class enjoyed only that part of the income attributable to the period during which he was alive.

However, for the purposes of taxation the rules differ from those laid **16–036** down by the Apportionment Act 1870; the whole of the dividend is treated as the income of the person who is entitled to the income of the trust on the day on which the income in question is payable.[48] Suppose that one of the assets of a fund held on trust for Roger for life, with remainder to Susan for life, is a holding of shares in a company which pays dividends in respect of years ending on March 31, and that in June 2009 the company declares a dividend for the year which ended on March 31, 2009. If Roger dies on February 15, 2009, his estate will be entitled to almost all the dividend by virtue of the Apportionment Act 1870; however, the whole of the dividend will form part of Susan's taxable income for the year of assessment 2009–2010.

2. *Scrip Dividends*

Companies sometimes give shareholders a choice between receiving their **16–037** dividends in cash and receiving additional shares. Dividends paid in the form of shares are known as scrip dividends. This choice does not pose any particular problems for the trustees if the value of the scrip offered is more or less the same as the cash dividend. In both cases the dividend will belong to the tenant for life and in such circumstances trustees have traditionally opted to take the dividend in cash. However, in the last few years there have

---

[45] *Re Wakley* [1920] 1 Ch. 205.
[46] [1967] Ch. 14.
[47] See *post*, para 17–035.
[48] I.R.C. *v. Henderson's Executors* (1931) 16 T.C. 282; *Bryan v. Cassin* [1942] 2 All E.R. 262; *Wood v. Owen* [1941] 1 K.B. 92; *Potel v. I.R.C.* [1971] 2 All E.R. 504.

been a large number of enhanced scrip dividends, under which the value of the scrip on offer can be as much as 50 per cent more than the cash dividend with, sometimes, the possibility of converting the scrip into cash by selling it on at a pre-arranged price, never as high as the value of the scrip but still substantially more than the cash dividend. Trustees are clearly under an obligation to consider whether to take up such an offer. If they decide to do so, the question arises as to whether the tenant for life is entitled to the whole of the scrip (or, where appropriate, the whole of any pre-arranged purchase price for which the trustees sell it). It was held at the end of the nineteenth century that in these circumstances an apportionment is necessary as between income and capital.[49] If this decision is still good law, the tenant for life will be entitled to no more than the amount of the cash dividend; the additional value of the scrip (or, where appropriate, of any pre-arranged price for which the trustees sell it) will therefore have to be added to the capital of the trust. If enhanced scrip dividends continue to be popular, it is likely that a test case will at some stage be necessary to establish definitively whether or not such an apportionment is indeed necessary.

3. Purchases and Sales Cum and Ex Dividend

16–038   On the face of things, an apportionment would appear to be appropriate where stocks and shares are bought and sold. There are obviously a number of factors which affect the price of stock exchange investments, such as the yield which is obtained,[50] the stability of the company concerned, the general economic condition of the country as a whole, and the future prospects of the company; however, an important short-term factor is the date when the dividend is to be paid. Any example is obviously artificial but, assuming that all other factors remain constant, if a dividend of £500 is payable on both January 1 and July 1 on a holding of stock worth £20,000, on January 2 the stock is worth £20,000 but its value on June 30, the day before the payment of the next dividend, will be £20,450 (£20,000 plus the net value of the dividend, £500 less the 10 per cent income tax retained out of the dividend[51]). If trustees purchase that stock on January 2 for £20,000 and sell it for £20,450 on June 30, does the whole of that £20,450 belong to capital or is the sum apportioned so as to attribute £20,000 to capital and £450 to income? After all, had the holding been kept for one day longer, the net payment of £450 would have been received as a dividend and treated as income. Somewhat surprisingly, there is in this case no rule providing for any apportionment and the whole amount received is deemed to be capital. The explanation for this apparently inequitable rule is that there are in practice so many factors which affect the value of shares that it is thought too difficult to lay down any set rules to govern how the apportionment is to be calculated. It has, however, been said that, in the event that the rule of

---

[49] *Re Malam* [1894] 3 Ch. 578.
[50] See *ante*, para 14–091.
[51] Further income tax will be payable if the holder of the stock is a discretionary trust or a higher rate tax payer but this does not affect the value of the stock.

non-apportionment leads to a "glaring injustice", apportionment will be ordered.[52]

4. *Bonus Shares*

Considerable difficulty has been caused where a company issues bonus shares. Suppose the capital of a company consists of 10,000 £1 ordinary shares and that the company has prospered and has retained accumulated profits of £5,000. If the company distributes the £5,000 to its shareholders, this sum is clearly income in the hands of any trustee shareholders. But the company may alternatively decide to retain the £5,000 permanently by using it to fund the issue of 5,000 additional shares to be distributed free to the existing shareholders in the company on the basis of one new share for each two shares already held. Are these new shares equally to be treated as income in the hands of any trustee shareholders?

16–039

The general rule is that the new shares are capital and must be held by the trustees as such; however, the tenant for life will of course obtain some benefit from them by virtue of the fact that he will be entitled to the dividends which they produce.[53]

16–040

However, where the company has no power under its articles of association to create new shares in this way and therefore ought to have distributed the accumulated profit in cash, the shares distributed are regarded as income; this was decided in *Bouch v. Sproule*.[54] That decision was considered by the Privy Council in *Hill v. Permanent Trustee Co. of New South Wales*,[55] where Lord Russell of Killowen laid down the following principles.[56]

16–041

(1) Where a company makes a distribution of money among its shareholders, it is not concerned at all with the way in which the shareholders deal with that money. Thus, where the shareholder is a trustee, the company is not itself concerned with whether the money is treated as capital or income.

(2) Unless a company is in liquidation, it can only make a payment by way of a return of capital under a scheme for the reduction of capital approved by the court[57] (restrictions are placed on a reduction of capital by a company so that creditors of the company are not prejudiced). In any other case, apart from liquidation, it follows that, if the company is able to distribute money, that money must be profit so far as the company is concerned.

(3) Where the shareholder is a trust, the trustees will therefore generally receive the money as income which as such will be payable to the tenant for life. This will not be the case, however, if there is some

---

[52] *Re MacLaren's Settlement Trusts* [1951] 2 All E.R. 414 at 420.
[53] *I.R.C. v. Blott* [1921] 2 A.C. 171.
[54] (1887) 12 App. Cas. 385.
[55] [1930] A.C. 720.
[56] *ibid.*, at 730–732.
[57] See now Companies Act 2006, Chapter 10.

provision in the trust instrument to the contrary, or if the following principle applies.

(4) Where the company has power under its articles of association to utilise its profits by adding them to capital and issuing bonus shares representing the amount of that additional capital to its shareholders, those shares are capital.

(5) Where the company's capital is increased in this way, its assets are undiminished (for the cash never leaves its hands) whereas, if a distribution of profits is made, the company's assets are consequently diminished.[58]

16–042 To these five principles a sixth was, in effect, added by Plowman J. in *Re Outen*,[59] namely that, where under a power in its articles of association a company capitalises profits, not by using the profits to issue new shares but by issuing some other investment in the company, that other investment is capital in the hands of a shareholder who is a trustee. This case arose out of a takeover bid made in 1962 by I.C.I. for Courtaulds. The bid was resisted by the directors of Courtaulds who, in order to persuade their stockholders not to sell their stock to I.C.I., capitalised £40 million of reserves, which represented capital profits, in accordance with the company's articles of association and used this sum to make a free issue of new loan stock to their stockholders. Before the takeover battle had commenced, a testatrix had left her holding of stock to trustees upon trust and in due course they, along with all the other stockholders in Courtaulds, were issued with a holding of the new loan stock. Was this to be treated as capital or as income? Plowman J. held that, although Courtauld's actions had not involved the creation of any new shares, that company had effected a capitalisation under which the assets which were its subject matter ceased to have the character of divisible profits. The company's decision to this effect was binding on its stockholders; consequently the loan stock was capital.

16–043 A further complication arises where a company gives its shareholders the option either to have bonus shares or cash. In such circumstances what is crucial is whether the company intends to make a capital distribution or whether it really intends to distribute income.[60] If the intention of the company is to make a capital distribution then, whether the trustees take the bonus shares or the cash, what is received by them will be capital (in fact the cash offer is usually inferior in value to the offer of bonus shares and so the trustees should normally take the bonus shares). If, on the other hand, the intention of the company is to distribute income, then what is received by the trustees will be income; if the trustees take the cash, this will obviously be payable to the tenant for life but, if they take the bonus shares (which is what they should normally do), it was held at the end of the nineteenth century that the tenant for life will still receive only the value of the cash offer, the remainder of the value of the shares being regarded as capital.[61]

---

[58] Though why this should be relevant to a trustee is difficult to understand.
[59] [1963] Ch. 291.
[60] *I.R.C. v. Fisher's Executors* [1926] A.C. 395.
[61] *Re Malam* [1894] 3 Ch. 578.

In summary, in the ordinary case where a company issues bonus shares, **16–044** the reserves or profits which are used within the company to back the bonus shares are retained by the company as long-term capital. Consequently, bonus shares are in general received by trustees as capital. Where, on the other hand, the company has no power under its articles of association to create new shares in this way, the shares distributed are received by trustees as income. This is also the case where the intention of the company was to distribute income.

5. *Capital Profits Dividends*

All forms of distribution by a company by way of money or money's worth **16–045** other than the issue of bonus shares or stock consist of the company passing on to its shareholders a profit which it has received without the company itself retaining any long-term benefit from the distribution. Therefore, in the ordinary case, such dividends are received by the trustees as income.

The best illustration of this is provided by capital profits dividends, the **16–046** distribution by a company of capital profits either in cash or in some other valuable form. A series of cases were decided around 1951 in relation to a capital profit dividend declared by Thomas Tilling & Co. A substantial part of the business of this company consisted of operating buses and coaches. When this part of its business was nationalised, the company received in compensation some British Transport stock, which it in turn distributed among its shareholders as a capital profits dividend. Was this stock to be regarded as capital or as income for the purposes of a trust? In *Re Sechiari*[62] and *Re Kleinwort*[63] it was held that trustees received the stock as income and so it belonged to the tenant for life. The position was not the same as that of bonus shares in the company making the distribution, where the increase in the number of shares entitles the holders to participate in future dividends; this was an isolated payment, complete in itself, from which no future benefit would accrue directly from the company.

Nevertheless, in *Re Kleinwort* Vaisey J. considered that, in special circum- **16–047** stances, the sum received was properly apportionable between capital and income. Such circumstances would arise where the trustees had committed a breach of trust, particularly in not maintaining a balance between the conflicting interests of different beneficiaries. Thus if the trustees acted solely with the intention of benefiting the tenant for life at the expense of the remainderman by investing in shares in a company in the expectation of a capital profits distribution, they would have committed a breach of trust and the court would undoubtedly apportion the capital profits dividend between income and capital. However, in *Re Rudd*,[64] it was held that a breach of trust had not been committed merely by virtue of the fact that trustees, who foresaw the capital dividend and so could have sold the stock with a large profit for capital, did not do so; consequently, the court refused to apportion the capital profit dividend received. This decision seems to be based entirely on the motive of the trustees which involved no intention of

---

[62] [1950] 1 All E.R. 417.
[63] [1951] Ch. 860.
[64] [1952] 1 All E.R. 254.

prejudicing the remainderman. Special circumstances were, however, found to exist in *Re MacLaren*.[65] The tenant for life consented to the purchase of stock in Thomas Tilling & Co. as a capital investment after it became known that that company intended to distribute the British Transport stock among its shareholders. It was held that he had to be regarded as having consented to the British Transport stock being regarded as capital and that it therefore was to be treated as capital.

16–048   The principle just illustrated by reference to the Thomas Tilling & Co. cases applies to any case where a company makes a capital profit and distributes it either in cash or in some other valuable form. That profit will, therefore, in normal circumstances be received by the trustees as income and so will be payable to the tenant for life. Where the distribution is as substantial as that made by Thomas Tilling & Co., the capital value of the fund will thereby be substantially reduced; in that case, the price of the shares fell by as much as 77 per cent, amount to an enormous windfall for the tenant for life and a substantial loss for the remaindermen.

6. Demergers

16–049   Similar potential difficulties are caused by the recently fashionable practice of demerging companies, that is to say hiving off some composite part of the businesses of a company into a new company and issuing all the shareholders of the original company with fully paid up shares in the new demerged company. This is done by the original company transferring the part of its assets which relate to the businesses which are to be demerged to a new subsidiary company and then declaring a dividend out of distributable profits. There are two ways of proceeding after that: the "direct" method is for the original company to satisfy the dividend directly by allocating to its shareholders shares in the subsidiary company, which then becomes the demerged company; the "indirect" method is for the shares in the subsidiary company to be transferred to a quite separate company, which then satisfies the dividend indirectly by allocating its own shares to the shareholders of the original company. Both of these methods appear to amount to a capital distribution which, in accordance with the principles just discussed, appears to be received as income for the purposes of a trust and will, therefore, be payable to the tenant for life. In one of the largest demergers of its time, that of the bioscience activities of I.C.I. into a new company, Zeneca Group, this potentially had the effect of halving the value of the capital investment in I.C.I. of any trust which held shares in that company and of providing the tenant for life with a windfall of half the capital value of those shares.

16–050   The companies involved were sufficiently anxious about this question to arrange for a test case, *Sinclair v. Lee*,[66] to be brought to establish how the shares allocated in the new company would be treated for the purposes of a trust. This demerger was to be carried out by the "indirect" method. Nicholls V.-C. stated that "no one, unversed in the arcane mysteries I shall be mentioning shortly, would have any doubt over the answer. Nobody

---

[65] [1951] 2 All E.R. 414.
[66] [1993] Ch. 497.

would think that the Zeneca Group shares could sensibly be regarded as income."[67] He relied on the fact that, since this demerger was to be carried out by the "indirect" method, the shares of the demerged company, Zeneca Group, would never be held or received by I.C.I.; this enabled him to distinguish the authorities discussed in the previous two sections of this chapter and he therefore held that the distribution of Zeneca Group shares would indeed be capital for the purposes of a trust.

This decision establishes that shares in a company which is demerged by   **16–051**
the "indirect" method will be capital for the purposes of a trust. However, the decision leaves completely open the position of shares in a company which is demerged by the "direct" method. Since the ground on which Nicholls V.-C. was able to distinguish the earlier authorities applies only to "indirect" demergers, it may well be that the opposite conclusion will be reached in respect of "direct" demergers. It may be that another test case will one day have to be brought in order to resolve this question.

7. Taxation Considerations

The treatment of the various types of dividends, distributions, and shares   **16–052**
which have just been considered for the general purposes of trust administration has to be distinguished from their treatment for the purposes of taxation.

Company distributions are normally paid with a tax credit of 10 per cent   **16–053**
so that the sum actually received has in effect suffered tax of 10 per cent, which is regarded as satisfying the basic rate of income tax. Trustees of fixed trusts need take no further action in respect of distributions paid over to a beneficiary who has a fixed interest; the distributions are taxed as his income so, if he is a higher rate taxpayer, he has to pay a further 30 per cent tax. However, discretionary trusts pay tax at a higher rate and so a further 22.5 per cent tax will be payable by the trustees of these settlements to bring the rate paid up to 32.5 per cent; distributions to beneficiaries will involve the trustees and any higher rate taxpayer beneficiaries in paying further tax (other beneficiaries will be able to reclaim tax[68]).

Where trustees elect to take scrip dividends rather than cash and where   **16–054**
shares are held which carry with them the right to receive bonus shares,[69] then, if the company is resident in the United Kingdom,[70] the shares received are treated as income. The usual 10 per cent tax credit will not be forthcoming from the company and so tax is payable as if a dividend had been paid of an amount which, after deducting income tax at 10 per cent, equals the value of the scrip dividend or other shares at the date of issue.[71] If the scrip dividend or shares are passed to an income beneficiary, the

---

[67] *ibid.*, at 504.

[68] The precise amount of tax payable and reclaimable is set out *ante*, para 15–028.

[69] That is, the terms upon which the shares are issued gives the shareholders the right to call for bonus shares.

[70] Income and Corporation Taxes Act 1988, s.349.

[71] If, therefore, an issue of scrip is made which is worth £100, the company will be treated as if it paid a dividend of £111.11 from which 10% income tax had been retained (£111.11 less £11.11 tax = £100).

notional amount of the dividend is treated as part of his income for income tax purposes. If the scrip dividend or shares are retained by the trustees as an accretion to capital for a remainderman there will be no further tax liability[72]; however, if the dividend or shares are retained by the trustees of a discretionary trust, they will have to pay a further 22.5 per cent tax to bring the tax paid up to 32.5 per cent.[73] Bonus shares and capital profits dividends are treated in the same way. Where, on the other hand, the company which pays the scrip dividend or in which the shares are held which carry with them the right to receive bonus shares is resident outside the United Kingdom, the shares which are received are treated as capital for taxation purposes if they would be so treated for the purposes of trust administration.[74]

16–055　　The transfer of shares in demerged companies is not a distribution and so does not give rise to any payment of income tax. However, there are potential difficulties as to precisely what the base cost of the shares is for the purposes of capital gains tax where the shares are treated as the property of a fixed interest beneficiary; this particular question awaits resolution.

IV. Apportionments in Respect of National Savings Certificates

16–056　　It has been seen[75] that, by virtue of the Apportionment Act 1870, it may be necessary to apportion by time dividends or other income between the person entitled to the income before an event, such as death, and the person entitled after that event. It is, however, first necessary to establish that the amount in question is of an income nature. This problem arises in particular with the increment over the purchase price which is payable on the encashment of National Savings Certificates. In *Re Holder*[76] the testator in his lifetime purchased National Savings Certificates for £375, which were encashed after his death for £534. Roxburgh J. held that, by virtue of the terms on which the certificates were issued by the Government, the increment up to the date of death was capital. It was conceded that the increment which arose between the date of death and the date of encashment was to be treated as income, but the point was not actually argued. Although the basis for the concession does not appear from the report of the case, it would appear to be a correct concession, following the rule in *Re Earl of Chesterfield's Trusts*.[77]

---

[72] Because, in general, income received by trustees subject to deduction of tax at source is not further taxable in their hands; see *ante*, para 15–023.

[73] This is the rate of tax payable on accumulated company distributions; see *ante*, para 15–028. In the example given *ante*, n.71, the trustees would therefore be liable to pay an additional 22.5% of £111.11 = £30.00.

[74] *I.R.C. v. Wright* (1926) 11 T.C. 181.

[75] See *ante*, para 16–034.

[76] [1953] Ch. 468.

[77] (1883) 24 Ch.D. 643; see *ante*, para 16–018.

V. Apportionment of Outgoings

Subject to contrary directions in the trust instrument, expenses which relate   **16–057**
solely to the income of a trust, such as the cost of making an income tax
return, are primarily payable out of income, and other expenses, such as the
cost of appointing new trustees or of bringing legal proceedings, are payable
out of capital. Where an audit takes place, however, the trustees may
apportion the cost of this between capital and income in such proportions as
they think fit.[78]

VI. Excluding Apportionments

The apportionment rules are designed to achieve fairness and in most cases   **16–058**
it is easy to see the logic behind them. Nevertheless, it is becoming increasingly common for them to be expressly excluded. This is partly due to
taxation considerations but in the main it is because the calculations which
have to be made under some of the rules are so complicated that it is far
simpler from an administrative point of view for apportionments to be
excluded. Ironically, then, the long-term effect of the rules has probably been
the reverse of what equity actually intended.

---

[78] Trustee Act 1925, s.22(4).

CHAPTER 17

INCOME FROM THE TRUST FUND

17–001 Five questions have to be considered about the income from a trust fund.

   (i)   What is the relationship between income received by the trustees from the assets which comprise the trust fund and the income to which the beneficiaries are entitled?

   (ii) Which beneficial interests under the trust carry the right to income?

   (iii) Are the trustees entitled to retain income?

   (iv) How are the trustees to apply income where the beneficiary is an infant?

   (v)   What are the taxation consequences of entitlement to income?

I. THE INCOME OF THE TRUST FUND

1. *The Accounting Period*

17–002 One of the fundamental elements in the concept of income is that of time; it is only possible to speak of the income of trustees, or indeed of any person, if the period of time which is to be considered is known. For taxation purposes, the period to be considered is, generally,[1] the fiscal year of assessment which ends on April 5. Where a trust is created (as a result of becoming completely constituted) on any date other than April 6, the first accounting period for taxation purposes will be from the date of the creation of the trust until the following April 5, and the final accounting period will be from the April 6 immediately prior to the date of termination of the trust until that date.

17–003 There are, however, no corresponding statutory rules for the purposes of general trust administration. The various Trustee Acts seem to proceed on the basis that the basic accounting period will be 12 months[2] but this is not expressly provided anywhere and so the trustees can in principle select any period which they wish.[3] In practice, however, most trustees adopt for the

---

[1] The general rule applies for income tax and capital gains tax.

[2] See, for example, Trustee Act 1925, s.22(4) authorising trustees to have the trust accounts audited once in every three "years".

[3] Unless the trust instrument itself prescribes the accounting period.

purposes of trust administration the same accounting period as that adopted for the purposes of taxation.

2. Gross and Net Income

The trustees may derive income from a number of sources during an **17–004** accounting period. For example, they may receive company distributions such as dividends, bank deposit interest, and rent. From this gross income, the expenses of the administration of the trust will be deducted in so far as those expenses are applicable to income; so will any other payments which the trustees may make in the exercise of administrative powers.

However, the net income will usually only be determined at some point of **17–005** time after the end of an accounting period. This is because trustees have a reasonable time[4] within which to exercise powers and discretions and they will often wish to wait until the end of an accounting period before so doing in order that they can take their decisions in the light of the amount of gross income received in the whole of that period.

3. Trust Management Expenses

Expenses of a recurrent nature are generally payable out of income, unless **17–006** the trust instrument provides otherwise. Thus, out of income is paid council tax and rates on any land owned by the trust[5]; rent payable in respect of leasehold property owned by the trust[6]; income tax[7]; and the cost of preparation of the annual accounts and the income tax returns.[8] The expenses which are payable from capital are discussed later.[9]

Although, in general, expenses are payable either from income or from **17–007** capital according to their nature, the trust instrument can direct how the expenses are to be borne[10] and, in certain instances, the trustees are given a discretion. Thus, where the trustees require the trust accounts to be audited under the statutory power so to do,[11] they have an absolute discretion to pay the fees of the auditor either from income or from capital, or partly from income and partly from capital.

4. Administrative Powers

In *Pearson v. I.R.C.*[12] the House of Lords drew a distinction between admin- **17–008** istrative powers and dispositive powers. Where payments are made by the

---

[4] See, for example, *Re Gulbenkian's Settlement Trusts (No.2)* [1970] Ch. 408.
[5] *Fountaine v. Pellet* (1791) 1 Ves. Jun. 337 at 342.
[6] *Re Gjers* [1899] 2 Ch. 54; *Re Betty* [1899] 1 Ch. 821.
[7] *Re Cain's Settlement* [1919] 2 Ch. 364. Capital gains tax is of course payable out of capital.
[8] See *Shore v. Shore* (1859) 4 Drew. 501. Strictly speaking, the costs of preparation of the capital gains tax return, which forms part of the same document as the income tax return, should be charged to capital; however, unless the time spent on doing this was very substantial, in practice the entire cost is likely to be paid out of income.
[9] See *post*, para 18–003.
[10] However, the court may override the direction in the trust instrument; *Re Tubbs* [1915] Ch. 137; *Re Hicklin* [1917] 2 Ch. 278.
[11] Trustee Act 1925, s.22(4).
[12] [1981] A.C. 753.

trustees out of income in the exercise of their administrative powers, these payments are treated in the same way as trust management expenses, that is to say they are deducted from the gross receipts in determining the amount of the net trust income. On the other hand, payments which are made in the exercise of a dispositive power are applications of net trust income.

17–009   There is in many respects no clear authority as to precisely which powers are to be regarded as administrative and which as dispositive. In the absence of authority, the following classification is suggested for present purposes; however, as will be seen in a later chapter,[13] different considerations, and therefore a slightly different classification as to which powers are and are not administrative, may be necessary when it has to be decided, as a matter of private international law, which of these powers are governed by what should, strictly speaking, now be known as the applicable law of a trust[14] and which are governed by a different law which, according to the trust instrument, governs that trust's administration.[15]

17–010   The following powers are classified as administrative powers for all purposes:

    (i) the power to engage and pay agents and professional advisers;

    (ii) the power to have investments held in the name of a nominee or by a custodian and to pay the nominee or custodian;

    (iii) the power to insure trust assets and to pay the premiums;

    (iv) the power to insure the life of the settlor or any beneficiary and to pay the relevant premiums;

    (v) the power to pay taxes and other duties[16]; and

    (vi) the power to use income to improve land.

---

[13] See *post*, para 23–058.

[14] Prior to the Recognition of Trusts Act 1987, the expression used was the "proper law" of a trust but The Hague Convention on the Law Applicable to Trusts and their Recognition, which that Act incorporated into English law, instead uses the expression "applicable law".

[15] The applicable law of a trust will govern the nature of the interests of the beneficiaries and the duties of the trustees towards them (including any powers which they have to determine the manner in which the income and capital of the trust is distributed and their duties to convert and apportion the trust property) and also the construction of the trust instrument (unless this has been expressly reserved to the law of some other jurisdiction). The trustees' duties to provide accounts and to give information to the beneficiaries are purely administrative, as are their powers to appoint and remove trustees and all the powers listed in the first group of powers below in the text. But a number of other powers which are, for other purposes, often classified as administrative are capable of affecting directly or indirectly the interests of the beneficiaries in the event that the provisions of the proper law and of the law specified as governing administration differ as to their existence or scope. The presence or absence of a power for the trustees to remunerate themselves (although such a power is now implied in the case of trustees acting in a professional capacity) clearly affects the income and capital available for the beneficiaries. So does the presence or absence of powers of advancement, maintenance and accumulation in the event that they are exercised. So too, to a lesser extent, do the trustees' powers of investment.

[16] As to which see *Pearson v. I.R.C.* [1981] A.C. 753 itself.

The following powers can also be classified as administrative powers for present purposes, although they may not be for the purposes of private international law: **17–011**

(i) the power to charge for services;

(ii) the power to retain commission, brokerage, and directors' fees; and

(iii) the power to advance capital.[17]

The following powers can be classified as dispositive powers for present purposes although it is not inconceivable that they could be classified as administrative for the purposes of private international law.[18] **17–012**

(i) the power to accumulate income;

(ii) the power to pay or apply income to or for the maintenance, education, or benefit of a beneficiary;

(iii) the power to allow a beneficiary to use trust assets (even if the exercise of that power does not result in the creation of an interest in possession in the assets in question);

(iv) the power to pay the premiums on a policy of assurance which is effected for the benefit of a beneficiary; and

(v) the power to pay or apply income in securing the discharge of an obligation owed by a beneficiary or in guaranteeing the performance of an obligation by a beneficiary.

5. Net Trust Income

The net trust income in respect of an accounting period may, therefore, be said to be the aggregate of the gross income received[19] in that period from all the trust assets, less the expenses of trust administration paid from income either by virtue of their nature or pursuant to a provision in the trust instrument, and less any other payments made from income in the exercise of an administrative power. In the remainder of this chapter, the net trust income in this sense is referred to as the trust income. **17–013**

II. GIFTS CARRYING INCOME

Once the amount of the trust income has been ascertained, it is then necessary to determine whether any beneficiary is entitled to that income. If he is, his interest is said to carry the intermediate income. The possibilities are: **17–014**

---

[17] In *Inglewood (Lord) v. I.R.C.* [1983] 1 W.L.R. 866, this power was treated as "similar" to an administrative power even though its exercise unquestionably affects beneficial entitlement.

[18] By analogy with the power to advance capital listed above.

[19] In many respects it is uncertain whether, in order for an amount to be taken into account, it must actually be received by the trustees or whether the fact that it is merely receivable suffices.

(i) a beneficiary is entitled to the income without any further decision of the trustees being necessary (this will usually be the case where trustees hold a fund upon trust to pay the income to Adam for life, with remainder to Eve);

(ii) no person is entitled to the income, because the trustees have the power to accumulate it and do so;

(iii) a beneficiary is entitled to the income but only as a result of the trustees exercising a discretion in his favour; and

(iv) the income has not been effectively disposed of and so is held on a resulting trust either for the settlor or, in the case of a trust *post mortem*, for the deceased's residuary beneficiaries or those entitled on his intestacy.

17–015   Vested gifts carry the intermediate income[20] unless the trust instrument provides either that it is to be paid to someone else[21] or that it is to be accumulated and added to capital. This is the case whether the trust is fixed or discretionary.[22]

17–016   The question of whether contingent gifts carry the intermediate income is more complex. In the case of wills, it is largely, but not entirely, governed by section 175 of the Law of Property Act 1925. This section[23] provides that, except in so far as the testator has otherwise expressly disposed of the income, the following types of gift carry the intermediate income as from the testator's death:

(i) contingent or future specific devises or bequests[24] of property, whether real or personal;

(ii) contingent residuary devises of freehold land; and

(iii) specific or residuary devises of freehold land to trustees upon trust for persons whose interests are contingent or executory.

17–017   The position in relation to vested and contingent interests under both *inter vivos* trusts and *post mortem* trusts,[25] in so far as the latter are not governed by section 175 of the Law of Property Act 1925, is as follows:

(1) The directions of the settlor or testator always prevail. Accordingly, if the trust instrument directs that the income is to be accumulated, that direction will prevent the gift from carrying the intermediate

---

[20] *Re Stapleton* [1946] 1 All E.R. 323.

[21] Thus in the case of the gift to Adam for life, with remainder to Eve, both gifts are vested but the gift to Eve does not carry the intermediate income because the trust deed provides that it is to be paid to Adam.

[22] Thus a discretionary trust of income for such of Adam, Eve, Abel and Cain as the trustees in their absolute discretion determine with a provision for accumulation in default does not carry the intermediate income during the accumulation period; once that period has ended, the gift does carry the intermediate income.

[23] Which applies only to wills coming into operation on or after January 1, 1926.

[24] A "devise" is a gift of realty by will; a "bequest" is a gift of personalty by will.

[25] In each case, when they take effect after 1925.

income.[26] Similarly, if there is a direction for the payment of the income to another, then even if the gift in question is vested that direction will prevail and the gift will not carry the intermediate income (an example would be where property was held in trust for a minor absolutely, subject to a provision that, until he attained the age of majority, the income should be paid to his cousin). Again, if the payment of income is expressly deferred until a future date, the gift will not carry the intermediate income.[27]

(2) In the absence of express directions from the settlor or testator, a vested interest will carry the intermediate income subject to just one exception, a testamentary gift of residuary personalty which is expressly deferred to a future date.[28]

(3) In the absence of express directions from the settlor, a contingent interest arising under an *inter vivos* settlement carries the intermediate income provided the contingency is attaining the age of majority or the happening of some event (usually but not necessarily his marriage) before he attains that age.

(4) In the absence of express directions from the testator, a contingent interest arising under a will carries the intermediate income if it is:

(i) a residuary gift of personalty[29] but not if the interest in question is expressly deferred to a future date[30];

(ii) a residuary gift of realty[31] but not if the interest in question is expressly deferred to a future date[32]; and

(iii) a specific gift of personalty, other than a pecuniary legacy,[33] even if the interest is expressly deferred to a future date.[34]

(5) In the absence of express directions from the testator, a pecuniary legacy does not generally carry the intermediate income. To this general principle there are two exceptions, when the gift does carry the intermediate income, namely:

(i) if the gift was to an infant by his parent or by some other person who stood *in loco parentis* to him, and

(a) if the gift is contingent, the contingency is not the attaining of an age greater than 18,[35] and

---

[26] *Re Turner's Will Trusts* [1967] Ch. 15; *Re Ransome* [1957] Ch. 348; *Re Reade-Revell* [1930] 1 Ch. 52.

[27] *Re Geering* [1964] Ch. 136.

[28] *Re Oliver* [1947] 2 All E.R. 162; *Re Gillett's Will Trusts* [1950] Ch. 102.

[29] *Re Adams* [1893] 1 Ch. 329 (unaffected by the 1925 legislation).

[30] *Re Geering* [1964] Ch. 136.

[31] Law of Property Act 1925, s.175.

[32] This situation is not covered by Law of Property Act 1925, s.175.

[33] There is little logic in the distinction between contingent pecuniary legacies and other contingent gifts of personalty.

[34] *Re McGeorge* [1963] Ch. 544.

[35] *Re Jones* [1932] 1 Ch. 642; Family Law Reform Act 1969, s.1.

(b) there is no other fund set aside for the maintenance of the infant[36]; or

(ii) the testator directs that the legacy to be set apart from the rest of his estate for the benefit of the legatee.[37]

17–018   It should be emphasised that, as has already been mentioned, where the intermediate income is not carried, it is undisposed of; consequently, it is held on resulting trust for the settlor or, in the case of a trust *post mortem*, for the deceased's residuary beneficiaries or those entitled on his intestacy.

III. The Retention of Income

17–019   Where trustees do not pay out or apply all the income, they will necessarily either have accumulated it or have retained it in its character as income.

1. *Accumulation*

17–020   Accumulation is the conversion of what was originally income into capital. It occurs at the moment at which the trustees decide to accumulate the income and, while no formality is required, it is desirable as a matter of practice for the decision to accumulate to be recorded carefully in the trust's minutes. Income can only be accumulated if, first, the trust instrument contains a trust or power enabling this to be done; secondly, that trust or power is not for an excessive period; and, thirdly, the trustees decide to give effect to the trust or to exercise the power.

2. *A Trust or Power to Accumulate*

17–021   Trustees have no general power to accumulate income. In *Re Gourju's Will Trusts*,[38] trustees held a fund upon protective trusts[39]; the fixed interest of the principal beneficiary having come to an end, the trustees sought to accumulate the income. However, Simonds J. said[40]:

"I come to the conclusion that the obligation of the trustees is to apply the trust income as and when they receive it for the purposes indicated in the subsection. . . . Putting it in a negative way, they are not entitled, regardless of the needs of the beneficiaries, to retain in their hands the income of the trust estate."

17–022   A trust or power to accumulate may arise either by virtue of the express provisions of the trust instrument or, in the case of income which is held for

---

[36] *Re West* [1913] 2 Ch. 245. This is the effect of the words in what is now section 31(3) of the Trustee Act that the section "applies to a future or contingent legacy by the parent of the legatee if and for such period as, under the general law, the legacy carries interest for the maintenance of the legatee".

[37] *Re Jones* [1932] 1 Ch. 642; Family Law Reform Act 1969, s.1.

[38] [1943] Ch. 24.

[39] Under Trustee Act 1925, s.33; see *ante*, para 8–003.

[40] [1943] Ch. 24 at 34.

the benefit of a minor beneficiary, by statute[41] to the extent that that income is not used for his maintenance.

3. Excessive Powers

Where a trust is subject to English law, accumulation can at present only be prescribed for a maximum of one of the following periods[42]: **17–023**

    (i) the life of the settlor;

    (ii) a period of 21 years from the death of the settlor;

    (iii) the duration of the minority or respective minorities of any person or persons living or *en ventre sa mère* at the death of the settlor;

    (iv) the duration of the minority or respective minorities of infant beneficiaries who, if of full age, would be entitled to the income;

    (v) a term of 21 years from the creation of the settlement; and

    (vi) the duration of the minority or respective minorities of any person or persons in being when the settlement is created, whether or not they are beneficiaries or have any other connection with the a settlement.

The period most commonly utilised is the term of 21 years from the creation of the settlement ((v) above). If, at the end of the prescribed period, the income is prima facie payable to a beneficiary who is a minor, then income can nevertheless still be accumulated, to the extent that it is not utilised for the minor's maintenance, under the statutory trust to accumulate; this is also possible if a minor becomes the beneficiary in possession at a later stage.[43] Outside the permissible accumulation periods, the income cannot be accumulated and must be distributed to someone; where no beneficiary of the trust is entitled to it, it will have to be paid to the settlor or to those entitled to his estate. **17–024**

Proposed new legislation will substitute all the above six possibilities for a period of 125 years (accumulation during the infancy of a beneficiary will obviously also continue to be possible).[44] **17–025**

If a trust prescribes accumulation for a period which is longer than that prescribed by statute, the whole gift is void if that period is longer than the appropriate perpetuity period[45] but if that period is less than that period, it is void only as to the excess.[46] However, where a settlor wishes income to be accumulated for a period longer than the maximum permitted by English law, this can be achieved by providing for the trust to have as its applicable **17–026**

---

[41] Trustee Act 1925, s.31.

[42] Law of Property Act 1925, s.164; Perpetuities and Accumulations Act 1964, s.13. These periods do not apply where the settlor is a body corporate; *Re Dodwell & Co. Ltd's Trust Deed* [1978] 3 All E.R. 738.

[43] Trustee Act 1925, s.31(2).

[44] See *ante*, para 7–053.

[45] See *ante*, para 7–012.

[46] *Re Joel's Will Trusts* [1967] Ch. 14.

law the law of a jurisdiction which permits a longer period. An on-shore jurisdiction which is popular for this purpose is Northern Ireland, which permits accumulation for the entire perpetuity period[47]; virtually all off-shore jurisdictions have longer accumulation periods, usually fixed periods of years, some even longer than the 125 years envisaged by the proposed new legislation, which is also proposed as the new perpetuity period.

4. *Exercise of Power*

17–027   Trustees must exercise any discretion within a reasonable time. What is reasonable depends on the facts of each case. In *Re Gulbenkian's Settlement Trusts (No.2)*[48] trustees learned in April 1957 of a decision[49] which cast doubt on the validity of a provision in the trust instrument and they then retained the income in their hands as income without accumulating it. The doubt as to validity was not resolved until the decision of the House of Lords in *Re Gulbenkian's Settlement Trusts*[50] in October 1968. Plowman J. held that in the circumstances the trustees' retention of the income was not unreasonable and they were therefore still able to exercise their discretion in respect of all the income which had arisen since 1957. Thus, provided that they act reasonably, trustees can clearly retain income as income for a considerable time and then accumulate it.

17–028   If the trustees are under a specific duty to accumulate income, that duty is not extinguished by lapse of time. In such circumstances, the trustees can carry out their duty long after the income has actually arisen; further, if they do not do so, the court will issue a direction to this effect.[51] If, on the other hand, the trustees have only a mere power to accumulate, that is a duty to consider whether to accumulate but without any duty to do so, their power to accumulate will be lost if they do not act within a reasonable time.[52]

5. *The Fiscal Effect of Accumulation*

17–029   Trust instruments which impose a duty or confer a power to accumulate frequently also confer a power for payments from capital to be made to beneficiaries. The trustees may thus have both a power in respect of income, under which they may either distribute income as it arises to members of a discretionary class or accumulate it, and a trust or power to distribute capital, including accumulated income, to the same persons. What difference does it make to the beneficiary whether he receives a distribution of income or capital? This is largely governed by fiscal considerations.

17–030   What is the position of trustees of a fund who receive gross income of £1,000 per annum which they have a discretion either to distribute as income or to accumulate? The following example proceeds on the basis, unlikely in

---

[47] For an example of the use of trusts governed by the law of Northern Ireland for this purpose, see *Vestey v. I.R.C.* [1980] A.C. 1148.

[48] [1970] Ch. 408.

[49] *Re Gresham's Settlement* [1956] 1 W.L.R. 573, subsequently overruled.

[50] [1970] A.C. 508.

[51] *Re Locker's Settlement Trusts* [1977] 1 W.L.R. 1323; see *ante*, para 14–025.

[52] *Re Gourju's Will Trusts* [1943] Ch. 24; *Re Wise* [1896] 1 Ch. 281; *Re Allen-Meyrick's Will Trusts* [1968] 1 W.L.R. 499.

practice, that there are no trust administration expenses and that the whole of the gross income is actually available for accumulation or distribution. Suppose that the trustees are considering making some form of distribution to two of the discretionary objects, George who pays income tax at the basic rate[53] of 20 per cent[54] and Harry who pays income tax at the higher rate of 40 per cent. The trustees will themselves be liable to pay income tax at a total rate of 40 per cent on any income which is capable of being accumulated,[55] although a different rate of 32.5 per cent is payable in respect of income from company distributions. On the assumption that none of the £1,000 is income from company distributions, the tax payable will be £400, although 20 per cent will already have been retained out of any bank interest.

The detailed provisions which apply when income which is capable of   **17–031** being accumulated is distributed are discussed in the chapter on the taxation of trusts.[56] On the assumption that none of the £1,000 is income from company distributions, in which case the situation is much more complicated, in broad outline the position is as follows. If the trustees distribute the net amount of £600 to one of the two potential beneficiaries as income without first accumulating it, the beneficiary is treated as having received a gross payment of £1,000, from which tax at 40 per cent has been deducted. In the case of George, his marginal rate of tax is 20 per cent so he will be able to recover from H.M. Revenue & Customs the difference between the tax which he ought to have suffered on the £1,000, namely £200, and the £400 tax which the income has actually borne; in the final result, he will therefore receive £800, £600 from the trustees and £200 by way of tax reclaim. On the other hand Harry, who is also liable to tax at 40 per cent, will not be able to recover anything from H.M. Revenue & Customs (indeed, when trusts paid a lower rate of tax than individuals taxed at the higher rate of income tax, a person such as Harry had himself to pay such additional tax as was necessary to bring the overall rate of income tax paid up to the higher rate of 40 per cent); Harry will therefore simply receive the £600 from the trustees.

If the trustees instead accumulate the net income of £600 and then at some   **17–032** later stage distribute it as a capital payment, it is treated as capital for all purposes relating to income tax; consequently, no repayment claims can be made nor can any further liability arise. Thus, George will be worse off because he will not be able to recover the £200 from H.M. Revenue & Customs but Harry will be in exactly the same position (however, when trusts paid a lower rate of tax than individuals taxed at the higher rate of income tax, a person such as Harry would have been better off since he would not have had to pay any additional income tax). However, such a distribution from capital which has been derived from accumulated income will be treated in the same way as any other distribution of capital and may therefore give rise to a liability to inheritance tax.[57]

---

[53] See *ante*, para 15–016.
[54] These examples assume that the top rate of tax payable by George will not alter as a result of him receiving another £1,000 gross income.
[55] The provision also applies to income subject to a discretion.
[56] See *ante*, para 15–030.
[57] Inheritance Tax Act 1984, s.65. See *ante*, para 15–092.

6. *Retained Income*

17–033 As income can be converted into capital as a result of a decision by the trustees to accumulate it, as a matter of strict theory the income can never be accumulated in the absence of such a decision. However, if the trustees are under a duty to accumulate, the longer the period which elapses the greater will be the willingness of the courts to hold that there has been an accumulation in any event. Similarly, the courts will infer that a decision to accumulate has been made if the trustees act in a manner which indicates that income has been accumulated; this will be the case, for example, where trustees complete an income tax return for the trust showing the income as having been accumulated.

7. *Beneficial Entitlement*

17–034 Special rules apply where income has been accumulated during the minority of a minor beneficiary.[58] Apart from these special rules, which will be considered below, and subject to any contrary provision in the trust instrument, income which has been accumulated will be added to capital and the beneficiary ultimately entitled to the capital will also become entitled to the accumulations. On the other hand, income which is retained by the trustees without being accumulated will belong to the beneficiary, if any, who is entitled to income.

IV. The Maintenance of Minor Beneficiaries

1. *The Trust Instrument Prevails*

17–035 Section 31 of the Trustee Act 1925 confers upon trustees a power to apply income in the maintenance of minor beneficiaries.[59] However, it was decided in *Re Turner*[60] that all the provisions of this section, irrespective of whether they are expressed as powers or as duties, are in fact only "powers conferred by this Act" for the purposes of section 69(2) of the Act (this subsection of course provides that "the powers conferred by this Act on trustees" apply only in so far as there is no intention expressed in the trust instrument that they should not apply). Therefore, although the general principle is that the statutory powers are additional to any powers in the trust instrument, any of the statutory powers, including the power of maintenance, may be expressly excluded, or varied, under section 69(2).

17–036 The statutory power of maintenance will be excluded: first, if and to the extent that the terms of an express power of maintenance are inconsistent with the statutory power; secondly, where any other provision in the trust instrument, such as a direction to accumulate the whole of the income, is

---

[58] See *post*, para 17–046.
[59] There is no statutory power to maintain adult beneficiaries.
[60] [1937] Ch. 15.

inconsistent with the statutory power; and, thirdly, where there is a provision expressly excluding the statutory power. *Re Erskine's Settlement Trusts*[61] provides an example of the second and third of these circumstances. The settlor created a settlement for the benefit of his grandson Richard, who was to become entitled to the capital of the fund upon attaining the age of 22. What was Richard's entitlement to income prior to attaining that age? The trust instrument provided that the income should be accumulated both during the lifetime of the settlor and thereafter until Richard reached the age of 22; it also provided that the statutory powers of maintenance and advancement should not apply. The provision for accumulation was in fact void[62] but Stamp J., following *Re Turner*,[63] held that the statutory power of maintenance was nevertheless effectively excluded. Consequently the income remained undisposed of until Richard reached the age of 22; it therefore belonged to the settlor's estate. While it is therefore possible to exclude the statutory power, that power will only be excluded if there is a clear expression of intention to that effect. If the trust instrument is silent on the point, then the statutory power will apply.

2. *The Statutory Power*

The statutory power of maintenance is contained in section 31 of the Trustee Act 1925. This provides[64] that, where property is held upon trust for any minor, then during the minority of that person the trustees may, if in their discretion they think fit, pay the whole or part of the income to the parent or guardian of the minor beneficiary or otherwise apply it for or towards his maintenance, education, or benefit. The trustees are under a duty to accumulate the whole of the income which is not paid or applied in this way.[65]   **17–037**

It follows from what has been said earlier in this chapter that the trustees will have a power to maintain a minor beneficiary unless the gift to the infant beneficiary does not carry the intermediate income[66] or the power has been excluded.[67] Where the statutory power arises, it is important to note that that power only applies while the beneficiary is under the age of 18[68] but, during that period, it applies whatever the nature of the property.[69] It also has the following further noteworthy features: **17–038**

(1) The statutory power applies where the interest of the beneficiary is vested and to this extent overrides the apparent provisions of the trust instrument. Where trustees hold a fund upon trust for Cedric   **17–039**

---

[61] [1971] 1 W.L.R. 162.
[62] Because it was contrary to the Law of Property Act 1925, s.164.
[63] [1937] Ch. 15.
[64] Trustee Act 1925, s.31(1).
[65] *ibid.*, s.31(2).
[66] See *ante*, para 17–014.
[67] See *ante*, para 17–036.
[68] Family Law Reform Act 1969, Sch.3, para.5. See *post*, para 17–044, as to the position when the beneficiary reaches the age of 18.
[69] *Stanley v. I.R.C.* [1944] K.B. 255; *Re Baron Vestey* [1951] Ch. 209.

for life, remainder to Edmund, the terms of the trust instrument would suggest that Cedric is entitled to the whole of the income. However, the effect of the application of the statutory power of maintenance, assuming that it has not been excluded, is to deprive Cedric of any right to the income while he is under the age of 18 except to the extent that the trustees decide to pay or apply the whole or any part of it for his maintenance.

17–040   (2) The statutory power also applies where the interest of the beneficiary is contingent. So where a fund is held upon trust for Fergus if he attains the age of 30, the trustees may use the whole or any part of the income for his maintenance while he is under the age of 18, provided that the gift carries the intermediate income.[70]

17–041   (3.) The reference in the statutory power to vested interests is sufficient to apply it to vested interests which are defeasible. Thus it applies where a fund is held upon trust for Solly but, if he dies under the age of 30, for Holly and the trustees may use the whole or any part of the income for the maintenance of Solly while he is under the age of 18.

17–042   (4) Where the statutory power has not been excluded, the trustees are under a duty to consider whether to exercise their power but are under no obligation to exercise it. In deciding whether, and, if so, to what extent, to exercise the power, the trustees are directed by section 31 to have regard: first, to the age of the minor; secondly, to what other income, if any, is available for his maintenance; thirdly, to his requirements; and, fourthly, "generally to the circumstances of the case". If the trustees know that other income is available for the maintenance of the minor and the total amount available exceeds the needs of the minor, then so far as is practicable a proportionate part only of each fund should be paid or applied for his maintenance. The trustees may pay any money which they decide to use either to the minor's parent or guardian[71] or apply it directly for his maintenance, education or benefit.

(5) Where the statutory power is to be exercised, the trustees must exercise it positively and not merely pay out the money for the minor's maintenance without considering whether or not it is desirable for them to do so. Thus, where[72] trustees made automatic payments to a minor's father without exercising any discretion, the court ordered that the money had to be repaid by them to the trust fund. But as long as the trustees exercise their discretion in good faith, the court will not interfere with their decision.[73]

---

[70] See *ante*, para 17–014. If the gift does not carry the intermediate income, there will obviously be no income available for the trustees to use.
[71] *Sowarsby v. Lacy* (1819) 4 Madd. 142.
[72] *Wilson v. Turner* (1883) 22 Ch.D. 521 and see *ante*, para 6–077.
[73] *Re Bryant* [1894] 1 Ch. 324; *Re Lofthouse* (1885) 29 Ch.D. 921.

3. *Accumulation of Surplus Income*

All income which is not paid to the parent or guardian of the infant   **17–043**
beneficiary or applied by the trustees for his maintenance, education, or
benefit must be accumulated.[74] Despite the fact that, by being accumulated,
the surplus income becomes capital, the trustees may nevertheless use the
income accumulated in previous years as if it were the income of a later year,
provided that the interest of the beneficiary in question actually continues
and he is still under 18 in that later year.[75]

4. *Income Arising After the Age of 18*

There is no statutory power to maintain an adult beneficiary. The general   **17–044**
principle is therefore that, once the beneficiary has reached the age of 18, he
is thereafter entitled either to the whole of the income[76] or to none of it. It is,
however, possible for the trust instrument to confer an express power to
maintain in these circumstances.[77] In *Re McGeorge*,[78] a testator devised land
to his daughter but declared that the devise should not take effect until the
death of his wife. It was held that this was a "future specific devise" within
section 175 of the Law of Property Act 1925 and so prima facie carried the
intermediate income. The daughter was over 18 and so claimed the income
of the property. Her claim was unsuccessful. Cross J. held that the testator,
by having deferred the enjoyment of the property until after the widow's
death, had expressed the intention that the daughter should not in fact have
the intermediate income; it therefore had to be accumulated.

Where, on attaining the age of 18, the beneficiary has only a contingent   **17–045**
interest in the trust property, he would, in the absence of any other provision, have no entitlement to anything until he had satisfied the contingency.
However, section 31(1)(ii) has the effect of accelerating the beneficiary's
interest. It provides that, once the beneficiary has attained the age of 18, the
trustees shall[79] thereafter pay to the beneficiary the income from the trust
fund and the income from any accumulations[80] until the contingency is
either satisfied or fails.

5. *Accumulated Income at the Age of 18*

When the minor beneficiary attains the age of 18, the trustees will hold the   **17–046**
accumulations, including income from the accumulated fund which has
itself been accumulated, in accordance with any provision of the trust
instrument and, if there is no such provision, either for the beneficiary

---

[74] Trustee Act 1925, s.31(2). The manner in which the accumulations are dealt with is
discussed *post*, para 17–046.
[75] *ibid*.
[76] *Re Jones' Will Trusts* [1947] Ch. 48.
[77] *Re Turner* [1937] Ch. 15.
[78] [1963] Ch. 544.
[79] Despite this apparently mandatory provision, the section can be excluded; *Re Turner* [1937]
Ch. 15.
[80] Trustee Act 1925, s.31(1)(ii).

absolutely or as an accretion to the capital of the trust property.[81] A beneficiary will become entitled to the accumulations in the following circumstances:

(i) in any circumstances in which the trust instrument so provides; or

(ii) if during his minority his interest was according to the settlement vested and he attains the age of 18[82]; or

(iii) if he attains the age of 18 and is then entitled to capital[83] (for this purpose, a beneficiary is entitled to capital if, where the property is realty, he is entitled to a fee simple absolute, a determinable fee simple, or an entailed interest[84] or if, where the property is personalty, he is entitled to the property absolutely or for an entailed interest).[85]

17–047   In any other case, the accumulations are added to the capital of the property from which they arose.[86] Where they arose from a share of a fund and that share continued to exist as a separate share, the accumulations are an accretion to that share and not to the fund as a whole.[87] This is in contrast with the position where a beneficiary dies before attaining the age of 18 (or marrying under that age), in which case, subject to any provision in the trust instrument, the accumulations are an accretion to the fund as a whole.[88]

17–048   This latter point arose for consideration in *Re Sharp's Settlement Trusts*.[89] A settlement had conferred a power of appointment, exercisable during the perpetuity period, over the trust property, to which in default of appointment the children of the settlor were entitled in equal shares if they attained the age of 21. The settlor had three children: Penelope, who attained the age of 21 in 1964; Russell, who attained the age of 21 in 1967; and Joanne, who was at all material times an infant. Income had arisen under the settlement since 1966 and the trustees had appointed it to the three children equally; it obviously had to be paid out to any child who was 21. Between 1966 and the date when Russell attained his majority in 1967, his share of accumulated income amounted to about £5,000. Between 1966 and the date of the hearing in May 1972, Joanne's share of accumulated income amounted to about £41,000 and accumulation was continuing. Did the accumulations of the income of the shares of Russell and Joanne pass to them absolutely when each attained the age of 21 or did they instead form part of the settled fund,

[81] *ibid.*, s.31(2).
[82] *ibid.*, s.31(2)(i)(a). This also applies if he marries under the age of 18 and had a vested interest until marriage.
[83] *ibid.*, s.31(2)(i)(b). This also applies if he marries under the age of 18.
[84] See *Re Sharp's Settlement Trusts* [1973] Ch. 331 at 338. Since January 1, 1997 no further entailed interests have been able to be created but it is unlikely that all such interests expressly created before that date have yet determined and there are anyway some statutory entailed interests which will continue indefinitely.
[85] *ibid.*
[86] Trustee Act 1925, s.32(2)(ii).
[87] *Re Sharp's Settlement Trusts* [1973] Ch. 331.
[88] See *Re Joel* [1967] Ch. 14; *ante*, para 16–035.
[89] [1973] Ch. 331.

in which case they would still be subject to the future exercise of the power of appointment? Since the fund was personalty, Pennycuick V.-C. held that Russell and Joanne were not absolutely entitled to the accumulations which were therefore subject to the power of appointment (this is admittedly anomalous[90]; had the property been realty and the interest of the beneficiaries a determinable fee,[91] they would have been entitled to the accumulations). The further question then arose as to whether the accumulations were accretions to their individual shares or accretions to the fund as a whole. Penelope argued for the latter (because she would therefore potentially become entitled to part of the income from them). However, Pennycuick V.-C. took the opposite view; thus the accumulations from Russell's share were held, with that share itself, for Russell subject to any future exercise of the power of appointment, and Joanne's share was held in the same way, contingently on her reaching the age of 21. Russell was therefore immediately entitled to the income from his share, including the income produced by the accumulations.

The manner in which trustees deal with accumulations when a beneficiary **17–049** reaches the age of 18 is illustrated by the following table. For the purposes of the table, "Conditions A" means that the beneficiary had a vested interest during infancy and attains the age of 18 and "Conditions B" means that the beneficiary attains the age of 18 and then becomes entitled to the capital.

Trust instrument provides for fund to be held for	Circumstances	Entitlement	Remarks
Andrew absolutely[92]	Andrew attains 18	Andrew	Conditions B
	Andrew dies under 18	Andrew's estate	The entitlement is by virtue of the original gift, not s.31
Brian for life	Brian attains 18	Brian	Conditions A
	Brian dies under 18	Added to capital	Neither Conditions satisfied
Charles for life if he attains 18	Charles attains 18	Added to capital	Charles' interest during infancy was contingent only and he does not become entitled to the capital

---

[90] *ibid.*, at 340.

[91] Although not a fee simple subject to a condition subsequent. As to the distinction, see *Megarry's Manual of the Law of Real Property*, 8th edn (London, Sweet & Maxwell, 2002), pp.51 *et seq.*

[92] Andrew's infancy being the only reason why he could not call for the capital to be transferred to him.

Trust instrument provides for fund to be held for	Circumstances	Entitlement	Remarks
(Charles for life if he attains 18)	Charles dies under 18	Added to capital	Neither Conditions satisfied
Douglas if he attains 18	Douglas attains 18	Douglas	Conditions B
	Douglas dies under 18	Added to capital	Neither Conditions satisfied
Edward if he attains 30	Edwards attains 18	Added to capital	Neither Conditions satisfied
	Edward dies under 18	Added to capital	Neither Conditions satisfied
Frank, but if he dies under 30, for George	Frank attains 18	Frank	Although Frank's interest was defeasible, it was vested and Conditions A is satisfied
	Frank dies under 18	Added to capital	Neither Conditions satisfied
Henry, but if he dies under 18 for Ian	Henry attains 18	Henry	Conditions A
	Henry dies under 18	Added to capital	Neither Conditions satisfied

It will be seen from this table: first, that where the beneficiary dies under the age of 18, the accumulations will always be added to capital, except where the property was held for a minor beneficiary absolutely (as in the case of Andrew); secondly, that where the beneficiary has a life interest which is contingent on his attaining the age of 18, or some later age, then, notwithstanding the fact that he satisfies the contingency, the accumulations are added to capital (as in the case of Charles and Edward); and, thirdly, that the distinction between a contingent interest (as in the case of Charles and Edward) and a vested interest which is defeasible (as in the case of Frank) is crucial.

V. TAXATION CONSEQUENCES

17–050   Section 31 and the actions taken by trustees pursuant to that section can have a considerable effect on the fiscal position of the beneficiary. In considering these fiscal consequences, two points must be kept in mind: first, that section 31 can be excluded by the trust instrument; and, secondly, that where, according to the trust instrument, a minor beneficiary has a vested life interest, section 31 converts that interest into a life interest contingent on his attaining 18 in respect of any income which is accumulated (this happens because, notwithstanding the terms of the settlement, during the minority of the beneficiary the trustees will have a power to maintain and a trust to accumulate the remaining income and the beneficiary (or his estate) will only become entitled to the accumulations if he attains the age of 18). The latter point can cause considerable confusion. In order to determine the destination of accumulations, then, whether or not a beneficiary had during his minority a vested interest, regard is paid to the terms of the trust instrument. For all other purposes, however, the nature of the beneficiary's interest is determined by the terms of the trust instrument as modified by the section itself.

It has already been seen[93] that the income tax is payable at the basic rate[94] **17–051** on all income which is received by trustees, regardless of whether that income is used for the payment of trust administration expenses, paid to a beneficiary, or accumulated but that, if the trustees have a discretion with regard to the distribution of income or are directed to accumulate it, they are liable to pay additional income tax at what is known as the rate applicable to trusts[95] so as to bring the total payable up a higher flat rate.[96]

If section 31 applies, then, whether the beneficiary's interest under the **17–052** terms of the trust instrument is vested or contingent, the trustees necessarily have a discretion in that they have a power to maintain; consequently, they are liable to pay tax at the rate applicable to trusts. However, there is no further liability on the beneficiary unless the income is actually paid out to him, or applied for his benefit.

There is, however, a further rule under which a beneficiary will be taxable **17–053** on the whole of the net trust income if he has a vested interest in it. He is taxable according to the rate of income tax applicable to his own income but he is entitled to a credit in respect of the income tax already paid by the trustees on the trust income paid to him. Suppose, therefore, that Harry, the beneficiary of a trust, has income apart from the trust of £45,000; that the income of the trust fund is £6,000 per annum gross, £2,000 from bank interest, and £4,000 from other sources (such as rent).[97] Twenty per cent tax (£400) will have been withheld at source on the bank interest. The trust administration expenses are £700.

---

[93] See *ante*, para 15–023.

[94] At present (2008–2009) the trustees have to pay the basic rate of tax, which in this particular year was reduced to 20% from 22%, on all income except for company distributions and bank interest, in respect of which tax is retained at source at 10% and 20% respectively and those retentions satisfy the basic rate of tax, in both cases quite irrespective of what the basic rate of tax actually is.

[95] The additional rate is not payable in respect of that part of the gross income which was paid out in trust administration expenses, which have in the first instance to be set against the income from company dividends taxed at 10%, then against income from bank interest taxed at 20% and only subsequently against other income taxed at 20%. Further, the first £1,000 of income after the payment of trust administration expenses is not liable to the additional rate.

[96] At present (2008–2009) 40% in respect of all income except for company distributions, which are taxable at 32.5%; credit is given for the 20% retained on bank interest, and the 10% retained on company distributions.

[97] In practice, the trust would be likely also to have some income from company distributions but the different tax treatment of this source of income would make the example excessively complicated if any income from it were included.

17–054 If Harry has a vested interest under the trust, his liability is as follows:

The trustees have received	£6,000	
less 20% tax withheld on bank interest of £2,000	£400	
leaving	£5,600	
from which they have paid trust administration expenses of	£700	
and paid 20% tax on the other income of £4,000	£800	
leaving net income paid to Harry of	£4,100	
This is treated as a gross sum of	£5,250	
from which income tax[98] has been retained of	£350	
and income tax has been paid of	£800	
	£4,100	
So Harry's trust income is:		
the amount paid to him	£4,100	
and the tax retained on that amount	£1,150	
	£5,250	£5,250
which is added to his other income of		£45,000
making a total income of		£50,250
On the "slice" of income between £45,000 and £50,250		
the present rate of income tax[99] is 40%, producing a total liability of (40% × £5,250.00		£2,100
The appropriate part of the retentions at source was		£1,150
So Harry has a further liability of		£950

The net benefit to Harry is therefore £3,150 (£4,100 minus £950). However, if he paid either no income tax or income tax at a lower rate, he could recover from H.M. Revenue & Customs all or some of the income tax which the trustees have paid on the sum which has then been paid to him.

17–055 If the facts are varied so that Harry will only receive any income if the trustees exercise a discretion in his favour, either because the trust is a

---

[98] In effect, the £400 tax retained out of the trust income is attributed: as to
700/5600 × 400 = £50.00 to trust administration expenses
4900/5600 × 400 = £350.00 to income paid to Harry.

[99] For 2008–2009 (this has been the higher rate of income tax for many years and is unlikely to be changed since successive governments have preferred to increase this rate indirectly by stealth taxes (such as the extra National Insurance Contributions which now apply to earned income at this level) rather than to raise it directly).

discretionary trust anyway or because he is a minor and section 31 applies, then the trustees can choose either to accumulate the income or to pay it (or some of it) to Harry. If they choose to accumulate the whole of the income, the total tax liability will be imposed on the trustees, as follows:

The trustees have received	£6,000	
less 20% tax withheld on bank interest of £2,000	£400	
leaving	£5,600	
from which they have paid trust administration expenses of	£700	
leaving a balance before the trustees pay any tax of	£4,900	£4,900
The first £1,000 income after the payment of administration expenses is free of tax at the rate applicable to trusts so:		
tax at the rate applicable to trusts (40%[100]) on £3,900	£1,560	
discounting the 20% retained at source on that part of the gross income of the trust of £6,000 not used in the payment of administration expenses, which as seen above was £350	£350	
so the tax payable by the trustees is	£1,210	£1,210
So the net income accumulated is		£3,690

If the trustees instead want to pay the whole of the income to Harry, the **17–056** amount which they can actually pay to him has to be calculated in the light of the fact that any payment to him is treated as if it were made after deduction of tax at the rate applicable to trusts and that the trustees will actually have to pay that tax to the extent that it is not "franked" (wiped out) by the tax which they have already paid (other than the irrecoverable 10 per cent retention on company distributions, which is of course not relevant to the present example). If they were to pay him the whole of the income of £3,690, the grossed up income tax payable thereon would be £2,460; since they have only actually paid £1,560 income tax in respect of the accumulated sum, they would have to pay a further £900 income tax and would have nothing with which to pay it. However, if they instead pay him £3,150, the grossed up income tax will be £2,100; the difference between that and the £1,560 tax which they have already paid is £540, exactly the same as the difference between £3,690 and £3,150. So they can pay Harry £3,150 and use the remaining £540 to pay the further tax.

---

[100] If any part of the income was from company distributions, then only a total of 32.5% income tax would be payable on that income; 10% retained and 22.5% by the trustees; see *ante*, para 15–028.

Harry's trust income then is:

the net income actually paid to him	£3,150	
the sum needed to gross it up at the rate applicable to trusts	£2,100	
	£5,250	£5,250
which is added to his other income of		£45,000
making a total income as before of		£50,250

On the "slice" of income between £45,000 and £50,250 the present rate of income tax is 40%, producing a total liability as before of (40% × £5,250.00) £2,100

Less the appropriate part of the retentions at source	£350
the tax paid at the rate applicable to trusts	£1,210
the further tax payable on the distribution to Harry	£140

The liability and the credit are the same so nothing is payable 0

So the net benefit to Harry is therefore once again £3,150. However, as before, if instead he paid either no income tax or income tax at a lower rate, he could recover from H.M. Revenue & Customs all or some of the income tax which the trustees have paid on the sum which has eventually been paid to him. Harry will therefore receive the same net benefit whether he has a vested interest under a fixed trust or an interest under a discretionary trust. But this would not be the case if the income of the trust included company distributions. The fact that the 10 per cent retention is not recoverable and therefore cannot be used to "frank" the tax payable on the distribution to Harry under a discretionary trust means that he will receive less under a discretionary trust than he would under a fixed trust.

17–057   The income will be treated as that of Harry, during Harry's minority: first, if he is absolutely entitled to both capital and income, so that his infancy is the sole reason why he cannot call for the capital to be transferred to him, and either he, if he lives, or his estate, if he does not, will be entitled to the accumulations[101]; and, secondly, if, according to the terms of the trust instrument, Harry is entitled to the whole of the income, section 31 therefore being excluded, so that the trustees do not have power to accumulate any part of it. In all other circumstances, only that income which is actually paid to Harry or applied for his benefit, is treated as his for the purposes of income tax.[102] The remainder of the income, which is accumulated, is taxable in the hands of the trustees at the higher flat rate of, at present, 40 per cent.

---

[101] *Roberts v. Hanks* (1926) 10 T.C. 351; *Edwardes-Jones v. Down* (1936) 20 T.C. 279.
[102] *Stanley v. I.R.C.* [1944] K.B. 255.

CHAPTER 18

APPLICATIONS OF TRUST CAPITAL

In general, entitlement to capital will, in the case of a fixed trust, depend on   **18–001**
the terms of the trust instrument and will, in the case of a discretionary trust,
depend on the decision of the trustees. However, as in the case of entitlement to income, the quantum of capital which is available for beneficiaries
will be determined only after the payment of those costs and expenses
which are attributable to capital.[1] Further, even in the case of a fixed trust,
the trustees may take decisions which have the effect of altering both the
time at which a beneficiary will take capital and the quantum of his entitlement.

The main powers which are capable of affecting the time and the quantum   **18–002**
of entitlement to capital are powers of advancement, powers of appointment, and powers of appropriation. Power of appointment have already
been considered.[2] This chapter will, after dealing with expenses payable
from capital, be concerned primarily with the powers of advancement and
powers of appropriation.

I. EXPENSES FROM CAPITAL

It has already been seen[3] that, in general, recurrent expenses are payable out   **18–003**
of the income of the trust fund. This is partly because of the nature of
recurrent expenses and partly because such expenses are generally incurred
primarily for the benefit of the beneficiary who is entitled to income. The
corollary of this is that, in principle, the capital of the trust fund generally
has to bear expenses which constitute capital expenditure on one or more of
the assets of the trust or which apply to the trust as a whole; this is because
these expenses can consequently be said to be for the benefit of all the
beneficiaries.

Examples of expenses which are treated as capital expenditure on a trust   **18–004**
asset are sums applied in discharging mortgage debts[4] and sums applied in
improving land and buildings.[5] Where a building is purchased by the
trustees when it is in a derelict state, the cost of putting it into good
condition at the outset will be treated as if it were part of the purchase price

---

[1] As to net income, see *ante*, para 17–013.
[2] See *ante*, para 6–013.
[3] See *ante*, para 17–016.
[4] *Whitbread v. Smith* (1854) 3 De G.M. & G. 727; *Marshall v. Crowther* (1874) 2 Ch.D. 199.
[5] *Earl of Cowley v. Wellesley* (1866) L.R. 1 Eq. 656; *Re Walker's Settled Estate* [1894] 1 Ch. 189.

and so will be chargeable to capital.[6] On the other hand, ordinary repairs are, in principle, payable out of income. However, where the repairs can be said to be for the benefit of all the beneficiaries, in certain circumstances the trustees and the court have a statutory power to direct that the whole or part of the cost is to be borne by capital.[7] It can also be expressly provided by the trust instrument that the trustees have a discretion over when the cost of such repairs should be charged to income or to capital.[8] Where any such power exists, it must be exercised in such a way that the costs in question will be borne equitably between beneficiaries with different interests.[9]

18–005   The second category of expenses which are borne by capital covers those items relating to the trust as a whole and which can be said to be for the benefit of all the beneficiaries. Examples are the costs of appointing new trustees,[10] of making changes in investments, of obtaining legal advice as to the extent of the trustees' powers,[11] and of taking or defending court proceedings for the protection of the trust assets.[12]

II. ADVANCEMENTS

1. The Concept

18–006   An advancement essentially consists of the payment or the application of a capital sum in order to establish a person in life or to make permanent provision for him.[13] An advancement is often of an amount which, in the light of the circumstances of the recipient, is large; where a payment is large in this sense, there is a presumption that it is made by way of advancement.[14] However, it is not now generally necessary to consider in relation to the administration of trusts[15] whether or not a payment is, strictly speaking, by way of advancement; this is because the trustees now usually have a power to apply capital for the advancement or other benefit of a beneficiary, either under the statutory power considered below or under an express power in the trust instrument.

---

[6] *Re Courtier* (1886) Ch.D. 136.

[7] Under the Settled Land and Trustee Acts (Courts' General Powers) Act 1943 and Emergency Powers (Miscellaneous Provisions) Act 1953.

[8] See paras 1.4 and 1.5 of the Precedents for Administrative Provisions set out and discussed in J. Kessler, *Drafting Trusts and Will Trusts: A Modern Approach*, 8th edn (London, Sweet & Maxwell, 2007). (It is particularly important always to use the most recent edition of this work; the current one is the 8th (2007) edition).

[9] *Re Lord De Tabley* (1896) 75 L.T. 328; *Re Earl of Stamford and Warrington* [1916] 1 Ch. 404.

[10] *Re Fulham* (1850) 15 Jur. 69; *Re Fellows' Settlement* (1856) 2 Jur. (N.S.) 62.

[11] *Poole v. Pass* (1839) 1 Beav. 600.

[12] *Re Earl of Berkeley's Will Trusts* (1874) 10 Ch. App. 56; *Re Earl De La Warr's Estates* (1881) 16 Ch.D. 587; *Stott v. Milne* (1884) 25 Ch.D. 710.

[13] *Boyd v. Boyd* (1867) L.R. 4 Eq. 305; *Taylor v. Taylor* (1875) L.R. 20 Eq. 155; *Re Hayward* [1957] Ch. 528; *Hardy v. Shaw* [1975] 2 All E.R. 1052.

[14] *Taylor v. Taylor* (1875) L.R. 20 Eq. 155 at 157; *Hardy v. Shaw* [1975] 2 All E.R. 1052 at 1056.

[15] The situation is different when an estate is being administered; see Administration of Estates Act 1925, s.46(1).

2. *The Statutory Power*

The statutory power of advancement is contained in section 32 of the Trustee   **18–007**
Act 1925. This section gives trustees a power to pay or apply capital for the
benefit of any beneficiary who is interested in the capital of the trust fund,
whether his interest is vested or contingent, and whether or not it is liable to
be defeated by the exercise of a power. Exercise of the power of advancement always has one and may have two important effects.

(1) The beneficiary who receives the advancement inevitably obtains a
    capital benefit from the trust earlier than he would otherwise have
    done. If trustees hold a fund on trust for Gerald for life, with
    remainder to Harry, and are able to pay part of the fund to Harry
    during the lifetime of Gerald,[16] Harry will take the benefit of that
    part at that time, rather than having to wait until the death of
    Gerald.

(2) The beneficiary who receives the advancement may well receive a
    capital benefit from the trust which he might otherwise might not
    have received at all. If trustees who hold a fund on trust for Ian if he
    attains the age of 30 but, if he dies under that age, for John pay part
    of the trust fund to Ian when he is aged 22, the subsequent death of
    Ian at the age of 25 means that he has obtained a capital benefit for
    which in the event he never actually qualified.

(A) The Extent of the Statutory Power
Under the statutory power, the trustees can make payments by way of   **18–008**
advancement or benefit to the same beneficiary on more than one occasion,
provided that the total which is paid or applied does not exceed one half of
the presumptive or vested share of the beneficiary.[17] It was decided in *The
Marquess of Abergavenny v. Ram*[18] that, if the trustees ever advance to a
beneficiary the whole of the permissible half of his presumptive or vested
share, their power of advancement in favour of that beneficiary is thereby
exhausted and no further advancement can be made to him even if the value
of the remaining trust assets subsequently appreciates.[19] If the trustees of a
trust out of which there have been no previous advancements made an
advancement of £25,000 in 2003 to its sole contingent beneficiary when the
value of the trust fund was £50,000 but by 2009 the value of the unadvanced
half has risen to £80,000, they will have fully exhausted their power in 2003
and can make no further advancement in 2009. If, on the other hand, they
only advanced £24,000 in 2003, so that their power was not fully exhausted,

---

[16] The consent of Gerald will be necessary, see *post*, para 18–011.
[17] Trustee Act 1925, s.32(1), proviso (a).
[18] [1981] 1 W.L.R. 843.
[19] The decision actually related to an express provision of the Marquess of Abergavenny's
Estate Act 1946 but it is equally applicable to s.32 of the Trustee Act 1925.

in 2009 they could advance the further sum of £28,000[20] (although it would again be better to advance only a lesser sum of (say) £27,000 so as to leave room for further advancements in the future).

(B) Bringing Advancements into Account

18–009 If, after a beneficiary has received an advancement, he is or becomes absolutely and indefeasibly entitled to the trust property or to a share in it, he must bring into account the amount of his advancement.[21] Suppose that trustees who hold a fund upon trust for James and John in equal shares if and when they attain the age of 30 paid £20,000 by way of advancement to James when he was aged 26; if, by the time when the fund is distributed to James and John, it is worth £100,000, the amounts which they will receive are:

Value of fund	£100,000
Amount advanced	£20,000
Total	£120,000

Entitlement

	James	John
$\frac{1}{2} \times £120,000$	£60,000	£60,000
Less: advancement	£20,000	—
Net entitlement	£40,000	£60,000

When an advancement was not made in cash but *in specie*, the amount to be brought into account is the value of the asset at the time when the beneficiary becomes absolutely and indefeasibly entitled to his share.[22]

18–010 However, if the beneficiary who received the advancement had only a contingent or defeasible interest and never becomes absolutely and indefeasibly entitled, the amount advanced to him cannot be clawed-back. Consequently, the trustees can, by making an advancement to a contingent beneficiary, partially defeat the interests of other beneficiaries.

(C) The Possible Need for Consents

18–011 Where the making of an advancement will prejudice the interest of a prior beneficiary, the advance can only be made if that beneficiary is of full age

---

[20] The calculation is:

Value of fund in 2009	£80,000
Add: amount previously advanced	£24,000
	£104,000
One half of that	£52,000
less: amount previously advanced	£24,000
Maximum further advance	£28,000

[21] Trustee Act 1925, s.32(1), proviso (b).
[22] See *Hardy v. Shaw* [1975] 2 All E.R. 1052.

and gives his consent in writing. Thus if £100,000 is settled upon trust for Mary for life, with remainder to Derek, the statutory power, if applicable, will enable the trustees to advance up to £50,000 to Derek but only if Mary consents. If Mary does consent and an advancement of the full £50,000 is made, thereafter her income will be that produced by the remaining £50,000 and not, as previously, by £100,000. It should be noted that a person on whom property is settled on protective trusts will not normally forfeit his life interest by consenting to an advancement.[23]

(D) The Nature of Property which can be Advanced
The statutory power of advancement applies only to money or securities or to land which is the subject matter of a trust of land. It therefore does not apply to capital money arising under a settlement subject to the Settled Land Act 1925 (no more such settlements can now be created).[24]   **18–012**

3. *Exclusion, Extension and Replacement of the Statutory Power*

The statutory power will apply even where there is no mention of it in the   **18–013** trust instrument. However, the power is one which falls within the scope of section 69(2) of the Trustee Act 1925[25]; consequently, the settlor or testator can exclude or extend or completely replace that power in the trust instrument. Thus, in *Re Evans's Settlement*[26] Stamp J. held that, where the trust instrument provided that the trustees could advance up to £5,000, this by implication excluded the statutory power of advancing up to one-half of the prospective interest. Further, in *I.R.C. v. Bernstein*,[27] where there was a direction to accumulate income during the settlor's lifetime, the Court of Appeal held that this was a sufficient indication that the settlor did not intend the statutory power of advancement to apply. However, in practice it is more likely that the statutory power will be extended or completely replaced. The most usual extensions give the trustees a power to advance up to the whole and not merely one half of the beneficiary's share, extend the power to the subject matter of settlements under the Settled Land Act 1925 (prospectively, of course, no longer necessary) and, in some cases, do away with the need to obtain the consent of beneficiaries with prior interests. But it is now more common completely to replace the statutory power by conferring on the trustees a totally unfettered power to make advancements as part of their overriding power of appointment.[28]

---

[23] See *ante*, para 18–016.
[24] Trustee Act 1925, s.32(2) (substituted by Trusts of Land and Appointment of Trustees Act 1996 Sch.3, para.3(8)). No further settlements under the Settled Land Act 1925 can now be created.
[25] See *ante*, para 17–035.
[26] [1967] 1 W.L.R. 1294.
[27] [1960] Ch. 444.
[28] See the overriding powers of appointment in the different precedents set out and discussed in J. Kessler, *Drafting Trusts and Will Trusts: A Modern Approach*, 8th edn (London, Sweet & Maxwell, 2007). (It is particularly important always to use the most recent edition of this work; the current one is the 8th (2007) edition).

4. *The Purpose of an Advancement*

18–014 It has already been seen[29] that a power of advancement had originally to relate to some substantial preferment in life. Examples were the purchasing of a commission in the Army[30] (the modern equivalent would be purchasing a partnership in a business or practice), the purchasing or furnishing of a house,[31] or even establishing the husband of a daughter in business.[32] It has also been seen that the need for a substantial preferment of this kind has been modified by the extension of the statutory power of advancement to payments which produce "benefit", a word of wide import. However, the trustees must nevertheless still consider whether a particular advancement is or is not for the benefit of the beneficiary in question. In *Lowther v. Bentinck*[33] it was held that the payment of his debts was not as such for the benefit of a beneficiary, though in special circumstances a payment to a beneficiary which enabled him to discharge his debts might be a benefit for this purpose.[34] Further, it is extremely clear that the trustees must not make an advancement which will benefit themselves. In *Molyneux v. Fletcher*,[35] the trustees made an advance to a beneficiary to enable her to pay the debts which her father owed to one of the trustees; unsurprisingly, this was held to be an improper exercise of the power of advancement.

18–015 In most cases the "benefit" for which an advancement is made is some form of material benefit. In some circumstances, however, the court will authorise an advancement to be made which is, at least to some extent, for the moral benefit of the beneficiary. In *Re Clore*[36] a beneficiary who was entitled to an interest in a trust fund of considerable value felt a moral obligation to make payments to charity. Pennycuick J. authorised an advancement to enable him to do so on the apparent basis that, since the beneficiary felt that he was subject to this obligation, the payment by the trustees was only relieving him of a financial obligation which he would otherwise have sought to meet from his personal funds. The judge made it clear, however, that the beneficiary must genuinely feel the moral obligation himself; the trustees were not at liberty to make payments in satisfaction of what they considered to be the beneficiary's moral obligations if the beneficiary did not himself share their view. Further, there must be some sense in which the advancement improves the material situation of the beneficiary. In *X v. A*,[37] the life tenant had requested the trustees to exercise an express power of advancement (which they were entitled to do without the consent of the remaindermen) by advancing the bulk of the trust assets to her so that she could apply them for charitable purposes. Unlike *Re Clore*, this would not have had the effect of relieving her from a financial obligation which she

---

[29] See *ante*, para 18–006.
[30] *Lawrie v. Bankes* (1857) 4 Kay & J. 142.
[31] *Perry v. Perry* (1870) 18 W.R. 482.
[32] *Re Kershaw's Trust* (1868) L.R. 6 Eq. 322.
[33] (1875) L.R. 19 Eq. 166.
[34] See *Re The Esteem Settlement* [2002] W.T.L.R. 337 (Jersey Court of Appeal).
[35] [1898] 1 Q.B. 648.
[36] [1966] 1 W.L.R. 955.
[37] [2005] EWHC 2706 (Ch), [2006] 1 W.L.R. 741.

would otherwise have sought to meet from her own funds. The consequential complete absence of any improvement to her material situation caused the court to decline to bless the advancement.[38] As these two decisions indicate, it is prudent for trustees to seek the prior sanction of the court before making advancements of this nature except, possibly, in the case of relatively small amounts.

Just as trustees cannot properly make an advancement in order to benefit themselves,[39] they cannot make an advancement with a view to benefiting some other person other than the beneficiary. In *Re Pauling's Settlement Trusts*[40] the bankers Coutts & Co. were trustees of a fund for a wife for her life, with remainder to her children. The trust instrument contained an express power for the trustees to advance to the children up to one-half of their share with the consent of the wife. The husband of the life tenant, who was the father of the children, regularly lived beyond his means and therefore sought to obtain part of the trust moneys. A series of advancements were made, nominally to the children. However, the money advanced was used for the benefit of the father or the family in general; the proceeds of one advance were used to purchase a house for the father in the Isle of Man and the proceeds of another one were used to discharge a loan incurred by the mother. **18–016**

Counsel had advised the trustees that, so far as they were concerned, they were advancing the money to the children for their own absolute use and that what the latter then did with the money was not the trustees' concern. This view was unanimously rejected by the Court of Appeal, who considered that: **18–017**

"the power [of advancement] can be exercised only if it is for the benefit of the child or remoter issue to be advanced or, as was said during argument, it is thought to be 'a good thing' for the advanced person to have a share of capital before his or her due time . . . . [A] power of advancement [can] be exercised only if there is some good reason for it. That good reason must be beneficial to the person to be advanced; [the power] cannot be exercised capriciously or with some other benefit in view."[41]

In their consideration of the circumstances in which an advancement could properly be made, the Court of Appeal drew a distinction between the situation where the beneficiary applies for an advancement for a particular purpose and the situation where the trustees themselves stipulate the purpose to which the advancement is to be put. As Willmer L.J. said: **18–018**

"if the trustees make the advance for a particular purpose which they state, they can quite properly pay it over to the advancee if they reasonably think

---

[38] Even if the proposed advancement had been held to be for the benefit of the life tenant, the Court would on the facts still have declined to bless it because there was insufficient evidence that the trustees had looked in sufficient detail into the individual circumstances of the remaindermen and the potential remaindermen, some of whom had not supported the making of the advancement.

[39] *Molyneux v. Fletcher* [1898] 1 Q.B. 648.

[40] [1964] Ch. 303.

[41] *ibid.*, at 333.

they can trust him or her to carry out the prescribed purpose. What they cannot do is to prescribe a particular purpose and then raise and pay the money over to the advancee, leaving him or her entirely free, legally and morally, to apply it for that purpose or to spend it in any way he or she chooses . . . . This much is plain, that if such misapplication [of the money advanced] came to [the trustees'] notice, they could not safely make further advances for particular purposes without making sure that the money was in fact applied to that purpose, since the advancee would have shown him or herself quite irresponsible."[42]

18–019   The court expressly left open the question whether, in the event that money advanced for a particular purpose was used for something quite different, that money could be recovered by the trustees. This possibility apart, the trustees certainly have no legal control over the money once they have paid it to the beneficiary; consequently, they must take pains to ensure that the beneficiary is under a moral obligation to apply the money to the purpose intended.

5. Adult beneficiaries

18–020   While, as has already been seen,[43] the statutory power of maintenance applies only to minor beneficiaries, the statutory power of advancement can be exercised in favour of beneficiaries of any age.[44]

6. Fiscal Considerations

18–021   Where an advancement is made, there is a potential liability both to capital gains tax and to inheritance tax.

18–022   If the advancement is made in cash, there can be no liability to capital gains tax in respect of the advancement itself although, if the trustees disposed of chargeable assets in order to produce funds with which to make the advancement, a liability to capital gains tax in respect of that disposal may have arisen according to general principles.[45] If, however, the advancement is made *in specie* then, at the time when the trustees decide to make the advancement, they will be deemed to have disposed of the asset at its market value at that time and then immediately to have re-acquired it at that value as nominees for the beneficiary.[46] If the asset has risen in value since it was acquired, the same capital gains tax will be payable as if the asset had actually been sold for that value. However, provided that the beneficiary is resident in the United Kingdom, the trustees and the beneficiary can elect for "hold-over" relief to apply if, first, the assets settled comprise business

---

[42] *ibid.*, at 334, 335.
[43] See *ante*, para 17–044.
[44] In *Hardy v. Shaw* [1975] 2 All E.R. 1052 there was an advancement, in the strict sense of the expression, in favour of persons who were middle-aged.
[45] See *ante*, para 15–130.
[46] Taxation of Chargeable Gains Act 1992, s.71(1).

assets[47] or if, secondly, the making of the advancement involves a chargeable transfer for the purposes of inheritance tax.[48]

With regard to inheritance tax, if the advancement is to a beneficiary who **18–023** immediately before the advancement had an interest in possession for the purposes of the inheritance tax regime, no liability to inheritance tax will arise as a result of that advancement; this is because, for the purposes of inheritance tax the beneficiary will be deemed to have been entitled to the capital already so the advancement will have made no difference.[49] If, where there is such an interest in possession, the advancement is to someone other than the holder of that interest, the latter will have made a potentially exempt transfer.[50] However, as has already been seen,[51] there are now very few types of trust where a beneficiary has an interest in possession for the purposes of inheritance tax. Where this is not the case, any advancement will potentially give rise to an exit charge.[52]

III. ADVANCEMENTS INTO SETTLEMENT

1. *Generally*

Originally, an advancement necessarily consisted of an outright payment of **18–024** money or the transfer of an asset to a beneficiary. However, during the twentieth century[53] it became established that a power of advancement could, in principle, be exercised so that the money or property was not transferred outright but became held on new trusts for the benefit of the beneficiary in question.[54] This is usually done in one of three ways.

(1) If the beneficiary is *sui juris*, the trustees may make an outright payment to him, thereby putting him into the position in which he can himself creating a new settlement.[55]

(2) The trustees may exercise a power given to them in the trust instrument in order to declare that from then on they will hold a part of trust fund on separate trusts for the benefit of one or more of the beneficiaries.[56]

(3) A new settlement may be created, either by the trustees or by some other person, usually with a nominal sum of money, so that a

---

[47] *ibid.*, s.165.
[48] See *ante*, para 15–137.
[49] Inheritance Tax Act 1984, s.49(2).
[50] Unless the advancement is into settlement; see *post, infra.*
[51] See *ante*, para 15–084.
[52] See *ante*, paras 15–097, 15–099.
[53] Following certain decisions at the end of the nineteenth century.
[54] The principle has long been established. See *Re Halstead's Will Trusts* [1937] 2 All E.R. 570; *Re Moxon's Will Trusts* [1958] 1 W.L.R. 165; *Re Ropner's Settlement Trusts* [1956] 1 W.L.R. 902; *Re Wills' Will Trusts* [1959] Ch. 1; *Re Abraham's Will Trusts* [1969] 1 Ch. 463; *Re Hastings-Bass (dec'd.)* [1975] Ch. 25; *Pilkington v. I.R.C.* [1964] A.C. 612.
[55] In *Roper-Curzon v. Roper-Curzon* (1871) L.R. 11 Eq. 452, where it was necessary for the court to give its sanction to an advancement, the court refused to give that sanction unless the beneficiary resettled the amount to be advanced.
[56] See *Hoare Trustees v. Gardner* [1978] 1 All E.R. 791.

convenient "vehicle" can be established. The trustees of the existing settlement then transfer the amount to be advanced to the trustees of the new settlement as an addition to the funds of that settlement to be held on the trusts declared by it.[57]

It will be apparent that the trustees of the original settlement may, but not necessarily will, be the trustees of new settlement created with the advanced fund. Whichever method is used, some aspects of the passing of funds from an existing settlement into a new settlement require consideration.

2. *Is the Proposed Advance for the Benefit of the Beneficiary?*

18–025   Any advancement, whether outright or into settlement, must be for the benefit of the beneficiary to be advanced. The following principles are established by the authorities.

18–026   In general, "benefit" means direct financial benefit, so that it is unlikely that there will have been a valid exercise of the power of advancement if the quantum of the beneficiary's interest is reduced. This point is most likely to arise where the trustees wish to make a settled advance on protective trusts for the beneficiary in question. In *Re Morris*[58] Jenkins L.J. laid down the principle that a "power of advancement is a purely ancillary power, enabling the trustee to anticipate by means of an advance under it the date of actual enjoyment by a beneficiary and it can only affect the destination of the fund indirectly in the event of the person advanced failing to attain a vested interest". He therefore held that an advancement into settlement on protective trusts was not valid because it altered the beneficial interests. However,[59] some advancements on protective trusts can nevertheless be held to be for the direct financial benefit of the beneficiary, provided that they comply with the remaining requirements.

18–027   An advancement on settlement will be for the benefit of the beneficiary if a fiscal liability which would otherwise arise in respect of the funds held for the beneficiary is mitigated.[60] The position was summarised by Viscount Radcliffe in *Pilkington v. I.R.C.*[61] when he said that "if the advantage of preserving the funds of a beneficiary from the incidence of [tax][62] is not an advantage personal to that beneficiary, I do not see what is". If, in order to effect the fiscal mitigation, it is necessary for the beneficiary not to take any, or any direct, financial interest in the advanced fund, the advancement may still be proper. *Re Clore's Settlement Trusts*,[63] which has already been mentioned,[64] concerned a transfer of funds into a charitable settlement under which the beneficiary took no beneficial interest.[65]

---

[57] See *Hart v. Briscoe* [1999] Ch. 1; *Pilkington v. I.R.C.* [1964] A.C. 612.
[58] [1951] 2 All E.R. 528.
[59] See *post, infra.*
[60] *Re Ropner's Settlement Trusts* [1956] 3 All E.R. 332; *Re Meux* [1958] Ch. 154; *Re Wills' Will Trusts* [1959] Ch. 1.
[61] [1964] A.C. 612 at 640.
[62] The tax in question was estate duty.
[63] [1966] 1 W.L.R. 955.
[64] See *ante*, para 18–015.
[65] This decision may depend on its particular facts.

In determining whether an advancement into settlement is for the benefit   **18–028**
of a beneficiary, all the terms of the instrument which constitutes the new
settlement, not merely those under which the trustees are in practice likely
to act, must be considered. In *Re Hunter's Will Trusts*,[66] a testator settled
property upon trust for his sister for life, with remainder to her children
with "such provision for their respective advancement maintenance and
education" as the sister should by will appoint; one of the sister's sons was
financially unstable and in fact became bankrupt shortly after she made her
will. In an attempt to enable her son to enjoy the benefit of part of the trust
property, she purported to appoint that property upon protective trusts for
him. Cross J. held the trust invalid, following the dictum of Jenkins L.J. in *Re
Morris*[67] that protective trusts should not be regarded:

"merely as a device to enable a forfeiting life-tenant to enjoy the income
notwithstanding purported alienation and so forth or the event of his or her
bankruptcy, and that the discretionary trust should be regarded merely as
machinery to that end and not as really designed to confer any beneficial
interest on the issue nominally included in it. The validity or otherwise of
the discretionary trust declared in the event of forfeiture must, in my view,
be determined by reference to what the trustees are empowered to do under
such a trust, and not by reference to what they would in fact be likely to do,
or be expected to do, under it."

A beneficiary may derive a benefit from knowing that financial provision   **18–029**
is being made for his wife and children. So, in *Re Halsted's Will Trusts*,[68]
Farwell J. held that trustees could in the exercise of a power of advancement
for a beneficiary properly settle funds on trust for the beneficiary, his wife
and his children. Nor is there any necessary connection between "benefit"
and "need". Thus, an advancement of funds may be valid if the trustees
consider that it is for the benefit of the beneficiary, irrespective of his
needs.[69]

3. *The Benefit of the Other Beneficiaries under the Advancement*

Property will only be settled if at least one person other than the beneficiary   **18–030**
receiving the advancement has some interest therein, either vested or contingent. The fact that one or more other persons will or might benefit does
not in itself make an advancement into settlement defective. This is one of
the several points which the House of Lords decided in *Pilkington v.
I.R.C.*[70]

A testator set up a will trust under which the trustees were directed to   **18–031**
hold the trust fund on trust, broadly, for the benefit of the testator's nephew

---

[66] [1963] Ch. 372.
[67] [1951] 2 All E.R. 528.
[68] [1937] 2 All E.R. 570.
[69] In *Re Pilkington's Will Trusts* [1961] Ch. 466 (not the same case), the Court of Appeal had
held that there could only be a valid advancement into settlement where the benefit to be
conferred was related to the real or personal needs of the beneficiary. This was rejected by the
House of Lords in *Pilkington v. I.R.C.* [1964] A.C. 612.
[70] [1964] A.C. 612.

Richard for life, with the remainder to such of Richard's children as he should appoint, or, in default of appointment, for all of his children in equal shares. Richard had three children, all born after the death of the testator, one of whom was his daughter Penelope. When Penelope was still very young, the trustees wished to advance funds into a new settlement for her benefit. What was proposed was the creation of a settlement under which the income would be accumulated or used for Penelope's maintenance until she reached the age of 21. Penelope was to be entitled to income on attaining that age and to the capital on attaining the age of 30; if she died under the age of 30, other members of the family were to benefit. One half of Penelope's share under the original settlement was to be transferred to the trustees of the proposed new settlement. The House of Lords held that, in principle,[71] this would be within the trustees' power of advancement, notwithstanding the fact that other members of the family might benefit instead of or as well as Penelope.

4. *Can Dispositive Discretions be Conferred under the New Settlement?*

18–032   In *Re Wills' Will Trusts*[72] Upjohn J. said that "a settlement created in exercise of the power of advancement cannot in general delegate any powers or discretions, at any rate in relation to beneficial interests, to any trustees or other persons, and in so far as the settlement purports to do so, it is pro tanto invalid". These remarks have given rise to the view that an advance into a discretionary settlement would be unauthorised; they have also given rise to the view that, if there is an effective advancement into a settlement on protective trusts, the discretionary trusts which would normally arise on the termination of the principal beneficiary's life interest would also be ineffective. Both the dictum of Upjohn J. and the views to which it has given rise follow from the maxim *delegatus non potest delegare*. However, the better view seems to be that discretions can be conferred on the trustees of the new settlement.

18–033   First, in *Pilkington v. I.R.C.*[73] Viscount Radcliffe said:

"I am unconvinced by the argument that the trustees would be improperly delegating their trust by allowing the money raised to pass over to new trustees under a settlement conferring new powers on the latter. In fact I think the whole issue of delegation is here beside the mark. The law is not that trustees cannot delegate: it is that trustees cannot delegate unless they have authority to do so. If the power of advancement which they possess is so read as to allow them to raise money for the purpose of having it settled[74] then they do have the necessary authority to let the money pass out of the old settlement into the new trusts. No question of delegation of their powers or trust arises."

---

[71] The actual appointment was void because it contravened the rule against perpetuities.
[72] [1959] Ch. 1 at 13.
[73] [1964] A.C. 612 at 639.
[74] Which was how the power was read by the House of Lords.

This seems to mean that, provided that the power in the original settlement is sufficiently wide, the advancement can properly be made into a new settlement which does confer dispositive powers on its trustees and, further, that the statutory power, or an express power with similar effect, will be construed as being sufficiently wide. Modern overriding powers of appointment generally expressly permit the conferring of dispositive powers on both trustees of new settlements and others.[75]

Secondly, where there is an advancement into settlement, the principle of *delegatus non potest delegare* is rarely observed in its entirety. It is clear that, even when the original settlement does not give its trustees any general right to confer dispositive powers on the trustees of a new settlement, powers of advancement can nevertheless be conferred and that those powers of advancement can be more extensive than those held by the trustees of the original settlement.[76] It has of course already been seen[77] that, while a power of advancement may conceptually be regarded as nothing more than a power to bring forward the date at which a beneficiary begins to enjoy the benefit of the trust property,[78] the exercise of such a power may well nevertheless alter the ultimate beneficial enjoyment of the funds advanced.   **18–034**

Thirdly, if in appropriate circumstances[79] there can be a valid advancement into a settlement under which the beneficiary whose interest is being advanced takes no interest whatever in the sum advanced, it would be quite absurd if there could not be a valid advance into a settlement under which he was a discretionary beneficiary.[80]   **18–035**

While it is therefore thought that there is no fundamental objection to a new settlement conferring dispositive powers on its trustees, it is nevertheless still necessary in any particular case to show that the creation of the new settlement is for the benefit of the beneficiary whose interest is being advanced.   **18–036**

5. *What Perpetuity Period Applies to the New Settlement?*

Where the trustees of an existing settlement make an advance into a new settlement, for the purposes of the rules against perpetuities the trustees are treated as if they had exercised a special power of appointment. Accordingly, the interests limited by the new settlement, when read back into the original settlement, must comply with the rule against perpetuities as it applied to the original settlement. It was on this ground that the House of   **18–037**

---

[75] See the overriding powers of appointment in the different precedents set out and discussed in J. Kessler, *Drafting Trusts and Will Trusts: A Modern Approach*, 8th edn (London, Sweet & Maxwell, 2006). (It is particularly important always to use the most recent edition of this work; the current one is the 8th (2007) edition).

[76] *Re Mewburn* [1934] Ch. 112; *Re Morris* [1951] 2 All E.R. 528; *Re Hunter's Will Trusts* [1963] Ch. 372.

[77] See *ante*, para 18–007.

[78] *Re Morris* [1951] 2 All E.R. 528; see *ante*, para 18–026.

[79] As in *Re Clore's Settlement Trust* [1966] 1 W.L.R. 955; see *ante*, para 18–015.

[80] Although the issues of benefit and delegation are separate, much greater tax mitigation may be achieved by using discretionary, rather than fixed, trusts.

Lords held that the proposed appointment in *Pilkington v. I.R.C.*[81] would have been void.

18–038   The Perpetuities and Accumulations Act 1964 will therefore only apply to the advancement if the original settlement itself was made after July 15, 1964[82]; this is why the pre-existing rules must even today still govern many advancements—powers of advancement can be exercised at any time until a beneficiary obtains an absolute vested interest in possession, which may not occur for well over 50 years. However, where the Perpetuities and Accumulations Act 1964 does apply, the interests under the new settlement will be treated as valid until, if at all, it becomes established that those interests will in fact vest outside the perpetuity period.[83] But under the proposed new legislation, all special powers, whenever created, will be permitted by the new 125-year fixed period measured from the date of the original creation of the power (this is one of only two provisions of that legislation which will affect gifts which have already come into effect).

18–039   If some of the interests purportedly created by the new settlement fall foul of the applicable rule against perpetuities, the validity of the advancement will depend on whether the provisions of the new settlement which are effective will, when taken by themselves, be for the benefit of the beneficiary whose interest is being advanced and will not have an effect totally different from what the trustees intended. This is shown by the decision in *Re Hastings-Bass (deceased)*,[84] where trustees transferred from an existing settlement the sum of £50,000 to be held upon the trusts of a new settlement by way of advancement for the primary benefit of one particular beneficiary, William. However, the trustees had misunderstood the effect of the new settlement, under which the life interest conferred on William was valid but all of the remaining beneficial interest were void for perpetuity.

18–040   The first question was whether an exercise of the statutory power of advancement could be valid when its effect was to give the beneficiary whose interest was being advanced, in this case William, only an interest in income and no interest in capital. The court held that this was a sufficient "application" of the funds and that the appointment was not necessarily defective on that ground.

18–041   The second question was of more general application. Was the purported exercise of the power effective when the trustees did not fully appreciate the effects of the new settlement and so could not take into account all the relevant circumstances? The court held that, where trustees purport to exercise a power in good faith, then, even if the effect of that purported exercise is different from that intended by the trustees, the court would only interfere with the purported exercise in two circumstances. First, the court would interfere if the result actually achieved was not authorised by the trustees' power. Secondly, the court would interfere if it was clear that the trustees would not have acted as they did had they not taken into account considerations which they ought not to have taken into account or if they

---

[81] [1964] A.C. 612; see *ante*, para 18–030.
[82] s.15(4) will apply to exclude the Act in the case of original settlements made before that date.
[83] s.3; see *ante*, para 7–020.
[84] [1975] Ch. 25.

had not failed to take into account considerations which they ought to have taken into account (there has since been considerable controversy both as to the correct formulation of this particular principle, which has become known as the Rule in *Re Hastings-Bass (deceased)*, and as to the circumstances which will bring that Rule into operation[85] but this is not relevant for present purposes). In this case, the effect of conferring an effective life interest on William was to achieve a substantial saving of estate duty.[86] It was likely, therefore, that the trustees would have acted broadly as they had even if they had appreciated the true effect of the advancement; consequently, the court held that the exercise of their power was valid. If, however, it had been held that the trustees would not have acted as they had if they had appreciated the true effect of the advancement, the purported exercise of their power would have been void.[87]

6. *Fiscal Considerations*

Just as a liability to capital gains tax may arise in the case of an ordinary advancement,[88] so it may arise in the case of an advance into settlement. The capital gains tax legislation treats most settlements as if they are each separate legal persons. Thus, if an asset is transferred from one settlement to another, that asset is deemed to have been disposed of by the trustees of the transferring settlement and to have been acquired by the trustees of the acquiring settlement. However, the capital gains tax legislation does not actually prescribe any rules for determining precisely what constitutes a separate settlement. Particular difficulties arise where the trustees of a settlement declare that they will themselves henceforth by way of advancement hold part of the trust fund on separate trusts for the benefit of one of the beneficiaries; when will that part of the trust fund become subject to a new settlement and when will it remain within the original settlement? In *Roome v. Edwards*[89] Lord Wilberforce said "Since 'settlement' and 'trusts' are legal terms, which are also used by businessmen or laymen in a business or practical sense, I think that the question whether a particular set of facts amounts to a settlement should be approached by asking what a person, with a knowledge of the legal context of the word under established doctrine and applying this knowledge in a practical and commonsense manner to the facts under examination, would conclude."   **18–042**

If the resettlement occurs only as the result of the exercise by the trustees of their powers under the original settlement, it seems that the exercise of a special power of appointment will not amount to a resettlement so that there will be no consequential deemed disposal of the property in question[90]; on the other hand, while the exercise of a wider power, such as a power of advancement, will not necessarily amount to a resettlement, it will have this effect if the new settlement is complete in itself and is sufficiently separate   **18–043**

---

85 See *ante*, para 6–087.
86 The inheritance tax rules are different; consequently no tax would be saved if the facts recurred at the present time.
87 *Re Abraham's Will Trust* [1969] 1 Ch. 463 but see now *ante*, para 6–100.
88 See *ante*, para 18–021.
89 [1981] 1 All E.R. 736 at 739.
90 *Roome v. Edwards* [1981] 1 All E.R. 736; *Bond v. Pickford* [1983] S.T.C. 517.

to require no further reference back for any purpose to the original settle-ment.[91] If there is such a resettlement, the trustees of the original settlement are deemed to dispose of all the assets which become subject to the new settlement at their market value at the time and the assets are then reac-quired at that value. However, if the acquiring settlement is resident in the United Kingdom, hold-over relief is available in the circumstances already discussed: if, first, the assets settled comprise business assets[92] or if, sec-ondly, the creation of the trust involves a chargeable transfer for the pur-poses of inheritance tax.[93]

18–044   There may also be a liability to inheritance tax if there was an interest in possession for the purposes of inheritance tax under the original settlement and the same beneficiary does not have an immediate interest in possession for the purposes of inheritance tax under the new settlement.[94] There will not usually be a liability if there was no interest in possession either under the original or the new settlement[95] but in other cases there usually will be.

IV. Other Applications of Capital

18–045   In some cases, the available powers of maintenance and advancement, whether they are the statutory powers or are contained in the trust instru-ment, will not be sufficient for a beneficiary's needs. Where this is the case, there are four other possibilities:

> (i) maintenance out of capital;
>
> (ii) an application to the court under section 53 of the Trustee Act 1925;
>
> (iii) an application to the court under its inherent jurisdiction; and
>
> (iv) an application to the court to vary the trust (this is considered in a later chapter[96]).

1. *Maintenance out of Capital*

18–046   Although, in principle, income is to be used for the maintenance of a beneficiary,[97] it is just about possible that the trustees can use capital for this purpose.

18–047   Section 31 of the Trustee Act 1925 clearly envisages that only income will be used for maintenance and it was said, in a note to the old case of *Barlow*

---

[91] *Swires v. Renton* [1991] S.T.C. 490.
[92] Taxation of Chargeable Gains Act 1992, s.165.
[93] See *ante*, para 15–137.
[94] Inheritance Tax Act 1984, ss.51, 52.
[95] *ibid.*, s.81; however, for tax purposes the property remains comprised in the first settle-ment.
[96] See *post*, para 21–018.
[97] See *ante*, para 17–014.

v. Grant,[98] that "the court will not permit executors and trustees to break in upon the capital of infants' legacies without the sanction of the court, and the court itself, though it will break in upon the capital for the purpose of advancement, will rarely do so for maintenance". But, no matter how rarely a court will exercise its power to use capital for an infant's maintenance, it undoubtedly does have such a power. Lord Alvanley L.C. said in *Lee v. Brown*[99] that "[t]he principle is now established that if an executor does without application what the court would have approved, he shall not be called to account, and forced to undo that merely because it was done without application". The precise extent of this dictum (the case actually concerned an advancement) is not entirely clear but it is just about possible that a trustee who had maintained out of capital would not be called upon to make good the capital if the court would itself have ordered maintenance out of capital.

However, quite apart from the doubtful legality of such a course of conduct, there would today be fiscal disadvantages in following it; in respect of every £1 taken out of capital for this purpose, the trustees would today have to deduct income tax at the basic rate and pay it over to H.M. Revenue & Customs.[100] In contrast, no income tax is payable where an advancement of capital is made; thus, by making an advancement, the result of a purported maintenance out of capital can be achieved much more advantageously.

18–048

2. *Section 53 of the Trustee Act 1925*

This section provides that, where a minor is beneficially entitled to any property, the court may, "with a view to the application of the capital or income thereof for the maintenance, education, or benefit of the" minor, make an order appointing a person to convey the minor's interest on his behalf. This section is chiefly used where the minor's interest is small and produces very little income and where, if the interest were sold, the proceeds could be used for the minor's maintenance or benefit.[101] It was, however, pointed out in *Re Meux*[102] that this section does not give the court power to dispose of the minor's interest whenever it is merely for the minor's benefit; there must be "a view to the application" of the capital or income for the maintenance, education or benefit of the minor. It therefore seems that it must be intended to apply the capital or income in some way for the benefit of the minor. In *Re Heyworth's Contingent Reversionary Interest*[103] the court refused to give its consent under section 53 to a proposal merely to sell the minor's interest and hand over a cash sum without there being any clear idea as to what was to happen to that money thereafter. On the other hand, where what is proposed is to resettle the money and the transaction as a whole is for the minor's benefit, the court has held that the

18–049

---

[98] (1684) 1 Vern. 255.
[99] (1798) 4 Ves. 362.
[100] See *ante*, para 15–023.
[101] *Ex parte Green* (1820) 1 Jac. & W. 253; *Ex parte Chambers* (1829) 1 Russ. & M. 577; *Ex parte Swift* (1828) 1 Russ. & M. 575.
[102] [1958] Ch. 154.
[103] [1956] Ch. 364.

fact that there was to be a resettlement was a sufficient "application" to come within this section.[104]

18–050   An example of the use of this power can be seen in *Re Bristol's Settled Estates*.[105] There were two tenants in fee tail of settled land, the Marquess of Bath and his infant son, Lord Jermyn. The estate was a large one and in order to save estate duty it was, in essence, proposed that the existing settlement should be terminated, part of the property paid absolutely to the Marquess of Bath, and the remaining part resettled. Provided the Marquess lived for a period of five years (and an insurance policy was to be taken out to cover the possibility of him failing to do so), both he and the ultimate beneficiaries would gain by the arrangement, the only loser being the Inland Revenue. Before the scheme could be put into operation, it was necessary for the estates in fee tail to be "barred" by being converted into estates in fee simple. The Marquess of Bath was entitled to carry out this process in respect of his own estate in fee tail and, had Lord Jermyn not been a minor, he could have done the same with the consent of his father, who was (in the original sense of the expression) the protector of the settlement.[106] The court made an order under section 53 appointing a named person to execute with the consent of the Marquess of Bath an assurance on behalf of Lord Jermyn "barring" his estate in fee tail; that way the capital and income could, under the proposed scheme, be appointed for his benefit.[107]

18–051   Schemes for raising money for the education of a minor, or to provide him with a house, or to purchase a share in a partnership for him clearly also fall within the terms of section 53 of the Trustee Act 1925.[108]

3. *The Inherent Jurisdiction of the Court*

18–052   In limited circumstances the court has an inherent jurisdiction (quite apart from the Variation of Trusts Act 1958[109]) to modify the terms of the trust. One of the occasions in which it will do so is where a settlor or testator has made some provision for a family but has postponed the enjoyment, for example, by directing accumulation of the income for a set period. Where this has been done, the trustees cannot themselves use the income to maintain a minor but the court will assume from the fact that the settlor has made provision for the family that he did not intend to leave the minor children inadequately provided for. The court has, therefore, in some cases directed that the income (or some part of it) is not to be accumulated but is instead to be used for the maintenance of the minor.[110]

---

[104] *Re Meux* [1958] Ch. 154.

[105] [1965] 1 W.L.R. 469.

[106] For the original and the modern sense of this expression, see *ante*, para 6–032.

[107] See also *Re Lansdowne's Will Trusts* [1967] Ch. 603.

[108] *Re Baron Vestey's Settlement* [1951] Ch. 209.

[109] See *post*, para 21–018, as to the circumstances in which the court may vary beneficial interests in this and other cases.

[110] *Havelock v. Havelock* (1881) 17 Ch.D. 807; *Re Collins* (1886) 32 Ch.D. 229; *Revel v. Watkinson* (1748) 1 Ves. Sen. 93; *Re Walker* [1901] 1 Ch. 879; *Greenwell v. Greenwell* (1800) 5 Ves. 194; *Cavendish v. Mercer* (1776) 5 Ves. 195; *Errat v. Barlow* (1807) 14 Ves. 202.

V. APPROPRIATION

Appropriation occurs when trustees effectively set aside part of the trust **18–053**
property and earmark it for a specific purpose. For the purposes of trust law
generally, the effect of appropriation is that beneficiaries who have an
interest in the appropriated fund have no rights in respect of the non-
appropriated property and the beneficiaries of the non-appropriated property have no rights in respect of the appropriated fund. The position is,
generally speaking, as follows:

(1) Trustees do not have any general power to appropriate.

(2) The trust instrument may direct appropriation or confer on the
trustees a power to appropriate.

(3) If the trust instrument directs that different property to be held on
different trusts, that will be treated as an implied direction to appropriate.[111] If, therefore, the trust instrument directs one quarter of the
trust property to be held on trust for Pinky for life, with remainder
to her issue, and the other three quarters to be held on trust for
Perky for life with remainder to her issue, then separate funds
should be appropriated.

(4) It seems that, if property is held on express trust for sale, the trustees
have an implied power to appropriate unless there is a direction to
the contrary in the trust instrument.[112]

(5) A mere power to appropriate, whether express or implied, will
require the consent of any adult beneficiaries affected, although not
of minor or unborn beneficiaries. However, the power may go
beyond one merely to appropriate, in which case it will be a power
to appropriate without any consent being required. In any event,
consents are not required where the trust instrument directs
appropriation.

(6) Personal representatives are given a statutory power of appropriation,[113] but this does not apply to trustees. Because the exercise of
the power can potentially require the consent of beneficiaries of the
estate, the normal practice is to modify it by removing the requirement for consent.

---

[111] *Fraser v. Murdoch* (1881) 6 App. Cas. 855; *Re Walker* (1890) 62 L.T. 449; *Re Nicholson* [1939]
3 All E.R. 832.
[112] *Re Nickels* [1898] 1 Ch. 630; *Re Brooks* (1897) 76 L.T. 771.
[113] By Administration of Estates Act 1925, s.41.

CHAPTER 19

THE POSITION OF A BENEFICIARY UNDER A TRUST

19–001   In general terms, as long as a trust is being properly administered and is continuing, a beneficiary has no right to interfere in its administration but has passively to wait to receive the benefits to which he is entitled under the trust. If, however, the trust is not being properly administered, the beneficiary can take steps to compel its proper administration, and in any case may take certain action to preserve his position. Ultimately, however, the destiny of the trust may well lie in the beneficiary's own hands since, if various conditions are fulfilled, he can bring the trust to an end even if this appears contrary to the wording of the trust instrument.

I. The Beneficiary's Right to Information

19–002   A beneficiary will obviously not be able to do anything unless he actually knows that he is a beneficiary in the first place. It has already been seen[1] that, while executors are under no duty to inform the beneficiaries of a will of their rights under that will,[2] trustees of both testamentary and *inter vivos* fixed trusts who have agreed to act are under a duty to inform the beneficiaries of the existence and nature of their interests under the trust.[3] The same principle presumably applies to discretionary trusts in favour of relatively small groups of beneficiaries. However, it is clearly impracticable to oblige or to expect trustees of the many modern discretionary trusts which have enormous classes of beneficiaries to notify every single potential member of his potential rights thereunder[4]; the most that they could conceivably be expected to do would be to advertise for potential beneficiaries to present themselves. But it cannot seriously be doubted that the need to compel the proper administration of trusts dictates that trustees should be obliged to give a truthful answer to any potential beneficiary who actually enquiries. Where a beneficiary knows that he is a beneficiary or a potential beneficiary of a discretionary trust but does not know the identity of the current

---

[1] See *ante*, para 14–026.
[2] *Re Lewis* (1868) 5 L.R. Eq. 545. This was a particularly strong case since the executor was entitled to the subject matter of a legacy in the event that the beneficiary in question failed to claim it and the failure to inform the latter of the existence of the legacy meant that he failed to do so prior to his death.
[3] *Hawkesley v. May* [1956] 1 Q.B. 304.
[4] See Davies (1995) 7 Bond Law Review 5, referring to the remarks of Mahoney J.A. in *Hartigan Nominees v. Rydge* (1992) 29 N.S.W.L.R. 405 at 425 & 432 (Court of Appeal of New South Wales).

trustees, he is able to oblige the settlor to disclose this information to him[5]; however, this right does not extend to trusts of which he merely suspects that he is a beneficiary or potential beneficiary.

When a beneficiary is or has become aware that he is a beneficiary or potential beneficiary, it has also already been seen[6] that there has until recently never been any doubt about the right of beneficiaries of both fixed trusts and small discretionary trusts to require information as to the state of the trust property and to any dealings with it and sight of the corresponding trust documents; nor was any distinction drawn between beneficiaries with interests in possession and those whose interests had either not yet vested or had not yet vested in possession.[7] Doubts had, however, been expressed both as to whether the right was or should be available to every single potential member of the enormous classes of beneficiaries which many modern discretionary trusts now have[8] and as to the position of persons who are not among the actual beneficiaries of a discretionary trust but are merely among the possible objects of a power of appointment. However, according to the Privy Council in *Schmidt v. Rosewood Trust*,[9] these distinctions no longer have any formal significance; the right to require information is instead now to be approached as merely one aspect of the court's inherent jurisdiction to supervise (and where appropriate intervene in) the administration of trusts. In practice, however, these distinctions will obviously remain highly relevant in the court's exercise of that inherent jurisdiction. The immediate beneficiaries of fixed trusts and of small discretionary trusts are bound in practice to be given exactly the same trust documents as hitherto. But disclosure to the beneficiaries of large discretionary trusts and potential beneficiaries of all types of trusts is likely to be restricted to those who in practical terms have a reasonable chance of receiving some part of the trust property at some point. This means that the rights of default beneficiaries, the ultimate beneficiaries of discretionary trusts who, although they are necessarily beneficiaries of fixed trusts, are only likely to take in the event of the death of all the other beneficiaries, may well now in practice be considerably restricted. **19–003**

II. THE CONTROL OF TRUSTEES' DISCRETIONS

Two fundamental principles govern the control of trustees by beneficiaries. First, so long as the trust continues, decisions which have to be made in the administration of the trust are to be made by the trustees alone. Secondly, all the beneficiaries under the trust, if they are *sui juris* and between them absolutely entitled to the trust property, may bring the trust to an end.[10] **19–004**

The court is jealous to preserve the trustees' powers, largely because the main function of trustees is to control the trust as a whole and the right to **19–005**

---

[5] *Murphy v. Murphy* [1999] 1 W.L.R. 282.
[6] See *ante*, para 14–032.
[7] *Re Londonderry's Settlement* [1965] Ch. 918.
[8] *Hartigan Nominees v. Rydge* (1992) 29 N.S.W.L.R. 405 (Court of Appeal of New South Wales).
[9] [2003] UKPC 26, [2003] 2 A.C. 709.
[10] See *post*, para 19–019.

exercise all the decisions necessary goes to the root of trusteeship. Thus, even where it has power to do so under the Variation of Trusts Act 1958, the court will not approve an arrangement which could override the discretionary powers which the trustees intend to exercise.[11] The leading case is *Re Brockbank*,[12] although the actual decision in that case has been abrogated by statute. It was seen in an earlier chapter[13] that, where the trust instrument does not expressly confer the power to appoint new trustees on anyone, then the existing trustee or trustees are given that power by section 36 of the Trustee Act 1925. In *Re Brockbank*, the beneficiaries, who were all *sui juris* and were between them absolutely entitled to the whole of the beneficial interest under the trust, wished to appoint a new trustee against the wishes of the existing trustee. It was held that the appointment of new trustees was a power given to the existing trustees and that this power could not be exercised by the beneficiaries. This principle survives in relation to powers in general; however, where section 19 of the Trusts of Land and Appointment of Trustees Act 1996 applies to the trust in question (which it will do unless it has been excluded by the settlor[14]), beneficiaries who are *sui juris* and between them absolutely entitled to the whole of the beneficial interest under the trust are now entitled to require the trustees to retire and to appoint the new trustees nominated by the beneficiaries.

19–006　　It has also been suggested,[15] probably correctly, that, while the beneficiaries cannot generally speaking cut down the trustees' powers, they can add to them. It must be stressed that this right, if it exists, is only to add to the powers of trustees, not to their duties; their existing discretions are, therefore, preserved intact but are enlarged.

19–007　　The main areas in which beneficiaries are likely to seek to control the trustees' discretions are with regard to investments and in respect of the exercise of their discretions under discretionary trusts. In both respects the trustees' position is essentially the same. They must take note of any representations made to them, for these representations may properly affect the exercise of their discretion. Thus, if one of the beneficiaries passes to the trustees confidential information that shares in a particular company are likely to improve rapidly, the trustees must give full consideration to that information in reaching their decision as to whether or not to buy. But the decision must be theirs, for they are the persons who can best judge the interests of all the beneficiaries and it will be them, not the beneficiary in question, who will be ultimately answerable for the decision reached.

19–008　　To the general rule that the trustees should listen, but must alone make the decisions, there are certain exceptions.

19–009　　(1) The trustees' discretions may be limited by contract; thus, where a person acts as nominee for another, the terms of the arrangement between them may require the trustee-nominee to act in accordance with the directions of the beneficiary.

---

[11] *Re Steed's Will Trusts* [1960] Ch. 407, also discussed *post*, para 21–028.
[12] [1948] Ch. 206.
[13] See *ante*, para 13–033.
[14] It is usually so excluded.
[15] Underhill & Hayton, *Law of Trusts and Trustees*, 17th edn (London, LexisNexis Butterworths, 2006), p.908.

(2) The trustees' discretions may be limited by the terms of the trust   **19–010**
instrument itself; the usual form of this limitation is to require the
consent of a beneficiary or other person to the sale of a particular
asset but there is no reason in principle why their discretions should
not be restricted in some other way.

(3) In the case of trusts of land, the trustees' discretions are, unusually,   **19–011**
restricted by statute, the Trusts of Land and Appointment of Trus-
tees Act 1996. This provides that, subject to any contrary provision
in the trust instrument,[16] trustees of land are under an obligation,
when exercising any of their functions relating to land which is
subject to the trust,[17] to consult, so far as is practicable, the beneficiaries of full age entitled to interests in possession in the land.[18]
The trustees must, so far as is consistent with the general interests of
the trust, give effect to the wishes of those beneficiaries or, in the
event that they are not all in agreement, to the wishes of the majority
by value.[19]

Obligations of this type were first introduced by the Law of
Property Act 1925[20] but only in the context of the statutory trusts for
sale implied by that statute in the case of co-ownership, a situation
in which the trustees will also normally be the beneficiaries anyway,
unless there are more than four beneficiaries[21]; consequently, this
was more a matter for land law than for the law of trusts.[22] But the
Trusts of Land and Appointment of Trustees Act 1996 modified the
obligation to consult in respect of the trusts implied in the case of
co-ownership and, more significantly for present purposes,
extended it to all trustees of land; however, the obligation is of
course limited to the exercise of functions relating to land and so
does not apply to any pure personalty which the trustees of land are
also holding on trust. Further, even when the obligation to consult
arises, the trustees are not actually obliged to follow the wishes of
the beneficiaries, nor need a purchaser be concerned to see that the
trustees have complied with the obligation.[23]

(4) There is also a further exception of somewhat uncertain extent,   **19–012**
which arises from the decision of the Court of Appeal in *Butt v.
Kelson*.[24] The trustees of a trust held a large proportion of the shares
in a private limited company, of which they were also directors by

---

[16] Trusts of Land and Appointment of Trustees Act 1996, s.11(2)(a).

[17] Other than their right to compel absolutely entitled beneficiaries to take a conveyance of
the legal title; *ibid.*, s.11(2)(c).

[18] Other than persons who are merely annuitants; *ibid.*, s.22(3).

[19] *ibid.*, s.11(1).

[20] Law of Property Act 1925, s.26(3) (now repealed).

[21] In which case only four of them will be able to be trustees; see Trustee Act 1925, s.34, *ante*
para 13–049.

[22] There was no such obligation in the case of express trusts for sale of land and, in the case
of settlements under the Settled Land Act 1925, the functions in question were vested in the
beneficiary of full age entitled to the interest in possession for the time being anyway.

[23] Trusts of Land and Appointment of Trustees Act, s.16(1); this was also the case under Law
of Property Act 1925, s.26.

[24] [1952] Ch. 197.

virtue of their trust shareholding. The question arose as to how far the beneficiaries could control the votes of the trustees both as directors and as shareholders. It was held that the trustees' votes as directors could not be controlled by the beneficiaries, while their votes as shareholders could be controlled.

The apparent inconsistency of this curious result may be explained by the fact that under company law directors have duties to all the shareholders, not only to those shareholders, if any, whom they represent; it would therefore have been inconsistent with this obligation if the trustees had been compelled to vote as directors solely in accordance with the wishes of the beneficiaries. On the other hand, their votes as shareholders were not subject to this conflict of duty. That does not alter the fact that at first sight it seems that the manner in which the voting power was to be exercised should have been a matter for the trustees' discretion, exercisable by them free from any interference by the beneficiaries. *Butt v. Kelson* was on this ground criticised by Upjohn J. in *Re Whichelow*[25] as being inconsistent with the principle laid down in *Re Brockbank*. It is, however, possible to regard a right to vote in a company as a property right and for special considerations to apply to such votes. Nevertheless, *Butt v. Kelson* is probably incorrect in so far as it allows beneficiaries to control the votes of trustee-shareholders and should not be extended.

III. The Right to Compel Due Administration

19–013 Whether or not a beneficiary suspects that there has been any improper conduct on the part of the trustees, he may nevertheless insist that the accounts of the trust are audited by any solicitor or accountant who is acceptable to the trustees. If agreement cannot be reached as to the identity of the auditor, the audit is carried out by the Public Trustee. Unless special circumstances exist, the audit cannot be carried out more than once in every three years; a beneficiary who does require more frequent audits will therefore be ordered personally to pay the costs.[26] Although this is not particularly relevant for present purposes, the position is exactly the same where the trustee requires an audit to be carried out.

19–014 Where the beneficiary thinks that the trust is not being properly administered, where there is some point of doubt relating to the administration of the trust, and in certain other circumstances, he may have recourse to the court. There are two possibilities: first, by issuing an application to the court for the determination of a specific question or questions (such applications used to be made by way of originating summons but, since the introduction of the Civil Procedure Rules 1998, they are instead made by application under Part 23 of those Rules); and, secondly, by issuing proceedings for the general administration of the trust. It is preferable that the former method is

---

[25] [1954] 1 W.L.R. 5.
[26] Trustee Act 1925, s.22(4); Public Trustee Act 1906, s.13(5).

used whenever possible, because it is cheaper, quicker and simpler than the latter method.

The following are examples of the circumstances in which it may be appropriate for the beneficiaries to apply to the court (the circumstances in which it may be appropriate for the trustees to apply to the court, some of which are comparable and some of which are quite distinct, have already been considered[27]): **19–015**

   (i) The court may be asked to approve a specific transaction for which permission is not given by the general law or by the trust instrument but which is thought to be in the interests of the beneficiaries as a whole[28] (in most cases, of course, this type of application will be made by the trustees).

   (ii) The court may be asked to direct the trustees to do a particular act which they ought to do or to refrain from doing a particular act which they ought not to do. The act referred to must be one which the trustees are under a definite obligation to do or not to do; it is not appropriate for a beneficiary to question by this means an act in respect of which the trustees have a discretion.[29]

   (iii) The court may be asked to direct the payment of money in the hands of the trustees into court.[30]

   (iv) The court may be asked to construe the provisions of the trust instrument or to ascertain the class(es) of beneficiaries (again, in most cases this type of application will be made by the trustees[31]).

   (v) The court may be asked to determine any other specific question which arises in the course of the administration of a trust.

It is not generally appropriate for the beneficiaries to make an application to the court in this way where its subject-matter will involve third parties or in any action against trustees for breach of trust where the facts are in dispute.

It will be seen that almost all the specific questions which arise in the administration of a trust can be dealt with by issuing an application to the court in this manner. Consequently, the alternative of issuing proceedings for the general administration of a trust, which is intended to lead to the court itself becoming responsible for the entire administration of the trust, is usually only necessary in three situations: first, where there have been constant disputes between the trustees; secondly, where the circumstances of the trust give rise to recurring difficulties which would require frequent **19–016**

---

[27] See *ante*, para 14–121.

[28] See *Phipps v. Boardman* [1967] 2 A.C. 46 (which was, at least in the opinion of the court, an example of the circumstances where an application should have been made); see *ante*, para 14–142.

[29] *Syffolk v. Lawrence* (1884) 32 W.R. 899.

[30] As to the circumstances in which money is payable into court, see Trustee Act. 1925, s.63.

[31] See *ante*, para 14–122.

single applications to the court; and, thirdly, where clear prima facie doubts exist as to the bona fides of the trustees.

IV. THE RIGHT TO ENFORCE CLAIMS

19–017   As part of his right to compel the due administration of the trust, a beneficiary can apply to the court if the trustees fail to take any action necessary to preserve the trust property.[32] A cause of action against a third party can itself be an item of trust property and the court may either direct the trustees to enforce that claim or allow the beneficiary to sue the third party directly for the benefit of the trust, where necessary using the name of the trustees.[33] Alternatively, a beneficiary can sue the trustees, making those who are alleged to be under obligations to the trust co-defendants.

19–018   In *Wills v. Cooke*[34] the trust property included a farm which was subject to a tenancy. The trustees had retained solicitors to advise them with regard to the administration of the trust but, it was alleged, the solicitors had failed to advise the trustees to take action to increase the rent in accordance with the Agricultural Holdings Act 1948. One of the beneficiaries sued the solicitors directly, claiming that the trustees had a right of action against them and that that right was an item of trust property. On what is now known as an interim application, Slade J. held that that right might be an item of trust property and that the statement of claim should not be struck out. He also said, however, that the right would not have been an item of trust property if the trustees had entered into the contract with the solicitors solely for their own protection and benefit.

V. THE RIGHT TO TERMINATE A TRUST

19–019   If there is only one beneficiary under a trust who is *sui juris*, or if there are two or more beneficiaries and they are all *sui juris* and all in agreement, he or they can bring the trust to an end irrespective of the wishes of the trustees or of the creator of the trust. This is what is known as the Rule in *Saunders v. Vautier*[35] and has two underlying bases.

(1) Equity regards the role of the trustees as primarily that of holding the balance between various beneficiaries with conflicting interests; where all the beneficiaries are of the same mind, the basic reason for the trustees' existence has therefore disappeared. If, on the other hand, the beneficiaries still want the trust to continue, it has already been seen that they cannot generally speaking control the trustees'

---

[32] *Fletcher v. Fletcher* (1844) 4 Hare 67.
[33] As in *Foley v. Burnell* (1783) 1 Bro. C.C. 274, a case of trespass to trust land.
[34] (1979) Law Soc. Gaz., July 11, 1979.
[35] (1841) Cr. & Ph. 240. See also *Josselyn v. Josselyn* (1837) 9 Sim. 63; *Gosling v. Gosling* (1859) Johns. 265; *Wharton v. Masterman* [1895] A.C. 186; *Re Johnston* [1894] 3 Ch. 204; *Re Smith* [1928] Ch. 915; *Re Lord Nunburnholme* [1911] 2 Ch. 510; *Berry v. Green* [1938] A.C. 575.

discretions; either the trust must be terminated or the trustees must be allowed to carry on with their task.

(2) Secondly, a voluntary trust is in equity the equivalent of a gift at common law[36] so that, as a general principle, once a trust has been created, the settlor has no longer any control over it; after all, if he had made instead an outright gift of property to the beneficiaries, he would thereafter have had no control over what his donees subsequently did with that property. Thus, if all the beneficiaries are *sui juris* and between them entitled to the whole of the beneficial interest in the trust property, the settlor's provisions as expressed in the trust instrument will not prevent those beneficiaries from bringing the trust to an end.

In *Saunders v. Vautier* itself, a trustee held a sum of money upon trust to accumulate the income until a specified date, and then to pay it to the nominated beneficiary. The beneficiary reached the age of 21, then the age of majority, and so became *sui juris*, before the date specified for payment to him. He successfully claimed that the capital and accumulated income to date should be paid over to him immediately. However, if the trust instrument had instead provided that the beneficiary would not obtain a vested interest unless and until he survived to the specified date, then he would not have been able to invoke the Rule without the concurrence of the person entitled in default of his attaining that age.[37] Similarly, in *Tod v. Barton*[38] property had been left to charity subject to the payment of an annuity of £20,000 a year to the testator's son from the age of 65 (he was about 50 at the time of the testator's death). The charity and the son agreed that the son should receive an immediate payment of £164,000 rather than the annuity and, despite a challenge by the testator's widow,[39] this agreement was upheld under the Rule in *Saunders v. Vautier*.

19–020

However, the Rule only applies if the beneficiary is entitled to wind-up the trust and to require the trustee to assign to him the subject matter of the trust. In *Don King Productions Inc. v. Warren*,[40] the subject matter of the trust was a non-assignable contract, under whose provisions the trustee had outstanding obligations to perform. Lightman J. held that, where the trustee has outstanding obligations under a contract which is held as a trustee and has no power to transfer the trust asset to the beneficiary or to his order, the trust cannot be determined and the Rule does not apply. It seems tolerably clear that the absence of any power to transfer the trust asset to the beneficiary would be sufficient on its own to prevent the Rule applying but it is doubtful whether the existence of outstanding obligations of the trustee would alone be sufficient if the beneficiary was able and willing to waive

19–021

---

[36] *Re Bowden* [1936] Ch. 71.
[37] *Gosling v. Gosling* (1859) Johns. 265; *Re Lord Nunburnholme* [1912] 1 Ch. 489.
[38] (2002) 4 I.T.E.L.R. 715.
[39] The challenge was made on the grounds that the testator's will was not, as it expressly provided, subject to English law but subject to the law of the jurisdiction where he had died domiciled, Texas, where beneficiaries can only terminate a trust once all its purposes have been fulfilled or become illegal or impossible to fulfil (*Lanius v. Fletcher* (1907) 101 S.W. 1076, *Frost National Bank v. Newton* (1977) 554 S.W. 2d 149). This challenge is considered *post*, para 23–047.
[40] [2000] Ch. 291 at 321 (Lightman J.); the point did not arise in the Court of Appeal, *ibid*.

them. In any event, this qualification of the Rule is clearly limited to trusts whose subject matter is the benefit of a contract.

19–022   The Rule can also be utilised in a number of further situations.

(1) The beneficiaries of a trust can break it before they have all fulfilled a contingency provided that they are all *sui juris*. If property is held on trust for such of two beneficiaries as attain the age of 25, then the two of them can agree to bring about the termination of the trust as soon as one has attained the age of 25 and the other has attained the age of 18; this is because, even if the younger beneficiary dies without attaining the age of 25, his potential share will then go to the older beneficiary and so between them they are the only persons who can conceivably ever become entitled to the trust property.

(2) Beneficiaries who are entitled by way of succession can also break the trust. If property is held on trust for Andrew for life, remainder to Brian for life, remainder to Charles absolutely, the three of them can bring the trust to an end if they are all alive and *sui juris* and they all join in.

(3) The beneficiaries of a discretionary trust can also break that trust in certain circumstances. If property is held on trust for such of David, Edward and Francis as the trustees in their absolute discretion decide, none of the three has any actual right to anything. Nevertheless, if there is no gift over in the event that the trustees fail to exercise their discretion, then the three of them can still bring the trust to an end if they are all alive and *sui juris* and they all join in. However, today the vast majority of discretionary trusts are subject to overriding powers of appointment and as a result have default beneficiaries, whose existence is sufficient to prevent the Rule being applied.

19–023   Whenever a trust is brought to an end under the Rule in *Saunders v. Vautier*, the beneficiaries can compel the trustees to convey the property to whoever they direct[41] and, if the trustees refuse, they will personally have to pay the cost of the beneficiaries' application to the court for a direction to this effect. This of course means that the beneficiaries can bring the trust to an end and compel the trustees to transfer the property to their own chosen trustees on the same trusts. This enables the beneficiaries to overcome the actual decision in *Re Brockbank*[42]; however, as has already been seen,[43] use of the Rule in *Saunders v. Vautier* for this purpose will now only be necessary if the settlor has excluded section 19 of the Trusts of Land and Appointment of Trustees Act 1996.

19–024   It should also be noted that, if a beneficial interest under a trust is sold, the purchaser stands in the same position as the vendor and, if the vendor could have brought the trust to an end, the purchaser will be able to do so if he is *sui juris*. But if the beneficial interest is question is merely mortgaged, the

---

[41] *Re Marshall* [1914] 1 Ch. 192; *Re Sandeman's Will Trusts* [1937] 1 All E.R. 368.
[42] [1948] Ch. 206; see *ante*, para 19–005.
[43] See *ante*, para 19–005.

mortgagee cannot bring the trust to an end for so long as the beneficiary still has a right under the mortgage to have his beneficial interest redeemed upon payment of the amount secured.[44]

However, exercising the Rule in *Saunders v. Vautier* and bringing a trust to an end may have negative consequences of a fiscal nature; this is because there will often be a liability both to capital gains tax and to inheritance tax on the termination of a trust.

19–025

If a trust is terminated and the trustees sell the investments comprising the trust fund, they will be liable to capital gains tax on any increase in value which has accrued while the investments have been subject to the trust. If they instead distribute the assets *in specie*, the beneficiaries will become absolutely entitled to the assets as against the trustees,[45] and in principle a liability to capital gains tax will again arise as if the trustees had disposed of the assets on the open market for their full value at the time when the beneficiaries became entitled.[46] However, if the beneficiaries are resident in the United Kingdom, they can claim holdover relief if the assets in question comprise business assets[47] or if the vesting of the property in the beneficiaries involves a chargeable transfer for the purposes of inheritance tax. When this relief is available, the beneficiaries are treated for capital gains tax purposes[48] as acquiring the assets at their base cost to the trustees. By claiming this relief, the liability for the tax is deferred until the beneficiaries actually dispose of the assets themselves.

19–026

The position with regard to inheritance tax is more complicated in one situation, namely where there are successive interests and the beneficiary in possession has an interest in possession for the purposes of inheritance tax. Since March 22, 2006 this has only been possible where that beneficiary has an immediate post-death interest, that is to say where an interest in possession under a trust has taken immediate effect as the result of a death.[49]

19–027

Suppose that a will has had the immediate effect of creating a trust whereby a fund of £100,000 is held on trust for Elizabeth for life and, subject to that, for Angela absolutely and it is agreed to bring the trust to an end by paying £40,000 to Elizabeth and £60,000 to Angela. It has already been seen[50] that, where a beneficiary has an interest in possession in settled property for the purposes of inheritance tax, he is treated for inheritance tax purposes as if he is beneficially entitled to the settled property itself.[51] Accordingly, immediately before the termination Elizabeth would be treated for inheritance tax purposes as being beneficially entitled to £100,000, whereas after the termination she would only be entitled to the actual sum of £40,000 paid to her. The making of these payments will, therefore, cause Elizabeth to make a potentially exempt transfer of £60,000, which will be potentially

---

[44] This is the conclusion derived from *Re Bell* [1896] 1 Ch. 1.

[45] This concept was considered *ante*, para 15–136.

[46] Taxation of Chargeable Gains Act, s.71(1).

[47] *ibid.*, s.165.

[48] See *ante*, para 15–137.

[49] The only other interest in possession for the purposes of inheritance tax which can now exist is an interest under a trust for a disabled person and there cannot be successive interests under such a trust.

[50] See *ante*, para 15–087.

[51] Inheritance Tax Act 1984, s.49.

subject to inheritance tax if she fails to survive for a further seven years.[52] In contrast, Angela has given up a reversionary interest in a fund of £100,000 in order to obtain an immediate outright payment of £60,000. However, there will be no liability to inheritance tax on her because in normal circumstances[53] no inheritance tax is payable where a person disposes of a reversionary interest.[54]

In every other situation where successive interests arise, there will not now be an interest in possession for the purposes of inheritance tax. Consequently, the beneficiary with the interest in possession in the settled property is not treated as if he is beneficially entitled to the settled property itself and so, on the same facts, will not be treated as having made a potentially exempt transfer.

---

[52] In the event that she fails to do so, the tax payable will be calculated by reference to her own lifetime transfers, not to those made by the settlement.

[53] The rule under discussion does not apply where the person disposing of the reversionary interest acquired it for value, or was himself the settlor: Inheritance Tax Act 1984, s.48(1).

[54] *ibid.*, ss.47, 48(1).

CHAPTER 20

TRUSTEES' REMUNERATION AND BENEFITS

Until the enactment of the Trustee Act 2000, the basic principle was that the **20–001** office of trustee was gratuitous, that is to say that its duties had to be performed by the trustee without remuneration or profit. The development of this rule was due in part to the fact that trustees were often members of the family and persons of substance, who were prepared to act as trustees as part of the general obligations of kinship. In more recent years, however, it has become recognised that the management of money and assets is an activity which requires skill, aptitude, and often considerable technical support. Accordingly, it became, and still is, very common for trustees to be either professional advisers, such as solicitors and accountants, who act as part of their ordinary professional practice, or banks and similar trust companies; such trustees are generally prepared to act only if given adequate recompense. This caused no difficulty when such persons were to be the original trustees of an *inter vivos* trust, since an appropriate charging clause could be inserted in the trust deed. However, very real difficulties arose if a will trust or an *inter vivos* trust did not contain an appropriate provision since this would generally preclude such persons from acting either as trustees of the will trust or as replacement trustees of the *inter vivos* trust.

The answer provided by the Trustee Act 2000[1] is to permit trust corpora- **20–002** tions and trustees other than sole trustees or charitable trustees who are "acting in a professional capacity" to receive "reasonable remuneration". The legislation also provides that such trustees can charge "reasonable remuneration" or charge the remuneration to which they are entitled under an express charging clause despite the fact that the services which they are providing "are capable of being provided by a lay trustee". Where the appointment of professional trustees is envisaged when the trust instrument is being drawn up, express charging clauses will undoubtedly continue to be utilised in order to avoid any difficulties about the definitions of "acting in a professional capacity" and "reasonable remuneration". However, the legislation has resolved the difficulties which formerly arose when there was no such charging clause. But the basic principle that the office of trustee is gratuitous continues to apply to trustees who are neither trust corporations nor "acting in a professional capacity".

---

[1] Trustee Act 2000, ss.28, 29.

20–003   Whatever the position regarding remuneration, however, a trustee is always entitled to reimburse himself for his expenses. This right has already been considered.[2]

I. Modern Commercial Remuneration Terms

20–004   Throughout this chapter, it will be helpful to keep in mind what types of remuneration a professional trustee or a commercial trust company may wish to obtain. The main items are as follows:

(i) fees for acting as a trustee, including the actual day to day administration of the trust;

(ii) fees for acting as a director where the trust property includes shares in a company and the trustees act as directors of that company;

(iii) commissions customarily paid by third parties in respect of business transacted on behalf of the trust (insurance companies and brokers both habitually pay commission to those who place business with them); and

(iv) profits made by the trustee from services performed for the trust as its customer (a banker trustee will wish to retain for itself its ordinary commercial profit derived from acting as banker).

The remainder of this chapter considers the extent to which a trustee can achieve these objectives.

II. Express Charging Clauses

1. The Nature and Effect of Charging Clauses

20–005   The settlor of any trust can authorise the trustees to be paid for their services and this is in practice what is invariably done when a trust corporation or a professional person is appointed as the original trustee of an *inter vivos* trust. Such express charging clauses are generally also inserted in *inter vivos* trusts even where the original trustees are not to be professional trustees and are included in virtually all professionally drawn wills because in such circumstances it is obviously less clear when the will is drawn up whether or not professional trustees will prove to be necessary. Express charging clauses have traditionally been construed strictly as against the trustee and this general practice will undoubtedly continue. However, the Trustee Act 2000 has now provided that trust corporations and trustees who are "acting in a professional capacity" are, in the absence of any contrary provision in an express charging clause, to be treated as being entitled to the remuneration envisaged by that clause despite the fact that the services which they are

---

[2] See *ante*, para 14–118.

providing "are capable of being provided by a lay trustee"[3] (this provision applies to trustees of charitable trusts only where they are not sole trustees and to the extent that a majority of the other trustees have agreed that it should be applicable[4]).

Express charging clauses have habitually been drawn up in formulations **20–006** something like the following one:

"Any trustee for the time being who is a solicitor accountant or other person engaged in any profession shall be entitled to charge and be paid all usual professional or other charges for business transacted, time expended and acts done by him or any partner of his in connection with these trusts including business and acts which a trustee not being engaged in a profession or business could have done personally."

This sort of formulation works when a professional person is acting as a trustee. However, for an express charging clause to enable a trust corporation to charge, a formulation specifically referring to trust corporations is necessary; it has been held[5] that the sort of formulation set out above does not permit such a corporation to charge.[6] Express charging clauses of these types will undoubtedly continue to be utilised despite the reforms made by the Trustee Act 2000 in order to avoid any difficulties about whether or not the criteria laid down by that legislation have been satisfied.

Further, where the express charging clause in question is sufficiently wide, **20–007** a trustee is entitled to engage a company which he controls to act on behalf of the trust and to pay that company for so doing. In *Re Orwell's Will Trusts*,[7] the will of the author George Orwell contained a clause authorising the trustee[8] of a trust created thereby to charge for services performed by him or by his company.[9] Vinelott J. held that the company could be paid and that the trustee need not account to the trust for the remuneration which he himself had received from the company.[10] On the other hand, he stated that "it has been said that a wider form of charging clause entitling a solicitor trustee to charge for such matters ought not to be included except under express instructions given by the client himself with full knowledge of its effect". It may be that not only this wider form of charging clause but also the fact that it will now enable the trustees to charge for services capable of

---

[3] Trustee Act 2000, s.28(1), (2). A lay trustee is defined in s.28(6) as a trustee who is not a trust corporation and "does not act in a professional capacity".

[4] *ibid.*, s.28(3).

[5] *Re Cooper* (1939) 160 L.T. 453.

[6] This was not in practice much of a problem even before the enactment of the Trustee Act 2000; the appropriate type of express charging clause could be used when a trust corporation was to be the original trustee and the court would almost invariably authorise the payment of remuneration on the subsequent appointment of a trust corporation. Now of course, in the absence of an effective charging clause, the trust corporation could charge reasonable remuneration under the Trustee Act 2000 anyway.

[7] [1982] 1 W.L.R. 1337.

[8] The case concerned the literary executor of the will who, for the purposes of remuneration, was held to be in the same position as a trustee.

[9] The clause authorised the trustee to charge for work done by him "or his firm' ". Although the expression "firm" generally denotes an unincorporated partnership, the court held that for the purposes of this clause the expression extended to a private company.

[10] Compare *Re Gee* [1948] 1 All E.R. 498; see *post*, para 20–051.

being provided by a lay trustee should be specifically drawn to the attention of the client in this way.

20–008   A trustee cannot charge exactly what he likes under these types of charging clauses. Where he is a solicitor presenting bills as such, the beneficiaries can insist on having his charges assessed, that is reviewed by a costs judge. A solicitor will normally charge by the hour. However, professionals other than solicitors generally charge on the basis of the value of the assets being administered or dealt with (the *ad valorem* fees charged by the Public Trustee are set out below[11]). Provided that such fees are the normal charges of the professional in question, they will be within the type of charging clause set out above. However, whether or not a trustee is a solicitor, if he takes from the trust fund an amount in excess of the amount to which the beneficiaries consider that he is entitled, they may bring an action against him for breach of trust,[12] although this is obviously more difficult where his charges are on *ad valorem* basis.

20–009   That is not to say that the remuneration payable must necessarily be the trustee's normal professional charges. It may be expressed to be a fixed amount (the position where trustees who have agreed a fixed level of remuneration subsequently wish to increase it is considered below[13]). Less commonly, it may be expressed to be the income from some proportion or part of the estate[14] or even, by virtue of the exercise of a power of appointment, part of the capital.[15] If this is indeed what the trust instrument has provided, there seems no reason why the beneficiaries should be able to object to this, provided of course that the trustee actually fulfils his functions as such.

2. *The Risks of Express Charging Clauses*

20–010   Express charging clauses in an *inter vivos* trust are normally effective; the only possible risk for a professional trustee is the relatively unlikely possibility of the trust being set aside for one of the reasons discussed in Chapter 7,[16] in which case there will of course be no trust property out of which his fees can be paid. This risk is very much more substantial in relation to express charging clauses in a will because of the possibility of the will being void or the estate having insufficient funds to pay the remuneration.

20–011   If the will turns out to be void, the express charging clause will obviously be void as well; a professional executor who has begun to administer the estate under the impression that he is to receive his normal fees will not be able to charge and will have to return any fees which he has already been paid. Thus in *Gray v. Richards Butler*,[17] executors obtained a grant of probate in respect of what was thought to be the testatrix's last will. This nominated as executor one of the partners in the defendant firm of solicitors; pursuant to an express charging clause, he paid his firm more than £25,000 for work

---

[11] See *post*, para 20–013.
[12] *Re Wells* [1962] 1 W.L.R. 784.
[13] See *post*, para 20–033.
[14] *Public Trustee v. I.R.C.* [1960] A.C. 398.
[15] *Re Beatty's Will Trusts* [1990] 1 W.L.R. 1503.
[16] See *ante*, para 7–001 *et seq.*
[17] (1996) [2001] W.T.L.R. 625.

done in the administration of the estate. When the will was subsequently held to be void because the two witnesses had not both witnessed it at the same time, the grant of probate was set aside and a grant was instead made to the plaintiff, who had been nominated as executor under the testatrix's previous will. He successfully claimed that the defendant solicitors were liable to repay this sum to the estate. However, the court exercised its inherent jurisdiction[18] to enable the solicitors to charge for such of their work as could properly have been undertaken for the purposes of the earlier will.[19]

Further, even when the will is valid, there may be no assets available out **20–012** of which the remuneration can be paid. Prior to the enactment of the Trustee Act 2000, an express charging clause ranked only as a pecuniary legacy; consequently, if the estate in question was insolvent or was exhausted by specific gifts, there would be no assets available out of which the trustees' remuneration could be paid and, if the estate was insufficient to pay all the pecuniary legacies, the fees payable would abate in the same proportions as those legacies.[20] This of course meant that a professional executor who had administered the estate under the impression that he was to receive his normal fees might find himself deprived of some or all of them because the estate turned out to be subject to some unexpected claim which had priority over his. However, the Trustee Act 2000 has provided[21] that any payments to which a trustee is entitled should be regarded as remuneration for services. Consequently, such payments now[22] constitute an expense of administering the estate and enjoy priority over the interests of all the beneficiaries of the will. It is, therefore, only in the event that the estate is insolvent that a professional trustee will be at risk and even then any payments to which he is entitled will rank equally with the sums owed to the unsecured creditors of the estate.[23]

3. The Ad Valorem Fees Charged by the Public Trustee

As an illustration of fees charged on an *ad valorem* basis, the following fees **20–013** are what the Public Trustee is at present charging,[24] in all cases subject to the addition of Value Added Tax at the rate in force when the fee becomes due (17.5 per cent in 2008–2009).

---

[18] See *post*, para 20–034.

[19] The court did not specify what work fell into this category but an obvious example would have been the preparation of the inheritance tax return, which would on the facts have been in exactly the same form no matter which of the two wills was effective.

[20] *Re White* [1898] 2 Ch. 217.

[21] Trustee Act 2000, s.28(4)(b).

[22] In respect of deaths occurring on or after February 1, 2001.

[23] Trustee Act 2000, s.28(4)(a) also removes another trap for professional trustees by providing that the fact that either they or their spouses have attested the will no longer prevents them from claiming their remuneration.

[24] As from April 1, 2007 (the percentages charged have recently been increased very substantially on several occasions; compare those set out in two previous editions of this work (7th edn, p.644; 8th edn, p.725). The basic legislation is the Public Trustee (Fees) Act 1957; Public Trustee (Fees) Orders are made from time to time under that legislation.

(A)   Executorship Fee

20–014   When the Public Trustee acts as an executor or administrator under a will or intestacy, an executorship fee is charged calculated on the gross capital value of the estate; this covers all work done during the executorship or administration period except for the same activity fees as those mentioned in (B)(1) below.

On the first £50,000	12.5%
On the excess over £50,000 up to £75,000	10%
On the excess over £75,000 up to £100,000	5%
On the excess over £100,000	3.8%
Minimum fee £1,250	

(B)   Trusts

(1)   Acceptance fee

20–015   This is due when the Public Trustee is appointed as original trustee of a new settlement or as trustee of an existing will or settlement. The fee is one half of the rate shown in the table above with a minimum fee of £550. However, when the Public Trustee is appointed under a declaration of trust to carry out investment portfolio management or by the Supreme Court under a Standard Trusts Order or as trustee for a single beneficiary or for an absolutely entitled infant beneficiary, the rates and minimum fee are lower: 1.25 per cent on the first £50,000 and 0.5 per cent on any excess over £50,000, the minimum fee being £175.

(2)   Administration fee

20–016   This is due annually on April 1 each year on the net capital value of funds under administration: the valuation date is whichever of the following dates most recently precedes the date on which the fee is payable: July 1, 1987, in the case of any estate or trust in which the Public Trustee was acting on that day; September 30, 1991, in the case of any estate or trust in which the Public Trustee was acting on that day; and, in any other case, the date of the acceptance of the trust by the Public Trustee or such convenient date as he may select.

On the first £30,000	4.65%
On the excess over £30,000 up to £150,000	2.70%
On the excess over £150,000 up to £375,000	2%
On the excess over £375,000 up to £2,500,000	1.25%
On any excess over £2,500,000 up to £3,000,000	0.6%
On any excess over £3,000,000	0.3%
Minimum fee £60	

(3) Activity fees

An income collection fee is charged of 7.5 per cent on the gross amount of the income actually received by the Public Trustee. There is no fee on income paid direct from source to a beneficiary. **20–017**

A reasonable additional fee may be charged according to the work involved for various matters including: dealing with a business, dealing with assets outside the United Kingdom, dealing with freehold or leasehold property or a mortgage, and for duties of an unusual, complex or exacting nature. When acting as a tax agent, the charges are commensurate with the work involved. **20–018**

(4) Withdrawal fee

There is now no withdrawal fee due on the retirement from the trusteeship of the Public Trustee in favour of new trustees; this is presumably because it is consistent with the present policy of the Public Trustee to refuse to act except as a last resort not to discourage his replacement by other trustees. **20–019**

However, a withdrawal fee is still in principle payable on the distribution or withdrawal from the trust of trust property, although no fee is actually charged where the total value of the trust did not exceed £30,000 on March 31, 2004. In all other cases, the withdrawal fee is charged at the same percentage rate as the effective rate of the administration fee due on the April 1 prior to retirement. **20–020**

III. No Express Charging Clause

Where there is no express charging clause, the statutory charging provisions of the Trustee Act 2000 come into play. These distinguish between a trust corporation, a trustee "acting in a professional capacity", and a lay trustee; reference is also made to charitable trustees and sole trustees, who can obviously fall into in any of the three basic categories. There is a quite separate statutory definition of a trust corporation,[25] while the Trustee Act 2000 unhelpfully defines[26] a lay trustee as a trustee who is not a trust corporation and "does not act in a professional capacity"; the crucial definition is therefore that of "acting in a professional capacity", which is provided by section 28(5) of the Trustee Act 2000: **20–021**

"a trustee acts in a professional capacity if he acts in the course of a profession or business which consists of or includes the provision of services in connection with—

(a) the management or administration of trusts generally or a particular kind of trust, or
(b) any particular aspect of the management or administration of trusts generally or a particular kind of trust,

and the services he provides to or on behalf of the trust fall within that description."

[25] See *ante*, para 13–007.
[26] Trustee Act 2000, s.28(6).

20–022   This definition is obviously intended to cover all cases where a professional person habitually acts as a trustee as part of his business; in particular, it does not appear to matter that the part of the person's business which consists of or includes the provision of the services in question is minimal provided, presumably, that he is providing these services for at least one trust other than the trust in respect of which he is endeavouring to charge. But the definition does not, unlike express charging clauses, the overwhelming majority of which are of the type set out above, cover a person who has not taken on a trusteeship as part of his business, even if he is a professional person with considerable expertise such as a practising Chancery barrister, an accountant or a surveyor. Such persons are, for the purposes of the Trustee Act 2000, just as much lay trustees as non-professionals.

20–023   It should also be remembered that the provisions of the Trustee Act 2000 governing remuneration do not enable remuneration to be claimed in respect of work done before February 1, 2001, the day on which the Trustee Act 2000 came into force.

1. Trust Corporations

20–024   As has already been seen,[27] a company which is appointed a trustee is not by virtue of that fact alone a trust corporation. This term is applied only to a body corporate, such as a bank or insurance company, which undertakes the business of acting as a trustee and which fulfils certain conditions. Where a trust instrument contains no express charging clause, a trust corporation can now charge "reasonable remuneration" out of the trust funds for any services which it provides to or on behalf of a private trust[28]; this is defined as "such remuneration as is reasonable in the circumstances for the provision of those services to or on behalf of that trust by that trustee".[29] This remuneration can be claimed even in respect of services which were capable of being provided by a lay trustee.[30]

20–025   Prior to this legislation, trust corporations other than the Public Trustee, which has always been entitled to charge,[31] were automatically entitled to charge only if they were acting as judicial trustees.[32] Otherwise, a trust corporation was in the same position as an ordinary trustee and was only entitled to remuneration pursuant to an express charging clause; this meant that in practice a trust corporation would not agree to act as an original trustee unless an express charging clause provided for its remuneration. This remains the position for trust corporations which are trustees of charitable trusts; such trustees cannot claim reasonable remuneration[33] and, although the Secretary of State may by regulations make provision for the

---

[27] See *ante*, para 13–007.

[28] Trustee Act 2000, s.29(1); this provision does not apply to charitable trusts.

[29] *ibid.*, s.29(3).

[30] *ibid.*, s.29(4).

[31] Public Trustee Act 1906, s.9; Administration of Justice Act 1965, s.2; Public Trustee (Fees) Act 1957.

[32] Judicial Trustees Act 1896, ss.1(5), 4(1).

[33] Trustee Act 2000, s.29(1) does not apply to charitable trusts.

remuneration of trustees of charitable trusts who are trust corporations,[34] no such regulations have yet been made.

It is obviously likely that trust corporations who are trustees of private   **20–026**
trusts will continue to insist on express charging clauses where they are in a position to do so; this will almost inevitably be the case where they are original trustees of *inter vivos* trusts or where they have been involved in the preparation of the will which creates testamentary trusts of which they are appointed trustees. They are likely to so insist in order to avoid any future disputes with the beneficiaries as to exactly what constitutes "reasonable remuneration"—express charging clauses oust the provisions relating to reasonable remuneration.[35]

It remains to be seen what attitude the courts will now adopt when   **20–027**
appointing a trust corporation to be a trustee, usually of course as a replacement trustee; the courts remain entitled to fix its remuneration[36] but may instead now prefer to leave the trust corporation to claim the reasonable remuneration to which it is entitled under the Trustee Act 2000. Until the attitude of the courts becomes clear, trust corporations who indicate their willingness to be appointed as replacement trustees[37] of trusts which do not have an adequate express charging clause would therefore be well advised to make that willingness expressly conditional on the court fixing their remuneration in accordance with their standard fees as charged from time to time.

2. *Trustees Acting in a Professional Capacity*

Where a trust instrument contains no express charging clause, a trustee who   **20–028**
is acting in a professional capacity and is not either a trust corporation, a charitable trust or a sole trustee is entitled to receive reasonable remuneration out of the trust funds for any services which he provides to or on behalf of the trust provided that each other trustee has agreed in writing that he may be remunerated for his services.[38] A trust corporation is excluded because it is in fact in a better position in that it does not need to seek the agreement of anyone. The prohibition on sole trustees is obviously in order to prevent a trustee from agreeing to pay himself and can in practice readily be circumvented when the power of appointing new trustees is in the sole trustee[39]; the latter can simply appoint as an additional trustee someone who is prepared to agree.[40] Trustees acting in a professional capacity who are trustees of charitable trusts cannot claim reasonable remuneration[41] and, although the Secretary of State may by regulations make provision for the

---

[34] *ibid.*, s.30(1).

[35] Trustee Act 2000, s.29(5).

[36] Trustee Act 1925, s.42.

[37] In practice, they will have to do so in a letter signed by their officers which will be put before the court when the application is made for their appointment.

[38] Trustee Act 2000, s.29(2).

[39] As it will be in the absence of contrary provision in the trust instrument; see *ante*, para 13–024.

[40] Given that the legislation expressly envisages trustees acting in a professional capacity being able to charge, it is hard to see how this manoeuvre could be impugned by the beneficiaries, except of course where the remuneration agreed was excessive.

[41] Trustee Act 2000, s.29(1) does not apply to charitable trusts.

remuneration of trustees of charitable trusts who are trust corporations,[42] no such regulations have yet been made.

20–029   While trustees who are acting in a professional capacity will certainly be protected by this provision where they are original trustees or where the original trustees were also acting in this capacity, lay trustees of a small trust who appoint a professional trustee for the first time may still be subject to criticism by virtue of the fact that his appointment has unduly increased the costs of administering the trust running and some of this criticism may rub off on the professional trustee if he continues to act and charge irrespective of the financial position of the trust. Nor is it clear whether the other trustees either can or should make an irrevocable agreement that a trustee acting in a professional capacity should be remunerated indefinitely. It may be that, at least in the case of small trusts, the trustees should agree to this only on the basis that this should be reviewed from time to time; however, it does not necessarily follow that a professional trustee will agree to be appointed on that basis.

20–030   As in the case of trust corporations, it is obviously likely that trustees of private trusts who are acting in a professional capacity will continue to insist on express charging clauses where they are in a position to do so; this will almost inevitably be the case where they are original trustees of *inter vivos* trusts or where they have been involved in the preparation of the will which creates testamentary trusts of which they are appointed trustees. They are likely to so insist in order to avoid any future disputes with the beneficiaries as to exactly what constitutes "reasonable remuneration"—express charging clauses oust the provisions relating to reasonable remuneration.[43]

3. *Lay Trustees*

20–031   The position of lay trustees is not affected by the Trustee Act 2000. They are still not entitled to claim any salary or remuneration for carrying out their trusteeship[44]; this is the case even where the trustee in question devotes a considerable amount of time and trouble to managing a business belonging to the trust. In *Barrett v. Hartley*,[45] a trustee had managed a business for six years with such success that a large profit accrued to the beneficiaries; however, his subsequent claim for remuneration was unsuccessful on the grounds that his efforts were merely part of the duties imposed upon him as a result of his acceptance of the trusteeship. The rule has always been harsh and is now also somewhat illogical in the light of the unlimited power of trustees to appoint agents to act on their behalf and to pay those agents out of the trust funds for so doing[46]; in these circumstances, why should a trustee not be paid if he instead does the work himself, as the settlor presumably intended at the time of his appointment? The general rule denying remuneration was established in the eighteenth century, a time

---

[42] *ibid.*, s.30(1).

[43] Trustee Act 2000, s.29(5).

[44] *Robinson v. Pett* (1734) 3 P. Wms. 249; *Re Thorpe* [1891] 2 Ch. 360; *Re Barker* (1886) 34 Ch.D. 77.

[45] [1866] L.R. 2 Eq. 789.

[46] See *ante*, para 14–101.

when agents could be employed only in very limited circumstances and it is arguable that both rules should have been changed at the same time. However, after very full consultation, the Law Commission decided that the right to charge "reasonable remuneration" introduced in the Trustee Act 2000 should not be extended to lay trustees and no further review of the position is now likely.

IV. Other Situations where a Trustee can Charge

There are a number of other situations where a trustee can charge. These apply both where a trustee is not able to charge at all and where the remuneration provided for by an express charging clause turns out to be inadequate.   20–032

1. *Authorisation from the Court*

The court may, under its inherent jurisdiction, first, authorise a trustee to be remunerated where there is no charging clause[47]; secondly, authorise a trustee to retain remuneration which he has already received[48]; and, thirdly, authorise a trustee to charge more than he agreed to receive when he accepted the appointment.[49]   20–033

In some of the older cases, the courts were not averse to allowing the trustee reasonable remuneration. In *Brown v. Litton*,[50] the captain of a merchant ship took with him on a voyage a sum of money to use in trade. During the voyage he died and his mate, on assuming command of the vessel, took possession of the money and with it made considerable profits in trade. The mate was ordered to account for his profits but Harcourt L.K. nevertheless held him to be entitled to a fair remuneration, which was to be fixed by the court, for his trouble. This attitude was also adopted recently in *Gray v. Richards Butler*,[51] where the firm of a solicitor-executor had carried out work pursuant to a charging clause in respect of what was thought to be the testatrix's last will but which turned out to be void. The firm was held liable to repay the fees received to the estate but the court exercised its inherent jurisdiction to enable it to charge for such of their work as could properly have been undertaken for the purposes of the earlier will.[52]   20–034

However, the recent policy of the courts has generally been to authorise the receipt of remuneration by a trustee only where his services have been of exceptional benefit to the trust.[53] Thus remuneration or increased remuneration in respect of future work will be ordered only if the court considers   20–035

---

[47] *Bainbridge v. Blair* (1845) 8 Beav. 558; *Re Freeman's Settlement Trusts* (1887) 37 Ch.D. 148; *Re Masters* [1953] 1 All E.R. 19; *Re Worthington (dec'd)* [1954] 1 All E.R. 677.

[48] *Forster v. Ridley* (1864) 4 De G.J. & Sm. 452.

[49] *Re Duke of Norfolk's Settlement Trusts* [1982] Ch. 61.

[50] (1711) 1 P.Wms. 140.

[51] (1996) [2001] W.T.L.R. 625.

[52] The court did not specify what work fell into this category but an obvious example would have been the preparation of the inheritance tax return, which would on the facts have been in exactly the same form no matter which of the two wills was effective.

[53] See, for example, *Protheroe v. Protheroe* [1968] 1 W.L.R. 519, *ante*, para 10–124, where the trustee was only entitled to reimbursement of his actual expenses.

that, having regard to the nature of the trust, the experience and skill of a particular trustee is of great importance for the interests of the beneficiaries, while remuneration will be authorised in respect of work already done only if the work in question was wholly outside what could have been anticipated at the time of appointment.

20–036   In *Foster v. Spencer*,[54] substantial remuneration for their past work was awarded to two of the trustees of a moribund cricket club who had over a 20-year period had to engage in repeated administrative procedures and various types of legal proceedings in order successfully to bring about a sale of the club's ground[55]; however, it was held that the remaining task of determining the beneficial interests and dealing with the proceeds of sale was insufficiently onerous to justify an order for future remuneration. On the other hand, future remuneration was ordered in *Re Duke of Norfolk's Settlement Trusts*,[56] where a trust company accepted the trusteeship of a discretionary trust on the basis that it would receive a low fixed annual fee. It became involved in an extensive re-development programme in the Strand and applied both for special remuneration in respect of the re-development, which was granted,[57] and for an increase in the ordinary standard of remuneration. The Court of Appeal held that it could authorise an increase in the agreed level of remuneration, but it would only do so if the experience and skill of the trustee made it in the interest of the beneficiaries to do so. The Court of Appeal also held that it was relevant to take into account remuneration charged by other trust companies although it is not yet clear how much reliance can actually be placed on that.

20–037   The inherent jurisdiction has also been used to award remuneration to those guilty of a breach of fiduciary duty or of undue influence where their conduct has produced a substantial benefit for the other party; however, none of the relevant authorities actually concern express trustees, as distinct from constructive trustees, and such situations are fortunately uncommon.

20–038   In *Phipps v. Boardman*,[58] Boardman was the solicitor to the trustees of a will, who held among other assets 8,000 out of an issued 30,000 shares in a private company. Boardman, thinking there was considerable scope for making a profit, considered with the trustees whether they should acquire the remaining shares in the company but the trustees refused, partly because under the terms of the trust instrument they had no power to acquire additional shares in the company.[59] Boardman, with the benefit of knowledge which he had gained as a result of representing the trust, then fought, on behalf of himself and one of the beneficiaries, a lengthy takeover battle for control of the company. As Wilberforce J. observed at first instance, "it is

---

[54] [1996] 2 All E.R. 672.

[55] One of the trustees, a chartered surveyor who had been principally engaged in dealing with the planning authorities and the prospective purchasers, was awarded 5% commission on the purchase price while the other, who lived near the ground and had had to bear the brunt of dealing with squatters, the neighbours and the municipal authorities, was awarded £5,000 per annum for the most crucial 10-year period.

[56] [1982] Ch. 61.

[57] At first instance ([1979] Ch. 37), and not reversed by the Court of Appeal.

[58] [1967] 2 A.C. 46; see *ante*, para 10–140.

[59] The Court of Appeal said that application should have been made to the court for permission to purchase these shares.

interesting, and at times fascinating to watch, through the long correspondence that has been put in [evidence], the manner in which [Boardman] drives [the chairman of the company] from one prepared position to another until the fruit is ready to drop into his hand."[60] Eventually the fruit did indeed drop. Boardman and the beneficiary acquired virtually all the shares in the company other than those held by the trust and, having gained control of the company, were able to dispose of some of the assets and to make a capital distribution to all the shareholders, obviously including the trust. The trust benefited to the tune of £47,000 and Boardman and the beneficiary obtained £75,000, of which one of the other beneficiaries subsequently claimed the proportion equivalent to his beneficial interest.

It was held on the facts that Boardman would not have been able to have conducted these negotiations without the knowledge which he had gained while representing the trust and, controversially,[61] that he and the beneficiary were liable as constructive trustees to account for their profit. Both the Court of Appeal and the House of Lords[62] however considered that Boardman was "a man of conspicuous ability, of great energy, clarity of mind and persistence with a flair for negotiation" and, although he and his associate were nevertheless made to disgorge their profit, he was allowed "generous remuneration" because he had exceptional abilities in this respect, and had exercised them for the benefit of the trust. In other words, the average trustee, and even the average professional trustee, would not have been able to have achieved the results which Boardman had achieved. **20–039**

Phipps v. Boardman was a case in which remuneration was awarded to a person who had committed a breach of fiduciary duty. In *O'Sullivan v. Management Agency and Music,*[63] remuneration was ordered even in favour of a fiduciary who had been guilty of undue influence. A fiduciary agent, whose contract with the singer Gilbert O'Sullivan was set aside for undue influence, was held to be entitled to remuneration, together with a reasonable sum by way of profit, on the basis that he had contributed significantly to the performer's success. This decision was subsequently applied in *Badfinger Music v. Evans*[64] where a former member of a rock group which had broken up in very acrimonious circumstances had retained some tapes of a live concert which, after a considerable amount of essential remixing and remastering, he succeeded in releasing in a form which achieved a commercial success. He did not dispute that he was in a fiduciary relationship with the other members of the group or that they were entitled to share in the profit. The question was whether he was entitled to remuneration for the work which he had done. This was not a case where a fiduciary had, as in *Phipps v. Boardman,* acted honestly and openly in the best interests of his principal, although there was no doubt that his work had ultimately benefited the others. However, the judge[65] held that he could award remuneration despite a lack of honesty and openness and did so because the work **20–040**

---

[60] [1965] Ch. 922 at 1014.
[61] See *ante,* para 10–140.
[62] Upholding Wilberforce J.
[63] [1985] Q.B. 428.
[64] [2001] W.T.L.R. 1.
[65] Lord Goldsmith Q.C., sitting as a Deputy Judge of the Chancery Division.

done was not only of a special character calling for the exercise of a particular kind of professional skill but also could realistically only have been
done by the fiduciary.

20–041   On the other hand, in *Guinness v. Saunders*,[66] a claim for remuneration by
a director who had acted in good faith but in a situation where there was a
clear conflict between his interest and his duty was denied by the House of
Lords; indeed the House of Lords doubted whether such remuneration
would ever be ordered in favour of a director.[67] Lord Goff felt that the
jurisdiction could not be exercised where it would encourage trustees to put
themselves into a situation of conflict; in this respect, however, his statement
does not appear consistent with the authorities already discussed.

2. *Agreement with All Beneficiaries*

20–042   If the beneficiaries of a trust are all *sui juris* and between them absolutely
entitled to the whole of the beneficial interest under the trust, they can
validly agree with the trustees that they shall be paid. Such agreements are
construed strictly, in the same way as provisions for payment in the trust
instrument.[68] Where all the beneficiaries do not agree, or some are not *sui
juris*, individual beneficiaries can agree with a trustee for his remuneration
but that agreement obviously binds only the individual beneficiary on a
personal basis and not the trust property as such.

3. *Custodian Trustees*

20–043   A custodian trustee is entitled to charge fees equivalent to those which the
Public Trustee could charge for acting as a custodian trustee.[69] However, this
only enables the custodian trustee to charge for the services which he
performs in that capacity. In *Forster v. Williams Deacon's Bank*[70] an attempt
was made to use the device of custodian trusteeship to overcome the
absence of a charging clause in the trust instrument. In that case Williams
Deacon's Bank had been appointed both managing trustee and custodian
trustee. It was appreciated that the bank could not charge as managing
trustee but it was anticipated that it could derive its remuneration from its
capacity as a custodian trustee. The Court of Appeal rejected the device,
however, holding that the deed merely constituted the bank the sole trustee
and so the inability to charge remained. A similar attempt in a later case was
held to be totally ineffective.[71] However, if the same situation recurred
today, it is obviously likely that the custodian trustee in this situation would
be able to charge reasonable remuneration under the Trustee Act 2000.

---

[66] [1990] 2 A.C. 663.
[67] On the grounds that this would constitute interference by the court in the administration
of the company's affairs.
[68] It seems that the agreement has to be concluded with the beneficiaries before the trustee
takes up his office; *Douglas v. Archbutt* (1858) 2 De G. & J. 148; *Re Sherwood* (1840) 3 Beav. 338.
This appears to be contrary to principle.
[69] Public Trustee Act 1906, s.4.
[70] [1935] Ch. 359.
[71] *Arning v. James* [1936] Ch. 158.

The fact that a validly appointed custodian trustee may always charge for **20–044** his services as such does not entitle him to profit in other ways from the trust either. Thus in *Re Brooke Bond*[72] an insurance company was a custodian trustee under the trust deed securing the pension scheme of Brooke Bond & Co. Under the terms of the trust deed the managing trustees were entitled to effect with any insurance company a policy assuring the payment of the pensions under the scheme. The managing trustees proposed to effect the policy with the custodian trustee. Cross J. held that the custodian trustee could not, without the authority of the court, contract with the managing trustee for its own benefit; however, when an application was made for the sanction of the court in this respect,[73] the managing trustees were authorised to effect the policy with the custodian trustee on the basis that the latter need not account for its profit on condition that the terms of the policy were approved by an independent actuary.

4. *The Rule in* Cradock v. Piper

Prior to the enactment of the Trustee Act 2000, a solicitor trustee, like any **20–045** other trustee, could not, in the absence of an express charging clause or authorisation from the court, pay either himself or another member of his firm for work done for the trust[74] save where he could properly employ an outside solicitor in which case he might employ and pay another member of his firm provided that it had been expressly agreed that the solicitor-trustee would not take any share in the profits.[75] The so-called Rule in *Cradock v. Piper*[76] is, or was, a curious exception to this principle; it establishes that, where a solicitor-trustee acts as a solicitor for himself and his co-trustees in litigation relating to the trust and the costs of acting for both of them do not exceed the expense which would have been incurred if he had been acting for the co-trustees alone, then he may be paid his usual costs.

The Rule in *Cradock v. Piper* became firmly established[77] but, despite some **20–046** feeble attempts at justification made by the court,[78] was always quite illogical. If it is proper for a solicitor to be paid his usual fees for litigation, why is it not proper for him to be paid his usual fees for non-litigious work? However, in the absence of an express charging clause, a solicitor-trustee will now almost always be able to claim reasonable remuneration under the Trustee Act 2000. Consequently, the Rule survives only to the extent that an express charging clause is construed as being too narrow to entitle a solicitor to pay either himself or another member of his firm for work done for the trust; in these admittedly unlikely circumstances, he will nevertheless be able to recover the costs of engaging in litigation on behalf of the trust if he can satisfy the conditions of the Rule.

---

[72] [1963] Ch. 357.
[73] In the manner envisaged *ante*, para 14–124.
[74] *Christophers v. White* (1847) 10 Beav. 523.
[75] *Clack v. Carlon* (1866) 30 L.J. Ch. 639.
[76] (1850) 1 Mac. & G. 664.
[77] *Broughton v. Broughton* (1855) 5 De G.M. & G. 160; *Lincoln v. Windsor* (1851) 9 Hare 158; *Re Baker* (1886) 24 Ch.D. 77.
[78] See *Re Corsellis* (1887) 34 Ch.D. 675 at 682.

5. *Trust Property Abroad*

20–047 Where the trust property is situated abroad and the law of the country where the property is situated allows the trustees to be remunerated, the trustees appear to be entitled to retain that remuneration. In *Re Northcote*[79] English executors had to get in assets of the deceased in America. To do so they had to obtain a grant of probate in the State of New York, under the law of which they were entitled to a commission on the value of the assets. They deducted this for themselves and the English court held they need not account for it to the trust. However, while lay executors could undoubtedly still rely on this decision, it is probable that professional trustees who did not have the benefit of an express charging clause would be limited to the reasonable remuneration to which they are entitled under the Trustee Act 2000.

V. Directors' Fees

20–048 The second type of remuneration which a trustee may seek to retain is fees paid to him as a director of a company in which the trust fund is invested. Three questions arise:

   (i) whether the trustee-director is in principle liable to account for his director's fees;

   (ii) whether there are any exceptions to the basic principle; and

   (iii) how, when the trustee-director does have to account, should the fees be treated in the administration of the trust.

1. *Liability in Principle to Account*

20–049 There are two preliminary points. First, in the case of private companies, the articles of association often endeavour to prevent the directors from acting contrary to the interests of shareholders by providing that any person who becomes a director must himself hold, or must within a short specified time acquire, a number of shares in that company. In this way it is hoped that, as the director will wish to advance the value of his own shares, he will also be acting in the interests of the other shareholders. Secondly, by section 126 of the Companies Act 2006,[80] a company is not allowed to take notice of the fact that shares might be held upon trust and, as far as the company is concerned, it deals with trustees who are registered holders of shares in exactly the same way as shareholders who are beneficially entitled. It will, therefore, be apparent that directors can use shares which they hold as trustees as their share qualification; if they do so, will they be allowed to keep their directors' fees?

---

[79] [1949] 1 All E.R. 442.
[80] Replacing provisions of previous Acts.

In *Re Francis*,[81] under the articles of association of a company, the holders   **20–050**
of a specified number of shares were entitled to vote themselves into directorships. Trustees held sufficient shares on behalf of their trust and duly
procured their appointment as directors. Kekewich J., following the general
principle that a trustee cannot profit from his trusteeship, held that they had
to account to the trust for their fees. This case, however, was not even cited
in *Re Dover Coalfield Extension*,[82] which introduced new considerations. The
company Dover Coalfield Extension held shares in the Consolidated Kent
Collieries Corporation, with whom they did business. In order to protect the
interests of the former company, one of its directors was appointed a director of the latter company; as such, he had a contract which governed the
services which he was to perform and also regulated his remuneration.
However, all directors were required to acquire 1,000 shares within one
month of appointment. Dover Coalfield Extension therefore transferred to
him this number of shares, which he held upon trust for that company. It
was not disputed that he had to account for the dividends on those shares
and he did in fact do so; however, he claimed that he did not have to account
for his directors' fees. The Court of Appeal held that, even though he could
not have continued in office without the shares, he could retain his fees; he
had been appointed a director by an independent board of directors before
he had acquired the shares and his directorship did not therefore automatically flow from his trusteeship.

In *Re Macadam*,[83] following *Re Francis*,[84] trustees who by virtue of the trust   **20–051**
shareholding were able to elect themselves directorships and did in fact do
so were held liable to account for their fees. However, this decision was
distinguished in *Re Gee*,[85] where Harman J. said that in some circumstances,
even where a trustee is able through his voting rights to compel his appointment as director, he is nevertheless entitled to retain his fees, if his appointment was in fact independent of his trust shareholding. He reviewed the
previous cases and concluded that the test was whether the trustee has used
powers vested in him as trustee to procure his appointment as a director. To
be liable to account the trustee therefore, first, must have powers vested in
him as trustee and, secondly, must have utilised those powers to procure his
appointment as director.

If any of these elements is missing, the trustee-director may retain his fees,   **20–052**
as in *Re Dover Coalfield Extension*, where the trustee has his directorship first
and, although he has powers as trustee, does not use those powers to
procure his appointment as a director. Similarly, if the trustee-director has a
majority shareholding in a company beneficially, as well as a minority
holding as trustee, and votes himself into a directorship, his directorship
will be the result of his beneficial voting power and not his voting power as
trustee. Similarly, where others hold the majority shareholding, the trustee
has a minority shareholding, and he is appointed a director by the votes of
the others, although he has powers as trustee he will not have used those

---

[81] (1905) 74 L.J. Ch. 198.
[82] [1908] 1 Ch. 65.
[83] [1946] Ch. 73.
[84] (1905) 74 L.J. Ch. 198.
[85] [1948] Ch. 284.

powers to procure his appointment. The court will consider all the circumstances to see whether or not the appointment was truly independent of the voting powers held as trustee.

20–053   In *Re Orwell's Will Trusts*,[86] the facts of which have already been considered,[87] Vinelott J. distinguished *Re Gee*. He held that, while the general rule is that a trustee must account for any benefit, such as remuneration, which he obtains from a company as a result of his position as a trustee, this rule does not apply if the company was properly entitled to be paid from the trust fund and there is no other nexus between the company with which the trustee is connected and the trust fund.

2. *Exceptions to the Basic Principle*

20–054   Where a trustee-director is, in principle, not entitled to retain his director's fees, there are two circumstances in which, nevertheless, he may do so.

   (1) The settlor can include an effective power in the trust instrument authorising the retention of directors' fees. This power may be express or implied. So in *Re Llewellin*,[88] where the testator had expressly provided that the trustees could use the trust shares to acquire directorships, it was held that he had also impliedly authorised them to retain their directors' fees.

   (2) The court can authorise a trustee-director to retain his director's fees. In deciding whether to exercise this power, it will consider the extent of the skill and effort which has been applied. The general rule is that a trustee is expected to exercise in the discharge of his trusteeship the effort and skill which a prudent man of business would in general undertake in the management of his own investments. A trustee-director is expected to exercise the same standard when acting as a director. So, in *Re Keeler's Settlement Trusts*[89] the court directed that an inquiry should be held as to the extent to which trustee-directors had exerted effort and skill above that standard and held that they could retain their directors' fees, but to that extent only.

3. *The Manner in which Forfeited Fees should be Applied*

20–055   Where a trustee-director is obliged to account for his directors' fees and does so, it seems that, notwithstanding the revenue character of those sums so far as the company is concerned, in the administration of the trust they are to be treated as an addition to the settled property and added to capital.[90]

---

[86] [1982] 1 W.L.R. 1337.
[87] See *ante*, para 20–007.
[88] [1949] Ch. 225.
[89] [1981] Ch. 156.
[90] *Re Francis* (1905) 74 L.J. Ch. 198.

VI. Commissions

The third category of payment which a trustee may seek to retain is commis-   **20–056**
sions paid by third parties.

1. *The General Rule*

The general rule is that the trustee is accountable for commissions which he   **20–057**
receives in respect of trust business.[91] The test is not whether the trust has
suffered a loss but whether the trustee has made a profit. Thus, in *Williams
v. Barton*[92] the trustee was a stockbrokers' clerk who was paid commission
earned on business introduced by him to his firm. He arranged for his firm
to value the trust assets and was duly paid his commission. It was held that
he had to account for that commission. There was no suggestion that the
valuation of the trust assets was improper or unnecessary but nevertheless
the trustee was not entitled to make a profit from it. Had this not been the
case, the trustee might have been tempted to have the assets valued more
frequently than was in fact necessary.

2. *Exceptions*

The trust instrument can, and often does, empower trustees to retain com-   **20–058**
missions. The court undoubtedly also has power to authorise this but there
does not seem to be any reported case in which it has exercised this power.
Further, the rule does not apply where the recipient of the commission is
discharging a duty imposed by statute and in so doing does not act harshly
or oppressively. So in *Swain v. The Law Society*[93] the House of Lords held that
The Law Society was entitled to retain the equivalent of commission paid in
respect of the compulsory insurance against professional negligence which
solicitors are obliged to maintain.[94] The Law Society was required to apply
that commission for the benefit of the profession as a whole.

VII. Commercial Profits

The last category of benefit which, in ordinary circumstances, a trustee may   **20–059**
seek to keep is profits derived by him in carrying on a business, where the
trust is a customer of that business. As in the case of commissions, it seems
that the general rule is that the trustee is liable to account for his profit.[95]
However, the trust instrument can empower trustees to retain their profit. So
in *Re Sykes*[96] two brothers who were wine merchants were appointed as
trustees of a will under which one of the assets of the trust was a public

---

[91] This question is discussed more fully *ante*, para 10–073.
[92] [1927] 2 Ch. 9.
[93] [1983] A.C. 598; see *ante*, para 10–049.
[94] Solicitors Act 1974, s.37. At that time they had to insure through The Law Society but this
is no longer the case.
[95] *Re Sykes* [1909] 2 Ch. 241.
[96] [1909] 2 Ch. 241.

house. Under the terms of the will, they were authorised to supply wine to the public house and they were held entitled to their usual profit for doing so. Similarly, in *Space Investments v. Canadian Imperial Bank of Commerce*,[97] a bank trustee was entitled under a settlement to deposit trust funds with itself on a normal commercial basis; it was held that no breach of trust had been committed by the bank in so doing and that the position of the trust was no better than any other depositor or general creditor, even when the bank went into liquidation. The court also has power to authorise trustees to retain a commercial profit.

VIII. Other Financial Benefits

20–060   Finally, quite apart from the specific examples already considered, there is anyway a general rule that a trustee is not to be entitled to profit in any way from his trusteeship unless he is authorised to do so by the trust instrument or by the court.

20–061   An extreme, if unusual, example is *Sugden v. Crossland*,[98] where a person was anxious to become a trustee of a will. He therefore paid the existing trustee £75 to retire and to appoint him in his place. It was held that the retirement and appointment was ineffective and also that the £75 so paid belonged to the trust. Similarly in *Webb v. Earl of Shaftesbury*,[99] Lord Eldon L.C. held that trustees were not entitled to exercise sporting rights over land held by them as trustees. He held that either the rights should be let for the benefit of the beneficiaries or, if they could not be let, should be held for the heirs of the settlor on a resulting trust. The trustees could not themselves derive any benefit.

20–062   In view of the above, it hardly needs to be said that, quite apart from the rules relating to investments,[100] a trustee must not use trust moneys in his own trade or business. If he does so, he will be liable to account for the profit he makes or, at the beneficiaries' option, the sum invested with compound interest.[101] The rule applies not only to profits which are made at the expense of the trust but also to profits which are made without any loss to the trust at all but which are derived by virtue of the trusteeship. This principle has already been considered.[102]

---

[97] [1986] 1 W.L.R. 1072. (Privy Council on appeal from The Bahamas).
[98] (1856) 3 Sm. & G. 192.
[99] (1802) 7 Ves. 480.
[100] See *ante*, para 14–054.
[101] See *post*, para 22–034.
[102] See *ante*, para 10–128.

CHAPTER 21

VARIATION OF TRUSTS

If all the beneficiaries of a trust are *sui juris* and absolutely entitled they can, if they think fit, terminate the trust and if they so choose, set up new trusts in respect of the trust property.[1] But if they are not all so qualified, it is necessary for an application to be made to the court for a variation of the trusts. It is important to make a distinction for this purpose between two classes of variation by the court: first, variations concerned with the management or administration of the trusts; and, secondly, variation of the beneficial interests arising under the trusts. **21–001**

I. MANAGEMENT AND ADMINISTRATIVE VARIATIONS

1. *The Inherent Jurisdiction of the Court*

The court has always had an inherent jurisdiction to sanction a departure from the terms of a trust; however, it is now clearly established that this jurisdiction applies only to the management or administration of the trust. It therefore does not apply to any rearrangement of the rights of the beneficiaries to the beneficial interests themselves,[2] with the sole exceptions of cases of "maintenance"[3] and "compromise",[4] assuming that the latter amounts to a variation in the true sense of the word.[5] **21–002**

The inherent jurisdiction, although still somewhat nebulous, was defined by Romer L.J. in *Re New*[6] to cover an "emergency" which has arisen in the administration of the trust, that is to say something for which no provision is made in the trust and which could not have been foreseen or anticipated by the settlor of the trust. The inherent jurisdiction is, therefore, of distinctly limited scope. In *Re New* itself the trustees of shares in a company were authorised by the court as a matter of emergency to concur in a scheme under which the shares were to be exchanged for more realisable shares in a new company. The sanction of the court was required because the trustees **21–003**

---

[1] See *ante*, para 19–019.

[2] *Chapman v. Chapman* [1954] A.C. 428 at 454, 455.

[3] See *post*, para 21–012.

[4] See *post*, para 21–013.

[5] This is rather doubtful because it seems that the court's sanction to a compromise of disputed rights (which is what "compromise" means in this context) does not actually result in a variation of the beneficial trusts but only brings to an end any dispute about what those rights are. See *post*, para 21–013, for further discussion of "compromise" in this sense.

[6] [1910] 2 Ch. 524.

had no power of investment in the new shares under the terms of the trust instrument. This was in the circumstances a transaction analogous to the "salvage" of the trust property.[7]

2. Section 57 of the Trustee Act 1925

21–004 One of the reasons why the inherent jurisdiction is so nebulous is that it has been largely superseded by section 57 of the Trustee Act 1925, which is based on a concept wider than that of "emergency". The basis of the section is instead expediency. It in effect provides that the court may empower trustees[8] to perform any act relating to the management or administration of the trust property which is not authorised by the trust instrument when in the opinion of the court that act is expedient. The ambit of the section was considered by the Court of Appeal in the conjoined appeals in *Re Downshire's Settled Estates, Re Chapman's Settlement Trusts* and *Re Blackwell's Settlement Trusts*.[9] According to Lord Evershed M.R. and Romer L.J. in a joint judgment:

"The object of section 57 was to secure that trust property should be managed as advantageously as possible in the interests of the beneficiaries, and, with that object in view, to authorise specific dealings with the property which the court might have felt itself unable to sanction under the inherent jurisdiction, either because there was no actual 'emergency' or because of inability to show that the position which called for intervention was one which the creator of the trust could not reasonably have foreseen but it was no part of the legislative aim to disturb the rule that the court will not rewrite a trust."

Moreover, the court must be satisfied that the proposed transaction is for the benefit of the trust as a whole and not simply for one of its beneficiaries.[10]

21–005 The section does not, therefore, confer on the court any general jurisdiction to vary beneficial interests; it is limited to the managerial supervision and control of trust property by the trustees and cannot be stretched further than that. However, subject to this decisive limitation, it is an overriding provision which is to be read into every trust.[11] It has been used for a number of purposes: to authorise the partitioning of land where a necessary consent could not be obtained[12]; to authorise the sale of a reversionary

---

[7] The principle was applied in *Re Tollemache* [1903] 1 Ch. 955.

[8] But not trustees under the Settled Land Act 1925; Trustee Act 1925, s.57(4).

[9] [1953] Ch. 218 (Denning L.J. dissented). On appeal to the House of Lords *sub nom. Chapman v. Chapman* [1954] A.C. 429, it was conceded that s.57 did not apply. In the House of Lords, the statement of law in the Court of Appeal regarding s.57 was neither approved or disapproved and is therefore still good law.

[10] *Re Craven's Estate (No.2)* [1937] Ch. 431.

[11] *Re Mair* [1935] Ch. 562.

[12] *Re Thomas* [1930] 1 Ch. 194.

interest which the trustees had no power to sell until it fell into possession[13]; and to blend two charitable trust funds into one.[14]

The section has also been used to extend trustees' investment powers,[15] most recently in *Mason v. Farbrother,*[16] and *Anker-Petersen v. Anker-Petersen*[17] (despite the fact that trustees now have the general power of investment conferred by the Trustee Act 2000,[18] such extensions may well still be sought where the trust instrument has cut down the statutory power of investment or when the trustees wish to enlarge that power to include, for example, non-income producing investments[19]). It used to be thought that applications for this purpose were better made under the Variation of Trusts Act 1958.[20] However, *Anker-Petersen v. Anker-Petersen*[21] has now established that, provided the beneficial interests are not also affected by the proposed extension of the trustees' investment powers, section 57 of the Trustee Act 1925 should be used in preference to the Variation of Trusts Act 1958.

21–006

II. Variation of Beneficial Interests

The rules already discussed relate only to variations relating to the management and administration of the trust. Variation of the beneficial interests of a trust obviously involves a much more drastic rewriting of its provisions.

21–007

1. *Under the Settled Land Act 1925*

Section 64 of the Settled Land Act 1925 provides that the court may sanction any transaction affecting or concerning the settled land or any part thereof or any other land (not being a transaction otherwise authorised by the Settled Land Act 1925 or by the terms of the settlement) which in the opinion of the court would be for the benefit of the settled land, or any part of that land, or the persons interested under the settlement.[22] The section used also to apply to land held on trust for sale,[23] but this is now no longer the case following the Trusts of Land and Appointment of Trustees Act 1996. The expression "transaction" is widely defined so as to include a "compromise

21–008

---

[13] *Re Cockerell's Settlement Trusts* [1956] Ch. 372; compare *Re Heyworth's Contingent Reversionary Interest* [1956] Ch. 364.

[14] *Re Shipwrecked Fishermen and Mariners' Benevolent Fund* [1959] Ch. 220.

[15] *Re Brassey's Settlement* [1955] 1 W.L.R. 192; *Re Shipwrecked Fishermen and Mariners' Benevolent Fund* [1959] Ch. 220, not following *Re Royal Society's Charitable Trusts* [1956] Ch. 87.

[16] [1983] 2 All E.R. 1078.

[17] (1990) [2000] W.T.L.R. 581.

[18] See *ante*, para 14–055.

[19] See *ante*, para 14–096.

[20] See *post*, p.742 and *Re Coates' Will Trusts* [1959] 1 W.L.R. 375; *Re Byng's Will Trusts* [1959] 2 All E.R. 54 at 57. In *Mason v. Farbrother* [1983] 2 All E.R. 1078, it was held that this was not possible because the parties were not fully representative.

[21] (1990) [2000] W.T.L.R. 581.

[22] Settled Land Act 1925, s.64(1). The powers were extended by Settled Land and Trustee Acts (Court's General Powers) Act 1943, s.1 as amended by Emergency Laws (Miscellaneous Provisions) Act 1953, s.9.

[23] Danckwerts J. so interpreted Law of Property Act 1925, s.28 in *Re Simmons* [1956] Ch. 125 but this section has now been repealed by Trusts of Land and Appointment of Trustees Act 1996, Sch.4.

or other dealing or other arrangement".[24] It is now clear[25] that the section confers a more ample jurisdiction than that conferred by section 57 of the Trustee Act 1925[26] which is not in any sense restricted to steps of a purely administrative character; the section therefore enables the beneficial interests under the settlement to be remoulded.[27] However, this jurisdiction is likely to become progressively less significant now that the Trusts of Land and Appointment of Trustees Act 1996[28] has prohibited the creation of any more settlements under the Settled Land Act 1925.[29]

2. Under Section 24 of the Matrimonial Causes Act 1973

21–009   Section 24 of the Matrimonial Causes Act 1973, which replaced earlier longstanding legislation, confers on the Family Division of the High Court a wide jurisdiction, after pronouncing a decree of divorce or nullity of marriage, to vary the trusts contained in any ante-nuptial or post-nuptial settlement which has been made for the benefit of the parties to the marriage or the children of that marriage. It is clearly established that the jurisdiction extends to a rearrangement of beneficial interests and the fact that a saving of inheritance tax or other taxes will result will have no bearing on the exercise of this jurisdiction.[30] A relatively recent application of this jurisdiction is the decision of the House of Lords in *Brooks v. Brooks*[31] that a pension scheme of which a former husband was the sole member could be varied to provide an immediate annuity and an eventual pension for the former wife.[32]

---

[24] Settled Land Act 1925, s.64(2); *Raikes v. Lygon* [1988] 1 W.L.R. 281.

[25] This was held by the majority of the Court of Appeal held in *Re Downshire's Settled Estates* [1953] Ch. 218.

[26] See *ante*, para 21–004.

[27] *Raikes v. Lygon* [1988] 1 W.L.R. 281.

[28] s.2(1). Existing settlements will continue only for as long as any land or heirlooms remain subject thereto.

[29] A relatively recent example of the utilisation of this jurisdiction is *Hambro v. Duke of Marlborough* [1994] Ch. 158. The Blenheim Estate is held by the successive Dukes of Marlborough for an estate in fee tail which is, by Act of Parliament, "unbarrable", that is to say incapable of being converted into an estate in fee simple. The Duke and the trustees of what was then a settlement under the Settled Land Act 1925 considered that the Duke's heir apparent, the Marquess of Blandford, would be incapable of managing the estate if and when he succeeded his father because of what were referred to as his "unbusinesslike habits and the lack of responsibility shown by him". They proposed to seek approval for the Duke to convey the estate to the trustees of a new settlement on trust for sale to pay the income to the Duke for life, subject thereto for the Marquess of Blandford on protective trusts, and subject thereto on the trusts of the pre-existing settlement (this would bring to an end the settlement under the Settled Land Act 1925 pursuant to s.1(7) and replace it by a trust of land pursuant to Trusts of Land and Appointment of Trustees Act 1996, s.1(2)(a)). The matter came before Morritt J. on the preliminary issue as to whether such a conveyance, which would clearly vary the Marquess of Blandford's existing beneficial interest, would be a "transaction" which the court could sanction under section 64. This question was answered in the affirmative and approval was subsequently given (see *The Times*, July 23, 1994).

[30] See *Thomson v. Thomson and Whitmee* [1956] P. 384.

[31] [1996] 1 A.C. 375.

[32] See *ante*, para 12–095.

3. Under the Inheritance (Provision for Family and Dependants) Act 1975

The Inheritance (Provision for Family and Dependants) Act 1975 confers on **21–010** the Chancery and the Family Divisions of the High Court jurisdiction to order reasonable financial provision out of the estate of a deceased person for any of a number of persons, including his spouse, civil partner, co-habitant, child or dependant, for whom such provision has not been made by the provisions of his will or as a result of the operation of the intestacy rules. In the event that the effect of the will or the intestacy rules has been the creation of a trust (as will inevitably be the case when anyone who is survived by both a spouse and one or more children dies intestate with an estate of more than £125,000), the orders which the court can make include any necessary variation of those trusts.

4. Under the Mental Capacity Act 2005

The Mental Capacity Act 2005, which replaced earlier legislation to the same **21–011** effect, confers on the Court of Protection a power to vary any settlement of the property of any person lacking capacity which that court has previously exercised its power to make if there was a material non-disclosure when the settlement was made or if there has been a material change of circumstances.[33]

5. Maintenance

The position here is and has long been that, where a testator or settlor has **21–012** made a settlement in such a way that the immediate beneficiaries have no funds out of which they can be maintained, something which is particularly possible where the settlement provides primarily for income to be accumulated, the court will assume that his intention to provide sensibly for the beneficiaries is so paramount that it will order maintenance in disregard of the trusts.[34] Any such order for maintenance will obviously result in a variation of the beneficial interests. The jurisdiction is not restricted to cases of "emergency",[35] nor is it dependent on the beneficiaries in question being infants.[36]

6. Compromise

It has long been clearly established that the court may sanction on behalf of **21–013** an infant or unborn person a "compromise" proposed by those persons

---

[33] Mental Capacity Act 2005, Sch.2, para.6. The power to make the settlement in the first place is conferred by *ibid.*, ss.16(1)(b), 16(2)(a), and 18(1)(h), replacing Mental Health Act 1983, ss.95 and 96.

[34] *Re Downshire Settled Estates* [1953] Ch. 218 at 238, *per* Evershed M.R. and Romer L.J., considered in *Chapman v. Chapman* [1954] A.C. 429 at 445, 455–457, 469, 471: see *post*, p.746. See also *Re Collins* (1886) 32 Ch.D. 229 at 232; *Havelock v. Havelock* (1881) 17 Ch.D. 807.

[35] See *ante*, para 21–002 and *Hayley v. Bannister* (1820) 4 Madd. 275.

[36] *Revel v. Watkinson* (1748) 1 Ves.Sen. 93.

beneficially interested in the trusts who are *sui juris*, thus protecting the trustees from subsequent liability to the infant or unborn person. This, like the power to award maintenance,[37] is part of the inherent jurisdiction of the court and, where applicable, clearly also enables beneficial interests to be varied.

21–014   In conjoined appeals in *Re Downshire Settled Estates, Re Chapman's Settlement Trusts* and *Re Blackwell's Settlement Trusts*,[38] the Court of Appeal had to consider the important question of what amounts to a "compromise" for this purpose. The majority, Lord Evershed M.R. and Romer L.J., held that the word "compromise" should not be construed narrowly so as to be confined to a compromise of disputed rights but covered any arrangement between a tenant for life and the remaindermen. The arrangements proposed in *Re Downshire Settled Estates* and *Re Blackwell's Settlement Trusts* were duly held to be in the nature of a compromise in this wider sense of the word and were accordingly sanctioned. But the majority refused to sanction the arrangement proposed in *Re Chapman's Settlement Trusts* because they involved no compromise even in this extended sense; the court was merely being asked to destroy trusts which had been expressly created. Denning L.J. dissented on the basis of a broad principle that the court had the power to deal with the property and interests of infants or other persons under disability in a manner not authorised by the trust whenever the court was satisfied that what was proposed was most advantageous for them, provided that everyone of full age also agreed. He was therefore prepared to give the inherent jurisdiction of the Court a very wide scope indeed.

21–015   However, when an appeal from the decision of the Court of Appeal was taken to the House of Lords in *Chapman v. Chapman*,[39] the House of Lords not only unanimously affirmed the decision of the Court of Appeal but, by a majority, adopted a considerably narrower meaning of "compromise" than that adopted by Lord Evershed M.R. and Romer L.J. The latter had shown that the inherent jurisdiction was limited to some degree by holding that the word "compromise", however widely construed, would not cover every kind of arrangement. But the majority of the House of Lords (Lord Simonds, Lord Morton and Lord Asquith) stated that the power of the court to sanction a compromise in a suit to which a person, such as an infant or unborn person, was not a party did not extend to cases where there was no real dispute between the parties. Lord Cohen alone was prepared to accept that the jurisdiction of the court extended to "compromises" in the wider sense accepted by the majority of the Court of Appeal. This decision clearly established that a "compromise" means a compromise of a disputed right and this is as far as the inherent jurisdiction of the court goes.[40] This decision led directly to the enactment of the Variation of Trusts Act 1958.[41]

21–016   It was therefore clear that in *Re Downshire Settled Estates* and *Re Blackwell's Settlement Trusts* the Court of Appeal had gone too far in giving the word

---

[37] See *ante*, para 21–012.

[38] [1953] Ch. 218 (CA).

[39] [1954] A.C. 429.

[40] It was subsequently held not to include a compromise of a simulated dispute (*Re Powell-Cotton's Resettlement* [1956] 1 W.L.R. 23) or a variation of the existing investment powers (*Mason v. Farbrother* [1983] 2 All E.R. 1078).

[41] See *post, infra*.

"compromise" an unnatural meaning, although that did not mean that those cases had actually been wrongly decided.[42] However, a number of schemes had been approved in the Chancery Division prior to the decision of the House of Lords on the basis of the wider principle upheld by the majority of the Court of Appeal which could not possibly be so justified; the orders made in those cases had accordingly been made without any jurisdiction.[43] Further, it immediately became fashionable to scrutinise settlements with a view to finding a provision of sufficient ambiguity or uncertainty in its effect on the beneficial interests to form a peg on which to hand a compromise of a "genuine" dispute, a clearly undesirable development susceptible of bringing the law into disrepute.

This bizarre situation clearly could not last for long so in 1957 the Law   **21–017** Reform Committee was invited to consider the position. They reached the conclusion that the result produced by *Chapman v. Chapman* was most unsatisfactory. It was pointed out that on the grant of a decree of divorce or nullity the court had the power to sanction variations in a marriage settlement even if these were designed to produce a saving of tax. The Committee fairly inquired why an infant whose parents were happily married should be in a worse position than an infant whose parents had just divorced. The recommendations of the Committee were accordingly given legislative effect in the Variation of Trusts Act 1958.

7. The Variation of Trusts Act 1958

The principal motive for the invocation of the inherent jurisdiction of the   **21–018** court to vary beneficial interests on the basis of a "compromise" was in order to minimise fiscal liabilities which would be incurred if the trust remained unaltered. The old-fashioned settlement with its succession of limited interests had, in particular, fallen out of favour because on the death of each limited owner estate duty (the predecessor of inheritance tax) was leviable on the value of the whole of the settled funds. A great deal of ingenuity had been and for that matter still is devoted to the formulation of schemes dividing up the trust funds between those interested in capital and income respectively in such a way that such fiscal liabilities were minimised.

(A) Permissible Motives
The schemes formerly presented to the court for its sanction under the head   **21–019** of "compromise" are therefore now presented to the court under the Variation of Trusts Act 1958. Although Lord Morton said in *Chapman v. Chapman*[44] that, if the court had power to approve and did approve schemes for the purpose of avoiding taxation, "the way would be open for a most undignified game of chess between the Chancery Division and the legislature", the

---

[42] They could probably have been justified under Settled Land Act 1925, s.64: see *ante*, para 21–008.

[43] See *Re Leeds (Duke) and Re The Coal Acts 1938 to 1943* [1947] Ch. 525. *Re Downshire Settled Estates* and *Re Blackwell's Settlement Trusts* [1953] Ch. 218 may also be taken to be overruled on this point, although these decisions could probably be justified under Settled Land Act 1925, s.64; see *ante*, para 21–008.

[44] See *ante*, para 21–013.

plain fact remains that very many applications under the Act have been made successfully for this very purpose alone.[45]

21–020 Yet despite these realities, echoes of judicial repugnance towards tax avoidance can still occasionally be heard and it is arguable, if only faintly, as a result of the controversial decision in *Re Weston's Settlements*,[46] that certain forms of tax avoidance may still be regarded as illegitimate. In this case the applicants applied for an order for approval of an arrangement by which property settled on English trusts should be freed from those trusts and settled on a Jersey settlement. The purpose of the exercise was to avoid a heavy liability to capital gains tax and estate duty.[47] Stamp J. said at first instance: "I am not persuaded that this application represents more than a cheap exercise in tax avoidance which I ought not to sanction, as distinct from a legitimate avoidance of liability to taxation."[48] The Court of Appeal however tended to place emphasis on other factors (not that Stamp J. ignored them). As has already been seen,[49] the primary basis of the Court of Appeal decision appears to have been that no administrative benefits would accrue in transferring the settlement to Jersey because the family had been living in Jersey for only a few months and probably would not stay there. There was also doubt as to the competence of the Jersey courts to administer trusts.[50] Finally the element of moral or social benefit was stressed. In the words of Lord Denning M.R.:

"There are many things in life more worthwhile than money. One of these things is to be brought up in this our England which is still 'the envy of less happier lands'. I do not believe that it is for the benefit of children to be uprooted from England and transported to another country simply to avoid tax. Children are like trees: they grow stronger with firm roots."[51]

The result of this case can be justified on the grounds just mentioned. But to introduce notions of "legitimate" and "illegitimate" tax avoidance seems to be not only uncontrollably vague but also wholly unworkable.[52]

(B) The General Scheme of the Act

21–021 The Variation of Trusts Act 1958, which came into force on July 23, 1958, applies to trusts of real and personal property, whether the trusts arise before or after the passing of the Act, under any will, settlement or other

---

[45] See *Re Norfolk's Will Trusts* (1966) *The Times*, March 23, 1966 (the purpose was to reduce duty on estates worth £3 million).

[46] [1969] 1 Ch. 223; see *ante*, para 13–055 for further discussion of this decision.

[47] Approximately £160,000.

[48] [1969] 1 Ch. 223 at 234.

[49] See *ante*, para 13–057.

[50] [1969] 1 Ch. 223 at 223 *per* Stamp J. (Chancery Division), at 247 *per* Harman L.J. (Court of Appeal); this doubt has certainly since been favourably resolved, see *ante*, para 13–054.

[51] [1969] 1 Ch. 223 at 245.

[52] The scheme was one of "tax avoidance", not "tax evasion". The latter amounts to a criminal offence and clearly a scheme which "evaded" tax could not be sanctioned. But to take advantage of the existing tax laws for a person's own benefit and thereby "avoid" tax is generally regarded as a legitimate exercise; see also Bretten [1968] 32 Conv. (N.S.) 194; Harris [1969] 33 Conv. (N.S.) 183 at 191.

disposition.[53] The court may, if it thinks fit, by order approve an arrangement varying or revoking all or any of the trusts, or enlarging the powers of the trustees to manage or administer any of the trust property, on behalf of four classes of beneficiaries or potential beneficiaries. These are as follows:

(i) by virtue of section 1(1)(a), persons having, directly or indirectly, a vested or contingent interest who by reason of infancy or other incapacity are incapable of assenting;

(ii) by virtue of section 1(1)(b), persons, whether ascertained or not, who may become, directly or indirectly, entitled to an interest at a future date or on the happening of a future event, if they then answer a specified description or qualify as members of a specified class, but not including such persons if the future event had happened at the date of application to the court[54];

(iii) by virtue of section 1(1)(c), persons unborn; and

(iv) by virtue of section 1(1)(d), persons who will be interested as discretionary beneficiaries under protective trusts[55] if the protected life interest of the principal beneficiary under should fail or determine.[56]

The court can only approve the arrangement on behalf of the persons listed in the first three classes if it is for their benefit. But the potential benefit of the persons listed in the final class does not need to be considered.[57] Further, if a beneficiary falls both within this final class and within one of the other classes, then because the four classes are alternatives it is only necessary to apply for approval on the basis of his membership of the final class and so no benefit needs to be established.[58] **21–022**

---

[53] Variation of Trusts Act 1958, a.1(1).

[54] For decisions on the meaning of this paragraph, see *Re Suffert's Settlement* [1961] Ch. 1; *Re Moncrieff's Settlement Trusts* [1962] 1 W.L.R. 1344. Briefly, if the class in question is, for example, the statutory next-of-kin of a living person, then the latter is treated as having died at the date of application to the court and the next-of-kin consequently become notionally ascertainable. Since the "future event", the death of that person, has notionally happened, a member of the class of next-of-kin who is in existence cannot be bound by an order for variation without his consent (see *Re Suffert's Settlement* [1961] Ch. 1). Further, persons who have contingent interests, however remote, are already entitled; they are not persons who "may become entitled". Consequently, in *Knocker v. Youille* [1986] 1 W.L.R. 934, it was held that consent could not be given on behalf of a very numerous class of contingently entitled beneficiaries, whose approval it was not practicable to obtain.

[55] See *ante*, para 8–003.

[56] Variation of Trusts Act 1958, s.1(2) defines "protective trusts" as the trusts specified in Trustee Act 1925, s.33(1)(i), (ii) or "any like trusts". For the meaning of this last expression, see *Re Wallace's Settlement* [1968] 1 W.L.R. 711 at 716, *per* Megarry J.: "The word 'like' requires not identity but similarity and similarity in substance suffices without the need for similarity in form or detail or wording." See also *Gibbon v. Mitchell* [1990] 1 W.L.R. 1304.

[57] *ibid.*, s.1(1), proviso; see also *post*, para 21–035.

[58] *Re Turner's Will Trusts* [1960] Ch. 122.

21–023   The Variation of Trusts Act 1958 thus largely gives to the court the jurisdiction for which Denning L.J. had contended in *Re Chapman's Settlement Trust*.[59] The Act has commendably done away with the hair-splitting technicalities involved in the precise nature of a "compromise" and has attracted a great many applications to the court since it was passed. However, it must be emphasised that, although the jurisdiction is wide in many respects, it is nevertheless limited in that it only empowers the court to authorise arrangements on behalf of the persons designated in the Act, as if they were all ascertained and *sui juris*. It does not enable the court to override any objection, no matter how unreasonable, or dispense with the consent, even if unreasonably withheld, of any beneficiary who is in fact ascertained and *sui juris*. In such circumstances, the Variation of Trusts Act 1958 simply cannot be invoked.

(C)   The Trusts to which the Act Applies

21–024   While, by virtue of section 1(1), the Variation of Trusts Act 1958 applies where "property, whether real or personal, is held on trusts arising under any will, settlement or other disposition", it nevertheless does not apply to every type of trust. *Allen v. Distillers Co. (Biochemicals)*[60] arose as a sequel to proceedings which had been commenced on behalf of children who were alleged to have been born with physical deformities as a result of their mothers having taken the drug thalidomide during pregnancy. These proceedings had been settled on the basis that the manufacturers of the drug paid into court nearly £6 million on terms that various sums should be paid out or applied "in such manner as the judge may direct to or for the benefit of each [deformed] child". An application was consequently made under the Variation of Trusts Act 1958 for the payment of money out of court to be held by trustees on the terms of a draft which was submitted to the court for approval. Under the terms on which the original proceedings had been settled, each child was entitled to payment on attaining the age of majority, whereas under the proposed draft, the trustees were to be empowered to defer the date upon which the child would be entitled. The court held that it had no jurisdiction under the Act to approve the "variation" of the terms upon which the money had been paid into court. Eveleigh J.[61] said[62] that the terms upon which the money had been paid into court was not "a trust of the kind referred to in the 1958 Act. The Act contemplates a situation where a beneficial interest is created which did not previously exist and probably one which is related to at least one other beneficial interest." Similarly in *Mason v. Farbrother*[63] an application under the 1958 Act for the variation of the existing investment powers of a pension fund was not pursued because of doubts about whether the parties were truly representative of the classes of beneficiaries whom they purported to represent.

---

[59] [1953] Ch. 218. In *Re Chapman's Settlement Trusts (No.2)* [1959] 1 W.L.R. 372, an application to create substantially the same scheme was granted under the Variation of Trusts Act 1958.

[60] [1974] 2 All E.R. 365.

[61] As he said in the judgment, "a common lawyer with this problem" of what constitutes a trust.

[62] [1974] 2 All E.R. 365 at 374.

[63] [1983] 2 All E.R. 1078.

The jurisdiction conferred by the Variation of Trusts Act 1958 may also **21–025** now be confined to trusts governed by English law. Prior to the enactment of the Recognition of Trusts Act 1987, the English courts asserted jurisdiction to vary trusts governed by any law provided, of course, that they had jurisdiction over their trustees. Thus, in *Re Ker's Settlement Trusts*[64] the court made an order varying the trusts of a settlement whose proper law was that of Northern Ireland and a similar order was made in *Re Paget's Settlement*[65] in respect of a settlement whose proper law was believed to be that of New York. However, as will be seen in Chapter 23,[66] the Hague Convention on the Law applicable to Trusts and their Recognition confers exclusive jurisdiction to vary trusts on the courts of the jurisdiction of their applicable law. Now that this convention has been incorporated into English law by the Recognition of Trusts Act 1987, it is therefore considered unlikely that English courts still have any jurisdiction to make orders under the Variation of Trusts Act 1958 varying any trust whose proper law is not English law; this seems to be the case even if the trustees of such a trust are personally susceptible to the jurisdiction of the English courts.

(D) Specific Considerations for the Court

(1) Benefit
The only essential guidance specifically provided in the Variation of Trusts **21–026** Act 1958 as to the principles on which the exercise of the jurisdiction is based is that, with the exception of discretionary beneficiaries under protective trusts, the arrangement proposed should be for the benefit of the persons designated in the Act[67] on whose behalf its approval is sought. A definite benefit, even if it is not purely financial, must be conferred on such persons. In *Re Van Gruisen's Will Trusts*[68] it was shown that the provisions for infants and unborn persons were from an actuarial point of view more beneficial to them under the proposed arrangement than under the trusts of the will. The arrangement was therefore approved but Ungoed-Thomas J. sounded a warning note by saying:

"The court is not merely concerned with the actuarial calculation ... the court is also concerned whether the arrangement as a whole in all the circumstances, is such that it is proper to approve it. The court's concern involves, inter alia, a practical and businesslike consideration of the arrangement, including the total amount of the advantages which the various parties obtain and their bargaining strength."

Similar reasoning was applied in the earlier decision of *Re Clitheroe's* **21–027** *Settlement Trusts*,[69] where the arrangement was designed to exclude any future wife from the class of objects of an immediate discretionary trust[70] but

---

[64] [1963] Ch. 553.
[65] [1965] 1 W.L.R. 1046.
[66] See *post*, para 23–012.
[67] Variation of Trusts Act s.1(1), proviso.
[68] [1964] 1 W.L.R. 449.
[69] [1959] 1 W.L.R. 1159.
[70] It was not a protective trust, so the proviso to s.1(1) did not apply.

in compensation gave her the benefit of a covenant by the settlor to pay the trustees an annual sum for her benefit. Danckwerts J. sanctioned the arrangements in principle but required evidence to show that it was in fact for the benefit of a future wife.

21–028   The rule that a "benefit" is all-important has caused some, though admittedly very few, applications to fail. Thus in *Re Steed's Will Trusts*,[71] the Court of Appeal refused to sanction a variation sought by the beneficiary enabling her to take the whole beneficial interest because it did not take sufficient account of a "spectral spouse" whom the trusts were also designed to benefit and whom the beneficiary in question might conceivably marry. Again, in *Re Tinker's Settlement*,[72] Russell J. declined to accept the argument that it was for the benefit of unborn persons as members of a family viewed as a whole that something should be done which, although reasonable and fair, was to their financial detriment.

21–029   The same test was applied in *Re T.'s Settlement Trusts*[73] although on this occasion this does not appear to have been the primary reason for the decision of Wilberforce J. to refuse to approve a proposed arrangement to transfer a minor female's share of settled funds to trustees to hold on protective trusts for her lifetime, with remainders over. The minor would otherwise have become absolutely entitled in possession to the funds on attaining 21 and the arrangement had been devised because she had shown herself to be irresponsible in matters of money. A secondary reason for this refusal was that the proposals were not confined simply to dealing in a beneficial way with the special requirements of the minor. Another proposal for variation was later approved; this was to the effect that the minor's right to capital should be deferred for a time, she being given a protected life interest in the meantime.

21–030   It must, however, be admitted that these authorities do not appear to be entirely consistent with the decision of Danckwerts J. in *Re Cohen's Will Trusts*.[74] It was contended that in the admittedly unlikely event of one of the testator's children predeceasing his widow, who was then aged nearly 80, the proposed arrangement would not be advantageous to his grandchildren, some of whom were minors. However, Danckwerts J. held that risk of some kind was inherent in every application under the Act and, since this risk was one which it would be reasonable for an adult to run, the court would run it on behalf of the minors.

21–031   This sort of attitude is clearly sound when a risk is non-existent. Indeed in such cases it may not even be necessary to apply to the court. Thus it has

---

[71] [1960] Ch. 407. See also *Re Cohen's Settlement Trusts* [1965] 1 W.L.R. 1229 (it was proposed to substitute June 14, 1973 in lieu of the applicant's death as the date when the persons to take were to receive the capital of the settled funds; Stamp J. refused the application on behalf of unborn beneficiaries because it could happen (although it was only a remote possibility) that the applicant might survive the proposed date and under the arrangement persons not born by then would have no interest in the fund, whereas they would have under the original settlement).

[72] [1960] 1 W.L.R. 1011.

[73] [1964] Ch. 158. The primary ground for the decision of Wilberforce J. is discussed *post*, para 21–032.

[74] [1959] 1 W.L.R. 865; compare *Re Cohen's Settlement Trusts* [1965] 1 W.L.R. 1229 (which concerned a completely different family), see *ante*, n.71).

been held[75] that trustees can properly and with complete safety deal with their funds on the basis that a woman of 70 will not have a further child and in such circumstances an application under the Act is inappropriate; "the Act is concerned to vary trusts applicable in events which will or may happen and not to cover impossible contingencies".[76] But where there is an identifiable risk, the more general attitude is to require it to be covered by insurance. This is particularly appropriate if the risk is that a beneficiary will die within a short time of the variation being made. In such circumstances, when the proposed variation is, when viewed broadly, for the financial benefit of the beneficiaries, the court will generally require the life of that beneficiary to be insured, even if the premiums have to be paid for out of income and are in that sense at the expense of a minor beneficiary.[77]

Finally, it should be emphasised that, although the settlor, if still alive, has to be made a party to any application under the Variation of Trusts Act 1958,[78] neither his wishes nor any wishes expressed earlier by a deceased settlor or by a testator prevent the court from concluding that an arrangement confers benefit. In *Goulding v. James*,[79] the testatrix left her residuary estate to her daughter for life, remainder to her 32-year-old grandson at the age of 40 absolutely, remainder to any of her great-grandchildren living at her grandson's death. An arrangement was proposed whereby 45 per cent was to be held for each of the daughter and the grandson absolutely, with the remaining 10 per cent held for the as yet unborn grandchildren, who even if born obviously only had a somewhat limited chance of receiving anything under the existing trusts.[80] Laddie J. refused to approve this on the grounds that the testatrix had, on the evidence, wished to prevent her daughter from having any access to capital because she did not trust her son-in-law and wished to defer her grandson's interest until the age of 40 because he had not yet "settled down".[81] This decision was reversed by the Court of Appeal. Mummery L.J. held that "the intentions and wishes of [the testatrix], expressed externally to her will in relation to the adult beneficiaries and an adult non-beneficiary, had little, if any, relevance or weight to the issue of approval on behalf of the future unborn great grandchildren, whose interest in residue was multiplied five-fold under the proposed arrangement".[82] Sir Ralph Gibson went even further, saying that it was not clear to him "why evidence of the intention of the testator can be of any relevance whatever if it does no more than explain why the testator gave the interests set out in the will and the nature and degree of feeling with which such provisions were selected".[83]

---

[75] *Re Pettifor's Will Trusts* [1966] Ch. 257.

[76] *ibid.*, at 260, 261. See also *Re Westminster Bank Ltd's Declaration of Trust* [1963] 1 W.L.R. 820, where an order was made under the Variation of Trusts Act 1958 in respect of a woman aged 50.

[77] For an example, see *Re Robinson's Settlement Trusts* [1976] 3 All E.R. 61.

[78] This is provided by the Civil Procedure Rules, Part 64.4(1)(a).

[79] [1997] 2 All E.R. 239.

[80] The actuarial valuation of their contingent interest was only 1.85%.

[81] [1996] 4 All E.R. 853.

[82] [1997] 2 All E.R. 239 at 251–252.

[83] *ibid.*, at 252.

21–032   The authorities considered thus far have, like the immense majority of all applications under the Variation of Trusts Act 1958, been concerned exclusively with financial benefit; this is a mundane consideration admitting of reasonable proof. But it has been clearly established that this is not necessarily the only consideration to be taken into account by the court. Thus in *Re T.'s Settlement Trusts*[84] the judge approved the alternative scheme of variation because on the special facts of the case the evidence showed that the minor beneficiary was irresponsible and immature; "there appears to me to be a definite benefit for this infant for a period during which it is to be hoped that independence may bring her into maturity and responsibility to be protected against creditors".[85] This decision was followed by Megarry J. in *Re Holt's Settlement*[86] where he said in relation to an arrangement postponing the vesting of interests in children from the ages of 21–30: "The word 'benefit' in the proviso to section 1 of the Act of 1958 is plainly not confined to financial benefit, but may extend to moral or social benefit".[87] This approach was confirmed by the decision of the Court of Appeal in *Re Weston's Settlement*,[88] where it was decided that it was for the benefit of children to be educated in England rather than in Jersey.

21–033   An even broader view of "benefit" in this context was taken in *Re Remnant's Settlement Trusts*,[89] where Pennycuick J. approved an arrangement deleting forfeiture clauses depriving certain children of their interests if they practised Roman Catholicism or married a Roman Catholic. This appears to have been on the basis that such provisions might operate as a deterrent to them in the selection of a husband and might also be a source of possible family dissension.

21–034   It is also clear that an arrangement which results in improvement in the general administration of the trust may also be a "benefit" within the meaning of the Act. As has already been seen,[90] it is on this ground that the courts have approved applications for the export of trusts to countries abroad where the beneficiaries are resident.

(2) The position of discretionary beneficiaries under protective trusts

21–035 It has already been stated that it is unnecessary to establish that an arrangement confers any benefit on discretionary beneficiaries under protective trusts.[91] Nevertheless, their interests cannot be simply ignored. As Wilberforce J. held in *Re Burney's Settlement Trusts*,[92] in approving an arrangement varying discretionary trusts, the discretionary power conferred on the court still has to be judicially exercised and it is incumbent on the applicant to make out a case for interfering with protective trusts. Indeed, the basic

---

[84] [1964] Ch. 158.
[85] *ibid.*, at 162.
[86] [1969] 1 Ch. 100.
[87] *ibid.*, at 121.
[88] [1969] 1 Ch. 223; for further discussion of this case, see *ante*, para 21–020. See also *Re C.L.* [1969] 1 Ch. 587, where a mental patient surrendered his protected life interest and contingent interest in remainder and Cross J. held that it was for the patient's benefit because in all probability it was what he would have done if he had been of sound mind.
[89] [1970] Ch. 560; compare *Re Tinker's Settlement* [1960] 1 W.L.R. 1011.
[90] See *ante*, para 13–052.
[91] Variation of Trusts Act 1958, s.1(1), proviso.
[92] [1961] 1 W.L.R. 545.

principle had been stated earlier, more generally, by Lord Evershed M.R. in *Re Steed's Will Trusts*,[93] where he said that "the court is bound to look at the scheme as a whole and when it does so, to consider, as surely it must, what really was the intention of the benefactor". The requirements were spelt out in *Re Baker's Settlement Trusts*,[94] where Ungoed-Thomas J. said that, where property was held on protective trusts for the benefit of the applicant and an application was made to vary those trusts, evidence (including in this case that of the financial position of the applicant and her husband) should be laid before the court to show to what extent the protective trusts continued to serve any useful purpose.

(3) Fraud and public policy
Obviously a variation which is fraudulent or contrary to public policy will not be sanctioned.   21–036

Fraud has only so far arisen in connection with the doctrine of fraud on a power.[95] In *Re Robertson's Will Trusts*,[96] the applicant had exercised a special power of appointment in favour of his children as a preliminary to the proposed arrangement. His purpose and intention in making the appointment was to benefit his children and not himself. Later he was advised that his own financial position would in fact be improved if the appointment were made and the scheme approved. But Russell J. held that to suppose his original purpose and intention had been changed or added to was unjustified. It followed that there was no fraud on the power, though, if there had been, the court would not have been able to approve the scheme.   21–037

However, subsequent case law appears to indicate a certain conflict as to the precise principles to be applied. In *Re Wallace's Settlement*[97] Megarry J. said that the fact that protected life tenants had executed appointments in favour of their children in itself raised a case for inquiry because the life tenants benefited by the arrangement; however, on the evidence he was satisfied that there was no fraud on the power because the benefit to the life tenants was not substantial and they had intended to make the appointment before the arrangement was approved. On the other hand, in *Re Brook's Settlement*[98] Stamp J. adopted a rather different approach. He held that the exercise of a special power of appointment amounted to a fraud on the power and as a result he was unable to approve the variation. Here one of the purposes of the appointment (by a protected life tenant in favour of his children from which he would also benefit as a result of a division of the settled capital) was to enable the life tenant to obtain what was not otherwise available to him, namely capital rather than income; this was enough to invalidate the appointment. The important feature of *Re Brook's Settlement* was that the judge emphasised that the question is whether the purpose of the appointment amounted to a fraud, not, as was apparently suggested in *Re Wallace's Settlement*, the effect of the appointment on the financial position   21–038

---

[93] [1960] Ch. 407 at 421.
[94] [1964] 1 W.L.R. 336.
[95] See *ante*, para 6–102.
[96] [1960] 1 W.L.R. 1050.
[97] [1968] 1 W.L.R. 711.
[98] [1968] 1 W.L.R. 1661.

of the appointor. It is thought that *Re Brook's Settlement* applies the correct principle.

21–039   The difficulties that may thus arise as a result of a fraud on the power, however inadvertent, may in some circumstances be avoided by releasing the power (no question of a fraud on a power normally arises on a mere release[99]). It has been held that, provided that the power in question can be released,[100] the court will approve an arrangement varying a settlement even though the objects of the power are ignored.[101] There appears to be some doubt as to whether the release has to be effected by deed or whether it can be inferred from the facts; the latter would seem to be sufficient.[102]

21–040   Even if the power cannot be released (because, for example, it is a fiduciary power[103]), it still seems possible to apply to the court for an arrangement either extinguishing the power outright or permitting its release simply because this amounts to varying or revoking a trust within section 1 of the Act. But because the power is not of itself capable of release, the court is likely to impose conditions on any subsequent release. Thus in *Re Drewe's Settlement*[104] Stamp J. insisted, when approving an arrangement, that the release of such a power could only be effected by deed and with the consent of the trustees.

21–041   The only reported case in which considerations of public policy have arisen is *Re Michelham's Will Trusts*,[105] where they were neatly sidestepped by Buckley J. Approval was sought to an arrangement whereby trust property was transferred to the applicants absolutely. The efficacy of the scheme depended on the applicants continuing to remain unmarried. Insurance policies were therefore to be effected which would ensure that, if either did in fact marry, certain sums would become available to replace the funds thus transferred. The policies included a stipulation that the insurers should be indemnified by a Swiss bank if the policy moneys became payable. The bank proposed to give the indemnity on terms that it, in turn, should be indemnified by one or other of the applicants if the moneys became payable. The judge, in approving the arrangement, held that, although the counter-indemnities given by the applicants to the bank ought to be regarded as tending to discourage the applicants from marrying, that would not affect the validity of the arrangement. This was the case because, in the event that the counter-indemnities proved to be unenforceable by the bank on grounds of public policy, something which was a question of Swiss law, that fact alone would not relieve the bank from its obligation to indemnify the insurers.

---

[99] See *ante*, para 6–119.

[100] The present rules emerge from *Re Wills's Trust Deeds* [1964] Ch. 219 and *Mettoy Pension Trustees v. Evans* [1990] 1 W.L.R. 1587; see *ante*, para 6–116.

[101] *Re Christie-Miller's Settlement* [1961] 1 W.L.R. 462; *Re Courtald's Settlement* [1965] 1 W.L.R. 1385; *Re Ball's Settlement* [1968] 1 W.L.R. 899.

[102] In *Re Ball's Settlement* [1968] 1 W.L.R. 462 Megarry J. insisted on a formal release but in *Re Christie-Miller's Settlement* [1965] 1 W.L.R. 462 and *Re Courtald's Settlement* [1965] 1 W.L.R. 1385 an inferred release was regarded as sufficient.

[103] See *ante*, para 6–124.

[104] [1966] 1 W.L.R. 1518.

[105] [1964] Ch. 550.

(4) Perpetuity

The Perpetuities and Accumulations Act 1964[106] applies only to instruments taking effect after the commencement of that Act[107] and the proposed new legislation on perpetuities will contain a similar provision in the event that it is enacted.[108] How far do provisions of this type affects variations made under the Variation of Trusts Act 1958? In *Re Holt's Settlement*[109] Megarry J. held that an arrangement, when taken with the court order[110] was an "instrument" for this purpose, with the result that provisions deriving their validity from the Perpetuities and Accumulations Act 1964 might be included in the arrangement and that this would apply not only to trusts created after the commencement of the 1964 Act but also to those created before that date.[111]

21–042

However, the question remains as to whether, for this to be the case, the instrument so formed must take effect as a "disposition"; the Perpetuities and Accumulations Act 1964 tends to suggest that this is indeed necessary.[112] The point did not arise in *Re Holt's Settlement* because there the applicant surrendered his life interest and so the arrangement clearly involved a "disposition". It seems, however, that if the arrangement does not involve a disposition, then the benefits of the Perpetuities and Accumulations Act 1964 cannot be utilised in respect of subsequent variations of the original trusts.[113]

21–043

(5) The precise meaning of "arrangement"

There is no doubt that this term has been widely construed to cover many classes of variation. As Lord Evershed M.R. said in *Re Steed's Will Trusts*,[114] "it is deliberately used in the widest possible sense to cover any proposal which any person may put forward for varying or revoking trusts". It need not, therefore, necessarily be *inter partes*. The views of the trustees are relevant but not conclusive and, if necessary, will be overridden.[115]

21–044

The wide meaning thus attached to an arrangement was, however, modified in *Re T.'s Settlement Trusts*,[116] whose facts have already been considered. Here Wilberforce J., as the primary ground for his decision, refused to sanction the arrangement initially proposed because it amounted to a completely new settlement and that was beyond the jurisdiction conferred by the Act. If this represents the true position, then there are limits to the conception of an "arrangement", although this does appear to be an unjustified abridgment of the court's jurisdiction. Nevertheless, subsequent case law does seem to have accepted the distinction between "variation" and

21–045

---

[106] See *ante*, para 7–007.
[107] Perpetuities and Accumulations Act 1964, s.15(5).
[108] See *ante*, para 7–007.
[109] [1969] 1 Ch. 100.
[110] See *post*, para 21–052.
[111] The same principle was applied but no reasons were given in *Re Lloyd's Settlement* [1967] 2 W.L.R. 1078 in relation to s.13 and to the accumulation periods.
[112] See Perpetuities and Accumulations Act 1964, ss.1, 3(5).
[113] See *Re Holmden's Settlement* [1968] A.C. 685, where it was suggested that a mere alteration of the period for which discretionary trusts should continue was not a "disposition".
[114] [1960] Ch. 407 at 419.
[115] *ibid.*, at 420.
[116] [1964] Ch. 158; see *ante*, para 21–029.

"resettlement". In *Re Ball's Settlement*[117] Megarry J. laid down the following test:

"If an arrangement changes the whole substratum of the trust, it may well be that it cannot be regarded as merely varying that trust. But if an arrangement, while leaving the substratum effectuates the purpose by other means, it may still be possible to regard that arrangement as merely varying the original trusts, even though the means employed are wholly different and even though the form is completely changed."

However, he actually held that, although the arrangement sought rescinded all beneficial and administrative trusts of the settlement and substituted new provisions, he could approve it because it preserved the "general drift" of the old trusts. The fact remains that a pedantic distinction has grown up between "variation'" and "resettlement" for which there appears to be neither any sanction in the words of the Variation of Trusts Act 1958 nor any practical justification.

(E)   Investment Clauses

21–046   Prior to the enactment of the now repealed Trustee Investments Act 1961,[118] the Variation of Trusts Act 1958 was frequently used to increase the then very restricted statutory powers of investment of trustees. The Trustee Investment Act 1961 itself expressly preserved the discretion of the court under the Variation of Trusts Act 1958 to extend these powers. However, the courts were initially not prepared to utilise their powers under the Variation of Trusts Act 1958 to sanction the grant to trustees of more extensive investment powers than those conferred by the Trustee Investment Act 1961 unless there were "special circumstances".[119] This remained the position until the courts came to recognise that the Trustee Investments Act 1961 had itself become outdated[120]; they then once again became readily prepared to authorise under the Variation of Trusts Act 1958 extensions to the investment powers of trustees.

21–047   Despite the fact that the provisions of the Trustee Investment Act 1961 have now been replaced by the general power of investment conferred on trustees by section 3 of the Trustee Act 2000,[121] extensions of investment powers may still be sought in at least two situations: first, where the powers of investment conferred by the trust instrument are less extensive than and therefore have cut down the statutory power of investment[122]; and, secondly, when the trustees wish to enlarge that power to include types of investments which are not within the general power of investment, the most obvious example being non-income producing investments.[123] Where variations of this type can be shown to be for the benefit of the beneficiaries

---

[117] [1968] 1 W.L.R. 899. See also *Re Holt's Settlement* [1969] 1 Ch. 100 at 117.
[118] See *ante*, para 14–069, n.145.
[119] *Re Cooper's Settlement* [1962] Ch. 826; *Re Kolb's Will Trusts* [1962] Ch. 531. Special circumstances were found in *Re University of London Charitable Trusts* [1964] Ch. 282.
[120] *Trustees of the British Museum v. Attorney-General* [1984] 1 W.L.R. 418.
[121] See *ante*, para 14–069.
[122] See *ante*, para 14–083.
[123] See *ante*, para 14–096.

(which will of course be considerably easier in the first situation than in the second one), there seems no reason why applications of this type should not succeed. However, *Anker-Petersen v. Anker-Petersen*[124] has now established that, provided the beneficial interests are not also affected by the proposed extension of the trustees' investment powers, section 57 of the Trustee Act 1925 should be used in order to obtain such extensions rather than the Variation of Trusts Act 1958.

(F) Procedure and Formalities

(1) Form of application

An application should normally be made by a life tenant or other person   **21–048** entitled to the income of the trust funds. It should only be made by the trustees, as Russell J. said in *Re Druce's Settlement Trusts*,[125] where "they are satisfied that the proposals are beneficial to the persons interested and have a good prospect of being approved by the court, and further, that if they do not make the application no one else will". As these principles were satisfied in this case, the application by the trustees was held to be proper.

In the ordinary way the trustees will be respondents, as will be all the   **21–049** existing beneficiaries, adult and minor, the settlor[126] and, if the existing settlement contains a charitable trust, the Attorney-General.[127] It is, moreover, the duty of persons appointed as litigation friends for any minor beneficiaries to take proper legal advice and to appraise themselves fully of the nature of the application and the manner in which the beneficial interest of the minor is proposed to be affected.[128] At the same time, it is recognised that there is a limit to the necessity for joinder of parties. It therefore seems unnecessary, for reasons of practicality and expense, to join persons who are merely potential members of a class and so it has been held that it is unnecessary to join persons who are only interested as the objects of a power which may never be exercised.[129] The same view has been taken in respect of persons interested under protective trusts which it is proposed to vary; as Wilberforce J. said in *Re Munro's Settlement Trusts*,[130] the court looks prima facie to the trustees as watchdogs to see that interested parties' interests are protected.

(2) Combined applications

Under section 53 of the Trustee Act 1925,[131] the court has power to make   **21–050** vesting orders in relation to a minor's beneficial interest. In some cases it may prove necessary to combine an application under this section with one under the Variation of Trusts Act 1958. This happened in *Re Bristol's Settled*

---

[124] (1990) [2000] W.T.L.R. 581.
[125] [1962] 1 W.L.R. 363.
[126] This is provided by the Civil Procedure Rules, Part 64.4(1)(a); see *Goulding v. James* [1997] 2 All E.R. 239.
[127] See *Re Longman's Settlement Trusts* [1962] 1 W.L.R. 455.
[128] *Re Whittall* [1973] 1 W.L.R. 1027.
[129] *Re Christie-Miller's Settlement* [1961] 1 W.L.R. 462.
[130] [1963] 1 W.L.R. 145; compare *Re Courtland's Settlement* [1965] 1 W.L.R. 1385.
[131] See *ante*, para 18–049.

Estates,[132] where Buckley J. authorised the execution of a deed "barring" (converting into an estate in fee simple) the estate in fee tail in remainder of a minor so that the property could be dealt with for his benefit under a proposed "arrangement" which the judge also approved.

(3) The effect of a variation

21–051   It now seems to be established that it is the arrangement itself and not the order of the court which effects the variation.[133] But it does seem necessary to regard the order of the court and the arrangement as having been made at the same time.[134] The arrangement will, however, be embodied in, or referred to in, the order and, where this causes a disposition of beneficial interests, stamp duty was formerly payable (however, such voluntary dispositions are at present not subject either to stamp duty or to stamp duty land tax). In *Thorn v. I.R.C.*,[135] Walton J. had to consider the nature of the disposition affected. A trust fund was held upon protective trusts for the settlor's wife for life, with remainder to the settlor's daughter for life, and ultimately for the children and remoter issue of the daughter. An order had been made under the Variation of Trusts Act 1958 approving a variation on behalf of the unborn and unascertained issue of the daughter. The trustees contended that, in giving its approval, the court in effect dealt with the interest of each unborn or unascertained person. Each interest, looked at separately, would have had almost no value. However, Walton J. held that the order affected the disposition of the totality of the separate interests which therefore fell to be valued as a composite whole. This decision will once again become important if *ad valorem* duty is ever reimposed on voluntary dispositions.

21–052   A further question is whether the trusts are effectively varied by the arrangement when the court order is made even though the arrangement does not comply with section 53(1)(c) of the Law of Property Act 1925. This section requires that the disposition of a subsisting equitable interest should be in writing.[136] In *Re Holt's Settlement*[137] Megarry J. answered this question in the affirmative. In coming to this conclusion, he relied on *Oughtred v. I.R.C.*,[138] on the basis that the arrangement amounted to a specifically enforceable oral contract and so gave rise to a constructive trust; this meant that the requirements of section 53(1)(c) could therefore be ignored because of section 53(2), which exempts constructive trusts from those requirements. In the House of Lords in *Oughtred v. I.R.C.*, this view was in fact adopted only by Lord Radcliffe, who was dissenting on the main issue, to which this

---

[132] [1965] 1 W.L.R. 469; see also *Re Lansdowne's Will Trusts* [1967] Ch. 603.

[133] *Re Holt's Settlement* [1969] 1 Ch. 100. See also *Re Holmden's Settlement* [1968] A.C. 685 at 701, 705, 713; *Spens v. I.R.C.* [1970] 1 W.L.R. 1173 at 1183, 1184. Megarry J. in *Re Holt's Settlement* followed *Re Joseph's Will Trusts* [1959] 1 W.L.R. 1019, not *Re Hambledon's Will Trusts* [1960] 1 W.L.R. 82, which had held that the court order effected the variation.

[134] *Re Holt's Settlement* [1969] 1 Ch. 100 at 115. The main reason for this requirement seems to be that decisions made on the basis of *Re Hambledon's Will Trusts* [1960] 1 W.L.R. 82 would have been made without jurisdiction.

[135] [1976] 2 All E.R. 622.

[136] For further discussion of this section and the authorities, see *ante*, para 4–008.

[137] [1969] 1 Ch. 100.

[138] [1960] A.C. 206; see *ante*, para 4–043.

point was, in the view of the majority, irrelevant.[139] However, Lord Radcliffe's view has since been expressly confirmed by the Court of Appeal in
Neville v. Wilson,[140] so that the decision of Megarry J. now clearly constitutes
the law in so far as the Variation of Trusts Act 1958 is concerned. However,
a variation will only take effect without formality on this basis where the
subject matter of the trusts which have been varied is entirely pure personalty; this is because all contracts for the sale of land are now required to be
in writing.[141]

---

[139] See *ante*, para 4–046.
[140] [1997] Ch. 144; see *ante*, para 4–047.
[141] Under the Law of Property (Miscellaneous Provisions) Act 1989, s.2.

CHAPTER 22

BREACH OF TRUST

22–001   A breach of trust occurs if a trustee does any act which he ought not to do, or fails to do any act which he ought to do with regard to the administration of the trust, or with regard to the beneficial interests arising under the trust. It would be undesirable to attempt an exhaustive list of circumstances in which a breach of trust can be committed, but the following are examples:

   (i) investing of trust moneys in unauthorised investments;

   (ii) taking a profit from the trust not authorised by the trust instrument or by the court;

   (iii) manipulating the investments to benefit one beneficiary at the expense of another;

   (iv) allowing trust property to remain under the control of one trustee only;

   (v) paying trust property to the wrong person;

   (vi) purchasing trust property without authority; and

   (vii) failing to exercise a proper discretion with regard to trust decisions.

22–002   Where there is an allegation of breach of trust, the following questions have to be considered:

   (i) whether a breach of trust been committed;

   (ii) whether the proposed defendant is liable;

   (iii) what the prima facie measure of liability is;

   (iv) whether there is any right to contribution or indemnity;

   (v) whether the proposed claimant is in time to sue; and

   (vi) whether the proposed defendant may be relieved from liability by the court or otherwise.

A consideration of these questions should be sufficient to ensure that no relevant point is overlooked when looking at the position from the point of view of the trustees.

22–003   However, when these questions are looked at from the point of view of the beneficiaries, it is also necessary to ask whether they can take any action against third parties if sufficient redress cannot be obtained from the trustees. Their possibilities are:

(i) a personal claim against a third party;

(ii) a legal proprietary claim in respect of the trust property; and

(iii) an equitable proprietary claim in respect of the trust property.

The two types of proprietary claims can be brought against the trustees as well as against third parties and often are when one or more of the trustees is insolvent.

I. THE LIABILITY OF A TRUSTEE FOR HIS OWN ACTS

There will usually be little difficulty in ascertaining whether a breach of trust   **22–004**
has been committed by a trustee during his trusteeship. Complications sometimes arise, however, in respect of acts done at the beginning and end of a trusteeship.

On appointment, a trustee should take certain steps. He should inspect   **22–005**
the trust instrument to ascertain the terms of the trust and to see whether any notices have been indorsed on it. He should ensure that all the trust property is transferred into his name jointly with the other trustees, for he may be liable if he allows the property to remain in the hands of another.[1] He may wish to go through the trust papers in order to familiarise himself with the circumstances of the trust. If in the course of doing so, or for that matter in any other way, he learns that a breach of trust has been committed, he must obtain satisfaction from the person responsible. Should the new trustee not do so, he will himself be liable for breach of trust for his own omission; the only exception to this principle is if the new trustee is reasonably satisfied that it would be useless to institute proceedings because, for example, the former trustee cannot be found, or is destitute.[2] On the other hand, unless a new trustee does acquire knowledge that a breach of trust has been committed or there are sufficient suspicious circumstances to place him on enquiry, he may assume that there have been no previous breaches of trust.[3]

When a trustee retires from a trust, in principle he remains liable for   **22–006**
breaches of trust committed during his trusteeship and his estate will be held liable if he has died by the time that the breaches come to light. He will only be relieved from liability if and to the extent that he may have been released by the continuing trustees or by the beneficiaries but, in the latter case, only where they were in possession of the relevant facts at the time of the release.

---

[1] He will only be liable if loss is caused as a result of the property being left in the hands of others; *Re Miller's Deed Trusts* (1978) Law Society Gazette, May 3, 1978.

[2] *Re Forest of Dean Coal Co.* [1878] 10 Ch.D. 450.

[3] *Re Stratham* [1856] 8 De G.M. & G. 291.

22–007   A breach of trust sometimes occurs shortly after the retirement of a
trustee. In such circumstances, the retiring trustee will be liable if he contemplated that a breach of trust would occur and he retired with the intention
of facilitating it or if, believing that it would occur, he retired to avoid being
involved in it. In such circumstances, he will be liable because his motive in
retiring was to enable the breach of trust to occur. If he merely realised that
his retirement would facilitate the breach of trust, he will not be liable just
for that reason[4] but he will be liable if, in addition to realising that his
retirement would facilitate the breach, he foresaw, or ought reasonably to
have foreseen, that such a breach would in fact take place. In this case he will
have failed in his duty to prevent a breach of trust occurring. It follows that,
if the retiring trustee did not foresee what would happen and the remaining
trustees have simply taken advantage of his absence to perpetrate the
breach, he will not himself have failed in any of his duties and so will not be
liable.[5] Apart from this, a trustee is not liable for breaches of trust which
occur after his retirement.

II. THE LIABILITY OF A TRUSTEE FOR THE ACTS OF HIS CO-TRUSTEES

22–008   A trustee can never be liable for the acts of his co-trustees as such but he will
be liable where a breach of trust is committed by his co-trustees if he himself
has breached the statutory duty of care imposed by the Trustee Act 2000.[6]
Until 1926 the position was governed by the general common law rule that
unpaid trustees were bound to use only such due diligence and care in the
management of the trust as an ordinary prudent man of business would use
in the management of his own affairs[7]; however, after 1925 the position was
held instead to be governed by the now repealed section 30 of the Trustee
Act 1925,[8] under which a trustee was only liable for losses which occurred
"through his own wilful default". The statutory duty of care clearly gives
rise to liability for conduct less than wilful default and it is, therefore, likely
that a trustee will now be liable for a breach of trust arising through the act
or default of his co-trustee in the same circumstances as he would have been
before 1926, that is to say:

(i)   where the trustee leaves a matter in the hands of his co-trustee
      without inquiry[9];

(ii) where he stands by while a breach of trust of which he is aware is
      being committed[10];

---

[4] *Head v. Gould* [1898] 2 Ch. 250.
[5] *ibid.*
[6] See *ante*, para 14–002.
[7] *Speight v. Gaunt* (1883) 9 App.Cas. 1.
[8] See *Re Vickery* [1931] 1 Ch. 572.
[9] *Chambers* v. *Minchin* (1802) 7 Ves. 186; *Shipbrook v. Hinchinbrook* (1810) 16 Ves. 477; *Hanbury
v. Kirkland* (1829) 3 Sim. 265; *Broadhurst v. Balguy* (1841) 1 Y. & C.C.C. 16; *Thompson v. Finch* (1865)
8 De G.M. & G. 560; *Mendes v. Guedalla* (1862) 8 Jur. 878; *Hale v. Adams* (1873) 21 W.R. 400; *Wynee
v. Tempest* (1897) 13 T.L.R. 360; *Re Second East Dulwich Building Society* (1899) 68 L.J.Ch. 196.
[10] In *Styles v. Guy* (1849) 1 Mac. & G. 422 at 433, Lord Cottenham stated that it is the duty of
executors and trustees "to watch over, and if necessary, to correct, the conduct of each other".
See also *Booth v. Booth* (1838) 1 Beav. 125; *Gough v. Smith* [1872] W.N. 18.

(iii) where he allows trust funds to remain in the sole control of his co-trustee[11]; and

(iv) where, on becoming aware of a breach of trust committed or contemplated by his co-trustee, he takes no steps to obtain redress.[12]

The circumstances in which a trustee is liable for the acts or defaults of his agents, as distinct from of his co-trustees, have already been considered.[13]

III. THE MEASURE OF LIABILITY

What is the measure of liability of a trustee who has committed a breach of trust? Leaving on one side the situation where the beneficiary seeks the imposition of a constructive trust on property which the trustee has himself obtained as a result of his breach of trust,[14] what the beneficiary will be seeking is an award of equitable compensation under *Nocton v. Lord Ashburton*[15]; the effect of that decision is that equitable compensation is available whether or not there has been a misappropriation of trust property.[16]

22–009

The primary means by which a beneficiary who is the victim of a breach of trust can obtain equitable compensation for that breach is by requiring the trustee to comply with his obligation to account for his stewardship.[17] This involves the trustee rendering an account of what he has done with the trust property which has been in his hands. If the beneficiary is dissatisfied with what the trustee has done, then he has the right to "surcharge" or "falsify" the account rendered. If the trustee has negligently failed to obtain all the income or capital that he should have done for the benefit of the trust, the beneficiary will surcharge the account, in other words claim a sum additional to the amount which the trustee actually obtained; in these circumstances, the excess is calculated on what is known as a footing of wilful default, in other words by reference to the specific amount of the loss occasioned by the trustee's lack of skill and care. If, on the other hand, the

22–010

---

[11] *English v. Willats* (1831) 1 L.J.Ch. 84; *Ex parte Booth* (1831) Mont. 248; *Child v. Giblett* (1834) 3 L.J.Ch. 124; *Hewitt v. Foster* (1843) 6 Beav. 259; *Wiglesworth v. Wiglesworth* (1852) 16 Beav. 269; *Byass v. Gates* (1854) 2 W.R. 487; *Trutch v. Lamprell* (1855) 20 Beav. 116; *Cowell v. Gatcombe* (1859) 27 Beav. 568; *William v. Higgins* (1868) 17 L.T. 525; *Rodbard v. Cooke* (1877) 25 W.R. 555; *Lewis v. Nobbs* (1878) 8 Ch.D. 591.

[12] *Boadman v. Mosman* (1779) 1 Bro.C.C. 68; *Wilkins v. Hogg* (1861) 8 Jur.(N.S.) 25 at 26, *per* Lord Westbury.

[13] See *ante*, para 14–111.

[14] This type of claim was considered in Chapter 10.

[15] [1914] A.C. 932, see *post*, para 22–011.

[16] Equitable compensation had always been available when there had been a misappropriation of trust property and in this respect the House of Lords did no more than reaffirm the continued existence of equity's jurisdiction to award it, then thought in some quarters to have been extinguished due to the very wide interpretation which was being given to *Derry v. Peek* (1889) 14 App.Cas. 337. However, the House of Lords went considerably further than this and upheld the existence of the same jurisdiction when there had been no misappropriation of trust property but merely a breach of fiduciary duty (in that case the fact that the defendant solicitor had failed adequately to disclose a conflict of interest).

[17] See Lord Millett, extrajudicially, (1998) 114 L.Q.R. 214.

trustee has made an unauthorised disbursement, the beneficiary has the option of falsifying the account in that respect, in other words of disallowing the expenditure in question; in that case, the trustee will then be treated as if he was still holding on trust the sum paid away and, once the account has been taken,[18] will be obliged to reimburse that sum to the trust.[19] However, where the disbursement was an unauthorised investment which has subsequently appreciated in value, it will not be in the interests of the beneficiary to falsify the account; he will, therefore, instead normally accept the unauthorised investment as part of the trust property and, in such circumstances, he is said to affirm or adopt the transaction. Whenever an account is surcharged or falsified, "the obligation of a defaulting trustee [to compensate the trust fund for such a loss] is essentially one of effecting restitution to the estate. The obligation is of a personal character and its extent is not to be limited by common law principles governing the remoteness of damage."[20]

22–011   However, the taking of an account will not necessarily or usually be appropriate where there has been neither a failure to obtain nor a misapplication of trust property. This will be the case where, for example, the breach of trust complained of relates to a conflict of interest and duty. In *Nocton v. Lord Ashburton*[21] itself, a solicitor was found to be in breach of fiduciary duty as a result of his failure adequately to disclose to his client a conflict of interest and duty arising out of the fact that he was interested in the proceeds of the investment in respect of which he was advising the client; when the investment proved to be unsuccessful, equitable compensation was awarded in respect of the client's loss. In *Longstaff v. Birtles*[22] a solicitor who had been representing a client in connection with the purchase of a hotel suggested to the client, after he had decided not to proceed, that he should instead invest in a different hotel owned by a partnership of which the solicitor was a member; the solicitor disclosed all the facts but his failure to insist that the client obtained independent legal advice was held to place him in a conflict of interest and duty and he was held liable to compensate the client for the losses arising out of his investment. A different conflict, one of preferential interest, potentially arises where a solicitor is representing more than one party to a transaction, typically both a purchaser and his mortgagee; in such circumstances, the solicitor will have committed a breach of fiduciary duty if he intentionally prefers the interests of one of his clients to those of the other.[23] However, it must always be remembered that, as the Court of Appeal emphasised in *Bristol and West Building Society v. Mothew*,[24] not every breach of duty by a fiduciary is a breach of fiduciary duty; the fiduciary's liability will be merely contractual or tortious unless he

---

[18] The obligation to reimburse the trust does not arise as soon as the unauthorised disbursement has been made but only when the beneficiary elects to falsify it; until then, the trustee does not know whether or not the beneficiary will choose to do so.

[19] *Clough v. Bond* (1838) 3 My. & Cr. 490 at 496–497, *per* Lord Cottenham L.C.

[20] *Re Dawson* [1966] 2 N.S.W.L.R. 211 at 214 (Supreme Court of New South Wales).

[21] [1914] A.C. 932, see *ante*, para 22–009, n.16.

[22] [2002] 1 W.L.R. 470.

[23] Such breaches of fiduciary duty were held to have arisen in *Nationwide Building Society v. Balmer Radmore* [1999] Lloyds Rep. P.N. 241.

[24] [1998] Ch. 1.

has preferred the interests of either himself or someone else to those of his principal.

In circumstances where there has been a breach of fiduciary duty of one **22–012** of these types, there will normally be nothing that can be surcharged or falsified and the quantum of recovery will, therefore, have to be established in some other way. Exactly how has been a matter of considerable debate but the general view is that in these circumstances it is appropriate to apply common law principles of remoteness of damages to the assessment of equitable compensation. This was the approach adopted by Lord Browne-Wilkinson in *Target Holdings v. Redferns*[25] when he applied the "but for" test of causation to the assessment of equitable compensation; although, as will be seen later on,[26] this was a case in which an account could appropriately have been taken, the beneficiary did not seek one. Lord Browne-Wilkinson's decision and the Commonwealth authorities on which he relied[27] were subsequently applied by Hobhouse L.J. in *Swindle v. Harrison*[28] where a solicitor had failed to disclose all the facts of a loan transaction between himself and his client; the client had suffered no loss as a result of the solicitor's breach of duty so no equitable compensation was awarded. Further, it was subsequently held in *Nationwide Building Society v. Balmer Radmore*[29] that a fiduciary who is liable for breach of fiduciary duty is entitled to prove that his principal's loss would have occurred, in whole or in part, irrespective of his breach of fiduciary duty[30] and, in the event that he can prove this, he will not be responsible for the loss, or the part of the loss, in question.[31]

It should be added that equitable compensation is not awarded in order **22–013** to punish the trustee; however, if he has been fraudulent or has otherwise behaved particularly badly, the court will reflect its displeasure by increasing the amount of interest payable by the trustee above that which he would otherwise have been ordered to pay.[32]

---

[25] [1996] 1 A.C. 421.

[26] See *post*, para 22–018.

[27] *Re Dawson* [1966] N.S.W.L.R. 211 (Supreme Court of New South Wales); *Canson Enterprises v. Boughton & Co.* (1991) 85 D.L.R.(4th) 129 (Supreme Court of Canada).

[28] [1997] 4 All E.R. 705 at 727–728.

[29] [1999] Lloyds Rep. P.N. 241 at 272–279.

[30] *Brickenden v. London Loan Savings Company* [1934] 3 D.L.R. 465 (Privy Council on appeal from Canada) had established that the principal is entitled to be put back into the position in which he was prior to the breach of fiduciary duty even if his loss or some part of it would have occurred even if there had been no breach of fiduciary duty; this view had subsequently been adopted in Australia (*Gemstone Corporation of Australia v. Grasso* (1994) 13 A.C.S.R. 695 (Supreme Court of South Australia)). But Blackburne J. preferred the more recent Canadian authorities (*Commerce Trust Co. v. Berk* (1989) 68 O.R.(2d.) 257 (Ontario Court of Appeal); *Hodgkinson v. Simms* (1994) 117 D.L.R. (4th) 161 (Supreme Court of Canada)) and the New Zealand authorities (*Everist v. McEvedy* [1996] 3 N.Z.L.R. 349 (High Court of New Zealand), applying *Haira v. Burbery Mortgage Finance and Savings* [1995] 3 N.Z.L.R. 396 (New Zealand Court of Appeal)).

[31] Blackburne J. rejected (*ibid.*, pp.279–282) the further contention that the fiduciary should be entitled to rely on the contributory negligence of his principal in the way that he can in New Zealand (*Day v. Mead* [1987] 2 N.Z.L.R. 443 at 451 (New Zealand Court of Appeal)) and in Canada (*Canson Enterprises v. Boughton & Co.* (1991) 85 D.L.R. (4th) 129 at 151–152 (Supreme Court of Canada)). He granted leave to appeal but the litigation as a whole was compromised.

[32] See *post*, para 22–032.

22–014   The following examples illustrate these principles. All are concerned with the prima facie liability of the trustee and do not take into account the possibility of some protection or relief being given to the trustee in the manner which will be discussed later on.[33]

1. *Improper Payments of Trust Money*

22–015   Where the trustees make an improper payment of trust money, the beneficiaries are clearly entitled to falsify the disbursement made; consequently, the trustees are liable to make good to the trust fund that amount, so that the income or capital sum wrongly paid, together with interest thereon,[34] can be paid out to the correct beneficiary.

22–016   An unusual illustration of the operation of this principle is provided by *Target Holdings v. Redferns*.[35] The plaintiff had agreed to lend £1,525,000 on the security of two properties which were in fact being acquired for £775,000 but, as a result of the interposition of two intermediate purchasers, appeared to be being purchased for £2,000,000. The defendant solicitors, who were acting in the normal way both for the purchasers and for the plaintiff mortgagee, were holding the mortgage advance on trust for the plaintiff with authority to release it to the vendor only upon receipt of the duly executed conveyances and mortgages of the properties. However, they released the funds to the intermediate purchasers several days before the execution of these documents. The plaintiff nevertheless obtained, admittedly after the release of the funds, the mortgage securities which it had instructed the defendants to obtain. However, those securities proved to be insufficient and their realisation produced for the plaintiff over £1,000,000 less than the sum advanced; this loss would of course have been incurred even if the defendants had complied with their instructions.

22–017   The plaintiff sought the reconstitution of the trust fund. On an application for summary judgment, the Court of Appeal[36] held that the obligation of a trustee who had committed a breach of trust was to put the trust fund in the same position as it would have been if no breach had taken place. Where the breach consisted in the wrongful payment of trust moneys to a stranger, there was an immediate loss which the trustee was immediately liable to reimburse; it was not necessary for there to be any inquiry as to whether the loss would have occurred if there had been no breach of trust. Summary judgment was therefore ordered. However, this decision was reversed by the House of Lords. Lord Browne-Wilkinson held that there was only any obligation to reimburse the trust fund at all when the trust in question was ongoing rather than where the beneficiary was, like the plaintiff, absolutely entitled; further, even when such an obligation arose, it was not possible to "stop the clock" at the moment when the wrongful payment occurred and ignore all subsequent events. He therefore held that the liability of a trustee

---

[33] See *post*, paras 22–046, 22–078.

[34] For the rate of interest, see *post*, para 22–032. See generally *Youyang v. Minter Ellison Morris Fletcher* [2003] W.T.L.R. 751.

[35] [1996] 1 A.C. 421. This case is analysed in detail in *Trends in Contemporary Trust Law* (ed. Oakley, 1996), p.217.

[36] [1994] 1 W.L.R. 1089.

to pay equitable compensation was subject to a "but for" test of causation. The defendants would consequently only be liable if it could be shown that the transaction would not have proceeded and the plaintiff's loss would therefore not have been incurred but for the payment by the defendants to the intermediate purchasers in breach of trust.[37] The defendants were therefore given leave to defend the action; however, because of the high probability that the test of causation would be satisfied, they were ordered to pay £1,000,000 into court as a condition of being allowed to do so. The case was subsequently settled without proceeding to trial on the basis that the plaintiff received the £1,000,000.

It has been contended[38] that this case would have been more appropriately decided on the basis of the defendant trustees' obligation to account. The plaintiff had authorised a payment only in exchange for the mortgage securities; consequently, it was entitled to "falsify" the defendants' account in respect of the payments to the intermediate purchasers since those mortgages had not yet been executed. Had an account been taken at that stage, the plaintiff would undoubtedly have been entitled to reimbursement of the whole sum paid away and could clearly have obtained summary judgment for that sum. However, the defendants had subsequently complied with their instructions by obtaining the mortgage securities, something which they were at that stage still authorised to do; this transformed their unauthorised payment into an authorised one. Consequently, nothing would be found to be due to the plaintiff on any subsequent taking of an account, which would thus have produced exactly the same result as that arrived at by the House of Lords. This analysis cannot be faulted but that does not alter the fact that no account was actually sought in the proceedings. The reason for this was that the plaintiff initially brought only proceedings for professional negligence; it was only in the course of the trial at first instance that the plaintiff discovered that the funds had been paid to the intermediate purchasers and realised that there had been a breach of trust. The decision of the House of Lords, therefore, remains a perfectly acceptable authority on the measure of equitable compensation available where no account is taken. However, the taking of an account is obviously the more appropriate method by which to proceed when trust funds have been paid to the wrong person. It is, therefore, inevitable that an account will normally be the means by which beneficiaries proceed in cases of this kind.

22–018

2. Failure Properly to Invest the Trust Property

(A) Investment in Unauthorised Investments
Where trustees invest the trust funds in unauthorised investments, the beneficiaries have the right to falsify the disbursement and require the trustees to replace the funds wrongfully invested. In such circumstances, the

22–019

---

[37] This had been able to be shown in *Alliance & Leicester Building Society v. Edgestop* (1991), unreported.
[38] By Lord Millett, extra-judicially, in (1998) L.Q.R. 214.

trustees will in effect have to sell the unauthorised investments and make good whatever loss results.[39] On the other hand, where the unauthorised investment has made a profit, it will not be in the interests of the beneficiaries to falsify the account and, provided that they are all ascertained and *sui juris*, they will, therefore, be able to adopt the unauthorised investment and take the profit. Where they do so, they clearly should not be entitled also to claim the difference between the value of the improper investment and any higher amount that would have been obtained by an authorised investment. However, there is in fact a conflict of authority on this point.[40]

22–020   A slightly different question arose in *Vyse v. Foster*,[41] where the unauthorised investment consisted, unusually, of an unauthorised improvement to other trust property; in such circumstances, the beneficiaries will of course have no real option but to adopt the investment. In that case trustees who held land and money upon a common trust expended, without authority, some of the money on erecting a bungalow on the land at a cost of £1,600; this benefited the trust by more than the £1,600 which had been expended. The beneficiaries argued that not only were the trustees liable to reimburse the £1,600 because this expenditure had been unauthorised but that they were also entitled to the benefit of the bungalow because it was an accretion to the trust property. The Court of Appeal and House of Lords rejected this argument and it is only surprising that it was accepted at first instance. However, had the erection of the bungalow benefited the trust by less than the cost of erecting it, the beneficiaries could undoubtedly have surcharged the disbursement and recovered the difference.

22–021   If trustees instead sell an authorised investment and reinvest the proceeds in an unauthorised one, the beneficiaries have the same choice as to whether to falsify or to adopt the unauthorised investment. If it is falsified, that is likely to be because it has resulted in a loss. In such circumstances, the beneficiaries have a further choice. They can compel the trustees either to make good the difference between the sale price of the authorised investment and the proceeds of sale of the unauthorised investment, or to repurchase for the trust the authorised security, taking credit for the proceeds of sale of the unauthorised security. Suppose, therefore, that the trustees sell an authorised investment, 4,000 shares, for £100,000 and reinvest that £100,000 in an unauthorised investment such as some gold bars.[42] If a year later the gold bars are sold at a loss for £80,000, the beneficiaries have a choice. They can compel the trustees to pay to the trust fund £100,000, the proceeds of the shares, less the £80,000 which the trustees will already have paid in from the sale of the gold bars. Alternatively, they can compel the trustees to purchase for the trust 4,000 shares in the company in question, however much they might then cost; if the shares have doubled in price, the trustees will

---

[39] *Re Salmon* (1889) 42 Ch.D. 351.

[40] The conclusion suggested in the text was adopted in *Thornton v. Stokill* (1855) 1 Jur. 151 but in *Re Lake* [1903] 1 K.B. 439 the beneficiaries were held to be entitled to the additional amount as well.

[41] (1872) L.R. 8 Ch. 309, affirmed (1874) L.R. 7 H.L. 318.

[42] In the absence of express authorisation in the trust instrument, these will not be an authorised investment because they are not income-producing.

therefore have to pay £200,000 for them but can utilise as part of that sum the £80,000 received from the sale of the gold bars.

This relatively unobjectionable principle was taken a stage further in *Re* **22–022** *Massingberd*.[43] In that case the trustees sold Consols and reinvested the proceeds of sale in an unauthorised security. This was in due course sold without loss but by this time the price of Consols had risen. The court held that the trustees should place the beneficiaries in the same position as they would have been had no sale taken place with the result that they had themselves to pay the increase in the price of the Consols.

Where an unauthorised investment is falsified, the trustees are not enti- **22–023** tled to take into account any loss which would have been sustained if they had strictly performed the trust.[44] Suppose, therefore, that trustees are directed to invest in one particular investment. They make that investment but later improperly sell it for £100,000 and invest that sum in another investment. The latter declines in value and is sold for £80,000 but by the time of that sale the investment which the trustees were directed to make has also declined in value since they sold it and its market price is now only £70,000. If the beneficiaries falsify the account, the trustees are liable to make good, at the option of the beneficiaries, the difference between £80,000 and £100,000 and they are not excused from liability by virtue of the fact that, if the investment which they had been directed to make had been retained, the holding would have been worth only £70,000. This is because the effect of falsifying the investment is that the trustees are treated as having held £100,000 on trust for the beneficiaries at all times.

Finally, it should be noted that, where a trust is for persons by way of **22–024** succession, an unauthorised investment which yields a very high income will have benefited the income beneficiary at the expense of the remainder-men. Consequently, whether the investment is falsified or adopted, it will be necessary for the income actually obtained to be apportioned between the income beneficiary and the remaindermen; the income beneficiary will be entitled to interest at the ordinary rate and the balance of the income will then be added to the trust fund as capital.[45]

(B) Leaving Trust Property Uninvested

The Trustee Act 1925[46] gave trustees the power to pay trust money into a **22–025** bank while an investment was being sought. This provision was necessary then because of the very restricted powers of investment which trustees had under that Act; however, it is no longer necessary now that the Trustee Act 2000 has conferred a general power of investment on trustees[47] and has consequently been repealed. However, it was never thought that this provision of the Trustee Act 1925 had affected the cases decided before 1926 to the

---

[43] (1890) 63 L.T. 296.
[44] *Shepherd v. Mouls* (1845) 4 Hare 500 at 504; *Watts v. Girdlestone* (1843) 6 Beav. 188; *Byrchall v. Bradford* (1822) 6 Madd. 235.
[45] *Re Emmet's Estate* (1881) 17 Ch.D. 142. As to the "ordinary" rate of interest, see *post*, para 22–033.
[46] Trustee Act 1925, s.11(1).
[47] Trustee Act 2000, s.3(1); *ante*, para 14–069.

effect that moneys must not be left uninvested for an unreasonable time[48] and this is clearly the case under the general power of investment. Where leaving trust property uninvested is held to amount to a breach of the statutory duty of care,[49] the beneficiaries will be entitled to the following equitable compensation (this will not be an appropriate case for the taking of an account). If the trustees ought to have invested in a range of investments, as will usually be the case, their liability is limited to making good the difference between any interest actually received and the rate of interest fixed by the court.[50] The trustees are not liable for any capital loss, because it is impossible to ascertain it.[51] If, on the other hand, the trustees ought to have invested in one specified security only but did not do so, in the event that its price rises they can be compelled to purchase such an amount of that specified security as they could have purchased with the trust fund at the proper time.

22–026   Trustees may erroneously regard their investment powers as more limited than they actually are and, as a result invest in a more restricted range of investments than they were actually obliged to. This occurred in *Nestlé v. National Westminster Bank*.[52] The Court of Appeal held that a beneficiary who could prove that loss had been suffered thereby could obtain equitable compensation. However, save in extreme cases (the court used as an example the investment of the entire trust fund in fixed interest securities when the trustees had power to invest in equities), such a loss will be extremely difficult to prove and could not be established in that case.

(C)   Use by Trustees of the Trust Funds for their Personal Purposes

22–027   If the trustees use the trust money for their personal purposes, the beneficiaries will clearly be entitled to falsify these disbursements. The trustees will consequently be liable to pay back the amount used, or the value[53] of any property improperly sold to provide the funds which the trustees have used. In these circumstances, special rules apply as to interest.[54] However, rather than receiving interest, the beneficiaries can instead require the trustees to pay over the actual profit which they have received.[55] Further, if a trustee has mixed the trust money with his own money and invested the whole in something which is still identifiable, the beneficiaries will normally be able to maintain an equitable proprietary claim[56] and recover, at their election,[57] either the amount of the trust money invested or a proportional

---

[48] *Cann v. Cann* (1884) 33 W.R. 40.
[49] See *ante*, para 14–002.
[50] As to which, see *post*, para 22–032.
[51] *Shepherd v. Mouls* (1845) 4 Hare 500 at 504.
[52] [1993] 1 W.L.R. 1260.
[53] Ascertained as at the date of judgment.
[54] See *post*, para 22–034.
[55] *Newman v. Bennett* (1784) 1 Bro.C.C. 359; *Ex parte Watson* (1814) 2 V. & B. 414; *Walker v. Woodward* (1826) 1 Russ. 107 at 111; *Att-Gen. v. Solly* (1829) 2 Sim 518; *Wedderburn v. Wedderburn* (1838) 4 My. & Cr. 41 at 46; *Jones v. Foxall* (1852) 15 Beav. 388; *Williams v. Powell* (1852) 15 Beav. 388; *Macdonald v. Richardson* (1858) 1 Giff. 81; *Townend v. Townend* (1859) 1 Giff. 201; *Re Davis* [1902] 2 Ch. 314.
[56] See *post*, para 22–133.
[57] *Foskett v. McKeown* [2001] 1 A.C. 102 at 131 *per* Lord Millett

share of whatever profit has been made[58]; they will obviously do the former if the investment has fallen in value and the latter if it has risen in value.

3. *How Losses are to be Assessed*

(A) The Date at which Losses are to be Assessed

Where a trustee improperly deals with an asset which as a result ceases to be under his control, it is necessary to determine the date at which the loss to the trust fund is to be measured. Previously, when the values of many assets were more stable than at the present time, the loss was ascertained at the date when proceedings were commenced. Thus in *Re Massingberd*,[59] where trustees improperly sold Consols, the Court of Appeal ordered them to pay the cost of replacing the Consols as at the date of the writ. Much more recently, in *Re Bell's Indenture*,[60] Vinelott J. said that this was incorrect, and that the general principle was that the loss should be ascertained at the date of judgment. Subsequently, in *Jaffray v. Marshall*,[61] it was held that this question had not actually had to be decided in either of these cases which were therefore of no assistance; however, the conclusion actually reached in this case, that where there had been a continuing breach of trust, the trustees were liable to compensate the trust at the highest intermediate value of the property between the date of breach and the date of judgment, was clearly inconsistent with the subsequent decision in *Target Holdings v. Redferns*[62] and the House of Lords duly held that *Jaffray v. Marshall* had been wrongly decided. The law is thus uncertain at present; however, the view of Vinelott J. seems preferable.

22–028

Once established, the liability of a defaulting trustee to make restitution continues until restitution is actually made; this is the case even if the settlement has in the meantime come to an end. In *Bartlett v. Barclays Bank Trust Co.*[63] a trust company had permitted a company in which the trust had a controlling interest to engage in two hazardous property speculations and was consequently held liable to compensate the trust for the loss which had ensued from the fall in the value of the shares in the company. The trust did not actually sell the shares until after the company had disposed of all its speculative investments; this was four years after three of the beneficiaries had became absolutely entitled to their shares and were, therefore, in control of their own destiny. It was nevertheless held that the loss suffered by the beneficiaries was to be assessed at the time when the shares were finally sold.

22–029

Whatever the general rule about the date at which losses have to be assessed actually is, it is at least clear that, if the trustees improperly dispose of an asset which, had they not disposed of it then, would have been properly disposed of at a later date, the loss is to be ascertained at that later

22–030

---

[58] In *Foskett v. McKeown* [2001] 1 A.C. 102, the beneficiaries recovered the proportion of the proceeds of a life insurance policy corresponding to the proportion of the premiums paid with their funds.
[59] (1890) 63 L.T. 296.
[60] [1980] 1 W.L.R. 1217 at 1233.
[61] [1993] 1 W.L.R. 1285.
[62] [1996] 1 A.C. 421.
[63] [1980] Ch. 515.

date and not at any date thereafter. In *Re Bell's Indenture*[64] the court was concerned with a marriage settlement made in 1907 and a voluntary settlement made in 1930, which had a common trustee who was also a common beneficiary. In 1947, the trustees of the marriage settlement improperly sold a farm for £8,200 to the trustees of the voluntary settlement. In 1949 the latter properly sold the farm to a third party for £12,400. If the trustees of the marriage settlement had not sold the farm in 1947, they would undoubtedly have done so when the trustees of the voluntary settlement did in 1949. Vinelott J. held that the liability of the trustees of the marriage settlement was to be limited to the value of the farm in 1949. He also held that their liability was not affected by the fact that, if they had sold in 1949, they would probably have reinvested the proceeds of sale in another farm, because it was impossible to determine how any such other farm would have appreciated or depreciated.

(B) The Absence of any Allowance in respect of Tax

22–031   Where a trustee takes trust moneys and applies them for his own purposes, he is liable to restore the moneys which he has taken and is not allowed to benefit from any reduction in the liability to tax which ensues from the misapplication.[65] A further point which arose in *Re Bell's Indenture*[66] was that, if the trustees of the marriage settlement had not improperly sold the farm in 1947 but had instead retained it until 1949, sold it then and reinvested the proceeds of sale, the value of the trust fund would have been much greater than it actually was. This would in turn have given rise to greater liabilities to estate duty[67] on the deaths of the successive income beneficiaries. It was held that the defaulting trustee was not entitled to reduce the amount which he had to pay to make good the breach of trust by the amount of that tax saving. This decision was followed in *Bartlett v. Barclays Bank Trust Co. (No.2)*.[68] Had the trustee in that case not permitted the company to engage in loss-making speculative property investments, the company would have made larger dividend payments. This would have increased the income and with it the income tax liability of the beneficiaries. Similarly, if the company had not sustained losses, the shares could have been sold for a higher price, which would probably have increased the liability of the beneficiaries to capital gains tax. Brightman J. however held that the trustees were liable to make good the gross loss and could not take into account the tax savings which had occurred, even though this produced "a somewhat unjust bias"[69] against the trustees.

(C) The Incidence of Interest

22–032   Where a trustee has misapplied trust funds, he is liable not only to replace those funds, but also to pay interest thereon. A trustee is similarly liable to pay interest where income is lost as a result of his failure to make an

---

[64] [1980] 1 W.L.R. 1217.

[65] Thus, the rule in *British Transport Commission v. Gourley* [1956] A.C. 185 does not apply.

[66] [1980] 1 W.L.R. 1217; see *ante*, para 22–030.

[67] The forerunner of inheritance tax, under which this would also be the case; see *ante*, para 15–059.

[68] [1980] Ch. 515.

[69] *ibid*. at 538.

investment.[70] In such circumstances, two questions arise: first, at what rate is the interest to be calculated; and, secondly, whether the interest is to be simple or compounded and, if the latter, at what frequency.[71] The approach of the courts, particularly with regard to the rate of interest, has changed in recent years. The present position appears to be as follows.

In the nineteenth century the ordinary interest rate was 4 per cent.[72] Subsequently,[73] the normal rate became that allowed from time to time on the court's special account, formerly the short-term investments account[74]; this rate, which is generally in line with that offered on National Savings investments, is varied from time to time by statutory instrument and, because changes do not tend to be made very often,[75] calculation of the interest payable is quite straightforward. More recently, it has been said[76] that the usual rate against trustees is now not more favourable than 0.5 per cent less than the Bank of England's base rate, which is now reviewed every single month and therefore tends to change quite often. These last two rates probably set the permissible range for awards of interest at the present time, subject to what follows.

22–033

It has long been clear that, if a trustee uses trust money for his own purposes, he will be ordered to pay a higher rate of interest where it can reasonably be concluded that he would himself have realised a higher rate[77]; this will be the case even in the absence of any evidence that the trustee did in fact derive a higher rate. More recently, this higher rate has also been regarded as available where the trust in question is a commercial concern rather than a trust for private individuals on the basis that commercial concerns can generally obtain higher rates of interest. When the ordinary interest rate was 4 per cent, this higher rate was 5 per cent. However, since 1975 it has instead been taken to be 1 per cent above the Bank of England's base rate.[78] However, this is no more than a presumption which can readily be displaced by evidence showing that it is unfair to one or other of the parties[79] and in this respect the court's discretion is unusually wide. In such circumstances an obvious alternative candidate is LIBOR, the rate at which banks lend to one another in London, which has often been used in commercial, as distinct from trusts, cases.

22–034

---

[70] *Stafford v. Fiddon* (1857) 23 Beav. 386.

[71] The differences are striking. On £10,000, 10% simple interest for 10 years will amount to £10,000, 10% compounded yearly will amount to £15,937 and 10% interest compounded half-yearly will amount to £16,533.

[72] *Att.-Gen. v. Alford* (1855) 4 De G.M. & G. 843; *Fletcher v. Green* (1864) 33 Beav. 426.

[73] *Bartlett v. Barclays Bank Trust Co (No.2)* [1980] Ch. 515; *Jaffray v. Marshall* [1993] 1 W.L.R. 1285 (overruled on other grounds by the House of Lords in *Target Holdings v. Redferns* [1996] 1 A.C. 421); *Mathew v. T. M. Sutton* [1994] 1 W.L.R. 1455.

[74] Established under s.6(1) of the Administration of Justice Act 1965.

[75] Certainly far less frequently than in the case of the Bank of England's base rate, which is now reviewed every single month.

[76] In *Re Duckwari (No.2)* [1999] Ch. 268 (CA) at p.273.

[77] *Att.-Gen. v. Alford* (1855) De G.M. & G. 852; *Mathew v. T. M. Sutton* [1994] 1 W.L.R. 1455.

[78] *Wallersteiner v. Moir (No.2)* [1975] Q.B. 373; *Belmont Finance Corporation v. Williams Furniture (No.2)* [1980] 1 All E.R. 393; *Guardian Ocean Cargoes v. Banco do Brasil (No.3)* [1992] 2 Lloyd's Rep. 193; *Re Duckwari (No.2)* [1999] Ch. 268 (CA) at p.273.

[79] *Shearson Lehman Hutton v. Maclaine Watson & Co. (No.2)* [1990] 1 Lloyd's Rep. 441 at 451–453.

22–035   Simple interest is the general rule in the absence of special circumstances.[80] However, the court has a discretion to order a trustee to pay compound interest. He will be ordered to pay interest compounded annually if he was under an obligation to accumulate the trust income.[81] If, however, he should have invested the fund in a specified investment and accumulated the income from that investment, then the interest must be compounded at the same intervals as interest or dividends would have been received on that investment.[82] A trustee will also be ordered to pay interest compounded annually if he has used trust money in his own business[83] or for his own commercial purposes but probably not if he has used it in his professional practice.[84] Although the purpose of ordering a trustee to pay compound rather than simple interest has been stated[85] not to be to punish the trustee, compounding does appear to have been used for this purpose in certain cases of active and deliberate fraud or misconduct.[86]

22–036   Where a trustee pays interest, it seems that it is for the court to decide whether or not the income beneficiaries are entitled to receive the whole of that interest. In *Bartlett v. Barclays Bank Trust Co. (No.2)*[87] Brightman J. said:

"To some extent the high interest rates payable on money lent reflect and compensate for the continual erosion in the value of money by reason of galloping inflation. It seems to me arguable, therefore, that if a high rate of interest is payable in such circumstances, a proportion of that interest should be added to capital in order to help maintain the value of the corpus of the trust estate. It may be, therefore, that there will have to be some adjustment as between life tenant and remainderman."

This approach, which reflects that adopted where there is an unauthorised investment in a high income producing security, was applied in *Jaffray v. Marshall*,[88] in which judicial notice was taken of the fact that high rates of interest contain a large element which merely preserves capital values (which should belong to the remaindermen) while, in times when inflation is at a less high level, the rate of return needed to preserve capital is not as high. Since in that case the period in question was of the latter kind, the interest (at the short-term investment account rate) was apportioned equally

---

[80] *Stafford v. Fiddon* (1857) 23 Beav. 386; *Burdick v. Garrick* (1870) 5 Ch. App. 233; *Vyse v. Foster* (1874) L.R. 7 H.L. 318; *Belmont Finance Corporation v. Williams Furniture (No.2)* [1970] 1 All E.R. 393. This was the basis on which the lower courts held the local authority liable to pay compound interest in *Westdeutsche Landesbank Girozentrale v. Islington L.B.C.* [1994] 4 All E.R. 890 (Hobhouse J.), [1994] 1 W.L.R. 938, CA. However, the House of Lords [1996] A.C. 669 held that the local authority was not a trustee and so this basis did not apply; the House also held, by a majority, that there was no equitable jurisdiction to order the payment of compound interest on a purely common law claim.

[81] *Raphael v. Boehm* (1805) 11 Ves. 92; *Re Barclay* [1899] 1 Ch. 674.

[82] *Re Emmet's Estate* (1881) 17 Ch.D. 142; *Gilroy v. Stephens* (1882) 30 W.R. 745.

[83] *Wallersteiner v. Moir (No.2)* [1975] Q.B. 373; *Guardian Ocean Cargoes v. Banco do Brasil (No.3)* [1992] 2 Lloyd's Rep. 193.

[84] *Burdick v. Garrick* (1870) 5 Ch. App. 233; *Hale v. Sheldrake* (1889) 60 L.T. 292.

[85] By Lord Hatherley in *Burdick v. Garrick* (1870) 5 Ch. App. 233.

[86] Such as *Jones v. Foxall* (1852) 15 Beav. 388; *Gordon v. Gonda* [1955] 1 W.L.R. 885.

[87] [1980] Ch. 515 at 538.

[88] [1993] 1 W.L.R. 1285.

between the tenant for life and the remainderman. It is to be hoped that the overruling of this decision on other grounds by the House of Lords in *Target Holdings v. Redferns*[89] does not prevent these helpful observations from being applied in future similar cases.

(D) The Right to Set-Off

If a trustee commits more than one breach of trust, he cannot set off a gain made in one transaction against a loss suffered in another. However, each transaction is considered as a whole. In *Fletcher v. Green*[90] trustees made an authorised investment on mortgage. The property was in due course sold at a loss and the proceeds were paid into court. The court authorities invested the money in Consols, which rose in price. It was held that the trustees could offset the gain in the Consols against the loss on the mortgage as both were incidents in the same transaction. On the other hand, in *Dimes v. Scott*[91] trustees committed a breach of trust in that they ought to have sold an unauthorised investment and invested the proceeds in Consols. Much later on, part of the unauthorised investment was sold and the proceeds were then invested in Consols. By that time the market price of Consols had fallen considerably from the price at which they had been standing when the investment should have been made. The trustees sought to offset the gain made by virtue of the fact that they had thus been able to buy a larger quantity of Consols against the loss which had been suffered on the sale of the unauthorised investment. It was held that they could not do so for these were two distinct transactions, not one; the breach of trust was in not realising the unauthorised investment while the gain arose from the authorised investment being at an unusually low figure. *Dimes v. Scott* was followed in *Wiles v. Gresham*,[92] where trustees of a marriage settlement committed a breach of trust by negligently failing to recover from the husband the sum of £2,000 which he had covenanted to pay to them. They then committed a further breach of trust by investing some of the other trust funds in the purchase of land without having any authority so to do. However, the husband considerably improved the land so purchased by the use of his own funds and it consequently became worth considerably more than the trustees had paid for it. When a claim was made against them for failure to recover the £2,000, the trustees sought to set-off the profit which had fortuitously been made on their unauthorised investment in the land; they also were held to be unable to do so because the two transactions were distinct. Both decisions, particularly that in *Dimes v. Scott*, are on the harsh side and it may be that if similar facts recurred today the court might strive to reach different conclusions.

22–037

While the rule established by these authorities is entirely clear, namely that a gain can only be set off against a loss if both occur in the same transaction, it is not always easy to decide whether two or more events are stages in the same transaction or separate transactions. The test seems to be whether all the individual steps taken in pursuance of a common policy can

22–038

---

[89] [1996] 1 A.C. 421.
[90] (1864) 33 Beav. 426.
[91] (1828) 4 Russ. 195.
[92] (1854) 2 Drew. 258; 24 L.J.Ch. 264.

be treated as one "transaction" for this purpose. Thus, in *Bartlett v. Barclays Bank Trust Co.*,[93] where the trustee allowed the company to embark on two speculative property developments as part of the company's policy of seeking to increase the cash funds available to it, the trustee was allowed to offset the profit from one development against the loss arising from the other.

IV. THE POSITION OF TRUSTEES *INTER SE*

22–039 Trustees are under a duty to act jointly; therefore they only have the authority to act individually if the trust instrument so provides. Decisions of trustees must usually be unanimous and, with very limited exceptions, there is no question of a vote of the majority binding them all.[94] They are also under an obligation to ensure that all the trust property and investments are placed in the names of all the trustees. In principle, each trustee, therefore, takes an equal part in the administration of the trust and has an equal say in what happens to the trust property. Thus, if a breach of trust has been committed, each trustee should be equally liable. However, the wronged beneficiary is not obliged to sue every single trustee; he can of course do so but is just as entitled to sue only one or two of them. For this reason the liability of trustees is joint and several.

22–040 Prior to the Civil Liability (Contribution) Act 1978, there was a absolute right of contribution as between the different trustees if an action was successfully brought against only one or some of them. Thus any trustee who was successfully sued had an absolute right of contribution against any trustee who had not been sued so that in the end each trustee would have contributed equally to the compensation paid to the beneficiary; the only exception to this was where the trustees had acted fraudulently.[95] This legislation made matters rather more flexible by giving the court power to award, in favour of one trustee against another, contribution of such amount as is found to be just and equitable, having regard to the extent of the responsibility of the other trustee for the loss.[96] This principle extends beyond express trustees to constructive trustees and to persons who are liable for dishonest assistance. Thus, in *Dubai Aluminium Co. v. Salaam*[97] a firm of solicitors who had settled proceedings in which it was claimed that they were vicariously liable for the alleged dishonest assistance of their senior partner in a fraudulent breach of trust, were held able to recover contribution from the persons who had actually benefited from the breach of trust.[98]

22–041 However, despite the principle of contribution, the trustee who is originally sued may nevertheless sometimes find himself in a very difficult position. Suppose that there are three trustees, Timothy, Titus and Tom, who

---

[93] [1980] Ch. 515. See also *ante*, para 14–066.
[94] See *ante*, para 14–013.
[95] *Bahin v. Hughes* (1886) 31 Ch.D. 390.
[96] ss.1(1), 2(1).
[97] [2003] UKHL 48, [2003] 2 A.C. 366.
[98] Controversially, they were awarded a contribution of 100% on the basis that this still left the contributers with some of the benefits of the breach of trust following their own settlement with the claimant.

commit a breach of trust involving the loss of £30,000. A beneficiary who chooses to sue Timothy alone has the right to recover the entire £30,000 from Timothy, the latter's right of contribution being completely irrelevant. Timothy can of course claim £10,000 from each of Titus and Tom but, if Titus has disappeared and Tom has gone bankrupt, Timothy's claim will remain unsatisfied; he will thus have paid out £30,000 without recovering any of it.

The Civil Liability (Contribution) Act 1978 has also made more flexible the circumstances in which a trustee who is successfully sued can claim a complete indemnity from one or more of his co-trustees. However, the three specific circumstances considered below in which a complete indemnity was available prior to the enactment of that legislation are all still thought to survive. These were, first, where the breach of trust was committed on the advice of a solicitor-trustee; secondly, where one trustee alone had benefited from the breach of trust; and, thirdly, where one of the trustees was also a beneficiary. **22–042**

Where one of the trustees was a solicitor and the breach of trust was committed solely in reliance on his advice, then the solicitor-trustee was obliged to indemnify his co-trustees.[99] It was not sufficient to show merely that one of the trustees at the time of the breach was a solicitor; it had to be shown that the other trustees were relying entirely on his advice. Thus in *Head v. Gould*[100] Miss Head and a solicitor, Mr Gould, were the trustees of a settlement. They sold a house forming part of the trust property and, instead of reinvesting the proceeds, in breach of trust paid the proceeds to the life tenant, Miss Head's mother. Following a successful action by the remainder-man against the two trustees, Miss Head unsuccessfully sought to be indemnified by Mr Gould. Kekewich J. found that she had not relied on Mr Gould but had actively urged him to commit the breach. Where the basic rule applied because the breach of trust was committed principally on the advice of the solicitor-trustee, in order successfully to resist a claim by his co-trustee for indemnity it was for the solicitor-trustee to show that his co-trustee was in full possession of all the relevant facts and made an independent judgment. In *Re Partington*,[101] which concerned improper investments, Stirling J. said: "I have got to consider the question, has [the solicitor] communicated what he did to [the co-trustee] in such a way as to enable her to exercise her judgment upon the investments, and to make them, really and in truth, her act as well as his own?" The judge found in favour of the co-trustee, who was therefore entitled to an indemnity. **22–043**

The situation where one trustee alone has benefited from the breach was considered in *Bahin v. Hughes*.[102] Cotton L.J. refused to limit the circumstances in which an indemnity would be ordered, saying "I think it wrong to lay down any limitation of the circumstances under which one trustee would be held liable to the others for indemnity, both having been held liable to the *cestui que trust* but so far as cases have gone at present, relief has only been granted against a trustee who has himself got the benefit of the **22–044**

---

[99] *Lockhart v. Reilly* (1856) 25 L.J.Ch. 697.
[100] [1898] 2 Ch. 250.
[101] (1887) 57 L.T. 654.
[102] (1886) 31 Ch.D. 390.

breach of trust, or between whom and his co-trustees there has existed a relation which will justify the court in treating him as solely liable for the breach of trust." In that case there were two trustees, one of whom was content to leave the administration of the trust to the other. The latter acted honestly but made an improper investment which resulted in a loss. The passive trustee unsuccessfully claimed an indemnity. It is by no means clear how far this dictum of Cotton L.J. was intended to go.

22–045   The situation where a trustee is also a beneficiary was considered in *Chillingworth v. Chambers*.[103] It was held that a trustee who was also a beneficiary and who had participated in a breach of trust must indemnify his co-trustee to the extent of his beneficial interest. However, this only applied if the trustee-beneficiary had, as between himself and his co-trustees, exclusively benefited from the breach of trust. Suppose that Abraham and Ambrose were the trustees of a trust, in which Ambrose had a beneficial interest worth £5,000 but in which Abraham had no interest. If the trustees were to invest in unauthorised securities in order to obtain a higher income and Ambrose, but obviously not Abraham, enjoyed the benefit of that higher income but the investment ultimately produced a capital loss of £8,000, Ambrose would be liable to indemnify Abraham to the extent of £5,000, leaving the remaining liability of £3,000 to be shared by them equally. It is not clear whether, for the rule in *Chillingworth v. Chambers* to apply, it is necessary for the trustee-beneficiary actually to receive a benefit from the breach, or whether it is sufficient if the breach was committed with the intention to give him a benefit; the latter view seems preferable.

V. LIMITATION OF ACTIONS

22–046   On the assumption that a breach of trust has been committed which has caused some loss, the further question arises as to whether the beneficiaries are in time to sue. The history of limitation of actions in respect of breaches of trust has been extremely complicated; however the position is now governed by the Limitation Act 1980, coupled with the application in certain respects of the equitable doctrine of laches (laches occurs where a wronged person has delayed so long in bringing his action that he is deemed by his conduct to have waived his claim). Two distinct situations have to be considered.

1. *Where there is No Statutory Period of Limitation*

22–047   Section 21(1) of the Limitation Act 1980 provides that there shall be no statutory period of limitation in respect of an action by a beneficiary under a trust if the action is one:

> "(a) in respect of any fraud or fraudulent breach of trust to which the trustee was a party or privy, or

---

[103] [1896] 1 Ch. 685.

(b) to recover from the trustee trust property or the proceeds thereof in the possession of the trustee, or previously received by the trustee and converted to his use."

It will be seen below that, where this subsection does not apply, a six-year limitation period applies to actions by beneficiaries for breach of trust although sometimes a different statutory limitation period will be applicable. However, the relevant period does not necessarily start running at the time when the trustees did whatever it is that the beneficiaries are complaining about.

(A) Fraud to which the Trustee was a Party

The meaning of the expression "any fraud or fraudulent breach of trust to   **22–048** which the trustee was a party or privy" in section 21(1)(a) has been considered relatively recently on a number of occasions by the Court of Appeal.

In *Armitage v. Nurse*[104] the paragraph was held to be "limited to cases of   **22–049** fraud or fraudulent breach of trust properly so called, that is to say to cases involving dishonesty". It follows that, whenever trustees have, in this sense, committed fraud or have retained any of the capital of the trust, there is no question of any defence under the statute. Thus, in *Re Howlett*[105] where a trustee occupied property belonging to the trust, he was held to be outside the scope of the Act and have no limitation defence. Likewise, in *Wassell v. Leggatt*,[106] where a husband forcibly took property belonging to his wife, thereby becoming a trustee of it for her, and kept it until his death, his executors were held to be unable to plead the statutory limitation period.

Subsequently, in *Paragon Finance v. D.B. Thakerar & Co.*,[107] the court had to   **22–050** consider whether paragraph (a) is restricted to fraudulent breaches of existing trusts, as in *Wassell v. Leggatt*, or whether it also applies to situations where the fraudulent act in question is the reason for the existence of the trust, in other words where the trust in question is a constructive trust which has only arisen because of the fraud of the constructive trustee. The expression "trust" in the Limitation Act 1980 does extend to constructive trusts.[108] However, the Court of Appeal held that this does no more than apply paragraph (a) to fraudulent breaches of already existing constructive trusts. Consequently, paragraph (a) does not apply to situations where the fraudulent act in question is the reason for the existence of the trust.

Millett L.J. referred to *Taylor v. Davies*,[109] where this conclusion had been   **22–051** reached in respect of a similar Canadian statute, and identified two different categories of constructive trusts. He said[110]:

---

[104] [1998] Ch. 241 at 260 *per* Millett L.J.
[105] [1949] Ch. 767.
[106] [1896] 1 Ch. 554; see also *Re Tufnell* (1902) 18 T.L.R. 705; *Re Eyre-Williams* [1923] 2 Ch. 533.
[107] [1999] 1 All E.R. 400.
[108] Because the definitions section of the Limitation Act 1980, (s.38) incorporates the definition of trust in the definitions section of the Trustee Act 1925 (s.68).
[109] [1920] A.C. 636 at 652–653 (Privy Council on appeal from Canada).
[110] [1999] 1 All E.R. 400 at 413–414. Compare *James v. Williams* [2000] Ch. 1.

"the distinction drawn in *Taylor v. Davies* . . . marks a real difference between trustees (whether or not expressly appointed as such) who commit a breach of trust (however created) and persons who are not trustees at all but who are described as trustees for the purpose of enabling equitable relief to be granted against them. Actions founded on tort are barred after six years, and there is no exception for actions founded on fraud, though the start of the limitation period may be deferred in such cases. There is no logical basis for distinguishing between an action for damages for fraud at common law and the corresponding claim in equity for 'an account as constructive trustee' founded on the same fraud. Section 21 of the 1980 Act can sensibly be limited to wrongs cognisable by equity in the exercise of its exclusive jurisdiction. It makes no sense to extend it to the exercise of its concurrent jurisdiction."

Therefore anyone who is a constructive trustee because, without having been appointed as such, he is acting as an express trustee and so is a trustee *de son tort* (or de facto trustee) falls within the first category and cannot rely on any statutory limitation period in relation to any fraudulent breach of trust. In contrast, someone who is not otherwise a trustee but has been held to be a constructive trustee because of his own fraudulent contract falls within the second category and can rely on the six-year limitation period.

22–052   Anyone who commits a fraudulent breach of a pre-existing fiduciary duty will be within the first category. This was held by the Court of Appeal in *Gwembe Valley Development Company v. Koshy*[111] where a director had failed fully to disclose his interest in a contract into which the company was entering; in the absence of fraud, the appropriate statutory limitation period would have applied[112] but, in the light of the trial judge's decision that he was guilty of dishonest and deliberate concealment of his secret profit, the Court of Appeal held that there was no applicable period of limitation. In contrast, someone who is held liable for dishonest assistance but was not previously a fiduciary will be within the second category; this was held expressly in *Cattley v. Pollard* but ths decision has since been doubted.[113]

(B)   Trust Property Received Beneficially by a Trustee
22–053   The distinction between the two categories of constructive trusts enunciated by Millett L.J. in *Paragon Finance v. D.B. Thakerar & Co.*[114] also applies to the provision in section 21(1)(b) that no statutory period will run in respect of trust property in the possession of the trustee or received by him. This time the distinction is between anyone who has beneficially received property which he was already holding on express or constructive trust, who is in the first category and cannot rely on any statutory limitation period, and someone who has beneficially received property which he was not previously holding on trust, who is in the second category and can rely on the six-year limitation period.

---

[111] [2003] EWCA Civ. 1478, [2004] W.T.L.R. 97.
[112] See below, para 22–060.
[113] [2006] EWHC 3130 (Ch), [2007] 3 W.L.R. 317. In *Statak Corporation v. Alford* [2008] EWHC 32 (Ch) Evans-Lombe J. stated that there was no applicable period of limitation for dishonest assistance and would not have followed *Cattley v. Pollard*.
[114] [1999] 1 All E.R. 400.

Consequently, a trustee who disposes of trust property to himself in **22–054** breach of the self-dealing rule will be within the first category. This was specifically held by the Court of Appeal in *J.J. Harrison v. Harrison*[115] in relation to a director who had a power to dispose of the property of the company in question and had disposed of it to himself. So will an inter-meddler. In *James v. Williams*[116] one of three intestate successors had taken possession of a house of the intestate, thereby becoming an executor *de son tort*, and remained in possession of it for longer than the normal statutory limitation period of 12 years; the Court of Appeal held that, since he had thus been holding the house on constructive trust, paragraph (b) applied to prevent a successful plea of limitation being raised by his successor in title to a claim brought by one of the other intestate successors.

In contrast, where the trust of the property whose recovery is being **22–055** sought arose merely as a result of the receipt of that property because, for example, it was a secret profit received by a pre-existing fiduciary or was knowingly received by a non-fiduciary, the recipient will be in the second category. This was specifically held by the Court of Appeal in *Gwembe Valley Development Company v. Koshy*,[117] which concerned a failure by a director fully to disclose his interest in a contract into which the company was entering, although in that case the director was actually caught by paragraph (a). Similarly, in *Halton International Inc v. Guernroy*,[118] the defendant had acquired further shares in a company by using a right to vote existing shares which were said to be subject to fiduciary duties although the latter shares were not themselves held on trust; more than six years later, the persons to whom the alleged fiduciary duties were owed claimed that some of the further shares were subject to a constructive trust in their favour. The Court of Appeal held that this claim fell within the second category and was therefore statute barred. However, the court dealt with an attempt to rely on the Rule in *Keech v. Sandford*[119] by stating that in such cases the property held on constructive trust "is treated as 'an accretion to or graft upon the original term arising out of the goodwill or quasi-tenant right annexed thereto' "[120]; it thus appears that the court would have regarded such a constructive trust as falling within the first category. This seems quite wrong as a matter of principle but it is bound to be contended that the constructive trusts imposed in all the situations to which the Rule in *Keech v. Sandford* has been extended are therefore also within the first category.[121]

---

[115] [2001] EWCA Civ. 1467, [2002] 1 B.C.L.C. 162.
[116] [2000] Ch. 1 (CA).
[117] [2003] EWCA Civ. 1478, [2004] W.T.L.R. 97.
[118] [2006] EWCA Civ. 801, [2006] W.T.L.R. 1241.
[119] (1726) Sel.Cas.Ch. 61; see *ante*, para 10–118.
[120] [2006] EWCA Civ. 801, [2006] W.T.L.R. 1241 at [24]; the sub-quotation is from *Re Biss* [1903] 2 Ch. 40 at 56.
[121] Examples are opportunities utilised by trustees to purchase the freehold reversions of property of which their trust is lessee (see *Thompson's Trustee v. Heaton* [1974] 1 W.L.R. 605), opportunities utilised by directors to subscribe for shares in subsidiaries for which their companies could not afford to subscribe (see *Regal (Hastings) Ltd. v. Gulliver* [1967] 2 A.C. 134N), and possibly even the use of information by agents of a trust to acquire a majority shareholding in a company in which the trust holds a minority holding (see *Phipps v. Boardman* [1967] 2 A.C. 46)

22-056   Where paragraph (b) is prima facie applicable, a special rule applies where the trustee is also a beneficiary. If the trustee distributed the trust fund honestly and reasonably but made an over-distribution to himself, the statutory period discussed below applies to the extent of his own share but only to that extent[122]; no limitation period is applicable to any excess in his hands over his own entitlement.

(C) Laches

22-057   Where an action is within either paragraph of section 21(1), there is no statutory period of limitation. Despite some indications to the contrary in *Gwembe Valley Development Company v. Koshy*,[123] the Court of Appeal confirmed in *Re Loftus*[124] that in those circumstances the trustee can nevertheless raise the defence of laches. The Court of Appeal went to state that the modern approach to that defence of laches is[125] to:

"require a broad approach, directed to ascertaining whether it would in all the circumstances be unconscionable for a party to be permitted to ascertain his beneficial right. No doubt the circumstances which gave rise to a particular result in the decided cases are relevant to the question whether or not it would be conscionable or unconscionable for the relief to be asserted, but each case has to be decided on its facts applying the broad approach."

22-058   The relevant decided cases show that, in order to establish the defence of laches, it is necessary to show that the beneficiary has known of the breach of trust for a substantial period of time and has acquiesced in it. There have never been, and in the light of *Re Loftus* there could not possibly now be, any fixed rules as to the period of time which must elapse; it must in the particular case be sufficiently long to enable the court to impute acquiescence and render the assertion of any claim unconscionable. On the other hand, if a beneficiary clearly acquiesces in the breach of trust in question after only a fairly short time, that will be a sufficient defence although such a defence failed on the facts in *Re Loftus*. What is essential is acquiescence on the part of the beneficiary when he has full knowledge of the facts; thus delay in taking action is merely evidence of acquiescence.[126] Further, delay is certainly not sufficient in itself since it has been held[127] that laches requires both unreasonable delay by the claimant and consequential substantial prejudice to the defendant which justifies the refusal of the equitable relief sought.

---

[122] Limitation Act 1980, s.21(2).

[123] [2003] EWCA Civ. 1478, [2004] W.T.L.R. 97 *per* Mummery L.J. at [140].

[124] [2006] EWCA Civ. 1124, [2007] 1 W.L.R. 591 *per* Chadwick L.J. at [40–41].

[125] *ibid.* at [42], quoting the passage in the text which is from the judgment of Aldous L.J. in *Frawley v. Neill* (1999) *The Times*, April 5, 1999.

[126] *Morse v. Royal* (1806) 12 Ves. 355; *Life Association of Scotland v. Siddal* (1861) 3 De G.F. & J. 58.

[127] In *Nelson v. Rye* [1996] 1 W.L.R. 1378 *per* Laddie J. at 1392. Although it was subsequently held, in *Paragon Finance v. D.B. Thackerar & Co* [1999] 1 All E.R. 400 (CA) *per* Millett L.J. at 415–416 that laches had not in fact been needed as a defence in *Nelson v. Rye* because there had been an applicable limitation period, that does not affect the utility of *Nelson v. Rye* as an authority on laches.

In the special circumstance already referred to where the trustee is also a   22–059
beneficiary, and has distributed the trust fund honestly and reasonably,
made an over-distribution to himself and as a result the statutory period
applies to the extent of his own share, he can raise the defence of laches in
respect of the excess.[128]

2. *Where there is a Statutory Period of Limitation*

(A) The General Position

Section 21(3) of the Limitation Act 1980, which applies both to express   22–060
trustees of private trusts[129] and to resulting and constructive trustees,[130]
provides that actions to recover trust property or in respect of breaches of
trust must be brought within six years from the date on which the right of
action accrued. In the case of breaches of trust, in principle the right of action
accrues on the date on which the breach in question occurred, not on the
date when the loss in question was sustained.[131] Suppose that a beneficiary
knows that the trustees invest in unauthorised investments and that at first
the investments do well but later lead to losses; even though the losses may
not be sustained for several years, the limitation period runs from when the
unauthorised investment was made. In *Re Swain*[132] trustees were under an
obligation to convert the deceased's assets into authorised investments but
in breach of trust continued to carry on the deceased's business until the
youngest beneficiary attained the age of 21. When, eight years later, one
of the other beneficiaries sought to make the trustees liable for the loss
caused through carrying on the business, they were held entitled to plead
limitation.

(B) Future Interests

Where a beneficiary has a future interest, an expression whose exact mean-   22–061
ing for the purposes of limitation will be considered below, a proviso to
section 21(3) applies. This specifically states that, for the purposes of the
Limitation Act 1980, his right of action is deemed not to have accrued until
his interest falls into possession; therefore time does not start to run against
him until then.

This does not actually prevent the beneficiary from suing before this point   22–062
if he wishes to do so. Consequently, a remainderman can take action in
respect of a breach of trust at any time during the subsistence of a prior life
interest, or within six years from becoming entitled to an interest in possession. This is the case even where the breach of trust consists of an improper

---

[128] Limitation Act 1980, s.21(2).

[129] The section does not apply to an action by the Attorney-General against the trustee of
charitable trusts which in this sense have no beneficiaries; *Att.-Gen. v. Cocke* [1988] Ch. 414.

[130] s.21(3) only applies where the action is against a "trustee" and not where the action is
against someone who, although in a fiduciary capacity, is not a trustee. In *Tito v. Waddell (No.2)*
[1977] Ch. 106 (see *ante*, para 1–037) the Crown was held not to be in a fiduciary position.
However, Megarry V.-C. said (at 249) that, even if the Crown had been in a fiduciary position,
it would not have been a trustee; consequently, the claim would not have been barred by the
predecessor of s.21(3) (Limitation Act 1939, s.19(2)). The doctrine of laches therefore applied but
was no bar in that case because it had not been pleaded.

[131] *Re Somerset* [1894] 1 Ch. 231.

[132] [1891] 3 Ch. 233.

advance to the remainderman during the lifetime of the tenant for life, something which can only be done with the tenant for life's consent. Both these latter points emerge from the decision of Wilberforce J. in *Re Pauling's Settlement Trusts*, his decision in this respect being simply affirmed by the Court of Appeal.[133] In that case improper advancements had been made in respect of the interests of minor beneficiaries and the trustees pleaded, among other defences, that the period of limitation ran in their favour from the time when the advancements were made. In rejecting this defence, Wilberforce J. held that the interests of the minors in respect of which the advancements had been made were future interests within the terms of the proviso to section 21(3) and that, if such an improper advancement was made while the interests were future interests, that did not start the limitation period running. Since the advancements were improper, they did not bind the minor beneficiaries at all and the latter could therefore sue at the time when they ought to have received the whole of their share, namely when their interests vested in possession.

22–063   However, the operation of the proviso to section 21(3) is restricted by section 21(4) which provides that, where limitation can be pleaded against any particular beneficiary, he cannot benefit from an action brought by a beneficiary against whom limitation cannot be pleaded.[134] Suppose that trustees who hold investments upon trust for Daphne for life, with remainder to Chloe, sell one of those investments and improperly hand over the proceeds to Daphne's daughter, who is not a beneficiary at all. In the absence of fraudulent concealment, Daphne will be debarred from suing after six years. Chloe is obviously entitled to wait until Daphne's death before suing but is not obliged to. If she does sue before then, she can compel the trustees to make good the capital loss. Assuming they do so, they can themselves retain the income from that property during the lifetime of Daphne; this is on the basis that Daphne, by not suing, has in effect consented to the breach of trust and so the trustees, having repaired the breach, are entitled to the income which she would otherwise have received.[135]

22–064   The precise meaning of "future interest" in the context of this proviso also had to be considered by the Court of Appeal in *Armitage v. Nurse*.[136] Trustees held income upon trust to accumulate it until the beneficiary in question reached the age of 25[137] subject to a power to pay it to her or apply it for her benefit. The Court of Appeal held that, while she was under the age of 25, she had a future interest for the purposes of the proviso, rejecting an argument by the trustees that the fact that she was entitled to see the trust documents was sufficient to give her an interest in possession under the trust. Millett L.J. held that the rationale of the proviso was that a beneficiary "should not be compelled to litigate (at considerable personal expense) in respect of an injury to an interest which he may never live to enjoy" and went on to say that "similar reasoning would apply to exclude a person who is merely the object of a discretionary trust or power which may never be

---

[133] [1964] Ch. 303.

[134] *Re Somerset* (1894) 1 Ch. 231.

[135] *Fletcher v. Collis* [1905] 2 Ch. 24.

[136] [1998] Ch. 241.

[137] She then acquired an absolute interest in the income but did not become entitled to the capital until she reached the age of 40.

exercised in his favour".[138] While it is clearly appropriate that a beneficiary of a fixed trust with a future interest should, when his interest vests in possession, be able to impeach any breaches of trusts committed at any time since the trust was originally created, it is superficially rather startling that a discretionary beneficiary or the object of a power to whom no income is appointed until (say) 20 years after the creation of the trust may at that point maintain an action for any breach of trust which has occurred during the previous 20 years. However, there seems no way of avoiding this conclusion since the wording of the statute provides no obvious means of distinguishing between the two cases.

This rationale enunciated by Millett L.J. may be extremely significant when the as yet unanswered question of how this proviso operates in the case of pension trusts has to be decided. Is the interest of a beneficiary of a pension trust a future interest in this sense until he becomes entitled to receive his pension? He will obviously not live to enjoy his pension if he dies before retirement age. On the other hand, his death before that time will inevitably lead to some form of payment being made, usually of both a lump sum death benefit and a pension for his surviving spouse and other dependants; he therefore certainly has an interest worth defending in the intervening period. The contention that his interest is indeed a future interest until he becomes entitled to his pension has been pleaded in a number of pension trust cases but does not appear yet to have been argued in court. If it is upheld, then the liability of the trustees of pension trusts for breach of trust will be to all intents and purposes indefinite. However, in that event, they will obtain at least some protection from section 21(4). **22–065**

(C) Concealment by Fraud

It has already been stated that there is no statutory period of limitation in respect of a fraudulent breach of trust. However, it is possible for a non-fraudulent breach of trust to have been committed which is subsequently concealed by fraud. Special provision is therefore made for actions based on fraud and for rights of actions concealed by fraud. Section 32 (which is of general application and is not confined to actions for breach of trust) provides that, where an action is based upon the fraud of the defendant or his agent and where a right of action is concealed by fraud, "the period of limitation shall not begin to run until the plaintiff has discovered the fraud ... or could with reasonable diligence have discovered it". For the purposes of this section, "fraud" is wider than the type of conduct which would give rise to an independent action. In *Beaman v. A.R.T.S.*[139] Lord Greene M.R. pointed out that the fraudulent conduct "may acquire its character as such from the very manner in which that act is performed". **22–066**

The scope of section 32 is illustrated by *Eddis v. Chichester Constable.*[140] One of the assets of a trust was a painting of St John the Baptist by Caravaggio which was normally hung in a stately home where the life tenant lived. However, in 1950 he lent the painting for an exhibition at Burlington House **22–067**

---

[138] [1998] Ch. 241 at 261.
[139] [1949] 1 K.B. 550.
[140] [1969] 2 Ch. 345. The decision concerned the predecessor of Limitation Act 1980 s.32, Limitation Act 1939, s.26.

and, during that exhibition, sold it to a consortium of art dealers, who subsequently sold it to an art gallery in Kansas City. The life tenant obviously had no title to the painting and, when the trustees discovered the loss of painting in 1963, they brought an action for breach of trust against the estate of the life tenant, who had by then died, and an action for conversion against the purchasers. The normal six-year limitation period for both of these actions was held not to apply. Lord Denning M.R. said[141]:

"one thing is quite clear: the right of action was 'concealed by the fraud' of the [life tenant]. I do not know that he did anything actively to deceive the trustees, but that does not matter. His wrongful sale of the heirloom was enough. It was a fraud and by saying nothing about it, he concealed the fraud."

22–068   However, in *Paragon Finance v. D.B. Thakerar & Co.*[142] the Court of Appeal emphasised that the question of whether section 32 will apply is determined not by whether the claimant should have discovered the fraud sooner but whether he could with reasonable diligence have done so; in this respect the burden of proof is on him to show that he could not have discovered the fraud without exceptional measures which he could not reasonably have been expected to take. In this context the fact that the applicable period of limitation is six years is irrelevant.[143]

3. *Other types of Actions*

(A)   Actions for an Account
22–069 Section 23 of the Limitation Act 1980 provides that "an action for an account shall not be brought after the expiration of any time limit under this Act which is applicable to the claim which is the basis of the duty to account". The section clearly prevents any action for an account being brought in respect of a breach of trust which is already statute-barred, even though a separate provision for this purpose hardly seems necessary. Until recently it was difficult to see what further purpose the section served. In *Attorney-General v. Cocke*[144] the Attorney-General brought an action against the executors and trustees of an estate held on charitable trusts, seeking accounts and enquiries as to the estate. Section 21(3) of the Limitation Act 1980 was clearly inapplicable: first, because the action was being brought by the Attorney-General and not by a beneficiary; and, secondly, because the claim was neither to recover trust property nor in respect of any breach of trust. Harman J. held that all fiduciaries were under a permanent duty to account arising out of their fiduciary relationships; such claims were not subject to

---

[141] *ibid.* at 356.

[142] [1999] 1 All E.R. 400 at 418.

[143] In this case, where the claimant was a mortgage lender, the court suggested that "the test was how a person carrying on a business of the relevant kind would act if he had adequate but not unlimited staff and resources and were motivated by a reasonable but not excessive sense of urgency". However, this is obviously not an appropriate test for a claimant who is a beneficiary under a trust.

[144] [1988] Ch. 414. This decision was applied in *Nelson v. Rye* [1996] 1 W.L.R. 1378.

any period of limitation under the Act and so there was no time limit to which section 23 could apply in respect of such a claim.

However in *Paragon Finance v. D. B. Thakerar & Co.*[145] Millett L.J. held that   **22–070**
"an action for an account brought by a principal against his agent is barred by the statutes of limitation unless the agent is more than a mere agent but is a trustee of the money which he received". This makes it clear that the purpose of section 23 is to protect fiduciaries who are not trustees from any additional liability to account; thus an agent who collects money on behalf of his principal without being under any obligation to segregate it will, in the event that an action under the contract of agency becomes statute barred, not be under any additional liability to account.

(B)   Actions for Breach of Fiduciary Duty
It has already been seen[146] that, where a breach of fiduciary duty is fraudu-   **22–071**
lent, section 21(1)(a) of the Limitation Act 1980 will apply and there will be no statutory limitation period. This was held by the Court of Appeal in *Gwembe Valley Development Company v. Koshy.*[147] However, the same decision establishes that section 21(1)(b) is limited to actions in respect of pre-existing trust property. It therefore does not apply to actions for breaches of fiduciary duty where there has been no misapplication of pre-existing trust property and the breach complained of relates to a conflict of interest and duty or of interest and interest[148] where the fiduciary did not act fraudulently. What limitation period is applicable in such circumstances?

In such circumstances, it must first be re-emphasised that breaches of duty   **22–072**
by a fiduciary which are not breaches of fiduciary duty sound only in tort or in contract[149] and are therefore governed by the provisions of the Limitation Act 1980 appropriate to such causes of action.[150] However, that Act contains no specific provision applying to claims relating to non-fraudulent breaches of fiduciary duty which have arisen as a result of the fiduciary in question preferring the interests of either himself or someone else to those of his principal. It was therefore contended in *Cia. de Seguros Imperio v. Heath (REBX)*[151] that there was no statutory period of limitation for such claims.

However, the Court of Appeal rejected this contention. Section 36(1) of the   **22–073**
Limitation Act 1980 provides that the time limits which apply to actions in tort and contract do not apply to any claim for "equitable relief, except in so far as any such time limit may be applied by the court by analogy in like manner as the corresponding time limit under any enactment repealed by the Limitation Act 1939 was applied before 1 July 1940". This provision had previously been considered in *Coulthard v. Disco Mix Club,*[152] where the judge[153] summarised the authorities prior to July 1, 1940 as follows:

---

[145] [1999] 1 All E.R. 400 at 415–416. Millett L.J. stated that *Nelson v. Rye* [1996] 1 W.L.R. 1378 had been wrongly decided.
[146] See *ante*, para 22–048.
[147] [2004] W.T.L.R. 97.
[148] See *ante*, para 22–011.
[149] *Bristol and West Building Society v. Mothew* [1998] Ch. 1.
[150] Limitation Act 1980, s.2 (tort) and s.4 (contract).
[151] [2001] 1 W.L.R. 112
[152] [2000] 1 W.L.R. 707 at 730.
[153] Jules Sher Q.C., sitting as a Deputy Judge of the Chancery Division.

"First, where the court of equity was simply exercising a concurrent jurisdiction giving the same relief as was available in the court of law the statute of limitation would be applied. But secondly, even if the relief afforded by the court of equity was wider than that available at law the court of equity would apply the statute by analogy where there was 'correspondence' between the remedies available at law or in equity."

The Court of Appeal held that there was the necessary "correspondence" between actions for breach of fiduciary duty of this type and actions for breach of contract; consequently, the court would have applied the contractual time limit to such actions for breach of fiduciary duty before July 1, 1940. Therefore, the period of limitation for such claims is still the six-year period which applies to actions for breach of contract.

(C) The Liability of Strangers as Constructive Trustees

22–074   So far as concerns intermeddlers, it has already been seen that in *Paragon Finance v. D.B. Thakerar & Co.*,[154] Millett L.J. specifically stated that anyone who is a constructive trustee because, without having been appointed as such, he is acting as an express trustee and so is a trustee *de son tort* (or de facto trustee) falls within the first category and cannot rely on any statutory limitation period in relation to any fraudulent breach of trust.

22–075   So far as concerns liability for dishonest assistance, in *Dubai Aluminium Co. v. Salaam*[155] Lord Millett said that a person who is held liable for dishonest assistance "is not in fact a trustee at all, even though he may be liable to account as if he were. . . . I think that we should now discard the words "accountable as constructive trustee" in this context and substitute the words "accountable in equity"." This terminology is clearly preferable but means that, for the purposes of limitation, liability for dishonest assistance does not fit into any of the categories discussed so far. However, in *Coulthard v. Disco Mix Club*,[156] it was held that such a claim for the imposition of accessory liability could not have a longer limitation period than that appropriate to the claim against whoever benefited from the dishonest assistance in question. This in practice meant that the period of limitation for such claims will be the six-year period provided for by section 21(3) of the Limitation Act 1980. Precisely this conclusion was expressly reached at first instance in *Cattley v. Pollard* but this decision has since been doubted.[157]

22–076   So far as concerns liability for knowing receipt, it follows from the decisions in *Gwembe Valley Development Company v. Koshy*[158] and in *Halton International Inc v. Guernroy*[159] that that liability falls into the second of the categories enunciated by Millett L.J. in *Paragon Finance v. D.B. Thakerar & Co.*[160] and that the knowing recipient is therefore entitled to rely on the six-year limitation period provided by section 21(3) of the Limitation Act 1980.

---

[154] [1999] 1 All E.R. 400.
[155] [2002] UKHL 48, [2003] 2 A.C. 366 at 404.
[156] [2000] 1 W.L.R. 707 at 730.
[157] [2006] EWHC 3130 (Ch), [2007] 3 W.L.R. 317, [2006] EWCA Civ 801, [2006] W.T.L.R. 1241.
[158] [2003] EWCA Civ. 1478, [2004] W.T.L.R. 97.
[159] See *ante*, para 22–052, n.113.
[160] [1999] 1 All E.R. 400.

Finally, so far as concerns liability for inconsistent dealing, the limitation **22–077**
position of the two types of inconsistent dealer described in this work[161] has
not been considered in any reported case; however, in principle his position
should be no worse than that of the knowing recipient, in which case he also
would be entitled to rely on the six-year limitation period provided by
section 21(3) of the Limitation Act 1980. However, an agent of a trust who
misapplies trust property which he has received from the trustees for the
legitimate purposes of the trust can obviously also be described as having
engaged in inconsistent dealing and is so described in *Lewin on Trusts*[162];
such a person is clearly within the first of the categories enunciated by
Millett L.J. in *Paragon Finance v. D.B. Thakerar & Co.*[163] and therefore cannot
rely on any statutory limitation period; this was specifically held in *Lee v.
Sankey.*[164]

VI. RELIEF OR EXEMPTION FROM PRIMA FACIE LIABILITY

Even if an action for breach of trust can prima facie be brought against a **22–078**
trustee, it may nevertheless be possible for him to claim total or partial relief.
He may be able to do so:

   (i) by virtue of a provision in the trust instrument;

   (ii) by means of an application to the court;

   (iii) by virtue of an act of the beneficiaries, either their concurrence in
         or their waiver of the breach; or

   (iv) by virtue of an indemnity obtainable from one or more of the
        beneficiaries.

1. *Provisions in Trust Instruments*

It has already been seen that a trust instrument can authorise a large number **22–079**
of acts which a trustee would not otherwise be able to do. If the trustee acts
in accordance with such authorisation, he is of course not guilty of a breach
of trust in the first place. However, even when a trustee has committed a
breach of trust, the provisions of the trust instrument may nevertheless be
effective to relieve him from liability if they include what is generally known
as a trustee exemption clause.

The Trustee Act 2000 specifically provides that the statutory duty of care **22–080**
imposed by that Act "does not apply if or in so far as it appears from the
trust instrument that the duty is not meant to apply".[165] Further the Court
of Appeal has held that the beneficiaries cannot invoke the Unfair Contract

---

[161] [2003] EWCA Civ. 1478, [2004] W.T.L.R. 97.
[162] 18th edn (London, Sweet & Maxwell, 2007) 42–88, 44–51.
[163] [1999] 1 All E.R. 400.
[164] (18710 L.R. 15 Eq. 204 at 211.
[165] Trustee Act 2000, Sch.1, para.7.

Terms Act 1977 either.[166] Nevertheless, there are inevitably some restrictions on the types of breaches of trust in respect of which liability can be excluded by a trustee exemption clause.

22–081   (1) In principle, the fundamental obligation of a trustee to account to his beneficiary cannot be excluded by a trustee exemption clause. This is part of the "irreducible core of obligations owed by the trustees to the beneficiaries and enforceable by them which is fundamental to the concept of a trust".[167] Thus, a provision in a trust agreement respecting an employee pension plan which prohibited any action against the trustees except by the employer-settlors was held to be unenforceable and did not deprive the court of jurisdiction to hear proceedings brought by the employees against the trustee.[168] However, it has been held that in special circumstances minimal accountability may subsist for a period[169] although possibly not in respect of the whole of the trust property.[170] Nor has any challenge ever been made to clauses providing that trustees have no duty or power either to inquire into or interfere with the running of companies in which the trust has a controlling shareholding unless they acquire actual knowledge of dishonesty or mental incapacity,[171] although that does not necessarily mean that such a challenge would not succeed.

22–082   (2) Trustee exemption clauses do not purport to exclude liability for dishonest and fraudulent breaches of trust anyway and it follows from the decision of the Court of Appeal in *Armitage v. Nurse*[172] that

---

[166] *Baker v. J.E. Clark & Co. (Transport) UK* [2006] EWCA Civ. 464, [2006] All E.R. (D) 337. However, it is thought that there might be some scope for a beneficiary who was a party to the trust deed containing the exemption clause to be able to rely on this legislation.

[167] *Armitage v. Nurse* [1998] Ch. 241 at 253 *per* Millett L.J. However, a custodian trustee appointed under the Public Trust Act 1906 is not liable for breach of trust where he follows the instructions of the managing trustee.

[168] *Jones v. Shipping Federation of British Columbia* (1963) 37 D.L.R. (2d) 273 (Supreme Court of British Columbia).

[169] In *Hayim v. Citibank* [1987] A.C. 730 (Privy Council on appeal from Hong Kong), the testator directed that, in respect of a house forming part of his estate, which he left on trust for sale with power to postpone sale and which was occupied by his elderly brother and sister (92 and 87 years old at the date of his death), his executor and trustee should "have no responsibility or duty with respect to such property... and my executor's and trustee's only duty and responsibility with respect thereto shall arise upon its receipt of proceeds of said residence or upon the death of the survivor of my said brother and my said sister, whichever shall first occur". The object of the exercise was clearly to prevent the brother and sister being cast on the mercy of the beneficiaries while at the same time avoiding them having a life interest in the property and so incurring a second liability to estate duty on the death of the survivor. The Privy Council upheld the validity of the clause, emphasising that it could only be used for the purpose for which it had been inserted in the will; had the trustee sought to obtain any personal advantage by its utilisation, it would have been void. The beneficiaries' action against the trustees for having failed to sell the property at the top of the market was therefore unsuccessful.

[170] The house in *Hayim v. Citibank* formed only a small part of the testator's estate.

[171] See Hayton in *Trends in Contemporary Trust Law* (ed. Oakley, 1996) 47. Clauses which merely provide that the trustees have no duty to do so are inherently vulnerable because of the existence of the trustees' power to do so.

[172] [1998] Ch. 241; see *infra*.

they could not validly do so. Usually such clauses expressly exclude such conduct from the exemption being conferred. In such a case, the Court of Appeal held in *Walker v. Stones*[173] that a solicitor-trustee will be dishonest and so unable to rely on a trustee exemption clause of this type if an honest belief, though actually held, is so unreasonable that, by any objective standard, no reasonable solicitor-trustee could have thought that what he did or agreed to do was for the benefit of the beneficiaries. This decision seemed inconsistent with the subsequent decision of the House of Lords in *Twinsectra v. Yardley*[174] as to the meaning of "dishonesty" for the purposes of liability for dishonest assistance but this is no longer a problem since *Walker v. Stones* is entirely consistent with the "clarification" of *Twinsectra v. Yardley* which has since been provided by the Privy Council in *Barlow Clowes International v. Eurotrust International*.[175]

(3) Statute prohibits trust instruments from exempting from liability for negligence trustees of debentures,[176] managers or trustees of unit trusts,[177] and, in respect of investment functions only, trustees of pension trusts.[178] Similar non-statutory restrictions have been introduced by the securities regulatory authorities, who have the sanction of withdrawing licences; thus the Securities and Investment Board prohibited custodian trustees from exempting themselves from liability in contracts entered into as from February 2, 1998 and the Investment Management Regulatory Organisation has prohibited investment managers licensed by them from exempting themselves from liability to their private clients.　　**22–083**

Otherwise it follows from *Armitage v. Nurse*[179] that there are at present no further restrictions on the contents of trustee exemption clauses. In particular it appears that liability for wilful default, defined in *Re Vickery*[180] as "consciousness of committing a wrong or recklessness as to whether or not a wrong was being committed", can be excluded. However, clauses in common use of the type set out below, do not purport to do so:　　**22–084**

"In the professed execution of the trusts of this deed no trustee shall be liable for any loss to the trust property arising by reason of any improper investment made in good faith or by reason of any mistake or omission made in good faith by any trustee of this deed or by reason of any other matter of thing except wilful and individual fraud or wrongdoing on the part of the trustee who is sought to be made liable."

---

[173] [2000] 4 All E.R. 412.
[174] [2002] UKHL 12, [2002] 2 A.C. 162; see *ante*, para 10–180.
[175] [2005] UKPC 37, [2006] 1 W.L.R. 1476.
[176] Companies Act 1985, s.192.
[177] Financial Services Act 1986, s.84.
[178] Pensions Act 1995, s.33.
[179] [1998] Ch. 241.
[180] [1931] 1 Ch. 572. This was actually a decision on the meaning of this phrase in the now repealed Trustee Act 1925, s.30(1) and in that respect, but not more generally, was highly controversial.

22–085   In *Armitage v. Nurse*, the clause did purport to exclude liability for wilful default: "No trustee shall be liable for any loss or damage which may happen to [the] fund or any part thereof or the income thereof at any time or from any cause whatsoever unless such loss or damage shall be caused by his own actual fraud". The court construed this clause as excluding any liability for breach of trust in the absence of dishonesty, which was held to mean "at the minimum an intention on the part of the trustee to pursue a particular course of action, either knowing that it is contrary to the interests of the beneficiaries or being recklessly indifferent whether it is contrary to their interests or not"[181] ("fraud" in the longer clause set out above would clearly be construed in the same way). The beneficiary contended[182] that clauses of this type were void, either for repugnancy or as contrary to public policy, in that they therefore excluded liability for gross negligence, a position which has been adopted by the legislature in some other jurisdictions.[183] However, the court held that this proposition was not supported by any English authority and, further, that "English lawyers have always had a healthy disrespect" for the distinction between negligence and gross negligence,[184] a distinction which is of course a necessary consequence of not permitting liability for gross negligence to be excluded. Exemption clauses of this kind are therefore valid, at least for the moment. However, the court "acknowledged that the view is widely held that these clauses have gone too far"[185] but held that only Parliament could deny them effect.

22–086   This indication that some form of legislation might be appropriate caused the Law Commission to publish a Consultation Paper in January 2003[186] recommending that professional trustees should no longer be able to exclude liability for negligence or be permitted to claim indemnity from the trust fund in respect of negligent breaches of trust. Since these proposals enabled lay trustees to continue to exempt themselves for liability for breach of trust up to and including wilful default, they seemed entirely consistent with the distinction drawn by the Trustee Act 2000 between professional and lay trustees in the context of remuneration and should certainly have been enacted. However, after consultation the Law Commission was persuaded to abandon their recommendations in favour of a rule of practice that any paid trustee who causes a settlor to include a clause in a trust instrument which excludes or limits liability for negligence should before the trust comes into effect take such steps as are reasonable to ensure that the settlor is aware of the meaning and effect of the clause.[187] There is of course no possibility of either monitoring or imposing any sanctions for failure to comply with any such rule of practice; consequently, this about turn was simply ludicrous and it is greatly to be regretted that the Law Commission

---

[181] [1998] Ch. 241 at 251.

[182] Relying on the view taken by Matthews [1989] Conv. 42.

[183] In Guernsey (Guernsey) Trusts Law 1988, s.34(7)) and Jersey (Trusts (Jersey) Law 1984, Art.26(9)). The Turks and Caicos Islands have gone even further and do not permit liability even for negligence to be excluded ((Turks & Caicos Islands) Trusts Ordinance 1990, s.29(10)).

[184] [1998] Ch. 241 at 254.

[185] *ibid.* at 256.

[186] Law Commission Consultation Paper No.171

[187] Law Com. No.301.

allowed itself to be persuaded by the wholly self-serving arguments of the largely self-appointed representatives of professional trustees.

Two further aspects of trustee exemption clauses have also been con-   **22–087**
sidered by the Court of Appeal. In *Bogg v. Raper*[188] the Court of Appeal was faced with an argument by the beneficiaries of a will which contained a clause almost identical with the one set out above where the solicitor-executor who had drawn up the will had been in a fiduciary relationship with the testator; namely that, by obtaining the benefit of exemption from the consequences of his own future negligence, he was obtaining a benefit at the testator's expense; and that, consequently, he could not rely on the clause unless he could show that the testator had received independent legal advice. This argument was rightly rejected.[189] In *Wight v. Olswang*[190] the court had to consider an argument that a rather different type of clause, providing that "Every discretion or power hereby or by law conferred on the Trustees shall be an absolute and uncontrolled discretion or power and no Trustee shall be held liable for any loss or damage accruing as a result of the Trustees concurring or failing to concur in the exercise of any such discretion or power", excluded liability for loss arising out of the exercise or non-exercise by the trustees of all powers and discretions, whether dispositive or administrative (this was crucial since it was a failure to sell trust investments at the right time which the beneficiaries were principally complaining about). However, the Court of Appeal, reversing Ferris J., held that the clause only prevented the court from interfering with the exercise of any discretion or power in circumstances where the court merely considered the trustees' grounds as unreasonable or would not have exercised the discretion or power in the same way; the clause did not actually confer any exemption on trustees who had committed a breach of trust. Consequently, such clauses cannot really be regarded as trustee exemption clauses at all.

2. *Applications to the Court*

It has already been seen[191] that the court has power to sanction in advance,   **22–088**
on an application by the trustees for directions, acts of a wide variety of types even if those acts would otherwise be breaches of trust. Where no such application to the court has been made prior to the act being carried out, the court also has, by virtue of section 61 of the Trustee Act 1925, a discretion to grant relief. This section provides that, if it appears to the court that a trustee is or may be personally liable for any breach of trust but has acted honestly

---

[188] (1998) 1 I.T.E.L.R. 267.

[189] Millett L.J. rejected this argument: first, because the exemption clause applied not just to the solicitor in question but to all possible trustees of the will; secondly, because it limited liability rather than conferring a benefit; thirdly, because the duty of the solicitor was to advise the testator on the terms on which his executors and/or trustees might properly accept office and so he could tell the testator that he would not accept office without such a clause; and, fourthly and in any event, any complaint that the solicitor was accepting a benefit under a will which he had prepared was a ground for opposing probate and, even if the grant of probate were now revoked for this reason, the solicitor would be able to rely on the exemption clause in respect of anything which he had done in the interim.

[190] (1999) 3 I.T.E.L.R. 352.

[191] See *ante*, para 14–142.

and reasonably and ought fairly to be excused for the breach of trust or for omitting to obtain the directions of the court in the matter in which he committed such breach, then the court may relieve him either wholly or partially from personal liability. Thus the trustee must, first, have acted honestly; secondly, have acted reasonably; and, thirdly, ought fairly to be excused.

22–089   "Honestly" here means in good faith. "Reasonably" is a question of fact which depends on the circumstances of each case. It does not follow that, whenever it is shown that a trustee has acted honestly and reasonably, he will automatically be excused; these conditions are a prerequisite of the court having discretion to grant relief, not a ground for the exercise of that discretion. The courts have consistently refused to lay down any rules[192] but there have been numerous applications under the section, and under the provisions which it replaced. A typical case where relief was granted was *Re Kay*,[193] where the applicant was an executor and trustee of a will of a testator who left over £22,000 with apparent liabilities of only about £100. Before advertising for claims, the executor paid to the widow a legacy of £300 and only afterwards learned that the liabilities of the estate exceeded its value. Relief was granted on the basis that it was reasonable for the executor to have assumed that with an estate of this size its liabilities would not be anywhere its total value, so that he could safely pay the legacy.

22–090   Difficulties sometimes arise where a trustee has taken legal advice which turns out to be wrong. Although it may appear hard on the trustee, the fact that he has taken and has followed legal advice does not automatically excuse him from liability. Where the advice given to a trustee by his solicitor is wrong, he should basically sue his solicitor; where he does not seek to recover the loss in this way (assuming the solicitor is in fact potentially liable for negligence), the court will generally not excuse him. In *National Trustee Co. of Australia v. General Finance Co. of Australia*,[194] trustees followed wrong advice given by their solicitors and it was held that in the special circumstances they should not be granted relief. In this connection, relevant factors are the value of the trust property, the appropriateness of the level of advice obtained in the light of that value,[195] and whether the trustees are lay or professional. In *National Trustee Co. of Australia v. General Finance Co. of Australia* the court clearly took into account the fact that the trustees were paid. But the fact that trustees are professional does not automatically disqualify them from relief. In *Re Pauling's Settlement Trusts*[196] the Court of Appeal held that relief under section 61 can be granted to a paid trustee if the circumstances are appropriate and a degree of relief was indeed granted in that case to paid trustees who were bankers. However, in its judgment the Court of Appeal stated that "Where a banker undertakes to act as a paid trustee of a settlement created by a customer, and so deliberately places itself in a position where its duty as trustee conflicts with its interest as a banker,

---

[192] *Re Turner* [1897] 1 Ch. 536; *Re Kay* [1897] 2 Ch. 518 at 524.
[193] [1897] 2 Ch. 518.
[194] [1905] A.C. 373.
[195] If the property is of low value, trustees would probably be acting reasonably in taking merely the advice of a solicitor, whereas if the trust fund were very large, only the advice of a Queen's Counsel might be sufficient.
[196] [1964] Ch. 303.

we think that the court should be very slow to relieve such a trustee under the provisions of the section."[197]

Two particular aspects of the section were considered in *Re Rosenthal*.[198]   **22–091**
The testator devised his house to his sister and left the remainder of his estate to his widow. The estate duty payable in respect of the house should have been paid by the sister, but the executors, who for this purpose were treated as trustees,[199] transferred the house to the sister without making any arrangements with her to secure the payment of the duty. They improperly paid £270 out of the residue on account of this liability and a further £1,500 plus interest was still outstanding. One of the trustees, who was a solicitor and who was acting in connection with the administration of the estate, claimed to be entitled to rely on section 61. Plowman J. rejected this contention on two grounds. First, although the trustee had acted honestly in paying the £270, he had not acted reasonably and had not shown that he ought fairly to be excused; in this respect, Plowman J. took account of the fact that he was a professional trustee,[200] for which reason he appears to have adopted a more stringent approach. Secondly, in respect of the question of whether section 61 could apply to an anticipated breach of trust, the future payment of the further sum due out of the residue, the solicitor was in effect seeking a declaration that he was entitled to take this sum from residue; Plowman J. held that relief could not be given under the section in respect of a breach of trust which had not yet occurred.

3. *Acts of the Beneficiaries*

A beneficiary who has once agreed to, or concurred in, a breach of trust   **22–092**
cannot afterwards sue the trustees in respect of it. This applies only if three conditions are satisfied:

   (i) that the beneficiary was of full age and sound mind at the time when he agreed or concurred;

   (ii) that he had full knowledge of all relevant facts and of the legal effect of his agreement or concurrence; and

   (iii) that he was an entirely free agent and was not under any undue influence.

A good example of the working of this rule is *Nail v. Punter*.[201] Trustees   **22–093**
held stock on trust for a married woman for life, with remainder to such

---

[197] See also *Re Windsor Steam Coal Company (1901)* [1929] 1 Ch. 151 and *Re Waterman's Will Trusts* [1952] 2 All E.R. 1054. In *Re Cooper (No.2)* (1978) 21 O.R. (2d) 579 (Ontario), the two trustees were the senior partner in a trustee law firm and one of his junior partners. The whole of the conduct of the administration was left in the hands of the senior partner, who stole Can$180,000 and was sentenced to seven and a half years imprisonment. The court found that the junior partner had no reason to suspect the fraud of his senior partner, and that he had acted honestly and reasonably. It therefore granted him relief under the Ontario equivalent of s.61.

[198] [1972] 1 W.L.R. 1273.

[199] One of the persons appointed as an executor had purported to resign from his office by means of the appointment of new trustees. This was probably invalid but the so-called new trustees were treated by the judge as trustees for the purposes of the case.

[200] [1972] 1 W.L.R. 1273 at 1278.

[201] (1832) 5 Sim. 555.

person as she should by will appoint. During her lifetime, the woman's husband persuaded the trustees to sell the stock and pay him the proceeds. She then brought an action against the trustees but died before it was concluded, having by her will appointed the stock to her husband. The husband endeavoured to claim the same remedy as his wife had sought. But, since he had become a beneficiary by virtue of the exercise of the power of appointment, it was held that he could not succeed because he had been a party to the breach.

22–094   A trustee is also protected from action if the beneficiaries subsequently learn of the breach and either acquiesce in it or give the trustee a release. The same three conditions apply. Releases are generally granted formally by deed but an informal release, if supported by consideration, will be effective. In *Ghost v. Waller*,[202] part of the trust property was lost through a breach of trust. The beneficiary agreed by letter through her solicitors that, in consideration of the trustees undertaking to assist in recovering part of the loss, she would "give up all claims if she has any against her trustees for negligence". This was held to be an effective release.

22–095   Neither a formal nor an informal release will be effective if the beneficiary was not in full possession of the facts. In *Thompson v. Eastwood*[203] the beneficiary was entitled to a legacy under a will. The trustee denied the beneficiary's right to that legacy on the grounds of alleged illegality and the dispute was settled on the payment by the trustee of a smaller sum than that to which the beneficiary was entitled. A formal deed of release was executed but, when the beneficiary discovered the true position, he was held entitled to claim the full legacy, despite the deed of release, and despite the fact that over 25 years had passed since the breach.

22–096   In *Re Pauling's Settlement Trusts*,[204] the bank Coutts & Co. was trustee of a fund for a mother for life, remainder to her children. The trustee had an express power, which would anyway have been implied by statute, to advance to each child up to half his share of the capital provided that the mother consented. The father habitually lived beyond his means and persuaded the bank to make a series of advances to which the mother consented. These, although nominally for the benefit of the child in question, as they were required to be, were in fact used for the benefit of the father or the family as a whole. The children now sought to recover from the bank the sums advanced. As has already been seen,[205] the bank's attempt to rely on limitation failed because of the proviso to what is now section 21(3) of the Limitation Act 1980. The children's interests were future interests until the death of the mother; she was still alive so time had not yet even started running against them. However, the bank also attempted to rely on section 61 of the Trustee Act 1925.

22–097   This attempt succeeded only to the very limited extent that, in respect of one clearly improper advance, the bank had been lulled into a false sense of security by a letter from the solicitors of the two children in question stating

---

[202] (1846) 9 Beav. 497.
[203] (1877) 2 App.Cas. 215 and see *Re Freeston's Charity* [1978] 1 W.L.R. 741 (no acquiescence in a breach of a charitable trust).
[204] [1964] Ch. 303, and see *ante*, para 18–016.
[205] See *ante*, para 22–062.

that it was satisfactory; it was, therefore, relieved to the extent that the children had at the time benefited from it. But the bank also contented that each advance had been made at a time when the beneficiary in question was over the age of majority (then 21) and had consented to the improper advances being made. It is clear that, had those consents been effective, the beneficiaries could not afterwards have succeeded in an action against the trustees. The Court of Appeal actually held that the children had not been fully aware of the nature of their rights at the time of these consents. This was enough to dispose of the defence but the court went on to consider the impact of undue influence. The presumption of undue influence which arises where an infant makes a gift to a parent[206] continues for a short time—the exact period is undefined and depends on the circumstances of each case—after the infant has attained his majority.[207] The court found that the presumption arose in respect of a series of advances in favour of a daughter just over the age of majority. This raised the question of what for the purposes of any liability of the trustees is the effect on an advancement which favours a parent and not a child of a consent given by that child which may be the result of undue influence. The Court of Appeal said: "Without expressing a final opinion, we think that the true view may be that a trustee carrying out a transaction in breach of trust may be liable if he knew, or ought to have known, that the beneficiary was acting under the undue influence of another, or may be presumed to have done so, but will not be liable if it cannot be established that he so knew or ought to have known." A trustee who is asked to commit a breach of trust for the benefit of a parent on the basis of consent by a beneficiary just turned 18 ought, therefore, to satisfy himself that the child is emancipated from the parent.

4. Indemnities Obtainable from Beneficiaries

It has already been shown that, subject to the conditions just mentioned, a **22–098** beneficiary who with full knowledge concurs in a breach of trust cannot afterwards sue his trustees. This does not, however, affect the right of other beneficiaries to take action and, in the event that such action is taken, the trustee may be able to claim an indemnity out of the beneficial interest of the beneficiary who has concurred in the breach. In particular, if the beneficiary who has concurred in the breach of trust is the tenant for life and the trustee repairs the breach at the behest of the remainderman, he is entitled to the income which the tenant for life would otherwise have received during the remainder of his lifetime.[208]

Outside this special situation, there are two rules which overlap. First, **22–099** under its inherent jurisdiction, the court has power to order a beneficiary to give the trustee an indemnity if he instigated[209] or requested[210] a breach of trust with the intention of obtaining a personal benefit (whether or not such personal benefit was in fact received) or if he concurred in a breach of trust

---

[206] *Huguenin v. Baseley* (1807) 14 Ves. 273.
[207] See *Lancashire Loans v. Black* [1943] 1 K.B. 380.
[208] *Fletcher v. Collis* [1905] 2 Ch. 24.
[209] *Trafford v. Boehm* (1746) 3 Atk. 440.
[210] *Fuller v. Knight* (1843) 6 Beav. 205.

and actually derived a personal benefit from it.[211] Secondly, under section 62 of the Trustee Act 1925, the court may impound the interest of a beneficiary in the trust fund if he instigates or requests or consents in writing to a breach of trust by the trustee. Where the section applies, the court has the discretion to impound, and, if so, whether to impound the whole or only part of the beneficiary's interest.

22–100   Section 62 applies irrespective of personal benefit, or of a motive for personal benefit. On the other hand, it only applies in the case of mere consent to a breach of trust if such consent was in writing, whereas the inherent jurisdiction of the court can be utilised whether or not the consent is in writing. The court will not exercise either power to impound the beneficiary's interest unless the trustee can show that the beneficiary fully appreciated that the proposed action would constitute a breach of trust. Further, as the result of a fairly robust construction, it was held in *Re Pauling's Settlement (No.2)*[212] that the power under section 62 can be exercised in favour of a person who is not a trustee at the time when the breach of trust occurred. In coming to this decision, Wilberforce J. was clearly influenced by the consideration that, if the section only applied to persons who were trustees at the time of the application, the court might be loath to remove trustees before such application has been made, even if in the other circumstances of the case their removal was desirable.

22–101   Where a beneficiary unsuccessfully brings proceedings against a trustee alleging breach of trust, the trustee will be entitled to take his costs out of the trust fund. This right is apparently not limited to the beneficiary's interest in the trust fund but extends to the whole of it; consequently, beneficiaries who have not taken part in the proceedings against the trustee can nevertheless be prejudiced if those proceedings are unsuccessful. Only in the event that the trust fund is insufficient will an order for costs be made personally against the beneficiary who brought the proceedings (obviously no such order can be made against any other beneficiary). All of these propositions were established in *Re Spurling's Will Trusts*.[213]

VII. PERSONAL CLAIMS AGAINST THIRD PARTIES

22–102   Thus far this chapter has been concerned with personal actions for breach of trust against the trustees who have committed those breaches. From the point of view of the beneficiaries, such claims may be inadequate and clearly will be if the trustees are insolvent. In these circumstances, the beneficiaries may additionally make either a personal claim against any third parties who have received the trust property in breach of trust or a legal or equitable proprietary claim in respect of the trust property against such third parties or against the trustees. This section is concerned with personal claims against third parties; the following two sections are concerned with legal and equitable proprietary claims.

---

[211] *Montford v. Cadogan* (1816) 19 Ves. 635.
[212] [1963] Ch. 576.
[213] [1966] 1 W.L.R. 920 (in this case the plaintiffs were between them absolutely beneficially entitled).

In the leading case of *Re Diplock*,[214] a testator by his will directed his   **22–103**
executors to apply his residuary estate "for such charitable institution or
institutions or other charitable or benevolent object or objects" as they
should in their absolute discretion think fit. His executors distributed the
residue, which amounted to the then very substantial sum of over £200,000,
among 139 charities. Subsequently, the testator's next-of-kin challenged the
validity of this gift. The House of Lords eventually held, in *Chichester
Diocesan Fund and Board of Finance v. Simpson*,[215] that it was ineffective. *Re
Diplock* was concerned with the next-of-kin's subsequent claims to recover
the money from the executors and the charities which had received it.

The claims of the next-of-kin against the executors were eventually com-   **22–104**
promised with the approval of the court. But actions continued for the
considerable balance of the funds distributed against the charities, who had
used the money paid to them for a variety of purposes. In the majority of
cases, the cheques sent to them had been paid into their general accounts at
the bank. Some of such accounts were in credit, while some were overdrawn
on either a secured or an unsecured basis. In a few cases payment had been
made into a special account, in some it had been earmarked for a designated
purpose, while in others the money had been spent on altering or enlarging
existing buildings owned by the charity. The next-of-kin based their claim to
recover the money on both personal and proprietary claims, both of which
succeeded. The personal claims were brought against the charities on the
basis of an alleged "equity" which the next-of-kin had to recover the money;
they contended that any unpaid (or underpaid) creditor, legatee or next-
of-kin possessed such an "equity" as against an overpaid beneficiary or
stranger to the estate. In respect of personal claims of this type, *Re Diplock*
remains the principal authority. The proprietary claims, which will be discussed later on, were to follow identifiable assets into the hands of the
charities on the basis that the charities were innocent volunteers who had
received assets paid away in breach of trust. In respect of proprietary claims
of this type, *Re Diplock* is only one of a number of leading authorities.

1. *The Personal Claim made in* Re Diplock

The next-of-kin sought to assert two distinct personal claims against the   **22–105**
charities. Their claim that the charities were liable for knowing receipt failed;
the Court of Appeal held that the charities had had no notice of the breach
of trust by the executors[216] and, as has already been seen, declined to impose
"the heavy obligations of trusteeship" upon recipients of trust property who

---

[214] [1948] Ch. 465, affirmed by the House of Lords *sub nom. Ministry of Health v. Simpson* [1951]
A.C. 251.
[215] [1944] A.C. 341 and see *ante*, para 11–104.
[216] The next-of-kin contended that, since the letter which accompanied all the executors'
payments to the charities set out, admittedly not entirely accurately, the terms of the gift in the
will, the charities had been given notice of the invalidity of the trusts, or at least were put on
enquiry as to their validity; at that time this would have amounted to sufficient knowledge for
the imposition of liability for knowing receipt. However, the Court of Appeal held ([1948] Ch.
465 at 478–479) that "persons in the position of the [charities], themselves unversed in the law,
are entitled in such circumstances as these to assume that the executors are properly administering the estate".

had no knowledge of the breach of trust in question. It is the alternative claim which is relevant for present purposes. This was, in the words of the court, that "apart from any notice which the [charities] may have had of the true effect of the testator's will, they had in truth no right to receive any of the moneys paid to them and that . . . the unpaid next-of-kin had a direct claim, recognised and established by the courts of equity, to recovery from the [charities] of the sums improperly paid to the [charities] and properly belonging to the next-of-kin."

22–106   The first question which had to be decided was whether it mattered that the mistake of the executors had been a mistake of law. The Court of Appeal acknowledged that the mistake was one of law and that common law claims for money had and received would not lie where money had been paid under a mistake of law (this was the certainly the law then, although this is no longer the case[217]). However, the court held that such common law claims were in no sense derived from equity but had developed entirely independently of equity.[218] The court took the view that there was no "necessity in logic for the claim as being clothed, as it were, with all the attributes or limitations appropriate to the common law action for money had and received"[219] and went on to consider the relevant authorities dating back as far as the days of Bridgman L.K. and Finch L.K. (afterwards Lord Nottingham L.C.) to see what principles had been established by them.[220] Having done so, the court rejected the contention that in equity the mistake under which the payment is made must be one of fact.

22–107   When the decision of the Court of Appeal was affirmed by the House of Lords, Viscount Simonds said in this respect[221]:

"It would be a strange thing if the Court of Chancery having taken upon itself to see that the assets of a deceased person were duly administered was deterred from doing justice to the creditor, legatee or next-of-kin because the executor had done him wrong under a mistake of law. If in truth this were so, I think that the father of Equity would not recognise his own child."

Further, the underpaid creditor, legatee or next-of-kin will necessarily not himself be a party to the wrongful payment; only the executor will be responsible for that. As Lord Simonds said, it is therefore difficult to see what relevance the distinction between mistake of fact and law can have to

---

[217] The general prohibition on the recovery of money paid under a mistake of law was rejected by the House of Lords in *Kleinworth Benson v. Lincoln City Council* [1999] 2 A.C. 349.
[218] [1948] Ch. 465 at 480.
[219] *ibid.* at 481.
[220] *ibid.* at 482. The cases cited and discussed at length included *Nelthrop v. Hill* (1669) 1 Ch.Cas. 135; *Grove v. Banson* (1669) 1 Ch.Cas. 148 at 148; *Chamberlain v. Chamberlain* (1675) 1 Ch.Cas. 256; *Noel v. Robinson* (1682) 1 Vern. 90; *Anon.* (1682) 1 Vern. 162; *Newman v. Barton* (1690) 2 Vern. 205; *Anon.* (1718) 1 P.Wms. 495; *Orr v. Kaines* (1750) 2 Ves.Sen. 194; *Walcot v. Hall* (1788) 2 Bro.C.C. 304; *Gillespie v. Alexander* (1827) 3 Russ. 130; *Greig v. Somerville* (1830) 1 Russ. & My. 338; *David v. Frowd* (1833) 1 My. & K. 200; *Sawyer v. Birchmore* (1836) 1 Keen 391; *Thomas v. Griffith* (1860) 2 Giff. 504; *Fenwick v. Clarke* (1862) 4 De G.F. & J. 240; *Peterson v. Peterson* (1866) L.R. 3 Eq. 111; *Rogers v. Ingham* (1876) 3 Ch.D. 351; *Re Robinson* [1911] 1 Ch. 502; *Re Hatch* [1919] 1 Ch. 351; *Re Rivers* [1920] 1 Ch. 320; *Re Mason* [1928] Ch. 385, [1929] 1 Ch. 1; *Re Blake* [1932] 1 Ch. 54.
[221] *Ministry of Health v. Simpson* [1951] A.C. 251 at 270.

such a situation (as has already been mentioned, the distinction is now no longer relevant at common law either).

The Court of Appeal also held, on the basis of the authorities already **22–108** referred to,[222] that it is irrelevant to the applicability of the remedy that the original recipient had no title at all and was a stranger to the estate.[223] While many of those authorities were undoubtedly concerned with providing equality between the original recipient and other persons having a title similar to that of the recipient, such as next-of-kin, that was not a good reason why the remedy should not also be applied against a stranger even though the effect of the refund would actually be to dispossess the stranger rather than to produce equality.

However, the court stated that there is one important pre-condition **22–109** which must be fulfilled before a claim by an underpaid beneficiary can succeed.[224]

"Since the original wrong payment was attributable to the blunder of the personal representatives, the right of the unpaid beneficiary is in the first instance against the wrongdoing executor or administrator and the beneficiary's direct claim in equity against those overpaid or wrongly paid should be limited to the amount which he cannot recover from the party responsible. In some cases the amount will be the whole amount of the payment wrongly made, e.g. where the executor or administrator is shown to be wholly without assets or is protected from attack by having acted under an order of the court."[225]

In *Re Diplock* the claims of the next-of-kin against the executors or their estates had already been compromised. Accordingly it was held that the amount recovered from the executors should be apportioned among the charities in proportion to the money the latter had wrongly received. This meant that the maximum recoverable from an individual charity by the next-of-kin would be rateably reduced.[226]

Finally, the Court of Appeal held that the recipients were only liable for **22–110** the principal sum claimed and not for any interest thereon.[227]

2. The Scope of the Personal Claim in Re Diplock

Re Diplock was a claim in respect of the administration of an estate and was **22–111** dealt with by the Court of Appeal and by the House of Lords[228] strictly on that basis. It is not, therefore, so clearly established that the principles laid down will apply with equal force between beneficiaries under an *inter vivos* trust, although there seems no cogent reason why they should not do. In

---

[222] See the authorities cited *ante*, n.220.

[223] [1948] Ch. 465 at 502.

[224] *ibid.* at 503.

[225] For early authority for this proposition, see *Orr v. Kaines* (1750) 2 Ves. Sen. 195; *Hodges v. Waddington* (1684) 2 Vent. 360.

[226] [1948] Ch. 465 at 506.

[227] The relevant authority is *Gittins v. Steele* (1818) 1 Swanst. 200.

[228] *Sub nom. Ministry of Health v. Simpson* [1951] A.C. 251.

Butler v. Broadhead,[229] the plaintiffs had purchased land from a company in the course of being wound up. Some years later, it transpired that the company had had no title to the land and so the plaintiffs, having been deprived of it, attempted to utilise the personal claim in *Re Diplock* in order to claim against the contributories of the company, to whom its surplus assets had been distributed when the winding-up had been concluded. They argued that such a personal claim was limited to the administration of estates; however, Templeman J. did not dismiss the claim on this ground but rather on the ground that it was barred by the Companies Act 1948[230] (it was assumed that the plaintiffs had failed to respond to the liquidator's advertisement seeking claims by the creditors of the company). This decision suggests that there is no reason in principle why the personal claim should not apply to *inter vivos* trusts. Subsequently, in *Re J. Leslie Engineers Company*,[231] Oliver J. accepted the theoretical availability of such a claim to the liquidator of a company who was attempting to recover payments made to a creditor by a director after the liquidation had commenced; however, he denied the claim because the creditor had given value and the liquidator had not exhausted his remedies against the director. These decisions suggest that, in an appropriate case, the personal claim could be applied at least to *inter vivos* trusts and possibly also to companies in liquidation.

22–112   Admittedly, the scope of the personal claim has now presumably been affected by the recognition by the House of Lords in *Lipkin Gorman v. Karpnale*[232] of a general defence of change of position but this is an entirely desirable development. It was the charities' contention that there was such a defence that had formed the sole grounds of the unsuccessful appeal to the House of Lords[233] against the decision of the Court of Appeal in *Re Diplock*; however, at that stage, the House of Lords had refused to recognise any such defence, a decision which produced very considerable hardship for those charities who had used the funds to improve their buildings and, consequently, provoked very considerable criticism. This relatively new defence will be considered in detail in the final section of this chapter.[234] However, now that it has been established, the personal claim which succeeded in *Re Diplock* will be able to operate in a much more reasonable manner. Consequently, there seems no reason whatever why it should not now be extended to *inter vivos* trusts and perhaps also to companies in liquidation.

22–113   The extension of the remedy to *inter vivos* trusts is also what is in effect being proposed by those who advocate the replacement of the present rules governing "liability for knowing receipt" by the introduction of a universal principle of strict liability for receipt of trust property transferred in breach of trust. As has already been seen,[235] the most significant advocate of this view has been Lord Nicholls of Birkenhead, writing extrajudicially,[236] and

---

[229] [1975] Ch. 97.
[230] Now Companies Act 1985, s.557.
[231] [1976] 1 W.L.R. 292.
[232] [1991] 2 A.C. 548.
[233] *Sub nom. Ministry of Health v. Simpson* [1951] A.C. 251.
[234] See *post*, para 22–194.
[235] See *ante*, para 10–228.
[236] In *Restitution—Past, Present and Future* (ed. Cornish, 1998) 231. See also Birks [1993] L.M.C.L.Q. 218; Harpum in *Frontiers of Liability* (ed. Birks, 1993), 9.

Lord Millett's apparent support for this view in *Twinsectra v. Yardley*[237] showed that a future reform of the law in accordance with that proposal certainly could not be discounted, particularly since that proposal was also subsequently supported by Lord Walker. But two of these three Law Lords have now retired and, in the light of the subsequent direct rejection of this argument by the High Court of Australia,[238] this reform now appears less likely, unless of course the Law Commission does eventually make proposals which are implemented by the legislature. In any event, for the reasons which have already been stated,[239] this reform is not the preferred option of this work.

VIII. LEGAL PROPRIETARY CLAIMS[240]

Proprietary claims have important advantages over any personal claim. If the claimant can identify his property in the hands of the defendant, he will generally[241] be entitled to recover that property in full in priority to the claims of the general creditors of the defendant.[242] He will also normally be able to take advantage of any increase in the value of the property.[243] Further, he will also be able to claim the income or fruits of the property from the date when it reached the hands of the defendant, either the income or fruits actually produced or, if the property in question is or becomes money, interest on that money[244] (the earliest date from which the payment of interest will be awarded in a personal claim is from the date when the claim form was issued[245] and, in many cases, the payment of interest will only be ordered as from the date of judgment[246]).

22–114

Before any proprietary claim can be brought, the claimant must identify his property in the hands of the defendant. The terminology which is at present fashionable is to describe this process of identification as "following and tracing" and to distinguish both from the proprietary claim itself. However, until relatively recently, the expression "tracing" was utilised to describe both the process of identification and the proprietary claim itself.

22–115

---

[237] [2002] 2 A.C. 164 at 194.

[238] In *Farah Construction Pty v. Say-Dee Pty* [2007] HCA 22, (2007) 81 A.L.J.R. 1107 at [148].

[239] See *ante*, para 10–231.

[240] The best short discussion of proprietary claims is found in Goff & Jones, *The Law of Restitution*, 7th edn (2007), pp.85–126. See also Birks, *An Introduction to the Law of Restitution* (1989), pp.358–401. Smith, *The Law of Tracing* (1997) is devoted entirely to this subject.

[241] This always occurs in the case of equitable proprietary claims but not always in the case of legal proprietary claims; see *post*, para 22–133.

[242] Insolvency Act 1986, s.283; *Chase Manhattan Bank v. Israel-British Bank (London)* [1981] Ch. 105 (which concerned an equitable proprietary claim).

[243] *Re Tilley's Will Trusts* [1967] Ch. 1179; *Papamichael v. National Westminster Bank* [2003] EWHC 164 (Comm), [2003] 1 Lloyd's Rep. 341 (both equitable proprietary claims; see *post*, para 22–176, n.414).

[244] In the case of an equitable proprietary claim, that interest will be compound interest; see *Westdeutsche Landesbank Girozentrale v. Islington L.B.C.* [1996] A.C. 669

[245] *Jaffray v. Marshall* [1993] 1 W.L.R. 1285 (overruled by the House of Lords on other grounds in *Target Holdings v. Redferns* [1996] 1 A.C. 421).

[246] *Re Diplock* [1948] Ch. 465.

The principal protagonist in this terminological change has been Lord Millett. In *Foskett v. McKeown*[247] he defined "following" and "tracing" in this way:

"These are both exercises in locating assets which are or may be taken to represent an asset belonging to the plaintiffs and to which they assert ownership. The processes of following and tracing are, however, distinct. Following is the process of following the same asset as it moves from hand to hand. Tracing is the process of identifying a new asset as the substitute for the old. Where one asset is exchanged for another, a claimant can elect whether to follow the original asset into the hands of the new owner or to trace its value into the new asset in the hands of the same owner. In practice his choice is often dictated by the circumstances."

22–116   Later in the same speech[248] he distinguished between the processes of identification and the proprietary claim itself, in this respect repeating his own earlier judicial[249] and extra-judicial[250] observations:

"Tracing is thus neither a claim nor a remedy. It is merely the process by which a claimant demonstrates what has happened to his property, identifies its proceeds and the persons who have handled or received them, and justifies his claim that the proceeds can properly be regarded as representing his property. Tracing is also distinct from claiming. It identifies the traceable proceeds of the claimant's property. It enables the claimant to substitute the traceable proceeds for the original asset as the subject matter of his claim. But it does not affect or establish his claim. That will depend on a number of factors including the nature of his interest in the original asset. He will normally be able to maintain the same claim to the substituted asset as he could have maintained to the original asset. If he held only a security interest in the original asset, he cannot claim more than a security interest in its proceeds. But his claim may also be exposed to potential defences as a result of intervening transactions."

22–117   This chapter will use the expressions "following" and "tracing" in the way in which Lord Millett has defined them and will use the expression "proprietary claim" to denote the substantive claim which is being brought by the claimant. However, it must be borne in mind that most of the authorities utilise the expression "tracing" to denote all of these things.

22–118   This section has been headed "legal proprietary claims" because the attitudes of the common law and of equity not only to following and tracing but also to proprietary claims have always been quite distinct and, despite judicial statements that one set of rules is enough,[251] for the moment they

---

[247] [2001] 1 A.C. 102 at 127.

[248] *ibid.* at 128.

[249] In *Boscawen v. Bajwa* [1996] 1 W.L.R. 328 at 334.

[250] (1998) 110 L.Q.R. 399.

[251] See *Foskett v. McKeown* [2001] 1 A.C. 102 at 128 *per* Lord Millett. In *Banque Belge pour l'Etranger v. Hambrouck* [1921] 1 K.B. 321, Atkin L.J. went so far as to say that the rules of tracing at law and equity were in fact the same but this view is generally regarded more as an expression of hope than as a statement of reality.

remain quite distinct. For this and other reasons, it is therefore necessary to consider legal and equitable proprietary claims separately.

1. *The Nature of Legal Proprietary Claims*

A person who seeks to assert a proprietary claim at law will use the action **22–119** appropriate to the type of property which he is claiming. If he is claiming land, he will use the action for the recovery of land; he merely needs to show a better title than the other party and, if he can do so, he will not be defeated by the defence of bona fide purchase for value without notice although his action may become statute-barred as a result of the other party's adverse possession. A successful claim will produce an order for the specific recovery of the land so that a legal proprietary right to land is indeed a right *in rem*. If the claim is instead for specific chattels, the claimant will use a tortious action for conversion under the Torts (Interference with Goods) Act 1977.[252] Bona fide purchase for value without notice will now[253] only be a defence to such a claim if the purchaser is protected by the provisions of the Sale of Goods Act 1979.[254] However, a successful claimant is not entitled to specific recovery of the chattel, although the court has a discretion to so order.[255] Thus a legal proprietary right to chattels will only rarely amount to a right *in rem*. Finally, if the claim is for a chose in action or money, the claimant will only be able to use the action for money had and received, which imposes only a personal liability on the defendant. Bona fide purchase for value without notice will apparently be a defence to such a claim.[256] Thus, a legal proprietary right to property of this type will never amount to a right *in rem*. An action for money had and received is certainly now subject to the defence of change of position, which will be discussed in detail at the end of the next section of this chapter[257]; however, it is questionable whether an action for the recovery of land or a tortious action for conversion are also subject to this defence, and it is anyway not easy to see how a relevant change of position could actually arise in either case.

2. *Who can Bring a Legal Proprietary Claim?*

Only a person who has some form of title to the property in question which **22–120** is recognised by the common law is entitled to bring a proprietary claim at

---

[252] Torts (Interference with Goods) Act 1977, s.1.

[253] It was formerly also a defence if the property had been purchased in market overt but this defence was removed by Sale of Goods (Amendment) Act 1994, which repealed Sale of Goods Act 1979, s.22(1).

[254] Sale of Goods Act 1979, s.23. See also Consumer Credit Act 1974, Sch.IV, Pt I, para.22.

[255] Torts (Interference with Goods) Act 1977, s.3.

[256] There is no justification in principle for this view but it must follow from *Lipkin Gorman v. Karpnale* [1991] 2 A.C. 548, where the plaintiff solicitors would not have been able to recover funds abstracted from their client account from the casino where those funds had been gambled and lost had the casino been able successfully to plead bona fide purchase for value without notice (it was unable to do so because of the nature of gaming contracts). See Halliwell [1992] Conv. 124.

[257] See *post*, para 22–194.

common law.[258] This was specifically held by the Court of Appeal in *MCC Proceeds v. Lehman Brothers International (Europe)*[259] where they rejected a claim by the beneficiaries of a bare trust to bring an action of conversion in respect of share certificates which their trustee had in breach of trust pledged to the defendant. As in that case and in cases such as *Re Diplock*, this requirement will generally prevent the beneficiaries of a trust from taking advantage of any potential legal proprietary claim to the trust property; the legal owner of property subject to a trust are the trustees who in such cases will themselves have been responsible for the property reaching the hands of the defendant and so are prevented from reclaiming it by the principle of non-derogation from grant. Consequently, it is only where the trustees have themselves been defrauded by the potential defendant to a legal proprietary claim that such a claim is likely to be available to a trust.

3. *What Property can be the Subject Matter of a Legal Proprietary Claim?*

(A) Property in its Original Form

22–121   Where the property which is the subject matter of the claim remains in its original form, the legal owner will, subject to the defences mentioned above, be able to follow it into the hands of anyone in the world, bring the appropriate legal proprietary claim and obtain the appropriate remedy.

22–122   Difficulties may arise, however, when chattels are intermingled with other chattels of the same nature so that it cannot precisely be ascertained which belong to the claimant.[260] In these circumstances, it seems that a tortious action will still be available despite the mixing. This follows from *Jackson v. Anderson*,[261] where it was held that an action of conversion could be maintained against someone who had mixed the plaintiff's gold coins in a barrelful of the same description. So far as ownership of the intermingled chattels is concerned, this has traditionally depended on whether the mixing was accidental or deliberate.

22–123   If chattels are mixed accidentally so that they cannot be separated or identified, then the original owners are treated as tenants in common of the whole in proportion to their contributions. This was held in *Spence v. Union Marine Insurance Co.*,[262] where bales of wool belonging to different owners became indistinguishable as the result of a shipwreck.

22–124   On the other hand, it has been stated[263] that, where a person deliberately mixed the property of another with his own, then the whole must be taken

---

[258] This form of title will normally be legal ownership but, in the case of personal chattels, in some circumstances the person entitled to maintain an action of conversion is the person with the immediate right to possession of those chattels rather than their legal owner; *International Factors v. Rodriguez* [1979] 1 Q.B. 351 (CA).

[259] [1998] 4 All E.R. 675.

[260] See Pearce 40 Conveyancer (N.S.) (1976) 277.

[261] (1811) 4 Taunt. 24.

[262] (1868) L.R. 3 C.P. 427.

[263] *Spence v. Union Marine Insurance Co.* (1868) L.R. 3 C.P. 427 at 437–438; *Sandeman & Sons v. Tyzack and Branfoot Steamship Co.* [1913] A.C. 680 at 695 *per* Lord Moulton. This is also the rule in equity; see *Lupton v. White* (1808) 15 Ves. 432; *Foskett v. McKeown* [2001] 1 A.C. 102 at 133 *per* Lord Millett.

to be the property of the other unless and until the mixer unmixes the chattels. This principle was applied by a Canadian court in *Jones v. De Marchant*[264] where a wife was held to be the owner of a fur coat which her husband had had made up out of 18 beaver skins belonging to her and four skins of his own and had then given to his mistress. The result of this case would undoubtedly still be the same today but, in so far as the principle concerns fungibles, it has now been described as no longer appropriate given the availability of modern and sophisticated methods of measurement. This was in *Indian Oil Corp. v. Greenstone Shipping Co.*,[265] where the owners of a vessel had mixed with their own crude oil a cargo of crude oil which they were shipping. The owners of the cargo claimed the whole of the crude oil. However, since it was possible to determine exactly the amounts of oil belonging to each party, it was held that the mixture was held in common and that the owners of the cargo were entitled to receive a quantity of the mixed oil equal to that which had gone into the mixture, any doubts being resolved in their favour, together with damages for any loss which they had suffered. While this view seems a more appropriate way of dealing with fungibles in modern conditions, it remains to be seen which way the conflict of authority thus produced is finally resolved.

Legal proprietary claims to money, on the other hand, suffer from the difficulty that money has no earmark (it is rare for a note to be taken of the numbers of banknotes and there is no way of doing so in the case of coins). Further, since money is the universal medium of exchange, the transferor of money normally makes that money the property of the transferee. However, if a claimant can identify money in the hands of another as belonging to him (as would be the case where bank notes of known serial numbers were stolen and found in the possession of the thief), then that money could be recovered by an action for money had and received.

22–125

(B) Property which is Identifiable Despite a Change of Form

Provided that property or its product has at all times remained identifiable, it can be traced at law despite a change of form and anything into which it is turned can be recovered. *Jackson v. Anderson*,[266] *Spence v. Union Marine Insurance Co.*,[267] and *Indian Oil Corp. v. Greenstone Shipping Co.*[268] are all still applicable for this purpose. In *Taylor v. Plumer*,[269] the defendant had given his stockbroker a draft for £22,000 to be disbursed on Exchequer Bills. The stockbroker, having cashed the draft and used £6,500 for this purpose, paid for certain American securities which he had already agreed to purchase and also obtained some bullion with a draft which he had exchanged for cash. He then attempted to flee the country but was intercepted by the defendant at Falmouth and surrendered to him the securities and the bullion. His trustee in bankruptcy tried to recover these assets or their value from the defendant on the basis that the latter's title could not survive these transactions; had he succeeded, the defendant would have had to take his turn with

22–126

---

[264] (1916) 28 D.L.R. 561.
[265] [1987] 2 Lloyd's Rep. 286.
[266] (1811) 4 Taunt. 24.
[267] (1868) L.R. 3 C.P. 427.
[268] [1987] 2 Lloyd's Rep. 286.
[269] (1815) 3 M. & S. 562.

the general creditors. However, Lord Ellenborough C.J. held that the defendant could at all times have traced the product of his draft into the hands of the stockbroker and brought a proprietary claim against him in respect of the assets in his hands; this was because the product of the defendant's original draft had at all times been completely identifiable. This meant that the defendant could still claim the assets in priority to the general creditors. Lord Ellenborough stated that only when property had been turned into money and mixed with other money did the right to trace and bring a legal proprietary claim in respect of it disappear.

22–127   Although it has been contended[270] that this decision is no authority for a legal proprietary claim surviving a change of form of the property unless the nature of the transaction by which the change of form occurs is such as to vest title in the new form of the property in the claimant, *Taylor v. Plumer* has been repeatedly followed. In *Re J. Leslie Engineers Co.*,[271] the liquidator of a company was held entitled to trace at law a cheque drawn on the company account to cash into the postal orders which had been purchased with the cash and sent to the defendant. Similarly, in *Lipkin Gorman v. Karpnale*,[272] the House of Lords held that the plaintiff firm of solicitors could trace at law its right of action against its bankers in respect of the credit balance of its client account into the funds drawn in cash from the account by one of its partners and exchanged for gaming chips at the defendant's casino. In *Trustee of the Property of F. C. Jones & Sons (a Firm) v. Jones*,[273] the Court of Appeal held that the trustee in bankruptcy of a partnership could trace cheques totalling £11,700 which one of the partners had after the act of bankruptcy drawn on the partnership account in favour of his wife; she had paid the cheques into a new account which she opened with commodity brokers and then, having traded profitably with this account, paid the commodity broker's cheque for the profit into another new account with a bank; the trustee in bankruptcy had at all times been the legal owner of the money, had at all times been able to identify it, and so could claim not only the £11,700 and interest thereon but also the profit made with it.

22–128   Further, *Taylor v. Plumer* was, if anything, extended in *Banque Belge pour l'Etranger v. Hambrouck*,[274] where the Court of Appeal emphasised that it is not the mere payment of money into a bank account which matters but the identifiability of the property. The defendant had fraudulently obtained £6,000 from the plaintiff bank by drawing cheques on his employers in favour of himself. He paid these cheques into his own account with another bank, an account into which no other substantial sums were ever paid. From this account, he drew out cash which he paid over to his mistress in consideration for the continuance of their relationship; she paid these sums into a deposit account, whose outstanding balance was successfully claimed

---

[270] By Khurshid & Matthews (1979) 95 L.Q.R. 78, who argue that the references in *Taylor v. Plumer* to the right of the defendant to trace were to tracing in equity, rather than to tracing at law. This argument is convincing historically and there is much to be said for it as a matter of principle; however, it is inconsistent with the many authorities in which *Taylor v. Plumer* has been applied.

[271] [1976] 1 W.L.R. 292.

[272] [1991] 2 A.C. 548.

[273] [1997] Ch. 159.

[274] [1921] 1 K.B. 321.

by the plaintiff. The majority of the Court of Appeal[275] held that the plaintiff was entitled at law to trace the money through the defendant's bank account into the hands of the mistress because it was possible to distinguish the money at every stage; the fact that, to all intents and purposes, no other sums had been paid into the defendant's account meant that the funds abstracted from the plaintiff had never lost their identity.[276]

(C) Property which is No Longer Identifiable Following a Change of Form

Where property is no longer identifiable following a change of form, it cannot be traced at law. Property is usually no longer identifiable because it or its product has been turned into money and mixed with other money. Payment into a mixed fund or through an inter-bank clearing system will clearly prevent a legal proprietary claim while, as *Banque Belge pour l'Etranger v. Hambrouck* clearly illustrates, payment into an unmixed bank account (other than through such a clearing system) will not. However, it is not at present entirely clear whether legal proprietary claims are limited to physical substitutions (where, as in all the cases discussed so far, cash is withdrawn from one bank account and used to acquire some other asset, including a credit balance in another bank account) or also extend to other forms of transfer, such as an electronic transfer from one bank account to another where the funds have not had to pass through an inter-bank clearing system. 22–129

In *Agip (Africa) v. Jackson*,[277] the name of the payee on a payment order issued by the plaintiff was fraudulently altered and the sum in question was transferred by the plaintiff's bank in Tunis through its correspondent bank in New York and then, presumably through the New York clearing system, to an account at Lloyds Bank in London in the name of a shell English company controlled by the defendants, a firm of accountants from the Isle of Man. The plaintiff subsequently claimed to be entitled to trace this payment through the account of the shell company into an account of the defendants in the Isle of Man, to which it had subsequently been transferred. The shell company's account had contained no other funds at the relevant time so there would have been no difficulty about tracing the funds from that account to the account of the defendants. However, Millett J. held that the funds could not be traced at law into the account of the shell company. Given that the money had been transmitted by telegraphic transfer and had almost certainly passed through the New York clearing system, 22–130

"nothing passed between Tunisia and London but a stream of electrons. It is not possible to treat the money received by Lloyds Bank in London or its

---

[275] Bankes and Atkin L.JJ. Scrutton L.J. held that the plaintiff was entitled only to trace in equity.

[276] Atkin L.J. went so far as to say that it was possible to trace at law even into a mixed fund. However, this view is generally regarded more as an expression of hope than as a statement of reality.

[277] [1990] Ch. 265.

correspondent bank in New York as representing the proceeds of the payment order or of any other physical asset previously in its hands and
delivered by it in exchange for the money."[278]

22–131   Millett J. thus seems to have restricted legal proprietary claims to cases of
physical substitutions; however, in the Court of Appeal,[279] Fox L.J., while
affirming the judgment of Millett J., placed a greater emphasis on the
clearing system limitation. The view of Millett J. was subsequently reiterated
in *Bank Tejerat v. Hong Kong and Shanghai Building Corp.*,[280] where Tuckey J.
refused a legal proprietary claim to funds which had been the subject of
telex instructions.

22–132   These decisions emphasise the restrictions of proprietary claims at law.
However, they do not necessarily mean that payments made by cheque can
never be traced at law; indeed the decision in *Trustee of the Property of F.C.
Jones & Sons (a Firm) v. Jones*,[281] where cheques were traced at law, suggests
quite the opposite. Consequently, where both payer and payee have their
accounts at the same branch, it will clearly be possible to trace the payment
at law from one account to another and this will almost certainly also be
possible where the accounts are at different branches of the same bank.
However, it is obviously likely that the intervention of any inter-bank
clearing system will cause the funds to lose their identity and be prevented
from being traced at law despite the existence of the original cheque; it will
be entirely fortuitous whether or not any funds were actually transferred
from the payer's bank to the payee's bank on the day in question since this
will depend on the overall balance of cleared transactions between the two
banks on that day. Whether or not the intervention of any inter-bank clearing system will actually have this effect, these restrictions on legal proprietary claims are clearly highly inconvenient; however, the difficulties have
been substantially alleviated by the intervention of equity.

IX. Equitable Proprietary Claims

22–133   A person who seeks to assert an equitable proprietary claim will be relying
on the existence of an equitable proprietary interest in the property in
question which he will be endeavouring to enforce against the defendant.
However, no such claim will be able to be made successfully against a
defendant who is a bona fide purchaser for value of a legal estate in the
property without notice of the interest of the claimant (or any statutory
equivalent); such a person inevitably takes the property free of such an
equitable proprietary interest. It has been contended, but has not yet
actually been held, that such a claim also cannot be made successfully
against any defendant who is able to invoke the recently recognised defence
of change of position. There are also some further defences open only to

---

[278] [1990] Ch. 265 at 286.
[279] [1991] Ch. 547.
[280] [1995] 1 Lloyd's Rep. 239.
[281] [1997] Ch. 159.

innocent volunteers. All these defences are discussed at the end of this section.[282]

1. *The Consequences of a Successful Equitable Proprietary Claim*

The consequences of a successful equitable proprietary claim are normally that the defendant will thereafter be bound by the equitable interest of the claimant and will therefore be treated as a trustee of the property in question for him. This trust is often said to be a constructive trust; this expression is not inaccurate but it is potentially confusing.[283] It does not mean that the defendant will automatically be regarded as having been subject to all the obligations of a trustee from the moment when he originally received the property in question; that will only be the case if "liability for knowing receipt" is also imposed on him under the rules which have already been discussed.[284] However, he will certainly be subject to such obligations thereafter and, if he does not comply with them, "liability for inconsistent dealing" will be imposed on him.[285] If the claimant is able to show that any particular item of property in the hands of the defendant is, in equity, either entirely his own property or entirely the product of his own property, then he will obviously be able to call for that property to be transferred to him.[286] If, on the other hand, he is able to show that any particular item of property in the hands of the defendant is only partially the product of his own property, then he will have an election between a lien or charge over it for the amount of his contribution to that property or, if it has gone up in value, for a beneficial interest in proportion to his contribution to it. This was specifically held by Lord Millett in *Foskett v. McKeown*.[287] In all cases, he will enjoy the rights appropriate to the holder of such an interest in the type of property in question[288] and his equitable proprietary right will amount to as much of a right *in rem* as any other proprietary right, something which is of course dependant on that right being enforceable against the defendant in the first place.

However, treating the defendant as a trustee is not the only possible consequence of a successful equitable proprietary claim. The claimant can alternatively be subrogated to rights which a third party has against the defendant. This happened in *Boscawen v. Bajwa*.[289] The Abbey National Building Society had agreed to make a mortgage advance to fund the purchase of a property belonging to the defendant. The purchasers' solicitors, who were as usual acting both for the building society and for the

22–134

22–135

---

[282] See *post*, para 22–191.

[283] See Lord Millett, extra-judicially, (1998) 114 L.Q.R. 399.

[284] See *ante*, para 10–199.

[285] See *ante*, para 10–234. *Sheridan v. Joyce* [1844] 1 Jo. & Lat. 41 (Court of Chancery of Ireland).

[286] *Foskett v. McKeown* [2001] 1 A.C. 102 at 130 *per* Lord Millett, who went on to say that the claimant could instead "bring a personal claim against the trustee for breach of trust and enforce an equitable lien or charge on the proceeds to secure restoration of the trust fund".

[287] [2001] 1 A.C. 102 at 131.

[288] Thus if it is land he will enjoy the same rights as any other beneficiary under a trust of land (see Trusts of Land and Appointment of Trustees Act 1996).

[289] [1996] 1 W.L.R. 328.

purchasers, transferred the amount advanced to the defendant's solicitors who used that sum to pay off the defendant's mortgage with the Halifax Building Society. However, although the defendant had executed an undated transfer in favour of the purchasers, a small outstanding balance of the price was never paid to him so this transfer was never dated or registered; the purchasers therefore never acquired legal title to the property. To make matters worse, the contract between the defendant and the purchasers did not comply with the necessary formalities[290] and so was void; consequently, the purchasers had never acquired any equitable interest in the property either. The Abbey National therefore had no valid mortgage over the defendant's property yet their money had been used to pay off his mortgage. Various creditors of the defendant then obtained a charging order over the property and sought an order for sale.

22–136   The Abbey National was able to comply with the requirements for an equitable proprietary claim and was able to demonstrate that its funds had in fact been used to discharge the mortgage. The Court of Appeal said this[291]:

"If the plaintiff succeeds in tracing his property, whether in its original or in some changed form, into the hands of the defendant, and overcomes any defences which are put forward on the defendant's behalf, he is entitled to a remedy. The remedy will be fashioned to the circumstances. The plaintiff will generally be entitled to a personal remedy; if he seeks a proprietary remedy he must usually prove that the property to which he lays claim is still in the ownership of the defendant. If he succeeds in doing this the court will treat the defendant as holding the property on a constructive trust for the plaintiff and will order the defendant to transfer it in specie to the plaintiff. But this is only one of the proprietary remedies which are available to a court of equity. If the plaintiff's money has been applied by the defendant, for example, not in the acquisition of a landed property but in its improvement, then the court may treat the land as charged with the payment to the plaintiff of a sum representing the amount by which the value of the defendant's land has been enhanced by the use of the plaintiff's money. And if the plaintiff's money has been used to discharge a mortgage on the defendant's land, then the court may achieve a similar result by treating the land as subject to a charge by way of subrogation in favour of the plaintiff."

The Abbey National was held to be entitled to be subrogated to the mortgage security of the Halifax which had been paid off with its money and therefore enjoyed priority over the plaintiffs' charging order. The facts of this case were very peculiar and it is not often that a claimant will need to have recourse to subrogation in order to enforce an equitable proprietary claim. However, there seems no reason why he should not be able to do so in the sort of circumstances which occurred in *Boscawen v. Bajwa*.

---

[290] For failure to comply with the Law of Property (Miscellaneous Provisions) Act 1989, s.2.

[291] [1996] 1 W.L.R. 328 at 334–335, *per* Millett L.J. In this passage, the references to the plaintiff are to the claimant in an equitable proprietary claim, not to the plaintiffs in *Boscawen v. Bajwa*.

2. What are the Prerequisites of an Equitable Proprietary Claim?

(A) An Equitable Proprietary Interest

It is hardly necessary to state that an equitable proprietary claim can only be   **22–137**
pursued if the claimant has an equitable proprietary interest in the property
in question. Although it is generally said that a claimant is able to trace an
equitable proprietary interest into its product only if he can point to the
existence of a fiduciary relationship, the converse is not true. Thus the fact
that funds have been deposited with a fiduciary agent pursuant to a contract
of loan does not entitle the depositor to bring an equitable proprietary claim;
he has retained no proprietary interest in the funds deposited.[292] Nor does
an agent who is retained to collect rents or other moneys on behalf of his
principal automatically become a trustee of them for the latter; this will only
be the case if he did or should have segregated the sums.[293]

(B) A Fiduciary Relationship

As has already been mentioned, it is generally said that a claimant is able to   **22–138**
trace an equitable proprietary interest into its product only if he can point
to the existence of a fiduciary relationship. In *Agip (Africa) v. Jackson*,[294]
Millett J. held that:

"the only restriction on the ability of equity to follow assets is the requirement that there must be some fiduciary relationship which permits the
assistance of equity to be invoked. The requirement has been widely condemned and depends on authority rather than principle."

Historically there was no such requirement. In *Re Hallett's Estate*,[295] the   **22–139**
defendant solicitor sold bonds belonging partly to his own marriage settlement and partly to a client and mixed the proceeds with his own funds in
a bank account. The beneficiaries of the marriage settlement could clearly
point to the existence of a fiduciary relationship but the client was also
permitted to maintain an equitable proprietary claim on the basis that she
was the legal and beneficial owner of the property which she had deposited
with the defendant. Similarly, in *Banque Belge pour l'Etranger v. Hambrouck*,[296]
Scrutton L.J., who had doubted the availability of a legal proprietary claim,
held that the plaintiff had an equitable proprietary claim and both the other
members of the court stated that, had they not held the plaintiff to have a
legal proprietary claim, they also would have permitted an equitable proprietary claim. None of the members of the court stated any requirement for the

---

[292] *Daly v. The Sydney Stock Exchange* (1986) 160 C.L.R. 371 (High Court of Australia).
[293] *Cohen v. Cohen* (1929) 42 C.L.R. 91 (High Court of Australia). However, any failure to
segregate means that no priority will be able to be obtained unless the whereabouts of the funds
can actually be established.
[294] [1990] Ch. 265.
[295] (1880) 13 Ch.D. 696. See [1975] C.L.P. 64.
[296] [1921] 1 K.B. 321.

existence of a fiduciary relationship as a prerequisite to an equitable proprietary claim. There is, of course, no doubt whatever that the necessary fiduciary relationship could have been found in both these cases had it been
necessary. As Millett J. went on to say in *Agip (Africa) v. Jackson*, "the
requirement may be circumvented since it is not necessary that the fund to
be traced should have been the subject of fiduciary obligations before it got
into the wrong hands; it is sufficient that the payment to the defendant itself
gives rise to a fiduciary relationship." Both the defaulting solicitor in *Re
Hallett's Estate* and the fraudulent employee in *Banque Belge pour l'Etranger v.
Hambrouck* could undoubtedly have been held to be constructive trustees of,
respectively, the proceeds of the bonds and the proceeds of the cheques. The
significant fact is that none of the judges felt it necessary to look for and find
such a fiduciary relationship.

22–140   However, it is generally thought that in *Re Diplock*[297] the Court of Appeal
interpreted the decision of the House of Lords in *Sinclair v. Brougham*[298] as
establishing, in the words of Goulding J. in *Chase Manhattan Bank v. Israel-
British Bank (London)*,[299] "that an initial fiduciary relationship is a necessary
foundation of the equitable right of tracing". It is questionable both whether
this was really the opinion of the Court of Appeal in *Re Diplock* and whether
Sinclair v. Brougham imposed any such requirement. As will be seen later on,
the actual decision reached in *Sinclair v. Brougham* itself has now been
overruled by the House of Lords in *Westdeutsche Landesbank Girozentrale v.
Islington L.B.C.*[300] However, the House did not consider the fiduciary relationship requirement, Lord Browne-Wilkinson merely saying the House
"should not be taken to be casting any doubt on the principles of tracing as
established in *Re Diplock*".[301]

22–141   In *Sinclair v. Brougham*[302] the House of Lords had had to look for and find
a fiduciary relationship, wrongfully as it has now been held, because that
was the only way of establishing that the depositors in an *ultra vires* banking
business had an equitable proprietary interest in the funds of the building
society which had been running it. This does not, however, of itself necessarily mean that a fiduciary relationship is required where the claimant has
a pre-existing equitable proprietary right. Indeed, in *Re Diplock*[303] the Court
of Appeal did no more than state that "equity may operate on the conscience
not merely of those who acquire a legal title in breach of some trust, express
or constructive, or of some other fiduciary obligation, but of volunteers
provided that as a result of what has gone before some equitable proprietary
interest has been created and attaches to the property in the hands of the
volunteer." It is not obvious that this passage has the effect of requiring a
fiduciary relationship where the claimant already has a pre-existing equitable proprietary interest. However, that is the way in which it has always

---

[297] [1948] Ch. 465.
[298] [1914] A.C. 398.
[299] [1981] Ch. 105.
[300] [1996] A.C. 669.
[301] *ibid.* at 714. This may well have been a reference to the mixed fund rules established in *Re
Diplock* (see *post*, para 22–187) rather than to its supposed enunciation of a fiduciary relationship
requirement.
[302] [1914] A.C. 398.
[303] [1948] Ch. 465 at 530.

been subsequently interpreted, both at first instance[304] and in the Court of Appeal.[305]

Whether or not such a requirement exists is not purely a technical issue. **22–142** Even though the courts have on occasions strained the concept of fiduciary relationship to its limits, if not well beyond them, in order to satisfy this requirement, an absolute legal and beneficial owner of property cannot possibly point to any such relationship and so, according to the present understanding of the law, is therefore apparently not entitled to maintain an equitable proprietary claim. Consequently, if the property of such a person is stolen and its product is mixed with other money in a bank account, the victim of the theft will prima facie not be entitled to maintain a proprietary claim either at law (because of the mixing) or in equity (because of the absence of a fiduciary relationship). This ridiculous anomaly could be rectified in any of the following ways.

First, the requirement for the existence of a fiduciary relationship could be **22–143** abolished. A challenge to the existence of this requirement has often been advocated but is realistically only possible in the House of Lords. It is thought that the House of Lords would if necessary abolish this requirement but this certainly cannot be assumed.

Secondly, the thief could be held to hold the stolen property on resulting **22–144** trust for his victim, thus providing both the fiduciary relationship and the equitable proprietary interest necessary for an equitable proprietary claim. Such a conclusion was reached by the High Court of Australia in *Black v. S. Freeman & Co.*,[306] a decision which was cited with approval by Lord Templeman in *Lipkin Gorman v. Karpnale*,[307] although the House of Lords was not considering any equitable proprietary claim. The difficulty about this view is that, since a thief does not acquire title to the stolen property, it is not easy to see exactly what he would actually be holding on trust.

Thirdly, the thief could be held to hold the stolen property on constructive **22–145** trust for his victim as a result of his fraudulent conduct, thus equally providing both the fiduciary relationship and the equitable proprietary interest necessary for an equitable proprietary claim. In *Westdeutsche Landesbank Girozentrale v. Islington L.B.C.*[308] Lord Browne-Wilkinson specifically envisaged this possibility and in *Twinsectra v. Yardley*[309] the Court of Appeal held that a constructive trust existed for this reason (this question was not considered on the subsequent appeal to the House of Lords[310]). While there is obviously not the slightest difficulty about imposing a constructive trust

---

[304] In *Agip (Africa) v. Jackson* [1990] Ch. 265, and in *Box v. Barclays Bank* [1998] Lloyd's Rep. Bank. 185. In the latter case Ferris J. denied the plaintiffs an equitable proprietary claim specifically because there was no fiduciary relationship (they had deposited money with a person running an unlicensed deposit taking business, a transaction which was classified as creating nothing more than a debtor-creditor relationship).

[305] In *Aluminium Industrie Vaassen v. Romalpa Aluminium* [1976] 1 W.L.R. 676 and in *Agip (Africa) v. Jackson* [1991] Ch. 547.

[306] [1910] 12 C.L.R. 105.

[307] [1992] 2 A.C. 548.

[308] [1996] A.C. 669 at 715–716.

[309] [2000] W.T.L.R. 527 at 567–568.

[310] [2002] 2 A.C. 162.

on this ground,[311] exactly the same difficulty arises as to what the thief would be holding on trust.

22–146   Fourthly, the thief could be held to hold the stolen property on constructive trust for his victim as a result of his fraudulent conduct in the way just envisaged but only if he steals money or if and when he turns other types of stolen property into money. Since money is the universal medium of exchange, it becomes his property and so can certainly become the subject matter of a trust without any of the difficulties referred to above (this argument was deployed in the House of Lords in *Twinsectra v. Yardley* in order to justify the conclusion reached by the Court of Appeal but in the event the House did not need to consider it[312]). It is suggested that this fourth possibility should be adopted in appropriate circumstances unless and until the unnecessary requirement for a fiduciary relationship is abolished.

3. *When will these Prerequisites be Satisfied?*

(A) Express Trusts

22–147   It is obvious that these requirements will be satisfied where the person against whom the equitable proprietary claim is being brought is an express trustee of the property in question and it was held in *Re Diplock*[313] that these requirements will also be satisfied where the property in question was originally subject to an express trust, even though the equitable proprietary claim is in fact being brought against a subsequent holder of that property. This was the case in *Foskett v. McKeown*,[314] where funds had been provided by a number of potential purchasers of plots of land in Portugal and were held on express trust to be used to make the payments necessary to bring about a transfer of the plot in question to its purchaser or, in the event that this did not happen within two years, to be returned to that purchaser. Some of the funds were misappropriated and used to pay the premiums on a life insurance policy and the purchasers were held to be entitled to bring an equitable proprietary claim against the trustees of that policy.[315]

(B) Resulting Trusts

22–148   These requirements will equally be satisfied where the person against whom the equitable proprietary claim is being brought is a resulting trustee of any of the traditional types.[316] They will also be satisfied in the event that a resulting trust arises as a result of the rescission of a transaction which is void or voidable. In *Shalson v. Russo (Mimran, Part 20 Claimant)*[317] it was specifically held that the effect of the rescission of such a transaction was to give rise to a trust on the basis of which the party rescinding the transaction was entitled to maintain an equitable proprietary claim. However, Rimer J.

---

[311] See *ante*, para 10–248.

[312] Given that the House of Lords upheld the existence of a *Quistclose* trust, there was no need for any constructive trust and so the House did not hear argument on whether or not one had arisen.

[313] [1948] Ch. 465.

[314] [2001] 1 A.C. 102.

[315] *ibid.* at 108 *per* Lord Browne-Wilkinson.

[316] See *ante*, Chap. 9.

[317] [2003] EWHC 1637 (Ch), [2005] Ch. 281 *per* Rimer J. at [121–127].

did not actually specify whether the trust in question was resulting or constructive and, since this is a matter of some controversy, trusts of this type will be considered separately below.

(C) Constructive Trusts
These requirements will again be satisfied where, as in *Attorney-General for*   **22–149**
Hong Kong v. Reid,³¹⁸ the person against whom the equitable proprietary claim is being brought has been held to be a constructive trustee of the property in question; this will clearly be the case even where, as in *Agip (Africa) v. Jackson*,³¹⁹ the property in question became subject to a constructive trust only as a result of an improper disposition of that property, if in other words, the act which has given rise to the equitable proprietary claim itself brought about the imposition of the constructive trust. They will also be satisfied in the event that a constructive trust arises as a result of a transaction which is void, voidable or mistaken; these situations are considered below.

(D) Void Transactions
Where a transfer of property is void *ab initio* for some reason such as   **22–150**
illegality, mistake or lack of capacity of the transferor, no title will generally have passed to the transferee; in that case the transferor will not need any trust as a prerequisite of asserting his title. Only where title has nevertheless passed to the transferee because the property in question was or has subsequently been turned into money is a trust necessary. In such circumstances, a constructive trust will be imposed where the money has been obtained as the result of a crime³²⁰ and as a result of fraud³²¹ or undue influence³²²; in this event, an equitable proprietary claim will obviously be available to the victim of the crime, fraud or undue influence.

However, it has now been established that no trust can arise where title has passed to the transferee under a transaction which is within the capacity of the transferor but beyond the capacity of the transferee. Admittedly a trust was held to arise in *Sinclair v. Brougham*,³²³ which concerned the liquidation of a building society in the course of which it became apparent that a banking business which it had been running was in fact *ultra vires*. When a question of priorities arose as between the shareholders of the society and the depositors in the banking business,³²⁴ a majority of the House of Lords held that the depositors did indeed have an equitable proprietary interest arising under a trust, variously identified as a resulting trust and a constructive trust.³²⁵ However, this decision was overruled by

---

³¹⁸ [1994] 1 A.C. 324.
³¹⁹ [1990] Ch. 265; [1991] Ch. 547.
³²⁰ See *ante*, para 10–241.
³²¹ See *ante*, para 10–249.
³²² See *ante*, para 10–255.
³²³ [1914] A.C. 398.
³²⁴ Both had agreed that the outside creditors should be paid off first.
³²⁵ Viscount Haldane L.C. and Lord Atkinson held that the trust in question was "a resulting trust, not of an active character" (whatever that may be), while Lord Parker of Waddington held that it was a constructive trust. Lord Sumner upheld the existence of a trust but did not indicate with which of these two views he agreed. Lord Dunedin reached the same result without recourse to an equitable proprietary claim.

the majority of the House of Lords in *Westdeutsche Landesbank Girozentrale v. Islington L.B.C.*[326] The parties had entered into an interest rate swap agreement, under which each agreed to pay to the other during a period of five-years at six-monthly intervals an amount calculated by reference to the interest which would have accrued over the previous six-monthly period on a notional principal sum, the interest rate being fixed in the case of the bank and floating in the case of the local authority. However, during the five-year period, such agreements were held[327] to be *ultra vires* local authorities and consequently void. The bank sought to recover the sums which it had paid to the local authority. In the lower courts,[328] it succeeded both at common law under an action for money had and received and on the basis of an equitable proprietary claim in accordance with *Sinclair v. Brougham.* However, the House of Lords held that, where title has passed to the transferee under a transaction which is within the capacity of the transferor but beyond the capacity of the transferee, the transferor retains no equitable proprietary interest therein under either a resulting trust or a constructive trust. Consequently, the bank was not entitled to an equitable proprietary claim.[329]

(E) Voidable Transactions

In *Shalson v. Russo (Mimran, Part 20 Claimant),*[330] the Part 20 claimant and the defendant had set up a company as the vehicle for joint ventures to which the Part 20 claimant had made a number of loans on the basis of fraudulent representations by the defendant that they were to be used joint venture property transactions. In fact the funds advanced were used for other purposes, including loan payments to another company which the defendant had set up with the claimant as a vehicle for the acquisition of a yacht. The Part 20 claimant now sought, by means of an equitable proprietary claim, to recover his loans by tracing them into the loans to the other company and on into the yacht which had been acquired (ultimately by yet another company). Rimer J. held[331] that the Part 20 claimant was able to maintain an equitable proprietary claim; the loan agreement was voidable because of the defendant's fraudulent misrepresentations and, as a result of having rescinded that agreement,[332] the Part 20 claimant had become entitled to a proprietary interest in the subject matter of the loans, which entitled him to trace the sums advanced into their product.[333] However, in the event, his equitable proprietary claim failed because the claimant was held to have

---

[326] [1996] A.C. 669.

[327] By the House of Lords in *Hazell v. Hammersmith and Fulham L.B.C.* [1992] A.C. 1.

[328] [1994] 4 All E.R. 890 (Hobhouse J.), [1994] 1 W.L.R. 938 (Court of Appeal).

[329] Consequently the bank was not entitled to compound interest on the sum, which the local authority accepted in the House of Lords that it was liable to repay at common law with simple interest thereon.

[330] [2003] EWHC 1637 (Ch), [2005] Ch. 281.

[331] *ibid.*, at [121–127].

[332] Rescission was held to have occurred as the result of the issue of the Part 20 proceedings seeking to trace the subject matter of the loans into their product.

[333] The Part 20 claimant had in fact relied on three different trusts as the basis for his equitable proprietary claim: a constructive trust which had arisen as a result of the defendant's fraud (whose existence Rimer J. rejected), the trust which had arisen as a result of the rescission of the loan agreement (on which the Part 20 claimant succeeded), and a *Quistclose* trust (whose existence Rimer J. also rejected).

been a bona fide purchaser for value of the loans without notice of the rights of the Part 20 claimant.

Rimer J. did not specifically state whether the trust which formed the basis **22–151** of this equitable proprietary claim was a resulting or a constructive trust (the heading of the section of his judgment in question is headed "Constructive/resulting trust"). It is obviously of not the slightest importance to the person who has an equitable proprietary claim on this basis whether that claim is based on a resulting or a constructive trust but the competing views must nevertheless be examined. In *El Ajou v. Dollar Land Holdings*,[334] the plaintiff had been induced to purchase shares by fraudulent misrepresentations and was seeking to impose "liability for knowing receipt" on the defendant, into whose hands the purchase moneys had come for value but, as the Court of Appeal subsequently held,[335] with sufficient knowledge of the fraud for the imposition of such liability. The imposition of liability for knowing receipt requires there to have been a disposition of property in breach of trust. Millett J. found such a trust on the basis of the principle which would later be adopted by Rimer J. and stated that "the trust which is operating in these cases is not some new model remedial constructive trust, but an old fashioned institutional resulting trust".[336] However, in *Papamichael v. National Westminster Bank*,[337] whose facts will be discussed below,[338] the judge[339] regarded this classification as inconsistent with some statements by Lord Browne-Wilkinson in *Westdeutsche Landesbank Girozentale v. Islington L.B.C.*[340] and held the statement that "the trust which is operating in these cases is . . . an old fashioned institutional resulting trust"[341] was "all very well, but Lord Browne-Wilkinson was specific in saying that what was being imposed was an institutional constructive trust not a resulting trust". However, the view expressed by Millett J. seems more in accordance with principle.

(F) Mistaken Transactions

In *Chase Manhattan Bank v. Israel-British Bank (London)*,[342] the plaintiff New **22–152** York bank had, as the result of a clerical error, made twice rather than once a payment of US$2,000,000 to another New York bank for the credit of the defendant London bank, which subsequently became insolvent. The plaintiff duly proved in the liquidation in respect of the second payment made under a mistake of fact but this gave no priority over the other creditors of

---

[334] [1993] 3 All E.R. 717, affirmed by the Court of Appeal without discussion of this particular point [1994] 2 All E.R. 685. See *ante*, para 10–207.

[335] [1994] 2 All E.R. 685, reversing Millett J. on this point.

[336] [1993] 3 All E.R. 717 at 734. The judge subsequently confirmed this view extra-judicially (114 L.Q.R. (1998) 399 at 416), stating that, "where the plaintiff pays away his money by a valid payment, fully intending to part with the beneficial interest to the recipient, but his intention is vitiated by some factor such as fraud, misrepresentation, mistake and so on . . . , the beneficial interest passes, but the plaintiff has the right to elect whether to affirm the transaction or rescind it. If he elects to rescind it, it is usually assumed that the beneficial title revests in the plaintiff, and the authorities suggest that it does so retrospectively."

[337] [2003] EWHC 164 (Comm), [2003] 1 Lloyd's Rep. 341.

[338] At para 22–156.

[339] Judge Chambers Q.C., sitting as a Judge of the Commercial Court.

[340] [1996] A.C. 669 at 716.

[341] [1993] 3 All E.R. 717 at 734.

[342] [1981] Ch. 105.

the defendant. The plaintiff therefore also claimed to be entitled to an equitable proprietary claim against the defendant. The legal effects of the mistaken payment had to be determined in accordance with the law of the State of New York, where a payment under a mistake of fact of money which the payee cannot conscientiously withhold gives rise to the imposition of a constructive trust. Goulding J. held, rather unexpectedly, that this was "also in accord with the general principles of equity as applied in England".[343] He justified this conclusion on the grounds that "a person who pays money to another under a factual mistake retains an equitable property in it and the conscience of that other is subjected to a fiduciary duty to respect his proprietary right".[344] This decision seems highly questionable. It is not obvious how either an equitable proprietary interest or a fiduciary duty could conceivably have arisen as the result of a payment made through a third party bank intended to be in settlement of a commercial debt.

22–153   The decision in *Chase Manhattan Bank v. Israel-British Bank (London)* was expressly applied in the Court of Appeal of New Zealand in *Liggett v. Kensington*.[345] A gold dealer had offered its purchasers the option of leaving their bullion in its custody on their behalf as "non-allocated bullion". Purchasers who did so were issued with a certificate of ownership and were entitled to take physical possession of their bullion on seven days' notice. The gold dealer subsequently became insolvent and the question arose as to whether these purchasers were entitled to an equitable proprietary claim in priority not only to its general creditors but also to a debenture holder. As has already been seen,[346] the majority of the Court of Appeal of New Zealand held that the gold dealer was in a fiduciary relationship with the purchasers, breach of which led to the imposition of a constructive trust and thus in turn to the purchasers having an equitable proprietary interest in the purchase moneys and their product, the remaining bullion. Cooke P., however, also held, applying *Chase Manhattan Bank v. Israel-British Bank (London)*, that the mistaken belief of the purchasers that they were acquiring gold, not merely contractual rights, meant that they had throughout retained an equitable proprietary interest in the purchase moneys.

22–154   However, when this case reached the Privy Council under the name of *Re Goldcorp Exchange*,[347] this decision was reversed. Lord Mustill held that there was no fiduciary relationship between the gold dealer and the purchasers so that no equitable proprietary interest could arise in that way. Further, in relation to the claim based on the retention by the purchasers of an equitable proprietary interest in the purchase money, Lord Mustill held that, whether this claim was based on mistake, misrepresentation or a total failure of consideration, the purchasers had at no time sought to rescind their contracts with the gold dealer on any of these grounds but had, on the contrary, "throughout the proceedings asserted various forms of proprietary interest in the bullion, all of them derived in one way or another from the contracts of sale". This stance was "wholly inconsistent with the notion that the

---

[343] *ibid.* at 118.
[344] *ibid.* at 119.
[345] [1993] 1 N.Z.L.R. 257.
[346] See *ante*, para 10–056.
[347] [1995] 1 A.C. 74.

contracts were and are so ineffectual that the customers are entitled to get their money back".[348] This of course meant that the Board did not have to consider the validity of the principle enunciated by Goulding J. in *Chase Manhattan Bank v. Israel-British Bank (London)* but Lord Mustill[349] declined to express an opinion as to whether or not that case was correctly decided.

Lord Mustill's clear doubts in this respect were confirmed by Lord   **22–155**
Browne-Wilkinson in *Westdeutsche Landesbank Girozentale v. Islington L.B.C.*[350] who specifically held that he did not accept the reasoning of Goulding J. Lord Millett has also stated, extra-judicially,[351] that he considers that *Chase Manhattan Bank v. Israel-British Bank* was wrongly decided. Unfortunately, however, in *Westdeutsche Landesbank Girozentale v. Islington L.B.C.*, Lord Browne-Wilkinson went on to say that *Chase Manhattan Bank v. Israel-British Bank (London)* nevertheless "may well have been rightly decided" on the basis that "although the mere receipt of the moneys, in ignorance of the mistake, gives rise to no trust, the retention of the moneys after the recipient bank learned of the mistake may well have given rise to a constructive trust".[352] Lord Browne-Wilkinson did not specify the basis of the imposition of such a constructive trust but this would presumably have been a remedial constructive trust of the type which he envisaged later in his speech.[353]

The issue arose again in the Commercial Court in *Papamichael v. National*   **22–156**
Westminster Bank.[354] The claimant's husband had deposited two billion Greek drachmas of the claimant's money with the bank; it was, as intended by everyone involved, converted into dollars, producing about US$6.5 million. The claimant thought that the dollars had been placed on fixed term deposit with the bank. However, unknown to her, her husband had fraudulently arranged for the dollars to be used as security for the operation by the bank of a foreign exchange margin account for his benefit. This account traded unsuccessfully and most of the dollars were lost. It was held that the claimant was entitled to the recovery of the two billion drachmas from the bank on the basis that she had been under a mistake of fact as to what would happen to that sum once it had been paid to the bank. However, because the drachma had depreciated by about 20 per cent as against the dollar during what she thought was the term of the fixed deposit, she was interested in recovering the US$6.5 million instead. This was only possible if the bank held the dollars on some form of trust for her, in which case the bank was potentially liable to account to the claimant for the whole of the dollars because it had dishonestly assisted in a breach of the trust or trusts in question.[355]

The judge[356] held that a trust had arisen (and so "liability for dishonest   **22–157**
assistance" was duly imposed on the bank) for three different reasons: breach of fiduciary duty by the husband; fraudulent conduct by the husband

---

[348] *ibid.*, at 102.
[349] *ibid.*, at 103.
[350] [1996] A.C. 669 at 715.
[351] 114 L.Q.R. [1998] 399 at 412–413.
[352] [1996] A.C. 669 at 715.
[353] *ibid.*, at 716. See *ante*, para 10–310.
[354] [2003] EWHC 164 (Comm), [2003] 1 Lloyd's Rep. 341.
[355] See *ante*, para 10–161.
[356] Judge Chambers Q.C., sitting as a Judge of the Commercial Court.

of which the bank was aware[357]; and[358] because the bank had received the dollars with knowledge of the claimant's mistake; in this respect, he relied on the explanation given by Lord Browne-Wilkinson of the decision in *Chase Manhattan Bank v. Israel-British Bank* but to do so was, as a matter of precedent, clearly wrong because of the repeated statements in the Court of Appeal[359] that the remedial constructive trust does not form part of English law and that the contention that it should be adopted by English law can only be maintained in the House of Lords. The judge therefore proceeded on the basis that both these trusts were constructive trusts rather than resulting trusts. He gave the bank leave to appeal to the Court of Appeal but the appeal was compromised.

22–158 It is considered that the better view is that *Chase Manhattan Bank v. Israel-British Bank* was wrongly decided both in its reasoning and in its result but, as is shown by *Papamichael v. National Westminster Bank*, the result, if not the reasoning, of that decision remains good law at present. Further developments in this respect are inevitable, if not before then when the House of Lords is called upon to decide, as it will undoubtedly have to do one day soon, "whether English law should follow the United States and Canada by adopting the remedial constructive trust".[360]

4. What Property can be the Subject Matter of an Equitable Proprietary Claim?

22–159 From its earliest days, equity has always been prepared to permit a beneficiary of a trust to enforce that trust against every transferee of the trust property save where the latter can show that he is a bona fide purchaser of a legal interest in that property for value without notice (or a statutory equivalent) or, possibly, can make out a defence of change of position. There seems no reason why such a claim should ever have been confined to the trust property in its original form for, otherwise, any alteration in the form of the trust property would have defeated the interests of the beneficiaries. Thus, equity was prepared to allow a beneficiary to trace the trust property into its product.[361] However, at this stage equity, like the common law, only permitted an equitable proprietary claim so long as the property or its product remained identifiable; consequently, the payment of the property or its product into a mixed fund was at this stage as fatal to an equitable proprietary claim as it was (and still is) to a legal proprietary claim. However, in 1852 in *Pennell v. Deffell*,[362] the Court of Appeal in Chancery held that the fact that property had become unidentifiable in a mixed fund was no bar to an equitable proprietary claim. The fact that it is thus possible to trace in equity property which has been mixed with the property of another has

---

[357] It was in this context that the judge made the observations about the correct classification of the trust which arises where a voidable transaction is rescinded.

[358] [2003] EWHC 164 (Comm), [2003] 1 Lloyd's Rep. 341 at 371.

[359] Most recently in *Twinsectra v. Yardley* [1999] Lloyd's Rep. Bank 438 and *Bank of Credit and Commerce International (Overseas) v. Akindele* [2001] Ch. 437.

[360] These are the words of Lord Browne-Wilkinson in *Westdeutsche Landesbank Girozentale v. Islington L.B.C.* [1996] A.C. 669 at 716.

[361] See *Ryall v. Ryall* (1739) 1 Atk. 59 and the other authorities cited in [1975] C.L.P. 64.

[362] (1853) De M. & G. 372.

made equitable proprietary claims attractive to the suppliers of goods to manufacturers. They have sought, by means of what are known as retention of title clauses, to ensure that title to the goods which they have supplied does not pass to the manufacturers until the goods have been paid for. This has meant that the rules of tracing property in equity have had to be applied in a commercial context very different from the trust context in which they were originally developed.

(A) Property in its Original Form

Where the claimant has an equitable proprietary interest in property which is still in its original form, he will be able to follow that property into the hands of anyone except a bona fide purchaser of a legal interest in that property for value without notice (or a statutory equivalent) or, possibly, able to make out a defence of change of position. In such circumstances, the claimant will often be able to compel the holder of the legal title to bring a legal proprietary claim. Thus, if property is stolen from a trust, the trustee will have the right to trace that property at law and the beneficiary will have the right to trace that property in equity. In such circumstances, because of the absence of a defence of bona fide purchase for value without notice at law, the beneficiary will be better advised to compel the trustee to trace the property or its product at law. However, this will not be possible where, as in *Re Diplock*,[363] the trustee has himself disposed of the property in question since he will be estopped from bringing a legal proprietary claim by the principle of non-derogation from grant. Nor will it be possible where the claimant is seeking to follow the property into the hands of someone who has acquired the property by operation of law, such as personal representatives who have acquired the property as a result of the trustee's death or a trustee in bankruptcy who has acquired it as a result of his insolvency. Where it is thus not possible for the claimant to trace the property at law, or he chooses not to do so, he will nevertheless be able to follow it in equity and call for it to be transferred to him.

22–160

(B) Property which is Identifiable Despite a Change of Form

Where the claimant has an equitable proprietary interest in property which is still identifiable despite a change in form, he will similarly often be able to compel the holder of the legal title to bring a legal proprietary claim. However, where this is not possible for one of the reasons stated above, or where the claimant chooses not to do so, he will be able to trace the property in equity. He will then be entitled to elect between calling for the property or its product to be transferred to him or taking a charge over that property to the extent of his contribution to its acquisition. This was stated by Jessel M.R. in *Re Hallett's Estate*[364] and was confirmed by the House of Lords in *Foskett v. McKeown*.[365]

22–161

Foskett v. McKeown[366] was a case where the change of form of the property was the result of a disposition of trust property in breach of trust. The

22–162

---

[363] [1948] Ch. 465.
[364] (1880) 13 Ch.D. 676 at 709.
[365] [2001] 1 A.C. 102 at 131, *per* Lord Millett.
[366] [2001] 1 A.C. 102.

deceased took out a life insurance policy for £1,000,000 and paid the first two annual premiums out of his own funds. However, subsequent annual premiums were paid in breach of trust[367] out of funds which were held on express trust for the claimants.[368] The deceased subsequently settled the life policy on trust for his mother and his children. Following the death of the deceased, the claimants wished to trace the premiums paid with their funds into the proceeds of the life policy and to recover from its trustees the proportion of those proceeds appropriate to the proportion of the premiums paid with their funds. The Court of Appeal[369] held, by a majority, that their rights were limited to following their funds into the premiums which they had been used to pay and to recovering the amount of those premiums with interest. Scott V.-C. held[370] that the payment of the later premiums was more akin to an improvement of existing property and had not in fact improved that property because, in the event, the £1,000,000 would have been paid out whether or not the later premiums had been paid.[371] Hobhouse L.J. similarly held[372] that the payment of the later premiums had not benefited the mother and children and had not affected the latter's right to the proceeds. But the House of Lords, by a bare majority, preferred the approach manifested in the dissenting judgment of Morritt L.J.; they rejected the improvement analogy[373] and held that the payment of the later premiums had benefited the mother and children at the time when they had been paid[374] and that was all that mattered; the fact that with the benefit of hindsight their payment had been unnecessary was irrelevant.[375] Consequently, the claimants were held to be able to trace into the proceeds of the policy.

22–163   *Russell-Cooke Trust Company v. Prentis*[376] was a case where the property in its changed form was in the hands of a successor trustee. The defendant solicitors ran an investment scheme whereby clients placed funds in the firm's client account with a view to those funds being combined and invested in short-term interest only loans secured against immoveable property by way of registered first charges. Some of these charges were taken in the name of the firm which therefore held them on resulting trust for the investors. When The Law Society subsequently became suspicious about the honesty of the firm and intervened in its practice, the claimant trustee company was appointed trustee of these resulting trusts. The trust company sought the directions of the court by means of an application to which representative investors were joined as defendants and was directed to distribute the proceeds of the loans to the investors in proportion to their

---

[367] The fourth and fifth annual premiums were certainly so paid; the source of the funds which had paid the third annual premium awaited determination at trial.
[368] See *ante*, para 22–147.
[369] [1998] Ch. 265.
[370] *ibid.*, p.278.
[371] If no further premiums had been paid after the first two, the policy would have been converted into a paid up policy and the later premiums would, in effect, have been deducted from the sum assured.
[372] [1998] Ch. 265 at 291.
[373] [2001] 1 A.C. 102 *per* Lord Browne-Wilkinson at 110, *per* Lord Millett at 137.
[374] Because it was likely that the assured would live long enough for the later premiums to be required to preserve the cover.
[375] [2001] 1 A.C. 102 *per* Lord Browne-Wilkinson at 111, *per* Lord Millett at 139.
[376] [2003] 2 All E.R. 478.

contributions to the sums lent. The principal issue in this litigation which is relevant for present purposes was the determination of which investors' funds had been invested in which loan, but there was not the slightest doubt about the right of the investors to trace their funds into their product in the hands of the replacement trustee.

Aluminium Industrie Vaassen v. Romalpa Aluminium[377] was a case in which a claimant with the benefit of what is known as a retention of title clause chose not to exercise a legal proprietary claim. A company selling aluminium foil was, under the terms of the contract of sale, expressed to remain the owner of the foil until such time as the purchaser had paid the purchase price in full (it was also provided that the vendor would become the owner of any new objects made as a result of mixing the foil with other materials). This did not prevent the purchaser from giving a good title to third parties but, as between vendor and purchaser, the goods remained the property of the vendor. The purchaser went into liquidation owing substantial sums in respect of unpaid foil. The vendor claimed to be entitled to such foil as remained in the possession of the purchaser and to the proceeds of sale of unmixed foil sold to third parties which had been paid by them to the receiver and had been placed by him in a separate bank account. Once it had been held that the terms of the contract were indeed as has been stated (this was in fact disputed by the purchaser), the vendor was clearly entitled to the foil which was still in the possession of the purchaser (the nature of this claim was not discussed at all but the vendor, as legal owner of the foil, was clearly entitled to recover this property at law). However, the vendor's claim to the proceeds of sale of the unmixed foil sold to third parties was based on *Re Hallett's Estate*.[378] The Court of Appeal held that the purchaser held the foil as a fiduciary agent of the vendor. Consequently, the vendor was entitled to trace the foil in equity into its product, the proceeds of sale.[379]

22–164

(C) Property which is No Longer Identifiable Following a Change of Form

It has already been seen that, where property is no longer identifiable following a change of form, this is usually because it or its product has been turned into money and mixed with other money. In such circumstances, if the mixed fund has subsequently remained intact, the claimant will clearly be entitled to a lien or charge on the mixed fund for the amount of his property and, presumably, in the event that any interest has been earned, to the part of the interest earned in respect of his property. (In practice, however, it is likely that sums will have been withdrawn from the mixed fund,

22–165

---

[377] [1976] 1 W.L.R. 676.
[378] (1880) 13 Ch.D. 696.
[379] Given that neither the foil nor its proceeds of sale had ever become unidentifiable by being mixed with other property, there seems no reason why the vendor should not equally have been able to trace the proceeds of sale at law. However, this decision establishes that a vendor with the benefit of a retention of title clause will be able to recover the product of the property subject to it by means of an equitable proprietary claim, provided that the necessary fiduciary relationship had been established (this has not been possible in a number of subsequent cases concerning retention of title clauses and, consequently, the vendors have necessarily had to trace at law; see *Clough Mill v. Martin* [1985] 1 W.L.R. 111 and *Hendy Lennox (Industrial Engines) v. Grahame Puttick* [1984] 1 W.L.R. 485).

in which case the result appears to depend on whether the mixing was authorised or unauthorised. If it was authorised, the claimant will inevitably be entitled to the appropriate proportion of the mixed fund or its product. If, on the other hand, the mixing was unauthorised, it is necessary to have recourse to a series of presumptions in order to establish whether such withdrawals have been made from the mixed funds rateably or from one or more of its component parts. These rules will be considered in detail later on.)

22–166   In the same way, at least in principle, a claimant who can show that his property has been mixed with other property to form a new object should be entitled to trace his property in equity into its product, provided that he can show the necessary fiduciary relationship. This has indeed been attempted in a number of cases concerning retention of title clauses. If, as in *Aluminium Industrie Vaassen v. Romalpa Aluminium*,[380] such a claimant can show both the necessary fiduciary relationship and a clear intention that any such new objects should become the property of the vendor in whole or in part, such a claim should in principle be able to succeed (no such claim was in fact brought in that case but in *Bordon (U.K.) v. Scottish Timber Products*[381] the formulation used was described as "presumably effective" for this purpose). However, for a variety of reasons, such claims as have been brought have been unsuccessful. It has sometimes[382] been held that the terms of the contract have not had the effect of giving the vendor any proprietary interest in the new object; it has sometimes[383] been held that there has been no sufficient fiduciary relationship; and it has sometimes[384] been held that any interest created in the new object amounts to a charge which should have been registered under what is now the Companies Act 2006[385] and in default is consequently void for non-registration.

(1) Identifiability
22–167   A claim to trace property in equity into a mixed fund has traditionally presupposed that the claimant can actually identify his property or its product in that fund, if necessary with the aid of the various rules and presumptions as to withdrawals to which reference has already been made. Thus, in *Re Hallett's Estate*,[386] the Court of Appeal held that the priority given to the claimants was limited to the extent that they were able to identify the product of their property in the mixed fund. However, in recent years, there have been some indications that the courts may be prepared to relax this requirement of identifiability.

22–168   In *Space Investments v. Canadian Imperial Bank of Commerce Trust Company*[387] the trust instrument authorised the trustee, a bank, to deposit trust funds

---

[380] [1976] 1 W.L.R. 676.
[381] [1981] Ch. 25.
[382] In *Borden (U.K.) v. Scottish Timber Products* [1981] Ch. 25 and *Re Peachdart* [1984] Ch. 131.
[383] In *Re Bond Worth* [1980] Ch. 228; *Re Andrabell* [1984] 3 All E.R. 407; *Hendy Lennox (Industrial Engines) v. Grahame Puttick* [1984] 1 W.L.R. 485.
[384] In *Re Bond Worth* [1980] Ch. 228; *Re Peachdart* [1984] Ch. 131; *Re Weldtech Equipment* [1991] B.C.C. 16; *Compaq Computer v. Abercorn Group* [1991] B.C.C. 484.
[385] Companies Act 2006, ss.860–862.
[386] (1880) 13 Ch.D. 696.
[387] [1986] 1 W.L.R. 1072.

with itself; it did so but subsequently went into liquidation. A person who deposits money with a bank necessarily makes the bank absolute legal and beneficial owner thereof; were this not the case, the bank would have considerable difficulty in earning the interest payable to the depositor since it would be unable to utilise the funds other than in accordance with the relevant rules governing trust investments and would certainly not be able to use the funds to make unsecured loans. The Privy Council[388] therefore held that, since the mixing of the trust funds with the trustee's own funds had been entirely lawful, the beneficiaries had retained no proprietary interest in the funds deposited and so could not bring an equitable proprietary claim; they were, therefore, no more than general creditors of the bank. However, Lord Templeman emphasised that, if the mixing had been carried out without such an express authorisation, it would have been unlawful. In such circumstances, he stated that the beneficiaries would have been allowed "to trace the trust money to all the assets of the bank and to recover the trust money by an equitable charge over all the assets of the bank".[389] In this hypothetical situation, it is inconceivable that the trust would have been able to identify its own funds within the general assets of the bank. Consequently, if the trust would indeed have been entitled to trace, then the rights to persons entitled to trace property in equity into a mixed fund are considerably wider than has previously been held. Giving such a claimant an equitable charge over all the assets of the bank converts him to all intents and purposes into a debenture holder since he obtains priority over the general creditors even in respect of assets which were not the product of the mixed fund. This seems wholly unfair to the general creditors.[390]

Lord Templeman's remarks have been considered in two decisions concerning payments into funds which subsequently became overdrawn, something which has traditionally been fatal to the right to trace in equity. In *Re Goldcorp Exchange*,[391] the Court of Appeal of New Zealand[392] applied Lord Templeman's remarks to this situation but the Privy Council, having held that the purchasers had no equitable proprietary interest at all, did not need to consider them. Lord Mustill, having referred with approval to the traditional rule, expressed the view that "the law relating to the creation and tracing of equitable proprietary interests is still in a state of development"[393]; however, he concluded that it was not "necessary or appropriate to consider the scope and ambit of the observations in *Space Investments* or their application to trustees other than bank trustees"[394] A similar approach was taken by the Court of Appeal in *Bishopsgate Investment Management v. Homan*,[395] where it was argued that the traditional rule should, on the strength of Lord

22–169

---

[388] On an appeal from the Court of Appeal of The Bahamas.

[389] [1986] 1 W.L.R. 1072 at 1074.

[390] See Goode (1987) 103 L.Q.R. 433. An equally unorthodox, but this time excessively narrow, view of equitable tracing claims of this type was taken in *Re Att.-Gen.'s Reference (No.1) 1985* [1986] Q.B. 491. However, this view was based on *Lister & Co. v. Stubbs* (1890) 45 Ch.D. 1 and therefore presumably cannot survive the criticism of that decision by the Privy Council in *Att.-Gen. for Hong Kong v. Reid* [1994] 1 A.C. 324, see *ante*, para 10–079.

[391] [1995] 1 A.C. 74. Lord Templeman was a member of the Board.

[392] [1993] 1 N.Z.L.R. 257.

[393] [1995] 1 A.C. 74 at 109.

[394] *ibid.*, at 110.

[395] [1995] Ch. 211.

Templeman's remarks, be overruled. The Court of Appeal rejected this argument, classifying the remarks as dicta, and holding that their extension to this situation had been rejected in *Re Goldcorp Exchange*; the traditional rule was therefore applied. In neither of these two decisions was a view expressed as to the situation specifically envisaged by Lord Templeman, where a bank trustee has unlawfully deposited with itself trust funds which can no longer be identified. However, the reliance placed in both cases on the traditional rules governing mixed funds suggests that these rules are likely to be followed in preference to the view expressed by Lord Templeman. It is hoped that this proves to be the case.

(2) Authorised Mixing

22–170 In the relatively unlikely situation where the mixing of trust property with the property of another has been specifically authorised by the trust instrument and the mixing occurs in precisely the manner envisaged, then the beneficiaries will inevitably be entitled to the appropriate proportion of the mixed fund. This somewhat obvious proposition does not appear to have been the subject of any English authority but was upheld in New South Wales in *Hagan v. Waterhouse*.[396] Following the death of their father, three brothers carried on the family bookmaking business as general partners. One having died, the other two, who were his executors and trustees, continued the partnership business and therefore necessarily mixed the assets of the estate with their own. Kearney J. held that this mixing had been authorised by the terms of the will and that, quite irrespective of the presumptions which apply where mixing is unauthorised, the estate was, therefore, entitled to a one-third interest in the income of the bookmaking business and the substantial investments which it had been used to purchase.

(3) Unauthorised Mixing

22–171 It is much more likely that any mixing which has occurred will have been unauthorised, either because it was not authorised at all or because it has not been carried out in the manner envisaged. Where this occurs and sums have subsequently been withdrawn from the mixed fund, it has traditionally been necessary to have recourse to a series of presumptions in order to establish whether such withdrawals have been made from the mixed funds rateably or from one or more of its component parts; the presumptions differ depending on whether the mixed fund consists of funds of the claimant and funds of a fiduciary, of funds of two claimants both entitled to trace in equity into the mixed fund, or of funds of the claimant and funds of an innocent volunteer (it is obviously also possible for a mixed fund to consist of the funds of two claimants and the funds of a fiduciary or of the funds of two claimants and the funds of an innocent volunteer; in these circumstances, the situation is resolved by treating the two claimants as one and ascertaining first what they together can recover out of the mixed fund and then what part of this sum can be recovered by each individual claimant).

---

[396] (1991) 34 N.S.W.L.R. 308.

(a) Unauthorised mixing of funds of the claimant and funds of a   **22–172**
fiduciary The traditional rules governing tracing into an unauthorised
mixed fund consisting of funds of the claimant and funds of a fiduciary are
based on the decision of the Court of Appeal in *Re Hallett's Estate*.[397] The
defendant solicitor sold bonds belonging partly to his own marriage settlement and partly to a client and mixed the proceeds with his own funds in
a bank account. Subsequently, he made various withdrawals from the mixed
fund, which on his death was insufficient to satisfy all the claims against it.
The Court of Appeal, having held unanimously that both the beneficiaries
and the client were entitled to bring equitable proprietary claims,[398] held by
a majority,[399] that the funds drawn out must be debited to Hallett's share of
the mixed fund on the basis that, where a man does an act which may be
rightfully performed, he cannot be heard to say that that act was intentionally and in fact done wrongfully. The balance left in the mixed fund was
sufficient to satisfy both claims so that it was not necessary to decide any
question of priorities as between them.[400] The presumption, therefore, is that
a fiduciary draws his own funds out first and so any balance left in the
mixed fund represents the property of the claimant. His claim to that
balance is of course limited to the amount of his funds which were originally
mixed (together with, presumably, any interest which has been earned in
respect of the part of the funds which is his property). This principle is not
limited to funds but also extends to other assets which are mixed such as
shares.

However, the claimant cannot normally assert a proprietary claim to   **22–173**
further sums or property which become part of the mixed assets after the
original mixing. In *James Roscoe (Bolton) v. Winder*,[401] the balance of the mixed
fund fell to £25 as a result of repeated dissipation by the fiduciary. However,
at his death the fund contained a balance of £358. Sarjant J. held the
beneficiaries entitled to trace only £25; the sums which had been paid in
after the balance fell to that amount went to the general creditors, with
whom the beneficiaries could of course prove for the remaining sum which
they were claiming. This conclusion was approved and applied both by the
Privy Council in *Re Goldcorp Exchange*[402] and by the Court of Appeal in
Bishopsgate Investment Management v. Homan,[403] both of which concerned
mixed funds which subsequently became overdrawn, thus barring any
equitable proprietary claim completely. However, in the latter case,
Dillon L.J.,[404] but not Leggatt L.J.,[405] was prepared to envisage the possibility

---

[397] (1880) 13 Ch.D. 696.
[398] See *ante*, para 22–139.
[399] Thesiger L.J. dissented, holding that payments out of the mixed fund should, in accordance with the decision of the Court of Appeal in Chancery in *Pennell v. Deffell* (1853) De M. &
G. 372, be governed by the Rule in *Clayton's Case* (*Devaynes v. Noble, Clayton's Case* (1816) 1 Mer.
572); (see *post*, para 22–179).
[400] Had this not been the case, priorities as between the two claimants would have been
determined by the Rule in *Clayton's Case* (see *post*, para 22–179), as had indeed been held by Fry
J. at first instance.
[401] [1915] 1 Ch. 62.
[402] [1995] 1 A.C. 74.
[403] [1995] Ch. 211.
[404] *ibid.*, at 216–217.
[405] *ibid.*, at 222.

of tracing funds through an overdrawn account where misappropriated funds are paid into the account in order to reduce the overdraft and so make finance available within the overdraft limits for the purchase of some particular asset. Provided that the link between the reduction of the overdraft and this subsequent purchase can be genuinely established, there seems no reason why this limited modification of the basic rule should not be adopted.

22–174   If the balance of the mixed fund is insufficient fully to discharge the liability of the fiduciary to the claimant, the latter can nevertheless trace the withdrawals into any identifiable product of the mixed fund and claim an equitable charge over that product. In *Re Oatway*,[406] a trustee, having mixed the trust money with his own, first withdrew sums which he invested and later withdrew and dissipated the remainder. His trustee in bankruptcy suggested that, according to *Re Hallett's Estate*, what he had first withdrawn was his own money; consequently, the investments belonged to him and it was the trust money which had been dissipated. This unmeritorious claim was predictably rejected; Joyce J. held that the beneficiaries were entitled to the investments on the basis that their claim must be satisfied from any identifiable part of the mixed fund or its product before the trustee could assert any claim to any of this property.

22–175   In *Bishopsgate Investment Management v. Homan*[407] Dillon L.J. was also prepared[408] to countenance the possibility of what Vinelott J. at first instance had called "backwards tracing". This novel concept envisages a situation where a fiduciary acquires an asset with borrowed money and it can be inferred that the borrowing was subsequently repaid by funds misappropriated from the claimant; in such circumstances, the claimant can apparently recover the asset even though it was acquired prior to the misappropriation in question. However, this seems contrary to the nature of proprietary claims; indeed Leggatt L.J. explicitly rejected "backwards tracing", holding that "there can be no equitable remedy against an asset acquired before misappropriation of money takes place, since *ex hypothesi* it cannot be followed into something which existed and so had been acquired before the money was received and therefore without its aid".[409] This view seems preferable. Indeed it was approved by two of the members of the Court of Appeal in *Foskett v. McKeown*,[410] however, the third member of the court[411] wished "to make it clear that I regard the point as still open and, in particular, that I do not regard the fact that an asset is paid for out of borrowed money with the borrowing subsequently repaid out of trust money as being necessarily fatal to an equitable tracing claim by the trust

---

[406] [1903] 2 Ch. 356.

[407] [1995] Ch. 211.

[408] *ibid.*, at 216–217.

[409] *ibid.*, at 221.

[410] [1998] Ch. 265 *per* Hobhouse L.J. (one of the majority on the main issue) at 289, *per* Morritt L.J. (dissenting on the main issue) at 296. This was an appeal against an order for summary judgment so it was not possible to reach a conclusion on whether the facts necessary to give rise to the possibility of "backwards tracing" had actually occurred.

[411] Scott V.-C. (the other member of the majority on the main issue) at 283–284. Scott V.-C. referred to Smith [1995] C.L.J. 290, who is in favour not just of "backwards tracing" but of general tracing into the payment of a debt.

beneficiaries". The point was not considered on the subsequent appeal to the House of Lords so the availability of "backwards tracing" therefore clearly still awaits definitive resolution.

The precise scope of this right to trace the withdrawals from the mixed **22–176** fund into their product was for long not entirely clear. In *Re Hallett's Estate*[412] Jessel M.R. stated that, where a claimant was seeking to trace into property which was the product of a mixed fund containing funds of the claimant and funds of a fiduciary, the only remedy available to him was to take a charge over that property for the amount of the property of his own which had been laid out in its acquisition. On this basis, the claimant's right to trace was limited to his original contribution to the purchase price of the property and did not extend to any increase in its value. This view was followed[413] but different views were also expressed[414] which have now been definitively upheld by the House of Lords. In *Foskett v. McKeown*[415] Lord Millett said:

"Accordingly, I would state the basic rule as follows. where a trustee wrong-fully uses trust money to provide part of the costs of acquiring an asset, the beneficiary is entitled *at his option* either to claim a proportionate share of the asset or to enforce a lien upon it to secure his personal claim against the trustee for the amount of the misapplied money. It does not matter whether the trustee mixed the trust money with his own in a single fund before using it to acquire the asset, or made separate payments (whether simultaneously or sequentially) out of the differently owned funds to acquire a single asset."

The claimant, therefore, now clearly has a choice between taking a charge on the property for the amount of his funds which were invested in that property (which will be to his advantage if its value has fallen) or claiming an interest in the property in proportion to his contribution to its purchase (which will be to his advantage if its value has risen).

Until recently there was no direct authority as to whether a claimant has **22–177** a similar choice between recovering an asset which is the product of the mixed fund and taking any balance of the mixed fund to which he is entitled. It will be of interest for him so to do the former if the asset in

---

[412] (1880) 13 Ch.D. 696 at 709.

[413] In *Re Oatway* [1903] 2 Ch. 356.

[414] In *Re Tilley's Will Trusts* [1967] Ch. 1179 at 1189 where Ungoed-Thomas J. regarded as good law a concession that, where property is the product of a mixed fund, the claimant has the right to "require the asset to be treated as trust property with regard to that proportion of it which the trust moneys contributed to its purchase". However, on the facts, he held that trust funds which an executrix who was also tenant for life had paid into her own bank account and used as part payment for two houses had not in fact been invested in those two properties since the use by the tenant for life of the estate's funds had merely prevented her from having to use more extensive overdraft facilities, which were clearly available to her; hence the remainder-men were entitled only to the funds of the estate which had been mixed together with interest thereon. It is questionable whether it should in fact be open to a fiduciary who has committed a clear breach of trust by mixing trust funds with his own successfully to contend that any profits so made were not actually due to the use of the trust funds; while *Re Tilley's Will Trusts* clearly establishes that such a contention is possible, the opposite view has been taken in other jurisdictions (in Australia in *Scott v. Scott* (1963) 36 A.L.J.R. 345 and in the United States of America in *Primeau v. Granfield* (1911) 184 Fed. 480).

[415] [2001] 1 A.C. 102 at 131.

question has increased in value or if any part of the mixed fund to which he is prima facie entitled has subsequently been invested in some other asset which has fallen in value or, for that matter, has been dissipated. In all the cases discussed so far, the observations of the judges, particularly those of Jessel M.R. in *Re Hallett's Estate*, had indicated that the mixed fund was the recourse primarily available to the claimant. This has indeed now been held by Patten J. in *Turner v. Jacob*.[416] A husband had paid £75,000 to his estranged wife to enable her to discharge the mortgage on a property on the basis that that amount of the eventual proceeds of its sale would go to her daughter (his step-daughter). Patten J. held that as a result the mother eventually came to hold £75,000 of a mixed fund on trust for the daughter. Subsequently, that balance was reduced to £10,339 before being replenished; under *James Roscoe (Bolton) v. Winder*[417] any equitable proprietary claim by the daughter therefore became limited to £10,339. Subsequently, funds from the replenished fund were used to purchase another property, which in the event was left away from the daughter, but the balance of the replenished fund never again fell as low as £10,339. Because the daughter had inherited the £10,339 anyway as her mother's residuary legatee, she sought to trace the £10,339 into the further property and so effectively recover it twice. However, Patten J. held that she was restricted to the £10,339. In such circumstances the interests of the claimant are very evenly balanced with the interests of whoever else is potentially entitled to the asset in question; normally of course this will be the general creditors of the fiduciary although that was not the case in *Turner v. Jacob*. But on the grounds of simplicity and consistency it is suggested that the conclusion reached by Patten J. was correct; on this basis, the claimant must take any balance of the mixed fund to which he is entitled before he can proceed to follow any withdrawals from the mixed fund into their product.

22–178   Finally, it must be emphasised that all the rules which have been discussed are no more than presumptions. Consequently, these presumptions can be rebutted in any given case if either the claimant or the fiduciary is able to establish to the satisfaction of the court that any particular withdrawal was intended to be made from some specific part of the mixed fund or that any subsequent payment back into the mixed fund was intended to replace a previous withdrawal.

22–179   **(b) Unauthorised mixing of funds of two claimants** Where an unauthorised mixed fund consists of the funds of two claimants, both of whom are entitled to trace in equity into the mixed fund, withdrawals from the mixed fund are presumed to be made rateably from the funds held by each claimant. Since each claimant necessarily has an equitable proprietary interest in his part of the funds which have been mixed, the attribution of profits and losses rateably between them is entirely in accordance with principle. However, in the event that the mixed fund in question is an active unbroken bank account (the only relevant example is a current, but not a deposit, account), then the presumption that withdrawals from the mixed fund are presumed to be made rateably is displaced by a principle enunciated by

---

[416] [2006] EWHC 1317 (Civ).
[417] [1915] 1 Ch. 62.

Grant M.R. in *Devaynes v. Noble, Clayton's Case*,[418] which is generally known as the Rule in *Clayton's Case*. In such an account,

"there is no room for any other appropriation than that which arises from the order in which the receipts and payments take place, and are carried into the account. Presumably, it is the sum first paid in, that is first drawn out. It is the first item on the debit side of the account, that is discharged, or reduced, by the first item on the credit side. The appropriation is made by the very act of setting the two items against each other. Upon that principle, all accounts current are settled, and particularly cash accounts."[419]

Devaynes v. Noble did not concern a tracing claim but rather a question as **22–180** to the appropriation of payments. The Rule in *Clayton's Case* was, however, applied to equitable tracing claims in the first case in which tracing was permitted in equity into a mixed fund, *Pennell v. Deffell*[420] in 1852. As has already been seen, the Court of Appeal decided by a majority in *Re Hallett's Estate*[421] that the Rule should no longer apply to mixed funds containing funds of a claimant and funds of a fiduciary. However, had any question of priorities between the two claimants in *Re Hallett's Estate* had to be determined, there is no doubt that the Rule in *Clayton's Case* would have been applied for this purpose, as it had indeed been applied by Fry J. in *Re Hallett's Estate* at first instance; this was expressly recognised by all three members of the court.[422] The same conclusion was reached in *Hancock v. Smith*.[423]

The effect of the application of the Rule in *Clayton's Case* can be quite **22–181** bizarre. Suppose that a trustee mixes the funds of two trusts in a current banking account, paying in £20,000 of the funds of Trust A on Day 1 and £10,000 of the funds of Trust B on Day 2. If on Day 3 he withdraws £20,000 from the mixed fund and invests it in securities, those securities will have been purchased entirely with the funds of Trust A. If on Day 4 he withdraws £7,000 from the mixed fund and loses this sum gambling at a casino, the entire loss will fall on the beneficiaries of Trust B, whose only right will be to the £3,000 left in the account. Were, on the other hand, the mixed fund a deposit account, both profits and losses would be shared rateably; the beneficiaries of Trust A and Trust B would respectively be entitled to two-thirds and one-third of the securities and £2,000 and £1,000 of the balance of the mixed fund. It is equally possible for the beneficiaries of Trust A to finish up worse off. If the payment on Day 3 is of £20,000 to a bona fide purchaser for value without notice and the payment on Day 4 is of the remaining £10,000 to an innocent volunteer, the entire loss will fall on the beneficiaries

---

[418] (1817) 1 Mer. 572.

[419] *ibid.*, at 608–609.

[420] (1853) De M. & G. 372.

[421] (1880) 13 Ch.D. 696.

[422] Jessel M.R. and Baggallay L.J., who had held that the Rule in *Clayton's Case* did not apply to a mixed fund consisting of funds of a claimant and funds of a fiduciary, agreed with Thesiger L.J., who had taken the opposite view, that the Rule in *Clayton's Case* clearly applied to mixed funds consisting of funds of two claimants.

[423] (1889) 41 Ch.D. 456, *per* Lord Halsbury L.C. and Cotton L.J. (Fry L.J. did not deal with the point).

of Trust A. As Hart J. held in *Campden Hill v. Chakrani*,[424] where the rule was
applied, once all the funds of a particular beneficiary have gone, his equitable charge over the mixed fund also disappears and there is nothing that
equity can do to assist him.

22–182   Fortunately, however, the Rule in *Clayton's Case* is no longer automatically
applied. In *Barlow Clowes International v. Vaughan*,[425] Woolf L.J. said that
there were three possible solutions: apart from applying the Rule in *Clayton's
Case*, these were: "the rolling charge or North American solution . . . [which]
involves treating credits to a bank account made at different times and from
different sources as a blend or cocktail with the result that when a withdrawal is made from the account it is treated as a withdrawal in the same
proportions as the different interests in the account . . . bear to each other at
the moment before the withdrawal is made"[426]; and "the *pari passu ex post
facto* solution . . . [which] involves establishing the total quantum of the
assets available and sharing them on a proportionate basis among all the
investors who could be said to have contributed to the acquisition of those
assets, ignoring the dates on which they made their investment".[427]

22–183   The Court of Appeal nevertheless confirmed that the Rule in *Clayton's Case*
provided a convenient method of determining competing claims where the
funds of several beneficiaries had been blended in one account and there
was a deficiency or where there had been a wrongful mixing of different
sums of trust money in a single account. However, they held that, where its
application would be impracticable or would result in injustice between the
investors, because a relatively small number of investors would obtain most
of the funds, or would be contrary to the express or implied intention of the
investors, the rule would not be applied if a preferable alternative method
of distribution was available. The case concerned the rights of the various
subscribers to a collective investment scheme, under which their money
would be mixed together and invested through a common fund, to the
assets which remained available for distribution. The Court of Appeal held
that, because of the shared misfortunes of these investors, they would be
presumed not to have intended the Rule in *Clayton's Case* to apply and the
court should, therefore, adopt whichever of the possible alternatives was
more satisfactory; because of the complications of applying the North American solution, the *pari passu ex post facto* solution was therefore applied.

22–184   Subsequently, in *Russell-Cooke Trust Company v. Prentis*,[428] the application
of the Rule in *Clayton's Case* was restricted still further at first instance. As
has already been seen,[429] this case concerned an investment scheme whereby
clients placed funds in a solicitor's client account with a view to those funds
being combined and invested in short-term interest only loans secured
against immoveable property by way of registered first charges. When The
Law Society subsequently intervened, some of the clients' funds had not yet
been invested and so were still in the client account; however, this account

---

[424] [2005] EWHC 911 (Ch), [2005] All E.R. (D) 238 (May) at [78–79].
[425] [1992] 4 All E.R. 22.
[426] *ibid.*, at 35.
[427] *ibid.*, at 36.
[428] [2003] 2 All E.R. 478.
[429] See *ante*, para 22–163.

contained insufficient to repay all those funds in full.[430] All three possible solutions were put before the court. Lindsay J. held[431] that the Rule in *Clayton's Case* "can be displaced by even a slight counterweight. Indeed, in terms of its actual application between beneficiaries who have in any sense met a shared misfortune, it might be more accurate to refer to the exception that is, rather than the rule, in *Clayton's Case*." He went on to hold that the prime reason to apply the North American solution falls away when *Clayton's Case* is not being applied in any event. He therefore adopted the *pari passu ex post facto* solution on the basis that it is "the system least unfairly distributing loss on an account that should have been dealt with in accordance with" the rules governing solicitors' client accounts.

Nor was *Clayton's Case* applied at first instance in *Commerzbank v. IMB* **22–185** *Morgan*[432] where the court had to decide how to distribute the contents of two correspondent bank accounts[433] which included the proceeds of what is known as "advance fee fraud"[434] and were the subject of claims whose amounts greatly exceeded the funds in the accounts. Lawrence Collins J. seems to have followed *Barlow Clowes International v. Vaughan* by declining to apply *Clayton's Case* on the basis that to do so "would be both impracticable and unjust".[435]

Consequently, although *Barlow Clowes International v. Vaughan* clearly did **22–186** not affect the prima facie applicability of the Rule in *Clayton's Case* to mixed funds consisting of the funds of a small number of claimants,[436] *Russell-Cooke Trust Company v. Prentis*[437] is likely to prevent the Rule applying whenever the mixed fund has fallen in value as the result of unprofitable investment or dissipation simply because the beneficiaries will have "met a shared misfortune". It also seems to follow from that decision that in such circumstances the *pari passu ex post facto* solution will virtually always be applied. This development is most welcome and it is to be hoped that the Rule in *Clayton's Case* will one day also be effectively abrogated in the

---

[430] Funds of different clients in the same client account are not treated as mixed funds because they have to be dealt with according to the strict rules governing solicitors' client accounts. However, when there is a shortfall as a result of non-compliance with those rules, the funds necessarily have to be treated as mixed funds.

[431] [2003] 2 All E.R. 478 at 495.

[432] [2004] EWHC 2771 (Ch), [2005] 1 Lloyd's Rep. 298.

[433] Accounts established to receive deposits and to make payments on behalf of the correspondent, usually a foreign institution such as a bank, without any indication being given as to which of the clients of the correspondent the funds being credited or debited actually belong to.

[434] Sums which victims of fraud have been induced to part with in the expectation that they will subsequently receive much larger sums.

[435] [2004] EWHC 2771 (Ch), [2005] 1 Lloyd's Rep. 298. at [50], the law was reviewed at [42–48].

[436] This was despite the fact that its applicability in this situation is just as capable of enabling a relatively small number of investors to obtain most of the funds as when it is applied to common funds in collective investment schemes. It is not obvious why the result of the example discussed above in the text is any less absurd than it would have been to have permitted the later investors in a collective investment scheme to have recovered almost all their investment and the earlier investors to have recovered almost none of theirs (the consequence of the application of the Rule in *Clayton's Case* which induced the Court of Appeal to find the implied intention necessary to displace it in *Barlow Clowes International v. Vaughan*).

[437] [2003] 2 All E.R. 478.

relatively unlikely situation where a mixed fund of this type has made a profit.[438]

22–187   (c) **Unauthorised mixing of funds of the claimant and funds of an innocent volunteer** Where an unauthorised mixed fund consists of the funds of a claimant and the funds of an innocent volunteer, withdrawals from the mixed fund are presumed to be made in exactly the same way as withdrawals from a mixed fund consisting of the funds of two claimants. In other words, withdrawals are presumed to be made rateably unless the mixed fund in question is an active unbroken bank account; in that case the Rule in *Clayton's Case* has been held to apply[439] but it is now probable that one of the other two solutions reviewed in *Barlow Clowes International v. Vaughan*[440] and *Russell-Cooke Trust Company v. Prentis*[441] will be applied instead.

22–188   However, while the basic attribution of profits and losses rateably is entirely in accordance with principle in the case of a mixed fund consisting of the funds of two claimants who both have equitable proprietary interests, it is highly questionable in the case of a mixed fund consisting of the funds of a claimant and the funds of an innocent volunteer. The claimant necessarily has an equitable proprietary interest in the mixed fund; if he did not, he would not be entitled to trace in equity. How can an innocent volunteer resist a claim by the holder of an equitable proprietary interest to recover his property? What defence, other than, perhaps, the defence of change of position, can an innocent volunteer possibly have to an equitable proprietary claim? In principle, the claimant should be able to recover his funds in full out of the mixed fund quite irrelevant of what withdrawals have been made from that fund by the innocent volunteer.

22–189   However, this is clearly not the law. In *Re Diplock*[442] Lord Greene M.R. held that the positions of the claimant and the innocent volunteer were equivalent.

"This burden on the conscience of the volunteer is not such as to compel him to treat the claim of the equitable owner as paramount. That would be to treat the volunteer as strictly as if he himself stood in a fiduciary relationship to the equitable owner which ex hypothesi he does not. The volunteer is under no greater duty of conscience to recognise the interest of the equitable owner than that which lies upon a person having an equitable interest in one

---

[438] There has been no reported case in which this has ever happened but examiners like questions in which the first withdrawal from the mixed fund referred to in the example above is invested in a painting which turns out to be an "Old Master" worth many times the sum paid for it while the second withdrawal is still dissipated. It is not immediately obvious that this can be described as "shared misfortune" and, if it cannot, in such circumstances the Rule in *Clayton's Case* would appear to be applicable so that Trust A makes an enormous profit while Trust B still bears all the loss. And where Trust A's investment made an enormous profit while Trust B's investment produced a more normal one or broke even, there could not really be said to have been any misfortune at all.

[439] *Re Diplock* [1948] Ch. 465 (in respect of the claim against the National Institute for the Deaf).

[440] [1992] 4 All E.R. 22.

[441] [2003] 2 All E.R. 478.

[442] *ibid.*, at 524.

of two trust funds of 'money' which have become mixed towards the equitable owner of the other. Such a person is not in conscience bound to give precedence to the equitable owner of the other of the two funds."

He therefore relied on *Sinclair v. Brougham*[443] as authority for the attribution of profits and losses rateably in mixed funds consisting of funds of a claimant and funds of an innocent volunteer. However, the analogy with *Sinclair v. Brougham* (which has now of course been overruled anyway[444]) is in fact unsound. The House of Lords indeed held that the shareholders and the depositors in the ultra vires banking business should share the remaining assets rateably but the depositors were held to be entitled to trace in equity by virtue of the existence of a trust in their favour. Therefore, both the depositors and the shareholders in fact had proprietary interests. This was not the case in *Re Diplock*, where only the claimants had an equitable proprietary interest.

It is of course highly unlikely, given the decision in *Re Diplock*, that an **22–190** innocent volunteer will ever be held liable for the whole of the losses suffered by a mixed fund. It seems generally to be accepted that, subject to the effect of the possible operation of the Rule in *Clayton's Case*, at present losses should be attributed rateably between the claimant and the innocent volunteer. Profits are also attributed rateably at present, subject, perhaps, to the defence of change of position, which if applicable will operate in an exceptionally favourable way in favour of an innocent volunteer. As will be seen later on, both these propositions are demonstrated by the decision of the Court of Appeal in *Foskett v. McKeown*[445] (the point did not arise in the House of Lords[446]). However, prior to this decision it had been suggested that, provided that the claimant was in a position to recover his original contribution to the mixed fund in full by means of a charge on the mixed fund or on the property which constituted its product, the innocent volunteer should be entitled to retain the benefit of any improvements which he had made or profits which he had obtained.[447] This suggestion is now unlikely to be taken up; what is surprising is the fact that it was ever made—depriving the holder of an equitable proprietary interest of profits while retaining his rateable liability for losses does not seem very consistent with the nature of an equitable proprietary claim. But suggestions of this type clearly demonstrate that the leniency shown at present towards innocent volunteers is more likely to be amplified than taken away.

5. *When will Priority be Lost?*

No equitable proprietary claim can succeed if the property in question has **22–191** simply disappeared as a result of dissipation. If, for example, funds which are susceptible of being traced are expended on a case of wine which is then

---

[443] [1914] A.C. 398.
[444] By the House of Lords in *Westdeutsche Landesbank Girozentrale v. Islington L.B.C.* [1996] A.C. 669.
[445] [1998] Ch. 265; see *post*, para 22–201.
[446] [2001] 1 A.C. 102.
[447] See Hayton (1990) 106 L.Q.R. 87 at 100.

consumed, no proprietary claim will be able to be brought against the person who has expended the funds (nor will any proprietary claim be able to be brought against the vendor of the wine, who will be a bona fide purchaser for value without notice). The disappearance of the property is not, formally, a defence to an equitable proprietary claim but its effect is the same as if it were a defence. Quite apart from this situation, there are of course a number of formal defences which can be made out to an equitable proprietary claim.

(A) Where a Recipient has Taken Free of the Interest of the Claimant

22–192   It is, of course, axiomatic that no equitable proprietary interest can survive the bona fide purchase for value of a legal estate or interest in the property in question to a person who has no notice of any kind of the equitable proprietary interest in question (or, in the case of registered land, the bona fide purchase for value of any interest by virtue of a duly registered disposition). This was the ground on which the equitable proprietary claim failed in *Shalson v. Russo (Mimran, Part 20 Claimant)*.[448] In that case the value in question had not been provided to the trustee but to a vendor further down the line. However, where trustees have actually received purchase moneys, the claimant will be able to pursue those funds. Thus, where trustees in breach of trust sell part of the trust property to a bona fide purchaser for value who has no notice of the interests of the beneficiaries, the beneficiaries will not be able to maintain any equitable proprietary claim against the purchaser but they will be able to attempt to recover or to follow or to trace the proceeds of sale.

22–193   On the other hand, an equitable proprietary interest will normally enjoy priority over any subsequent holder of the property who has acquired only an equitable, rather than a legal interest therein. This is the case except that "where the merits are unequal and favour the later interest, as for instance where the owner of the later equitable interest is led by conduct on the part of the owner of the earlier interest to acquire the later interest in the belief or on the supposition that the earlier interest did not then exist, priority will be accorded to the later interest".[449] Save in the relatively unlikely event of this exception applying, there is no doubt whatever that a beneficiary of an express or resulting trust will, by virtue of this rule, enjoy priority over the holder of any later equitable interest in the property in question. So will a beneficiary of a constructive trust, once the existence of that trust has actually been upheld by the court in question. What is less clear is the position of a potential beneficiary of a constructive trust, someone who is entitled to seek the imposition of a constructive trust but who has not yet obtained the necessary court order; this depends on whether his interest prior to the court order is classified as a full equitable interest, in which case he will enjoy the same priority, or a mere equity, in which case a bona fide purchaser for value of any later equitable interest without notice will take

---

[448] [2003] EWHC 1637 (Ch), [2005] Ch. 281.
[449] *Heid v. Reliance Finance Corporation* (1983) 154 C.L.R. 326 at 339, *per* Mason & Deane JJ. (High Court of Australia). The facts of this case provided a good example of the operation of this exception.

free.[450] In principle, it is suggested that his interest should be classified as a full equitable interest, giving him the same priority, but the matter awaits decision.[451]

(B) Where there has been a Change of Position

English law has traditionally denied any general defence of change of   **22–194**
position[452] although in *Re Diplock*[453] the Court of Appeal held that innocent volunteers could rely on two limited (and controversial) manifestations of this defence as against equitable proprietary claims. However, in *Lipkin Gorman v. Karpnale*[454] the House of Lords upheld for the first time the existence of such a defence. All the members of the House of Lords agreed that, on the facts, the defendant casino could invoke the defence of change of position against the claim by the plaintiff solicitors to recover funds which had been stolen from its client account and subsequently lost at the casino but only to the extent that the casino had paid out winnings to the gambler.

However, the House took considerable care not to pre-empt the sub-   **22–195**
sequent development of the defence. Lord Bridge stated[455] that "in expressly acknowledging the availability of this defence for the first time it would be unwise to attempt to define its scope in abstract terms". Lord Goff said this[456]:

"I am most anxious that, in recognising this defence to actions of restitution, nothing should be said at this stage to inhibit the development of the defence on a case by case basis, in the usual way. It is, of course, plain that the defence is not open to one who has changed his position in bad faith, as where the defendant has paid away the money with knowledge of the facts entitling the plaintiff to restitution and it is commonly accepted that the defence should not be open to a wrongdoer. These are matters which can, in due course, be considered in depth in cases where they arise for considera-tion. It is not appropriate in the present case to identify all those actions in restitution to which change of position may be a defence. At present I do not wish to state the principle any less broadly than this: that the defence is available to a person whose position has so changed that it would be inequitable in all the circumstances to require him to make restitution, or alternatively to make restitution in full. I wish to stress, however, that the mere fact that the defendant has spent the money, in whole or in part, does not of itself render it inequitable that he should be called upon to repay, because the expenditure might in any event have been incurred by him in the ordinary course of things.

---

[450] *Latec Investments v. Hotel Terrigal* (1965) 113 C.L.R. 265 (High Court of Australia).

[451] The only relevant authority is *Re Jonton* [1992] 1 Qd.R. 105 (Supreme Court of Queensland) where the conclusion suggested in the text was reached; however, this case cannot be regarded as decisive since the holder of the later interest would, if necessary, almost certainly have been held to have constructive notice anyway.

[452] See particularly *Ministry of Health v. Simpson* [1951] A.C. 251.

[453] [1948] Ch. 465 at 546–548.

[454] [1991] 2 A.C. 548.

[455] *ibid.*, at 558.

[456] *ibid.*, at 579–580.

I wish to add two further footnotes. The defence of change of position is akin to the defence of bona fide purchase but we cannot simply say that bona fide purchase is a species of change of position. This is because change of position will only avail a defendant to the extent that his position has been changed whereas, where bona fide purchase is invoked, no inquiry is made (in most cases) into the adequacy of the consideration. Even so, the recognition of change of position as a defence should be doubly beneficial. It will enable a more generous approach to be taken of the recognition of the right of restitution, in the knowledge that the defence is, in appropriate cases, available and, while recognising the different functions of property at law and in equity, there may also in due course develop a more consistent approach to tracing claims, in which common defences are recognised as available to such claims, whether advanced at law or in equity."

22–196   It is clear from the final passage of this quotation that Lord Goff envisaged the application of the defence of change of position to both legal and equitable proprietary claims and that he did not regard this defence as supplanting the defence of bona fide purchase for value without notice. However, in *Foskett v. McKeown*[457] Lord Millett stated that the only defence to an equitable proprietary claim is bona fide purchase of a legal estate for value without notice, from which it must obviously follow that change of position is not a defence to such a claim. This seems consistent neither with Lord Goff's remarks nor with the earlier remarks of Lord Millett in *Boscawen v. Bajwa*.[458] But this means, as Hart J. expressly acknowledged in *Campden Hill v. Chakrani*,[459] that it is at present controversial whether the general defence of change of position applies to all legal and equitable proprietary claims.[460] It is clearly a defence to all restitutionary personal claims and for that reason necessarily applies to legal proprietary claims to a chose in action and to money because the claimant will have to use a personal action, the action for money had and received; indeed *Lipkin Gorman v. Karpnale* was such a claim. But it does not necessarily follow that the right of a claimant to recover by means of a proprietary, as distinct from a personal, claim what he has necessarily proved to be his own property should be adversely affected by what the defendant has done with that property in good faith. In this respect, the commentators have also expressed conflicting views.[461] In principle, there seems much to be said for the view that the defence should not apply and this was expressly stated by Arden L.J. very recently in *Charter v. City Index*. In practice, however, it may well be that the defence will be held to be applicable.

22–197   Given the possibility that the general defence of change of position is applicable to legal and equitable proprietary claims (and it is certainly applicable where a legal proprietary claim is maintained by means of an action for money had received), the subsequent development of the defence

---

[457] [2001] 1 A.C. 102 at 129. See also *Charter v. City Index* [2007] EWCA Civ 1382, [2008] 2 W.L.R. 950 *per* Arden L.J. at [74].

[458] [1996] 1 W.L.R. 328 at 334–335.

[459] [2005] EWHC 911 (Ch), [2005] All E.R. (D) 238 (May).

[460] In that case, the applicability of the defence was not disputed and anyway Hart J. held that there had been no change of position.

[461] See, on the one hand, Fox [2000] R.L.R. 465 and Goff & Jones, *op. cit.* [2–043].

must clearly be considered here, albeit briefly. In *Lipkin Gorman v. Karpnale*, only Lord Templeman[462] added to Lord Goff's broad statement of principle by way of illustration of circumstances in which the defence of change of position would be available. He envisaged a situation in which a donee of stolen money has expended it

"in reliance on the validity of the gift before he receives notice of the victim's claim for restitution. Thus if the donee spent £20,000 in the purchase of a motor car which he would not have purchased but for the gift, it seems to me that the donee has altered his position on the faith of the gift and has only been unjustly enriched to the extent of the second hand value of the motor car at the date when the victim of the theft seeks restitution. If the donee spends the £20,000 on a trip round the world, which he would not have undertaken without the gift, it seems to me that the donee has altered his position on the faith of the gift and that he is not unjustly enriched when the victim of the faith seeks restitution."

Subsequent authorities have established that there must be some causal **22–198** link between the receipt of the claimant's property and the change of position by the defendant; the fact that the defendant's general financial position has worsened since the receipt is not in itself sufficient.[463] However, it does now appear also to suffice if the defendant relied on the validity of a void transaction rather than an actual receipt of property.[464] Nor does it now seem to matter that the change of position involved the defendant passing up an opportunity to earn income or acquire assets rather than engaging in outright expenditure.[465] The most difficult question concerns the requirement of good faith. The Privy Council has held[466] that mere negligence on the part of the recipient is not sufficient to deprive him of the defence of change of position. On the other hand, lack of good faith is not limited to subjective dishonesty in the sense identified in *Twinsectra v. Yardley*[467] but also extends to "failure to act in a commercially acceptable way and sharp practice of a kind that falls short of outright dishonesty".[468] It has also been stated that constructive notice of the true facts ought to amount to a lack of good faith for this purpose[469] although the judge in

---

[462] [1991] 2 A.C. 548 at 560.

[463] *Scottish Equitable v. Derby* [2001] EWCA Civ. 369, [2001] 3 All E.R. 818.

[464] *Dextra Bank & Trust Co. v. Bank of Jamaica* [2001] UKPC 50, [2002] 1 All E.R. (Comm.) 193 at 215 (Privy Council on appeal from Jamaica); *Scottish Equitable v. Derby* [2001] EWCA Civ. 369, [2001] 3 All E.R. 818 at 827. The opposite view appears to have been expressed earlier in *National Westminster Bank v. Somer International (U.K.)* [2001] EWCA Civ. 970, [2002] Q.B. 1286.

[465] This seems to follow from *Dextra Bank & Trust Co. v. Bank of Jamaica* [2001] UKPC 50, [2002] 1 All E.R. (Comm.) 193 at 215 (Privy Council on appeal from Jamaica) but the opposite view was taken in *South Tyneside M.B.C. v. Svenska International* [1995] 1 All E.R. 545.

[466] *Dextra Bank & Trust Co. v. Bank of Jamaica* [2001] UKPC 50, [2002] 1 All E.R. (Comm.) 193 at 207 (Privy Council on appeal from Jamaica).

[467] [2002] UKHL 12, [2002] 2 A.C. 164; see *ante*, para 10–175.

[468] *Niru Battery Manufacturing Co. v. Milestone Trading* [2002] EWHC 1425 (COMM), [2002] 2 All E.R. (Comm.) 705 *per* Moore-Bick J. at [135]; the decision was affirmed at [2004] EWCA Civ. 487, [2004] 1 Lloyd's Rep. 344.

[469] *Papamichael v. National Westminster Bank* [2003] EWHC 164 (Comm), [2003] 1 Lloyd's Rep. 341 at 369, citing *Re Montagu* [1987] 1 Ch. 264 (see *ante*, para 10–219).

question[470] was "content to proceed upon the basis of a requirement of actual knowledge . . . which would include wilfully and recklessly failing to make such inquiries as an honest and reasonable man would make".[471]

22–199   If the general defence of change of position is applicable to legal and equitable proprietary claims, there will have to have been a receipt of property for such a proprietary claim to be available in the first place and it is obviously unlikely that any defendant will have passed up an opportunity to earn income or acquire assets in reliance on such a receipt. It is clear that a defaulting fiduciary will never himself be able to utilise the defence of change of position since he will necessarily have actual knowledge of the true facts and so cannot possibly be held to have acted in good faith. On the other hand, a person other than a fiduciary who has received property in good faith and subsequently engaged in some expenditure which he would not otherwise have made will be entitled to invoke the defence of change of position to the extent that he is worse off as a result of the transaction. At law, if a person purchases stolen property in good faith and subsequently sells it on at a loss, he will be entitled to invoke the defence of change of position to the extent of his loss on the sale and repurchase. In equity, if an innocent volunteer receives in good faith property transferred to him in breach of trust, he will be able to invoke the defence of change of position to the extent that he has spent the property or its product in ways which have provided no lasting benefit to him, provided that he would not have engaged in the expenditure in question in any event. Thus a charity which, as in *Re Diplock*, receives in good faith a payment which has been made in breach of trust, will be able to invoke the defence of change of position to the extent that it discharges unsecured debts[472] or spends the funds on improvements to its properties which increases their value by less than the amount expended. A private individual will additionally be able to invoke the defence to the extent that he has spent the sum received on some item of one-off expenditure, such as a holiday, which he would not otherwise have made. If the defence of change of position is applicable to proprietary claims, its effect therefore seems likely to be confined to cases of resales at a loss and of one-off non-productive expenditure.

(C)   Where a Proprietary Claim would be Inequitable

22–200   In *Re Diplock*[473] the Court of Appeal held that it would be inequitable for a claimant to maintain an equitable proprietary claim where an innocent volunteer had used the claimant's property either to alter or improve his land or to pay off his debts. If the defence of change of position does now apply to equitable proprietary claims, these further defences must have been subsumed within it to the extent that the expenditure has produced no lasting benefit for the innocent volunteer and would not have been engaged

---

[470] Judge Chambers Q.C., sitting as a Judge of the High Court.

[471] [2003] 1 Lloyd's Rep. 341 at 369. This apparent recourse to the categories of knowledge identified by Peter Gibson J. in *Baden v. Société Générale* (1983) [1993] 1 W.L.R. 509N at 575–576 is not of course consistent with the recent authorities on "liability for dishonest assistance" and "liability for knowing receipt"; see *ante*, paras 10–173, 10–223.

[472] Unless Smith [1995] C.L.J. 290 is right in his contention that the proceeds of unsecured debts can be traced.

[473] [1948] Ch. 465 at 546–548.

in but for the receipt of the claimant's property. However, the defences enunciated by the Court of Appeal are not limited to this situation.

The Court of Appeal clearly envisaged that improvements made to land **22–201** would constitute a complete defence whether or not the value of the land had thereby increased in value. If it has indeed increased in value, there seems no reason why the claimant should not be entitled to obtain a charge over the land for the amount by which its value has increased. Nevertheless the decision of the Court of Appeal in *Re Diplock* was approved, applied, and extended to property other than land by Scott V.-C. in the Court of Appeal in *Foskett v. McKeown*.[474] It has already been seen[475] that the majority of the Court of Appeal restricted the claimants' equitable proprietary claim to the recovery of the premiums on the life insurance policy which had been paid with their funds and interest thereon and were subsequently reversed by the House of Lords, where the point at present under discussion was not considered. Scott V.-C. proceeded on the basis that the claimants' funds had been used to improve an asset which was already[476] vested in the defendants, who were of course innocent volunteers. He consequently stated that, even if the improvements had conferred any benefit on the defendants (in fact both he and Hobhouse L.J. held that this was not the case[477]), the claimants could not, in accordance with *Re Diplock*,[478] have traced their funds into the asset so improved.[479]

Further, although it is of course axiomatic that the payment of unsecured **22–202** debts prevents any subsequent equitable proprietary claim (because the discharged creditor will be a bona fide purchaser for value without notice), there seems no reason why secured debts should be treated in the same way. If secured debts of an innocent volunteer are discharged by the use of the funds of the claimant, why should the claimant not be subrogated to the security discharged with his money and be entitled to enforce that security against the innocent volunteer? In *Boscawen v. Bajwa*[480] Millett L.J. justified the decision actually reached in *Re Diplock* on the basis that the claimants were seeking the immediate realisation of the security to which they claimed to be subrogated; however, he expressed the view that "justice did not require the withholding of any remedy, but only that the charge by subrogation should not be enforceable until the [innocent volunteer] had had a reasonable opportunity to obtain a fresh advance on suitable terms from a willing lender, perhaps from the bank which had held the original security". Such a view seems much more consistent both with principle and with the general defence of change of position, which is what Millett L.J. said would be regarded as relevant today.[481]

However, for the moment it is clear that the defences enunciated by the **22–203** Court of Appeal in *Re Diplock* have survived the enunciation of the general

---

[474] [1998] Ch. 265.
[475] See *ante*, para 22–162.
[476] At any rate by the time of the payment of the fourth and fifth years' premiums.
[477] [1998] Ch. 265 at 282, *per* Scott V.-C.; at 291–292, *per* Hobhouse L.J.
[478] [1948] Ch. 465.
[479] [1998] Ch. 265 at 278.
[480] [1995] 4 All E.R. 769 at 782–783.
[481] See Goff & Jones, *op. cit.*, paras 2–042 to 2–043.

defence of change of position and extend well beyond the scope of that general defence.

(D)   Where Compensation has been Recovered from a Fiduciary

22–204   It has already been seen[482] that any personal claim available against an innocent volunteer will be reduced to the extent that compensation can be obtained from any fiduciary responsible for having made any relevant disposition of trust property in breach of trust. In *Re Diplock*,[483] the Court of Appeal took the view that "prima facie and subject to discussion" any equitable proprietary claim should similarly be reduced by any amounts which the claimant had recovered from any fiduciary responsible for having made such a disposition. The court did not actually suggest that it was necessary for the claimant to sue any such fiduciary prior to embarking on an equitable proprietary claim, merely that if any compensation had been recovered it should constitute a rateable bar to any such equitable proprietary claim.[484]

22–205   It is, frankly, difficult to see why the existence of a personal liability should constitute a bar to a proprietary claim.[485] However, if it is ever held that it is in fact necessary for such a claimant to sue any fiduciary first, it is to be hoped that the fiduciary will be subrogated to that part of the claimant's claim against the innocent volunteer claim which represents the difference between the total of the sum recovered from the fiduciary and the innocent volunteer and the loss suffered by the claimant.[486] It would in fact be preferable to require the claimant to proceed against the innocent volunteer before suing the fiduciary, who would then be liable only for any amount which cannot be recovered from the innocent volunteer; however, such a solution could only be imposed by statute.[487]

---

[482] See *ante*, para 22–109.

[483] [1948] Ch. 465 at 556.

[484] *Re J. Leslie Engineers* [1976] 1 W.L.R. 292.

[485] The argument that it should be specifically rejected in *Hagan v. Waterhouse* (1991) 34 N.S.W.L.R. 308 at 369–370, per Kearney J. (Supreme Court of New South Wales).

[486] Goff & Jones, *op. cit.*, para.2–047.

[487] As in New Zealand (Administration Act 1952, s.30B(5)) and in Western Australia (Trustee Act 1962, s.65(7)). However, Queensland has gone even further than the Court of Appeal in *Re Diplock* and prohibits, except by leave of the court, any claim against any transferee of trust property transferred in breach of trust until the claimant has exhausted his remedies against the fiduciary responsible (Trusts Act 1973, s.109(2); see Lee (1981) 1 O.J.L.S. 414).

CHAPTER 23

TRUSTS IN THE CONFLICT OF LAWS

The rules of the conflict of laws, often also known and described throughout **23–001** this chapter as the rules of private international law, determine the jurisdiction by whose laws any legal relationship is governed. Its rules are relevant whenever a legal relationship, be it a contract, a tort, a marriage, a trust or an inheritance, has an international element. Taking an admittedly artificial example from outside the law of trusts, suppose that a Frenchman and a German make a contract for the sale and purchase of shares in a Spanish company on board a ship flying the Liberian flag which at that time happens to be moored in the Port of Amsterdam, Holland; the law of any one of the five jurisdictions mentioned could govern that contract in the event that the parties do not expressly provide what law is to constitute what is known as the proper law of the contract, which does not actually have to be any of those five (many commercial contracts, particularly shipping contracts, provide that they are to be governed by English law even though none of the parties or the subject matter of the contract has ever had any connection with the United Kingdom). In the context of trust law, if an English settlor creates a trust whose trustees are two Canadians who live and work in Bermuda, whose beneficiaries live either in Florida or in California, and whose assets consist of shares in companies constituted in various tax havens and land in other jurisdictions scattered around the world, there are an equally large number of possible jurisdictions by whose law that trust may be governed and which may therefore constitute what is now known as the applicable law of the trust (formerly known as the proper law of the trust).[1] That is not to say that any necessary proceedings have to be brought in the jurisdiction whose law constitutes the proper law of the contract or the applicable law of the trust in question; there are a variety of reasons why those proceedings may be brought elsewhere. In such circumstances, while that other jurisdiction will have to apply the proper or applicable law when determining questions of substance, all questions of procedure will be governed by its own law, by what is known as the law of the forum, the jurisdiction in which any proceedings are being brought.

---

[1] Prior to the Recognition of Trusts Act 1987, which was passed in order to incorporate into English law the Hague Convention on the Law Applicable to Trusts and their Recognition ("the Hague Convention"), the relevant law was always known as "the proper law" of the trust in question but the Hague Convention instead uses the expression "applicable law". The expression "proper law of the trust" is still invariably utilised in jurisdictions which have not incorporated the Hague Convention into their law.

23–002   An additional complication is that countries often contain more than one jurisdiction. The United Kingdom has three, England and Wales,[2] Scotland, and Northern Ireland while each of the offshore islands of Guernsey, Jersey and the Isle of Man also has a separate jurisdiction, to which must be added the further separate jurisdictions of each of the United Kingdom's dependant territories such as The Cayman Islands and Gibraltar (to mention two which are important tax havens and so are relevant to the law of trusts). Federal countries, such as the United States of America, Australia and Canada, have as many jurisdictions as there are individual states, provinces or territories plus, in each case, an additional federal jurisdiction whose rules, which are admittedly unlikely to be applicable to many matters in which private international law is relevant, apply to the entire country. Even some basically unitary countries, such as Spain, have distinct rules governing such matters as matrimonial property regimes and rights of inheritance which apply in different parts of that country.

23–003   The situation is complicated still further by the fact that the application of the rules of private international law of different jurisdictions not infrequently produces different answers to the question of which jurisdiction's laws govern the transaction in question. This is because the common law jurisdictions, such as England and the majority of the United Kingdom's former colonies, tend to determine the applicable law by the use of connecting factors which differ in almost every respect from those utilised by civil law jurisdictions such as those of mainland Europe. The common law jurisdictions tend to utilise connecting factors such as the domicile of the persons involved (a highly technical concept[3]) and the location of any relevant assets, whereas the civil law jurisdictions tend instead to utilise connecting factors such as habitual residence and nationality (in the case of a United Kingdom national, nationality presumably means the United Kingdom jurisdiction with which he has the closest connection[4]). Even worse,

---

[2] Throughout this chapter, references to "England" and "English law" therefore mean "England and Wales" and "the law of England and Wales". This is in the interests of brevity and no disrespect is thereby intended to the inhabitants of the Principality of Wales.

[3] Domicile has nothing to do with habitual residence. A person's domicile of origin is the jurisdiction in which one of his parents (usually his father) was domiciled at the time of his birth. He will only be held to have given up that domicile of origin in favour of a domicile of choice if he goes to another jurisdiction with the intention of remaining there permanently or if, having gone to another jurisdiction without any such intention, he subsequently decides to remain there permanently; whether he so intended or decided is a question of fact, often an extremely difficult one. However, once a person has obtained a domicile of choice, he can give up that domicile of choice up simply by leaving the jurisdiction in question with the intention of ceasing to reside there permanently. He can give up that domicile of choice simply by leaving the jurisdiction in question with the intention of ceasing to reside there permanently. There is no requirement that he must then also intend to reside somewhere else permanently. If he does have such an intention, he will obtain a further domicile of choice wherever he intends to reside permanently; if he does not have such an intention, his domicile of origin will then automatically revive. See J. Collier, *Conflict of Laws*, 3rd edn (Cambridge, CUP, 2001) pp.37–60.

[4] This at least was what was held in the highly criticised but undoubtedly pragmatic decision in *Re O'Keefe* [1940] Ch. 124. This case is a good illustration what can actually happen in practice. The question was what law governed the intestate succession to the moveable property of a someone with United Kingdom nationality who had died with a domicile of choice in Italy. The English court initially applied Italian law on the grounds that the relevant connecting factor under English private international law was domicile. However, the relevant

some but by no means all jurisdictions accept a reference back to their own law where the law which they regard as prima facie applicable so dictates and some common law jurisdictions also accept a reference on to the law of a third jurisdiction (both types of reference are technically known as *"renvoi"*). All this means that the law applicable to any given transaction is likely to differ depending on which jurisdiction's courts have to decide the question. Consequences of this type can only be avoided if the different rules adopted by the common law and the civil law jurisdictions can be synthesised in an international convention; this obviously involves both groups of jurisdictions giving way in substantial respects. The effect of such a convention will be that those states who sign and ratify it will then all apply the same rules to the same legal transaction.

Fortunately, the law of trusts is governed by such a convention, The Hague Convention on the Law Applicable to Trusts and their Recognition ("the Hague Convention"), which was incorporated into English law by the Recognition of Trusts Act 1987. This now largely governs the question of which jurisdiction is the applicable law of the trust; that law will determine at the very least the nature of the interests of the beneficiaries under the trust and the duties owed by the trustees to them (it is, however, possible for the trust instrument to provide for other questions to be governed by the law of some other jurisdiction). The incorporation of the Hague Convention into English law certainly means that it is no longer necessary (if indeed it ever was) for the student of the English law of trusts to master the intricacies of doctrines of private international law such as domicile and *renvoi*. Nor need such a student try to work out what would happen if proceedings were brought in the courts of any jurisdiction other than England, although this is obviously relevant to anyone setting up a trust governed by the law of some other jurisdiction.   23–004

This chapter, after a brief discussion of the situations in which the rules of private international law governing trusts may be relevant, therefore needs to consider only two questions: first, in what circumstances an English court has jurisdiction to hear trust proceedings and, secondly, which jurisdiction's rules of substantive law it will apply when doing so. It cannot be emphasised too often that these two questions are wholly independent of one another[5] and must therefore always be considered separately. Hereafter, a trust whose applicable law is English law will be described as "an English trust", a trust whose applicable law is not English law will be described as "a foreign trust" and a trust whose applicable law is that of another specific jurisdiction will be described as, for example, "a Jersey trust".   23–005

---

connecting factor under Italian private international law was nationality. The English court therefore accepted Italian law's reference back to the law of the United Kingdom under the doctrine of *"renvoi"* (discussed in the next sentence of the text) and then decided that in this case the law of the United Kingdom meant Irish law (which was duly applied) on the grounds that the deceased's domicile of origin had been what is now the Republic of Ireland (part of the United Kingdom at the time of her birth); it made no difference that she had only ever paid one short visit there. See J. Collier, *Conflict of Laws*, 3rd edn (Cambridge, CUP, 2001) pp.23–24.

[5] The distinction emerges clearly in *Macmillan v. Bishopsgate Trust (No.3)* [1995] 1 W.L.R. 978 at 989.

I. SITUATIONS WHERE PRIVATE INTERNATIONAL LAW IS RELEVANT

23–006   There are at least five situations in which the rules of private international law governing trusts are relevant in the English courts.

1. *Proceedings Brought in England to Enforce a Foreign Trust*

23–007   The most straightforward situation in which the rules of private international law governing trusts are relevant in the English courts are where proceedings are brought in England to enforce a trust which is (or may be) a foreign trust. The most likely scenario is where the beneficiaries bring proceedings in England against the trustees for breach of trust in England because either the trustees themselves and/or some part of the trust property are physically present in this jurisdiction. However, it is also possible that for one or both of the same reasons the settlor or the protector might bring such proceedings or that new trustees might bring proceedings in England against former trustees who are physically present in this jurisdiction.

23–008   An example is the leading case of *Chellaram v. Chellaram*.[6] The settlors of the discretionary trusts in question were almost certainly domiciled in India at the time of the settlements, which were drawn up in India in English form and executed by them respectively in Singapore and in Lagos. Two of the original trustees were permanently resident in England and the third had a United Kingdom passport and spent some months each year here in a house of his ownership. The trust property was shares in Bermudan companies whose assets were situated in many parts of the world but not in India. Some of the beneficiaries brought proceedings in England seeking the removal of the then trustees, who were all born and domiciled in India but were not all resident there and all of whom visited London on a regular basis; all the trustees entered an appearance but subsequently sought a stay on the basis that England was not the most appropriate forum.[7] However, even on the basis that the trusts were Indian trusts, the court was held to have jurisdiction over those particular proceedings. But, in subsequent proceedings for breach of trust by effectively the same beneficiaries many years later, the trusts were held to be Bermudan trusts; since none of the then trustees had entered an appearance or was domiciled here, the court was held not to have jurisdiction and service out of the jurisdiction on the trustees was set aside. The court held that, even if it had had jurisdiction and the trusts had been English trusts, India not England would have been the most appropriate forum.

2. *Other Types of Proceedings in England to which a Foreign Trust is Relevant*

23–009   The rules of private international law can also be relevant where the nature, beneficial interests, and assets of a foreign trust affect other types of proceedings in respect of which the English courts clearly have jurisdiction.

---

[6] [1985] Ch. 409, *(No.2)* [2002] 3 All E.R. 17; see *post*, para 23–052.
[7] In technical terms, that England was not the *forum conveniens*.

A straightforward illustration is where the trustees and/or a beneficiary   **23–010**
of a foreign trust have brought proceedings in England in which the nature
of the foreign trust or the rights of its beneficiaries are relevant. In *Neumann
v. Azon Anstalt*,[8] a Liechtenstein company which was the tenant of a flat in
London declared a trust of that flat in favour of its occupier in order to
enable the company to obtain a new lease to which it was entitled provided
that, first, the beneficiary had occupied the flat as his only or principal home
for three out of the previous 10 years and, secondly, that the declaration of
trust was actually valid; the latter question turned on whether the trust was
an English trust, in which case it was clearly valid, or a Liechtenstein trust,
in which case it was arguably invalid on the basis that the Liechtenstein trust
legislation only envisages trusts created by transfer. It was held[9] that the
trust was a Liechtenstein trust[10] and that Liechtenstein law does indeed only
envisage trusts created by transfer; the declaration of trust was therefore
invalid and so the claim for a new lease failed.

Foreign trusts can also be relevant to proceedings for the reallocation of   **23–011**
property following a divorce. One of the former spouses may claim assets to
which the other former spouse is entitled under a foreign trust. Such claims
have been successful in the past[11] but, following the incorporation of the
Hague Convention into English law, it was questioned whether the English
courts still had jurisdiction over foreign trusts in this respect.[12] There has
never been any difficulty in practice where the trustees of the foreign trust
are within the English jurisdiction or can be controlled by a respondent who
is himself within the English jurisdiction; in such circumstances the trustees
or the respondent will be susceptible to the personal jurisdiction of the
English courts. However, the Court of Appeal has now held in *Charalambous
v. Charalambous*[13] that English law is the designated law for proceedings of
this type and that, pursuant to Article 15 of the Hague Convention,[14] its
power to vary settlements cannot be derogated from by voluntary act. In
policy terms, this can certainly be justified on the grounds that otherwise
putting assets in a foreign trust would be far too easy a way of protecting
them from potential claims by former spouses. This of course does not
necessarily mean that the courts of the jurisdiction of the applicable law of

---

[8] (2001) unreported. The author of this edition was junior counsel for the landlord.

[9] By Judge Levy Q.C. in the Central London County Court.

[10] Because in the absence of an express clause selecting an applicable law other than Liechtenstein law, a trust created by a Liechtenstein company was, as a matter of Liechtenstein law, necessarily a Liechtenstein trust.

[11] Claims to vary pre-nuptial or post-nuptial settlements of property abroad governed by foreign law with exclusively foreign trustees were successfully made in *Nunneley v. Nunneley* (1890) 15 P.D. 186, *Forsyth v. Forsyth* [1891] P. 363, and *Goff v. Goff* [1934] P. 107. More recently, claims for the reallocation of property on divorce were successfully made in *Browne v. Browne* [1989] 1 F.L.R. 291 (Jersey discretionary trust, Liechtenstein trust), *E v. E (Financial Provision)* [1990] 2 F.L.R. 233 (Guernsey discretionary trust), and *T v. T* [1996] 2 F.L.R. 357 (Jersey discretionary trust); however, in these proceedings no reference was made to the Recognition of Trusts Act 1987.

[12] It had been argued in unreported proceedings that the English courts no longer have jurisdiction to make orders governing such trusts but such arguments had never been the subject of a reasoned judgment until recently.

[13] [2004] EWCA Civ. 1030, [2005] Fam. 250 (*sub nom. C. v. C.*, but reported under the names of the parties elsewhere).

[14] See *post*, para 23–065.

the settlement in question will take any notice of the order of the English courts purporting to vary it. The Royal Court of Jersey, which is the applicable law of most of the settlements which have so far been the subject of orders of this type, does generally make the variation which has been ordered as a matter of comity.[15] But a foreign court from a jurisdiction whose links with the United Kingdom are less close than those of Jersey may not feel obliged to act as a matter of comity at all; in this respect, proceedings are at present pending in Bermuda seeking the enforcement of an order of an English court in an extremely high profile divorce case which purported to vary a Bermudan trust and the outcome may well be instructive.

23–012   In the past English courts have also been prepared to make orders under the Variation of Trusts Act 1958[16] in respect of foreign trusts but it is extremely doubtful whether the English courts still have jurisdiction in such proceedings following the incorporation of the Hague Convention into English law[17]; even if they do they may well now not feel inclined to make such orders and the courts of the foreign jurisdiction may well decline to enforce them.

3. Proceedings to Enforce an English Trust against Foreign Trustees and Beneficiaries

23–013   The rules of private international law can also be relevant where proceedings are brought in the English courts relating to an English trust all of whose trustees and/or some or all of whose beneficiaries are domiciled or habitually resident outside the United Kingdom. Such proceedings may be for the purpose of establishing the correct interpretation of the trust instrument, in which case the proceedings are likely to be brought by the trustees, joining representative beneficiaries as defendants, or for the enforcement of the trusts, in which case the proceedings are likely to be brought by one or more of the beneficiaries against the trustees and/or against the other beneficiaries.

23–014   Such a case was *González Gómez v. Gómez-Monche Vives*[18] which concerned a trust created in 1984 whose only connection with England was that English law was expressly stated to be its applicable law. The settlor and all the beneficiaries were Spanish; the trust property was a substantial 14 per cent shareholding in a Cayman Island company, the holding company of the González Byass sherry group; and the trustees had at all times been offshore companies, at the time of the proceedings from the British Virgin Islands and from Liechtenstein. The income of the trust was undisposed of, at least following the end of the accumulation period in 2005, and was therefore held on resulting trust for the settlor; the capital could not be appointed out until the death of the survivor of the settlor and his widow. Nevertheless, following the death intestate of the settlor in 1991, the trustees had paid all the income and appointed some of the capital to the widow. She was entitled to some of the income under the resulting trust pursuant to the Spanish

---

[15] One of many cases of this kind is *Compass Trustees v. McBarnett* [2003] W.T.L.R. 461.
[16] *Re Ker's Settlement* [1963] Ch. 553; *Re Paget's Settlement* [1965] 1 W.L.R. 1046.
[17] See *post*, para 23–055.
[18] [2008] EWHC 259 (Ch), [2008] 3 W.L.R. 309.

intestacy rules but her sons were entitled to the remainder of that income and were also the default capital beneficiaries. Three of them therefore brought proceedings in England[19] against her and the trustees claiming repayment by her of the sums to which she had not been entitled and the reconstitution of the trust fund. They also challenged her exercise of a power to nominate herself as the person capable of appointing the capital with effect from her death. As will be seen below, she successfully challenged the jurisdiction of the English court but an appeal is pending which will have been heard by the time that this edition is published.

4. *Proceedings to Set Aside an English Trust*

The rules of private international law can also be relevant where proceed-   **23–015**
ings are brought in the English courts to set aside an English trust created by a settlor who is domiciled or habitually resident outside the United Kingdom. Such proceedings may be brought on a number of grounds: first, on the grounds that the creation of the trust amounted to a fraud on the settlor's creditors under foreign legislation analogous to the English legislation which has already been considered[20]; secondly, on the grounds that its creation breached the terms of his matrimonial property regime (this would, for example, be the case if a person married under French law settled property on his spouse[21]); or, thirdly, on the grounds that its creation deprived his forcible heirs of their rights (the civil law systems of continental Europe require that a substantial percentage (generally at least two-thirds) of the deceased's lifetime assets passes to any descendants and sometimes that, in default of descendants, a lower percentage passes to any ascendants, subject in both cases to provision for surviving spouses; the Muslim legal systems have similar provisions limited to the assets held at the time of death).

5. *Dispositions of Trust Property in Breach of Trust*

Finally, the rules of private international law can also be relevant where the   **23–016**
assets of an English trust have been disposed of in breach of trust to persons in other jurisdictions or the assets of a foreign trust have been disposed of in breach of trust to persons in England and the beneficiaries are trying to maintain equitable proprietary claims or to impose "liability for knowing receipt" or "liability for dishonest assistance".

In this respect, it can sometimes be difficult to determine whether assets   **23–017**
were actually subject to a foreign trust in the first place. In *Kuwait Oil Tanker Company v. Al Bader*[22] it had to be decided whether the directors and other

---

[19] The proceedings were brought in England because Spanish law does not recognise trusts and so the changes of obtaining a judgment against the widow there were minimal, while a judgment against her in either the British Virgin Islands or Liechtenstein would not have been enforceable in Spain; in contrast, a judgment in England would have been automatically enforceable against her in Spain.

[20] See *ante*, para 7–056.

[21] Under French law (*Code Civile*, Art. 1096) all gifts between spouses are void so a settlement by one spouse of property on trust for the other spouse would also be void.

[22] (2000) *The Times*, May 30, 2000.

officers of companies incorporated in non-common law jurisdictions can be regarded as owing fiduciary duties to those companies. The defendants were various officers of the plaintiff Kuwaiti company who had interposed off-shore companies between the plaintiff and the owners of ships which it had chartered and, by the use of back to back charterparties, had creamed off the difference between the rates of hire paid by the plaintiff and the rates of hire received by the owners. The plaintiff contended that the defendants were constructive trustees, first, because they had obtained property from the plaintiff by fraud and, secondly, because they had obtained property in breach of their fiduciary duties to the plaintiff; both contentions succeeded.[23] In *Arab Monetary Fund v. Hashim (No.8)*[24] Chadwick J. had held that in such circumstances what the English court has to do is to decide whether the duties which arise under the relevant foreign law are capable of being classified by the English court as fiduciary. In *Kuwait Oil Tanker Company v. Al Bader* both Moore-Bick J. and the Court of Appeal held that exactly the same attitude should be adopted in deciding whether a person is a constructive trustee of property which he has received. Under Kuwaiti law, anyone who receives property in bad faith is obliged to return both that property and its fruits; consequently, the defendants were held to be constructive trustees of the proceeds of their fraud. Similarly, their relationship to the plaintiff under Kuwaiti law was clearly classifiable by an English court as fiduciary and so they were held to be constructive trustees on this ground as well.

23–018   Where there is a trust, there is no difficulty about either equitable proprietary claims or claims to impose liability for knowing receipt where the claims are being brought against a person to whom the property subject to the trust was directly transferred. Assuming that that person is susceptible to the jurisdiction of the English courts in the first place, English law will clearly apply to the claims against him because he can be shown to have received the property in question. This was also held by Chadwick J. in *Arab Monetary Fund v. Hashim (No.8)*.[25] Difficulties do however arise where either of these types of claim is being brought against someone to whom the original recipient has transferred the trust property on, the principal problem being that of determining by what law the second or subsequent transfer is governed. There is also some controversy as to what law governs liability for dishonest assistance.

23–019   For the purposes of an equitable proprietary claim against a subsequent recipient of the trust property, it appears that the effect of a transfer of that property between persons who are both in a jurisdiction other than England will be governed by the law of that jurisdiction. This seems to follow from the judgments of the members of the Court of Appeal in *MacMillan v.*

---

[23] The defendants had been held liable for conspiracy so the existence of a constructive trust was relevant only to the question of whether or not the plaintiff was entitled to compound interest (see *Westdeutsche Landesbank Girozentrale v. Islington L.B.C.* [1996] A.C. 669).

[24] (June 13, 1994) unreported (there are several unreported judgments in this interminable case).

[25] *ibid.* ("liability for knowing receipt").

Bishopsgate Trust (No.3).[26] Consequently, such a claim will only be able to be maintained against the later recipient if under the law of that jurisdiction the equitable interests of the beneficiaries continue to affect the property transferred to him. If they do not, as would be the case where, for example, funds were transferred to a Swiss bank,[27] then the beneficiaries will be unable to demonstrate that any of their property ever reached the hands of the recipient and so will not possibly be able to maintain an equitable proprietary claim in respect of it.

For identical reasons, the result ought to be exactly the same in the case of a claim to impose liability for knowing receipt against a subsequent recipient. However, the rules by which English law traces property into its product appear to be more flexible in cases of this kind,[28] although they certainly should not be! If such rules are classified as procedural rather than substantive (which they could conceivably be[29]) and so apply irrelevant of where any transfer took place, then the beneficiaries may nevertheless be able to demonstrate that the recipient actually received their property. It is to be hoped that this latter view is not adopted.   **23–020**

Liability for dishonest assistance is less straightforward. Although this liability has been held[30] to be a matter "relating to tort, delict or quasi delict" for the purposes of the allocation of jurisdiction as between European countries,[31] it has been held by the Court of Appeal[32] not to be tortious for the purpose of service of proceedings out of the jurisdiction, although the rules have now been changed[33] to permit service out of the jurisdiction in such cases. Liability for dishonest assistance has also been held not to be tortious for the purposes of the rules of private international law—this was in *Arab Monetary Fund v. Hashim (No.9)*.[34] The judge in question, Chadwick J., then stated that whether or not a person can be held liable for dishonest assistance "where the fault alleged lies wholly in things done or not done in a foreign jurisdiction . . . is a question to which the authorities provide no ready answer".[35] However, he went on to hold that the matter was governed by a rule of private international law which at one time used   **23–021**

---

[26] *MacMillan v. Bishopsgate Trust (No.3)* [1995] 1 W.L.R. 978 (Millett J.), [1996] 1 W.L.R. 387 (Court of Appeal). The conclusion in the text seems to follow from the statements in the Court of Appeal at 399 *per* Staughton L.J., at 410 *per* Auld L.J., and at 424 *per* Aldous L.J., each of whom held that the effect of such transfers was governed by the law of the place where it took place. At first instance, Millett J. reached the same conclusion for a different reason, namely that this was the place where the enrichment of the recipient took place.

[27] Under Swiss law deposits in banks become the property of the depositee and no proprietary interest in the depositor or anyone claiming through him can survive. See *Arab Monetary Bank v. Hashim (No.8)* (June 13, 1994) unreported, transcript at 316.

[28] *El Ajou v. Dollar Land Holdings* [1993] 3 All E.R. 717 at 736, *per* Millett J.; see *ante*, para 10–207.

[29] This point was left open by Millett J. (it did not have to be decided because in that case the property had been received here). The point also arose, and was again left open, in *Chase Manhattan Bank v. Israel-British Bank (London)* [1981] Ch. 105 at 127.

[30] In *Casio Computer v. Sayo* [2001] I.L.Pr. 594.

[31] Then under the Brussels and Lugano Conventions, art.5(3); since March 1, 2002, also under Council Regulation (E.C.) 44/2001, art.5(3); *post*, para 23–035.

[32] In *Metall & Rohstoff v. Donaldson Lufkin & Jenrette* [1990] 1 Q.B. 391 at 474.

[33] Civil Procedure Rules 1998, Part 6.20, paras 14, 15; see *post*, para 23–028.

[34] (October 11, 1994) unreported, transcript at para.22–23.

[35] *ibid.*, at 24.

to govern liability for tort[36] but has long since ceased to do so.[37] On this basis, liability depends, first, on whether the alleged accessory is liable under English law and, secondly, on whether he is exempted from liability under the law of the jurisdiction where the assistance took place. Only if he is both liable under English law and not exempted by the law of the other jurisdiction, will he be liable for dishonest assistance. This decision was criticised[38] on the basis that it seems at best an unsatisfactory half way house first to hold that liability for dishonest assistance is not tortious for the purposes of private international law and then to return to and adopt as of general application an abrogated rule of private international law on tort which has long since been rejected by the House of Lords. However, this decision of Chadwick J. was subsequently followed and applied by Rix J. in *Dubai Aluminium Co. v. Salaam*[39] (the point did not arise on appeal) and both at first instance and in the Court of Appeal in *Grupo Torras v. Al-Sabah*.[40] Consequently, this view must clearly now be regarded as constituting English law.

II. The Jurisdiction of the English Courts

23–022   The rules governing the jurisdiction of the English courts differ depending on the applicability of the European legislation which governs the allocation of jurisdiction between the courts of the various countries who are bound by it (the legislation will collectively be described as "the European Conventions"). Prior to March 1, 2002, the relevant legislation was the Brussels and Lugano Conventions. However, the Brussels Convention is now[41] virtually defunct[42] and the Lugano Convention applies only as between, on the one hand, all the members of the European Union and, on the other hand, Iceland, Norway, Poland and Switzerland.[43] As between the whole of the members of the European Union,[44] the relevant legislation is now Council Regulation (E.C.) 44/2001 ("the Council Regulation"), which came into force on March 1, 2002. The Brussels and Lugano Conventions were incorporated into English law by the Civil Jurisdiction and Judgments Acts of 1982 and 1991 respectively, which have been modified to incorporate the

---

[36] The principle enunciated in *The Halley* (1868) L.R. 2 P.C. 193 (a decision of the Privy Council but, because it was on appeal from the Court of Admiralty, an English precedent).

[37] It was rejected by the House of Lords in *Boys v. Chaplain* [1971] A.C. 356, where a different rule was adopted. This has in turn been replaced by yet a further rule contained in Private International Law (Miscellaneous Provisions) Act 1995.

[38] In the 7th edition of this work, p.748.

[39] [1999] 1 Lloyd's Rep. 415 at 452.

[40] [1999] C.L.C. 1469 (Mance L.J., sitting in the Commercial Court), [2001] Lloyd's Rep. Bank 36 (C.A.).

[41] In April 2008. Until 2007 the Brussels Convention also applied as between Denmark and the remaining members of the European Union.

[42] The Brussels Convention still applies as between a few small overseas territories of Member States which are members of the European Union and all the remaining members of the European Union. Not all overseas territories of Member States are members of the European Union; for example, Guernsey, Jersey and the Isle of Man are not members.

[43] The members of the European Free Trade Association other than Liechtenstein (which has not ratified the Lugano Convention and has no intention of doing so).

[44] Other than the few small overseas territories of member states which are still governed by the Brussels Convention.

Council Regulation by statutory instrument.[45] The situation where the European Conventions do not apply will be considered first.

1. *Jurisdiction when the Applicable Law is Specified*

Most well-drawn trust instruments today contain a clause specifying the applicable law of the trust, which will govern all questions concerning that trust unless any of them is stated to be governed by the law of some other jurisdiction. Where English law is specified as the applicable law of a trust, there can be no doubt whatever that the English courts have jurisdiction over all questions concerning that trust (other of course than any which is stated to be governed by the law of another jurisdiction). Indeed, many trust instruments contain a further clause specifically conferring that jurisdiction on the courts in question. It is of course theoretically possible for a trust to contain both a clause specifying English law as the applicable law of the trust and a clause giving jurisdiction over all questions concerning the trust to some other jurisdiction. The latter clause would presumably have to be upheld in proceedings between the trustees and the settlor, all of whom would obviously have agreed to it by executing the trust instrument. However, the most likely parties to any proceedings are the trustees and the beneficiaries and it is improbable that the latter will have executed the trust instrument. In such circumstances, it is inconceivable that the English courts would decline jurisdiction to hear proceedings brought by any beneficiary of a trust who had not executed the trust instrument where English law was specified as the applicable law.

23–023

As has just been indicated, a trust instrument can also specify that some questions concerning its trusts are to be governed by the law of some jurisdiction other than that of its applicable law. The administration of a trust is what is most often excluded from the ambit of its applicable law, although in this and in all other cases it is usually prudent also to define extremely precisely exactly what has been so excluded. Many modern trust instruments expressly envisage the possibility of the applicable law and the law governing the administration of the trust being different by referring to them in separate clauses, even if both are initially to be governed by the law of the same jurisdiction (this is in order to enable the two to be separated later under the change of law clauses which such instruments tend also to contain). Occasionally a trust instrument will also specify that it should be construed in accordance with the law of a particular jurisdiction, usually that of the jurisdiction in which it is being drawn up; this can be advantageous since it enables technical expressions such as "issue" to be given the meaning which the draftsman intended them to have and permits presumptions which the draftsman will consciously or unconsciously have had in mind to be carried into effect. If the law chosen to govern the construction of the trust instrument or the administration of the trust or anything else is English law, there is equally no doubt that the English courts have jurisdiction in that respect.

23–024

---

[45] SI 2001/3929.

23–025   However, the fact that a court has jurisdiction by virtue of an express provision of the trust instrument in question does not mean that it will necessarily exercise it. It may nevertheless decline to hear the proceedings under what is known as the doctrine of forum *non conveniens* if it is satisfied that the courts of another jurisdiction constitute a more appropriate forum. In *Chellaram v. Chellaram (No.2)*,[46] the facts of which have already been considered,[47] it was held that, on the hypotheses that, contrary to earlier findings, the court had jurisdiction and the trusts were English trusts, England was not an appropriate forum.[48] The forum *conveniens* was India: first, there were already proceedings there between the same parties involving other trusts and an Indian court was far better equipped to understand the intricacies of the parties' family relationships; and, secondly, several of the most important witnesses were there and the only important witnesses who were non-compellable there were English solicitors who would in practice attend if asked to do so by their clients.

2. Jurisdiction when the Applicable Law is not Specified

23–026   Where a trust instrument contains no clause specifying the applicable law, the English courts will equally have jurisdiction where the applicable law is nevertheless English law; this will be determined pursuant to the Hague Convention[49] A straightforward example where this would be the case is where all the relevant parties and the relevant property are habitually physically within the jurisdiction; more complex situations are considered later on.[50] Further, in relation to proprietary claims, the English courts are likely to assume jurisdiction if only the property and none of the parties is within the jurisdiction in this sense. It is also possible for defendants outside the jurisdiction to submit to the jurisdiction of the English courts by giving someone within the jurisdiction authority to accept service on their behalf.[51] The crucial question is obviously in what other circumstances the English courts will assume jurisdiction.

23–027   The basic rule is that the physical presence of the defendant within the jurisdiction, no matter how fleeting it may be, is sufficient to confer jurisdiction on the English courts even if the proper law of the trust is not English law. In *Ewing v. Orr-Ewing*[52] an order was sought by an English minor beneficiary against English and Scottish executors, all of whom were regarded as having been properly served,[53] for the administration by the English court of both the English and Scottish assets of the estate of a Scottish domiciliary. Part of the assets had originally been within the jurisdiction but had been removed to Scotland by the time that the action commenced. The House of Lords made the order sought. In *Cook Industries*

---

[46] [2002] EWHC 632 (Ch), [2002] 3 All E.R. 17.
[47] See *ante*, para 23–008.
[48] [2002] EWHC 632 (Ch), [2002] 3 All E.R. 17 at 50.
[49] See *post*, para 23–039.
[50] See *post*, para 23–039.
[51] As some of the trustees had in *Chellaram v. Chellaram* [1985] Ch. 409.
[52] (1883) 9 App.Cas. 34.
[53] The Scottish executors seem to have been served in Scotland without any special leave of the court but no objection was taken.

v. Galligher,[54] an order was sought by and granted to the plaintiff, a New York creditor under a New York judgment, for the inspection of a property in France which the defendant, an American who lived in England for approximately six months a year, was alleged to hold on trust for the plaintiff's judgment debtor. These, and other authorities not involving trusts, were relied on by Millett J. in *El Ajou v. Dollar Land Holdings*[55] in support of the proposition that "liability for knowing receipt" could be imposed on an English company in respect of assets which it had knowingly received abroad.[56] Similarly, in *Chellaram v. Chellaram*,[57] whose facts have already been considered,[58] the English court clearly had jurisdiction in the first proceedings by virtue of the fact that all the trustees had been served in England, some as a result of having submitted to the jurisdiction.

Further, jurisdiction can also arise as a result of service of the proceedings on defendants who are out of the jurisdiction; whether or not service out of the jurisdiction is possible is determined as at the date of the proceedings rather than as at the date when the cause of action arose.[59] The leave of the court is usually, but not always, required.[60] It is not required for service out of the jurisdiction in certain circumstances covered by the European Conventions.[61] It is always available for service out of the jurisdiction of any claim against a defendant domiciled in the jurisdiction.[62] Otherwise the relevant situations in which leave can be granted for service out of the jurisdiction are:

    23–028

(i) where "the whole subject matter of a claim relates to property located within the jurisdiction"[63] (in *Banca Carige v. Banco Nacional*[64] Lightman J. confirmed that this provision extended to all property within the jurisdiction, including shares in an English company and held that leave could in principle be given to an Italian bank to serve out of the jurisdiction in respect of a challenge under the Insolvency Act 1986 to a sale of such shares by the former national bank of Cuba to its successor[65]);

---

[54] [1979] Ch. 439.

[55] [1993] 3 All E.R. 717 at 737.

[56] This proposition does not form part of his ratio since the company had actually received the assets in England. Millett J. was using this proposition based on hypothetical facts in order to establish that, if the company was potentially liable for knowing receipt if the assets had been received abroad, it was *a fortiori* potentially liable if they had been received in England.

[57] [1985] Ch. 409.

[58] See *ante*, para 23–008.

[59] *Chellaram v. Chellaram (No.2)* [2002] EWHC 632 (Ch), [2002] 3 All E.R. 17 at 46.

[60] Civil Procedure Rules 1998, Part 6, Sect. III. This was formerly governed by Rules of the Supreme Court, Ord. 11.

[61] See *post*, para 23–038.

[62] Civil Procedure Rules 1998, Part 6.20, para. 1; this was also the case under Rules of the Supreme Court, Ord. 11.

[63] Civil Procedure Rules 1998, Part 6.20, para.10. This is broader than Rules of the Supreme Court, Ord. 11, r.1(1)(g), which applied only where the whole subject-matter of the action was land within the jurisdiction.

[64] [2001] 3 All E.R. 923 at pp.937–938.

[65] In the light of the facts, leave was not actually granted.

> (ii) in respect of claims "made for any remedy which might be
> obtained in proceedings to execute the trusts of a written instru-
> ment where (a) the trusts ought to be executed according to Eng-
> lish law; and (b) the person on whom the claim form is to be served
> is a trustee of the trusts"[66];
>
> (iii) where "a claim is made for a remedy against the defendant as
> constructive trustee where the defendant's alleged liability arises
> out of acts committed within the jurisdiction"[67]; and
>
> (iv) where "a claim is made for restitution where the defendant's
> alleged liability arises out of acts committed within the jurisdic-
> tion".[68]

23–029   Where a court has jurisdiction under these rules, then, just as in the
situation where a court has jurisdiction by virtue of an express provision of
the trust instrument in question, it may also decline to hear the proceedings
under the doctrine of *forum non conveniens*. An example of a situation where
a court might well decline jurisdiction in proceedings involving a trust
would be where the trustees had been served on a casual visit to the
jurisdiction in question and had no assets within it, none of the trust
property was within the jurisdiction, and it was clear that the judgment of
the court in question would not be enforced in the jurisdiction(s) where the
trustees and the trust property were physically present; in such circumstances, the latter jurisdiction(s) would clearly constitute a more appropriate
forum.

3. *Jurisdiction when the European Conventions Apply*

23–030   The rules discussed so far do not, however, apply when the proceedings in
question fall within the scope of the European Conventions. The countries
who are bound by the relevant legislation ("European Convention States")
have already been considered.[69] But, by virtue of Article 1,[70] the European
Conventions never apply to, among other things, revenue, customs or
administrative matters, or the status or legal capacity of natural persons,

---

[66] Civil Procedure Rules 1998, Part 6.20, para.11. Effectively the same provision was included
in Rules of the Supreme Court, Ord. 11, r.1(1)(j).
[67] Civil Procedure Rules 1998, Part 6.20, para.14; this provision will presumably cover "liability for dishonest assistance" despite the view that this does not lead to the imposition of a
construction trust (see *ante*, para 10–161). A similar provision was included in Rules of the
Supreme Court, Ord. 11, r.1(1)(t), which was added in 1990 as a result of the decision in *Metall
& Rohstoff v. Donaldson Lufkin & Jenrette* [1990] 1 Q.B. 391 at 474; this certainly covered "liability
for dishonest assistance". Under that provision, provided that at least some of the acts which
gave rise to the claim occurred within the jurisdiction, it did not appear to matter that others
and the acquisition of any knowledge necessary for liability, occurred elsewhere (dicta in *ISC
Technologies v. Guerin* [1992] 1 Lloyd's Rep. 430, confirmed by dicta in *Polly Peck International v.
Nadir* (1993) *The Times*, March 22, 1993).
[68] Civil Procedure Rules 1998, Part 6.20, para.15; no similar provision was included in Rules
of the Supreme Court, Ord.11. If para.14 above does not cover "liability for dishonest assistance", this paragraph may do so.
[69] See *ante*, para 23–022.
[70] Both of the Brussels and Lugano Conventions and the Council Regulation.

rights in property arising out of a matrimonial relationship, wills and succession, or to bankruptcy. Consequently, they do not apply to claims concerning trusts in favour of individual creditors, testamentary trusts and ante-nuptial or post-nuptial settlements or to claims to set aside a trust on the grounds that its creation amounted to a fraud on the settlor's creditors, breached the terms of his matrimonial property regime, or deprived his forcible heirs of their rights. Such claims are therefore still governed by the rules which have already been considered.

Article 3 of the European Conventions[71] prohibits the exercise of jurisdiction on the basis of the temporary physical presence of the defendant or of his property within a particular jurisdiction. Article 2[72] provides that a person who has his domicile (which means a habitual residence, not the technical English private international law concept of domicile) in a European Convention State can only be sued in the courts of that state; the only exception is where the European Conventions confer jurisdiction on the courts of another European Convention State.[73] A court must decline jurisdiction where a defendant is sued other than in accordance with these provisions.[74] When proceedings involving the same cause of action and the same parties are brought in more than one European Convention State (such a situation is possible because most of the provisions of the European Conventions do not confer exclusive jurisdiction), any court other than the court where the proceedings started first must stay its proceedings while the jurisdiction of the court where the proceedings started first is established and, if it is established, must decline jurisdiction in favour of that court.[75] When proceedings in different European Convention States are related, in that it is expedient to hear and determine them together, any court other than the court where the proceedings started first may similarly first stay the proceedings and then decline jurisdiction.[76]

23–031

Proceedings brought pursuant to the European Conventions cannot be stayed on the ground of *forum non conveniens*. It was initially held[77] that an action in respect of which a court has jurisdiction under the European Conventions can nevertheless be stayed on the grounds of *forum non conveniens* when the alternative forum is not a European Convention State. However, this argument was rejected in *Owusu v. Jackson*[78] by the European Court of Justice, which reaffirmed the inapplicability of the doctrine of *forum non conveniens* to all proceedings brought pursuant to the European Conventions. In *González Gómez v. Gómez-Monche Vives*,[79] whose facts have already been considered,[80] it was contended that this prohibition applies only to the Article 2 prohibition on suing a person other than in the courts of his

23–032

---

[71] Both of the Brussels and Lugano Conventions and the Council Regulation; the provisions are not in the same form.

[72] Both of the Brussels and Lugano Conventions and the Council Regulation.

[73] Art.3 of both the Brussels and Lugano Conventions and the Council Regulation.

[74] Brussels and Lugano Conventions, Arts 19, 20; Council Regulation, Arts 25, 26.

[75] Brussels and Lugano Conventions, Arts 21, 23; Council Regulation, Arts 27, 29.

[76] Brussels and Lugano Conventions, Art.22; Council Regulation, Art.28.

[77] *Ace Insurance v. Zurich Insurance Company* [2001] 1 All E.R. (Comm.) 802.

[78] Case C-281/02, [2005] Q.B. 801.

[79] [2008] EWHC 259 (Ch), [2008] 3 W.L.R. 309.

[80] See *ante*, para.23–014.

domicile and not to the exceptions to that prohibition contained in Article 5, discussed in the next paragraph. However, Morgan J. rejected this argument and that decision is not being appealed.

23–033   Article 5 contains a number of exceptions to the basic rule in Article 2, providing a jurisdiction alternative to that of the jurisdiction of the defendant's domicile. One of these exceptions relates to proceedings involving trusts. By Article 5(6),[81] a person with a domicile (which again means a habitual residence, not the technical English private international law concept of domicile) in a European Convention State may be sued in another European Convention State if he is "settlor, trustee or beneficiary of a trust created by the operation of a statute, or by a written instrument, or created orally and evidenced in writing, in the courts of the [European Convention State] in which the trust is domiciled". Because trusts do not have legal personality and cannot really be said to have a habitual residence and because the United Kingdom is not a sole jurisdiction, specific provision has had to be made as to when and where a trust is domiciled in the United Kingdom; a trust is domiciled in the United Kingdom if it is domiciled in any part of the United Kingdom and is domiciled in a part of the United Kingdom "if and only if the system of law of that part is the system of law with which the trust has its closest and most real connection".[82]

23–034   These were the relevant provisions in *González Gómez v. Gómez-Monche Vives*[83] whose facts have already been considered.[84] The claim by some of the beneficiaries to recover payments of income and capital made to the settlor's widow who was entitled to some of the income under a resulting trust but was not otherwise entitled was resisted on the grounds that she was being sued not "as beneficiary" of the trust in question but because, so far as the sums being claimed from her were concerned, she was not a beneficiary at all. This contention was upheld by Morgan J. This narrow interpretation of Article 5(6) produces the unsatisfactory result that, where there are doubts about beneficial entitlements to an English trust with foreign beneficiaries domiciled in another Member State, proceedings will be necessary in England to determine the entitlements of the beneficiaries and, in the event that payments have been made to persons who turn out not to have been entitled, those payments will only be able to be recovered in the jurisdiction of the beneficiary in question. Morgan J. also held that the other claim, the challenge to the conduct of the widow as donee of a power, could not be made in the English courts either since in that capacity she was not being sued "as trustee" even if the power was a fiduciary power. The widow had also challenged the jurisdiction on the grounds that, even if she was being sued as beneficiary and as trustee, the trust was not domiciled in England. However, Morgan J. rejected this objection, holding that a trust will normally be domiciled in the jurisdiction of its applicable law and that this trust

---

[81] Both of the Brussels and Lugano Conventions and of the Council Regulation.
[82] Civil Jurisdiction and Judgments Act 1982, s.45.
[83] [2008] EWHC 259 (Ch), [2008] 3 W.L.R. 309.
[84] See *ante*, para.23–014.

was. All these decisions are being challenged in an appeal which will have been heard by the time that this edition is published.[85]

The extent to which resulting and constructive trusts are within Article 5(6) is not entirely clear at present. It follows from *González Gómez v. Gómez-Monche Vives*[86] that the position of the beneficiary of a resulting trust is the same as that of the beneficiary of an express trust but that is obviously being challenged on appeal. As for constructive trusts, although in *Chellaram v. Chellaram (No.2)*[87] Lawrence Collins J. twice stated that constructive trusts were outside the scope of Article 5(6), it is in fact clear that actions against trustees *de son tort*, or de facto trustees, are within that article and in *González Gómez v. Gómez-Monche Vives*[88] Morgan J. stated that actions against express trustees in respect of secret profits are as well. On the other hand, in *Casio Computer Co. v. Sayo*,[89] the Court of Appeal held that actions seeking to impose liability for dishonest assistance are within not Article 5(6) but within Article 5(3); this means that the choice of jurisdictions is between that of the domicile of the accessory and that where the dishonest assistance occurred. The Court of Appeal specifically left open the question of jurisdiction over actions seeking to impose liability for knowing receipt; however, it seems likely that this will be held also to fall within Article 5(3).

Whatever rule has been established by Article 5(6), but not whatever rule has been established by Article 5(3), is overridden where any jurisdiction has been the subject of a choice of law clause in a trust instrument.[90] In this case exclusive jurisdiction is conferred on the jurisdiction so selected.

There are, however, two exceptions which are of general application so that they override Article 5 as a whole and any provisions by which it is overridden. Where proceedings relate to the title to immoveable property or to a leasehold interest in that property, the courts of the state where the immoveable property is situated have exclusive jurisdiction.[91] This provision was applied in *Re Hayward (dec'd)*,[92] where a trustee in bankruptcy was trying to assert in an English court a claim to an undivided one half share of a property in Spain which had belonged to the bankrupt but which had since been transferred by his widow into and registered in the name of the other co-owner; the claim was struck out for lack of jurisdiction. However, this provision does not prevent the English courts from having jurisdiction over proceedings relating to purely beneficial interests in such property. Thus in *Webb v. Webb*[93] the European Court of Justice held that the English courts were entitled to exercise jurisdiction over proceedings in which the plaintiff was claiming that the defendant, his son, was holding land in France on resulting trust for him. These proceedings did not concern the

23–035

23–036

23–037

---

[85] No appeal is being made against the decision on *forum conveniens* discussed *ante*, para.23–032. The Court of Appeal confirmed the decision on domicile. Judgment on the remaining points is awaited.
[86] [2008] EWHC 259 (Ch), [2008] 3 W.L.R. 309.
[87] [2002] EWHC 632 (Ch), [2002] 3 All E.R. 17 at para.49–50.
[88] [2008] EWHC 259 (Ch), [2008] 3 W.L.R. 309.
[89] [2001] I.L.Pr. 594.
[90] Brussels and Lugano Conventions, Art.17; Council Regulation, Art.23.
[91] Brussels and Lugano Conventions, Art.16(1)(a); Council Regulation, Art.22(1).
[92] [1997] 1 All E.R. 32.
[93] *Webb v. Webb* [1994] Q.B. 696

legal title to the land in question and consequently the English courts were held to be able to exercise jurisdiction by virtue of the physical presence of the son in England. This jurisdiction was held not to be restricted to declaring the existence of the beneficial interest in question but also to extend to ordering the execution by the son of the notarial conveyance necessary under French law to transfer title to the land to his father. *Webb v. Webb* was applied in *Ashurst v. Pollard*,[94] where the Court of Appeal held that the trustee in bankruptcy of an English bankrupt was entitled to claim and the bankrupt was obliged to transfer to him an interest held by the bankrupt in immoveable property situated in Portugal.

23–038   These provisions of the European Conventions are also reflected in the rules governing service out of the jurisdiction.[95] No leave is required for service out of the jurisdiction against a defendant in another European Convention State in three alternative circumstances provided that no proceedings between the parties in respect of the claim are already pending in any other European Convention State: either, first, where the defendant is domiciled in the United Kingdom or another European Convention State (this again means a habitual residence, not the technical English private international law concept of domicile); or, secondly, in a number of situations of which the only one which is relevant for present purposes is where the subject matter of the dispute is rights *in rem* in English immoveable property or in tenancies in English immoveable property[96]; or, thirdly, where the defendant is a party to an agreement conferring exclusive jurisdiction on the English courts (this last exception would presumably apply to proceedings between a settlor and his trustees where the trust deed conferred such jurisdiction on the English courts, although such proceedings are relatively unlikely).

III. WHAT LAW WILL THE ENGLISH COURTS APPLY?

23–039   As has already been mentioned, the rules of English law governing the applicable law of a trust are now contained in the Hague Convention, incorporated into English law by the Recognition of Trusts Act 1987.[97] As the title of the Hague Convention suggests, it actually had two broad purposes: that of determining the law by which different aspects of trusts are governed and of enabling the recognition of trusts in jurisdictions where the trust concept is unknown; indeed it was the authorities of the latter jurisdictions who suggested to the Hague Secretariat that a convention should be prepared. The sort of potential problems which the provision of such recognition was intended to resolve have already been considered.[98] This chapter is

---

[94] [2001] 2 All E.R. 75.

[95] Civil Procedure Rules 1998, Part 6.19, repeating earlier provisions in the Rules of the Supreme Court.

[96] Rule 6.19 specifically refers to Brussels and Lugano Conventions, Art.16(1)(a) and to Council Regulation, Art.22(1), discussed *supra*.

[97] See Hayton (1987) 36 I.C.L.Q. 260 (Prof. Hayton was the head of the U.K. delegation to the body which produced the Convention and is therefore uniquely qualified to comment on its background and provisions); see also generally Harris, *The Hague Trusts Convention* (2002).

[98] See *ante*, para 1–027.

only concerned with the determination of the law by which trusts are governed.

The Recognition of Trusts Act 1987 "is obscure as to its retrospective **23–040** effect".[99] Article 22 of the Hague Convention provides that it "applies to trusts regardless of the date on which they were created" while section 1(5) of the Recognition of Trusts Act 1987 provides that "Article 22 shall not be construed as affecting the law to be applied in relation to anything done or omitted before the coming into force of this Act". In *Re Carapiet's Trusts*[100] the settlement had been created before the coming into force of the Act but the provisions under review only became operative afterwards on the death of the life tenant. Whether the Hague Convention applied was not decided because all parties agreed that the applicable law was the same at common law as under the Hague Convention. However, section 1(5) can only disapply the Hague Convention in actions for breach of trust and not many breaches of trust committed before the Recognition of Trusts Act 1987 are now likely to come before the courts. The Hague Convention will therefore clearly apply to all other trust proceedings, no matter when the trust in question was created.

1. *Situations where the Applicable Law is Irrelevant*

Preliminary issues concerning the question of whether a trust has actually **23–041** been created are not governed by its applicable law but by whatever system of law governs the capacity of the settlor to create the trust and the means by which the trust property is vested in the trustees. This is expressly provided by Article 4 of the Hague Convention and would be the case even if the Convention contained no such provision. The Hague Convention does not as such deal with trusts created orally or by declaration (see Article 3) but section 1(2) of the Recognition of Trusts Act 1987 applies the Hague Convention to all English trusts however created. There is, however, no reason why a civil law jurisdiction which had ratified the Hague Convention could not restrict its recognition of trusts to trusts created by transfer and/or in writing if it chose to do so. This would be particularly likely if that jurisdiction had itself enacted legislation envisaging only the creation of such trusts; an English court has held[101] that a Liechtenstein trust can only be created by transfer (however, Liechtenstein had not then ratified the Hague Convention but has done so since).

Under English law a minor, that is anyone under 18, has the capacity **23–042** neither to create a trust nor to transfer property to its trustees and, in the admittedly unlikely event that he purported to do so, the property would remain vested in whoever had previously held it and no trust would have been created because it would not have become completely constituted; the fact that the trust instrument provided that the applicable law was that of

---

[99] *Re Carapiet's Trusts* [2002] EWHC 1304 (Ch), [2002] W.T.L.R. 989 at 993.
[100] [2002] EWHC 1304 (Ch), [2002] W.T.L.R. 989 at 993.
[101] In *Neumann v. Azon Anstalt* (2001) unreported.

some jurisdiction where the law was in some way different[102] would have no effect whatever, at least in an English court. Similarly, transfers of property to trustees can be set aside under the Insolvency Act 1986, the Matrimonial Causes Act 1973 and the Inheritance (Provision for Family and Dependants) Act 1975, notwithstanding the fact that the trust in question is a foreign trust.

23–043   Further, an English trust will be invalid if its foreign settlor lacked capacity to create it under his own personal law. In *Neumann v. Azon Anstalt*[103] a Liechtenstein company which was the tenant of a flat in London declared a trust of that flat in favour of its occupier in order to enable the company to obtain a new lease to which it was entitled if the beneficiary had occupied the flat as his only or principal home for three out of the previous 10 years and if the trust was actually valid. The trust declared was in English law form but did not contain an express choice of law clause. In the absence of such a clause Liechtenstein law provides that the proper law will be that of the jurisdiction where the trustees (or a majority of the trustees) are domiciled or resident; a Liechtenstein company is necessarily both domiciled and resident in Liechtenstein. The judge[104] held that, if the trust was indeed an English trust, it was invalid because, in the absence of a choice of law clause, the Liechtenstein company did not have the capacity to create an English trust.[105]

23–044   Similar questions of capacity also arise where foreign settlors transfer property to the trustees of an English trust in breach of the rules of their matrimonial property regime or of their home jurisdiction's forcible heirship provisions.[106] Whether the English trust is valid will depend on whether the relevant foreign law makes the transfer by the foreign settlor void, thus affecting his capacity and rendering the English trust void, or merely voidable, in which case his capacity will not be affected and the English trust will be valid. In the case of French law, the settlement of property by a person married under French law on trust for his spouse would be wholly void from the outset,[107] while a settlement of property on trust by a person habitually resident in France which left insufficient assets for his forcible heirs would be merely voidable and would only be able to be avoided in the

---

[102] Because the age of majority was lower there. It is difficult to think of any jurisdiction where this is the case; however, if a 19-year-old from Jersey (where the age of majority is 20) tried to create a trust, the fact that it was expressly subject to English law would not make it valid in Jersey; nor, if he purported to transfer English land vested in him to the trustees of the English trust, would the transfer be held to be effective even in an English court if its validity was subsequently challenged (by the minor's parents or guardian, or indeed by the minor himself immediately after he obtained the age of majority).

[103] (2001) unreported.

[104] Judge Levy Q.C. in the Central London County Court.

[105] The judge went on to hold that, on the alternative hypothesis that the trust was a Liechtenstein trust, it was also invalid because Liechtenstein law does not envisage the creation of trusts by declaration, only by transfer.

[106] The ability to impeach such transactions does of course depend on the property in question still being within the reach of those seeking to set the transfers aside. It will not be if it is in the control of trustees of another jurisdiction which does not recognise and enforce the judgments of courts in the jurisdiction where any such transfer is set aside; this is the case in many off shore trust jurisdictions.

[107] (French) *Code Civile*, Art.1096.

event that there were still insufficient assets to fund their percentage of his lifetime assets on his death.[108]

Nor is the applicable law of the trust likely to be applied if the trust created is contrary to English public policy. If English land were settled on a form of trust which is prohibited by English law but permitted by the law of the jurisdiction whose law was chosen as its applicable law, such as a trust for the settlor for life or until bankruptcy[109] or on trusts which can last for ever and so blatantly infringe the rule against perpetuities,[110] an English court would be highly likely to apply English law and declare the trust to be void (it would of course have jurisdiction so to do because the subject matter was land within the jurisdiction). This would also be the case with moveable property which was actually within the jurisdiction at the time of the proceedings. It is less certain how the English courts would react to the various types of purpose trusts which have recently become fashionable in many off-shore trust jurisdictions[111] which are contrary to the rules of English trust law because they have no beneficiaries or to the more extreme trusts (or so-called trusts) which deprive their beneficiaries of any right to enforce them.[112]

23–045

2. *What is the Applicable Law?*

Article 6(1) of the Hague Convention provides that:

23–046

"A trust shall be governed by the law chosen by the settlor. The choice must be express or be implied in the terms of the instrument creating or the writing evidencing the trust, interpreted, if necessary, in the light of the circumstances of the case."

The only restriction placed by Article 6 on the settlor's choice is the requirement that the law chosen "provides for trusts or the category of trust involved"; if it does not do so, Article 6 does not apply to the trust in question, and the applicable law is determined by recourse to Article 7.

It was held in *Tod v. Barton*[113] that Article 6 contemplates two different situations: first, where there is an express choice of applicable law; and, secondly, where there is an implied choice of applicable law. Only in the second of those two situations can recourse be had to the circumstances of the case. Consequently in *Tod v. Barton*, where the testator had expressly chosen English law, there was held to be no legal basis for the argument that in the circumstances of the case that choice could and should be disregarded

23–047

---

[108] (French) *Code Civile*, Art.1097.

[109] Permitted in The Cook Islands.

[110] Permitted in The Cayman Islands. However, it is unlikely that there would be any difficulty about perpetuity and accumulation periods which are merely longer than the maximum period at present permitted by English law, which the proposed new legislation will extend anyway; most off-shore trusts jurisdictions at present have longer perpetuity periods than the present English law and even Northern Ireland has a longer accumulation period.

[111] Pioneered by Bermuda but now relatively common. See *ante*, para 3–139.

[112] This is now permitted in The Cayman Islands. See *ante*, para 3–145.

[113] (2002) 4 I.T.E.L.R. 715 at [para 32–35].

(the circumstances in question were that under English law the testator's provision that his son could not take the annuity given to him by the will until he attained the age of 65 could be and was to be circumvented by recourse to the Rule in *Saunders v. Vautier*,[114] something which would not have been possible under the law of the testator's last domicile[115]). Where there is no express choice of applicable law, the settlor will be found to have made an implied choice if the trust instrument contains other references to a particular jurisdiction. In *Tod v. Barton*, had the testator not made an express choice of applicable law, he would have been held to have made an implied choice by virtue of the fact that the will contained a provision restricting the gift over to educational purposes which were charitable according to English law. The circumstances of the case referred to would not have prevented this conclusion, which indicates that recourse to such circumstances will only be necessary if the provisions of the trust instrument are much less clear. It must also follow that the factors which determine the applicable law in default of an express or implied choice do not constitute relevant circumstances of the case either.

23–048   Where there is no express or implied choice of applicable law, the Hague Convention provides in Article 7:

"Where no applicable law has been chosen, a trust shall be governed by the law with which it is most closely connected.

In ascertaining the law with which a trust is most closely connected reference shall be made in particular to—

(a) the place of the administration of the trust designated by the settlor;

(b) the situs of the assets of the trust;

(c) the place of residence or business of the trustee;

(d) the objects of the trust and the places where they are to be fulfilled."

23–049   The delegations negotiating the terms of the Hague Convention decided to restrict themselves to these four factors. The need for both common law and civil law jurisdictions to make concessions meant the former had to accept the absence of domicile and the latter the absence of nationality, factors which are generally all important in these respective jurisdictions; these factors must presumably therefore be disregarded. However, as the wording of Article 7 itself recognises, the four factors actually listed do not constitute an exclusive list. Admittedly, the actual language of the trust instrument, and in particular any references which it may make to the law

---

[114] (1841) Cr. & P. 240; see *ante*, para 19–019. The son and the Royal Chemical Society, which was otherwise entitled to the testator's residuary estate, agreed that the son should receive an immediate payment of £164,000 rather than the annuity.

[115] The testator had died domiciled in Texas, where beneficiaries can only terminate a trust once all its purposes have been fulfilled or become illegal or impossible to fulfil (*Lanius v. Fletcher* (1907) 101 S.W. 1076, *Frost National Bank v. Newton* (1977) 554 S.W. 2d 149).

or the specific statutory provisions of any particular jurisdiction, will point towards an implied choice of applicable law under Article 6 rather than constitute an additional factor under Article 7. But the habitual residence of persons other than the trustee may be significant. The habitual residence of the testator will clearly be a key factor in testamentary trusts, although the habitual residence of the settlor will obviously be less relevant in *inter vivos* trusts if different from the place of residence or business of the trustee. However, the extent to which the habitual residence of the beneficiaries should be relevant, if different from the place of residence or business of the trustee (which it always will be in the case of an off-shore trust), is much more questionable.

In *Tod v. Barton*,[116] it was held that recourse to Article 7 would also have led to the conclusion that the applicable law was English law; the situs of the assets and the place where the trust was to be fulfilled were in England, as was the residence of one of the trustees, and the fact that the testator and the other trustee were resident and domiciled in Texas would not have displaced English law as the law with which the trust was most closely connected.

In *Re Carapiet's Trusts*,[117] the settlor was born in Iraq and as a result of successive marriages acquired British nationality and an Indian domicile. The settlement had been made in England, where the settlor was apparently then resident, as a result of litigation in India between her and the Armenian Patriarch of Jerusalem; the settlor had been given special permission to remove the assets from India to England. The trustee was an English bank and the settled property was held on trust for the settlor for life and subject to that to apply the income in accordance with the directions of the Armenian Patriarch for the education and advancement in life of Armenian children. Jacob J. held that this was an Article 7 case and that English law was the applicable law; it was abundantly clear from the transfer of the assets to England and the appointment of an English trustee that the settlor had wanted the trust controlled from England.

In *Chellaram v. Chellaram (No.2)*,[118] the facts of which have already been considered,[119] there was initially no express choice of an applicable law but the court upheld the validity of a decision of the trustees to change the applicable law to Bermudan law. Had it been necessary to apply Article 7, the court would have held Indian law to be the applicable law because the trusts had been drafted in India by Indian lawyers for a family of Indian origin with strong Indian ties and it was very doubtful that English law would have been the applicable law merely because two of the original trustees were in London and it was contemplated but not required that the trusts would, at least initially, be administered in London.

If whatever factors are decided to be relevant in any given case point towards the law of two different jurisdictions, one under which the trust

23–050

23–051

23–052

23–053

---

[116] (2002) 4 I.T.E.L.R. 715 at [36].
[117] [2002] EWHC 1304 (Ch), [2002] W.T.L.R. 989.
[118] [2002] EWHC 632 (Ch), [2002] 3 All E.R. 17 at 49–50.
[119] See *ante*, para 23–008.

would be valid and one under which it would be void, English law at least would be likely to opt for the jurisdiction in which it is valid.[120]

3. *What is the scope of the Applicable Law?*

23–054   Article 8 of the Hague Convention provides that the applicable law shall govern "the validity of the trust, its construction, its effect, and the administration of the trust" (although this is subject to Article 9 which permits "a severable aspect of the trust, particularly matters of administration" to be governed by a different law; this possibility is considered below). There then follows a non-exhaustive list of what the applicable law will govern. This contains nearly everything which could be expected. The only significant omission appears to be powers vested in persons other than the trustee such as the settlor or a protector. However, it cannot seriously be contended that these would not be governed by the applicable law (unless, of course, their subject matter related to "a severable aspect . . . governed by a different law").

23–055   The inclusion in the list of what the applicable law will govern of "(h) the variation or termination of the trust" leads to the conclusion that, as has already been mentioned,[121] the English courts no longer have the jurisdiction which they have previously arrogated[122] to approve applications under the Variation of Trusts Act 1958[123] in respect of foreign trusts; even if they do, they may well now not feel inclined to make such orders and the courts of the foreign jurisdiction in question may well decline to enforce them.

23–056   On the face of things, paragraph (h) also applies to claims for the variation of a trust in proceedings for the reallocation of property following a divorce in which one of the former spouses claims assets to which the respondent former spouse is entitled under a foreign trust. Such claims had also been successful in the past[124] and there has never been any difficulty in practice where the trustees of the foreign trust are within the English jurisdiction or can be controlled by a respondent who is himself within the English jurisdiction; in such circumstances the trustees or the respondent will be susceptible to the personal jurisdiction of the English courts. However, as has already

---

[120] In accordance with the decision of the majority of the Court of Appeal in *Re Baden's Deed Trusts* [1969] 2 Ch. 126, see *ante*, para 6–064, that, where the considerations were evenly balanced in arriving at one or other conclusion, the court was at liberty to lean towards the conclusion which might effectuate rather than frustrate the settlor's intentions (the point did not arise on the subsequent appeal to the House of Lords (*McPhail v. Doulton* [1971] A.C. 424)). This case concerned a private trust but the existence of a similar attitude towards charitable trusts was confirmed by the House of Lords in *I.R.C. v. McMullen* [1981] A.C. 1, see *ante*, para 11–008, although the House did not need to resort to it in that case.

[121] See *ante*, para 23–012.

[122] *Re Ker's Settlement* [1963] Ch. 553; *Re Paget's Settlement* [1965] 1 W.L.R. 1046.

[123] See *ante*, para 21–018.

[124] Claims to vary pre-nuptial or post-nuptial settlements of property abroad governed by foreign law with exclusively foreign trustees were successfully made in *Nunneley v. Nunneley* (1890) 15 P.D. 186, *Forsyth v. Forsyth* [1891] P. 363, and *Goff v. Goff* [1934] P. 107. More recently, claims for the reallocation of property on divorce were successfully made in *Browne v. Browne* [1989] 1 F.L.R. 291 (Jersey discretionary trust, Liechtenstein trust), *E v. E (Financial Provision)* [1990] 2 F.L.R. 233 (Guernsey discretionary trust), and *T v. T* [1996] 2 F.L.R. 357 (Jersey discretionary trust); however, in these proceedings no reference was made to the Recognition of Trusts Act 1987.

been seen, this question has been resolved by the decision of the Court of Appeal *Charalambous v. Charamboulous*,[125] where it was held that English law is the designated law for proceedings of this type and that, pursuant to Article 15, its power to vary settlements cannot be derogated from by voluntary act.[126] In policy terms, this can certainly be justified on the grounds that otherwise putting assets in a foreign trust would be far too easy a way of protecting them from potential claims by former spouses. This of course does not necessarily mean that the courts of the jurisdiction of the applicable law of the settlement in question will take any notice of the order of the English courts purporting to vary it. The Royal Court of Jersey, which is the applicable law of most of the settlements which have so far been the subject of orders of this type, does generally make whatever variation has been ordered as a matter of comity.[127] But a foreign court from a jurisdiction whose links with the United Kingdom are less close than those of Jersey may not feel obliged to act as a matter of comity at all; in this respect, proceedings are at present pending in Bermuda seeking the enforcement of an order of an English court in an extremely high profile divorce case which purported to vary a Bermudan trust and the outcome may well be instructive.

Where a settlement takes advantage of Article 9 of the Hague Convention **23–057** to provide that a severable aspect of the trust is to be governed by a different law (and most precedents now envisage this being done by providing both separate choice of law clauses for the applicable law and the law governing the administration of the trust and for the two to be independently changed), considerable difficulties can be encountered in determining precisely what is to be governed by the law of which jurisdiction unless the trust instrument has defined extremely precisely what is to be regarded as constituting whatever has been excluded from the ambit of its applicable law.

The applicable law will govern at the very least the nature of the interests **23–058** of its beneficiaries and the duties of the trustees towards them; this was specifically stated in *Chellaram v. Chellaram*.[128] It will also govern all other questions concerning the trust other than any which has been stated to be governed by the law of some other jurisdiction so that, in the event that it cannot be decided whether or not the trust instrument has provided for a severable aspect of the trust is to be governed by a different law, the applicable law will apply. The construction of the trust instrument and the administration of the trust are what are most commonly excluded from the ambit of its applicable law. There is no difficulty whatever in defining the scope of the former exclusion but very considerable difficulties can be encountered in defining precisely what constitutes administration in the absence of an express definition. Prior to the incorporation of the Hague Convention into English law, Dicey & Morris,[129] the leading practitioners' text, drew a distinction between, on the one hand, the validity, interpretation and effect of a trust and, on the other hand, its administration; the former

---

[125] [2004] EWCA Civ. 1030, [2005] Fam. 250 (*sub nom. C. v. C.*, but reported under the names of the parties elsewhere).

[126] See *post*, para 23–065.

[127] One of many cases of this kind is *Compass Trustees v. McBarnett* [2003] W.T.L.R. 461.

[128] [1985] Ch. 409 at 432.

[129] Conflict of Laws (10th edn (1980)), Rules 120 and 121.

were said to be governed by what was then known as its proper law and the latter was said to be governed by the law of its place of administration. This distinction was rejected by Scott J. in *Chellaram v. Chellaram*,[130] who expressed the view that all four were governed by its proper law.[131] However, that does not answer the question of what is to be regarded as administration when the settlor has stated that administration is to be governed by a law other than the proper law without defining what he means by administration.

23–059   It has already been stated that the proper law of the trust will at the very least govern the nature of the interests of the beneficiaries and the duties of the trustees towards them (the latter will clearly include any powers which they have to determine the manner in which the income and capital of the trust is distributed and their duties to convert and apportion the trust property). The proper law will also undoubtedly govern the construction of the trust instrument if this has not been expressly reserved to the law of some other jurisdiction. At the other extreme, there can be no doubt that the trustees' duties to provide accounts and to give information to the beneficiaries are purely administrative; so are some of their powers, such as the power to appoint and remove trustees, to appoint agents, and to insure. But a number of other powers which are, for other purposes, often classified as administrative are capable of affecting directly or indirectly the interests of the beneficiaries in the event that the provisions of the proper law and of the law specified as governing administration differ as to their existence or scope. The presence or absence of a power for the trustees to remunerate themselves clearly affects the income and capital available for the beneficiaries. So does the presence or absence of powers of advancement, maintenance and accumulation in the event that they are exercised. So too, to a lesser extent, do the trustees' powers of investment. And where powers exercisable by persons other than the trustees, such as the settlor or the protector, fit in is anyone's guess; the law applicable will presumably (or at any rate should) be determined by the nature of the power in question. There therefore seems no sensible way of drawing a line in the absence of a precise definition in the trust instrument and it is consequently impossible to predict what would happen in the event that an English court had to decide by which law such powers were governed.

23–060   Such a situation would open the way for the court to ignore the provisions of the trust instrument completely and simply apply English law. Indeed, this is precisely what Scott J. did in *Chellaram v. Chellaram*,[132] which was admittedly decided before the incorporation of the Hague Convention into English law. In this case, the facts of which have already been considered,[133] the beneficiaries were seeking the removal and replacement of the trustees. Scott J. was prepared to apply the provisions of English law to this question even if both the applicable law and the law under which the trust was being administered turned out to be Indian law. He said this[134]:

---

[130] [1985] Ch. 409 at 432.
[131] The current edition of Dicey, Morris & Collins (14th edn, London, Sweet & Maxwell, 2007) Rule 151 states the law in accordance with the Hague Convention.
[132] [1985] Ch. 409.
[133] See *ante*, para 23–008.
[134] [1985] Ch. 409 at 432–433.

"The function of English courts in trust litigation is to enforce or protect the rights of the beneficiaries which bind the conscience of the trustee defendants. The identification and extent of those rights is a matter for the [applicable] law of the settlement, but the manner of enforcement is, in my view, a matter of machinery which, under English domestic law, can be exercised by English courts where necessary in order to enable the rights of beneficiaries to be enforced or protected .... Accordingly, except where rights conferred by the settlement are under consideration, the removal of trustees and the appointment of new ones are not, in my judgment, a matter to be governed by the [applicable] law of the settlement. Nor, in my opinion, is it a matter to be governed by the law of the place where the administration of the settlement has taken place. It is, in my judgment, a matter to be governed by the law of the country whose courts have assumed jurisdiction to administer the trusts of the settlement in question."

The last sentence of this passage suggests, without actually stating, that **23–061** English law was applicable simply because it was the law of the forum. If English domestic law is indeed applicable whenever it is necessary to protect the interests of the beneficiaries, then the possibilities for its application are infinite. It is of course possible that this approach would be held no longer to be appropriate in the light of the subsequent incorporation of the Hague Convention into English law. But in the event that this approach is still applicable, it is at least theoretically possible that the provisions of the Hague Convention could be ignored in any proceedings brought by beneficiaries against trustees to enforce their interests in which the English courts have jurisdiction; such a contention could obviously most easily be made in a case where, as in *Chelleram v. Chellaram*, the beneficiaries were seeking a change of trustees.

4. *Changing the Applicable Law*

Article 10 of the Hague Convention deals with changes of the applicable law **23–062** (or for that matter of any other governing law) by providing that the question of whether such a change is possible shall be determined by "the law applicable to the validity of the trust". This presumably means the applicable law but it would have been more helpful if the Hague Convention had actually said so specifically. Such changes of governing law will require, at least under English law, either a provision in the trust instrument expressly permitting this[135] or the agreement of all the beneficiaries which, if any of them is not *sui juris*, will require an order of the court under the Variation of Trusts Act 1958.[136] That a change of governing law is not otherwise possible seems to have been confirmed by the courts of The Cayman Islands in *Wahr-Hansen v. Bridge Trust Co.*,[137] which concerned a

---

[135] This follows from the authorities referred to *post*, n.137.

[136] See *ante*, para 21–018.

[137] 1997 C.I.L.R. 527 (Court of Appeal); the question was discussed more fully at first instance *sub nom. Bridge Trust Co. v. Attorney-General* 1996 C.I.L.R. 52 but did not arise on the further appeal to the Privy Council *sub nom. Attorney-General of the Cayman Islands v. Wahr-Hansen* [2001] 1 A.C. 75.

change of what in the two jurisdictions in question is still known as the proper law from the law of The Bahamas to the law of The Cayman Islands pursuant to a clause expressly permitting such a change.[138]

23–063   A change of the applicable law of a trust away from English law will often take place as part of an arrangement by which a trust changes its fiscal status from a resident to a non-resident trust,[139] in which case the latter change will produce a deemed disposal for the purposes of capital gains tax.[140] Where a trust remains resident for fiscal purposes despite a change of applicable law, there will nevertheless be a deemed disposal for the purposes of capital gains tax where the change of applicable law is made pursuant to the agreement of the beneficiaries; this is because for at least for a moment of time the beneficiaries will be absolutely entitled to the trust property as against the trustees.[141] However, it is not thought that a deemed disposal would be a consequence of a change of applicable law pursuant to an express provision in the trust instrument.

23–064   Surprisingly Article 10, unlike the provisions governing the choice of the original applicable law, does not restrict changes of applicable law to changes to jurisdictions whose laws "provide for trusts or the category of trusts involved". A change to a jurisdiction which did not recognise trusts could lead to the settlor being regarded as absolutely entitled to the trust property or as being entitled to revoke the trusts in favour of himself; this could have disastrous fiscal consequences,[142] as could a change to a jurisdiction which recognised trusts but only of a type which English law regarded as void for public policy. Presumably, the Convention assumes that the trustees will be sensible! However, serious consideration should be given by draftsmen to restricting the scope of clauses permitting a change of law to, at the very least, jurisdictions which recognise trusts. The relevant Cayman Islands legislation requires any new applicable law to recognise both the validity of the trust and the respective interests of the beneficiaries. However, it may be that this is implied at common law anyway since in *Bridge Trust Co. v. Attorney-General*[143] the Chief Justice of The Cayman Islands held

---

[138] The plaintiffs contended that the change of proper law was ineffective because, as the Privy Council subsequently held, the entire trust was void and so the clause permitting a change of proper law was void as well. However, at first instance, it was held that all that was necessary was that Bahamian law recognised the possibility of a change in the proper law and that, given that it did, the change of law was, therefore, valid because it satisfied the legislation of The Cayman Islands governing changes of proper law. While it must admittedly be possible for such a clause permitting a change of applicable or proper law to survive the invalidity of one or more of the individual provisions of the trust, it is hard to see how such a clause can continue to exist, like the grin of the Cheshire Cat, in a trust which has been declared to be entirely void. However, the Court of Appeal confirmed the decision at first instance in this respect and the point was not pursued further.

[139] See *ante*, para 15–146.

[140] See *ante*, para 15–160.

[141] See *ante*, para 15–143.

[142] Because the settlor would under English law be regarded as being beneficially entitled to the trust property and, if he was subject to English taxation, would therefore become liable to income tax and capital gains tax on its assets. This would also stop any seven-year period running for the purposes of inheritance tax.

[143] 1996 C.I.L.R. 52 (the question did not arise on appeal; see n.137 above).

that at common law[144] a change of what is still known there as the proper law will not be recognised unless the new proper law chosen recognises both the validity of the trusts and the original interests of the beneficiaries.

6. *Mandatory Provisions of the Hague Convention*

The Hague Convention describes Articles 15 and 16 as mandatory provisions. Article 15 provides that the Hague Convention "does not prevent the application of provisions of the law designated by the conflicts rules of the forum, in so far as those provisions cannot be derogated from by voluntary act" referring in particular to, among other things,[145] "(a) the protection of minors and incapable parties (b) the personal and proprietary effects of marriage; (c) succession rights, testate and intestate, especially the indefeasible share of spouses and relatives ... (e) the protection of creditors in matters of insolvency".   **23–065**

In *Tod v. Barton*,[146] it was contended that Article 15 required the court to apply the rules of private international law relating to succession and, therefore, the law of the testator's domicile, Texas, which would have prevented the beneficiaries agreeing to exercise the Rule in *Saunders v. Vautier*[147] and so frustrating his wishes.[148] Lawrence Collins J. rejected this argument, holding that "the purpose of article 15 is to preserve the mandatory effect of the rules of the law designated by the conflict of laws rules for matters other than trusts". He gave as an example the rule of English law that succession to personal property is governed by the law of the deceased's domicile at the date of his death, saying that, if the law of that domicile contains forcible heirship provisions, those provisions must be given effect to notwithstanding the creation of a trust which purports to override them. But in *Tod v. Barton* the testator's domicile was relevant only for the purposes of determining the essential validity of his will. Given that it was valid and had been carried into effect, no rule of English private international law referred the validity of the agreement to vary it to Texan law.   **23–066**

This decision indicated that Article 15 might be a means by which English law could justify a decision to avoid a foreign trust made in fraud of creditors, spouses, and dependants[149]. That article did indeed subsequently prove to be the ground on which the Court of Appeal held in *Charamboulos v. Charamboulas* that English courts still have a jurisdiction to order the reallocation, following divorce, of property held under a foreign trust not subject to English law.[150] It remains to be seen whether this article is also deployed in less straightforward situations.   **23–067**

---

[144] This was what applied in The Bahamas, the jurisdiction from which the proper law was being changed, at the relevant time.

[145] Those not listed are not relevant to English law, although "(d) the transfer of title to property ... " may well confirm the conclusions which have already been expressed (*ante*, para 23–019) about the limitations on equitable proprietary claims and "liability for knowing receipt".

[146] (2002) 4 I.T.E.L.R. 715 at [39–42].

[147] (1841) Cr. & P. 240; see *ante*, para 19–019.

[148] See *ante*, para 23–050.

[149] See *ante*, para 23–045.

[150] [2004] EWCA Civ 1030, [2005] Fam. 250; *ante*, para 23–056.

23–068   Article 16 (the second paragraph of which does not form part of English law) similarly provides that "those provisions of the law of the forum which must be applied even to international situations, irrespective of" its rules of private international law are also applicable despite the provisions of the Hague Convention. The only obvious situation to which this would apply (and this is fairly far-fetched) would be if the trustees, beneficiaries, settlor or protector of a foreign trust brought in an English court proceedings which were connected in some way with assets whose sale, purchase or ownership was permitted by its applicable law but prohibited by English law (examples would be arms, drugs, classical architectural artefacts, and protected species).

IV. THE ENFORCEMENT BY ENGLISH COURTS OF FOREIGN TRUSTS JUDGMENTS

23–069   Any judgment in proceedings involving a trust given by a court which has jurisdiction under the European Conventions[151] will be automatically recognised and enforced by the English courts[152] unless it falls foul of a further provision of the European Conventions[153] for one of the following reasons:

   (i)   because it is contrary to public policy;

   (ii) because judgment was given in default of appearance in circumstances where the defendant was not properly served in sufficient time to prepare his defence;

   (iii) if the judgment cannot be reconciled with a judgment already given by an English court in a dispute between the same parties;

   (iv) (only under the Council Regulation) if the judgment cannot be reconciled with an earlier judgment already given in any country (whether a European Convention State or not) involving the same cause of action and between the same parties and that earlier judgment is entitled to be recognised by the English court; and

   (v)   (only under the Brussels and Lugano Conventions), if the judgment was given pursuant to a rule of private international law as to capacity, matrimonial property rights, or succession which produced a result different from that which would have been reached under English private international law.

23–070   Any judgment in proceedings not subject to the European Conventions will also be recognised and enforced if it is within any bilateral or multilateral convention for the enforcement of judgments between the state where the judgment was given and the United Kingdom and is duly registered in the High Court of England and Wales. If no such convention is

---

[151] See *ante*, para 23–022.
[152] Brussels and Lugano Conventions, Arts 26 and 31; Council Regulation, Arts 33 and 38.
[153] Brussels and Lugano Conventions, Art.27; Council Regulation, Art.34.

applicable, then the foreign judgment will not be recognised or enforced by the English courts; it will merely create an obligation binding on the defendant which the successful claimant will have to enforce by bringing a separate action in the English courts.[154] This is still the position where a successful claimant in any of the jurisdictions of the United States of America seeks to enforce his judgment in the English courts.[155]

---

[154] Since he will normally be able to obtain summary judgment, this is not usually any slower than the process of registering a judgment under a bilateral or multi-lateral convention.

[155] And of course vice-versa.

INDEX